FOREIGN AND COMMONWEALTH OFFICE

A
YEAR BOOK
OF THE
COMMONWEALTH

1972

LONDON
HER MAJESTY'S STATIONERY OFFICE
1972

© *Crown copyright* 1972

Published by
HER MAJESTY'S STATIONERY OFFICE

To be purchased from
49 High Holborn, London WC1V 6HB
13a Castle Street, Edinburgh EH2 3AR
109 St Mary Street, Cardiff CF1 1JW
Brazennose Street, Manchester M60 8AS
50 Fairfax Street, Bristol BS1 3DE
258 Broad Street, Birmingham B1 2HE
80 Chichester Street, Belfast BT1 4JY
or through booksellers

Price £5·50 net

PREFACE

THIS is the Fourth edition of *A Year Book of the Commonwealth* under its present title.

While every effort has been made to ensure that the information contained in this volume is correct at the time of going to press (September 1971) the Editor would be grateful if his attention could be drawn to any errors or omissions that may be noted.

LIBRARY AND RECORDS DEPARTMENT
FOREIGN AND COMMONWEALTH OFFICE
SANCTUARY BUILDINGS
GREAT SMITH STREET
LONDON S.W.1.

CONTENTS

Contents

PART I

PART 1

THE CONSTITUTIONAL DEVELOPMENT
OF THE COMMONWEALTH

THE present Commonwealth as a free association of sovereign nations is the outcome of the development of self-government in the older British Dominions and, more immediately, of their demand during the First World War for an equally full control of their own foreign policy. Recognition was given to this in the resolution of the Imperial War Conference 1917, that 'the constitutional relations of the component parts of the Empire ... should be based upon a full recognition of the Dominions as autonomous nations of an Imperial Commonwealth'. Accordingly, the Dominions* and India signed the Versailles Peace Treaty individually, and had their own representation in the League of Nations. The Inter-Imperial Relations Committee of the 1926 Imperial Conference, under the Chairmanship of Lord Balfour, made the first formal attempt to describe the resultant status and mutual relationship of the Members in what came to be known as the 'Balfour formula'. The Committee's report declared that 'They are autonomous communities within the British Empire, equal in status, in no way subordinate one to another in any aspect of their domestic or external affairs, though united by a common allegiance to the Crown and freely associated as Members of the British Commonwealth of Nations'. This principle was legally formulated in the Statute of Westminster of 1931 which gave effect to this fully independent status of the Dominions in relation to Great Britain and, by implication, in relation to each other.

The progress which India had already made towards a similar status was completed in 1947 when India and Pakistan became independent and Members of the Commonwealth. The Second World War had hastened this development with the remaining dependencies and the next two decades saw Ceylon become independent and a Member of the Commonwealth in 1948, then Ghana and Malaya in 1957, Nigeria and Cyprus in 1960†, Sierra Leone and Tanganyika in 1961, Jamaica, Trinidad and Tobago, and Uganda in 1962, Zanzibar and Kenya, together with Sabah, Sarawak and Singapore (as parts of the Federation of Malaysia) in 1963‡, Malawi, Malta and Zambia in 1964, The Gambia in 1965, Guyana (formerly British Guiana), Botswana (formerly the Bechuanaland Protectorate), Lesotho (formerly Basutoland) and Barbados in 1966, Mauritius and Swaziland in 1968, and Tonga and Fiji in 1970. Nauru became independent in 1968 and joined the Commonwealth as a 'special member'. Western Samoa became independent in 1962 and a Commonwealth member in 1970.

India's decision to become a republic in 1949 marked a further step in the development of the Commonwealth. The definition in the Balfour formula of the Commonwealth as an association of states 'owing a common allegiance to

---

* *Other than Newfoundland.*

† Cyprus became a member of the Commonwealth six months after her Independence, i.e. in March, 1961.

‡ Singapore subsequently became independent as a separate state by her secession from the Federation of Malaysia in 1965.

1

the Crown' could not be applied to a republican Member and the Commonwealth Prime Ministers at their meeting in 1949 agreed to accept India's continued membership on the basis of her expressed 'acceptance of the King as the symbol of the free association of the independent Member Nations and as such the Head of the Commonwealth'. Following this precedent Pakistan (1956) and Ghana (1960) both adopted republican constitutions, while Cyprus, Zambia and Botswana became republics upon achieving independence. Tanganyika became a republic in 1962, and in 1964 united with Zanzibar to form the United Republic of Tanzania. Nigeria and Uganda became republics in 1963, Kenya in 1964 and Malawi in 1966. Singapore became a republic upon its withdrawal from the Malaysian Federation (1965) and Guyana became a republic on 23rd February 1970 in accordanace with a provision in the independence constitution of Guyana (1966). The Gambia became a republic on 24th April 1970 after a plebiscite, and Sierra Leone became a republic on 19th April 1971.

Malaysia, Swaziland, Lesotho, Western Samoa and Tonga provide further variations. Malaysia is an elective monarchy and the Head of State is the Yang di Pertuan Agong, whom the Malay Rulers of nine of the States of Malaya elect from among their number to hold office for five years. Swaziland and Lesotho are monarchies where the King is designated by the Chiefs in accordance with the customary law of the country. Tonga is a hereditary monarchy, and Western Samoa is ruled by a Head of State analogous to a constitutional monarch, who has been elected for life.

No functions attach to the title of Head of the Commonwealth and it has no strict constitutional significance. But, as the sole symbolic link uniting all the Members of the Commonwealth, it is the outward and visible mark of the special relationship which exists between them.

A further departure from the Statute of Westminster is the decline of the use of the term 'Dominion'. Although the Indian Independence Act, 1947 provided for the creation of two new 'Dominions', the use of the term had already begun to disappear after the Second World War even in describing those independent Commonwealth countries which already had 'Dominion Status'. In 1947 the Dominions Office was re-named the Commonwealth Relations Office, and Commonwealth countries which have become independent since 1947 do not call themselves, and are not referred to, as 'Dominions'. As a result of discussions at the Prime Ministers' Meeting of 1952 the term was also dropped from the Royal Titles. The term would indeed be inappropriate for such Commonwealth countries as no longer have the Queen as their Head of State.

For some years after the 1926 Imperial Conference apprehension was felt in some quarters lest the Balfour formula did not imply the right of secession, and the Union of South Africa, in approving the report of the Conference on the Operation of Dominion Legislation in 1929, expressly affirmed 'the right of any member of the British Commonwealth of Nations to withdraw therefrom'. The Union Prime Minister (Gen. Hertzog) in fact brought this resolution to the notice of the Imperial Conference of 1930, which took note of it without discussion.

In 1947 the view of the British Government that there was a full right of secession was clearly indicated in the statement of the Prime Minister (Mr Attlee) on the Burma Independence Bill, where he pointed out that 'The British Commonwealth of Nations is a free association of peoples, not a collection of subject nations'; hence, in view of Burma's desire to become an independent state outside the Commonwealth, 'it was the duty of His Majesty's Government . . . to implement their decision'. The Secretary of State for Burma (the Earl of Listowel) endorsed this with the statement in the House of Lords, that 'We do not regard membership of the Commonwealth as something to be thrust by force upon a reluctant people'. That members of the Commonwealth were considered as independent and as free as those nations who chose to break all links with the United Kingdom and the Commonwealth, was given further emphasis by the fact that the same title was used for the Burma Independence Act as had been used for the Independence Acts of India and Ceylon.

The Burma Independence Act (1947) was followed by the Ireland Act of 1949, which recognised that Eire, or the Republic of Ireland as it now came to be known, had ceased to be part of His Majesty's dominions.

During 1960 the Union of South Africa decided, after a referendum, to become a republic from 31st May 1961. In accordance with precedents set by India, Pakistan and Ghana, the South African Government enquired whether South Africa as a republic would be accepted as a Member of the Commonwealth. After considerable discussion at the Prime Ministers' Meeting in March 1961, largely concerning the Union's racial policies, the Prime Minister of the Union of South Africa withdrew his application. When South Africa became a republic on 31st May 1961, she therefore ceased to be a Member of the Commonwealth.

Certain other territories, formerly British dependencies, left the Commonwealth on becoming independent. Besides Burma in 1948, the Sudan became an independent sovereign state outside the Commonwealth in 1956. In 1960 British Somaliland joined with its neighbour, the former United Nations Trust Territory of Italian Somaliland, to form the independent Somali Republic. Similarly in 1961 the Southern Cameroons, on becoming independent, moved out of the Commonwealth to join the neighbouring French Cameroons to form the Federal Republic of Cameroun. The Maldive Islands ceased to be a protected state in 1963. With the end of the South Arabian Federation in 1967, the independent sovereign state of the People's Republic of South Yemen was established outside the Commonwealth.

Western Samoa, formerly a Trust Territory administered by New Zealand, became independent in 1962. She did not join the Commonwealth until 1970, although she was treated in the intervening period by New Zealand in all except nationality matters as though she were a Member of the Commonwealth, and in certain respects this was true also of her relations with other Commonwealth countries.

The Cook Islands, formerly a dependency of New Zealand, became fully self-governing internally in July 1965 and chose to remain in free association with New Zealand, 'free association' being one of the three ways recognised by the United Nations General Assembly by which a territory reaches a full measure of self-government. The New Zealand Government remains responsible for the conduct of the external affairs and defence of the islands. Early in 1967 five former British colonies in the Eastern Caribbean (St Christopher, Nevis and Anguilla, Antigua, Dominica, St Lucia and Grenada) received constitutions similar to that of the Cook Islands. The Associated States (as they are now known) are fully self-governing while Britain remains responsible for their external affairs and defence. St Vincent became an Associated State on 27th October 1969.

Nauru, formerly a Trust Territory administered by Australia on behalf of the Governments of Australia, New Zealand and Britain, became independent in

January 1968. The Republic of Nauru became the first 'Special Member' of the Commonwealth with the right to participate in all functional meetings and activities of the Commonwealth, the only limitation being that she does not attend Meetings of Prime Ministers.

The Commonwealth has no legal definition although a statement of principles which all members hold in common was made in the Commonwealth Declaration, January 1971. Until recently it had no formal institutional expression. Intergovernmental consultation is its principal mode of operation, and this is carried on both by direct inter-governmental correspondence and by the periodic Commonwealth Prime Ministers' meetings. While some of the Members of the Commonwealth have been inflexibly opposed to the establishment of any centralised machinery for the consideration of political questions, particularly foreign policy and defence, the Prime Ministers' Meeting in 1964 favoured the institution of more formal machinery to promote closer and more informed understanding between their governments. After a report by officials on the matter, the Prime Ministers agreed in June 1965 to set up a Commonwealth Secretariat for this purpose. Its headquarters are at Marlborough House and its chief official is the Secretary-General, who is appointed by the Prime Ministers. The Secretariat is staffed from Member countries and financed by their contributions, and is at the service of all Commonwealth governments. Its functions are principally the circulation of information to Commonwealth governments and the organisation of such meetings as those of the Prime Ministers and Commonwealth Finance Ministers. It has no executive functions. The Secretariat is described in detail in a separate section of this Year Book.

There has recently been a further sharp reduction in the number of the remaining British dependencies. In 1966 four more became independent, and five others reached Associated status in February 1967. Mauritius and Swaziland became independent in March and September 1968. Tonga became independent on 4th June 1970 and Fiji on 10th October 1970. The remainder vary from wealthy and populous Hong Kong to the tiny island of Pitcairn with fewer than one hundred inhabitants; but most are small and have very limited natural resources.

ORGANISATION OF BRITISH GOVERNMENT RELATIONS WITH OTHER COMMONWEALTH COUNTRIES

CONSTITUTIONAL responsibility to Parliament for British relations with other Members of the Commonwealth and for relations with the Governments of Brunei, Tonga, the Associated States in the Caribbean*, and Rhodesia, rested until October 1968, with the Secretary of State for Commonwealth Affairs†, who was also responsible for the good government of the remaining British dependent territories. The Prime Minister announced on 15th March 1968, that the Commonwealth Office, which was the Department of

---

* *At that time these were: Antigua, Dominica, Grenada, St Christopher, Nevis and Anguilla, and St Lucia.*

† *Relations with certain non-Commonwealth countries (the Republic of Ireland and the Maldive Islands) were also handled by the Secretary of State for Commonwealth Affairs.*

State responsible to the Secretary of State for the conduct of these relations and the administration of the dependencies, would merge with the Foreign Office during the year. The two Offices were merged as the Foreign and Commonwealth Office on 17th October 1968.

The new Secretary of State has now assumed all responsibility for Foreign and Commonwealth Affairs. While there is no minister in the new Office solely in charge of Commonwealth matters, each minister has responsibility for the Commonwealth aspects of the work under his control. Each department in the new Office is also responsible for ensuring that the Commonwealth interest is fully taken into account when appropriate. There is also a Commonwealth Coordination department which is responsible for advising ministers and departments on matters affecting the Commonwealth and a Dependent Territories General Department which performs the same functions for Dependent Territories.

Overseas, responsibility to the Secretary of State for the conduct of British relations with other Commonwealth countries rests with British High Commissioners, whose offices are situated in Commonwealth capitals and in some other major towns. In the countries to which they are accredited the High Commissioners are the representatives of the British Government; and in those countries whose Head of State is other than Her Majesty The Queen they are her representatives. They have a status equivalent to Ambassadors. They advise the Secretary of State either direct or through the Foreign and Commonwealth Office on the policies of, and British relations with the countries to which they are accredited, interpret and project British policies and way of life to the Governments and people there and at the same time look after British interests and foster Commonwealth links.

Other Commonwealth countries likewise have government departments which include among their responsibilities that for Commonwealth relations and have High Commissioners resident in London and in other Commonwealth capitals. Although British and Commonwealth Ministers sometimes correspond direct the normal channel of communication between the British Government and the Governments of other Commonwealth countries is between the Foreign and Commonwealth Office in London and the government departments responsible for Commonwealth relations in those other countries. Communication is not direct but passes either through the British High Commissioners overseas or through Commonwealth High Commissioners in London. British High Commissioners, unlike Ambassadors, often deal with government departments other than those dealing with Commonwealth relations—as do Commonwealth High Commissioners in London.

Except for the specialist advisers, the staffs in London and of British High Commissioners' offices and British Embassies are members of H.M. Diplomatic Service, which was formed on 1st January 1965 to take over the duties and posts of the former Foreign Service, the Commonwealth Relations Office at home and overseas, and the Trade Commission Service.

The Secretary of State also has responsibility for Britain's overseas aid programme. This is administered by the Overseas Development Administration of the Foreign and Commonwealth Office under the Minister for Overseas Development, who exercises powers delegated to him by the Secretary of State. Further details about the Overseas Development Administration are contained in Appendix A.

The administration of the dependent territories is carried out by the various territorial Governments, the Governor in each territory being the representative of the Sovereign. Subject to the overriding authority of Parliament, the territorial Governments enjoy a large and increasing measure of autonomy. Each territory has its own legislature and its own civil service, which is paid from local revenue and is not part of the Home Civil Service. The Secretary of State for Foreign and Commonwealth Affairs is responsible for transfers, promotions and discipline of members of Her Majesty's Overseas Civil Service serving in dependent territories; appointments to senior posts such as Governorships and Chief Justiceships; and for compensation schemes and pensions payable by the governments of dependent territories. He is advised and assisted in these matters by the appropriate departments of the Foreign and Commonwealth Office.

PART II

BRITISH REPRESENTATIVES
IN OTHER COMMONWEALTH COUNTRIES

COMMONWEALTH OF AUSTRALIA

BRITISH HIGH COMMISSION
Commonwealth Avenue, Canberra, A.C.T.
(Tel. 7–0422; Cable UKREP, Canberra; Telex 29–AA 62043)
(Office Hours: 08.45–17.00 Monday–Friday)
High Commissioner: His Excellency The Rt Hon. Sir Morrice James, KCMG, CVO, MBE
Minister: D. P. Aiers, CMG

Sydney
Gold Fields House, Sydney Cove, Sydney, 2000, New South Wales
(Tel. 27–7521; Cable UKREP, Sydney; Telex AA 20680)
(Office Hours: 08.45–17.00 Monday–Friday)
Deputy High Commissioner: G. Booth, CMG

Melbourne
C.M.L. Building, 330 Collins Street, Melbourne, Victoria
(Tel. 67–7254 and 67–8601; Cable UKREP, Melbourne; Telex AA 30660)
(Office Hours: 08.45–17.00 Monday–Friday)
Deputy High Commissioner: R. W. B. Carter, CMG

Commercial Section
339 Swanston Street, Melbourne, Victoria
(Tel. 32–026)
(Office Hours: 08.45–17.00 Monday–Friday)
Civil Aviation Adviser to the British High Commissioner,
C.M.L. Building, 330 Collins Street, Melbourne, Victoria, 3000.
(Tel. 677254 and 678601; Cable CIVATT Melbourne; Telex AA 30660)
(Office hours: 0845–1700 Monday to Friday)
Civil Aviation Adviser: Norman W. Walker, DFC

Brisbane
6th Floor, M.L.C. Building, Corner Adelaide & Edward Streets, Brisbane, Queensland
(Tel. 2–2307: Cable UKREP, Brisbane)
(Office Hours: 08.45–17.00 Monday–Friday)
Deputy High Commissioner: F. S. Fielding, OBE

Perth
7th Floor, A.N.Z. Building, 84 St George's Terrace, Perth, Western Australia
(Tel. 21–5128; Cable UKREP, Perth)
(Office Hours: 08.45–17.00 Monday–Friday)
Deputy High Commissioner: A. H. Birch, CMG, OBE

Adelaide
4th Floor, F.C.A. Building, 15 Franklin Street, Adelaide, South Australia
(Tel. 51–4011; Cable UKREP, Adelaide)
(Office Hours: 08.45–1700 Monday–Friday)
Deputy High Commissioner: H. O'Brien

BRITISH COUNCIL
18 Greenoaks Avenue, Edgecliff, Sydney, N.S.W., 2027
(Tel. 32–3773)
Representative: E. R. H. Paget, OBE

BARBADOS
BRITISH HIGH COMMISSION
Barclay's Bank Building, 147–149 Rosebuck Street, (P.O. Box 676c), Bridgetown
(Tel. 3525; Cable UKREP, Bridgetown)
High Commissioner: His Excellency Mr D. A. Roberts
Deputy High Commissioner and Head of Chancery: J. A. B. Stewart

BOTSWANA
BRITISH HIGH COMMISSION
The Mall, Gaborone, (Private Bag No. 23)
(Tel. 483–4–5; Cable UKREP, Gaborone)
(Office Hours: 08.30–16.30 Monday–Friday)
High Commissioner: His Excellency Mr G. D. Anderson, C M G
First Secretary and Head of Chancery: W. F. Grieve

BRUNEI
HER MAJESTY'S HIGH COMMISSION
Jalan Residency, Bandar Seri Begawan
(Tel. 2231; Cable HIGHCOMA, Brunei)
(Office Hours: 07.30–12.30 and 13.30–16.00 Monday–Thursday and Saturday)
High Commissioner in the State of Brunei: A. R. Adair, C V O, M B E

CANADA
BRITISH HIGH COMMISSION
80 Elgin Street, Ottawa 4
(Tel. 237–1530; Cable UKREP, Ottawa; Telex 013266)
(Office Hours: 08.30–17.00 Monday–Friday)
High Commissioner: His Excellency Sir Peter Hayman, K C M G, C V O, M B E
Deputy High Commissioner and Minister (Commercial): G. S. Whitehead, C M G, M V O

BRITISH GOVERNMENT OFFICE
Edmonton
Suite 600, Bank of Montreal Building, Jasper Avenue (for Alberta)
(Tel. 424–0481; Cable UKREP Edmonton; Telex 037-2421)
(Office Hours: 09.00–17.15 Monday-Friday)

BRITISH GOVERNMENT OFFICE
Halifax
10th Floor, Centennial Building, 1645 Granville West (for Atlantic Provinces)
(Tel. 422–7488; Cable UKREP, Halifax; Telex 014–42634)
(Office Hours: 09.00–17.00 Monday–Friday)

BRITISH GOVERNMENT OFFICE
Montreal
635 Dorchester Boulevard West, Montreal 2 (for Province of Quebec)
(Tel. 866–5863; Cable UKREP, Montreal; Telex 0126437)
(Office Hours: 09.00–17.00 Monday–Friday)

BRITISH GOVERNMENT OFFICE
Quebec
500 Grande-Allée Est, Suit 707, Quebec 4 P.Q.
(Tel. 525–5187; Cable UKREP, Quebec; Telex 011–246)
(Office Hours: 09.00–17.00 Monday–Friday)

BRITISH GOVERNMENT OFFICE
Regina
8th Floor, 815 Avord Tower, 2002 Victoria Avenue
(Tel. 527–6459 and 527–6350; Cable UKREP, Regina)
(Office Hours: 08.30–17.30 Monday–Friday)

BRITISH GOVERNMENT OFFICE

Toronto

8th Floor, 200 University Avenue
(Tel. 362–1223; Cable UKREP, Toronto; Telex 02–29060)
(Office Hours: 08.30–17.30 Monday–Friday)

BRITISH GOVERNMENT OFFICE

Vancouver

4th Floor, Bank of Nova Scotia Building,
602 West Hastings Street, Vancouver 2
(Tel. 683–4421; Cable UKREP, Vancouver; Telex 045–481)
(Office Hours: 09.00–17.15 Monday–Friday)

BRITISH GOVERNMENT OFFICE

Winnipeg

4th Floor, Monarch Life Building, 333 Broadway Avenue
(Tel. 942–3151; Cable UKREP, Winnipeg; Telex 03–5465)
(Office Hours: 08.30–17.30 Monday–Friday)

BRITISH COUNCIL

c/o British High Commission, 80 Elgin Street, Ottawa 4 (Tel. 237-1530)
(Office Hours: 08.30–17.00 Monday–Friday)
Representative: J. A. Cayton, OBE

CEYLON

BRITISH HIGH COMMISSION

Galle Road, (P.O. Box 1433), Kollupitiya, Colombo 3
(Tel. 27611/8, Cable UKREP, Colombo; Telex 101)
(Office Hours: 08.30–12.30 and 14.00–16.30 Monday–Friday; 08.30–12.30 Saturday)
High Commissioner: His Excellency Mr A. M. MacKintosh, CMG†
Deputy High Commissioner and Counsellor (Commercial): J. W. Nicholas

BRITISH COUNCIL

P.O. Box 753, Steuart Lodge, 154 Galle Road, Colombo 3
Representative: W. R. McAlpine, OBE

REPUBLIC OF CYPRUS

BRITISH HIGH COMMISSION

Alexander Pallis Street, (P.O. Box 1978), Nicosia
(Tel. 73131–7; Cable UKREP Nicosia, Telex 2208 UKREPNIC).
(Office Hours: *1st October–31st May 08.00–12.30 and 14.00–1630 Monday–Friday; 08.00–12.30 Saturday;
*1st June–30th September 07.30–13.30 Monday–Friday; 07.30–12.30 Saturday)
(*Depending on Cyprus Government dates)
High Commissioner: His Excellency Mr R. H. G. Edmonds, CMG, MBE
Counsellor: M. Scott, MVO
British Information Services:
Christodoulos Sozos Street, No. 2, Nicosia
(Tel. 74341–5)

BRITISH COUNCIL

17/19 Archbishop Makarios III Avenue, Nicosia
Representative: R. K. Brady, OBE

FIJI

BRITISH HIGH COMMISSION

Civic Centre, Stinson Parade, (PO Box 1355), Suva
(Tel. 311033)

(Office Hours:)
High Commissioner: His Excellency Mr J. R. Williams
First Secretary and Head of Chancery: J. R. W. Parker, OBE

† Also Ambassador to the Republic of Maldives.

THE GAMBIA

BRITISH HIGH COMMISSION
78 Wellington Street, (P.O. Box 507), Bathurst
(Tel. Bathurst 244/5/6; Cable UKREP, Bathurst)
(Office Hours: 08.00–16.00 Monday–Saturday)
High Commissioner: His Excellency Mr J. G. W. Ramage
First Secretary (Head of Chancery): M. B. Collins, MBE

GHANA

BRITISH HIGH COMMISSION
Barclays Bank Building, High Street (P.O. Box 296), Accra
(Tel. 64651; Cable UKREP, Accra, Telex Accra 239)
(Office Hours: 07.30–13.30 Monday–Friday; 07.30–12.00 Saturday)
(Commercial Section: 07.30–12.00 and 14.00–16.15 Monday–Friday)
High Commissioner: His Excellency Mr H. S. H. Stanley, CMG
Counsellor and Head of Chancery: R. M. Blaikley

BRITISH COUNCIL
Liberty Avenue (P.O. Box 771), Accra
(Tel. 21766–7)
(Office Hours: 08.00–12.15 and 13.30–16.00 Monday–Friday; 08.30–12.00 Saturday)
Representative: H. C. Burrow, OBE

Cape Coast
P.O. Box 324, UAC Building, Jackson Avenue, Cape Coast
(Tel. 2348)
(Office Hours: 08.00–12.15 and 13.30–16.00 Monday–Friday; 08.00–12.00 Saturday)
Regional Director: G. I. Michael, OBE

Kumasi
P.O. Box 1996, Bank Road, Kumasi
(Tel. 3462)
(Office Hours: 09.30–12.30 and 14.30–17.00 Monday–Friday; 08.00–12.00 Saturday)
Regional Director: D. R. Howell

GUYANA

BRITISH HIGH COMMISSION
44 Main Street, (P.O. Box 625), Georgetown
(Tel. 2881–2–3; Cable UKREP, Georgetown)
(Office Hours: 08.00–16.00 Monday–Friday; 08.00–11.30 Saturday)
High Commissioner: His Excellency Mr W. S. Bates CMG
First Secretary and Head of Chancery: R. M. James
Information Section:
Palm Court, Main Street, Georgetown
(Tel. 2881/2/3)

BRITISH COUNCIL
P.O. Box 365, 125 Carmichael Street, Georgetown
(Tel. 4448)
(Office Hours: 08.00–11.30 and 13.00–16.00 Monday–Friday; 08.00–11.30 Saturday)
Representative: J. M. G. Halsted

INDIA

BRITISH HIGH COMMISSION
Chanakyapuri, New Delhi 21
(Tel. 70371; Cable UKREP, New Delhi)
(Office Hours: 09.00–13.00 and 14.30–17.30 Monday–Friday; 09.00–13.00 Saturday)
High Commissioner: His Excellency Sir Terence Garvey, KCMG
Minister: P. J. E. Male, CMG, MC

Calcutta
1 Ho Chi Minh Sarani, Calcutta 16
(Tel. 44–5171–8; Cable UKREP, Calcutta)
(Office Hours: 08.30–12.45 and 14.15–17.00 Monday–Friday; 09.00–13.00 Saturday)
Deputy High Commissioner: F. S. Miles, CMG

Bombay
Mercantile Bank Buildings, P.O. Box 815, Mahatma Gandhi Road, Bombay 1
(Tel. 259952 and 259981/5, Cable UKREP, Bombay)
(Office Hours: 08.45–13.00 and 14.30–17.15 Monday–Friday; 09.00–13.00 Saturday)
Deputy High Commissioner: **M. H. G. Rogers**

Madras
150A Mount Road, (P.O. Box 3710), Madras 2
(Tel. 83136/9; Cable UKREP, Madras)
Office Hours: 08.00–13.00 and 14.00–16.00 Monday –Friday; 09.00–12.30 Saturday)
Deputy High Commissioner: **J. E. A. Miles**, OBE

BRITISH COUNCIL

21 Jor Bagh, New Delhi 3
(Tel. 618341–4)
(Office Hours: 09.00–13.00 and 14.00–17.00 Monday–Friday)
Representative: **S. E. Hodgson**, OBE

Bombay
French Bank Building, Homji Street, Bombay 1
(Tel. 255736/737 and 255743)
(Office Hours: 09.15–13.00 and 14.00–17.15 Monday–Friday; 09.15–13.00 Saturday)
Regional Representative: **Dr D. S. Coombs**

Calcutta
5 Shakespeare Sarani, Calcutta 16
(Tel. 44–5370 and 44–5378/79)
(Office Hours: 09.00–13.00 and 14.00–17.00 Monday-Friday)
Regional Representative: **T. F. S. Scott**

Madras
105A Mount Road, Madras 2
(Tel. 86152–5)
(Office Hours: 07.30–13.20 Monday–Saturday)
Regional Representative: **J. D. L. Hughes**

JAMAICA
BRITISH HIGH COMMISSION
58 Duke Street, (P.O. Box 628), Kingston
(Tel. 22106–10; Cable UKREP, Kingston; Telex 2110 UKREPKIN JA)
(Office Hours: 08.30–16.30 Monday–Friday)
High Commissioner: His Excellency Mr E. N. Larmour, CMG†
Counsellor: Mrs M. B. Chitty

Commercial Section
Barclays Bank Building, King Street, (P.O. Box 393), Kingston
(Tel. 22461–3; Telegraphic Address: BRITCOM, Kingston)
(Office Hours: 08.30–16.30 Monday–Friday; 08.30–12.00 Saturday)

Information Section
6th Floor, Bernard Sunley Building, 32 Duke Street, (P.O. Box 410), Kingston
(Tel. 24135 and 22711; Cable BRITINFORM, Kingston)
(Office Hours: 08.30–16.30 Monday–Friday)

Passport and Entry Certificate Section
111–115 Harbour Street, (P.O. Box 628), Kingston
(Tel. 222106–10)
(Office Hours: 09.00–16.00)

† Also Ambassador to Haiti.

KENYA

BRITISH HIGH COMMISSION
Shell-B.P. Building, Harambee Avenue, (P.O. Box 30465), Nairobi
(Tel. 28001, Nairobi; Telex 20219)
(Office Hours: 08.15–12.30 and 14.00–16.30 Monday–Friday; 08.30–12.30 Saturday)
High Commissioner: His Excellency Sir Eric Norris, KCMG
Deputy High Commissioner and Counsellor (Economic and Commercial):
R. Walker

Commercial Department:
Cotts House, Wabera Street, (P.O. Box 30133), Nairobi
(Tel 28791)

Economic Department:
(P.O. Box 30133)
(Tel. 28001)

Passport Section:
Cotts House, Wabera Street, (P.O. Box 8543), Nairobi
(Tel. 28791)

British Information Services:
(P.O. Box 4779)
(Tel. 25805)

Mombasa
Edinburgh House, Kilindini Road, (P.O. Box 2070), Mombasa
(Tel. 6684)

BRITISH COUNCIL
Kenya Cultural Centre, (P.O. Box 751), College Road, Nairobi
(Tel. 24805)
(Office Hours: 08.00–12.30 and 14.00–16.45 Monday–Friday; 08.00–12.30 Saturday)
Representative: R. A. Hack

Kisumu
P.O. Box 454, Old Barclays Bank Building, Oginga Odinga Road, Kisumu
Director: J. F. Perret

Mombasa
P.O. Box 2590, City House, Nyerere Avenue, Mombasa
Director: P. I. Hill, MBE

LESOTHO

BRITISH HIGH COMMISSION
P.O. Box 521, Maseru
(Tel. 2961; Cable UKREP, Maseru; Telex 2MS Maseru)
(Office Hours: 08.15–12.45 and 14.15–16.45 Monday–Friday)
High Commissioner: His Excellency Mr H. G. M. Bass
First Secretary and Head of Chancery: M. F. Chapman

BRITISH COUNCIL
P.O. Box No. 429, Hobson's Square, Maseru
(Tel. 2609; Cable BRITCOUN, Maseru)
(Office Hours: 08.00–12.45 and 14.00–16.30 Monday–Friday)
Representative: G. C. Thomas

MALAWI

BRITISH HIGH COMMISSION
Victoria Avenue, (P.O. Box 479), Blantyre
(Tel. 8456; Cable UKREP, Blantyre; Telex 5)
(Office Hours: 07.30–12.00 and 13.30–15.30 Monday–Friday; 07.30–12.00 Saturday)
High Commissioner: His Excellency Mr W. R. Haydon, CMG
Deputy High Commissioner and Head of Chancery: H. M. S. Reid

BRITISH COUNCIL
P.O. Box 456, Lalji Kurji Building, Glyn Jones Road, Blantyre
(Tel. 410 and 460)
(Office Hours: 07.30–12.00 and 13.00–16.00 Monday–Friday; 07.30–12.00 Saturday)
Representative: G. C. Thomas

MALAYSIA

BRITISH HIGH COMMISSION
Bangunan Sharikat Polis, (P.O. Box 1030), 1 Jalan Suleiman, Kuala Lumpur
(Tel. 81901; Cable UKREP, Kuala Lumpur)
(Office Hours: 08.00–12.30 and 14.00–16.30 Monday–Friday)
High Commissioner: His Excellency Sir John Johnston, KCMG
Deputy High Commissioner: A. A. Duff, CMG, DSO, DSC

Information Section
Hwa-Li Building, 63–65 Jalan Ampang, Kuala Lumpur
(Tel. 25503)
(Office Hours: 08.00–12.30 and 14.00–16.30 Monday–Friday)

Sarawak
Overseas Chinese Bank Building, Khoo Hun Yeang Street, Kuching
(Tel. 3373; Cable UKREP, Kuching)
(Office Hours: 08.00–12.00 and 13.30–16.30 Monday–Friday)
First Secretary in Charge: E. G. Lewis, OBE

Sabah
Wing-on-Life Building, 1 Chester Street, (P.O. Box 824), Kota Kinabalu
(Tel. Jesselton 4424, 4456 and 4457; Cable UKREP, Kota Kinabalu)
(Office Hours: 08.00–12.00 and 13.45–16.30 Monday–Friday; 08.00–12.00 Saturday)
First Secretary in Charge: G. H. Grubb

BRITISH COUNCIL
Jalan Bluff, (P.O. Box 539), Kuala Lumpur
(Tel. 22601–3; Cable BRITCOUN, Kuala Lumpur)
(Office Hours: 09.00–17.00 Monday–Friday; 09.00–13.00 Saturday)
Representative: J. Goatly, OBE

Penang
87 Bishop Street, (P.O. Box 595), Penang
(Tel. 61152)
(Office Hours: 09.00–17.00 Monday–Friday; 09.00–13.00 Saturday)
Director: K. R. Hunter

Kuching
Sarawak Library Building, Jalan Tun Haji Openg, Kuching, Sarawak
(Tel. 2632 and 2637; Cable BRITCOUN, Kuching)
(Office Hours: 08.30–16.30 Monday–Friday; 08.30–12.30 Saturday)
Regional Representative: L. C. K. Smith

Kota Kinabalu
Wing-on-Life Building, 1st Floor, 1 Chester Street, (P.O. Box 746), Kota Kinabalu, Sabah
(Tel. 4056; Cable BRITCOUN, Kota Kinabalu)
(Office Hours: 08.30–16.30 Monday–Friday; 08.30–12.30 Saturday)
Regional Representative: L. K. S. Lambert

MALTA
BRITISH HIGH COMMISSION
7 St Anne Street, Floriana, Malta, G.C.
(Tel. Central 21285–6–7; Cable UKREP, Floriana)
(Office Hours: October–mid-June 08.30–12.45 and 14.15–1700 Monday–Friday;
08.30–12.45 Saturday; Mid-June–October 08.30–13.30 Monday–Friday; 08.00–12.45
Saturday)
High Commissioner: His Excellency Sir Duncan Watson, KCMG
Deputy High Commissioner: J. S. Arthur

BRITISH COUNCIL
Pjazza Indipendenza, Valletta
(Tel. Central 25038)
(Office Hours: 08.30–12.30 and 14.30–17.30 Monday–Friday; 08.30–12.30. Saturday
(Winter); 08.00–12.30 Saturday (Summer))
Representative: I. P. Allnutt

MAURITIUS
BRITISH HIGH COMMISSION
Cerne House, Chaussee, Port Louis
(Tel. 20201/5 Cable UKREP, Portlouismauritius)
High Commissioner: His Excellency Mr P. A. Carter, CMG
Deputy High Commissioner (Head of Chancery): R. G. Giddens

BRITISH COUNCIL
Royal Road, Rose Hill
(Tel. 4-2034 and 4-2035)
(Office Hours: 0900–1530 Monday–Friday; 0900–1200 Saturday)
Representative: P. J. C. Dart

NEW ZEALAND
BRITISH HIGH COMMISSION
Government Life Insurance Building, Customhouse Quay, (P.O. Box 1812), Wellington C.1
(Tel. 46–060; Cable UKREP, Wellington; Telex NZ 3325)
(Office Hours: 08.45–17.00 Monday–Friday; 09.00–12.30 Saturday)
High Commissioner: His Excellency Sir Arthur Galsworthy, KCMG
Minister (Commercial and Economic): R. A. Daniell, CBE

Auckland
9th Floor, Norwich Union Building, Queen Street, (or Private Bag), Auckland C.1
(Tel. 42–833 and 49–646; Cable UKREP, Auckland)
British Information Services: P.O. Box 2857
(Tel. 48–060; Cable UKIO, Auckland)
Counsellor in Charge: C. E. Dymond, CBE

Christchurch
Bank of New Zealand Building, Corner of Colombo and Hereford Street (or P.O. Box 1762)
Christchurch (Tel. 30–142/3)
First Secretary (Commercial) in Charge: W. J. Rumble

BRITISH COUNCIL
c/o British High Commission, P.O. Box 1812, Government Life Insurance Building,
Customhouse Quay, Wellington, C1.
(Tel. 46–000)
(Office Hours: 08.45–17.00 Monday–Friday; 09.00–12.30 Saturday)
Representative: J. H. Grimes

FEDERAL REPUBLIC OF NIGERIA
BRITISH HIGH COMMISSION
Kajola House, 62–64 Campbell Street, (Private Mail Bag 12136), Lagos
(Tel. 26441; Cable UKREP, Lagos; Telex Lagos 247)
(Office Hours: 08.00–14.00 Monday–Friday; 08.00–12.00 Saturday)
High Commissioner: His Excellency Sir Cyril Pickard, KCMG.
Minister: K. A. East, CMG

Northern Nigeria
United Bank of Africa Building, Hospital Road, (P.M.B. 2096), Kaduna
(Tel. Kaduna 2573; Cable UKREP, Kaduna)
Office Hours: 08.00–14.00 Monday–Thursday; 08.00–13.30 Friday; 08.00–1300 Saturday)
Deputy High Commissioner: The Hon. I. T. M. Lucas

Western Nigeria
Finance Corporation Building, Lebanon Street, (P.M.B. 5010), Ibadan
(Tel. 21551; Cable UKREP, Ibadan)
(Office Hours: 08.00–14.00 Monday–Friday; 08.00–12.00 Saturday)
Deputy High Commissioner: J. A. Pugh, OBE

Mid-western Nigeria
1st Floor, U.A.C. Main Building Premises, Siluko Road, (P.M.B. 1094), Benin City
(Tel. Benin 805)
(Office Hours: 08.00–14.00 Monday–Friday; 08.00–12.00 Saturday)
Deputy High Commissioner: G. D'Arnaud-Taylor, OBE

BRITISH COUNCIL, NIGERIA
P.O. Box 3702, Western House, Yakubu Gowon Street, Lagos
(Tel. 20205; Cable BRITCOUN, Lagos)
(Office Hours: 08.00–14.00 Monday–Friday; 08.00–13.00 Saturday)
Representative: R. A. F. Sherwood

Kaduna
P.O. Box 81, Yakubu Gowon Way, Kaduna
(Tel. 2521)
(Office Hours: 08.00–14.00 Monday–Thursday; 08.00–13.30 Friday; 08.00–13.00 Saturday)
Regional Representative: I. I. L. Watts

Enugu
P.O. Box 330, 15 Ogui Road, Enugu
(Tel. 2005)
(Office Hours: 08.00–14.00 Monday–Friday; 08.00–13.00 Saturday)
Regional Representative: G. W. Shaw

Ibadan
P.M.B. 5103, Dugbe, Ibadan
(Tel. 21354)
(Office Hours: 08.00–14.00 Monday–Friday; 08.00–13.00 Saturday)
Regional Representative: A. P. Weaver

Kano
P.M.B. 3003, Kano City, Kano
(Tel. 2055)
(Office Hours: 07.30–13.30 Monday–Thursday
07.30–13.00 Friday and Saturday)
Regional Representative: K. Nicholson)

PAKISTAN

BRITISH HIGH COMMISSION
Diplomatic Enclave, Ramna 5, (PO Box 1122), Islamabad, West Pakistan
(Tel. 22131/5)
(Office Hours: 07.30–14.00 Monday–Friday; Saturday 08.30–12.30)
High Commissioner: His Excellency Mr J. L. Pumphrey, CMG
Deputy High Commissioner: R. A. Burrows, CMG

Dacca
D.I.T. Building, Dilkusha, (P.O. Box 90), Dacca, 2
(Tel. 43251–3/44216–7)
(Office Hours: 08.00–14.00 Monday–Friday; 08.00–12.30 Saturday)
Deputy High Commissioner: R. G. Britten
Information Centre and Reading Room
14/2 Topkhana Road, Dacca 2

Karachi
Finlay House, McLeod Road, Karachi
(Tel. 230921–8)
(Office Hours: 08.00–12.30 and 14.00–16.30 Monday–Thursday;
08.00–12.30 Friday–Saturday)
Deputy High Commissioner: A. J. Brown

British Information Services:
Finlay House, MacLeod Road
(Tel. 222641)
and
Mandviwalla Chambers, Wood Street
(Tel. 221316–7 and 221307)

Lahore
4 Racecourse Road, P.O. Box 416, Lahore
(Tel. 60141)
(Office Hours: April–September, 07.30–13.00 Monday–Saturday; September–April, 08.00–
12.30 and 14.00–16.30 Monday–Friday; 09.00–12.30 Saturday)
Deputy High Commissioner: P. R. Oliver, CMG
Commercial Division: Gardee Trust Building, Napier Road
(Tel. 62266)

BRITISH COUNCIL
P.O. Box 47, 56–A Satellite Town, Rawalpindi
(Tel. 6439 and 63141; Cable BRICOUNCIL, Rawalpindi)
(Office Hours: April–September, 07.30–13.00 Monday–Saturday; September–April, 08.00–
13.30 Monday–Saturday)
Representative: D. A. Smith, OBE
Deputy Representative: E. J. Rayner

Lahore
32–A Mozang Road, P.O. Box 88
(Tel. 2337 and 2338)
(Office Hours: April–September, 07.30–13.00 Monday–Saturday; September–April, 08.00–
13.30 Monday–Saturday)
Regional Representative: D. D. Reid

Dacca
P.O. Box 161, 5 Sir Syed Ahmed Road, Ramna, Dacca 2
(Tel. 43356, 45383, 46743 (Library))
(Office Hours: 08.00–13.30 Monday–Friday; 08.00–12.30 Saturday)
Regional Representative: P. B. Naylor

Karachi
P.O. Box 146, 6–10 Sarnagati Building, Pakistan Chowk, Karachi 1
(Tel. 225551–3 and 230172)
(Office Hours: 08.00–13.30 Monday–Friday; 08.00–12.30 Saturday)
Regional Representative: C. Somerville

Peshawar
P.O. Box 49, 35(M) The Mall
(Tel. 2756)
Director: C. P. Carter

SIERRA LEONE

BRITISH HIGH COMMISSION
Standard Bank of West Africa Building, Oxford Street, Freetown
(Tel. 3961–6; Cable UKREP, Freetown)
(Office Hours: 08.00–14.00 Monday–Friday; 08.00–12.00 Saturday)
High Commissioner: His Excellency Mr S. J. L. Olver, CMG, MBE
Deputy High Commissioner: J. Brasnett

Information Section
4th Floor, Leone House, Westmoreland Street, Freetown
(Tel. 4096; Cable UKREP, Freetown)
(Office Hours: 08.00–14.00 Monday–Friday; 08.00–12.00 Saturday)

BRITISH COUNCIL
P.O. Box 124, Tower Hill, Freetown
(Tel. 2223)
(Office Hours: 08.00–16.00 Monday–Friday; 08.00–12.00 Saturday)
Representative: J. A. B. Smith

SINGAPORE

BRITISH HIGH COMMISSION
Maritime Building, Collyer Quay, Singapore 1
(Tel. 95011; Cable UKREP, Singapore)
High Commissioner: His Excellency Mr S. Falle, CMG, DSC
Counsellor: W. J. Watts, OBE

British Information Services:
Clifford House, Collyer Quay, Singapore 1
(Tel. 79108)
(Office Hours: 08.30–12.30 and 14.00–14.30 Monday, Tuesday, Thursday and Friday;
08.30–13.00 Wednesdays and Saturdays)

BRITISH COUNCIL
Amber Mansions, 1a Orchard Road, Singapore 9
(Tel. 26145)
(Office Hours: 09.00–16.30 Monday–Friday; 09.00–13.00 Saturday)
Representative: T. J. Rutter

SWAZILAND

BRITISH HIGH COMMISSION
Allister Miller Street, Mbabane
High Commissioner: His Excellency Mr P. Gautrey, CVO
Head of Chancery: A. G. Elgar, OBE

UNITED REPUBLIC OF TANZANIA

BRITISH HIGH COMMISSION
Permanent House, Independence Avenue, P.O. Box 9200, Dar-es-Salaam
(Tel. 23366–9; Cable UKREP, Dar-es-Salaam)
High Commissioner: His Excellency Mr Horace Phillips, CMG
Counsellor and Head of Chancery: M. K. Ewans

BRITISH COUNCIL
P.O. Box 9100, Independence Avenue, Dar-es-Salaam
(Tel. 21955)
(Office Hours: 08.00–12.30 and 14.00–16.30 Monday–Friday; 08.00–12.30 Saturday)
Representative: W. M. Emslie, OBE

Moshi
P.O. Box 426, Boma Road, Moshi
Regional Director: Miss J. H. Malcolm

TONGA

BRITISH HIGH COMMISSION
Nuku'alofa
High Commissioner: His Excellency Sir Arthur Galsworthy, KCMG
(Resides in Wellington, New Zealand)
Deputy High Commissioner (and Consul for Pacific Islands under United States
Sovereignty South of the Equator): H. A. Arthington-Davy, OBE

TRINIDAD AND TOBAGO
BRITISH HIGH COMMISSION
4th Floor, Furness House, 90 Independence Square, (P.O. Box 778), Port of Spain
(Tel. 52861–6; Cable UKREP, Port of Spain; Telex 52342)
(Office Hours: 08.30–16.30 Monday–Friday; 08.30–12.30 Saturday)
High Commissioner: His Excellency Mr R. C. C. Hunt, CMG
Deputy High Commissioner and Counsellor (Commercial): B. A. F. Pennock, OBE

UGANDA
BRITISH HIGH COMMISSION
10–12 Obote Avenue, (P.O. Box 7070), Kampala
(Tel. 57054–59; Cable UKREP, Kampala, Telex 4106)
(Office Hours: 08.00–12.30 and 14.00–16.30 Monday–Friday)
High Commissioner: His Excellency Mr R. M. K. Slater, CMG
Deputy High Commissioner and Counsellor (Commercial): A. H. Brind

BRITISH COUNCIL
P.O Box 7014, National Cultural Centre, Kampala
(Tel. 4230 and 56350)
(Office Hours: 08.15–12.45 and 14.00–1600 Monday–Friday; 08.30–12.00 Saturday)
Representative: A. G. Hamer, MBE

Fort Portal
Plot 31, Delhi Street, P.O. Box 28
(Tel. 115)
Regional Director: W. M. Snee

WEST INDIES ASSOCIATED STATES
OFFICE OF THE BRITISH GOVERNMENT REPRESENTATIVE
The George Gordon Building, Bourbon Street, (P.O. Box 227), Castries, St Lucia,
West Indies
(Tel. 2482; Cable UKREP, Castries, St Lucia)
British Government Representative: J. E. Marnham, CMG, MC, TD
Deputy British Government Representative: R. A. R. Barltrop

ZAMBIA
BRITISH HIGH COMMISSION
Waddington Road, (P.O. Box R.W. 50), Lusaka
(Tel. Lusaka 51122; Cable UKREP, Lusaka; Telex 4115)
(Office Hours: 07.45–16.00 Monday–Friday; 07.45–12.30 Saturday)
High Commissioner: His Excellency Mr J. S. R. Duncan, CMG, MBE
Counsellor (Economic and Commercial): C. E. Diggines
Information Section: Codrington Street, P.O. Box 1918, Lusaka
(Tel. Lusaka 72946)

BRITISH COUNCIL
P.O. Box 3571, Grosvenor Court, Cairo Road, Lusaka
(Tel. 82120)
(Office Hours: 08.00–13.00 and 14.00–16.30 Monday–Friday; 08.00–12.00 Saturday)
Regional Director: J. Lawrence

Ndola
P.O. Box 415, Capital House, Buteko Avenue, Ndola
Regional Director: D. M. Waterhouse

REPRESENTATIVES IN BRITAIN
OF OTHER COMMONWEALTH COUNTRIES

COMMONWEALTH OF AUSTRALIA
Australia House, Strand WC2
(01–836 2435)
High Commissioner: His Excellency the Hon. Sir Alexander Downer, KBE
Deputy High Commissioner: R. W. Boswell, OBE
Deputy High Commissioner: W. B. Pritchett
Official Secretary: W. R. Cumming, CVO
Head, Australian Defence Staff and Defence Adviser: Rear Admiral G. V. Gladstone, DSC
Special Commercial Adviser: F. P. Donovan
Economic Adviser (Treasury): I. Castles
Australian Army Adviser Brigadier L. I. Hopton, MBE
Australian Naval Adviser: Commodore K. D. Gray, DFC
Australian Air Adviser: Air Commodore E. W. Tonkin, OBE
Scientific Adviser: Dr. E. G. Hallsworth
Public Service Board Representative: T. F. Paterson
Atomic Energy Adviser: R. M. Fry
Senior Representative, Department of Supply: R. S. McIntyre
Migration Adviser: R. F. Harris
Medical Adviser: Dr. B. E. Welton
Adviser: P. G. M. Gilbert
Postal Services Adviser: J. M. Ryan
Customs and Excise Adviser: B. A. Bissaker
Public Relations Adviser: R. D. Harris
Audit Adviser: C. A. Harrington
Taxation Adviser: J. W. Toolin
Civil Aviation Adviser: F. E. Parker
Education Adviser: D. W. Hood
Chief Purchasing Officer: R. Suzor
Chief Finance Officer: R. V. Hutchinson, MBE

AGENTS-GENERAL FOR THE AUSTRALIAN STATES

NEW SOUTH WALES
56–57 Strand, WC2
(01–839 6651)
Agent-General: Sir John Pagan, CMB MBE E G KB
Official Secretary: W. A. Butterfield

VICTORIA
Victoria House, Melbourne Place, Strand WC2
(01–836 2656)
Agent-General: Hon. Sir Murray Porter
Official Secretary: J. N. McAuley

QUEENSLAND
392–3 Strand, WC2
(01–836 3224)
Agent-General: N. C. Seeney
Official Secretary: B. A. Putnam

SOUTH AUSTRALIA
South Australia House, 50 Strand, WC2
(01–930 7471)
Agent-General: R. C. Taylor
Official Secretary: A. N. Deane

WESTERN AUSTRALIA
Savoy House, 115 Strand, WC2
(01–240 2881)
Agent-General: Hon. W. S. Bovell
Official Secretary: F. W. G. Andersen

TASMANIA
458–9 Strand, WC2
(01–839 2291)
Agent-General: R. R. Neville
Official Secretary: R. J. Garrad, OBE

BARBADOS
6 Upper Belgrave Street, SW1
(235-8686-9)
High Commissioner: (Vacant)
Deputy High Commissioner: S. C. Corbin
Counsellor: F. Brewster

BOTSWANA
3 Buckingham Gate, SW1
(01–828 0445)
High Commissioner: Her Excellency Miss G. K. T. Chiepe, MBE
First Secretary: B. M. Setshogo
Second Secretary: M. T. Modisanyane

CANADA
Canada House, Trafalgar Square, SW1
(01–930 9741)

Commercial Section
Macdonald House, 1 Grosvenor Square, W1
(01–629 9492)
High Commissioner: His Excellency Mr C. S. A. Ritchie
Deputy High Commissioner: R. L. Rogers
Minister (Commercial): C. G. van Tighem
Minister-Counsellor (Economic): R. M. Tait
Counsellor (Commercial): I. R. Smyth
Counsellor (Administration): F. M. Meech
Counsellor: A. D. Small
Counsellor: D. R. Hill
Counsellor: A. Potvin
Counsellor: J. W. Graham
Counsellor: D. M. Miller
Counsellor (Information/Cultural): I. C. Clark
Attaché: M. K. Nelles
Counsellor (Agricultural): G. E. Blackstock
Counsellor (Commercial): K. D. Taylor
Counsellor (Commercial): T. D. McGee
Counsellor: A. de W. Mathewson
Commander. Canadian Defence Liaison Staff: Brigadier – General D. W. Cunnington, GM

AGENTS-GENERAL FOR THE CANADIAN PROVINCES

ALBERTA
Alberta House, 37 Hill Street, W1
(01–499 3061)
Agent-General: Rene Albert McMullen

BRITISH COLUMBIA
British Columbia House, 1–3 Regent
Street, SW1
(01–930 6857)
Agent-General: Rear Admiral Michael
Grote Stirling

ONTARIO
Ontario House, 13 Charles II Street,
SW1
(01–930 6404)
Agent-General: A. A. Rowan-Legg

QUEBEC
12 Upper Grosvenor Street, W1
(01–629 4155)
Agent-General: Guy Roberge

SASKATCHEWAN
28 Chester Street, Belgrave Square, SW
(01–235 1871)
Agent-General: Frederick H. Larson

NOVA SCOTIA
60 Trafalgar Square, WC2
(01–930 6864)
Agent-General: Charles A. Richardson

NEW BRUNSWICK
60 Trafalgar Square, WC2
(01–930 6881)
Agent-General: John A. Paterson

CEYLON
13 Hyde Park Gardens, W2
(01–262 1841–7)
High Commissioner: His Excellency T. E.
Gooneratne
Deputy High Commissioner: J. J. G.
Amirthanayagam
First Secretaries: A. Nesaratnam, S.
Gautamadasa
Trade Commissioner: S. C. A. Nanayakkara
First Secretary (Information): D. L. D.
Samarasekera
Second Secretary: W. M. G. Abeyaratne
Commercial Attaché: Mrs M. V. Aranwela

CYPRUS
93 Park Street, W1
(01–499 8272)
High Commissioner: His Excellency Mr
Costas Ashiotis, MBE
Counsellor: D. Papasavvas
First Secretary: A. Vakis
Commercial Counsellor: M. R. Erotokritos
Cultural Attaché: P. Vanezis
Welfare Attachés: A. Savvides; Hussein Siret
Administration Attaché: Munir Essel

FIJI
25 Upper Brook Street, W.1.
(01–493 6516/9)
High Commissioner: His Excellency Josua
R. Rabukawaqa, MVO, MBE
Counsellor: K. R. Bain
Private Secretary to the High Commissioner:
Mrs K. R. Bain
Second Secretary: Mrs A. V. Dreunamisimisi

THE GAMBIA
The Gambia House, 28 Kensington Court,
W8
(01–937 0800)
High Commissioner His Excellency Mr.
B. O. Semega-Janneh, MBE
First Secretary: O. A. Sallah
Second Secretary: Abdou Janha

GHANA
13 Belgrave Square, SW1
(01–235 4142)
High Commissioner: His Excellency Mr
A. B. Attafua
Deputy High Commissioner: S. A. Sykes
Head of Chancery: K. F. Prah
Counsellors: G. R. Nipah (Welfare)
J. A. Brobbey (Economic)
G. O. Lamptey (Political)
Director of Education: W. L. Tsitsiwu
Director of Recruitment: W. K. Djan
Trade Commissioner (Acting): Issac Dakwa
Defence Adviser: Col (AF) O. K. Bonsu
Press Attaché: Henry Thompson

GUYANA
28 Cockspur Street, SW1
(01–930 1994/5/6)
High Commissioner: His Excellency Mr
John Carter, SC
Deputy High Commissioner: P. A. Thierens
First Secretary (Commercial): Ashik Altaf
Mohamed
First Secretary (Consular): A. N. Storey
Second Secretary (Information and Educa-
tion): R. E. Chandisingh
Attaché: D. T. Wray

INDIA
India House, Aldwych, WC2
(01–836 8484)
High Commissioner: His Excellency Mr
Apa B. Pant
Deputy High Commissioner: P. N. Kaul
Minister (Economic): B. D. Jayal
Counsellor: I. Singh
Counsellor: A. Madhavan
Minister (Educational and Scientific Affairs):
A. J. Kidwai
Military Adviser: Maj. Gen. Amreek Singh
Naval Adviser: Commodore N. P. Datta
Air Adviser: Air Commodore H. K. Bose
Minister (Accounts Adviser): A. Mozoomdar
Ordnance Consulting Officer: Brigadier
S. G. Payara
First Secretary (Commercial): Surendra
Singh
Legal Adviser: N. L. Vaidyanathan
Public Relations Officer: M. R.
Sivaramakrishnan
First Secretary (Protocol): V. P. Marwah
First Secretary (Shipping): S. Bannerjee
First Secretary (Consular): S. L. Kaul

JAMAICA
48 Grosvenor Street, W.1.
(01–499 8600)

High Commissioner: His Excellency Sir Laurence Lindo, CMG
Deputy High Commissioner: R. E. K. Philips
Deputy High Commissioner: J. K. M. Pringle
Counsellor: K. G. A. Hill
Legal Attaché: A. E. Alberga
First Secretaries: D. O'N. Lindsay (Commercial); D. E. Davidson

KENYA
45 Portland Place, W1
(01–636 2371–5)

High Commissioner: His Excellency Mr Ng'ethe Njoroje
Counsellor: O. A. Fakih
First Secretary: J. B. K. Mwaura
Commercial Attaché: W. A. Kisiero
Press Attaché: S. L. Muhanji

LESOTHO
16A St James's Street, SW1
(01–839 1154)

High Commissioner: His Excellency Chief C. M. Molapo
Counsellor: T. E. Ntlhakana
Third Secretary: B. C. Mokhele

MALAWI
47 Great Cumberland Place, W1
(01–723 6021–3)

High Commissioner: His Excellency Mr B. W. Katenga

MALAYSIA
45 Belgrave Square, SW1
(01–245 9221/5)

Trade Section: Malaysia House,
57 Trafalgar Square, WC2
(01–930 9837)

Education Section: Malaysia Hall,
44–46 Bryanston Square, W1
(01–723 2265)

High Commissioner: His Excellency Tan Sri Aziz Bin Yeop
Deputy High Commissioner: J. D. de Silva, KMN
Information Attaché (Minister): Soon Cheng Hor
Services Adviser: Brigadier General Ungku Ahmad bin Abdul Rahman
Counsellor and Head of Chancery: Razali bin Ismail
Trade Commissioner: Burhanuddin bin Mohd. Saman Rais
Education Adviser: Chang Min Kee

MALTA, G.C.
Malta House, 24 Haymarket, SW1
(01–930 9851)

High Commissioner: His Excellency Mr Arthur J. Scerri
Deputy High Commissioner: H. Borg Cardona

First Secretary: P. P. Vassallo
First Secretary: E. Gerada Azzopardi
Second Secretary: G. N. Busuttil
Second Secretary: M. Mallia
Second Secretary: C. Sammut
Second Secretary: M. J. Lubrano

MAURITIUS
Mezzanine Suite, Grand Buildings,
Trafalgar Square, WC2
(01–930 2895/6)

High Commissioner: His Excellency Dr L. Teelock, CBE
Second Secretary: D. G. Facknath

NEW ZEALAND
New Zealand House, Haymarket, SW1
(01–930 8422)

High Commissioner: His Excellency Sir Denis Blundell, KBE
Deputy High Commissioner: R. M. Miller
Minister: N. V. Farrell
Counsellor (Economic): E. Farnon
First Secretary: J. D. L. Richards
Head, New Zealand Defence Liaison Staff, Naval Liaison Officer and Defence Adviser: Commodore E. C. Thorne
Deputy Head of Defence Liaison Staff, Army Liaison Officer and Assistant Defence Adviser: Colonel H. L. Jones
Deputy Head of Defence Liaison Staff, Air Liaison Officer, and Assistant Defence Adviser: Group Capt. A. F. Tucker, DFC
Administrative Secretary: B. R. Finny
Minister (Commercial) and Senior Trade Commissioner: A. E. Monaghan
First Secretary (Commercial): J. D. Kerr
Financial Secretary: R. G. de Jardine
Public Relations Officer: G. W. Symmans
Chief Migration Officer: R. D. G. Nicholson
Scientific Adviser: Dr V. Armstrong
Customs Adviser: S. G. Marshall
Agricultural Adviser: G. J. Batten
Inspector of Dairy Products: I. Willis
Tourist Adviser: W. F. Bern
Veterinary Adviser: Dr A. Ginsberg

NIGERIA
Nigeria House, 9 Northumberland Avenue WC2
(01–839 1244)

High Commissioner: His Excellency Mr Sule Dede Kolo
Deputy High Commissioner: J. A. O. Akadiri
Counsellor and Head of Chancery: Isa Modibo
Counsellor (Information): Magaji Dambatta
Counsellor (Education): C. C. Uchuno
First Secretary (Consular): J. Ogunkeye
First Secretary (Political): A. Adekuoye
First Secretary (Commercial): U. K. Bello
First Secretary (Recruitment and Establishment): P. C. Omilegan
Financial Attaché: S. L. Alli
Defence Adviser: Lt.-Col. B. M. Usman

B

PAKISTAN
35 Lowndes Square, London SW1
(01-235 2044)
High Commissioner: His Excellency Mr Salman A. Ali, SQA
Deputy High Commissioner: Selimuz Zaman, SK TPk
Minister: Dr Maqbool Ahmad Bhatty, TPk
Economic Minister: A. F. M. Ehasanul Kabir
Counsellor: Bakhtiar Ali
Counsellor: Rao Abdur Rashid Khan
Head of Military Mission and Naval Adviser: Commodore L. N. Mungavin, SK
Air Adviser: Group Captain Mohammed Aslam
Press Counsellor: Abdul Qayyum, TQA
Education Counsellor: Tanvir Ahmad Khan
Commercial Counsellor: (Vacant)
First Secretaries: M. M. Rezaul Karim; Mujahid Husain; M. Sarwar Khan
Army Adviser: Colonel Agha Asad Raza Khan
Pakistan Army Technical Liaison Officer: Colonel Mirza M. Siddique
Attaché, Defence Procurement: Commander Tajammul Hossain
Technical Attaché: S. A. Hussain
Labour Attaché: Aga Kamran
Director of Audit and Accounts: M. A. L. Matin

SIERRA LEONE
33 Portland Place, W1
(01-636 6483-6)
(01-636 0400: Information only)
High Commissioner: (Vacant)
Counsellor: H. M. Lynch-Shyllon
First Secretary: S. M. Jonjo
First Secretary: S. K. Bart-Williams
Information Attaché: John Bankole-Jones
Education Attaché: E. J. Gabbidon
Recruitment Attaché: M. Munu
Trade Attaché: S. G. Carew (Acting)
Financial Attaché: A. C. O. Hollist

SINGAPORE
2 Wilton Crescent, SW1
(01-235 8315/8)
Student's Department:
16 Northumberland Avenue, WC2
(01-839 5061/2)
High Commissioner: His Excellency Dr Lee Yong Leng
Counsellor: Anthony Tan Song Chuan

SWAZILAND
58 Pont Street, SW1)
(01-589 5447/8
High Commissioner: His Excellency Dr A. B. Gamedze

TANZANIA
43 Hertford Street, Mayfair, W1
(01-499 8951)
High Commissioner: His Excellency Mr P. P. Muro

TONGA
New Zealand House, 17th Floor, Haymarket, SW1
(01-839 3287)
High Commissioner: His Excellency Baron Vaea
First Secretary: D. Tupou

TRINIDAD AND TOBAGO
42 Belgrave Square, SW1
(01-245 9351)
High Commissioner: His Excellency Dr P. V. J. Solomon
Deputy High Commissioner: E. Seignoret
Information Attaché: A. Charles
First Secretary: C. Alleyne
First Secretary: Mrs L. S. Dorset

UGANDA
Uganda House, Trafalgar Square, WC2
(01-839 1963)
High Commissioner: His Excellency Lieutenant-Colonel S. E. Lukakamwa, Paul O. Etiang
Counsellor (Commercial): S. M. Musoke
Counsellor (Education): J. C. Katuramu

ZAMBIA
7-11 Cavendish Place, W1
(01-580 0691)
High Commissioner: His Excellency The Hon. Ammock Israel Phiri, MP
Deputy High Commissioner: P. W. Lumbi
Trade Commissioner: E. S. Kapotwe

GOVERNMENT OFFICES IN LONDON

BRUNEI GOVERNMENT AGENCY

101 Grand Buildings, Trafalgar Square, WC2 (01–839 1355)

Agent: Sir Dennis White, KBE, CMG, DK

6, GRAFTON ST, LONDON WIX 3LB

HONG KONG GOVERNMENT OFFICE

~~54 Pall Mall, S.W.1 (01–839 6721)~~ *499 – 9821*

Administrative Commissioner for the Government of Hong Kong in London:
A. M. J. Wright, CMG
Assistant Commissioner (Commercial): D. M. Sellers

The principal function of the office is to liaise with H.M. Government Departments on matters of concern to Hong Kong. It has sections dealing with Commercial Relations, the Hong Kong Chinese Community in Britain, Students from Hong Kong, the Training in Britain of Hong Kong Government Officers and the Dissemination of Information.

THE COMMISSION IN THE UNITED KINGDOM FOR THE EASTERN CARIBBEAN GOVERNMENTS

Kings House, 10 Haymarket, S.W.1 (01–930 7902/4)

Commissioner: N. G. F. Taylor, CMG, JP

The Associated States of Antigua, Dominica, Grenada, St Kitts-Nevis-Anguilla St Lucia and St Vincent with the Government of Montserrat have established an office in London. It is concerned with:—

(a) the furthering of commercial, economic, cultural and scientific relations with the United Kingdom; and

(b) representing and safeguarding the interests of Nationals of the Associated States whether as individuals or bodies corporate.

GOVERNMENT TOURIST, TRADE AND TRAVEL AGENCIES IN LONDON

BAHAMAS MINISTRY OF TOURISM

23 Old Bond Street, W.1 (01–629 5238)

Regional Sales Manager: Robert E. Duffett

The Primary function of this office is to promote tourism and give information to intending visitors to the Bahama Islands.

BERMUDA TRAVEL INFORMATION OFFICE

Sackville House, 40 Piccadilly, W1V 0NU (01–734 1412/3)

Manager: M. F. Gregg

The office is maintained by the Department of Tourism and Trade Development; the Department of the Bermuda Government responsible for the development of the tourist trade. The Department, which also maintains information offices in the United States and Canada, first established an office in London in 1925. The purpose of the office is to assist the development of the tourist trade and to provide intending visitors and travel agents with information and literature about Bermuda. Limited information is also available on exempted companies and banking facilities.

GIBRALTAR TOURIST OFFICE
15 Grand Buildings, Trafalgar Square, W.C.2 (01–930 2284)

HONG KONG TRADE DEVELOPMENT COUNCIL
55/58 Pall Mall, S.W.1 (01–930 7955)
Representative: F. McKellar

The office is responsible for activities on behalf of the Hong Kong Trade Development Council designed to assist promotion of Hong Kong exports to the United Kingdom.

CHRONOLOGICAL LIST OF BRITISH HIGH COMMISSIONERS AND REPRESENTATIVES IN OTHER COMMONWEALTH COUNTRIES

AUSTRALIA
REPRESENTATIVE
1931. (May) E. T. Crutchley, CB, CMG, OBE.

HIGH COMMISSIONERS
1936. (March) Sir Geoffrey Whiskard, KCMG, CB (later KCB).
1941. (July) Sir Ronald Cross, Bt., PC, MP (later KCVO).
1946. (July) E. J. Williams, PC (later Sir Edward Williams, KCMG).
1952. (October) Sir Stephen Holmes, KCMG, MC.
1956. (November) Peter Alexander Rupert Carrington, MC, 6th Baron Carrington (later KCMG).
1959. (November) Lieutenant-General Sir William Oliver, KCB, OBE, DL (later GBE, KCMG).
1965. (June) Sir Charles Johnston, KCMG.
1971. (April) The Rt Hon. Sir Morrice James, KCMG, CVO, MBE.

BARBADOS
HIGH COMMISSIONERS
1966. (November) J. S. Bennett, CVO, CBE.
1971. (March) D. A. Roberts.

BOTSWANA
HIGH COMMISSIONERS
1966. (September) J. S. Gandee, CMG, OBE.
1969. (November) G. D. Anderson, CMG

BRUNEI
HIGH COMMISSIONERS
1963. (December) E. O. Laird, MBE, (later CMG).
1965. (July) F. D. Webber, CMG, MC, TD.
1968. (May) A. R. Adair, CVO, MBE.

CANADA
HIGH COMMISSIONERS
1928. (September) Sir William Clark, KCSI, KCMG (later GCMG).
1935. (January) Sir Francis Floud, KCB, KCMG (later KCSI).
1938. (October) Sir Gerald Campbell, KCMG (later GCMG).
1941. (April) Malcolm MacDonald, PC, MP.
1946. (May) Sir Alexander Clutterbuck, GCMG, MC.
1952. (August) Lieutenant-General Sir Archibald Nye, GCSI, GCMG, GCIE, KCB, KBE, MC.
1956. (November) Sir Saville Garner, KCMG (later GCMG).
1961. (October) Derick Heathcoat-Amory, 1st Viscount Amory, PC, GCMG.
1963. (October) Sir Henry Lintott, KCMG.
1968. (September) Sir Colin Crowe, KCMG.
1970. (October) P. T. Hayman, CMG, CVO, MBE (later Sir Peter Hayman, KCMG).

CEYLON
HIGH COMMISSIONERS
1948. (January) Sir Walter Hankinson, KCMG, OBE, MC.
1951. (October) Sir Cecil Syers, KCMG, CVO.
1957. (December) A. F. Morley, CMG, CBE (later Sir Alexander Morley, KCMG).
1962. (November) C. M. Walker, CMG (later Sir Michael Walker, KCMG).
1966. (March) F. S. Tomlinson, CMG (later Sir Stanley Tomlinson, KCMG).
1969. (March) A. M. Mackintosh, CMG.

REPUBLIC OF CYPRUS
REPRESENTATIVE
1960. (August) W. A. W. Clark, CMG, CBE (later Sir Arthur Clark, KCMG).
COUNSELLOR
1960. (August) I. F. Porter, OBE (later CMG).
HIGH COMMISSIONERS
1961. (March) W. A. W. Clark, CMG, CBE (later Sir Arthur Clark, KCMG).
1964. (April) Major-General W. H. A. Bishop, CB, CMG, CVO, OBE (later Major-General Sir Alec Bishop, KCMG).
1965. (April) Sir David Hunt, KCMG, OBE.
1967. (January) Sir Norman Costar, KCMG.
1969. (April) The Hon. P. E. Ramsbotham, CMG
1971. (June) R. H. G. Edmonds, CMG, MBE.

FIJI
HIGH COMMISSIONER
1970. (October) J. R. Williams.

THE GAMBIA
HIGH COMMISSIONERS
1965. (February) G. E. Crombie, CMG.
1968. (January) J. G. W. Ramage.

GHANA
HIGH COMMISSIONERS
1957. (March) Sir Ian Maclennan, KCMG.
1959. (September) A. W. Snelling, CMG (later Sir Arthur Snelling, KCMG, KCVO).
1961. (December) Sir Geoffrey de Freitas, KCMG.
1964. (January) H. Smedley, MBE (later CMG).
1967. (December) H. K. Matthews, CMG, MBE.
1970. (November) H. S. H. Stanley, CMG.

GUYANA
HIGH COMMISSIONERS
1966. (May) T. L. Crosthwaite, CMG, MBE.
1967. (August) K. G. Ritchie, CMG.
1970. (November) W. S. Bates, CMG.

INDIA
HIGH COMMISSIONERS
1946. (November) Sir Terence Shone, KCMG.
1948. (October) Lieutenant-General Sir Archibald Nye, GCSI, GCMG, GCIE, KCB, KBE, MC.
1952. (October) Sir Alexander Clutterbuck, GCMG, MC.
1955. (September) Malcolm MacDonald, PC.
1960. (November) Sir Paul Gore-Booth, KCMG (later GCMG, KCVO).
1965. (April) Rt Hon. J. Freeman, MBE.
1968. (October) The Rt Hon. Sir Morrice James, KCMG, CVO, MBE.
1971. (April) Sir Terence Garvey, KCMG.

JAMAICA
HIGH COMMISSIONERS
1962. (August) Sir Alexander Morley, KCMG, CBE.
1965. (May) J. D. Murray, CMG.
1970. (April) E. N. Larmour, CMG

KENYA
REPRESENTATIVE
1963. (June) H. S. H. Stanley.

HIGH COMMISSIONERS
1963. (December) Sir Geoffrey de Freitas, KCMG.
1965. (February) Malcolm MacDonald, PC.
1966. (March) Sir Edward Peck, KCMG.
1968. (September) E. G. Norris, CMG (later Sir Eric Norris, KCMG).

LESOTHO
HIGH COMMISSIONERS
1966. (October) I. B. Watt, CMG.
1970. (May) H. G. M. Bass.

MALAWI
HIGH COMMISSIONERS
1964. (July) D. L. Cole, MC (later CMG).
1967. (October) T. S. Tull, CBE, DSO.
1971. (April) W. R. Haydon, CMG.

MALAYA
HIGH COMMISSIONER
1957. (August) G. W. Tory, CMG (later Sir Geofroy Tory, KCMG) *see* Malaysia
below).

MALAYSIA
HIGH COMMISSIONERS
1963. (September) Sir Geofroy Tory, KCMG.
1963. (November) Anthony Henry Head, 1st Viscount Head, PC, GCMG, CBE,
MC.
1966. (January) Sir Michael Walker, KCMG.
1971. (March) Sir John Johnston, KCMG.

MALTA
HIGH COMMISSIONERS
1964. (September) Sir Edward Wakefield, Bt., CIE.
1965. (January) Sir John Martin, KCMG, CB, CVO.
1967. (February) Sir Geofroy Tory, KCMG.
1970. (March) Sir Duncan Watson, KCMG.

MAURITIUS
HIGH COMMISSIONER
1968. (March) A. Wooller, CBE.
1970. (September) P. A. Carter, CMG.

NEW ZEALAND
HIGH COMMISSIONERS
1939. (March) Sir Harry Batterbee, KCMG, KCVO (later GCMG).
1945. (July) Sir Patrick Duff, KCB, KCVO.
1949. (September) Sir Roy Price, KCMG.
1953. (September) General Sir Geoffry Scoones, KCB, KBE, CSI, DSO, MC.
1957. (May) H. G. C. Mallaby, CMG, OBE (later Sir George Mallaby, KCMG.)
1959. (December) The Hon. F. E. Cumming-Bruce, CMG (later The Hon. Sir
Francis Cumming-Bruce, KCMG).
1964. (March) Sir Ian Maclennan, KCMG.
1969. (October) Sir Arthur Galsworthy, KCMG.

NIGERIA
HIGH COMMISSIONERS
1960. (October) Anthony Henry Head, 1st Viscount Head, PC, CBE, MC (later
GCMG).
1964. (February) The Hon. Sir Francis Cumming-Bruce, KCMG.
1967. (February) Sir David Hunt, KCMG, OBE.
1969. (June) Sir Leslie Glass, KCMG.
1971. (July) Sir Cyril Pickard, KCMG.

PAKISTAN
HIGH COMMISSIONERS
1947. (August) Sir Laurence Grafftey-Smith, KBE (later KCMG).
1951. (August) Sir Gilbert Laithwaite, KCMG, KCIE, CSI (later GCMG, KCB).
1954. (December) Sir Alexander Symon, KCMG, OBE (later KCVO).
1961. (October) J. M. C. James, CMG, CVO, MBE (later Sir Morrice James, KCMG).
1966. (February) C. S. Pickard, CMG (later Sir Cyril Pickard, KCMG).
1971. (June) J. L. Pumphrey, CMG.

RHODESIA
(Following the illegal Declaration of Independence on 11th November 1965, the High Commission was closed. A residual staff remained, but they were finally withdrawn on 14th July 1969).

HIGH COMMISSIONERS
1951. (March) I. M. R. Maclennan, CMG (later Sir Ian Maclennan, KCMG) (*see* Federation of Rhodesia and Nyasaland (*below*).
1964. (January) J. B. Johnston, CMG.

FEDERATION OF RHODESIA AND NYASALAND
(*Formed* 3.9.53. *Dissolved* 31.12.63)
HIGH COMMISSIONERS
1953. (October) I. M. R. Maclennan, CMG (later Sir Ian Maclennan, KCMG) (*see* Rhodesia *above*).
1955. (August) M. R. Metcalf, CMG, OBE.
1961. (March) Cuthbert James McCall Alport, Baron Alport, PC, TD.
1963. (July) J. B. Johnston, CMG (*see* Rhodesia *above*)

SIERRA LEONE
HIGH COMMISSIONERS
1961. (April) J. B. Johnston (later CMG).
1963. (September) D. J. C. Crawley, CVO (later CMG).
1966. (July) S. J. G. Fingland, CMG.
1969. (September) S. J. L. Olver, CMG, MBE.

SINGAPORE
REPRESENTATIVE
1965. (August) J. V. Rob, CMG.
HIGH COMMISSIONERS
1965. (October) J. V. Rob, CMG.
1968. (January) A. J. de la Mare, CMG (later Sir Arthur de la Mare, KCMG).
1970. (December) S. Falle, CMG, DSC.

TANGANYIKA
HIGH COMMISSIONER
1961. (December) N. Pritchard, CMG (later Sir Neil Pritchard, KCMG) (*see* Tanganyika and Zanzibar *below*).

TANGANYIKA AND ZANZIBAR
(*United as Tanzania in April* 1964)
HIGH COMMISSIONERS

1964. (April) Sir Neil Pritchard, KCMG.
1964. (August) R. W. D. Fowler, CMG (later Sir Robert Fowler, KCMG) (*see* Tanzania *below*).

TANZANIA
HIGH COMMISSIONERS

1964. (October) R. W. D. Fowler, CMG (later Sir Robert Fowler, KCMG).
1968. (September) H. Phillips, CMG.

TONGA
REPRESENTATIVE

1965. (June) A. C. Reid, CMG, CVO.

HIGH COMMISSIONER

1970. (June) Sir Arthur Galsworthy, KCMG. (Resides in Wellington, New Zealand).

TRINIDAD AND TOBAGO
HIGH COMMISSIONERS

1962. (August) N. E. Costar, CMG (later Sir Norman Costar, KCMG).
1966. (December) G. P. Hampshire, CMG (later Sir Peter Hampshire, KCMG).
1970. (May) R. C. C. Hunt, CMG.

UGANDA
HIGH COMMISSIONERS

1962 (October) D. W. S. Hunt, CMG, OBE (later Sir David Hunt, KCMG).
1965. (May) R. C. C. Hunt, CMG.
1967. (July) D. A. Scott, CMG.
1970. (March) R. M. K. Slater, CMG.

WEST INDIES ASSOCIATED STATES
(ANTIGUA; DOMINICA; GRENADA; ST CHRISTOPHER, NEVIS AND ANGUILLA; ST LUCIA; ST VINCENT)
BRITISH GOVERNMENT REPRESENTATIVE

1967. (February) C. S. Roberts.
1970. (April) J. E. Marnham, CMG, MC, TD.

ZAMBIA
HIGH COMMISSIONERS

1964. (October) W. B. L. Monson, CB, CMG (later Sir Leslie Monson, KCMG.)
1967. (January) J. L. Pumphrey, CMG.
1971. (June) J. S. R. Duncan, CMG, MBE.

ZANZIBAR
HIGH COMMISSIONER

1963. (December) T. L. Crosthwait, MBE (later CMG).
(*Post terminated with effect from 1st July* 1964, *see* Tanganyika and Zanzibar *above*).

B*

TANGANYIKA AND ZANZIBAR

(1964) ... Tanganyika and Zanzibar ...

First Day Covers

1964 (1 Dec.) Post Office opening ...

Add. 1s. and 8c., 2s. T. ... , ...

TANZANIA

First Day Covers

1965 ... 10c., 30c., 70c., 1s.30 ... Kenya, Uganda, Tanzania ...
1966 (July) ... 1s.30 ...

TRINIDAD AND TOBAGO

First Day Covers

1969 (1 Aug.) ... The Cocoa ... the State Sir Norman ... County Council ...
1966 (Dec.) ... (1 P.) Independence ... Port of Spain ...
1976 ... R. F. Calhart ...

GRAND TURK

First Day Covers

1967 (October) ... U.S. flight ...
19... , ... B. C. C. ...
1967 ... ... Stamps ...
1968 ... R.A.F. S. ...

WEST INDIES ASSOCIATED STATES

ANTIGUA, DOMINICA, ... ST CHRISTOPHER NEVIS AND
ANGUILLA, ... ST VINCENT

First Day Covers

1969 ... , C. S. Brown ...
1969 ... ... Postmaster General, ...

ZAMBIA

First Day Covers

1967 (October) ... R. L. Vernon, The Controller, Stamp Bureau, P.O.
1968 (January) ... , ...
1972 ... ...

ZANZIBAR

First Day Covers

1963 (Dec.) ... , The Postmaster, Revenue Stamp ...
... ... Zanzibar.

PART III

PART III

PRIME MINISTERS' MEETINGS

FROM 1911 to 1937, Imperial Conferences of the Prime Ministers and other Ministers of Britain and the Dominions were held periodically to discuss matters of common concern, particularly constitutional questions, foreign affairs, defence and economic policy. At the end of each conference full reports of the proceedings and conclusions were published. A brief account of the Imperial Conferences during these years was included in the 1955 *Commonwealth Relations Office List.*

When meetings were resumed in 1944 the old Imperial Conferences gave place to the more informal exchanges of views on issues of first importance provided by the present Commonwealth Prime Ministers' Meetings, and *ad hoc* conferences of other Ministers for the discussion of particular questions. Details of the proceedings of these meetings are not published, but it is the practice for a *communiqué* to be issued at the close of each meeting summarising its results. Brief outlines of the *communiqués* issued from 1944 to 1962 may be found in the *Commonwealth Relations Office Lists* of 1961 to 1964. The *communiqués* issued after the Prime Ministers' Meetings of 1964 and 1965 were published in the *Commonwealth Relations Office Year Book*, 1966.

There were two Prime Ministers' Meetings in 1966. The earlier of these, at Lagos, was the first meeting to be held in a Commonwealth capital other than London and the first devoted to a single subject (Rhodesia). The *communiqués* of both the 1966 meetings were published in the *Commonwealth Office Year Book*, 1967.

There were no Prime Ministers' Meetings during 1967 or 1968. In January 1969 there was a Meeting of Commonwealth Heads of Government in London. The *communiqué* was published in *A Year Book of the Commonwealth*, 1970.

Commonwealth Heads of Government met in Singapore in January 1971. This was the first full Prime Ministers' Meeting to be held outside London. The Meeting issued a communiqué and also the Commonwealth Declaration; both are printed below.

PRIME MINISTERS' MEETING, JANUARY 1971—COMMUNIQUÉ

The following communiqué was issued on 22nd January 1971 at the end of the meeting.

Commonwealth Heads of Government met in Singapore from 14 to 22 January. All Commonwealth countries were represented, seven by their Presidents, seventeen by their Prime Ministers, one by the Vice-President, and six by senior Ministers. The Prime Minister of Singapore was in the Chair.

2. This was the first Heads of Government Meeting to be held in Asia. Heads of Government welcomed this and expressed gratitude to the Government of Singapore for the hospitality it had provided.

3. The Meeting expressed a warm greeting to the Prime Ministers of Tonga, Western Samoa and Fiji whose countries had become members of the Commonwealth during 1970, and particularly welcomed their membership as it brought to Commonwealth consultations additional views of the peoples of the south-west Pacific.

COMMONWEALTH DECLARATION

4.   Heads of Government approved unanimously and issued a Commonwealth Declaration.

INTERNATIONAL AFFAIRS

5.   Heads of Government reviewed the world political situation and trends. Views were exchanged on: East-West relations; Chinese representation in the United Nations; the steps required to end the conflict in Indo-China; the neutralisation of south-east Asia; the conditions necessary for achieving a durable settlement in the Middle East; the violation of the security and sovereignty of the Republic of Guinea by the military and naval forces of Portugal in conjunction with other elements; the need for general and complete disarmament under effective international control, the cessation of the nuclear arms race and the conclusion of collateral measures with particular attention to nuclear disarmament until general and complete disarmament is achieved; the staging of nuclear weapons tests and the dumping of chemical weapons in the peaceful south-west Pacific area; and the complementary role of regional organisations and such trans-regional groupings as the Commonwealth.

SOUTHERN AFRICA

6.   The Meeting reviewed major developments in southern Africa, including in particular those in South Africa and Namibia (South West Africa), the Portuguese colonies and Rhodesia, and noted that tensions in that region were likely to increase rather than decrease unless there were fundamental changes in the conditions now prevailing. Earlier discussions on NIBMR were recalled. There was unanimous reaffirmation of the importance of the principle that any proposals for settlement must be acceptable to the people of Rhodesia as a whole.

7.   The Meeting had before it the report of the Commonwealth Sanctions Committee which reviewed the working of economic sanctions over the last two years. Heads of Government authorized the Committee to continue to review the situation.

8.   Heads of Government discussed fully the question of the sale of arms to South Africa.

9.   Heads of Government considered the factors affecting the security of maritime trade routes in the South Atlantic and Indian Oceans, which are of vital importance for a large number of Commonwealth countries. They decided to set up a Study Group, consisting of representatives of Australia, Britain, Canada, India, Jamaica, Kenya, Malaysia and Nigeria, with instructions to consider the question further and report to them through the Secretary-General as soon as possible.

10.   Certain Heads of Government stipulated the understandings on which they agreed to support the proposal to set up the Study Group.

THE SECURITY OF THE INDIAN OCEAN

11.   In their discussion of a paper presented by the Prime Minister of Ceylon on the security of the Indian Ocean, Heads of Government agreed on the desirability of ensuring that it remains an area of peace and stability.

ECONOMIC AFFAIRS

12. Heads of Government held a full and frank discussion on the world economic situation and broadly reviewed recent developments and trends. Among the items discussed were: liberalisation of trade and access to markets; the special problems relating to exports of developing countries; the generalised preferences system and the problems connected with it; international commodity problems; high freight rates, inflation and its consequences; debt servicing problems of developing countries; targets for the transfer of resources to developing countries; terms and conditions of assistance, including the untying of aid; supplementary financing; the possibility of a link between Special Drawing Rights and development finance; and, the lending policies of international financial institutions.

13. Heads of Government expressed their satisfaction that agreement was reached on the International Development Strategy for the Second Development Decade at the United Nations General Assembly. They reaffirmed their Governments' resolve to take the measures to translate into reality the goals and objectives of the Decade. In summarising their discussions, they also reaffirmed their conviction that fulfilment of the economic and social aspirations of the peoples of the developing countries was a matter of vital concern not only to the developing nations but to the world at large.

POSSIBLE BRITISH ENTRY INTO THE EEC

14. Heads of Government discussed Britain's possible entry into the European Economic Community and the implications of this for other Commonwealth members. Among the matters dicussed were the questions of: the effect of the Common Agricultural Policy on the exports of Britain's traditional suppliers; the need for any enlarged Community to be outward looking; standstill arrangements for those countries which desired or may be offered association or other trading arrangements with an enlarged Community; reverse preferences and their impact on international trading arrangements; the potential advantages and disadvantages for the Commonwealth in the event of Britain's accession; and methods of consultation during negotiations. They welcomed the resolve of the British Government to continue to press during the negotiations for measures to safeguard the interests of Commonwealth countries.

COMMONWEALTH CO-OPERATION FOR DEVELOPMENT

15. Heads of Government welcomed the establishment of the Commonwealth Fund for Technical Co-operation and noted that the way was now open for it to be made operational.

16. Heads of Government discussed the recommendations embodied in a study on Commonwealth Export Market Development. They decided that these recommendations should be given further consideration at an early meeting of trade and finance officials.

COMMONWEALTH INFORMATION PROGRAMME

17. Heads of Government agreed in principle on the proposals submitted to them for a Commonwealth Information Programme.

COMMONWEALTH CO-OPERATION ON YOUTH QUESTIONS

18. Heads of Government noted with approval the Secretariat's activities in the youth field and agreed that such activities be expanded. They noted that a number of related matters would be discussed at the forthcoming Commonwealth Education Conference in Canberra. They decided that a meeting of Ministers concerned with Youth matters be convened as early as possible.

COMMONWEALTH BOOK DEVELOPMENT AND GIFT VOUCHER SCHEME

19. Heads of Government approved in principle the establishment of a Commonwealth Book Voucher Scheme.

SPECIAL COMMONWEALTH PROGRAMME FOR ASSISTING THE EDUCATION OF RHODESIAN AFRICANS

20. Heads of Government took note of the development of the programme and supported its continuation.

COMMONWEALTH FOUNDATION

21. Heads of Government noted the progress of the Commonwealth Foundation and agreed to its proposed expansion.

COMPARATIVE TECHNIQUES OF GOVERNMENT

22. The Conference agreed that the item on "Comparative Techniques of Government", which was introduced by the Prime Minister of Canada, should be the subject of further discussion at the next meeting of Commonwealth Heads of Government. It was proposed that the Secretary-General should facilitate such discussion by arranging for preliminary study of the subject by appropriate officials.

REPORT OF THE COMMONWEALTH SECRETARY-GENERAL

23. Heads of Government took note of the Third Report of the Commonwealth Secretary-General.

COMMONWEALTH DECLARATION

The Commonwealth of Nations is a voluntary association of independent sovereign states, each responsible for its own policies, consulting and co-operating in the common interests of their peoples and in the promotion of international understanding and world peace.

Members of the Commonwealth come from territories in the six continents and five oceans, include peoples of different races, languages and religions, and display every stage of economic development from poor developing nations to wealthy industrialised nations. They encompass a rich variety of cultures, traditions and institutions. Membership of the Commonwealth is compatible with the freedom of member governments to be non-aligned or to belong to any other grouping, association or alliance.

Within this diversity all members of the Commonwealth hold certain principles in common. It is by pursuing these principles that the Commonweath can continue to influence international society for the benefit of mankind.

WE BELIEVE that international peace and order are essential to the security and prosperity of mankind; we therefore support the United Nations and seek to strengthen its influence for peace in the world, and its efforts to remove the causes of tension between nations.

WE BELIEVE in the liberty of the individual, in equal rights for all citizens regardless of race, colour, creed or political belief, and in their inalienable right to participate by means of free and democratic political processes in framing the society in which they live. We therefore strive to promote in each of our countries those representative institutions and guarantees for personal freedom under the law that are our common heritage.

WE RECOGNISE racial prejudice as a dangerous sickness threatening the healthy development of the human race and racial discrimination as an unmitigated evil of society. Each of us will vigorously combat this evil within our own nation. No country will afford to regimes which practise racial discrimination assistance which in its own judgment directly contributes to the pursuit or consolidation of this evil policy. We oppose all forms of colonial domination and racial oppression and are committed to the principles of human dignity and equality. We will therefore use all our efforts to foster human equality and dignity everywhere and to further the principles of self-determination and non-racialism.

WE BELIEVE that the wide disparities in wealth now existing between different sections of mankind are too great to be tolerated; they also create world tensions; our aim is their progressive removal; we therefore seek to use our efforts to overcome poverty, ignorance and disease, in raising standards of life and achieving a more equitable international society. To this end our aim is to achieve the freest possible flow of international trade on terms fair and equitable to all, taking into account the special requirements of the developing countries, and to encourage the flow of adequate resources, including governmental and private resources, to the developing countries, bearing in mind the importance of doing this in a true spirit of partnership and of establishing for this purpose in the developing countries conditions which are conducive to sustained investment and growth.

WE BELIEVE that international co-operation is essential to remove the causes of war, promote tolerance, combat injustice and secure development amongst the peoples of the world; we are convinced that the Commonwealth is one of the most fruitful associations for these purposes.

In pursuing these principles the members of the Commonwealth believe that they can provide a constructive example of the multi-national approach which is vital to peace and progress in the modern world. The association is based on consultation, discussion and co-operation. In rejecting coercion as an instrument of policy they recognise that the security of each member state from external aggression is a matter of concern to all members. It provides many channels for continuing exchanges of knowledge and views on professional, cultural, economic, legal and political issues among member states. These relationships we intend to foster and extend for we believe that our multi-national association can expand human understanding and understanding among nations, assist in the elimination of discrimination based on differences of race, colour or creed, maintain and strengthen personal liberty, contribute to the enrichment of life for all, and provide a powerful influence for peace among nations.

COMMONWEALTH CONFERENCES 1971

January	2nd Commonwealth Students' Conference	Kumasi
	Commonwealth Heads of Government Meeting	Singapore
	Association of Commonwealth and Language Studies Conference	Kingston, Jamaica
	4th Quinquennial Commonwealth Law Conference	New Delhi
February	5th Commonwealth Education Conference	Canberra
May	Commonwealth Meteorological Conference	Bracknell
	20th Parliamentary Seminar of the Commonwealth Parliamentary Association	London
	Pre-World Health Assembly Meeting of Commonwealth Health Ministers and Officials	Geneva
June	Commonwealth Engineering Conference	London
July	3rd Quinquennial Conference of the Commonwealth Council of the Royal Life Saving Society	London
	Commonwealth Asian and Pacific Countries' Regional Seminar on Youth	Kuala Lumpur
August	Commonwealth Survey Officers' Conference	Cambridge
	Commonwealth Military Survey and Mapping Conference	London
	Annual Conference of the Commonwealth Parliamentary Association	Kuala Lumpur
September	Commonwealth Librarians' Conference	London
	Commonwealth Finance Ministers' Meeting	Nassau
October	Conference of Commonwealth Postal Administrations	London
	Conference on Consular Relations in the Commonwealth	London
	Commonwealth Information Officials' Conference	London
November	3rd Commonwealth Medical Conference	Port Louis
	Commonwealth Youth Officials' Conference	London

THE COMMONWEALTH SECRETARIAT

THE Commonwealth Secretariat was established by the Commonwealth Prime Ministers at their Meeting in London in June 1965 (see pages 25–31 of the *Commonwealth Relations Office Year Book*, 1966). The following is a list of the senior officers of the Secretariat:

Arnold C. Smith	Commonwealth Secretary-General
Azim Hussain	Deputy Secretary-General
R. H. Wade	Deputy Secretary-General
Y. K. Lule, CBE	Assistant Secretary-General
N. Salter	Special Assistant
D. McDowell	Special Assistant
Dr. R. Glen	Scientific Adviser

General, Trade & Commodities Division

D. K. Srinivasachar	Director
H. Brewster	Assistant Director

Development, Aid & Planning Division

A. F. Hussain	Director
N. Agathocleous	Assistant Director

Education Division

Dr J. A. Maraj	Director
(vacant)	Assistant Director

Information Division

T. Eggleton	Director
(vacant)	Assistant Director

Legal Division

T. Kellock	Director

International Affairs Division

E. C. Anyaoku	Director
(vacant)	Assistant Director
Mrs. S. Kochar	Assistant Director
D. W. Sagar	Assistant Director

Establishment & Finance Division

J. W. Nicholas	Director

Medical Division

Dr V. Kyaruzi	Medical Adviser

Commonwealth Fund for Technical Co-operation

G. Kidd	Managing Director
A. B. Pusar	Director, Transport and Project Appraisal Programmes
J. B. Kaboha	Director, Public Administration Programmes
S. M. Ikhtiar Ul Mulk	Director, Statistical Programmes

1971 saw Commonwealth countries looking to the Secretariat for increased activity in several areas, principally technical assistance, education and information.

The Secretariat was also responsible for the organisation of an extensive schedule of conferences during the year, beginning with the Commonwealth Heads of Government Meeting in Singapore in January.

The scope and variety of Commonwealth co-operation was reflected in the nine other conferences arranged and serviced by the Secretariat during the year, ranging from meetings of Finance and Health Ministers to an Asian Pacific Regional Youth Seminar.

It was at their meeting in Singapore that Heads of Government decided that the Secretariat should step up its role in a number of fields.

The Heads of Government Meeting (14th–22nd January) was organised by the Secretariat in close collaboration with the Government of Singapore whose Prime Minister, Mr. Lee Kuan Yew, was host and Chairman. All 31 member countries of the Commonwealth were represented, with 25 delegations being led either by their Presidents or Prime Ministers. (see *communiqué* page 35).

A feature of the meeting was the desire of many delegations to reiterate the basic principles which all members held in common. The Meeting approved unanimously a Commonwealth Declaration, which sets out these principles and beliefs. (See page 38 for Declaration).

International political trends were reviewed by Heads of Government with special attention being paid to Southern Africa and the question of the sale of arms to South Africa. Factors affecting the security of the maritime trade routes in the South Atlantic and the Indian Ocean were discussed.

After reviewing recent developments and trends in the world economic situation, Heads of Government discussed the implications for Commonwealth members of Britain's application for membership of the European Economic Community. The Meeting welcomed the resolve of the British Government to continue to press for measures to safeguard the interest of Commonwealth countries.

The Meeting also reviewed the extensive range of co-operation which exists in such fields as development and education and approved a number of schemes strengthening this co-operation. These included the establishment of the Commonwealth Fund for Technical Co-operation, the Commonwealth Information Programme, and a Book Voucher Scheme. Heads of Government also supported the continuation of the Special Commonwealth Programme for Assisting the Education of Rhodesian Africans.

The Book Development Programme approved by the Heads of Government is designed to facilitate the flow of books throughout the Commonwealth and to promote local production of books in developing countries. This programme incorporates an exchange voucher scheme which is expected to assist research institutes in developing countries to obtain scientific and technical periodicals.

The Singapore Conference also agreed to a Commonwealth Information Programme, providing for the establishment of an Information Division within the Secretariat. The main aim of this Programme is to increase the flow of information about Commonwealth affairs. A meeting of Senior Information Officers of the Commonwealth was held in London in October to fill in details of the new Information Programme. It is expected that the scheme will take some years to develop fully.

Another meeting resulting directly from the Heads of Government Conference was a gathering of trade officials in London (June) to give further consideration to the Secretariat's study on Commonwealth Export Market Development (more details to come later).

Educational co-operation within the Commonwealth was reviewed at the Fifth Commonwealth Education Conference held in Canberra from 3rd–17th February. A review of existing schemes revealed various ways in which co-operation could be improved and strengthened, and several new initiatives were agreed upon. One of the decisions taken at the meeting was that the next regional seminar to discuss youth and development should cover the Asian and the Pacific Region, and this seminar was held in Kuala Lumpur in July-August.

On the economic front, there were the annual meetings of Finance Officials and Ministers (Bahamas – September). They welcomed the fact that the way was open for the establishment of the Commonwealth Fund for Technical Cooperation, and this Fund was formally inaugurated on 1st April. The establishment of the Fund meant that the bilaterally financed Commonwealth Programme for Technical Cooperation operating for the past three years, had become truly multilateral with contributions from both developed and developing members. This new arrangement represented a move towards real Commonwealth partnership and a blurring of the distinction between "donor" and "recipient". The first year's pledges to the Fund totalled in the region of £300,000.

The Fund is governed by a Board of Representatives drawn from all participating countries and at the first Board meeting on 29th March, the High Commissioner for Cyprus, Mr. Costas Ashiotis, was elected Chairman and the High Commissioner for Canada, Mr. C. S. A. Ritchie as Vice-Chairman. The meeting also elected Britain, Canada, Fiji, Ghana, Guyana, India, Kenya, Malawi, New Zealand and Pakistan to the Committee of Management of the Fund. The Commonwealth Secretary-General is also a member.

The Third Commonwealth Medical Conference – a ministerial level meeting – was held in Mauritius in November. It reviewed progress made since the first of these meetings in Edinburgh in 1965, and discussed plans for further improving health facilities in the Commonwealth, particularly in the developing countries.

A Budget of £690,937 was approved by Commonwealth Governments for 1971/72. The scale of contribution is:—

					Per cent
Australia	..	..	..	..	9·00
Barbados	..	..	..	..	·75
Botswana	..	..	..	..	·75
Britain	..	..	..	..	30·00
Canada	..	..	..	..	17·87
Ceylon	..	..	..	..	1·50
Cyprus	..	..	..	..	·75
Fiji	..	..	..	..	·75
The Gambia	..	..	..	..	·75
Ghana	..	..	..	..	1·50
Guyana	..	..	..	..	·75
India	..	..	..	..	10·30
Jamaica	..	..	..	..	1·50
Kenya	..	..	..	..	1·50
Lesotho	..	..	..	..	1·50

					Per cent
Malawi	..	..	..	..	·75
Malaysia	..	..	..	..	1·50
Malta	..	..	..	..	·75
Mauritius	..	..	..	..	·75
New Zealand	..	..	..	..	2·14
Nigeria	..	..	..	..	1·50
Pakistan	..	..	..	..	2·19
Sierra Leone	..	..	..	..	1·50
Singapore	..	..	..	..	1·50
Swaziland	..	..	..	..	·75
Tanzania	..	..	..	..	1·50
Tonga	..	..	..	..	·75
Trinidad and Tobago		..	..	..	1·50
Uganda	..	..	..	..	1·50
Western Samoa	..	..	..	..	·75
Zambia	..	..	..	..	1·50

100.00

MARLBOROUGH HOUSE

AT the Commonwealth Economic Conference in Montreal in September 1958 the British Government offered to provide, for the many Commonwealth activities and meetings which are held in London, suitable premises which might be regarded as a Commonwealth centre. This suggestion was welcomed by the Conference and in February 1959 the Prime Minister announced in the House of Commons that Her Majesty The Queen, who had shown a close personal interest in this project, had placed her Palace of Marlborough House at the disposal of the Government so that it might be available for this purpose.

Few structural alterations were needed but some adjustment and modernisation was required to adapt the building to its new purpose and new furnishings and equipment were installed. The initial cost of adapting the building was met by the British Government, who also bear the cost of maintenance. The Governments of the twelve countries then Members of the Commonwealth each presented six chairs for the main conference room.

On 28th March 1962 Marlborough House came into use as a Commonwealth centre.

The main purpose of Marlborough House is to serve as a centre for Commonwealth meetings in London. The most important of these meetings are the Commonwealth Prime Ministers' Meetings. Fifteen Meetings of Commonwealth Prime Ministers have been held in London since 1944; the 1962 Commonwealth Prime Ministers' Meeting was the first to be held at Marlborough House.

Marlborough House stands to the east of St. James's Palace, between the Mall and Pall Mall. The main central part of the house now provides on the ground floor a suite of conference rooms for Commonwealth Prime Ministers' Meetings and other Commonwealth meetings, together with secretariat offices and reception rooms. On the upper floors there are offices for Prime Ministers and their accompanying delegations and staffs. A small radio and television studio is in the basement. The East and West Wings contain the offices of the Commonwealth Secretariat and the Commonwealth Foundation.

The Commonwealth Secretariat maintains a Commonwealth Information Centre and Reading Room, on the ground floor of the West Wing, which is open to the public from 10 a.m. to 5 p.m. Mondays to Fridays. Adjoining is a Press Conference room used for briefings during official conferences, and available at other times to Commonwealth organisations for exhibitions, discussion groups, film showings, etc.

When Marlborough House is not in use for Commonwealth meetings the assembly and conference rooms and other former state apartments are open to the public at stated times from Easter Sunday until the last Sunday in September.

COMMONWEALTH MEMBERSHIP OF UNITED NATIONS BODIES AND SPECIALISED AGENCIES

	Principal Organs of the United Nations	General Assembly	Security Council	Economic and Social Council	Trusteeship Council	International Court of Justice	Functional Commissions of Economic and Social Council	Commission on Human Rights	Commission on Narcotic Drugs	Commission on the Status of Women	Population Commission	Commission on Social Development	Statistical Commission	Sub-Commission on Prevention of Discrimination and Protection of Minorities
Britain		A	A	B	A	C		B	B	B	B	B	B	D
Canada		A								B	B			D
Australia		A			A									
New Zealand		A		B							B			
India		A						B	B	B				
Pakistan		A				C		B	B					D
Ceylon		A		B										
Ghana		A		B				B						
Malaysia		A		B						B				
Nigeria		A				C				B				D
Cyprus		A										B		
Sierra Leone		A	B									B		
Tanzania		A						B						D
Jamaica		A							B		B			
Trinidad and Tobago		A												
Uganda		A											B	
Kenya		A		B							B			D
Malawi		A												
Malta		A												
Zambia		A												
The Gambia		A												
Singapore		A												
Guyana		A												
Botswana		A												
Lesotho		A												
Barbados		A										B		
Mauritius		A						B						
Swaziland		A												
Fiji		A												

A Permanent Member. B Elected Member C National as Judge.
D National as Member

	Regional Economic Commissions	Economic Commission for Africa	Economic Commission for Asia and the Far East	Economic Commission for Europe	Economic Commission for Latin America	Specialised Agencies the IAEA and GATT	Food and Agriculture Organisation (FAO)	FAO Council	General Agreement on Tariffs and Trade (GATT)	International Atomic Energy Agency (IAEA)	IAEA Board of Governors	International Bank for Reconstruction and Development (IBRD)	International Civil Aviation Organisation (ICAO)
Britain		C	A	A	A		A	B	A	A	B	A	A
Canada					A		A	B	A	A	B	A	A
Australia			A				A		A	A	B	A	A
New Zealand			A				A	B	A	A		A	A
India			A				A	B	A	A	B	A	A
Pakistan			A				A	B	A	A	B	A	A
Ceylon			A				A	B	A	A		A	A
Ghana		A					A		A	A		A	A
Malaysia			A				A		A	A		A	A
Nigeria		A					A	B	A	A	B	A	A
Cyprus				A			A		A	A		A	A
Sierra Leone		A					A		A	A		A	A
Tanzania		A					A	B	A			A	A
Jamaica					A		A		A	A		A	A
Trinidad and Tobago					A		A		A			A	A
Uganda		A					A		A	A		A	A
Kenya		A					A		A	A		A	A
Malawi		A					A		A			A	A
Malta				A			A		A				A
Zambia		A					A	B	†	A		A	A
The Gambia		A					A		A			A	
Singapore			A						†	A		A	A
Guyana					A		A		A			A	A
Botswana		A					A		†			A	A
Lesotho		A					A		†			A	
Barbados					A		A		A				A
Mauritius		A					A		A			A	A
Swaziland		A							†			A	
Fiji									†				
Tonga			A						†				

A Permanent Member.   B Elected Member.   C Associate Member.
†Applying GATT *de facto* pending final decision as to their future commercial policy.

	ICAO Council	International Development Association (IDA)	International Finance Corporation (IFC)	International Labour Organisation (ILO)	ILO Governing Body (Government Members)	Inter-Governmental Maritime Consultative Organisation (IMCO)	IMCO Council	International Monetary Fund (IMF)	IMF Executive Directors	International Telecommunication Union (ITU)	ITU Administrative Council	U.N. Educational, Scientific and Cultural Organisation (UNESCO)	UNESCO Executive Board	Universal Postal Union (UPU)	UPU Executive Council	World Health Organisation (WHO)
Britain	B	A	A	A	A	A	B	A	D E	A	B	A	B	A		A
Canada	B	A	A	A	A	A	B	A	D	A	B	A	B	A		A
Australia	B	A	A	A		A	B	A	D	A	B	A		A	B	A
New Zealand		A	A	A				A		A		A		A		A
India	B	A	A	A	A	A	B	A	D E	A	B	A	B	A	B	A
Pakistan		A	A	A	F	A		A		A	B	A	B	A	B	A
Ceylon		A	A	A				A		A		A	B	A		A
Ghana		A	A	A		A	B	A		A		A	B	A		A
Malaysia		A	A	A				A		A		A		A		A
Nigeria	B	A	A	A	B	A		A		A	B	A		A	B	A
Cyprus		A	A	A				A		A		A		A		A
Sierra Leone		A	A	A				A	E	A		A		A		A
Tanzania	B	A	A	A				A		A		A	B	A		A
Jamaica		A	A					A	E	A		A	B	A		A
Trinidad and Tobago			A		A			A		A		A		A	B	A
*Uganda	B	A	A	A	F			A		A	B	A		A		A
Kenya		A	A	A	B			A	D	A		A		A		A
Malawi		A	A	A				A		A		A		A		A
Malta		A		A				A		A		A		A		A
Zambia		A	A	A				A		A		A	B	A		A
The Gambia		A						A								
Singapore			A	A		A		A		A		A		A		A
Guyana		A	A	A				A		A		A		A		A
Botswana		A						A		A				A		
Lesotho		A		A				A		A		A		A		A
Barbados			A		A			A		A		A		A		A
Mauritius		A	A	A				A		A		A		A		A
Swaziland		A	A					A		A				A		

A Permanent Member.   B Elected Member.   D Executive Director.
E Alternate Director.   F Deputy Member.   *In rotation with Tanzania.

	WHO Executive Board	World Meteorological Organisation (WMO)	WMO Executie Committee								
Britain		A	B								
Canada	B	A	B								
Australia		A	B								
New Zealand		A									
India		A	B								
Pakistan		A	B								
Ceylon		A									
Ghana		A	B								
Malaysia		A									
Nigeria		A									
Cyprus	B	A									
Sierra Leone		A									
Tanzania		A	B								
Jamaica		A									
Trinidad and Tobago	B	A									
Uganda		A	B								
Kenya	B	A	B								
Malawi		A									
Malta											
Zambia		A									
The Gambia											
Singapore		A	B								
Guyana		A									
Botswana		A									
Lesotho	B										
Barbados		A									
Mauritius		A									
Swaziland											

A Permanent Member.   B Designated by Elected Countries.

The British Government is responsible for the international relations of Antigua, Dominica, Grenada, St Christopher, Nevis and Anguilla, St Lucia, St Vincent, Brunei and the British dependent territories. Some are members of the specialised agencies and United Nations Regional Economic Commissions, *viz:*

Economic Commission for Asia and the Far East—Hong Kong, Fiji, Brunei and British Solomon Islands Protectorate (Associate Members).

Economic Commission for Latin America—British Honduras and the Eastern Caribbean Group (Associate Members).

IMCO—Hong Kong (Associate Member).

ITU and UPU—Collective Member (known as 'Overseas territories for the international relations of which the Government of the U.K. is responsible').

UNESCO—Eastern Caribbean Group (Antigua, Dominica, Grenada, Montserrat, St Kitts, St Lucia, St Vincent) (Associate Members).

WMO—Hong Kong (Member), British Caribbean Territories (Collective Member), Bahamas.

The British Government may also, when appropriate, include territorial representatives in United Kingdom Delegations at meetings of agencies which do not provide for direct territorial representation.

Each member country of the IBRD appoints one Governor. Most of the authority of the Board of Governors for each institution in the World Bank Group (IBRD, IBA, IFC) is delegated to the Executive Directors. Each of the five largest share holders (India, Britain, France, Germany, United States of America) appoints a single Executive Director; the remaining 15 Executive Directors are elected for two-year terms. Each Director appoints his own alternate.

Rhodesia is a member of *GATT* and *ITU*, an Associate Member of *ECA* and *WHO*, and a component of the British Overseas Territories Member of *UPU* and *WMO*. Since the illegal declaration of independence in November 1965, however, when the former Rhodesian ministers were dismissed from office, and pending the restoration of constitutional government, the British Government have withheld authority for Rhodesian representation at meetings of these organisations.

PART IV

MEMBER COUNTRIES OF THE COMMONWEALTH

THE COMMONWEALTH OF AUSTRALIA

THE Commonwealth of Australia is situated in the Southern Hemisphere and lies between meridians of longitude 113° 9′ E. and 153° 39′ E. Its northern and southern limits are the parallels of latitude 10° 41′ S. and 43° 39′ S. It is bounded on the west by the Indian Ocean and on the east by the Coral and Tasman Seas of the South Pacific Ocean, to the north by the Timor and Arafura Seas and to the south by the Indian Ocean. The name Australia is derived from the Latin *australis*, meaning southern, a name commonly used in early times for regions south of the equator. In the sixteenth century geographers used the name 'Terra Australis' to describe a continent which they thought must exist in the South Pacific. The east coast of Australia was named New South Wales by Captain Cook but when it was realised that this and New Holland, the name by which the west coast was known, formed one land mass, the word Australia began to be used, and was first given official recognition in April 1817 when Governor Macquarie of New South Wales used the word in his correspondence.

The Commonwealth of Australia comprises the six federated States of New South Wales, Victoria, Queensland, South Australia, Western Australia and Tasmania, each of which has its own Government, and two internal territories, the Australian Capital Territory, which is the seat of the Commonwealth Government, and the Northern Territory which includes also the Ashmore and Cartier Islands. Responsibility for the administration of these two internal territories is vested in the Department of the Interior. Macquarie Island, about 1,000 miles South East of Tasmania, is administered by Tasmania.

Australia's external territories are Norfolk Island, the Territory of Papua (formerly British New Guinea); the Territory of New Guinea (under Trusteeship Agreement with the United Nations; the Territory of Cocos (Keeling) Islands; the Territory of Christmas Island; the Territory of Heard and McDonald Islands; the Australian Antarctic Territory. Responsibility for the general administration of these external territories is vested with the Australian Department of External Territories with the exception of the last two (Antarctic and Heard and McDonald) which are administered by the Australian Department of Supply. (*The external territories are dealt with in Part VI of this volume*).

The total area of the Commonwealth is 2,967,909 square miles. Almost three-quarters of the land mass is a vast ancient plateau, averaging about 1,000 feet above sea level. There is a large portion of lowland with an elevation of less than 500 feet which is, in one place, below sea level. A third division is the eastern highlands belt, featuring a chain of elevated plateaux extending from north to south along the eastern boundary. This highland is known as the Great Dividing Range. The dominating structural division—the Great Western Plateau—has a few high tablelands and ridges such as the Kimberleys Region, Hamersley, Macdonnell and Musgrave Ranges. The Hamersley Range contains Western Australia's highest peak, Mount Bruce (4,024 feet). The Northern Territory's highest point is Mount Zeil (4,950 feet) in the Macdonnell Ranges, and South Australia's highest is Mount Woodroffe (5,000 feet) in the Musgrave Ranges. Ayers Rock, 1,100 feet high, a huge monolith rising from the central Australian desert with a circumference of six miles, is sometimes referred to as the 'largest stone in the world'. The Great Dividing Range stretches from Cape York in Queensland to the southern seaboard of Tasmania, but despite the name the mountains of the Divide are relatively low. In the north and central sections they rarely exceed 5,000 feet. The rugged south-eastern area, known as the Australian Alps, is higher with peaks of over 6,000 feet. This area contains some of Australia's highest land, together with its highest peak, Mount Kosciusko (7,316 feet). The Great Divide also provides the highest points in Queensland, Victoria and Tasmania. These peaks are respectively Mount Bartle Frere (5,287 feet); Mount Bogong (6,516 feet) and Mount Ossa (5,305 feet).

Australia does not possess any extensive inland river system. The greater part of the continent lies within the southern arid belt between latitudes 15° and 35° S. The largest river system is the Murray River and its tributaries which drain about 414,000 square miles, including a large part of southern Queensland, the major part of New South Wales and much of Victoria. The river rises in the Australian Alps and flows westward to form for 1,200 miles the boundary between New South Wales and Victoria. After flowing 400 miles through South Australia it discharges into the sea at Lake Alexandrina. With its tributaries (the Darling, the Murrumbidgee, the Lachlan and many smaller rivers in New South Wales, and the Goulburn, Ovens, Campaspe and other rivers in Victoria) the Murray has an estimated flow of some 12,500,000 acre feet annually. Most of the rivers of the central interior flow only after heavy rains, while the majority of Australia's coastal rivers are short with moderate rates of flow, although the monsoon season in the north of the country can augment the discharge rate enormously. Australia's largest reservoir is the man-made Lake Eucumbene in the Snowy Mountains area of New South Wales with a useful storage capacity of 3,890,000 acre feet. Other major reservoirs are Eildon Weir, Victoria, 2,750,000 acre feet; Hume Reservoir, N.S.W., 2,500,000 acre feet; Warragamba Dam, N.S.W., 1,670,000 acre feet; Menindee Lakes, N.S.W., 2,000,000 acre feet and Great Lake, Tasmania, 1,300,000 acre feet. Other large lakes include Lake Corangamite (Victoria) 80 square miles in area; Great Lake (Tasmania) and the Gippsland Lakes (Victoria). The largest lake in Australia is Lake Eyre which covers an area of about 4,000 square miles with neighbouring Lake Eyre South. However, this lake in central Australia is generally dry with its bed covered with salt. This is true of many of the lakes of inland Australia, which, although big in area, often contain no water except after infrequent rain. The four seasons in Australia are: Spring, September to November; Summer, December to February; Autumn, March to May; and Winter, June to August. In most parts January is the hottest month but in Tasmania and Southern Victoria February is hotter while in the tropical north (probably because of the cooling monsoon rains occurring in late summer) December is the hottest month. In northern Australia the year is divided into the usual tropical divisions of dry and wet seasons, with the wet season occurring in summer and the heaviest rain in January, February and March. On the coast, where rainfall is often abundant, the temperature extremes are limited by the moist atmosphere whereas in the dry inland areas the extremes extend in proportion to the distance from the seaboard. Central and southern Queensland are sub-tropical. Farther south there are the warm temperate regions of north and central New South Wales and the cooler areas of Victoria, south-west Western Australia and Tasmania, with rainfall distributed throughout the year and increasing in winter. Australia's coldest regions are the highlands and tablelands of Tasmania and the south-east corner of the mainland. Australia's regular winter snowfalls occur in the highlands of these areas. Mean maximum temperatures (Fahrenheit) of the various state capitals, showing the mean minimum in brackets, are: Sydney 70·4 (56·3); Brisbane 77·8 (59·8); Perth 73·6 (55·4); Darwin 90·3 (74·1); Melbourne 67·4 (49·7); Adelaide 72·4 (53·2); Hobart 62·0 (46·5); and the Federal Capital, Canberra 66·7 (43·1). The heaviest rainfall occurs on the north coast of Queensland (up to 160 inches) and in western Tasmania (up to 140 inches). A vast area of the interior, however, stretching from the far west of New South Wales and south-west Queensland to the western seaboard of Western Australia has a rainfall below 10 inches a year. Between these regions of heavy and very low rainfall are the extensive areas which experience useful to good rains, ranging from 10 to 50 inches a year.

The flora and fauna of Australia include many groups which do not occur elsewhere. Vegetation is colourful and varied. Forests are relatively small in area and occur mainly in the coastal area of high rainfall. The dominant tree is the eucalyptus, a hardwood of which there are more than 500 species, ranging from small shrubs to some of the tallest trees in the world; many are renowned for the strength and durability of their timber. Other hardwoods include the red cedar, Queensland maple, silky oak, walnut, rosewood and blackwood. The indigenous softwoods are limited; they include the kauri and bunya pines of Queensland, the hoop pine of Queensland and northern New South Wales, the huon, celery-top and King William pines of Tasmania and the cypress pines of the inland. Australia is also the home of a wide range of acacias.

The native animals of Australia are of primitive types. The land species are chiefly marsupial and include the kangaroos, native cats, opossums, koala, pouched mice and wombats. There are also two species of egg-laying mammals, the platypus and the spiny anteater. The dingo, or wild dog, is believed to have been introduced from Asia. Sheep, cattle, horses and other domestic animals have been introduced since the European settlement; imported animals also include rabbits, which have become pests. Birds, often more conspicuous for their gorgeous plumage than their song, include the emu, kookaburra, lyre bird, rosella and many kinds of parrots and cockatoos. Fish abound in the rivers and coastal waters.

At 31st December 1968 the population was estimated to be 12,173,300. This included an estimated 40,000 to 45,000 full blood aborigines, whose nomadic habits, and in some cases remoteness, have prevented a complete census. In 1968 the birth and death rates were 20 per 1,000 and 9·1 per 1,000 respectively. English is the official language and used by the population except for small minorities of the foreign-born. There are, however, many aboriginal languages: it is believed that at the time of the beginning of white settlement there were about 500. Many attempts have been made in the past to link the Australian languages with other parts of the world, i.e., South India, the Andaman Islands and Africa, but without success. It is now considered possible to explain the multiple form of languages on the basis of a single original. As yet a final grouping of the languages among themselves has not been achieved, and the following are the main groups which are clear at present: the prefixing languages of the Kimberleys and North Australian Regions; the languages of the Western Desert; the Aranda Group of Central Australia; the Victorian languages and the languages of Eastern Australia. In the 1961 census 88 per cent of the population acknowledged the Christian faith, 0·7 per cent were non-Christians and the balance were either indefinite, had no religion or made no reply. Primary educa-

C

tion is available free throughout Australia. Education is compulsory between the ages of 6 and 14–16 years; the permissible school-leaving age varies slightly between State and State. Education, except in the Territories, is controlled by the State Governments. In addition to the free Government schools, there are church and private schools, most of which charge fees. There are special schools, Government and non-Government, for the handicapped. Secondary education throughout Australia is extensive, covering a period of five to six years (again varying between the States) and including High (Grammar) and Technical schools to University entrance, plus numerous specialist schools and colleges in such particular fields as business and commerce, agriculture and home science. University and other tertiary education, including post-graduate institutions, is also extensive. Illiteracy is virtually non-existent in Australia, except for a minute percentage of persons so handicapped as to be ineducable. Some newly arrived immigrants know little English, but literacy in their own language is one of the requirements for entry to the country. A special education system helps them adjust to the new language.

There are about 66 ports of commercial significance in Australia, the principal being associated with State capital cities and industrial centres. In terms of cargo tonnage (weight and measurement combined) discharged and shipped in 1967–68, the 15 largest ports are:— Sydney (including Botany Bay) 16,998,000 tons, Melbourne 10,567,000 tons; Newcastle 10,499,000 tons; Port Kembla 9,509,000 tons; Fremantle (including Kwinana) 9,210,000 tons; Dampier 7,052,000 tons; Geelong 5,984,000 tons; Whyalla 5,623,000 tons; Brisbane 4,525,000 tons; Port Headland 4,057,000 tons; Gladstone 3,103,000 tons; Port Adelaide 2,713,000 tons; Port Stanvac 2,353,000 tons; Yampi 2,085,000 tons; Westernport 1,682,000 tons. The principal shipping companies are: The Australian National Line, the Union Steamship Co. of New Zealand, the Associated Steamships Pty. Ltd., the Broken Hill Proprietary Co. Ltd., Messrs. Burns Philp & Co. Ltd., The State Shipping Service of Western Australia, Messrs. Wm. Holyman and Sons Pty., Ltd., and Ampol Petroleum Ltd.

There are major airports at, or near, all capital cities and most of the larger cities and towns. All capital city airports cater for inter-State and intra-State services. The armed services—Navy, Army and Air Force—maintain their own bases, catering for their special needs. Thirteen major international airlines operate regular services to and from Australia. At June 1968 there were 670 licensed civil airports. The principal airports, with length of main runway in feet and distance from the centre of the city in miles, are Sydney, 9,100 (5): Essendon 6,300 (8); a second major airport of international standard was completed at Tullamarine near Melbourne in 1970; it occupies an area of 5,300 acres and has runways of 8,500 feet and 7,500 feet with fast turn-outs, modern terminal buildings and the latest in air navigation facilities—Melbourne's present airport, Essendon, cannot be further extended because of the surrounding city; Brisbane 7,760 (4); Perth 10,300 (6·5); Darwin 11,000 (3·5); Adelaide 6,850 (4); Canberra 6,800 (4); Hobart 6,500 (10). The principal Australian airline is Qantas Airways Limited based in Sydney, operating services around the world of 83,054 miles. Ten airlines operate inter-State, intra-State and feeder services throughout Australia and the Territory of Papua and New Guinea, over a network of 100,000 miles. Two major operators are Trans-Australia Airlines (TAA) owned and operated by the Australian National Airlines Commission, a statutory body formed for the purpose by the Federal Government, and Ansett/ANA, the major airlines subsidiary of Ansett Transport Industries Ltd., (ATI), a multi-company organisation engaged in road and air travel, hotels and motels, tourism, manufacturing and television. TAA operates a fleet of about 60 aircraft (including one helicopter) over a route network of 46,000 miles and carrying over 2,000,000 passengers a year. The ATI airlines group consists of six airlines with a fleet of more than 105 aircraft, covering about 59,000 miles, carrying more than two million passengers a year. Connellan Airways Pty. Limited operates a fleet of 18 aircraft over a network of 11,251 miles; East-West Airlines Ltd. operates a fleet of about five aircraft over a network of 3,960 miles and Papuan Airlines Pty. Ltd. operate nine aircraft over a network of 1,945 miles in the Territory of Papua and New Guinea.

Australia has 561,000 miles of highways and roads. Road transport, freight and passenger, is a major industry. Apart from the freight and passenger carrying services, Australian highways and roads carry a heavy traffic of private automobiles: the ratio of automobiles to population is approximately 1:2½.

The various Government Railway Systems operating at 30th June 1968 had 25,146 route-miles of track open for traffic as follows: New South Wales, 6,061 miles of 4 feet 8½ inches gauge; Victoria, 4,216 miles comprising 4,005 miles of 5 feet 3 inches gauge, 202 miles of 4 feet 8½ inches gauge, and 9 miles of 2 feet 6 inches gauge; Queensland, 5,825 miles comprising 5,726 miles of 3 feet 6 inches gauge, 69 miles of 4 feet 8½ inches gauge from Brisbane to the New South Wales border, and 30 miles of 2 feet gauge line; South Australia, 2,481 miles comprising 1,652 miles of 5 feet 3 inches gauge and 829 miles of 3 feet 6 inches gauge; Western Australia, 3,815 miles comprising 3,502 miles of 3 feet 6 inches gauge and 313 miles of 4 feet 8½ inches gauge and Tasmania, 500 miles of 3 feet 6 inches gauge. The Commonwealth Railways System comprises four separate railways. The Trans-Australian Railwy, 1,108 miles of 4 feet 8½ inches gauge between Port Pirie (South Australia) and Kalgoorlie (Western Australia). This railway was completed in 1970. The Central Australia Railway, 217 miles of 4 feet 8½ inches gauge between Port Augusta and Maree (South Australia) and 605 miles of 3 feet 6 inches gauge between Maree and Alice Springs (Northern Territory); the North Australia Railway, 317 miles of 3 feet 6 inches gauge between Darwin and Birdum (Northern Territory) and the Australian Capital Territory Railway, 5 miles of 4 feet 8½ inches gauge between Queanbeyan (New South Wales) and Canberra (Australian Capital Territory).

Under various Commonwealth-State Standardisation Agreements approximately 1,100 route-miles of standard (4 feet 8½ inches) gauge track have been completed since 1956.

At 30th June 1968 there were 78 national broadcasting stations and 114 commercial stations; with 39 national stations providing television facilities and 42 commercial television stations. More television stations are being developed with the aim of bringing this medium to more than 95 per cent of the population.

A wide range of primary and secondary industry products is produced in Australia. The main primary products are wool, wheat and flour, meat, dairy products, sugar, fruit and a number of minerals including lead, zinc, copper, coal, iron ore, gold and bauxite. Secondary industry production is diverse and includes engineering products, motor vehicles, chemicals, textiles, domestic appliances, newsprint and petroleum products.

Total expenditure of the Federal Government in 1967–68 was $6,558 m.

and receipts were $5,962 m. Consolidated Revenue Funds of the States for 1967–68 totalled revenue $2,463·3 m. and expenditure $2,468·6 m.

Australia has under way a programme of about 400 major national development works at an estimated cost on completion of $2,441,000,000. The types of project and their estimated cost are as follows: water conservation, supply, irrigation and drainage (73) $536,000,000; electricity generation (15) $918,000,000; electricity transmission (65) $85,000,000; gas (4) $3,000,000; railways (32) $195,000,000; roads and bridges (98) $251,000,000; ports (63) £302,000,000; airports (13) $40,000,000; telecommunications (35) $69,000,000. These are in addition to the $800,000,000 Snowy Mountains Hydro-electric Scheme in southern New South Wales, which is now over three-quarters complete, ahead of schedule, and on which some $665,000,000 to 30th June 1968 had already been expended. Latest estimated completion date for the undertaking, which began in 1949, is 1974. The Snowy Scheme will provide about 6,800,000 acre feet of storage in 15 large dams with 100 miles of tunnels, more than 80 miles of aqueducts and seven power stations in addition to making 2,000,000 acre feet of irrigation water available each year. The planned capacity of the Snowy Hydro-electric Scheme is 3,740,000 Kw of which 1,610,000 are already available.

Some of the larger single development projects under construction are the Munmorah and Liddell power stations in New South Wales, the Hazelwood power station in Victoria and the Ord River Irrigation Project in Western Australia. Munmorah will cost $140,000,000, Hazelwood $232,000,000 and Liddell, with a capacity of 2,000,000 Kw, $200,000,000. At present there are plans for the expenditure of about $48,000,000 on the Ord River Project.

Australia Day, 26th January, commemorates the landing and commencement of settlement at Sydney Cove by Governor Philip on 26th January 1788. It is celebrated as a public holiday throughout Australia.

HISTORY

The first known landing by a European on the shores of Australia was by William Jansz who, in the service of the Dutch, came ashore on the west coast of Cape York Peninsula in 1606 in the belief that it was part of New Guinea. At about the same time Louis de Torres, a Spaniard from Peru, passed through the straits which now bear his name. A few years later the Dutch discovered that it was quicker and healthier to approach Java by sailing with the westerly trade winds, 3,000 miles eastwards from the Cape and then turning north. It was not long before one of their Captains, Dirk Hartog, overshot his turning point and sighted the west coast of Australia at Shark Bay. Thenceforth a number of ships touched on the coast, which was found to be barren and inhospitable. The Dutch named it New Holland.

In 1642 the Dutch sent Abel Tasman to explore further. Picking up the westerlies south of Mauritius, he sailed past the south coast without sighting it and landed on what is now Tasmania, which he named Van Diemen's Land after the Governor-General in Batavia. Continuing eastwards, he discovered New Zealand before returning to Java round the north of New Guinea. A further voyage in the following year to the north coast confirmed the Dutch East India Company's view that no profit was to be obtained from the new land, and further exploration was abandoned. The British Admiralty were equally unimpressed by reports of the voyages of Dampier to the west and north-west in 1688 and 1699.

For seventy years no further exploration took place, but at the end of that period a growing interest in Pacific exploration led the British Admiralty to send an expedition under James Cook, with the scientist Sir Joseph Banks, to look for the fabled southern Continent, the *Terra Australis*, in the south Pacific. Failing to find this, Cook charted the shores of New Zealand and then made a landfall at Botany Bay. Sailing north along the coast, he took possession of the land as New South Wales. The British Government at first doubted the value of the new land, but later, on favourable reports by Sir Joseph Banks of its fertility, decided that it would be a suitable place to which to send convicts who could no longer be sent to the American colonies. On 18th January 1788 Governor Philip and the first party of convicts arrived at Botany Bay but, after a few days, moved to Sydney Cove in Port Jackson. A secondary settlement was made at Norfolk Island.

The land was found to be less fertile than Sir Joseph Banks had reported, and at first there was a danger of starvation. Once the settlements were reasonably secure, exploration continued and further settlements were established. Bass in 1798 and Flinders in 1803 completed the exploration of the south and southeast coast and the latter confirmed that New Holland and New South Wales formed part of one continent. It is believed to have been Flinders who first used the term Australia to describe this continent. Three strategic settlements were established on Sydney's lines of communications in 1803 and 1804, two of which developed into Hobart and Launceston in Van Diemen's Land, and were used for the worst convicts. In 1824 to 1828, because of fears of French landings, three other settlements were made in the north and south-east and at Albany in the south-west. The latter alone survived. Another station was established in 1824 at Moreton Bay, on the Brisbane River.

Meanwhile free settlers had begun to change the Colony's character. Some of these were former members of the New South Wales Corps, which arrived in 1790; others were persons attracted by cheap or free land. Another section of the population was formed of freed convicts. Initially, although some of the larger farmers made a success of growing for the local market, the Colony produced little or nothing for export. This was changed when Captain John Macarthur demonstrated that the Colony was very suitable for sheep rearing and that the wool would find a ready market in Britain. The discovery by Lawson, Blaxland and Wentworth of a way through the Blue Mountains, which had previously confined settlement to the coast, allowed rapid expansion of this industry. Many exploring expeditions followed, and although these opened up the country they also revealed its aridity. From then on settlement was a voluntary movement, often carried on without the approval of the government, which wished to limit expenditure. Examples of this were the settlements of Henty at Portland and Batman at Port Phillip in 1834 and 1835. Although the Government at first disapproved, Captain Lonsdale was put in charge in 1836 and Melbourne was officially named in 1837. Swelled by settlers who had come overland from the east coast, the settlements became the District of Port Phillip and, in 1851, the Colony of Victoria.

Meanwhile opportunity in Australia and distress in Britain led to the formation of companies to exploit new areas. In 1829 a settlement was started at Swan River on the west coast under Governor Stirling, and although many at first found life there too difficult the settlement later developed and, when incorporated with Albany in 1831, became the second Australian Colony, Western Australia.

The next voluntary settlement was due to the activities of Edward Gibbon Wakefield whose *Letter from Sydney* (which he had never visited) drew attention to his new scheme for financing settlement by the sale of land. The South Australia Company was formed in 1836 and a settlement was made at Adelaide. Land for the new Colony, South Australia, was taken from New South Wales whose boundaries in the west had been extended up to the boundary of Western Australia in 1835. Land speculation and a division of authority between the Governor and the Land Commissioners led to the appointment of Captain (later Sir George) Grey as Governor in 1841 and to his assumption of the powers of the Land Commissioners in 1842. His vigorous and economical administration, the development of sheep farming and agriculture and the opening of copper mines at Burra in 1843, set the new Colony on a firm basis.

During the 'hungry forties' immigration to all the Australian Colonies quickened until by 1850 the convicts accounted for less than 15 per cent of the population. Local agitation forced the Government to abandon the transportation of convicts to New South Wales in 1840, and frustrated attempts to introduce convicts into Victoria. When transportation to Van Diemen's Land stopped in 1853, Western Australia remained the only Colony to which convicts continued to be sent until the system's final abolition in 1868. Van Diemen's Land, which had been separated from New South Wales in 1825, was, on 1st January 1856, formally renamed Tasmania.

The settlement founded at Moreton Bay was abandoned in 1839, but news of the fertility of the land attracted settlers, and, after the founding of the town of Gladstone in 1853, settlement was rapid. On 6th June 1859 the territory from Point Danger north to Cape York was separated from the Colony of New South Wales to become the sixth Colony in Australia under the name of Queensland. The western boundary was moved further west in 1862.

With the creation of Queensland, the whole of Australia was divided up among the six colonies with the exception of that part to the north of South Australia. In theory this was part of New South Wales, but when the explorations of Stuart showed that much of it could be settled, it was put under the administration of South Australia, under the name of the Northern Territory, and remained under that administration until 1911, when it was transferred to the Commonwealth Government.

So long as Port Jackson remained a penal settlement, it was ruled autocratically by the Governor. To begin with he had the New South Wales Corps to enable him to keep order, but the Corps eventually took up trade, and attempts by the Governor to keep the Corps under control led to their deposing Governor Bligh in 1808. Bligh was later reinstated, the Corps disbanded and replaced by regular troops. As the proportion of free settlers increased, so did agitation for limitation of the Governor's powers. In 1823 a start was made in the process of introducing democratic institutions by the passing of the New South Wales Judicature Act setting up a nominated Legislative Council with advisory functions. Enlarged in 1828, the Council became partly elective in 1842. Similar Councils were set up over the years in the other Colonies. The changed ideas in Britain resulting from the Durham Report, and the agitation by the District of Port Phillip for full colony status, led in 1850 to the Australian Colonies Government Act, which created the Colony of Victoria and set up partly elective Legislative Councils in all the five Colonies and, furthermore, permitted them to make amendments to their own constitutions. Led by William Charles Wentworth, the Colonies one by one brought in new constitutions on the Westminster model, New South Wales obtaining responsible government in 1855, Tasmania and Victoria in 1856, South Australia in 1857, Queensland, on separation from New South Wales, in 1860, and finally Western Australia in 1890. In each of the Colonies there was established a bi-cameral legislature, the Upper House being elective except in New South Wales and Queensland, where its members were nominated by the Crown. The ballot was early introduced, together with the payment of members of the lower house and the grant of universal adult male franchise; and towards the end of the century the vote was extended in South Australia to women also.

Meanwhile the economy of Australia had been further strengthened by the discovery of gold and other minerals—the discovery of gold, in particular, leading to a great inrush of population, not all of whom were of British stock, and to a great movement of population within Australia, a movement which tended to disrupt other industries. By 1891 this country, whose exploration had hardly been completed, had already over three million inhabitants, living in the six self-governing Colonies. The export of wheat to Europe and Britain began in about 1870, Australia rapidly becoming one of the leading wheat-producing countries. The invention of refrigeration led to an export trade in dairy products and mutton. The basis of a railway system was laid.

As communications improved, and as the population increased and land was opened up, it slowly became realised that the community of interest between the colonies justified some closer union. When the proposals to confer self-government on the Colonies were being discussed in 1849, there had been proposals that there should be a General Assembly for the whole of Australia, whose members should be elected by the Colonial Parliaments. But the idea was then unpopular, and was dropped. However it soon became clear that some form of consultation was required, and this was provided on an *ad hoc* basis by inter-colonial conferences. In 1883 Henry Parkes of New South Wales suggested that there should be a Federal Council, and the British Parliament passed a bill in 1885 giving power to the six Colonies, and to Fiji and New Zealand, to pass acts to enable each of them to send representatives to a central Council. This Council first met in 1886, New Zealand never sending representatives and Fiji only sending representatives on the first occasion. More important, Parkes and his government in New South Wales did not take part. Later Parkes began to press for a Federation of the six Colonies, and the first Australian Convention of Members of Parliaments was held in Sydney in 1891 and prepared a draft. But again Parkes withdrew his support. Thenceforth it was the people who took the lead. From 1893 there was a great public movement for Federation, leading to a Convention in 1897–98 attended by 10 persons from each Colony, other than Queensland. Except in the case of Western Australia, whose representatives were chosen by Parliament, these representatives were elected by the people. The Convention drafted a Federal Constitution under which each self-governing Colony voluntarily surrendered to the Federal Government certain of its powers, ensuring at the same time that the Federal Government was in itself a democratic Government of the type which they themselves had developed on the British model. For this new Federation they adopted the name of the Commonwealth, a name suggested by Parkes in 1891, a name with a long history in British political thought beginning long before the time of Cromwell. A Commonwealth Bill, based on the proposals o the Convention, was prepared and agreed not only by the Parliaments but by an affirmative vote of all the peoples in the Colonies; and in July an Act to constitute the Commonwealth of Australia was passed by the British Parliament, and the Commonwealth of Australia, by proclamation of 17th September 1900, came into existence on 1st January 1901.

Many of the bases of modern Australian social policy were established between Federation and the First World War. The social and industrial legislation which had begun in Victoria in the 1870s, with the introduction of free, secular and compulsory education and the passing of the first Factory Act, and which had gathered momentum during the eighties and nineties, was now continued in the Federal sphere. With the steady increase in the number of wage-earners, trade unionism had spread rapidly. Arbitration in industrial disputes had been introduced in Victoria and New South Wales after a general strike in 1890. In 1903 the Commonwealth Court of Conciliation and Arbitration was created to cover disputes extending outside the borders of a single State; in 1906 Chief Justice Higgins declared that it was for the Court to determine the minimum wage necessary for 'the normal needs of an average employee regarded as a human being in a civilized country'. Invalid and old-age pensions were introduced two years later, followed by maternity allowances.

While the foundations of a welfare state were being laid, a policy of protection was adopted to further national development and maintain full employment. By this and other means Federal and State Governments helped to reduce the dependence of the economy on primary production. Although iron and steel were manufactured as early as 1848, the modern industry in Australia dates from 1915, when the Broken Hill Proprietary, a Company formed originally to develop the Broken Hill silver mines, 'blew in' its first blast furnace at Newcastle. By 1939 the Company was producing the world's cheapest iron and steel. This helped to develop other industries, as well as mining. The older industries expanded and new industries such as the manufacture of glass, chemicals and electrical goods, were added. Industry, which in 1911 had accounted for only one fifth of the value of total production, by 1939 accounted for two fifths.

After the Second World War expansion and diversification accelerated. Australia became virtually self-sufficient in iron and steel in 1958. The car manufacturing industry developed and this in turn encouraged the development of oil refining. The mining of uranium and bauxite was developed as well as the mining of coal. Commercial oil fields were discovered. A rocket-launching site was constructed at Woomera.

Nevertheless, agriculture, and particularly sheep rearing, remained the mainstay of the country. From 1890 the expansion of Australian agriculture depended on improvements in method, in particular on the discovery of means of farming areas of low rainfall. The extended use of dry-farming techniques and the production in 1902 by William Farrer of a wheat resistant to both drought and rust made possible the rapid expansion of the wheat export trade. In 1886 the first major irrigation scheme was begun in Victoria, and, after Federation, major schemes were developed elsewhere. The Snowy Mountains scheme, although better known as a scheme for generating hydro-electricity, was primarily intended to divert easterly flowing rivers to irrigate areas to the west of the Blue Mountains. Elsewhere the discovery of artesian wells, particularly in the Great Artesian Basin of Queensland, made possible a further advance inland for the sheep and cattle rearing industries. In the north the increase in the area under sugar cane led to the temporary immigration of Chinese and Pacific Island labour.

The achievements of Australian troops in the 1914–18 War, particularly in the Gallipoli campaign (still commemorated on the public holiday of 'Anzac Day'), fostered a sense of nationhood. At the Peace Conference at Versailles, the Australian Prime Minister, W. M. Hughes, played a prominent part. By the Peace Treaty Australia was entrusted with the administration of the former German Pacific colonies south of the Equator, and German New Guinea (renamed New Guinea) was later joined with Papua, which had become a Commonwealth territory in 1906, in an administrative union known as the Territory of Papua and New Guinea. In domestic politics, the war had stimulated the growth of sectional organisations outside the towns, and this led to the formation of the Country Party, which has remained one of the three major Federal political parties.

The depression of 1929 severely checked the pace of Australian development, which did not pick up again until shortly before the 1939 War, and reduced the inflow of immigrants. The Second World War and the Japanese advances in 1941 and 1942 made the Australians acutely aware of the inadequacy of their resources and manpower to fill the whole continent. The Australian Government therefore instituted a vigorous migration programme aimed at maintaining a high level of settler movement from the United Kingdom and other countries. By 31st December 1967 an estimated 2,260,000 settlers had entered Australia, of whom 1,140,000 were of British nationality.

CONSTITUTION

THE PARLIAMENT OF THE COMMONWEALTH

The Commonwealth of Australia Constitution, which was enacted by the Commonwealth of Australia Constitution Act 1900 (U.K.), established a Federal Parliament called the Parliament of the Commonwealth, consisting of the Queen, the Senate and the House of Representatives. A Governor-General appointed by the Queen is Her Majesty's representative in the Commonwealth. The Constitution requires that a session of the Parliament be held once at least in every year.

THE SENATE

The Senate is composed of an equal number of senators for each of the six States of the Commonwealth, it having been the intention of the framers of the Constitution that the Senate should be both a States' House and a House of Review. Although originally there were thirty-six senators, this number has been increased to the present number of sixty (ten from each State) in pursuance of the Parliament's power under the Constitution to increase or diminish the number of senators for each State, but so that equal representation of the original States is maintained and no original State has less than six senators. The Senate is presided over by the President who is chosen by the senators from their own members. Senators are chosen for a term of six years. The places of one half of the Senators become vacant every three years. Immediately prior to the Commonwealth Electoral Act 1948 the method of electing senators was

C*

in general the 'preferential block majority system' under which as a general rule all seats in any one State went to the party or combination of parties favoured at the time by a simple majority of the electors, leaving the minority without any representation at all in the Senate. The 1948 Act altered the system of Senate elections to one of proportional representation. The franchise for the election of senators is on the basis of adult suffrage, subject to electors being British subjects and having lived in Australia continuously for six months.

Where the place of a senator becomes vacant before the expiration of his term ot office, the House or Houses of Parliament for the State for which he was chosen, sitting and voting together may choose a person to hold the place until either the expiration of the term, the next general election of the House of Representatives or the next election of senators of the State, whichever event first happens, at which time a senator is elected to hold the senate place until the expiration of the term.

THE HOUSE OF REPRESENTATIVES

The House of Representatives is presently composed of 124 members, and, although the number of members may be increased or decreased by the Parliament, such changes must comply with the requirement that the number of members shall, as nearly as practicable, be twice the number of senators. Unlike the Senate, which has equal representation for each State, the number of members of the House of Representatives chosen in the respective States is required to be in proportion to the respective numbers of their people, subject to certain guaranteed numbers of members from original States. The House of Representatives is presided over by the Speaker who is chosen by the members from their own numbers. Every House of Representatives continues for three years from the first meeting of the House, and no longer, but may be sooner dissolved by the Governor-General. Members of the House of Representatives are elected for electoral Divisions on a preferential voting system by adult British subjects who have lived in Australia for at least six months.

A casual vacancy occurring in the House of Representatives is filled by by-election, the member so returned holding his place until the expiration or prior dissolution of that House of Representatives. Voting is compulsory in elections for both Houses of Parliament.

QUALIFICATIONS OF SENATORS AND MEMBERS

To qualify for election as a member of the Senate or House of Representatives a person must be a British subject of the full age of twenty-one years, be an elector entitled to vote at the election of members of the House of Representatives, or a person qualified to become such an elector, and have been for three years at least a resident within the limits of the Commonwealth of Australia as existing at the time he is chosen. A member of either House of Parliament is incapable of being chosen or of sitting as a member of the other House.

POWERS OF THE PARLIAMENT

The Constitution confers on the Parliament two classes of powers; those in respect of which the Parliament alone has power to legislate, i.e. exclusive powers, and those in respect of which the States retain power to legislate concurrently, i.e. concurrent powers. When a concurrent State law is inconsistent with a Commonwealth law, the Commonwealth law prevails and the State law is, to the extent of the inconsistency, invalid.

The matters in respect of which the Constitution expressly provides that the Parliament has exclusive power include the seat of Government of the Commonwealth and all places acquired by the Commonwealth for public purposes, the departments of the Commonwealth Public Service, the imposition of duties of customs and excise and, subject to limited exceptions, the granting of bounties on the production or export of goods.

The concurrent powers given to the Parliament include the power to make laws for the peace, order and good government of the Commonwealth with respect of international and inter-State trade and commerce, taxation, defence, banking and insurance (other than State banking and State insurance), industrial property, immigration and emigration, aliens and naturalisation, marriage, divorce and matrimonial causes, social services, external affairs and conciliation and arbitration for the prevention and settlement of industrial disputes extending beyond the limits of any one State.

With certain exceptions, proposed laws may originate in either House which, for most purposes, have equal power in respect of all proposed laws. Proposed laws appropriating revenue or money or imposing taxation, however, may originate only in the House of Representatives and the Senate may not amend proposed laws imposing taxation or appropriating revenue or moneys for the ordinary annual services of the Government. Such proposed laws may deal only with appropriation of revenue or with the imposition of taxation as the case may be and laws imposing taxation, except those imposing duties of customs or of excise, may deal with one subject of taxation only. The Senate may not amend any proposed law so as to increase any proposed charge or burden on the people but may, at any stage, return to the House of Representatives a proposed law that the Senate is not permitted to amend, requesting the omission or amendment of any item or provision therein. In such event the House of Representatives may, if it thinks fit, make any such omission or amendments, with or without modifications.

If a deadlock between the Senate and the House of Representatives occurs over a proposed law passed by the House of Representatives and if, after three months from the disagreement, the House of Representatives again passes the proposed law and the Houses again fail to agree, the Governor-General may dissolve both Houses immediately. If, after the double dissolution, the House of Representatives again passes the proposed law and a deadlock again occurs, the Governor-General may convene a joint sitting of Members and Senators and if the proposed law is passed by an absolute majority of Members and Senators sitting together it shall be taken to have been duly passed by both Houses.

When a proposed law has been passed by both Houses, it is presented to the Governor-General who is empowered to assent to the bill in the Queen's name, withhold assent or reserve the law for the Queen's pleasure. Additionally, the Queen is empowered to disallow any law within one year from the Governor-General's assent.

THE EXECUTIVE POWER

The executive power of the Commonwealth is vested in the Queen and is exercised by the Governor-General as the Queen's representative. In the Government of the Commonwealth, the Governor-General is advised by the Federal Executive Council, the members of which are appointed by him. By constitutional convention the Governor-General summons to meetings of the

Executive Council only such members of the Council as are Ministers of State of the Government of the day. All Ministers of State, of which there are at present 26, are required to be members of the Executive Council.

THE JUDICIAL POWER

The judicial power of the Commonwealth is vested in the federal courts, namely, the High Court of Australia, the Commonwealth Industrial Court, the Commonwealth Court of Conciliation and Arbitration and the Federal Court of Bankruptcy and in certain courts of the States and Territories when exercising federal jurisdiction conferred upon them by Commonwealth law.

The High Court of Australia, which is the federal supreme court, consists of the Chief Justice and six other justices all of whom are, in common with justices of the Commonwealth Industrial Court, the Commonwealth Court of Conciliation and Arbitration and the Federal Court of Bankruptcy, appointed by the Governor-General in Council and are removable by the Governor-General in Council only on an address by both Houses of the Parliament on the ground of proved misbehaviour or incapacity.

The High Court has both original and appellate jurisdiction. The Constitution confers original jurisdiction on the High Court in respect of matters (1) arising under any treaty, (2) affecting consuls or other representatives of other countries, (3) in which the Commonwealth is a party, (4) between States, or between residents of different States, or between a State and a resident of another State and (5) in which a writ of Mandamus or prohibition or an injunction is sought against an officer of the Commonwealth. In addition, the Parliament is empowered to make laws conferring original jurisdiction on the High Court in any matter (1) arising under the Constitution, or involving its interpretation, (2) arising under any laws made by the Parliament, (3) of Admiralty and maritime jurisdiction and (4) relating to the same matter claimed under the laws of different States.

The Parliament may, with respect to matters in which the High Court has or may be invested with original jurisdiction, make laws defining the jurisdiction of any federal court other than the High Court and the extent to which the jurisdiction of any federal court shall be exclusive of that which belongs to or is invested in the courts of the States, and investing any court of a State with federal jurisdiction.

The appellate jurisdiction of the High Court is to hear and determine appeals from (1) any justice or justices exercising the original jurisdiction of the High Court, (2) any other federal court or court exercising federal jurisdiction, (3) the Supreme Court or any other Court of any State from which at the establishment of the Commonwealth an appeal lay to the Queen in Council and (4) the Inter-State Commission, but as to questions of law only.

In 1968 appeals from decisions of the High Court to the Queen in Council were abolished. It is now not possible to ask for special leave to appeal to Her Majesty in Council against decisions of the High Court except decisions on appeals from State Supreme Courts on matters that do not involve the exercise of federal jurisdiction, or on matters that do not involve the application or interpretation of (1) the Constitution, (2) a law made by the Commonwealth Parliament or (3) an instrument made under such a law. It is also not possible to appeal to Her Majesty in Council from any decisions of Federal Courts other than the High Court.

The Constitution guarantees that the trial on indictment of an offence against any law of the Commonwealth shall be by jury, and that every such trial shall be held in the State where the offence was committed, and that if the offence was not committed within any State the trial shall be held at such place as the Parliament prescribes.

FINANCE AND TRADE

Upon the establishment of the Commonwealth, the collection and control of duties of customs and excise, and the control of the payment of bounties passed to the Government of the Commonwealth and uniform duties of customs were required to be imposed within two years. With the imposition of uniform duties in 1901 the power of the Commonwealth Parliament to impose duties of customs and excise, and to grant bounties on the production or export of goods became exclusive and all laws of the States with respect to these matters ceased to have effect. A further consequence of the imposition of uniform duties was that trade, commerce, and intercourse among the States became 'absolutely free'.

Under a financial agreement entered into by the Commonwealth and the States in 1927, provision was made first for the taking over by the Commonwealth of the public debts of the States and the payment of interest thereon and for the reimbursement of the Commonwealth by the States in respect thereof, and second, for the establishment of the Australian Loan Council, consisting of a Minister from the Commonwealth and each of the States, to regulate borrowing by the Commonwealth and the States so as to avoid competition between the respective governments for loan funds. Among the terms of the agreement was one requiring the Commonwealth to submit certain proposals to the Parliament and the people for the amendment of the Constitution to give the Commonwealth clear constitutional authority to enter into and carry out the terms of the agreement. The agreement was approved by the Financial Agreement 1928 and the proposal for the amendment of the Constitution was passed by both Houses and approved by referendum in 1929. As a consequence of this constitutional amendment the Parliament passed the Financial Agreement Validation Act 1929 validating the 1927 agreement.

In 1933 the Parliament enacted the Commonwealth Grants Commission Act 1933 which established, in the same form as it exists today, a three-member Commission appointed by the Commonwealth Government to enquire into claims made by the States for financial assistance and to make recommendations to the Government in respect thereof, Parliament being empowered to grant financial assistance to any State on such terms and conditions as the Parliament thinks fit.

TAXATION

The power of the Commonwealth Parliament to make laws with respect to taxation is one which is exercisable concurrently with the taxing powers of the several States. Prior to 1942 the amount of tax payable in each State under the respective State income tax laws was considerably in excess of that levied by the Commonwealth in respect of the same income. In 1942, the Commonwealth Government, in the light of the exigencies of the wartime financial position, secured the passage through Parliament of a scheme comprising four bills the nature of which was such as to increase the rate of Commonwealth income tax to a level that would make further State taxation of income virtually impossible. One of the Acts forming part of the scheme provided for the making of grants to the States by way of taxation reimbursements calculated on a formula related to the income tax that each State would have received had it continued to levy taxation. Although the constitutional authority of the scheme, known as Uniform Taxation was challenged by the States in High Court proceedings, it was, for the most part, upheld and now forms the basis of income taxation in Australia, although the formula for reimbursement of States has been varied.

THE STATES

Provision was made for the saving of the Constitutions of the States and the powers of the Parliaments of the States, except those powers exclusively vested in the Commonwealth Parliament, and for the saving of State laws relating to any matter within the powers of the Commonwealth Parliament until provision is made in that behalf by the Commonwealth Parliament. The Parliaments of the States are also empowered to surrender any part of the State to the Commonwealth whereupon that part of the State is to become subject to the exclusive jurisdiction of the Commonwealth.

States may not, without the consent of the Commonwealth Parliament, raise or maintain any naval or military forces or impose any tax on property of any kind belonging to the Commonwealth, and the Commonwealth, in turn, is required to protect every State against invasion and, on the application of the Executive Government of the State, against domestic violence, and is not permitted to impose any tax on property of any kind belonging to a State.

The States are required to make provision for the detention in State prisons of persons accused or convicted of offences against the law of the Commonwealth and for the punishment of persons convicted of such offences.

Full faith and credit must be given throughout the Commonwealth to the laws, the public Acts and records, and the judicial proceedings of every State.

The Commonwealth is expressly prohibited from making laws establishing any religion or for imposing any religious observance or for prohibiting the exercise of any religion, and no religious test is permitted to be required as a qualification for any office or public trust under the Commonwealth.

The Constitution guarantees that a subject of the Queen, resident in any State, shall not be subject in any other State to any disability or discrimination which would not be equally applicable to him if he were a subject of the Queen resident in such other State.

NEW STATES

The Commonwealth Parliament may admit to the Commonwealth, or establish, new States and may upon such admission or establishment impose such terms and conditions, including the extent of representation in either House of Parliament, as it thinks fit. A new State formed by separation of territory from a State may only be so formed with the consent of the Parliament of the State concerned and a new State formed by the union of two or more States or parts of States may only be so formed with the consent of the Parliaments of the States affected. Furthermore, the Commonwealth Parliament may increase, diminish, or otherwise alter the limits of a State only with the approval of the majority of the electors of the State voting upon the question and upon such terms and conditions as may be agreed on, and may, with the like consent, make provision respecting the effect and operation of any increase, diminution or alteration of territory in relation to any State affected.

TERRITORIES

The Commonwealth Parliament alone has power to make laws for the government of any territory surrendered by a State to, and accepted by, the Commonwealth, or of any territory placed by the Queen under the authority of and accepted by the Commonwealth or otherwise acquired by the Commonwealth, and may allow the representation of a territory in either House of Parliament to the extent and on the basis it thinks fit. In 1922, the Parliament exercised this latter power to permit the representation of the Australian Capital Territory and the Northern Territory in the House of Representatives by one member for each territory, either member being entitled to vote on any question arising in the House except on a motion for the disallowance of any Ordinance of the Territory which the member represented. Full voting rights were extended to the member for the Australian Capital Territory in 1966 and to the member for the Northern Territory in 1968. The Commonwealth Parliament has exercised its power with respect to Territories to create a Supreme Court of the Australian Capital Territory and a Supreme Court of the Northern Territory which have jurisdiction in their respective territories comparable to that exercised by the Supreme Court of each State. Appeals lie from Territory Supreme Courts to the High Court of Australia.

THE SEAT OF GOVERNMENT

The Constitution directed the Commonwealth Parliament to determine the Seat of Government, subject, however, to the requirements that it be situated in territory within the State of New South Wales to be granted to or acquired by the Commonwealth and that it be situated not less than one hundred miles from Sydney, the capital city of New South Wales. Provision was made for the Parliament to sit at Melbourne, the capital city of Victoria, until it met at the Seat of Government. In 1908 the Parliament determined the situation of the Seat of Government in the place now known as the Australian Capital Territory although it was not until 1927 that the Parliament first met in Canberra, the National Capital situated in that Territory.

ALTERATION OF THE CONSTITUTION

A proposed amendment of the Constitution must be passed by an absolute majority of both Houses of Parliament and must, not less than two or more than six months after its passage through both Houses, be submitted in each State to electors qualified to vote for the election of members of the House of Representatives. If, however, one House refuses twice to pass a proposed amendment that has been passed by the other House twice in the same session with an interval of not less than three months between each passage, the Governor-General may, notwithstanding such refusals, submit the proposed amendment to the electors. A proposed amendment submitted to the electors must be passed by an absolute majority of all electors voting and absolute majorities of the electors in a majority of the States. When so passed, the proposed law must be presented to the Queen for her assent.

Since 1901 twenty-six proposals have been passed by both Houses and submitted to the electors, the most recent being two proposals submitted on 27th May, 1967, and, of these, five only have been approved by the electors. In 1906 minor alterations were made to the provisions for the election of Senators; in 1910 the power of the Commonwealth to take over the debts of the States, which had hitherto been limited to debts existing at the establishment of the Commonwealth, was extended; in 1928 provisions empowering the Commonwealth to make agreements with the States with respect to the public debts of the States were inserted (see 'Finance and Trade' *supra*); in 1946 the Commonwealth Parliament was given concurrent powers with respect to social services; and in 1967 provisions (1) precluding the counting of aboriginals in reckoning the numbers of the people of the Commonwealth, or of a State or other part of the Commonwealth, and (2) excluding the aboriginal race from the races in respect of whose people the Commonwealth Parliament may make special laws, were deleted.

HISTORICAL LIST

GOVERNORS-GENERAL

John Adrian Hope, 7th Earl of Hopetoun, KT, PC, GCMG, GCVO, DL (later 1st Marquess of Linlithgow), 1st January 1901 to 9th January 1903

†Hallam Tennyson, 2nd Baron Tennyson, PC, GCMG, 17th January 1902 to 9th January 1903

Hallam Tennyson, 2nd Baron Tennyson, PC, GCMG, 9th January 1903 to 21st July 1904

Henry Stafford Northcote, 1st Baron Northcote, PC, GCIE, GCMG, CB, 21st January 1904 to 9th September 1908

William Humble Ward, 2nd Earl of Dudley, PC, GCB, GCMG, GCVO, 9th September 1908 to 31st July 1911

†Frederick John Napier Thesiger, 3rd Baron Chelmsford, PC, KCMG (later 1st Viscount Chelmsford, GCSI, GCMG, GCIE, GBE), 21st December 1909 to 27th January 1910

Thomas Denman, 3rd Baron Denman, PC, GCMG, KCVO, 31st July 1911 to 18th May 1914

Ronald Craufurd Munro-Ferguson, 1st Viscount Novar, PC, GCMG, 18th May 1914 to 6th October 1920

Henry William Forster, 1st Baron Forster of Lepe, PC, GCMG, 6th October 1920 to 8th October 1925

John Lawrence Stonehaven, 1st Baron Stonehaven, PC, GCMG, DSO, DL (later 1st Viscount Stonehaven) 8th October 1925 to 22nd January 1931

†Lieutenant-Colonel Arthur Herbert Tennyson Somers, 6th Baron Somers, KCMG, DSO, MC, 3rd October 1930 to 22nd January 1931

Sir Isaac Isaacs, PC, KCMG, KC (later GCB, GCMG), 22nd January 1931 to 23rd January 1936

Brigadier-General Alexander Gore Arkwright Hore-Ruthven, 1st Baron Gowrie of Canberra, VC, PC, GCMG, CB, DSO (later 1st Earl of Gowrie), 23rd January 1936 to 29th January 1945

†William Charles Arcdeckne Vanneck, Bt., 5th Baron Huntingfield, KCMG, 29th March to 24th September 1938

†Major-General Sir Winston Dugan, GCMG, CB, DSO, 5th September 1944 to 29th January 1945

His Royal Highness The Duke of Gloucester, KG, KT, KP, GMB, GCMG, GCVO, 30th January 1945 to 10th March 1947

†Major-General Sir Winston Dugan, GCMG, CB, DSO, 19th January 1947 to 10th March 1947

Sir William McKell, QC (later PC, GCMG), 11th March 1947 to 8th May 1953

†Lieutenant-General Sir John Northcott, KCMG, KCVO, CB, 19th July 1951 to 14th December 1951 and 30th July 1956 to 2nd October 1956 (Honorary rank of General whilst administering the Government)

Field-Marshal Sir William Slim, GCB, GCMG, GBE, DSO, MC (later 1st Viscount Slim of Yarralumba, KG, GCVO) 8th May 1953 to 31st January 1960

---

† Administering the Government

William Shepherd Morrison, 1st Viscount Dunrossil, PC, GCMG, MC, QC, 2nd February 1960 to 3rd February 1961
†General Sir Dallas Brooks, KCB, KCMG, KCVO, DSO, 4th February to 3rd August 1961
William Philip Sidney, 1st Viscount De L'Isle, VC, PC, GCMG (later GCVO), 3rd August 1961 to 6th May 1965
†Colonel Sir Henry Abel Smith, KCMG, KCVO, DSO, 7th May 1965 to 21st September 1965
Lord Casey, KG, CH, DSO, MC, 22nd September 1965 to 28th April 1969
The Rt Hon. Sir Paul Hasluck, GCVO, GCMG from 30th April 1969

MINISTRIES

E. Barton, PC, KC (later Sir Edmund Barton, GCMG, KC), 1st January 1901 to 24th September 1903
A. Deakin, 24th September 1903 to 27th April 1904
J. C. Watson, 27th April 1904 to 18th August 1904
G. H. Reid, PC, KC (later Sir George Reid, GCMG, GCB), 18th August 1904 to 5th July 1905
A. Deakin, 5th July 1905 to 13th November 1908
A. Fisher (later PC), 13th November 1908 to 2nd June 1909
A. Deakin, 2nd June 1909 to 29th April 1910
A. Fisher, PC, 29th April 1910 to 24th June 1913
J. Cook, PC (later Sir Joseph Cook, GCMG), 24th June 1913 to 17th September 1914
A. Fisher, PC, 17th September 1914 to 27th October 1915
W. M. Hughes, PC, CH, KC, 27th October 1915 to 9th February 1923
S. M. Bruce, PC, CH, MC (later Viscount Bruce of Melbourne), 9th February 1923 to 22nd October 1929
J. H. Scullin, PC, 22nd October 1929 to 6th January 1932
J. A. Lyons, PC, CH, 6th January 1932 to 7th April 1939
Sir E. C. G. Page, PC, GCMG, CH, 7th April to 26th April 1939
R. G. Menzies, PC, CH, KC, 26th April 1939 to 29th August 1941
A. W. Fadden, PC (later Sir Arthur Fadden, KCMG), 29th August to 7th October 1941
J. Curtin, PC, 7th October 1941 to 6th July 1945
F. M. Forde, PC, 6th July to 13th July 1945
J. B. Chifley, PC, 13th July 1945 to 19th December 1949
R. G. Menzies, PC, CH, QC (later Sir Robert Menzies, KT), 19th December 1949 to 26th January 1966
H. E. Holt, PC, CH, from 26th January 1966 to 19th December 1967
J. McEwen, from 19th December 1967 to 10th January 1968
J. G. Gorton, from 10th January 1968 to 10th March 1971
W. McMahon, from 10th March 1971

GOVERNMENT

After the general election held in November 1969, the composition of the political parties in the House of Representatives became: Liberal Party 46; Country Party 20; Australian Labour Party 59. The Government was formed by a coalition of the Liberal and Country Parties.

GOVERNOR-GENERAL

His Excellency The Right Honourable Sir Paul Hasluck, GCVO, GCMG

McMahon Ministry

*Prime Minister: The Rt. Hon. William McMahon, MP
*Deputy Prime Minister and Minister for Trade and Industry: The Rt. Hon J. D. Anthony, MP
*Minister for Defence: The Rt. Hon. David Fairbairn, DFC, MP
*Minister for Primary Industry: The Hon. Ian Sinclair, MP
*Minister for Supply and Leader of the Government in the Senate:
Senator The Hon. Sir Kenneth Anderson
*Minister for National Development and Leader of the House:
The Hon. R. W. C. Swartz, MBE, ED, MP
*Treasurer: The Hon. B. M. Snedden, QC, MP
*Attorney-General: The Hon. N. H. Bowen, QC, MP
*Minister for Education and Science: The Hon. Malcolm Fraser, MP

* Denotes Minister in Cabinet
† Administering the Government

*Postmaster-General and Vice-President of the Executive Council:
The Hon. Sir Alan Hulme, KBE, MP
*Minister for Foreign Affairs: The Hon. L. H. E. Bury, MP
*Minister for Shipping and Transport: The Hon. P. J. Nixon, MP
*Minister for Labour and National Service: The Hon. Phillip Lynch, MP
Minister for External Territories: The Hon. C. E. Barnes, MP
Minister for Immigration: The Hon. A. J. Forbes, MC, MP
Minister for Social Services and Minister in Charge—Aboriginal Affairs:
The Hon. W. C. Wentworth, MP
Minister for Works and Minister in Charge—Tourist Activities:
Senator The Hon. R. C. Wright
Minister for Civil Aviation: Senator The Hon. Robert Cotton
Minister for Customs and Excise: The Hon. D. L. Chipp, MP
Minister for Air: Senator The Hon. Tom Drake-Brockman, DFC
Minister for the Army and Minister assisting the Prime Minister:
The Hon. Andrew Peacock, MP
Minister for Repatriation: The Hon. R. McN. Holten, MP
Minister for Health: Senator The Hon. I. J. Greenwood, QC
Minister for the Navy: The Hon. Malcolm Mackay, MP
Minister for the Interior: The Hon. Ralph J. Hunt, MP
Minister for Housing: The Hon. Kevin Cairns, MP
Minister for the Environment, Aboriginal Affairs and the Arts: The Hon. Peter Howson, MP
*Minister in the Cabinet

LEADER OF OPPOSITION
E. G. Whitlam, QC, MP

SENATE
President: Senator the Hon. Sir Alister McMullin, KCMG
Chairman of Committees: Senator the Hon. T. C. Drake-Brockman, DFC
Clerk of Senate: J. R. Odgers, CBE

HOUSE OF REPRESENTATIVES
Speaker: The Hon. Sir William Aston, KCMG, MP
Chairman of Committees: P. E. Lucock, MP
Clerk of House of Representatives: A. G. Turner, CBE

JUDICIARY

HIGH COURT OF AUSTRALIA
Chief Justice: Rt. Hon. Sir Garfield Barwick, GCMG

Justices:

Rt. Hon. Sir Edward A. McTiernan, KBE	Rt. Hon. Sir William F. L. Owen, KBE
Rt. Hon. Sir Douglas I. Menzies, KBE	The Hon. Sir Cyril A. Walsh, KBE
Rt. Hon. Sir Victor Windeyer, KBE, CB, DSO, ED	Hon. Sir Harry Talbot Gibbs, KBE

Principal Registrar: A. N. Gamble

COMMONWEALTH INDUSTRIAL COURT
Chief Judge: The Hon. Sir John A. Spicer

Judges:

Hon. Mr. Justice E. A. Dunphy	Hon. Mr. Justice R. A. Smithers
Hon. Mr. Justice P. E. Joske, CMG	Hon. Mr. Justice J. R. Kerr, CMG
Hon. Mr. Justice R. M. Eggleston	Hon. Mr. Justice J. A. Nimmo, CBE, OStJ

FEDERAL COURT OF BANKRUPTCY
Judge:
Hon. Mr. Justice C. A. Sweeney

SUPREME COURT OF THE AUSTRALIAN CAPITAL TERRITORY
Judges:

Hon. Mr. Justice R. W. Fox	Hon. Sir Richard Eggleston
Hon. Mr. Justice R. A. Blackburn, OBE	Hon. Mr. Justice R. A. Smithers
Hon. Mr. Justice E. A. Dunphy	Hon. Mr. Justice J. R. Kerr, CMG
Hon. Mr. Justice P. E. Joske, CMG	Hon. Mr. Justice J. A. Nimmo, CBE, OStJ

* Denotes Minister in Cabinet

SUPREME COURT OF THE NORTHERN TERRITORY OF AUSTRALIA
Judges:
Hon. Mr. Justice W. Forster
Hon. Mr. Justice E. A. Dunphy
Hon. Mr. Justice P. E. Joske, CMG

Hon. Mr. Justice R. A. Smithers
Hon. Mr. Justice J. A. Nimmo, CBE, OStJ

CHAIRMAN OF THE LAW REFORM COMMISSION
Hon. Mr. Justice R. A. Blackburn, OBE

GOVERNMENT DEPARTMENTS

THE DEPARTMENT OF THE PRIME MINISTER AND CABINET
Secretary: Sir John Bunting, Kt, CBE

Public Service Board
Chairman: Sir Frederick Wheeler, CBE
Commissioners: J. E. Collings; A. B. McFarlane, CBE, DFC
Secretary: H. B. McDonald

Auditor-General's Office
Auditor-General: V. J. W. Skermer, CBE

*Commonwealth Grants Commission**
Chairman: Sir Leslie Melville, KBE

DEPARTMENT OF TRADE AND INDUSTRY
Secretary: Mr. D. H. McKay, OBE

Tariff Board
Chairman: G. A. Rattigan, CBE

TREASURY
Secretary: Sir Richard Randall

Bureau of Census and Statistics
Commonwealth Statistician: J. P. O'Neill

Reserve Bank of Australia†
Governor: J. G. Phillips, CBE

Commonwealth Banking Corporation†
Chairman: Sir Roland Wilson, KBE

Commonwealth Taxation Office
Commissioner of Taxation: E. T. Cain, CBE

Australian Government Publishing Service
Controller: P. A. Nott

Superannuation Board
President: L. K. Burgess

DEPARTMENT OF NATIONAL DEVELOPMENT
Secretary: L. F. Bott, DSC

Australian Atomic Energy Commission†
Chairman: Professor Sir Philip Baxter, KBE, CMG

DEPARTMENT OF DEFENCE
Secretary: Sir Arthur Tange, CBE

DEPARTMENT OF EXTERNAL TERRITORIES
Secretary: D. O. Hay, CBE, DSO

DEPARTMENT OF LABOUR AND NATIONAL SERVICE*
Secretary: Dr. P. H. Cook, OBE
Public Service Arbitrator: E. A. C. Chambers, CBE

DEPARTMENT OF CIVIL AVIATION*
Director-General: Sir Donald Anderson CBE

POSTMASTER-GENERAL'S DEPARTMENT*
Director-General, Posts and Telegraphs: Sir John Knott, CBE

DEPARTMENT OF IMMIGRATION
Secretary: R. E. Armstrong, OBE

DEPARTMENT OF FOREIGN AFFAIRS
Secretary: Sir Keith Waller, CBE

ATTORNEY-GENERAL'S DEPARTMENT
Solicitor-General: R. J. Ellicott, QC
Secretary: C. W. Harders, OBE
Crown Solicitor: R. B. Hutchison, OBE
Commissioner and Registrar of Patent, Trade Marks, Designs and Copyright Offices: K. B. Petersson
Commissioner of Trade Practices: R. M. Bannerman
Inspector-General in Bankruptcy: J. T. Johnston
Commissioner of Police, Commonwealth Police Force: J. M. Davis, QPM

OFFICE OF PARLIAMENTARY COUNSEL‡
First Parliamentary Counsel: J. Q. Ewens, CBE
Second Parliamentary Counsel: C. K. Comans, OBE, B. C. Quayle, OBE

DEPARTMENT OF PRIMARY INDUSTRY
Secretary: W. Ives

---

*Head Office in Melbourne   † Head Office in Sydney
‡Now a separate Dept. *not* under Attorney-General's.

DEPARTMENT OF THE ARMY

Military Board President: The Hon. Andrew Peacock, MP, Minister for the Army
Chief of the General Staff: Lieutenant-General M. F. Brogan, CB, CBE
Adjutant-General: Major-General D. Vincent, CB, OBE
Quartermaster-General: Major-General G. F. T. Richardson, CBE
Master-General of the Ordnance: Major-General T. F. Cape, CBE, DSO
Deputy Chief of the General Staff: Major-General S. C. Graham, DSO, OBE, MC
Citizen Military Forces Member: Major-General A. C. Murchison, MC, ED
Judge Advocate General: Major-General B. M. Hogan, ED
Secretary, Department of the Army: B. White, CBE

DEPARTMENT OF SOCIAL SERVICES*

Director-General: L. B. Hamilton, OBE

DEPARTMENT OF CUSTOMS AND EXCISE

Comptroller- General: A. T. Carmody, CBE

DEPARTMENT OF THE INTERIOR

Secretary: G. Warwick Smith, CBE

DEPARTMENT OF WORKS*

Director-General: A. S. Reiher

DEPARTMENT OF THE NAVY

Naval Board, President: The Hon. Dr. M. McKay, MP, Minister for the Navy
1st Naval Member: Vice-Admiral R. I. Peek, CB, OBE, DSC
2nd Naval Member: Rear-Admiral H. D. Stevenson, CBE
3rd Naval Member: Rear-Admiral B. J. Castles, CBE
4th Naval Member and Chief of Supply: Rear-Admiral W. D. H. Graham, CBE
Secretary, Department of the Navy: S. Landau, CBE

DEPARTMENT OF SHIPPING AND TRANSPORT*

Secretary: M. M. Summers

DEPARTMENT OF HEALTH

Director-General of Health and Director of Quarantine: Major-General Sir William Refshauge, CBE, ED

DEPARTMENT OF SUPPLY*

Secretary: A. S. Cooley

REPATRIATION DEPARTMENT*

Chairman of Repatriation Commission: R. Kingsland, CBE, DFC
Secretary to Commission: R. G. Kelly

DEPARTMENT OF AIR

Air Board, Chief of Air Staff: Air Marshal Sir Colin Hannah, KBE, CB
Air Member for Personnel: Air Vice-Marshal B. A. Eaton, CB, CBE, DSO, DFC
Air Member for Supply and Equipment: Air Vice-Marshal C. G. Cleary, CBE
Air Member for Technical Services: Air Vice-Marshal E. Hey, CB, CBE
Secretary, Department of Air: F. J. Green

DEPARTMENT OF HOUSING

Secretary: J. F. Nimmo, CBE

DEPARTMENT OF EDUCATION AND SCIENCE

Secretary: Professor Sir Hugh Ennor, CBE

AUSTRALIAN UNIVERSITIES COMMISSION

Chairman: Professor P. H. Karmel, CBE

COMMONWEALTH SCIENTIFIC AND INDUSTRIAL RESEARCH ORGANISATION

Chairman of Executive Committee: Dr. J. R. Price, FAA

DIPLOMATIC REPRESENTATION

AUSTRALIAN HIGH COMMISSIONERS IN OTHER COMMONWEALTH COUNTRIES

Britain: Hon. Sir Alexander Downer, KBE (High Commissioner); Canada: D W. McNicol, CBE (High Commissioner); New Zealand: Dame Annabelle Rankin (High Commissioner); India: P. Shaw, CBE (High Commissioner); Pakistan: F. H. Stewart (High Commissioner); Ceylon: H. D. White (High Commissioner); Fiji: R. F. Osborn (Commissioner); Ghana: J. M. McMillan (High Commissioner); Hong Kong: R. J. Barcham (Senior Trade Commissioner); Malaysia: J. R. Rowland (High Commissioner); Malta G.C.: Hon. Sir Hubert Opperman, OBE (High Commissioner); Nigeria: P. Hutton (High Commissioner); Tanzania: W. G. A. Landale (High Commissioner); Uganda: K. H. Rogers (resident in Nairobi) (High Commissioner); Kenya: K. H. Rogers (High Commissioner); Singapore: N. S. Parkinson (High Commissioner); Trinidad and Tobago: T. N. Cronin (Trade Commissioner); Nauru: R. K. Bate (Representative).

---

* Head Office in Melbourne

COMMONWEALTH HIGH COMMISSIONERS
IN AUSTRALIA

Britain: Rt. Hon. Sir Morrice James,
KCMG, CVO, MBE; Canada: A. R. Menzies;
Ghana: J. Owusu-Akyeampong; New
Zealand: A. J. Yendell; India: M.
Krishnamorti; Pakistan: M. M. Abbas;
Ceylon: J. Siriwardene; Singapore: A. P.
Rajah; Malaysia: Tan Sri Dato Mohamed
Fuad Stephens, PSM, PDK, PNBS; Malta
G.C.: J. M. Dingli.

AUSTRALIAN REPRESENTATION IN
NON-COMMONWEALTH COUNTRIES

Afghanistan: (Ambassador) (resident in
Islamabad); Argentina: (Ambassador);
Austria: (Ambassador); Belgium: (Ambassador);
Brazil: (Ambassador); Burma:
(Ambassador); Chile: (Ambassador); Denmark:
(Ambassador) (resident in The
Hague); Ethiopia: (Ambassador) (resident
in Nairobi); Finland: (Ambassador) (resident
in Stockholm); France: (Ambassador);
Germany: (Ambassador); Greece: (Ambassador);
Indonesia: (Ambassador); Iran:
(Ambassador); Israel: (Ambassador); Italy:
(Ambassador); Japan: (Ambassador);
Khmer Republic: (Ambassador); Korea:
(Ambassador); Laos: (Ambassador); Lebanon:
(Ambassador); Mexico: (Ambassador);
Nepal: (Ambassador) (resident in New
Delhi); Netherlands: (Ambassador); New
Caledonia: (Consul); Norway: (Ambassador)
(resident in Stockholm); Peru:
(Ambassador) (resident in Buenos Aires);
Philippines: (Ambassador); Portugal:
(Ambassador) (resident in Paris); Portuguese
Timor: (Consul); Republic of Ireland:
(Ambassador); Republic of South Africa:
(Ambassador); Romania: (Ambassador)
(resident in Belgrade); Spain: (Ambassador);
Sweden: (Ambassador); Switzerland: (Ambassador);
Thailand: (Ambassador);
Turkey: (Ambassador); U.S.S.R.: (Ambassador);
United Arab Republic: (Ambassador);
United Nations: (Ambassador,
New York); (Permanent Representative in
Europe, Geneva); United States: (Ambassador);
Uruguay: (Ambassador) (resident
in Buenos Aires): Viet Nam: (Ambassador);
Yugoslavia: (Ambassador).

STATES OF THE COMMONWEALTH AND AUSTRALIAN TERRITORIES
NEW SOUTH WALES

The State of New South Wales lies on the eastern (Pacific) coast of Australia, almost entirely between the 29th and 36th parallels of south latitude. To the south it is separated from Victoria by the Murray River, but the boundary with South Australia to the west and the greater part of that with Queensland to the north is merely a straight line on the map.

The area of New South Wales (inclusive of a dependency, Lord Howe Island, five square miles, but exclusive of the Australian Capital Territory, 910 square miles) is 309,433 square miles, a little over two and a half times that of Great Britain and Ireland. The estimated population as at 30th June 1970 was 4,567,000 of whom an estimated 2,780,310 lived in Sydney, the State capital.

HISTORY

The name New South Wales was given to the eastern part of Australia on its discovery by Captain Cook in 1770, but the first settlement was not formed until 1788, at Sydney under Captain Phillip.

Settlement for a time was slow, because a passage over the Blue Mountains, giving access to the interior plains, was not discovered until 1813. In 1828 the total population was only 36,598, but the discovery of gold in 1851 attracted many settlers. Responsible Government was established in 1856. In 1901 the Colony of New South Wales federated with the Colonies of Victoria, Queensland, South Australia, Western Australia and Tasmania to form the Commonwealth of Australia.

CONSTITUTION

The Constitution Act of 1902 (No. 32 of 1902) provides that the Legislature

For further information about New South Wales see the *Official Year Book of New South Wales* of New South Wales 'shall, subject to the provisions of the Commonwealth of Australia Constitution Act, have power to make laws for the peace, welfare and good government of New South Wales in all cases whatsoever'. The Legislature consists of the Crown and two Houses; the Legislative Council and the Legislative Assembly.

The Governor is the local representative of the Crown. His functions are defined partly by statutes and partly by Letters Patent and Instructions to the Governor issued under the Royal Sign Manual. He acts on the advice of the Executive Council or of a Minister of the Crown, except in limited spheres where he possesses discretionary power, *e.g.* in regard to the dissolution of Parliament.

The Executive Council consists of members of the Ministry formed by the leader of the dominant party in the Legislative Assembly, and the Governor presides over its deliberations.

In compliance with a referendum assented to in May 1933, the Legislative Council was reconstituted on 23rd April 1934. The new House consisted of sixty members, elected by the combined vote of members of the existing Legislative Council and Legislative Assembly, provision being made for the retirement of fifteen members in rotation every three years, and the members being therefore initially elected in groups for three, six, nine and twelve years respectively.

The Legislative Assembly consists of ninety-six members elected under a system of universal adult suffrage for up to three years. By Act No. 33 of 1950 any bill prolonging the life of the Assembly beyond the period of three years cannot be presented for the Royal Assent until it has been approved by a referendum. The Act also provides that any bill repealing or amending its provisions similarly requires approval by referendum. Any person enrolled as an elector may be elected to the Assembly, except members of the Legislative Council or of the Federal Legislature. Bills appropriating money or imposing taxation and bills affecting the Assembly itself must originate in the Assembly, and by its power over supply this House controls the Executive.

Adult British subjects, men and women, are qualified for enrolment as electors when they have resided in the Commonwealth for a period of six months, in the State for three months, and in any sub-division of an electoral district for one month preceding the date of claim for enrolment. Since 1894 each elector has been entitled to one vote only, and voting has been compulsory since 1928.

The electoral law provides that electorates are to be redistributed whenever directed by the Governor. In the event of there being no direction by the Governor, a distribution must take place on the expiration of five years from the date of the last redistribution. The redistribution is made by the Electoral Districts Commissioners, who may make use of the services of any of the officers and employees of the Public Service.

GOVERNMENT

At the Legislative Assembly election in February 1971 the Liberal Party secured 33 seats, the Country Party 16, the Labour Party 45, and seats were gained by two Independents. The Government was formed by a coalition of the Liberal and Country Parties.

The Legislative Council comprised in April 1971: 17 Liberal Party members: 12 Country Party; 26 Labour Party; 5 Independents.

GOVERNOR

His Excellency Sir Arthur Roden Cutler, VC, KCMG, KCVO, CBE, KStf

THE MINISTRY

Premier and Treasurer: The Hon. Robin William Askin, MLA
Deputy Premier, Minister for Education and Minister for Science:
The Hon. Charles Benjamin Cutler, ED, MLA
Chief Secretary and Minister for Tourism and Sport:
The Hon. Eric Archibald Willis, BA, MLA
Minister for Decentralisation and Development and Vice-President of the Executive Council:
The Hon. John Bryan Munro Fuller, MLC
Minister for Public Works: The Hon. Davis Hughes, MLA
Attorney-General: The Hon. Kenneth Malcolm McCaw, MLA
Minister for Local Government and Minister for Highways:
The Hon. Philip Henry Morton, MLA
Minister for Transport: The Hon. Milton Arthur Morris, MLA
Minister for Lands: The Hon. Thomas Lancelot Lewis, MLA
Minister for Environment Control: The Hon. Jack Gordon Beale, ME, MLA
Minister for Agriculture:
The Hon. Geoffrey Robertson Crawford, DCM, MLA
Minister for Housing and Minister for Co-operative Societies:
The Hon. Stanley Tunstall Stephens, MLA
Minister of Justice: The Hon. John Clarkson Maddison, BA, LLB, MLA
Minister for Health: The Hon. Arnold Henry Jago, MLA
Minister for Mines and Minister for Conservation: The Hon. Wallace Clyde Fife, MLA
Minister for Labour and Industry: The Hon. Frederick Maclean Hewitt, MLC
Minister for Child Welfare and Minister for Social Welfare:
The Hon. John Lloyd Waddy, OBE, DFC, MLA
Minister for Cultural Activities and Assistant Treasurer:
The Hon. George Francis Freudenstein, MLA

OPPOSITION

Leader of the Opposition: Patrick Darcy Hills, MLA

LEGISLATIVE COUNCIL

President: The Hon. Sir Harry Vincent Budd, MLC
Chairman of Committees: The Hon. Thomas Sidney McKay, MLC
Clerk: Major-General J. R. Stevenson, CBE, DSO, ED

LEGISLATIVE ASSEMBLY

Speaker: The Hon. Sir Kevin Ellis, KBE, MLA
Chairman of Committees: Leon Ashton Punch, MLA
Clerk of the Legislative Assembly: I. P. K. Vidler

SUPREME COURT

Chief Justice: The Hon. Sir Leslie Herron, KBE, CMG
President, Court of Appeal: The Hon. Sir Bernard Sugerman, Kt

JUDGES OF APPEAL

Hon. C. McLelland	Hon. A. F. Mason, CBE
Hon. K. S. Jacobs	Hon. J. K. Manning
Hon. K. W. Asprey	Hon. A. R. Moffitt
Hon. J. D. Holmes	

PUISNE JUDGES

Hon. J. H. McClemens	Hon. J. O'Brien
Hon. R. Le G. Brereton	Hon. S. Isaacs
Hon. H. Maguire	Hon. N. A. Jenkyn
Hon. M. F. Hardie	Hon. L. W. Street
Hon. W. H. Collins	Hon. J. A. Lee
Hon. R. Else-Mitchell	Hon. R. G. Reynolds
Hon. B. P. Macfarlan, OBE	Hon. M. M. Helsham
Hon. J. F. Nagle	Hon. C. L. D. Meares
Hon. R. L. Taylor	Hon. P. B. Toose, CBE
Hon. D. M. Selby, ED	Hon. M. Hope
Hon. C. E. Begg	Hon. G. Carmichael
Hon. P. H. Allen	Hon. J. P. Slattery

LORD HOWE ISLAND

This island lies 436 miles north-east from Sydney. Its area is five square miles and its estimated population as at 30 June 1970 was 270. For purposes of representation in Parliament it is included in one of the Sydney electorates. A Board of Control under the Chief Secretary's Department, Sydney, administers the island.

VICTORIA

Victoria is situated at the south-east of the continent of Australia, and lies between the 34th and 39th parallels of S. latitude. The area is 87,884 square miles. The latest official estimate of Victoria's population (at 30th June 1970) was 3,443,800, published in the Victorian monthly statistical review, issued by the Bureau of Census and Statistics, in February 1971.

The other principal urban areas in Victoria are Geelong (pop. 105,059), Ballarat (pop. 56,290) and Bendigo (pop. 42,208). Principal seaports are Melbourne and Geelong. There is an international airport at Tullamarine nine miles from Melbourne.

The principal products are wool, cereals, dairy products, meat, fruits (fresh, canned and dried) and a wide range of manufactured goods.

HISTORY

It is believed that the first Europeans to sight the Victorian coast were Captain Cook and the crew of His Majesty's ship *Endeavour*. The first permanent settlement was formed at Portland in 1834 by Edward Henty from Van Diemen's Land (Tasmania). Melbourne, later to be the capital, was founded at the northern end of Port Phillip Bay in 1835.

In 1851 the District of Port Phillip, which had previously formed part of New South Wales, was separated from that State by an Act of the Parliament at Westminster and became a separate Colony under the name of Victoria with a Legislative Council of its own.

Shortly afterwards, rich deposits of gold were discovered in Victoria which led to a great influx of population.

PRESENT CONSTITUTION

The Constitution Act (13 & 14 Vict. c. 59. s.32) was assented to by Her Majesty in Council, pursuant to the provisions of Statute 18 & 19 Vict. c. 55.s. 1, on 21st July 1855 and was proclaimed and came into operation on 23rd November 1855. It is generally referred to as Schedule (1) of the Imperial Act 18 & 19 Vict. c. 55.

Under the Constitution the Parliament of Victoria comprises a Legislative Council, or Upper House, and a Legislative Assembly, or Lower House. It has power to alter the Constitution in any way. The Constitution Act Amendment Act 1958 dated 30th September 1958 consolidated previous amending Acts and consolidated the law relating to the amendment of the Constitution. There have been further amendments between 1958 and 1970.

The Legislative Council consists of 36 members elected for 18 provinces and the Legislative Assembly consists of 73 members elected for 73 electoral districts

For further information about Victoria see the *Victorian Year Book*

One of the two members of the Legislative Council returned for each province retires in rotation at three-yearly intervals so that the tenure of office of each is ordinarily six years.

The duration of the Assembly and the tenure of office of its members is ordinarily three years but it may be dissolved by the Governor in accordance with Parliamentary convention at any time.

Persons over 21 years of age of either sex are eligible to vote at both Council and Assembly elections. Voting was made compulsory at Assembly elections in 1926 and at Council elections in 1935. At elections each elector has only one vote.

Under the Constitution the ultimate executive power is vested in the Crown and is exercised by the Governor as the Queen's representative.

As the Queen's representative the Governor summons and prorogues Parliament, gives Assent to Bills which have passed all stages in Parliament, with the exception of those required to be specially reserved for the Royal Assent, and exercises the Royal prerogative of mercy.

The Governor, upon the advice of the Executive Council, also exercises many powers conferred by numerous Victorian Statutes.

The Executive Council is a body created under the Governor's Instructions which in practice gives formal effect to Cabinet and ministerial decisions. There are at present 15 Ministers of the Crown, who are the only active members of the Executive Council.

GOVERNMENT

At the Assembly election in May 1970 the Liberal Party secured 42 seats, the Labour Party 22 seats, the Country Party 8 seats and Independent Labour 1 seat. In the Legislative Council the Liberal Party has 19 seats; the Labour Party 8; and the Country Party 9.

GOVERNOR
His Excellency Major-General Sir Rohan Delacombe, K CMG, K CVO, K BE, CB, DSO, KStJ

THE LIEUTENANT-GOVERNOR
Lieutenant-General the Honorable Sir Edmund Herring, K CMG, K BE, DSO, MC, ED

THE MINISTRY
Premier and Treasurer: The Hon. Sir Henry Bolte, K CMG, MP
Chief Secretary, and Attorney-General: G. O. Reid, MP
Minister of Agriculture: G. L. Chandler, CMG, MLC
Minister for Local Government: R. J. Hamer, ED, MLC
Minister of Education: L. H. S. Thompson, MP
Minister of Housing, Minister of Forests, and Minister for Aboriginal Affairs:
E. R. Meagher, MBE, ED, MP
Minister for Fuel and Power, and Minister of Mines: J. C. M. Balfour, MP
Minister of Health: J. F. Rossiter, MP
Minister of Transport: V. F. Wilcox, MP
Minister of State Development, Minister for Tourism, and Minister of Immigration:
V. O. Dickie, MLC
Minister of Lands, Minister of Soldier Settlement, and Minister for Conservation:
W. A. Borthwick, MP
Minister of Labour and Industry, and Assistant Minister of Education:
J. A. Rafferty, MP
Minister of Public Works: Murray Byrne, MLC
Minister for Social Welfare: Ian Winton Smith, MP
Minister of Water Supply: Robert Christian Dunstan, DSO, MP
Parliamentary Secretary of the Cabinet: A. H. Scanlan, Esquire, MP

LEADER OF THE OPPOSITION
A. C. Holding, MP

LEGISLATIVE COUNCIL
President: Hon. R. W. Garrett, AFC, AEA, MLC
Chairman of Committees: Hon. G. J. Nicol, MLC
The Clerk of Parliaments and Clerk of the Legislative Council:
A. R. B. McDonnell

LEGISLATIVE ASSEMBLY
Speaker: Hon. Vernon Christie, MP
Chairman of Committees: Sir Edgar Tanner, CBE, ED, MP
The Clerk of the Legislative Assembly: J. H. Campbell

SUPREME COURT
Chief Justice: Hon. Sir Henry Winneke, KCMG, OBE, QC

Puisne Judges:

Hon. T. W. Smith	Hon. M. V. McInerney
Hon. Sir George Pape	Hon. G. H. Lush
Hon. A. D. G. Adam	Hon. C. I. Menhennitt
Hon. D. M. Little	Hon. H. R. Newton
Hon. U. G. Gowans	Hon. F. R. Nelson
Hon. O. J. Gillard	Hon. K. V. Anderson
Hon. J. E. Starke	Hon. W. C. Crockett
Hon. E. H. E. Barber	Hon. N. M. Stephen

QUEENSLAND

Situated within the parallels of 10 and 29 degrees S. latitude and the meridians of 138 and 154 degrees E. longitude the State of Queensland occupies an area of 667,000 square miles (being more than equal to the combined areas of France, Germany, Italy and the British Isles). The breadth of the territory near the southern boundary is about 900 miles. As at 31 December 1970 the estimated population was 1,819,800 of whom some 860,000 resided in the Brisbane Statistical Division. In Queensland the population of assisted and non-assisted aborigines, part aborigines and Torres Strait Islanders, is estimated to be over 60,000. All have full citizenship rights.

The number of assisted persons is 30,500 of whom 7,000 reside in Government communities, 13,000 in country reserves, 2,500 in Church sponsored communities, and 8,000 in the Torres Strait Islands. The non-assisted aboriginal and Island Queenslanders (approx. 30,000) live in the general community.

HISTORY

Captain Cook discovered Moreton Bay in 1770, but the Brisbane River, running into it, was not located until 1823. The Moreton Bay Settlement was formed in New South Wales in 1824. The Darling Downs were explored in 1827 and squatters began to settle there soon afterwards. The territory was not, however, thrown open to colonisation until 1842. It was separated from New South Wales in 1859, to become a separate colony with about 25,000 inhabitants. It received responsible government at the same time.

CONSTITUTION

The constitution is regulated by the Letters Patent of 6 June 1859 and Queensland Act 31, Vict. No. 38. The legislature consists of one House, the Legislative Assembly, the members of which are elected (since 1905) by male and female adult franchise on residential qualifications only (three months' continuous residence in the State, and six months' within the Commonwealth). By the

Electoral Districts Act of 1958 the State is divided into 78 districts, each returning one member. It is compulsory for all duly qualified persons to vote at State and Local Authority Elections.

The Upper House, or Legislative Council, was abolished by an Act passed in 1922 (12 Geo. V. c. 32). Its members were nominated by the Governor-in-Council and held office for life.

GOVERNMENT

Following the election of May 1969 and subsequent bye-election the Country Party holds 25 seats, the Liberal Party 20 seats, the Australian Labor Party 31 seats, the Queensland Labor Party 1 seat and the North Queensland Labor Party 1 seat. The Country and Liberal parties, with a total of 45 seats, form a coalition Government.

GOVERNOR
His Excellency The Hon. Sir Alan James Mansfield, KCMG, KCVO

CABINET
Premier and Minister for State Development: Hon. J. Bjelke-Petersen, MLA
Treasurer: Hon. G. W. W. Chalk, MLA
Minister for Mines and Main Roads: Hon. R. E. Camm, MLA
Minister for Justice and Attorney-General: Hon. Dr. P. R. Delamothe, OBE, MLA
Minister for Education and Cultural Activities: Hon. A. R. Fletcher, MLA
Minister for Primary Industries: Hon. J. A. Row, MLA
Minister for Health: Hon. S. D. Tooth, MLA
Minister for Labour and Tourism: Hon. J. D. Herbert, MLA
Minister for Transport: Hon. W. E. Knox, MLA
Minister for Industrial Development: Hon. F. A. Campbell, MLA
Minister for Lands: Hon. V. B. Sullivan, MLA
Minister for Works and Housing: Hon. A. M. Hodges, MLA
Minister for Conservation, Marine and Aboriginal Affairs: Hon. N. T. E. Hewitt, MLA
Minister for Local Government and Electricity: Hon. W. A. R. Rae, MLA

LEADER OF THE OPPOSITION
J. W. Houston, MLA

LEGISLATIVE ASSEMBLY
Speaker: The Hon. D. E. Nicholson, MLA
Chairman of Committees: K. W. Hooper, MLA

SUPREME COURT
Chief Justice: The Hon. Mostyn Hanger
Senior Puisne Judge: The Hon. C. G. Wanstall

Puisne Judges:

The Hon. N. S. Stable	The Hon. M. B. Hoare, CMG
The Hon. R. W. Skerman	The Hon. W. B. Campbell
The Hon. G. L. Hart	The Hon. R. H. Matthews
The Hon. G. A. C. Lucas	The Hon. D. M. Campbell (Central Judge)
The Hon. J. B. G. Kneipp (Northern Judge)	The Hon. E. S. Williams
The Hon. J. A. Douglas	The Hon. D. G. Andrews

DISTRICT COURT
Judges:

W. M. Grant-Taylor (Chairman)	L. L. Byth
R. F. J. Cormack	E. G. Broad, DFC
R. F. Carter	B. M. McLoughlin
G. Seaman	V. M. Nicholson
V. M. Mylne	A. K. McCracken
E. J. Moynahan	

SOUTH AUSTRALIA

South Australia consists of that portion of Australia bounded on the east by the 141st meridian of East longitude, on the north by the 26th parallel of South latitude, on the west by the 129th meridian of East longitude, and on the south by the Southern Ocean. The northern boundary is therefore approximately 746 miles long, while the distance from north to south varies from 391 miles near the western extremity to approximately 823 miles near the eastern boundary. Excluding minor indentations, the coast line runs for 2,100 miles. The total area of the State is approximately 380,070 square miles, of which roughly 23,300 square miles are closely settled (principally near the coast), while 218,300 square miles are under sparse occupation, mainly pastoral. The State was constituted a British colony by Act of Parliament 4 and 5 William IV, Cap. 95, under the designation of South Australia, the western boundary then being defined as the 132nd meridian of East longitude. In 1861 the boundary of South Australia on the western side was extended to the 129th meridian of East longitude by Act 24 and 25 Vict. Cap. 44.

The country known as the Northern Territory from the 26th parallel of south latitude to the Indian Ocean, between the 129th and 138th meridians of East longitude, was annexed to South Australia in 1863 by Letters Patent, but on 1st January 1911 this portion of the State was taken over by the Commonwealth of Australia.

All the adjacent islands on the south coast, including Kangaroo Island with an area of 1,700 square miles, are included in the State.

The estimated population of the State at 31st December 1969 was 1,155,300 of whom over 808,000 live in the capital, Adelaide. The larger country centres include Whyalla, population at 30th June 1969, 28,900, Mount Gambier 17,550, Port Pirie 13,850, and Port Augusta 11,050.

The major seaports are Port Adelaide and Port Stanvac on Gulf St Vincent, Whyalla, Port Pirie, Wallaroo and Port Lincoln on Spencer Gulf, and Thevenard on the Great Australian Bight. Adelaide Airport, located about five miles west of the centre of the city, is the main commercial airport while the main military airport is Edinburgh, near Salisbury, about fifteen miles north of Adelaide.

Principal primary products are wool, wheat, barley, oats, grapes, oranges, apples and pears, apricots and peaches. The approximate livestock population at 31st March, 1969 was sheep 18.4 million, cattle for meat production 631,000, cattle for milk production 234,000, and pigs 288,000.

The principal industries include a fully integrated iron and steel industry, the largest shipbuilding industry in Australia, production of motor vehicle panels, bodies and engines, materials handling equipment, agricultural machinery, a highly developed domestic appliance industry, ferrous and non-ferrous pipes and tubes and a complete range of engineering industries, a complex electronics industry, a large alkali industry and solar salt fields, oil refining, the largest lead smelting plant in the world and a modern timber and paper industry.

Electricity generated during the year ended 30th June 1970 by the main power stations at Osborne and Torrens Island on the outskirts of Adelaide, and Port Augusta, amounted to 4,162 million kilowatt hours. The power station at Port Augusta at the head of Spencer Gulf uses low grade coal mined by open cut at Leigh Creek, approximately 160 miles north of Port Augusta and 360 miles north

---

For further information about South Australia see *The South Australian Year Book.*

of Adelaide. During the production period two million tons of this fuel were used. A major power station on Torrens Island located near Osborne, was brought into full service in 1968 using fuel oil.

Natural gas in the north of the State, is being brought to Adelaide by a recently completed pipeline from large deposits. The gas is being used as a fuel by the major industries, by domestic users, and also in the Torrens Island Power Station.

The Whyalla shipyards are the largest in Australia. Since 1948, 51 vessels, including five of 55,000 tons and one, an oil tanker, the *Amanda Miller*, of 62,000 tons have been built there. An off-shore drilling rig "Ocean Digger" standing 310 feet high which involved completely new techniques in Australia, was launched in August 1967 and is undertaking drilling for oil in South Australian and adjacent waters.

Extensive radiata pine plantations in the south-east of the State support saw-milling and paper-pulp industries. A State-owned sawmill at Mount Gambier is the largest in Australia and one of the largest in the southern hemisphere, having an annual intake of 57 million super feet of logs.

HISTORY

The south coast was explored by Flinders in 1802 and in 1830 Captain Charles Sturt navigated the River Murray from its junction with the Murrumbidgee to its mouth.

The colony of South Australia was founded in 1836 on a scheme of colonisation expounded by Edward Gibbon Wakefield. The general principle, as set out in the Ripon Regulations, was that the Government should sell colonial lands and use the proceeds for emigration to the colony, and that Britain should later grant some measure of self-government. Under the Foundation Act the control was divided between the Colonial Office and a Board of Commissioners for Land Sales and Emigration. The Board of Commissioners was wound up in 1841, and in 1842 a nominated Legislative Council was set up. Responsible government was established in 1856.

The task of choosing the site for the first settlement in the colony was entrusted to Colonel William Light. After landing on Kangaroo Island he rejected this site, Port Lincoln and the eastern shore of Spencer Gulf, in favour of the east coast of Gulf St Vincent where he surveyed the present site of Adelaide on the coastal plains at the foot of the Mount Lofty Ranges.

CONSTITUTION

The Parliament of South Australia consists of a Legislative Council and a House of Assembly, created by South Australia Act No. 2 of 1855–56, which was proclaimed on 24th October 1856. This Act, commonly called the Constitution Act, was passed by virtue of Imperial Act 13 and 14 Vict. Cap. 59.

The Legislative Council and House of Assembly as originally constituted consisted of eighteen and thirty-six members respectively. By South Australia Act No. 27 of 1872 the House of Assembly was increased to forty-six members, representing twenty-two electoral districts. By Act No. 236 of 1881 six members were added to the Legislative Council, and the colony was divided into four electoral districts for the purpose of Council elections. In 1882 the House of Assembly was further increased to fifty-two members, representing twenty-six electoral districts. Act No. 450 of 1888 constituted Northern Territory an electoral district to return two members, thus increasing the number of members to 54 as from April 1890. By Act 779 of 1901 the number of members was reduced to eighteen in the Legislative Council and forty-two (representing thirteen districts) in the House of Assembly. Act No. 1029 of 1910 repealed Act No. 450 of 1888 and the House of Assembly was reduced to forty members from twelve districts from 5th January 1911, on severance of Northern Territory. By Act 1148 of 1913 the Assembly districts were increased to nineteen, returning forty-six members. Act 2336 of 1936 divided the State into thirty-nine electoral districts, each returning one member. Act 110 of 1969 divided the State into 47 electoral districts, each returning one member to the House of Assembly. Elections are conducted by preferential ballot and since 1942 voting at elections has been compulsory. Each of the five electoral districts of the Legislative Council returns four members for six years, two of those members being elected every three years (section 10 of Act 959 of 1908 and section 15 of Act 1148 of 1913).

Judges, Ministers of Religion, Members of either House of the Commonwealth Parliament and persons holding an office of profit under the Crown, are ineligible for membership of either House of the South Australian Parliament. Qualifications for a Member of the Legislative Council are that he or she shall have attained the age of 30 years, be a British subject, and have resided in the State for three years. An elector for the Legislative Council must be 21 years of age, be a natural-born or naturalised British subject, have resided in South Australia for at least six months, and, in addition, possess certain property or war service qualifications specified in the Constitution Act.

The House of Assembly is elected for a term of three years but may be dissolved earlier by the Governor. Any person who is qualified and entitled to be registered as an elector for the House of Assembly is eligible for membership of it, provided he or she is not disqualified by holding one of the offices mentioned in the preceding paragraph. The qualifications of an elector for the House of Assembly are that he or she be at least 21 years of age and a natural-born or naturalized British subject and have resided in South Australia for six months, and in the subdivision for one month.

The franchise for both Houses was extended to adult women by Act 613 of 1894. South Australia was the first Australian State to extend the franchise to adult women.

GOVERNMENT

The Election for the House of Assembly in South Australia held on Saturday 30th May 1970 resulted in the defeat of the Liberal Country League Government by the Labour Party. The state of the Parties is: Labour 27; Liberal Country League 20.

GOVERNOR

His Excellency Major-General Sir James Harrison, KCMG, CB, CBE

LIEUTENANT-GOVERNOR

The Hon. Sir John Mellis Napier, KCMG

CABINET

Premier, Treasurer, Minister of Mines and Minister of Development:
The Hon. D. A. Dunstan, QC, LLB, MP
Deputy Premier, Minister of Works and Minister of Marine: The Hon. J. D. Corcoran, MP
Chief Secretary and Minister of Health: The Hon. A. J. Shard, MLC
Attorney-General and Minister of Social Welfare and Minister of Aboriginal Affairs:
The Hon. L. J. King, QC, MP

Minister of Education: The Hon. H. R. Hudson, MP
Minister of Roads, Transport and Minister of Local Government: The Hon. G. T. Virgo, MP
Minister for Conservation and Assisting the Premier: The Hon. G. R. Broomhill, MP
Minister of Labour and Industry: The Hon. D. H. McKee, MP
Minister of Agriculture and Forests: The Hon. T. M. Casey, MP
Minister of Lands, Repatriation and Irrigation: The Hon. A. F. Kneebone, MLC

LEADER OF OPPOSITION
The Hon. R. Steele-Hall, MP

SUPREME COURT
The Hon. The Chief Justice: Dr J. J. Bray

Judges:

The Hon. Mr Justice R. R. St. C. Chamberlain	The Hon. Mr Justice G. H. Walters
The Hon. Mr Justice D. S. Hogarth	The Hon. Mr Justice H. Zelling
The Hon. Mr Justice C. H. Bright	The Hon. Mr Justice A. N. Wells
The Hon. Mr. Justice Roma F. Mitchell	The Hon. Acting Mr. Justice A. K. Sangster

WESTERN AUSTRALIA

Western Australia comprises nearly one-third of the Australian continent. The total area is 975,920 square miles (more than one-fourth the area of Europe). It is the fastest growing Australian State with a population growth rate currently twice the national average. Perth, the capital city, is situated on the Swan River, twelve miles from the river mouth at Fremantle, the State's principal port.

Western Australia's principal exports are minerals, wheat, wool, fish, meat and raw chemicals. The Pilbara region in the North-West contains one of the world's largest resources of high grade iron ore with estimated reserves of over 20,000 million tons of ore averaging more than 50 per cent iron.

The population reached 1,000,000 at the end of 1970, of whom some 663,000 live in the Perth Statistical Division which is the main urban area of Western Australia. The principal cities and towns outside the Perth and Fremantle urban area are:—

Kalgoorlie and Boulder	23,200
Bunbury	17,600
Geraldton	14,900
Albany	12,700

HISTORY AND CONSTITUTION

The first authentic record of European explorers visiting any portion of Western Australia is in 1616. In 1791 Vancouver, in the *Discovery*, took formal possession of the country about King George Sound. In 1826 a small settlement, subsequently named Albany, was formed on King George Sound.

In 1829 Captain Fremantle took formal possession of the territory, and in the same year Captain Stirling founded the Swan River Settlement and the towns of Perth and Fremantle and was appointed Lieutenant-Governor.

In 1870, a 'Representative' constitution was established by Imperial Act 33, Vict. Cap. 13. The Governor was assisted by an Executive Council composed of the principal officers of the Government and two unofficial members appointed by him. There was also a Legislative Council, consisting then of three official members of the Executive Council, three unofficial nominees of the Governor and twelve elected members.

For further information about Western Australia see the *Official Year Book of Western Australia*

Responsible government was granted to Western Australia in 1890 (53 and 54 Vict. Cap. 26).

The Legislature consists of two Houses: The Legislative Council, of 30 members, and the Legislative Assembly, of 51 members. The members of both Houses are elected. By an amendment in 1936 of the Electoral Act voting for the Legislative Assembly is compulsory, and in December 1964 voting for the Legislative Council was also made compulsory.

GOVERNMENT

In February 1971, after twelve years of Liberal and Country Party coalition government, the Australian Labor Party was returned with a majority of 1 in the Legislative Assembly. In the Assembly the Labor Party has 26 seats, the Liberal Party has 17 seats and the Country Party 8 seats. In the Legislative Council the position is Liberal Party 13, Labor Party 10 and the Country Party 7.

GOVERNOR
His Excellency Major-General Sir Douglas Kendrew, KCMG, CB, CBE, DSO

CABINET
Premier and Minister for Education, Environmental Protection and Cultural Affairs: The Hon. J. T. Tonkin, MLA
Deputy Premier and Minister for Industrial Development and Decentralisation and Town Planning: The Hon. H. E. Graham, MLA
Treasurer and Minister for Forests and Tourism: The Hon. T. D. Evans, MLA
Minister for Community Welfare and Leader of the Government in the Legislative Council: The Hon. W. F. Willesee, MLC
Minister for Police and Transport: The Hon. J. Dolan, MLC
Minister for Mines and the North West: The Hon. D. G. May, MLA
Minister for Works, Water Supplies and Electricity: The Hon. C. J. Jamieson, MLA
Minister for Lands, Agriculture and Immigration: The Hon. H. D. Evans, BA, MLA
Minister for Prices Control, Consumer Protection, Health, and Fisheries and Fauna: The Hon. R. Davies, MLA
Minister for Housing and Labour: The Hon. A. D. Taylor, BA, MLA
Attorney-General and Minister for Railways: The Hon. R. E. Bertram, AASA, MLA
Minister for Local Government and Chief Secretary: The Hon. R. H. C. Stubbs, MLC

LEADER OF THE OPPOSITION
The Hon. Sir D. Brand, KCMG, MLA

LEGISLATIVE COUNCIL
President: The Hon. L. C. Diver, MLC

LEGISLATIVE ASSEMBLY
Speaker: The Hon. J. M. Toms, MLA

SUPREME COURT
Chief Justice: Hon. Sir Lawrence W. Jackson, KCMG
Senior Puisne Judge: Hon. J. E. Virtue

Puisne Judges:

2nd Hon. J. Hale	4th Hon. J. M. Lavan
3rd Hon. F. T. P. Burt	5th Hon. J. L. C. Wickham

TASMANIA

Tasmania, the smallest State of the Australian Commonwealth, is an island at the southern extremity of the continent of Australia, from which it is divided by Bass Strait, 140 miles wide. The area is 26,383 square miles.

The population figures as at 30th June 1970 are State of Tasmania 392,458; Hobart 127,260; Launceston 62,500; Burnie 19,710; Devonport 17,120. Main seaports are Hobart, Launceston, Beauty Point, Burnie, Devonport and Port Latta. Principal airports are Hobart, Launceston, Devonport and Wynyard.

The principal products of Tasmania are timber, newsprint, zinc, confectionery, calcium-carbide, apples, canned fruits, hand-tools, wool and textiles from Hobart; iron ore in pellets from Port Latta; aluminium, ferro-alloys, fruit, wool, textiles and meat from Launceston; butter, potatoes, paper pulp and timber from Burnie, and textiles, frozen foods, paper products, potatoes and dairy products from Devonport.

HISTORY

Tasmania was discovered in 1642 by the Dutch navigator, Abel Jan Tasman, and by him named Van Diemen's Land, the name by which it was known down to 1856. Captain Cook landed in 1777 on his third voyage. It was formally taken possession of by England in 1803 and made auxiliary to the settlement at Botany Bay, from which it was separated in 1825.

The name of the island was officially changed to Tasmania by proclamation from the 1st January 1856 in accordance with Her Majesty's Order in Council dated 21st July 1855.

CONSTITUTIONAL DEVELOPMENT

In 1851 a partly elective legislature was inaugurated and responsible government was introduced in 1856. The colony, together with the mainland States, entered the Australian Commonwealth Federation in 1901.

CONSTITUTION

The main lines of the present Constitution were laid down by a local Act in 1855. These have been amended from time to time and modified by Federation.

The State Executive Authority is vested in a Governor appointed by the Crown, aided by an Executive Council of Ministers responsible to the Legislature.

Parliament consists of two elected Houses. The Legislative Council of 19 members is elected by owners of freehold estate, occupiers of property and the spouse of any owner or occupier of property. In addition the franchise is granted to university graduates, officiating ministers of religion, and ex-members of the Australian Imperial Forces who served outside Tasmania. Three members retire annually except that in each sixth successive year from 1953 onwards four members retire. The Council cannot be dissolved as a whole. The House of Assembly is elected on adult suffrage for a maximum of three years. The House consists of 35 members returned for five seven-member constituencies, which are the same as the Commonwealth electoral divisions. The system of voting is substantially the Hare-Clark system of single transferable vote, with obligations to record at least three preferences. After an earlier partial trial, it was applied to the whole State in 1909, and all subsequent general elections have been held under it.

The power of the Upper House to amend Money Bills sent up from the Assembly has always been a matter of some doubt, and at the end of 1924 was successfully challenged by the House of Assembly in respect both of the Appropriation Bill and of an Income Tax Bill. The controversy on the subject was in 1926 settled by a compromise, by which the Upper House gave up any claim to amend the Appropriation Bill or bills imposing a rate of income tax, but maintained full powers of amendment of other Money Bills.

Voting is compulsory at elections for both Houses of the State Parliament.

D

GOVERNMENT

At the election in May 1969 the Liberal and Labour Parties each secured 17 seats, and the Centre Party one seat. The Government is a Liberal/Centre Party coalition.

The Legislative Council comprises 2 Labour Party and 17 Independent members.

GOVERNOR

His Excellency Lieutenant-General Sir Edric Montague Bastyan, KCMG, KCVO, KBE, CB

MINISTRY

Premier, Treasurer, Minister in Charge of the Hydro-Electric Commission:
The Hon. W. A. Bethune, MHA
Deputy Premier, Chief Secretary and Minister for Tourism:
The Hon. K. O. Lyons, MHA
Minister for Agriculture and Forestry: The Hon. E. W. Beattie, MHA
Minister for Education: The Hon. R. Mather, MHA
Minister for Lands and Works and for Local Government:
The Hon. W. G. Barker, MHA
Minister for Development, Housing and Sea Fisheries: The Hon. D. F. Clark, MHA
Minister for Transport, Racing and Gaming and for Mines:
The Hon. L. H. Bessell, MHA
Minister for Health and Road Safety: Dr The Hon. N. D. Abbott, MHA
Attorney General, Minister for Police and Licensing: The Hon. E. M. Bingham, MHA

LEADER OF THE OPPOSITION
The Hon. E. E. Reece, MHA

LEGISLATIVE COUNCIL
President: The Hon. W. B. T. Davis, MLC
Clerk of the Council: G. W. Brimage

HOUSE OF ASSEMBLY
Speaker: The Hon. C. R. Ingamells, MHA
Clerk of the House: B. G. Murphy

THE NORTHERN TERRITORY OF AUSTRALIA

The Territory consists of that part of the Australian mainland lying to the north of latitude 26° S. (the northern border of South Australia) and bounded on the west by longitude 129° E. (Western Australia border) and on the east by longitude 138° E. (Queensland border). The Territory also comprises the adjacent islands lying between those longitudes.

The total area of the Territory is 520,280 square miles, the coastline being 1,040 miles in length. Darwin is the principal town and the centre of the Administration of the Territory, as well as the main port. The estimated non-Aboriginal population at 30th June 1966 was 21,119. Alice Springs, about 950 miles south of Darwin, had a non-Aboriginal population of 6,000 at 30th June 1966.

At 30th December 1969 the population of the Territory as a whole was estimated at 68,042 including Aborigines.

Mining surpasses the pastoral industry as the Territory's chief producer of wealth, the latter having been the mainstay of the Territory's economy for the past half-century. Copper is the chief mineral being mined; others are manganese ore, iron ore, gold, uranium, and tin. Important mining development projects are now under investigation in bauxite, manganese, and lead-zinc. Tourism is an important and growing industry.

HISTORY AND ADMINISTRATION

The first attempt at settlement in northern Australia was made in 1824. In 1827 a portion of north Australia extending to the border of Western Australia was included within New South Wales. In 1862 the western boundary of Queensland was altered by Letters Patent from 141° E. longitude to its present position at 138° E. longitude. In 1863 the portion subsequently known as Northern Territory was annexed by Letters Patent to the Colony of South Australia. However, as from the 1st January 1911, the Territory, with its adjacent islands, was transferred to the Commonwealth by the Northern Territory Acceptance Act, 1910. One of the conditions of the transfer was that such of the laws of South Australia as were applicable to the Territory at the time of transfer were to continue in force until such time as they were altered or repealed by or under any law of the Commonwealth.

The Northern Territory (Administration) Act, 1910–1969, provides that there shall be an Administrator appointed by the Governor-General to administer the Territory on behalf of the Commonwealth, subject to any instructions given him by the Minister for Territories from time to time.

The Northern Australia Act, 1926, provided for the division of the Territory for administrative purposes into North Australia and Central Australia, separated by the 20th parallel of S. latitude; however, in 1931 this Act was repealed and as from that year the Territory was reunited and administered as before.

There is a Legislative Council for the Northern Territory with power to make ordinances for the peace, order and good government of the Territory, subject to assent by either the Administrator or the Governor-General as provided in the Act. The Council consists of six official members and eleven elected members representing the electorates of Alice Springs, Arnhem, Barkly, Elsey, Fannie Bay, Nightcliff, Port Darwin, Stuart, McMillan, Victoria River and Ludmilla. The official members hold office during the Governor-General's pleasure. Elected members hold office for a maximum period of three years and may then seek re-election. The President of the Legislative Council is elected from among the elected members of the council.

Persons who, under Part V of the Northern Territory Electoral Regulations made under the Northern Territory Representation Act 1922–1959 and the Commonwealth Electoral Act 1918–1966, are qualified to vote at an election for a member to represent the Northern Territory in the House of Representatives of the Commonwealth Parliament are qualified to vote at an election of a member to the Legislative Council.

Aborigines may enrol, and having enrolled are entitled to vote at Federal and Northern Territory Legislative Council elections.

Under the procedures for assent to ordinances, the Administrator or the Governor-General (as appropriate) may return ordinances with suggested amendments for reconsideration by the Council. Every ordinance, whether assented to or disallowed, must be laid before each House of Parliament within fifteen sitting days of that House. When assent is withheld from an ordinance, the Minister is obliged to lay the reasons before each House as soon as possible, but in any case within fifteen sitting days of that House. A statement of reasons for withholding assent is also presented to the Legislative Council.

The Northern Territory (Administration) Act also provides for an Administrator's Council consisting of the Administrator, and two official and three elected members of the Legislative Council. Each member of the Administrator's Council (other than the Administrator) is appointed by the Minister on the nomination of the Administrator and, subject to the Act, holds office during the pleasure of the Minister. The Council's function is to advise the Administrator on any matters referred to it by the Administrator and on other matters as provided in the Ordinances of the Territory.

The Supreme Court of the Northern Territory is the highest judicial tribunal in the Territory and is the only court possessing jurisdiction over civil and criminal matters, and appeals from its judgement may be taken to the Full Court of the High Court of Australia. Federal jurisdiction in bankruptcy is exercised by the Supreme Court through the Bankruptcy Act 1924–1960. There are of course courts of summary jurisdiction and local courts with limited jurisdiction in civil matters. There are also wardens' courts constituted by the mining laws, and licensing courts having jurisdiction in liquor licensing matters, etc.

The Social Welfare Ordinance provides for care and assistance to all persons socially and economically in need, including Aborigines. There is no legislative discrimination against Aborigines.

Most land held from the Crown is held on leasehold, as provided for by the Crown Lands, Darwin Town Area Leases, Special Purposes Leases, Church Lands Leases and Agricultural Development Leases Ordinances. Provision is made for the control of mining, fisheries and pearling. The Director of Agriculture and Animal Industry has wide powers in regard to the movements of stock, control of stock routes, disease prevention, etc.

Local government was reconstituted in Darwin on the 1st July 1957. Darwin is now a city with a Council consisting of the Mayor and eight aldermen elected by electors of the municipality.

PARLIAMENTARY REPRESENTATION

The Northern Territory Representation Act 1922–1959 provides for the election of a member for the Territory to the House of Representatives. For some years prior to an amendment of the Act in 1959 the member had no vote in the House, although he could take part in debates in the House. Amendments passed in 1959 gave the member limited voting rights in respect of matters which relate solely to the Northern Territory. The Act was further amended in 1968 and the member representing the Northern Territory now has the same voting rights as other members of the House of Representatives.

BARBADOS

BARBADOS is the most easterly of the Caribbean islands and lies between latitudes 13° and 14° N. and longitudes 59° and 60° W. Its total area is 166 square miles.

It is comparatively flat, rising in a series of tablelands marked by well-defined terraces to the highest point (1,104 feet) at Mount Hillaby. The north-east corner of the island, the Scotland area, is broken country, much eroded and rather barren. The formation of the rest of the island is coral limestone. There are no rivers, but deep gullies which fill with water during heavy rain have cut their way through the coral terraces in many places. Indigenous forest covers about 46 acres.

The climate is more equable than the tropical latitude would suggest. North-easterly trade winds blow steadily from December to June but during the remainder of the year, the wet season, the wind moves to the south-east and is less strong, resulting in humid, hotter conditions. The average temperature is 26·5°C (79·8°F). The rainfall is very varied: in the high central district the yearly average is 75 inches while in some of the low-lying coastal areas the average is 50 inches.

The population of Barbados at the census of 1960 was 232,820. The population of the parishes were: Bridgetown, the capital, and St Michael 94,209; Christ Church 33,425; St George 17,075; St Philip 17,255; St John 10,967; St James 13,611; St Thomas 10,026; St Joseph 8,582; St Andrew 7,813; St Peter 10,860; St Lucy 8,997. The main population divisions were Negro 207,156; White 10,083; Mixed 13,993; Others 1,588. The estimated population in 1970 was 238,000. The birth rate, based on 1969 figures, is 20.9 per 1,000 and the death rate 8.0 per 1,000. The main religious denominations are Anglican 133,772; Methodist 18,403; Roman Catholic 6,429; Others 74,216.

Education (primary and secondary) is free in Government aided schools.

Bridgetown is the only port of entry, but oil is pumped ashore at Spring Gardens and at an Esso installation on the West Coast.

The main shipping companies visiting Barbados are Harrison Line, Geest Line, Royal Netherlands Steamship Company, *Compagnie Générale Transatlantique*, Saguenay Shipping Ltd, Booth Line, Lamport and Holt Line, Moore McCormack Line, Hamburg-Amerika Line, Caribbean-Hamburg Line (formerly Three Bays Line) and Federal Shipping Service. Companies calling less frequently include Linea 'C', Delta Line, Blue Ribbon Line, Atlantic Line, and Blue Star Line.

An international airport is situated at Seawell, 12 miles from Bridgetown, Air France, British Overseas Airways Corporation, British West Indian Airways, International Caribbean Airways, Leeward Island Air Transport, Pan American World Airways, Air Canada, Caribair and the Netherlands Antilles air line A.L.M. operate frequent scheduled services connecting Barbados with the major world air routes.

There are 800 miles of roads, of which approximately 720 miles are asphalted.

Barbados has a colour television service, a wireless broadcasting service and a wired broadcasting service. The first two are operated by the Caribbean Broadcasting Corporation, a corporate body set up by Order-in-Council of the Barbados Government in 1963. The wired system, which covers the whole island, is operated by Barbados Rediffusion Service Limited, a local subsidiary of Rediffusion Limited.

The economy of the island is based on sugar and the tourist industry is also an important source of revenue. Total exports in 1969 were valued at $EC68,824,293, of which $EC27,797,770 worth were to the United Kingdom.

The imports in 1969 were valued at $EC194,589,761, of which $EC56,158,529 came from Britain.

In 1970/71 Government revenue was estimated to be $EC92,442,414 and expenditure $EC128,976,304.

Barbados National Day is Independence Day, which commemorates the achievement of Independence on 30th November 1966.

HISTORY

The first inhabitants of Barbados were Arawak Indians but the island was uninhabited when the first British landings took place some time between 1620 and 1625.

The first British settlements in the island were established between 1625 and 1628. The first group of settlers was led by Captain Henry Powell, representing the interests of Sir William Courteen. Other groups were sponsored by the Earl of Carlisle who in 1628 was granted a patent by King Charles I in respect of the whole of the Barbados settlements. This was subsequently leased by Carlisle's son to Lord Willoughby of Parham who during the Civil War became Governor of the island and continued to hold it in the Royalist interest until 1652, when he capitulated to a Cromwellian fleet. The terms of this capitulation, however, guaranteed the rights of the settlers and became known as the Charter of Barbados.

At the Restoration, the Carlisle/Willoughby interests were renewed, but the patent was surrendered to the Crown in exchange for a provision entitling Lord Willoughby and his heirs to a duty of $4\frac{1}{2}$ per cent on Barbados exports. Although this agreement marked the end of proprietary rule, the export duty was sorely resented by the islanders and remained a source of grievance until it was abolished by Act of Parliament in 1838.

CONSTITUTIONAL DEVELOPMENT

The island has one of the oldest constitutions in the Commonwealth. The office of Governor and a Legislative Council were established in 1627. The House of Assembly was formally constituted in 1639.

A distinctive feature of the constitutional development of Barbados has been that it has progressed and been regulated largely by convention, rather than by formal legislation. It is nevertheless convenient to trace, by reference to the latter, the steps by which the island progressed through widening forms of representation and suffrage and through modifications of policy-making and legislative powers, successively to a ministerial form of government, to a cabinet system and finally, through full internal self-government, to independence.

The first of these steps was the creation in 1876 of an Executive Council which in 1881 became the nucleus of an Executive Committee, some of whose functions and powers developed into forms analogous to those of Ministerial government.

A widening of the franchise in 1944 was to prove the start of a quickening process towards full internal self-government: a party political system and a modified form of ministerial government in 1946; universal adult suffrage in 1951; a full ministerial system in 1954; cabinet government in 1958.

By the end of 1957, Barbados had in practice progressed to virtual self-government. This status was formally achieved in 1961, when the post of Chief Secretary was abolished, nominated members ceased to sit in the Executive Committee and provisions were made under which the Governor, subject to one reference back, was bound to accept the advice of the Ministers in the Executive Committee. At the same time, the powers and responsibilities of Ministers were widened and the island assumed control over its own public service. Arrangements were made for appeals on matters of discipline, which formerly went to the Secretary of State, to be dealt with by the Executive Council, which was re-named the Privy Council.

The final stage of constitutional advance before Independence was reached in 1964, when the Executive Committee was abolished and its powers and functions transferred entirely to the Cabinet. Among other changes, the Legislative Assembly was also abolished and replaced by a Senate.

Barbados had been a member of the Federation of the West Indies, which was set up in 1958 but which was dissolved in 1962. In August 1965 the Barbados Government announced its intention to seek separate Independence. At a conference held in London in June-July 1966, arrangements were agreed under which Barbados became an independent Sovereign State within the Commonwealth on 30th November 1966.

CONSTITUTION

The Constitution of Barbados, contained in the Barbados Independence Order 1966 provides for a Governor-General appointed by Her Majesty the Queen and for a bi-cameral Legislature. The Senate consists of 21 Senators appointed by the Governor-General, 12 on the advice of the Prime Minister, two on the advice of the Leader of the Opposition and seven by the Governor-General acting in his own discretion. The House of Assembly consists of 24 elected members but provision is made for a greater number of members as may be prescribed by Parliament. The President and Deputy President of the Senate and speaker and Deputy Speaker of the House of Assembly are elected, respectively by the Senate and the House of Assembly from within their own membership.

The normal life of Parliament is five years. The Cabinet consists of the Prime Minister who must be a Member of Parliament and such other ministers as the Governor-General, acting on the advice of the Prime Minister, appoints from among the Senators and Members of Parliament. The Member of Parliament, who in the judgement of the Governor-General is the Leader in the House of the party commanding the support of the largest number of Members of Parliament in opposition to the Government, is appointed by him Leader of the Opposition.

Apart from the entrenched provisions, the Constitution may be amended by an Act of Parliament passed by both Houses. The entrenched provisions which relate to citizenship, rights and freedom, the establishment of the office of the Governor-General, his functions, the composition of the two Houses of Parliament, Sessions of Parliament, the Prorogation and Dissolution of Parliament, General Elections, the appointment of Senators, the executive Authority of Barbados, the Judicature, the Civil Service and Finance, can only be amended by a vote of two-thirds of all the members of both Houses.

There is a Supreme Court of Judicature consisting of a High Court and a Court of Appeal, and in certain cases a further appeal lies to the Judicial Committee of Her Majesty's Privy Council. The Chief Justice is appointed by the Governor-General acting on the recommendation of the Prime Minister after consultation with the Leader of the Opposition. Puisne Judges are appointed by the Governor-General, acting in accordance with the advice of the Judicial and Legal Service Commission.

The Constitution also contains provisions relating to citizenship and the fundamental rights and freedoms of the individual.

HISTORICAL LIST

GOVERNOR-GENERAL

Sir John Montague Stow, GCMG, KCVO, from 30th November 1966 to 15th May 1967
Sir Winston Scott, GCMG, from 15th May 1967

GOVERNMENT

The last general election took place on 3rd November 1966 and as a result the composition of the political parties in the House of Representatives was: Democratic Labour Party 14; Barbados Labour Party 8; Barbados National Party 2.

GOVERNOR-GENERAL
His Excellency Sir Winston Scott, GCMG

MINISTRY
Prime Minister, Minister of Finance and Minister of External Affairs:
The Rt. Hon. E. W. Barrow
Deputy Prime Minister, Minister of State for Caribbean and Latin American Affairs
also Leader of the House of Assembly: The Hon. J. Cameron Tudor
Minister of Education: Senator The Hon. Erskine Sandiford
Minister of Home Affairs and Leader of the Senate: Senator the Hon. P. M. Greaves
Minister of Health and Social Welfare: The Hon. C. E. Talma
Minister of Trade, Tourism, Community Development and Youth Affairs:
The Hon. K. N. R. Husbands, MP
Minister of Agriculture, Science and Technology: The Hon. A. DaC. Edwards
Minister of Communications and Works: The Hon. G. G. Ferguson
Minister of Labour, National Insurance and Housing: The Hon. N. W. Boxhill, MP
Minister of State designated Attorney-General: The Hon. F. G. Smith, QC

PARLIAMENTARY SECRETARIES
Ministry of Education: Senator Odessa Gittens
Ministry of Communications and Works: W. R. Lowe, MP
Ministry of Agriculture, Science and Technology: J. W. Corbin, MP
Ministry of Health and Social Welfare: R. St C. Weekes, MP
Ministry of Labour, National Insurance and Housing: Senator Le Roy Brathwaite

LEADER OF THE OPPOSITION IN THE HOUSE OF REPRESENTATIVES
H. B. St John, MP, Barbados Labour Party

SENATE
President of the Senate: Senator Sir Stanley Robinson, KT, CBE
Clerk of the Senate: L. H. Clarke

HOUSE OF REPRESENTATIVES
Speaker: The Hon. Sir Theodore Brancker, KT, QC
Clerk: H. O. St C. Cumberbatch

JUDICIARY
Chief Justice: The Hon. Sir William Douglas, KT

COURT OF APPEAL
Puisne Judges:
Mr Justice A. J. H. Hanschell
Mr Justice D. H. L. Ward
Mr Justice D. A. Williams
Registrar of the Supreme Court: C. A. Rocheford

MINISTRIES AND GOVERNMENT DEPARTMENTS

PRIME MINISTER'S OFFICE
Permanent Secretary (Cabinet Affairs): F. M. Blackman, OBE
Permanent Secretary (General): A. N. Forde

MINISTRY OF FINANCE
Financial Secretary: N. D. Osborne, OBE

MINISTRY OF EXTERNAL AFFAIRS
Permanent Secretary: C. B. Williams, OBE

MINISTRY OF EDUCATION
Permanent Secretary: Major H. R. Daniel

MINISTRY OF HOME AFFAIRS
Permanent Secretary: A. W. Symmonds

MINISTRY OF HEALTH AND
SOCIAL WELFARE
Permanent Secretary: C. A. Burton, OBE

MINISTRY OF TRADE, TOURISM,
COMMUNITY DEVELOPMENT AND
YOUTH AFFAIRS
Permanent Secretary: C. H. Clarke

MINISTRY OF AGRICULTURE,
SCIENCE AND TECHNOLOGY
Permanent Secretary: C. M. Thompson

MINISTRY OF LABOUR,
NATIONAL INSURANCE AND HOUSING
Permanent Secretary: A. S. Howell, MBE

MINISTRY OF COMMUNICATIONS AND WORKS
Permanent Secretary: C. R. E. Edwards

DIPLOMATIC REPRESENTATION

BARBADIAN HIGH COMMISSIONERS IN
OTHER COMMONWEALTH COUNTRIES
Britain: W. E. W. Ramsey
Canada: O. H. Jackman

COMMONWEALTH HIGH COMMISSIONERS
IN BARBADOS
Britain: D. A. Roberts; Canada: G. A. Rau
(resident in Port of Spain); India: L. N. Ray
(resident in Port of Spain); Jamaica: Ivo de
Souza (resident in Port of Spain)

BARBADIAN REPRESENTATIVES IN
NON-COMMONWEALTH COUNTRIES
Permanent Mission to the United Nations:
G. C. R. Moc (Permanent Representative);
A. A. Brathwaite (Acting Deputy Permanent
Representative); United States: Valerie T.
McComie (Ambassador in Washington);
B. M. Taitt (Consul-General, New York)

BOTSWANA

THE Republic of Botswana lies between latitudes 18° and 27° S. and longitudes 20° and 28° W. The area of the country, which has not yet been wholly surveyed, is estimated to be 220,000 square miles, about the size of France, and has a mean altitude of 3,300 feet. Entirely landlocked, its neighbours are the Republic of South Africa to the south and east, Rhodesia to the northeast, Zambia and the Caprivi Strip (part of South West Africa) to the north, and South West Africa to the west.

A plateau at a height of about 4,000 feet, which forms the watershed between the Molopo and Notwani Rivers in the south and swings northward from a point about 20 miles west of Kanye all the way to the border of Rhodesia, divides the country into two dominant topographical regions, characterised by two drainage systems. To the east of the plateau, streams flow into the Marico, Notwani and Limpopo Rivers; to the west is an inactive internal system, which at one time drained this tableland into the great Makarikari Flats. Within this flat region there are three sub-regions: the Kalahari Desert, the Okavango Swamps and the Northern State Lands area.

Eastern Botswana is broken by a series of rocky hills and is covered, particularly along its eastern margin and over its northern half, by relatively dense bush, but its rainfall is sufficient to produce good pasturage. The existence of grasses of high food value in many parts, the easily tapped underground watertable and the presence of water at shallow depths in the sand beds of the rivers and streams for most of the year, combine to make this an excellent cattle-rearing region. Most of the arable land is also situated in this area, where a mean annual rainfall of 20 inches is normally sufficient for the production of grain sorghum. In the south-east, climate and soils are suitable for the production of maize under dryland cultivation. Eighty per cent of the population lives in this region.

West of the plateau which marks the boundary of Eastern Botswana the ground falls to the great expanse of the Kalahari Desert, a level tract closely covered with thorn bush and grass, extending 300 miles to the west and bounded by the Makarikari salt pans and the Botletle River in the north. Rainfall in the Kalahari Desert varies from 20 inches in the east to a scant 9 inches in the south-west. Precipitation, however, tends to be erratic and is frequently of a local nature. Surface water is absent except for limited accumulations in flat, sandy clay-floored depressions in the sandveld, known as pans, and in dams built as a result of tribal initiative or the provision of post-war development funds. Along the eastern margin of this region, where the sand mantle thins out, and in the north-west on the Ghanzi plateau which extends into the desert from South West Africa, potable underground water supplies have been developed. Elsewhere underground water tends to be saline and sweet water supplies are rare. Where potable water is found in the desert small Bakgalagadi communities gather with their cattle, but there is virtually no arable land. For the most part, this region is inhabited only by shy bands of Bushmen.

The 6,500 square miles of the Okavango swamps lie in the remote north-western corner of Botswana known as Ngamiland. Apart from the Limpopo and Chobe Rivers, this area is the only source of permanent surface water in the country. The Okavango River, which flows into the swamps, is estimated to have an average flow of 9,000 cubic feet per second at Shakawe, but most of this flow is either trapped in the *sudd*-like swamps where it evaporates, or disappears in the sand beds of the Botletle and Thamalakane Rivers. The swamps are infested with tsetse fly which is harboured by the shade trees and dense undergrowth, and is spread beyond the margins of the swamp by wild game. However, the advance of the insect has been successfully arrested by insecticide spraying at selected breeding sites. The perimeter of this area is inhabited by the Batawana and allied tribes, numbering 42,000. They are chiefly pastoralists and the cattle population of the district is 120,000, but crops can be produced utilising the residual moisture of the soil in areas which are subject to seasonal flooding, or in other areas under normal rainfall conditions.

The Kalahari Desert extends north of the Botletle River and the Makarikari depression into the Northern State Lands where it gives way to belts of indigenous forest and dense bush sustained by the higher rainfall of the region. Valuable stands of *mukwa* (Rhodesian teak) and *mukusi* cover extensive areas, whilst in other parts, where poorer soils are found, *mopane* forest predominates. The availability of ground water resources, particularly in the southern and eastern sections, and the existence of suitable soils and reliable rainfall in the north-eastern corner of this sub-region indicates a favourable development potential. The remaining areas are populated only by vast herds of game, in whose migratory path the Northern State Lands lie. Elephant numbers alone are estimated at over 10,000. As in the case of the Kalahari Desert, the human population is sparsely scattered around the perimeter.

The climate of the country is generally sub-tropical, but varies considerably with latitude and altitude. The Tropic of Capricorn passes through Botswana, and the northern part therefore lies within the tropics. The southern and south western areas vary between hot steppe with summer rains to desert or semi-desert climate.

During the winter the days are pleasantly warm and the nights cold, with occasional frosts in the north, and heavy frost in the semi-desert areas. The summer is hot but tempered by a prevailing north-easterly breeze which generally springs up during the night and usually lasts until mid-morning.

The annual seasonal winds from the West Coast begin in August and with every drop of humidity extracted during the Kalahari crossing, sweep across the country raising dust and sandstorms. The normally dry atmosphere helps to mitigate the high temperatures throughout the year, though this consistent dryness and constant glaring sunlight added to the effect of altitude can prove trying, particularly to those whose occupation is sedentary. The whole territory lies in the summer rainfall belt, the rains generally beginning in late October and ending in April. May to September are usually completely dry months.

The mean maximum temperature at Gaborone, the capital, which is 3,339 feet above mean sea level, is about 32·5° C (90·5° F). The mean annual rainfall at Gaborone is 21·26 inches.

A census of the population of Bechuanaland held between 13th January and 10th June 1964 showed that the country's total population was 543,105, comprising 535,275 Africans, 3,921 Europeans, 3,489 persons of mixed race, 382 Asians, and 38 others. Overall population density is 2·5 persons per square mile; it varies from 57·5 per square mile in the Gaborone District to less than 0·5 per square mile in areas such as Ghanzi. The annual rate of population increase is believed to be at least 3 per cent.

The eight principal Botswana tribes are the Bakgatla (32,118), Bakwena (73,088), Bangwekatse (71,289), Bamalete (13,861), Bamangwato (199,782), Barolong (10,662), Batawana (42,347) and Batlokwa (3,735).

The four largest towns are Serowe (34,182), Kanye (34,045), Molepolole (29,625) and Mochudi (17,712). The national census to be held in 1971, the first since 1964 on a nationwide basis, is expected to show considerable alterations in these figures.

The main business centres are Lobatse (11,000), Gaborone (estimated 15,000) and Francistown (17,800).

In July 1969, the Botswana Airways Corporation took over responsibility for civil aviation from Botswana National Airways, who started operations in November 1965. The external services have not proved viable and from May 1971 Botswana Airways Corporation is only operating internal services to Maun five times weekly. The service to Johannesburg, five times weekly, is at present being undertaken by South African Airways.

There are eighteen government owned airfields and twelve emergency landing grounds in Botswana. The airfield at Gaborone is 5,820 feet in length and capable of accepting DC4 aircraft.

The main railway line from Cape Town to Rhodesia passes through Botswana running practically due north, entering at Ramathlabana, 866 miles from Cape Town, and leaving at Ramaquabane, 394 miles further north. The single track runs roughly parallel to the eastern boundary of Botswana at an average distance from it of about 50 miles. The gauge of the track is 3 ft 6 in. The line is owned and operated by Rhodesia Railways.

The total road mileage in Botswana is 4,847, of which 2,753 miles are trunk and main roads. Apart from tarmac-surfaced roads at Gaborone, Lobatse and Francistown, all roads are gravel.

Radio Botswana is the only broadcasting service in the country. It broadcasts in the 31, 49, 60 and 90 metre bands, short wave and also in the medium wave band and on VHF.

The economy of Botswana is based on its cattle industry. Following about five years of below average rainfall, there was a total failure in 1965 which caused the worst crop failure and drought which the territory had experienced for 25 years. It is estimated that approximately 200,000 head of cattle died of starvation. Farmers were handicapped by the fact that their oxen were in very weak condition as a result of the previous season's droughts and in many cases were unable to take advantage of the early rains for ploughing. Large-scale importations of maize and sorghum were necessary, and during 1965 and 1966 emergency measures had to be taken to alleviate what threatened to become a serious famine. The rains and the harvest were good in 1966/67 but in 1967/68 and again in 1968/69 the rains came too late and poor crops necessitated the introduction of emergency feeding measures in certain parts of the country, but the harvest improved in 1969/70.

The development of mineral deposits which have been discovered in the north-eastern area of the country will lead to the diversification of the economy, and improvement of Botswana's financial position. After some years of exploration work, Bamangwato Concessions Ltd., a subsidiary of Botswana R.S.T. Ltd., announced in February 1967 that they had at that time proved a total of some 33 million tons of potential copper ore at Matsitama and copper/nickel ore at Selibe/Phikwe. Mining is expected to commence in 1973. The World Bank, Canada and the United States have agreed to provide approximately $58.5 million for the necessary infrastructure. Coal deposits at Monipule near Palapye will be used for the supply of power to serve the mining areas.

Exploitation of the diamond deposits discovered at Orapa by De Beers Prospecting Company is proceeding satisfactorily and full scale mining started in July 1971. A further smaller pipe containing a higher percentage of gem stones is also being investigated.

There was a considerable increase in customs revenue accruing to Botswana account following the 1969 revision of the 1910 Customs Agreement between South Africa, Botswana, Lesotho and Swaziland. In 1969/70 the revenue from this source was R.5,141,921. The estimate for 1971/72 is R.8,287,000.

The total value of exports in 1969 was R.13,060,031, the bulk of which consisted of animal produce (R.10,351,693). Imports for 1969 totalled R.30,833,366.

Following independence, the British Government continued to provide Botswana with budgetary and development aid. For the current three years period 1970-1973, Development Aid up to a maximum of £6.8 million has been agreed plus Budgetary Aid of up to £4.2 million for the two years 1970-1972. If the mining developments proceed according to plan, and as a result of the revised Customs Agreement, it is hoped that no Budgetary aid will be needed after 1971/72.

In addition Britain is providing technical assistance including OSAS, experts and advisers, consultancies, training and the services of the Directorate of Overseas Surveys. This is running at over £600,000 per annum. Britain has offered to take over responsibility for the payment of pensions of British officers earned by pre-independence service and to convert the loans provided under the General Compensation Scheme to grants.

The first schools were established by the London Missionary Society during the first half of the last century. As the number of schools increased so did administrative problems and in 1910 the Society and the Chief of the Bangwaketse tribe formed a committee to administer schools in that tribal area. This committee included representatives of the tribe, the Mission and the District Administration. Other tribes followed suit and the system of committee management proved so useful and popular that it was extended to cover practically all educational work being done in tribal areas. Local District Councils were formed in 1966 and today most primary schools are controlled by the local authorities. All professional matters are controlled by the Ministry of Education.

About 22 per cent of the total population are literate in Setswana, and 15 per cent are literate in English.

The national day of the Republic of Botswana is the 30th September, commemorating the achievement of Independence in 1966.

HISTORY

The picture presented by most parts of Southern Africa in the first quarter of the 19th century was one of tribal wars, pillage and bloodshed, caused mainly by the expansion of the Zulus under Chaka. This warrior chief had succeeded in welding his people into a disciplined and warlike nation who fell upon everyone unfortunate enough to be within their reach. Their neighbouring tribes therefore fled to all points of the compass, despoiling on their way the peoples in their path and thereby setting up a general movement of destructive migration.

Among these migratory bands were the followers of an amazon called Mma-Ntatisi and her son Sekonyela, who came from tribes living in the neighbourhood of what is now Lesotho. They united to form a kind of cohesive army, and advanced northwards and westwards, attacking the tribes along their way.

In a different category were the Matabele. These were originally a group of Chaka's people under Mzilikazi, one of Chaka's principal captains. On one of his raids it is said that Mzilikazi embezzled the booty and decided not to return home. He moved north-westwards and, after a destructive march, established himself near what is now the town of Zeerust, from where he made warlike raids on the tribes within his reach.

Among the victims of Mzilikazi's onslaughts were those known as Batswana, of Western Sotho stock—and hence related to the people of what is now Lesotho —who lived in the western Transvaal and westwards towards the Kalahari. Like other Sotho peoples, their early history is shrouded in legend.

The generally accepted tradition is that the principal tribes of the group are descended from a people ruled by a chief named Masilo who lived about the middle of the 17th century. Masilo had two sons, Mohurutshe and Malope. The former founded the line of the chiefs of the Bahurutshe, while the latter had three sons, Kwena, Ngwato and Ngwaketse. Ngwato and Ngwaketse at different times broke away from Kwena's tribe and went with their followers to live at a distance from each other. The Bahurutshe were set upon first by Mma-Ntatisi's people and then by the Matabele. The home of the Bahurutshe is in the western Transvaal but scattered elements have attached themselves to the present tribes of Botswana. The Bangwaketse, after several migrations, finally settled in their present country around Kanye, while the Bamangwato founded a colony in the vicinity of Shoshong in the area occupied by the tribe today. The descendants of the Kwena section now live around Molepolole. Among the Bamangwato a further split occurred; Tawana, one of the Chief Mathiba's sons seceded at the end of the 18th century and formed a settlement in Ngamiland. The Batswana are still the ruling community in that area.

The Barolong, the greater number of whom today live in the Republic of South Africa, trace the genealogy of their chief to one Rolong, who lived at a time even more remote than did Masilo. The Barolong are settled along the southern border of Botswana and round Mafeking.

Other important tribes of the Batswana are the Bakgatla, the Bamalete, and the Batlokwa. These arrived in Botswana from the Western Transvaal in the 19th century.

The years between 1820 and 1870 saw a number of intertribal disputes. These were complicated by the impact of the Boer trekkers, who did, however, rid the Zeerust area of the Matabele: after losing several engagements with the Boers, Mzilikazi trekked northwards in 1838, attacking the less warlike Batswana and Makalanga on the way. Few of the Batswana chiefs were able to make effective resistance, but in 1840 Chief Sekgoma of the Bamangwato defeated several Matabele raiding parties. About this time, David Livingstone established a mission among the Bakwena, where he stayed until the early fifties.

In 1872 one of the most remarkable Africans of his time succeeded to the chieftainship of the Bamangwato. This was Khama III (the son of Sekgoma), whose youth had been much troubled by dissensions within the tribe and by the ever-present peril of the Matabele. During the first few years of his reign Khama greatly enhanced the standing of his tribe. He was a capable general, and formed a small but well-trained army. With this he earned the respect of Lobengula, son of Mzilikazi, thus obtaining immunity from the depredations of the Matabele. A lifelong and firm adherent of Christianity, Khama introduced many reforms into the life of the tribe, of which the most important, and the one on which he himself set most store, was the total prohibition of alcoholic liquor. A capable if occasionally a harsh administrator, he devoted himself with energy to the organisation of his people.

Though the weaker tribes still suffered at the hands of Lobengula's Matabele, by the middle eighteen seventies there was some stability and order in the life of the Bamangwato and the other Batswana tribes.

At this time, the Batswana had seen little of the white man. A few traders and hunters had penetrated into their territories, but, except at centres like Shoshong, no permanent relations had been established. The only Europeans who had lived among the Batswana were the missionaries, men like Moffat and Livingstone. Now began the exploration of Africa and the division of the continent among the European Powers. Embittered relations between the Boers from the Transvaal and the Batswana people (particularly the Barolong and the Batlhaping) prompted the latter to address appeals for assistance to the Cape authorities, while Khama, shortly after his accession, also asked for his country to be taken under British protection.

The British Government showed no anxiety to assume such new responsibilities, and it was not until 1884 that the missionary John Mackenzie was sent to Bechuanaland as Deputy Commissioner. Finally in 1885 Sir Charles Warren, with the concurrence of Khama and the other principal chiefs, proclaimed the whole of Bechuanaland to be under the protection of the Queen.

The part of the Territory to the south of the Molopo River, which included Mafeking, Vryburg and Kuruman, was constituted a Crown Colony, called British Bechuanaland, in 1885, and became part of the Cape Colony (now the Cape Province of the Republic of South Africa) in 1895. The northern part, the Bechuanaland Protectorate, remained under the protection of the British Crown.

The colony and the protectorate were at first both administered from Vryburg; but on the incorporation of the Colony in the Cape, the headquarters of the protectorate were moved to Mafeking, the nearest convenient centre to the protectorate.

The British expansion northwards continued, under the powerful inspiration of Cecil John Rhodes, who had in 1889 obtained a Royal Charter for his British South Africa Company organised 'for the development of the Bechuanaland Protectorate and the North'. With the occupation in 1895 of what is now Rhodesia, Rhodes's description of Botswana as the 'Suez Canal to the North' was seen to be an apt one.

In 1894 the British Government showed itself in favour of handing the administration of the protectorate to the British South Africa Company. Chiefs Khama of the Bamangwato, Bathoen of the Bangwaketse and Sebele of the Bakwena went to England to protest against the suggested transfer. A compromise was reached whereby the tribal lands would be demarcated, with the understanding that all other lands not specifically reserved would come under the control of the British South Africa Company and a strip of land on the eastern side of the protectorate would be ceded for the building of a railway. In the event, the diminution of Rhodes's influence which followed the failure of the Jameson Raid in December 1895, led to postponement and eventual abandonment of the plan to hand over the administration of the non-tribal lands of the protectorate to the British South Africa Company.

The South Africa Act of Union of 1909, which established the Union of South Africa, included provisions for the possible inclusion in South Africa of the three territories of Basutoland, Bechuanaland and Swaziland, which were administered by the High Commissioner for South Africa.

When the South African Constitution was being drawn up the Chiefs in Basutoland, Bechuanaland and Swaziland objected to any scheme which would bring their territories under the rule of South Africa. Assurances were given that no immediate change would be made in the administration of these territories, but provision was made for the possible eventual transfer subject to certain conditions for the protection of African rights embodied in the Act. From 1909 on successive South African Governments asked for the implementation of the transfer, which was understood to be provided for by the Schedule to the South African Act of Union. The British Government reiterated that it alone bore the ultimate responsibility in the question of a decision about transfer and that no such transfer could take place until the wishes of the inhabitants had been ascertained and considered. For many years past the records of the African Advisory Council, African Council, and Legislative Council have left no doubt of the opposition of the African people of Botswana to any such transfer. The question of handing over the administration of the three countries to South Africa ceased to be a serious issue in 1960. In February 1965 the headquarters of the Administration was transferred from Mafeking in the Cape Province of South Africa, which had been its home since 1895, to Gaborone.

CONSTITUTIONAL DEVELOPMENT

From 1891 to 1960, the constitutional position of the protectorate was governed by various Orders in Council and Proclamations of which the most important was the Order in Council of Queen Victoria dated 9th May 1891 which empowered the High Commissioner to exercise on her behalf all the powers and jurisdiction of the Queen, subject to such instructions as he might receive from Her Majesty or through a Secretary of State.

Since about the mid-thirties necessary intervention in tribal affairs by the central authority, financial and economic development, the growth of export and import trade, technical advances and ever-increasing demands for more and better services brought about an inevitable and intensifying extension of central government activity. The expansion of central authority was accompanied by the steady evolution of local tribal government. In 1934, the promulgation of the African Courts and African Administration Proclamation set out to regularise the position of the chiefs, to provide for the proper exercise of their powers and functions, to define the constitution and functions of the Courts and to establish their powers and jurisdiction on a proper legal footing. The actions of African Authorities and African Courts were consequently henceforward governed by law.

In 1960 a new constitution was introduced providing for an advisory Executive Council consisting of the Resident Commissioner (or the High Commissioner), three *ex-officio* members (The Government Secretary, the Finance Secretary and the Attorney-General), two official members appointed by the High Commissioner, and four nominated members appointed by the High Commissioner who were members of the Legislative Council not holding any public office, two of them African and two Europeans; a representative Legislative Council, consisting of the Resident Commissioner as President, the three *ex-officio* members of the Executive Council, seven official members holding public office appointed by the High Commissioner, twenty-one elected members, and not more than four nominated members, not holding any public office, appointed by the High Commissioner, who had to be either one African and one European or two Africans and two Europeans; and an advisory African Council partly official, partly *ex-officio*, and partly elected. The Constitution also established a judicature consisting of a High Court comprising a Chief Justice and puisne judges.

By Order in Council signed on 27th September 1963 the territory was made independent of High Commission rule by the transformation of the post of Resident Commissioner into that of Her Majesty's Commissioner, with the status and rank of a Governor. Her Majesty's Commissioner assented to laws and was directly responsible to the Secretary of State for the Colonies. Certain powers retained by the High Commissioner ceased to exist when the office was abolished on 1st August 1964.

During 1963 and early in 1964 a series of constitutional discussions took place to determine the form of further constitutional advance.

Unanimously agreed proposals for internal self-government based on universal adult suffrage and a ministerial form of government were put forward to Her Majesty's Government and were accepted in June 1964.

The new Constitution contained in the Bechuanaland Protectorate (Constitution) Orders 1965 (S.I. 1965 Nos. 134 and 1718) as modified by the Bechuanaland Protectorate (Constitution) (Amendment) Order 1965 (S.I. 1965 No. 1718) and by Her Majesty's Commissioner's order in terms of section 12(7) of the Bechuanaland Protectorate (Constitution) Order 1965 (G.N. No. 99 of 1965), came into effect on the 3rd March 1965. This Constitution granted to the country a form of responsible government upon which the present Constitution is based.

The executive government of Bechuanaland was controlled by a Cabinet presided over by the Prime Minister, consisting of the Deputy Prime Minister and six other members chosen by the Prime Minister from the Legislative Assembly. Under the Constitution, the Prime Minister was the member of Legislative Assembly who appeared to Her Majesty's Commissioner to command the support of the majority of the Members of the Assembly, i.e. the leader of that political party which obtained the largest number of seats in the General Election.

CONSTITUTION

The President of Botswana is Head of State, in whom is vested the executive power of the Republic. The Vice-President is appointed by the President from among members of the National Assembly and is the principal assistant to the President and leader of Government business in the National Assembly. The Cabinet, which advises the President on Government policy, consists of not more than seven ministers, appointed by the President.

The Botswana Parliament consists of the President and the National Assembly. The Assembly is made up of 31 elected members and four specially elected members, the Attorney-General, who does not have a vote in the Assembly and the Speaker. The Assembly is elected on the basis of universal adult suffrage.

The House of Chiefs consists of eight *ex-officio* members, who are the chiefs of the eight principal Batswana tribes, four members elected from among their own number by the Sub-Chiefs who reside in the State Land areas, and three specially elected members, elected by the *ex-officio* and elected members. The House of Chiefs considers draft bills which are referred to it by the National Assembly, and which if enacted would alter any of the provisions of the Constitution or affect a defined range of subjects relating to tribal matters. The House of Chiefs is also entitled to discuss any matters affecting the tribes and tribal organisations and may make representations to the President, and through him to the Cabinet, and may send messages to the National Assembly.

GOVERNMENT

For the first general election in the Bechuanaland Protectorate, roughly 80 per cent of the potential electorate registered as voters in 1964; of those nearly 5/6ths actually voted in 1965. The result was an overwhelming victory for the Bechuanaland Democratic Party led by Sir Seretse Khama, who won 28 seats in the Legislative Assembly. The remaining 3 seats went to the Bechuanaland People's Party led by Mr Philip Matante.

Sir Seretse Khama became the first Prime Minister of Bechuanaland and subsequently the first President of the Republic of Botswana on 30th September 1966.

On 18th October 1969, the first general elections since the achievement of Independence in 1966 were held, and about one-half of the registered voters of Botswana went to the polls. The result was a victory for the Botswana Democratic Party, led by Sir Seretse Khama, which won 24 seats in the Legislative Assembly. The Botswana People's Party and the Botswana National Front won 3 seats each, and the Botswana Independence Party gained 1 seat.

A Presidential Candidate who is supported by more than one-half of elected MPs is automatically declared as President. As his party had a clear majority, Sir Seretse Khama therefore retained the Presidency and was sworn in by the Chief Justice on 22nd October 1969.

PRESIDENT AND CABINET

President: Sir Seretse Khama, KBE
Vice-President and Minister of Finance and Development Planning:
The Hon. Dr Q. K. J. Masire, MP
Minister of State in the Office of the President: The Hon. E. S. Masisi, MP
(with responsibility for external affairs and information and broadcasting)
Minister of Health, Labour and Home Affairs: The Hon. M. P. K. Nwako, MP
Minister of Education: The Hon. B. C. Thema, MBE, MP
Minister of Agriculture: The Hon. A. M. Dambe, BEM, MP
Minister of Works and Communications: The Hon. J. G. Haskins, OBE, JP, MP
Minister of Commerce, Industry and Water Affairs: The Hon. M. K. Segokgo, MP
Minister of Local Government and Lands: The Hon. E. M. K. Kgabo, MP

JUDICIARY

Chief Justice: J. R. Dendy Young, QC.
Attorney-General: M. D. Mokama
Registrar: F. X. Rooney

NATIONAL ASSEMBLY

Speaker: Reverend A. A. F. Lock

MINISTRIES AND DEPARTMENTS

PRESIDENT'S OFFICE

Assistant Minister: K. P. Morake, MP
Permanent Secretary to the President: A. M. Mogwe, MBE
Administrative Secretary: P. L. Steenkamp, MBE
Under Secretary, External Affairs: N. E. K. Sebele
Commissioner of Police: Lt.-Col. J. T. A. Bailey, CBE, QPM
Director of Personnel: D. L. Pilane

MINISTRY OF HEALTH, LABOUR AND HOME AFFAIRS

Permanent Secretary: M. T. M. Kgopo, MBE
Director of Prisons: R. N. Bowers, BEM
Chief Information Officer: M. Galetshage
Director of Medical Services: Dr D. G. Standing

MINISTRY OF FINANCE AND DEVELOPMENT PLANNING

Assistant Minister: Mr Bakwena K. Kgari
Permanent Secretary: C. Hermans
Accountant-General: C. Griffith, OBE

MINISTRY OF AGRICULTURE

Permanent Secretary: G. W. Winstanley, MBE
Director of Veterinary Services: J. Falconer, OBE

MINISTRY OF LOCAL GOVERNMENT AND LANDS

Permanent Secretary: R. Mannothoko
Director of Surveys and Lands: W. L. Dickson

MINISTRY OF WORKS AND COMMUNICATIONS

Permanent Secretary: L. D. Laxalare
Permanent Secretary: M. O. S. Hawkins
Director of Public Works: W. D. Scott, MBE
Director of Civil Aviation: N. A. Baguley
Director of Posts and Telegraphs: M. Cromarty

MINISTRY OF COMMERCE, INDUSTRY AND WATER AFFAIRS

Permanent Secretary: S. T. Ketlogetswe
Director of Geological Survey: C. Boocock, OBE
Director of Water Affairs: C. J. Lang
Registrar of Companies, Trade Marks, Patents and Designs: H. B. Mannothoko

MINISTRY OF EDUCATION

Permanent Secretary: B. Mookodi
Chief Education Officer: A. W. Kgarebe

AUDIT DEPARTMENT

Director: J. C. Northway, OBE

DIPLOMATIC REPRESENTATION

High Commissioner in the United Kingdom: Miss G. K. T. Chiepe; The High Commissioner in London is also non-resident High-Commissioner to Nigeria; High Commissioner in Zambia: P. P. Makepe; The High Commissioner in Lusaka is also non-resident High Commissioner to Kenya, Malawi, Uganda and Tanzania.

COMMONWEALTH HIGH COMMISSIONERS IN BOTSWANA

Britain: G. D. Anderson, CMG; Canada: H. H. Carter (resident in South Africa); Zambia: M. Sokoni

BOTSWANA REPRESENTATIVES IN NON-COMMONWEALTH COUNTRIES

Denmark, France, Germany, Norway, Sweden: Miss G. K. T. Chiepe (resident in London); Ethiopia: P. P. Makepe (resident in Lusaka); United Nations: T. J. Molefhe; United States: Chief Linchwe II

NON-COMMONWEALTH REPRESENTATION IN BOTSWANA

Austria (Ambassador) (resident in South Africa); Belgium (Ambassador) (resident in South Africa); Czechoslovakia (Chargé d'Affaires) (resident in Lusaka); France (Ambassador) (resident in Lusaka); Italy (Ambassador) (resident in Lusaka); Israel (Ambassador) (resident in Lusaka); Japan (Consul-General) (resident in South Africa); Korea (Ambassador) (resident in Nairobi); Netherlands (Ambassador) (resident in South Africa); Republic of China (Ambassador); Switzerland (Ambassador) (resident in South Africa); United States (Ambassador); West Germany (Ambassador) (resident in Lusaka)

CANADA

CANADA occupies the northern half of the North American Continent with the exception of Alaska, which is part of the United States, Greenland which belongs to Denmark, and the small islands of St Pierre and Miquelon off the coast of Newfoundland which belong to France. In latitude the country stretches from Middle Island in Lake Erie, at 41° 41' N., to Cape Columbia on Ellesmere Island, at 83° 07' N. It thus includes the islands immediately North of the mainland such as Victoria Island and Baffin Island as well as those in the extreme North known collectively as the Queen Elizabeth Islands. Other islands of importance are Vancouver Island and the Queen Charlotte Islands off the West Coast; the island of Newfoundland forming part of the Province of Newfoundland; the Province of Prince Edward Island; Cape Breton Island forming part of the Province of Nova Scotia; Grand Manan and Campobello Islands forming part of the Province of New Brunswick; Anticosti Island and the Magdalen group included in the Province of Quebec. Canada is the largest country in the Western Hemisphere and second largest country in the world, comprising an area computed at 3,851,809 square miles of land and fresh water, over forty times the area of Britain.

The predominant geographical feature is the Great Cordilleran Mountain System which contains many peaks over 10,000 feet in height. The highest peak in Canada is Mount Logan, in the St Elias Mountains of Yukon Territory, which rises 19,850 feet above sea level. The highest elevations in the country are to be found in Yukon (19 other peaks over 10,000 feet), Alberta (32 peaks over 10,000 feet in the Rockies) and British Columbia (32 peaks over 10,000 feet).

Another geographical feature of note is the area known as the great Canadian Shield. This is a vast area of ancient rocks occupying the greater part of the territory north of the River St Lawrence. It consists of plateau-like highlands, made up of a great mass of ancient, very hard rocks, which present a rough,

For further information about Canada see *Canada Year Book*.

broken surface strewn with lakes and varying in height from 1,000 to 3,000 feet above sea level with a few higher peaks. It contains rich mineral deposits, and its vast forest and water power resources contribute much to the wealth of the country.

Canada's inland waters are very extensive, constituting about 7·6 per cent of the total area of the country. The Great Lakes are the outstanding lakes of the country, their total Canadian area being almost 36,000 square miles. Other large lakes ranging in area from 9,500 to 12,300 square miles are Lake Winnipeg, Great Slave Lake and Great Bear Lake. In addition there are innumerable lakes scattered over that major portion of Canada lying within the Canadian Shield; in an area of 6,094 square miles south and east of Lake Winnipeg there are 3,000 lakes. Eastern Canada is dominated by the Great Lakes–St Lawrence system which drains an area of about 678,000 square miles and forms an unequalled navigable inland waterway through a region rich in natural and industrial resources. From the head of Lake Superior to the entrance to the Gulf of St Lawrence the distance is 2,280 miles. In the mid-west two main branches of the Saskatchewan River, tributary to the Nelson flowing into Hudson Bay, drain one of Canada's great agricultural regions and are now the bases of important irrigation projects. North-westward, one of the world's longest rivers, the Mackenzie, flows 2,635 miles to the Arctic Ocean and drains an area in the three westernmost provinces of approximately 700,000 square miles.

There are great differences in the weather throughout Canada at any given time, as there are many climates. Because Canada is situated in the northern half of the hemisphere, most of the country loses more heat annually than it receives from the sun. The general atmospheric circulation compensates for this and at the same time produces a general movement of air from west to east. Migrant low pressure areas move across the country in this 'westerly zone', producing storms and bad weather. In intervals between storms there prevails the fair weather associated with high pressure areas. The physical geography of North America also contributes greatly to the climate. On the west coast, the western Cordillera limits mild air from the Pacific to a narrow band along the coast, while the prairies to the east of the mountains are dry and have extreme temperatures. The prairies are part of a wide north-south corridor open to rapid air flow from either north or south which often brings sudden and drastic weather changes. On the other hand, the large water surfaces of eastern Canada produce a considerable modification to the climate. In south-western Ontario winters are milder with more snow, and in summer the cooling effect of the lakes is well illustrated by the number of resorts along their shores. On the east coast the Atlantic Ocean has considerable effect on the immediate coastal area where temperatures are modified and conditions made more humid when the winds blow inland from the ocean. The following figures give some indication of the varying temperatures (Fahrenheit): Newfoundland (Gander) January 20·8, July 62·3; Nova Scotia (Halifax) January 26·0, July 65·3; Quebec (Montreal) January 16·3, July 70·8; Prairie Provinces (Regina) January 1·6, July 66·7; British Columbia (Vancouver) January 37·2, July 63·8; (Smith River) January 11·4, July 57·3; Yukon (Whitehorse) January 0·6, July 57·5.

The Canadian federal state was established by the British North America Act, 1867, and now consists of ten Provinces and two Territories. The Provinces, with the date on which they joined the Confederation, are: Ontario (1867), Quebec (1867), Nova Scotia (1867), New Brunswick (1867), Manitoba (1870),

British Columbia (1871), Prince Edward Island (1873), Saskatchewan (1905), Alberta (1905) and Newfoundland (1949). The Territories are the Northwest Territories (1870) and the Yukon Territory (1898). The Northwest Territories were divided in 1920 into the Districts of Mackenzie, Keewatin and Franklin.

As recorded at the Census of 1966, the population of Canada was 20,014,880, of whom 74 per cent were classed as urban dwellers; 56 per cent lived in or on the fringes of urban centres having a population of 30,000 or more and less than 10 per cent lived on farms. Of the total population, 32·9 per cent were under 15 years of age and 59·4 per cent were in the working age group 15 to 64 years; 7·7 per cent were 65 years of age or over. The 5-year average birth and death rates are 24·2 and 7·7 per 1,000 respectively. The two basic ethnic groups in the Canadian population are the British Isles group and the French. In 1961 43·8 per cent of the population belonged to the former group and 30·4 per cent to the latter. The next largest ethnic group was German with 5·8 per cent of the total population, followed by Ukrainian with 2·6 per cent, Italian with 2·5 per cent and the Netherlands with 2·4 per cent. Asians made up only 0·7 per cent of the population. (On 1st June 1968 the population was estimated to be 20,744,000.)

At the time of the 1961 Census the native peoples of Canada, the Indians and Eskimos, together made up only 1·2 per cent of the total population. The Indian population numbered 191,709 (the estimated 1968 figure was 218,000) including all persons with a paternal ancestor of Indian race who have chosen to remain under Indian legislation. About 74 per cent of the Indians live on reserves having a total area of 6,000,735 acres. The remainder reside away from reserves, including those in the Yukon and Northwest Territories for whom reserves have not been set aside. In the northern and other outlying areas, hunting, fishing and trapping remain an important means of livelihood for them but in the more settled areas many Indians have fitted into the economy of the communities in which they live in a wide range of occupations. Subject to special provisions in the Indian Act, all laws of general application are applicable to Indians, and they may vote in federal elections on the same basis as other citizens and in provincial elections where the electoral laws of the provinces permit. Indian affairs are administered by the Federal Government and are conducted in a manner that will enable the Indians to participate fully in the social and economic life of the country. A wide range of programmes has been brought into effect in the fields of education, economic development, social welfare and community development; nearly 65,000 Indians are enrolled in schools throughout the country.

The affairs of approximately 15,000 Canadian Eskimos living in the North-west Territories, northern Quebec and Labrador are also administered by the Federal Government. While many of them still hold to the traditional way of life, an ever-increasing number are making the change from a nomadic existence to regular wage employment. Continued development in the north, coupled with a decrease in some types of game, is resulting in more and more Eskimos settling in modern communities with schools, health and transportation facilities and wage employment opportunities. The Canadian Government is helping this transition by providing such forms of assistance as education and welfare services, vocational training and economic development programmes. About 3,000 Eskimo children now regularly attend schools.

Under the provisions of the British North America Act, 1867, either the English or the French language may be used in debates in the Parliament of Canada and in the Legislature of Quebec and either of these languages may be used by any person or in any Pleading or Process in or issuing from any Court of Canada established under the Act and in or from all or any of the Courts of Quebec. Results of the 1961 census showed that 12,284,762 persons spoke English only, 3,489,866 spoke French only, 2,231,172 spoke both English and French and 232,447 spoke neither English nor French. The main religious denominations as recorded in the 1961 census were: Roman Catholic 8,342,826; United Church of Canada 3,664,008; Anglican Church of Canada 2,409,068; Presbyterian 818,558; Baptist 593,553 and Lutheran 401,836, Information on religious affiliations was not recorded in the 1966 census.

Primary education is free and universal.

Total tonnages handled in 1970 in the principal ports, including those on the St Lawrence River and the Great Lakes, were, in millions of tons; Montreal (22·2); Vancouver (26·7); Thunder Bay (20·7); Sept Îles (29·9); Hamilton (12·6); Halifax (11·1); Port Cartier (16·0); Baie Comeau (7·6); Toronto (5·5); Sault Ste Marie (5·6); Quebec (8·4); Saint John (6·3). The principal Shipping Line is Canadian Pacific Steamships Ltd.

There are two major Canadian air lines Air Canada and Canadian Pacific Airlines Limited. There are also five domestic air carriers licensed to operate scheduled commercial air services in Canada, namely, Eastern Provincial Airways (1963) Limited, Gander, Newfoundland; Quebecair, Montreal, Quebec; Nordair Ltée-Ltd., Dorval, Quebec; Transair Limited, Winnipeg, Manitoba; and Pacific Western Airlines Limited, Vancouver, British Columbia.

The 1967 road mileage figure was 449,561 (328,288 surfaced and 123,273 earth) and there were 43,168 miles of railway track.* The Canadian Broadcasting Corporation provides coast to coast radio and television services with 431 radio stations and 92 television stations in operation in 1968. There were also 343 privately owned radio stations and 239 television stations.

Exports and re-exports for the calendar year 1970 were valued at $16,458·2 million, and imports at $13,939·4 million.

The National Day of Canada is 1st July, Dominion Day.

HISTORY
Discovery and Exploration. The original inhabitants of North America migrated from Asia across the Bering Strait over twenty-five thousand years ago, gradually dispersing themselves throughout the continent. The first Europeans known to have landed on Canadian shores were the Vikings under Leif Ericson who founded short-lived settlements, probably in Newfoundland or Labrador, about A.D. 1000. Thereafter contact was lost between Europe and the New World.

The re-discovery of North America by Columbus encouraged other mariners to sail westward, among them John Cabot who, in the service of King Henry VII, made a landfall in the Gulf of St. Lawrence in 1497. Cabot's reports of the abundance of fish off Newfoundland attracted French, Spanish, Portuguese and English fishermen, who have continued to frequent these fishing grounds ever since. As early as 1534 Jacques Cartier, in the service of France, visited the Gulf of St Lawrence and in 1535 sailed up the St Lawrence River, where he visited Indian villages on the sites of present-day Quebec and Montreal. The name

---

* There are two trans-continental railway systems in Canada, Canadian National Railways (government-owned) and the Canadian Pacific Railway Company.

'Canada' may be derived from the Indian word *kanata*, meaning a town, applied to one of these villages.

Seeking a north-west passage to the Orient, Frobisher in 1576 and Davis in 1585 penetrated into the Frobisher and Davis Strait, and in 1602 Hudson Strait was discovered, and Hudson himself explored Hudson Bay in 1610. But the explorations of Baffin and others eventually persuaded the explorers that there was no suitable north-west passage. It was not until the nineteenth century that the explorations of Parry, Ross and Franklin enabled the passage to be passed by Roald Amundsen in 1906. The Pacific coast of Canada was explored by the Russians from Siberia, and by the Spaniards from Mexico, in the eighteenth century. It was left to Captain Cook to make a more thorough survey in 1778-79 and to Captain George Vancouver to complete his work in 1792-94.

The exploration of the interior of northern North America was impelled by the requirements of the fur trade. Samuel de Champlain of France reached the shores of Lake Huron in 1615 and laid the basis for the exploration of the Great Lakes. Other French traders turned south to the Mississippi or traversed the wilderness north of the Great Lakes to reach the western prairies. The Hudson's Bay Company also sent explorers into the Saskatchewan country. Alexander Mackenzie, a Montreal fur trader, was the first man to travel overland across northern North America. He reached the Pacific Coast in 1793.

Settlement. The main English settlements in North America were those along the Atlantic seaboard which later became the United States. Settlements in the northern part of the continent emerged through the need for bases for the fisheries and the fur trade. The English settlements were centred in Newfoundland, but the Hudson's Bay Company, founded by Royal Charter in 1670, claimed trading rights over Rupert's Land, defined as the area whose rivers drained into Hudson Bay. The father of the French empire in North America, Samuel de Champlain, founded Quebec at the narrows of the St Lawrence in 1608. A riverine colony, New France or Quebec became the base for a chain of fur trading posts that reached south to the Gulf of Mexico (to the landward of the English Atlantic colonies) and westward to the Rocky Mountains.

Until 1663 Quebec was governed autocratically by a trading company; in that year it became a Royal Province, under a Governor to whom was entrusted the general policy of the colony, the direction of its military affairs and its relations with the Indian tribes. A Superior Council also existed with certain administrative powers more formal than real. This system continued until the end of the French régime.

Meanwhile the English North American colonies established along the Atlantic seaboard were growing in population and wealth. Economic rivalry in the fishing and fur trades between the two European empires was reinforced by dynastic struggles in Europe. Four major wars were fought between 1689 and 1763, each with its North American sphere of operations. By the Treaty of Utrecht which, in 1713, ended the second of these wars, France surrendered all claims to Rupert's Land, to Acadia 'within its ancient limits' and to her settlements in Newfoundland, retaining, however, two small islands, St Pierre and Miquelon (which she still possesses) and some controversial fishing rights which remained in dispute until 1904. France, however, only surrendered that part of Acadia which is now Nova Scotia, keeping that part which is now New Brunswick as well as Isle St Jean (Prince Edward Island) and Isle Royale (Cape Breton Island) on which was constructed the fortress of Louisburg.

That part of Acadia which was surrendered was renamed Nova Scotia, and possessed few British settlers until the strategic base at Halifax was established in 1749. The fourth war, the Seven Years War, reached its North American culmination in Wolfe's victory at the Plains of Abraham outside Quebec (1759), which led to the conquest of Quebec and Montreal and the fall of the French empire in North America. By the Treaty of Paris of 1763 New France ceased to exist and all French territory east of the Mississippi was transferred to British sovereignty.

From 1763 until the outbreak of the American War of Independence in 1775, the whole of North America to the east of the Mississippi was held by Britain, the various colonies having a population of nearly 2,000,000 persons. In the north was Rupert's Land, under the jurisdiction of the Hudson's Bay Company; Newfoundland, still sparsely inhabited by fishermen; Nova Scotia, including Cape Breton Island and what is now New Brunswick and Prince Edward Island; and the Province of Quebec, comprising the area of the former French settlements along the St Lawrence and the Great Lakes.

The final partition of North America occurred as a result of the American War of Independence, which in some respects reflected the old economic rivalry between French and English in North America. An attempt by the American colonies to invade Quebec was unsuccessful and the Treaty of Paris, 1783, established what was to become the definitive boundary in eastern North America from the St Croix River in the Bay of Fundy to the Lake of the Woods. Various adjustments were, however, later made in the boundary, notably the Maine-New Brunswick boundary settlement (the Webster-Ashburton Treaty) of 1842.

From 1763 to 1774 Quebec was governed in the main by military authority. In the latter year the Quebec Act, passed by the British Parliament, secured for the French colonists the right to retain their language, religion and civil law. Roman Catholics were allowed the free exercise of their religion and were relieved of all civil disabilities. An appointed Council was created to advise the Governor. The Quebec Act, laid the legal basis for the survival of French culture and institutions in North America. Its embodiment of the principle of toleration for non-British elements in the colonies represented the emergence of a policy that was to be highly significant for the later Commonwealth.

The British character of the remaining North American colonies was strengthened as a result of the American Revolution. A considerable migration of Loyalists, perhaps 35,000 in number, moved north to remain under the rule of the Crown. Many of these people went to Nova Scotia, from which Prince Edward Island had been detached in 1769, while others settled in Cape Breton Island (a separate colony from 1784 to 1820 when it again became part of Nova Scotia) or established the new colony of New Brunswick. Still others entered Quebec, the majority settling in the western reaches of the colony. Objecting to the authoritarian rule of the Quebec Act, the Loyalists and other British residents petitioned for representative institutions. In 1791 Parliament passed the Constitutional Act to meet their wishes. Quebec was divided along the Ottawa River into two provinces: Upper Canada (now Ontario) and Lower Canada (Quebec). An elected Assembly was provided for each province, though the Governors, appointed by the Crown, and the nominated Legislative Councils retained control. Thus the Canadas followed Nova Scotia, which had been granted an Assembly in 1758, in taking the first step towards democratic institutions. Assemblies were also authorised for New Brunswick and Prince Edward Island, but Newfoundland, with its large transient fishing population, did not gain a legislature until 1832.

The economic life of the British North American colonies in the early nineteenth century was based on several great staple trades. Fishing, the oldest of these activities, continued to be pursued all along the coasts of the Maritime colonies and Newfoundland and around the Gulf of St Lawrence. The Napoleonic Wars produced a great demand for timber and a flourishing export in square timbers and naval stores grew up in New Brunswick and Quebec. All the Maritime colonies, but particularly Nova Scotia, built wooden ships for sale or for their own carrying trade. The Canadas exported wheat to Britain and, under the protection of the British preferential system, engaged in a large milling industry. The fur trade continued to be the dominant activity in the vast interior, where the Hudson's Bay Company (which by absorbing rival Montreal fur trading interests in 1821 monopolised trade throughout the West to the Pacific) exercised semi-governmental powers over the traders and the Indian population. Efforts were made to improve the transportation system of the Great Lakes-St Lawrence route, first by canals and then by railways, in an attempt to channel the export trade of the American mid-West through British North American ports.

The British North American colonies gained a considerable increase in population through the waves of immigration that flowed out from Europe in the 1830s, '40s and '50s. By 1851, the year of the first decennial census, the population of the colonies stood at 2·4 million. The colonies suffered economic dislocation in 1846, when Britain embarked upon the policy of free trade, and in 1849, when the Navigation Laws were repealed. The search for assured markets turned their eyes to the south, where the United States economy was advancing rapidly during this period. The Governor-General of British North America, Lord Elgin (8th Earl of Elgin and Kincardine), was successful in negotiating a Reciprocity Treaty (the Elgin-Marcy Treaty) in 1854. This provided for the free exchange of natural products and opened the Maritime inshore fisheries to American vessels. Although the treaty was abrogated by the United States in 1866, the demands of the Civil War created a large interchange of goods under it and brought prosperity to British North America.

In Upper and Lower Canada the constitution of 1791 did not prove a success. A struggle soon developed between the elected Assembly and the executive composed of the Governor and his advisers; this conflict was exacerbated in Lower Canada by friction between the French-speaking majority, who dominated the assembly, and the English minority, whose representatives surrounded the Governor. Disputes over the control of finance led to a small and ineffectual rebellion in Upper Canada in 1837 and to more serious uprisings in Lower Canada which lasted into 1838. The Melbourne government in Britain sent Lord Durham to the Canadas to investigate and report on the situation.

Durham was in North America for only five months, but his *Report on the Affairs of British North America* is one of the great landmarks in the history of Britain's relations with her colonies. His solution of the problem of how to preserve the relationship between Britain and her empire was to urge that the colonies be given self-government in all matters except those, such as foreign relations, regulation of commerce, the disposal of public lands and the determination of constitutions, which then appeared essential for the maintenance of imperial unity. At the same time he recommended the union of Upper and Lower

Canada under one government in the hope that this might help to assimilate the French population. His recommendations were partly embodied in the Union Act of 1840, which set up a single Province of Canada. The common government was to consist of the Governor, a nominated Legislative Council and an Assembly of 84 members, 42 to be elected from each part. The new constitution did not correct what Durham saw as the basic weakness of government in British North America—the lack of conformity between the executive and the legislature.

The struggle to establish the practice of responsible or cabinet government in British North America continued for the next eight years. The principle was first achieved in Nova Scotia, following instructions sent to Sir John Harvey, the Lieutenant-Governor, by Lord Grey (3rd Earl Grey), the Colonial Secretary: 'It cannot be too distinctly acknowledged that it is neither possible nor desirable to carry on the government of any of the British provinces in North America in opposition to the opinion of the inhabitants'. As a result Nova Scotia witnessed the accession to office, early in 1848, of a reform ministry which enjoyed the confidence of the majority of the legislature. In Canada the principle was affirmed in 1849 when Lord Elgin, despite riots and the burning of the Parliament buildings, refused to veto an unpopular bill which had been sponsored by the Baldwin-Lafontaine ministry and passed by the legislature. The Governor-General's decision to withdraw from meetings of his cabinet was a further confirmation of the principle. New Brunswick gained responsible government more peacefully, in 1854; Newfoundland in 1855.

For the first century after the English victory at Quebec, the British colonies shared the continent uneasily with their expanding neighbour, the United States. The War of 1812 marked a renewal of the American efforts of 1775-83 to expel Britain from the continent. The Canadas were invaded during each of the three years of the war.

The War was followed by two notable events which pointed the way towards a permanent settlement in North America. One was the Rush-Bagot Agreement of 1817, by which Britain and the United States limited naval vessels on the Great Lakes. This agreement removed a source of friction, even if it did not apply to land fortifications. These continued to be built until the Civil War, and it was not until 1871 that there can be said to have been 'an undefended border' between the United States and Canada. A second agreement, the Convention of 1818, fixed the international boundary along the 49th parallel of latitude from the Lake of the Woods to the Rockies. The Oregon territory, lying between the Rocky Mountains and the Pacific, was left in joint ownership at this time. However the migration of American settlers into the southern part of the territory determined its political disposition. The Treaty of Washington (1846) confirmed a continuation of the 49th parallel as the boundary west to the Pacific.

Relations between the United States and British North America were strained again during the American Civil War when border troubles, ship seizures, privateering and smuggling were rife. After the war the victorious North assumed an expansionist attitude, which expressed itself in threats and pressures on Canada. There was concern in Canada that the Hudson's Bay Company territories might be occupied by the same process that had determined the fate of Oregon. There was also fear that the United States might insist on the cession of Canada in the post-Civil War settlement with Britain. These anxieties were intensified by the withdrawal of the British garrisons from the North American colonies, a process which had been temporarily interrupted by the Civil War emergency. With Britain reducing her commitments in North America it seemed as if the colonies would have to look to each other for more of their security. Thus the Civil War, and the mood which followed it, provoked the discussions for a union of the British North American colonies.

The initiative for the confederation of British North America came from the province of Canada, where the mechanism of government had broken down by 1864. Neither Canada East nor Canada West had been happy in the union, and each had given support to political groups which found it impossible to co-operate for common purposes. The prospect of a wider union offered an escape from this political deadlock. Thus a coalition was formed in Canada to explore a plan of federation with the Maritime colonies. At a conference in Charlottetown in 1864 delegates from the colonies met to consider the practicability of union. The discussion was resumed at the Quebec conference in October, where a scheme of union, the Seventy-Two Resolutions, was drafted. Accepted by the British government and modified by later meetings, the Seventy-Two Resolutions became the basis of the British North America Act, 1867. Under this imperial statute the three colonies of Canada, Nova Scotia and New Brunswick were 'federally united' to form 'One Dominion under the name of Canada'. Self-government and union had produced the first colonial state and given rise to yet another line of growth that led to the Commonwealth.

In 1867 Canada consisted of only four provinces: Quebec and Ontario (the historic divisions of the Province of Canada), New Brunswick and Nova Scotia. It was imperative that steps be taken to secure the annexation of the West, still a fur trader's preserve under the authority of the Hudson's Bay Company. In 1869 the Company formally relinquished its charter, under compensation, to the Crown; and the whole of the vast territory over which the Company had exercised trading rights, known as Rupert's Land and the North-Western Territory, was in 1870 transferred to the Dominion of Canada. This territory did not include Alaska, purchased by the United States from the Russians in 1867. The transfer was opposed by some of the settlers, the Métis, who succeeded in having a new province, Manitoba, created in the lower Red River valley. Manitoba entered the Dominion in 1870 to become Canada's fifth province.

Beyond the Rockies existed the crown colony of British Columbia, with a history extending from the days of the maritime fur trade in the last part of the eighteenth century. Vancouver Island had been created as a colony in 1849, while the mainland area, British Columbia, was made a colony in 1858, as a means of maintaining order during the troubled period of a gold rush. The two jurisdictions were joined in 1866 under the name of British Columbia. However, the decline of the gold fields rendered the new colony's financial position precarious and in 1871 it was induced to become part of the Canadian union. The little colony of Prince Edward Island, which had held aloof from the earlier scheme of union, also cast in its lot with the new Dominion in 1873. Thus Canada extended from the Atlantic to the Pacific, the interior prairie region being administered as a federal territory. Sovereignty over the Arctic archipelago was formally transferred from Britain to Canada in 1880, giving the Dominion jurisdiction to the Pole.

The growth of settlement on the prairies led, in 1905, to the creation of two new provinces, Alberta and Saskatchewan. Their northern boundary was set at the 60th parallel, so that north of them the federal government still retained control of two regions, the Yukon Territory and the North-West Territories. Newfoundland, obliged to give up its powers of self-government in 1934 because of the impact of the world depression, voted to join Canada in 1948. Together with its dependency of Labrador, it became Canada's tenth province a year later. The inclusion of Newfoundland fulfilled the original design of the Canadian confederation.

Since 1867 the history of Canada has been a record of steady and substantial progress. Population growth, while slow in the last three decades of the nineteenth century, increased rapidly during a period of active immigration and Western settlement lasting from 1896 to the outset of the First World War. A similar period of rapid growth, this time associated with industrial advance, followed the Second World War, leading to a Canadian population of over 20 millions by 1961. Transportation, the sinew of Canada, has shown a continuous development since 1867. The country's first transcontinental railway, the Canadian Pacific Railway, was completed in 1885; by the First World War two other transcontinental lines were in operation. Air routes and gas and oil pipe lines now span the country and the opening of the St Lawrence Seaway in 1959 allowed ocean-going vessels to sail into the heart of the continent. New resources—pulp and paper, base metals, oil, uranium and iron—have joined the traditional export staples of Canada. Secondary industry has advanced rapidly, particularly around Canada's largest cities, Montreal and Toronto.

The Treaty of Washington, 1871, ended the American hopes of Canada eventually becoming part of the United States. Although Canadians rejected a comprehensive offer of trade reciprocity with the United States in 1911, favourable commercial arrangements in the 1930s allowed a growing measure of economic interdependence to develop between the two countries. The Boundary Waters Treaty of 1909 created an International Joint Commission for the solution of border problems of all kinds. Association in two world wars has strengthened the mutual confidence across the border, which is now symbolized by such military arrangements as the Permanent Joint Board on Defence (1940), the North Atlantic Treaty Organization (1949) and the North American Air Defence Command (1958).

CONSTITUTIONAL DEVELOPMENT

The machinery of government set up by the British North America Act of 1867 has remained basically unchanged to the present day; the principal change being the introduction of universal adult franchise in 1921. But the area over which the Canadian government exercises jurisdiction has greatly increased not only by the addition of new Provinces, increasing the number from 4 to 10, but by the transfer to the Canadian Government of vast areas which it rules directly. This increase in the area of Canadian governmental jurisdiction has resulted in an increase in the number of the Members both of the Senate and of the House of Commons.

The 1867 Act included within its provisions lists of subjects over which the Canadian Parliament and Provincial Legislatures respectively had exclusive legislative authority. Broadly speaking the Federal Government was given jurisdiction over all subjects of general interest and the Provincial Governments jurisdiction over subjects of local concern. But the lists were not comprehensive and there have, over the years, been jurisdictional disputes between the two levels of government.

After 1867 there still remained a number of limitations on the internal self-governing powers of the Canadian Government. By section 55 of the Act, the

Governor-General had the power, at his discretion, to withhold consent to Bills passed by the Canadian Parliament. In fact he was instructed to do so if the Bills were repugnant to the laws of Britain or if they concerned certain subjects which were reserved to the British Parliament. However these powers ceased to be used after 1875, and the Governor-General became less and less the representative or agent of the British Government. In 1926 it was finally confirmed that his status was only that of personal representative of the Crown and that he was bound to act on the advice of his Canadian Ministers. British garrisons remained on Canadian soil until 1906, and Canadian troops served under British generals up to the 1914 war. Another restriction on Canadian internal self-government was the appellate jurisdiction of the Judicial Committee of the Privy Council, and this was abolished in 1949. Yet another restriction arose from the fact that the British North America Act was an Act of the British Parliament and could only be amended by another Act of that Parliament. This remains the position until the present day, but the British Parliament only acts at the request of the Canadian Government, and the right to amend the Act in respect of certain internal matters was granted to the Canadian Parliament by the British North America Act (No. 2) of 1949. Except for the restriction on the power to amend its constitution, all the remaining legal and other restrictions on Canadian sovereignty were swept away as a result of the Imperial Conferences of the 1920s and the Statute of Westminster of 1931.

It was in the matter of the conduct of her foreign affairs that Canada from 1867 had the least self-government. The British North America Act left foreign affairs to the British Foreign Office, which was responsible for the conduct of foreign affairs of the Empire as a whole. Canada was not, in the eyes of Britain and the world, a sovereign state. Although Canadian representatives might sit with their British colleagues in discussions with foreign countries on matters concerning Canada, the resultant agreements or treaties were at first signed only by Britain. Until 1877 Canada was bound by British commercial treaties, but from that year she could choose whether to be bound or not; and from 1899 could withdraw from a commercial treaty. Later she was permitted to make her own commercial treaties, but the first non-commercial treaty to be made and signed by the Canadian Government was the Halibut Fishery Treaty with the United States in 1923. Although permitted to appoint to Britain in 1880 a semi-diplomatic representative, named a High Commissioner, Canada had no foreign affairs department until 1909, and did not appoint diplomatic representatives to other countries until 1927. As the population of Canada increased and as her influence grew, her subordinate status became more irksome to her, and the 1914-18 war, in which half a million Canadians took part, brought a realisation to Britain and to other countries that Canada had an independent part to play in world affairs. That the organisation of the Empire was based on equality of manhood was recognised in 1917 by the Imperial War Conference, on which Canada was represented, and Canada played an important and independent part in the Peace Conference, signed the Peace of Versailles, and became a member not only of the International Labour Organization but of the League of Nations, to whose Council she was elected for 1927.

Finally the Balfour formula of 1926, endorsed by the Statute of Westminster in 1931, set the seal on Canada's complete independence within the Commonwealth and on her status as a sovereign country.

CONSTITUTION

The Executive Government is vested in the Crown and is exercised by a Governor-General appointed by the Queen on the recommendation of Her Majesty's Canadian Prime Minister. The Governor-General exercises his executive powers on the advice of his Cabinet, which is formed of the principal members of the Government, chosen by the Prime Minister and responsible to the Parliament of Canada. The Cabinet is a Committee of the Queen's Privy Council for Canada, which has at present about 127 Members. Membership of the Privy Council is for life; so that Privy Councillors include both former and present Ministers of the Crown as well as a number of persons who have been, from time to time as an honour, sworn as Privy Councillors; these include members of the Royal Family, past and present Commonwealth Prime Ministers, and former Speakers of the Senate and of the House of Commons of Canada. The Council seldom meets as a body and its constitutional responsibilities as adviser to the Crown in respect to Canada are performed exclusively by a Committee; whose membership, with a few historical exceptions, is identical with that of the Cabinet of the day. A clear distinction between the functions of the Committee of the Privy Council and the Cabinet is rarely made and actually the terms 'Council' and 'Cabinet' are commonly employed as synonyms.*

The supreme legislative power in the field of jurisdiction assigned to the federal legislature by the British North America Act is vested in a Parliament, consisting of the Queen (represented by the Governor-General), a Senate and a House of Commons. The Senate now consists of 102 members: 24 representing Ontario, 24 Quebec, 24 the Maritime Provinces, 24 the Western Provinces and 6 Newfoundland. Until 1965, Senators were appointed for life but in accordance with an Act passed on 2nd June 1965, Senators appointed after that date will cease to hold their position on reaching 75 years of age. The qualifications for Senator include the possession of property worth $4,000, age not less than 30 years and residence within the province for which he is appointed. The House of Commons consisted originally (1867) of 181 elected members. This number has been increased by additions on the accession of new provinces and as the result of increase in population. Representation in the House is reviewed decennially, and a new Act was passed in 1966, to take effect upon the dissolution of the 27th parliament. The provincial and territorial representation as it now stands is given below: Ontario 88; Quebec 74; Nova Scotia 11; New Brunswick 10; Manitoba 13; British Columbia 23; Prince Edward Island 4; Saskatchewan 13; Alberta 19; Newfoundland 7; Yukon Territory 1; Northwest Territories 1; Total 264. There is no property qualification; the age qualification is 21 years. A Parliament lasts five years if not sooner dissolved.

The Parliament of Canada has exclusive legislative power in certain specified matters; these include public finance, trade regulations, postal services, currency, coinage, banking, navigation, defence, criminal law, bankruptcy, copyright, patents, naturalization and Indian affairs.

The Judges are appointed by the Governor-General in the superior, district and county courts throughout Canada, except in the probate courts of Nova Scotia and New Brunswick.

---

* The Governor General, the Prime Minister and the Chief Justice of Canada enjoy the style 'Right Honourable' for life. Otherwise in Canada the prefix 'Rt. Hon.' indicates membership of the British Privy Council and the suffix 'PC', if used, indicates membership of the Canadian Privy Council. In the historical lists in this section of the Year Book the suffix 'PC' denotes membership of the British Privy Council. Elsewhere in the section it indicates membership of the Canadian Privy Council.

CONSTITUTIONAL CONFERENCES

The first Federal Provincial Conference to review the Constitution was held in Ottawa in February 1968 under the Chairmanship of the then Prime Minister, Mr Pearson. A Continuing Committee of Officials and a Secretariat were established to help the process of review which has been carried forward since that time in further conferences, meetings of Ministers, and meetings of officials.

The second Conference held in February 1969 under the Chairmanship of Mr Trudeau reached agreement that the process of the Constitutional review should be carried on at an accelerated pace. It was agreed in particular that Committees of Ministers and of officials should examine specific aspects of the review, especially in regard to financial issues and the distribution of powers generally; official languages; fundamental rights; regional disparities; reform of the Senate; reform of the judiciary; and the establishment of a Canadian Capital Region. A working session of the Conference at Prime Minister level held *in camera* in June 1969 resulted in a measure of agreement on the distribution of taxing and spending powers. A third public Conference was held in December 1969. The main item discussed was income security and social services, the Federal Government's views on which were incorporated in a white paper published before the Conference. The various aspects of the subject were referred to Committees of Ministers and of Officials for further study. Items on taxation and regional economic disparities were referred to the Continuing Committee of Officials. The Conference also considered progress reports from the Committees of Ministers on Fundamental Rights, the Judiciary and Official Languages.

In 1970 there was one Constitutional Conference: a working session held *in camera* in Ottawa on 14th and 15th September. This session considered reports from the Committee of Ministers on Official Languages, and from the Continuing Committee of Officials on taxing power, regional economic disparities and public retirement insurance. It also examined the question of environmental management and the capital market and financial constitutions. On the question of the process of constitutional review, the Conference concluded that it was important to continue and complete the task undertaken in 1968 as quickly as practicable, but it recognised that in view of the need for thoroughness, it would be unrealistic to expect an early completion of the task. The Conference agreed that at the same time attention should be given to the question of amending procedures for the constitution.

A further working session of the Constitutional Conference was held *in camera* in Ottawa on 8th and 9th February, 1971. Priority in discussion was given to the question of an amending formula and the early patriation of the constitution. Agreement was reached on a procedure for patriating the constitution and transferring to the people of Canada, through their elected representatives, the exclusive powers to amend and to enact constitutional provisions affecting Canada. This procedure would involve agreement among the Federal and Provincial governments on changes and procedure, a resolution of the two Houses of Parliament in Ottawa concerning a proclamation by the Governor General, a recommendation to the British Parliament to enact appropriate legislation and the issuance of the proclamation by the Governor General on a date to coincide with the effective date of the British law.

On the question of an amending formula, it was agreed that future constitutional amendments (with the exception of some amendments concerning federal or provincial constitutions and others of concern to only Canada plus one or more but not all provinces) would require consent at the Federal level and a majority of the provincial legislatures including (a) any legislature of a province which now or in the future contains 25% of the population of Canada and (b) the legislators of at least two provinces west of Ontario providing that the consenting provinces comprise 50% of the population of the provinces west of Ontario and the legislatures of at least two provinces east of Quebec.

The Conference also agreed that certain basic political rights should be entrenched in the constitution, that English and French should be declared the official languages of Canada, that the existence and independence of the Supreme Court should be entrenched in the constitution, that the reduction of regional disparities should be referred to both in a new preamble and in the body of the constitution, that the revised Constitution should contain a provision recognising the important role of intergovernmental consultation and co-operation and that specific proposals for alteration to the Constitution should be prepared in time for the next session of the Conference planned to be held in Victoria, British Columbia, in June.

The Conference also discussed social policy (in particular income security) interprovincial marketing, environmental management and public retirement insurance.

THE GOVERNMENT

Pierre Elliott Trudeau succeeded Lester Bowles Pearson as Leader of the Liberal Party and as Prime Minister on 20th April 1968. In the General Election on 25th June 1968 the Liberal Party, which previously had operated as a minority Government, was returned with an overall majority. Members returned were Liberals 154, Progressive Conservatives 72, New Democrats 23, Creditistes 14, Independent (the Speaker) 1.

GOVERNOR-GENERAL AND COMMANDER-IN-CHIEF
His Excellency the Rt Hon. Roland Michener, CC, CD
Secretary to the Governor-General: Esmond Butler

THE MINISTRY
According to precedence
Prime Minister: The Rt. Hon. Pierre Elliott Trudeau
Leader of the Government in the Senate: The Hon. Paul Joseph James Martin
Secretary of State for External Affairs: The Hon. Mitchell Sharp
Minister of Public Works: The Hon. Arthur Laing
President of the Queen's Privy Council for Canada: The Hon. Allan Joseph MacEachen
President of the Treasury Board: The Hon. Charles Mills Drury
Minister of Finance: The Hon. Edgar John Benson
Minister of Industry, Trade and Commerce: The Hon. Jean-Luc Pepin
Minister of Regional Economic Expansion: The Hon. Jean Marchand
Minister of Energy, Mines and Resources: The Hon. John James Greene
Minister of Communications: The Hon. Joseph Julien Jean-Pierre Côté
Minister of Justice: The Hon. John Napier Turner
Minister of Indian Affairs and Northern Development: The Hon. Jean Chrétien
Minister of Labour: The Hon. Bryce Stuart Mackasey
Minister of National Defence: The Hon. Donald Stovel Macdonald
Minister of National Health and Welfare: The Hon. John Carr Munro
Secretary of State for Canada: The Hon. Gérard Pelletier
Minister of Environment: The Hon. Jack Davis
Minister of Agriculture: The Hon. Horace Andrew Olson
Minister of Veterans' Affairs: The Hon. Jean-Eudes Dubé
Minister of Consumer and Corporate Affairs: The Hon. Stanley Ronald Basford
Minister of Transport: The Hon. Donald Campbell Jamieson
Minister without Portfolio: The Hon. Robert Knight Andras
Minister of Supply and Services: The Hon. James Armstrong Richardson
Minister of Manpower and Immigration: The Hon. Otto Emil Lang
Minister of National Revenue: The Hon. Herb Gray
Minister without Portfolio: The Hon. Robert Douglas George Stanbury
Solicitor General of Canada: The Hon. Jean-Pierre Goyer

LEADER OF THE OPPOSITION
Hon. Robert Stanfield, PC, QC, MP

SENATE OF CANADA
Speaker: Hon. Jean-Paul Deschatelets, PC
Leader of the Government in the Senate: Hon. Paul Martin, PC, QC
Leader of the Opposition in the Senate: Hon. Jacques Flynn, PC, QC
Clerk of the Senate and Clerk of the Parliaments: Hon. Robert Fortier, QC
Gentleman Usher of the Black Rod: A. G. Vandelac
Parliamentary Librarian: Erik J. Spicer

HOUSE OF COMMONS
Speaker: Hon. Lucien Lamoureux, PC, QC, MP
Clerk of the House of Commons: A. Fraser
Sergeant-at-Arms: Lt.-Col. D. V. Currie, VC

SUPREME COURT OF CANADA
Chief Justice of Canada: Rt Hon. J. H. G. Fauteux

Puisne Judges:

Hon. D.ʳC. Abbott, PC	Hon. E. M. Hall
Hon. Ronald Martland	Hon. W. F. Spence
Hon. Wilfred Judson	Hon. Philippe Pigeon
Hon. Roland A. Ritchie	Hon. Bora Laskin

Registrar: K. J. Matheson, QC

EXCHEQUER COURT OF CANADA
President: Hon. W. R. Jackett

Puisne Judges:

Hon. Jacques Dumoulin	Hon. H. F. Gibson
Hon. Arthur Thurlow	Hon. Camil Noel
Hon. Allison A. M. Walsh	Hon. Roderick Kerr
Hon. A. A. Cattanach	

Registrar: A. E. G. R. Belleau, QC

COURT MARTIAL APPEAL COURT
President: Hon. H. F. Gibson

Judges:

Hon. W. R. Jackett	Hon. A. A. Cattanach
Hon. Jacques Dumoulin	Hon. Allison A. M. Walsh
Hon. Arthur Thurlow	Hon. Roderick Kerr
Hon. Camil Noel	

Hon. G. E. Tritschler (Manitoba)
Hon. L. McC. Ritchie (New Brunswick)
Hon. T. G. Norris (British Columbia)
Hon. Y. Bernier (Quebec)
Associate Registrar: A. E. G. R. Belleau, QC

GOVERNMENT DEPARTMENTS

PRIME MINISTER'S OFFICE
Principal Secretary: Marc Lalonde

PRIVY COUNCIL OFFICE
Clerk of the Privy Council and Secretary to
the Cabinet: R. G. Robertson
Chief Science Adviser: (vacant)
Economic Adviser: R. B. Bryce, CC

DEPARTMENT OF TRANSPORT
Deputy Minister: O. G. Stoner

DEPARTMENT OF EXTERNAL AFFAIRS
Under-Secretary of State for External
Affairs: A. E. Ritchie
Associate Under-Secretary: Paul Tremblay

CANADIAN INTERNATIONAL DEVELOPMENT
AGENCY
President: P. Gérin Lajoie

DEPARTMENT OF THE SOLICITOR-GENERAL
Deputy Solicitor-General: E. A. Côté
Commissioner of Penitentiaries: A. J.
MacLeod, QC

DEPARTMENT OF PUBLIC WORKS
Deputy Minister: J. A. MacDonald

DEPARTMENT OF ENERGY, MINES AND
RESOURCES
Deputy Minister: J. Austin, QC

E

DEPARTMENT OF MANPOWER AND
IMMIGRATION
Deputy Minister: L. E. Couillard

TREASURY BOARD
Secretary: A. W. Johnson

DEPARTMENT OF FINANCE
Deputy Minister: S. S. Reisman
Comptroller of the Treasury: H. R. Balls
Master of the Royal Canadian Mint:
Gordon W. Hunter

DEPARTMENT OF NATIONAL DEFENCE
Deputy Minister: E. B. Armstrong
Chief of Defence Staff: General F. R. Sharp,
DSO, CD
Chairman, Defence Research Board: Dr L.
L'Heureux

DEPARTMENT OF INDUSTRY, TRADE AND
COMMERCE
Deputy Minister: J. H. Warren

DEPARTMENT OF NATIONAL REVENUE
Deputy Minister (Customs and Excise):
R. C. Labarge
Deputy Minister (Taxation): Sylvian Cloutier

DEPARTMENT OF JUSTICE
Deputy Minister and Deputy Attorney-
General of Canada: D. S. Maxwell, QC

DEPARTMENT OF INDIAN AFFAIRS AND
NORTHERN DEVELOPMENT
Deputy Minister: H. B. Robinson

DEPARTMENT OF LABOUR
Deputy Minister: Douglas Love

DEPARTMENT OF NATIONAL HEALTH AND
WELFARE
Deputy Minister of National Health:
J. Maurice Leclair
Deputy Minister of Welfare: Joseph W.
Willard

DEPARTMENT OF THE SECRETARY OF STATE
Under-Secretary of State: Jules Léger

DEPARTMENT OF FISHERIES AND FORESTRY
Deputy Minister: R. Shaw

DEPARTMENT OF AGRICULTURE
Deputy Minister: S. B. Williams

DEPARTMENT OF VETERANS' AFFAIRS
Deputy Minister: J. S. Hodgson, OBE

DEPARTMENT OF CONSUMER AND
CORPORATE AFFAIRS
Deputy Minister: J. F. Grandy

DEPARTMENT OF SUPPLY AND SERVICES
Deputy Minister (Supply): Jean Boucher
Deputy Minister (Services): H. R. Balls

DEPARTMENT OF COMMUNICATIONS
Deputy Minister: A. E. Gotlieb

POST OFFICE DEPARTMENT
Deputy Postmaster-General: J. A. H.
Mackay

ANTI-DUMPING TRIBUNAL
Chairman: W. W. Buchanan

ATOMIC ENERGY CONTROL BOARD
President: Donald G. Hurst

ATOMIC ENERGY OF CANADA LTD.
President: J. L. Gray, CC

AUDITOR-GENERAL'S OFFICE
Auditor-General: A. M. Henderson, OBE

BANK OF CANADA
Governor: Louis Rasminsky, CC, CBE
Inspector-General of Banks: W. E. Scott

CANADA COUNCIL
Director: Peter Dwyer

CANADA DEPOSIT INSURANCE
CORPORATION
Chairman: Antonio Raninville

CANADIAN ARSENALS LTD
General Manager: K. G. Price

PRICES AND INCOMES COMMISSION
Chairman: J. H. Young

DEPARTMENT OF REGIONAL ECONOMIC
EXPANSION
Deputy Minister: Tom Kent

CANADIAN BROADCASTING CORPORATION
President: Dr G. F. Davidson

CANADIAN DAIRY COMMISSION
Chairman: S. C. Barry

CANADIAN PENSION COMMISSION
Chairman: T. D. Anderson

CANADIAN RADIO-TELEVISION
COMMISSION
Chairman: Pierre Juneau

CANADIAN TRANSPORT COMMISSION
President: Hon. J. W. Pickersgill, PC, QC

CENTRAL MORTGAGE AND HOUSING
CORPORATION
President: H. W. Hignett, MBE

OFFICE OF THE CHIEF ELECTORAL OFFICER
Chief Electoral Officer: J. M. Hamel

COMPANY OF YOUNG CANADIANS
Executive Director: P. D. Brodhead

CROWN ASSETS DISPOSAL CORPORATION
President: J. Miquelon, QC

DOMINION BUREAU OF STATISTICS
Dominion Statistician: W. E. Duffett

DEPARTMENT OF INSURANCE
Superintendent of Insurance: Richard Humphrys

ECONOMIC COUNCIL OF CANADA
Chairman: Arthur J. Smith

EXPORT DEVELOPMENT CORPORATION
President: H. T. Aitken

FARM CREDIT CORPORATION
Chairman: G. Owen

IMMIGRATION APPEAL BOARD
Chairman: Miss J. V. Scott

INFORMATION CANADA
Director: J.-L. Gagnon

INTERNATIONAL DEVELOPMENT RESEARCH CENTRE
President: Dr W. D. Hopper

INTERNATIONAL JOINT COMMISSION
Chairman (Canadian Section): A. D. P. Heeney, CC, QC

MEDICAL RESEARCH COUNCIL
Chairman: Dr G. Malcolm Brown

NATIONAL ARTS CENTRE
Director-General: G. Hamilton Southam

NATIONAL CAPITAL COMMISSION
Chairman: Douglas Fullerton

NATIONAL ENERGY BOARD
Chairman: R. D. Howland

NATIONAL FILM BOARD
Chairman and Government Film Commissioner: Sydney Newman

NATIONAL GALLERY
Director: Dr Jean S. Boggs

NATIONAL HARBOURS BOARD
Chairman: H. A. Mann

NATIONAL LIBRARY
National Librarian: Dr J. G. Sylvestre

NATIONAL MUSEUMS OF CANADA
Secretary-General: C. J. Mackenzie, CC

NATIONAL PAROLE BOARD
Chairman: T. G. Street, QC

NATIONAL RESEARCH COUNCIL
President: W. G. Schneider

PUBLIC ARCHIVES
Dominion Archivist: Dr. W. I. Smith

PUBLIC SERVICE COMMISSION
Chairman: J. J. Carson

PUBLIC SERVICE STAFF RELATIONS BOARD
Chairman: Jacob Finkelman, QC

REPRESENTATION COMMISSION
Commissioner: N. J. Castonguay

RESTRICTIVE TRADE PRACTICES COMMISSION
Chairman: R. S. MacLellan, QC

ROYAL CANADIAN MOUNTED POLICE
Commissioner: W. L. Higgitt

ST. LAWRENCE SEAWAY AUTHORITY
President: P. Camu

SCIENCE COUNCIL OF CANADA
Chairman: Dr O. M. Solandt, OBE

TARIFF BOARD
Chairman: L. C. Audette, QC

TAX APPEAL BOARD
Chairman: R. S. W. Fordham, QC

UNEMPLOYMENT INSURANCE COMMISSION
Chief Commissioner: J. M. DesRoches

VETERAN AFFAIRS DEPARTMENT
Deputy Minister: J. S. Hodgson, OBE

WAR VETERANS' ALLOWANCE BOARD
Chairman: D. M. Thompson

DIPLOMATIC REPRESENTATION

CANADIAN REPRESENTATIVES IN OTHER COMMONWEALTH COUNTRIES
Australia: A. R. Menzies (High Commissioner); Barbados: G. A. Rau (High Commissioner) (resident in Port of Spain); Botswana: H. H. Carter (High Commissioner) (resident in Pretoria); Britain: C. S. A. Ritchie (High Commissioner); Ceylon: R. M. MacDonnell (High Commissioner); Cyprus: C. E. McGaughey (High Commissioner) (resident in Tel Aviv); The Gambia: G. G. Riddell (High Commissioner) resident in Dakar); Ghana: D. B. Hicks (High Commissioner); Guyana: J. A. Stiles (High Commissioner); India: James George (High Commissioner); Jamaica: V. C. Moore (High Commissioner); Kenya: J. M. Cook (High Commissioner); Lesotho: H. H. Carter (High Commissioner) (resident in Pretoria); Malaysia: J. G. Hadwen (High Commissioner); Malta, G.C.: E. B. Rogers; (High Commissioner) (resident in Rome): Mauritius: J. A. Irwin (High Commissioner) (resident in Dar-es-Salaam); New Zealand;

J. A. Dougan (High Commissioner); Nigeria: A. S. McGill (High Commissioner); Pakistan: C. J. Small (High Commissioner); Sierra Leone: A. S. McGill (High Commissioner) (resident in Lagos); Singapore: J. G. Hadwen (High Commissioner) (resident in Kuala Lumpur); Swaziland: H. H. Carter (High Commissioner) (resident in Pretoria); Tanzania: J. A. Irwin (High Commissioner); Trinidad and Tobago: G. A. Rau (High Commissioner); Uganda: J. M. Cook (High Commissioner) (resident in Nairobi); Zambia: J. A. Irwin (High Commissioner) (resident in Dar-es-Salaam); West Indies: (Associated States): G. A. Rau (Commissioner) (resident in Port of Spain); Hong Kong: C. R. Gallow (Senior Trade Commissioner).

COMMONWEALTH REPRESENTATION IN CANADA

Australia: D. W. McNicol, CBE (High Commissioner); Barbados: (vacant) (High Commissioner); Botswana: Chief Linchwe II Molefhi Kgafela (High Commissioner) (resident in Washington); Britain: Sir Peter Hayman KCMG, CVO, MBE (High Commissioner); Ceylon: P. H. William de Silva (High Commissioner); Cyprus: Zenon Rossides (High Commissioner) (resident in Washington); Ghana: Seth K. Anthony, MBE (High Commissioner); Guyana: Rahman Baccus Gafraj (High Commissioner) (resident in Washington); India: Ashok Balkrishna Bhadkamkar (High Commissioner): Jamaica: V. C. Smith (High Commissioner); Lesotho: Mothusi Thamsanqa Mashologu (High Commissioner) resident in Washington; Malaysia: H. M. A. Zakaria (High Commissioner); Mauritius: P. G. G. Balancy, CBE (High Commoisier) (resident in New York); Malta, G.C.: Dr Arvid Pardo (High Commissioner) (resident in Washington); New Zealand: The Honourable Dean J. Eyre (High Commissioner); Nigeria: E. O. Enahoro (High Commissioner); Pakistan: M. S. Shaikh (High Commissioner); Sierra Leone: John J. Akar, MBE (High Commissioner) (resident in New York); Singapore: T. T. B. Koh (High Commissioner) (resident in New York); Swaziland: Dr S. T. M. Sukati (High Commissioner) (resident in Washington); Tanzania: A. K. Sykes (High Commissioner) Trinidad and Tobago: Matthew Ramcharen (High Commissioner) Uganda: Erifasi Otema-Allimadi (High Commissioner)r (e-sident in New York); Eastern Caribbean: Novelle H. Richards (Commissioner); Zambia: V. J. Mwaanga (High Commissioner) (resident in New York).

CANADIAN REPRESENTATIVES IN NON-COMMONWEALTH COUNTRIES

Afghanistan (Ambassador) (resident in Karachi); Algeria (Ambassador) (resident in Berne); Argentina (Ambassador); Austria (Ambassador); Belgium (Ambassador); Bolivia (Ambassador) (resident in Lima);

Brazil (Ambassador); Burma (Ambassador) (resident in Kuala Lumpur); Cameroun (Ambassador); Central African Republic (Ambassador) (resident in Yaounde); Chad (Ambassador) (resident in Yaounde); Chile (Ambassador); Colombia (Ambassador); Congo (Brazzaville) (Ambassador) (resident in Kinshasa); Congo (Kinshasa) (Ambassador); Costa Rica (Ambassador); Cuba (Ambassador); Czechoslovakia (Ambassador); Dahomey (Ambassador) (resident in Lagos); Denmark (Ambassador); Dominican Republic (Ambassador) (resident in Caracas); Ecuador (Ambassador) (resident in Bogota); El Salvador (Ambassador) (resident in San José); Ethiopia (Ambassador); European Communities (Economic, Atomic Energy, Coal and Steel) (Representative and Ambassador) (resident in Brussels); Finland (Ambassador); France (Ambassador); Gabon (Ambassador) (resident in Yaounde); Germany, Federal Republic (Ambassador) (also Head of Canadian Military Mission, Berlin); Greece (Ambassador); Guatemala (Ambassador) (resident in Mexico City); Guinea (Ambassador) (resident in Dakar); Haiti (Ambassador) (resident in Havana); Honduras (Ambassador) (resident in San José); Hungary (Ambassador) (resident in Prague); Iceland (Ambassador) (resident in Oslo); Indonesia (Ambassador); International Atomic Energy Authority, Vienna (Permanent Representative); Iran (Ambassador); Iraq (Ambassador) (resident in Teheran); Irish Republic (Ambassador); Israel (Ambassador); Italy (Ambassador); Ivory Coast (Ambassador); Japan (Ambassador); Jordan (Ambassador) (resident in Beirut); Korea (Ambassador) (resident in Tokyo); Kuwait (Ambassador) (resident in Teheran); Lebanon (Ambassador); Luxembourg (Ambassador) (resident in Brussels); Malagasy Republic (Ambassador) (resident in Addis Ababa); Mexico (Ambassador); Morocco (Ambassador) (resident in Madrid); Nepal (Ambassador) (resident in New Delhi); Netherlands (Ambassador); Nicaragua (Ambassador) (resident in San José); Niger (Ambassador) (resident in Lagos); North Atlantic Council, Brussels (Permanent Representative and Ambassador); Norway (Ambassador); Organisation for Economic Co-operation and Development, Paris (Permanent Representative); Panama (Ambassador) (resident in San José); Paraguay (Ambassador) (resident in Buenos Aires); Peru (Ambassador); Philippines (Consul General); Poland (Ambassador); Portugal (Ambassador); Rumania (Ambassador) (resident in Belgrade); Rwanda (Ambassador) (resident in Kinshasa); Senegal (Ambassador); Somali Republic (Ambassador) (resident in Addis Ababa); South Africa (Ambassador); Spain (Ambassador); Sudan (Ambassador) (resident in Cairo); Sweden (Ambassador); Switzerland (Ambassador) Syria (Ambassador) (resident in Beirut); Thailand (Ambassador) (resident in Kuala Lumpur); Togo (Ambassador) (resident in Accra); Tunisia (Ambassador); Turkey (Ambassador); United Arab Republic (Ambassador); United

Nations (Permanent Representative and Ambassador); European Office of the United Nations, Geneva (Permanent Representative and Ambassador); U.N.E.S.C.O., Paris (Permanent Delegate); U.N.I.D.O., Vienna (Permanent Representative); United States (Ambassador); Upper Volta (Ambassador) (resident in Accra); Uruguay (Ambassador) (resident in Buenos Aires); U.S.S.R. (Ambassador); Vatican (Ambassador); Venezuela (Ambassador); Yugoslavia (Ambassador); Conference of the Committee on Disarmament, Geneva (Ambassador).

THE PROVINCES OF CANADA

Canada consists of ten Provinces and two Territories. The Provinces comprise the Atlantic Provinces of Newfoundland, Prince Edward Island, Nova Scotia and New Brunswick; the Provinces of Quebec and Ontario; the Prairie Provinces of Manitoba, Saskatchewan and Alberta; the Pacific Province of British Columbia.

Prior to the British North America Act of 1867, British North America consisted of the Colonies of Canada (the provinces of Ontario and Quebec), New Brunswick, Nova Scotia, Prince Edward Island and Newfoundland in the east and the Colony of British Columbia in the west, the vast central and northern territory being known as Rupert's Land (the territory which drained into the Hudson Bay) and the North-Western Territory. There were also lands to the north which were virtually unexplored.

In 1867 the British North America Act divided Canada into the two Provinces of Quebec and Ontario and joined these with the colonies of New Brunswick and Nova Scotia to form a confederation, to which was given the name of Canada. This Act was brought into force on 1st July 1867 by Royal Proclamation dated 22nd May 1867.

By Order in Council dated 23rd June 1870, following the introduction of the Rupert's Land Act, 1868, Rupert's Land and the North-Western Territory were transferred to Canada with effect from 15th July 1870. The combined territories were designated as The North-West Territories.

On the date of the transfer a part of the North-West Territories, by the Manitoba Act, 1870, was formed into a new province called the Province of Manitoba (its boundaries being later extended in 1881). On the same day the new Province was admitted separately into the Union of Canada. A Lieutenant-Governor was appointed to govern Manitoba, and by a separate commission the Governor of Manitoba was appointed as the Lieutenant-Governor of the North-West Territories.

By Order in Council dated 16th May 1871 the Colony of British Columbia was admitted into the confederation on 20th July 1871.

Prince Edward Island was admitted by Order in Council of 26th June 1873 on the 1st July of that year.

On 31st July 1880, in compliance with the prayer of an Address from the Parliament of Canada dated 3rd May 1878, Her Majesty issued an Order in Council annexing to Canada from 1st September 1880 all British Territories in North America not already included within Canada and all islands adjacent thereto, with the exception of the Colony of Newfoundland and its dependencies. These additional territories were formally included in the North-West Territories.

The Keewatin Act, 1876, provided for the formation of a separate district of the North-West Territories, to be known as the District of Keewatin, to the north of Manitoba. By Order in Council of 8th May 1882 the southern part of the North-West Territories was divided into the provisional Districts of Assiniboia, Saskatchewan, Alberta and Athabasca and by Order in Council of 2nd June 1895 further provisional Districts of Ungava, Franklin, Mackenzie and Yukon were created in the north of the Territories, the boundaries being redefined by Order in Council of 18th December 1897. Yukon was created a separate Territory, distinct from the North-West Territories, by the Yukon Territory Act, 1898.

On 1st September 1905, by the Alberta Act, 1905, and the Saskatchewan Act, 1905, the Provinces of Alberta and Saskatchewan were formed from the provisional Districts of Alberta, Assiniboia, Saskatchewan and Athabasca, the dividing line running north and south.

The remainder of the North-West Territories were re-designated the Northwest Territories in 1906.

By a Federal Act of 1912 the boundaries of the Provinces of Ontario, Quebec and Manitoba were extended, the whole of Ungava being transferred to Quebec and parts of Keewatin to Ontario and Manitoba. However the Newfoundland Government objected to the transfer of the whole of Ungava to Quebec. By the decision, on 1st March 1927, of the Judicial Committee of the Privy Council, Newfoundland was confirmed in the ownership of the Atlantic watershed of the Labrador peninsula, including the basin of the Hamilton River, an area of about 112,000 square miles. The decision was the outcome of a dispute between Canada and Newfoundland as to the ownership of this region which had lasted for 25 years and was ultimately by agreement submitted to the arbitrament of this Tribunal.

In 1949 Newfoundland, including Labrador, was joined by the British North America Act, 1949, with the existing nine Provinces as a tenth Province after the people of Newfoundland had by a majority voted in favour in a referendum held in 1948.

For each province there is a Lieutenant-Governor, appointed by the Governor-General in Council and holding office during pleasure, but not removable within five years of appointment except for cause assigned.

Each province has a 'Legislative Assembly'. The Provincial Legislatures possess the power of altering their own constitutions. The territory not comprised within any province (Yukon and the Northwest Territories) is very thinly inhabited. The Yukon Territory is governed by an appointed Commissioner (under instructions from the Governor-General in Council or the Minister of Northern Affairs and National Resources) and an elective legislative council of seven members. The Northwest Territories are similarly governed by a Commissioner and nine councillors, of whom four are elected and the rest appointed by the Governor-General in Council.

The Provincial Legislatures have powers to legislate in respect of certain specified subjects, of which the chief are property and civil rights, the alteration of their own constitutions, direct taxation within the province and provincial loans, the management of provincial public lands, provincial and municipal offices, hospitals, gaols, licences, local works, and the general civil law and procedure. Over education they have full powers, subject only to certain provisions to secure protection to religious minorities. In agricultural, quarantine and immigration matters they possess concurrent legislative powers with the Parliament of Canada.

By the provisions of the British North America Act and subsequent arrangements entered into from time to time, the Canadian Government is required to make certain annual payments to the individual Provinces. These payments (subsidies) are of four kinds:

(*a*) *Interest on Debt Allowances.* This is based on payment of interest at 5 per cent per annum on the amount by which the actual debts of the Provinces on their entering into Confederation fall short of a prescribed debt allowance.

(*b*) *Allowances for Government and Legislature.* These are fixed amounts based on the population of the Province concerned and range from $100,000 to $240,000.

(*c*) *Allowances per Head of Population.* Grants are paid at the rate of 80 cents a head up to a population of 2½ million, and at 60 cents a head for so much of the population as exceeds that number.

(*d*) *Special Grants.* A number of special grants have been sanctioned for various reasons.

NEWFOUNDLAND AND LABRADOR

SITUATION AND POPULATION

The Province of Newfoundland and Labrador consists of the island of Newfoundland and the mainland of Labrador. The island, with an area of 43,359 square miles, lies between the Gulf of St Lawrence and the Atlantic Ocean. It is triangular in shape, each side being about 320 miles long. The mainland consists of that part of the Ungava peninsula which drains into the Atlantic Ocean as distinct from Hudson Bay or the Gulf of St Lawrence; its area is 112,826 square miles.

The estimated population of Newfoundland in April 1970 (including Labrador) was 517,000. The capital is St John's, with a population in the Metropolitan Area of 112,100 in April 1970.

HISTORY

The island of Newfoundland, according to the Icelandic saga, was sighted in A.D. 1001 by a merchant of Iceland, voyaging in search of trade. John Cabot discovered the island in 1497, but no permanent settlement resulted. The lasting results of Cabot's discovery sprang from a revelation of the riches of the sea, and the island was frequented as early as 1500 by British, Portuguese, Spanish, Basque and Breton fishermen, the Portuguese being the first to exploit the new fishing grounds. In the reign of Queen Elizabeth I several attempts were made to colonise the island, but these were unsuccessful. The interior was explored by Anthony Parkhurst in 1578, but the first attempt at formal annexation, made by Sir Humphrey Gilbert in 1583, had no direct effect on subsequent history. In 1610 a Charter was granted to the 'Treasurer and Company of Adventurers and Planters for the Colony or Plantation in Newfoundland', and colonists were established by the company in Conception Bay, mainly for the purpose of improving the fishing industry. In 1623 Sir George Calvert (afterwards Lord Baltimore) obtained grants from the Crown for the establishment of a settlement in the south-eastern peninsula of the island, which he named the Province of Avalon. In 1633 the Privy Council issued an order which, known as the 'Western Charter' or the 'Fishing Charter', lay at the base of all regulations concerning Newfoundland for more than 150 years. The first permanent colony was founded by Sir David Kirke, who was granted two Patents in 1637 for the colonisation of the whole of Newfoundland, and by 1774 a true colony had grown up, after which the island proceeded to develop more normally as compared with its previously amphibious character as 'a great English ship moored near the Banks during the fishing season for the convenience of fishermen'.

By the Treaty of Utrecht in 1713, subsequently ratified by the Treaty of Paris, the French, who in 1662 had established a base at Placentia, acknowledged British sovereignty over the whole of Newfoundland. Certain rights were granted to French fishermen under the Treaty, the extent of which long remained in dispute until settled by the Anglo-French Convention of 1904, by which France renounced her privileges under Article XIII. The Convention was of great benefit to Newfoundland, since it removed an obstruction to local development, to mining and other industrial enterprises, over some two-fifths of the whole coast-line. French sovereignty over the islands of St Pierre and Miquelon 15 miles off the tip of the Basin peninsula remains however and this now gives rise to the question of demarcation of undersea mineral rights, a matter of growing importance with the upsurge of off-shore oil exploration.

The mainland of Labrador, discovered by the Norseman Leif, son of Eric the Red, in A.D. 1000, was early frequented by Basque and subsequently by Breton fishermen. In 1763 the Atlantic coast was annexed to Newfoundland but was temporarily re-annexed to Quebec from 1774 to 1809.

CONSTITUTIONAL DEVELOPMENT

Newfoundland has had a Legislature since 1832, but it was the last of the old North American Colonies to which responsible government was conceded, in 1855. The island was subsequently administered by a Governor, aided by a responsible Executive Council in which the Governor presided, a Legislative Council appointed for life (17 members in 1932) and an elected House of Assembly (27 members in 1932).

The British North America Act, 1867, made provision for the accession of Newfoundland to Canada, but Newfoundland voted against confederation in 1869. Talks between Governments of Canada and Newfoundland with a view to confederation broke down in 1895. Newfoundland was separately represented at Imperial Conferences and enjoyed Dominion status, but did not become a separate member of the League of Nations and was not responsible for its own international relations.

Owing to the world depression and inability to meet the interest charges on the Public Debt, the Legislature in 1933 prayed His Majesty The King to suspend the constitution and appoint six Commissioners who, with the Governor as Chairman, would administer the government under the supervision of the British Government until Newfoundland became self-supporting again. His Majesty thereupon appointed three Commissioners from Newfoundland and three drawn from Britain, who took office in 1934. In 1945 it was announced that an elected National Convention would meet in 1946 to make recommendations as to the forms of future government which might be put before the people at a national referendum. The Convention met in September and sent fact-finding delegations to London and Ottawa in 1947. In the course of the discussions at Ottawa the Canadian Government agreed provisionally that if the people of Newfoundland should vote in favour of confederation with Canada, the Canadian Government would conclude a taxation agreement on a 'most favoured Province' basis, would service the sterling debt, would take over the Newfoundland railroad and would make a special confederation grant to Newfoundland. The issue was decided by referendum in 1948 when the final votes were 78,323 in favour of confederation with Canada and 71,334 for responsible government. A delegation of seven was sent to Ottawa to discuss the terms of union with Canada, and agreement was reached on the 11th December 1948.

The union of Newfoundland and Canada took effect immediately before the expiration of the thirty-first day of March 1949 (North America Act, 1949).

CONSTITUTION

Under the Terms of Union the Province of Newfoundland (embracing Labrador and the island of Newfoundland, with their existing boundaries) became part of Canada with provision for the application of the British North America Acts, 1867 to 1946, to Newfoundland as if the latter had been one of the Provinces originally united, but subject to the modifications mentioned in the terms of agreement and to the omission of such provisions as were specially applicable to or only intended to affect one or two but not all of the original Provinces. By an Act passed in 1964 the name of the province was changed to "Newfoundland and Labrador." Provision was made for Newfoundland to be represented in the Senate of Canada by six members and in the House of Commons by seven, subject to subsequent readjustment in accordance with the provisions of the British North America Acts.

As Newfoundland was governed by a Commission of Government (1934-1949) rather than by an elected legislature and executive responsible to it, as was the case in all existing Canadian provinces, and as the newest or tenth provincial member in the Canadian confederation should have a constitution similar to that of the other provinces, provision was made under the Terms of Union for the revival of the constitution of Newfoundland as it existed prior to 16th February 1934, subject to the terms of the British North America Acts 1867 to 1946 (which largely defined the Constitution of Canada) and excepting that there should be no legislative council; thus provision was made for the establishment of the usual institutions of provincial government comprising a Lieutenant-Governor, an Executive Council or Cabinet and a Legislative Assembly elected by adult suffrage, and for the continuation of Newfoundland laws until altered or repealed by the Parliament of Canada or by the Legislature of the Province of Newfoundland in accordance with their respective authorities under the British North America Acts, 1867 to 1946.

Under Article XXIX of the Terms of Union a Royal Commission of three members was appointed on 21st February 1957 to review the financial position of the Province.

In its Report dated 31st May 1958 the Commission made recommendations for additional financial assistance and in consequence the Parliament of Canada made provision for the payment to the Province of additional grants, rising to a level of $8 million a year terminating in the fiscal year 1966/67, was provided, under the Federal-Provincial Fiscal Arrangements Act, for the years 1962-63 to 1966-67 inclusive.

The present Government of Newfoundland consists of a Lieutenant-Governor, an Executive Council and a Legislative Assembly of 42 members, elected for a term of five years.

THE GOVERNMENT

At the last General Election held on 8th September 1966 the Liberal Party secured 39 seats and the Progressive Conservative Party 3.

E*

GOVERNMENT OF NEWFOUNDLAND AND LABRADOR
The Lieutenant Governor: Hon. E. John A. Harnum
The Premier: Hon. Joseph R. Smallwood, PC, DCL, LLDLitt
Minister of Justice: Hon. Leslie R. Curtis, QC
Minister of Labour: Hon. Stephen A. Neary
Minister of Public Works: Hon. J. R. Chalker
Minister of Education and Youth: Hon. Dr F. W. Rowe
Minister of Provincial Affairs: Hon. G. A. Frecker
Minister of Finance: Hon. E. S. Jones
Minister of Labrador Affairs and Acting Minister of Fisheries:
Capt. the Hon. Earl W. Winsor
Minister of Social Services and Rehabilitation: Hon. Stephen A. Neary
Minister of Health: Hon. Edward M. Roberts
Minister of Mines, Agriculture and Resources: Hon. W. R. Callahan
Minister of Supply and Services and Minister of Economic Development:
Hon. John A. Nolan
Minister of Community and Social Development: Hon. William N. Rowe
Minister of Highways: Hon. Harold E. Starkes
Minister of Municipal Affairs and Housing: (vacant)
Ministers without Portfolio: Hon. P. J. Lewis, QC, Hon. G. I. Hill

SUPREME COURT
Chief Justice: Hon. R. S. Furlong, MBE

JUDGES:
Hon. H. G. Puddester; Hon. J. D. Higgins; Hon. A. S. Mifflin

DISTRICT JUDGES IN ADMIRALTY:
Hon. R. S. Furlong, MBE; Hon. H. G. Puddester; Hon. J. D. Higgins, Hon. A. S. Mifflin

PRINCE EDWARD ISLAND

SITUATION AND POPULATION

Prince Edward Island lies in the southern part of the Gulf of St Lawrence.
Its area is 2,184 square miles. The estimated Provincial population in 1970 was
109,000 of whom 18,300 lived in Charlottetown, the capital city.

HISTORY AND CONSTITUTIONAL DEVELOPMENT

Prince Edward Island, formerly the Isle St Jean and a dependency of Cape
Breton Island (Isle Royale), formed part of the French province of Acadia. It was
ceded to Britain in 1763 by the Treaty of Paris and formed part of the colony of
Nova Scotia. It was separated from Nova Scotia and formed into a separate
colony in 1769 and shared in the influx of Loyalists from the American colonies
during and after the Revolutionary War. The problem of absentee proprietors be-
devilled the relations of Governor and Assembly for the next 60 years, but
responsible government was established in 1851. The colony was not one of the
original provinces of Canada but joined the federation in 1873.

CONSTITUTION

The Government of the Province of Prince Edward Island consists of a
Lieutenant-Governor, an Executive Council and a Legislative Assembly of 32
members, elected for a statutory term of five years.

THE GOVERNMENT

At the last General Election held on 11th May 1970 the Liberal Party obtained
27 seats and the Progressive Conservative Party 5 seats.

LIEUTENANT GOVERNOR
The Hon. J. George MacKay

EXECUTIVE COUNCIL
Premier and Minister of Development: Hon. Alex B. Campbell, PC, QC
Minister of Education and Minister of Justice: Hon. Gordon L. Bennett, MSC
Minister of Tourist Development: Hon. M. Lorne Bonnell, MD, CM
Minister of Community Services: Hon. Robert Sherman
Minister of Fisheries and Minister of Labour, Industry and Commerce: Hon. Bruce L. Stewart
Minister of Health and Welfare: Hon. John H. Maloney, MD
Minister of Public Works and Highways: Hon. George J. Ferguson
Minister of Agriculture and Forestry: Hon. Daniel J. MacDonald
Minister of Finance and Provincial Secretary: Hon. T. Earle Hickey, FCA
Minister without Portfolio: Hon. Robert E. Campbell

SUPREME COURT
Chief Justice: C. St Clair Trainor
Assistant Justice and Master of Rolls: Hon. R. R. Bell
Assistant Justice and Vice-Chancellor: Hon. George J. Tweedy
District Judge in Admiralty: Hon. Gordon R. Holmes, QC
COURT OF CHANCERY
Master of the Rolls: Hon. R. R. Bell
Vice-Chancellor: Hon. G. J. Tweedy

NOVA SCOTIA

SITUATION AND POPULATION
Nova Scotia consists of the peninsula of Nova Scotia and the island of Cape Breton, both lying between the Gulf of St Lawrence and the Atlantic Ocean. The area is 21,425 square miles. The estimated population of the province in April 1970 was 765,000, of whom 205,300 lived in the metropolitan area of Halifax, the capital city.

HISTORY AND CONSTITUTIONAL DEVELOPMENT
Nova Scotia was first discovered by the Norsemen and rediscovered by John Cabot in 1497; it was colonised by the French in 1598; was taken by the English, and a grant of it made to Sir W. Alexander by James I in 1621. In 1632 it was restored to France, with Quebec, by the Treaty of St Germain-en-Laye, but again ceded to England at the Peace of Utrecht in 1713. After the Peace of Aix-la-Chapelle in 1748, a settlement for disbanded troops was formed there by Lord Halifax, and the city which now bears his name is the capital of the province. Cape Breton Island was not finally taken from the French until 1758, in which year the first Assembly was summoned. Many Loyalists moved to Nova Scotia from the former American colonies to the south when the independence of the latter was recognised in 1783 and the last British troops withdrawn. In 1769 Prince Edward Island became a separate colony and in 1784 New Brunswick and Cape Breton Island were also separated from the rest of Nova Scotia to which Cape Breton Island was later reunited. In 1848 responsible government was established, and in 1867 Nova Scotia was one of the three colonies which united to form Canada, of which it became a Province.

CONSTITUTION
The Government of Nova Scotia consists of a Lieutenant-Governor, an Executive Council and a House of Assembly. The Legislature has 46 members elected for a maximum term of five years.

THE GOVERNMENT
After 14 years of Conservative rule the Liberal Party formed the present

Government following a general election on 13th October 1970. Party standings are Liberal 23, Conservative 20, New Democratic Party 2, vacant 1.

LIEUTENANT-GOVERNOR
Brigadier the Hon. Victor deBedia Oland

EXECUTIVE COUNCIL
Premier and Chairman, Nova Scotia Power Commission: Hon. Gerald A. Regan, QC
Minister of Finance and Economics and Minister of Education:
Hon. Peter M. Nicholson, QC
Minister of Highways and Minister of Public Works: Hon. A. Garnet Brown
Attorney General and Minister of Labour: Hon. Leonard L. Pace, QC
Minister of Lands and Forests, Minister of Fisheries, Minister i/c of administration of
Emergency Measures Act: Hon. Benoit Comeau
Minister of Agriculture and Marketing, Minister of Municipal Affairs and Minister i/c of
Administration of Nova Scotia Liquor Control Act: Hon. J. William Gillis
Minister of Public Welfare, Minister of Mines and Minister i/c of Administration of the
Water Act: Hon. Allan E. Sullivan
Minister of Trade and Industry and Provincial Secretary:
Hon. Ralph F. Fiske
Minister of Public Health, Minister i/c of Administration of Housing Development Act and
Minister i/c of Administration of Human Rights Act: Hon. D. Scott MacNutt

SUPREME COURT
Appeal Division: Chief Justice: The Hon. Alexander H. MacKinnon
The Hon. Mr Justice A. Gordon Cooper
The Hon. Mr Justice Thomas H. Coffin

Trial Division: Chief Justice: The Hon. Gordon S. Cowan

Puisne Judges:
The Hon. Mr Justice Frederick W. Bissett
The Hon. Mr Justice M. C. Jones
The Hon. Mr Justice J. Dubinsky
The Hon. Mr Justice Gordon L. S. Hart
The Hon. Mr Justice Donald J. Gillis

District Judge in Admiralty: Hon. Gordon S. Cowan

NEW BRUNSWICK

SITUATION AND POPULATION

New Brunswick consists of the mainland between Quebec and Nova Scotia. The area of the Province is 28,354 square miles, and the estimated provincial population in April 1970 was 623,000. The provincial capital is Fredericton, with a population in 1970 of 24,300.

HISTORY AND CONSTITUTIONAL DEVELOPMENT

New Brunswick was part of the ancient French Province of Acadia and was ceded to England by the Treaty of Utrecht in 1713. Great Britain, however, did not obtain full possession of the country until after the fall of Quebec in 1759. It was first colonised by British subjects from New England in 1761, and in 1783, at the close of the Revolutionary War, it received a large body of Loyalists from the Thirteen Colonies. In 1784 it was separated from Nova Scotia, of which it had formed a part, and given a separate Governor and Assembly. The colony remained quiet and prosperous, largely free from the conflicts between Executive and Legislature which vexed the other North American colonies until 1837. In 1854 responsible government was established, and in 1867 New Brunswick was one of the colonies which agreed to form the Dominion of Canada, of which it became an original Province.

CONSTITUTION

The Government of New Brunswick consists of a Lieutenant-Governor, an Executive Council and a House of Assembly. The Legislature has 58 members who are elected for a statutory term of five years.

THE GOVERNMENT

At the last General Election held on 26th October 1970 the Progressive Conservative Party secured 32 seats and the Liberal Party 26 seats exactly reversing the previous standing.

LIEUTENANT-GOVERNOR
Hon. Wallace Samuel Bird

EXECUTIVE COUNCIL
Premier: Hon. Richard B. Hatfield
Minister of Justice: Hon. John B. M. Baxter, QC
Minister of Finance: Hon. Jean-Maurice Simard
Provincial Secretary and Minister of Labour: Hon. Rodman E. Logan
Minister of Highways and Minister of Public Works: Hon. J. Stewart Brooks
Minister of Natural Resources: Hon. Wilfred G. Bishop
Minister of Economic Growth and Minister of Agriculture and Rural Development:
Hon. A. Edison Stairs
Minister of Health: Hon. Paul Creaghan
Minister of Education: Hon. Lorne McGuigan
Minister of Municipal Affairs: Hon. Jean-Paul LeBlanc
Minister of Fisheries and Environmental Affairs: Hon. G. W. N. Cockburn
Minister of Welfare and Youth: Hon. Mrs. Brenda Robertson
Chairman, N. B. Electric Power Commission: Hon. George E. McInerney, QC
Minister of Tourism: Hon. J. C. Van Horne
Ministers without Portfolio:
Hon. Cyril B. Sherwood, Hon. Dr G. Everett Chalmers, Hon. Horace B. Smith

SUPREME COURT
Appeal Division and Chancery Division
Chief Justice: Hon. G. F. G. Bridges

Puisne Judges:
Hon. Charles J. A. Hughes; Hon. R. V. Limerick
Queen's Bench Division
Chief Justice: Hon. A. J. Cormier

Puisne Judges:
Hon. J. McL. Prescott; Hon. Albany M. Robichaud; Hon. J. A. Pichete;
Hon. David M. Dickson; Hon. J. Paul Barry
District Judge in Admiralty: (Vacant)

QUEBEC

SITUATION AND POPULATION

Quebec lies on both sides of the Lower St Lawrence and extends from the New England states of the U.S.A. to the Davis Straits. Its area is 594,860 square miles. The population on 1st June 1966 was 5,780,845 of whom 2,436,817 lived in greater Montreal, the world's largest inland port, which is located at the confluence of the Ottawa and St Lawrence Rivers 1,000 miles from the Atlantic Ocean. The capital city is Quebec, which had a population of 166,984 in 1966. The population of greater Quebec was 413,397 in 1966 and the provincial population was estimated at 5,927,000 on 1st June 1968.

HISTORY

(For the history of Quebec see page 108 *et seq.*)

CONSTITUTION

The Government of Quebec consists of a Lieutenant-Governor, an Executive Council and since 1969, a uni-cameral legislature, called the National Assembly. The Legislative Council was abolished by the legislature at the end of 1968, and the name of the Assembly changed. The National Assembly has 108 elected members.

THE GOVERNMENT

At the last General Election held on 29th April 1970 the Liberal Party obtained 72 seats, the Union Nationale 17, the Ralliement des Créditistes 12, and the Parti Quebécois 7.

LIEUTENANT-GOVERNOR
Hon. Hugues Lapointe, P C, Q C

EXECUTIVE COUNCIL
Premier: Hon. Robert Bourassa
Minister of Labour and Manpower: Hon. Jean Cournoyer
Minister of Roads and Minister of Public Works: Hon. Bernard Pinard
Minister of Industry and Commerce: Hon. Gérard D. Lévesque
Minister of Tourism, Fish and Game: Hon. Mrs Claire Kirkland-Casgrain
Minister of Social Affairs: Hon. Claude Castonguay
Minister of Justice: Hon. Jérome Choquette
Minister of Education and High Commissioner of Youth, Leisure and Sports:
Hon. Guy Saint-Pierre
Minister of Education and High Commissioner of Youth, Leisure and Sports:
Hon. Guy Saint-Pierre
Minister of Public Service and Minister of Communications and Minister responsible for the
Office Franco-Québécois: Hon. Jean-Paul L'Allier
Minister of Municipal Affairs- Hon. Maurice Tessier
Minister of Revenue: Hon. Gerald Harvey
Minister of Agriculture and Colonization: Hon. Normand Toupin
Minister of Natural Resources: Hon. Gilles Masse
Minister of Lands and Forests: Hon. Kevin Drummond
Minister of Transport: Hon. Georges-E. Tremblay
Minister of Cultural Affairs and Minister of Immigration: Hon. François Cloutier
Minister of Finance: Hon. Raymond Garneau
Minister of Intergovernmental Affairs: Hon. Oswald Parent
Minister of Financial Institutions, Companies and Co-operatives: Hon. William Tetley
Minister of State responsible for the Environment: Hon. Victor Charles Goldbloom
Minister of State (Industry and Commerce Department): Hon. Claud Simard
Minister of State (Health Department: Hon. Robert Quenneville

COURT OF QUEEN'S BENCH
Chief Justice: Hon. Lucien Tremblay

Puisne Judges (Quebec)
Hon. Andre Taschereau; Hon. F. L. Choquette; Hon. Antoine Rivard;
Hon. Jean Turgeon

Puisne Judges (Montreal)
Hon. Paul C. Casey; Hon. G. Miller Hyde; Hon. Edouard Rinfret;
Hon. George R. Owen; Hon. George-H. Montgomery; Hon. Elie Salvas;
Hon. Roger Brossard

SUPERIOR COURT
Quebec
Chief Justice: Hon. Frédéric Dorion
Associate Chief Justice: Hon. George S. Challies

Judges:

Hon. Sam S. Bard	Hon. Jacques Dufour	Hon. Eugene Marquis
Hon. J-Robert Beaudoin	Hon. George-René Fournier	Hon. Vincent Masson
Hon. Jean-Jacques Bédard	Hon. Antoine Lacourciére	Hon. Yvan Mignault
Hon. Yves Bernier	Hon. Gérard Lacroix	Hon. Paul Miquelon
Hon. Gérard Corriveau	Hon. Edouard Laliberté	Hon. Georges Pelletier
Hon. Pierre Coté	Hon. Paul Lesage	Hon. Gabriel Roberge
Hon. André Dubé	Hon. Pierre Letarte	

Montreal
Associate Chief Justice: Hon. G. S. Challies

Judges:

Hon. Harry L. Aronovitch
Hon. Maurice Archambault
Hon. François Auclair
Hon. Alphonse Barbeau
Hon. Harry Batshaw
Hon. Laurent-E. Bélanger
Hon. Claude Bisson
Hon. Bernard deL Bourgeois
Hon. Paul Carignan
Hon. Frederick T. Collins
Hon. J-Maurice Cousineau
Hon. André Demers
Hon. Guy-Merrill Desaulniers
Hon. Ignace-J. Deslauriers
Hon. René Duranleau
Hon. F. Raymond Hannen

Hon. W. Austin Johnson
Hon. Réjane Laberge Colas
Hon. Léon Lalande
Hon. Philippe Lamarre
Hon. Ruston B. Lamb
Hon. Antonio Lamer
Hon. Paul Langlois
Hon. Albert Leblanc
Hon. Yves Leduc
Hon. L-Fernand Legault
Hon. Kenneth C. Mackay
Hon. Edouard Martel
Hon. Guoy Mathieu
Hon. Albert Mayrand
Hon. James E. Mitchell
Hon. Amédée Monet

Hon. André Montpetit
Hon. André Nadeau
Hon. Marcel Nichols
Hon. John A. Nolan
Hon. J. Brendan O'Connor
Hon. Roger Ouimet
Hon. Rodolphe Paré
Hon. Chateauguay Perralut
Hon. Philippe Pothier
Hon. Claude Prévost
Hon. G. B. Puddicombe
Hon. Jean St Germain
Hon. Peter V. Shorteno
Hon. Edouard Tellier
Hon. Paul Trepanier

Rimouski District
Judge: Hon. J. T. Arthur Gendreau

Sherbrooke District
Judges:
Hon. W. E. Mitchell; Hon. Evender Veilleux: Hon. Carrier Fortin;
Hon. G. C. R. Desmarais

Three Rivers District
Judges:
Hon. Jean Louis Marchand; Hon. Roger Laroche;
Hon. J. A. M. Crete

Rouyn District
Judges:
Hon. Camille-L. Bergeron; Hon. Jean-Paul Bergeron

Hull District
Judges:
Hon. Paul Ste Marie; Hon. J. N. R. Boucher; Hon. François Chevalier

Chicoutimi District
Judge: Hon. T. McNicoll

Shawinigan District
Hon. René Hamel

Amos District
Hon. C-Noel Barbes; Hon. Henri Drouin

ONTARIO

SITUATION AND POPULATION

The Province stretches 1,000 miles from east to west, from Quebec to the Prairies, and 1,050 miles from south to north, from the Great Lakes to Hudson Bay. Its area is 412,582 square miles, and the population in 1966 was 6,960,870, thirty-five per cent of the total population of Canada. The population of the Province at January 1970 was estimated to be 7,753,000. The capital is Toronto, the population of which was 664,584 in 1966, metropolitan Toronto having a population of 2,158,496. At June 1970, the population of Metropolitan Toronto, including the City of Toronto, was estimated at 2,366,000.

134 *Canada*

HISTORY
(For the history of Ontario see page 108 *et seq.*)

CONSTITUTION
The Government of Ontario consists of a Lieutenant-Governor, an Executive Council and a House of Assembly. The House of Assembly, the single-chamber Legislature of the province, is composed of 117 members elected for a statutory term of five years.

GOVERNMENT
The last election was held on 17th October 1967, the Progressive Conservative Party obtaining 69 seats, the Liberal Party 27, the New Democratic Party 20, Liberal-Labour 1, but due to by-elections the Progressive Conservative Party now has 68 seats, the Liberal Party 27, the New Democratic Party 21, Independent 1.

LIEUTENANT-GOVERNOR
Hon. W. Ross Macdonald, PC, QC

EXECUTIVE COUNCIL
Prime Minister and President of the Council: Hon. William G. Davis, QC
Minister of Justice and Attorney General: Alan F. Lawrence, QC
Treasurer of Ontario and Minister of Economics: Hon. W. Darcey McKeough
Minister of Education: Hon. Robert Welch, QC
Minister of Health: Hon. Bert Lawrence, QC
Provincial Secretary and Minister of Citizenship: Hon. John Yaremko, QC
Minister of Trade and Development: Hon. Alan Grossman
Minister of Agriculture and Food: Hon. William A. Stewart
Minister of Highways and Minister of Transport: Hon. Charles MacNaughton
Minister of Public Works: Hon. James A. C. Auld
Minister of Financial and Commercial Affairs: Hon. Arthur A. Wishart, QC
Minister of Lands and Forests: Hon. René Brunelle
Minister of Municipal Affairs: Dalton A. Bales, QC
Minister of Social and Family Services: Thomas L. Wells
Minister of Tourism and Information: Fern Guindon
Minister of University Affairs: John White
Minister of Energy and Resources Management: Hon. George A. Kerr, QC
Minister of Correctional Services: Hon. C. J. S. Apps
Minister of Labour: Gordon Carton, QC
Minister of Mines and Northern Affairs: Hon. Leo Bernier
Minister of Revenue: Hon. Eric A. Winkler
Ministers without Portfolio:
Hon. James W. Snow; Hon. Richard T. Potter, MD; Hon. Edward Dunlop
Secretary to the Cabinet: Dr. J. K. Reynolds

SUPREME COURT OF ONTARIO

COURT OF APPEAL FOR ONTARIO

Toronto
Chief Justice of Ontario: Hon. G. A. Gale

Justices of Appeal:

Hon. John B. Aylesworth	Hon. G. A. McGillivray	Hon. A. R. Jessop
Hon. F. G. MacKay	Hon. Arthur Kelly	Hon. J. W. Brooke
Hon. Walter Frank Schroeder	Hon. G. T. Evans	Hon. John Arnup

HIGH COURT OF JUSTICE FOR ONTARIO
Chief Justice: Hon. D. C. Wells

Justices:

Hon. John Leonard Wilson	Hon. E. A. Richardson	Hon. E. P. Hartt
Hon. J. M. King	Hon. Neil C. Fraser	Hon. D. A. Keith
Hon. Charles D. Stewart	Hon. Campbell Grant	Hon. G. A. Addy
Hon. Eric C. Moorhouse	Hon. H. S. Hughes	Hon. L. T. Pennell, P C
Hon. E. G. Thompson	Hon. E. L. Haines	Hon. P. T. Galligan
Hon. N. M. Lacourciere	Hon. A. H. Lieff	Hon. L. W. Holden
Hon. J. F. Donnelly	Hon. W. A. Donohue	Hon. J. H. Osler
Hon. D. R. Morand	Hon. W. J. Henderson	Hon. T. Wright
Hon. W. D. Parker	Hon. H.A. Stark	

District Judge in Admiralty: Hon. D. C. Wells
Surrogate Judge in Admiralty: (Vacant)

MANITOBA

SITUATION AND POPULATION

Manitoba was the first of the prairie Provinces to be formed, and when created in 1870 included only a small area south of Lake Winnipeg. In 1912 it was increased to its present size of 251,000 square miles. The population of the Province in 1969 was 979,000 and of metropolitan Winnipeg, the provincial capital 534,000.

HISTORY

Manitoba was formed from the territory, including the Red River Colony, which formed part of Rupert's Land, granted to the Hudson's Bay Company when it received a Royal Charter in 1670. It became a Province of the Canadian Federation by legislative enactments taking effect on the 15th July 1870.

CONSTITUTION

The Government of Manitoba consists of a Lieutenant-Governor, an Executive Council, at present composed of 14 members, and a Legislative Assembly of 57 members elected for a statutory term of five years.

THE GOVERNMENT

As a result of the last General Election held on 25th June 1969, and subsequent by-elections, the new Democratic Party hold 30 seats, the Progressive Conservative Party 21, the Liberal Party 3, the Social Credit Party 1, and Independent 2.

LIEUTANT-GOVERNOR
Hon. W. J. McKeag

EXECUTIVE COUNCIL
Premier, President of the Council, Minister of Dominion-Provincial Relations, Minister charged with the administration of the Manitoba Development Act, Minister responsible for Manitoba Hydro: Hon. Edward Richard Schreyer
Minister of Finance: Hon. Saul Mark Cherniack
Minister of Labour: Hon. A. Russell Paulley
Attorney-General: Hon. Alvin H. Mackling
Minister of Mines, Resources and Environmental Management; Commissioner of Northern Affairs: Hon. Sidney Green
Minister of Agriculture: Hon. Samuel Uskiw
Minister of Health and Social Development: Hon. Rene Toupin
Minister of Industry and Commerce: Hon. Leonard Evans
Minister of Tourism, Recreation and Cultural Affairs; Minister responsible for Manitoba Telephone System: Hon. Peter Burtniak
Minister of Youth and Education: Hon. Saul A. Miller
Minister of Public Works and Highways: Hon. Joseph P. Borowski
Minister of Municipal Affairs: Hon. Howard Pawley
Minister of Consumer, Corporate and Internal Services: Hon. Ben Hanuschak
Minister without Portfolio: Hon. Russell Doern

COURT OF APPEAL
Chief Justice: Hon. Samuel Freedman

Judges:

Hon. Robert Duval Guy   Hon. R. G. B. Dickson
Hon. Alfred Maurice Monnin

COURT OF QUEEN'S BENCH
Chief Justice: Hon. G. E. Tritschler

Puisne Judges:

Hon. J. E. Wilson   Hon. G. C. Hall
Hon. F. M. Bastin   Hon. J. M. Hunt
Hon. I. Nitikman   Hon. R. J. Matas
Hon. L. Deniset

District Judge in Admiralty: Hon. G. E. Tritschler

SASKATCHEWAN

SITUATION AND POPULATION

Saskatchewan lies between Manitoba and Alberta. It has an estimated area of 251,700 square miles. The population in 1966 was 955,344 of whom 131,127 lived in the provincial capital, Regina. The estimated provincial population on 1st June 1968 was 960,000.

HISTORY

Rupert's Land and the North-Western Territories, the vast area under the jurisdiction of the Hudson's Bay Company, in 1870, extended from Labrador to the Rockies and from the headwaters of the Red River to Chesterfield Inlet on Hudson Bay. When the Province of Manitoba was established in 1870, the Hudson's Bay Company surrendered to the Government of Canada its territorial rights to the entire area. In 1882, the provincial districts of Assiniboia, Saskatchewan, Alberta and Athabaska were created from the southern portion of the North-West Territories. Population in the districts increased rapidly during the last two decades of the nineteenth century and with it the desire for provincial status. This was achieved in 1905 when approximately four-fifths of the districts of Assiniboia and Saskatchewan and one half of the district of Athabaska were merged to form the present Province of Saskatchewan.

CONSTITUTION

The Government of Saskatchewan consists of a Lieutenant-Governor, an Executive Council and a Legislative Assembly of 59 members, elected for a statutory term of five years.

THE GOVERNMENT

At the last General Election held in October 1967 the Liberal Party secured 36 seats and the New Democratic Party 23 seats.

LIEUTENANT-GOVERNOR
Hon. Stephen Worobetz, MC, MD, CRCS(C)

EXECUTIVE COUNCIL

Premier, President of the Executive Council, Minister of Industry and Commerce, Minister responsible for the Saskatchewan Economic Development Corporation, the Liquor Licensing Commission and the Liquor Licensing Board and Provincial Treasurer: Hon. Allan Blakeney
Minister of Mineral Resources, Minister responsible for the Water Resources Commission and Water Supply Board, and in charge of Indian and Metis Affairs: Hon. Ted Bowerman

Attorney General, Minister responsible for the Local Government Board, Surface Rights Arbitration Board and the Public and Private Rights Board, and Provincial Secretary:
Hon. Roy Romanow
Minister of Agriculture and Minister responsible for the Saskatchewan Power Corporation:
Hon. Jack Messer
Minister of Highways, Minister responsible for Saskatchewan Government Telephones and Saskatchewan Government Transportation: Hon. Neil Byers
Minister of Health and Minister in charge of the Public Service Commission-
Hon. Walter Smishek
Minister of Public Works and Municipal Affairs and Minister in charge of the Central Vehicle Agency and Saskatchewan Government Printing: Hon. Everett Wood
Minister of Labour and Welfare and Minister responsible for Saskatchewan Minerals Corporation: Hon. Gordon Snyder
Minister of Education and Minister in charge of the Saskatchewan Research Council and the Provincial Library with special responsibilities to the University of Saskatchewan:
Hon. Gordon MacMurchey
Minister of Natural Resources, Minister responsible for Co-operation and Co-operative Development and Minister in Charge of Saskatchewan Fur Marketing Services:
Hon. Eiling Kramer

COURT OF APPEAL
Chief Justice of Saskatchewan: Hon. E. M. Culliton

Puisne Judges of Appeal:
Hon. M. J. Woods   Hon. P. H. Maguire
Hon. R. L. Brownridge   Hon. R. N. Hall

COURT OF QUEEN'S BENCH
Chief Justice: Hon. A. H. Bence

Puisne Judges:
Hon. C. S. Davis   Hon. W. A. Tucker   Hon. F. W. Johnson
Hon. D. C. Disbery   Hon. A. L. Sirois   Hon. Raymond A.
Hon. M. A. MacPherson, Jr.   MacDonald

ALBERTA

SITUATION AND POPULATION
Alberta lies between Saskatchewan and the Rocky Mountains. Its area is 255,285 square miles, and the population in 1966 was 1,463,203 of whom 376,925 lived in the provincial capital, Edmonton. The estimated provincial population on 1st June 1968 was 1,526,000 and of metropolitan Edmonton 401,299 in 1966.

HISTORY
Alberta was created a Province, by an enactment of the Parliament of Canada, on 1st September 1905 out of territory that previously had formed part of the North-West Territories.

CONSTITUTION
The Government of Alberta consists of a Lieutenant-Governor, an Executive Council and a Legislative Assembly of 65 members, elected for a maximum period of five years.

THE GOVERNMENT
At the last General Election held on 23rd May 1967 the Social Credit Party secured 55 of the 65 redistributed seats, the Progressive Conservative Party 6, Liberal Party 3 and Independent 1 seat.

LIEUTENANT-GOVERNOR
Hon. J. W. Grant MacEwan

EXECUTIVE COUNCIL

Premier and President of the Council: Hon. Harry Edwin Strom
Minister of Highways and Transport: Hon. Gordon Edward Taylor
Hon. Gordon Edward Taylor
Provincial Treasurer: Hon. Anders Olav Aalborg
Minister of Municipal Affairs: Hon. Frederick Charles Colborne
Minister of Mines and Minerals: Hon. Allen Russell Patrick
Minister of Labour and Minister of Telephones: Hon. Raymond Reierson
Minister of Lands and Forests: Hon. Joseph Donovan Ross
Minister of Culture, Youth and Recreation: Hon. Ambrose Holowach
Minister without Portfolio: Hon. Mrs Ethel S. Wilson
Minister of Agriculture: Hon. Henry A. Ruste
Minister without Portfolio: Hon. Adolph O. Fimrite
Minister of Education: Hon. Robert C. Clark
Attorney-General: Hon. Edgar H. Gerhart
Minister of Health and Social Development: Hon. Raymond A. Speaker
Minister of the Environment: Hon. James Douglas Henderson
Minister of Industry and Tourism: Hon. Raymond Samuel Ratzlaff
Minister of Public Works: Hon. Albert Ludwig

SUPREME COURT

Appellate Division
Chief Justice of Alberta: Hon. S. Bruce Smith

Judges of Appeal:

Hon. Carlton W. Clement	Hon. N. D. McDermid
Hon. Horace G. Johnson	Hon. James M. Cairns
Hon. E. W. Kane	Hon. Gordon H. Allen

Trial Division
Chief Justice: Hon. J. Valentine Milvain

Puisne Judges:

Hon. Neil Primrose	Hon. Marshall E. Manning	Hon. M. B. O'Byrne
Hon. Peter Greschuk	Hon. W. J. C. Kirby	Hon. Hugh J. McDonald
Hon. Harold W. Riley	Hon. W. R. Sinclair	Hon. Samuel S. Lieberman
Hon. Alan J. Cullen	Hon. Andre M. Déchené	

BRITISH COLUMBIA

SITUATION AND POPULATION

British Columbia is the westernmost Province in Canada and lies between the Rocky Mountains and the Pacific Ocean. The area (including Vancouver Island and Queen Charlotte Islands) is 366,255 square miles. The population in 1966 was 1,873,674, of whom 892,286 lived in the metropolitan Vancouver area and 173,455 in metropolitan Victoria, the capital city. The estimated provincial population at 1st April 1970 was 2,128,000.

HISTORY

British Columbia is an amalgamation of four Colonial jurisdictions. Vancouver Island was granted to the Hudson's Bay Company by Royal Charter in 1849, at which time the Crown Colony was established. In 1852 the Queen Charlotte Islands were established as a Lieutenant-Dependency of Vancouver Island. In consequence of a large migration on the discovery of gold on the Fraser and Thompson Rivers in 1858, the mainland Crown Colony of British Columbia was constituted, comprising roughly the southern half of the mainland. In 1862 the northern half of the mainland, including part of the present Yukon Territory, was established as the Territory of Stikine. In 1863 the Queen Charlotte Islands, British Columbia and the Stikine Territory were united under the name of British Columbia. In 1866 this colony of British Columbia and Vancouver Island were united under the former name and in 1871 British Columbia became a province of Canada.

CONSTITUTION

The Government of British Columbia consists of ? Lieutenant-Governor, an Executive Council and a Legislative Assembly of 55 members elected for a statutory term of five years.

THE GOVERNMENT

At the last General Election held on 27th August 1969 the Social Credit Party secured 39 seats, the New Democratic Party 11 seats and the Liberal Party 5 seats.

LIEUTENANT-GOVERNOR
Hon. John Nicholson, PC, OBE, QC

EXECUTIVE COUNCIL
Premier, President of the Council, and Minister of Finance:
Hon. W. A. C. Bennett, PC
Deputy Premier: Hon. L. J. Wallace
Provincial Secretary and Minister of Highways: Hon. Wesley Drewett Black
Attorney-General: Hon. Leslie Raymond Peterson, QC
Minister of Labour: Hon. James Chabot
Minister of Lands, Forests and Water Resources: Hon. Ray Gillis Williston
Minister of Agriculture: Hon. Cyril Morley Shelford
Minister of Mines and Petroleum Resources, and Minister of Commercial Transport:
Hon. Francis Xavier Richter
Minister of Industrial Development, Trade and Commerce:
Hon. Waldo McTavish Skillings
Minister of Education: Hon. Donald Leslie Brothers, QC
Minister of Municipal Affairs: Hon. Daniel Robert John Campbell
Minister of Health Services and Hospital Insurance: Hon. Ralph Raymond Loffmark
Minister of Public Works: Hon. William Neelands Chant
Minister of Recreation and Conservation, and Minister of Travel Industry:
Hon. William Kenneth Kiernan
Minister of Social Improvement, Rehabilitation and Human Development:
Hon. P. A. Gaglardi
Members of the Executive Council without Portfolio:
Hon. Grace McCarthy   Hon. Patricia Jordan
Hon. Isabel Pearl Dawson

COURT OF APPEAL
Chief Justice of British Columbia: Hon. H. W. Dave

Justices of Appeal:

Hon. J. D. Taggart	Hon. H. A. Maclean	Hon. A. E. Branca
Hon. C. W. Tysoe	Hon. M. M. McFarlane	Hon. Bruce Robertson
Hon. N. T. Nemetz	Hon. Ernest B. Bull	

SUPREME COURT
Chief Justice: Hon. J. O. Wilson

Puisne Judges:

Hon. J. G. Ruttan	Hon. V. L. Dryer	Hon. G. Gould
Hon. E. E. Hinkson	Hon. W. K. Smith	Hon. Thomas A. Dohm
Hon. D. R. Verchere	Hon. G. G. S. Rae	Hon. J. A. Macdonald
Hon. F. C. Munroe	Hon. A. B. McFarlane	Hon. P. D. Seaton
Hon. R. A. Wootton	Hon. G. F. Gregory	Hon. W. R. McIntyre
Hon. J. S. Aikins		

District Judge in Admiralty: Hon. T. G. Norris

THE TERRITORIES OF CANADA

The areas over which the Hudson's Bay Company had trading rights, known as Rupert's Land and the North Western Territory were transferred by Britain to the Dominion of Canada with effect from 15th July 1870 and were administered by the Federal Government. To this was added on 1st September 1880 all the remaining British territories to the north, including the polar islands. As set out on page 128, several Provinces were formed from this vast area, and other parts of it were transferred to existing Provinces. However, one third of the area of Canada still lies outside the Provinces, and is divided into two Territories, each administered directly by the Canadian Government.

YUKON TERRITORY

SITUATION AND POPULATION

The Yukon Territory covers 207,076 square miles. The population of the Territory has remained almost static during the past few years. It was 14,628 at the 1961 Census, including 2,167 Indians and decreased to 14,382 on 1st June 1966. The capital city is Whitehorse which contains roughly half the population.

ADMINISTRATION

The Yukon was created a separate Territory in June 1898 as the result of development in the mining industry, the Klondike gold strike and the consequent influx of population. The local Government consists of a Federal Government Commissioner and an elected Council of seven members with a three-year tenure of office. The members shown below were elected in 1967. The Council, which was increased from five to seven under an Amendment of the Yukon Act in 1960, usually meets twice a year in Whitehorse, which is the seat of local government. The Council elects its own Speaker. A Territorial Ordinance passed at the Third Session 1960 provides for seven electoral districts. The Commissioner administers the government of the Territory under instructions from the Governor-General in Council or the Minister of Indian Affairs and Northern Development. The Commissioner in Council has power to make ordinances dealing with the imposition of local taxes, sale of liquor, preservation of game, establishment of territorial offices, maintenance of municipal institutions, education, issue of licences, incorporation of companies, solemnisation of marriage, property and civil rights, administration of justice, and generally dealing with matters of a local and private nature in the Territory. One member represents the interests of the Yukon in the Federal House of Commons.

The Northern Administration Branch, Department of Indian Affairs and Northern Development, has the responsibility for the general administration of the natural resources of the Yukon Territory, except game. The Department maintains lands and mining offices at four points in the Territory. Other departments and agencies of the Federal Government, including the Department of Justice, the Royal Canadian Mounted Police, the Departments of National Defence, Energy, Mines and Resources, National Revenue, Transport, Post Office, Agriculture, Fisheries, Public Works, and the Unemployment Insurance Commission also maintain offices in the Yukon Territory.

Commissioner: J. Smith
Executive Assistant: R. A. Hodgkinson

Members of Council:
J. O. Livesay (Carmacks-Kluane); G. O. Shaw (Dawson); Mrs G. Jean Gordon (Mayo); D. Taylor (Watson Lake); N. S. Chamberlist (Whitehorse East); J. K. McKinnon (Whitehorse North); J. Dumas (Whitehorse West)

Officers of Council:
Territorial Secretary: H. J. Taylor
Legal Adviser: P. O'Donaghue
Territorial Treasurer: K. McKenzie

Territorial Court:
Judge: H. C. B. Maddison

COURT OF APPEAL
Chief Justice of British Columbia
Justices of Appeal of British Columbia
Judges of the Territorial Courts of the Northwest Territories and the Yukon Territory

NORTHWEST TERRITORIES

SITUATION AND POPULATION

The Northwest Territories comprise those parts of the former Rupert's Land and the North-West Territories which remained after the formation of the Yukon Territory, the formation of Manitoba, Alberta and Saskatchewan, and the expansion of British Columbia, Manitoba, Ontario and Quebec. It consists of the greater part of Canada which lies to the north of 60°N. latitude. It includes the principal islands in Hudson and James Bays, the Canadian Arctic Archipelago and the Queen Elizabeth Islands, which stretch to 83°N. latitude. The total area is about 1,304,903 square miles and the population at the 1961 census was 22,998, of which 5,256 were Indians and 7,977 were Eskimos. On 1st June 1966 the population reached 28,738, a twenty-five per cent increase. The estimated population at 1st June 1968 was 31,000.

ADMINISTRATION

The seat of government of the Northwest Territories moved from Ottawa to Yellowknife in the autumn of 1967. For administrative purposes the Territories were subdivided into the Districts of Mackenzie (the western mainland), Keewatin (the eastern mainland) and Franklin (the northern islands) by Order in Council of the 16th March 1918 which became effective on 1st January 1920. Under the Canadian Northwest Territories Act (RSC 1952, c. 331, and as amended in 1966), the Government of the Territories is administered by a Commissioner, appointed by the Governor-General in Council, aided by a Council of 12 members, 7 of whom are elected and 5 appointed by the Governor-General in Council. The territorial administration will assume responsibility for most provincial-type services except education, welfare, engineering, health services and natural resources. It is expected that within a few years the territorial administration will take over all provincial functions except natural resources. Meetings of the Council, which formerly met once each year in Ottawa and once in the Territories, will all take place in Yellowknife. The Northwest Territories elects one Member to the Federal House of Commons.

The resources of the Territories, except game, remain under the control of the Federal Government. The administration of legislation passed by the Commissioner in Council and the management of resources under federal legislation are conducted by the Northern Administration Branch of the Department of Indian Affairs and Northern Development. Administrative offices are located at a number of centres in the Territories including Fort Smith, Yellowknife, Hay River, Inuvik and Frobisher Bay.

CEYLON

THE island of Ceylon lies in the Indian Ocean off the southern extremity of the Indian sub-continent, between latitudes 5° 55′ and 9° 50′ N. and longitudes 79° 42′ and 81° 53′ E. It is separated from Cape Cormorin by the Palk Strait. The maximum length of the island from north to south is 270 miles and its greatest width is 140 miles. Its area is 25,332 square miles, about half the size of England.

From a central massif of mountains composed of almost solid gneiss and of outstanding scenic beauty the land slopes down to the sea on all sides in a series of three terraces or peneplains. The third of these lies at approximately 6,000 feet, the second at 1,600 feet and the first at 100 feet. The first peneplain or coastal plain is broadest towards the north.

The highest peak in the central massif is Pidurutalagala (8,292 feet). The other major peaks are Kirigalpota (7,837 feet), Totapella (7,733 feet), Adams' Peak (7,341 feet) and Great Western (7,258 feet). Although not particularly high, the fourth of these, Adam's Peak, is probably the most famous and spectacular mountain in Asia south of the Himalayas. It has been likened in outline to the Matterhorn and the pinnacle can be seen far out to sea in all directions. A mark on the summit which resembles a gigantic human footprint has made it since very early times one of the great places of pilgrimage in the world, revered by Buddhists, Hindus and Muslims. For Buddhists, the footprint is that of Gautama, for Hindus that of Vishnu, and in Muslim tradition it was made by Adam when he was cast down from paradise.

Rivers radiate from the central massif in all directions, the longest of which, Mahaweli Ganga (more than 200 miles long), drains into Trincomalee Bay. None of the rivers is navigable to ocean-going vessels. Ceylon has an excellent natural harbour at Trincomalee; it was an important naval base from the sixteenth to the nineteenth centuries and was again in use as such during the Second World War.

The climate is hot in the low country, particularly from March to May. The average mean temperature is 79°–82°F and the humidity in the wet zone is high. In the hills it is pleasantly temperate, and at resorts such as Nuwara Eliya near Pidurutalagala there may be frost at night in December and January but no snow or ice. There are two main seasons, that of the south-west monsoon from mid-May to September and that of the north-east monsoon from November to March. The average temperature in Colombo throughout the year is 80°F ranging to a maximum of 95°F. The annual rainfall ranges from 43 inches in the dry Northern Province to 218 inches in the central massif. The inland average is 99·49 inches.

A national census conducted in July 1963 found the total population to be 10,590,000. The provisional estimate in 1969 was 12,245,000. The distribution of the main ethnic groups at the time of the 1963 census was (per cent):

Sinhalese ..	..	..	..	..	71·0
Ceylon Tamils	..	..	..	..	11·0
Indian Tamils	..	..	..	..	10·6
Moors	..	..	..	..	6·5
Burghers and others	..	..	..		0·9

There is a census every ten years. In 1967 the estimated birth and death rates were 31·6 per thousand and 7·5 per thousand respectively. The net annual increase in population in 1968 was 2·4 per cent. It is estimated that 66·3 per cent of the population are Buddhists, 18·4 per cent Hindus, 8·3 per cent Christians and 6·9 per cent Muslims.

Primary education is free and compulsory, but there are not yet enough school places to enable all children to attend. About 29 per cent of the population attend secondary schools, and the literacy figure for 1966 was 82·2 per cent. (IBRD Report). There were 13,005 students attending university in 1968/69.

Ceylon is divided into eight provinces, these (with population figures according to the 1963 census) being: Western (2,845,408), Central (1,710,136), Southern (1,433,781), Northern (741,802), Eastern (547,000), North-Western (1,157,082), North-Central (394,282), Uva (665,538) and Sabaragamuwa (1,128,668). For administrative purposes, the provinces are divided into districts (22 in all), each of which is administered by a Government Agent, who is a member of the Ceylon Administrative Service.

The capital of Ceylon is Colombo, with an estimated population, in 1968 of 561,000. Other major towns are Dehiwela/Mt. Lavinia, a suburb of Colombo, (122,000), Jaffna (101,000), Kandy (78,000) and Galle (73,000). Colombo, Trincomalee and Galle Port are the principal ports, Colombo handling 3,074,747 tons of cargo during 1968. The principal local shipping line is Ceylon Shipping Lines Ltd. A new body, the Ceylon Shipping Corporation, has been established by the authorities to set up a national shipping line to handle a proportion of Ceylon's exports and imports. It is expected that the Corporation will purchase a small number of cargo vessels to start the new line.

The principal airports are the Bandaranaike International Airport at Katunayake, 19 miles to the north of Colombo, with a runway of 11,000 feet, and Ratmalana, 9 miles south of Colombo, with a runway of 6,000 feet. A new passenger terminal building at Katunayake, built with substantial assistance from the Canadian Government, was opened for use in June 1968, Ceylon's national airline is Air Ceylon.

The railway system, operated by Ceylon Government Railways, has (excluding sidings) 845 miles of broad gauge line and 87 miles of narrow gauge. At its highest point the railway reaches 6,200 feet above sea level. At the end of 1967 the total road mileage was some 13,000, of which 10,780 miles were motorable. Of the motorable roads, 7,670 miles were bitumen surfaced and the rest were tarred.

The Ceylon Broadcasting Corporation, a public corporation since 5th January 1967, provides services in Sinhala, Tamil and English for the whole island. There is no television service at present but the possibility of introducing television on a limited scale is under consideration.

Principal products include, tea, rubber, copra, spices and gems. There is increasing emphasis on local production of food, particularly rice. Plans also exist for large-scale production of sugar cane, cotton and citrus fruits.

Government revenue for the financial year 1970/71 is estimated at Rs.2,878 million or Rs.142 million more than the provisional estimate for 1969/70. Estimated total Government expenditure for 1970/71 is Rs.4,058 million—an increase of Rs.172 million on the 1969/70 provisional revised total of Rs.3,886 million. A gross budget deficit of Rs.1,180 million is forecast for 1970/71 compared with the provisional figure of Rs.1,150 million for 1969/70.

The economy of Ceylon has traditionally been based on export agriculture, particularly tea production and to a lesser extent, rubber and coconut products. Although production of these commodities has expanded, falling world prices have resulted in a severe foreign exchange shortage. Export earnings which had been improving steadily from the low levels of 1963 declined in the years 1966 and 1967. Even in 1968, although as a result of the devaluation of the rupee terms increased substantially, in terms of US dollars the decline continued. In 1969 the value of Ceylon's exports was Rs.119 less than that for 1968—a decline of US$20 million to US$322 million or Rs.1,916 million.

Since 1965, successive World Bank missions have discussed with the Government possible lines along which Ceylon's economy could be stimulated. Five meetings of aid-giving countries have been convened in consequence of which various countries have granted commodity and project aid designed to make it possible for Ceylon to devote more resources to productive capital investment. The Ministry of Planning and Economic Affairs in August 1967 issued 'Economic Development 1966–68 Review and Trends' which gives an analysis of the economic progress of the country as seen at that date. Following a World Bank mission in October/November 1967, the International Bank of Reconstruction and Development and the International Development Association published the 'Problem of Foreign Exchange and Long-Term Growth of Ceylon' containing recommendations on future policy. This publication also contains a useful assessment of Ceylon's economic progress in the public and private sector.

In 1967, following the devaluation of sterling, Ceylon devalued her currency by 20%. May 1968 saw the introduction of the Foreign Exchange Entitlement Certificate Scheme. This provided for the issue of Foreign Exchange Entitlement Certificates against certain specified exports and inward rmittances. The Certificates could also be bought from recognised Commercial Banks at a premium subsequently fixed at 55%. The Certificates carried an entitlement to the use of foreign exchange for approved purposes which included payment for imports of a wide range of goods which were then made available on Open General Licence. The Foreign Exchange Entitlement Certificate Scheme remains in force and its scope is being extended to cover a yet wider range of payments despite the replacement of the Open General Licensing system by a comprehensive quota system of licensing.

Since the change of Government in May 1970, there has been a move to expand the public sector at the expense of the private sector, inter alia, the Sri Lanka State Trading Corporation has been established with the avowed intention of eventually taking over all the import and export trade.

Ceylon's National Day is Independence Day, the anniversary of which is the 4th February.

EXPORTS AND IMPORTS
By Country

Exports 1969 Rs.m.	Exports 1970 Rs.m.		Imports 1969 Rs.m.	Imports 1970 Rs.m.
379	455	United Kingdom	443	330
79	72	Australia	104	112
49	52	Canada	34	68
6	7	Hong Kong	15	15
25	21	India	213	226
2	2	Malaysia	7	13
1	1	Maldive Islands	10	15
40	34	New Zealand	8	20
48	42	Pakistan	75	58
8	13	Singapore	18	31
60	63	Other Commonwealth Countries	72	31
1	—	Austria	3	3
1	1	Argentine Republic	—	—
6	6	Belgium	22	19
2	2	Bulgaria	1	1
2	2	Burma	30	89
240	252	China	282	289
4	4	Czechoslovakia	13	30
6	6	Denmark	11	11
45	56	United Arab Republic	18	36
17	17	France	70	62
14	20	Democratic Republic of Germany	85	10
77	81	Federal Republic of Germany	160	140
1	2	Hungary	11	8
—	—	Indonesia	3	3
—	—	Iran	40	19
12	17	Ireland	1	2
35	39	Italy	37	27
45	67	Japan	187	195
20	15	Mexico	—	—
35	34	Netherlands	35	26
27	41	Poland	23	48
20	19	Rumania	15	18
7	7	Spain	1	1
2	2	Switzerland	10	12

EXPORTS AND IMPORTS—*continued*
By Country

Exports			Imports	
1969	1970		1969	1970
Rs.m.	Rs.m.		Rs.m,	Rs.m.
1	1	Thailand	27	29
64	56	Iraq	—	—
84	80	South Africa	11	11
149	144	USA	213	132
89	82	USSR	51	40
7	4	Yugoslavia	51	30
169	176	Other Foreign Countries and Miscellaneous	127	103
1,879	1,995	Total	2,537	2,313

EXPORTS

Commodity	Value Rs.m.	
	1969	1970
Tea	1,062	1,120
Rubber	431	440
Coconut and Coconut Products	221	237
Other Products	161	236
Total	1,875	2,033

IMPORTS

Commodity	Value Rs.m.	
	1969	1970
I. CONSUMER GOODS	1,218	1,294
of which (a) Food and Drink	976	1,069
(i) Rice	257	318
(ii) Flour	255	260
(iii) Sugar	115	170
(b) Textiles and Clothing.. ..	122	124
II. INTERMEDIATE GOODS	592	451
of which (a) Fertilisers	66	81
(b) Petroleum Products	156	58
(c) Chemicals	66	56
(d) Paper and Paperboard ..	55	45
(e) Yarn and Thread	80	41
III. INVESTMENT GOODS	700	546
of which (a) Building Materials	99	119
(b) Transport Equipment.. ..	213	126
(c) Machinery and Equipment ..	368	276
IV. UNCLASSIFIED	33	22
Total	2,543	2,313

HISTORY

The earliest known inhabitants of Ceylon were aborigines who migrated, about five thousand years ago, from the pre-Dravidian tribes which populated the Deccan. The most important of these early settlers were the Nagas, a tribe which ruled the northern and north-eastern coasts of Ceylon, and the Yakkas, who dominated the interior. Their descendants, the primitive Veddhas, are still to be found in small numbers in the remote forests of the interior. The ancient Sanskrit name of Ceylon was Lanka.

The chronological sequence of the earliest Sinhalese kings is confused and open to some doubt. Vijaya I, the traditional founder of the Great Dynasty in 543 B.C., was the son of Sinha Bahu (the lion), a petty nobleman of Bengal. Expelled from India for lawlessness, Vijaya landed in the island and soon became the King of Ceylon. Vijaya's followers were called Sihala, or Sinhala (lion race) after Vijaya's father, and are now known as Sinhalese.

Vijaya and his successors organised the country on a patriarchal village system and colonists from southern India were encouraged to settle. The civilization of Ceylon from the earliest times up to the twelfth century was centred on the dry zone; the wet zone in the south-west part of the island was the least developed. The whole surface of the northern plains, comprising some twelve thousand square miles of jungle and semi-desert, was converted to cultivated land by means of a vast irrigation system, which was to last for fifteen centuries, involving the construction of huge tanks or reservoirs, supplying an intricate system of canals which watered every village.

Buddhism was introduced into Ceylon during the reign of Tissa, *circa* 247-207 B.C., by the son of the Emperor Asoka, Prince Mahinda, who planted at Anuradhapura the sacred Bo-tree which survives to this day. Successive kings constructed tanks for irrigation and built dagobas. Monasteries and Buddhist temples were constructed in every important village and became centres of spiritual life, education and culture.

The country flourished for several centuries until it was invaded from southern India. The history of Ceylon thereafter is largely a succession of invasions from southern India and of internal strife fomented by Sinhalese chiefs who employed Tamil mercenaries in their conflicts with the royal line. From the seventh century onwards the Tamils came in increasing numbers and they filled all the principal offices, including that of Prime Minister. In the eighth century they forced the king to leave Anuradhapura, which had been the Sinhalese royal seat for almost a thousand years, and the capital was moved to Polonnaruwa. In 1017 the whole of Ceylon was subdued by a great invasion from the Chola Empire but sixty years later a Sinhalese prince of the exiled royal house succeeded it restoring part of the Sinhalese kingdom. The exploits of a successor, King Parakrama Bahu I, who became ruler of the entire island and reduced the Chola and Pandya Empires to the position of tributaries, are among the most notable in the history of Ceylon. Thirty years after his death invaders from Kalinga in southern India appeared and under their leader Magha the north of Ceylon became a Tamil kingdom. This kingdom, which came to be known as the Jaffna Kingdom, survived successive invasions from India and remained separate from the Sinhalese kingdoms. Magha's invasion compelled the Sinhalese rulers to move south and a new capital was eventually established in 1410 at Kotte, near Colombo.

The Sinhalese kings who followed Parakrama were weak and exercised little control over their semi-independent chiefs, who, beyond acknowledging the nominal supremacy of the Kotte king, usually obeyed no other authority than their own. This led, at the end of the fifteenth century, to the rise of an independent kingdom of Kandy, dividing the inhabitants into low-country and up-country Sinhalese. The high-country kingdom of Kandy comprised the present North-Central and Eastern Provinces and Hambantota District. The low-country kingdom of Kotte covered the present North-Western, Western and Sabaragamuwa Provinces and the Galle and Matara Districts. In the sixteenth century the low-country was divided between the Sinhalese king at Kotte and Sitavaka, a relative and rival to the throne.

The Portuguese first visited the island in 1505 and were granted permission to build a fort at Colombo. At this period the commerce of Ceylon was in the hands of the Ceylon Moors, so-called by the Portuguese, who were Muslims of Arab stock and had traded with Ceylon for centuries before the birth of Muhammad. The principal trade of the island was centred on Galle.

The Portuguese returned in 1517 and built the fort, and later named the township the City of St. Lawrence. The Sinhalese king at Kotte was persuaded to submit to Portuguese protection and gave them the cinnamon trade, for the collection of which Sinhalese villagers were organised into forced labour. Despite the defection of their king the Sinhalese people resisted the Portuguese as far as they were able and Portuguese records later showed that Ceylon was 'gradually consuming her Indian revenues, wasting her forces and artillery, and causing a greater outlay for the government of that single island than for all her other conquests of the East'. The last legitimate king of Ceylon ruling from Kotte was Dharmapala, a protégé of the Portuguese. He died in 1597 bequeathing Ceylon to King Philip II of Spain (Philip I of Portugal), who thus gained control of the island except for the Tamil kingdom of Jaffna, which the Portuguese took in 1621, and the territory of the king of Kandy. The Portuguese introduced monopolies on cinnamon, areca and pepper, precious stones, elephants and the pearl fishery. They also introduced Roman Catholicism, which to-day has more than three quarters of a million adherents in Ceylon.

The Dutch from 1602 began to take an interest in the island and from 1634, with help from the king of Kandy, gradually overran the Portuguese possessions. A Dutch Governor arrived for the new settlements in 1640 and a truce with the Portuguese was reached in 1646. This was broken in 1652 by the Dutch and on 11th May 1656 the Portuguese capitulated, the Dutch becoming masters of the island except for the kingdom of Kandy, and the Portuguese fort at Jaffna, which they took in 1658.

Throughout the Dutch occupation there was constant trouble with the king of Kandy. Following an abortive attempt to treat with the British at Madras in 1762 the king attacked the Dutch settlements, without success. In 1766 he was compelled to sign a treaty relinquishing to the Dutch not only the settlements they already held but also the remaining districts bordering the coast, the Kandyans being thus cut off from the outer world. The confinement of the Kandyans was the prime reason for further attacks on the Dutch. The expense of maintaining an inner ring of defence around the Kandyan kingdom as well as round the coast was a cause of great concern to the Dutch and to the British who succeeded them. The Dutch retained the monopolies and divided their settlements between Colombo, Jaffna and Galle, building a track round the coast. Tamil laws were codified and where there was any conflict between them and the Sinhalese usages and customs, Roman-Dutch law was introduced. The Dutch Reformed Church was installed in Ceylon and severe measures were taken against Roman Catholics. The Ceylon Moors and Chetties (Indian Moors of Malabar stock) were treated as foreigners, liable to compulsory service which was, however, commutable on cash payment. The Malays, imported by the Dutch from the archipelago, were bound to military service. Education was placed in the hands of the Protestant Church and many schools were opened. Numerous canals between Puttalam, Negombo and Kalutara were constructed. These canals, together with Roman-Dutch law, the forts and the Burghers, who are the descendants of the Dutch colonists, are the principal legacies of Dutch rule in Ceylon.

Whilst Britain and Holland were at war over Britain's insistence on the right to search neutral vessels during the American War of Independence, a British Fleet captured Trincomalee in January 1782. The British force was dislodged eight months later by a French fleet which held Trincomalee until it was returned to the Dutch at the Peace of Paris in the following year.

France declared war on Britain and Holland on 1st February 1793 and during the next two years overran Holland. In January 1795 the Dutch Stadtholder, William IV of Orange, fled to England and called upon the Dutch overseas possessions to seek British protection. To forestall French designs on India and to acquire a safe naval base as near as possible to the harbourless Coromandel coast, the British Government in July 1795 ordered Lord Hobart, the Governor of the Madras Presidency, to secure the Dutch possessions. Disobeying the orders of the Stadtholder, the Dutch in Ceylon refused British protection. An expedition from Madras captured Trincomalee on 26th August 1795. Other Dutch posts were soon captured and Colombo was placed under siege. By the terms of capitulation, signed on 15th February 1796, Colombo and the remaining Dutch settlements were surrendered to Britain on the following day.

Britain originally had no intention of retaining the settlements and intended to hand them back to the Dutch at the end of the war. Later, however, Britain decided to retain the settlements and the possession of Ceylon by Britain was confirmed at the Peace of Amiens, signed on 27th March 1802. Difficulties with the Kandyan kingdom of the interior continued up to 1815 when the king was deposed and whole island came under the control of Britain.

The Kandyans had succeeded in defying the Portuguese and the Dutch largely by reason of the inaccessibility of their country. With the object at first of facilitating military movements, therefore, the British built a network of roads which by the middle of the 19th century gave Ceylon one of the best road systems in Asia. The development of roads was followed between 1864 and 1885 by the construction of railways linking the interior with Colombo and with the south-west coast. In 1858 the first telegraph line was constructed.

These improvements in communications, coupled with reforms in the ancient Sinhalese systems of land tenure, contributed very largely to the complete transformation of the economy of Ceylon which was one of the most significant results of British rule. Before the British arrived, the economy of the island was based on subsistence agriculture supplemented by a long-established export trade in gems, coconut products and, above all, spices. Beginning in the 1830s, however, the British introduced plantation crops, coffee, coconuts, rubber and, after coffee was wiped out by disease, tea, with such success that by the end of the 19th century the export of these crops formed the mainstay of Ceylon's economy. There was some Ceylonese participation in the coconut and rubber industries but by far the greater part of the capital for the development of the plantations, and of the ancillary services such as banking, insurance and shipping which grew in the wake of the export trade, was provided from Britain. Particularly in the case of those at the higher altitudes, in which the best tea is produced, the estates were developed mainly with the use of labour brought in from Southern India. The descendants of these Tamil labourers (known as Indian Tamils to distinguish them from the long-settled Ceylon Tamils) still provide the bulk of the estate labour force and their presence in Ceylon has proved a considerable irritant both in internal Ceylonese politics and in Indo/Ceylonese relations. An Agreement, providing for the repatriation to India of a large number of these labourers, was reached between the Indian and Ceylon Government in October 1964. Now in the first stages of implementation, it offers prospects of a solution to this problem.

The British brought with them to Ceylon their ideals of justice and the English common law—although some difficulty was encountered at first in assimilating this with the legacy of Roman-Dutch Law left behind by the Dutch. In 1801 a Supreme Court of Justice and a High Court of Appeal were established from both of which appeal lay to the Privy Council. A few years later trial by jury was introduced. In 1883 the judiciary was declared independent of the executive and common courts were instituted for the whole island, their jurisdiction covering expatriates and Ceylonese alike.

From 1834 onwards, as a result of a recommendation in the Colebrooke Report, the Government actively encouraged the spread of education, at first in the English medium but later in Sinhala and Tamil also. The Government both established its own schools and assisted financially the more numerous schools founded by the Christian missionary bodies and, after 1886, by Buddhist and Hindu associations. In 1921 University College was set up which became in 1942 the University of Ceylon. Three more Universities have since been established.

As education became more widespread, so political consciousness grew among the Ceylonese, which led in turn to increasing pressure for them to be given a greater voice in the affairs of the Government. In 1908 the Ceylon National Association was appointed to forward this cause. The Association was succeeded in 1917 by the Ceylon Reform League which, in the following year, developed into the Ceylon National Congress. The efforts of these bodies culminated on 4th February 1948 in the achievement by Ceylon of complete independence as a sovereign monarchical member of the Commonwealth of Nations. (The actual constitutional stages by which independence was attained are described in the succeeding section.)

From 1948 to 1956 Ceylon was governed by the United National Party, which had its origins in the National Congress, supported by the Tamil Congress and, at first, the Indian Congress (representing the Tamil labourers). At first the Opposition consisted of the (Trotskyist) Marxist Lanka Sama Samaja Party and the Communists; from 1951 onwards its ranks were augmented by the Sri Lanka Freedom Party led by Mr S. W. R. D. Bandaranaike who had, with several others, broken away from the United National Party. The first Prime Minister was Mr D. S. Senanayake who had been prominent in the Ceylonese independence movement from its earliest days. In 1952 Mr Senanayake died and was succeeded in the Premiership by his son, Mr Dudley Senanayake. Dudley Senanayake resigned on grounds of ill-health in 1953 and the reins of office passed to Sir John Kotelawala—another veteran politician.

In the 1956 General Election Mr Bandaranaike joined hands with Mr Philip Gunawardena and Mr W. Dahanayake, to form the Mahajana Eksath Peramuna (M.E.P.) or People's United Front with a socialist and Sinhalese nationalist programme. Assisted by dissension among the Marxist groups, and by the fact that the Tamil constituencies in the north and north-east of Ceylon were contested almost entirely on a communal basis between the Tamil Congress and the Federal Party who, under the leadership of Mr S. J. V. Chelvanayakam, had previously broken away from the Congress, the M.E.P. won a sweeping victory, reducing the U.N.P. to eight seats in the House of Representatives.

The year marked a watershed in Ceylonese politics. The policies of the U.N.P. Governments had been moderately conservative in internal and economic affairs, and western-aligned in foreign affairs. The policies of the M.E.P. Government were based upon the three pillars of linguistic and racial nationalism in internal affairs, socialism in economic affairs and non-alignment in foreign affairs. One of the first acts of Mr Bandaranaike's Government was to negotiate with the British Government for the handing over to Ceylon of the naval base at Trincomalee and the airfield at Katunayake which had been retained under a Defence Agreement entered into on Independence. They were handed over in 1957.

In July 1959 Mr Philip Gunawardena, the leader of the left wing of the M.E.P., was expelled from the Government and in September 1959 Mr Bandaranaike was assassinated. He was succeeded in the Premiership by Mr Dahanayake who called a General Election in March 1960. This returned to power the U.N.P. of which Mr Dudley Senanayake had resumed the leadership. Although the U.N.P. were the largest single party, however, they were outnumbered by the Opposition parties and were defeated immediately on the Vote on the Address. A further General Election was therefore held in July 1960.

At this stage Mrs Sirimavo Bandaranaike agreed to assume the leadership of her late husband's original Party, the S.L.F.P. Assisted by a no-contest pact with the Trotskyist L.S.S.P. and the orthodox Communist Party, the S.L.F.P. won an overall majority in the House of Representatives. In June 1964 Mrs Bandaranaike entered into a coalition with the Lanka Sama Samaja Party led by Dr N. M. Perera to strengthen her administration and to combat mounting industrial unrest. The policies of the Coalition Government, however, aroused considerable uneasiness both within the S.L.F.P. and in the country at large. This culminated in December 1964 in the defection of a section of the S.L.F.P., under the leadership of Mr C. P. de Silva, the Minister of Lands, Irrigation and Power, which in turn led to the Government being defeated in the House of Representatives. Parliament was dissolved and a General Election was called for in March 1965, at which the United National Party emerged the largest single party with 66 seats. Mr Dudley Senanayake was able to form a government with the support of the two Tamil Parties (17), Mr C. P. de Silva's breakaway group the Sri Lanka Socialist Party (5) and other groupings. Although losing the support of the Tamil Party in 1969, Mr Senanayake remained in power until the General Election of May 1970, the results of which are shown below.

CONSTITUTIONAL DEVELOPMENT

Under the Sinhalese Kings, under the Portuguese and Dutch, and initially under the British, Ceylon, or as much of it as they controlled, was governed autocratically by kings or governors, usually with the assistance of an advisory council. The country was administered through a complicated hierarchy of provincial governors, district chiefs and village heads; most land was held on feudal tenure and compulsory service was general. The first British Civil Governor, appointed on 16th March 1798, and invested with complete legislative power, was responsible partly to the Crown and partly to the East India Company Court of Directors and Governor-General at Calcutta. On 13th March 1801 Ceylon became a Crown Colony and the Governor, whilst retaining complete legislative authority, was thereafter responsible only to the Crown. The Kingdom of Kandy was taken over in 1815, but was administered separately from the rest of the country.

The history of the present Constitution of Ceylon can be said to start with the setting up of the Colebrook Commission in 1829 to examine every matter concerning the administration of the island. Following the Commission's Report, Kandy was amalgamated with the rest of the country in a uniform administration. Executive and Legislative Councils were established in March 1833, compulsory service abolished, Ceylonese admitted to the Civil Service and plans laid for an educational system and the encouragement of a free press. The Judicature was declared independent of the Executive, Common Courts constituted for the whole island and the jurisdiction of the Courts extended to Europeans and Ceylonese alike.

The Legislature set up in 1833 consisted of 9 official members and 6 unofficial members to represent the principal communities. Demands by the unofficial members for representative and responsible Government led to their resignation in 1864 and in 1865 the Ceylon League was formed with the object of securing an unofficial majority in the Council. The number of unofficials was increased by stages and by 1924 the Council consisted of 12 official and 37 unofficial members of whom 34 were elected and 3 appointed by the Governor. Of the elected members 23 were elected for territorial constituencies and the remainder for communal electorates.

The practical working of the Constitution was examined by the Donoughmore Commission in 1927-28. The Commission reported (Cmd. 3131) that the Executive was ineffectual owing to the opposition of the Legislature while at the same time the Ceylonese members of the Legislative Council were receiving no experience in the responsibility of government. The Commission advised that extensive responsibility should be transferred to the Ceylonese members. The new Constitution, promulgated in the Ceylon (State Council) Order in Council 1931, together with the franchise and election law, dealt with in the Ceylon (State Council Elections) Order in Council 1931, made on the same day, and based on the recommendations of the Commission, provided for virtually universal suffrage, the abolition of communal electorates and the creation of seven Executive Committees composed of groups of the elected members of the Legislature. The single-chamber Legislature was named the State Council and was composed of fifty elected members, eight members nominated by the Governor and three *ex-officio* Officers of State. A system of dyarchy was set up by dividing the administration into reserved and transferred subjects, the former under control of the three Officers of State (the Chief Secretary, the Legal Secretary and the Financial Secretary) and the latter under the respective Executive Committees. The seven Chairmen of the Executive Committees with the three Officers of State (who had no voting powers) constituted the Board of Ministers.

In a Declaration of May 1943, the British Government promised to grant Ceylon at the end of the war fully responsible government under the Crown in all matters of internal civil administration, the British Government retaining control only of defence and foreign affairs. The Ceylon Board of Ministers was invited to draw up a constitutional scheme on this basis and a Commission under the Chairmanship of Lord Soulbury was sent to Ceylon in 1944 to advise the British Government on the measures necessary to give effect to the Declaration. A new Constitution based on the Commission's recommendations was approved in May 1946 and in June of the following year the British Government announced that steps would be taken to confer on Ceylon full self-governing status as soon as the necessary agreements had been negotiated. Ceylon accordingly attained complete independence and became a fully self-governing Member of the Commonwealth on 4th February 1948.

CONSTITUTION

The Constitution of Ceylon is contained in the Ceylon Independence Act of 1947 and in the Ceylon (Constitution and Independence) Orders in Council 1946/47 and subsequent amendments. The Constitution followed closely the Soulbury Commission's recommendations (Cmd. 6677) in providing for a bicameral Legislature. The House of Representatives consists of 151 elected members (originally 95) representing territorial constituencies and six members appointed by the Governor-General to represent important interests not otherwise adequately represented. The House of Representatives has a maximum term of five years. (The present House was elected in 1970.) The Senate consists of fifteen Senators elected by the House of Representatives and fifteen appointed by the Governor-General. The term of office for Senators is six years and one-third of their number retire every second year.

The Orders in Council define the position, powers and privileges of the Governor-General and Parliament and lay down rules for the functioning of Parliament and the conduct of business. Under the Constitution a Judicial Service Commission and a Public Service Commission are established. No change may be made to the Orders in Council without the consent of two-thirds of the members of the House of Representatives.

Shortly after the 1970 election a Constituent Assembly was formed to draft a new constitution. At 1st June 1971 it had not completed its work.

HISTORICAL LIST OF MINISTRIES

D. S. Senanayake, PC, 4th February 1948 to 22nd March 1952
Dudley Senanayake, 26th March 1952 to 12th October 1953
Sir John Kotelawala, PC, CH, KBE, 12th October 1953 to 12th April 1956
S. W. R. D. Bandaranaike, 12th April 1956 to 26th September 1959
W. Dahanayake, 26th September 1959 to 20th March 1960
Dudley Senanayake, 21st March 1960 to 20th July 1960
(Mrs) Sirimavo R. D. Bandaranaike, 21st July 1960 to 24th March 1965
Dudley Senanayake, 25th March 1965 to 28th May 1970
(Mrs) Sirimavo R. D. Bandaranaike, from 29th May 1970

GOVERNMENT

Ceylon's seventh General Election, held on 27th May 1970, returned the Sri Lanka Freedom Party as the largest single party with 91 seats—an overall majority. In 1968, however, Mrs Bandaranaike's Party had formed a united front with the Communist Party and the Trotskyist Lanka Sama Samaja Party which won 6 and 19 seats respectively in this election. Three Cabinet portfolios were therefore given to the L.S.S.P. and one to the C.P. The support of these Parties will among other things enable the Government to alter the Constitution as they are pledged to do.

The United National Party was reduced at the election to 12 seats; the Tamil Federal Party won 13 seats and the Tamil Congress 3 seats. 2 Independents were elected.

GOVERNOR-GENERAL AND COMMANDER-IN-CHIEF
His Excellency Mr William Gopallawa, MBE

THE CABINET
Prime Minister, Minister of Defence and External Affairs, Minister of Planning and Employment:
The Hon. Mrs S. R. D. Bandaranaike
Minister of Irrigation, Power and Highways: The Hon. Maitripala Senanayake
Minister of Foreign and Internal Trade: The Hon. T. B. Illangaratne
Minister of Education: The Hon. B. Mahmud
Minister of Shipping and Tourism: The Hon. P. B. G. Kalugalle
Minister of Labour: The Hon. M. P. de Z. Siriwardene
Minister of Public Administration, Local Government and Home Affairs:
The Hon. F. R. D. Bandaranaike
Minister of Industries and Scientific Affairs: The Hon. T. B. Subasinght
Minister of Finance: The Hon. Dr N. M. Perera
Minister of Communications: The Hon. L. S. Goonewardene
Minister of Plantation Industry and Constitutional Affairs: The Hon. Dr C. R. de Silva
Minister of Justice: The Hon. J. M. Jayamanne
Minister of Agriculture and Lands: The Hon. H. S. R. B. Kobbekaduwa
Minister of Fisheries: The Hon. G. Rajapakse
Minister of Housing and Construction: The Hon. P. G. B. Keuneman
Minister of Posts and Telecommunications: The Hon. C. Kumarasurier
Minister of Health: The Hon. W. P. G. Ariyadasa
Minister of Information and Broadcasting: The Hon. R. S. Perera
Minister of Social Services: The Hon. T. B. Tennekoon
Minister of Cultural Affairs: The Hon. S. S. Kulatilake
Minister of Parliamentary Affairs and Sports and Chief Government Whip:
The Hon. K. B. Ratnayake

CABINET OFFICE
Director, Cabinet Affairs and Secretary to the Cabinet: M. S. Alif
Leader of the Opposition: J. R. Jayewardena

THE SENATE
President: Senator The Hon. A. Ratnayake
Deputy President and Chairman of Committees: Senator The Hon. S. D. S. Somaratne
Clerk of the Senate: P. Weerasinghe

HOUSE OF REPRESENTATIVES
Speaker: The Hon. S. Tillekaratne
Deputy Speaker and Chairman of Committees: I. A. A. Cader
Clerk of the House of Representatives: S. S. Wijesinha

JUDICIARY
Supreme Court
Chief Justice: Hon. H. N. G. Fernando, OBE

Puisne Judges:

Hon. G. P. Silva	Hon. C. G. Weeramantry
Hon. A. L. Sirimanne	Hon. O. L. de Kretser
Hon. A. C. A. Alles	Hon. S. R. Wijayatillake
Hon. G. T. Samerawickrame	Hon. V. T. Thamotheram

Registrar: N. Navaratnam

Commander of the Army: Major-General D. S. Attygalle, MVO
Commander of the Air Force: Air Commodore P. H. Mendis
Captain of the Navy: Commodore D. V. Hunter
Inspector-General of Police: Stanley Senanayake

ADMINISTRATION

The central administration of Ceylon is provided by the Ministries and Government Departments set out below.

Below the centre, Ceylon is divided into 22 administrative Districts each under the authority of a Government Agent whose headquarters is traditionally known as the 'Kachcheri'. The Government Agents are supported by one or more Assistant Government Agents and by Divisional Revenue Officers for the sub-Divisions of their Districts. All these officers are members of the Ceylon Administrative Service (formerly the Ceylon Civil Service), which also staffs the Ministries and non-technical departments, and are fully transferable. At the foot of the administrative 'pyramid' are the Grama Sevakas, a new class of full-time civil servants established in 1963 to replace the old part-time Village Headmen.

The basic function of Government Agents and District Revenue Officers is land administration. But in addition to other administrative functions directly vested in them by legislation they are the principal executive officers and representatives of Government in their respective areas and, as such, are responsible for the co-ordination and general supervision of the work of the local representatives of specialist and technical departments such as Health Services, Public Works, Education and Irrigation.

Local Government in the usual sense of the term is in the hands of elected bodies: Municipal Councils in the ten largest towns, Urban Councils in the bigger towns and Town Councils in the smaller, and Village Councils for villages or groups of villages. The staffs of these local authorities with the exception of those at the lower salary levels, are recruited centrally and their terms and conditions of service are centrally regulated by the Local Government Service Commission. Local authorities derive their revenue in part direct, *e.g.* from the rating of property, and in part from block and specific groups from the Central Government.

Co-ordination between the Provincial Administrations and the Local Authorities is achieved by the District Co-ordinating Committees of which there is one in each Administrative District. These comprise on the one hand the Government Agent and all local Heads of Government Departments and, on the other, representatives of all local authorities in the District together with those members of Parliament whose constituencies lie within the District.

MINISTRIES AND GOVERNMENT DEPARTMENTS

Secretary to the Governor-General: N. Wijewardane

MINISTRY OF DEFENCE AND EXTERNAL AFFAIRS
Permanent Secretary: A. R. Ratnavale
Captain of the Navy: Commodore D. V. Hunter
Commander of the Army: Major-General D. S. Attygalle, MVO
Commander of the Air Force: Air Vice-Marshal E. R. Amerasekera, DFC
Inspector-General of Police: Stanley Senanayake

Department of Immigration and Emigration
Controller: W. T. Jayasinghe

MINISTRY OF PLANNING AND EMPLOYMENT
Permanent Secretary: Prof. H. A. de S. Gunasekera

MINISTRY OF INFORMATION AND BROADCASTING
Permanent Secretary: S. Dassanayake

MINISTRY OF FINANCE
Permanent Secretary and Secretary to the Treasury: M. Rajendra

MINISTRY OF IRRIGATION, POWER AND HIGHWAYS
Permanent Secretary: M. Chandrasena

MINISTRY OF PUBLIC ADMINISTRATION, LOCAL GOVERNMENT AND HOME AFFAIRS
Permanent Secretary: B. Mahadeva

MINISTRY OF HEALTH
Permanent Secretary: Dr S. Weeratunga

MINISTRY OF INDUSTRIES AND SCIENTIFIC AFFAIRS
Permanent Secretary: J. V. Fonseka

MINISTRY OF FISHERIES
Permanent Secretary: E. G. Gunawardene

MINISTRY OF FOREIGN AND INTERNAL TRADE
Permanent Secretary: Dr J. B. Kelegama

MINISTRY OF JUSTICE
Permanent Secretary: N. Jayawickreme
Attorney-General: The Hon. V. Tennekoon, Q C

MINISTRY OF AGRICULTURE AND LANDS
Permanent Secretary: A. T. M. Silva

MINISTRY OF EDUCATION
Permanent Secretary: Dr P. P. Udugama

MINISTRY OF LABOUR
Permanent Secretary: A. E. Gogerly Moragoda

MINISTRY OF POSTS AND TELECOMMUNICATIONS
Permanent Secretary: S. J. Serasinghe

MINISTRY OF COMMUNICATIONS
Permanent Secretary: J. H. Lanerolle

MINISTRY OF SOCIAL SERVICES
Permanent Secretary: P. D. Udawela

MINISTRY OF HOUSING AND CONSTRUCTION
Permanent Secretary: Dr Nath Amerakoon

MINISTRY OF SHIPPING AND TOURISM
Permanent Secretary: P. Kandarawela

MINISTRY OF PLANTATION INDUSTRY
Permanent Secretary: Dr A. T. A. de Sousa

MINISTRY OF CULTURAL AFFAIRS
Permanent Secretary: N. Wijeratne

MINISTRY OF PARLIAMENTARY AFFAIRS
Permanent Secretary: Dr N. S. R. Gunawardene

DIPLOMATIC REPRESENTATION

CEYLON REPRESENTATIVES IN OTHER COMMONWEALTH COUNTRIES

Britain: (High Commissioner); Canada: (High Commissioner); Australia: (High Commissioner); New Zealand: (High Commissioner) (resident in Canberra); India: (High Commissioner); Pakistan: (High Commissioner); Ghana: (High Commissioner); Malaysia: (High Commissioner)

COMMONWEALTH HIGH COMMISSIONERS IN CEYLON

Britain: A. M. MacKintosh, C M G; Canada: R. M. Macdonnell; Australia: H. D. White; New Zealand: B. S. Lendrum (resident in New Delhi); India: Y. K. Puri; Pakistan: Altaf Ahmed Shaikh; Malaysia: Tungku Indra Petra; Ghana: P. K. Owusu-Ansah resident in New Delhi)

CEYLON REPRESENTATIVES IN NON-COMMONWEALTH COUNTRIES

Afghanistan: (Ambassador) (resident in Delhi); Belgium: (Ambassador) (resident in Bonn); Brazil: (Ambassador); Burma: (Ambassador); Cambodia: (Ambassador) (resident in Peking); China: (Ambassador); Cuba: (Ambassador) (resident in Ottawa); Czechoslovakia: (Ambassador) (resident in Moscow); France: (Ambassador); Germany: (Ambassador); Greece: (Ambassador); Indonesia: (Ambassador) (resident in Karachi); Iran: (Ambassador) (resident in Karachi); Israel: (Minister); Italy: (Ambassador); Japan: (Ambassador); Lebanon: (Ambassador) (resident in Cairo); Mexico: (Ambassador) (resident in Washington); Mongolia: (Ambassador) (resident in Peking); Nepal: (Ambassador) (resident in Delhi); Netherlands: (Ambassador) (resident in Bonn); Philippines: (Ambassador) (resident in Tokyo); Poland: (Ambassador) (resident in Moscow); Rumania: (Ambassador) (resident in Moscow); Sudan: (Ambassador) (resident in Cairo); Switzerland: (Ambassador) (resident in Paris); Thailand: (Ambassador); United Arab Republic: (Ambassador); United Nations: (Permanent Representative); United States: (Ambassador); U.S.S.R.: (Ambassador); Yugoslavia: (Ambassador) (resident in Cairo)

REPUBLIC OF CYPRUS

THE island of Cyprus, latitude 35° N., longitude 33° 30' E., lies in the eastern Mediterranean and has an area of 3,572 square miles. The territory of the Republic of Cyprus comprises the whole of the island with the exception of the two Sovereign Base Areas of Akrotiri and Dhekelia in the south, which have a combined area of 99 square miles. These have been retained under British sovereignty. Mount Olympus rises 6,403 feet above sea level and is the highest peak situated in the Troodos Massif in the south-west of the island. Cyprus has an intense Mediterranean climate with a hot dry summer and a variable winter. July and August are the hottest months with a maximum temperature of 44·5°C (112°F) while December and February are the coldest with a minimum temperature of —5·5°C (22°F). The annual rainfall varies between 27·1 inches maximum and 9·7 inches minimum.

A census was last taken in 1960 and showed a total population of 577,615 consisting of the two major racial communities: the Greek Cypriots 441,656 and the Turkish Cypriots 104,942; Armenians 3,378, Maronites 2,752 and other nationalities 23,887. In mid-1969 the population was estimated to be 630,000. The birth rate in 1965 was estimated to be 24·4 and the death rate 6·1 per thousand. The official languages are Greek and Turkish. The main religious groups, with some indication of relative numbers, are Greek Orthodox (441,656), Muslim (104,942), Armenian Gregorian (3,378), Roman Catholic (4,505), Maronite (2,752). Primary education is free and universal and the extent of secondary education is 70 per cent. More than 80 per cent of the population aged seven and over is literate.

For administrative purposes the Republic is divided into six districts which, with population, are: Nicosia (228,500); Kyrenia (33,000); Famagusta (126,000); Larnaca (61,500); Limassol (118,000); Paphos (63,000). Nicosia (population including suburbs 115,000) is the largest town in Cyprus and is the capital of the Republic. It is situated in the central plain of the Messaoria. Other principal towns are Limassol (51,000); Famagusta (42,000); Larnaca (21,500); Paphos (12,000) and Kyrenia (5,000). Famagusta, Limassol and Larnaca, with nett registered tonnage 1,834,000, 1,743,000 and 519,000 respectively, are all ports of call for ocean-going shipping, but only at Famagusta are there berths at which ships of moderate size (with a draft not exceeding 30 ft) can come alongside.

At Limassol and Larnaca ships anchor in the open roadstead and goods are transported to and from shore by lighters. The construction of new ports at Larnaca and Limassol is under way. Extensions and improvements at Famagusta are planned.

Nicosia International Airport is situated five miles from the town centre and has runway lengths of 8,000 and 6,000 feet. The new terminal buildings were opened in March 1968. Work is in progress to extend the runway to 9,700 feet. The principal airline is Cyprus Airways Limited. There are no public railways in Cyprus (Cyprus Mines Corporation operates a private railway to facilitate its mining operations) and the road mileage consist of 2,154 miles of asphalt and 2,629 miles of gravel. A road development programme provides for the expenditure of £6·2 million. The island's broadcasting and television facilities are supplied by the Cyprus Broadcasting Corporation.

Cyprus is predominantly an agricultural country; agriculture and mining account for more than ninety per cent of exports. Receipts from the supply of goods and services to the Sovereign Base Areas are important to the Republic's economy. The principal agricultural products are wheat and barley, carobs, citrus, grapes and other soft fruits, potatoes, carrots, cauliflowers and other vegetables, olives, almonds, tobacco, hides and skins. Mining is carried on in various parts of the island, the most valuable minerals being pyrites and copper concentrates. Other minerals extracted are asbestos, chrome, gypsum and pigment earths. There is no heavy industry in Cyprus other than electricity generating and cement production. Work has begun on the construction of an oil refinery at Larnaca, scheduled to come on stream at the end of 1971 and designed to make the island self-sufficient in most petroleum products. There are many small and medium sized industries which manufacture a wide range of foodstuffs and consumer goods. Manufacturing industries will become the cornerstone of the development effort; this sector is targeted to increase its G.D.P. from 12·2 per cent in 1966 to about 14 per cent in 1971. Exports under the Second Five Year Plan are anticipated to expand by 74 per cent, with major industrial projects including meat canning, saw milling, cement, asbestos pipes and the extension of industrial estates.

The tourist industry, which until 1963 had been expanding steadily, suffered considerably as a result of the political unrest. Apart from one-day tourists, the number of visitors fell from 75,900 in 1963 to 16,000 in 1964. With quieter conditions however the industry has gradually regained the ground lost and in 1970 there were 126,580 visitors, a record figure.

The Second Five Year Plan was published in April 1968 and aims at securing an average *per caput* income of £335 in 1971 compared with £258 at the end of 1966; it also envisages an annual growth rate of 7 per cent and total investment of over £200 million, an unprecedented figure in the island's history. Government development expenditure is projected at £57 million while the private sector is called upon to play a decisive role by investing £136 million. The plan's major objectives offer the prospect of a broad advance in economic development and social progress.

The Government Revenue and Expenditure Estimates for 1970 and 1971 were as follows:—Revenue (1970) £31,200,000 and (1971) £37,900,000; expenditure (1970) £27,600,000 ordinary and £13,000,000 development; (1971) £32,300,000 ordinary and £14,000,000 development.

The crude trade deficit continues to be a striking feature of the Cyprus economic scene, but it is comfortably bridged by foreign military expenditure, earnings from tourism, official and private transfer payments and inflow of investment capital. By the end of 1970 Cyprus' foreign exchange reserves had risen to a record level of £94·6 million, representing nearly twelve months value of exports. Britain continues to be Cyprus' leading trading partner; since independence, Britain's share of the island's import trade has remained fairly constant between 30 and 37 per cent, with British exports in 1970 reaching an estimated total of £28,700,000 compared with £26,300,000 in 1969. Over the past four years, the values of imports and exports were as follows:—

£ million	1967	1968	1969	1970 (est.)
Imports	59·2	70·9	84·6	98·2
Exports	29·9	36·9	40·9	44·4
Balance	—29·3	—34·0	—43·7	—53·8

HISTORY

Extensive archaeological finds going back to the fifth millenium B.C. testify to the existence of cultures in Cyprus in the earliest times. By the beginning of the first millenium, Greek-speaking Achaean colonies had been established, and in the 8th century B.C. the island appears to have been divided into a series of independent Greek and Phoenician kingdoms, tributaries of the Assyrian Empire. From the Assyrians, Cyprus passed successively to the Egyptians and the Persians. In 391 B.C. Evagoras of Salamis, having made himself master of almost the whole of Cyprus, raised the island to a position of virtual independence, but was unable long to sustain his position. On the division of the Empire of Alexander the Great, Cyprus passed to the Ptolemaic Kingdom of Egypt. It became a Roman province in 58 B.C., was early converted to Christianity and, on the partition of the Roman Empire, fell under the rule of the Byzantine Emperor. From an early date the Church of Cyprus has been autocephalous. In 478 A.D., following the discovery of the remains of St Barnabas, the Emperor bestowed certain privileges on the Archbishop of Cyprus including the right to sign his name in red ink. These privileges have been retained to this day. From the 7th to the 10th centuries Cyprus was ravaged intermittently by the Arabs. Only in 965 A.D. was Byzantine rule re-established, but it endured for another 200 years, a period marked by much church building.

In 1185 Isaac Comnenos usurped the Governorship of Cyprus and proclaimed his independence. In 1191 ships of the fleet of Richard Coeur de Lion, who was on his way to take part in the Third Crusade, were wrecked on the coast of Cyprus and their crews maltreated by Isaac. To avenge the wrongs done to his men, Richard attacked and defeated Isaac and conquered the island. Shortly afterwards he celebrated his marriage to Berengaria of Navarre at Limassol. Richard sold Cyprus after a few months to the Knights Templar, but they found the task of government beyond their powers and the next year with Richard's agreement, it was transferred to Guy de Lusignan, the dispossessed King of Jerusalem. Thereafter Kings of the House of Lusignan ruled Cyprus until 1489, although from 1373 to 1464 the Genoese Republic held Famagusta and exercised suzerainty over a part of the country.

The 300 years of Frankish rule were a great epoch in the varied history of Cyprus. The little kingdom played a distinguished part in several aspects of mediaeval civilization. Its constitution, inherited from the Kingdom of Jerusalem, was the model of that of a mediaeval feudal state. In the Abbey of Bellapaix and in the cathedrals of Nicosia and Famagusta it could boast examples of Gothic architecture without equal in the Levant. But such achievements were only attained through the introduction of an alien nobility and the ruthless subjugation of the Greek Church to a Latin hierarchy. The fall of Acre in 1291 left Cyprus the outpost of Christendom in the Levant. With the diversion of the Syrian trade to its ports, Cyprus prospered for a period and under Pope Peter I Alexandria was sacked and towns on the Turkish coast were occupied. But towards the end of the 14th century, with the Black Death and plagues and the Genoese invasion of 1373, the power of the Lusignans began to wane.

In 1489 Cyprus fell to the Republic of Venice, which held it until it was conquered by the Turks in 1571. The Venetian administration was elaborate, but often inefficient and corrupt. The population increased to about 200,000, but the former prosperity did not return.

F*

The Turkish conquest was welcomed by many Cypriots, particularly since the liquidation of the Latin Church ensued. Serfdom disappeared, the Orthodox Archbishopric was restored after having been in abeyance since about 1275, and the Christian population was granted a large measure of freedom. The power and authority which passed into the Archbishop's hands were particularly significant. As time went on, the Church acquired much influence. In 1821 the Archbishop, Bishops and leading personages of the Orthodox community were arrested and executed on a charge of conspiring with the insurgents in Greece. This proved to be only a temporary check.

In 1878, in exchange for a promise of British assistance to Turkey against Russian encroachment on her eastern provinces, Cyprus passed under the administration of Britain, although nominally it was still Ottoman territory and its inhabitants Ottoman subjects. At the outbreak of war with Turkey in 1914 Cyprus was annexed to the British Crown. The annexation was recognised by Greece and Turkey under the Treaty of Lausanne and in 1925 Cyprus became a Crown Colony.

The movement among the Greek population in Cyprus for the union (*Enosis*) of Cyprus with Greece was a constant feature of local political life during the British period. In 1915 Britain offered Cyprus to Greece on condition that Greece went forthwith to the aid of Serbia. Greece declined the offer, which subsequently lapsed. In October 1931 the Enosis movement led to widespread disturbances. The Greek Government's action in 1954 in taking the question of self-determination for Cyprus to the United Nations, and Her Majesty's Government announcement in July of the same year that it was intended to introduce a constitution as a first step towards self-government, gave added impetus to local political activities. The Church and local politicians advocated a boycott of the plans for introducing self-governing institutions, which they stigmatised as a betrayal of Enosis. In April 1955 the Greek Cypriot underground organisation, EOKA (*Ethniki Organosis Kyprion Agoniston*—National Organisation of Cypriot Combatants) launched an armed campaign in support of the demand for Enosis. This led to the declaration of a State of Emergency, which was to last four years.

The Emergency ended only on the signature in February 1959 of the Agreements of Zürich and London regarding the establishment of the Cyprus Republic. A further eighteen months of preparation for independence and of detailed negotiations (particularly over the provisions of the Treaty concerning the Establishment of the Republic) led to the transfer of power by Britain and to the declaration of the Republic on 16th August 1960. In February 1961, following a resolution by the House of Representatives, the Republic applied to become a Member of the Commonwealth; and at the Meeting of Commonwealth Prime Ministers on 13th March 1961 Cyprus was welcomed as a Member of the Commonwealth.

CONSTITUTIONAL DEVELOPMENT

In 1881, three years after the British occupation of Cyprus, a constitution was introduced under which there was an Executive Council to advise the High Commissioner and a partly elective Legislative Council. The legislature consisted of six official non-elected members and twelve elected members, three of whom were elected by the Turkish inhabitants and nine by the non-Turkish, with the High Commissioner as President. In 1925, when the island became a Crown

Colony, the Legislative Council was enlarged by the addition of three officially nominated members, and three elected members. After the disturbances of 1931 the Government was re-constituted without a Legislative Council; and the legislative authority, subject to the power of His Majesty to disallow local legislation or to legislate for the colony by Order in Council, was entrusted to the Governor. The Executive Council was retained and, before Independence, consisted of five official members. Its function was to advise the Governor on new legislation, on the exercise of the powers reposed in the Governor-in-Council under existing laws, and on major policy.

After the end of the second world war a number of unsuccessful attempts were made by Britain to introduce a constitutional Government, among them being the proposals prepared in 1956 by Lord Radcliffe, which outlined a very wide measure of self-government.

On 5th February 1959, after informal negotiations between the Greek and Turkish Foreign Ministers, the Prime Ministers and the Foreign Ministers of Greece and Turkey arrived in Zürich to begin a series of meetings lasting six days. At the end of the conference the Prime Ministers initialled a document which proposed that Cyprus should become an independent Republic and which set out the basic articles of the Constitution of the new Republic. The Foreign Ministers of Greece and Turkey flew on from Zürich to London, where they were joined by Archbishop Makarios and Doctor Kutchuk as the representatives of the Greek Cypriot and Turkish Cypriot communities. At the opening session of the London Conference the Foreign Secretary stated that the British Government accepted the Zürich Agreement, subject to the requirements that two areas should be retained under full British Sovereignty, together with the rights necessary to ensure their effective use as military bases, and that satisfactory guarantees should be given by Greece and Turkey and the Republic of Cyprus for the integrity of these areas. Britain also stipulated that a number of other points should be met regarding the rights of the various communities of the island, the Public Service, nationality and the assumption of certain obligations by the Republic. On 19th February the instruments recording the Agreement of all parties to the Conference on the settlement of the Cyprus problem were initialled.

During the period between the signature of the London Agreement and the declaration of Independence on 16th August 1960 a Transitional Committee was appointed in preparation for the transfer of power. This Transitional Committee consisted of Archbishop Makarios, Doctor Kutchuk and ten Cypriots appointed as Ministers in Provisional Ministries. Throughout the period the Transitional Committee met regularly with the Governor's Executive Council under the chairmanship of the Governor as a Joint Council. Elections for the offices of President and Vice-President of the Republic took place in December 1959. Elections of members of the House of Representatives and of the Communal Chambers took place immediately before Independence.

CONSTITUTION

The English text of the Constitution of the Republic of Cyprus is contained in the July 1960 White Paper on Cyprus (Cmnd. 1093). The Constitution is based on the document setting out the basic structure of the Republic of Cyprus which was initialled by the Prime Ministers of Greece and Turkey at Zürich on 11th February 1959.

Executive authority is vested in the President, who must be a Greek Cypriot, and the Vice-President, who must be a Turkish Cypriot. Both are elected by universal suffrage by the members of their respective communities. The President and Vice-President work through a Council of Ministers consisting of ten members, of whom seven must be Greek-Cypriot and three Turkish Cypriot Ministers. These are not in the House of Representatives, and are appointed jointly by the President and Vice-President. It is provided that the Ministry of Foreign Affairs or the Ministry of Defence or the Ministry of Finance, shall be entrusted to a Turkish Cypriot. (The President and Vice-President, as also the Greek and Turkish Ministers, have had no common dealings since December 1963). In the event of the temporary absence or temporary incapacity of the President the President of the House of Representatives acts for him. Similarly in the absence or incapacity of the Vice-President, the Vice-President of the House of Representatives acts for him.

Legislative authority other than in matters expressly reserved to the Communal Chambers is vested in the House of Representatives, whose 50 members are elected for a period of five years by universal suffrage. Each of the two communities elect their separate representatives, there being 35 Greek Cypriot members and 15 Turkish Cypriot members. The Greek and Turkish Cypriot members have not sat together since December 1963. The President and Vice-President of the Republic, separately and conjointly, have the right of veto on any law or decision of the House concerning foreign affairs, and certain questions of defence and security, and may also return all laws and decisions to the House of Representatives for reconsideration. In matters where laws and decisions of the House are considered by the President or Vice-President as discriminating against either of the two communities, the Supreme Constitutional Court may annul, confirm or return the measures to the House for reconsideration in whole or in part.

The Greek Cypriot and Turkish Cypriot communities each have a Communal Chamber (but see below) which exercises authority in such matters as religion, education, co-operative societies and other questions of a communal nature. Citizens of the Republic who are neither of Greek origin nor of Turkish origin are required to opt to belong either to the Greek Cypriot or the Turkish Cypriot community. The Communal Chambers have the right to impose taxes and levies on the members of their community.

The judicial provisions of the Constitution concern the Supreme Constitutional Court, the High Court and the Subordinate Courts. The Supreme Constitutional Court consists of a Greek Cypriot judge, a Turkish Cypriot judge and a neutral judge, the neutral judge being President of the Court. The High Court is composed of two Greek Cypriot judges, one Turkish Cypriot judge and a neutral judge, the neutral judge being the President of the Court and having two votes. (These provisions are, however, in abeyance at present).

Other provisions of the Constitution concern fundamental rights and liberties, the Public Service, the independent officers of the Republic, the armed forces of the Republic, financial procedures, and various miscellaneous and transitional matters. It is provided that the Civil Service should be composed of 70 per cent Greek Cypriots and 30 per cent Turkish Cypriots, with this quantitative distribution applying as far as possible in all grades of the hierarchy. Other sections of the Constitution provide for the establishment of separate Greek Cypriot and Turkish Cypriot municipalities in the main towns, for the use of Greek and

Turkish as official languages, for the right of the Greek Cypriot and Turkish Cypriot communities to celebrate the Greek and Turkish national holidays, for the regulation of broadcasting, and for the constitutional validity of the Treaty of Guarantee concluded between the Republic, Greece, Turkey and Britain and the Treaty of Military Alliance concluded between Greece, Turkey and Britain. The Constitution provides further that the territory of the Republic should be one and indivisible and excludes the integral or partial union of Cyprus with any other state.

The basic articles of the Constitution cannot be amended, although other articles may be modified by a majority of two-thirds of each of the representatives of the two communities in the House of Representatives. Despite this the Greek Cypriot members of the House have legislated on several occasions in the past five years on grounds of 'necessity' to amend basic articles of the Constitution.

HISTORICAL LIST
President
Archbishop Makarios, from 16th August 1960
Vice-President
Dr Fazil Kutchuk, from 16th August 1960

GOVERNMENT

Archbishop Makarios was elected by the Greek Cypriot community first President of the Republic of Cyprus on 13th December 1959. He received 144,501 votes against 71,753 cast for the rival candidate, John Clerides, who had the support of his own right-wing Democratic Union Party and also of AKEL (the Communist party). Dr Fazil Kutchuk was nominated to the office of Vice-President in the absence of any opposing Turkish Cypriot candidate.

The first election to the House of Representatives took place on 31st July 1960. Under an electoral arrangement AKEL were allowed five seats in the House in exchange for an undertaking not to contest the other thirty Greek Cypriot seats against the Patriotic Front, the loosely organised supporters of Archbishop Makarios. The 15 Turkish Cypriot members returned were all members of the National Party supporting Dr Kutchuk. The terms of office of the President, Vice-President and members of the House of Representatives were extended annually for a period of one year at a time from 16 August 1965 until fresh elections were held in 1968 and 1970 (see below). Elections for the Presidency and the Vice-Presidency were held in February 1968 for a further five-year term of office. In a contested election Archbishop Makarios received 95·45 per cent of the Greek Cypriot vote while Dr Kutchuk was returned unopposed.

Elections to the two Communal Chambers took place on 7th August 1960. The majority of the candidates to the Greek Cypriot Communal Chamber were returned unopposed. In the Turkish Cypriot Communal Chamber all 30 members returned were members of the National Party. The Greek Cypriot Communal Chamber by its own motion dissolved itself on 23rd March 1965 and the Greek Cypriot members of the House of Representatives on 30th March legislated to dispose of its functions. A Ministry of Education was subsequently set up.

Futher elections to the House of Representatives took place on 5 July 1970. The 35 Greek-Cypriot seats were contested by five parties—all, with the exception of AKEL, the Cyprus Communist Party, of recent formation. The results were: Unified Party (15 seats), AKEL (9 seats), Progressive Front (7 seats), Unified Democratic Union (2 seats), Independents (2 seats). The Turkish Cypriots held

separate elections on the same day for the 15 Turkish-Cypriot seats in the House
of Representatives and 15 seats in the Communal Chambers. All candidates stood
on the same platform.

The Breakdown of Law and Order, December 1963

Throughout 1963 there was a steady deterioration in political relations
between the Greek Cypriot and Turkish Cypriot Communities in Cyprus and it
was apparent that the constitutional settlement resulting from the Zürich and
London Agreements was in danger of breaking down. A principal source of contention were the constitutional provisions regarding municipal government in
the main towns. Events were precipitated by the summary rejection in early
December by the Turkish Government of certain proposals for constitutional
reform which were presented by Archbishop Makarios to Dr Kutchuk on 30th
November 1963. These proposals were designed to give the Greek Cypriots a
greater control over the Government of the Republic.

Following a succession of violent incidents, particularly in Nicosia, armed
fighting broke out in the island on 22nd December. Four days later the Cyprus
Government accepted an offer that the forces of the United Kingdom, Greece
and Turkey, stationed in Cyprus, and placed under British Command, should
assist them to secure the preservation of a ceasefire and the restoration of peace.
A Joint Force Headquarters under British Command was established forthwith
in Nicosia and carried out peacekeeping operations in the island.

In January 1964 the London Conference, attended by delegates of Greece,
Turkey, the United Kingdom and representatives of the Greek and Turkish
communities in Cyprus, met to find a solution to the problem. No agreement
was reached. Meanwhile the island remained in a very disturbed state and
there were fresh outbreaks of fighting. The problem was eventually referred to
the Security Council of the United Nations. On 4th March the Security Council
passed a Resolution to set up a United Nations Peace-keeping Force in Cyprus
for three months and this replaced the British Command on 27th March. Meanwhile, the United Nations Secretary-General appointed Mr Tuomioja to act as
the United Nations Mediator in Cyprus and to attempt to evolve a satisfactory
solution to the Constitutional problem. Under his chairmanship, unsuccessful
talks were held in Geneva in July/August 1964 between representatives of the US.,
Greek and Turkish Governments. He died on 9th September and was succeeded
by Senor Galo Plaza. On 26th March 1965 Senor Plaza presented his report. It
recorded the views of the interested parties and expressed the Mediator's personal
opinion that settlement should be on the basis of an independent unitary state
with a new constitution in which guarantees for the Turkish Cypriots would be
incorporated. These were, however, no more than guide lines and not a firm
recommendation. The Turkish Government declared that the Mediator had
exceeded his mandate and the mediation effort lapsed. After meetings between
the Greek and Turkish Foreign Ministers in London representatives of the Greek
and Turkish Governments started discussions in June 1965 in Athens and
Ankara. These discussions were suspended in July 1965, resumed in July 1966
and suspended again in December 1966 following a further Greek political crisis.

A final abortive attempt was made by Greece and Turkey to settle the Cyprus
problem when Colonel Papodopoulos, who came to power in the Greek military
coup in April 1967, met the Turkish Prime Minister at Euros in Thrace in
September of the same year. This meeting was a failure. In November 1967 a

long dispute about the right of the Cyprus police to patrol two Turkish villages in the Larnaca District came to a head and Greek Cypriot forces under General Grivas attacked the villages inflicting more than twenty casualties. Turkey reacted vigorously and a full scale international crisis resulted. Forceful intervention by Mr Cyrus Vance the Special Representative of President Johnson was successful in preventing a Turkish invasion of Cyprus. Following the crisis General Grivas was recalled to Athens (whence he has not returned) and several thousand Greek mainland soldiers in excess of the National contingent laid down in the Treaty of Alliance were withdrawn. Greek mainland officers serving with the National Guard remain.

At a meeting of the Security Council held in December 1967, U Thant offered his good offices in helping to bring about a political settlement. The Cyprus Government subsequently lifted the economic blockade that had been maintained on Turkish Cypriot areas and lifted the restrictions on the freedom of movement of Turkish Cypriots. They also permitted the return of Mr Rauf Denktash, the President of the Turkish Cypriot Chamber from exile in Ankara.

Contacts subsequently took place between the Communities and in June 1968 Mr Denktash and Mr Clerides (President of the House of Representatives) began unofficial talks aimed at finding a basis for a new Constitution for Cyprus. These talks, now in their fourth phase, are still continuing. Two sub-committees were set up to examine the functioning of the Legislature and the Para-statal organisations, but are dormant.

The UN Force in Cyprus has had its mandate renewed eighteen times; it was last renewed on 26th May 1971 for a further period of six months. The Force has been able, with exceptions, to maintain the peace in the island. The major exception was in August 1964 when fighting between Turkish Cypriots in enclaves in the north-west part of the island and numerically superior Greek Cypriot forces, led to limited air strikes by the Turkish Air Force; and in November 1967 when the possibility of Turkish intervention was narrowly averted.

THE PRESIDENT
His Beatitude Archbishop Makarios

VICE-PRESIDENT
His Excellency Dr Fazil Kutchuk

MINISTRY*
Minister of Commerce and Industry: Andreas Loizides†
Minister of the Interior (and Acting Minister of Defence):
Epaminondas Komodromos†
Minister of Foreign Affairs: Spyros Kyprianou
Minister of Health: Dr Niazi Maniera
Minister of Health: Michael Glykys†
Minister of Defence: Osman Orek
Minister of Communications and Works: Nicos Roussos†
Minister of Labour and Social Insurance: Andreas Mavrommatis†
Minister of Agriculture and Natural Resources: Fazil Plumer
Minister of Agriculture and Natural Resources: Panayiotis Toumazis†
Minister of Finance: Andreas Patsalides†
Minister of Justice: Georghios Ioannides†
Minister of Education: Frixos Petrides†

TURKISH COMMUNAL CHAMBER
President of the Chamber: Rauf Denktash

---

* The prefix 'His Excellency' is generally used for Ministers.
† Appointed by President acting alone. (This also includes the additional acting capacities of the Minister of the Interior.)

PRESIDENT'S STAFF
Under-Secretary: Patroclos Stavrou

VICE-PRESIDENT'S STAFF
Under-Secretary: H. K. Nidai

HOUSE OF REPRESENTATIVES
President: Glafcos Clerides
Director-General: Chr. Haji Ioannou (acting)

COUNCIL OF MINISTERS SECRETARIAT
Joint-Secretary: A. Andronikou

JUDICIARY
SUPREME CONSTITUTIONAL COURT
(In Abeyance)

HIGH COURT
(In Abeyance)

SUPREME COURT
President: The Hon. Mr Justice G. Vassiliades

Judges:
The Hon. Mr Justice M. Triantafyllides
The Hon. Mr Justice J. P. Josephides
The Hon. Mr Justice M. N. Munir, OBE
The Hon. Mr Justice A. S. Stavrinides
The Hon. Mr Justice Loizos N. Loizou
The Hon. Mr Justice T. Hadjianastassiou
Registrar: A. S. Olympios

THE INDEPENDENT OFFICERS OF THE REPUBLIC
Attorney-General: C. Tornaritis, QC
Deputy Attorney-General: O. Feridun
Auditor-General: R. Z. Tatar
Deputy Auditor-General: I. Stathis

MINISTRIES AND GOVERNMENT DEPARTMENTS

MINISTRY OF AGRICULTURE AND
NATURAL RESOURCES
Director-General: R. Michaelides
Director of Agriculture: Dr A. A. Papasolomontos
Director of Animal Husbandry: I. Papadopoulos
Director of Veterinary Services: K. Polydorou

Forest Department
Director: G. Secaphim

Water Development Department
Director: Chr. Konteatis

Agricultural Research Institute
Director: Th. Christou

MINISTRY OF COMMUNICATIONS
AND WORKS
Director-General: P. M. Kazamias

Department of Civil Aviation
Director of Civil Aviation: L. Xenopoulos

Public Works Department
Chief Engineer: E. L. Symeonides

Department of Antiquities
Director of Antiquities: Dr V. Karagheorghis

Post and Telegraphs Department
Director of Posts and Telegraphs: P. Hadjioannou

Ports Services
Director of Ports: A. Kantounas

MINISTRY OF COMMERCE AND INDUSTRY
Director-General: G. Eliades
Senior Officer, Internal Trade, Imports: A. Thrasyvoulides
Senior Officer, Exports, Marketing and Quality Control: A. Koupparis
Senior Officer, Tourism: C. Montis
Senior Officer, Industries: A. Kontolemis
Official Receiver and Registrar: T. L. Christodoulides
Co-operative Development Department Commissioner: A. Azinas

Department of Geological Survey
Director of Geological Survey: Y. Hadjistavrinou (acting)

Mines Department
Senior Mines Officer: P. G. Petropoulos

MINISTRY OF DEFENCE
Director-General: A. Olgun

MINISTRY OF FINANCE
Director-General: G. T. Phylaktis
Director-General, Planning Commission: (vacant)

Treasury
Accountant-General: S. Z. Nathanael

Department of Customs
Director: T. Georghiou

Department of Inland Revenue
Commissioner of Taxes: A. N. Apostolides

Establishment Department
Director of the Department of Personnel: G. S. Olympios

Department of Statistics
Director of Statistics and Research: A. Menelaou

Printing Department
Government Printer: (vacant)

MINISTRY OF FOREIGN AFFAIRS
Director-General: Chr. Veniamin
Deputy Director-General: G. Pelaghias

MINISTRY OF HEALTH
Director-General: Dr V. Vassilopoullos
Director of Medical Services: Dr M. Economo-Poulos

MINISTRY OF THE INTERIOR
Director-General: A. Anastasiou
Migration Officer: D. Karakoulas

Department of Lands and Surveys
Director of Lands and Surveys: G. Ph. Avraamides

Department of Town Planning and Housing
Director: C. Ioannides (acting)

Police
Commander of Police: S. Antoniou (Acting)

Public Information Office
Director: M. Christodoulou

Cyprus Broadcasting Corporation
Director-General: A. Christofides
Director of Television: G. Mitsides

District Officers
Nicosia and Kyrenia: Chr. Kythreotis
Famagusta: D. Paralikis
Larnaca: Z. Vyronides
Limassol: Ph. Zachariades
Paphos: K. Stefanides

MINISTRY OF JUSTICE
Director-General: A. Kephalas (acting)

Prisons
Chief Superintendent of Prisons: O. Antoniou

MINISTRY OF LABOUR AND SOCIAL INSURANCE
Director-General: M. D. Sparsis
Senior Employment Officer: A. Protopapas
Senior Inspector of Factories: G. M. Callimachos
Senior Industrial Relations Officer: E. Constantinides
Director of Social Insurance Officer: J. Robson
Cyprus Productivity Centre Director: S. Theocharides

Department of Welfare
Chief Welfare Officer: C. Vakis

CYPRUS ARMY
Commander, Cyprus Army: (vacant)

MINISTRY OF EDUCATION
Director-General: P. K. Adamides

Director of Education: A. Kouros

Cultural Development Department
Director: Chr. Papachrysostomou

DEPARTMENT OF TURKISH COMMUNAL CHAMBER
Co-operatives Department
Director: Djahit Tilki

Education Office
Acting Director: M. A. Raif

Finance Department
Director of Finance: Selcuk Egemen

DIPLOMATIC REPRESENTATION

CYPRUS REPRESENTATIVES IN OTHER COMMONWEALTH COUNTRIES
Britain: Costas Ashiotis, MBE (High Commissioner); Canada: Zenon Rossides (resident in New York); Ghana: G. M. Nicolaides (Hon. Consul); Nigeria: C. P. Leventis (Hon. Consul); Uganda: Andreas N. Roussos (Hon. Consul).

COMMONWEALTH HIGH COMMISSIONERS IN CYPRUS
Britain: R. G. H. Edmonds, CMG, MBE; Canada: G. E. McGaughey; (resident in Tel Aviv); India: Avatar Krishna Dar (resident in Beirut); Pakistan: M. Rabb (resident in Beirut).

CYPRUS REPRESENTATION IN NON-COMMONWEALTH COUNTRIES
Argentina (Hon. Consul), (Ambassador—non-resident); Austria (Hon. Consul); Brazil (Ambassador) (resident in New York); Cameroons (Hon. Consul); Chile (resident in New York); Congo (Lubumbashi) (Hon. Consul); Congo (Kinshasa) (Hon. Consul); Czechoslovakia (resident in Moscow); Denmark (Hon. Consul-General); Ethiopia (Hon. Consul); Finland (Hon. Consul), Ambassador (resident in Moscow); France (Hon. Consul General) Paris, (Hon. Consul) Marseilles, (Hon. Consul) Lyons; Germany (Ambassador), (Hon. Consul General)

Hamburg; Ghana (Hon. Consul); Greece (Ambassador); Italy (Ambassador) (resident in Athens), (Hon. Consul General); Rome, (Hon Consul) Genoa; Ivory Coast (Hon. Consul); Kuwait (Hon. Consul); Mexico (Hon. Consul) resident in New York); Norway (Hon. Consul); Panama (Hon. Consul); Paraguay (resident in New York);

Sweden (Hon. Consul); Switzerland (Hon. Consul General); Turkey (Ambassador); United Arab Republic (Ambassador); United Nations (Permanent Representative); United States (Ambassador), (Hon. Consul) Boston; Uruguay (resident in New York); U.S.S.R. (Ambassador); Yugoslavia (Ambassador) (resident in Athens).

FIJI

FIJI has a total area of approximately 7,095 square miles and comprises 844 islands and islets including numerous atolls and reefs. About 100 islands are permanently inhabited but many more are used by Fijians for planting food crops or as temporary residences during the turtle fishing season.

The largest islands are Viti Levu, 4,010 square miles, and Vanua Levu 2,137 square miles. The main archipelago lies between latitudes 15° and 22° South and longitudes 175° East and 177° West. The island of Rotuma (17 square miles) and its dependencies were added to the territory in 1881 and are geographically separate. They lie between latitudes 12° and 15° South and longitudes 175° and 180° East.

Suva, the capital and chief port, is 1,148 miles by air from Auckland, 1,738 from Sydney, 3,183 from Honolulu and 5,611 miles from San Francisco.

With the exception of the islands of Kadavu and of the Koro Sea, the islands of Fiji rise from two submerged platforms. The western platform is the broader and from it rise the islands of Viti Levu, Vanua Levu, Taveuni, Kadavu, and the Lomaiviti and Yasawa groups. The numerous islands of the Lau group are scattered across more than 44,000 square miles, and are based on the elongated and narrower eastern platform. The two platforms are joined by a narrow ridge which lies athwart the deep Nanuku Passage; north of this passage the ocean floor drops steeply to depths of over 5,000 feet.

Most of the larger islands are 'high' islands with sharp peaks and crags, but they have conspicuous areas of flat land as many of the rivers have built extensive deltas.

Viti Levu is the third largest island in the 'open Pacific' (only New Caledonia and Hawaii are larger). The interior is mountainous. The highest peak is Mount Victoria (4,341 feet) but 29 other peaks exceed 3,000 feet. The main axis trends north-south across the island. On both sides of the mountain axis are tracts of broken highland, rimmed in many places by ranges of hills with precipitous seaward-facing slopes. The main rivers are the Rewa, Sigatoka, Navua, Nadi and Ba. The largest of these, the Rewa, is formed of four main streams—the Wainibuka, Wainimala, Waidina and the Waimanu, and a multitude of minor tributaries. It drains a third of the island of Viti Levu and is navigable for about 70 miles by small boats. The lower reaches of the main rivers provide fertile alluvial flats and fan out into substantial deltas. The island of Vanua Levu is also mountainous. The most intensively cultivated areas are in the lower reaches of the Labasa valley which drains northwards. The island of Taveuni (168 square miles), a wholly volcanic island, has rich deep soils and is noted for its flourishing coconut plantations.

The innumerable small islands vary considerably in structure and form and a great number consist wholly or partly of limestone. They generally rise steeply from the shore and have flat-topped profiles; wherever the limestone is exposed it is eroded into pinnacles or deeply honeycombed. Coral reefs surround many of the islands. In Fiji barrier reefs occur at the seaward edge of the submarine platform and on the outer margins of the large shore flats; the most extensive is the Great Sea Reef which extends with only a few navigable passages for nearly 300 miles along the western fringe of the archipelago.

Temperatures at Suva and at other sea-level stations are high throughout the year but are tempered by the ocean and the territory has all the advantages of a tropical climate without undue extremes of heat. At Suva the mean maximum temperature is 86·6°F (February) and the mean minimum is 68·1°F (July). The prevailing winds are the Trades which blow steadily and with little interruption throughout the greater part of the year and are generally easterly or south-easterly. Wind direction is more variable in the so-called wet season, between November and March or April, when the inter-tropical front reaches farthest south. It is during these months that tropical cyclonic storms or hurricanes are most likely to develop.

The annual rainfall totals vary according to exposure and the windward areas enjoy abundant rainfall, well distributed throughout the year. The leeward (that is north-western) sides have well defined wet and dry seasons.

Conditions at Suva are typical of windward locations not only on Viti Levu but also on Vanua Levu, Kadavu and Taveuni. Its average annual rainfall is 123 inches, most of which falls between November and March. Stations at sea level on the leeward sides have mean annual totals of between 70 and 80 inches, most of which fall during the hurricane season when variable winds blow. In the dry season the leeward sides, particularly on Vanua Levu and Viti Levu, have clear skies, low humidity and a considerable diurnal range of temperatures so that the evenings are quite cool.

The mountains on the larger islands are often shrouded in mist and cloud and receive annual rainfall totals of 300 inches. On the other hand, the small low islands have a moderate rainfall evenly distributed throughout the year and temperatures are more equable. There is a great contrast in vegetation cover between the windward sides of the larger islands with its evergreen rain forest, and the dry leeward sides with its mainly treeless 'talasiga' land. Tropical rain forest extends up the sides of even the highest mountains. Much however has been destroyed and much cultivated and allowed to revert to secondary forest, bamboo and reeds. Mangrove swamps flourish in the deltas and along the shores. The many small coral and limestone islands have little spontaneous vegetation because of their thin sandy soils.

The total population at the last census, which was on 12th September 1966, was 476,727. This was made up as follows: Fijian 202,176 (42·41 per cent), Indian 240,960 (50·55 per cent), European 6,590 (1·38 per cent), Part-European 9,687 (2·03 per cent), Chinese 5,149 (1·08 per cent) and other Pacific Islanders 12,165 (2·55 per cent). At the end of 1970, the estimated total population was 524,457, an increase of about 9·8 percent. This was made up as follows: Fijians: 225,102 (43 per cent); Indians: 266,189 (51 per cent); Europeans: 5,286 (1·01 per cent); Part-Europeans: 9,523 (1·82 per cent); Rotumans: 6,512 (1·24 per cent); Chinese: 5,008 (0·95 per cent); Other Pacific Islanders: 6,837 (1·30 per cent).

English, Fijian and Hindustani are the main languages. English is the official language and the medium of instruction in all secondary schools.

The main religions are Christianity, Hinduism and Islam.

Registration of births in 1970 totalled 15,546. This was made up as follows: Fijian 6,303; Indian 8,144 and 1,099 others. These figures emphasised the success of the family planning campaign and represented a birth rate of 28·97 per 1,000. A target birth rate of 25 per 1,000 by 1972 has been set.

Fiji's isolation has kept it free from the major tropical diseases and the general health of the population is good. Tuberculosis, though waning, is still the main public health problem in the territory and the total number of new cases registered in 1969 was 358, a decrease from 541 cases in 1968. The decrease emphasised the success of the mobile Survey Units which have now covered the whole colony.

Clinical services are provided almost entirely by the Medical Department and the few private practitioners have concentrated mainly in the larger centres of population. The facilities available for the provision of services consist of 45 health centres in the charge of locally qualified medical officers, eight rural hospitals, six district hospitals which provide services similar to those of rural hospitals but at a slightly higher level, and four divisional hospitals which admit patients from the immediate area and also act as centres of referral from the rural and district hospitals with their divisions. In addition, there are three special hospitals in the territory for the treatment respectively of tuberculosis, leprosy and mental illness and a further hospital which is maintained by the Methodist Mission. Clinical servies are also provided by district nurses in the more sparsely populated rural areas of the territory. These nurses provide midwifery and child health services and emergency first aid treatment where no doctor is available. Consolidation of nursing stations with dispensaries to form health centres has permitted the reduction of the number of nursing stations from about 120 to 70. In urban and the more thickly populated rural areas, maternal and child health services, with which are integrated family planning facilities, are provided in hospitals and health centres and through mobile clinics.

Government spending on medical services in 1969 was estimated at $3,145,737.

Voluntary bodies are responsible for the maintenance of the great majority of the territory's schools and while education is not yet free it is heavily subsidised by the Government.

Primary schools are staffed in the main by government teachers and grants are paid towards the salaries of untrained teachers where trained ones are not available. Grants are also payable to controlling authorities to enable them to remit fees in necessitous cases, and supplies of basic textbooks are issued free to all primary schools. At the secondary level assistance takes the form of grant-in-aid including the posting of government teachers to non-government schools, and provision for free or partly free places. All schools are eligible to receive building grants and there is provision for some assistance for school hostels.

While primary education is not universal, an estimated 86 per cent of children of school age were in school in 1969 and it is estimated that a further 3 per cent of these children will be admitted in future while a considerable, though steadily declining proportion of them have attended school but have left before completing the eight-year course.

The secondary academic course lasts for 4 to 5 years, leading through the Fiji Junior Certificate examination in the second year to the New Zealand or Cambridge School Certificate examination in the 3rd or 4th year and the New Zealand

University Entrance examination in the 4th or 5th year. Post University Entrance courses are provided at the University of the South Pacific.

In 1969 there were six government, 26 grant-aided and 23 private secondary schools, attended by 13,795 pupils. In addition 951 followed technical or vocational courses at this level and 322 attended the three primary teacher-training colleges.

The labour force is comprised mainly of Fijians and Indians and in 1970 there were approximately 34,200 people in paid employment, excluding domestic servants and casual labourers. The construction and engineering industries employ the largest percentage of the labour force, but large percentages are also employed in manufacturing and crafts, agriculture and fishing.

At the end of 1969 there was a total of 30 registered trade unions and it is estimated that more than half of the persons in wage-earning employment were members of one or the other.

The main crops produced are sugar, copra and bananas. During the year 1970 cane crops harvested were 2,840,395 tons; about 355,147 tons of raw sugar were produced and 324,785 tons valued at approximately F$31,492,228 were exported.

Production of copra in 1970 was 28,000 tons of which 1,060 tons valued at F$180,000 were exported. About 7,073 tons of oil-seed cake and meal valued at F$383,000 and 18,704 tons of coconut oil valued at F$5,130,000 were exported. Banana exports to New Zealand in 1970 totalled 79,740 cases valued at $253,000.

Figures for livestock are: cattle 140,447; pigs 24,448; goats 66,151 and 24,769 horses. Beef production in 1970 totalled 8,089,000 lbs; an increase of 3 per cent from the total output in 1969 (7,878,000 lbs). The total pork output in 1970 was 558,000 lbs, an increase of 1 per cent from the 1969 output of 553,000 lbs.

During 1970 about 3,881,000 cubic feet of round timber was produced.

The principal mineral resources at present being exploited are gold, silver and manganese ore.

Exports in 1970 were as follows:

				Value ($ f.o.b.)	Unit Price ($ f.o.b.)
Raw Sugar	..	tons	..	328,819	31,799,078	96·71
Coconut Oil	..	tons	..	18,704	5,130,000	274·27
Gold, Refined	..	fine oz.	..	107,632	3,349,000	31·12
Molasses	..	tons	..	91,381	479,536	5·25
Expeller Pellets	..	tons	..	7,073	383,000	54·15
Bananas	..	Case (72 lb)	..	79,740	235,000	3·17
Copra	..	tons	..	1,060	180,000	169·81
Silver	..	fine oz.	..	26,983	42,000	1·56

PROVISIONAL TRADE FIGURES 1970

					($F)
Total Imports	..	..	..	..	88,540,427
Total Exports (Inc. Re-exports)			..		58,939,473
Trade Deficit	..	..	..	..	—29,600,954

The trade deficit was offset by earnings of $24·3 million from tourism.

Copper metal is contained in telluride concentrates exported from the Emperor Gold Mine. Copper concentrates were produced from the Udu Copper Mine which was closed down due to the exhaustion of ore reserves.

The ports of entry of the territory are Suva, Lautoka and Levuka. Other places of call are Labasa, Vuda Point, Vatia, Ellington, Savusavu and Naikorokoro. During 1970 Suva handled 433,632 tons of cargo and the remainder of the ports 774,551 tons.

During the year 1969 the main imports were: food, drink and tobacco F$16,965,412; mineral fuels, lubricants etc. F$8,376,461; chemicals F$5,116,522; fibres, yarns, textiles and related products F$15,316,276; machinery and transport equipment F$16,760,933; miscellaneous manufactured articles F$11,548,284. The principal countries of origin of imports during 1969 were: Australia F$19,654,448; United Kingdom F$15,456,791; Japan F$11,058,639; New Zealand F$7,264,726; USA F$3,690,196; Hong Kong F$2,804,066; Iran F$2,656,643; Singapore F$2,546,217; South Korea F$1,895,109; India F$1,375,812; Aden F$1,084,376; Federal Germany F$903,714; Canada F$835,688 and Switzerland F$667,653. In February 1969, decimal currency was introduced into Fiji. The Fiji dollar has parity with the Australian dollar. (F$2.09=£ stg 1).

Nadi International Airport, some four miles from Nadi township on the western coast of Viti Levu, comprises one of the largest airport complexes in the South Pacific. The airport has two runways, one 10,700 feet and the other 7,000 feet by 150 feet in width. Located in the airport control tower is the Fiji Flight Information Centre which is responsible for all flights within the airspace of the Fiji Flight Information Region. The South Pacific main meteorological office is situated on the airport and apart from collecting weather observations over a large area of the South Pacific on a 24-hour basis provides route and terminal forecasts for all trunk route regional aircraft operating in the area. Weather forecasts are provided for shipping as well as weather information for Fiji and other territories in the area. A Rescue Co-ordination Centre forms part of the airport complex and the whole is served by a comprehensive communications centre which provides communication connections on a world-wide basis. The trunk route operators providing services through Nadi Airport are Qantas, Air New Zealand, BOAC, Pan American, UTA, Air India, American Airlines and CPA. Connections are provided to Sydney, Auckland, Hawaii, Tahiti, New Caledonia on routes East and West to Europe via USA, Canada, Mexico and the Middle and Far East, and services via Sydney—Perth to South Africa, Sydney to the Far East or Middle East and Noumea to Singapore, the Middle East and Europe. Nadi Airport is the traffic centre of the South Pacific.

Suva, which is approximately 132 miles from Nadi by road, is served by Nausori Airport which is 14 miles from Suva. Nausori Airport is an international, regional and domestic airport and the operational and maintenance base of Air Pacific. It has a runway 6,000 feet in length and equipped for night operations. Air Pacific operates regional services to Western Samoa, the Kingdom of Tonga and the Western Pacific High Commission territories of the British Solomon Islands Protectorate, the Gilbert and Ellice Islands, the New Hebrides, Port Moresby in Papua, New Guinea and the newly independent island of Nauru. Polynesian Airlines of Western Samoa operates services between Apia, Nadi and Tonga using DC.3 aircraft. Air Pacific operate a fleet comprising three HS.748s, two DC.3s and three Herons. In the Gilbert Islands, Air Pacific operate domestic services, using a Heron aircraft based at Tarawa.

The major shareholders of Air Pacific are Qantas, BOAC, Air New Zealand and the Fiji Government. The Western Pacific High Commission, Kingdom of Tonga and the Republic of Nauru have now taken up shares in the Airline. There has been an exchange of shares between Air Pacific and Polynesian Airlines with Air Pacific having taken over the management of Polynesian Airlines. All the new shareholders have representation on the Board of Air Pacific which is now regarded as the Airline of the territories which it serves. Domestic services are operated from Nausori to Nadi, Labasa and Savusavu on Vanua Levu and Matei on Taveuni.

Fiji Air Services now have a fleet of three Beech 'Baron' aircraft. These aircraft provide a 'second line' operation within Fiji and permit services to outer islands, and give connections to Ovalau, Ba, Korolevu and Natadola. The 'Baron' aircraft are used for aerial photography and geological survey on behalf of the Government.

The South Pacific Sugar Mills Limited owns the only railway in the territory, which consists of approximately 400 miles of permanent line with a 2 feet gauge, and about 260 miles of portable line. The territory possesses 664 miles of main roads, 230 miles of secondary roads, 526 miles of country roads and 18·5 miles of residential roads, all of which are maintained by the Government. In addition to these roads there are approximately 86 miles of urban roads which are maintained by local authorities.

Broadcasting is conducted by the Fiji Broadcasting Commission which was established by statute.

Individuals are liable for the payment of income tax which ranges from 6·25c. to 30c. in the dollar. There is a basic tax of 2·5c. in the dollar on all income, both individual and company, before any deduction for personal allowance. Provision is made for personal, married, dependent children and widows' allowances and contributions to approved superannuation funds and life insurance premium payments may be claimed up to a maximum amount of one-fifth of the income. The P.A.Y.E. system operates in respect of earned income and a provisional tax system in respect of other income of individuals. Surtax is charged on the chargeable income of individuals in excess of $4,000 commencing at the rate of 5c. in the dollar of incomes between $4,000 and $8,000 the rate increasing by 5c. in stages until the maximum surtax payable is 30c. in the dollar on income in excess of $40,000. In addition, a surcharge of 5 per cent is at present payable on all normal tax, surtax and company tax.

Non-Fiji shipping companies pay 2c. in the dollar on total outward freight and passages earned. Non-Fiji mutual insurance companies pay 22·5c. in each dollar of chargeable income in respect of mutual life insurance business. Other companies pay 28·75c. in the dollar on all income whether distributed or not.

A dividend tax at the rate of 5 per cent of the gross amount of the dividend is deducted by a company incorporated in Fiji upon payment of the dividend to its shareholders who are resident in Fiji. Where shareholders are not resident in Fiji a dividend tax at the rate of 15 per cent of gross amount of dividend is deducted by a company upon payment of dividend to shareholders. This is the final charge to Fiji income tax upon such a dividend.

Any company whose operations are considered by the Governor to contribute to the economic development of Fiji is exempted from the payment of company and basic tax on all its profits from the approved enterprise for a five-year period, from the date of commencement of production.

In 1970 Government revenue was F$42,089,000 and expenditure F$39,854,000.

DEVELOPMENT PLANNING

Performance of Development Plan V (1966–1970)

The overall growth of the economy during the Development Plan V period was close to the target set. The rates of growth of the tourist and services sectors were much higher than envisaged in Development Plan V. Agriculture achieved an average rate of growth of only 2·7 per cent but a target rate of 5·4 per cent had been set.

Following the sugar boom of 1963–64 the economy went into a slight recession during 1965–66. The upturn in economic activity since 1967 was due to three main factors:—

    (i) a continued increase in government expenditure;

    (ii) the rapid expansion of the tourist industry; and

    (iii) the rapid expansion in the building and construction sector.

It is significant that this upturn occurred despite low international prices for sugar and poor results from the other principal agricultural crops.

The annual rate of growth in population was 2·5 per cent as against a projected rate of 2·8 per cent. The continuing fall in population growth will only begin to affect the growth in the labour force in the eighties. During the plan period itself, the employment situation deteriorated. This problem now demands urgent consideration.

Development Plan VI (1971–75)

A Development Plan for the period 1971–1975 has been prepared. The experiences of the Development Plan V period have been valuable and Development Plan VI will attempt to avoid some of the important factors that were overlooked.

The target rate of growth of gross domestic product for the 1971–1975 development period is 6·5 per cent per annum. This implies an increase in GDP from about F$169 million in 1970 to F$234 million in 1975 (at 1970 prices). The Plan places high priorities on the objectives of increasing employment and improving the present unequal distribution of income in Fiji. In particular improvement in the standard of living in rural areas will be given special emphasis. A detailed rural development programme is under way. Emphasis will be given to agricultural development. Such a programme, by making life in rural areas more attractive, will help to contain the drift to urban areas.

Agriculture is expected to grow at an average annual rate of 3·5 per cent. Tourism and Building and Construction are expected to be particularly buoyant and a growth rate at 17 per cent and 11 per cent per annum respectively is predicted.

Private consumption is projected to grow at about 5·9 per cent per annum. The target annual rate of growth of total investments is 11·8 per cent. Government consumption will grow at about 9·0 per cent annually. Since population growth rate is expected to be about 2·5 per cent during the Development Plan period, private consumption per head will grow at about 3·4 per cent.

The commodity trade deficit is expected to worsen and will be over $60 million by 1975 (imports calculated on f.o.b. basis). Because of the expected rapid growth in tourist receipts, the balance in the goods and services account will be more favourable although still in deficit. This deficit balance is expected to be slightly more than $20 million by 1975. Fiji will therefore continue to be heavily dependent on capital inflow in order to be able to implement its plan.

Slightly more than 60 per cent of total investment will be financed through domestic sources. A revision of the tax system is called for. This revision will aim at increasing government savings for developmental purposes. Personal and corporate savings will account for a large proportion of total resources for investment.

Public investment will account for about 30 per cent of total investment during the plan period. Local borrowing will finance about 20 per cent of the government investment programme. A further 13 per cent will be met through government savings and the bulk of the remaining 67 per cent will depend on external resources for its implementation.

The plan emphasises the need for accelerating industrial development in Fiji. Government will continue to do all it can to improve the industrial investment climate. Generous concessions are available and will be given to investors according to laid down criteria.

Agriculture and Forestry will receive increased government attention during the plan period. Substantial increases in outputs of rice and copra are envisaged. Other minor crops will continue to be actively encouraged. The Forestry programme has the long-term aim of achieving internal self-sufficiency and building up an export market for local timber. An extensive planting programme will therefore be implemented during the plan period and beyond.

Tourism will receive every encouragement and is expected to continue its present high growth rate. Its impact on employment and in providing foreign exchange will be substantial.

Surveys

Plans for land surveys are in course of being formulated in co-operation with the Overseas Development Administration, Foreign and Commonwealth Office in London. They will include the establishment of a hydrological network.

A pre-investment survey of the Navua Plains has recently been completed by Huntings Technical Services; the recommendations include rice production under drainage and irrigation for some 5,000 acres. A UNDP/FAO team is currently undertaking a similar survey of the Rewa area. This project includes a 250-acre pilot irrigated rice scheme on the left bank of the Rewa River. It is hoped to make Fiji self-sufficient in rice before 1980 with irrigated production of up to some 13,000 acres at Navua and in the Rewa area.

It seems satisfactorily established that forestry and the further processing of forestry products offer one of Fiji's major development potentials. Fiji is endowed with the necessary conditions in the way of suitable land, favourable climatic and ecological conditions and suitable quick-growing species tested locally. It is estimated that there are up to 3,000 square miles of land having no competing agricultural claims which would support a planting programme of up to 50,000 acres per year of softwoods and hardwoods. The produce from plantings would have an annual export value of at least $40 million as roundwood, and if exported as processed products as pulp, paper or board would generate annual earnings of more than $200 million. A UNDP/FAO project is currently under way to investigate the forestry potential of Fiji. The purpose of the project was to prepare development plans and feasibility studies for the rational utilisation of forests and for the expansion of forest industries.

Transport presents one of the basic problems of Fiji. Due to the country's size, geographical structure and location, an efficient and co-ordinated transport infra-structure is an important development factor. Roads, air transport and inter-insular shipping must be fully integrated. The coastlines of the islands are still virtually undeveloped. Wharves, coastal roads and storage facilities are lacking or do not co-exist in an effective manner and shipping operations are therefore difficult, slow and expensive. A closer economic and social knitting-together of the islands will help in bringing about a more balanced development of the archipelago. A request to the United Nations Special Fund by the Fiji Government for a pre-investment survey of the national transport system was accepted and the survey was started late in 1966. The general purpose of the project was to assist in the fomulation of a phased programme for transport development during the next thirty years. The UN survey team has completed its survey and its report is now under consideration.

With the exception of a gold mine employing some 1,600 men and productive exports worth $3,349,000 there has been little mining activity in Fiji. In recent years, however, there has been a considerable increase in exploration activity. The Government encourages exploration by well-established and experienced companies and care is taken to avoid undue fragmentation. A number of large overseas mining companies are now engaged in exploration programmes involving relatively high levels of expenditure and increasing use is being made of advanced geochemical and geophysical techniques. Airborne geophysics are currently being employed for the first time in Fiji in a regional exploration programme undertaken by a private exploration company in association with the Government.

Consequent on the reports of oil seepages in Tonga several oil companies applied for the right to search for oil in off-shore areas of Fiji. One oil exploration licence had been issued by the end of 1969 and several others were under consideration. The off-shore oil exploration policy has the objective of obtaining a diversified exploration programme by several separate exploration companies each holding a licensed area of some 3,000 sq. miles and committed to expenditure of some $2,000,000 in the first five years.

HISTORY

The first European navigator to discover the Fiji islands was Abel Tasman, whose two little ships, the *Heemskerck* and the *Zeehaen*, sailed through the north-eastern part of the archipelago in 1643. They sighted about a dozen islands but found no anchorage and did not land. The Dutch authorities at Batavia showed little interest in the discovery. In 1774, after visiting Tonga, Captain James Cook sighted the lone southern island of Vatoa while bound for the New Hebrides. A landing party left gifts for the natives, who had fled from the shore, and Cook sailed off to the south-west, passing south of the Moala and Kandavu groups without seeing them.

In April 1789, the crew of H.M.S. *Bounty* mutinied near Tofua, Tonga. Lieutenant Bligh and 18 loyal officers and men were cast off in the ship's launch with a meagre supply of bread and water and four cutlasses. The launch could not be sailed against wind and sea back to Tahiti and Bligh set course for Timor in the Dutch East Indies, 3,600 miles to the west. The party sailed right through the Fijis, chased on several occasions by sailing canoes. Despite the hardships of the voyage, the overcrowding and the tossing of the 23-foot craft, Bligh managed to make rough charts of 39 of the islands, including Viti Levu. His observations were later shown to be substantially correct.

In the early years of the 19th century, 'Bligh's Islands' were still scarcely known. The search for sandalwood brought many ships to Vanua Levu, but although the course there from Tonga was known and regularly followed, it was only a narrow lane through a maze of unknown reefs and islands. No systematic survey of the archipelago was made until the middle of the century. Soon American ships and East Indiamen were competing for sandalwood cargoes. The trade lasted less than 10 years but it left its mark. Deserters and shipwrecked men stayed as beachcombers; firearms salvaged from wrecks were used in native wars with startling effect; new diseases swept through the islands; and rum and muskets became regular articles of trade.

Firearms, and white men to use them, were for a time the monopoly of the chiefs of Bau who, using muskets against clubs and spears, raised themselves to a dominant position which they held even after their rivals also had obtained firearms. Soon the political scene changed. The earlier native states had been small, and patriarchal in structure; their noisy quarrels had been the quarrels of children brandishing sticks, but now greedy men had given these children firearms. Fighting became more bloody and more general. Large confederacies or kingdoms grew up on the windward coasts and islands and their rivals fed the flames of war.

For nearly thirty years the only Europeans known to the Fijians were beachcombers and the crews of visiting ships. Then a different type of man appeared. Traders settled at Levuka and built small schooners for trading among the islands. Missionaries from Tonga arrived at Lakeba in 1835, having already reduced the language to writing, and soon young and old were learning to read. Other missionaries followed, bringing a printing press, but for more than 10 years there were few converts. When a few of the high chiefs were won over progress was more rapid.

Meanwhile, ships came seeking bêche-de-mer and whalers called to take on supplies. There were attacks by Fijians, not always unprovoked, and there were inquiries and reprisals by French, American and British warships. Then, during the early fifties, the native wars reached a climax in the conflict between Bau and Rewa, in which Cakobau, at this time the most powerful chief in the islands, was driven back on Bau, deserted by many of his followers, and threatened with defeat and death. He renounced his ancient gods in April 1854, and thereafter the character of the war changed. It became a struggle between the old ways and the new with Cakobau now the champion of the missionaries. The issue was decided by the timely arrival of King George of Tonga with 2,000 warriors and at Kaba in April 1855 the combined forces of Bau and Tonga were completely successful and Cakobau became the paramount chief of western Fiji. But he owed his position to Tongan help, and for 20 years he lived under the shadow of Tongan domination. The Tongan prince, Ma'afu who came to Fiji in 1848, gained within a few years a position equal to that of Cakobau himself. As for the issue between the old ways of life and the new, the religion of the Chief became the religion of the people. Cannibalism and savage practices ceased in western Fiji.

In 1857 a British Consul was appointed at Levuka. Within a month of his arrival an American warship came to demand of Cakobau the payment of indemnities fixed three years before for outrages suffered by American citizens.

The harassed chief sought relief by offering to cede the government of his dominions to Great Britain, the principal condition being the payment of the American claims (about £9,000) in consideration of which he offered 200,000 acres of land. The consul went to London, taking a deed of cession. A year later he returned to find the islands in a state of turmoil owing to Tongan aggressions. Having restored order he went far beyond his powers as consul in assuming administrative responsibilities, generally with good results. In 1860 an officer was sent from England to investigate the offer of cession, but advised against its acceptance. In 1862 it was declined and the consul was recalled.

Meanwhile, settlers had been arriving from the Australasian colonies. A few returned when they saw the true state of things, but many stayed to establish the first cotton plantations or to pasture sheep. All needed land and labour and difficulties arose owing to the lack of any organised government. In 1865 the high chiefs were induced to unite in a confederacy of independent chiefs, but this fell to pieces after a year or so. The need for some form of government was now greater than ever, and in 1867 Ma'afu successfully established the Confederation of North and East Fiji. Cakobau replied by setting up a Kingdom of Bau on an ambitious scale, but after a few years the constitution was largely a dead letter. An attempt was made two years later to revive it, but without success.

The American civil war caused a boom in cotton prices and exports rose rapidly. New settlers arrived and to augment local labour supplies men were imported from the New Hebrides and the Solomon Islands. This prosperity brought problems with which the native government was unable to deal. There were abortive attempts by the settlers to establish some form of government, but these were largely concerned with security of life and property.

The merchants and middlemen of Levuka had most to gain from a stable government and in June 1871 a small group of them staged a *coup d'état*, setting themselves up as an administration under Cakobau's doubtful authority. Such an attempt by a few white men to govern their compatriots without their consent was bound to be resisted, and the main body of settlers opposed it from the first and with increasing bitterness. The Fijians for their part were passive. Their chiefs were relegated to a nominal position in the government; their people were treated merely as a source of revenue and of labour; and within two years whole districts had been reduced to a deplorable state.

By the end of 1873 a constitutional crisis developed: trade was almost at a standstill; the Treasury was empty and the country on the verge of bankruptcy; and some of the highest chiefs were considering secession. On three previous occasions, the intervention of British warships had kept the government from falling to pieces: now the chiefs appealed to Britain to bring order out of chaos. Sir Hercules Robinson thereupon visited Levuka as the Queen's representative. An unconditional deed of cession was drawn up and completed and in October 1874 Fiji was proclaimed a possession and dependency of the British Crown.

For about a year the new colony was administered by a provisional government with a skeleton staff of officials. However, early in 1875 an epidemic of measles raged through the islands, carrying off about a third of the population and when Sir Arthur Gordon arrived in June he found the Fijians generally dispirited and the hill tribes angry and unsettled. Trade was depressed, and the settlers' high hopes of annexation were unrealised. Revenue was far short of expectation, although temporary relief was given by an Imperial advance. In the face of so many pressing problems Gordon gave first place to restoring the confidence of the Fijians and his success was apparent when, early in 1876, a rebellion among the hill tribes of Viti Levu brought offers of help from loyal chiefs and people everywhere. The problem of native taxation was solved by a novel system of communal plantations, the taxes being paid in kind, but the settlers complained that this policy restricted their labour supply and robbed traders of their profits. Gordon, however, refused to sacrifice the interests of the Fijians to the immediate needs of planters and middlemen, and throughout his term he was subjected to bitter attack and obloquy. Nevertheless, he accomplished what he set out to do, confirming and protecting the Fijians in the ownership and occupancy of their lands, and ensuring for them a rightful place in their own country.

With loan money exhausted and sugar not yet fully replacing cotton as the main plantation crop, the early eighties were years of depression and of discontent among the planters. Efforts to secure a change of government by federation with Australia or New Zealand failed in 1883 and again in 1885. By that time, however, larger sugar mills were in operation and indentured labourers from India had been introduced. Despite a sharp fall in prices during 1886-87 exports of sugar reached 15,291 tons in 1890 and by 1900 they were twice as much and valued at £394,000. Exports of copra and bananas rose rapidly. In the general prosperity opposition was quieted and the attention of the Government was directed towards preventing the decline of the Fijian people. Among other measures adopted, Fijian youths were given a limited training as medical practitioners and by 1906 a sustained upward trend of the population became evident.

The turn of the century brought renewed agitation for federation with New Zealand, and when this issue was seen to be impracticable there was a demand for elective representation in the Legislative Council. This was granted for the European population in 1904. The improved economic position made other reforms possible: new lands were opened up, native taxation was lightened and a school was established for the sons of the chiefs. While much was also done to ameliorate the lot of the Indian indentured labourers, nevertheless there were alarming reports of social and moral evils among them. Investigators found that these evils were inherent in the indenture system and in 1917 the Government of India abolished it. All unexpired contracts were cancelled from the 1st January 1920 and after a period of unrest, owing mainly to the high cost of food, the Indians settled down as free cane-growers and farmers. The planters, on the other hand, fell on hard times: the price obtainable for their copra was uneconomic; an Australian tariff excluded their bananas; and their sugar estates were being cut up into small holdings for Indian growers.

The last forty years have seen considerable development, mainly along the lines suggested by these events. So far as the European section of the population is concerned, the centre of gravity has shifted from the plantations to the towns and industrial centres. The development of mining and secondary industries, and of special services, has brought many trained men from overseas: nevertheless, while the total population has increased substantially since 1921, the European section of it has increased to a lesser extent. The Fijians for their part have maintained a steady rate of increase. The coming into operation of the Fijian Affairs Ordinance in 1945 marked the beginning of a period in native administration when the Fijian people assumed greatly increased responsibility for the management of their own affairs, each province becoming in effect a unit of local government with its own councils, courts, treasury and executive officers.

The co-operative movement, which is gaining momentum, offers a practical means of enabling the people to retain the essential features of their traditional way of life and at the same time play their part in the economic life of the country and meet the impact of modern commerce.

The Indians, too, have prospered greatly. In twenty-five years their numbers doubled without any significant accretions from immigration and they are now the largest single section of the population. They are still settled mainly in or near the sugar producing areas, where there has been an increasing shortage of agricultural land for occupation by tenant farmers. Measures to make suitable land available, and at the same time to protect the interests of the Fijian owners by reserving amply for their present and future needs, were proposed by the Fijian Council of Chiefs and embodied in 1940 in an ordinance under which all Fijian lands were vested in a Board to be administered on behalf of and for the benefit of the native owners.

In the constitutional field there has been considerable progress. In 1929 Letters Patent granted elective representation in the Legislative Council to the Fiji Indians and eight years later they were granted equal representation with the Fijians and Europeans.

Economically there have been important changes. What was for long virtually a sugar economy has been broadened by the development of dairying and mixed farming; mining has become one of the principal industries, the Tavua field being among the major finds of the period anywhere in the world; and secondary industries have been soundly established. These developments have been reflected in increased revenue, making possible an extension of public works, education, sanitation, and medical services. In at least some of these fields Fiji has assumed a regional role in the south-western Pacific. The Fiji School of Medicine, the Fiji School of Agriculture, and the newly opened University of the South Pacific in Suva, all draw students from other English-speaking territories in the region; while the leprosy hospital at Makogai provides (though on a diminishing scale as the incidence of the disease declines) for patients from many other Pacific territories, and the Colonial War Memorial Hospital in Suva takes occasional patients from territories where medical facilities are less advanced than in Fiji. This central position has been strengthened by recent developments in sea and air communications, and Fiji has become a crossroads of the Pacific.

Rotuma, a dependency of Fiji discovered in 1791 when a search was being made for the mutineers of the *Bounty*, was offered to Great Britain by the three principal Rotuman chiefs in 1879 and was formally annexed on 13th May 1881.

CONSTITUTION

The Constitution is set out in the Fiji (Constitution) Order 1970. The Constitution contains provisions relating to the protection of fundamental rights and freedoms, the powers and duties of the Governor-General, the Cabinet, the House of Representatives, the Judiciary, the Public Service, and finance.

It provides that every person in Fiji regardless of race, place of origin, political opinion, colour, creed or sex is entitled to the fundamental rights of life, liberty, security of the person and the protection of the law, freedom of conscience, expression, assembly, and association; protection for the privacy of his home and other property and for the deprivation of property without compensation.

The enjoyment of these rights, however, is subject to the proviso that they do not prejudice the rights and freedom of others, or the public interest.

The Legislative Council is presided over by a Speaker who may be elected either from within the Council or from persons outside who are qualified to be elected to the Council. A Deputy Speaker must be elected from among the Legislative Council members.

Justice is administered by the Fiji Court of Appeal, the Supreme Court, the Magistrates' Courts of the First, Second and Third Classes and Provincial and Tikina (District) Courts. Appeals from the Courts of the territory in criminal and civil cases lie to the Judicial Committee of the Privy Council. At present the Constitution provides for the constitution of the Supreme Court of Fiji as a superior court of record presided over by the Chief Justice and such other Judges called Puisne Judges as may be appointed from time to time by Letters Patent.

The Supreme Court exercises within the territory all the jurisdiction, powers and authority which are vested in or capable of being exercised by Her Majesty's High Court of Justice in England.

The Fiji Court of Appeal has jurisdiction to hear and determine appeals from the Supreme Court and from the High Court of the Western Pacific. The Governor-General appoints legally qualified persons to hold Magistrates' Courts of the first class and fit and proper persons to hold courts of the second and third classes.

Charges against children and young persons unless they are jointly charged with adults are brought to juvenile courts. Provincial and Tikina (District) Courts constituted under the Fijian Affairs Ordinance exercise limited civil and criminal jurisdiction.

CONSTITUTIONAL DEVELOPMENT

A Constitutional Conference was held at Marlborough House in London from 20th April to 5th May 1970, attended by members of the British Government and Fiji political leaders at which it was agreed that Fiji would become independent on 10th October 1970—the 96th Anniversary of the Deed of Cession. The Fiji Delegation informed the Conference that Fiji would apply for membership of the Commonwealth on becoming independent. The Conference resulted in agreement on an Independence Constitution of which the main provisions are as follows:

Governor-General. The Queen will appoint a Governor-General as Her representative in Fiji.

The Cabinet. The Cabinet will consist of the Prime Minister, the Attorney-General, and any other Ministers whom the Governor-General might appoint on the advice of the Prime Minister. The Governor-General will also be required to appoint as Leader of the Opposition in the House of Representatives either the leader of the largest Opposition party or, if there were no such party, the person whose appointment would be most acceptable to the leaders in the House of the Opposition parties.

Parliament. The Fiji Parliament will consist of a Senate and a House of Representatives. The Senate will consist of 22 members—eight nominated by the Council of Chiefs, seven nominated by the Leader of the Opposition and one nominated by the Council of the island of Rotuma. Their appointments will be for a six-year term, except that, of the 22 nominated after independence, 11 will be appointed for a term of only three years. The President and Vice-President of the Senate will be elected from members who were neither Ministers nor Assistant Ministers. Upon Independence, the existing Legislative Council will become the

House of Representatives. Parliament will be dissolved five years after the date of the first sitting of the existing Legislative Council and a general election will be held for the 52 members of the new House of Representatives. They will be elected on the following basis: Fijian—12 members elected on the Fijian Communal Roll; 10 members elected by voters on the National Rolls. (The National Roll will consist of all registered electors on the three communal rolls). Indian—12 members elected by voters on the Indian Communal Roll; 10 members elected by voters on the National Roll. General—3 members elected by voters on the General Communal Roll; 5 members elected by voters on the National Roll. ('General' means persons who are neither Fijian nor Indian, e.g. Europeans). The House will elect a Speaker and a Deputy Speaker from among its non-ministerial members. The official language of Parliament will be English, but any member may also address the Chair in Fijian or Hindustani.

Constituencies. Fiji will be divided into 12 constituencies, each returning one communally-elected Fijian member; into 12 constituencies each returning one communally-elected Indian member; and into three constituencies each returning one communally-elected General member. For the National Roll elections there will be 10 constituencies, each returning a Fijian and an Indian member, and these will be combined into five pairs for the purpose of each returning one General member. Constituency boundaries will be delimited by a Constituency Boundaries Commission.

The Fiji Independence Bill was given an unopposed Second Reading by the newly elected House of Commons on 14th July 1970, and the Bill received the Royal Assent on 23rd July 1970.

LAND POLICY

Land in Fiji is owned by the Crown, private freeholders, and Fijians. The Crown owns 87,000 acres of freehold land plus a further 85,000 acres of land declared vacant by the Native Lands Commission and commonly known as Crown Land Schedule B, and 147,000 acres of Fijian land whose owning units have become extinct, known as Schedule A land. Much of the Schedule A land, plus some of the Schedule B, has been recommended for reservation for Fijian units which are short of land. Crown freehold may not be sold except in very special circumstances and only then with the approval of the Secretary of State. Crown land may be obtained by way of lease.

The area of land owned by Fijians is 3,748,000 acres, owned communally by more than 6,600 recognised land-owning units. Administrative control of it is vested in the Native Land Trust Board by virtue of the Native Land Trust Ordinance. The Board is presided over by the Governor and contains a majority of Fijian members. A proportion of Fijian land has been reserved from leasing under a policy of securing to the owners adequate lands to provide for their future needs. This reserved land may be leased only to members of the Fijian race. Fijian owned land outside reserve may be leased by the Native Land Trust Board to anyone.

In July of 1966 new legislation was passed giving tenants of agricultural land better security of tenure, protection against unduly high rents and certain rights of compensation when leases are not renewed to them on expiry. A minimum period of ten years is prescribed both for original leases and also for renewals of leases (of which there can be two).

GOVERNORS

1874	Sir Hercules Robinson, GCMG	1929	Sir Murchison Fletcher, KCMG. CBE
1875	The Hon. Sir Arthur Gordon, (later Lord Stanmore) GCMG	1936	Sir Arthur Richards (later Lord Milverton, GCMG)
1880	Sir George William Des Voeux, KCMG	1938	Sir Harry Luke, KCMG
		1942	Sir Phillip Mitchell, GCMG, MC
1887	Sir Charles Mitchell, KCMG	1945	Sir Alexander Grantham, GCMG
1888	Sir John Thurston, KCMG	1948	Sir Brian Freeston, KCMG, OBE
1897	Sir George O'Brien, KCMG	1952	Sir Roland Garvey, KCMG, KCVO, MBE
1902	Sir Henry Jackson, KCMG		
1904	Sir Everard Im Thurn, KCMG, KBE, CB	1958	Sir Kenneth Maddocks, KCMG, KCVO
1911	Sir Henry May, KCMG	1964	Sir Derek Jakeway, KCMG, OBE
1912	Sir Bickham Sweet-Escott, KCMG	1968	Sir Robert Foster, KCMG, KCVO
1918	Sir Cecil Rodwell, GCMG		(Governor-General since Independence on 10th October 1970)
1925	Sir Eyre Hutson, KCMG		

GOVERNMENT

THE CABINET

The Hon. Ratu Sir Kamisese Mara, KBE, Prime Minister
The Hon. J. N. Falvey, OBE, Attorney-General
The Hon. Ratu Sir E. T. T. Cakobau, KBE, OBE(Mil), MC, ED, Minister for Labour
Senator Ratu P. K. Ganilau, CMG, CVO, DSO, OBE, Minister for Home Affairs, Lands and Mineral Resources
The Hon. Vijay R. Singh, Minister for Commerce, Industry and Co-operatives
The Hon. C. A. Stinson, OBE, Minister for Communications, Works and Tourism
The Hon. D. W. Brown, MBE, Minister for Agriculture, Fisheries and Forests
The Hon. J. Mavoa, Minister for Social Services
The Hon. Ratu G. K. Cakobau, OBE, Minister for Fijian Affairs and Local Government
The Hon. W. M. Barrett, Minister for Finance
The Hon. Jone Naisara, Minister for Youth, Sports and Rural Development
The Hon. K. S. Reddy, Assistant Minister for Social Services
Mr R. T. Sanders, Secretary to the Cabinet

MEMBERS OF THE HOUSE OF REPRESENTATIVES

Speaker, the Hon. R. G. Q. Kermode
The Hon. Ratu Sir Kamisese Mara, KBE, Prime Minister
The Hon. J. N. Falvey, Attorney-General
The Hon. Ratu Sir E. T. T. Cakobau, KBE, OBE(Mil), MC, ED, Minister for Labour
The Hon. Vijay R. Singh, Minister for Commerce, Industry and Co-operatives
The Hon. C. A. Stinson, OBE, Minister for Communications, Works and Tourism
The Hon. D. W. Brown, MBE, Minister for Agriculture, Fisheries and Forests
The Hon. J. Mavoa, Minister for Social Services
The Hon. Ratu G. K. Cakobau, OBE, Minister for Fijian Affairs and Local Government
The Hon. W. M. Barrett, Minister for Finance
The Hon. Jone Naisara, Minister for Youth, Sports and Rural Development
The Hon. K. S. Reddy, Assistant Minister for Social Services
The Hon. Ratu D. Toganivalu, Assistant Minister, Prime Minister's Office
The Hon. E. Vuakatagane, Assistant Minister for Commerce, Industry and Co-operatives
The Hon. P. D. Naqasima, Assistant Minister for Communications, Works and Tourism
The Hon. Ratu W. Tonganivalu, Assistant Minister for Home Affairs, Lands and Mineral Resources
The Hon. Adi Losalini Dovi, Second Council of Chiefs Member
The Hon. H. B. Gibson, OBE, General Member Northern
The Hon. A. Lateef, MBE, Indian Member Central
The Hon. Mrs B. C. Livingston, General Member Western
The Hon. S. S. Momoivalu, Fijian Member for Lomaiviti/Kadavu
The Hon. U. Koroi, Fijian Member for Rewa/Suva
The Hon. Ratu J. B. Toganivalu, Fijian Member Western
The Hon. Ratu W. B. Toganivalu, Fijian Member for Tailevu
The Hon. S. N. Waqanivavalagi, Fijian Member for North-West Viti Levu
The Hon. R. H. Yarrow, JP, General Member for West Viti Levu
The Hon. H. W. W. Yee, Second General Member for Suva
The Hon. Dr W. L. Verrier, General Member Northern and Eastern
The Hon. S. M. Koya, Leader of the Opposition
The Hon. J. Madhavan, Indian Member for North-East Vanua Levu
The Hon. C. A. Shah, Indian Member for North-East Viti Levu
The Hon. Mrs I. Jai Narayan, Indian Member for Suva
The Hon. R. D. Patel, Indian Member for North-West Viti Levu
The Hon. K. C. Ramrakha, Indian Member for Tailevu/Rewa
The Hon. Ramjati Singh, Indian Member North-Eastern
The Hon. Ujagar Singh Indian Member for South Central Viti Levu.

G

CIVIL ESTABLISHMENT

Governor-General of Fiji: His Excellency Sir Robert Foster, GCMG, KCVO

OFFICE OF THE PRIME MINISTER
Secretary, Prime Minister's Office: R. T. Sanders
Secretary for the Public Service: C. Walker
Public Relations Officer: G. Rawnsley
Controller of Organisation and Establishments: V. D. Prasad
Commissioner: Northern Division: R. D. Dods
Commissioner: Central Division: A. F. Varea
Commissioner: Eastern Division: G. Mataika
Commissioner: Western Division: J. B. Takala
Commissioner of Police: R. T. M. Henry, MVO, OBE, QPM
Government Printer: T. Sanerive

CROWN LAW OFFICE
Attorney-General: J. N. Falvey, OBE
Solicitor-General: D. McLoughlin
Registrar-General: A. D. S. Anderson
Registrar of Titles: M. T. Khan

MINISTRY OF FINANCE
Secretary for Finance: M. Qionibaravi
Deputy Secretary (Finance and Treasury): G. Singh
Government Statistician: M. A. Sahib
Comptroller of Customs: C. F. Wooley
Commissioner of Inland Revenue: S. Singh
Controller of Government Supplies: W. B. Tagilala

MINISTRY OF FIJIAN AFFAIRS AND LOCAL GOVERNMENT
Secretary, Fijian Affairs and Local Government: J. Kamikamica

MINISTRY OF AGRICULTURE, FISHERIES AND FORESTS
Secretary for Agriculture, Fisheries and Forests: B. Vunibobo
Director of Agriculture: B. Vunibobo
Conservator of Forests: G. Watkins

Director of Geological Survey: D. Green.

MINISTRY OF HOME AFFAIRS, LANDS AND MINERAL RESOURCES
Secretary for Lands and Mineral Resources: R. H. Regnault
Secretary for Home Affairs: R. J. Ackland

MINISTRY OF SOCIAL SERVICES
Secretary for Social Services: R. W. Baker
Secretary, Medical Services: Dr C. H. Gurd
Director of Education: J. D. Gibson
Director of Medical Services: Dr Dharam Singh

MINISTRY OF COMMUNICATIONS, WORKS AND TOURISM
Secretary for Communications, Works and Tourism: R. M. Jenkins, MBE
Postmaster-General: K. E. Miles
Controller of Transport and Civil Aviation: J. V. Verran, DFC
Director of Public Works: J. P. Barron
Director of Marine: Captain P. G. Hough

MINISTRY OF LABOUR
Secretary/Commissioner of Labour: T. R. Vakatora

MINISTRY OF COMMERCE, INDUSTRY AND CO-OPERATIVES
Secretary for Commerce, Industry and Co-operatives: S. Nand

AUDIT DEPARTMENT
Director: T. Bhim

JUDICIARY
Chief Justice: Sir Clifford Hammett, KBE
Puisne Judge: M. Tikaram

DIPLOMATIC REPRESENTATION

FIJI REPRESENTATIVES IN OTHER COMMONWEALTH COUNTRIES
Britain: Josua R. Rabukawaqa, MVO, MBE (High Commissioner; Australia: Raman Nair MVO (High Commissioner); Canada: Semesa K. Sikivou, MBE (High Commissioner) (resident in New York).

COMMONWEALTH HIGH COMMISSIONERS IN FIJI
Australia: Rowen F. Osborn; Britain: J. R. Williams; Canada: A. R. Menzies (resident in Canberra); India: Bhagwan Singh; New Zealand: Sir John Te H. Grace, KBE, MVO; Pakistan: M. M. Abbas (resident in Canberra).

FIJI REPRESENTATIVES IN NON-COMMONWEALTH COUNTRIES
European Economic Community: Josua R. Rabukawaqa, MVO, MBE (Ambassador) (resident in London); United Nations (Permanent Representative) and United States (Ambassador); S. K. Sikivou, MBE (resident in New York).

FOREIGN REPRESENTATIVES IN FIJI
South Korea: Choon Sik Min (resident in Canberra); France: Count Christian de Nicolay (resident in Wellington); Israel: Mr Moshe Erell (resident in Canberra).

READING LIST

DERRICK, R. A. The Fiji Islands. *Government Printer*, Suva, Revised edition, 1957.

FURNAS, J. C. Anatomy of Paradise. *Gollancz*, London, 1950.

BELSHAW, Professor Cyril S. Under the Ivi Tree. *Routledge and Kegan Paul*, London, 1964.

BURNS, Sir Alan. Fiji. *H.M. Stationery Office*, London, 1963.

Handbook of Fiji, 1965, edited and compiled by Judy Tudor. *Pacific Publications Pty Ltd*, Sydney.

DERRICK, R. A. A History of Fiji, which deals with the period up to 1874. *Government Printer*, Suva.

LEGGE, J. D. Britain in Fiji, 1858-1880. *Macmillan*, London, 1958.

MILNER, G. B. Fijian Grammar. *Government Printer*, Suva, 1956.

SNOW, P. A. A Bibliography of Fiji, Tonga and Rotuma. *University of Miami Press*.

THOMSON, Basil. The Fijians. *Heineman*, London, 1908.

THE GAMBIA

THE GAMBIA lies on the west coast of Africa between latitudes 13° and 14° north of the equator. Surrounded by Senegal except at the coast, it is called after the River Gambia which it straddles for over 200 miles (as the crow flies) eastwards from the Atlantic Ocean to longitude 13° 45′ west of Greenwich. At the estuary its northern and southern boundaries are 30 miles apart, but from about 90 miles inland these narrow to enclose two ribbons of land, each only about 6 miles wide, which faithfully follow the winding course of the river, forming its north and south banks. The country's total area, land and water, is just over 4,000 sq. miles.

The river, one of the finest waterways in Africa, is The Gambia's principal geographical feature and indeed the background to its history and the source of its life. The capital and seaport of Bathurst, on the island of Banjul near its mouth, can accommodate ocean-going vessels of up to 26 feet draught, while smaller freighters of up to 17 feet draught can sail 120 miles upstream to the groundnut-handling township of Ka-ur.

The Gambian climate is of the two-season type. It is cool and dry from November to April, with temperatures sometimes as low as 60°F, but during the other half of the year it is hot and humid, the thermometer at midday up-river often going well beyond 100°F. The rain falls almost exclusively during the hot season, the annual average being about 40 inches although considerable fluctuations occur both from year to year and from place to place.

The city of Bathurst has its own form of local government. The rest of the country is divided for administrative purposes into five Divisions each with a Commissioner. The Divisions are sub-divided into Districts. The growth of representative local government is being fostered by gradually increasing the responsibilities of Area Councils, of which there are six. The names of these administrative units (with their headquarter towns indicated within brackets) and their populations at the last census in 1963 are:—

Bathurst	27,809
Western Division (Brikama)	67,601
Lower River Division (Mansakonko) ..	97,272
MacCarthy Island Division (Georgetown)	64,755
Upper River Division (Basse)	58,049
Total population	315,486

There is also an Assistant Commissioner situated at Kerewan for the North Bank section of the Lower River Division.

There are a number of tribes, the most important being the Mandingo (128,807); Fula (42,723); Woloff (40,805); Jola (22,046); and Serahuli (21,318). In Bathurst the Woloffs form the largest element, numbering 11,311. An influential community is that of the Akus (2,974), mainly descended from detribalized Africans liberated in the early nineteenth century during the campaign against the slave trade.

The official language is English and all State education, both at primary and secondary level, is in English, but each tribe has its own language. The principal vernacular languages are Mandinka and Woloff. There are numerous Muslim schools in which Arabic is taught for the better understanding of the Koran. The Christian Mission schools are Anglican, Methodist and Roman Catholic. There are relatively few Christians outside the Bathurst area, and in the Provinces there are large numbers of Muslims and some sections of the population retain their original animist beliefs.

There are 95 Primary Schools with an enrolment figure, for the 1970/71 school year, of 17,140, of whom 5,251 were girls. Secondary education is provided by three Senior Secondary Schools in Bathurst and one in Georgetown, with an enrolment of 1,494, of whom 418 were girls; by 15 Junior Secondary Schools providing education up to Form 4. There were 3,218 pupils, of whom 747 were girls. There is a Teachers' Training College in Yundum with 135 students of whom 104 were men and 29 women, and a Vocational Training Centre in Bathurst. Literacy rate is not known: in English it is estimated at 15 per cent; in Arabic 20 per cent.

The principal sea port at Bathurst has two Government-owned wharves for ocean-going vessels and a number of private jetties used mainly for the river trade. In 1970, 279 ocean-going ships, trawlers and yachts of a net registered tonnage of 579,211 tons called there.

Bathurst airport is at Yundum, 17 miles away from the town. The main runway is now 7,300 feet long. Internal communications are by road and river. There are 730 miles of motorable roads, of which 330 rank as all-season. There is no railway. Gambia Airways is a handling agency but owns no aircraft.

Bathurst port is served principally by ships of Elder Dempster Lines and other lines of the West African Shipping Conference (Palm Line, Guinea Gulf, Hoegh Line and Nigeria and Ghana national lines). Airlines flying scheduled services to Yundum airport are BUA Caledonian, Nigeria Airways and Air Senegal.

The Gambian Broadcasting Service opened in 1962 and is known as Radio Gambia. There is also a commercial broadcasting station called Radio Syd.

Well over 90 per cent of exports from The Gambia consists of groundnut products. The following table shows the exports during 1969/70:

	Nuts (shelled)	Oil	Meal	Other	Total
£	3,064,977	2,293,189	894,013	169,998	6,422,177

Imports in 1969/70 were valued at £7,123,146. In addition to groundnuts, Gambia farmers grow sorghum, millet and rice, the latter having now superseded millet in most of The Gambia as the principal crop for local consumption.

The Government financial year runs from July to June. The budget of the 1970/71 financial year proposed an expenditure of £4·04m. and revenue of £3·7m., the balance to be made up by surpluses from the 1969/70 account. The Development Programme to cover the four years from 1st July 1967 to 30th June 1971 proposes expenditure of up to £5 million, of which aid from Britain will account for £3·2 million in the form of an interest-free loan repayable over 25 years. In the Development Programme emphasis is being laid on agriculture and communications.

The Gambia Government contributes towards the following Commonwealth Institutions:

The Rothamstead Experimental Station
The Commonwealth Agricultural Bureau and Associated Activities.
The Committee of Information Phytosanitary Convention
The Commonwealth Forestry Association
The International African Migratory Locust Organisation
The West African Institute of Oil Palm Research
The United Nations Desert Locust Project
The Tropical Diseases Bureau
The London School of Hygiene and Tropical Medicine
The Liverpool School of Tropical Medicine
The British Leprosy Relief Association
The British Tuberculosis Association
The Commonwealth Broadcasting Conference

The Gambia's National Day is on 18th February, Independence Day.

HISTORY

The banks of the Gambia River have been inhabited for many centuries and a number of stone circles of ancient origin exist, but there is insufficient archaeological or written evidence to throw much light on the early history of the country.

During the fifth to eighth centuries A.D. most of the Sene-Gambian area was part of the empire of Ghana, whose rulers were of the Serahuli tribe, still strongly represented in The Gambia, and had their seat north of the Upper Niger (not in the country now known as 'Ghana', of which only a small sector was an outlying part of the empire). The Ghana empire was gradually superseded by the kingdom of the Songhais, based on the bend of the Niger south of Timbuktu. The Songhai rulers were also of the Serahuli tribe. They became Muslims and vigorously promoted Islam.

About the thirteenth century A.D. tribes of Mandingo and Susus from the Futa Jallon plateau of Guinea shook off Songhai rule and established themselves in what is now Mali, from Bamako to Timbuktu. They assumed overlordship over the whole Gambia basin. What is now The Gambia was then probably mainly inhabited by Woloffs on the north bank and by Jolas on the south bank. The Mali rulers' names, Keita and Sonko, are still prominent names among Gambian Mandingos.

The Mali empire declined by about A.D. 1500 and its Mandingo leaders retired to their former lands in Futa Jallon, but they held influence over The Gambia as recently as the early eighteenth century. Later in that century the area was penetrated by Fula invaders, whose ancestors had come from North Africa and who went on to found the Emirates of Northern Nigeria.

The first Europeans to visit the River Gambia were a Venetian and a Genoese, commissioned by Prince Henry the Navigator of Portugal to lead an expedition along the African coast to the south of Cape Verde. They arrived in the River Gambia in 1455, but only proceeded a short way upstream. In the following year they proceeded farther up the river and got in touch with some of the native chiefs. When they were near the river's mouth 'they cast anchor at an island in the shape of a smoothing iron, where one of the sailors, who had died of fever, was buried. As his name was Andrew, being well loved, they gave the island the name of St Andrew'. For some three centuries afterwards the history of the European occupation of The Gambia was largely the history of this island.

This discovery was followed by attempts on the part of the Portuguese at settlement along the river banks. The number of settlers never appears at any time to have been large and such few as there were intermarried with the African races. The European strain in their descendants rapidly diminished, but Christian communities of Portuguese descent continued to live on the banks of the Gambia in separate villages well into the middle of the eighteenth century.

In 1580 a number of Portuguese took refuge in England, one of whom piloted two English ships to the Gambia and returned with a profitable cargo of hides and ivory in 1587. Thereafter certain London and Devon merchants purchased the exclusive right to trade between the Rivers Senegal and Gambia; this grant was confirmed to the grantees for a period of 10 years by letters patent of Queen Elizabeth. The patentees reported that the Gambia was a river of secret trade and riches, concealed by the Portuguese. In 1612 another attempt by the French to settle in The Gambia ended disastrously owing to sickness and mortality.

Letters patent were subsequently granted other adventurers, but no attempt was made by the English to explore the river until 1618. The expedition in that year had for its objective the opening of trade with Timbuktu. Leaving his ship in the estuary the commander proceeded with a small party in boats. During his absence the crew of his ship were massacred by the Portuguese, but some of the party managed on their return to make their way overland to Cape Verde and thence to England. In the meantime a relief expedition had been sent out under command of Richard Jobson, who gave a glowing account of the commercial potentialities of the River Gambia in his *Golden Trade*. But his expedition had resulted in considerable losses and a subsequent voyage, which he made in 1624, proved a complete failure. The patentees made no further attempt to exploit the resources of The Gambia.

In 1651 Cromwell granted a patent to certain London merchants who established a trading post at Bintang. Members of the expedition proceeded as far as the Barokunda Falls in search of gold, but Prince Rupert entered the

Gambia with three Royalist ships and captured the patentees' vessels. After this heavy loss the patentees abandoned further enterprise in The Gambia.

In the meantime, James, Duke of Courland had obtained from various chiefs the cession of St Andrew's Island and land which is now the Half-Die quarter of Bathurst. Settlers, merchants and missionaries were sent out by Courland and forts were erected.

After the Restoration, English interest in The Gambia was revived as the result of information which Prince Rupert had obtained in 1652 regarding the reputed existence of gold. A new patent was granted to a number of persons, who were styled the 'Royal Adventurers Trading to Africa' and of whom the most prominent were James, Duke of York and Prince Rupert. The Adventurers sent an expedition to the Gambia which arrived in the river at the beginning of 1661. It occupied what is now 'Dog Island' and erected a temporary fort there. This expedition seized St Andrew's Island from the Courlanders and gave it the name of James Island, which it retains.

In 1677 the French seized the island of Gorée near Dakar, and the history of the next century and a half is the history of a continuous struggle between England and France for political and commercial supremacy in the regions of the Senegal and the Gambia. By 1681 the French had acquired a small enclave at Albreda opposite James Island. Except for short periods, during which trouble with the natives of Barra or hostilities with England compelled them temporarily to abandon the place, they retained their foothold there until 1857.

In the wars with France James Fort was captured on four occasions by the French, namely, 1695, 1702, 1704 and 1708, but no attempt was made by them to occupy the fort permanently. At the treaty of Utrecht in 1713 they recognised the right of the English to James Island and their settlements in the River Gambia. In 1779 the French captured James Fort for the fifth and last time. They so successfully demolished the fortifications that at the close of the war it was found impossible to rebuild them, and thereafter James Island ceased to play any part in the history of The Gambia. After further fighting St Louis and Gorée were handed back to France in 1783·and Senegambia ceased to exist as a British Colony. The Gambia was once more entrusted to the care of the African Company which, however, made no attempt to administer it.

When the African slave trade was abolished by Act of Parliament in 1807, the British were in possession of Gorée. With the co-operation of the Royal Navy, the garrison of that fort made strenuous efforts to suppress the traffic in the River Gambia which was being carried on by American and Spanish vessels, but the slavers offered stubborn resistance.

At the close of the Napoleonic Wars Gorée was returned to France. On the recommendation of Sir Charles MacCarthy and in order to suppress the traffic in slaves, Captain Alexander Grant of the African Corps was despatched to establish a military post in The Gambia. James Island was found to be unsuitable, and on 23rd April 1816 Grant entered into a treaty with the Chief of Kombo for the cession of the island of Banjul. It was renamed St Mary's Island, and the settlement, which was established there, was called Bathurst after the then Secretary of State for the Colonies. In 1821 The Gambia was placed under the Government of Sierra Leone and was administered from Freetown until 1843, when it was created a separate colony. Again in 1866 The Gambia and Sierra Leone were united under a single administration until 1888.

Groundnuts first appear as an export from Bathurst in 1835. Thereafter they rapidly replaced the beeswax, ivory and skins, which had hitherto formed the main items of external trade.

From the late eighteenth century and throughout the early and middle nineteenth century there was bitter and protracted religious dissension in the rural areas, cutting across tribal groups, between the Marabouts, strict followers of Islam, and the Soninkis, who were not prepared to abjure animist customs and liquor. As a consequence of this civil strife various chiefs sought protection from the British established at Bathurst and treaties between the British and the chiefs were concluded. In 1826 a strip along the north bank of the River opposite Bathurst was ceded to Britain by the Chief of Barra. In 1823 Grant had acquired Lemain Island, about 170 miles up the River, to be made into a settlement for liberated African slaves. He renamed it MacCarthy Island and it became the headquarters of a Wesleyan Mission. In 1840 and 1853 areas of the mainland adjoining St Mary's Island were obtained from the Chief of Kombo for the settlement of discharged soldiers of the West India Regiment and of liberated Africans. In 1857 Albreda, the French enclave in The Gambia which had proved a constant source of friction, was handed over to Britain in return for concessions up the coast. The British Government was at this period desiring to reduce its liabilities and consolidate its areas of influence in West Africa. In 1870, and again in 1876, it entered into negotiations with the French for the exchange of The Gambia for territory further down the coast, but the proposal aroused such opposition in England and in The Gambia that it was decided to drop the scheme.

The modern history of The Gambia dates from 1888, when the administration was once again separated from Sierra Leone and a Gambia legislature was established. In the following year delimitation of the boundaries between The Gambia and Senegal was put in hand. For several years thereafter much of the country was unsettled but gradually the Government negotiated treaties of British protection with all the principal chiefs along the River. The last, and most important, was the treaty concluded in 1901 with Musa Mullah, Chief of Fulladu. Thereby it became possible to pass the Protectorate Ordinance of 1902, under which the whole of The Gambia was brought under the 'protectorate system' except Bathurst and Kombo St Mary, which continued to be termed the 'Colony'. Between 1902 and the end of the war in 1945 the history of The Gambia was uneventful. There were years of booming trade during and directly after the 1914-18 war and a period of deep depression during the 1930s, but the general picture was one of political tranquillity and very gentle economic advance. The pattern of the single cash crop, the busy 'trade season', and the wet season, slack in business but devoted to farming, soon became established and has remained very much unchanged ever since.

CONSTITUTIONAL DEVELOPMENT

When the small British settlements on the Gambia River were again formed into a separate Colony in 1888, the usual form of Crown Colony government was set up, with an Executive Council and a Legislative Council. The Executive Council consisted of the Administrator and three other officials; the Legislative Council consisted of the Administrator as President, the three other members of the Executive Council and two nominated unofficial members. In 1893, after the creation of an administration in the Protectorate, the Legislative Council of the Colony was empowered to make rules by Ordinance for the government of the Protectorate, subject to the understanding, as expressed in the Protectorate Ordinance of 1894, that 'all native laws and customs in force in the Protected Territories which are not repugnant to natural justice nor incompatible with any laws of the Colony which applies to the Protectorate shall have the same effect as regulations' made under Colony Ordinances. However the Protectorate did not at first have any representative on the Legislative Council.

The title of 'Administrator' was changed to that of 'Governor' in 1901. By 1902 the only settlement remaining under direct Crown Colony government was the Island of St Mary, of about five square miles; the remaining territories of what was then known as the Colony being administered under the Protectorate system together with the rest of the Protectorate. In 1915 the Legislative Council was enlarged, there being in addition to the Governor, four officials and three nominated unofficial members one of whom was to be a person to represent the business community and the other two were to be African Christians from Bathurst. In 1921 one of the latter was replaced by an African Muslim. In 1932 the Council was further enlarged by the inclusion of an African member nominated by the Bathurst Urban District Council (formed in 1931) and by the inclusion also, of one of the Commissioners from the Protectorate. Thus the Protectorate was represented for the first time on the Council. Until the end of the 1939/45 war, the Legislative Council continued to consist of the Governor, the Colonial Secretary, five official members (one of whom was a Commissioner from the Protectorate), and four unofficial members.

Under a new Constitution agreed in 1946 the principle of election was introduced for the first time, the Legislative Council consisting of the Governor, the Colonial Secretary, three official members, six unofficial nominated members and one elected member to represent Bathurst and Kombo St Mary which now together formed the Colony for administrative purposes. Of the six unofficial members, two were to represent the Colony and four the Protectorate. There was thus an unofficial majority. In 1947 the membership of the Executive Council was also enlarged to consist of the official members of the Legislative Council and three nominated unofficial members, of whom one was normally the elected member for the Colony. A second elected member was added in 1951.

The first Gambian political party, the Democratic Party, was formed in 1951 by the Reverend John C. Faye, and two others, the Muslim Congress Party and P. S. N'Jie's United Party, in 1952. In May 1953 the Governor invited thirty-four leading members of the community to meet to consider proposals for a new constitution; and from this resulted the constitution of 1954. Under this the Legislative Council was composed of the Governor, five *ex officio* members, two nominated unofficial members, seven elected members from the Colony (four directly and three indirectly) and seven elected members from the Protectorate, four of these being chosen by the Divisional Councils and three by the Chiefs. For the first time there was also an unofficial majority on the Executive Council, and three of the six unofficial members were appointed to act as Members to head Ministries.

There was criticism of this constitution because it gave too much power to the District Commissioners and chiefs of the Protectorate; and in 1959 representatives of the political parties made proposals which resulted in the 1959 Constitution which came into operation in 1960. The Legislative Council was replaced by a House of Representatives of thirty-four persons, with four *ex officio* members, three nominated members, seven directly elected members from the Colony,

G*

twelve directly elected members from the Protectorate and eight representatives of the Chiefs. There was an elected Speaker and Deputy Speaker. At the same time all six of the unofficial members of the Executive Council were given Ministerial posts. The elections which took place in May 1960 saw the rise of the Progressive People's Party under the leadership of D. K. (now Sir Dawda) Jawara. Dissatisfaction with the continuing influence of the chiefs, and also with the appointment by the Governor of P. S. N'Jie as Chief Minister in 1961, resulted in the Secretary of State agreeing to further constitutional changes and these came into operation in April 1962. The office of Premier was created, and the Executive Council consisted of the Governor as Chairman, the Premier and eight other Ministers. The House of Representatives had seven elected members from the Colony and twenty-five from the Protectorate, two members nominated by the Governor after consultation with the Premier (without voting rights), the Attorney-General (also without voting rights) and four members elected by the Chiefs. Finally, under the Gambia Constitution (Amendment) Order in Council 1963, The Gambia attained full internal self-government on 4th October 1963. The Governor withdrew from the Executive Council which became a Cabinet with a Prime Minister and eight other Ministers.

CONSTITUTION

The Gambia Independence Act, 1964, laid down that on and after 18th February 1965 all those territories which had been comprised in the Colony of The Gambia or in the Protectorate of The Gambia should form part of the independent sovereign country of The Gambia. The Gambia Independence Order, 1965, set out the Constitution. It provided for a Parliament consisting of Her Majesty The Queen, who was represented in The Gambia by a Governor-General appointed by her, and a House of Representatives. A new Republican Constitution was passed by Parliament in December 1969 by 27 votes to 5 and endorsed in a national referendum held in April 1970 by 84,968 votes in favour to 35,638 against. This provides for a President, with both executive and ceremonial functions, who becomes such at a general election in virtue of being the leader of the party with a majority in the House. The Vice-President and other Cabinet Ministers are chosen by the President from among elected MPs. The Vice-President is also leader of the House. In accordance with the new Constitution's transitional provisions Sir Dawda Jawara, who had held chief executive authority initially as Premier and then as Prime Minister since 1962, became the first President of the Republic on 24th April 1970.

The House of Representatives consists of a Speaker and the following other members; 32 members, who are known as "elected members" and who are elected on the basis of universal adult suffrage in 32 single-member constituencies whose boundaries are prescribed by a Constituency Boundaries Commission to contain as nearly equal numbers of inhabitants as the Commission deems practicable; four members who are elected by the Head Chiefs from among their own number by secret vote and who are known as Chiefs' Representative Members; the Attorney-General; and three members who are known as "nominated members" and who are appointed by the President; but these three nominated members do not have a vote. Members must have attained the age of 21 years, and be able to speak English well enough to take part in the proceedings of the House, which are conducted in that language. All except the nominated members must be citizens of The Gambia. Certain persons are debarred from membership, as for example, persons of unsound mind and those who owe allegiance to a foreign power or state, those who are undischarged bankrupts and those who are serving or who have within five years of the date of their nomination or appointment completed serving a sentence of imprisonment for a term of six months or more. The Speaker of the House of Representatives is elected from among the members of the House or from persons who are qualified to be elected as members; and when elected from among the former, the Speaker must vacate his seat in the House. The Speaker has neither an original nor a casting vote. A voting member must vacate his seat in the House, if in the case of an elected member, he ceases to be registered as a voter in elections of elected members to the House of Representatives or he ceases to be qualified to vote in such election; in the case of a Chiefs' Representative Member, he ceases to be a Head Chief; or, in the case of the Attorney-General, if he is not an elected member, if he is removed from office.

Subject to the provisions of the Constitution, Parliament may make laws for the peace, order and good government of The Gambia, and may alter the Constitution provided that the bill for this purpose is supported on the final reading in the House by the votes of two-thirds of all the voting members of the House. In addition, to alter certain provisions of the Constitution, the bill, after having been passed by the House, must be submitted to and be approved at a referendum by a majority vote of the whole electorate or by two-thirds of all the votes validly cast at the referendum.

The President may at any time prorogue or dissolve Parliament. If the House of Representatives passes a resolution which is supported by the votes of a majority of all the voting members of that House, and of which not less than seven days' notice has been given in accordance with the procedure of that House, declaring that it has no confidence in the Government of The Gambia and the President does not, within three days of the passing of that resolution, dissolve Parliament, Parliament shall stand dissolved on the fourth day following the day on which that resolution was passed. Parliament, unless sooner dissolved, shall continue for five years from the date of the first sitting of the House of Representatives after any dissolution and shall then stand dissolved. At any time when The Gambia is at war, Parliament may extend the period of five years for not more than twelve months at a time, provided that the life of Parliament shall not be extended in this case for more than another five years. If after a dissolution of Parliament and before the holding of a general election of members of the House of Representatives, the President considers that owing to a state of emergency arising or existing in The Gambia or any part thereof, it is necessary to recall Parliament, the President may summon the Parliament which has been dissolved to meet, and the Parliament shall be deemed to be the Parliament for the time being, but the general election of members of the House of Representatives shall proceed and the Parliament that has been recalled shall, if not sooner dissolved, again stand dissolved on the day appointed for the nomination of candidates in that general election.

There is a Supreme Court which has unlimited original jurisdiction to hear and determine any civil or criminal proceedings under any law. The Court consists of the Chief Justice and such number of Puisne Judges as may be prescribed by Parliament. The Chief Justice is appointed by the President, and the Puisne Judges are also appointed by him, but acting on the advice of a Judicial

Service Commission. In addition there is a Court of Appeal and various subordinate courts.

The Judicial Service Commission consists of the Chief Justice as Chairman, the Chairman of the Public Service Commission and a member appointed by the President. There is also a Public Service Commission consisting of a Chairman, Deputy Chairman and four other members appointed by the President.

An important part of the Constitution consists of provisions for the protection of fundamental rights and freedoms. Article 11 of the Constitution reads as follows:

"Whereas every person in The Gambia is entitled to the fundamental rights and freedoms, that is to say, the right, whatever his race, place of origin, political opinions, colour, creed or sex but subject to respect for the rights and freedoms of others and for the public interest, to each and all of the following, namely:

(*a*) life, liberty, security of the person and the protection of the law;

(*b*) freedom of conscience, of expression and of assembly and association;

and

(*c*) protection for the privacy of his home and other property and from deprivation of property without compensation."

In addition to specific provisions for the protection of each of these liberties, the Constitution also provides that a person charged with a criminal offence shall be presumed innocent until proved guilty and shall be given full facilities for defending himself. If any person alleges that any of the provisions of the Constitution relating to these matters are being or are likely to be contravened in relation to him, he has the right of application to the Supreme Court to seek redress.

GOVERNMENT

The House of Representatives comprises 32 elected members, three nominated members, the Attorney-General and four Chiefs' Representative members. The People's Progressive Party forms the Government.

PRESIDENT

His Excellency Sir Dawda Kairaba Jawara, Kt

THE CABINET

Vice-President and Minister of Finance: His Excellency Mr Sheriff M. Dibba, MP
Minister of External Affairs: The Honourable Andrew D. Camara, MP
Minister for Local Government, Lands and Mines:
Alhaji The Honourable Yaya Ceesay, MP
Minister of Works and Communications:
Alhaji The Honourable Kalilu Singhateh, MP
Minister of Education, Health and Social Welfare: Alhaji I. M. Garba-Jahumpa, MP
Minister of Agriculture and Natural Resources:
The Honourable Howsoon O. Semega-Janneh, MP
Attorney-General: Alhaji The Honourabel M. L. Saho, MP
Minister of State in the President's Office: Alhaji A. B. N'Jie, MBE, MP

LEADER OF THE OPPOSITION

P. S. N'Iie (United Party)

HOUSE OF REPRESENTATIVES

Speaker: Alhaji The Honourable Sir Alieu Jack
Deputy Speaker: Seyfu Kebba Janneh, MP
Clerk of the House: B. O. Jobe

Chief Justice: The Hon. P. R. Bridges, CMG, QC
President of Court of Appeal: The Hon. Mr Justice G. F. Dove-Edwin
Judge of Appeal: J. B. Marcus Jones

MINISTRIES AND GOVERNMENT DEPARTMENTS

PRESIDENT'S OFFICE

Secretary-General, Permanent Secretary, Ministry of External Affairs and Secretary to the Cabinet: E. H. Christensen, CMG
Deputy Secretary-General: M. M. Sosseh
Establishments Secretary: C. M. Cham
Commissioner of Labour: T. B. Foon
Director of Information and Broadcasting: Dr L. A. M'Bye

MINISTRY OF AGRICULTURE AND NATURAL RESOURCES

Permanent Secretary: F. A. J. M'Boge
Director of Agriculture: Dr L. J. Marenah

ATTORNEY-GENERAL'S OFFICE

Attorney-General: Alhaji The Honourable M. L. Saho
Solicitor-General, Legal Secretary and Director of Public Prosecutions: S. H. A. George

MINISTRY OF EDUCATION, HEALTH AND SOCIAL WELFARE

Permanent Secretary: H. B. Semega-Janneh
Chief Education Officer: S. H. M. Jones
Director of Medical Services: Dr J. A. Mahoney

MINISTRY OF FINANCE, TRADE AND DEVELOPMENT

Permanent Secretary: D. A. N'Dow
Accountant-General: D. T. Davies
Comptroller of Customs: G. P. F. Mendy, OBE
Commissioner of Income Tax: M. A. Ceesay

CENTRAL BANK OF THE GAMBIA

Governor: H. R. Monday Jr

MINISTRY OF LOCAL GOVERNMENT, LANDS AND MINES

Permanent Secretary: E. C. Sowe

MINISTRY OF WORKS AND COMMUNICATIONS

Permanent Secretary: F. Savage
Director Public Works and Controller of Civil Aviation: J. P. Moran
Director of Marine: Capt. B. M. Sallah
Postmaster-General: A. J. Senghore, OBE, JP

* * * *

PUBLIC SERVICE COMMISSION

Chairman: Dr S. H. O. Jones, CBE
Deputy Chairman: M. O. Manga, MBE, JP

AUDIT

Auditor General: V. J. Kennard

DIPLOMATIC REPRESENTATION

REPRESENTATIVES OF THE GAMBIA IN OTHER COMMONWEALTH COUNTRIES

High Commissioner in the United Kingdom: B. O. Semega-Janneh, MBE; Sierre Leone: Sam J. Sarr, MBE

COMMONWEATH HIGH COMMISSIONERS IN THE GAMBIA

United Kingdom: J. G. W. Ramage; Canada: G. Riddell (resident in Dakar); India: H. K. Krishan Singh (resident in Dakar); Pakistan: A. Haq (resident in Dakar); Ghana: K. Brew (resident in Dakar); Nigeria: Alhaji B. A. T. Balewa (resident in Dakar)

REPRESENTATIVES OF THE GAMBIA IN COUNTRIES OTHER THAN COMMONWEALTH COUNTRIES

High Commissioner to the Republic of Senegal: Sam J. Sarr, MBE (also accredited to Mali and Guinea)

REPRESENTATIVES OF THE GAMBIA OF COUNTRIES OTHER THAN COMMONWEALTH COUNTRIES

(All resident in Dakar, Senegal, unless otherwise stated); Austria (Ambassador); Belgium (Ambassador); China (Taiwan) (Ambassador, resident in Abidjan); Egypt (Ambassador); France (Ambassador); Germany (Federal Republic) (Ambassador); Guinea (Ambassador); Israel (Ambassador); Italy (Ambassador); Japan (Ambassador); Korea (Republic of) (Ambassador, resident in London); Lebanon (Ambassador); Mauritania (Ambassador); Morocco (Ambassador); The Netherlands (Ambassador); Senegal (High Commissioner, resident in Bathurst); Spain (Ambassador); Switzerland (Ambassador); Sweden(Ambassador,resident in Rabat); Tunisia (Ambassador); USA (Ambassador); USSR (Ambassador)

GHANA

GHANA, named after the ancient African Empire in which, it is thought by some historians, the people of the country had their origins, comprises the area in West Africa formerly known as the Gold Coast (the Gold Coast Colony, Ashanti and the Northern Territories) together with that part of Togoland which had been administered by the British Government under United Nations trusteeship. Its area is 91,843 square miles, almost the same as that of the United Kingdom of Great Britain and Northern Ireland. The whole area lies in the tropics. In the Northern Territories, the country is open and undulating and the climate is hot and dry. Further south, in the forest lands of Ashanti and in the south-west coastal area, the climate is hot and humid. The flat eastern coastal belt is warm and fairly dry. In most areas the mean maximum temperature is highest in March (absolute maximum 109°F) and lowest in August (absolute minimum 44°F). Coastal regions normally enjoy temperatures between 24°C (75°F) and 35°C (95°F) throughout the year. Annual rainfall varies in the different regions from 28 inches to 86 inches. The main river system of the country is that of the Volta River which is formed by the junction of the Black and White Voltas both of which rise in the Republic of Upper Volta. There are no high mountains but several ranges of hills rise to a maximum of about 3,000 feet. The central forest area is broken up into heavily wooded ridges and valleys.

At the time of the census taken in 1960 the population was estimated to be 6,726,815 and at June 1966 7,945,000. A further census was held in 1970 and the published figure was 8,545,561. The country is divided into eight regions: Eastern (including Accra); Ashanti; Volta; Upper; Central; Western; Brong-Ahafo; and Northern.

English is the official language and is used for instruction in schools from Primary Class II upwards. Other languages used are: Twi, in the Ashanti Region, the most widely spoken of all African languages in Ghana; Fanti, used in the coastal region, except the Accra plain where Ga is spoken; and Ewe in the Volta Region. Subsidiary languages are Nzima, used in the region west of Takoradi; Dagomba, Dagbani, Hausa and Moshie, used in the Northern Region, and many others. The principal religions are: Christianity 42·8 per cent; Traditional 38·2 per cent; Islam 12 per cent; others 7 per cent. Primary education is free and universal and in 1964, 35,000 students were enrolled for secondary education.

The capital city of Ghana is Accra (population estimated in 1966 at 532,600). Other main towns with population figures are: Sekondi/Takoradi 112,800 (1966 est.); Cape Coast 41,230 (1960); Koforidua 34,856 (1960); Kumasi 252,900 (1966 est.); Sunyani 12,160 (1960); Tamale 40,443 (1960); Bolgatanga 5,513 (1960); Ho 14,519 (1960). The principal ports are Tema in the Eastern Region (approximately 20 miles from Accra) and Takoradi in the Western Region (approximately 140 miles from Accra). The main shipping line is the Black Star Line. The only international airport is at Accra, six miles from the city centre (length of runway 9,600 feet) and the country's airline is Ghana Airways Corporation. There are also internal airports at Takoradi (runway 5,700 feet); Kumasi (runway 4,500 feet); Tamale (runway 4,200 feet). There are 749 miles of 3 ft 6 in. gauge railway and the road mileage is 20,000 of which 2,053 miles are bitumen-covered trunk road and 3,277 gravel trunk road. Broadcasting and television facilities are provided by the Ghana Broadcasting Corporation. Ghana is provided with electricity by the hydro-electric scheme at Akosombo on the Volta river.

HISTORY

There is no recorded history of the Gold Coast before the coming of the Europeans. The oral traditions of the tribes at present occupying the country indicate that their arrival there was only comparatively recent, historically speaking. They appear to have originated to the north of the present boundaries of Ghana and to have migrated southwards, under the pressure of various circumstances, roughly over the period A.D. 1200 to 1600. The identity of the previous inhabitants can only be conjectured; it is certain, however, that the country has been occupied by peoples of Negro stock since before the dawn of historical consciousness in Europe. The discovery of neolithic and, more rarely, palaeolithic relics points to the country having been occupied at an even earlier date by peoples of a different race; but no clues have been found to the physical type of these prehistoric inhabitants.

The Gold Coast first became known in Europe through Portuguese navigators who visited the country in the second half of the 15th century in search of gold, ivory and spices. The first recorded English trading voyage to the Coast was made by Thomas Windham in 1553 and in the course of the next three centuries the English, Danes, Dutch, Germans and Portuguese all controlled various parts of the Coast at different periods. By 1750 only the English, the Dutch and the Danes had settlements on the Coast. In 1821 the British Government assumed control of the British trading settlements and on 6th March 1844 the Chiefs in the immediate neighbourhood agreed to adhere to a Bond from which British power and jurisdiction were generally derived. The British settlements were at that time under the control of the Government of Sierra Leone. The Danes relinquished their settlements in 1850 and in 1871 the Dutch ceded theirs to the British. Under a new Charter in 1874 the Colony was still limited to the forts and settlements, but other territory under British influence was declared a Protectorate. In 1896 treaties of trade and protection were concluded with several tribes north of Ashanti and a Protectorate over the area now known as the Northern Territories was established. Boundary Commissions in 1898 and 1899 delimited the borders of the Gold Coast and neighbouring French and German African territories, and the area of British jurisdiction was clarified in 1901 by Orders in Council which declared as a Colony by settlement all territories in the Gold Coast south of Ashanti, declared Ashanti a Colony by conquest, and the Northern Territories a Protectorate under the Foreign Jurisdiction Act of 1890. It was thus not until 1901 that Britain assumed full responsibility for the government of the Gold Coast and its hinterland. In 1922 a part of the adjoining German territory of Togoland was placed under British administration by a League of Nations Mandate and after the Second World War was placed by agreement under the trusteeship system of the United Nations. From that time it was administered by Britain as part of the Gold Coast up to the date of independence.

CONSTITUTIONAL DEVELOPMENT

Constitutional advance has been continuous since 1850 when the first Legislative Council was set up in what was then the Colony Area; the first African unofficial member was appointed to the Legislative Council in 1888 and by 1916 the unofficial side of the Council consisted of three Europeans, three Paramount

Chiefs and three other Africans. In 1925 a new Constitution was promulgated which introduced the principles of direct election in municipalities and indirect election in the provinces of the Colony area.

The next major advance was the Burns Constitution of 1946. Until then Ashanti, and until 1951 the Northern Territories, were administered directly by the Governor; the 1946 Constitution brought in the first Legislative Council in British Africa to have a majority of African members and it represented Ashanti as well as the Colony. The peaceful progress of the Gold Coast was marred in 1948 by disturbances which occurred in the southern parts of the country and a Commission of Enquiry (the Watson Commission) was set up to make a thorough investigation into the general conditions in the country. In its Report the Commission made a number of proposals for constitutional reform, in particular that Africans should play a larger part in the proceedings of the Executive Council. As a result an all-African Committee—the Chairman was Mr Justice (later Sir Henley) Coussey—was set up in 1949. This Committee dealt in detail with the whole structure of government machinery from village area councils to the Executive Council and the Governor's reserved powers. The proposals of the Coussey Committee were generally accepted by the British Government and in 1951 elections took place under a new Constitution based on its recommendations. This provided for an Executive Council or Cabinet with the Governor as President, and a Legislative Assembly with some members representing special interests and 75 elected members with a fixed ratio between the Colony, Ashanti and the Northern Territories. In 1952 the office of Prime Minister was created; in 1953 proposals for further constitutional reform were submitted to the British Government and a new Constitution was introduced in 1954 with an all-African Cabinet and a Legislature of 104 members elected by direct suffrage. This was the Constitution in force up to the date of Independence. The Governor retained only certain reserved powers, including responsibility in his discretion for external affairs (including Togoland under United Kingdom trusteeship) defence and the police. In 1955 Sir Frederick Bourne, a former Governor of East Bengal, was, at the request of the Gold Coast Government, appointed Constitutional Adviser and in December of that year he published his recommendations which were mainly concerned with safeguarding the interests of the Regions. On 11th May 1956 the Colonial Secretary announced that if a general election were held in the Gold Coast the British Government would be prepared to accept a motion calling for independence within the Commonwealth passed by a reasonable majority in a newly elected Legislature, and then to declare a firm date for the attainment of independence within the Commonwealth. A general election was accordingly held in July 1956, and Dr Nkrumah's Party (the Convention People's Party) was returned with a majority of over two-thirds of the Legislative Assembly. The new Assembly approved a motion requesting the British Government to initiate legislation 'to provide for the independence of the Gold Coast as a sovereign and independent State within the Commonwealth under the name of Ghana'; on 18th September the Colonial Secretary announced the British Government's intention to do so and that, subject to Parliamentary approval, independence should come about on 6th March 1957. In May 1956 a plebiscite was held under United Nations' auspices in the Trust territory of Togoland as a result of which the United Nations agreed that the Trusteeship Agreement should end on the attainment of Independence by the

Gold Coast. On the 6th March 1957 Ghana attained complete independence as a fully self-governing Member of the Commonwealth with the Queen as Sovereign.

Following a plebiscite held in April 1960 a Republican Constitution was adopted by the National Assembly on 29th June 1960. On 21st February 1964, Ghana formally became a one-party state, the national party being the Convention People's Party. A general election was held in June 1965 and all 198 candidates nominated by the C.P.P. were returned unopposed.

On 24th February 1966 a *coup d'état* by the army and the police overthrew President Nkrumah while he was visiting Peking. The National Liberation Council consisting of four representatives each from the army and police was set up under the chairmanship of Major-General J. A. Ankrah, subsequently appointed Lieutenant-General. (Lieutenant-General E. K. Kotoka, one of the members of the N.L.C. was killed on 17th April 1967 in an abortive coup. He was not replaced on the N.L.C.). The N.L.C. dissolved the National Assembly and the C.P.P. and repealed the Constitution. On 18th November 1966, the N.L.C. appointed a Constitutional Commission, headed by the Chief Justice, to draft a new Constitution. This finished its work in January 1968, and the draft Constitution was published the next month. In December of that year the N.L.C. set up a Constituent Assembly to amend and approve the draft.

In April 1969 General Ankrah, after admitting involvement in the financing of politicians, resigned from the N.L.C. and was replaced as Chairman by Brigadier A. A. Afrifa.

The ban on political activity was lifted on 1st May 1969 and in the general elections held on 29th August 1969, Dr K. A. Busia's Progress Party won 105 seats, and the National Alliance of Liberals, led by Mr K. A. Gbedemah 29, the remaining 6 seats being won by minority parties. Dr Busia was sworn in as Prime Minister. On 22nd August 1969, the Constituent Assembly promulgated the new Constitution and approved the setting-up of a three-man Presidential Commission, which was inaugurated on 3rd September. The N.L.C. formally handed over to the Civilian Government on 1st October 1969.

The Presidential Commission was dissolved on 30th July 1970 and, in accordance with the Constitution, the functions of President were performed in the interim by the Speaker of the National Assembly, Mr Justice N. A. Ollennu, until Mr E. A. Akufo-Addo was elected President by a Presidential Electoral College on 31st August 1970.

The opposition Parties merged in October 1970 into one group called the Justice Party, comprising the National Alliance of Liberals, the United Nationalists Party and the All Peoples Party. Mr E. R. T. Madjitey, leader of the Parliamentary opposition was appointed leader of the new Party, the Chairman of which is Mr Joe Appiah.

HISTORICAL LIST

GOVERNORS GENERAL
Sir Charles Noble Arden-Clarke, GCMG, 6th March to 5th May 1957
William Francis Hare, 5th Earl of Listowel, PC, GCMG, 5th May 1957 to 30th June 1960

PRIME MINISTER
Dr Kwame Nkrumah, 6th March 1957 to 30th June 1960

PRESIDENT
Dr Kwame Nkrumah, from 1st July 1960 to 24th February 1966

CHAIRMAN OF NATIONAL LIBERATION COUNCIL
Major-General J. A. Ankrah, OOV, MC, 24th February 1966 to 2nd April 1969
Brigadier A. A. Afrifa, DSO, 2nd April 1969 to 30th September 1969

GOVERNMENT
President: Mr E. A. Akufo-Addo, MV

COUNCIL OF STATE
Lt-Gen. A. A. Afrifa, CV, DSO
Otumfuo Nana Opoku Ware II
Nana Kwamina Anaisie IV
Abudulai Mahamadu IV
Togbe Adza Tekpor VI
Nene Azzu Mate Kole
Mr E. R. T. Madjitey, MP
His Grace J. Kodwo Amissah, GM
Mrs Emily Naa Hesse
Mrs Agnes Owusu-Nyantakyi
Mr D. J. Buahin

CABINET
PRIME MINISTER
Dr K. A. Busia

MINISTERS
Minister responsible for Parliamentary Affairs: Hon. J. K. Lamptey
Minister of Foreign Affairs: Hon. William Ofori Atta
Minister of Trade, Industries and Tourism: Hon. R. A. Quarshie
Minister of Health: Hon. S. D. Dombo
Minister of Education and Sports: Hon. R. R. Amponsah
Minister of Justice and Attorney-General: Hon. Victor Owusu
Minister of Finance: Hon. J. H. Mensah
Minister of Works and Housing: Hon. S. W. Awuku Darko
Minister of Lands and Mineral Resources: Hon. T. D. Brodie-Mends
Minister of Transport and Communications: Hon. Jatoe Kaleo
Minister of Internal Affairs: Hon. N. Y. B. Adade
Minister of Labour and Co-operatives: Hon. Dr W. G. Bruce-Konuah
Minister of State and Chief of State Protocol (not in the Cabinet): Hon. K. G. Osei-Bonsu
Minister of Rural Development and Social Welfare: Hon. A. A. Munufie
Minister of Agriculture: Hon. Dr K. Safo Adu
Minister of Defence: Hon. B. K. Adama

NATIONAL ASSEMBLY
Speaker: Mr Justice N. A. Ollennu
Deputy Speaker: Mr I. Amissah-Aidoo
Leader of the Opposition: Mr E. R. T. Madjitey

THE JUDICIARY
Chief Justice: Mr E. A. L. Bannerman

SUPREME COURT JUDGES

Justice K. Bentsi-Enchill
Justice P. D. Anin
Justice K. O. Larbi
Justice J. B. Siriboe

Justice V. C. R. A. C. Crabbe
Justice S. Azu Crabbe
Justice F. K. Apaloo
Justice H. K. Prempeh

APPEAL COURT JUDGES

Justice A. N. P. Sowah
Justice G. S. Lassey
Justice Annie Jiagge
Justice P. E. N. K. Archer

Justice A. N. E. Amissah
Justice J. Kingsley-Nyinah
Justice F. Annan

HIGH COURT JUDGES

Justice J. N. K. Taylor
Justice C. E. H. Coussey
Justice G. Koranteng-Addoh
Justice G. R. M. Francois
Justice Quarshie Sam
Justice J. H. Griffiths Randolph
Justice J. S. A. Anterkyi
Justice S. Baidoo

Justice E. Edusei
Justice C. A. Owusu
Justice Wiredu
Justice Mensa Boison
Justice Doris Owusu-Addo
Justice P. V. Osei-Hwere
Justice K. Ata-Bedu
Justice F. P. Sarkodee

ARMED FORCES

Acting C.D.S.: Major-General D. K. Addo
Commander Ghana Army: Brigadier Acquah
Commander Ghana Navy: Commodore P. F. Quaye
Commander Ghana Air Force: Brigadier C. Beausoleil (Acting)

POLICE

Inspector-General: R. D. Ampaw

BANK OF GHANA

Governor: J. H. Frimpong Ansah

DIPLOMATIC REPRESENTATION

GHANIAN HIGH COMMISSIONERS IN
OTHER COMMONWEALTH COUNTRIES

Australia: J. Owusu-Akyeampong; Canada: Major S. K. Anthony; India: P. K. Owusu-Ansah; Kenya: E. K. Otoo; Malaysia: J. Owusu-Akyeampong (resident in Canberra); Nigeria: Major-General N. A. Aferi; Pakistan: Major-General C. C. Bruce; Sierra Leone: E. P. Awoonor-Williams; United Kingdom: A. B. Attafuah; Uganda: A. E. K. Ofori-Atta.

COMMONWEALTH HIGH COMMISSIONERS
IN GHANA

Australia: J. M. McMillan; Britain: H. S. H. Stanley, CMG; Canada: D. K. Doherty (Acting); India: A. S. Mehta; Malaysia:

T. H. Yogaratnam (Acting); Nigeria: P. U. Onu (Acting); Pakistan: S. A. Moid; Sierra Leone: L. H. O. Randall; Uganda: Brig. S. O. Opolot.

GHANAIAN REPRESENTATION IN
NON-COMMONWEALTH COUNTRIES

Algeria; Belgium; Brazil; Congo (Kinshasa); Czechoslovakia; Dahomey; Denmark; Ethiopia; France; Geneva; Federal Republic of Germany; Israel; Italy; Ivory Coast; Japan; Lebanon; Liberia; Mali; Mexico; Morocco; New York (United Nations); Netherlands; Senegal; Switzerland; Togo; U.S.S.R.; U.A.R.; U.S.A.; Upper Volta; Yugoslavia.

GUYANA

GUYANA lies on the north-east shoulder of the South American continent between latitudes 1° and 9° N. and longitudes 56° and 62° W. It is 83,000 square miles in area. The Atlantic sea-coast stretches for 270 miles; from it the land extends southwards into the interior for about 450 miles. Its borders are with Venezuela to the west, Brazil to the south and Surinam to the east. The country has three distinct geographical areas—the coastal belt, the forest area and the savannah zone. The narrow coastal belt, which is generally about 10 miles in width (though it runs inland for up to 40 miles along the banks of the main rivers), and which accounts for only 4 per cent of the total area, is intensively cultivated and contains 90 per cent of the population. It lies 4 to 5 feet below sea level at high tide and is dependent upon an elaborate system of dams, walls and groynes to protect it from the sea. The flatness of the coast necessitates an equally elaborate system of drainage canals.

Behind the coastal zone the land rises, gently at first, to an area of dense rain forest and mountains. Minerals are found in this area, the most valuable being bauxite, diamonds, gold and manganese. In the south-west the forest gives way to some open savannah country, usually known as the Rupununi, although the Rupununi District is much more extensive than the savannah area. The highest point is Mount Roraima (9,094 feet) in the Pakaraima range. The sparse population of this area is predominantly Amerindian.

Guyana is notable for its mighty rivers, the four best known being the Demerara, Berbice, Essequibo and Corentyne. They are of limited navigational value because of the many rapids, bars and falls. By far the largest river is the

Essequibo. Georgetown, the capital, lies at the mouth of the Demerara. The left bank of the Corentyne forms the boundary with Surinam. The most spectacular of the numerous waterfalls and rapids is Kaieteur Falls on the Potaro River which has a drop of 741 feet, nearly five times the height of Niagara Falls. In the north-west several rivers flow north-west towards the mouth of the Orinoco.

The climate is tropical, and there is very little temperature variation at the coast, where temperatures above 32°C (90° F) or below 24°C (75°F) at any time of the day or night are rare. There are greater temperature variations inland. Annual rainfall at the coast averages 90 inches. It is generally less in the interior but varies with altitude.

The last full census of the country took place in April 1970 when the total population was 714,233. Guyanese of East Indian descent account for over half the population, those of African descent for about a third; the remainder are composed of Amerindians (the aboriginal inhabitants of the country), Portuguese, Chinese and people of mixed race. Guyanese of African descent provide most of the urban and industrial community while those of East Indian descent provide most of the labour force in the sugar and rice industries. The Amerindian people live mainly in the west and south and there are a number of reserved areas for their protection.

Communications throughout the country are difficult. As mentioned above, the rivers are obstructed by rapids and falls not far from the coast. They are therefore of very limited value for communication though they do provide some sort of link with the timber and mining areas of the interior. There are roads along the coast from Charity in the Essequibo District to Springlands on the Corentyne and from Georgetown to Mackenzie and there are plans for further extensions. Air transport is the easiest means of communication between the coast and the interior and there are some 70 landing strips and landing pools in the country.

Georgetown is the main seaport, followed by New Amsterdam. Bauxite ships sail up the Demerara river as far as Mackenzie. There are 26 miles of railway track between Georgetown and Mahaica and 18 miles between Vreed-en-Hoop (across the Demerara River from Georgetown) and Parika on the Essequibo river. It was the first railway to be constructed in South America.

Education is free and universal, while free secondary education is available by competitive examination at the age of 11 years. The literacy rate is about 80 per cent. The University of Guyana, which recently moved into new buildings, has a total enrolment of about 1,800. Guyana has two broadcasting stations, the Government-operated Guyana Broadcasting Service and Radio Demerara, which is operated by a local associate of Rediffusion Ltd.

Guyana's economy is based on sugar, bauxite and rice together with gold, diamonds, timber, cattle ranching and some small scale industry.

Total exports in 1970 were G$266 million which included (in millions of Guyana dollars):

Bauxite	141·0
Sugar	72·4
Rice	18·0
Fish (mostly shrimp)	8·6
Precious and semi-precious stones	3·2
Rum	3·2
Timber	3·6

In 1970 the value of Guyana's imports was G$269·8 million, of which the largest items were machinery and transport equipment. Britain, the U.S.A., Trinidad and Tobago and Canada are the major suppliers.

In 1970 Government revenue and receipts were G$170·7 million and expenditure G$176·1 million.

HISTORY

Guyana is an Amerindian word meaning Land of Waters. This name was originally given to the territory on the north east of the South American continent which is drained by several large rivers, the most important being the Amazon, Orinoco, Demerara, Berbice, Essequibo and Corentyne. From this territory, five Guianas emerged: Spanish Guiana (now Venezuela), Portuguese Guiana (now Brazil), French Guiana, Dutch Guiana (now Surinam) and British Guiana (now Guyana).

The coastline was first traced by Spanish sailors in 1499 and 1500 and the first European settlements were almost certainly Spanish or Portuguese. The Dutch established a settlement on the Pomeroon in 1581 but were evicted by Spanish and Amerindians about 1596, after which they retired to a settlement up the Essequibo River. In 1627 Dutch merchants settled on the Berbice River. The Dutch West India Company, formed in 1621, controlled these settlements.

British attempts at settlement were made in 1604, 1609 and 1629, but no permanent settlements were established. A British settlement was founded in Surinam in 1651 but this was captured by the Dutch in 1667. In October of the same year it was recaptured by a British expedition. The Dutch finally obtained possession of Surinam in mid-1668 in accordance with the Treaty of Breda.

Meanwhile, the Dutch were in possession of that part of the area which is now Guyana. Although yielding intermittently to Britain, France and Portugal, they retained their hold on the territory until 1796 when it was captured by the British. It was restored to the Dutch in 1802, but in the following year was retaken by Great Britain. At that time the territory comprised the separate colonies of Essequibo, Demerara and Berbice. These were finally ceded to Great Britain in 1814.

The Courts of Policy and the Combined Courts, the legislature and executive bodies created by the Dutch remained in operation under British rule for another century. In 1831 the three Colonies merged to become British Guiana.

CONSTITUTIONAL DEVELOPMENT

A new Constitution with universal adult suffrage at the age of 21, two-Chamber Legislature and a ministerial system was introduced in 1953 and a General Election was held, at which the People's Progressive Party (P.P.P.) won a majority. Later in 1953, Her Majesty's Government suspended the Constitution in circumstances which were subsequently analysed in a report by a Constitutional Commission consisting of Sir James Robertson, GCVO, GCMG, KBE, Sir Donald Jackson (then Chief Justice of the Windward and Leeward Islands) and Mr George Woodcock, CBE (then Assistant General Secretary of the Trades Union Congress).

After the Commission's report was published in November 1954 Her Majesty's Government accepted its recommendation for a period of "marking time" in the advance towards self-government. In the meantime the Colony continued to be administered in accordance with the British Guiana (Constitution) (Temporary Provisions) Order in Council of 22 December, 1953, which provided for an Executive Council of three *ex officio* Members and not more than seven Nominated Members; and a Legislative Council of a Speaker, the same three *ex officio* Members and not more than twenty-four Nominated Members.

Constitutional changes were introduced by the British Guiana (Constitutional) (Temporary Provisions) (Amendment) Order in Council 1956, providing for a Legislative Council of not more than 28 Members (excluding the Speaker) comprising three *ex officio* Members, not less than 14 Elected Members and not more than 11 Nominated Members. At the first election held under the amended constitution in August 1957 the number of Elected Members was 14, and six other Members were nominated by the Governor.

As a result of a resolution passed by the Legislative Council in June 1958, a Constitutional Conference was convened in London in March 1960. Following the decisions of this Conference, the British Guiana (Constitution) Order in Council, 1961 was passed, providing for a new constitution giving full internal self-government to British Guiana.

The new constitution, which came into effect on 18th July 1961, provided for a bi-cameral Legislature—a Legislative Assembly of 35 members, elected by universal adult suffrage, and a nominated Senate of 13 members, eight appointed on the advice of the Premier, three after consultation with such persons as could speak for the differing political views of opposition groups in the Assembly, and two by the Governor in his discretion. The life of the legislature was to be for four years unless dissolved before. The Legislative Assembly was presided over by a Speaker who was not a member of the Assembly. The Senate was presided over by a President chosen by members from among their own number.

The Council of Ministers consisted of a Premier and not more than nine other Ministers and the Governor was required to exercise all his powers in accordance with the advice of the Council except where otherwise expressly stated (the notable exception being defence and external affairs).

In the elections under the new constitution held on 21st August 1961, the People's Progressive Party under Dr Cheddi Jagan obtained twenty seats and formed a government.

In January 1962, Her Majesty's Government announced its willingness to hold a Constitutional Conference to discuss the date and arrangements to be made for the achievement of independence by British Guiana. The Conference was held in October but was unable to reach agreement and was adjourned to allow for further discussions between the parties in British Guiana. Since these discussions did not lead to agreement the Secretary of State reconvened the Conference in 1963.

At the resumed Conference the Leaders of the three parties reported that they had failed to reach agreement between themselves on the terms of a constitution for independence and asked the British Government to settle on its own authority all the outstanding political issues. The then Secretary of State for the Colonies (the Right Honourable Duncan Sandys, MP) announced his decisions on 31st October 1963 at the closing session of the Conference. The most important item was that elections would be held on a new basis as soon as possible under a system of proportional representation.

In spite of renewed disturbances in the course of 1964 the elections were duly held under the proportional representation system in December 1964 as a result of which Mr L. F. S. Burnham, Leader of the People's National Congress (P.N.C.), formed a Government in coalition with the United Force (U.F.).

A final Constitutional Conference was held in London in November 1965 when agreement was reached on the outline of a Constitution under which British Guiana should become independent under the name of Guyana on 26th May 1966 (Cmnd. 2849, December 1965). The Leader of the People's Progressive Party (P.P.P.), Dr Cheddi Jagan declined to attend the Constitutional Conference or to be associated with its conclusions.

The British Parliament gave effect to the decisions of the Constitutional Conference in the Guyana Independence Act (1966 Ch. 14) of 12th May 1966. The Act gave power to provide a constitution for Guyana by Order in Council. An Order in Council was accordingly made on 16th May 1966 (S.I. 1966 No. 575) containing in a Schedule the Constitution of Guyana. The country became independent on 26th May 1966, and became a Republic within the Commonwealth on 23rd February 1970.

THE CONSTITUTION

The Constitution provides for a uni-cameral Legislature, which is referred to throughout the Constitution as the National Assembly but is now more usually known simply as Parliament. Members of Parliament are elected under a system of proportional representation by which those qualified to vote may cast a single vote in favour of lists of candidates. The seats in Parliament are then allocated between the lists in proportion to the numbers of votes cast. There is universal adult suffrage.

The normal life of Parliament is five years. The Cabinet consists of the Prime Minister, who must be an elected Member of Parliament and such other Ministers as the President, acting on the advice of the Prime Minister, may appoint. Provision is made for the appointment of up to four Ministers who have not been elected. Such Ministers become Members of Parliament but have no right to vote.

There is an office of Leader of the Opposition to which appointments are made by the President. The Prime Minister is required to consult the Leader of the Opposition before advising the President on certain senior appointments.

The Independence Constitution provided for a Governor-General to be appointed by the Queen but also gave Parliament the power after 31st December 1968 to declare Guyana a Republic if Parliament by a simple majority of all elected members passed a resolution to that effect. The motion that Guyana should become a Republic was adopted by Parliament on 29th August 1969, and the Republic was inaugurated on 23rd February 1970. Mr Arthur Chung was elected first President on 17th March 1970 for a six-year term.

There is a Court of Appeal and High Court. The Judges of the Court of Appeal are the Chancellor, who is President, the Chief Justice and such number of Justices of Appeal as Parliament prescribes. The Judges of the High Court are the Chief Justice and such number of Puisne Judges as Parliament prescribes. The Constitution provides for an Ombudsman to investigate actions taken by Government departments or other authorities.

The Constitution also contains provisions relating to human rights, citizenship, the functions of the executive, Parliamentary procedure and elections, and procedures for appointments in the Judicature, Public Service and Police. Parliament has power to alter the Constitution but certain provisions are entrenched.

HISTORICAL LIST
GOVERNORS-GENERAL

Sir Richard Luyt, G CMG, K CVO, D CM, 26th May 1966 to 31st October 1966
Sir Kenneth Stoby, 1st November 1966 to 15th December 1966 (Acting)
Sir David Rose, G CMG, CVO, MBE, 16th December 1966 to 10th November 1969
Sir Edward Luckhoo, QC, 11th November 1969 to 22nd February 1970 (Acting)

PRESIDENT
His Excellency Mr Arthur Chung
(Assumed office on 17th March 1970)

GOVERNMENT
At the elections in December 1968 the People's National Congress (P.N.C.)
won 30 seats, the People's Progressive Party (P.P.P.) 19 seats and the United
Force (U.F.) 4 seats.

CABINET
Prime Minister and Minister for External Affairs, Defence, Economic Development,
the Public Service, Public Corporations and Co-operatives: The Hon. L. F. S. Burnham
Deputy Prime Minister and Minister of Agriculture: Dr the Hon. P. A. Reid
Attorney-General and Minister of State: The Hon. S. S. Ramphal
Minister of Communications: The Hon. M. Kasim
Minister of Education, Information and Culture:
The Hon. Miss S. Field-Ridley (Mrs Hamilton Green)
Minister of Finance: The Hon. H. D. Hoyte
Minister of Health: The Hon. Mrs S. Talbot
Minister of Home Affairs: The Hon. O. E. Clarke
Minister of Housing and Reconstruction: The Hon. David Singh
Minister of Local Government: The Hon. C. V. Mingo
Minister of Labour and Social Security: The Hon. W. Carrington
Minister of Mines and Forests: The Hon. H. O. Jack
Minister of Trade and Leader of the House: The Hon. B. Ramsaroop
Minister of Works, Hydraulics and Supply: The Hon. Hamilton Green

PARLIAMENTARY SECRETARIES
Ministry of Agriculture: A. Salim; P. Duncan (for Interior Development)
Ministry of Finance: J. G. Joaquin, OBE JP
Ministry of Works, Hydraulics and Supply: C. Wrights
Office of the Prime Minister: J. R. Thomas; W. Haynes

LEADER OF THE OPPOSITION IN THE NATIONAL ASSEMBLY
Dr C. B. Jagan

NATIONAL ASSEMBLY
Speaker: His Honour Sase Naraine
Deputy Speaker: D. C. Jagan
Clerk of the Legislature: F. A. Narain

JUDICIARY
Court of Appeal

President The Chancellor: The Hon. E. V. Luckhoo, SC
Members The Chief Justice: The Hon. Harold B. S. Bollers
Justices of Appeal: Mr Justice P. A. Cummings,
Mr Justice V. E. Crane,
Mr Justice G. L. B. Persaud

High Jourt
The Chief Justice

Mr Justice Akbar Khan
Mr Justice K. M. George
Mr Justice R. M. Morris
Mr Justice J. Gonsalves-Sabola
Mr Justice L. F. Collins

Mr Justice F. Vieira
Mr Justice D. Jhappan
Mr Justice C. J. E. Fung-a-Fatt
Mr Justice H. Mitchell

REGISTRAR OF THE SUPREME COURT OF JUDICATURE
K. Barnwell

OMBUDSMAN
G. A. S. Van Sertima

MINISTRIES AND GOVERNMENT DEPARTMENTS

OFFICE OF THE PRIME MINISTER
Permanent Secretary: O. L. Henry
Chief of Staff, Guyana Defence Force:
Colonel C. A. L. Price

ATTORNEY-GENERAL'S CHAMBERS
Solicitor-General: M. Shahabuddeen
Chief Parliamentary Counsel: B. T. I. Pollard

MINISTRY OF AGRICULTURE
Permanent Secretary: F. A. Noel
Chief Agricultural Officer: B. W. Carter

MINISTRY OF COMMUNICATIONS
Permanent Secretary: R. A. Cheong (Acting)
General Manager, Transport and Harbours
Department: W. H. Griffith
Director of Civil Aviation: E. A. Phillips

MINISTRY OF ECONOMIC DEVELOPMENT
Permanent Secretary: B. Crawford
Chief Planning Officer: W. M. King

MINISTRY OF EDUCATION
Permanent Secretary: W. O. Agard
Chief Education Officer: G. O. Fox

MINISTRY OF EXTERNAL AFFAIRS
Permanent Secretary: R. E. Jackson
Chief of Protocol: Miss E. A. Mansell

MINISTRY OF FINANCE
Permanent Secretary and Secretary to the
Treasury: F. A. Hope
Deputy Secretary of the Treasury: H. A.
Wilkinson
Controller of Customs and Excise: D. F.
Corlette
Accountant General: S. Seymour (Acting)
Commissioner of Inland Revenue: W. R.
Devonish

MINISTRY OF HEALTH
Permanent Secretary: M. H. Ali
Chief Medical Officer: R. L. S. Baird

MINISTRY OF HOME AFFAIRS
Permanent Secretary: J. S. M. Worrell
(Acting)
Commissioner of Police: C. E. B. Austin
Director of Prisons: H. A. Davis
Chief Fire Officer: E. A. Spellen

MINISTRY OF HOUSING
Permanent Secretary: V. J. Correia

MINISTRY OF INFORMATION
Permanent Secretary: P. Dyal (Acting)
Chief Information Officer: V. L. C. Forsythe

MINISTRY OF LABOUR
Permanent Secretary: C. E. Douglas
Chief Labour Officer: L. A. Dyal

MINISTRY OF LOCAL GOVERNMENT
Permanent Secretary: T. B. Richmond

MINISTRY OF MINES AND FORESTS
Permanent Secretary: C. E. Barker
Director of Geological Survey: Dr S. Singh
Conservator of Forests: L. E. Dow

MINISTRY OF PUBLIC CORPORATIONS
Permanent Secretary: D. Yankana

MINISTRY OF THE PUBLIC SERVICE
Permanent Secretary (and Head of the Civil
Service): E. E. Burke

MINISTRY OF TRADE
Permanent Secretary: L. E. Mann

MINISTRY OF WORKS, HYDRAULICS AND
SUPPLY
Permanent Secretary: G. A. Marshall
Chief Works and Hydraulics Officer: P.
Allsopp (Acting)

SERVICE COMMISSIONS
Chairman, Public Service Commission:
W. G. Stoll
Chairman, Judicial Service Commission:
E. V. Lucknoo
Chairman, Police Service Commission:
W. G. Stoll
Chairman, Elections Commission: Sir Donald
Jackson

AUDIT DEPARTMENT
Director of Audit: R. P. Farnum

DIPLOMATIC REPRESENTATION

GUYANESE REPRESENTATIVES IN OTHER
COMMONWEALTH COUNTRIES
High Commissioner in the United Kingdom:
John Carter, S C
High Commissioner in Canada: R. B. Gajraj
(resident in Washington)
High Commissioner in Barbados, Jamaica
and Trinidad, and Commissioner to the
Associated States: Mrs W. Gaskin
(resident in Kingston).

COMMONWEALTH HIGH COMMISSIONERS
IN GUYANA
Britain: W. S. Bates, CMG; Canada:
J. A. Stiles; Trinidad and Tobago: Eric

Murray; India: D. Hejmadi; Jamaica: Ivo
S. De Souza, O B E (resident in Port of Spain);
Pakistan: (vacant).

GUYANESE REPRESENTATIVES IN
NON-COMMONWEALTH COUNTRIES
United States: R. B. Gajraj
Germany; France; Netherlands; Soviet
Union: John Carter S C (resident in
London)
Venezuela: Dr Ann Jardim
Surinam (Consul-General): W. O. R.
Kendall
United Nations: P. Thompson
Brazil: E. Drayton

INDIA

INDIA is bounded to the north-west by West Pakistan, to the north by Tibet, Nepal, Bhutan and Sikkim, and to the north-east by East Pakistan, China and Burma; Ceylon lies off the south-east coast. India also includes the Andaman and Nicobar Islands in the Bay of Bengal and the Laccadive Islands off the south-west coast. The mainland can be divided into three well-defined regions: (a) the mountain zone of the Himalayas; (b) the Indo-Gangetic Plain and (c) the Southern Peninsula. The main mountain ranges are the Himalayas in the north (over 29,000 ft), the Aravallis and Vindhyas (up to 4,000 ft) in central India, and the Western and Eastern Ghats (over 8,000 ft). The most important rivers are the Ganges, Jumma, Brahmaputra, Indus, Godavari, Krishna, Mahanadi, Nerbudda and Cauvery which are all navigable in parts.

There are four distinct seasons: (i) the cold season (December–March); (ii) the hot season (April–May); (iii) the rainy season (June–September); and (iv) what is known as the season of the retreating S.W. monsoon (October–November). The mean temperatures range at Delhi from 50°F to 92°F, at Calcutta from 65°F to 86°F and at Madras from 75°F to 89°F Maximum temperatures of about 100°F. and 115°F. are reached during May in Madras and Delhi respectively. Annual rainfall varies widely; as little as four inches falls in the Thar desert, but parts of Assam experience more than 300 inches.

India is the world's second most populous country. A census is taken every ten years and at the time of the 1961 census the population was estimated to be 439 million, an increase of 20 per cent during the previous decade. The preliminary estimate from the 1971 census (relating to 1st April) is 547 million, an increase of 24·7 per cent since 1961. The birth rate is about 39 per 1,000 (1968 figure), and the death rate about 12 per 1,000 (1967). The numbers of adherents to the main religions practised in India at the time of the 1961 census were: Hindus 366,500,000; Muslims 47,000,000; Christians 10,725,000; Sikhs 7,850,000; Buddhists 3,250,000 and Jains 2,000,000. Primary education is free but not yet universal. In the year 1965/66 there were 30,906,208 secondary school students. About 30 per cent of the population was literate according to the 1971 census, but estimates for 1969/70 showed about 79 per cent of children receiving some primary education.

Information about the division of the country into States and about the various languages used in India will be found in the sections dealing with Constitutional Development and the Constitution below. New Delhi is the capital of the country with an estimated population of 3·9 million. Other principal cities are Calcutta (5·4 million), Great Bombay (5·5 million) and Madras (2·0 million). The States with the largest populations are Uttar Pradesh (about 88 million), Bihar (about 56 million) and Maharashtra (about 48 million).

Major ports, showing some of the available tonnage figures for the years 1968–69 are: Calcutta 10,316,000, Bombay 18,630,000, Madras 9,430,000, Cochin 8,452,000, Visakhapatnam, Kandla (Gujarat), Marmagoa and Paradip. The principal shipping lines are: Shipping Corporation of India and Scindia Steam Navigation Company. The main airports are: Palam (Delhi), Bombay, Calcutta, Madras. The main airlines are: Indian Airlines (internal) and Air India

For further information about India see *India, a Reference Annual*, published by the Indian Ministry of Information and Broadcasting. An outline of the history and constitutional development of the Indian sub-continent prior to August 1947 may be found in the *Commonwealth Office Year Book*, 1967.

(International). Main runway lengths are: Palam, 10,000 ft., Santa Cruz, 10,925 ft.; Dum Dum, 10,500 ft.; and St Thomas' Mount, 10,050 ft. In 1966 road mileage outside towns was over 560,000. There are 60,014 kilometres of railway, of which 28,350 kilometres are of broad gauge (1·67 metres). Broadcasting service is provided for the entire country by All India Radio but the television service of All India Radio is at present confined to Delhi only. However, new television stations are planned in several localities.

India's main crops are rice, wheat and other cereals (*jowar, bajra*, maize etc.), gram, *tur* and other pulses, sugarcane, jute, cotton and tea. Other agricultural products include oil seeds, spices, groundnuts, tobacco, rubber and coffee. Among principal manufactures are textiles, jute goods, sugar, cement, paper and industrial and consumer goods. Industries include iron and steel, heavy and light engineering, drugs and chemicals, fertilisers, oil and petroleum and their products, coal and lignite. Among other minerals produced are iron, manganese, copper, gold, limestone mica and salt. The revised budget estimates for 1970/1 give Government revenue as Rs 4,147 crores (£2,300 million) including state's share of central revenues (Rs 755 crores) and expenditure as Rs 3,193 crores (£1,720 million). There are also substantial receipts and expenditure on capital account. Gross aid receipts in 1970/1 were estimated at over $1,000 million but external debt service amounted to about $580 million. The third Five Year Development Plan, completed in 1965–66, cost £5,953,000,000. For three years, 1966/67 to 1968/69, annual plans were in force. The Fourth Five Year Plan, covering the period 1969/70–1973/74, is now the basic document on the Government's economic strategy; it envisages expenditure over the five years of Rs 24,882 crores (£13,500 million), of which Rs 8,980 crores (£499 million) represents private sector investment. Food grain production in 1970/71 is expected to be of the order of £105 million tonnes, a record figure. The achievement of this total is largely due to the use of high yielding varieties of wheat and certain other crops. Irrigation and power projects include the Rajasthan Canal and the Bhakra-Nangal Project. The former will be 425 miles long, from Harika in the Punjab to Jaisalmer in Rajasthan and will irrigate some 3 million acres of land. In about 18 years, 10,000 square miles of the area served by the canal will be transformed from desert into a settled and productive region. The latter project, in the Punjab, is now nearing completion. It will be one of the largest multi-purpose river valley schemes in Asia and will eventually irrigate some 10 million acres of land and build up an ultimate power potential of 1,204 Mw. The expansion of the steel industry is playing a fundamental part in India's industrial development. Steel production increased from under 2 million tonnes in 1950 to 6·5 million tonnes in the financial year 1968/69. Hindustan Steel Limited, a Government undertaking set up in 1954 to augment the country's steel production, now has three plants in production. These are at Durgapur, Rourkela and Bhilai. A fourth steel plant is under construction at Bokaro. The Government of India has announced that three new steel plants will be established in Tamilnadu, Andhra Pradesh and Mysore. The plant in Tamilnadu will produce special steels and have a capacity of 250,000 tonnes, the other two will be conventional 2 m. tonne mills.

The production of oil is also playing an important part in India's programme of industrial development and reached about 5·85 million tonnes of crude oil and 15·4 million of refined products in 1968/69. Exploration is carried out mainly by the Oil and Natural Gas Commission who have discovered promising fields in Gujarat and a recent survey suggests major deposits also in the Gulf of Cambay:

offshore exploration has now begun. In association with E.N.I. of Italy and Philips Petroleum of U.S.A., the Commission has offshore drilling rights in the Persian Gulf. India is also increasing her refinery capacity in order to save foreign exchange on imported petroleum products and broaden her industrial base. In addition to the four oil refineries maintained by private firms, a Government undertaking, the Indian Oil Corporation Limited, is now operating refineries at Barauni, Gauhati, Koyali and Cochin. One more is under construction, at Madras, and a sixth is planned at Haldia. In the engineering industry machine tool production is being developed. In 1953 a public sector company, Hindustan Machine Tools Limited, was set up in Bangalore. Production started in 1956 and the firm now has three more factories in production, at Pinjore (Haryana), Kalamassery (Kerala), and Hyderabad (Andhra Pradesh). The manufacture of heavy electrical equipment is also being undertaken. At Bhopal the Heavy Electrical Industries (India) Ltd, a British-aided project, is manufacturing turbines, switchgear and generating equipment. Bharat Heavy Electricals Ltd (a Public Sector undertaking) have three manufacturing units at Tiruchirappalli (Madras), Ramachandrapuram (Andhra Pradesh) and Hardwar (Uttar Pradesh). The manufacturing programme includes steam turbo sets, hydro turbo sets, and medium A.C. and D.C. electric motors, heavy boilers, steam turbines heavy and turbo-alternators.

India's National Day is 26th January (Republic Day).

CONSTITUTIONAL DEVELOPMENT

Under the Indian Independence Act, power was transferred to the first government of the new Dominion of India on 15th August 1947: on that day Lord Mountbatten relinquished the office of Viceroy and was appointed, on the advice of the Indian Government, first Governor-General of independent India. Since then, the principal constitutional developments in India have been the integration of the Indian Princely States, the adoption of a Republican Constitution and the reorganisation of State boundaries.

The Princely States. One of the major problems involved in the transfer of power was the future of the Indian Princely States which numbered about 560 and comprised two-fifths of the area of the sub-continent. During the period of British rule, the Princely States had preserved a large measure of internal autonomy subject only to the paramountcy of the British Crown expressed in the form of many separate treaties and agreements entered into with the Rulers concerned. Under the Indian Independence Act this paramountcy was declared to have lapsed and with it the existing treaties between the Rulers and the Crown.

During the final preparations for the transfer of power, the Rulers of the States were advised by the Viceroy to accede to one or other of the two successor Dominions. In the event nearly all the Rulers accepted this advice; and, by the date of the transfer, practically all the States whose territory lay within or contiguous to the boundaries of the new Dominion of India had signed Instruments of Accession, the only major exceptions being Kashmir and Hyderabad. In October 1947 the Maharajah of Kashmir signed an Instrument of Accession to India. Pakistan did not accept the validity of this accession and fighting broke out between the two countries after partition and again in the latter part of 1965. There is now a cease-fire line between the Indian and Pakistan forces in Kashmir. Hyderabad was occupied by Indian forces in September 1948 after a long dispute between the Government of India and the Nizam.

The Instruments which the Rulers signed provided for accession in a limited number of subjects only. The larger and more important States (about 140 in all) acceded in respect of External Affairs, Defence and Communications; but in the case of the smaller States (which had had less autonomy under British rule), other subjects were added to the list. During the two years following the transfer of power, the Indian Government energetically pursued a policy of persuading the Rulers to agree to the complete integration of their States with the body politic of India and the consequent surrender of their remaining Princely powers. This aim was successfully achieved, and by the end of 1949 all the 554 States which had acceded to India (with the exception of Jammu and Kashmir which retained a special status) had been integrated with India. The Rulers signed individual agreements under which, in return for giving up their States, the Indian Government agreed to pay them privy purses for life and to grant certain other personal privileges. These purses and privileges were abolished by a Presidential order in September 1970 which "de-recognised" the former Rulers. In December 1970 however this Presidential Order was struck down by the Supreme Court of India as being *ultra vires* of the Constitution. But it is still a part of the policy of the ruling Congress Party to abolish the purses and privileges.

The constitutional arrangements for administering the Princely States after integration varied according to geographical and other circumstances. Some were incorporated in the former British Provinces; others were grouped into new composite political units (Rajasthan, Madhya Bharat, Patiala and East Punjab States Union, Saurashtra, Travancore-Cochin, Vindhya Pradesh, and Himachal Pradesh); and others retained their separate identities (Mysore, Hyderabad, Bhopal, Kutch, Manipur, Tripura, and Bilaspur). The larger States or groups of States in the two latter categories (Rajasthan, Madhya Bharat, P.E.P.S.U., Saurashtra, Travancore-Cochin, Mysore and Hyderabad) eventually became, under the 1950 Constitution, Part B States, with parliamentary institutions on the same lines as those possessed by the former British Provinces (Part A States), except that they had at their head a senior Princely Ruler—a Rajpramukh— rather than a Governor. The smaller units became Part C States and as such were placed under various forms of central administration.

The States Reorganisation Act, 1956. Soon after the Constitution (*see below under* 'Constitution') came into force in 1950 a movement gathered impetus for the redrawing of State boundaries on a more rational and in particular on a linguistic basis. (In several of the existing States the population was divided into two or three major language groups.) The first fruit of the linguistic campaign was the decision in 1953 to separate the Telugu-speaking areas of Madras to form a new State called Andhra: this came into being in October 1953. In December 1953 the first official move towards a more comprehensive reorganisation of the States was made with the appointment by the Government of a States Reorganisation Commission which was charged with a detailed examination of the whole problem. In its Report, submitted in September 1955, the Commission recommended a radical re-drawing of State boundaries. In September 1956, after prolonged public and parliamentary debate, the decisions of the Government on this Report, incorporated in the States Reorganisation Bill and the consequential Constitution (Seventh Amendment) Bill, were passed by the Indian Parliament, and the reorganisation of States became effective on 1st November 1956.

Under the new Acts, the former categories of States and with them the office of Rajpramukh were abolished, and the component parts of the Indian Union were reduced to 13 States (apart from Jammu and Kashmir) and 6 Union Territories, the revised division being mainly on a linguistic basis. Perhaps the most striking territorial change was the disappearance of Hyderabad and the incorporation of its parts in Andhra, Bombay and Mysore. Another major change was the re-shaping of Bombay which, as a bilingual Marathi-Gujarati-speaking State, lost its Kannada-speaking areas in the south to Mysore, but acquired Saurashtra, Kutch and extensive territories from Madhya Pradesh and Hyderabad. Travancore-Cochin, enlarged to include the Malabar District of Madras, was renamed Kerala. The union of former Punjab Princely States known as P.E.P.S.U. was merged with Punjab. Madhya Pradesh (the former Central Provinces) was extensively reshaped, losing a large area to Bombay, but incorporating Madhya Bharat, Vindhya Pradesh and Bhopal, all of which were former Princely States or unions of such States. Mysore was substantially enlarged to include Coorg and parts of Bombay and Hyderabad. Thus, under this comprehensive reorganisation, the political map of India was radically changed and in many places (with important exceptions like the States of Uttar Pradesh and Bihar) the old boundaries of the major Princely States and provinces of British India were no longer recognisable. In March 1960, following persistent agitation against its bilingual structure, Bombay State was, by the terms of the Bombay Reorganisation Act, 1960, divided into the separate unilingual States of Maharashtra and Gujarat. In 1961 Nagaland (comprising the Naga Hills area of Assam and the Tuensang area of the North East Frontier Agency) was accorded the status of a separate State of the Indian Union.

One bilingual State which the States Reorganisation Commission had left untouched was the Punjab, where both Hindi and Punjabi were joint official languages. In 1966, following prolonged pressure from some Punjabi-speakers, the Indian Government decided to split the Punjab on a linguistic basis. Part of its territory was incorporated into the Union Territory of Himachal Pradesh, and the remainder has been divided between a greatly contracted area which preserves the name 'Punjab', and a completely new Hindi-speaking State, Haryana. In January 1971 Himachal Pradesh was granted full Statehood.

INDIA AND THE COMMONWEALTH

The relationship between India and the other Members of the Commonwealth was settled at the Prime Ministers' Meeting held in London in April 1949. This Meeting had been arranged to consider the constitutional issues arising from the decision of the Indian Constituent Assembly to adopt a republican form of Government. The final *communiqué* stated that 'The Government of India have informed the other Governments of the Commonwealth of the intention of the Indian people that under the new Constitution which is about to be adopted, India shall become a sovereign independent Republic. The Government of India have, however, declared and affirmed India's desire to continue her full membership of the Commonwealth of Nations and her acceptance of the King as the symbol of the free association of its independent member-nations and as such the Head of the Commonwealth. The Governments of the other countries of the Commonwealth, the basis of whose membership of the Commonwealth is not hereby changed, accept and recognise India's continuing membership in accordance with the terms of this declaration'.

CONSTITUTION

The Indian Independence Act (*see above under* 'Constitutional Development') provided that the Government of India Act, 1935, should remain in force in the two new Dominions as their Constitutions, subject to any modifying Orders made by their Governors-General. Under this latter provision, the Governor-General of India made the India (Provisional Constitution) Order, 1947, to serve as a Constitution for India until a fresh Constitution had been drafted and put into force.

Meanwhile a Constituent Assembly, elected in 1946 from the existing Provincial Legislatures and intended to serve also as a Provisional Parliament, had begun drafting a Constitution. This new Constitution, which describes India as a 'Union of States' and as a 'Sovereign Democratic Republic' with a President as its constitutional head, was finally adopted in November 1949, and came into force on 26th January 1950. On that day the last Governor-General of India (Mr C. Rajagopalachari) relinquished his office and Dr Rajendra Prasad assumed office as the first President. Broadly speaking the Constitution provides, both at the Centre and in the States, for a system of Parliamentary and Cabinet government on the British model, though in a republican form.

Under the Constitution, the executive power is vested in the President, who is elected for a period of five years by an electoral college consisting of the elected members of the Union and State Legislatures, the voting strength of the Central Legislature in the college being equal to that of all the States put together. In his absence his functions are performed by the Vice-President, who at other times acts as Chairman of the Rajya Sabha (the Upper House). The President is 'aided and advised' in his functions by a Council of Ministers (the Cabinet). He appoints the Prime Minister and, on the latter's advice, the other Ministers, and can dismiss them. The Council of Ministers is collectively responsible to the Lok Sabha (the Lower House) and all Ministers must be or become Members of Parliament.

The legislative power vests in Parliament which comprises the President, the Rajya Sabha and the Lok Sabha. The Rajya Sabha consists of not more than 250 members, 12 nominated by the President, the rest elected by the members of the State legislatures or representing the Union Territories (*see below*) on a population basis; they hold office for six years, one-third retiring every two years. The Lok Sabha originally consisted of not more than 500 members. But this figure was adjusted in 1956 to take account of the reclassification of States and Territories and it now consists of not more than 525 members, of whom not more than 500 represent territorial constituencies in the States and not more than 25 represent the Union Territories. The members from the States are chosen by direct election under universal adult franchise; those from the Union Territories are chosen 'in such manner as Parliament may by law provide'. The Lok Sabha is elected for a maximum of five years though this may be extended during a State of Emergency. For a period of twenty years from 26th January 1950 seats are reserved in the Lok Sabha for the Scheduled Castes and Scheduled Tribes, and not more than 2 members of the Anglo-Indian Community may be nominated to fill additional seats.

There is a Supreme Court of not more than fourteen judges (including the Chief Justice) appointed by the President and only removable by his order following an address passed by each House of Parliament. The Court has sole jurisdiction in virtually all disputes between State and Union or between State and State. It is also the final Court of Appeal from other Courts.

The Constitution laid down that after 1965 Hindi should be used for all official purposes. The Official Languages Act, 1963, however, provided for the continued use after 1965 of English, in addition to Hindi, for all official purposes of the Union and for the transaction of business in Parliament. Under this Act a Parliamentary Committee is to be set up in 1975 to review the progress made in the use of Hindi. Article 345 of the Constitution provided for the adoption by States Legislatures, for official purposes of the State, of any of the fourteen regional languages listed in the Eighth Schedule to the Constitution. These are Assamese, Bengali, Gujarati, Hindi, Kannada, Kashmiri, Malayalam, Marathi, Oriya, Punjabi, Sanskrit, Tamil, Telugu and Urdu. Sanskrit, which is a scholarly language widely used throughout India, has not been adopted for official use by any State. Urdu also, although not adopted officially by any State, is spoken in the Punjab, Uttar Pradesh, Bihar, Delhi and Himachal Pradesh. The areas in which the other regional languages are used are indicated in the notes on the States and Territories of the Union at the end of this chapter.

The Constitution can be (and has on eighteen occasions already been) amended by a Bill passed in each House of the Union Parliament by a majority of its total members and not less than two-thirds of its members present and voting. Amendments to certain Articles must however also be ratified by the legislatures of a majority of the States.

CHINESE ATTACK, 1962

On the 26th October 1962 the President of India declared a National Emergency following the Chinese invasion which had taken place in N.E.F.A. and Ladakh earlier the same month. After the Chinese had made a further extensive attack in November, they announced a cease-fire along the entire Sino-Indian border on 21st November and withdrew from some of the territory which they had occupied since the beginning of October. The terms which the Chinese suggested at the same time for negotiations were unacceptable to the Indian Government, and the cease-fire has not yet been stabilised by any truce agreement. The state of emergency was lifted on 10th January 1968.

INDO-PAKISTAN HOSTILITIES, 1965

A dispute over the ownership of a part of the Rann of Kutch resulted in a minor outbreak of hostilities between India and Pakistan on 4th April 1965. Following the intervention of the British Prime Minister, a *de facto* cease-fire came into effect on 30th April 1965, and was confirmed under an agreement signed on 30th June 1965. The agreement also provided for a withdrawal of forces and the appointment of a tribunal for the settlement of the dispute. The tribunal's decision was announced on 19th February 1968, and accepted by both sides.

A more serious conflict between the two countries occurred in August/September 1965, when the armed forces of India and Pakistan were heavily engaged. After three United Nations Security Council Resolutions calling for a cease-fire and withdrawal, the two countries agreed to a cease-fire on 22nd September. Withdrawals did not follow until the Prime Minister of India and the President of Pakistan had signed an Agreement at Tashkent, U.S.S.R., on 10th January 1966.

HISTORICAL LIST OF HEADS OF STATE
GOVERNORS-GENERAL
(Dominion of India)
Louis Francis Albert Victor Nicholas Mountbatten, 1st Earl Mountbatten of Burma, KG, PC, GCSI, GCIE, GCVO, KCB, DSO (later GCB), 15th August 1947 to 20th June 1948
Chakravarty Rajagopalachari, 21st June 1948 to 26th January 1950

PRESIDENTS
(Republic of India)
Dr Rajendra Prasad, 26th January, 1950 to 6th May 1952
Dr Rajendra Prasad, 6th May 1952 to 11th May 1957
Dr Rajendra Prasad, 11th May 1957 to 13th May 1962
Dr S. Radhakrishnan, 13th May 1962 to 13th May 1967
Dr Zakir Husain 13th May 1967 to 3rd May 1969
V. V. Giri 3rd May 1969 to 19th July 1969 (Acting President)
Mr Justice M. Hidayatullah from 20th July 1969 to 23rd August 1969 (Acting President)
V. V. Giri from 24th August 1969

HISTORICAL LIST OF MINISTRIES
Jawaharlal Nehru, 15th August 1947 to 13th May 1952
Jawaharlal Nehru, 13th May 1952 to 17th April 1957
Jawaharlal Nehru, 17th April 1957 to 9th April 1962
Jawaharlal Nehru, 9th April 1962 to 27th May 1964
Gulzarilal Nanda, 27th May 1964 to 9th June 1964 (Acting Prime Minister)
Lal Bahadur Shastri, 9th June 1964 to 11th January 1966
Gulzarilal Nanda, 11th January 1966 to 24th January 1966 (Acting Prime Minister)
Shrimati Indira Gandhi. from 24th January 1966 to 12th March 1967
Shrimati Indira Gandhi, from 12th March 1967 to 18th March 1971
Shrimati Indira Gandhi from 18th March 1971

GOVERNMENT

The first general elections based on universal adult franchise in accordance with the new Constitution were held in 1952 and resulted in a sweeping victory for the Congress Party which won 75 per cent of the seats in the Lok Sabha (Lower House of the Central Parliament). The Communist Party and their allies with some 30 seats and the Praja Socialist Party (formed from the merger of two other left wing parties) with 26 seats were the most important elements in the Opposition.

The second series of general elections to the Lok Sabha and the Vidhan Sabhas (State Assemblies) were held in 1957. In the Lok Sabha the Congress Party maintained their position with another decisive victory, securing 371 out of a total of 494 seats filled by direct election and increasing their share of the poll from the 45 per cent they obtained in the first general elections to some 48 per cent on this occasion. The position of the Communist Party was also virtually unchanged; they and their allies won a total of 29 seats and were still the largest single Opposition group. The Praja Socialist Party lost some ground and won only 19 seats.

In the Vidhan Sabhas the Congress Party won absolute majorities in 11 out of 13 States and formed Governments in 12 States, including Orissa where they emerged as the largest single Party but without an overall majority. In May 1959 in Orissa they formed a coalition government sharing power with the Ganatantra Parishad, the largest of the Opposition parties. In Kerala the Communist Party won 60 out of 126 contested seats in the Assembly. They governed with the support of 5 Independents until July 1959, when the Communist Ministry was dismissed by the President under his emergency powers (*see above under* 'The Constitution') pending fresh elections in the State. In the subsequent mid-term elections to the Kerala State Assembly in February 1960, the main non-Com-

H

munist parties formed an electoral alliance and, despite a considerable increase in the Communist poll, succeeded in winning 94 out of a total of 126 contested seats. Thereafter, the Congress and Praja Socialist Parties, who controlled between them 83 seats, formed a coalition government until October 1962, when the Praja Socialists withdrew from the coalition, leaving the Congress Party to form the government by themselves.

In the third General Elections in February 1962, the Congress Party won another decisive victory in the Lok Sabha, although losing a little ground compared with 1957. They received just over 45 per cent of the votes cast in 1962 as against nearly 48 per cent in 1957, and obtained 361 seats as against 371 in 1957. The Communist Party remained the largest Opposition party with 30 seats, one more than in 1957. The Praja Socialist Party lost further ground, winning only 12 seats, but the Swatantra Party, formed since the 1957 elections, won 22 seats, and the Jan Sangh won 14 seats compared with 4 in 1957.

In 1962 simultaneous elections to the Vidhan Sabhas were held in all the States other than in Kerala and Orissa, which had had mid-term elections, *see above*. In these elections, the Congress won a majority in 10 out of 12 States but although they lost an overall majority in the other two, Rajasthan and Madhya Pradesh, they continued to form the Governments there. In 1964 the first elections were held in the new State of Nagaland. Congress did not contest the elections, which were won by the Naga Nationalist Organisation. In the mid-term election in Kerala in 1965 no one party secured a majority, and President's Rule, imposed in 1964, was continued.

Mr Nehru, who had been Prime Minister of India since Independence, died on 27th May 1964. The President of India swore in Mr Nanda, the senior member of Mr Nehru's Cabinet, as Prime Minister pending the election of a new leader by the Congress Party. On 9th June 1964 Mr Lal Bahadur Shastri, who had been unanimously elected as leader by the Congress Parliamentary Party, was sworn in as Prime Minister. He died at Tashkent on 11th January 1966. The Congress Parliamentary Party elected Mrs Indira Gandhi (daughter of Jawaharlal Nehru) as its new leader, and she was sworn in as Prime Minister on 24th January 1966.

General Elections held in February 1967 resulted in a setback for Congress, which was returned to power with 280 seats out of 521 compared with 365 out of 500 in the last Parliament. The Swatantra and Jana Sangh increased their representation to 44 and 35 respectively. The Communist Party had split in 1964 into a Right and a Left party, i.e., the CPI and CPI (Marxist) respectively. The CPI won 22 seats, the CPI (Marxist) 19 seats. The Samyukta Socialist Party increased their number of seats from 6 to 23 and the Praja Socialists won 13. The Dravida Munnetra Kazhagam (DMK)—a regional party based in Tamil Nadu (the former Madras State)—increased their number of seats from 7 to 25.

In the simultaneous 1967 elections to the Vidhan Sabhas, the Congress Party won an absolute majority in only eight States. It failed to win an absolute majority in Uttar Pradesh, Bihar, West Bengal, Rajasthan and Punjab and was defeated in Orissa, Madras and Kerala.

By the beginning of 1969, four States—West Bengal, Bihar, Uttar Pradesh and Punjab—were under President's Rule. In February 1969 mid-term elections were held in these States. The Congress Party was defeated in West Bengal and Punjab. A Communist/Socialist coalition Government was formed in the former and in the latter a coalition dominated by the regional and predominantly Sikh Akali

Dal. The Congress Party formed Governments in Uttar Pradesh and Bihar. By March 1970, all four of these Governments had fallen and had been replaced by new Ministries (Punjab, Uttar Pradesh, Bihar) or President's Rule (West Bengal).

In November 1969 the Congress Party split into two wings, the Congress (Ruling) and the Congress (Opposition). The former, led by Mrs Gandhi, had a strength of 228 in the Lok Sabha, the latter, led by Dr Ram Subhag Singh and Mr Morarji Desai, 64. In March 1970 the biennial elections to the Rajya Sabha reduced Congress (R) strength from 103 to 88 in a House totalling 240. The Congress (O) strength remained the same at 42.

In December 1970, the President, on the advice of Mrs Gandhi, dissolved the Lok Sabha and a General Election was held in March 1971, a year earlier than necessary under the Constitution. In this General Election Mrs Gandhi's Congress Party achieved an overwhelming victory and got more than two thirds of the seats in the Lok Sabha. The Congress (Ruling) now have 350 seats out of 521. The position in the Rayja Sabha remains as before, except in three States elections to the State Assemblies were not held. But Opposition Governments collapsed in a number of states immediately after the General Election and the Congress (Ruling) party now control, or are the dominant coaliton partner in 9 states. Mysore is under President's Rule (fresh elections are due towards the end of the year) and 7 states are controlled by other parties or coalitions. The Opposition parties were largely routed in the General Election and only the CPI (Marxist) increased its seats. It now has 25. The CPI and DMK got 23 each; the Jana Sangh 22; the Congress (O) 16; and the Swantantra 8. The Samyukta and Praja Socialists were reduced respectively to 3 and 2.

PRESIDENT
V. V. Giri

VICE-PRESIDENT
G. S. Pathak

CABINET
Prime Minister, Minister for Atomic Energy, Minister for Home Affairs and Minister for Information and Broadcasting: Mrs Indira Gandhi
Minister for Agriculture: Mr Fakhruddin Ali Ahmed
Minister for Finance: Mr Y. B. Chavan
Minister for Defence: Mr Jagjivan Ram
Minister for External Affairs: Mr Swaran Singh
Minister for Railways: Mr K. Hanumanthaiya
Minister for Tourism and Civil Aviation: Dr Karan Singh
Minister for Parliamentary Affairs, and Shipping and Transport: Mr Raj Bahadur
Minister for Industrial Development: Mr Moinul Haq Chaudhuri
Minister of Education and Social Welafre, who will also be in charge of the Department of Culture: Mr Sidhartha Shankar Ray
Minister for Law and Justice: Mr H. R. Gokhale
Minister for Steel and Mines: Mr S. Mohan Kumaramangalam
Minister for Health and Family Planning: Mr K. K. Shah
Minister for Planning, who will be concurrently in charge of the Department of Science and Technology: Mr C. Subramaniam
Minister for Works and Housing: Mr Uma Shankar Dikshit

MINISTERS OF STATE
Minister for Irrigation and Power: Dr K. L. Rao
Minister for Foreign Trade: Mr L. N. Mishra
Minister for Labour and Rehabilitation: Mr R. K. Khadilkar
Minister for Company Affairs: Mr K. V. Raghunath Reddy
Minister for Supply: Mr D. R. Chavan
Minister for Petroleum and Chemicals: Mr P. C. Sethi

Minister for Communications: Mr H. N. Bahuguna
Minister of State in the Ministry of Works and Housing: Mr I. K. Gujral
Minister of State in the Ministry of Agriculture: Prof. Sher Singh
Minister of State in the Ministry of Law and Justice: Mr Nitiraj Singh Chaudhuri
Minister of State in the Department of Parliamentary Affairs and the Ministry of Shipping and Transport: Mr Om Mehta
Minister of State in the Ministry of Home Affairs and in the Deparment of Personnel: Mr Ram Niwas Mirdha
Minister of State in the Ministry of Home Affairs who will also assist the Prime Minister in Parliamentary work relating to the Departments of Atomic Energy and Electronics: Mr K. C. Pant
Minister of State in the Ministry of Information and Broadcasting: Mrs Nandini Satpathy
Minister of State (Defence Production) in the Ministry of Defence: Mr V. C. Shulka
Minister of State in the Ministry of Agriculture: Mr Annasaheb P. Shinde
Minister of State in the Ministry of Finance: Mr K. R. Ganesh
Minister of State in the Ministry of Steel and Mines: Mr Shah Nawaz Khan
Minister of State in the Ministry of Health and Family Planning: Prof. D. P. Chattopadhyaya
Minister of State in the Ministry of Industrial Development: Mr Ghanshyam Oza
Minister of State in the Ministry of Planning: Mr Mohan Dharia
Minister of State in the Ministry of Tourism and Civil Aviation: Dr Sarojini Mahishi

Deputy Ministers

Deputy Minister in the Ministry of Health and Family Planning: Mr A. K. Kisku
Deputy Minister in the Ministry of Agriculture: Mr Jagannath Pahadia
Deputy Minister in the Ministry of Railways: Mr Mohd Shafi Qureshi
Deputy Minister in the Ministry of Education and Social Welfare: Mr K. S. Rameswamy
Deputy Minister in the Ministry of Industrial Development: Mr Sidheshwar Prasad
Deputy Minister in the Ministry of External Affairs: Mr Surendra Pal Singh
Deputy Minister in the Department of Parliamentary Affairs: Mr B. Shankaranand
Deputy Minister in the Department of Parliamentary Affairs: Mr Kodar Nath Singh
Deputy Minister in the Department of Company Affairs: Mr Bodabrata Barua
Deputy Minister in the Ministry of Education and Social Welfare: Prof. D. P. Yadav
Deputy Minister in the Ministry of Labour and Rehabilitation: Mr Balgovind Verma
Deputy Minister in the Ministry of Petroleum and Chemicals: Mr Dalbir Singh
Deputy Minister in the Ministry of Irrigation and Power: Mr Baijnath Kureel
Deputy Minister in the Ministry of Information and Broadcasting: Mr Dharamvir Singh
Deputy Minister in the Ministry of Communications: Mr Kartik Oraon
Deputy Minister in the Ministry of Foreign Trade: Mr A. C. George
Deputy Minister in the Ministry of Finance: Mrs Sushila Rohtagi
Deputy Minister in the Ministry of Home Affairs: Mr F. H. Mohsin

Note.

Mr K. K. Shah is expected to leave the Cabinet shortly on appointment as Governor of Tamilnadu. His portfolio will be added to that of Mr U. S. Dikshit. Mr K. Oraon has yet to take the Oath of Office (as of 4/5/71).

President's Staff
Secretary: Dr Nagendra Singh
Military Secretary: Major-General Amreek Singh

Rajya Sabha (Council of States)
Chairman: G. S. Pathak
Deputy Chairman: B. D. Khobragade, MP
Secretary: B. N. Banerjee

Lok Sabha (House of the People)
Speaker: G. S. Dhillon, MP
Deputy Speaker: G. G. Swell, MP
Secretary: S. L. Shakdher

Prime Minister's Secretariat
Secretary: P. N. Haksar
Joint Secretary: B. N. Tandon

Cabinet Secretariat
Secretary: T. Swaminathan

Judiciary
Supreme Court of India
Chief Justice of India: Mr Justice Sl M. Sikri

Judges:

Mr Justice J. M. Shelat	Mr Justice A. N. Ray
Mr Justice G. K. Mitter	Mr Justice P. J. Reddy
Mr C. A. Vaidialingam	Mr Justice I. D. Dua
Mr Justice K. S. Hegde	Mr Justice V. Bhargava
Mr Justice A. N. Grover	(2 vacancies)

Registrar: C. V. Rane

Each State has a separate High Court, the Judges of which are appointed by the President.

MINISTRIES AND GOVERNMENT DEPARTMENTS

DEPARTMENT OF ATOMIC ENERGY
Secretary: Dr Vikram A. Sarabhai

MINISTRY OF EXTERNAL AFFAIRS
Foreign Secretary: T. N. Kaul
Secretary (West): S. Krishnamurti
Secretary (East): S. K. Banerji

MINISTRY OF HOME AFFAIRS
Secretary: Govind Narain

MINISTRY OF FINANCE
Secretary: B. D. Pande

Department of Economic Affairs
Secretary: Dr I. G. Patel

Department of Banking
Secretary: A. Baksi

Bureau of Public Enterprises
Director-General: A. N. Banerji

Department of Revenue
Additional Secretary: D. P. Anand; R. N. Muttoo

MINISTRY OF RAILWAYS
Chairman, Railway Board: B. C. Ganguli

MINISTRY OF INDUSTRIAL DEVELOPMENT
AND INTERNAL TRADE
Secretary: B. B. Lall

MINISTRY OF FOREIGN TRADE
Department of Foreign Trade
Secretary: H. Lal

MINISTRY OF LABOUR, EMPLOYMENT
AND REHABILITATION
Secretary: P. M. Nayak

MINISTRY OF STEEL AND MINES
Secretary: H. C. Sarin

Department of Mines
Secretary: N. Subrahmanyam

MINISTRY OF SUPPLY
Secretary: K. Ram

MINISTRY OF PETROLEUM AND CHEMICALS
Secretary: B. Mukherji

MINISTRY OF DEFENCE
Secretary: K. B. Lall

MINISTRY OF AGRICULTURE
Department of Agriculture
Secretary: B. R. Patel
Department of Food
Secretary: A. L. Dias

MINISTRY OF IRRIGATION AND POWER
Secretary: K. P. Mathrani

MINISTRY OF LAW AND JUSTICE
Attorney-General: Niren De
Department of Legal Affairs
Secretary: R. S. Gae

DEPARTMENT OF PARLIAMENTARY AFFAIRS
Secretary: H. N. Trivedi

MINISTRY OF INFORMATION AND
BROADCASTING
Secretary: K. K. Das

MINISTRY OF HEALTH AND FAMILY
PLANNING
Secretary: K. K. Das

MINISTRY OF EDUCATION AND
YOUTH SERVICES
Secretary: T. P. Singh

MINISTRY OF TOURISM AND
CIVIL AVIATION
Secretary: N. Sahgal

MINISTRY OF WORKS AND HOUSING
Secretary: R. Mathews

ARMED FORCES HEADQUARTERS
Chief of Army Staff:
General S. Manekshaw, MC
Chief of Naval Staff: Admiral S. M. Nanda
Chief of Air Staff: Air Chief Marshal
P. C. Lal, DFC

* * * * *

Comptroller and Auditor-General:
S. Ranganathan

DIPLOMATIC REPRESENTATION OVERSEAS

INDIAN REPRESENTATIVES IN OTHER COMMONWEALTH COUNTRIES

Britain: A. B. Pant (High Commissioner); Canada: A. B. Bhadkamkar (High Commissioner); Australia: A. M. Thomas (High Commissioner); New Zealand: P. S. Naskar (High Commissioner); Pakistan: B. K. Acharya (High Commissioner); Ceylon: Y. K. Puri (High Commissioner); Ghana: A. S. Mehta (High Commissioner); Malaysia: K. C. Nair (High Commissioner); Singapore: Prem Bhatia (High Commissioner); Federal Republic of Nigeria: A. N. Mehta (High Commissioner); Cyprus: A. K. Dar (High Commissioner) (resident in Beirut); Sierra Leone: A. G. Mehta (High Commissioner) (resident in Accra); United Republic of Tanzania: J. S. Mehta (High Commissioner); Jamaica: Syed Muzaffar Aga (High Commissioner) (resident in Port o Spain); Trinidad and Tobago: Syed Muzaffar Aga (High Commissioner); Uganda: Dharam Deva (High Commissioner); Kenya: Gurbachan Singh (High Commissioner); Malawi: S. K. Chowdhry (High Commissioner); Malta: J. R. Atal (High Commissioner) (resident in Rome); Zambia: Vacant (High Commissioner); The Gambia: H. K. Singh (High Commissioner) (resident in Dakar); Guyana: D. Hejmadi (High Commissioner); Barbados: Syed Muzaffar Aga (High Commissioner) (resident in Port of Spain); Mauritius: D. S. Kamtekar (High Commissioner); Fiji: A. D. Venkateswaran (High Commissioner); Hong Kong: V. Siddharthacharry (Commissioner); Tonga: A. D. Venkateswaran (High Commissioner) (resident in Suva); Antigua, Dominica, Grenada, St Christopher, Nevis, Anguilla, St Lucia, St Vincent, The Bahamas, The Cayman Islands, Montserrat, Turks and Caicos Islands: Syed Muzaffar Aga (Commissioner) (resident in Port of Spain); Swaziland: S. K. Chowdhry (High Commissioner) (resident in Blantyre).

COMMONWEALTH HIGH COMMISSIONERS IN INDIA

Britain: Sir Terence Garvey, KCMG; Canada: James George; Australia: Patrick Shaw; New Zealand: Brian S. Lendrum; Pakistan: Sajjad Hyder; Ceylon: Siri Perera, QC; Ghana: P. K. Owusu-Ansah; Malaysia: Raja Aznam bin Raja Haji Ahmad; Federal Republic of Nigeria: J. N. Ukegbu; Singapore: P. Coomaraswamy; United Republic of Tanzania: Sebastian Chale; Uganda: E. Wapenyi (acting); Mauritius: Rabindrah Ghurburrun; Kenya: S. K. Kimalel; Trinidad and Tobago: Ashford S. Sinahan.

INDIAN REPRESENTATION IN NON-COMMONWEALTH COUNTRIES

Afghanistan (Ambassador); Algeria (Ambassador); Argentine (Ambassador); Austria (Ambassador); Belgium (Ambassador) (also India's Special Representative for Economic, Financial and Commercial Affairs and concurrently accredited to the EEC and the ECSC); Bolivia (Ambassador) (resident in Rio de Janerio); Brazil (Ambassador); Bulgaria (Ambassador); Burma (Ambassador); Burundi (Ambassador) (resident in Kampala); Cambodia (Ambassador); Cameroon (Ambassador) (resident in Lagos); Chile (Ambassador); China (Chargé d'Affaires); Colombia (Ambassador) (resident in Santiago); Congo (Kinshasa) (Ambassador); Congo (Brazzaville) (Ambassador) (resident in Kinshasa); Costa Rica (Ambassador) (resident in New York); Cuba (Ambassador) (resident in Mexico City); Czechoslovakia (Ambassador); Dahomey (Ambassador) (resident in Lagos); Denmark (Ambassador); Ecuador (Ambassador) (resident in Santiago); Ethiopia (Ambassador); Finland (Ambassador); France (Ambassador); Gabon (Ambassador) (resident in Kinshasa); Germany (Ambassador); Greece (Ambassador) (resident in Belgrade); Guinea (Ambassador); Holy See (Ambassador) (resident in Berne); Hungary (Ambassador); Indonesia (Ambassador); Iran (Ambassador); Iraq (Ambassador); Ireland (Ambassador); Italy (Ambassador); Ivory Coast (Ambassador) (resident in Dakar); Japan (Ambassador); Jordan (Ambassador) (resident in Beirut); Kuwait (Ambassador); Laos (Ambassador); Lebanon (Ambassador); Liberia (Ambassador) (resident in Accra); Libya (Ambassador) (resident in Cairo); Luxembourg (Ambassador) (resident in Brussels); Malagasy Republic (Ambassador); Maldives (Ambassador) (resident in Colombo); Mali (Ambassador) (resident in Conakry); Mauritania (Ambassador) (resident in Dakar); Mexico (Ambassador); Mongolia (Ambassador) (resident in Moscow); Morocco (Ambassador); Nepal (Ambassador); Netherlands (Ambassador); Norway (Ambassador); Panama (Ambassador) (resident in Mexico City); Paraguay (Ambassador) (resident in Buenos Aires); Peru (Ambassador) (resident in Santiago); Philippines (Ambassador); Poland (Ambassador); Rumania (Ambassador); Rwanda (Ambassador) (resident in Kampala); Saudi Arabia (Ambassador); Senegal (Ambassador); Somalia (Ambassador); Southern Yemen (Ambassador); Spain (Ambassador); Sudan (Ambassador); Surinam (Consul-General) (resident in Port of Spain); Sweden (Ambassador); Switzerland (Ambassador); Syrian Arab Republic (Ambassador); Thailand (Ambassador); Togo (Ambassador) (resident in Lagos); Tunisia (Ambassador) (resident in Rabat); Turkey (Ambassador); United Arab Republic (Ambassador); United Nations (Permanent Representative, New York); United States (Ambassador); Upper Volta (Ambassador) (resident in Dakar); Uruguay (Ambassador) (resident in Buenos Aires); U.S.S.R. (Ambassador); Venezuela (Ambassador) (resident in Rio de Janeiro); Vietnam (North) (Consul General); Vietnam (South) (Consul General); Yemen (Ambassador) (resident in Cairo); Yugoslavia (Ambassador).

THE STATES AND TERRITORIES OF THE UNION

The Executive of each State consists of a Governor appointed by the President and normally holding his office for a period of five years, and a Council of Ministers who must be, or within six months become, members of the Legislature of the State. In some States the Legislature consists of a single House only, the Legislative Assembly, but in other States there is an Upper House as well, the Legislative Council. Each assembly is elected directly by adult suffrage and has a maximum life of five years and strict limits as to maximum and minimum membership.

The legislative field is divided explicitly between the Union and the States, the residual powers belonging to the Union. In case of conflict, Union law overrides State law. Subject to the provisions of the Constitution, the Union Parliament may make laws for the whole or any part of the territory of India, and the Legislature of a State may make laws for the whole or any part of the State. The Union Parliament has exclusive powers to make laws with respect to matters grouped under 97 headings in the Constitution, including, *e.g.*, foreign affairs, defence, citizenship, currency, banking, railways, aviation, shipping, communications and trade and commerce with other countries. The State Legislatures have exclusive power to make laws for their own States with respect to matters grouped under 66 headings in the Constitution, *e.g.*, public order and police, education, public health, the administration of justice, elections to the Legislature, excise and taxes, water, land and forests. The Union Parliament and, subject to the exclusive powers referred to above, the State Legislatures have concurrent powers to make laws with respect to certain matters which are grouped under 47 headings in the Constitution, including criminal law and procedure, marriage and divorce, civil procedure, social security, labour, trade and commerce.

The Judges of the High Court of a State are appointed by the President, not by the Governor.

The President may proclaim an emergency which empowers the Union Government to assume executive and financial control of any State, but the proclamation must be approved subsequently by the Union Parliament. For up to three years the President may, if satisfied that the State cannot be governed in accordance with its constitution, himself assume the functions of Government subject to his proclamations (each valid for six months) receiving the subsequent approval of the Union Parliament.

The Union Territories are administered, save as otherwise provided by Parliament, by the President acting through an Administrator or other authority appointed by him.

Population figures mentioned below are based on the 1961 census.

ANDHRA PRADESH

The State of Andhra was formed in 1953 out of the Telugu-speaking parts of Madras State. Under the States Reorganisation Act, 1956, its size was almost doubled by the incorporation of the Telugu-speaking areas of the former Princely State of Hyderabad and its name was changed to Andhra Pradesh. Its area is about 106,000 square miles and its population about 40 million. The State capital is Hyderabad. The Congress Party (Ruling) form the State Government.

Governor: Khandubhai K. Desai
Chief Minister: Brahmananda Reddy
Chief Secretary: M. T. Raju

ASSAM

The State of Assam comprises the former Province of Assam, the North East Frontier Agency (N.E.F.A.), and a number of small Princely States. Its borders were affected by the States Reorganisation Act, 1956. Its principal language is Assamese. Its area is about 85,000 square miles and the population excluding tribal areas is nearly 14 million. The State capital is Shillong. The Congress Party (Ruling) form the State Government.

Governor: B. K. Nehru
Chief Minister: M. M. Choudhury
Chief Secretary: N. K. Rustomji

Within the State of Assam is the sub-state of Meghalaya which was formed in April 1970 and is formed from the two Assam hill Districts of Garo and United Khasi and Jaintia Hills. Its population is just under one million. The All Party Hill Leaders Conference party form the State Government. In November 1970 the Union Government agreed that Meghalaya should acquire full statehood.

Governor: B. K. Nehru
Chief Minister: Captain Sangma
Chief Secretary: K. L. Pasricha

BIHAR

The State of Bihar comprises the former Province of Bihar and the two small Princely States of Kharsawan and Seraikella. Under the States Reorganisation Act, 1956, it lost some territory to the neighbouring State of West Bengal. Its principal language is Hindi. Its area is about 67,000 square miles and its population about 52 million. The state capital is Patna. The State Government is a Coalition of Parties opposed to the Congress Party (Ruling) and led by a Samyukta Socialist Party Chief Minister.

Governor: Nityanand Kanungo
Chief Minister: Karpuri Thakur
Chief Secretary: B. S. Mandal

GUJARAT

Established on 1st May 1960, following the division of the bi-lingual Bombay State, Gujarat comprises the former States of Saurashtra and Kutch and the Gujarati-speaking area in the north of the former Bombay State reaching as far south as Surat. The area of the new State is about 72,000 square miles and its population about 24 million. The temporary State capital is Ahmedabad pending the completion of a new capital to be called Gandhinagar some 15 miles further north. The Congress Party (Opposition) form the State Government.

Governor: Shriman Narayan
Chief Minister: Hitendra Desai
Chief Secretary: L. R. Dalal

HARYANA

Haryana was established as a separate State in 1966 following the reorganisation of the Punjab (of which it was previously a part) on linguistic lines. Its principal language is Hindi. Its area is about 17,000 square miles and its population about 8 million. The Union Territory of Chandigarh is the State capital of Haryana as well as Punjab. In January 1970 however the Union Government decided that within 5 years Haryana would have to find another capital and Chandigarh would become the capital of Punjab alone. The Congress Party (Ruling) form the State Government.

Governor: B. N. Chakravarty
Chief Minister: Bansi Lal
Chief Secretary: Saroop Krishen

HIMACHAL PRADESH

The State of Himachal Pradesh comprises a number of former Princely States in the Punjab Hill area, plus six districts formerly belonging to the Punjab but allotted to Himachal when the Punjab was reorganised in 1966. Himachal Pradesh was a Union Territory until January 1971 when it acquired full Statehood. The State's area is about 19,500 square miles and its population about 2·5 million. Its capital is Simla. The Congress Party (Ruling) forms the State Government.

Governor: S. Chakavarti
Chief Minister: Dr Y. S. Parmar
Chief Secretary: K. N. Channa

KERALA

The State of Kerala was formed in 1956 out of most of the former Malayalam-speaking State of Travancore-Cochin (originally a Union of Princely States) together with the Malabar District of Madras, also Malayalam-speaking. Its area is about 15,000 square miles and its population nearly 19 million. The State capital is Trivandrum. The State Government is a coalition led by the CPI.

Governor: V. Viswanathan
Chief Minister: Acutha Menon
Chief Secretary: K. P. K. Menon

MADHYA PRADESH

The State of Madhya Pradesh originally comprised the former Central Provinces and Berar and 15 Princely States. In 1956 its borders were substantially redrawn. It lost territory in the south-west (Berar) to Bombay and acquired the former States of Bhopal, Madhya Bharat and Vindhya Pradesh, all originally Princely States or unions of such States. Its principal language is Hindi. Its area is about 171,000 square miles and its population about 37 million. Its capital is Bhopal. The Congress Party (Ruling) form the State Government.

Governor: Satya Narain Sinha
Chief Minister: S. C. Chukla
Chief Secretary: R. P. Naik

MAHARASHTRA

Established on 1st May 1960 following the division of the bi-lingual Bombay State, Maharashtra comprises the area of the former Bombay State south and east of Surat District (including Vidarbha). The area of the new State is about 118,500 square miles and its population about 45 million. The principal language is Marathi. The State capital is Bombay City. The Congress Party (Ruling) form the State Government.

Governor: Dr Nawab Ali Yavar Jung
Chief Minister: V. P. Naik
Chief Secretary: B. B. Paymaster

H*

MYSORE

The State of Mysore comprises the former Princely State of Mysore, more than doubled in size in 1956 by the addition of the Kannada-speaking areas of Bombay, Hyerabad, Madras and Coorg. Its area is about 74,000 square miles and its population about 26 million. The State capital is Bangalore. The State is at present under President's Rule and fresh elections are due towards the end of 1971.

Governor: Dharma Vira
Chief Minister: vacant
Chief Secretary: R. N. Vasudeva

NAGALAND

Under the Constitution (Thirteenth Amendment) Act 1962, the areas comprised in the Naga Hills-Tuensang Area, known by the name of Nagaland, became a separate State of the Indian Union. The State has an area of 6,236 square miles and the population number about 400,000. The State capital is Kohima.

As a result of elections held in February, 1969 the Naga Nationalist Organisation won an overall majority in the State Assembly, and form the State Government.

Governor: B. K. Nehru
Chief Minister: Hokishe Sema
Chief Secretary: R. Khathing

ORISSA

The State of Orissa comprises the former Province of Orissa and 24 former Princely States. Its borders were unaffected by the States Reorganization Act, 1956. Its principal language is Oriya. Its area is about 60,000 square miles and its population about 20 million. The State capital is Bhubaneshwar. The State Government is a coalition dominated by the Swantantra Party, but with an outside Chief Minister.

Governor: Shaukatullah Shah Ansari
Chief Minister: Biswanath Das
Chief Secretary: G. C. L. Joneja

PUNJAB

The Punjab lost its strict claim to the name (which means 'Five Rivers') when it was partitioned in 1947. In 1956 it was enlarged by the incorporation of a group of former Princely States. In 1966 it was reorganised and divided on linguistic lines. The present Punjab, the main language of which is Punjabi, thus represents only a small portion of the original Punjab. Its area is about 19,500 square miles, and its population about 15 million. The State capital is in Chandigarh (a city which is now a Union Territory). The Akali Dal (a regional predominantly Sikh party) form the State Government.

Governor: D. C. Pavate
Chief Minister: P. S. Badal
Chief Secretary: S. S. Grewal

RAJASTHAN

The State of Rajasthan was formed by the union of 18 minor and four major Princely States, including Jaipur, Bikaner, Jodhpur and Udaipur. It was enlarged in 1956 by the addition of Ajmer. Its principal language is Hindi. Its area is about 132,000 square miles and its population about 23 million. The State capital is Jaipur. The Congress Party (Ruling) form the State Government.

Governor: Sardar Hukam Singh
Chief Minister: Mohan Lal Sukhadia
Chief Secretary: Z. S. Jhala

TAMIL NADU

The State of Madras was re-named Tamil Nadu in 1968 and comprises the large Tamil-speaking remnant of the former Province of Madras. In 1953 it lost its northern areas to Andhra and in 1956 some of its western districts to Mysore and Kerala. It acquired, however, in 1956 a small Tamil-speaking portion of Travancore-Cochin. Its area is about 50,000 square miles and its population about 37 million. The State capital is Madras. The Dravida Munnetre Kazhagam form the State Government.

Governor: K. K. Shah (designate)
Chief Minister: Karunanidhi
Chief Secretary: E. P. Royappa

UTTAR PRADESH

The State of Uttar Pradesh comprises the former United Provinces and the Princely States of Benares, Tehri-Garhwal and Rampur. Its boundaries were unaffected by the States Reorganisation Act, 1956. Its principal language is Hindi. Its area is about 113,000 square miles and its population is about 82 million. The State capital is Lucknow. The Congress Party (Ruling) form the State Government.

Governor: B. Gopala Reddy
Chief Minister: Kamlapati Tripathi
Chief Secretary: M. Lal

WEST BENGAL

The State of West Bengal comprises the western part of the former Bengal Province and the Princely State of Cooch Behar. Under the States Reorganisation Act, 1956, it was enlarged to include certain contiguous areas of Bihar. Its principal language is Bengali. Its area is about 34,000 square miles and its population about 40 million. The State capital is Calcutta. The State Government is a Congress (Ruling) dominated coalition with an outside Chief Minister.

Governor: B. S. Dhawan
Chief Minister: Ajoy Mukerjee
Chief Secretary: M. M. Basu

DELHI

The Territory of Delhi (formerly a Part C State) comprises the cities of Old and New Delhi and the area immediately surrounding them. Its area is 573 square miles and its population about 3·5 million.

Lieutenant-Governor: A. N. Jha
Chief Executive Counsellor: V. K. Malhotra
Chief Secretary: S. C. Verma

MANIPUR

The Territory of Manipur was formerly a Princely State and then a Part C State of the same name. Its area is about 8,600 square miles and its population is about 950,000. Its capital is Imphal. The Territory has been under President's Rule since March 1970. The Union Government has promised Manipur full Statehood.

Lieutenant-Governor: D. R. Kohli
Chief Minister: M. Koireng Singh
Chief Secretary: D. G. Bhave

TRIPURA

The Territory of Tripura was formerly a Princely State and then a Part C State of the same name. Its area is about 4,000 square miles and its population about 130,000. Its capital is Agartala. The Union Government has promised Tripura full Statehood.

Lieutenant-Governor: A. L. Dias
Chief Minister: S. L. Singh
Chief Secretary: I. P. Gupta

THE ANDAMAN AND NICOBAR ISLANDS

This chain of islands, with an area of 3,215 square miles, lies in the eastern part of the Bay of Bengal about 800 miles to the east and south-east of Madras. The total population is about 78,000 of whom two thirds are to be found in the Andamans, where the majority live within a radius of 15 miles of Port Blair, the capital.

Chief Commissioner: H. S. Bhutalia
Chief Secretary: B. R. Basu

THE LACCADIVE, MINICOY AND AMINDIVI ISLANDS

This group of very small islands lies between 100 and 200 miles off the south-west coast of India. The islands were, prior to 1956, administered by the State of Madras. The total area of the group is 11 square miles and the population about 26,000. The Administrative Headquarters is at Kozhikode (formerly known as Calicut) in Kerala.

Administrator: K. D. Menon

DADRA AND NAGAR HAVELI

The area became a Union Territory, under the terms of the Constitution (Tenth) Amendment Act, 1961, on the 11th August 1961. It has an area of 189 square miles, and a population of 65,000.

Administrator: K. R. Damle

GOA, DAMAN AND DIU

Goa, Daman and Diu became a Territory of the Indian Union according to the provisions of the Constitution (Twelfth) Amendment Act, 1962. In the General Elections held in December 1963 the Maharashtrawadi Gomantak obtained a majority in the Goa Assembly, and now form the Government. The territory has a total area of 1,431 square miles (Goa 1,394 square miles) and the population is 660,000 of which some 600,000 live in Goa.

Lieutenant-Governor: Nakul Sen
Chief Minister: D. B. Bandodkar
Chief Secretary: K. N. Shrivastava

PONDICHERRY

The Government of India, in agreement with the Government of France, took over the administration of the French Establishments in India (Pondicherry, Karaikal, Yanam and Mahe) in 1954, and a Treaty ceding these territories to India was signed in 1956 and ratified by the French Assembly in 1962. The total area is 186 square miles and the population 410,000. The former French settlements now form one Territory of the Union under the collective name of Pondicherry.

Lieutenant-Governor: B. D. Jatti
Chief Minister: Marikar Farook
Chief Secretary: Mrs J. A. Dayanand

— — —

SIKKIM AND BHUTAN

SIKKIM

The area of the Himalayan State of Sikkim is 2,745 square miles and its population, enumerated in the 1961 census of India, 161,080. Its capital is Gangtok. The State is a protectorate of India. The Government of India is responsible for its external relations, defence and communications, while as regards internal government the State enjoys autonomy, subject to the ultimate responsibility of the Government of India for the maintenance of good administration and law and order.

BHUTAN

The State of Bhutan, near the eastern end of India's Himalayan frontier, is in treaty relations with the Government of India, under which, while the Government of India undertakes to exercise no interference in the internal administration of the State, the Government of Bhutan agree to be guided by the Government of India's advice in regard to external affairs. Its area is about 18,000 square miles and its population about 300,000. The capital is Thimpu. Following the submission in December 1970 of Bhutan's application to join the United Nations, the Security Council unanimously recommended to the General Assembly on 10th February 1971 that Bhutan be admitted to the membership of the United Nations.

TITLES IN INDIA

Prefixes to Indian names

Indian prefixes (to be used instead of, and not in addition to, Mr, Mrs, and Miss) are for men, Shri; for married women, Shrimati; and for unmarried women, Kumari. In the case of Sikhs the prefixes are Sardar, Sardarni and Biba respectively.

The suffix 'ji' is frequently added to Indian names as a term of respect. This can either be to the first name (Indiraji) or to the last name (Gandhiji).

Indian Honours

There are four awards given for eminent public service:—
1 Bharat Ratna
2 Padma Vibhushan
3 Padma Bhushan
4 Padma Shri

Titles

Under the Indian Constitution, 'no title, not being a military or academic distinction shall be conferred by the State'.

Titles received before Independence, or hereditary titles, may be retained, but they are not used in official communications.

JAMAICA

JAMAICA lies between longitudes 76° 11′ W. and 78° 21′ W. and between latitudes 17° 43′ N. and 18° 32′ N. The name is derived from the aboriginal Arawak name Xaymaca. It is 100 miles west of Haiti, 90 miles south of Cuba, 445 miles north of Cartagena and 540 miles from Colon. The island's greatest length is 146 miles and its greatest width about 51 miles, and with an area of more than 4,400 square miles it is the third largest island in the Caribbean Sea. The capital is Kingston.

Jamaica is mountainous; the main range runs from east to west, with numerous subsidiary ranges, some parallel to the main range, others spreading out north-west and south-east from it. The highest point is Blue Mountain Peak (7,402 feet), in the east of the island. From these mountains a number of streams flow to the north and south shores, but none is navigable except the Black River, and that only for small craft. The island is indented with many bays and harbours, notable among which are Port Antonio at the eastern end, Montego Bay at the western end of the north coast, and Kingston on the south side of the island.

Jamaica has a tropical climate of considerable variety. On the coast, high daytime temperatures (maximum 94° F., minimum 70° F.) are usually mitigated by sea breezes, while in the uplands of the interior the altitude brings a refreshing drop in humidity and temperature, particularly at night (maximum 81° F., minimum 43°F.). The island lies in the hurricane zone, and although the last hurricane to hit the island severely was in 1951 a number have threatened Jamaica since then. Lying close to the course of 'Flora', the hurricane of 1963, the island suffered great damage from floods and heavy rains. Most of Jamaica has a good rainfall, Kingston 60·35 inches, Port Antonio 153·83 inches representing respectively low and high rainfall areas, and although rain occurs at all times of the year, it is heaviest in May and from August to November.

The preliminary estimate of the population at the census of 7th April 1970 was 1,861,300. The preliminary estimate of the population of the main towns on 7th April 1970 was: Kingston and St Andrew (Metropolitan Area) 506,200; Montego Bay 42,800; Spanish Town 41,600; May Pen 26,200. The birth-rate in 1969 was 33·1 per 1,000 and the death-rate 7·2 per 1,000. In 1963 76·3 per cent of the population were of African descent, 15·1 per cent of Afro-European, 1·7 per cent of Indian (mainly from South India), 0·8 per cent of European and 0·6 per cent of Chinese descent. The main language is English and religion is mainly Christian with 317,600 Anglicans, 306,000 Baptists, 191,200 Church of God, 115,300 Roman Catholics, 107,900 Methodists and 82,700 Presbyterians. Primary education is free but not yet compulsory. About 10 per cent of the total school population receive secondary education. The literacy figure is approximately 59 per cent. For administrative purposes the island is divided into three counties (Surrey, Middlesex and Cornwall) and fourteen parishes.

In 1969 a total of 1,088,092 tons of cargo were imported into Jamaica through the Kingston Wharves, excluding petroleum products. During the same year 537,370 tons were exported over the Kingston Wharves.

Jamaica has international airports at Palisadoes, 11 miles from Kingston (length of runway 7,600 feet), and at Montego Bay (length of runway 8,500 feet), three miles from the town. The principal airline is Air Jamaica Ltd.

The principal shipping lines are Elders and Fyffee's Line, Harrison Line and Jamaica Banana Producers Steamship Company Limited. There are 205 miles of standard gauge railway and road mileage is 2,682. There are two broadcasting companies in the country: the Jamaica Broadcasting Corporation and Radio Jamaica Limited. The Jamaica Broadcasting Corporation provides television facilities.

The main agricultural products are sugar, rum and molasses, bananas and citrus fruit.

Jamaica is the largest exporter of bauxite in the world. The deposits are worked by five American and one Canadian companies; the latter and two others processing bauxite into alumina. The most recent to start production, May 1969, is the Alpart Consortium, comprising Reynolds Metal Co., the Kaiser Aluminium & Chemicals Corporation and the Anaconda Company of the United States. The total bauxite production in 1970 was 11,819,000 long dry tons compared with 10,333,000 long dry tons in 1969. A very significant increase took place in the production of alumina during 1970; from an output of 2,731,000 tons in 1969, the 1970 output rose to 4,244,000 tons—a 70% increase. By 1973 alumina production in Jamaica should be trebled; by 1974 it should be quadrupled according to the projections of the bauxite and alumina industry. Gypsum is also mined. Cement is manufactured locally.

The main exports in 1969 were bauxite and alumina £59,300,000; sugar and sugar preparations £16,500,000; bananas £6,800,000; tobacco products £1,053,732; citrus, cocoa, coffee £5,800,000. Total exports in 1969 were £103,497,792 and total imports £184,696,868.

For the year 1970/71 Government revenue is estimated at £124,900,000 and expenditure £133,000,000.

Development continues apace with Government schemes for schools, hospitals, water supply and tourist facilities and the private sector concentrating on industry, services, port facilities, hotels and houses.

National Day, Independence Day, which is celebrated on the first Monday in August, commemorates the achievement of Independence on 6th August 1962.

HISTORY

When Columbus discovered Jamaica on 4th May 1494 he found it peopled by Arawak Indians, estimated to number some 60,000. No pre-Arawak remains have been found, and it would appear that Jamaica was uninhabited before about A.D. 1000. Columbus took possession of the island in the name of the King and Queen of Spain, but it was not until Juan de Esquivel was appointed the first Governor in 1509 that European occupation began. The island became a fief held on special terms by the descendants of Columbus as Marquises of Jamaica; but it was never a large or flourishing colony and served little more than as a supply base for expeditions to the mainland. The first capital at Sevilla Nueva near the modern St Anne's Bay was soon abandoned in favour of Villa de la Vega, on the site of the present Spanish Town. Under the Spanish the Arawak Indians died out and had disappeared entirely by the time the English arrived.

It was in 1655 that an English expedition under Admirals Penn and Venables, after failing in their objective of capturing Hispaniola, landed at Passage Fort on 10th May. They met with little resistance, Villa de la Vega falling quickly, but Spanish guerrillas held out in the interior until 1660 when the Spanish Governor and his followers escaped to Cuba. They took with them most of the slaves whom they had imported from Africa; but some of these remained in the fastnesses of the interior, forming the nucleus of what were later known as the Maroons.

General Edward D'Oyley was appointed the first civil Governor in 1661 and was succeeded the following year by Lord Windsor, who brought with him a Royal Proclamation giving the people of Jamaica the rights of citizens of England and the right to make their own laws. Although Port Royal was the first capital, in 1664 much of the administration was removed to Spanish Town, where the first House of Assembly, comprising 23 freeholders, met on 20th January that year.

During the early years colonisation was slow, although the population was increased by 1,600 immigrants from Nevis in 1656 and 1,000 from Barbados in 1664. In 1670 the Treaty of Madrid recognised English sovereignty over all American territories in English possession, and removed the pressing need for constant defence against Spanish attack. Using slaves brought from Africa, sugar, cocoa, indigo and later coffee were planted, and Jamaica became a land of large estates often with absentee landlords. Although a further 1,200 settlers arrived from Surinam, the European population began to diminish again. Meanwhile, with official encouragement, Port Royal became the base and stronghold of the English buccaneers who, under Henry Morgan, roved widely over the Caribbean raiding Spanish territory. The plunder which they captured greatly enriched the town until it became the finest town in the West Indies, only to be destroyed by an earthquake on 7th June 1692. In its place Kingston, the modern capital, was developed.

At the beginning of the eighteenth century difficulties arose with the Maroons whose numbers had been increased by fugitive slaves. Aided by the difficult terrain of the interior, they took heavy toll of the English troops and militia sent against them; and what is known as the Maroon War lasted for many years, until in 1737 those in the west of the island accepted honourable terms which guaranteed them liberty and certain lands. A similar agreement in 1740 ended the rebellion in the Blue Mountains.

Port Royal recovered from the earthquake to become an important naval base associated with such names as Benbow, Parker, Rodney and Nelson. It was Rodney's victory over the French in 1782 at the Battle of the Saints which saved Jamaica from possible capture by the French; and from that date neither the French nor the Spanish ever again made a serious attempt to capture the island.

During the eighteenth century thousands more slaves were brought from Africa, many from the Gold Coast; and a high proportion of the African words which now survive in Jamaican speech, and much of the folk-lore, are of Ashanti origin. Slave ownership was governed by Slave Laws; at first these were principally concerned with the interests of the owners but they gradually evolved until, in the period immediately preceding emancipation, the protection of the slaves was given greater emphasis. Agitation against the slave trade and against slavery itself began during the last half of the eighteenth century and had its origin in England, being part of the great humanitarian movement. As a result of the efforts of Clarkson, Wilberforce and others, the slave trade was abolished by the British Parliament in 1807. Slavery was abolished in August 1834 and complete freedom for the slaves was declared in August 1838.

During the early years of the nineteenth century Nonconformist missionaries came out in increasing numbers and worked to prepare the people for emancipation and to remove the civil disabilities endured by the free coloureds. Their efforts were rewarded when full citizenship was granted to all free people of colour in 1832.

The abolition of slavery, coming at a time when Jamaica's importance as a military and naval station was declining, caused a great decrease in the wealth of the island. The decline was quickened by the free-trade policy of the British government which, from 1846, allowed slave-produced sugar from Cuba and elsewhere to enter the British market on equal terms with sugar from Jamaica. The abolition of the slave trade on the other hand led to a shortage of labour, and Indian immigrants were introduced in 1842 to be followed by Chinese in 1854. In 1869 the system of indentured labour was established, attracting considerable numbers of East Indians. Yet a further result of this great social change was that the estate ceased to be the main social unit; and the population began to re-form itself into new communities and new settlements.

In the 1860s disputes between the planters and their labourers grew increasingly bitter and culminated in an organized rebellion at Morant Bay in 1865. The severity with which this was crushed led to the recall of Governor Eyre and Crown Colony Government replaced the old representative system.

From this date prosperity began gradually to return. In 1860 a steamer service was opened between Jamaica and New York, offering facilities for the profitable export of Jamaican fruits which had previously only been used for local consumption. The first shipment of bananas was made in 1868, and the trade was soon firmly established. The economy of the country was helped by the building of railways and by the improvement and development of roads; and by the close of the century a spirit of self-confidence had been created and the small farmers were probably at the height of their prosperity. The Great Exhibition of 1891, opened by the future King George V and attended by over 300,000 people, expressed the confident mood of the island.

The disastrous earthquake of 1907 damaged every building in Kingston and killed some 800 people; the lower part of the city was completely destroyed. A new city of reinforced concrete rose in its place.

After the First World War came a time of fluctuating prosperity; but the rapid increase in the population, the onslaught of disease in the banana plantations and a series of storms, together with the effect of the world-wide slump of the '30s, brought another period of economic distress culminating in riots in 1938, a great increase in trade union activity, and the beginnings of rival political parties.

By the end of the Second World War Jamaica's trade was almost entirely with Britain; the production of sugar had expanded, and the export of bananas had recovered in importance as the result of the development of disease-resistant varieties. Travel restrictions elsewhere led to people in North America turning to the West Indies for their vacation, and led people in Britain to seek holidays within the sterling area. Bauxite was first mined on a commercial basis in 1952 and by 1957 Jamaica had become the world's largest producer. In 1960 bauxite and alumina together accounted for half Jamaica's exports. By that year also for the first time the contribution of manufacturing industries to the gross national income was equal to that of agriculture. But despite all this, unemployment and under-employment have remained problems, aggravated by the great population increase. Emigration which at first was directed towards the United States changed its course, encouraged by the labour shortage in Britain, and in 1961 37,202 emigrants reached Britain from Jamaica.

In 1948 the University College of the West Indies was established outside Kingston and in 1953 the University College Hospital of the West Indies was opened. In November of the same year Her Majesty Queen Elizabeth visited Jamaica. On 2nd April 1962 the University College was granted a Royal Charter and became the University of the West Indies and now grants its own degrees.

The formation of modern political parties can be dated from 1938 when the People's National Party was formed under the leadership of Mr N. W. Manley, with the aim of establishing representative and responsible government for Jamaica within the Commonwealth. It is supported by the National Workers Union to which it is affiliated. The P.N.P. held office from 1955 until April 1962, Mr Manley being Chief Minister and later the first Premier.

The second major political party, the Jamaican Labour Party, was formed in 1943 by Sir Alexander Bustamante. Like the P.N.P. it derives support from labour, the Bustamante Industrial Trades Union being affiliated to the J.L.P. The J.L.P. won a majority of seats in the 1944 General Election and continued to provide the elected members in the Government until a ministerial system was introduced. Sir Alexander Bustamante was Chief Minister from 1953 to 1955, and returned to office after the elections of April 1962. In the last General Election held on 21st February 1967, the J.L.P., led by Mr D. B. Sangster, who had been Acting Prime Minister was again returned to office. On 22nd February Mr Sangster (later to be awarded a Knighthood) became Prime Minister when Sir Alexander Bustamante retired from the position because of ill health. On the death of Sir Donald Sangster in April, 1967, Mr Hugh Shearer was sworn in as Prime Minister. The J.L.P. is still the ruling party.

CONSTITUTIONAL DEVELOPMENT

For the first few years after its capture by an English expedition, Jamaica was under military Government, but in 1662 the first constitution was introduced by Lord Windsor, the second civil Governor. This provided for an Executive consisting of a Governor, appointed by the Crown, acting with the advice of a nominated Council, and a Legislature consisting of the Governor, the Council and a representative Assembly. This constitution was modified in 1854, and immediately prior to its suspension in 1865 the Executive consisted of the Governor assisted by the Privy Council whose members were appointed by the Crown and included the Chief Justice and other officials, the Bishop of Kingston, all the members of the Executive Council, and representatives of the Legislative Council and Legislative Assembly. The Executive Committee, forming a link between the Governor and the Assembly, consisted of four persons nominated by the Governor of whom one was from the Legislative Council and three were unofficials from the Legislative Assembly. Formerly the Assembly had been able to originate and appropriate grants of money; but from 1854 no grant could originate except by message from the Governor or through the Executive Committee. The Legislature consisted of the Legislative Council and the Legislative Assembly. The members of the Legislative Council, which formed the Upper Chamber, were appointed by the Crown. There were 17 members, four of whom were official and 13 unofficial. The House of

Assembly consisted of 47 elected members, two from each of the 22 Parishes and one from each of the three main towns. They were elected by some 1,800 electors with income or property qualifications.

In 1866, after the Morant Bay uprising, this constitution was replaced by Order in Council of the 11th June of that year by a Crown Colony Government, with the legislative power vested in the Governor acting with the advice and consent of a nominated Legislative Council consisting of 6 Official Members and not more than 5 Non-official Members. Three years later the stipulation requiring there to be 6 Official Members was dropped, the number being left to the discretion of the Crown.

Further changes were made by Orders in Council dated 19th May 1884 and 3rd October 1895.

Under the Constitution introduced in 1944, the functions and membership of the Legislative Council remained unchanged. The Lower House, now known as the House of Representatives, was composed of 32 members all elected by universal adult suffrage. No legislation could be passed and no money voted without the approval of the House of Representatives.

Although the Privy Council continued to exist to advise the Governor on such matters as the exercise of the Royal Prerogative of Mercy, the remission of sentences and the discipline of the Civil Service, its other functions were taken over by an Executive Council formed of the Governor, three *ex-officio* members, two nominated members and five members elected by the House of Representatives. These elected members were styled Ministers, but although they were required to answer for certain subjects and Departments in the House of Representatives they had no executive responsibility.

In 1951 discussions with the two political parties and with the non-official members of the Legislative Council were held to consider what further reforms should be undertaken in the constitution. With general agreement, changes were introduced to take effect in June 1953.

The 1953 Constitution provided for the appointment of a Chief Minister and seven other Ministers (all Ministers being drawn from the House of Representatives), thus increasing from five to eight the number of members of the House of Representatives in the Executive Council and giving them a majority over the official and nominated members. Thenceforth the Ministers exercised wide responsibility in the management of the internal affairs of the island, and had executive functions in regard to nearly all Departments of Government. The Colonial Secretary however remained responsible for defence, public security and the public service and the Attorney-General was responsible for public prosecutions.

Apart from minor modifications and amendments the next important change came in 1957. The 1957 Constitution provided for the withdrawal of all official members from the Executive Council, which thereafter became known as the Council of Ministers, presided over by the Chief Minister. It consisted of ten members of the Government charged with responsibility for specific subjects, and two Ministers without Portfolio chosen from among the non-official members of the Legislative Council, all appointed by the Governor on the recommendation of the Chief Minister. The Governor could, however, at his discretion, summon special meetings of the Council of Ministers and attend and preside at such meetings.

Official members, with the single exception of the Attorney-General, also withdrew from the Legislative Council and were replaced by two more non-official members, the total thus remaining at 15, the permissible minimum.

The newly-created Ministry of Home Affairs became responsible for matters affecting internal security, police and immigration, while the Attorney-General continued to exercise control over public prosecutions. The Governor was not obliged to assign to any Minister responsibility for any business relating to defence, external affairs, dependencies, personnel matters and the audit of Government accounts, and these subjects, with the exception of audit, remained the responsibility of the Chief Secretary.

Jamaica became a member of the Federation of the West Indies on 23rd February 1958. By the Jamaica (Constitution) Order in Council, 1959, which came into operation on 4th July 1959, Jamaica became self-governing in its internal affairs, although its position as a unit territory of the Federation of The West Indies remained unchanged. The new constitution provided for a Privy Council, a Cabinet, a Legislative Council and a House of Representatives.

The Privy Council, consisting of six members, advised the Governor in the exercise of his disciplinary powers over members of the Government Service and in the exercise of the royal prerogative of mercy.

The Cabinet consisted of the Premier and not less than eleven other Ministers, drawn from the House of Representatives, charged with the general control and direction of the Government. There were also two or three Ministers without Portfolio who sat in the Legislative Council. The Governor was required to act in accordance with the advice of the Cabinet, except where the matter was the responsibility of some other body (*e.g.*, the Public Service Commission) or where the constitution specifically provided for him to act in his discretion.

The Legislative Council consisted of eighteen members appointed by the Governor after consultation with persons speaking for the differing political points of view of groups represented in the House of Representatives, and two or three members nominated by the Premier. The Legislative Council was essentially a revisionary Chamber with powers to delay bills for a limited period of time. The House of Representatives consisted of forty-five members elected by universal adult suffrage.

The constitution established Judicial Service, Public Service and Police Service Commissions with executive responsibility for appointments, discipline and dismissals in the Services for which they were responsible. Officers in the Public Service and the Police Service against whom disciplinary action was taken had the right of appeal to the Privy Council. Judicial officers had no right of appeal to the Privy Council. Judges of the Supreme Court could be removed from office only on the advice of the Judicial Committee of the Privy Council in Britain after investigation by a locally-appointed Judicial tribunal.

As a result of the Referendum held on 19th September 1961, Jamaica applied for withdrawal from the West Indies Federation to seek independence alone in 1962. At a Conference held in Lancaster House in February 1962 full agreement was reached between the British and Jamaican delegations on the date for Jamaican independence and on the form and content of the new constitution. Jamaica became an independent sovereign country and a Member of the Commonwealth on 6th August 1962.

CONSTITUTION

The Constitution of Jamaica, contained in the Jamaica (Constitution) Order in Council, 1962, provides for a Governor-General appointed by Her Majesty The Queen and for a bi-cameral Legislature. The Senate consists of 21 Senators appointed by the Governor-General, 13 on the advice of the Prime Minister and 8 on the advice of the Leader of the Opposition. The House of Representatives consists of 53 elected members, but provision is made for an increase up to 60 members. The President and Deputy President of the Senate and the Speaker and Deputy Speaker of the House of Representatives are elected, respectively, by the Senate and the House of Representatives from within their own membership.

The qualification for appointment to the Senate or for election to the House of Representatives is to be a citizen of Jamaica or another Commonwealth country of the age of 21 or more and to have been ordinarily resident in Jamaica for the immediately preceding twelve months. It is provided that persons holding or acting in public offices, judges of the Supreme Court and the Court of Appeal and persons of unsound mind, are disqualified for appointment to the Senate or election to the House of Representatives.

Apart from certain entrenched provisions, the Constitution may be amended by a majority of all the members of each House. There are ordinarily entrenched and specially entrenched provisions. The first group may be amended by an affirmative vote of not less than two-thirds of all the members of each House, provided that there shall be a period of three months between the introduction of the Bill seeking to amend the Constitution and the commencement of the debate on it in the House of Representatives and a further period of three months between the conclusion of that debate and the passing of the Bill by the House. The specially entrenched provisions (which relate to the legal force of the Constitution, Parliament, Sessions of Parliament, the Prorogation and Dissolution of Parliament, General Elections and the appointment of Senators, and the Executive Authority of Jamaica, and which include the section providing for the alteration of the Constitution) may be amended by the same procedure as that required for the ordinarily entrenched provisions with the additional requirement that such amendment shall be approved by the electorate by referendum. Should the Senate not approve a Bill amending any of the specially entrenched provisions by a two-thirds majority of all its members the matter may be referred to the electorate by referendum in which case a majority of two-thirds of the electorate voting shall be required before the Bill may be presented to the Governor-General for assent. As regards any ordinarily entrenched provision the required majority is three-fifths of the electorate voting.

The Privy Council consisting of six members appointed by the Governor-General after consultation with the Prime Minister, of whom at least two are persons who hold or have held public office, advises the Governor-General on the exercise of the Royal Prerogative of Mercy and on appeals on disciplinary matters from the three Service Commissions.

The Governor-General appoints as Prime Minister the member of the House of Representatives who, in his judgement, is best able to command the support of the majority of the members of the House. The Governor-General also appoints the Leader of the Opposition.

Executive responsibility rests with a Cabinet consisting of the Prime Minister and not less than eleven other Ministers. Not less than two, nor more than three, Ministers (without Portfolio) may be members of the Senate. The Governor-General is required to act on the advice of the Cabinet except in respect of any function conferred upon him in his discretion or any function exercisable on the advice or recommendation of, or after consultation with, persons or authorities other than the Cabinet.

Provision is made for the appointment of an Attorney-General, a Director of Public Prosecutions, an Auditor-General, a Public Service Commission, a Police Service Commission and a Judicial Service Commission.

There is a Supreme Court and a Court of Appeal. The President of the Court of Appeal and the Chief Justice of the Supreme Court are appointed by the Governor-General on the advice of the Prime Minister after consultation with the Leader of the Opposition.

HISTORICAL LIST OF GOVERNORS-GENERAL

Sir Kenneth Blackburne, GBE, KCMG (later GCMG), 6th August 1962 to 30th November 1962
Sir Clifford Campbell, GCVO, GCMG, from 1st December 1962

HISTORICAL LIST OF MINISTRIES

Sir Alexander Bustamante, 6th August 1962 to 21st February 1967
Hon. D. B. Sangster (Sir Donald Sangster, KCMG, from 7th April 1967), February 1967 to 11th April 1967
Hon. H. L. Shearer from 11th April 1967 (Rt. Hon. H. L. Shearer, PC from 6th January, 1969).

GOVERNMENT

After the election held on 21st February 1967 the composition of the political parties in the House of Representatives was: Jamaica Labour Party 33 seats, People's National Party 20 seats.

GOVERNOR-GENERAL
His Excellency Sir Clifford Campbell, GCMG, GCVO

CABINET
Prime Minister, Minister of External Affairs and Minister of Defence: The Rt. Hon. Hugh Shearer, PC
Minister of Trade and Industry: The Hon. R. C. Lightbourne
Minister of Labour and National Insurance: The Hon. L. G. Newland
Minister of Education: The Hon. E. L. Allen
Minister of Finance and Planning: The Hon. E. P. G. Seaga
Minister of Health: The Hon. Dr H. W. Eldemire
Minister of Agriculture and Fisheries: The Hon. J. P. Gyles
Minister of Home Affairs: The Hon. R. A. McNeill
Minister of Communications and Works: The Hon. N. C. Lewis
Minister of Local Government: The Hon. L. A. Lynch
Attorney-General and Minister of Legal Affairs: The Hon. V. B. Grant, QC
Minister of Youth and Community Development: The Hon. A. M. W. Douglas
Minister of Public Utilities and Housing: The Hon. Wilton O. Hill
Minister of Rural Land Development: The Hon. W. G. McLaren
Minister Without Portfolio: Senator The Hon. Sir Neville Ashenheim, CBE
Minister of State for Youth and Community Development: Senator The Hon. H. L. Wynter
Minister of State for Education: Senator the Hon. Dr A. E. Burt

PARLIAMENTARY SECRETARIES
Ministry of Education: A. H. Williams
Ministry of Communications and Works: W. T. Martin
Ministry of Agriculture and Fisheries: C. V. Atkinson
Ministry of Local Government: Arnold S. Jackson
Ministry of Trade and Industry: Alva E. Ross and David Lindo
Ministry of Labour and National Insurance: Mrs Esme M. Grant
Ministry of External Affairs: Dr Neville Gallimore

LEADER OF THE OPPOSITION
Michael N. Manley

SENATE
President: Senator The Hon. George S. Ranglin
Deputy President: Senator G. A. L. Mair, CBE
Clerk of the Legislature: H. D. Carberry
Deputy Clerk of the Legislature: Edley Deans

HOUSE OF REPRESENTATIVES
Speaker: Hon. E. C. L. Parkinson, QC
Deputy Speaker: C. A. Stanhope

JUDICIARY
Chief Justice: The Hon. Sir Herbert Duffus
President of the Court of Appeal: The Hon. Sir Cyril Henriques, CBE

Members of the Court of Appeal
Mr. Justice G. E. Waddington
Mr Justice L. J. Moody
The Hon. Sir Joseph Luckoo
Mr. Justice H. J. Shelley
Mr Justice I. D. Eccleston

Puisne Judges:
Senior Puisne Judge: Hon. Mr Justice A. M. Edun
Hon. Mr Justice K. G. Smith
Hon. Mr Justice R. M. Hercules
Hon. Mr Justice U. N. Parnell
Hon. Mr Justice Edward Zacca
Hon. Mr Justice K. C. Henry
Hon. Mr Justice C. H. Graham-Perkins
Hon. Mr Justice L. G. Robinson
Hon. Mr Justice H. S. Grannum
Hon. Mr Justice V. L. Lopez
Hon. Mr Justice V. C. Melville
Registrar of the Supreme Court: H. V. T. Chambers

MINISTRIES AND GOVERNMENT DEPARTMENTS

KING'S HOUSE
Governor General's Secretary: N. H. Smith, MVO
A.D.C. to the Governor-General: Captain O. H. Jobson.

AUDIT
Auditor-General: R. V. Irvine

PRIME MINISTER'S OFFICE
Permanent Secretary and Secretary to the Cabinet: J. B. McFarlane, MBE
Personal Assistant to P.M.: Lorrell Bruce
Director Jamaica Information Services: Carey Robinson

MINISTRY OF EXTERNAL AFFAIRS
Permanent Secretary: J. M. Lloyd, CMG

MINISTRY OF DEFENCE
Permanent Secretary: J. H. Clerk

MINISTRY OF FINANCE AND PLANNING
Financial Secretary: P. W. Beckwith, OBE
Accountant-General: W. C. Jervis, MBE
Collector-General: A. L. Baugh (Acting)
Commissioner of Income Tax: A. F. Smith
Manager, Government Savings Bank: (Acting) C. A. Hudson
Director, Central Planning Unit: Dr G. G Bonnick
Director of Statistics: Dexter Rose
Government Town Planner: D. McLaren
Director of Geological Surveys: H. R. Versey

MINISTRY OF TRADE AND INDUSTRY
Permanent Secretary: H. S. Walker
Chief Engineer, Electricity Division, W. M. Howell
Trade Administrator: W. T. Miller
Commissioner of Mines: (Acting) W. Gillett-Chambers

MINISTRY OF EDUCATION
Permanent Secretary: A. W. G. Shaw
Director, Institute of Jamaica: C. Bernard Lewis, OBE
Director, Jamaica Library Service: Mrs J. L. Robinson, MBE

MINISTRY OF PUBLIC UTILITIES AND HOUSING
Permanent Secretary: W. McDonald

MINISTRY OF YOUTH AND COMMUNITY DEVELOPMENT
Permanent Secretary: A. P. Clerk
Director of Prisons: Lt.-Col. G. Mignon

MINISTRY OF HEALTH
Permanent Secretary: H. H. Haughton
Chief Medical Officer: Dr Samuel Street
Registrar- General: (Acting) G. C. Pantry
Senior Medical Office, Bellevue Hospital: Dr V. Williams
Government Archivist: Clinton Black
Government Chemist: Dr A. C. Ellington

MINISTRY OF LABOUR
Permanent Secretary: Major E. H. Grell

MINISTRY OF AGRICULTURE AND FISHERIES
Permanent Secretary: R. T. Cousins
Commissioner of Valuations: W. C. Chang
Manager, Agricultural Credit Board: G. C. L. Gordon
Registrar of Co-operatives: J. W. Kirlew
Registrar of Titles: E. L. Miller

MINISTRY OF HOME AFFAIRS
Permanent Secretary: I. Lloyd Collins
Commissioner of Police: J. H. Middleton
Government Printer: C. S. Markland
Chief Electoral Officer: R. C. Roxburgh

MINISTRY OF COMMUNICATIONS
AND WORKS
Permanent Secretary: O. H. Goldson
Director of Civil Aviation: G. B. Morris
General Manager, Jamaica Railway Corporation: U. H. Salmon
Harbour Master: Capt. S. H. Willers
Postmaster-General: Winston Brown
Supervisor of Traffic and Transport: E. A. Marshall

MINISTRY OF LOCAL GOVERNMENT
Permanent Secretary: N. O. Glegg
Secretary, Board of Supervision: (acting) Mrs P. Constantine

MINISTRY OF LEGAL AFFAIRS
Permanent Secretary: N. A. Tomlinson
Director of Public Prosecutions: J. M. Kerr
Administrator-General: Louis Mendes
Crown Solicitor: V. K. G. McCarthy
Trustee in Bankruptcy: E. S. Hall

MINISTRY OF RURAL LAND
DEVELOPMENT
Permanent Secretary: Deryck Dyer
Commissioner of Lands: C. C. Langford
Conservator of Forests: K. Hall
Director of Surveys: E. A. Tate
Superintendent, Royal Botanic Gardens, Hope: Basil Collins (acting)

DIPLOMATIC REPRESENTATION

JAMAICAN HIGH COMMISSIONERS IN
OTHER COMMONWEALTH COUNTRIES
Britain: Sir H. L. Lindo, CMG (High Commissioner); Canada: V. H. McFarlane, CBE (High Commissioner); Trinidad and Tobago and Guyana and Barbados: I. S. DeSouza, OBE (High Commissioner) (and Commissioner to the Associated States) (resident in Port of Spain)

JAMAICAN REPRESENTATIVES IN NON-
COMMONWEALTH COUNTRIES
Argentina (Ambassador) (resident in New York); France (Ambassador) (resident in London); Germany (Ambassador) (resident in London); Mexico (Ambassador) (resident in Washington); Permanent Mission to the European Office and Specialised Agencies at the United Nations, Geneva (Permanent Representative); Mission to the European

Economic Community, Brussels (Minister Counsellor); Switzerland (Ambassador); United Nations (Permanent Representative); United States (Ambassador); Venezuela (Ambassador) (resident in Port of Spain); Yugoslavia (Ambassador) (resident in Geneva); Panama (Ambassador) (resident in Ottawa).

COMMONWEALTH HIGH COMMISSIONERS
IN JAMAICA
Britain: E. N. Larmour, CMG; Canada: Victor C. Moore; Ghana: Major-General N. Aferi, DSO (resident in Mexico City); Guyana: Mrs Winnifred Gaskin; India: Lakshmi Narayan Ray (resident in Port of Spain); Nigeria: Edwin O. Ogbu (resident in New York); Pakistan: Agha Hilaly (resident in Washington); Trinidad and Tobago: Anthony Khalil Sabga-Aboud.

KENYA

KENYA has a total area of about 224,960 square miles, including 5,171 square miles of water. The territory lies astride the equator and extends from the Indian Ocean in the east to Uganda in the west, from Tanzania in the south to Ethiopia and Sudan in the north, while the north-east frontier runs with Somalia.

Physically, Kenya may be divided into four areas. The north-east is an arid plain, mostly covered with thorn bushes, less than 2,000 feet above sea level, with a small nomadic population; the south-east is similar but practically uninhabited except along the banks of the Tana River and in the coastal strip and the Taita Hills, which rise to 7,000 feet above sea level, and where the rainfall is adequate. The north-west is also generally low and arid, but includes Lake Rudolf (160 miles long), and many mountains, including Nyiru (9,200 feet). The south-west quarter, in which 85 per cent of the population and practically all the economic production is concentrated, comprises a plateau rising to 10,000 feet, and includes Mount Kenya (17,058 feet), Mount Elgon (14,178 feet) and the Aberdare Range (13,104 feet). Much of the area between 7,000 and 11,000 feet above sea level (some 5,000 square miles) is forest. The plateau is bisected from north to south by a part of the Great Rift Valley, thirty to forty miles wide and 2,000 to 3,000 feet below the plateau on either side. The Rift floor rises from 1,280 feet above sea level at Lake Rudolf to 7,000 feet near Naivasha, and falls again to 2,000 feet at Lake Natron. West of the Rift the plateau falls to Lake Victoria (3,720 feet above sea level) and eastward the Tana (length 440 miles) and Athi (length 340 miles) rivers flow to the Indian Ocean. The Athi river changes its name to the Galana at Tsavo. Neither river is navigable except by local craft.

Rainfall in Kenya ranges from a mean annual figure of 6 inches at Lodwar to 58 inches at Kisumu. There is a fairly close inverse correlation between altitude and temperature: at Mombasa, 53 feet above sea-level, the mean annual temperature is 27°C (80°F); at Nairobi, the capital, 5,495 feet, 19°C (67° F); on the equator at 9,062 feet, the mean temperature is 13°C (56°F). Glaciers are found on Mount Kenya down to 15,000 feet above sea level.

The 1969 census shows a total population of 10,956,501 (including the population of Karapokot, transferred from Ugandan to Kenyan administration in 1970). This indicates a growth rate for population of about 3 per cent per annum.

Comparative figures for population by race in 1962 and 1969, and the number of Kenyan citizens in each category in 1969 are:—

	1962 Census	1969 Census	Citizens (1969)
African (including Somali)	8,365,942	10,733,202	10,673,770
Asian	176,613	139,037	60,994
European	55,759	40,593	3,889
Arab	34,048	27,886	24,199
Other	3,091	1,987	339
TOTAL	8,636,263	10,942,705	10,763,191

The overall birth rate per thousand head of the population is 50. The death rate is 17 per thousand.

There are four main races: African, Asians, Arabs and Europeans. The Africans consist of four main ethnic groups which, with the estimated populations at the time of the 1969 census are: Bantu, Kikuyu, Kamba, Luyha, etc. 7,096,404; Nilotic (Luo) 1,521,595; Nilo-Hamitic (Masai, Samburu, Nandi, Kipsigis, etc.) 1,716,442; Hamitic (Somali, Boran, Rendille, etc.) 339,329. In addition to this there are 59,432 other Africans, mainly immigrants from neighbouring countries. The Bantu inhabit the land to the south of the Tana River, including the coastal strip. The main tribe is the Kikuyu, numbering approximately 2,201,632. The Bantu are in the main agriculturists, traditionally living by intensive subsistence cultivation mainly of maize and beans, but this is rapidly giving way to the production of cash crops such as coffee, tea, wheat and dairy products which are marketed through co-operatives. The Nilotics occupy the highlands in western Kenya bordering on Lake Victoria. The main tribe is the

Luo, comprising some 1,521,595 people. The Masai (of the Nilo-Hamitic group) are also to be found in Tanzania. They are nomads, their lives being centred round their livestock although they are beginning to take part in the growing of wheat commercially. Also cattle-rearing nomads are the closely allied Hamitic groups of the north and north-east, from the Ethiopian and Somali borders to the shores of Lake Rudolf, where the Boran tribe merges with the Nilo-Hamitic group of the Rendille and with the Samburu. Much of the African livestock marketed through the Kenya Meat Commission comes from these areas. The Asians and Arabs are essentially town dwellers and own many of the shops. The European population is mainly in Nairobi and Mombasa and upcountry in the former White Highlands. Here, despite the intensive programme of transfer of European-owned farms to African ownership, European farmers still contribute substantially to agricultural output.

There are numerous vernaculars spoken in Kenya, of which Kikuyu and Luo are the most important. Somali is spoken in the north and north-east, and Arabic is widely used by educated Muslims both in the coastal region and elsewhere. Swahili is the most important language, being the *lingua franca* of the semi-literate and educated sections and generally understood throughout the country. English is also fairly widely understood. Gujarati and Urdu are used by many of the Asian population. The official language is English but there is a proposal to introduce Swahili by 1974. Newspapers are published in English and in Swahili and broadcasts are made in the same languages; there are also some programmes in other African languages.

Christianity is the predominant religion, there being in 1962 approximately 2,896,900 Protestants and 1,756,800 Roman Catholics. There are 309,100 Muslims, but this figure excludes the Somalis and those Africans in the north who are members of the Sunni sect. Among the Asian community there are Hindus, Sikhs, Jains, Muslims and Ismailis (followers of H.H. the Aga Khan), but the Goans are Roman Catholics.

Although the Government's long term objective of universal free primary education has not yet been achieved in Kenya, considerable advances have been made in recent years and it is estimated that over 60 per cent of those in the 7-13 age group are now attending primary school. Enrolment in primary schools rose from 891,553 in 1963 to approximately 1,278,850 in 1969, when there were 6,132 primary schools in existence. Secondary schools increased in number from 142 in 1962 to 708 in 1969. Secondary enrolment (excluding technical schools) was 114,567 in 1969 divided between Government aided schools and unaided schools, including 'Harambee' self-help schools. Enrolment in teacher training colleges was 7,145 in the same year. It is estimated that about 30 per cent of the total population are literate.

The University of Nairobi, formerly a constituent College of the University of East Africa, became an autonomous university in July 1970. It has Faculties of Arts, Science, Engineering, Law, Agriculture, Veterinary Science, Commerce, Medicine, Education and Design and Development. Also part of the University are the Institute of Development Studies, the Institute of African Studies and the Institute for Adult Studies. There is also a School of Journalism. There are 2,613 undergraduate students at the University.

The Kenya Government's Development Plan, 1970–74, does not envisage any dramatic changes in the scope and execution of health services but rather a general improvement in the standard of services through more effective co-ordination and consolidation of existing units and a steady increase in facilities, especially in rural and pastoral areas of the country. Work began, however, in 1969 on major extensions to the Kenyatta National Hospital in Nairobi. These extensions will provide an additional 1,100 beds and out-patient facilities for an anticipated one million patients per annum. The first phase, to which Britain contributed £1·7 million was completed in 1971 and includes clinical teaching facilities for the University of Nairobi Medical School. The first graduates, numbering 28, are expected in 1972 and an annual intake of 100 students is planned. The number of hospital beds in Kenya, including maternity beds, totalled about 13,600 in 1967 and it is expected that this will increase to 16,000 by 1974. Development expenditure on health services over the Plan period is estimated at K£19·6 million and recurrent costs K£43 million.

Kenya is divided into seven Provinces and the Nairobi Extra Provincial District, comprising Nairobi and its environs. The Provinces are: Central, Coast, North-Eastern; Eastern; Western; Nyanza; and Rift Valley. The racial populations of the Provinces, based on the 1969 census, are:

	Kenyan African	Other African	Asian	Euro-pean	Arab	Others	Total (1969)
CENTRAL ..	1,665,810	1,298	4,680	3,594	141	124	1,675,647
COAST ..	848,213	21,292	41,867	8,310	23,987	413	944,082
EASTERN ..	1,900,983	1,632	2,750	1,067	804	65	1,907,301
NORTH-EAST ..	241,400	3,460	75	28	708	86	245,757
NYANZA ..	2,106,357	3,856	8,994	2,090	437	311	2,122,045
RIFT VALLEY..	2,179,361	12,423	12,135	5,677	507	186	2,210,289
WESTERN ..	1,323,910	2,128	1,347	542	231	40	1,328,298

The capital of the country is Nairobi with a population of 509,286 (1969 census).

The principal cities and towns, with comparative population figures based on the 1962 and 1969 census, and racial population figures (1969) where available, are:—

	TOTAL (1962)	TOTAL (1969)	Africans	Asians	Euro-peans	Arabs
NAIROBI	266,794	509,286	421,079	67,189	19,185	1,071
MOMBASA	179,575	247,073	187,147	39,049	4,925	15,863
NAKURU	38,181	47,151				
KISUMU	23,526	32,431				
ELDORET	19,605	18,196				
THIKA	13,952	18,387				
NANYUKI	10,448	11,624				
KITALE	9,342	11,573				
NYERI	7,857	10,004				
ISIOLO	5,445	*8,201				
KERICHO	7,692	10,144				
GIGGIL	6,452	4,178				
FORT HALL ..	5,389	4,750				
THOMSON'S FALLS..	5,316	7,602				
ATHI RIVER ..	5,510	5,343				

(*including Meru concessional area)

The main port is Mombasa, which has 14 operational deep-water berths with extensions now under construction. Net registered tonnage in 1969 was 7,583,000 and the port is served by many steamship companies. Other ports of importance to the dhow traffic from India and the Arabian Peninsula are Lamu and Malindi. There is considerable traffic in livestock between Lamu and Mombasa. The Kenya shipping line, Southern Line, operates in East African waters carrying cargo to and from Mombasa, and the recently established East African Shipping Line is at present operating four cargo vessels between Europe and East African ports.

The principal international airport is Nairobi (Embakasi) (runway 13,500 feet), $8\frac{1}{2}$ miles from Nairobi. There is a small airport nearer Nairobi at Wilson, with a runway length of 4,800 feet, 3 miles from the city centre. Mombasa has an airport $4\frac{1}{2}$ miles from the town, with a 6,200 feet runway. The airport at Kisumu is two miles from the town, and has 6,000 feet of runway. Extensions are planned to both Nairobi and Mombasa airports. East African Airways Corporation, which has its headquarters in Nairobi, operates both internal and international scheduled flights. Several air charter companies also operate in Kenya.

There are about 1,270 miles of railway laid in Kenya, with a narrow gauge of 3 ft. $3\frac{3}{8}$ in. The railway in Kenya forms part of the East African railway system. The tonnage of public railway traffic amounted to 5,363,000 in 1969 and 5,470,000 passengers were carried during the same period. No separate figures exist for Kenya. There are about 27,500 miles of roads in Kenya, of which 1,740 miles are bitumen surfaced. Of the remaining 25,000 miles some are only tracks suitable for four-wheel-drive traffic.

Broadcasting services are provided by the 'Voice of Kenya' which is Government controlled. All production emanates from Nairobi at present and is boosted by 28 transmitting stations. Broadcasts are made in English, KiSwahili, twelve African vernaculars, Somali and Hindustani. T.V. broadcasting (government controlled) opened in 1962. Despite difficult reception conditions T.V. coverage extends over a considerable area around Nairobi as far west as Kisumu. There is also a separate television station operating from Mombasa for the Coast region.

The economy of Kenya is essentially agricultural but secondary industry is being encouraged. The principal exports during 1969 were: coffee (K£16,837,000); tea (K£11,271,000); petroleum products (K£7,623,000); fruit and vegetables (K£2,861,000); unmilled maize (K£2,772,000); meat and meat preparations (K£2,595,000); pyrethrum extract (K£2,224,000); undressed hides and skins (K£1,871,000); sisal fibre (K£1,717,000); cement (K£1,435,000) and wattle bark extract (K£1,144,000).

Britain is Kenya's major trading partner, taking in 1969 K£14,786,756 (21·8 per cent) of her exports and supplying K£36,453,305 (31·2 per cent) of her imports. Britain's principal imports from Kenya are tea, sisal, coffee, meat preparations, fruit and vegetables; main exports to Kenya are transport equipment, machinery, metals and chemicals.

For the year 1970/71, the net appropriations in aid on the Government appropriation account show an estimated total revenue of K£124,608,000 and estimated total expenditure of K£123,779,000.

Details of the National Power Development Plan (1966–1986) have been published, under which electric power potential would rise from 135 MW (1967) to 853 MW. At 1966 prices this will cost some K£170 million of which K£70 million can be attributed to the cost of building generating stations on the Tana River.

Kenya's mining industry has not yet been greatly developed. Total production of all minerals in 1969 was valued at K£2·2 million, over half of which is accounted for by soda ash production. Geological exploration is continuing, and deposits of lead, silver, fluorite and rare earths show prospects of becoming economically exploitable. Extensive surveys in the search for oil have taken place, and although no 'strikes' have been announced, expenditure on this is expected to continue at the rate of £1 m. per annum for the next few years.

At the end of 1969 Kenya's forest land covered 4,152,000 acres, of which the plantation area accounted for 277,000 acres. Exotic softwoods cover 230,000 acres, exotic hardwoods 24,700 acres, indigenous softwoods 12,400 acres and indigenous hardwoods 9,900 acres. A pulp and paper mill is to be constructed at Broderick Falls in the Western Province. Plantations of softwood species are being developed to support the industry and forest roads are under construction.

Tourism is Kenya's fastest growing industry, and is expected to overtake coffee as the country's principal foreign exchange earner. The number of holiday visitors to Kenya totalled over 186,000 in 1969 (a rise of 37,000 on the 1968 total) and receipts from tourism were estimated at about K£16·6 million. The 1970–74 Development Plan anticipates further expenditure on the development of the industry of about £14 m., and hopes that gross foreign exchange earnings will rise to £36·5 m. in 1974.

Jamhuri Day, 12th December, celebrates both the attainment of Independence and the adoption of a republican constitution in 1964. Kenyatta Day, 20th October, being the anniversary of the detention of President Kenyatta in 1952, is now a day of celebration and of re-dedication to the service of the nation. Madaraka Day on 1st June is also a public holiday to mark the anniversary of the attainment of internal self-government.

PRE-INDEPENDENCE HISTORY

Apart from knowledge of successive tribal migrations, little information is available regarding the early history of Kenya's interior. The coastal area has, however, been known for at least 2,000 years to Arabian merchants, who during the 7th century A.D. began to settle it with trading posts. The Portuguese explorer Vasco da Gama landed at Malindi, at the mouth of the Sabaki River, in 1498, after sailing round the Cape, and was welcomed by the Sultan. Subsequently the Portuguese established trading posts and gained for a time a monopoly of coastal trading. The Arabs appealed for help and their kinsmen from Oman drove out the Portuguese; Fort Jesus, in Mombasa, being taken in 1698. Although all important Portuguese possessions had gone by 1740, stability did not return to the coast until the rule of Seyyid Said (1806-1856).

The interior remained largely unknown to the West until the arrival of the first explorers in the middle of the 19th century.

Following German interest in East Africa, Britain and Germany concluded an agreement in 1886 regarding their respective spheres of influence. Britain was not, however, prepared to intervene directly, so in 1887 the British East Africa Association obtained from the Sultan of Zanzibar a concession of the mainland between the Umba and Tana Rivers. In 1888 the Imperial British East Africa Company was incorporated under Royal Charter.

Difficulties of administration in, and communication with, Uganda led to the construction of a railway linking the port of Mombasa with Kisumu on Lake Victoria. Construction commenced in 1895, and Kisumu was reached by 1901. During 1895 a Protectorate was declared over what is now Kenya and Uganda, the properties of the Imperial British East Africa Company being bought up.

European settlement took place between 1897 and the start of the First World War, following a survey made by Lord Delamere. Conditions of land alienation were laid down in 1902. There was also a large influx of Asians, in particular to work on the construction of the railway.

In 1905 the Protectorate was transferred from the authority of the Foreign Office to that of the Colonial Office, and a Governor and Commander-in-Chief, and Legislative and Executive Councils, were appointed in 1906. The Protectorate developed steadily prior to the First World War, settlement making good progress and exports of coffee, wool and wheat seemed promising.

The Germans in East Africa took the offensive at the start of the First World War, and penetrated Kenya's southern border. The British forces, under General Smuts, counter-attacked in 1916 and by the end of 1917 had driven the Germans out of the area.

Many more settlers arrived after the War, special schemes being launched for ex-soldiers. The early 1920s were marked by financial and economic crises, and Kenya was still on the road to recovery when the effects of the world depression of the early 1930s were felt. Economically, the story of the later 1930s is one of gradual recovery.

The defence forces in Kenya were strengthened after the Italian occupation of Ethiopia in 1936. Italy entered the Second World War in 1940, and British forces, under General Cunningham, took the offensive in 1941. Italian resistance in East Africa ceased when Gondar fell in November 1941.

Between October 1952 and January 1960 a State of Emergency existed, during the period of the Mau Mau uprising.

After a final constitutional conference in September 1963 at which it was agreed that Kenya would assume sovereignty over the coastal strip, previously subject to the sovereignty of Zanzibar, Kenya became a sovereign independent Member of the Commonwealth on 12th December 1963. On 12th December 1964 Kenya became a Republic within the Commonwealth with Mr Kenyatta as its first President.

CONSTITUTIONAL DEVELOPMENT

The first Legislative and Executive Councils were appointed in 1906, following the transfer of the Protectorate from the authority of the Foreign Office to that of the Colonial Office.

After the First World War, controversy raged over the question of representation on the Legislative Council. In 1919 the number of Nominated Unofficial Europeans was increased from four to eleven and an elective basis established. The grant of the franchise to Europeans called forth a demand from the more numerous Indian community for equal privileges on a common roll with educational qualifications. The matter was resolved by the Devonshire White Paper of 1923 which granted the Indians five seats on a communal basis and also made provision for an Arab Elected Member and a Nominated Unofficial Member to represent African interests. The settlement was accepted by the Europeans, but the Indians launched a campaign of non-co-operation and did not fill the full number of seats allotted to them until the 1930s. A second Unofficial Member was later nominated to represent African interests.

Further constitutional changes took place after the Second World War. Mr Eliud Mathu was nominated in 1944 as the first African to represent his people on the Legislative Council, and a reorganisation of government in 1945 grouped the main departments under Members of the Executive Council.

Constitutional changes proposed by the Secretary of State for the Colonies, Mr Griffiths, were brought into force in 1951. The appointment of ten Nominated Members of the Legislative Council raised the numbers of the 'government' side from sixteen to twenty-six. At the same time the number of European Elected Members was raised from eleven to fourteen, of Asian Elected Members from five to six, of African Representative Members from four to six, with Arabs having one Representative and one Elected Member.

In 1954 a new constitution was introduced. It provided for a Council of Ministers, exercising collective responsibility, to consist of the Governor, the Deputy Governor, six Official, six Unofficial and two Nominated Members. The Government was reformed on this basis, the six Unofficial Ministers consisting of three European Elected Members, two Asians and one African Representative Member. Three Parliamentary Secretaries were appointed, two Africans and one Arab. At a later date the Governor appointed the Liwali for the Coast as his Personal Adviser on Arab Affairs, and the Liwali was admitted to meetings of the Council of Ministers.

Further changes took place in 1956, when the six Representative African Members were replaced by eight Elected Members. The first African elections took place in March 1957, but deadlock ensued when the African Minister was defeated and none of the newly-elected Members were prepared to accept office. The Secretary of State for the Colonies, Mr Lennox-Boyd, held talks in Nairobi in November 1957 with the various groups involved. As agreement did not seem possible, the European and Asian Elected Ministers resigned and the Secretary of State came to the conclusion that the 1954 Constitution had become unworkable.

Following new proposals by the Secretary of State for the Colonies, the number of African Elected Members in the Legislative Council was increased from eight to fourteen. Elections for these new seats were held in March 1958. The Kenya Constitution Order in Council 1958, which came into force on 5th April, created Specially Elected Seats in the Legislative Council and set up a Council of State, designed to protect communities from harmful discriminatory legislation. Certain changes were made to the 1958 Constitution in December 1960, following a conference in London during January and February of that year.

Full internal self-government followed a conference in London in early 1962. A National Coalition Government supported by the two main political parties, the Kenya African National Union and the Kenya African Democratic Union, was set up. The chief instrument of government was the Council of Ministers, consisting of sixteen Ministers of whom two were civil servants. Of the fourteen unofficial Ministers, eleven were African, two European and one Asian. Parliamentary Secretaries were appointed by the Governor. Upper and Lower Houses of Parliament were established, the former consisting of one member from each existing District and certain non-voting members representing special interests, and the latter consisting of members elected by universal adult suffrage.

Ministerial talks were held in London in June 1963 to consider the question of Kenya's independence. During the discussions the Kenya Ministers outlined the progress made in working out the constitution for a proposed East African Federation, which it was hoped might comprise Kenya, Tanganyika and Uganda, and possibly also Zanzibar if it so wished. It was agreed that it was desirable that Kenya should become independent before a Federation could be inaugurated. A conference was held in London in September and October 1963 to settle the final form of Kenya's constitution and Kenya became an independent Member of the Commonwealth on 12th December 1963.

POST INDEPENDENCE HISTORY AND THE CONSTITUTION

The Independence Constitution provided for a Governor-General to be appointed by Her Majesty The Queen and a Parliament consisting of Her Majesty and a bi-cameral legislature, the National Assembly, comprising a Senate and a House of Representatives. The constitution also provided for Regional Assemblies for each of the seven regions, each with a President and a Vice-President elected from within their own membership. The Regional Assemblies were given exclusive legislative competence in some matters and concurrent legislative competence with Parliament in others.

The Constitution (Amendments) Act 1964 and 1965 provided for Kenya to become a Republic with a President as Head of State, Head of the Cabinet and Commander-in-Chief of the Armed Forces, choosing his Vice-President and Cabinet from among the members of the National Assembly to whom they are collectively responsible. The President would also appoint the Chief Justice, Chief Commissioner of Police and most senior civil servants. The first President was to be the Prime Minister in office immediately before 12th December 1964 (i.e. Mr Kenyatta) and was thereafter to be chosen by a majority of members of the House of Representatives. These acts also drastically reduced the powers and financial resources given to the Regional Assemblies by the Independence Constitution. These became Provincial Councils and were eventually abolished altogether by a further amendment in July 1967. During the passage of the 1964 Amendment Act the KADU opposition party, which had favoured the regional constitution, dissolved itself and joined the governing party KANU.

A further amendment in May 1965 reduced the majorities needed in the House of Representatives and the Senate to amend any clauses of the Constitution to a 65 per cent majority of all members of each House and provided that thenceforth no clauses should be specially entrenched as certain clauses had been in the Independence Constitution.

Following the resignation in April 1966 of the Vice-President, Mr Odinga, and his formation of a new Opposition Party, the K.P.U. (Kenya People's Union), a Constitutional Amendment Act was passed requiring those members who changed their party allegiance to seek re-election. In the "Little General Election" held in June 1966, KANU gained a majority of the contested seats but Mr Odinga was returned to lead the KPU, later recognised as the official Parliamentary Opposition.

Another Constitutional Amendment Act was passed in December 1966 to enable the Senate to be amalgamated with the House of Representatives as a unicameral National Assembly with 158 elected Members and 12 specially elected members chosen by the elected members. The constituency boundaries were redrawn to give each Senator a constituency including at least a part of his former district. The Act also provided for the postponement of the General Election due in 1968 until June 1970.

Yet another Constitutional Amendment Act was passed in June 1968. This provided that the President would in future be elected by popular vote and that, should the President die or become incapacitated in office, a general election to choose a new President must be held within 90 days. It is also laid down that in future both Presidential and Parliamentary candidates must be nominated by a registered political party. It further provided that the 12 specially elected members of the National Assembly should in future be nominated by the President.

The remaining clauses of the Independence Constitution and the subsequent amendments were consolidated into the Constitution of Kenya Bill 1968 which was passed by the National Assembly in December 1968.

A bill which introduced the primary system for the selection of party parliamentary candidates was passed in 1969. This system has now been extended to local Government elections.

In October 1969 following the disturbances during President Kenyatta's visit to Kisumu, the KPU was banned and its leaders detained making Kenya a *de facto* one party state. Many of these detainees have now been released including Mr Odinga himself.

The first post-independence General Election held in December 1969 resulted in the unopposed return of President Kenyatta and of those parliamentary candidates who had suceeded in the KANU party primary elections. The new administration was formed on 22nd December 1969.

LAND TRANSFER AND SETTLEMENT SCHEMES

Starting in 1961 and 1962 when Kenya was approaching Independence, several schemes for the transfer of mixed farming land from European to African ownership were put into operation with a view to increasing African participation in all sectors of Kenya's economic life and satisfying the aspiration to land ownership among the landless and unemployed.

The British and Kenya Governments agreed on a programme almost entirely financed by British loans and grants for the purchase of approximately one million acres of European-owned mixed farming land and its division into smallholdings for settlement by African farmers. Parallel with the Million Acre Settlement Scheme, the Agricultural Finance Corporation and Land Bank operated schemes to assist African farmers to purchase former European-owned farms.

The programme of land transfer and settlement is a continuing one for which the British Government has to date provided over £32 million in grants or loans. It is generally recognised that Kenya's land reform programme is one of the most successful ever.

HISTORICAL LIST

PRIME MINISTER

The Hon. Mzee Jomo Kenyatta, MP, 12th December 1963 to 11th December 1964
(re-elected 20th December 1969)

PRESIDENT

The Hon. Mzee Jomo Kenyatta, MP, from 12th December 1964
(re-elected 20th December 1969)

I

GOVERNMENT

The Government Party, the Kenya African National Union, holds all 170 seats in the National Assembly.

PRESIDENT AND CABINET

President: His Excellency The Hon Mzee Jomo Kenyatta, CGH, MP
Vice-President and Minister for Home Affairs:
His Excellency The Hon D. T. Arap Moi, EGH, EBS, MP
Minister for Defence: The Hon. James Samuel Gichuru, EGH, MP
Minister for Foreign Affairs: The Hon. Dr Njoroge Mungai, EGH, MP
Minister for Agriculture: The Hon. J. J. M. Nyagah, EGH, MP
Minister for Finance and Economic Planning: The Hon. Myai Kibaki, EGH, MP
Minister for Local Government: The Hon. Dr J. K. Kiano, EGH, MP
Minister for Labour: The Hon. E. N. Mwendwa, EGH, EBS, MP
Minister for Lands and Settlement: The Hon. J. H. Angaine, EGH, EBS, MP
Minister for Housing: The Hon. P. J. Ngei, EGH, MP
Minister for Works: The Hon. James Nyamweya, EGH, MP
Attorney General: The Hon. Charles Njonjo, EGH, MP
Minister for Commerce and Industry: The Hon. J. C. N. Osogo, EGH, MP
Minister for Power and Communications: The Hon. R. G. Ngala, EGH, EBS, MP
Minister for Information and Broadcasting: The Hon. Dr Z. Onyonka, MP
Minister for Co-Operatives and Social Services:
The Hon. Henry Masinde Muliro, EBS, MP
Minister for Health: The Hon. Isaac Omolo-Okero, MP
Minister for Natural Resources: The Hon. W. O. Omamo, MP
Minister for Tourism and Wildlife: The Hon. J. L. M. Shako, MP
Minister for Education: The Hon. Taita Arap Towett, MP
Minister for Common Market and Economic Affairs: The Hon. R. J. Ouko, MLA

MINISTER OF STATE

President's Office: The Hon. Mbiyu Koinange, EGH, MP

ASSISTANT MINISTERS

President's Office: The Hon. Kamwithi Munyi, EBS, MP
Vice-President's Office:
The Hon. R. S. Matano, MP; The Hon. Joseph Martin Shikuku, MP
Ministry of Defence: The Hon. J. Njeru, MP
Ministry of Foreign Affairs: The Hon. B. Nabwera, MP; The Hon. L. Oguda, MP
Ministry of Agriculture: The Hon. Maina Wanjigi, MP; The Hon. J. W. Khaoya, MP
Ministry of Finance: The Hon. Sheikh M. Balala, EBS, MP; The Hon. W. Cherono, MP
Ministry of Local Government:
The Hon. M. J. Ogutu, MP; The Hon. N. W. Munoko, MP
Ministry of Labour: The Hon. F. P. K. Kubai, EBS, MP; The Hon. P. F. Kibisu, MP
Ministry of Lands and Settlement:
The Hon. G. G. Kariuki, MP; The Hon. S. Mohamed Amin, MP
Ministry of Housing: The Hon. A. S. Khalif, MP; The Hon. E. K. K. Bomett, MP
Ministry of Works: The Hon. John Keen, MP; The Hon. D. N. Kuguru, MP
Ministry of Commerce and Industry:
The Hon. M. B. Wood, MP; The Hon. Z. M. Anyieni, MP
Ministry of Power and Communications:
The Hon. D. C. N. Moss, MP; The Hon. H. J. Onamu, MP
Ministry of Information and Broadcasting:
The Hon. J. Z. Kase, MP; The Hon. O. Makone, MP
Ministry of Co-Operatives and Social Services:
The Hon. L. K. Ngureti, MP; The Hon. S. Choge, MP
Ministry of Health:
The Hon. S. C. Ole Oloitipitip, EBS, MP; The Hon. Mohamed Jahazi, MP
Ministry of Natural Resources:
The Hon. A. A. Ochwada, MP; The Hon. S. M. Kioko, MP
Ministry of Tourism and Wildlife:
The Hon. Jan Mohamed, MP; The Hon. J. M. Kariuki, MP
Ministry of Education: The Hon. P. N. Mbai, MP; The Hon. C. W. Rubia, EBS, MP
East African Affairs: The Hon. G. N. Kalya, MP, MLA

NATIONAL ASSEMBLY

Speaker: The Hon. F. M. G. Mati, MP
Deputy Speaker: The Hon. Dr F. L. M. Waiyaki, MP
Clerk to the National Assembly: L. J. Ngugi
First Clerk Assistant: J. O. Kimoro
Second Clerk Assistant: H. B. N. Gicheru
Sergeant-at-Arms: J. Baraza

JUDICIARY

Chief Justice: Mr Justice M. Kitili Mwendwa, MA, LLB, DPA, DipEd, Barrister at Law

Puisne Judges:

Mr Justice J. Wicks
Mr Justice C. B. Madan
Mr Justice E. Trevelyan
Mr Justice Chanan Singh
Mr Justice A. A. Kneller

Mr Justice C. H. E. Miller
Mr Justice L. G. E. Harris
Mr Justice A. H. Simpson
Mr Justice K. G. Bennett
Mr Justice L. P. Mosdell

Registrar: J. O. Nyarangi

MINISTRIES AND GOVERNMENT DEPARTMENTS

PRESIDENT'S OFFICE

Permanent Secretary and Secretary to the Cabinet: G. K. Karrithi, CBS
Director of Personnel: J. A. Gethenji

VICE-PRESIDENT'S OFFICE

Permanent Secretary: G. S. K. Boit
Ministry of Defence: Permanent Secretary: J. G. Kiereini
Ministry of Foreign Affairs: Permanent Secretary: D. C. Mlamba
Ministry of Agriculture: Permanent Secretary: J. B. Kibe
Ministry of Finance: Permanent Secretary: P. Ndegwa
Ministry of Local Government: Permanent Secretary: A. J. Omanga
Ministry of Health: Permanent Secretary: J. M. Kyalo
Ministry of Natural Resources: Permanent Secretary: J. M. Ojal

Ministry of Labour: Permanent Secretary: G. I. Othieno
Ministry of Lands and Settlement: Permanent Secretary: S. Kungiu
Ministry of Housing: Permanent Secretary: A. Abutti
Ministry of Works: Permanent Secretary: P. Shiyukah
Attorney General's Chambers: Registrar General: D. J. Coward, CMG OBE
Ministry of Commerce and Industry: Permanent Secretary: J. W. Mureithi
Ministry of Power and Communications: Permanent Secretary: S. B. Ogembo
Ministry of Information and Broadcasting: Permanent Secretary: T. C. J. Ramtu
Ministry of Co-operatives and Social Services: Permanent Secretary: J. N. Oluoch
Ministry of Tourism and Wildlife: Permanent Secretary: J. K. Arapkoitie; G.M. Matheka
Ministry of Education: Permanent Secretary: P. J. Gachathi

DIPLOMATIC REPRESENTATION

KENYAN REPRESENTATIVES IN OTHER COMMONWEALTH COUNTRIES

High Commissioner in the United Kingdom: Ng'ethe Njoroge; High Commissioner in India: S. K. Kimalel; High Commissioner in Zambia: L. P. Odero

COMMONWEALTH HIGH COMMISSIONERS IN KENYA

United Kingdom: Sir Eric Norris, KCMG; Canada: J. M. Cook; Australia: K. H. Rogers; India: Gurbachan Singh; Pakistan: Air Vice-Marshal M. K. Khan; Ghana:

E. K. Otoo; Nigeria: I. C. Olisemeka; Malawi: J. Kachingwe; Zambia: A. N. Kalyati; Lesotho: D. P. Makoae; Botswana: P. P. M. Makepe; Swaziland: M. B. Mdiniso; Ceylon: I. B. Fonseka

KENYAN AMBASSADORS IN NON-COMMONWEALTH COUNTRIES

Congo (Kinshasa); France; Germany; Somali Republic; Sweden; United Arab Republic; United Nations (Representative); United States; U.S.S.R.; Ethiopia

LESOTHO

LESOTHO lies between latitudes 28° 35′ and 30° 40′ S. and longitudes 27° and 29° 30′ E. It is a mountainous country wholly surrounded by South Africa, with Natal to the east, Cape Province to the south and the Orange Free State to the north and west. Out of the total area of 11,716 square miles, about one-third lying along the western and southern boundaries, is classed as 'lowland' and is between 5,000 feet and 6,000 feet above sea level. The remainder of the country, the 'highlands', is mostly between 7,000 feet and 9,000 feet above sea level. The two main mountain ranges are the Maluti Mountains and the Drakensberg range, which run from north to south. The Maluti, in the central part of the country, are spurs of the main Drakensberg range, which they join in the north forming a high plateau. The highest mountains are in the Drakensberg range, which forms the border with Natal, where Cathkin Peak, Giant's Castle and Mont-aux-Sources are all over 10,000 feet high. The highest mountain is Thabana Ntlenyana, 11,425 feet high.

Two of the largest rivers in the Republic of South Africa, the Orange and the Tugela, and the tributaries of the Caledon, have their sources in the mountains of Lesotho. The climate is generally healthy and pleasant. Rainfall is variable and averages about 29 inches a year over the greater part of the country. Most of the rain falls during the summer months between October and April but there is normally no month which has less than half an inch of rain. The winters are normally dry with heavy frosts in the lowlands. Temperatures in the lowlands vary from about 32·2°C (90°F) in summer to a minimum of —6·7°C (20°F) in winter. In the highlands the range is much wider and temperatures below freezing point are common. Snow falls frequently in the highlands in winter but only rarely in the lowlands.

The results of a census taken in 1966 show a total population present in the country of 852,000 persons. The number of persons believed to be absent from Lesotho at the time of the census was 115,000, giving a total population of 967,000 persons. Of the 852,000 people in the country in 1966 the census shows that 849,986 were African, 1,593 European and 799 Asiatic. The Europeans are mainly civil servants, traders and missionaries and the Asiatics are mainly traders. The African population has more than quadrupled since an early census taken in 1891.

The language of the Basotho is Sesotho (or southern Sotho). Some small tribal units speak also vernaculars of the Nguni group, including Zulu and Xhosa. The official languages are English and Sesotho. About 70 per cent of the population are Christians. The non-Christians hold to their traditional beliefs.

Lesotho is divided into nine districts, each with the same name as the district town; Butha-Buthe, population 55,000; Leribe, population 139,000; Berea, population 100,000; Maseru, population 182,000; Mafeteng, population 103,000; Mohale's Hoek, population 97,000; Quthing, population 65,000; Qacha's Nek, population 57,000; Mokhotlong, population 55,000; the capital is Maseru with a population estimated in 1968 to be 14,000.

There are three weekly scheduled air flights (Mondays, Wednesdays, and Fridays) from Johannesburg to Maseru and back. Apart from the Maseru airfield, there are some thirty airstrips in Lesotho, the main ones being at Mokhotlong, Sehonghong, Semonkong and Qacha's Nek. Most of these are suitable only for the lightest type of aircraft. The country is linked for passenger and goods services with the rail system of South Africa by a short line (gauge 3 feet 6 inches) from Maseru to Marseilles on the Bloemfontein-Natal main line. One mile of the line is in Lesotho. Elsewhere the railway runs close to the border and goods are transported by road to and from the nearest station across the frontier. There are some 1,200 miles of gravelled and earth roads and vehicle tracks, and a few miles of bitumenised roads in urban areas. A 90-mile tarred road links Maseru to several of the main lowland towns in Lesotho.

Radio Lesotho is a broadcasting station operated by the Government Department of Information.

Lesotho has few natural resources and no significant industrial development. The economy is based on agriculture and animal husbandry, and the adverse balance of trade (mainly consumer and capital goods) is offset in part by the earnings of the large numbers of Basotho who work in South Africa. Apart from some diamonds, no mineral deposits have so far been discovered. With the setting up in 1967 of the Lesotho National Development Coroporation, the Government of Lesotho hopes to encourage industrial development which will provide local employment opportunities. The utilisation of Lesotho's great potentialities as a source of water supply are under study, and surveys have been made. Agreement has been reached in principle between Lesotho and the Republic of South Africa to go ahead with the Malibamatso (formerly the Oxbow) water supply scheme. This project is expected to add substantially to Lesotho's revenue if South Africa takes advantage of this new source of water.

British financial assistance towards the economic and social development of Lesotho includes the provision of capital for development and of aid for the recurrent budget. Under the Colonial Development and Welfare Acts grants totalling £4·9 million were provided between 1945–46 and 1965–66. Until 1956 the extra and increasing recurrent expenditure incurred from the expansion of social services, and even some development capital expenditure, was provided out of the country's revenues. From 1957 onwards, the annual budgetary deficits increased and in 1960 Britain began giving annual grants in aid of administration to balance the budget. In the period 1960–61 to 1966–67 these grants totalled some £11·5 million.

In the financial talks which took place immediately after independence, Britain offered a forward commitment to provide financial aid up to a total of £11 million in the period 1967–68 to 1969–70, to be allocated between development expenditure and budgetary aid as might subsequently be agreed between the Governments of Great Britain and Lesotho. Following the devaluation of the pound sterling in 1967 the British Government informed the Government of Lesotho that the Rand equivalent of the British aid would be maintained at the pre-devaluation value for the years 1967/68 and 1968/69. British budgetary and development aid up to a total of approximately £2 million was allocated in 1970/71 and up to £2·35 and £2·1 million respectively will be provided in 1971/72 and 1972/73.

Lesotho's well developed education system owes much to missionary work. Most schools are mission-controlled, the Government providing grants for salaries and buildings. Despite the mountainous countryside, few areas lack a school, a fact reflected in the high literacy rate of approximately 70 per cent. There were 35 secondary schools in 1970, 11 of which offered a full five-year course leading to the Cambridge Overseas School Certificate. The University of

Botswana, Lesotho and Swaziland was established by Royal Charter at Roma, 22 miles from Maseru, on 1st January 1964.

HISTORY

In the early nineteenth century some of the leading tribal groups which were later to form part of the Basotho nation were settled along the present-day north-western borders of Lesotho near Leribe. Among these were the Bakwena, led by Moshesh, then a young man who, though only a minor chief, had shown outstanding qualities of leadership and gathered a following from other tribes. This was the period of the "Wars of Calamity" when Chaka's Zulu *impis* raided across the Drakensburg from Natal, driving before them the remnants of other tribes. In 1824 Moshesh, who now was the leader of some 5,000 persons, sought refuge at Thaba Bosiu, a virtually impregnable flat-topped hill near Maseru. From this base he was able, by a judicious mixture of firmness and diplomacy, to avert further Zulu and Matabele attacks. By 1831 he had become the acknowledged chief of the local Basotho clans and had gained the allegiance of other tribal groups.

Within a few years, however, an even greater threat to Moshesh's people arose in the form of the emigrant Boers of the Great Trek of 1834. These Voortrekkers, seeking homes and grazing for their herds, encroached on the level lands around the Caledon river where the Basotho were already established.

From then on, until his death in 1870, Moshesh was engaged in a struggle involving both border warfare and negotiation to preserve the territorial integrity and independence of the Basotho homeland. In this he was ably assisted by the French Protestant missionary Eugene Casalis, who from his arrival in 1833 with two companions identified himself with the Basotho and acted as Moshesh's adviser in relations with the outside world.

For over 30 years the western and southern marches of the customary lands of the Basotho were in a state of constant unrest. While the Boer farmers continually encroached into Moshesh's territory, the Basotho retaliated by raiding their cattle. By adopting the horse as a means of transport and by acquiring firearms the Basotho were able to inflict severe reverses on the Boer commandos, but the creation of the independent Orange Free State (OFS) in 1854 led to increased pressure and in 1858 to inconclusive warfare.

Advised by Casalis, Moshesh had from as early as 1842 sought the protection of the British Crown; in the following year he signed an agreement by which he became "a friend and ally" of the Cape Colony, but this agreement was later cancelled. In 1861, under further pressure from the OFS, Moshesh again petitioned the British High Commissioner in South Africa, saying that his country could only be secure if the Basotho were to be recognised as the Queen's subjects. The British Government continued to be unwilling to assume further responsibilities in South Africa until renewed hostilities between the OFS and the Basotho from 1865 onwards, which seemed likely to result early in 1868 in the complete defeat of the Basotho and the total annexation of their country, led to a change of policy. On 12th March 1868 the British High Commissioner issued a proclamation declaring the Basotho to be British subjects and their territory to be British territory.

There remained the immediate cause of the conflict, the lack of a defined and accepted frontier between the OFS and the Basotho. The Convention of Aliwal North, concluded on 12th March 1869 confirmed to the OFS the recently conquered lands west of the Caledon River but restored to the Basotho other lands east of the Caledon which had been lost in the recent fighting. The frontier laid down by the convention has remained substantially unchanged to the present day.

For three years Basutoland was administered by the High Commissioner, but in 1871 it was formally annexed, with the agreement of Britain, to Cape Colony which had recently been granted responsible government. Although material conditions quickly improved under a rule of law and order, there was a legacy amongst the minor chiefs of insubordination to the Paramount Chief (as Moshesh's successors were entitled) and of apprehension amongst the people about the future. Much of the proceeds of the sales of their livestock or from their earnings by service in the Kimberley diamond fields (which from about 1870 began to provide a market for expatriate Basotho labour) were invested in firearms. An attempt by the Cape Colony Government in 1880 to enforce a policy of disarmament on the Basotho tribesmen, led to several years of desultory and inconclusive fighting—the so-called Gun War. In 1883 the Cape Government asked Britain to be relieved of the charge of Basutoland. The British Government thereupon offered the Basotho the choice of returning to the position they had occupied before being taken under the protection of the Crown or of coming under direct British rule. In November 1883 the major Basotho chiefs signified their wish to become British subjects 'under the direct rule of the Queen'. In March 1884 Basutoland was brought by proclamation and Order in Council under the direct control of the Crown, through the High Commissioner in South Africa.

CONSTITUTIONAL DEVELOPMENT

When the four provinces of South Africa came together in 1908 to discuss the possibility of a federation or union, the Basotho chiefs sent a deputation to England asking that Basutoland should not be incorporated in any future union. Accordingly when the Act of Union was passed Basutoland remained a British colony.

In 1910 an advisory body known as the Basutoland Council consisting of the Resident Commissioner as President, the Paramount Chief as Chief Councillor and 99 Basuto members (94 nominated by the Paramount Chief and 5 by the Resident Commissioner) was constituted by proclamation of the High Commissioner. Later on, the constitution of the 99 Basotho members was changed: 42 were elected, 52 were nominated by the Paramount Chief and 5 were nominated by the Resident Commissioner. In 1944 the High Commissioner formally declared that it was 'the policy of His Majesty's Government to consult the Paramount Chief and the Basutoland Council before proclamations closely affecting the domestic affairs and welfare of the Basotho people or the progress of the Basotho Native Administration are enacted'. At the same time, the Paramount Chief confirmed that it was the policy of the Paramountcy 'to consult the Basutoland Council before issuing orders or making rules closely affecting the life or welfare of the Basotho people and the administration of the Basotho'. In 1945 a small elected standing committee was created to deal with important matters between sessions of the full Council. In 1946 a Basotho National Treasury was established and a new system of some 122 courts, held by Basotho stipendiary magistrates, replaced the 1,340 courts previously held by chiefs in their own name. Fines and fees from these courts now went to the National

Treasury. By 1949 the number of these courts had been further reduced to 107. In 1960 a legislature—the Basutoland National Council—and an executive Council were formed. In 1962 a Constitutional Commission was appointed by the Paramount Chief to formulate proposals for the amendment of the 1960 Constitution. The Commission reported in 1963 and its report was adopted in February 1964 by the National Council as a basis for negotiation with the British Government. A Constitutional Conference was held in London in 1964 and agreement was reached on a new pre-independence constitution on lines recommended by the Constitutional Commission. The new Constitution was brought into operation on 30th April 1965. The Paramount Chief became the Queen's Representative. The legislature became bi-cameral; the Senate consisting of 22 Principal and Ward Chiefs and 11 other persons nominated by the Paramount Chief and the National Assembly consisting of 60 elected members. The Resident Commissioner became the British Government Representative retaining responsibility for defence, external affairs, internal security and the public service and for proper financial administration. At the 1964 Conference, the Secretary of State gave a formal undertaking that if at any time not earlier than one year after the new elections the people of Basutoland should ask for independence the British Government would seek to give effect to their wishes as soon as possible.

The first elections took place on the 29th and 30th April 1965 and were narrowly won by the National Party which won 31 of the 60 seats giving it a majority of 2 over the combined strength of the Congress Party (25 seats) and the Marema Tlou Freedom Party (4 seats). The deputy leader of the National Party held office as Prime Minister until 1st July 1965 when he was succeeded in office by Chief Leabua Jonathan who had entered the National Assembly after winning a by-election.

At further talks held in London in November 1965, between the British and Basutoland Governments, the Basutoland Prime Minister confirmed that a formal request for independence would be submitted immediately after 29th April 1966 and asked the British Government to accept that the conditions attached to the Colonial Secretary's undertaking of 24th April 1964 were likely to be fulfilled. The British Government accepted the Prime Minister's statement of intention and his assurances on the fulfilment of the stipulated conditions.

On the 18th and 19th April 1966 the Basutoland Government moved resolutions in the Senate and the National Assembly asking the British Government to grant independence to Lesotho in the terms of the agreement reached in London in 1964 and in terms of a White Paper of the 8th March 1966 in which the Basutoland Government had set out the conditions under which it proposed to seek independence. The resolutions were eventually passed and the Basutoland Independence Conference was held in London from the 8th to 17th June 1966 under the chairmanship of the Secretary of State for the Colonies. At the conclusion of the Conference the Colonial Secretary confirmed that the British Government accepted the independence resolutions of the Basutoland Government and that it would take the necessary steps to grant independence to Basutoland in accordance with the undertaking given at the 1964 Conference. The Conference agreed that Basutoland should become independent under the name of Lesotho on the 4th October 1966. Parliament gave effect to this decision by the Lesotho Independence Act 1966, enacted on 3rd August.

CONSTITUTION

The Constitution which was granted to Lesotho on Independence is set out in the Lesotho Independence Order 1966 (S.I. 1172). The Lesotho Order 1970, made by Chief Leabua Jonathan at Maseru on 10th February 1970, states that the Lesotho Independence Order 1966 was suspended on 30th January 1970.

GOVERNMENT

HEAD OF STATE
His Majesty King Moshoeshoe II

COUNCIL OF MINISTERS
Prime Minister, Minister of Foreign Affairs, Minister of Defence and Internal Security:
The Hon. Chief Leabua Jonathan
Deputy Prime Minister and Minister of Agriculture:
The Hon. Chief N. S. 'Maseribane
Minister to the Prime Minister: The Hon. Chief Selbourne R. Letsie
Minister of Finance, Commerce and Industry: The Hon. P. N. P. Peete
Minister of the Interior: The Hon. Chief P. M. Majara
Minister of Works and Communications: The Hon. A. C. Manyeli
Minister of Health and Education: The Hon. M. B. Leseteli
Minister of Justice and Tourism: The Hon. Chief P. Mota
Minister of State: The Hon. Chief Sotho M. Letsie

JUDICIARY
Chief Justice: The Hon. Mr Justice H. R. Jacobs

COURT OF APPEAL
President: Mr Justice O. D. Schreiner, MC
Mr Justice I. A. Maisels
Mr Justice A. Milne
Registrar: E. T. Kotelo

MINISTRIES AND GOVERNMENT DEPARTMENTS

PRIME MINISTER'S PORTFOLIO
Permanent Secretary: J. T. Mapetla, MBE
Director of Information: G. Geldenhuys
Chief Passport Officer: E. T. Matsau

CABINET OFFICE
Secretary to the Cabinet and Head of the Civil Service: J. T. Mapetla, MBE

MINISTRY OF FOREIGN AFFAIRS
Permanent Secretary: P. M. Mabathoana

MINISTRY OF FINANCE
Permanent Secretary: E. Waddington, OBE
Accountant-General: D. K. Noto (acting)

MINISTRY OF HEALTH AND EDUCATION
Permanent Secretary: J. R. L. Kotsokoane

AUDIT DEPARTMENT
Auditor-General: N. Harrison

MINISTRY OF THE INTERIOR
Permanent Secretary: P. Rasokoai

MINISTRY OF AGRICULTURE
Permanent Secretary: A. S. Mohale
Director of Veterinary Services: Dr N. N. Raditapole, OBE

MINISTRY OF WORKS AND COMMUNICATIONS
Permanent Secretary: H. Ntsaba
Director of Posts and Telecommunications: A. C. Heathcote, OBE

MINISTRY OF JUSTICE
Permanent Secretary: L. Qhobela

PUBLIC SERVICE COMMISSION
Chairman: S. M. Lepolesa, MBE

I*

DIPLOMATIC REPRESENTATION

LESOTHO REPRESENTATIVES IN OTHER COMMONWEALTH COUNTRIES

High Commissioner in Canada: M. T. Mashologu (resident in U.S.A.); High Commissioner in Ghana, Kenya, Sierre Leone and Tanzania: D. P. Makoae (resident in Kenya); High Commissioner in the United Kingdom: C. M. Molapo.

COMMONWEALTH HIGH COMMISSIONERS IN LESOTHO

Britain: H. G. M. Bass; Canada: H. H, Carter (resident in Republic of South Africa).

LESOTHO REPRESENTATIVES IN NON-COMMONWEALTH COUNTRIES

Austria, France, Germany, Vatican: C. M. Molapo (Ambassador) (resident in London); Cameroon, Ivory Coast: D. P. Makoae (Ambassador) (resident in Kenya); United Nations: M. T. Mashologu (Permanent Representative); United States: M. T. Mashologu (Ambassador).

NON-COMMONWEALTH REPRESENTATION IN LESOTHO

Austria (Ambassador) (resident in South Africa); Belgium (Ambassador) (resident in South Africa); Federal Republic of Germany (Ambassador) (resident in Malawi); France (Ambassador) (resident in Zambia); Israel (Ambassador) (resident in Malawi); Italy (Ambassador) (resident in South Africa); Japan (Consul General) (resident in South Africa); Netherlands (Ambassador) (resident in South Africa); Republic of China (Ambassador); South Korea (Ambassador) (resident in Kenya); Sweden (Ambassador) (resident in South Africa); Switzerland (Ambassador) (resident in South Africa); United States (Ambassador); Vatican (Pro-Nuncio) (resident in South Africa).

MALAWI

MALAWI is entirely land-locked and lies between 9° 25′ and 17° 07′ S. latitudes and between 33° 40′ and 35° 55′ E. longitudes. Malawi's neighbours are Tanzania on the north and east, Mozambique from the south-east to south-west and Zambia on the west. When the country became independent—at the last stroke of midnight on 5th/6th July 1964—it changed its name from Nyasaland to Malawi. 'Malawi' is the modern spelling of 'Maravi'. the name used in ancient times not only geographically to denote a large area in Central Africa, but also sociologically to describe the widespread groups of closely-associated Bantu peoples whose domain it was. This area included all of what used to be Nyasaland, together with much of present-day Zambia and Mozambique. Etymologically, the word 'Malawi' has associations with a general meaning of reflected light or bright haze, an appropriate name for a country containing African's third largest lake.

Malawi has an area of 45,411 square miles, of which one quarter is water. Lake Malawi, formerly known as Lake Nyasa, covers an area of 8,870 square miles and is 355 miles long; it varies in width from 10 to 50 miles and forms the southern end of the Great Rift Valley which runs through East Africa.

Internal traffic on Lake Malawi is moved by the Malawi Railways operating a fleet of tugs and barges, two 200-ton cargo vessels, M.V. *Mpasa* and *Nkwazi*, the small passenger and cargo M.V. *Chauncy Maples* and the larger *Ilala II*. The *Chauncy Maples*, a former missionary vessel, has recently been rebuilt to a new design and now has accommodation for 190 passengers and 10 tons of cargo. The *Ilala II* carries 80 tons of cargo and accommodates 12 first-class, 28 third-class and up to 460 fourth-class passengers. The *Chauncy Maples* maintains a regular service from Monkey Bay in the south to Nkhata Bay and the *Ilala II* from Monkey Bay to Kambwe (port for Karonga) in the north. The round trip for each vessel takes seven days.

Geographically the country may be divided into four main zones: (i) Lake Malawi and the Great Rift Valley—the surface of the lake is about 1,550 feet above sea level, and its depth is 2,300 feet at its northern end; (ii) the high table-land between Lake Malawi and the basin of the Luangwa River, ranging from 4,500 feet above sea level in the Central Plateau to 8,000 feet in the Nyika Plateau in the north; (iii) the southern or Shire Highlands Plateau, bounded on the west by the Shire River and on the south-east by the Ruo River, having a general elevation of 2,000-3,500 feet above sea level and rising to the mountain masses of Mlanje, 10,000 feet, and Zomba 7,000 feet; (iv) the lowlands of the Lower River Shire Basin in the extreme south. This area contains much marsh-land and is liable to extensive flooding.

The dry season lasts from May to October and the wet season from November to April. Rainfall has been very variable in past years, but usually ranges between 29 inches annually at Fort Johnston, and 102 inches at the Lujeri Tea Estate on the slopes of Mlanje mountain. Mean Annual Temperatures range from Nsanje with a maximum of 89°F and a minimum of 67°F to Bvumbwe with a maximum of 75°F and a minimum of 58°F.

At the last complete census, held in 1966, the population totalled 4,039,583, comprising 4,020,724 Africans, 7,375 Europeans, 11,299 Asians and 165 of other races. With an annual increase of 3 per cent, the population in 1970 is estimated at over 4·5 million. Approximately 92 per cent of the population live in villages while 52 per cent live in the Southern region, 36 per cent in the Central region and 12 per cent in the Northern region. The main languages spoken are Chichewa, Yao and Tumbuka, and the official languages are Chichewa and English. The main religious groups are Protestant, Roman Catholic and Muslim. Primary education is a responsibility of local authorities in both rural and urban areas. In 1969 there were approximately 343,000 pupils in over 2,000 primary schools, representing 37 per cent of children of primary school age. So far as secondary education is concerned, 32,780 school leavers competed for 3,412 places in the academic year 1969/70. There are 18 boarding schools, both Government operated and Government assisted; 26 Government day schools and four un-assisted schools. A £2·6 million loan has been provided by I.D.A. to extend and add a technical stream to all secondary schools and to provide a new national Primary Teacher Training College at Lilongwe. The University of Malawi came into being in 1965 and at present comprises four colleges in the Blantyre area and one in Lilongwe. Degrees were awarded to the first graduates in 1969. Construction on the new University site at Zomba began in 1971 and it is intended even-tually to concentrate most of the colleges on a central campus. Current expenditure on education in 1970 amounted to K8·1 million, representing 5·6 per cent of monetary gross domestic product at market prices, 18·1 per cent of Government revenue account expenditure and 9·4 per cent of development account.

The Capital is Zomba (population in 1966, 19,666) but construction has commenced in preparation for the Government's plan to move the capital to a new site near Lilongwe (population in 1966, 19,425). The chief commercial centre is the city of Blantyre (population in 1966, 109,461) comprising the towns of Blantyre and Limbe.

There are 352 miles of railway line and in 1970 the railways carried 108 million short tons of freight and 735,000 passengers. In August 1970 the opening of a rail link connecting Malawi's system to the Portuguese railway system at Nyuci provided a new outlet to the Indian Ocean via the port of Nacala. The main airport at Chileka, 11 miles from Blantyre, can now handle international jet flights. A further international airport will eventually be built at Lilongwe. Air Malawi, the national airline, operates an internal network and also international flights to Johannesburg, Nairobi and Salisbury. The total road mileage in Malawi is over 6,500 of which more than 400 miles are tarred. The Malawi Broadcasting Corporation provides country-wide coverage in the official languages.

The economy of Malawi is largely agricultural, the main crops being tea, tobacco, cotton, maize and groundnuts for which there are a number of development projects aimed at substantially increasing production. There is extensive fishing in Lake Malawi; the country is nearly self-sufficient in high-grade building timber and exports a small surplus in sugar production. A number of secondary industries have been established in recent years, mainly of an import-saving nature, including textiles, beer, holloware and agricultural hand tools and implements.

In February 1971 Malawi converted to a decimal currency: 1 Kwacha is worth fifty new pence. Gross domestic product at market prices totalled K258 million in 1970 (K235 million in 1969), providing a monetary *per capita* income of K57. Exports rose in value from K44 million in 1969 to K49 million in 1970, while Government revenue increased from K33 million to K39 million over the same period. Britain's contribution to the current account budget was reduced from K5·6 million for 1969/70 to K4·2 million for 1970/71 and will be phased out completely by 1973/74. Malawi Government current expenditure in 1970 amounted to K47 million. Development loans totalling K33 million were received in 1970, including K6·4 million from Britain. The economy's real growth of monetary output in 1970 is estimated to have been 5 per cent.

The National Day of Malawi is 6th July, which commemorates the attainment of independence on 6th July, 1964 and Republican status on the same day in 1966.

HISTORY

The latest archaeological evidence available indicates occupation by people of succeeding Stone Age cultures from about 50,000 B.C. in the northern part of Malawi, and from considerably later in the rest of the country. The earliest settlement by Bantu-speaking peoples appears to have been about the first century A.D., and there was a further influx of these peoples in the fifteenth and sixteenth centuries. Apart from the odd mention of the region in early Arab writing the first written records of Malawi come from Portuguese journals of the seventeenth and eighteenth centuries. It is also indicated on several early maps.

The modern history of Malawi may be said to have begun with the visit of David Livingstone to Lake Nyasa in 1859. British interest in the area was sustained by the missionary work of the Universities Mission to Central Africa (Anglican) from 1861, the Free Church of Scotland from 1875, and the established Church of Scotland from 1876. The country during these years was disturbed by warlike invaders, and Arab and Portuguese slave dealers took advantage of the confusion to involve the warring parties in the slave trade. The missionary pioneers were followed by traders, hunters and planters, and the steadily-growing British interests began to demand some sort of support from the home Government.

The first step was taken in 1883 when a British Consul was established at Blantyre, accredited to the 'Kings and Chiefs of Central Africa'. With the growing tide of the "scramble for Africa" it became clear to the British Government that British interests were in danger and in 1889 H. H. Johnston was entrusted with the task of making treaties with the Chiefs of the Shire river and Lake Nyasa regions. With the help of Sharpe and others he was successfully carrying out his task when events were forced by a clash between one of the treaty chiefs and a Portuguese expedition in the Lower Shire valley. The then Acting Consul proclaimed a British Protectorate over the southern part of what is now Malawi, on 21st September 1889. An Anglo-Portuguese convention subsequently defined the spheres of the two countries and on 15th May 1891, a British Protectorate was declared over the "Nyasaland districts", that is, present-day Malawi. Johnston was appointed as Her Majesty's Commissioner and Consul General for the new territory, which in 1893 was renamed the British Central Africa Protectorate, and he proceeded to set up an administration and pacify those areas still affected by wars and slave-trading. He was knighted for his services in 1896. By the Nyasaland Order in Council dated 6th July 1907 the name of the territory was again changed, this time to Nyasaland Protectorate, and Legislative and Executive Councils were set up and a Governor appointed in place of the Commissioner. The first Governor was Sir Alfred Sharpe, who had succeeded Sir Harry Johnston as Commissioner in 1897.

CONSTITUTIONAL DEVELOPMENT

The first Legislative Council met on 4th September 1907 and an Executive Council of senior officials was established at the same time.

The possibility of associating Nyasaland with one or more of its neighbours had been considered at various times between the two World Wars. In 1951, 1952 and 1953 a series of conferences worked out the implications and detailed organisation of a federal form of government for Nyasaland, Southern Rhodesia and Northern Rhodesia. By the Constitution Order in Council of 1953 (S.I. 1953 No. 1100) the Federation of Rhodesia and Nyasaland came into existence on 3rd September 1953. As a result audit, civil aviation, customs, immigration, income tax, posts and telecommunications, prisons, public health and certain categories of education were transferred to the control of the Federal Government.

Further constitutional advance in the territorial sphere followed in 1955 when the Legislative Council was reconstructed to comprise the Governor as President, four *ex-officio* members, seven official members, six non-African members elected by voters on a non-African electoral roll, and five Africans elected by the African Provincial Councils.

The State of Emergency declared in March 1959 temporarily precluded further constitutional advances. However, two more African members and two more official members were introduced into the Legislative Council in August 1959, and two African members were appointed to the Executive Council in August 1959, for the first time.

In July 1960 a new Constitution was agreed upon at a Conference held in London. This came into force in 1961 and provided, for the first time, for direct election of Africans to the Legislative Council and introduced a higher, and lower, qualitative franchise for voters. Elections took place in August 1961 resulting in a majority for Dr H. Kamuzu Banda's Malawi Congress Party. The Executive Council was appointed with three *ex-officio* members, two nominated civil servants and five elected members, all of whom were to be known

as Ministers. A conference held in November 1962 was followed by the introduction of a new Constitution on 1st February 1963 under which internal
self-government was achieved in the spring of 1963 with Dr Banda as the first
Prime Minister. As a result of the Victoria Falls Conference held between
28th June and 3rd July 1963 the Federation of Rhodesia and Nyasaland was
dissolved on 31st December 1963.

At a conference in September 1963 it was agreed that Nyasaland should
become the fully independent State of Malawi on 6th July 1964. On that date
Malawi attained complete independence as a fully self-governing Member of
the Commonwealth.

CONSTITUTION OF THE REPUBLIC OF MALAWI

Malawi became a Republic on the second anniversary of its independence
with Dr Banda as President. The constitution provides that the President is
both Head of State and Head of Government. In 1971 Dr H. Kamuzu Banda
was appointed President for life. As President he has, at any time, the right to
participate in the debates of Parliament and may refuse his assent to any Bill;
but, if the Bill is passed again within six months he must either assent or dissolve
Parliament and thus submit himself to a new election. Future Presidential candidates will be nominated by Malawi's only political party, the Malawi Congress
Party, and will be elected by the people for a five-year term. On the death of a
President, a Presidential Commission will be appointed consisting of the Secretary-General of the Party and two Cabinet Ministers.

Parliament consists of 75 members of whom 60 are elected in general-roll
constituencies and 15 nominated by the President—five of the nominated
members are of European race. The President may appoint and dismiss Cabinet
Ministers; he may appoint Ministers who are not Members of Parliament, who
may attend Parliament and debate but not vote.

The constitution continues to recognise the valuable part played by the chiefs
in their own traditional fields, but by the Chiefs Act, 1967, their power to issue
Rules or Orders having legislative effect is removed.

The Chief Justice is now appointed by the President. On the advice of the
Judicial Service Commission, the President also appoints other judges, and he
has the power to delegate to the Commission the appointment and dismissal of
more junior judicial posts. A judge of the High Court cannot be removed from
office unless Parliament petitions his removal on the grounds of incompetence
or misconduct.

The President personally makes senior appointments in the public service,
but he is empowered to delegate to the Public Service Commission appointments
to any other class of public services. Similarly, the President has the power to
make or terminate all appointments in the armed forces, but he may delegate
these powers to any member of the armed forces.

The President may issue a Proclamation enabling him to take emergency
measures.

The Constitution may only be amended by a majority of at least two-thirds
of all Members of Parliament.

Unlike some other Republics, Malawi does not have a Vice-President or
Prime Minister.

The Republic Constitution, unlike its predecessor, contains no Bill of Rights.

HISTORICAL LIST
GOVERNOR-GENERAL
Sir Glyn Jones, KCMG (later GCMG), MBE, from 6th July 1964 to 5th July 1966

PRIME MINISTER
Dr H. K. Banda, from 6th July 1964 to 5th July 1966

PRESIDENT
Dr H. K. Banda, from 6th July 1966—Life President March 1971

GOVERNMENT

As a result of the change to republican status, new elections were held in 1966. 50 candidates were returned on the general roll and 5 were nominated by the President to represent minority interests. As Malawi is a one-party state, all 50 general-roll candidates belong to that party, the Malawi Congress Party. At elections held in April 1971, 10 further constituencies were created and the President given the power to appoint a total of 15 nominated Members of Parliament. All MCP candidates for the elected constituencies were elected unopposed.

THE PRESIDENT
His Excellency, Ngwazi Dr H. Kamuzu Banda
(The President is responsible for External Affairs, Defence, Justice,
Works & Supplies, Agriculture and Natural Resources)

CABINET
Minister of Finance; Minister of Information and Tourism: The Hon. A. K. Banda
Minister of Trade and Industry: The Hon. J. D. Msonthi
Minister of Transport and Communications; Minister of Labour: The Hon. J. W. Gwengwe
Minister of Education; Minister of Health and Community Development:
The Hon. M. M. Lungu, MP
Minister of Local Government: The Hon. R. J. Sembereka, MP
Ministers of State in the President's Office:
The Hon. A. A. Muwalo, The Hon. A. B. J. Chiwanda, MP
Minister for the Northern Region: The Hon. M. Q. Y. Chibambo
Minister for the Central Region: The Hon. J. T. Kumbweza, MP
Minister for the Southern Region: The Hon. G. Chakuamba

PARLIAMENTARY SECRETARIES
Office of the President: Mrs J. M. Mlanga, MP

NATIONAL ASSEMBLY
Speaker: The Hon. A. M. Nyasulu

Deputy Speaker: (vacant)
Clerk of Parliament: L. M. Khofi

JUDICIARY
Chief Justice: The Hon. J. Skinner
Mr Justice L. Weston
Mr Justice L. A. Chatsikah

AUDIT DEPARTMENT
Auditor-General: G. T. C. Morris, OBE, TD

MINISTRIES AND GOVERNMENT DEPARTMENTS

OFFICE OF THE PRESIDENT AND CABINET
Secretary to the President and Cabinet:
B. C. Roberts, CMG, QC
Permanent Secretary (Administration).
B. L. Walker
Chief Personnel Officer: A. Panje
Under Secretary (Development): R. B. S.
Purdy
Army Commander: Brigadier J. B. Clements
Commissioner of Police: P. Long, CBE
Chief Agent, Malawi Buying and Trade
Agency, London: Sir Glyn Jones, GCMG:
MBE

OFFICE OF THE PRESIDENT (JUSTICE)
Attorney-General: B. C. Roberts, CMG, QC
Solicitor-General and Secretary for Justice:
D. R. Barwick
Director for Public Prosecution: R. Banda

MINISTRY OF EXTERNAL AFFAIRS
Permanent Secretary: J. R. Ngwiri
Chief of Protocol: F. W. Ntonya

MINISTRY OF FINANCE
Secretary to the Treasury: G. Jaffu
Deputy Secretary: C. W. Collings, MBE
Under Secretary (Revenue): H. W. Foot
Accountant General: R. G. A. Parvin
Commissioner of Taxes: G. W. Brake, DFC
Controller of Customs and Excise: B. D.
D'Urban Jackson

MINISTRY OF AGRICULTURE AND
NATURAL RESOURCES
Permanent Secretary: P. Bannister, OBE
Deputy Secretary: E. Wilmot
Director of Forestry and Game: B. R. Fuller,
MBE
Director of Geological Survey: G. Carter
Commissioner for Lands: P. D. Lucas
Director of Surveys: R. A. Minchell

MINISTRY OF EDUCATION
Permanent Secretary: L. P. Anthony
Chief Education Officer: L. B. Mallungu

MINISTRY OF HEALTH
Permanent Secretary: R. P. Chisala
Under Secretary: H. Y. S. Dickson

MINISTRY OF INFORMATION AND
TOURISM
Director of Information: N. M. Mwaungulu
Director of Tourism: J. Muwamba

MINISTRY OF LABOUR
Permanent Secretary: (vacant)

MINISTRY OF LOCAL GOVERNMENT
Permanent Secretary: G. P. Bandawe
Director of Antiquities and Culture: P. A.
Cole-King
Director, Department of Archives: J. D. C.
Drew

MINISTRY OF TRADE AND INDUSTRY
Permanent Secretary: K. W. Katenga-
Kaunda
Commissioner for Industrial Development:
J. S. Magombo

MINISTRY OF TRANSPORT AND
COMMUNICATIONS
Permanent Secretary: F. P. Kalilombe
Director of Civil Aviation: S. W. F. Palmer,
DFC
Road Traffic Commissioner: K. M. Luwani
Postmaster-General: R. E. Raby

MINISTRY OF WORKS AND SUPPLIES
Secretary for Works and Supplies: E. G.
Richards
Deputy Secretary: J. S. Pullinger, OBE, GM
Director of Buildings: R. J. King
Director of Roads: H. G. Brind
Director of Plant and Vehicles: C. H. A.
Lane

DIPLOMATIC REPRESENTATION

MALAWI REPRESENTATION IN OTHER
COMMONWEALTH COUNTRIES
Britain: B. W. Katenga (High Commissioner); Kenya: J. Kachingwe (High Commissioner).

MALAWI REPRESENTATION IN
NON-COMMONWEALTH COUNTRIES
Ethiopia; W. Germany; United States
(Ambassadors); Holy See; Belgium; The
Netherlands; Portugal (Ambassador)
(resident in London); Austria; Denmark:
Norway; Sweden; Switzerland (Ambassador)
(resident in Bad Godesberg); Israel (Ambassador) (resident in Addis Ababa); United
Nations (Permanent Representative); South
Africa (Chargé d'Affaires).

COMMONWEALTH HIGH COMMISSIONERS
IN MALAWI
Britain: W. R. Haydon, CMG; India: M. M.
Khurana; Botswana: M. F. Makepe (resident
in Lusaka).

NON-COMMONWEALTH REPRESENTATION
IN MALAWI
France, United States, Republic of China,
Israel, Germany, Portugal, Germany (Ambassadors); Norway, Austria, Switzerland,
Japan, Korea (Ambassadors) (resident in
Nairobi); Sweden, Holy See, The Netherlands, Italy (Ambassadors) (resident in
Lusaka); Belgium (Ambassador) (resident in
Bujumbura); South Africa (Chargé
d'Affaires); United Nations (Resident
Representative).

MALAYSIA

MALAYSIA is a federation consisting of the eleven States of West Malaysia, namely Johore, Kedah, Kelantan, Malacca, Negri Sembilan, Pahang, Penang, Perak, Perlis, Selangor and Trengganu and the two States of East Malaysia, namely Sabah and Sarawak. The States of West Malaysia are situated in that part of the Malay Peninsula which lies to the south of the Isthmus of Kra between latitudes 1° and 7° North and longitudes 100° and 105° East. They are bordered on the north by Thailand, on the west by the Straits of Malacca, on the east by the South China Sea and to the south by Singapore. The States of East Malaysia are situated on the North and West Coasts of Northern Borneo being bounded by the South China Sea to the West, the Sulu and Celebes Sea to the East and Indonesia to the South. The British protected state of Brunei is an enclave within Sarawak. Sabah lies between latitudes 4° and 7° North and longitudes 115° and 120° East, while Sarawak lies between latitudes 1° and 5° North and longitudes 109° and 116° East.

The total area of Malaysia is about 128,308 square miles, divided as follows:—

	Sq. miles
West Malaysia	50,670
East Malaysia	77,638

Malaysia includes a number of islands, none of which is far distant from its shores. In addition to the large island of Penang, the most important are the Langkawi Islands off the coast of Kedah, the Pangkor Islands off the coast of Perak, and the Tioman Islands administered by Pahang and Labuan off the coast of Sabah.

The greater part of Malaysia is covered by dense tropical jungle, the only generally cleared areas being in the west and north-east of West Malaysia and along the principal river valleys. Large areas of Pahang are gradually being cleared. In West Malaysia the mountain range runs along the spine of the country from the north-west to the south-east, the highest mountain being Gunong Tahan (7,186 feet). The main rivers are the Perak and the Pahang. In Sabah the central range rises to heights of from 4,000 to 6,000 feet and culminates in Mount Kinabalu (13,455 feet), the highest mountain in the region. The principal river is the Kinabatangan. The highest mountain in Sarawak is Murud (7,950 feet), and the main river the Rejang.

Both West and East Malaysia are open to maritime influences and are subject to the interplay of the wind systems which originate in the India Ocean and the South China Sea. The year is divided into the south-west and north-east monsoon seasons which in time correspond roughly with the summer and winter of northern latitudes. In West Malaysia the months between the two monsoon periods are generally the wettest, though on the east coast the period of the north-east monsoon brings the greatest amount of rain. In Sarawak, from the beginning of October until nearly the end of February, the north-east monsoon brings heavy rainfall, particularly in the coastal belt. From April to July there is a mild south-east monsoon and during the period rainfall often occurs in the form of afternoon thunderstorms. In Sabah the north-east monsoon lasts from late November and December until March and April, and the south-west monsoon from May to August with interim periods of indeterminate winds between the two monsoons. On the west coast the wetter seasons occur during the south-west monsoon period and the interim periods, while on the east coast the heaviest rainfall occurs during the north-east monsoon. Humidity is generally high.

Throughout Malaysia average daily temperature varies from about 21°C (70°F) to 32°C (90°F) though in higher areas temperatures are lower and vary more widely. In the Cameron Highlands in Pahang the extreme temperatures recorded are 26·5C (79°F) and 2°C (36°F). Rainfall averages about 100 inches throughout the year, though the annual fall varies from place to place and from year to year. The driest part of West Malaysia is Jelebu in Negri Sembilan with an average of 65 inches, and the wettest place Maxwell's Hill in Perak with 198 inches a year. A large area of Sarawak receives between 120 and 160 inches of rain. In Sabah rainfall varies from 60 to 160 inches.

Malaysia is a multi-racial state. The principal racial groups are the Malays, the Chinese and various communities from the Indian sub-continent and Ceylon. Other numerically significant groups are: the indigenous races of Sarawak and Sabah, of whom the Dayaks, Kadazans (Dusuns), Bajaus, Melanaus and Muruts are the most numerous; the aboriginal peoples who live in West Malaysia; Europeans and Eurasians. The population is increasing rapidly and at the end of 1968 was estimated to be:

WEST MALAYSIA

Malays	4,351,000	
Chinese	3,157,000	
Indians	958,000	
Others	189,000	
		8,655,000

SABAH

Kadazans (Dusuns) ..	175,907	
Chinese	130,268	
Muruts	258,859	
Bajaus	68,997	
Other Indigenous	105,364	
Europeans	2,331	
Others (inc. Malays, Indians etc.)	81,934	
		823,660

SARAWAK (Estimated at 31st December 1969)

Melanaus	53,599	
Ibans (Sea Dayaks) ..	269,148	
Land Dayaks	81,118	
Malays	176,178	
Chinese	318,078	
Others (inc. Europeans) ..	57,744	
		955,865

Total		10,434,525

Actual population figures at the time of the last census were: West Malaysia (1957)—6,279,000; Sabah (1960)—454,000; Sarawak (1960)—744,000, making a total of 7,477,000. The birth and death rates for the year 1966 were 34·1 per 1,000 and 6·1 per 1,000 respectively. A census was conducted in 1970, and preliminary results are listed below.

The languages mainly spoken are Malay, English, Chinese (various dialects) and Tamil. There are a few indigenous tongues spoken widely in East Malaysia. Hokkien and Cantonese are the main Chinese dialects. The national language of Malaysia is Malay and since 1967 it has also been the sole official language in West Malaysia, although English is still permitted in some fields (such as the law). English will remain an official language in East Malaysia until at least 1973. Islam is the official religion of Malaysia, but Confucianism, Buddhism, Taoism, Hinduism and Christianity are also widely practised. Six years of primary education are given free at public expense to all children throughout Malaysia. In West Malaysia they receive at least three years secondary schooling as well. The percentage of children attending secondary schools in East Malaysia has increased rapidly and in Sabah, enrolment is now 150,000 of which over 25,000 are in new secondary schools.

The following is a list of the States and their capitals with population figures (1970 Census preliminary figures).

State	Capital	Total population
Johore	Johore Bahru	1,291,648
Kedah	Alor Star	926,873
Kelantan	Kota Bharu	689,523
Malacca	Malacca	407,250
Negri Sembilan	Seremban	485,308
Pahang	Kuantan	503,088
Penang	Georgetown	777,104
Perak	Ipoh	1,589,513
Perlis	Kangar	124,158
Sabah	Kota Kinabalu	628,269
Sarawak	Kuching	1,007,502
Selangor	Kuala Lumpur	1,657,333
Trengganu	Kuala Trengganu	413,174

The capital of Malaysia is Kuala Lumpur situated in West Malaysia halfway between Penang and Johore and 27 miles inland from Port Swettenham. The town was founded in 1857, succeeded Klang as the capital of Selangor in 1895 and became the capital of the Federated Malay States. In 1948 it became the capital of the Federation of Malaya and in 1963 the capital of Malaysia. Under the Federal Capital Act of 1960 the previously elected Municipal Council was abolished and Kuala Lumpur is now Federal Territory, being administered on behalf of the Malaysian Government by a Commissioner with an Advisory Board of six official and five unofficial Members.

The principal sea ports in West Malaysia are Port Swettenham and Penang. Those of East Malaysia are Kuching, Sibu, Kota Kinabalu, Sandakan, Tawau and Labuan. Cargo loaded at West Malaysian ports during 1970 totalled over 10 million freight tons; cargo discharged, almost 8 million freight tons. Cargo loaded at East Malaysian ports during 1970 totalled over 11·4 million freight tons (an increase of over 1 million freight tons over 1968 mainly due to increased shipments of timber). Cargo discharged in East Malaysian ports in 1970 totalled almost 8 million freight tons.

The principal airports are at Kuala Lumpur, 14 miles from town (runway 11,400 feet); Penang 9½ miles from town (runway 7,000 feet); Labuan (runway 6,700 feet); Kota Kinabalu, 4 miles from town (runway 6,300 feet); Sandakan, 7 miles from town (runway 4,500 feet); Tawau (runway 4,500 feet); Kuching, 7 miles from town (runway 6,300 feet); Sibu (runway 4,500 feet); Miri (runway 4,500 feet). There are many others suitable for small aircraft. All parts of Malaysia (and Brunei) are linked by air services provided at present by Malaysia-Singapore Airlines Limited, the joint national airline of the Malaysian and Singapore Governments, which also operates international services to and from Bangkok, Manila, Hong Kong, Taipei, Djakarta, Tokyo, Perth and Sydney.* A new service is now being operated by M.S.A. in which Britten Norman Islanders are used to serve rural areas in the Third, Fourth and Fifth Divisions of Sarawak, and in Sabah. However Malaysia and Singapore have agreed to break up M.S.A. into two separate airlines. The split is scheduled to be completed by 1st January 1973. Malaysia's new airline, Malaysia Airlines Ltd. (MAL) was registered in April 1971. Plans are under consideration for extension to the runways at Penang, Kuala, Trengganu, Kota Kinabalu, and new or longer runways at Kuching, Sibu, Bintulu, Miri, Sandakan and Lahat Datu. The Penang runway is being extended to 9,400 feet, and that at Kota Kinabalu to 9,400 feet. There are 1,035 miles of main running railway lines and 1,340 miles of loops, sidings and yard lines. The road mileage is 13,475.

Radio Malaysia (a Government service) broadcasts programmes in Malay, English, Chinese (various dialects) and Tamil; in Sabah and Sarawak it broadcasts in several of the local languages as well. It provides facilities for commercial advertising to West Malaysia only. Approximately sixty per cent of all households in West Malaysia have a mains radio set; the percentage is however much smaller in Sabah and Sarawak. In addition, Rediffusion Ltd., a private commercial enterprise operate a wired service in the major urban areas of West Malaysia and provide advertising facilities in each of the three main languages. There are approximately thirty thousand subscribers to Rediffusion in West Malaysia.

Television (also a Government service) was introduced to Kuala Lumpur in December 1963 since when its coverage has been progressively extended to the whole of the West Coast of West Malaysia. A pilot service was extended into Kelantan State on the East Coast in July 1966 and has operated satisfactorily. A second channel, covering all the areas of the first channel, was introduced in November 1969 and an approximate total of 77½ hours transmission per week is now achieved. The opening of the earth-satellite station at Kuantan in 1970 gives Television Malaysia the opportunity to broadcast important world events live.

Plans to extend television to the whole East Coast of West Malaysia are in hand and it is hoped that in the near future more areas in the East Coast will be covered by television. Television is not yet fully available in East Malaysia but a television service is being tested in the Kota Kinabalu area and part of the West Coast is expected to be covered once the tests have proved successful.

There were 151,017 licensed television sets in Malaysia at the end of 1970.

Malaysia is a producer of primary commodities and the economy of the

---

* A service has recently opened to London.

country is largely dependent on exports. The main products are natural rubber, tin, palm oil, timber and rice. Despite diversification programmes rubber is the chief export and is still of major importance to the country's economy. Production is rising steadily though the price has fallen from an average of 74 cents a lb. in 1966 to 58 cents a lb. in 1970. The outlook for 1971 is that the average will drop below 50 cents a lb. (110 cents a kilo). Rubber exports during 1970 were 1,324,100 tons, worth M$1,723,800. Malaysia is the world's largest producer of tin, and in 1970 produced 72,630 tons. Exports including metal derived from imported concentrates amounted to 91·0 thousand tons valued at M$1,013·3 million. Timber is of considerable importance, particularly in the East Malaysian States of Sabah and Sarawak. Exports of round and sawn timber from Sabah in 1970 totalled 3,411,635 tons, worth M$395,806,801, while exports of round and sawn timber from Sarawak in 1970 totalled 1,954,900 tons worth M$198,217,000. Both production and exports have been expanding rapidly. Exports of round and sawn timber in 1970 totalled 7,248,800 tons, worth M$843·7 million. Exports of palm oil during 1970 from Malaysia were 393·8 thousand tons. Other export commodities are pepper, copra, coconut oil, canned pineapple, tea and bauxite. Rice is produced for local consumption and the production in West Malaysia during the 1968/69 season was 1,332,774 tons of padi and production of milled rice amounted to 866,840 tons. The corresponding figures for East Malaysian milled rice production was 113,716 tons. Malaysia is now producing 75 per cent of the country's requirements and hopes, through double cropping, to be producing 90 per cent of her requirements by the end of 1972. The manufacturing sector, which accounted for 11·9 per cent of the GDP in 1970 which is slightly higher than 1969, though still relatively small, has shown strong growth in the past few years and may be expected to provide substantial stimulus to the economy in the years to come. Malaysia enjoys a surplus on visible trade account. In 1970 total imports and exports on balance of payments merchandise basis were M$5,150·7 million and M$4,265·1 million respectively with a visible balance in Malaysia's favour of $885·6 million.

The estimate of Central Government ordinary expenditure for 1970 has been fixed at M$3,243·4 million and revenue is estimated to total M$2,130 million. These figures include Development Fund expenditure.

The First Malaysian Plan (1966-1970) incorporating an earlier Sabah Six Year Plan (1965-1970) and a Sarawak Five Year Plan (1964-1968), envisaged a total development expenditure during the period of the Plan of about M$4,550 million, as compared with an estimated development expenditure of about M$3,110 million in 1961-1965.

A mid-term review of the Plan was published in February 1969, and recorded an achievement of just under fifty per cent in the first three years 1966-68. Of the revised plan target of M$4,838 million in public development expenditure, M$2,329 million of which agriculture and rural development (M$621 million) transport (M$373 million), public utilities (M$339 million) and education (M$200 million) were the main components—remained to be spent. Details of the Second Malaysian Plan will become available during 1971.

SOME IMPORTANT NATIONAL DEVELOPMENT PROJECTS

In Agriculture

The Federal Land Development Authority which was established in 1956 is now responsible for rubber and oil palm smallholder development on over one hundred major schemes having about 400,000 acres under development. Included in this is the opening up of a 150,000 acre integrated development scheme in the Jenka Triangle region where the agricultural clearing is being preceded by large scale exploitation of the standing forest and industrial processing of the timber wealth. This is being financed by a series of loans from the World Bank, the first of which amounted to M$42,000,000. It will eventaully provide land settlements for twelve to fifteen thousand families. The Government is also planning to develop a further three large natural resources opportunist regions, and considerable economies in scale can be expected from concentrated development over a number of years. These areas include a region in south east Pahang which covers 1·3 million acres of potential agricultural land, most of which will be used for rubber and palm oil, two smaller regions totalling 300,000 acres in south east Johore. In 1970 some 70,000 acres of oil palm were planted on freshly cleared jungle or as a replacement crop on old rubber-producing land. There are two large double cropping irrigation schemes being gradually commissioned in the two main padi growing areas, namely the 210,000 acre Muda Scheme in Kedah and the 30,000 acre Kemubu irrigation scheme in Kelantan. Considerable exploitation is taking place in the forests of Pahang, Johore and Trengganu, as well as in Sabah and Sarawak.

In Industry

It is the Government's policy to promote the growth of secondary industry in order to diversify the economy and to attract the investment of local and foreign capital. To assist in this object tax concessions have been offered through Pioneer Industry legislation, industrial sites provided, and industrial credit institutions established. In 1966 tariff and taxation modifications were made with the object of encouraging the local assembly of motor vehicles. As a result a number of plants for the local assembly of motor vehicles in Malaysia have now commenced production. The Malaysian Government is encouraging the manufacture of component parts and accessories for this industry. Industries established during the last few years are (a) oil refining; (b) cement manufacture; (c) veneer production; (d) ship breaking and steel rolling; (e) galvanised steel production; (f) container manufacture; (g) sugar refining; (h) tyre manufacture; (i) textile manfacture; (j) cable and wire making; (k) carbon paper manufacture.

The $72 million Malayawata Steel Mill in Prai is to have a second blast furnace costing about $10-million by the end of 1971. When in operation, it will double present production of the plant, Malaysia's first and the only one in South-East Asia to have a blast-furnace. The first blast-furnace was installed in 1968 and started production in August 1969. A second blast furnace is being installed and it is not expected to be completed until some time towards the end of 1971 as it normally takes one and a half years to construct and set up the furnace. The present plant produces 6,000 tons of pig iron a day. The mill, in which the Government has invested $3.45 million, when in full production, will produce 124,000 tons of iron, 121,000 tons of steel and 111,000 tons of rolled products a year.

A new town for 60,000 people at Petaling Jaya some five miles from Kuala Lumpur is now almost complete and a new industrial site at Batu Tiga is well under way. Some industrial estates have been or are being established in Negri Sembilan (Senawang), Johore (Tampoi), Perak (Tasek and Menglembu), Province Wellesley (Mak Mandim) and Ayer Kroh near Malacca.

Malaysia is now producing about 40 per cent of the total manufactured consumer goods on the domestic market.

In the Public Sector

A number of large electricity projects have been or are being started in West Malaysia. The Cameron Highlands Hydro-Electric Scheme (106 megawatts) was completed in 1963. The second phase of the Sultan Ismail Power Station, Johore Bahru (initial capacity of 60 megawatts and an ultimate capacity of 150 megawatts) in 1967; the Prai Power Station (90 megawatts) in 1967; the Batang Padang Hydro-Electric Scheme (154 megawatts capacity) was completed in 1967.

Work is now in progress for the extension of three of the existing major thermal power stations by the installations of another 30,000 kW sets at Prai Power Station in the North which will be completed this year, another two 60,000 kW sets at Port Dickson Power Station, expected to be ready by 1972; and another 30,000 kW sets to be ready this year at Johore Bahru Power Station in the South. With these extensions there will be sufficient capacity to make the demand up to about early 1973.

To meet future demands the Board has planned for the extension of the Port Dickson Power Station by another 3 × 120,000 kW sets at a cost of $160 million. Work on this extension has already begun. The Board will also start work on the biggest hydro-electric power project in West Malaysia known as the Upper Perak River Hydro-Electric Scheme in the State of Perak. It is expected that, by the end of 1977, the first stage of this scheme will be completed thus adding another 260,000 kW to the generating capacity of the Western Network now stretching from Perlis in the North to Johore Bahru in the South. The potential capacity of the Upper Perak Hydro-Electric Scheme is 600,000 kW.

To meet the demand for power in the East Coast of West Malaysia the Board is constructing a 132 kV transmission line from Kuala Lumpur across the mountains of the main range to Bentong, Raub and Mentakab in the State of Pahang. This inter-connection will enable these towns to receive bulk supply some time in 1972 from the Western Network. This line will also be extended to Kuantan in the State of Pahang by 1974. The existing isolated diesel power stations at Kuantan, Kuala Trengganu and Kota Bahru will be augmented with 3,000 kW diesel sets to meet the increasing load demand in these areas until they could be supplied from the interconnected network.

Four new deep-water berths at North Klang Straits, four miles from Port Swettenham, were completed at the end of 1963. Included in Malaysia's Five Year Plan are proposals for further reconstruction of two berths in the old port, now under way and due to be completed by 1972, and construction of two additional berths on reclaimed land in the North Klang Straits. These berths will be able to handle container cargo. A new deep-water port has been constructed at Butterworth, and new port facilities are to be constructed at Kuching (Sarawak). Expanded port facilities are also planned for Sibu (Sarawak) and Sandakan and Kota Kinabalu (Sabah).

HISTORY

West Malaysia

Archaeological research in West Malaysia, although far from complete, has furnished proof of occupation of the peninsula at least five thousand years ago.

Enough has been uncovered to show that the peninsula was one of the routes by which the pre-historic populations of Indonesia, Melanesia and Australia travelled on their way south to their ultimate homes. Evidence of a later Bronze Age culture dating from about 250 B.C. has also been found.

From very early in the Christian era trading ships were sailing between India and China, some of which touched at river mouths in the Malay peninsula. The Chinese traders made no attempt to settle but Indian traders opened trading posts on the Merbok estuary in Kedah and elsewhere on the west coast, bringing with them both the Buddhist and Hindu religions. From the 7th to the 13th centuries the Indo-Malay empire of Sri Vijaya centred on south-east Sumatra controlled both sides of the Straits of Malacca. It was destroyed by the expanding Thais and Javanese. It is probable that settlers from Sri Vijaya founded Temasek (Tumasik) (later known as Singapore). Between 1331 and 1351 the whole of the Malay peninsula was temporarily overrun by the Javanese.

Malacca rose as a result of the destruction of Temasek, receiving large numbers of fugitives, amongst them Parameswara, exiled ruler of Temasek, who became ruler of Malacca. The conversion of the Malays to Islam also began in the early 15th century. Parameswara, although a Hindu when he came to Malacca, embraced the Muslim faith late in life, about 1411, and was known as Megat Iskander Shah. His example was rapidly followed and Malacca soon became an important Muslim missionary centre. Malacca's growth was rapid and, in the reign of the fourth Sultan, Kedah, Kelantan and Patani (now in Thailand) came under its rule.

In 1509 the first European fleet sailed into Malacca under the Portuguese flag but it was not until 1511 that Malacca became a Portuguese possession, which it stayed for 130 years. The Portuguese did not attempt to administer their conquered territory but held trading suzerainty and allowed a wide measure of self-government. Malacca was conquered by the Dutch in 1641.

During the period of the Portuguese possession of Malacca the Malay Kingdom of Johore held suzerainty over the remainder of the peninsula. From 1722 Bugis chiefs from the Celebes held a dominant position in the Riau-Johore Kingdom and later in Selangor and Perak. Although temporarily ousted from power in Riau by an alliance of the Dutch and the Johore Sultan and his chiefs, the Bugis continued to rule in Selangor and to exercise control in Kedah. As Dutch influence declined, however, the Bugis became once again the dominant power. The Malay kingdom of Riau-Johore now consisted of little more than the Riau-Lingga group of islands. The former capital of Johore was abandoned and the territories of Johore and Pahang were each normally supervised by a major chief on behalf of the Sultan. Selangor was an independent state under a Bugis ruler and Minangkabau settlers from Sumatra created a new territorial unit, south of Selangor, later to be known as Negri Sembilan.

The history of the British connection with West Malaysia began with the establishment of three British trading settlements at Penang, Malacca and Singapore. The earliest was established on Penang Island in 1786, when Capt. Francis Light obtained for the East India Company a grant of the island from the Sultan of Kedah; in 1800 Province Wellesley on the mainland was added. Until 1806 the settlement was governed by Superintendents and Lieutenant-Governors under the Presidency of Bengal. In 1806 Penang was made a Presidency of equal rank with Madras and Bombay.

Malacca, which had been occupied by the Portuguese from 1511 and then by the Dutch from 1641, came into British hands in 1795 during the Napoleonic Wars, but was returned to the Dutch by the Convention of London of 1814. It was finally ceded to Britain (in exchange for the East India Company's settlement at Bencoolen on the west coast of Sumatra) by the Anglo-Dutch Treaty of London of 17th March 1824.

It was the temporary loss of Malacca and the transfer back to the Dutch of Java in 1814 which caused Stamford Raffles to found a trading post on the sparsely inhabited island of Singapore as a rival to Malacca. In return for support for his claim to the disputed throne, the Temenggong of Johore signed a Treaty in 1819 granting Raffles permission to establish a settlement, and in 1823 the island of Singapore was transferred to Britain. As a free port, Singapore at once began its phenomenal development as a centre of *entrepôt* trade. From 1819 to 1823 Singapore was subordinate to the East India Company's settlement at Bencoolen but in the latter year it was placed under the Presidency of Bengal.

In 1826 Singapore and Malacca were incorporated with Penang to form the Straits Settlements. The seat of Government remained at Penang until 1832 when it was transferred to Singapore. With the reorganisation of the government of Bengal and the creation of the office of Governor-General of India on 22nd April 1834 the Straits Settlements came under the direct control of the Governor-General. On the same day the 'United Company of Merchants of England Trading to the East Indies' officially became 'The East India Company' and it was ordered that their exclusive trading with China and the tea trade were to cease. Act 29 & 30 Vict. cap. 115 of 1866 provided for the separation of the Straits Settlements, comprising Prince of Wales Island (Penang), the island of Singapore, the town of Malacca, and their dependencies, from Indian control and by virtue of an Order in Council dated 28th December 1866 the Straits Settlements became a Crown Colony in 1867. The extension of British authority into the peninsula was hastened by unsettled conditions in the Malay States which had deteriorated in some cases into civil war. In 1873 the new Governor of the Straits Settlements went out with authority for more active intervention. The first result was the Treaty of Pangkor with Perak in 1874, and in the next decade there followed agreements with Selangor, with the States of Negri Sembilan and with Pahang. In 1909 Siam transferred to Britain her rights in Kedah, Perlis, Kelantan and Trengganu by the Treaty of Bangkok. In 1910 agreements were concluded with Kelantan and Trengganu (the latter amended in 1919); in 1914 with Johore; in 1923 with Kedah, and in 1930 with Perlis. All these treaties were similar in their main features. The Malay States agreed to accept British protection and to have no dealings with foreign powers except through Britain, and were in turn guaranteed protection against attack by foreign powers; to each State there was appointed, as Resident or Adviser, a British Officer whose advice the Rulers agreed to follow in all matters except those of the Muslim religion or Malay custom. The foundations of good government and friendly relations laid by such early Residents as Sir Hugh Low and Sir Frank Swettenham made possible the great economic development of this century, when European and Chinese capital built up the rubber and tin industries and made of the Malay Peninsula one of the most prosperous territories in the Commonwealth. On 1st July 1896 Perak, Selangor, Negri Sembilan and Pahang became a Federation (the Federated Malay States) with a Resident-General as chief executive officer, and a system of centralised government was inaugurated. This system lasted in varying forms until 1932, when there was a measure of decentralisation by which legislative powers were to some extent restored to the States and the authority of the Rulers and Residents was re-inforced. The Federated Malay States, being Protected States, did not form part of the Colony of the Straits Settlements, but the Governor of the Colony was concurrently the High Commissioner of the Federated Malay States. The remaining five Malay States did not join the Federation and were hence known as the Unfederated Malay States. In addition to Penang, Malacca and Singapore, the Straits Settlements included the mainland opposite Penang Island, known as Province Wellesley (ceded in 1796), the Dindings, including Pangkor Island, ceded by the Treaty of Pangkor in 1874 and returned to Perak in 1935, Labuan in what is now Sabah (from 1905) and the Indian Ocean islands of Christmas Island and Cocos (Keeling) Islands (from 1882 and 1888 respectively).

In December 1941 progress and prosperity of all the territories which now form part of Malaysia were interrupted by the Japanese invasion and subsequent occupation, which lasted until the unconditional surrender of the Japanese and the British re-occupation in 1945. In September a British Military Administration was established in Malaya and Singapore. This was followed by the publication in January 1946 of a British Government White Paper setting out proposals for a Malayan Union which would unite Malaya, including the four Federated Malay States, the five Unfederated Malay States and the Settlements of Penang and Malacca, but excluding Singapore, Labuan, Christmas Island and the Cocos (Keeling) Islands, under a Governor and a strong unitary government. Because of opposition throughout the country, principally by the Malays organised under Dato Onn's leadership in the United Malays National Organisation, the Malayan Union, which was established on 1st April 1946, was soon abandoned. In its place the Federation of Malaya Agreement, which was concluded in January 1948, created the Federation of Malaya consisting of the same territories as the Malayan Union.

An attempt by Dato Onn in 1951 to widen the membership of the U.M.N.O. in the Federation of Malaya by admitting members of other races led to his displacement as President of the party by Tunku Abdul Rahman, who became the Chief Minister of the first elected government in 1955, and led the negotiations with the British which culminated in the attainment of independence by the Federation of Malaya in 1957.

The Emergency in Malaya. During the Japanese occupation, the Malayan Communist Party had carried on guerrilla warfare in the jungle, and had been able to build up a powerful organisation and to collect quantities of arms and equipment. These arms and equipment were not given up after the defeat of the Japanese. In June 1948, after a period of legal and semi-legal activity, the Party decided to resort to armed terrorism, and a State of Emergency was declared by the Federation Government. The communist terrorists failed, however, to disrupt the economy of the country, and the Federation's armed forces and police, assisted by overseas Commonwealth forces from Britain, Australia, New Zealand, Fiji, and elsewhere, gradually eliminated them, with the result that the Federation Government was able to declare the Emergency officially over on 31st July 1960. By that time virtually the sole remaining communist terrorists on Malayan soil were a few scattered bands in the neighbourhood of the Thai border.

Sabah

The earliest artefacts so far discovered in Sabah date from the mesolithic period about 8,000 years ago. Later neolithic tools have been found in relative abundance and are kept as charms by the Dusuns and Bajaus of the Kota Belud district. Fragments of Ming, Sung and other pottery indicate that there was trade with China from the seventh century onward.

Early in the fifteenth century the Sultan of Brunei was the overlord of most of Sabah but the Sultan of Sulu may have exercised the rights of suzerainty over some of the northern parts. The area was visited by the Portuguese, the Spaniards and by the Dutch, who eventually became the most important European nation in the East Indies. The British first visited Borneo in 1609. The Sultan of Sulu later ceded to the East India Company all the territory obtained from the Sultan of Brunei and shortly afterwards the Company opened a trading station in Balembangan Island. This settlement existed from 1773 until 1775 and from 1803 to 1804. Although the Dutch never occupied the whole of the island, European intervention weakened the power of the Sultan of Brunei, and there was much lawlessness and piracy. After the founding of Singapore, British interest in north Borneo revived, mainly because of the need to protect the trade routes from the pirates. Sir James Brooke established himself in Sarawak and in 1847 the island of Labuan was ceded to Britain by the Sultan of Brunei. In 1872 the Labuan Trading Company was established in Sandakan; and in 1878 the Sultan of Sulu again ceded his territory in north Borneo in perpetuity to Mr (later Sir Alfred) Dent and his associates, who also obtained certain areas from the Sultan of Brunei. In 1881 a Company was formed and was granted a Royal Charter. In 1882 the British North Borneo (Chartered) Company was formed and took over all the sovereign and territorial rights ceded by the original grants, and proceded to organise the administration of the territory. The territory of the Company was subsequently extended by further grants from the Sultan of Brunei, and, by agreement, was made a British Protectorate in 1888, remaining, however, under the administration of the Company until January 1942, when it fell to the Japanese. Labuan was put under the jurisdiction of the Company in 1890 but was removed from that jurisdiction in 1905 and transferred to the Straits Settlements. The British North Borneo Company was the last of the Chartered Companies to administer British territory. When British North Borneo was liberated by the Australians who landed in June 1945 it was first placed under Military Administration, but on 15th July 1946 it became a Crown Colony. Labuan was also incorporated in the new colony to form the Colony of North Borneo.

Sarawak

Archaeological excavations in the Niah Caves, in the Fourth Division, have produced artefacts dating from the Middle Palaeolithic period of about 40–50,000 B.C. Other sites have produced ceramics and stone and metal objects dating from the first millenium of this era; but few objects which can be dated from between A.D. 1450 to modern times have been discovered.

When the ships of Magellan reached Brunei in 1521, after the death of their leader in the Philippines, they found a rich and powerful Brunei Sultanate controlling most of Borneo including what is now Sarawak. Islam had reached this Sultanate in the previous century. But the history of Sarawak as an integral state began in 1839, when the Malays and Land Dayaks of the southern province of Brunei were in revolt against the Sultan of Brunei. James Brooke intervened in this dispute and brought about a settlement, being rewarded for his services by being installed in 1841 as Rajah of the territory from Cape Datu to the Samarahan River. Thereafter Rajah Brooke devoted himself to the suppression of piracy and head-hunting, often with the assistance of ships of the Royal Navy. Sarawak was recognised as an independent state by the United States of America in 1850 and by Britain in 1864. In 1861 the territory was enlarged by the cession by the Sultan of Brunei of all rivers and lands from the Sadong River to Kidurong Point.

At his death in 1868 Sir James Brooke bequeathed to his nephew and successor Charles Brooke a country paternally governed with a solid foundation of mutual trust and affection between ruler and ruled. In 1882 the frontier was advanced beyond the Baram River; in 1885 the valley of the Trusan River was ceded; and in 1890 the Limbang River was annexed at the request of the inhabitants. In 1905 the Lawas River area was purchased from the British North Borneo Company, with the consent of the British Government. British protection was accorded to Sarawak in 1888.

The third Rajah, Sir Charles Vyner Brooke, succeeded his father in 1917 and progress continued in all spheres. In 1941, the centenary year of Brooke rule, the state was in a sound economic position with large reserves. To celebrate the centenary, the Rajah enacted a new constitution, and set his people on the first stage of the road to democratic government.

During the Japanese occupation social services and communications were neglected; education ceased; health precautions were ignored; sickness and malnutrition spread throughout the country. After the surrender of Japan the Australian forces entered Kuching on the 11th September 1945 and Sarawak was for seven months under a British Military Administration, which began the rehabilitation of the country. On 15th April 1946 the Rajah resumed the administration; but is was evident to him that greater resources and more technical and scientific experience were needed to restore to Sarawak her former prosperity, and he therefore decided to hand over the country to the British Crown. A Bill for this purpose was introduced into the Council Negri in May 1946 and passed by a small majority. By an Order in Council the State became a British Colony on 1st July 1946.

CONSTITUTIONAL DEVELOPMENT OF THE FEDERATION OF MALAYA

Under the Federation of Malaya Agreement, 1948, between the British Crown and the Rulers of the nine Malay States, the Federation of Malaya, comprising the nine Malay States of Johore, Pahang, Negri Sembilan, Selangor, Perak, Kedah, Perlis, Kelantan and Trengganu and the two British Settlements of Penang and Malacca, was constituted on the 1st February 1948. The Agreement, as from time to time amended, provided for an Executive Council presided over by the High Commissioner, and for a Legislative Council presided over by a Speaker with a majority of elected members. Because of the outbreak of the communist terrorism in 1948, it was not practicable to hold the first Federal Elections until the 27th July 1955. These were based on the principle of universal adult franchise for all Federal citizens on a common electoral roll. The Alliance Party, formed by the combination of the United Malays National Organisation, the Malayan Chinese Association and the Malayan Indian Congress, won 51 out of 52 elective seats. In each of the Malay States there was a State Executive Council and a Council of State, which was the legislative body, and in the two Settlements a Settlement Executive Council and a Settlement Council. Elections to these Councils were held also in 1955, the elected members, together with un-official members, being in a majority in each Council. In all of them the over-whelming majority of elected seats were held by members of the Alliance Party.

At a Conference held in London in January/February 1956, attended by rep-resentatives of the British Government, of the Rulers of the Malay States and of the elected Government of the Federation, agreement was reached on certain changes in the Constitution of the Federation and also on the appoint-ment of an independent Constitutional Commission to make recommendations for the constitution of the Federation of Malaya after independence, which was to be achieved, if possible, by the 31st August 1957. The Commission, under the chairmanship of Lord Reid and including three members from other Commonwealth countries, began work on Malaya in July 1956. A further conference held in London in May 1957 broadly accepted the recommendations in the Commission's report. Thereafter steps were taken to bring the new Constitution into effect on the 31st August 1957, on which day the Federation of Malaya gained independence. The Federation was, with the agreement of the other Members, recognised as a Member of the Commonwealth. The Queen relinquished sovereignty of the two former Settlements of Penang and Malacca, each of which became a State on a parity with the other nine States.

THE MALAYSIA ARRANGEMENTS

The idea of a political association between the Federation of Malaya, Singa-pore and the British territories in Borneo (the Colonies of North Borneo and Sarawak and the Protected State of Brunei) had been mooted for some years. It was not, however, until 1961 that it became a practicable proposition when in May the Prime Minister of the Federation of Malaya, in a public speech, spoke favourably about the possibility of such an association. His proposals were welcomed by the British Government. In November the Malayan Government reached an agreement with the Government of Singapore on the broad terms for their countries' merger. Soon afterwards, following talks in London, the British and Malayan Prime Ministers issued on 22nd November a joint statement to the effect that they had agreed that Malaysia was a desirable aim but that before coming to a decision it would be necessary to ascertain the views of the people of North Borneo and Sarawak. A joint Anglo-Malayan Commission was to be set up to ascertain these views and to make recommendations; and the views of the Sultan of Brunei were sought.

The Commission, under Lord Cobbold's chairmanship, spent two months travelling widely throughout the two territories and made careful enquiries amongst all sections of the population, interviewing not only large numbers of individuals but also many associations and organisations of all types. The Commission's report concluded that a substantial majority of the people in both territories were in favour of Malaysia in principle, given suitable conditions and safeguards, that it was in the interests of both territories to join, and that an early decision to proceed with Malaysia was essential.

On 1st August 1962 the British and Malayan Governments announced their acceptance of the Cobbold Report and their agreement in principle to the arrange-ments for Malaysia coming into force by 31st August 1963. The detailed constitu-tional arrangements, including safeguards for the special interests of North Borneo and Sarawak, were to be drawn up by an Inter-Governmental Committee, with representatives of the Governments of Eritain, Malaya, North Borneo and

Sarawak, under the chairmanship of Lord Lansdowne (Minister of State at the Colonial Office). The Committee was charged with the task of working out the detailed terms under which North Borneo and Sarawak would join Malaysia. The British and Malayan Governments informed the Sultan of Brunei of their agreement and made it clear that their Governments would welcome the inclusion of the State of Brunei in Malaysia.

In September 1962 a referendum was held in Singapore resulting in a decisive majority in favour of accepting the broad terms agreed in 1961 for merger with the Federation of Malaya. In the same month the general concept of joining Malaysia was debated by the legislatures of Sarawak and North Borneo and both passed resulutions (unanimously in the case of North Borneo: without dissentient vote in Sarawak) welcoming the decision in principle to establish Malaysia by 31st August 1963 provided that their interests could be safeguarded. The Legislative Council of Brunei had previously also adopted a Resolution supporting Brunei's entry in principle, but negotiations between the Brunei Government and the Malayan Government on this were broken off temporarily by a revolt which broke out in Brunei on 8th December. They were resumed later in 1963 but agreement did not prove possible.

The detailed proposals made by the Lansdowne Committee were approved in February by the Legislatures of North Borneo and Sarawak which had unofficial majorities. In London on 9th July 1963 Britain, the Federation of Malaya, North Borneo, Sarawak and Singapore signed the Malaysia Agreement. In accordance with this Agreement, Britain would relinquish sovereignty over the Colonies of North Borneo and Sarawak and the State of Singapore, and these would thereupon be federated with the existing States of the Federation of Malaya as the States of Sabah, Sarawak and Singapore, the federation thereafter being called Malaysia. The Agreement also provided that the federation of the new States would be in accordance with draft constitutional instruments annexed to the Agreement, of which the principal ones were new constitutions for Singapore, Sabah and Sarawak (Sabah being the new name for North Borneo) and a draft Bill to be enacted by the Malayan Parliament amending the constitution of the Federation of Malaya. In another annex, Annex J, were set out the terms of an agreement between the Federation of Malaya and Singapore on common market and financial arrangements, providing *inter alia* for the progressive establishment of a common market within Malaysia for local manufactures for local consumption. A Malaysia Act, providing for the relinquishment of sovereignty, was passed by the British Parliament in July 1963; the Federation of Malaya enacted its legislation during August; and an Order in Council containing the constitutions of Sabah, Sarawak and Singapore was made on 29th August.

However, at a Meeting held in Manila from 30th July to 6th August, the Presidents of Indonesia and of the Philippines and the Prime Minister of Malaya agreed to invite the Secretary-General of the United Nations Organisation to send working teams to North Borneo and Sarawak to ascertain, in the light of the United Nations Resolution on Self-Determination, whether the people of North Borneo and Sarawak wished to join Malaysia. To enable this enquiry to be carried out, the date of the coming into force of the Malaysia arrangements was postponed from 31st August until 16th September. The Secretary-General said that a sizeable majority of the peoples of each territory wished to join.

On 7th August 1965 the Prime Ministers of Malaysia and Singapore concluded an agreement of the separation of Singapore from Malaysia as an independent sovereign state from 9th August. On 9th August the Malaysian Parliament passed the Constitution and Malaysia (Singapore Amendment) Act, 1965, providing for Singapore to become independent on that date.

CONSTITUTION

The Constitution is to be found in the original constitution for Malaya as set out in the Schedule to the Federation of Malaya Independence Order in Council 1957 as subsequently amended, in particular by the *Malayan* Malaysia Act, 1963. A consolidated version of the Constitution compiled in the Attorney-General's Chambers, Kuala Lumpur, was published in May 1964.

The Head of the State is the Yang di-Pertuan Agong who is elected for a period of five years from among their own number by the nine hereditary Malay Rulers of West Malaysia. These nine Rulers also elect, in similar manner, a Timbalan Yang di-Pertuan Agong (Deputy Supreme Head of State). The present Yang di-Pertuan Agong (the Sultan of Kedah) was installed on 20th February, 1971.

There is a Conference of Rulers consisting of the nine Malay Rulers already mentioned, the Governors of Malacca, Penang and Sarawak and the Yang di-Pertua Negara of Sabah. The Conference of Rulers has the power to elect the Yang di-Pertuan Agong and the Timbalan Yang di-Pertuan Agong, and to agree or disagree the extension of any religious acts, observances or ceremonies (except in Sabah and Sarawak), to consent or withhold consent to any law and to make, or give advice on, certain appointments; but only the nine Malay Rulers attend those Meetings of the Conference which deal with matters directly relating to Their Royal Highness the Rulers themselves (including the election of the Yang di-Pertuan Agong and Timbalan Yang di-Pertuan Agong).

There is a federal form of government with a bi-cameral legislature, residual legislative power resting with the States. The Malaysian Parliament consists of the Yang di-Pertuan Agong and two Houses of Parliament (Majlis), known as the Senate (Dewan Negara) and the House of Representatives (Dewan Ra'ayat). The Senate consists of 58 Members of whom 2 are elected by the Legislative Assembly of each State and 32 are nominated by the Yang di-Pertuan Agong. The House of Representatives consists of 144 Members, 104 being from West Malaysia, 16 from Sabah and 24 from Sarawak. Of these Members those from West Malaysia are directly elected. Those from East Malaysia are ultimately also to be directly elected but they have until now been elected indirectly by the Legislative Assemblies of the States. The term of office of members of the Senate is six years and is not affected by the dissolution of Parliament. The maximum life of the House of Representatives if five years. Bills have to be passed by both Houses and assented to by the Yang di-Pertuan Agong. A bill may originate in either House, with the exception of a money bill which may not be introduced in the Senate. A money bill, which has been passed by the House of Representatives and which the Senate fails to pass without amendment within a month, is presented to the Yang di-Pertuan Agong for his assent unless the House of Representatives otherwise directs. The Senate has the power to hold up for one year a bill which is not a money bill and which has been passed by the House of Representatives.

The Yang di-Pertuan Agong appoints as Prime Minister a member of the House of Representatives, who, in his judgment, is likely to command the confidence of the majority of the members of that House. On the advice of the Prime Minister he appoints other Ministers from among the members of either House of Parliament. Every member of the Cabinet has the right to take part in the proceedings of either House of Parliament, but may not vote in the House of which he is not a member. The Yang di-Pertuan Agong exercises his functions generally in accordance with the advice of Ministers. Cases in which he may act at his discretion include the appointment of a Prime Minister and the withholding of consent to a request for the dissolution of Parliament.

The Malaysian Constitution can only be altered by a two-thirds majority in each of the two Houses of Parliament.

On 15th May 1969 after disturbances in the capital a State of Emergency was declared and a National Operations Council set up. Its Director was given supreme power to administer the country. The Council contained civil, police and military representatives and was paralleled by State and District Operations Councils at the lower level. Parliament and State Assemblies were suspended at the same time, although an interim emergency Cabinet and the State Executive Councils remained in being. The State of Emergency was brought to an end and the National Operations Council dissolved, in February 1971. Parliament was reconvened and executive power returned to the Cabinet.

Islam is the religion of Malaysia, but the Constitution provides that other religions may be practised in peace and harmony. The Ruler is the Head of the Muslim religion in his State. In States not having a ruler the Yang di-Pertuan Agong holds that position.

The judicial power is vested in two High Courts of co-ordinate jurisdiction and status, namely:—

The High Court in West Malaysia, with its principal Registry in Kuala Lumpur.

The High Court in East Malaysia with its principal Registry in Kuching.

There is also a Federal Court, with its principal Registry in Kuala Lumpur, which is the Court of Appeal from the High Courts or a Judge of the High Courts and also has certain original and consultative jurisdiction. In particular the Federal Court has jurisdiction to determine whether any law made by Parliament or a State Legislature is invalid as being *ultra vires*, and to determine disputes between States or between the Central Government and a State.

Judges are appointed by the Yang di-Pertuan Agong on the advice of the Prime Minister after consulting the Conference of Rulers, but before tendering his advice, the Prime Minister is required to consult the Lord President of the Federal Court, and, in certain cases, the Chief Justices of the High Courts and the Chief Ministers of the East Malaysia States.

There is a Judicial and Legal Service Commission whose jurisdiction extends to all members of the judicial and legal service. There is also a Public Services Commission.

The National Language is Malay. Since September 1967 it has also been the sole official language, but English is still permitted in the Courts, and in certain other fields at the discretion of the Yang di-Pertuan Agong. No Act of Parliament terminating the use of English by Members from East Malaysia in either House of Parliament or the use of English for official purposes in East Malaysia shall come into operation until after ten years after Malaysia Day.

HISTORICAL LIST OF MINISTRIES

Tunku Abdul Rahman Putra Al-Haj, KOM, CH, 31st August 1957 to 16th April 1959
Tun Abdul Razak bin Dato Hussein, SMN, 16th April 1959 to 19th August 1959
Tunku Abdul Rahman Putra Al-Haj, KOM, CH, from 19th August 1959 to 22nd September 1970
Tun Haji Abdul Razak bin Dato Hussein, SMN, from 22nd September, 1970

The West Malaysian elections (104 seats) were completed on 10th May 1969. East Malaysian elections (40 seats), suspended on 15th May 1969, were held during June and July 1970. One by-election has still to be held in West Malaysia, at the resumption of Parliament. The state of the parties then was:

Government	93 seats	
comprising		
West Malaysian Alliance Party ..	68 seats	
Sabah Alliance Party	16 seats	
Sarawak Alliance Party	9 seats*	
Opposition	50 seats	
comprising		
Pan-Malaysian Islamic Party.. ..	12 seats	
Democratic Action Party	13 seats	
Malaysian People's Movement		
(Gerakan)	7 seats	
People's Progressive Party	4 seats	
Sarawak National Party	9 seats	
Sarawak United People's Party ..	5 seats	

GOVERNMENT

HEAD OF STATE
The Sultan of Kedah,
His Royal Highness Sultan Abdul Halim Muadzam Shah Ibni Al-Marhum
Sultan Badlishah, DK, DMN, DUK, SPMK
(The full name and style of His Majesty's Consort is Her Majesty the Raja Permaisuri Agong Tengku Bahiyah binti Al-Marham Tuanku Abdul Rahman).

DEPUTY HEAD OF STATE
The Sultan of Kelantan,
His Royal Highness Tuanku Yahya Petra Ibni Al-Marhum
Sultan Ibrahim, DR, SPMR, SJML, DMN, DK, Brunei SMN

CABINET
Prime Minister, Minister of Foreign Affairs and Minister of Defence:
Y.A.B. Tun Haji Abdul Razak bin Dato Hussein, SMN, SPMP
Deputy Prime Minister, Minister of Home Affairs:
Y.A.B. Tun Dr Ismail bin Dato Abdul Rahman, SMN, PMN
Minister of Finance: Y. A. B. Tun Tan Siew Sin, SSM, JP
Minister of Works, Posts and Telecommunications:
Y.A.B. Tun V. T. Sambanthan, SSM, PMN
Minister of Health: Y.B. Tan Sri Haji Sardan bin Haji Jubir, PMN
Minister of Commerce and Industry: Y.B. Enche Mohamed Khir Johari
Minister of Labour: Y.B. Tan Sri V. Manickavasagam, JMN, PJK, SPMS
Minister of Agriculture and Co-operatives:
Y.B. Tan Sri Haji Mohd. Ghazali bin Haji Jawi, PMN, DPCM
Minister of National and Rural Development: Y.B. Senator Abdul Ghafar bin Baba
Minister of Transport: Y.B. Dato Abdul Ganie Gilong
Minister for Sarawak Affairs:
Y.B. Tan Sri Temenggong Jugah anak Barieng, PMN, PDK, PNBS
Minister of Information and Minister with Special Function:
Y.B. Tan Sri Muhammad Ghazali bin Shafie, PMN, DIMP, PDK
Minister of Culture, Youth and Sport: Y.B. Dato Hamzah bin Dato Abu Samah, SHK
Minister of Welfare Services: Y.B. Tan Sri Fatimah binte Haji Hashim, PMN
Minister of Education: Y.B. Enche Hussein bin Onn
Minister of Technology, Research & Local Government: Y.B. Dato Ong Khee Hui
Attorney General: Y.B. Tan Sri Abdul Kadir bin Yusuf, PMN, PJK
Minister without Portfolio: Y.B. Enche Lee Siok Yew, AMN, PJK

---

* An independent member in Sarawak subsequently joined the Sarawak Alliance Party, giving them 10 seats.

DEPUTY MINISTERS

Deputy Minister of the Prime Minister's Department: Y.B. Enche Abdul Taib bin Mahmud
Deputy Minister of Finance: Y.B. Enche Ali bin Haji Ahmad
Deputy Minister of National and Rural Development:
Y.B. Dato Abdul Samad bin Idris, JMN, PJK
Deputy Minister of Labour: Y.B. Enche Lee San Choon, KMN
Deputy Minister of Defence:
Y.M. Tengku Ahmad Rithauddeen bin Tengku Ismail, PMK, Tengku Sri Mara Raja
Deputy Minister of Home Affairs: Y. B. Tuan Haji Mohamed bin Yaacob

THE SENATE

President: Y.B. Tan Sri Haji Abdul Hamid Khan bin Haji Sakhawat Ali Khan, PMN, JP

Clerk to the Senate: Lim Joo Keng

HOUSE OF REPRESENTATIVES (Dewan Ra'ayat)

Speaker: The Hon. Dato C. M. Yusuf bin Abdul Rahman, SPMP, JP
Clerk to the House: Enche Ahmad bin Abdullah

THE JUDICIARY
THE FEDERAL COURT
Lord President of the Federal Court:
The Hon. Tun Azmi bin H. Mohamed, SSM, PMN, DPMK, PSB

Federal Judges:
The Hon. Tan Sri M. Suffian, PMS, JMN, SMB, PJK (Brunei)
Dato Ali bin Hassan, DPMJ, SN (Brunei)
The Hon. Mr Justice S. S. Gill
Registrar of the Federal Court: Tuan Haji Azmi

THE HIGH COURT IN WEST MALAYSIA
Chief Justice of the High Court:
The Hon. Tan Sri Justice Ong Hock Thye, PSM, DPMS

Judges:

Y.A. Dato Sri Raja Azlan Shah Ibni Almarhum Sultan Sir Yusof Issudin Shah, DPMP
Y.A. Dato Justice S. M. Yong, DSP, JMN, SMS
Y.A. Tan Sri Abdul Aziz bin Mohd Zain, PSM, DJMK, PMK, PJK
Y.A. Tuan Hakim Dato Abdul Hamid bin Haji Omar, DPMP
Y.A. Tuan Hakim Haji Azmi bin Dato Kamaruddin
Y.A. Tan Sri Ismail Khan, PSM, DMK, PPT, BKT
Y.A. Tuan Hakim Harun bin Hashim.

THE HIGH COURT IN EAST MALAYSIA
Chief Justice of the High Court in East Malaysia:
Dato Ismail Khan, DMK, PPT, BKT

Judges:
The Hon. Mr Justice Lee Hun Hoe
The Hon. Mr Justice B. T. H. Lee
Mr Justice George Seah Kim Seng

Acting Registrar of the High Court in East Malaysia: Chew Kui Sang

FEDERAL MINISTRIES AND GOVERNMENT DEPARTMENTS

PRIME MINISTER'S DEPARTMENT
Chief Secretary to the Government and Secretary to the Cabinet: Abdul Kadir bin Shamsuddin, PSM, JMN, AMN, LLB

MINISTRY OF AGRICULTURE AND CO-OPERATIVES
Secretary General: Chong Hon Nyan, KMN

MINISTRY OF COMMERCE AND INDUSTRY
Secretary General: Nasruddin bin Mohamed

MINISTRY OF CULTURE, YOUTH AND SPORTS
Secretary General: Sulaiman bin Amin

MINISTRY OF DEFENCE
Secretary General: Abu Bakar Samad bin Mohamed Noor, JMN
Chief of Armed Force Staff: General Tan Sri Ibrahim Sin Ismail, PMN, DPMJ, PDK, JMN, PIS
Chief of General Staff: Lt General Dato Ungku Nazaruddin bin Ungku Mohammed, DIMP, PNBS, JMN, PJK
Chief of Air Staff: Air Commodore Dato Sulaiman bin Sujak, DPMS, DMN
Chief of Naval Staff: Commodore Dato K. Thanabalasingam, DPMT, JMN, SMJ

MINISTRY OF EDUCATION
Secretary General: Dato Sheikh Hussein bin Sheikh Mohammed

MINISTRY OF FOREIGN AFFAIRS
Secretary General: Tan Sri Zaiton Ibrahim bin Ahmad, PSM

MINISTRY OF FINANCE
Secretary General: Y.M. Raja Tan Sri Mohar bin Raja Badiozaman, PSM, DMN

MINISTRY OF HEALTH
Secretary General: Y.M. Raja Zainal Abdidin bin Raja Haji Tackik

MINISTRY OF HOME AFFAIRS
Secretary General: Tan Sri Sheikh Abdullah bin Sheikh Abu Bakar, JMN
Inspector General of Police: Tan Sri Mohamed Salleh bin Ismail, PMN, PDK, OStJ

MINISTRY OF INFORMATION AND BROADCASTING
Secretary General: Mohd. Osman bin Kassim, KMN

MINISTRY OF LABOUR
Secretary General: Abdul Kadir bin Talib, KMN

MINISTRY OF LANDS AND MINES
Permanent Secretary: Mahyuddin bin Haji Mohd. Zain

MINISTRY OF TECHNOLOGY RESEARCH AND LOCAL GOVERNMENT
Secretary General: Hassan bin Haji Mohd. Noh, JSM

MINISTRY OF NATIONAL AND RURAL DEVELOPMENT
Secretary General: Dato Harun bin Ariffin, PNBS

MINISTRY OF WELFARE SERVICES
Permanent Secretary and Director of Welfare Services: Enche Idris bin Mohd. Zabibin

MINISTRY OF TRANSPORT
Secretary General: Ramli bin Abdul Hamid KMN

MINISTRY OF WORKS, POSTS AND TELECOMMUNICATIONS
Secretary General: Alias b. Yassin, JSM

PUBLIC SERVICES COMMISSION
Chairman: Tan Sri (Dr) Haji Abdul Aziz bin Haji Abdul Majid, PMN, CBE, DPMK, PJK

LEGAL SERVICES COMMISSION
Chairman: Tan Sri (Dr) Haji Abdul Aziz bin Haji Abdul Majid, PMN, DPMK, PJK

ELECTION COMMISSION
Chairman: Tan Sri Ahmad bin Perang

DIPLOMATIC REPRESENTATION

MALAYSIAN HIGH COMMISSIONERS IN COMMONWEALTH COUNTRIES

Britain: Tan Sri Abdul Jamil bin Abdul Rais, PMN, PJK; Canada: Enche Zakaria Ali bin Haji Mohamed Ali, PDK; Australia: Dato Fuad Stephens; New Zealand: Lim Taik Choong; India: Raja Azram bin Raja Haji Ahmad; Ceylon: Tengku Indra Petra, DK, PMN; Pakistan: Mohamed Sopiee; Ghana and Nigeria: Enche T. H. Yogaratnam (resident in Lagos); Singapore: Abdullah bin Ali.

COMMONWEALTH HIGH COMMISSIONERS IN MALAYSIA

Britain: Sir John Johnson, KCMG; Canada: J. G. Hadwen; Australia: J. R. Rowland; New Zealand: R. L. Hutchens; India: Shri K. C. Nair; Pakistan: S. Irtiza Hussain; Ceylon: A. C. L. Ratwatte; Ghana: H. van Hien Sekyi (resident in Canberra); Singapore: Maurice Baker.

MALAYSIAN REPRESENTATION IN NON-COMMONWEALTH COUNTRIES

Belgium (Ambassador) (resident in The Hague); Burma (Ambassador); Eire (Ambassador) (resident in London); Ethiopia (Chargé d'Affaires); France (Ambassador); Germany (Federal Republic) (Ambassador); Italy (Ambassador); Japan (Ambassador); Jordan (Ambassador) (resident in Cairo); Korea (Ambassador); Kuwait (Ambassador) (resident in Cairo); Laos (Ambassador) (resident in Bangkok); Lebanon (Ambassador) (resident in Cairo); Morocco (Chargé d'Affaires); Nepal (Ambassador) (resident in New Delhi); Netherlands (Ambassador); Saudi Arabia (Ambassador); Sudan (Ambassador) (resident in Cairo); Switzerland (Ambassador) (resident in Paris); Thailand (Ambassador), (Consul at Songkhla); U.S.S.R. (Ambassador) United Arab Republic (Ambassador); United Nations (Permanent Representative); United States (Ambassador); Vietnam (Chargé d'Affaires).

THE STATES OF MALAYSIA

Each State has its own constitution, which must be compatible with the constitution of Malaysia. The constitutions of all the States are similar. In the East Malaysia States there are certain differences in nomenclature, and these are also mentioned in the articles on those States.

In each of the States there is a Head of State. In nine of the States of West Malaysia (those nine which were originally the Federated and Unfederated Malay States) the Head of State is a Malay Ruler. The Malay Rulers are either chosen or succeed to their position in accordance with the custom of the particular State. In other States the Head of State is appointed by the Yang di-Pertuan Agong acting in his discretion but after consultation with the Chief Minister of the State. In Sarawak and Sabah the Heads of State are, respectively, the Governor and the Yang di-Pertua Negara. They hold office for four years.

The executive authority in a State is vested in the Head of the State but he is advised by an Executive Council (Cabinet in Sabah and Supreme Council in Sarawak) in the exercise of his functions. The Executive Council consists of a Chief Minister (Mentri Besar) who is a Member of the State Legislative Assembly and who is likely to command the confidence of the majority of the Members of that Assembly; not more than eight or less than four other Members (in the case of Sarawak the number of other Members is fixed at five), appointed by the Head of State from among the Members of the Assembly on the advice of the Chief Minister. Portfolios may be allotted to members of the Supreme Council in Sarawak or Cabinet in Sabah as 'ministers'. The Head of State is required to act in accordance with the advice of the Executive Council (or Cabinet or Supreme Council) except in certain matters. These exceptions include the appointment of the Chief Minister and the withholding of consent to a request for the dissolution of the Legislative Assembly. A Malay Ruler may also act otherwise than in accordance with the advice of the Executive Council in matters which fall within his purview as Head of the Muslim Religion or relate to the customs of the Malays.

The Legislature of the State consists of the Head of State and one House, known as the Legislative Assembly (in Sarawak the Council Negri). The Legislative Assembly (Dewan Negri) consists of a Speaker, elected Members and Members nominated by the Head of State. The maximum life of the Assembly is five years.

The distribution of legislative powers between the Central Government and the States is set out in a Federal List, a State List and a Concurrent List. Any matter not enumerated in any of the Lists falls to the States. The main subjects in the Federal List are external affairs, defence, internal security, civil and criminal law, citizenship, finance, commerce and industry, shipping, communications, education, health and labour. The most important general State subject is land. Some matters such as religion, language, immigration and citizenship, are subject to special constitutional safeguards in their application to Sabah and Sarawak. The Malaysian Parliament may make laws with respect to any matter in the State List for the purpose of promoting uniformity of the laws of two or more States, and may legislate on any State subject if so requested by the Legislative Assembly of the State.

Each of the States of West Malaysia receives from the Federal Government an annual capitation grant at the rate of M\$15 per person for the first 50,000 persons, M$10 for the next 200,000 and M$4 per person for the remainder. Each State also receives a State road grant. Sources of revenue assigned to the States include revenue from land, mines and forests, from certain licences, court fees and receipts from land sales of State property. In the case of Sabah and Sarawak sufficient revenues are secured to them to meet the cost of State services at the level existing immediately before joining Malaysia and to provide for their reasonable expansion. Consequently certain revenues additional to those assigned to the States of West Malaysia are assigned to the two East Malaysia States, such as customs duties on petroleum products, timber and minerals, and revenue from State sales taxes and port dues. In the case of Sabah 30 per cent of all other customs revenue is assigned for as long as responsibility is retained by the State for medical and health expenditure. In addition to these assignments, a number of different grants from federal funds are made to the two East Malaysia States. These grants are to be subject to review.

The Malaysian Parliament may, by a simple majority, admit other States to the federation.

JOHORE

The most southerly State of West Malaysia, Johore, is separated from Singapore by the Straits of Johore which are crossed by a causeway carrying a road and railway. Its area is about 7,500 square miles and at the 1957 Census its population was 926,850 (Malays 444,618, Chinese 392,568, Indian 70,948, others 18,716). The capital is Johore Bahru.

The composition of the State Legislative Assembly, elected in May 1969, is as follows:—

Alliance Party	..	..	..	30
Democratic Action Party		..	..	1
Independent	..	..	..	..	1

Ruler: His Royal Highness Sultan Ismail ibni Al Marhum
Sultan Ibrahim, DMN, SMN, SPMJ, SPMK, DK (Brunei)
Mentri Besar (Chief Minister):
Dato Haji Othman bin Haji Mohammed Sa'at, DPMJ, PIS (Alliance)

KEDAH

This State lies on the north-west coast of West Malaysia and includes the Langkawi group of islands. It has a common frontier with Thailand and was subject to Thai suzerainty from 1511–1909 when an Anglo-Siamese Treaty transferred suzerainty from Thailand to Britain. The total area is 3,660 square miles. Its population at the 1957 Census was 701,964 (Malays 475,563, Chinese 144,057, Indians 67,094, others 15,250 mainly Thais). The capital is Alor Star.

The composition of the State Legislative Assembly, elected in May 1969, is as follows:—

Alliance Party	..	..	..	14
Pan-Malayan Islamic Party	..		..	8
Malaysian Peoples' Movement (Gerakan)	..	..	..	..	2

Ruler: His Royal Highness Sultan Abdul Halim Muadzam Shah ibni Al-Marhum
Sultan Badlishah, DMN, KOM
Mentri Besar (Chief Minister): Tan Sri Syed Omar bin Syed Abdullah Shahabudin,
PMN, JP (Alliance)

KELANTAN

This State lies in the north-east of West Malaysia bordered on the north by Thailand. Its total area is about 5,700 square miles. Its population at the 1957 Census was 505,522 (Malays 463,118, Chinese 27,861, Indians 5,665, others 7,878 mainly Thais). The capital is Kota Bharu.

The composition of the State Legislative Assembly, elected in May 1969, is as follows:—

Pan-Malayan Islamic Party	19
Alliance Party	11

Ruler: His Royal Highness Sultan Yahya Petra ibni Al-Marhum
Sultan Ibrahim, DK, SMN, SPMK, SJMK, DMN, DK (Brunei)
Mentri Besar (Chief Minister): Dato Mohamed Asri bin Haji Muda, DPMK (PMIP)

MALACCA

This State lies on the west coast of West Malaysia bounded to the north by Negri Sembilan and to the east by Johore. It was one of the two former British Straits Settlements which were incorporated in the former Federation of Malaya. Its area is 640 square miles. Its population at the 1957 Census was 291,211 (Malays 143,128, Chinese 120,759, Indians 23,266, others 4,058). The capital is Malacca.

The composition of the State Legislative Assembly, elected in May 1969, is as follows:—

Alliance Party	15
Democratic Action Party	4
Malaysian Peoples' Movement (Gerakan)	1

Governor: His Excellency Tun Haji Abdul Malek bin Yusuf, SMN
Chief Minister: Haji Talib bin Karim (Alliance)

NEGRI SEMBILAN

This State also lies on the west coast of West Malaysia and is bordered to the north by Selangor and to the south by Malacca and Johore. Its total area is about 2,500 square miles and its population at the 1957 Census was 364,524 (Malays 151,408, Chinese 150,055, Indians 54,399, others 8,662). The capital and seat of government is Seremban but the principal Royal Palace is at Sri Menanti about 25 miles to the east. In Negri Sembilan (which is in itself a confederation of six states) the Ruler is elected from the male issue of the Royal Family.

The composition of the State Legislative Assembly, elected in May 1969, is as follows:—

Alliance Party	16
Democratic Action Party	8

Ruler: His Royal Highness the Yang di-Pertuan Besar, Tuanku Ja'afar ibni Al-Marhum Tuanku Abdul Rahman
Mentri Besar (Chief Minister): Mansor bin Othman (Alliance)

PAHANG

This is the largest State in West Malaysia. It has a coastline of 130 miles on the east coast. Its area is about 13,800 square miles. Its population at the 1957 Census was 313,058 (Malays 179,088, Chinese 108,226, Indians 21,838, others 3,906). The seat of Government is Kuantan on the east coast but the Sultan's residence is at Pekan, about 20 miles to the south.

The composition of the State Legislative Assembly, elected in May 1969, is as follows:—

Alliance Party	20
Partai Rakyat Malaya	2
Malaysian Peoples' Movement (Gerakan)	1
Independent	1

Ruler: His Royal Highness Sultan Abu Bakar Riayatuddın Almuadzam Shah ibni Al-Marhum Almutasim Billah Sultan Abdullah, DMN, DK (Brunei)
Mentri Besar (Chief Minister): Tan Sri Haji Yaha bin Mohamed Seh (Alliance)

PENANG

This consists of the Island of Penang and Province Wellesley on the mainland of West Malaysia. It was one of the British Straits Settlements which were incorporated in the former Federation of Malaya. Its area is 388 square miles. Its population at the 1957 Census was 572,100 (Malays 165,092, Chinese 327,240, Indians 69,035, others 10,733).

The composition of the State Legislative Assembly, is now as follows:—

Malaysian Peoples' Movement (Gerakan)	16
Democratic Action Party	3
Partai Rakyat Malaya	1
Alliance Party	4

Governor: Tan Sri Syed Sheh Barakbah Al-Haj, PMN, DPMK, PSB
Chief Minister: Dr Lim Chong Eu (Gerakan)

PERAK

This State, lying on the west coast to the north of Selangor and to the south of Kedah and the Thai border, has some of the richest tin deposits in West Malaysia, particularly in the Kinta district. Its total area is 8,000 square miles. Its population at the 1957 Census was 1,221,446 (Malays 484,530, Chinese 539,334, Indians 178,623, others 18,959). The capital of the State is Ipoh but the seat of the Ruler is Kuala Kangsar about 30 miles to the north-west.

The composition of the State Legislative Assembly, is now as follows:—

Alliance Party	19
People's Progressive Party	12
Democratic Action Party	6
Malaysian Peoples' Movement (Gerakan)	2
Pan-Malayan Islamic Party	1

Ruler: His Royal Highness Sultan Idris Al-Mutawakil Alallahi Shah ibni Al-Marhum Sultan Iskandar Shah Kadasallah, DMN, DK, SPMP
Mentri Besar (Chief Minister): Dato Haji Kamaruddin bin Mohamed, ISA

PERLIS

This is the smallest State in Malaysia. It lies in the north-west tip of the country bounded by the sea, Thailand and Kedah. Its total area is 316 square miles. Its population at the 1957 Census was 90,885 (Malays 71,272, Chinese 15,771, Indians 1,539, others 2,303). The capital is Kangar.

The composition of the State Legislative Assembly, is now as follows:—

Alliance Party	11
Pan-Malayan Islamic Party ..	1

Ruler: His Royal Highness Raja Syed Putra ibni Al-Marhum Syed Hassan Jamalullail, D M N, S M N, D K (Brunei)

Mentri Besar (Chief Minister): Tan Sri Sheikh Ahmad bin Mohamed Hashim, P M N, P J K, J P (Alliance)

SABAH

Formerly known as North Borneo, Sabah became a State of Malaysia on 16th September 1963. The name Sabah is an old one, but apparently was originally the name for only the northern part of the area, being commonly used for the whole only after the beginning of the British occupation. The State, which includes the whole northern portion of the island of Borneo and also the island of Labuan, is largely covered by tropical jungle and contains the highest mountain in the region, Mount Kinabalu (13,455 feet). The most extensive plain is that on the east coast irrigated by the Kinabatangan River. In the interior are the Keningau and Tambunan plains which are traversed by the Pelangan River. The Keningau plain consists of wide stretches of grassland while Tambunan maintains a large rice-producing population. Labuan, 35 square miles in area, lies six miles off the coast and has an excellent harbour.

Sabah is divided into four Residencies: Sandakan, Tawau, Interior and West Coast. The capital is Kota Kinabalu (formerly known as Jesselton).

CONSTITUTIONAL DEVELOPMENT

At first the Colony of North Borneo was administered by the Governor with the aid of an Advisory Council, but Executive and Legislative Councils were established in October 1950.

During 1960 the Royal Instructions and Orders in Council were amended to provide for an unofficial majority in the Legislative Council and in 1961 they were further amended to provide an increased unofficial majority.

Elections to District Councils and Town Boards under a franchise of universal adult suffrage subject to a residence qualification took place between December 1962 and May 1963. These Councils formed the basis of an electoral college system which in July 1963 elected the eighteen unofficial Members of the Legislative Council.

With the establishment of Malaysia, a Head of State, the Yang di-Pertuan Negara, was appointed. There is a State Cabinet which is headed by a Chief Minister and has up to eight members. The State Cabinet is collectively responsible to the Legislative Assembly which comprises 32 elected members and up to six members nominated by the Yang di-Pertuan Negara.

In June 1970 elections were held. The United Sabah National Organisation (USNO) has all 32 seats.

GOVERNMENT

HEAD OF STATE
The Yang di-Pertuan Negara: H.E. Tun Pengiran Ahmad Raffae bin Orang Kaya Kaya Pengiran Haji Omar, SMN, PDK

CHIEF MINISTER
The Hon. Tun Datu Haji Mustapha bin Datu Harun, SMN, PDK, OBE

SARAWAK

Sarawak became a State of Malaysia on 16th September 1963. The State consists of a coastal strip 450 miles long and varies from 40 to 120 miles wide. The State is divided into three main zones, firstly an alluvial and coastal plain in which isolated mountains and mountain groups rise to 2,000 feet or more; then rolling country of yellow, sandy clay intersected by ranges of mountains; and finally a mountainous area in the interior. The Rejang and Sarawak Rivers are navigable for ocean-going ships for 170 and 22 miles respectively. For administrative purposes, the State is divided into five Divisions, known as the First, Second, Third, Fourth and Fifth Division. The capital is Kuching.

CONSTITUTIONAL DEVELOPMENT

In 1941, to celebrate the centenary of Brooke rule, His Highness the Rajah decided to grant a constitution which would give to the people of Sarawak a say in their own government. Although the Japanese invasion followed almost immediately, the new constitution was introduced when Sarawak became a Crown Colony in 1946, and a Supreme Council (Executive) and a Council Negri (Legislative) were set up.

A new constitution was granted in 1956 and came into force on 1st April 1957. This provided for a reformed legislature of forty-five Members of whom twenty-four were to be elected, fourteen to be *ex-officio* Members, four were to be nominated by the Governor, and three were to be Standing Members for life. The Supreme Council was to consist of three *ex officio* Members, two Nominated Members and five Elected Members.

Orders in Council made in 1962 and 1963 provided for the Supreme Council to consist of a Chief Minister, three *ex officio* Members and five Members appointed on the advice of the Chief Minister from among the Members of the Council Negri, and for the Council Negri to consist of a Speaker, three *ex officio* Members, thirty-six elected Members and not more than three Nominated Members and one Standing Member. The latter seat was abolished in September 1963, on the establishment of Malaysia.

In May and June 1963 direct elections were held to the District and Municipal Councils, which in turn elected representatives to the five Divisional Councils. The latter in July 1963 acted as electoral colleges for the Council Negri. Direct elections to the Council Negri which were suspended in May 1969, were held in June 1970.

The composition of the Council Negri (48 seats(elected in June 1970 was as follows:—

Government	34 seats
comprising	
Sarawak Alliance Party	15 seats
Sarawak United Peoples' Party ..	11 seats
Party Pesaka	8 seats

Opposition	13 seats
comprising	
Sarawak National Party	12 seats
Independent	1 seat

A subsequent by-election resulted in a further seat for the S.U.P.P., and the Independent joined the Sarawak Alliance Party. A by-election is still to be held following the death in 1971 of a Party Pesaka Member.

GOVERNMENT

HEAD OF STATE
Governor: H. E. Tun Datu Tuanku Haji Bujang bin Tuanku Othman, PSM, OBE

SUPREME COUNCIL
The State Constitution provides for up to nine Ministers but for the time being the number of Ministers in the Government will be limited to six.

Chief Minister:
The Hon. Dato Haji Abdul Rahman bin Ya'akob

Deputy Chief Minister:
The Hon. Stephen Yong

Deputy Chief Minister:
The Hon. Simon Dambab Maja

Ministers:
The Hon. Ikhwan Zaini
The Hon. Sim Khen Hong
The Hon. Penghulu Abok Anak Jalin

COUNCIL NEGRI
Speaker: The Hon. Senator William Tan, JMN, CBE
Clerk: Mazlan bin Hamdan

MINISTRIES AND GOVERNMENT DEPARTMENTS

CHIEF MINISTER'S OFFICE
State Secretary: Dato Gerunsin Lembat, PBS
Deputy State Secretary: Abang Yusof Putch, ABS

ATTORNEY-GENERAL'S OFFICE
Attorney-General: Tan Chiaw Thong

MINISTRY OF FINANCE
State Financial Secretary: Bujang Moh'd Nor, AMN (Acting)
Accountant-General: T. A. Scrimshaw

MINISTRY OF AGRICULTURE AND MINISTRY OF DEVELOPMENT AND FORESTRY
Permanent Secretary: Peter Tinggom
Director of Agriculture: B. Balbernie
Conservator of Forests: L. V. S. Murthy

MINISTRY OF COMMUNICATIONS AND WORKS
Permanent Secretary: Arni Haji Lampam, PBS
Director of Public Works: Ng Siak Khee, PBS

MINISTRY OF LANDS AND MINERAL RESOURCES
Permanent Secretary: Peter Tinggom
Director of Lands and Surveys: Song Thiam Hock (Acting]

MINISTRY OF LOCAL GOVERNMENT
Permanent Secretary: Mohammed Aton bin Saji

MINISTRY OF SOCIAL WELFARE, YOUTH AND CULTURE AND LOCAL GOVERNMENT
Permanent Secretary: Mohamad Aton bin Saji.
Director, Borneo Literature Bureau: Leo Moggie anak Irok Edward Enggu
Curator, Sarawak Museum: Benedict Sandin

SELANGOR

This west coast State of West Malaysia is bounded on the north by Perak, on the east by Pahang and on the south by Negri Sembilan. Its area is 3,160 square miles. Its population at the 1957 Census was 1,012,929 (Malays 291,411, Chinese 488,657, Indians 201,048, others 31,813). The State capital is Kuala Lumpur, which is also the capital of Malaysia. The seat of the Ruler is Klang, 25 miles to the west. The State contains Malaysia's port of Port Swettenham.

The composition of the State Legislative Assembly, elected in May 1969, is as follows:—

Alliance Party	16
Democratic Action Party	9
Malaysian Peoples' Movement	
(Gerakan)	3

Ruler: His Royal Highness Sultan Salahuddin Abdul Aziz Shah ibni Al-Marhum Sultan Hisammuddin Alam Shah Al-Haj, DMN, DK, SPMS, DK (Brunei)
Mentri Besar (Chief Minister): Dato Harun bin Idris SMS (Alliance)
State Secretary: Megat Mahmud bin Haji Megat Ismail

TRENGGANU

This State lies on the east coast of West Malaysia bordered to the north by Kelantan and to the south by Pahang. Its area is about 5,000 square miles. Its population at the 1957 Census was 278,269 (Malays 256,246, Chinese 18,228, Indians 2,731, others 1,064). The capital is Kuala Trengganu. The Sultan of Trengganu is the present Yang-di Pertuan Agong.

The composition of the State Legislative Assembly, elected in May 1969, is as follows:—

Alliance Party	14
Pan-Malayan Islamic Party	10

Regent: Yang Teramat Mulia Tengku Mahmud ibni Sultan Ismail Nasaruddin Shah
Mentri Besar (Chief Minister): Tan Sri Ibrahim Fikri bin Mohamed, PMN, SPMT, PPT
(Alliance)
State Secretary: Dato Bendang Setia Ibrahim bin Mohd. Salleh, PJK

MALAYSIAN TITLES, ORDERS, DECORATIONS AND MEDALS

A detailed list of Malaysian titles, orders, decorations and medals may be found in the *Commonwealth Relations Office Year Book*, 1966.

MALTA, G.C.

MALTA lies in the Mediterranean, latitude 35° 8′ N., longitude 14° 5′ E., 58 miles south of Sicily and approximately 180 miles east of Tunisia. The Maltese archipelago consists of the islands of Malta (94·4 square miles), Gozo (25·9 square miles) and Comino (1·1 square miles) together with four uninhabited islets, Cominotto, St. Paul's Islands and Filfla. The name Malta is derived from the Roman name for the island, Melita.

The highest point in Malta is just over 800 feet above sea level. The islands enjoy an average winter temperature of 55°F while in summer the average is 80°F. The mean annual rainfall is 20 inches, falling mainly between October and March. The soil, which contains much lime, is shallow except in low-lying places.

There are 34,314 acres of arable land, the main crops being potatoes, onions, tomatoes, grapes, wheat, barley and oranges.

The total population of the Maltese Islands at the end of 1970 was estimated to be 322,173 of which about 40 per cent live in the nine main towns. Valletta, the capital, has a population of 15,547 while Sliema is the largest town with a population of 21,983. Other towns are Qormi (15,761), Hamrun (14,910), Paola (12,197), Birkirkara (17,767), and Rabat (12,399). The capital of Gozo is Victoria (5,498). Emigration between 1946 and 1970 totalled 124,327 and was mainly directed to Australia, followed by the U.K. and Canada.

The population is mainly European, speaking the Maltese and English languages, and 90–95 per cent of the people are Roman Catholic. The birth and death rates in 1969 were 13·2 and 9·3 per thousand respectively.

Primary education is free and compulsory. There are two Government Grammar Schools for boys and four for girls; three Government Secondary Technical Schools for boys and one for girls. There are two Technical Institutes and a third is in an advanced state of construction. Secondary education in Government Schools is free and students are selected by examination. There are also two Government Industrial Training Centres. In addition to the Government Schools there are 68 fee paying private colleges, schools and convents of which 22 are Secondary Schools. In October 1970 30 new Government Secondary Schools will be opened and these will ensure that all boys and girls receive free secondary education according to their ability and aptitude.

Two Colleges of Education train male and female students for the Primary/Secondary Schools. The Malta College of Arts, Science and Technology prepares students who have completed their secondary education for a variety of examinations. The faculties of Civil, Electrical and Mechanical Engineering are also situated in the above college. Degrees are conferred by the Royal University of Malta.

The Grand Harbour is the main port. Traffic handled (excluding mineral oils) was 915,526 tons in 1970. Anchorage exposed to the S.E. is provided at Marsaxlokk Bay and anchorage exposed to N.E. is provided at St Paul's Bay. A yachting centre is established at Marsamextt Harbour. The airport at Luqa (runway, 7,800 feet), 5 miles from Valletta, is used by both civil and military aircraft. The principal airlines are British European Airways, Malta Airlines, Alitalia and Libyan Arab Airlines. Scheduled services are operated between Malta and U.K., Italy and Libya. There are no railways, and there are 710 miles of surfaced road. Broadcasting facilities are provided on behalf of the Broadcasting Authority by Rediffusion (Malta) Ltd., and by the Malta Television Services Ltd.—which, under the overall supervision of the Authority, are responsible for the provision of most of the programmes. The Authority itself produces and prescribes programmes on Sound and Television.

The Malta Development Corporation was constituted by virtue of Act No. XVII of 1967. The Board of the Corporation was appointed as from 1st January 1968. The Corporation took over the responsibility of executing the Aids to Industries Scheme by virtue of an Agency Agreement signed between the Malta Government and the Malta Development Corporation on the 27th April 1968. The Corporation is also a development bank and has received from Government an equity capital of £1 million for the purpose.

By the end of December 1970, 361 applications from 224 firms were approved since the inception of the Aids to Industries Scheme; 152 firms are in operation and have created some 9,400 new jobs. The commitment by way of grants and loans in respect of approved projects up to 31st December 1970 amounted to £5·0 million and £2·5 million respectively. The turnover value was £17·6 million of which £11·8 million were export sales.

There is a factory building programme in operation.

The industries cover a wide range of products such as bacon, canned foods, poultry packing, margarine, cooking fats and ghee, savoury foods, pasta, custards, compound fodder, wine, yarns, fabric and made-up textiles articles (including knitwear, shirts, stockings, tights, jeans, protective clothing, gloves etc.) mattresses, furniture, cardboard containers, files and similar products, type-setting and printing of books, sporting prints, synthetic rubber seals, Polyure-thane foam, paints, detergent, medicinals and toilet preparations, plastic goods, fibre glass building materials and gift merchandise, pottery, tiles, glass, machine knives, iron and steel rods, steel furniture, high precision tools, stainless steel sinks, electro-plating, light engineering products, electrical heating elements, electronic components, toys, wigs and musical instruments, assembly of vehicles, horticultural projects produce flowers, cuttings, tomatoes, mushrooms, straw-berries, and courgettes for export markets.

Tourism is assuming primary importance, and a number of new hotels have been built to cater for the ever-growing number of tourists. There are now more than 8,448 tourist beds in Malta, Gozo and Comino. By the end of 1971 it is hoped that there will be about 115 hotels providing accommodation for 9,039 visitors.

Stern to quay berthing facilities for about 350 yachts are provided at Marsamxett Harbour which lies to the West of Valletta. This is only part of the general plan to develop the whole of this harbour into a yachting centre.

The two thermal Power Stations supplying the electricity requirements of the Maltese Archipelago have capacities of 85 Megawatts and 30 Megawatts, respectively. The System Maximum Demand realised so far is 65·4 Mega watts.

All areas in the Maltese Islands are served with electricity supply which is transmitted by a primary system operating at 33,000 Volts and a secondary network at 11,000 Volts. The supply at the consumer's terminals is 415/240 Volts, 50 Cycles.

The electricity distribution system is capable of supplying efficiently the power requirements throughout the country. However, works on the reinforcement of the system are regularly carried out to maintain this capability.

The major Power Station also incorporates four sea-water desalination plants with a total production of 4·5 million gallons of potable distillate per day. This water supplements the supplies obtained from natural resources to meet the Island's water requirements.

Malta's National Day is 21st September, the anniversary of Independence.

HISTORY

There are notable stone-age survivals in Malta, but its history begins with settlement by the Phoenicians. After Phoenicia was conquered by the Persians, Carthage became the capital of the Punic Empire, and from Carthage Malta was colonised and received the earliest known form of its language. Malta re-mained under Carthaginian control until Hamilcar's surrender to the Roman Consul, Titus Sempronius, in 216 B.C.

The best known event during Malta's occupation by the Romans was St Paul's shipwreck in the bay which now bears his name, and the conversion of the Maltese to Christianity. After the collapse of the Western Roman Empire, Malta remained within the jurisdiction of the Byzantine Emperors in Constantinople until it was taken by the Arabs in 870. The Arabic occupation, which lasted for two centuries, served to introduce into the Maltese language a vocabulary of contemporary Arabic words which did not, however, destroy the earlier related Punic words. This produced a blend which still forms the core of modern Maltese and into this framework fresh words, mostly English or Italian, have been fitted.

After the expulsion of the Arabs by Roger the Norman, Malta remained in the hands of successive Sicilian rulers until it passed to the Holy Roman Emperor Charles V, who, in 1530, gave it as a sovereign fief to the Order of the Hospital of St John of Jerusalem, which had been homeless since its eviction by the Turks from Rhodes in 1523. The gift was conditional on the Knights of the Order assuming the defence of Tripoli as a Christian outpost in North Africa. Tripoli was lost to the Turks in 1551, but when the Turks tried to capture Malta itself they were eventually repelled in 1565, after the Great Siege. Soon after this victory, the Knights set about building Valletta within an impressive system of fortifications. At first Malta flourished as a bastion of Christendom and developed as a centre of trade and communications; but its importance declined after the Ottoman sea-power was broken at the battle of Lepanto in 1571. Thenceforth the Knights turned their activities to politics, and by the eighteenth century the Order had declined and become an anachronism, dependent on the support of other countries rather than on its own resources.

Napoleon Bonaparte regarded Malta as a vital link in a route to the East and in his designs on Egypt and India. The French met with no resistance when they landed at Valletta in June 1798 and Bonaparte departed for Egypt leaving a force of 6,000 troops on the island. The Maltese, however, soon rose against the French, offended by their pillaging of churches and encouraged by the defeat of Bonaparte at the Nile. In response to an appeal from the Maltese people for help Admiral Nelson set up a blockade and on 9th September 1798 sent Captain Ball, R N, to assume responsibility for the administration of the island. The French were driven into the fortified towns where they remained until they capitulated in 1800 whereupon they were evicted from the island. In May 1801 the administration of Malta was divided between the British Military Commander and a British Civil Commission. In 1802 the Treaty of Amiens provided for the Maltese administration to revert to the Knights of St John but the Maltese people petitioned Britain to place the island under British sovereignty and protection. The first British Governor was appointed in July 1813 and Malta formally became British by the Treaty of Paris in 1814.

Recognising Malta's strategic importance, Britain introduced a garrison which not only protected the islands but provided a source of income for their inhabitants. British trade with the Near East and the Adriatic began to pass through Malta, which was made a free port; and by 1812 there were some 60 British and 20 Maltese middlemen in business there. The port services required by ships engaged in this trade provided additional employment and with increasing prosperity agriculture was also stimulated.

Thenceforth Malta depended on shipping, military and civil. In 1827 the British Mediterranean Fleet was based on Malta and in 1832 the Admiralty started a packet service to the island. A few years later the ships of the P and O Shipping Company and other Companies began to use Malta as a port of call on their runs to Egypt and the Levant. The volume of shipping greatly increased with the opening of the Suez Canal in 1869: by 1882 some 80 per cent of the recorded tonnage there had cargoes for other than Mediterranean ports.

The boom in shipping caused a movement to the towns, and in the decade 1871-80 urban employment increased by 6,000, mainly in the docks. However, as larger merchant ships were introduced, the boom declined, for their longer range made it less necessary for them to call at Malta. But British Government expenditure bridged the gap, and by 1905 over 9,000 men were employed in her Naval Establishments in Malta. The Naval Dockyard and the income from the Defence services became the mainstay of Malta's economy.

Malta was an important base in the First World War; and in the Second World War the heroic garrison and the indomitable people of Malta were exposed to frequent and heavy air attacks and to an intense blockade. In recognition of their courageous resistance and of the exceptional hardships and privations which they endured, Malta was awarded the George Cross in 1942. A representation of this decoration appears in the National Flag of independent Malta.

The long-term changes in British defence policy announced in 1958, necessitated a major change in the traditional pattern of the Maltese economy which had previously depended on Service expenditure. In particular, in view of the decline in the use of Malta for Naval repair work which would take place after 1960, the British Government decided that the Naval Dockyard should be converted to commercial use.

The Dockyard was accordingly leased to Messrs Bailey, a firm of dry docks operators established in Britain, and financial assistance was provided to enable the transition to commercial operation to take place. In 1963 Messrs Bailey were deprived of control over the running of the Dockyard and a Council of Administration was appointed to keep things going pending the outcome of court proceedings instituted by and against Messrs Bailey. The Council of Administration were assisted by Messrs Swan Hunter and Wigham Richardson as Managing Agents. In April 1968 legislation was enacted by the Maltese Parliament under which the Dockyard was nationalised and control over the assets of the Yard was vested in a new Drydocks Corporation. The Drydocks Corporation has made arrangements for Messrs Swan Hunter to continue to assist them as Managing Agents of the dry docks.

The Maltese nation is almost wholly Roman Catholic. The Archbishop of Malta has always been recognised and treated as the spiritual head of the nation. Roman Catholic Canon law is the law of the land in such matters as marriage, and there is no civil marriage or divorce.

CONSTITUTIONAL DEVELOPMENT

During the period that Malta was a Crown Colony, the usual Advisory Councils to the Governor had contained a number of Maltese Members. In 1921 a constitution was introduced which established a limited form of self-government. A dyarchical system of Government was set up in which the Maltese Government, composed of a bi-cameral legislature and Ministry, was responsible for local affairs while the Maltese Imperial Government, composed of the Governor advised by a nominated Council, had full control of reserved matters including, in particular, defence, foreign affairs and language questions. In the Maltese Government, ten of the seventeen Senators were nominated or elected to represent special classes, and the others were returned by the general electorate. Members of the Legislative Assembly were elected by proportional representation, each voter having a single, transferable vote. However in 1930 the constitution was suspended, and again in 1933, owing to political crises, and was finally revoked in 1936. Crown Colony rule was resumed in 1939. Self-government was restored in 1947.

The constitution of 1947 provided for a uni-cameral legislature of 40 Members, elected under a system of proportional representation, with a Prime Minister and a Cabinet. The Assembly was empowered to legislate for the peace, order and good government of Malta, but certain matters, including defence, civil aviation, currency, immigration and nationality, were reserved to the Maltese Imperial Government under the Governor.

Elections under the new constitution gave Malta its first Labour Government. The election of 1950 returned a Nationalist Coalition Government which, in 1953, put forward proposals for Dominion status for Malta. Because of Malta's strategic importance and inability to be financially self-supporting, these proposals were unacceptable to the British Government, which suggested that Malta's status might be improved if responsibility for the islands were transferred to the Home Office. In 1955 a Labour Ministry was formed by Mr Dominic Mintoff and arrangements were made for a Round Table Conference in December of that year. Representatives of all the Maltese political parties and the Archbishop of Malta attended the Conference, and all accepted that the British Government needed to retain ultimate responsibility for Defence and foreign affairs. All wished to enhance the status of the Maltese Parliament and Government, and agreed that the position of the Roman Catholic Church should not be diminished; but the Maltese Government and Opposition were unable to agree on what should be Malta's ultimate constitutional status. The Labour Party wanted representation at Westminster, whereas the Nationalists wanted independence within the Commonwealth.

In a referendum held in February 1956, 76 per cent of the votes cast (44 per cent of the electorate) favoured integration with Britain and Maltese representation at Westminster. This was accepted in principle by the British Government but the consequent negotiation as to details broke down in March 1958, both the governing Malta Labour Party and the Opposition demanding independence. The Labour Party resigned; and the Opposition party, the Nationalists, led by Dr Borg Olivier, refused to form a caretaker Government. Shortly afterwards, disturbances took place, and the Government was compelled to institute direct rule once again. In 1959 an interim constitution was introduced under which executive authority was vested in the Governor who was advised by a nominated Executive Council which included Maltese non-official members, an arrangement similar to that which had been in force between 1936 and 1939.

As a result of the report of the Malta Constitutional Commission, 1960, which was appointed under the Chairmanship of Sir Hilary Blood, a new constitution, giving internal self-government was put into operation in March 1962. Foreign Affairs and Defence remained the ultimate responsibility of the British Government, which was represented in Malta by a United Kingdom Commissioner. A Consultative Council was established to provide for consultation between the Governments on matters of mutual concern. The Legislative Assembly consisted of 50 Members elected under the single, transferabl.e vote system. A Cabinet, consisting of a Prime Minister and not more than seven other Ministers, was appointed from the Legislative Assembly, and was collectively responsible to it. The Governor was appointed by the Crown and generally acted on the advice of the Maltese Ministers.

In 1962 the Nationalist Party under Dr Borg Olivier was successful at the polls, and after talks with the Colonial Secretary constitutional amendments were made giving wider powers to the Maltese Government. But this constitution was acceptable to neither of the major parties both of whose electoral programmes had included independence for Malta; and in August 1962 Dr Borg Olivier again called for independence. After further discussions in December 1962 and following a visit to Malta by the Colonial Secretary in June 1963 when he met representatives of all the political parties, the Malta Independence Conference took place in London in July 1963. This broke up without settling the final details of an independence Constitution, but the Commonwealth and Colonial Secretary suggested that the various Maltese parties should return to Malta to settle their constitutional differences in preparation for Independence by 31st May 1964. After further talks in London and Malta Dr Borg Olivier produced a new Constitution which was approved by the Malta Legislative Assembly and later by an island-wide referendum. A majority of the valid votes cast in the referendum were in favour of independence under the new constitution. After further talks in London, the Secretary of State for Commonwealth Relations and for the Colonies was able to announce in the House of Commons on 21st July 1964 that negotiations had been completed on the question of Malta's Independence and the form of Malta's new Constitution settled.

Under a Defence Agreement (Cmnd. 2410) signed at independence, British forces are entitled to remain in Malta for ten years. Under a Finance Agreement (Cmnd. 2423) Britain has undertaken to provide, during the same period, capital aid for diversification of the economy and for assistance to emigration up to a total of £50 million. Malta became independent on 21st September 1964.

A General Election was held in March 1966, which resulted in the return to power of Dr G. Borg Olivier and the Nationalist Party.

CONSTITUTION

The Malta Independence Constitution is set out in the Malta Independence Order 1964 (S.1. No. 1398).

The Governor-General of Malta is appointed by Her Majesty The Queen and is the representative of Her Majesty in Malta.

The Parliament of Malta consists of Her Majesty and a House of Representatives, and, subject to the provisions of the Constitution, is empowered to make laws for the peace, good order and good government of Malta. The fifty Members of the House of Representatives are elected by those citizens of Malta who have attained the age of 21 years and are not otherwise disqualified. There are ten electoral divisions and voting is by the single transferable vote system of proportional representation. The House elects its own Speaker and Deputy Speaker from among its own Members or from among persons who are qualified to be Members. The conduct of elections is placed under the direction and supervision of an Electoral Commission, which is also required to review the boundaries of the electoral divisions from time to time. Parliament, unless previously dissolved, has a life of five years.

The executive authority in Malta is vested in Her Majesty but the authority is normally exercised by the Governor-General on Her Majesty's behalf. The Governor-General is required to act in accordance with the advice of the Cabinet except in certain specified cases. The Prime Minister is appointed by the Governor-General, and must be the Member of the House of Representatives who, in the judgement of the Governor-General is able to command the confidence of a majority of the Members of that House. Other Ministers are also appointed by the Governor-General on the advice of the Prime Minister, and portfolios are allocated to them by the Governor-General on the same advice. The Cabinet of Malta consists of the Prime Minister and the other Ministers and has the general direction and control of the Government of Malta and is collectively responsible to Parliament.

The Leader of the Opposition is appointed by the Governor-General, who appoints to this post either the leader of the main opposition party or, if there are two or more opposition parties, the person who, in his judgment, commands the support of the largest single group of members of the House in opposition to the Government.

The Constitution provides for Superior Courts, one of which is known as the Constitutional Court and which has jurisdiction to hear and determine disputes over Membership of the House of Representatives and appeals from other courts on constitutional and certain other matters. The Chief Justice and the Judges are appointed by the Governor-General on the advice of the Prime Minister. There is appeal to the Judicial Committee of the Privy Council from the decisions of the Constitutional Court and, in the case of certain civil proceedings, from the decision of the Court of Appeal. Parliament may prescribe that appeal may also lie in other cases. The Crown Advocate-General is appointed by the Governor-General on the advice of the Prime Minister.

The Public Service Commission for Malta consists of a Chairman, Deputy Chairman and from one to three other Members. These are appointed by the Governor-General on the advice of the Prime Minister. Subject to the provisions of the Constitution, power to make appointments in public offices and to remove and to exercise disciplinary control over persons holding such offices rests with the Prime Minister acting on the recommendations of the Public Service Commission.

The Constitution provides that the religion of Malta is the Roman Catholic Apostolic Religion, and the State guarantees to the Roman Catholic Apostolic Church the right freely to express its proper spiritual and ecclesiastical functions and duties and to manage its own affairs.

The national language of Malta is Maltese, but English and Maltese are the official languages. The Language of the Courts is Maltese.

The Constitution contains a Declaration of Principles concerning the right to work, compulsory and free primary education, hours of work, the safe-guarding of rights of women workers, the encouragement of private economic enterprise, the encouragement of co-operatives, the provision of social assistance and insurance, and so on; and it also includes a Chapter on the Fundamental Rights and Freedoms of the Individual, such as the protection of the right to life, freedom from arbitrary arrest or detention, protection of freedom of conscience, protection from discrimination on the grounds of race, etc.

GOVERNMENT

The distribution of seats in the House of Representatives, as a result of the General Election held in June was: Malta Labour Party 28; Nationalist Party 27.

GOVERNOR-GENERAL
His Excellency Professor Sir Anthony Mamo, OBE, QC

CABINET
Prime Minister, Minister of Commonwealth and Foreign Affairs:
The Hon. Mr Dom Mintoff, BSC, BE & A, MA(Oxon.), A. & CE
Minister of Justice and Parliamentary Affairs:
The Hon. Dr Anton Buttigieg, BA, LLD
Minister of Education and Culture: The Hon. Miss Agatha Barbara
Minister of Finance and Customs: The Hon. Not. Dr J. Abela, LLD
Minister of Development: The Hon. Dr Albert V. Hyzler, MD
Minister of Health: The Hon. Dr D. Piscopo, BSC, MD
Minister of Trade, Industry, Agriculture, and Tourism:
The Hon. Dr J. Micallef Stafrace, BA, LLD
Minister of Public Building and Works: The Hon. Mr L. Sant
Minister of Labour, Employment and Welfare: The Hon. Dr Jos Cassar, BA, LLD
Commissioner of Police: A. J. Bencini Esq

HOUSE OF REPRESENTATIVES
Speaker: E. Attard Bezzina, MP
Deputy Speaker: N. Laivera, MP
Clerk of the House of Representatives: Maurice Gregory

LEADER OF THE OPPOSITION
The Hon. Dr Giorgio Borg Olivier, MP

JUDICIARY
Chief Justice:
The Hon. Mr Justice Professor J. J. Cremona
(President of the Constitutional Court and of the Court of Appeal)
Vice-President of the Constitutional Court and of the Court of Appeal:
The Hon. Mr Justice Professor J. J. Cremona.

Judges:

The Hon. Mr Justice J. Flores
The Hon. Mr Justice J. Xuereb
The Hon. Mr Justice A. P. Gauci Maistre

The Hon. Mr Justice M. Caruana Curran
The Hon. Mr Justice E. Magri
The Hon. Mr Justice V. R. Sammut

MINISTRIES AND GOVERNMENT DEPARTMENTS

OFFICE OF THE PRIME MINISTER

Administrative Secretary: The Hon. Edgar Cuschieri, CBE
Under Secretary: Chev. Edgar Cassar
Principal Assistant Secretaries: J. Carabott; M. Abela, MBE; J. V. Bonello, MBE
Director of Civil Aviation: Gerald H. Ferro, MVO, MBE
Commissioner of Civil Defence: E. S. Tonna, MBE
Commissioner for Gozo: J. Micallef
Director of Information: Chev. Paul J. Naudi, MBE
Commissioner of Police: A. J. Bencini
Principal Government Statistician: Henry A. Frendo.

MINISTRY OF COMMONWEALTH AND FOREIGN AFFAIRS

Secretary: J. M. Rossignaud

MINISTRY OF FINANCE, CUSTOMS AND PORTS

Financial Secretary: Richard Soler
Principal Assistant Secretary: Ronald Chalmers, MBE
Accountant-General: J. Camilleri
Commissioner of Inland Revenue: A. Agius Ferrante
Director of Audit: Carmel Naudi
Director of Public Lotto: O. Arrigo
Comptroller of Customs and Superintendent of Ports: A. Laurenti

MINISTRY OF TRADE, INDUSTRY AND AGRICULTURE

Secretary: A. Wirth
Director of Trade: L. Sammut Briffa, MBE
Director of Industry: Wilfred Podesta, MBE
Director of Agriculture: Anthony S. Farrugia
Manager, Water Works: O. Agius
Postmaster-General: Joseph Buttigieg
Manager, Milk Marketing Undertaking: Cosimo Montebello

MINISTRY OF EDUCATION, CULTURE AND TOURISM

Secretary: Major V. J. Castillo, E D
Director of Education: Miss M. Mortimer
Librarian, Royal Malta Library: Dr Vincent Depasquale
Director of Museum: Captain Charles G. Zammit

MINISTRY OF JUSTICE AND PARLIAMENTARY AFFAIRS

Crown Advocate General: Dr Michele Tufigno
Registrar of the Superior Courts: Dr V. Borg Costanzi
Director of Public Registry: Dr Vladimir Formosa
Notary to Government: Victor Miller
Director of Prisons: Joseph Tonna
Commissioner of Land and Chief Land Registrar: Dr J. Pullicino

MINISTRY OF PUBLIC BUILDING AND WORKS

Director of Public Works: Salvino J. Mangion, O B E
Housing Secretary: Salvino Bugeja

MINISTRY OF LABOUR, EMPLOYMENT AND WELFARE

Secretary: A. Laurenti
Director of Emigration and Labour: E. Vassallo
Director of Social Services: J. Vella Bonnici

MINISTRY OF HEALTH

Chief Government Medical Officer: Anthony Cuschieri, MP

Independent Statutory Bodies

THE GAS BOARD

Chairman: G. Craig

THE MALTA BROADCASTING AUTHORITY

Chairman: Judge A. J. Montanaro Gauci, C B E

TOURIST BOARD

Chairman: J. Pollacco

MALTA ELECTRICITY BOARD

Chairman: C. J. Mallia

THE GOZO CIVIC COUNCIL

President: Chev. Dr A. Tabone, O B E

PUBLIC SERVICE COMMISSION

Chairman: Judge W. Harding, C B E, KM
Secretary: George Soler

CENTRAL BANK

Governor: Dr P. L. Hogg

MALTA DEVELOPMENT CORPORATION

Chairman: Sir Sadler Forster, C B E

MALTA DOCKYARD CORPORATION

Chairman: O. Fenselav

DIPLOMATIC REPRESENTATION

MALTESE HIGH COMMISSIONERS IN OTHER COMMONWEALTH COUNTRIES

Britain: Mr Arthur Scerri (High Commissioner); Australia: J. L. Forace (High Commissioner).

COMMONWEALTH HIGH COMMISSIONERS IN MALTA

Australia: Sir Hubert Opperman, O B E; Britain: Sir Duncan Watson, K C M G; Canada: B. Rogers (Resident in Rome); India: Raja J. K. Atal (Resident in Rome); Pakistan: Hamid Nawaz Khan (Resident in Rome).

MALTESE REPRESENTATIVES IN NON-COMMONWEALTH COUNTRIES

Council of Europe (Permanent Representative resident in Malta); United Nations (Permanent Representative resident in Washington); The Holy See and Sovereign Military Hospitaller Order of St John of Jerusalem, of Rhodes and of Malta (resident in Malta); Italy, Israel, Greece, Austria and Switzerland (resident in Rome); Tunis, Libya and United Arab Republic (resident in Tripoli); Belgium, N.A.T.O.; E.E.C., Spain, Netherlands, West Germany, France and Luxembourg, (resident in Brussels); U.S.A. (resident in Washington); and U.S.S.R. (resident in London).

MAURITIUS

MAURITIUS lies 500 miles off the east coast of the Malagasy Republic between latitudes 19° 58′ and 20° 32′ S. and longitudes 57° 17′ and 57° 46′ E. It owes its name to the Dutch settlers who landed there in 1598 and who named the island after their ruler, Prince Maurice de Nassau. It is 1,551 miles from Durban, 2,094 from Colombo and 3,182 from Perth, Australia.

The territory includes Rodrigues Island, 350 miles to the east, with an area of 40 square miles and a population of about 26,000.

Mauritius, which is roughly pear-shaped, is 38 miles long by 29 miles broad. From the north an extensive undulating plain rises gently towards the central plateau, where it reaches a height of about 2,200 feet before dropping sharply to the southern and western coast. There are three main groups of mountains—the Port Louis group running in an east-north-easterly direction, the Black River-Savanne group massed in a north to south direction, and the Bambous group with an east-west trend. The highest peaks are Piton de la Rivière Noire (2,711 feet), Pieter Both (2,690 feet) and Le Pouce (2,661 feet). The main watershed of the island runs northwards across the central plateau for a distance of about 20 miles. From this ridge the ground slopes towards the coast, except where interrupted by the mountain ranges or by isolated peaks. The rivers consequently tend to run westward or eastward. Most of them are short and fast flowing, generally at the bottom of deep ravines and interrupted by waterfalls. The longest river is Grand River South East (24·5 miles). No river in the island is navigable but some of the larger have been harnessed for hydro-electric purposes. True crater lakes are found at Bassin Blanc and Grand Bassin, but in general water conservation is achieved by man-made reservoirs, of which there are now eight, the most important being Mare aux Vacoas. The mountains are a striking feature of the landscape, rising abruptly from the surrounding plain, with their lower slopes covered with dense vegetation—now being replaced by sugar cane or tea—and their upper slopes ending in precipitous rocky peaks. The island is almost completely encircled by coral reefs, within which are lagoons and a succession of beaches of white coral sand.

The island enjoys a sub-tropical maritime climate, with sufficient difference between summer and winter to avoid monotony: further variation is introduced by the wide range of rainfall and temperature resulting from the mountainous nature of the island. The south-east trade winds blow most of the year and the climate is generally humid. The summer season runs from November to April, and the winter from June to October, though April-June and September-November can be looked upon as transitional periods and are usually the most pleasant in the year. Rain falls mainly in summer, but there is no well-defined dry season. At sea the annual rainfall near Mauritius is about 40 inches, but the uplift of the moisture-laden maritime air caused by the mountains results in an annual rainfall varying from about 60 inches on the south-east coast to 200 inches on the central plateau. On the west coast the annual fall is 35 inches. Variation from year to year is not large, but is nevertheless sufficiently great to reduce considerably the size of the sugar and other crops when the year is dry.

In Port Louis the day maximum and night minimum temperatures during the hottest months average 31°C (87·8°F) and 24°C (75·2°F) respectively; in the winter they average 25°C (77°F) and 20°C (68°F). The highest and lowest reached are:

	Maximum	*Minimum*
Port Louis..	36°C (96·8°F)	12°C (53·6°F)
Curepipe (1,850 feet above mean sea level)	32°C (89·6°F)	7°C (44·6°F)

A complete census of the population is made every ten years. The last census took place in 1962 and showed a population of 681,619. In June 1970 the population was estimated at 811,280.

The following table gives the ethnic distribution of the population in 1969.

	Urban Area	*Rural Area*	*Total*	*Total Population* %
Hindus	128,465	292,925	421,390	52·2
Muslims	66,440	67,000	133,440	16·5
Total Indo-Mauritians ..	194,905	359,925	554,830	68·7
General Population..	142,355	84,775	227,130	28·2
Sino-Mauritians ..	19,560	5,510	25,070	3·1
Total	356,820	450,210	807,030	100·0

The term 'General Population' refers to people of European descent and of mixed and African descent.

The population of Mauritius being made up of people of European, Indian, African and Chinese ancestry, the number of languages in use among the various ethnic groups is necessarily large. The 1962 census classified the population by mother tongue as follows:—

English	1,606
French	47,109
Creole	199,091
Hindi	248,359
Marathi	11,533
Telegu	16,181
Tamil	44,044
Gujarati..	1,306
Urdu	92,276
Chinese	19,484
Other Languages ..	588
Language not stated ..	42

The number of live births during 1969 was 21,719, corresponding to a birth rate of 27·2 per thousand while deaths registered during the same year numbered 7,126, corresponding to a crude death rate of 8·0 per thousand.

The official language of the country is English, but French may be used in the Legislative Assembly and in the lower courts of law. Creole is, however, the *lingua franca*.

The capital of Mauritius is Port Louis, population 139,390, in the north west. Other important towns are: Curepipe, population 51,370; Beau Bassin-Rose Hill, population 70,640; Quatre Bornes, population 44,915; and Vacoas-Phoenix, population 48,320.

The Public Sector Development Plan (1971–75) provides for expenditure of Rs 660 million over the four-year period. For the year ending 30th June 1972 capital expenditure is expected to be Rs 126 million. Of this sum Rs 17 million is to be spent on the "Work for All" programme under which it is hoped to provide substantial relief of unemployment. Other expenditure is concentrated mainly on water and sewerage projects, harbour developments in Port Lewis and agricultural and fisheries projects.

The projections of potential resources for the financing of the four-year plan are as follows:

		Rs million
Domestic Sources		
a. Transfers from Recurrent Budget	.. ..	16
b. Backlog of resources ..	.. .. ..	69
c. Surplus of Semi Government Institutions	..	30
d. Domestic Borrowings ..	.. .. ..	200
Foreign Sources		
e. Anticipated loans and Grants including Food aid		400
Total	.. .. ..	715

British and and technical assistance to Mauritius, including food aid, has been of the order of Rs 33 million per annum over the last four years, partly loan and partly grant funds. These funds have been allocated primarily to water, sewerage and harbour projects and to the capital costs of the new University of Mauritius.

Retail price indices for the period 1963-1970 are shown in the following table:

Period	*Clerical* Rs 300-500 p.m.		*Manual Workers*
		1939=100	
	Urban	*Rural*	*Combined*
	January-June 1962		100(*a*)
1963 ..	98·5	98·5	98·5
1964 ..	101	100	100
1965 ..	102	102	102
1966 ..	105	105	105
1967 ..	106·6	106·6	106·6
1968 ..	113·0	114·9	114·1
1969 ..	115·6	117·6	116·7
1970 (Jan-June)	118·6	120·9	119·9

(*a*) Three new indices were introduced in July 1962, with January to June 1962=100, and cover households whose main wage earner draws an income of less than Rs 1,000 per month.

The main industry of the island is the growing of sugar as a plantation crop· Some 70,000 workers are employed in this industry during the harvest or 'crop' season, from July to December, and 60,000 during the intercrop season. The whole of the production with the exception of some 29,000 metric tons consumed locally, is exported, mainly to Britain, Canada and the U.S.A.

In 1970 the production of sugar reached 567,130 metric tons obtained from a harvested area of about 196,500 acres. The average yield of cane per acre over the whole island was 29·6 metric tons. Sugar produced per acre was 3·40 metric tons.

Although an important proportion of cane land is under peasant ownership, mostly Indo-Mauritian, the bulk of the sugar is produced on a plantation scale. The large plantations with factories produced about 60 per cent of the total crop. The smaller peasant owners, some 26,000 of whom cultivate altogether about 19 per cent of the land under cane, often work their land with the assistance of their families, employing extra labour only at peak periods such as planting and harvesting. Many of these small planters have grouped themselves into co-operative societies for the purpose of consigning their canes to factories. The whole of the sugar manufactured is marketed by the Mauritius Sugar Syndicate.

In 1969 exports of molasses amounted to 125,200 metric tons. Alcohol of different strengths was produced, equivalent to a production of 1,366,000 litres of pure alcohol. The greater part of this production was used locally as rum and denatured spirits.

Three other crops are grown industrially, but on a small scale compared with sugarcane. These are tea, tobacco and aloe fibre.

OVERALL TRADE

	IMPORTS £m.	EXPORTS £m.
1964	29·2	27·3
1965	27·5	24·1
1966	25·0	25·6
1967	27·8	22·9
1968	31·5	26·5
1969	28·2	26·9

Tea production rose from 5,054,579 lb in 1968 to 7,050,242 lb. in 1969. About 5,600,000 lb. of black tea were exported in 1969, 73·9 per cent of the total production, compared with about 2,480,625 lb. exported in 1965. 48·2 per cent of the tea exported was sold at the London auctions. Exports of tea to South Africa have increased considerably in recent years. (49·2 per cent in 1969). The International Development Association has approved a credit of US$5·2 million, for the extension of Mauritius tea production by another six million 165 per annum.

Tobacco was grown on 1,006 acres in 1969, a decrease of 329 acres compared with 1968. Total production amounted to 742,476 Kgs. compared with 528,308 Kgs. in 1968.

The entire 1969 fibre crop was purchased by the Government sack factory for manufacture into sacks for bagging sugar. In addition, the sack factory imported 198 tons of jute cuttings.

The commercial production of food crops and vegetables in 1969 was approximately 48,637 tons from a harvested area of about 10,554 acres. The production was higher than the year before mainly because of higher yields.

The control of the Mauritius Fisheries is exercised by the Fisheries Division of the Ministry of Agriculture and Natural Resources. About 2,750 fishermen with some 2,256 light fishing boats and a number of deep-sea pinnaces, together produce an annual catch of some 1,500 tons. Usually middlemen supply the boats and gear to the fishermen who in return bring in their catch at an agreed price. The middleman is expected to make advances during periods of enforced idleness occasioned by adverse weather. Loans are granted from Government funds either for the construction of boats or repairs to those damaged during cyclones.

Local industries produce beer, cigarettes, matches, aloe-fibre bags for sugar, rum, aerated minerals, country liquor, leather, rubber, leather and plastic footwear, thread, metal doors and windows, wooden and steel furniture, soap, toothpaste, margarine, spring mattresses, fibre glass manufactures, furniture polish, louvre windows, paints, retread tyres, nails, chain link fencing, welding electrodes, confectionery and car batteries. The bulk of the needs of the territory are met by importation from other countries. In November 1970, Government established Export Processing Zones in which overseas investors are offered a number of attractive duty and other concessions while manufacturing for the world market.

Imports of rice, the staple food of Mauritius, were 64,830 metric tons in 1969. Flour was imported mainly from Australia and France, beef on the hoof from Madagascar, and considerable quantities of foodstuffs from Britain, South Africa and Australia.

Port Louis, the capital is also the only port. It can accommodate eleven ocean-going vessels at any one time and six smaller vessels. The island is served by an international airport situated at Plaisance, some five miles from Mahébourg. It is managed and operated by the Department of Civil Aviation of the Mauritius Government. There are no other airfields nor are there any locally registered aircraft or operators. Scheduled air services are operated by Air France, Qantas, South African Airways, B.O.A.C., Air India, Air Madagascar, Lufthansa, East African Airways and Zambia Airways. The Island has an excellent system of road communications.

The broadcasting service in Mauritius is now run by an independent body, the Mauritius Broadcasting Corporation, which has a monopoly in the territory. The station at Malherbes operates on 439 metres, 9,710 and 4,850 kc/s with powers of 10 kW in both cases. In February 1965 a television service was introduced. The main transmitters, (5 kW vision and 1 kW sound) at Malherbes operate on Channel 4. To provide full coverage over the island three repeater stations have been erected at Jurançon (Channel 9), Fort George (Channel 7) and Motte Therese (Channel 11). In June 1970 there were 82,278 radio and 15,539 T.V sets duly licensed.

The main sources of recurrent revenue are income tax and customs and excise duties, mainly on imports; there is also an export tax on sugar.

Free primary education is provided for all children between the ages of five and twelve, but it is not compulsory. Secondary education is almost exclusively of the grammar school type leading to the School Certificate and Higher School Certificate. Apart from school libraries, there are extensive public library services in most townships. The Natural History Museum in Port Louis is mainly regional in character and contains representative collections of the fauna, flora and geology of Mauritius and of the neighbouring islands. The Historical Museum devoted to local history is at Mahébourg in the south east.

HISTORY

Mauritius was probably first visited by Arab sailors and Malays during the Middle Ages. During the early sixteenth century Portuguese sailors visited the island several times and the first European to discover it is believed to have been

Domingos Fernandez. The Portuguese used it merely as a port of call without making any settlement. The first settlers were the Dutch who landed in 1598 and gave the island the name Mauritius in honour of their ruler, Prince Maurice of Nassau. Settlements were established from 1638 onwards but did not prosper and the island was abandoned in 1710. In 1715 the island was formally taken possession of by the French. A small first contingent of colonists was sent in 1721 from the neighbouring island of Réunion (then called Bourbon), but it was not actually occupied until 1722 when a small party of colonists was sent out on behalf of the French East India Company. The island was then named Isle de France. From 1722 until about 1767 it was governed by that Company. From 1767 to 1810, apart from the brief period of independence under the Colonial Assembly during the French Revolution, it was in charge of officials appointed by the French Government.

During the long war between England and France, French men-of-war and privateers based on the Isle de France were a source of great mischief to the English merchant vessels. The British Government decided to capture the island and in 1810 a strong British expedition was eventually successful. The former name of Mauritius was then restored to it, and, with its dependencies, including Rodrigues, it was ceded to Great Britain by the Treaty of Paris in 1814. It was from Mauritius in 1642 that Tasman set out on his most important voyage of Australian discovery.

CONSTITUTIONAL DEVELOPMENT

From 1810 to 1903 Mauritius and Seychelles were administered as a single British colony. The administration at first consisted of a Governor, assisted by a number of British officials. In 1825 a Council of Government was established which consisted of the Governor and four officials nominated by him. In 1832 an equal number of officials and non-officials were appointed to the Council.

The constitution was amended in 1885 and in 1886 elections were held on a limited franchise for a Council of Government in which there were 8 officials, 9 other members (some of them officials) chosen by the Governor, and 10 members elected by the various districts of the island. Elections were subsequently held every five years until 1936. Seychelles became a separate colony in 1903.

In 1947 a new constitution granted a wide measure of enfranchisement on the basis of a 'simple literacy' requirement. A general election was held in August 1948 and the first Legislative Council met on 1st September. In 1957 the Governor appointed a Speaker to preside in the Legislative Council. In the same year a ministerial system was introduced. In 1958 the constitution was amended again to provide for universal suffrage and following elections in 1959 the Legislative Council was expanded.

In the last few years constitutional development in Mauritius has proceeded rapidly and at a constitutional conference held in London in September 1965 the Secretary of State for the Colonies announced that it was right that Mauritius should be independent and take her place among the sovereign nations of the world. It was then decided that after a general election had been held and a new Government formed, Her Majesty's Government would be prepared to fix a date and take the necessary steps to declare Mauritius independent after a period of six month's full internal self-government, provided a resolution to this effect were passed in the Legislative Assembly.

GOVERNMENT

The General Election was held on 7th August 1967, when the Independence Party, under Sir Seewoosagur Ramgoolam, was returned to power and a new constitution granting full internal self-government was introduced. The Independence motion was passed in the Mauritius Legislative Assembly on 22nd August 1967 and the island became independent on 12th March 1968. The Governor, Sir John Rennie, became the first Governor-General. A coalition Government was formed on 2nd December 1969 between the Labour Party, The Muslim Committee of Action and the Parti Mauricien Social Democrate.

GOVERNOR-GENERAL
Sir Leonard Williams, GCMG

CABINET
Prime Minister, Minister of Defence and Internal Security, and Minister of Information and Broadcasting and Civil Aviation:
Dr the Rt Hon. Sir Seewoosagur Ramgoolam, Kt, MLA
Minister of Finance: The Hon. Veerasamy Ringadoo, MLA
Minister of Housing, Lands, and Town & Country Planning:
The Hon. Sir Abdul Razak Mohamed, Kt, MLA
Minister of External Affairs, Tourism & Emigration: The Hon. Charles Gaetan Duval, MLA
Minister of Agriculture & Natural Resources: The Hon. Satcam Boolell, MLA
Minister of Health: The Hon. Harold Edward Walter, MLA
Minister of Works: The Hon. Abdool Hak Mahomed Osman, MLA
Minister of Education & Cultural Affairs: The Hon. Rajmohunsing Jomadar, MLA
Minister of Labour & Social Security: Dr the Hon. Beergoonath Ghurburrun, MLA
Minister of Economic Planning & Development: The Hon. Keharsingh Jagatsingh, MLA
Minister of Communications: The Hon. Pierre Gérard Raymond Rault, MLA
Minister of State in the Prime Minister's Office
(special responsibility probation and prison reform):
The Hon. Rameshwar Jaypal, MLA
Minister of Youth & Sports: The Hon. Dayanundlall Basant Rai, OBE, MLA
Minister of Local Government: The Hon. Jean Etienne Moi Lin Ah Chuen, MLA
Minister of Cooperatives & Cooperative Development:
The Hon. Hurrypersad Ramnarain, OBE, MLA
Minister of Commerce & Industry: The Hon. Jean Marie Michel Guy Marchand, MLA
Minister for Employment: The Hon. Jean Alex Rima, MLA
Attorney-General & Minister of Justice: The Hon. Jacques Paul Hein, MLA
Minister of State (External Affairs, Tourism & Emigration):
The Hon. Soobramanien Aroonassala Patten, MLA

LEGISLATIVE ASSEMBLY
Speaker: The Hon. Sir Harilall R. Vaghjee
(70 members)
Clerk: G. T. d'Espaignet

DIPLOMATIC REPRESENTATION

MAURITIAN REPRESENTATIVES IN
OTHER COMMONWEALTH COUNTRIES
United Kingdom: High Commissioner Dr L. Teelock, CBE; India: High Commissioner; Pakistan: High Commissioner.

COMMONWEALTH REPRESENTATIVES
IN MAURITIUS
United Kingdom: High Commissioner P. A. Carter, CMG; India: High Commissioner; Pakistan: High Commissioner; Australia: High Commissioner (resident in Dar-es-Salaam); Canada: High Commissioner (resident in Dar-es-Salaam);

MAURITIAN REPRESENTATIVES IN
NON-COMMONWEALTH COUNTRIES
France: Ambassador; Holy See, Belgium,

E.E.C.: Dr. L. Teelock, CBE (resident in London); United Nations: Permanent Representative; United States: Ambassador.

NON-COMMONWEALTH REPRESENTATIVES
IN MAURITIUS
Belgium: Ambassador (resident in Nairobi); France: Ambassador; Germany: Ambassador (resident in Tananarive); Holy See.: Apostolic Nuncio (resident in Tananarive); Israel: Ambassador (resident in Tananarive); Japan: Ambassador (resident in Tananarive); Malagasy: Ambassador; Netherlands: Ambassador (resident in Nairobi); Switzerland: Ambassador Mr H. Lagenbacher (resident in Addis Ababa); United States: Ambassador; U.S.S.R.: Ambassador, Mr V. A. Roslavtsev

REPUBLIC OF NAURU

The Republic of Nauru consists of a single island of approximately 8·2 square miles lying 26 miles south of the equator at 0° 32′ S. and 165° 55′ E. Nauru's nearest neighbour, 190 miles to the east, is Ocean Island, a part of the Gilbert and Ellice Islands Colony. The island is 2,500 miles from Sydney, 2,600 miles from Honolulu, and 3,000 miles from Tokyo.

Approximately oval and about 12 miles in circumference, the island is surrounded by a coral reef, which is exposed at low tide, and by a sandy beach from which the ground rises forming a fertile belt between 150 and 300 yards wide encircling the island. Inland coral cliffs rise to a height of up to 100 feet and merge with the central plateau, the highest point of which is 213 feet above sea level. The plateau is largely composed of phosphate rock and, where this has been removed, there is a rugged terrain of coral pinnacles up to 50 feet high.

The climate is tropical but is tempered by sea breezes. Average annual rainfall since 1950 has been 81 inches but there have been marked deviations from this average; as many as 180 inches and as few as 12 inches have been recorded since 1940. The only fertile areas are the narrow coastal belt where coconut palms and pandanus trees grow and the land surrounding Buada lagoon where bananas, pineapples and some vegetables are grown. Erratic rainfall and the highly porous nature of the soil severely restrict cultivation and local requirements of fruit and vegetables are mostly met by imports from Australia and New Zealand. Some sparse secondary vegetation grows over the coral pinnacles left by the removal of phosphate. There are few indigenous animals and birdlife is not plentiful. At times fish are abundant in the deep waters surrounding the island.

The Nauruan people are mainly of mixed Polynesian, Micronesian and Melanesian origin but are most closely related to the Polynesians. Their origin is uncertain and the Nauruan language provides no information about the origin of the people. English is used freely by educated (and is understood by all) Nauruans. Of the population of 6,927 on 23rd April 1971, 3,462 were temporary immigrants, recruited to work on the phosphate deposits and in the Public Service, and their dependants. Of these some 939 were Chinese, 1,954 Gilbert and Ellice Islanders and 571 Europeans.

ECONOMY

The economy of Nauru is wholly bound up with the extraction of phosphate from what is one of the world's richest deposits (averaging 37% to 37·5% phosphorous pentoxide (P_2O_5) with few impurities). 3,658 of the island's 5,263 acres are classified as phosphate bearing and represent a total of more than 90 million tons. A further area of 585 acres of rocky land is estimated to contain a further million tons. Up until 30th June 1970, 1,734 acres had been mined, and 116 acres partly mined, which has produced a total raising of 46½ million tons. It has been estimated that some 50 million tons of phosphate remain to be worked, representing a life span of approximately 22 years at the present rate of extraction. The Nauru Phosphate Corporation was established to run the industry from the 1st July 1970.

The phosphate industry provides employment for 117 Nauruans, 750 Gilbert and Ellice Islanders, 480 Chinese and 140 Europeans. The majority of Nauruans not employed in the phosphate industry are employed in either the Public Service or by the Nauru Local Government Council and the Nauru Co-operative Society.

HISTORY

The first European to visit Nauru was Captain John Fearn of the whaling ship *Hunter* in 1798. He called it Pleasant Island and noted that it was "extremely populous" with "houses in great numbers". During the 19th century various traders, beachcombers, etc., established themselves on the island without it coming under the formal control of any of the European powers. By the Anglo-German Convention of 1886 the island was allocated to the German sphere of interest and reverted to its native name of Nauru. German occupation began on 1st October 1888 when the gunboat *Eber* arrived carrying a German Commissioner, whose initial task was the restoration of peace between the twelve tribes living on the island. The earlier arrival of firearms and alcohol had upset the balance between the tribes and precipitated a ten years war which reduced the population from about 1,400 in 1842 to little over 900 in 1888. Apart from banning alcohol and restoring order the Germans did little to foster the development of Nauru until after the arrival of missionaries in 1899 who introduced Christianity as well as education.

During World War I the Germans surrendered Nauru to an Australian Expeditionary Force on 6th November 1914 and the island passed under British administration. The Germans formally renounced their title to Nauru by the Treaty at Versailles in 1919 and in 1920 Nauru became a British mandated territory under the League of Nations. Although Britain, Australia and New Zealand accepted the Trustee Mandate jointly, the administration of the island was conducted on their behalf by Australia. The three Governments established the British Phosphate Commissioners, which bought out the existing Pacific Phosphate Company and ran the industry.

Nauru was extensively damaged in World War II. While the allies still controlled the island in 1940, it was damaged by German naval gunfire and, following the Japanese occupation, the allies bombed the airfield. 1,200 Nauruans were deported by the Japanese to Truk in the Carolines where 463 died of starvation, disease, bombing and brutality. Only 591 Nauruans remained on Nauru when the Japanese surrendered on 13th September 1945 and the 737 survivors from Truk were returned to Nauru on 31st January 1946, which is remembered in Nauru as the 'Day of Deliverance'. On 1st November 1947 the General Assembly of the United Nations approved a Trusteeship Agreement for the Territory of Nauru submitted by the Governments of Australia, New Zealand and the United Kingdom on the same lines as the Mandate under the League of Nations.

CONSTITUTIONAL DEVELOPMENT

The first elections to be held on Nauru took place on 15th December 1951 for the Nauru Local Government Council, which elected Timothy Detudamo as Head Chief. The Council was, however, advisory only and in 1953 the United Nations Mission to the territory pressed for Nauru to have increased self-government.

In the period from 1951 until 1964 discussion of Nauru's future centred on the possibility of resettling the island's population on another island, whose economic future would not be clouded by the eventual exhaustion of the phosphate deposits. Many locations, including sites on the Australian mainland near Brisbane and Sydney, Prince of Wales Island and Fraser Island off Maryborough in Queensland, and, later, Curtis Island in Gladstone Harbour, were discussed as sites for possible resettlement. The proposal was abandoned in 1964 because the Nauruans under the leadership of Hammer DeRoburt, who had been elected Head Chief in 1955, were unhappy about a solution under which they did not retain some measure of sovereignty.

After 1964 discussions of Nauru's future were closely bound up with the Nauruan efforts to gain control of the phosphate extraction industry. In June 1967 the British, Australian and New Zealand Governments reached agreement in principle with the Nauruans for the sale to Nauru of the assets of the British Phosphate Commissioners. The details were subsequently incorporated in the Nauru Island Industry Agreement, 1967, which provided for payment over the three years ending June 1970. The price was later agreed at about \$A21 million, which was paid by April 1969. Earlier, in December 1965, the Australian Parliament passed legislation establishing the Nauru Legislative Council, the first elections for which were held on 25th January 1966 and whose first session was held on the 20th anniversary of Nauru's Day of Deliverance from Japanese Occupation, 31st January 1966. In October 1967 Agreement was reached for Nauru to become an independent Republic on 31st January 1968. The UN General Assembly agreed to terminate the Trusteeship Agreement the same day. A Parliament of 18 members was elected and Hammer DeRoburt was elected the Republic's First President in May 1968 for a term of three years, and was re-elected in January 1971 for a further term of three years. Nauru has not applied for membership of the United Nations, but plays an active part in several United Nations agencies.

NAURU AND THE COMMONWEALTH

In November 1968, in response to a request by the Government of Nauru, Commonwealth Heads of Government agreed that Nauru should be accorded the status of a special member of the Commonwealth. This "special membership" was devised in close consultation with the Government of Nauru; under it Nauru has the right to participate in all functional meetings and activities of the Commonwealth and is eligible for Commonwealth technical assistance. Nauru does not participate in meetings of Commonwealth Heads of Government.

Nauru is a member of the South Pacific Commission, the Universal Postal Union and the International Telecommunications Union.

GOVERNMENT (CABINET)

President, Minister of External Affairs and Minister of Industry and Island Development:
H. E. Hammer De Roburt, OBE, MP
Minister of Finance: The Hon. J. A. Bop, MP
Minister of Justice: The Hon. J. Detsimea Audoa, MP
Minister of Health and Education: The Hon. A. Bernicke, MP
Minister of Works and Community Services: The Hon. R. B. Detudamo, MP
Chief Justice: The Hon. Mr Justice I. R. Thompson

GOVERNMENT DEPARTMENTS

CHIEF SECRETARY'S DEPARTMENT
Chief Secretary: H. B. Connell

DEPARTMENT OF FINANCE
Acting Secretary: A. Gilroy

DEPARTMENT AND INDUSTRY AND
ISLAND DEVELOPMENT
Secretary: A. Carter

DEPARTMENT OF JUSTICE
Secretary: D. J. Dowdall

DEPARTMENT OF HEALTH AND EDUCATION
Secretary: J. R. Ayers

DEPARTMENT OF WORKS
Secretary: T. E. Spencer

DIPLOMATIC REPRESENTATION

OVERSEAS REPRESENTATION:
Nauru representative to Australia and New Zealand (resides in Melbourne): J. F. Pilbeam, ED BA; Nauru representative in the United Kingdom: Q. V. L. Weston, OBE

REPRESENTATION IN NAURU
Australia (Permanent Representative): Mr R. K. Gate

NEW ZEALAND
AND ISLAND TERRITORIES

THE boundaries of New Zealand were defined in 1863 as lying between 33° and 53° S. latitude and 162° E. and 173° W. longitude. New Zealand therefore consisted of the North Island and the South Island together with the smaller and sparsely-populated Stewart Island, which lies south of the South Island. The boundaries included the Chatham and Pitt Islands, some 467 miles east of Christchurch, and the Auckland Islands, which are south of the South Island. Other islands lying within this group were Three Kings Islands, Great Barrier Island, Solander Island, The Snares, Campbell Island, Bounty Island and the Antipodes Islands. The North Island, the South Island and Stewart Island extend over a distance of 1,100 miles.

By Proclamation dated 21st July 1887 the group of islands called the Kermadec Islands, lying between 29° and 32° S. latitude and 177° and 180° W. longitude, was annexed to New Zealand. The principal islands are Raoul Island or Sunday Island, and Macauley Island. The other islands are Curtis Island and L'Esperance Rock. Raoul Island, comprising an area of 11 square miles, rises to a height of 1,723 feet and is covered with forest.

The coasts of the Ross Sea and adjacent islands, south of 60° S. latitude and between 160° E. and 150° W. longitude, were brought within the jurisdiction of New Zealand by Order in Council on 30th July 1923.*

Niue (Savage) Island, 170° 20′ W., 19° S., was discovered by Captain Cook in 1774. The island became a British Protectorate in 1900 and was annexed to New Zealand in 1901. It is administered under the supervision of the New Zealand Department of Maori and Island Affairs.

The Tokelau Islands (formerly Union Islands), lying between 8° and 10° S. latitude and 170° and 173° W. longitude, became a British Protectorate in 1877. In 1916 the islands became part of the Gilbert and Ellice Islands Colony. In 1925 New Zealand assumed responsibility for the administration of the group, and in 1948 the Tokelau Islands were included within the boundaries of New Zealand.

The total area of New Zealand, exclusive of the Island territories and the Ross Dependencies, is 103,736 square miles. Less than one quarter of the land surface lies below 650 feet. In the North Island the mountain system runs generally in a south-westerly direction parallel to the coast from East Cape to Turakirae Head. Approximately one-tenth of the surface is covered by the following mountain ranges: Raukumara, Huiarau, Ruahine, Tararua and Rimutaka. Except for the volcanic peaks Egmont (8,260 feet), Ruapehu (9,175 feet), Ngauruhoe (7,515 feet) and Tongariro (6,458 feet) the mountains do not exceed 6,000 feet. In the South

---

For further information about New Zealand, see *New Zealand Official Year Book*
* The Ross Dependency (*q.v.*).

Island the Southern Alps run almost the entire length of the island and include the Victoria Range (W. and N.W.), St Arnaud (N.), Richmond and the Kaikoura Range (N.W.). Mount Cook (12, 349 feet) is in the centre and 15 peaks are over 10,000 feet. There are numerous swift flowing rivers some of which are used to provide hydro-electricity but most of which, being obstructed at their mouths by bars, are useless for navigation. The main rivers in the North Island are the Waikato, the Wangaehu, the Wanganui, the Rangitikei and the Manawatu. In the South Island the rivers Waitaki, Cobb, Clutha, and Waipara support hydro-electric projects. Two other rivers of importance are the Buller and Rangitata. A scheme has been agreed to use the waters of Lake Manapouri in the extreme south to power an aluminium smelter at Bluff. There are numerous lakes, mostly at high altitude in remote and rugged country. These are important as reservoirs and for the prevention of flooding but are of little use for communication. The most important lakes are Lake Taupo (234 square miles) in the North Island and Lake Wakatipu (113 square miles) and Te Anau (133 square miles) in the South Island. The islands of New Zealand are part of the unstable circum-Pacific mobile belt, a region where volcanoes are active and where the earth's crust has long been buckling and breaking at a geologically rapid rate of change. The Rotorua area of the North Island is world famous for its geo-thermal activities, boiling lakes, boiling mud, geysers, etc.

The climate is temperate and changeable, very similar to that in Britain except that winds are more frequent and there is a higher average sunshine. Normal temperatures range from 43·6° in June to 61·3° in January. The average rainfall for the greater part of the country is from 25–60 inches, but because of the mountain ranges can vary from as much as 300 inches to 13 inches.

There are 23 million acres of occupied farm land of which about half are in native and improved grass. There are 2·4 million dairy cows, 60·3 million sheep and 4·9 million beef cattle.

A census of population is taken every five years, the last being in March 1971. At 31st December 1970 the population was provisionally estimated at 2,857,862. In 1970 the birth rate was 22·02 per 1,0000 and the death rate 8·79 per 1,000. English is the official language and used by all, but a large proportion of the Maori population of 232,000 are bi-lingual in English and Maori. Christianity is the main religion and the 1966 census showed the chief groups to be Church of England 33·7 per cent, Presbyterian 21·8 per cent, Roman Catholic 15·9 per cent and Methodist 7·0 per cent; other denominations and sects include Ratana (Maori). Primary and secondary education is free and universal. University education is free to all holders of the University Entrance Examination and about one tenth of pupils leaving Secondary Schools go to Universities. Technical education is being developed. There is no illiteracy.

The urban areas which have the main concentrations of population are, in the North Island, Auckland (population 603,500), Wellington (179,300), Hutt (122,000), Hamilton (71,900), and Palmerston North (52,700); and in the South Island, Christchurch (260,200), Dunedin (110,100) and Invercargill (49,300).

Cargo statistics from the main ports for 1970 are: Whangarei 6,534,000 tons, Auckland 4,658,000, Taurange 2,530,000, Napier 940,000, Wellington 3,477,000, Lyttelton (Christchurch) 1,806,000, Port Chalmers (Dunedin) 646,000, Bluff (Invercargill) 673,000.

The principal airports are Auckland International Airport at Mangere with 8,500 feet of runway, Christchurch with 8,014 feet and 5,700 feet, and Wellington with 5,600 feet. Air New Zealand operates an international service and the National Airways Corporation provides a domestic service. In 1970 road mileage was 58,266, and there were 3,063 miles of 3 feet 6 inches gauge railway. The New Zealand Railways operate road/rail ferries between Wellington and Picton (in the South Island) and the Union Steam Ship Company operates a car ferry between Wellington and Lyttelton, the port of Christchurch. The New Zealand Broadcasting Corporation provides universal radio and television coverage.

The principal products and exports receipts for the year ending June 1970 were: wool ($205·0 million), meat ($369·3 million), butter ($109·7 million), cheese ($44·3 million), and hides, skins and pelts ($48·8 million). In the year ending March 1970 Government revenue was $1,282·5 million and expenditure $1,275·1 million. New Zealand is one of the largest exporters in the world of meat, dairy produce and wool and is heavily dependent on the export of pastoral products. There are probably more farm animals in proportion to population than in any other country. The value of goods exported forms a much higher percentage, about 20 per cent, of the gross national product than for most countries.

The Government plans to spend $870 million on power schemes during the 10-year period ending in 1976. This includes the completion of works already started and the capital expenditure on new works. Works in progress include the Manapouri (South Island) and Tongariro (North Island) hydro-electric projects. A 600 Mw station at New Plymouth in the North Island, the estimated cost of which is $134 million, is being constructed to burn oil or natural gas. Investigations are being made to further the development of power from geothermal sources in the North Island.

Other developments already under way include: a $20 million natural gas project at Kapuni in the North Island: an iron and steel works near Auckland using iron sand from West coast beaches as raw material (stage one costing approximately $35 million); major port developments in the four main ports in connection with container handling, and a $95 million aluminium smelter at Bluff.

HISTORY

New Zealand was first discovered and settled by the ancestors of its present Polynesian inhabitants some time before A.D. 1000. Over the centuries further immigrants arrived; and as their numbers increased they spread over the North Island until the whole island was divided up among a number of tribal communities, each under its own chief, each claiming descent from one or other of the crews of the canoes which had brought their ancestors from overseas. The South Island, where the climate was less congenial, was more sparsely inhabited; but at the time when contact with Europe began, it is estimated that the total population may have been more than 100,000 persons. The name Maori, meaning 'normal' (indigenous) person, used to describe these peoples, did not come into use until the nineteenth century.

The first European to sight New Zealand, on 13th December 1642, was the Dutchman Abel Janzoon Tasman. An employee of the Dutch East Indian Company, he was searching on behalf of the Company in Java for the legendary southern continent which geographers then believed must exist in the southern hemisphere. He charted part of the west coast of the South Island, and, hoping that he had found part of the continent he was seeking, named it Staaten Landt, that being the name of land discovered south of South America and believed to be part of the same continent. When the latter land was found to be an island, the new land was renamed Niew Zeeland, after the Dutch province. Although he did not land, Tasman found the inhabitants hostile and the land poor; no further European visitor touched its shores for over a century.

The next visitor was Lieutenant, later Captain, James Cook, preceding the Frenchman de Surville by only two months. Cook, who was sailing under the auspices of the Royal Society and the Admiralty, with the scientist Joseph Banks on board, had made a further search for the legendary continent before sailing west to look for the land which Tasman had discovered. On 7th October 1769 he sighted the eastern shores of the North Island, and in the months that followed circumnavigated the country and brilliantly charted its shores, proving that it consisted of two main islands. He was followed later by other explorers, Marion du Fresne, Crozet, d'Entrecasteaux and Vancouver, among others.

Cook found the inhabitants generally friendly; and his reports of good harbours, of the abundance of seals, and of the existence of timber and flax, attracted the attention of sealers and traders. Many of these came from the flourishing community growing up at Sydney across the Tasman Sea; but the existence of whales brought also whalers from America, Britain and France. Among the first settlers were the missionaries, organized initially by the Reverend Samuel Marsden from New South Wales, who aimed to assist the Maoris and to introduce European farming. At the end of the 1830s a slump in New South Wales increased the inflow of settlers, and by 1839 it was estimated that there were 2,000 of them, and that 130 ships were calling annually at the Bay of Islands.

The arrival of sailors, traders, missionaries and settlers in a land lacking an established administration and a rule of law, and their inter-relationship with the Maoris, whose traditional customs began to break down under the impact of association with the West, gave rise to problems which the British Government were at first reluctant to face. Cook's declarations of British sovereignty in 1769 and 1770 were repudiated; and as late as 1828 New Zealand was named in a British Act as a place not under British sovereignty. However, the need for action led the Governor of New South Wales to take, or be given, powers to try to maintain order. In 1814 Thomas Kendall, a missionary, was made a Justice of the Peace to assist in bringing British offenders to justice in the courts of New South Wales; and the Reverend John Gare Butler was made a Magistrate in 1819 with jurisdiction over the British settlements. In 1828 the jurisdiction of the courts of New South Wales was extended to deal with all kinds of offences committed by British subjects within the islands of New Zealand. In 1832 James Busby was appointed as British Resident at the Bay of Islands. His appointment indicated that the British Government still looked upon New Zealand as an independent country, but legislation to give him authority failed on the grounds that it was not lawful to legislate for an independent country. Two years later, in 1835, as a counterblast to the activities of the French Baron de Thierry, Busby convened an assembly of chiefs who signed a Declaration of Independence which was recognised by the Crown. Finally, pressure by settlers, traders and missionaries, and the clear need to protect the Maoris and to control the settlers, who were about to be re-inforced by settlers sent by Edward Wakefield's New Zealand Association, together with a suspicion that other nations had become interested, led the British Government to intervene more directly. Letters Patent of

5th June 1839 authorised the Government of New South Wales to include within the boundaries of that Colony any territory in New Zealand that might be acquired in sovereignty; and Captain Hobson landed in the Bay of Islands on 29th January 1840 and assumed the office of Lieutenant-Governor. Hobson was instructed to treat with the Maoris as an independent nation for recognition of the Queen's sovereignty over the whole of the country or over any parts which they might be willing to cede. A meeting of Chiefs was held at Waitangi on 5th February, and on the 6th February 1840 forty-six chiefs signed the Treaty of Waitangi ceding sovereignty to Queen Victoria; and their example was followed by many others. Finally, on 21st May, Hobson issued two proclamations, one declaring British sovereignty over the North Island by virtue of the cession of the Treaty of Waitangi, and the other over all the islands of New Zealand from 34° 30′ N. to 47° 10′ S., and from 166° 5′ E. to 179° E. by virtue of the right of discovery by Cook. This strip in fact included not only Fiji but the Marshall Islands and even Wake. New Zealand remained as part of New South Wales until 16th November 1840, when Letters Patent made it a separate colony. The boundaries were corrected by the charter of April 1842.

The signing of the Treaty of Waitangi is celebrated annually on 6th February (Waitangi Day).

The date on which Queen Victoria assumed the sovereignty of New Zealand also marked the beginning of the 'hungry forties' in Britain where many of those displaced by the industrial revolution felt that their only hope for the future was to emigrate. The propaganda of the New Zealand Company, which had obtained a Royal Charter in 1840, turned attention to the opportunities which might exist in the new Colony with its temperate climate; and the stream of immigrants into New Zealand was such that by 1858 the newcomers had begun to outnumber the Maoris. Many of these settlers were assisted by the New Zealand Company until it lost its Charter in 1850. These European New Zealanders pressed in on the Maoris, not all of whom wished to sell land under the crown pre-emption system inaugurated by the Treaty of Waitangi. Disputes arose, resulting in greater unity among the Maoris, in a stiffening of their resistance to encroachment and finally in the Maori wars from 1860 to 1872. The defeat of the Maoris appeared likely at first to be disastrous for them; but the realisation by the now much more populous race that both had their part to play in the future of the country led to improved relations, to the greater integration of the Maori people into the life of the country, to returning pride in their Maori heritage and to an increased birthrate.

The hopes of quick prosperity held out to its settlers by the New Zealand Company were not at first realised. Timber and flax remained important articles of export, but wool soon became still more important. Meat was exported to the gold miners in Australia; and the discovery of gold in Otago in 1865 not only itself increased prosperity but led to an influx of miners to provide an additional market for the farmers. The slump of the 1880s was lightened by the departure to England in 1882 of the first ship carrying refrigerated meat, and this was the herald of a prosperity built on wool, meat and dairy produce which, with an interval during the great slump, has continued until the present.

The development of the country was furthered during the 1870s by the financial policy of Julius (later Sir Julius) Vogel who borrowed on a large scale to develop government-controlled communications and to double the population through immigration schemes; but this policy, while bringing the provinces closer together, also aggravated the effects of the slump. During the 1890s Richard (later Sir Richard) Seddon brought in a series of laws dealing among other things with land, income tax, old age pensions, factory conditions, and industrial arbitration; laws which were to make New Zealand for a time the most radical state in the world. The Boer War and the First World War brought New Zealand on to the world stage and to a full realization of her nationhood. The development of New Zealand into the first Welfare State gained momentum from 1936. The Second World War brought New Zealand still more into the world arena, and the war with Japan stressed the importance of her role in East Asia and the Pacific. This was reinforced by participation in military operations in Korea, Malaysia, and Vietnam. New Zealand has taken her full part in United Nations Affairs. Under the Colombo Plan substantial assistance has been given to the developing countries of South East Asia.

A British Protectorate was established over the Cook Islands in 1888, and the group was administered through the Governor of New Zealand until October 1900. These islands lie between 8° and 22° S. latitude and 156° and 167° W. longitude. The group was annexed to Her Majesty's dominions in October 1900. By a Proclamation dated 10th June 1901 the boundaries of New Zealand were further extended from 11th June 1901 by inclusion of the Cook Islands. Niue (Savage) Island, geographically within the Cook group, although administered separately by New Zealand, was also included. The Cook Islands became self-governing in July 1965, but remain in free association within New Zealand.

Western Samoa (or Navigators' Islands), together with some small islets, lying between 13° and 15° S. latitude and 171° and 173° W. longitude, formerly in the possession of Germany, was occupied by New Zealand in August 1914. A Mandate for the government of the Territory by New Zealand was approved by the Council of the League of Nations in December 1920. In December, 1946 the General Assembly of the United Nations approved a Trusteeship Agreement which replaced the Mandate. Western Samoa ceased to be a Trust Territory and became an independent country on 1st January 1962. Under a Treaty of Friendship which came into force on 8th March 1962, New Zealand affords Western Samoa assistance in the conduct of foreign relations.

CONSTITUTIONAL DEVELOPMENT

By the Proclamation of 21st May 1840 New Zealand became British Territory. On 16th June 1840 the laws of New South Wales were, so far as they were applicable, extended to New Zealand by Act of the New South Wales Legislative Council. However, by Letters Patent of 16th November in the same year, made under a Statute passed on 17th August, New Zealand became a separate colony, although the laws of New South Wales remained temporarily in force. The North Island, the South Island and Stewart Island (named after an unsuccessful flax planter) were renamed New Ulster, New Munster and New Leinster; an Executive Council, consisting of the Governor, the Colonial Secretary, the Attorney-General and the Treasurer was formed; and the Governor was authorised to set up a Legislative Council to make laws and ordinances for the peace and good government of the Colony. This Charter was promulgated on 3rd May 1841, and the Legislative Council was duly formed, consisting of three officials and three senior Justices of the Peace. The Council met on twelve occasions, and passed a total of one hundred and twenty-nine ordinances.

When Captain (later Sir George) Grey became Governor in 1845 there was pressure for a greater measure of popular representation, and a new Charter, dated 23rd December 1846, proposed to divide the Colony into two Provinces, one being named New Ulster, consisting of the whole of North Island other than the district around Wellington, and the other New Munster, which covered the rest. It was the intention to appoint Lieutenant-Governors to each Province and to set up not only a central General Assembly, with an elected House of Representatives, but also Provincial Councils, which, too, would have elected Houses of Representatives. In 1848 a suspending Act of the Imperial Parliament delayed the creation of both General and Provincial assemblies for a period of five years. The Colonial Legislative Council was therefore revived and in 1848 passed the Provincial Legislative Councils Ordinance, setting up nominated Provincial Councils with unofficial majorities. Since the composition of the New Ulster Provincial Legislative Council was almost the same as that of the Colonial Legislative Council, the former never met. That of New Munster met once, in 1849.

On 30th June 1852 the British Parliament passed an Act to 'Grant a Representative Constitution to the Colony of New Zealand'. The number of Provinces was increased from two to six, the Provinces being Auckland, New Plymouth, Wellington, Nelson, Canterbury and Otago. In the centre, the General Assembly consisted of the Governor, a nominated Legislative Council and an elected House of Representatives. In each of the Provinces there was an elected Superintendent and an elected Provincial Council with defined, if limited, powers. The General Assembly, and the Provincial Councils, were expressly debarred from regulating Crown Lands or lands in the possession of the Maoris; and the laws, customs and usages of the Maoris were 'for the present to be maintained for the Government of themselves, in all their Relations to and Dealings with each other, and that particular Districts should be set apart within which such Laws, Customs and Usages should be observed'. There were also a number of other restrictions on the legislative capacity of the General Assembly; and the laws passed by it required the Royal Assent and were not to be repugnant to the laws of England. Thus the constitutional picture of New Zealand as a result of this Constitution was that of six small scattered European settlements each with its own Provincial Government and having a central Parliament; the Maori-occupied country between the settlements having no part in this representative Government but governing itself according to Maori custom, subject to the overriding authority of the Governor in Council. In 1867 four Maori seats were established in the General Assembly on the basis of manhood suffrage.

No provision was made in the Constitution for a responsible Executive, and although three Members of the House of Representatives and two Members of the Legislative Council took office without portfolio, effective power remained in the hands of the three officials, who, with the Governor, still continued to sit in the Executive Council. This arrangement led to disputes between the legislature and the executive, the resulting deadlock only being resolved when, on 7th May 1856, Henry Sewell took office as the first Premier of a fully responsible administration. The title of Prime Minister, although in common use from that date, was not officially assumed until 1899.

The name of the Province of New Plymouth was changed in 1858 to Taranaki, and new Provinces of Hawke's Bay, Marlborough, Southland and Westland were formed in 1858, 1859, 1861 and 1864 respectively. Southland, however, was re-united with **Otago** in 1870. The system of having both central and provincial governments led, as the Provinces developed, to friction between them; and in 1875 the Provincial organisation was brought to an end by the Abolition of Provinces Act, which became operative in 1876.

Some of the restrictions placed on the powers of the New Zealand General Assembly were removed by the New Zealand Constitutional Amendment Act of 1857, which gave power to the Assembly to amend, alter, suspend or repeal the majority of the provisions of the Act of 1852. Responsibility for Maori affairs remained with the Governor until 1864, when it was finally handed over to the New Zealand Government; and from that date the New Zealand central Government was responsible for the whole of New Zealand. By a Royal Proclamation of 9th September 1907 it was declared that after 26th September 1907 the Colony of New Zealand should be known by the title of the Dominion of New Zealand. The few remaining restrictions on the powers of the New Zealand Parliament to change the constitution remained, and were confirmed by Section 8 of the Statute of Westminster (1931). This Statute was not, however, adopted by New Zealand until 1947, when the New Zealand Statute of Westminster Adoption Act was passed, to be followed by the New Zealand Constitution (Request and Consent) Act, which, after implementary legislation had been passed by the British Parliament, finally removed the last restrictions on the right of the New Zealand Parliament to amend the constitution.

As originally provided, the Legislative Council which formed the Upper House, had a maximum of 15 members, but this number was slowly increased until 1885 when it had 53 members, which included two Maori Members from 1871. From that time the maximum number of Councillors was generally kept at half the membership of the House of Representatives. Legislative Councillors were at first appointed for life, by the Governor. In 1891 their term of appointment was reduced to five years, but they were eligible for re-appointment. In 1914 it was proposed that Councillors should become elective, but although an Act to this effect was passed it was never brought into force. Women were entitled to be Councillors from 1941.

In 1950 the Legislative Council was abolished by the Legislative Council Abolition Act; and the New Zealand Parliament thenceforth consisted of a single chamber only.

The first House of Representatives had only 40 Members, but the number slowly increased until 1881, when it had 95 Members. In 1887 the number was reduced to 74 and in 1900 increased to 80. Since the passing of the Maori Representation Act in 1867 four Maori Members have been elected by the Maori people. Four additional seats were added in 1969 and the Membership of the House therefore now stands at 84. Women have been eligible for election since 1919. Under the 1852 Constitution a vote could be exercised by any male person over the age of 21 years who possessed certain property qualifications. By the Qualification of Electors Act of 1879 every male person over the age of 21 years was entitled to vote, and women's suffrage was introduced in 1893. By the Legislative Act of 1908 the second ballot was introduced to ensure that elected Members had an absolute majority of the votes polled; but this was repealed in 1913. By the constitution of 1852 the House of Representatives was elected for five years, but this period was reduced to three years in 1879. In 1934 it was increased to four years, but reduced again to three years in 1937. The Electoral Amendment Act, 1969, reduced the voting age to 20 years.

HISTORICAL LIST

GOVERNORS

Sir George Gipps, Governor, 30th January 1840 to 3rd January 1841

Captain William Hobson, RN, Lieutenant-Governor 30th January 1840 to 3rd January 1841; Governor 3rd January 1841 to 10th September 1842

Lieutenant Willoughby Shortland, RN, Administrator 10th September 1842 to 26th December 1843

Captain Robert R. Fitzroy, RN, Governor 26th December 1843 to 17th November 1845

Captain George Grey (later Sir George Grey, KCB), Lieutenant-Governor 18th November 1845 to 1st January 1848; Governor-in-Chief over the Islands of New Zealand, Governor of the Province of New Ulster and Governor of the Province of New Munster 1st January 1848 to 7th March 1853; Governor of New Zealand 7th March 1853 to 31st December 1853

*Lieutenant-Colonel Robert Henry Wynyard, CB, 3rd January 1854 to 6th September 1855

Colonel Sir Thomas Gore Browne, CB, 6th September 1855 to 2nd October 1861

Sir George Grey, KCB, 4th December 1861 to 5th February 1868 (Administrator from 3rd October 1861)

Sir George Ferguson Bowen, GCMG, 5th February 1868 to 19th March 1873

*Sir George Alfred Arney, Chief Justice, 21st March to 14th June 1873

Sir James Ferguson, Bt., PC (later GCSI, KCMG, CIE), 14th June 1873 to 3rd December 1874

George Augustus Constantine Phipps, 2nd Marquess of Normanby, PC, GCB, GCMG, 9th January 1875 to 21st February 1879 (Administrator from 3rd December 1874)

*James Prendergast, Chief Justice, 21st February to 27th March 1879

Sir Hercules George Robert Robinson, GCMG (later 1st Baron Rosmead, PC), 17th April 1879 to 8th September 1880 (Administrator from 27th March 1879)

*James Prendergast, Chief Justice, 9th September to 29th November 1880

Sir Arthur H. Gordon, GCMG, 29th November 1880 to 23rd June 1882

*Sir James Prendergast, Chief Justice, 24th June 1882 to 20th January 1883

Lieutenant-General Sir William Francis Drummond Jervois, GCMG, CB, 20th January 1883 to 22nd March 1889

*Sir James Prendergast, Chief Justice, 23rd March to 2nd May 1889

William Hillier Onslow, 4th Earl of Onslow, PC, GCMG, 2nd May 1889 to 24th February 1892

*Sir James Prendergast, Chief Justice, 25th February to 6th June 1892

David Boyle, 7th Earl of Glasgow and 1st Baron Fairlie, GCMG, 7th June 1892 to 6th February 1897

*Sir James Prendergast, Chief Justice, 8th February to 9th August 1897

Uchter John Mark Knox, 5th Earl of Ranfurly, GCMG, 10th August 1897 to 19th June 1904

William Lee Plunket, 5th Baron Plunket, GCMG, KCVO, KBE, 20th June 1904 to 8th June 1910

*Sir Robert Stout, KCMG, Chief Justice, 8th to 22nd June 1910

Sir John Poynder Dickson-Poynder, Bt., 1st Baron Islington, PC, KCMG, DSO (later GCMG, GBE), 22nd June 1910 to 2nd December 1912

*Sir Robert Stout, KCMG, Chief Justice, 3rd to 19th December 1912

Arthur William de Brito Savile Foljambe, 2nd Earl of Liverpool, PC, GCMG, MVO (later GCB, GBE), 19th December 1912 to 28th June 1917

GOVERNORS-GENERAL

Arthur William de Brito Savile Foljambe, 2nd Earl of Liverpool, PC, GCB, GCMG GBE, MVO, 28th June 1917 to 7th July 1920

*Sir Robert Stout, PC, KCMG, 8th July to 26th September 1920

Admiral of the Fleet John Rushworth Jellicoe, 1st Viscount Jellicoe of Scapa (later 1st Earl Jellicoe and 1st Viscount Brocas), GCB, OM, GCVO, 27th December 1920 to 25th November 1924

*Sir Robert Stout, PC, KCMG, 26th November to 13th December 1924

General Sir Charles Fergusson, Bt., GCMG, DSO, MVO (later GCB), 13th December 1924 to 8th February 1930

*Sir Michael Myers, Chief Justice, 8th February to 18th March 1930

Charles Bathurst, 1st Baron Bledisloe (later 1st Viscount Bledisloe), PC, GCMG, KBE, 18th March 1930 to 15th March 1935

*Sir Michael Myers, PC, KCMG, Chief Justice, 15th March to 12th April 1935

George Vere Arundel Monckton-Arundell, 8th Viscount Galway, PC, GCMG, DSO, OBE, 12th April 1935 to 3rd February 1941

*Sir Michael Myers, PC, GCMG, Chief Justice, 3rd to 21st February 1941

Marshal of the Royal Air Force Sir Cyril Louis Norton Newall, 1st Baron Newal, GCB, OM, GCMG, CBE, 21st February 1941 to 19th April 1946

---

* Administering the Government

*Sir Michael Myers, PC, GCMG, Chief Justice, 19th April to 17th June 1946
General Sir Bernard Cyril Freyberg, 1st Baron Freyberg, VC, GCMG, KCB, KBE, DSO (3 Bars), 17th June 1946 to 15th August 1952
*Sir Humphrey Francis O'Leary, PC, KCMG, Chief Justice, 15th August to 2nd December 1952
Lieutenant-General Sir Charles Willoughby Moke Norrie (later 1st Baron Norrie), GCMG, GCVO, CB, DSO, MC, 2nd December 1952 to 24th July 1957
*Major-General Sir Harold Barrowclough, PC, KCMG, CB, DSO, MC, Chief Justice, 24th July 1957 to 3rd September 1957 and 7th April to 16th June 1960
Charles John Lyttelton, 10th Viscount Cobham, PC, GCMG, TD (later KG) 3rd September 1957 to 13th September 1962
*Major-General Sir Harold Barrowclough, PC, GCMG, CB, DSO, MC, Chief Justice, 13th September 1962 to 9th November 1962
Brigadier Sir Bernard Fergusson, GCMG, GCVO, DSO, OBE, from 9th November 1962 to 20th October 1967
*Rt Hon. Sir Richard Wild, KCMG, Chief Justice, 20th October 1967 to 27th November 1967
Sir Arthur Porritt, Bt., GCMG, GCVO, CBE, from 1st December, 1967

MINISTRIES

Henry Sewell, 7th May to 20th May 1856
William Fox, 20th May to 2nd June 1856
Edward William Stafford, 2nd June 1856 to 12th July 1861
William Fox, 12th July 1861 to 6th August 1862
Alfred Domett, 6th August 1862 to 30th October 1863
Frederick Whitaker, 30th October 1863 to 24th November 1864
Frederick Aloysius Weld, 24th November 1864 to 16th October 1865
Edward William Stafford, 16th October 1865 to 28th June 1869
William Fox, 28th June 1869 to 10th September 1872
Edward William Stafford, 10th September to 11th October 1872
George Marsden Waterhouse, 11th October 1872 to 3rd March 1873
William Fox, 3rd March to 8th April 1873
Julius Vogel, CMG, 8th April 1873 to 6th July 1875
Daniel Pollen, 6th July 1875 to 15th February 1876
Sir Julius Vogel, KCMG, 15th February to 1st September 1876
Harry Albert Atkinson, 1st September to 13th September 1876
Harry Albert Atkinson (Ministry reconstituted), 13th September 1876 to 15th October 1877
Sir George Grey, KCB, 15th October 1877 to 8th October 1879
John Hall, 8th October 1879 to 21st April 1882
Frederick Whitaker, 21st April 1882 to 25th September 1883
Harry Albert Atkinson, 25th September 1883 to 16th August 1884
Robert Stout, 16th August to 28th August 1884
Harry Albert Atkinson, 28th August to 3rd September 1884
Sir Robert Stout, KCMG, 3rd September 1884 to 8th October 1887
Sir Harry Atkinson, KCMG, 8th October 1887 to 24th January 1891
John Ballance, 24th January 1891 to 1st May 1893
R. J. Seddon, PC, 1st May 1893 to 21st June 1906
William Hall-Jones, 21st June to 6th August 1906
Sir Joseph George Ward, Bt., PC, KCMG, 6th August 1906 to 28th March 1912
Thomas Mackenzie, 28th March to 10th July 1912
Wm. Ferguson Massey, PC, 10th July 1912 to 12th August 1915
Wm. Ferguson Massey, PC, (National Ministry), 12th August 1915 to 25th August 1919
Wm. Ferguson Massey, PC, 25th August 1919 to 14th May 1925
Sir Francis Henry Dillon Bell, GCMG, QC, 14th May to 30th May 1925
Joseph Gordon Coates, PC, MC, 30th May 1925 to 10th December 1928
Sir Joseph George Ward, Bt., PC, GCMG, 10th December 1928 to 28th May 1930
George William Forbes, PC, 28th May 1930 to 22nd September 1931
George William Forbes, PC, (Coalition Ministry), 22nd September 1931 to 6th December 1935
Michael Joseph Savage, PC, 6th December 1935 to 1st April 1940
P. Fraser, 1st April to 30th April 1940
P. Fraser, PC, CH, 30th April 1940 to 13th December 1949
Sir Sidney G. Holland, PC, CH, 13th December 1949 to 20th September 1957
Sir Keith J. Holyoake, PC, 20th September to 11th December 1957
Sir Walter Nash, PC, 11th December 1957 to 12th December 1960
Sir Keith J. Holyoake, GCMG, PC, CH, from 12th December 1960

---

*Administering the Government.

GOVERNMENT

At the General Election in November 1969 the National Party secured 45 seats and the Labour Party 39. After a by-election in 1970 the Labour Party gained a seat at the expense of the National Party. The final division of votes between the parties was National 605,960, Labour 592,055, Social Credit 121,576 and others 20,577.

GOVERNOR-GENERAL
His Excellency Sir Arthur Porritt, Bt, GCMG, GCVO, CBE

CABINET
Prime Minister, Minister of Foreign Affairs, Minister of State Services, Minister in Charge of the Legislative Department, Minister in Charge of the Audit Department, Minister in Charge of the New Zealand Security Intelligence Service:
Rt Hon. Sir Keith Holyoake, GCMG, CH
Deputy Prime Minister, Minister of Overseas Trade, Minister of Labour, Minister of Immigration:
Rt Hon. J. R. Marshall
Minister of Industries and Commerce, Minister of Mines: Hon. N. L. Shelton
Minister of Education, Minister of Science: Hon. B. E. Talboys
Minister of Finance, Minister in Charge of the Department of Statistics, Minister in Charge of Friendly Societies: Hon. R. D. Muldoon
Minister of Housing, Minister in Charge of the State Advances Corporation, Minister in Charge of the Public Trust Office, Minister in Charge of the Government Life Insurance Office, Minister in Charge of the State Insurance Office, Minister in Charge of the Earthquake and War Damage Commission: Hon. J. Rae
Minister of Health, Minister of Social Security, Minister in Charge of the Child Welfare Division, Minister for the Welfare of Women and Children: Hon. D. N. McKay
Minister of Internal Affairs, Minister for Local Government, Minister of Civil Defence:
Hon. D. C. Seath
Minister of Works, Minister of Electricity: Hon. P. B. Allen
Minister of Agriculture: Hon. D. J. Carter
Minister of Transport, Minister of Railways: Hon. J. B. Gordon
Minister of Forests, Minister of Lands, Minister of Maori Affairs, Minister of Island Affairs, Minister in Charge of Valuation Department: Hon. D. MacIntyre, DSO, OBE, ED
Minister of Defence, Minister of Police, Associate Minister of Labour and Immigration, Minister in Charge of War Pensions, Minister in Charge of Rehabilitation:
Hon. D. S. Thomson, MC, ED
Minister of Customs, Associate Minister of Industries and Commerce:
Hon. L. R. Adams-Schneider
Postmaster General, Minister of Marine and Fisheries, Minister in Charge of the Government Printing Office: Hon. A. McCready
Attorney-General, Minister of Justice: Hon. D. J. Riddiford
Minister of Tourism, Minister in Charge of Publicity, Minister of Broadcasting:
Hon. H. J. Walker
Associate Minister of Finance: Hon. H. E. L. Pickering

Parliamentary Under-Secretaries
Parliamentary Under-Secretary to Minister of Agriculture: A. D. Dick
Parliamentary Under-Secretary to Minister of Education and Science: G. F. Gair

LEADER OF THE OPPOSITION
N. E. Kirk

HOUSE OF REPRESENTATIVES
Speaker: Sir Roy Jack, KB
Chairman of Committees: A. E. Allen, MP

JUDICIARY
Chief Justice: Rt Hon. Sir Richard Wild, KCMG

Court of Appeal:
Rt Hon. Sir Richard Wild, KCMG (ex-officio); Rt Hon. Sir Alfred North (President); Rt Hon. Sir Alexander Turner; Rt Hon. Sir Thaddeus McCarthy

L*

Judges of the Supreme Court:

Rt Hon. Sir Richard Wild, KCMG
(ex-officio)
Hon. Sir Trevor Henry
Hon. Mr Justice Haslam
Hon. Mr Justice Macarthur
Hon. Mr Justice Richmond
Hon. Mr Justice Woodhouse
Hon. Mr Justice Perry

Hon. Mr Justice Wilson
Hon. Mr Justice Moller
Hon. Mr Justice Speight
Hon. Mr Justice Roper
Hon. Mr Justice White
Hon. Mr Justice Beattie
Hon. Mr Justice Quilliam
Hon. Mr Justice McMullin

GOVERNMENT DEPARTMENTS

PRIME MINISTER'S DEPARTMENT
Permanent Head (also Secretary of Foreign Affairs): G. R. Laking, CMG
Chief Private Secretary: H. S. Wells
Secretary of the Cabinet: P. J. Brooks

MINISTRY OF FOREIGN AFFAIRS
Secretary (Permanent Head, Prime Minister's Department): G. R. Laking, CMG
Deputy Secretary: G. D. L. White, MVO

Legislative Department
Clerk of the House of Representatives and Clerk of Parliament: E. A. Roussell

AUDIT DEPARTMENT
Controller and Auditor-General: K. Gillies

DEPARTMENT OF INDUSTRIES AND COMMERCE
Secretary: M. J. Moriarty
President of Price Tribunal: S. T. Barnett

CUSTOMS DEPARTMENT
Controller: V. W. Thomas

ATTORNEY-GENERAL'S DEPARTMENT

Crown Law Office
Solicitor-General: J. C. White, QC

Law Drafting Office
Counsel and Compiler of Statutues: D. A. S. Ward

DEPARTMENT OF JUSTICE
Secretary for Justice and Controller-General of Prisons: E. A. Missen
Registrar-General of Births, Deaths and Marriages: J. L. Wright

DEPARTMENT OF MAORI AND ISLAND AFFAIRS
Secretary: J. M. McEwen
High Commissioner of the Cook Islands at Rarotonga: L. J. Davis
Resident Commissioner at Niue Island: S. D. Wilson
Administrator of the Tokelau Islands: R. B. Taylor

MINISTRY OF TRANSPORT
Secretary: R. J. Polaschek

RAILWAYS DEPARTMENT
General Manager: I. Thomas

DEPARTMENT OF LABOUR
Secretary of Labour: E. G. Davey

Court of Arbitration
Judges: A. P. Blair

Compensation Court
Judge: J. B. Thomson

MINES DEPARTMENT
Under-Secretary: I. D. Dick

TOURIST AND PUBLICITY DEPARTMENT
General Manager: J. E. Hartstonge

MINISTRY OF WORKS
Commissioner: J. H. Macky

ELECTRICITY DEPARTMENT
General Manager: E. B. Mackenzie

THE TREASURY
Secretary: H. G. Lang

DEPARTMENT OF INLAND REVENUE
Commissioner: D. A. Stevens

DEPARTMENT OF STATISTICS
Government Statistician: J. P. Lewin

MINISTRY OF DEFENCE
Secretary: J. F. Robertson
Chairman of the Chiefs of Staff Committee: Lieutenant-General Sir Leonard Thornton, KCB, CBE
Chief of the Naval Staff: Rear-Admiral L. G. Carr, CB DSC
Chief of the General Staff: Major-General R. J. H. Webb, MBE
Chief of the Air Staff: Air Vice-Marshal W. H. Stratton, CBE, DFC

POLICE DEPARTMENT
Commissioner of Police: W. H. A. Sharp

DEPARTMENT OF AGRICULTURE
Director-General: Dr A. T. Johns

DEPARTMENT OF LANDS AND SURVEY
Director-General of Lands: R. J. Maclachlan

NEW ZEALAND FOREST SERVICE
Director-General: A. P. Thomson

NEW ZEALAND SECURITY SERVICE
Director of Security: Brigadier H. E. Gilbert

VALUATION DEPARTMENT
Valuer-General: J. B. Brown

MARINE DEPARTMENT
Secretary: R. N. Kerr

DEPARTMENT OF INTERNAL AFFAIRS
Secretary and Clerk of Writs: P. J. O'Dea, CVO

STATE ADVANCES CORPORATION OF NEW ZEALAND
Managing Director: C. J. Ashton

PUBLIC TRUST OFFICE
Public Trustee: J. M. Fielder

GOVERNMENT LIFE INSURANCE OFFICE
Commissioner: A. C. Paine

GOVERNMENT PRINTING OFFICE
Government Printer: A. R. Shearer

DEPARTMENT OF EDUCATION
Director-General:

Child Welfare Division
Superintendent: L. G. Anderson

RESERVE BANK OF NEW ZEALAND
Governor: A. R. Low

DEPARTMENT OF SCIENTIFIC AND INDUSTRIAL RESEARCH
Director-General: Dr E. I. Robertson, OBE

SOCIAL SECURITY DEPARTMENT
Director: G. J. Brocklehurst

POST OFFICE
Director-General: G. Searle

NEW ZEALAND BROADCASTING CORPORATION
Director-General: L. Sceats

STATE SERVICES COMMISSION
Chairman: I. G. Lythgoe

DIPLOMATIC REPRESENTATION

NEW ZEALAND REPRESENTATIVES IN OTHER COMMONWEALTH COUNTRIES

Australia: H.E. Mr A. J. Yendell (High Commissioner); Barbados: Mr D. J. Walker (Trade Commissioner) (resident in Trinidad); Britain: H.E. Sir Denis Blundell, KBE (High Commissioner); Canada: H.E. the Hon. D. J. Eyre (High Commissioner); Ceylon: (vacant) (High Commissioner) (resident in New Delhi); Fiji: Sir John Grace, KBE (High Commissioner); Guyana: Mr D. J. Walker (Trade Commissioner) (resident in Trinidad); Hong Kong: Mr W. G. Thorp (Commissioner); India: (vacant); Jamaica: Mr D. J. Walker (Trade Commissioner) (resident in Trinidad); Malaysia: H.E. Mr R. L. Hutchens (High Commissioner); Singapore: H.E. Mr H. H. Francis (High Commissioner); Trinidad and Tobago: Mr D. J. Walker (Trade Commissioner); Western Samoa: H.E. Mr R. B. Taylor (High Commissioner)

COMMONWEALTH HIGH COMMISSIONERS IN NEW ZEALAND

Australia: H.E. Sir Edwin Hicks, CBE; Britain: H.E. Sir Arthur Galsworthy, KCMG;

Canada: H.E. Mr J. A. Dougan; Ceylon: H.E. Mr J. Siriwadene (resident in Canberra); India: H.E. Mr P. S. Naskar; Malaysia: H.E. Mr Lim Taik Choon; Pakistan: H.E. Mr M. Aslan Malik (resident in Canberra); Singapore: H.E. Mr K. M. Byrne

NEW ZEALAND REPRESENTATION IN NON-COMMONWEALTH COUNTRIES

Austria: (Ambassador) (resident in Bonn); Belgium: (Ambassador); E.E.C.: (Ambassador); France: (Ambassador); Germany: (Ambassador); Greece: (Consul-General); Indonesia: (Ambassador); Ireland: (Ambassador) (resident in London); Italy: (Ambassador); Japan: (Ambassador); Korea: (Ambassador) (resident in Tokyo); Laos: (Ambassador) (resident in Bangkok); Nepal: (Ambassador) (resident in New Dehli); Netherlands: (Ambassador); Philippines: (Minister) (resident in Hong Kong); Switzerland: (Consul-General); Thailand: (Ambassador); United Nations: (Permanent Representative); U.S.A.: (Ambassador); Vietnam: (Ambassador)

ISLAND TERRITORIES

NIUE

Niue is situated at 169° W. 19° S. and has an area of 100 square miles. At 31st December 1971 the estimated total population was 5,183.

The island was discovered by Captain Cook in 1774. British sovereignty was proclaimed over the island in 1900 and in 1901 Niue was annexed to New

Zealand. The Resident Commissioner is responsible to the New Zealand Minister of Island Affairs for the executive government of Niue. He is assisted by an Executive Committee comprising four members elected by the Legislative Assembly, which has fourteen elected members. The Resident Commissioner presides over the Assembly and is Chairman of the Executive Committee. The Niuean members of the Assembly are elected by universal suffrage and represent all villages on the island. Under a full member system of Government which was introduced in 1968, the Resident Commissioner has delegated some of his powers and functions to members of the Executive Committee, who hold portfolios covering various functions of government.

The principal exports are passionfruit pulp, copra, honey, kumaras, limes and plaited ware. Export revenue in 1970 totalled approximately $NZ177,000. Annual Niue Government expenditure slightly exceeds $NZ2 million, the bulk of the income being by way of New Zealand Government grants and loans.

Niue is linked with New Zealand and neighbouring Pacific islands by a weekly air service and a monthly shipping service.

Resident Commissioner: S. D. Wilson
Leader of Government Business: Hon. R. R. Rex

TOKELAU ISLANDS

This Group consists of three islands, or groups of islets, Atafu (500 acres), Nukunono (1,350 acres) and Fakaofo (650 acres), and lies about 4° due north of Apia, Western Samoa. On 25th September 1970 the total population was 1,687.

The three islands became a British Protectorate in 1877, and formal declarations were made at each atoll in 1889. At the request of the inhabitants, Britain annexed the islands (then known as the Union Islands) in 1916 and included them within the boundaries of the Gilbert and Ellice Islands Colony. In 1925, at the request of the British Government, New Zealand assumed responsibility for the administration of the Group, and as a result the islands were separated from the Gilbert and Ellice Islands Colony. In 1946 the Tokelau Nomenclature Ordinance officially designated the Group as the Tokelau Islands. The islands were included within the territorial boundaries of New Zealand by the Tokelau Islands Act, 1948.

The islands are administered by an Administrator in whom all administrative and executive functions are vested. Local public services are carried out on each island by appointed Tokelau officials. Of these officials the Faipule is the most important; he is the chief representative of the Government and acts in a supervisory capacity over other officials on his island.

As the economic and social future of the Islands seemed uncertain and overpopulation had already become a problem, the New Zealand Government suggested to the Tokelauans, in 1966, a scheme of progressive resettlement in New Zealand. A limited start was made with single Tokelauans being accepted under Government sponsorship for resettlement in various parts of New Zealand.

Administrator: R. B. Taylor

SELF-GOVERNING TERRITORY
COOK ISLANDS

The fifteen islands of the Cook Group (Rarotonga, Mangaia, Atiu, Mauke, Mitiaro, Aitutaki, Palmerston Atoll (Avarau), Penrhyn (Tongareva), Suwarrow (Suvorov), Manihiki (Humphrey Island), Rakahanga (Rierson Island), Pukapuka (Danger Islands), Nassau, Manuae and its twin islet Te Au o tu (Hervey Islands) and Takutea) have a total area of approximately 57,000 acres. A census of the Cook Islands taken on 1st September 1966 recorded a total population (exclusive of Niue) of 19,251. At 31st December 1969 the total population was 21,260.

Various islands of the Group were placed under British protection between 1888 and 1901.

Until 1901 British authority was represented by a Resident, who was paid by the Government of New Zealand and reported direct to the Governor. The first British Resident succeeded in 1891 in arranging for the establishment of an Elective Federal Parliament to make laws for the whole Group. Each island, however, continued to enjoy self-government in such purely local affairs as it could properly manage for itself. The Federal Executive Council or Government was composed of the Arikis, who were also the principal landowners. A Supreme Court was established. All laws and administrative acts were subject to the approval of the Resident, who was also a Deputy and Judicial Commissioner for the Western Pacific and Chief Justice of the High Court of the Cook Islands.

In 1900 a petition from leading islanders requested the abolition of the Federal Parliament and the annexation of the islands by New Zealand. An Imperial Order in Council was accordingly made on 13th May 1901, and on 11th June 1901 the Cook Islands were declared to lie within the boundaries of New Zealand. The administration and laws were continued in force subject to the provisions of the Cook Islands Government Act passed in that year.

In 1915 an Act was passed by the New Zealand Parliament consolidating the laws relating to the Cook Islands and Niue Island and providing for the appointment of a member of the Executive Council of New Zealand as the Minister for the Cook Islands charged with the administration of the government of the Islands. By the Cook Islands Amendment Act, 1932, the administration of Niue Island was transferred to the Minister of External Affairs.

The 1915 Act also made provision for the constitution of Island Councils for the establishment of public schools, Courts of Justice, Native Land Courts, etc. The Island Territories Act, 1943, established a Ministry of Island Territories and charged the Minister with the administration of the government of any territory outside of New Zealand which may at any time be a dependency or mandated territory of New Zealand, or otherwise be under the jurisdiction of the Government or Parliament of New Zealand.

The enactment of the Cook Islands Amendment Act, 1957, marked a major step forward in the constitutional development of the Cook Islands. The most important provision of the Act was the replacement of the Legislative Council by a reconstituted Legislative Assembly of the Cook Islands consisting of fourteen members elected by universal suffrage by the electors of the various islands—seven members elected by the various island councils, one European member and four officials nominated by the Administration. In 1962 the New Zealand Government placed before the Legislative Assembly four possible schemes for political development—complete independence, full internal self-government, integration with New Zealand or ultimate integration into a Polynesian Federation—and asked them to decide which course they would most favour. The Assembly chose full internal self-government with continuing association with New Zealand.

In 1963 three constitutional advisers were appointed to hold discussions with the Assembly on the form of the Cook Islands Constitution, and in November 1964 a draft Constitution, having already been accepted by the Legislative Assembly, was enacted by the New Zealand House of Representatives. In order to put this constitution before the people of the Cook Islands, general elections were held on 20th April 1965 to elect a new Legislative Assembly equipped with a special mandate to accept or decline the constitution. They were conducted in the presence of a United Nations Mission which observed the elections at the invitation of the New Zealand Government.

The elections were won by Mr Albert Henry's Cook Islands Party, which gained fourteen of the twenty-two seats in the new Legislative Council. The Cook Islands Party had already accepted the principle of full internal self-government and continuing association with New Zealand. Mr Albert Henry informed the New Zealand Government, however, that his party wished to propose a number of amendments to the draft constitution. The most important of these were:

(*a*) An amendment to the existing electoral regulations on residential qualifications. This enabled Mr Henry (who had not been eligible to stand at the elections) to be elected to the Assembly in a by-election; and

(*b*) An amendment to form a House of Arikis or Upper House on which the Arikis from all the islands would be represented.

The Cooks Islands Constitution Amendment Act was passed by the New Zealand House of Representatives in May 1965, and the new Constitution proclaimed on 8th August 1965.

The Cook Islands now have complete control of their own affairs in free association with New Zealand, but with the added special feature that they can at any time move into full independence by a unilateral act if they so wish. New Zealand will continue to be responsible for external affairs and defence while the Cook Islands retains this special relationship.

At a General Election held in May 1968, Mr Henry's Cook Island Party won 16 seats against the United Cook Islanders' Party's 6.

Premier: Mr Albert Henry
High Commissioner: Mr L. J. Davis

FEDERAL REPUBLIC OF NIGERIA

NIGERIA, which takes its name from the Niger, or 'great', river which flows through it to the sea, is situated on the west coast of Africa on the shores of the Gulf of Guinea and lies between 4° and 14° N. latitude and 2° and 15° E. longitude. It is bounded on the west by Dahomey, on the north by Niger and on the east by the Republic of Cameroun. It includes part of Lake Chad on the north-east. The total area is 356,669 square miles. It is 650 miles from the coast to the farthest point on the northern border and its greatest width is 700 miles. It is not a mountainous country: the only high ground is the plateau area near Jos and along the eastern border. There is one other navigable river of importance, apart from the Niger, the River Benue. There are two well-marked seasons, the rains lasting from April to October, and the dry season from November to March. Temperatures at the coast seldom rise above 32°C (90°F) but the humidity is high. Farther north the climate is drier and the temperature range greater, the extremes being 43°C (110°F) and 10°C (50°F) although it is occasionally lower in certain areas.

Nigeria is the most populous state in Africa. At the time of the 1952–53 census the population stood at 30,417,000. The census held in late 1963 recorded a total population of 55,654,000.

The main tribal groups are Fulani, Hausa, Yoruba and Ibo. The non-African population does not exceed 30,000. The principal languages in Nigeria are English, Hausa, Yoruba and Ibo. Primary education is not yet universal. In 1966 there were 2,907,745 primary pupils and 132,912 pupils in secondary schools and colleges.

Over half the population are Muslims, these being concentrated in the north and west. In the southern areas in particular there are many Christians.

The capital of the Republic is Lagos with an estimated population in 1967 of 680,000. Lagos also acts as capital of the Lagos State.

The principal seaports are served by a number of shipping lines including the Nigerian National Shipping Lines, Elder Dempster and Palm Lines. Several international airlines operate frequent services to the main international airports at Kano and Lagos. Regular internal air services by Nigeria Airways connect these two airports with Ibadan, Benin, Calabar, Port Harcourt, Jos, Kaduna, Maiduguri, Sokoto and Yola. Passenger and freight services are operated by the Nigeria Railway Corporation over a total of 2,178 route miles.

The Nigerian Broadcasting Corporation, a statutory body, covers the whole of the Republic through a chain of radio stations. In Lagos State the N.B.C. Television Service runs in association with it. There are separate State-owned companies for sound and television broadcasting in Kaduna (BCNN), Ibadan (WNBS/WNTV) and, before the civil war, Enugu (ENBS/ENTV). The Mid-Western State plans to establish its own radio and television station in Benin. A new and more comprehensive national radio network was approved in principle by Federal and State Information Commissioners in November, 1968.

Nigeria has a predominantly agricultural economy: farming, forestry, and fishing activities contribute over half of the country's gross domestic product but mining and industry are gaining in importance. The export structure is very diversified. Mineral oil forms the largest item, but cocoa, palm products, groundnut produce, tin, rubber, timber, cotton and hides and skins are also important.

Overseas investment, of which over half was British, stood at over £N400 million at the end of 1966, and heavy investment in the oil sector continued throughout the war and is still increasing. Crude oil production in mid-1971 was at the rate of 1·5 million barrels per day, making Nigeria the world's tenth largest producer.

In 1970/71 the combined estimated revenues of the Federal and State Governments totalled about £N318 million. The second National Development Plan was issued in November 1970. It calls for an investment programme of £N1,596 million.

The sharp upsurge in economic activity continues, with imports rising in 1970 by 52 per cent and exports by 39 per cent above the level of 1969, and with domestic demand buoyant. The increase in receipts from oil production should enable a high growth rate to be sustained.

HISTORY

The Nigerian plateau in the area around Jos is now regarded as a focal point in early Nigerian history; here was a meeting point for influences from the upper Niger valley, where agriculture had been independently invented around 5000 B.C., and from the civilization of Egypt. We know that the Plateau people practised agriculture by 3000 B.C., and it would seem that increased food supplies allowed the development of more complex societies which pushed their way southward. The Bantu, who subsequently conquered most of eastern and southern Africa with their iron weapons, are thought by some authorities to have originated on the Plateau. By 500 B.C. the remarkable Nok culture had emerged, controlling an area around the Plateau of some 400 square miles, a culture characterized by terra-cotta heads and figurines of a high technical and artistic standard, which reveal an agricultural people, who knew iron-working and had developed a specialised society. The culture lasted for some seven centuries, spread southwards, and influenced the art of Benin and Ife.

Nigerian history is characterised by this pressure of northern peoples on the southern forest belt. The northerners exploited geographical advantages, for their climate allowed them to domesticate cattle and horses and grow cotton and cereals, so that textiles, leather-working and smithing were able to develop. In the southern tropical forest agriculture depended on root crops and palm products until the later entry of Indonesian and American crops. The north was also in contact with Egypt and North Africa, and strong political state systems, often based on the concept of divine kingship, emerged early in the Christian era. Two main systems emerged in the north. In the area around Lake Chad the shadowy Zaghawa kingdom had by the eleventh century become the Kanem-Bornu empire, the Bornu section of which later became a separate state. The Hausa Bokwoi dominated the area further west as a loose confederation of several states which probably originated at different times between A.D. 100 and the tenth century. These states dominated the politics of the north until the nineteenth century. Both states were profoundly, though never completely, influenced by Islam, brought in by desert traders and later by Fulani immigrants. Both developed extensive foreign trade across the Sahara in leather goods, salt, cloth, slaves and gold. They were intermittently torn by internal civil wars, they fought each other, were invaded from outside (parts of Hausaland were forced to submit to the Songhai empire in the sixteenth century) and menaced by the Jukun state, centred upon Ibi on the River Benue, during the sixteenth century.

As yet little is known of events in the south in mediaeval times. Of the Ibo, the dominant linguistic group in Eastern Nigeria, we know little beyond shadowy legends indicating struggles with invaders from north and west. Though without centralized monarchical institutions, the Ibo survived and multiplied, developing agriculture to support a dense population which by the eighteenth century became a magnet for slave traders. Rather more is known of the Yoruba, the predominant group in the Western State. Their cultural history originated in the founding before A.D. 1000 of Ife, still the spiritual centre of Yorubaland, despite the fact that its political control was eclipsed in the fourteenth century by Oyo, which was in turn displaced by Ibadan and Abeokuta in the nineteenth century. The origins of Benin are also connected with Ife, and the claim of both upon the attention of historians lies in their magnificent sculpture, now regarded by some authorities as a major contribution to mankind's artistic spirit; its humanism and naturalism reflects a highly developed and sophisticated society. The bronze sculptures demonstrate great technical aptitude by the mastery of the complicated 'lost wax' process of casting.

Contact with Europe began in the fifteenth century with the Portuguese, and at first this contact seemed likely to have profound results, for it brought missionaries to Benin, who introduced the art of writing, and made converts among the royal family. Benin's territory expanded when the lucrative spice trade allowed her to purchase firearms, and, after the discovery of America, new plants revolutionised the diet of all the forest peoples. But by the seventeenth century the Portuguese began to lose interest, developing the richer trade of the Indian Ocean. Moreover, with the development of plantations in America and the West Indies, the demand for slaves from West Africa rapidly began to overshadow all other activities. The effects of the slave trade were overwhelmingly negative, for it could easily be developed from existing forms of slavery, using African middlemen. It needed no technical innovations, and as the slaves were bought from coastal states without the buyers penetrating inland there was very little external influence of new ideas. The firearms which were exchanged for the slaves strengthened and made aggressive the southern states; Benin expanded from Lagos to Bonny, and her influence on the Niger was felt as far north as Onitsha; and Oyo fought her Yoruba brothers to carve a way to the sea.

In this trade Britain had by the eighteenth century secured the major share, yet this had resulted in no colonial activity in Nigeria. Paradoxically it was the movement in Britain against the slave trade which began to involve the British in Nigerian affairs. In 1807 the slave trade was made illegal for British subjects, the Royal Navy began to patrol the coast, and the Sierra Leone colony became the resettlement area for slaves liberated at sea, the majority of whom were Nigerians. The anti-slavery groups, however, were sceptical of blockade, and pressed instead for the development of missionary work and 'legitimate commerce' to check the trade at its source in the interior. At the same time the rise of the British chemical and soap industries created a demand for palm oil and other vegetable oils capable of providing a substitute traffic. Missionaries settled in Abeokuta in the 1840s to begin a 'sunrise within the tropics' through 'the Bible and the Plough'. Africans liberated at sea from the slave ships played a major role in this process. Samuel Adjai Crowther, a liberated Yoruba, accompanied the British Niger Expedition of 1841, later returning to found a chain of Anglican missions on the Niger, staffed entirely by liberated Africans. In 1846 he became the first African Bishop of the Anglican communion. Such African Christians may be described as the first modern Nigerian nationalists; they had a vision of a united Christian country, transcending tribal divisions, in the valley of the Niger. Crowther, though a Yoruba, worked for most of his life among the Efik, Ibo, Ijaw, Ibibio and Nupe people.

Whilst missionary penetration of the Niger proceeded so did the commercial. After 1854, when W. B. Baikie demonstrated that quinine could reduce European mortality from malaria, shallow-draught trading steamboats annually ascended the river.

Meanwhile events had occurred in the north profoundly affecting the history of modern Nigeria. In May 1804 Shelu Usuman dan Fodio, a Fulani religious teacher, declared a jihad or holy war upon the Hausa state of Gobir. Giving flags to his generals he succeeded during the next thirteen years of his life in overthrowing most of the Hausa rulers, replacing them with Fulani Emirs. The impulse of the movement was Muslim reforming zeal, and it led to the creation of an empire with many features of Islamic administrative character, the lasting value of which was proved in the subsequent history of the area. When Usuman died his son Bello was left as Sultan of Sokoto, with his brother Abdullahi as Emir of Gwandu, twin suzerains of the state. The effects of this revolution might well be compared to those of the Norman Conquest of England. A state-system was created which transcended tribal loyalties, possessing a common religious and judicial basis, an aristocratic *lingua franca* and a system of education through Koranic schools. Though some Hausa states, notably Gobir, resisted successfully, the Fulani movement spread beyond Hausaland; a new Emirate in Adamawa was established, Nupe conquered, the Yoruba state of Ilorin made Muslim, and the Yoruba capital of Oyo destroyed. The Yoruba might well have been crushed between the Fulani in the north and Dahomey to the west had not Ibadan and Abeokuta beaten them off with the help of liberated slaves and European weapons.

With missionaries and traders moving into the south and up the Niger, it was inevitable that the British Government should become involved. British Consuls were appointed, and in 1861, after ten years of fitful interference in its affairs, Lagos was annexed partly at the behest of the Christian party in Abeokuta, who desired a docile and friendly port. Thereafter it was impossible to keep out of local politics, despite the Parliamentary Select Committee of 1865, which decreed no more expansion but eventual withdrawal. Further involvement arose on the Niger from the opposition of African middlemen to British trade in the oil-producing regions, and naval expeditions on the river became annual from the 1860s.

Before 1880, however, the British were reluctant to extend political control; the climate was still deadly to European officials, and trade and missions seemed to flourish without the expense of a colonial régime. After 1880 the situation changed rapidly with the arrival of missionaries, traders, and treaty-making explorers in the service of both France and Germany. The British responded with three methods of extending control; Lagos, ruled by the Colonial Office, expanded by treaties with Yoruba states; areas under consular rule were transformed by treaties into the Oil Rivers Protectorate in 1884; and on the Niger, where Sir George Goldie had amalgamated the British traders and bought out the French firms, his company was given a Royal Charter granting administrative powers in 1886. Renamed the Royal Niger Company it was placed under the somewhat sketchy control of the Foreign Office. From these bases British control was extended gradually in the next twenty years. The rule of the African middlemen in the Oil Rivers was broken by the deposition of rulers like King Jaja of Opopo, who opposed the penetration of British traders and missions into his markets. Force was used against Benin in 1897, and by the Niger Company against Ilorin and Nupe in the same year. The Ijebu were conquered by force in the 1890s, but elsewhere in Yorubaland treaties were the more usual method of control. A renewed period of rivalry with France resulted in the creation of much more direct control during the Colonial Secretaryship of Joseph Chamberlain (1895–1902). The frontiers were settled by agreements with France, the West African Frontier Force was established under Colonel (later Lord) Lugard, the

Royal Niger Company was deprived of its administrative powers in 1900 and, northern and eastern Nigeria placed under Colonial Office supervision. Lugard was made Governor of Northern Nigeria, and gradually occupied the Emirates militarily. Similar military moves led to the gradual conquest of the Ibo people.

Despite this forceful assertion of control, the British rejected, where they could, the idea of ruling directly, and thereby destroying indigenous political institutions. 'Indirect rule' had been practised by both the Royal Niger Company and the Lagos authorities, and it was cheaper, more economical in men and less likely to provoke opposition than direct administration. The classic system was developed by Lord Lugard in the north, where the area continued to be ruled by the Fulani Emirs, with their systems of justice and taxation reformed of their more unsatisfactory characteristics and developed to suit the colonial régime. In Yorubaland a similar policy was attempted, especially after 1914 when Nigeria was united administratively into one dependency. In the west, however, the system was more difficult to administer for the chiefs were not feudal rulers and did not fit easily into the hierarchical system. Among the Ibo indirect rule was almost impossible, and the British resorted to the expedient of creating warrant chiefs, a policy which contributed to widespread rioting in the 1920s. Among many educated Africans indirect rule became unpopular for its emphasis on preserving traditional culture, excluding them from administration and the native courts. Probably the policy was maintained after it had served its purpose; yet it did protect Africans; its corollary was the British refusal to allow white settlement or plantations such as those demanded by Lord Leverhulme in the 1920s. This protective element allowed economic development, especially in agriculture, to take place through Nigerian enterprise. Transported by a new network of railways, or carried in Nigerian owned lorries on a vastly extended road system, a large export trade in cocoa, groundnuts, leather, cotton and vegetable oils developed.

After the 1914–1918 War, part of the adjacent German colony of Kamerun was placed under British mandate by the League of Nations, and renamed the British Cameroons. It was administered as an integral part of Nigeria. On the formation of the United Nations, the Cameroons became a Trust territory. At a plebiscite held in the Northern Cameroons in November 1959 the territory voted to defer a decision on its own future and did not therefore achieve independence in 1960 as part of Northern Nigeria. The Cameroons ceased to be a part of Nigeria when Nigeria became independent but a plebiscite was held in February 1961 to decide whether the Cameroons should join Nigeria or the Cameroun Republic. At this second plebiscite the Northern Cameroons voted to become part of Nigeria and formally became part of the Federation on the 1st June 1961 and is now the Sardauna Province of the North Eastern State. The Southern Cameroons at the same plebiscite opted to join the Republic of Cameroun and did so on the 1st October 1961.

From 1960 to 1967 Nigeria was originally a Federation of three and subsequently four regions (after the creation of Mid-Western Nigeria following a referendum held on 13th July 1963). On 27th May 1967, regions were abolished and 12 states were created.

CONSTITUTIONAL DEVELOPMENT

When in 1914 Northern and Southern Nigeria were amalgamated, a Nigerian Council, consisting of six African and thirty European members, but without executive or legislative authority, was set up alongside the Lagos Executive Council. The Governor was not bound to give effect to any Resolution of the Council unless he thought fit to do so.

In 1922 a new constitution was introduced, providing for a Legislative Council of 46 members, of whom ten were Africans, four of these being elected. The Council was empowered to legislate for the Colony and for the Southern Provinces of Nigeria, while the Governor continued to legislate by proclamation for the Northern Provinces.

No further changes in the Constitution were made until 1947, when the 'Richards Constitution' was introduced (so-called after the Governor, Sir Arthur Richards, later Lord Milverton). The objects of this Constitution were to promote the future unity of the country, to express its diversity and to increase discussion and management by Nigerians of their own affairs. A Legislative Council was set up for the whole of Nigeria, with 45 Members, of whom 28 were Africans (4 elected and 24 nominated) while the Executive Council was still composed mainly of official members. But the biggest change brought about by the 1946 Constitution was the setting up of Regional Houses of Assembly in Eastern, Western and Northern Nigeria, with a House of Chiefs for the Northern Region. These Assemblies were created for the purpose of linking the Central Legislative Council and the Native Authorities, and were required to consider and advise by resolution on any matters referred to them by the Governor. Executive functions were not provided for, but estimates of annual and supplementary expenditure and bills whose terms were applicable to a Region were placed before the Houses of Assembly. Their recommendations were considered by the Governor-in-Council and were placed before the Central Legislative Council. The importance and uniqueness of the 'Richards Constitution' was its introduction of the policy of regionalisation which has since been developed in successive constitutions. Provision was included in the constitution for its operation to be reviewed after three-year and six-year periods and to be revised after nine years, but in fact the constitution worked so well that before the end of the first three-year period discussions on a new constitution began, and this constitution was introduced in January 1951.

The 1951 Constitution provided for a Council of Ministers of 18 members (12 African and 6 officials), a House of Representatives of 142 members (136 Africans and 6 officials) and for a House of Assembly in each of the three Regions and a House of Chiefs in Northern and Western Nigeria. Apart from the official members, members of the Houses of Assembly were elected through electoral colleges, and members of the House of Representatives were elected by each Regional House of Assembly on the basis of 34 members each from Eastern and Western Nigeria and 68 from Northern Nigeria. Increased powers were given to the Regional Houses to make laws covering a restricted range of subjects, mainly concerned with local social services, local courts and local taxation, subject to reference to the Governor-in-Council. Nominations to the Central Council of Ministers were subject to approval by a joint council of the Regional Houses in the North and West and to a session of the House of Assembly in the East. There was equal representation for each Region in the Council of Ministers.

Throughout its life of 27 months the 1951 Constitution was subject to stresses and strains and in March 1953 a crisis developed which made it clear that further constitutional revision had become necessary.

In August 1953 delegates of all political parties met in London to consider the problems involved in creating a new constitution. They met again in Lagos, in January 1954, and on 1st October 1954 a new constitution was brought into operation which recognized to a limited extent the autonomy of Regional Governments for their internal administration and affairs. The 1954 Constitution retained the framework of its predecessor but carried regionalization a stage further by declaring Nigeria a Federation. It also gave responsibilities to Nigerian Ministers for the formulation and execution of policy.

At the centre, the House of Representatives was enlarged to 184 directly elected members, and the Council of Ministers was composed of 10 African Ministers and 3 *ex officio* Ministers. In the Eastern and Western Regions all *ex officio* representation ceased both in the Regional Executive and in the Regional House of Assembly. In the Regions, the members of the Executive Councils were appointed from the party having a majority in the Regional House of Assembly. At the centre, appointment to the Council of Ministers was on the basis of three members from Eastern, Northern and Western Nigeria, and one member from the Southern Cameroons. Nominations were made by the party having a majority of seats in a Region at the Federal elections. These were separate from, and independent of, elections to the Regional House of Assembly, and no one could serve as a member both of a Regional and the Federal Legislature.

The review of the 1954 Constitution, scheduled for 1956, was deferred until May and June 1957. The delegates, who again met in London, pressed for a firm date for the grant of full independence for the Federation, but in view of the many unresolved questions the British Government were unable to give a firm undertaking to this effect. An undertaking was, however, given that sympathetic consideration would be given to the matter after a new Federal House had been elected in 1959. In the meantime it was agreed that Commissions should be set up to inquire into the fears of minorities, the fiscal arrangements for the Federation, and the delimitation of constituencies for the proposed new Federal House of Representatives of 320 members. It was also agreed that the office of Federal Prime Minister should be created; and in August 1957 the first Federal Prime Minister was appointed. *Ex officio* members disappeared from the Federal Council of Ministers, except for the President (the Governor-General). The Prime Minister formed a coalition Government of the principal parties in the House, and the Council was composed of the Governor-General, as President, the Prime Minister and 10 other Ministers. Agreement was reached also on the establishment of an Upper House—the Senate.

Internal self-government was granted to the Eastern and Western Regions on 8th August 1957, as a result of decisions taken at the 1957 Conference, and to Northern Nigeria on 15th March 1959, as a result of the Conference of 1958.

In September and October 1958 the Constitutional Conference was resumed in London and the British Government agreed to grant independence to the Federation of Nigeria as from 1st October 1960, if the Federal House of Representatives, to be elected at the end of 1959, so requested. The Conference accepted the reports of the Commissions set up as a result of the 1957 Conference on the question of minorities and the question of the allocation of revenue, decided to incorporate provisions for fundamental human rights in the Constitution, and agreed a number of other matters, including, in particular, arrangements relating to the Police. Those constitutional amendments which were not actually dependent upon independence came into operation during 1958, 1959 and 1960.

New elections to the Federal House of Representatives were held in December 1959. At its first meeting in January 1960 the new House passed a resolution requesting Her Majesty's Government to introduce the necessary legislation to enable Nigeria to become an independent sovereign state with effect from 1st October 1960, and seeking the support of Britain for Nigeria's request that she should be accepted as a Member of the Commonwealth on Independence. The Senate endorsed the resolution a few days later.

Further amendments to the Constitution were made in January 1960.

At the end of the 1958 Conference the Secretary of State for the Colonies assumed that there would be further discussions in London in order to go over any detailed points outstanding in the Constitution. Such discussions were held in May 1960, and were attended by the Prime Minister and some Federal Ministers as well as the Regional Premiers with some Regional Ministers and the President of the Senate. A full agreement was reached on outstanding points in the Federal Constitution.

At a brief further Conference in Lagos in July 1960 details of the Regional Constitutions were agreed.

The Independence Act was passed by both Houses of the British Parliament in July 1960 and received the Royal Assent on 29th July. Accordingly the Federation of Nigeria achieved independence and became a Member of the Commonwealth on 1st October 1960. In 1963 it was decided that Nigeria should become a republic within the Commonwealth. The Federal Republic of Nigeria was duly inaugurated on 1st October 1963 with Dr Nnamdi Azikiwe as the first President.

CONSTITUTION

The constitution of the Federation Act was passed by the Nigerian Parliament on 19th September 1963 and provided for a Federal Government at Lagos and for Regional Governments in the four regions. Certain subjects were reserved exclusively for the Federal Government and certain were included in a concurrent list which could be dealt with either by the Federal or Regional Legislature, residual powers resting with the Regions.

The era of the first Republic came to an end on 15th January 1966 when a *coup d'état* was staged by a small group of Army officers. The Prime Minister of the Federation, the Federal Minister of Finance, the Premiers of the Northern and Western Regions and a number of Army officers were all murdered. Major-General J. T. U. Aguiyi-Ironsi at the time General Officer Commanding the Nigerian Army was invited by members of the Federal Cabinet in Lagos to head a Military Government to maintain law and order and to prevent further bloodshed. He established a Supreme Military Council for the maintenance of law and order and a National Executive Council to deal with other matters and appointed four Army officers as Military Governors in the Regions. The office of President of the Federation and all political offices were suspended. The former Governors of the Regions were invited to serve as advisers to the Regional Military Governors. All political activities were banned and Study Groups were established to advise on the future constitution of Nigeria.

However, before these Study Groups had reported, the Supreme Commander and Head of the Military Government published a Decree on 24th May abolishing the Federation and the Regions and establishing a unitary state. The

Military Government was designated the National Military Government and former regions were designated Groups of Provinces, administered however, by the same four Military Governors. This Decree was subsequently claimed by the National Military Government to be a temporary measure to facilitate the workings of the Government. On 29th July a second *coup d'état* was staged, this time by Northern Army officers, in which the Supreme Commander, Major-General Aguiyi-Ironsi and the Governor of the Western Group of Provinces, Lt-Col. Fajuyi, were abducted and killed. Lt-Col. Y. Gowon was subsequently invited by the majority of the surviving members of the Supreme Military Council to become Supreme Commander. One of his first acts was to abolish the unitary Decree of 24th May and to re-establish Nigeria as a Federation.

On 12th September 1966 a Constitutional Conference began in Lagos with representatives from each of the Regions, to try to reach agreement on a new Constitution acceptable to all Nigerians. No agreement had been reached by November 1966 when the Conference was adjourned, and on 27th May 1967, Lt-Col. Gowon—since promoted to Major-General—announced the abolition of the regions and the creation of 12 states in their place. He has incorporated civilians within the Federal Executive Council and reaffirmed his intention to restore civilian rule as soon as practicable.

On 30th May 1967 the Military Governor of Eastern Nigeria, Lt-Col. Ojukwu, declared the Region an independent sovereign state under the name of the Republic of Biafra. The Federal Government declared this step illegal and took immediate steps to bring the rebellion to an end. Fighting broke out in July.

Peace talks, under the auspices of the Commonwealth Secretariat, opened in Kampala on 23rd May 1968. No agreement was reached and the talks collapsed on 31st May. Subsequently, the Consultative Committee on Nigeria of the Organisation for African Unity (O.A.U.) succeeded in arranging further peace talks between the two sides. These took place in Niamey, Niger, from 15–26th July and continued from 5th August to the 6th September in Addis Ababa, still under O.A.U. auspices and under the Chairmanship of Emperor Haile Selassie.

An O.A.U. Summit Meeting at Algiers (13–16th September 1968) appealed unsuccessfully to the secessionist authorities "to restore peace and unity in Nigeria" and a further meeting of the O.A.U. in Monrovia (18–20th April 1969) again failed to produce a peace formula acceptable to both sides. The secessionist forces were defeated in a series of military actions in late December 1969 and early January 1970. Former secessionist officers formally surrendered to the F.M.G. on 15th January 1970.

On the tenth anniversary of Nigeria's Independence, in October 1970, General Gowon announced that it was the duty of the military to carry out nine basic tasks before handing over to civilian government. The target date for completing these—1976—was also announced.

Britain's concern for Nigeria has been demonstrated in many ways. The then British Prime Minister, Mr Harold Wilson, visited Lagos and the war-affected areas in 1969, and at the end of the Civil War he announced that up to £5 million would be made available to Nigeria for relief and rehabilitation. Some of this was spent on the massive airlift by which urgently needed transport and medical personnel were flown into Nigeria from Britain. By mid-1971, the balance of this special allocation had been committed for the provision of a great variety of medical, building, agricultural and fishing equipment. A seed-planting programme was also undertaken with the assistance of British voluntary agencies, which also made large contributions to the relief/rehabilitation effort.

As part of her normal aid programme H.M,G. announced in June 1971 that she would be contributing an additional £13 million to assist Nigeria in the implementation of her Second National Development Plan (1970-74). Taking into account her on-going commitments, this means that Britain will be providing over £37 million in aid to Nigeria during the period of this Plan.

HISTORICAL LIST

GOVERNORS-GENERAL

Sir James Robertson, KT, GCMG, GCVO, 1st October 1960 to 15th November 1960
Dr Nnamdi Azikiwe, 16th November 1960 to 30th September 1963

PRESIDENT

Dr Nnamdi Azikiwe, from 1st October 1963 to 17th January 1966

MINISTRIES

Alhaji Sir Abubakar Tafawa Balewa, KBE, MP, from 1st October 1960 to 15th January 1966

HEAD OF THE MILITARY GOVERNMENT AND SUPREME COMMANDER OF THE ARMED FORCES

Major-General J. T. U. Aguiyi-Ironsi from 17th January 1966 to 1st August 1966
Major-General Y. Gowon, from 1st August 1966

GOVERNMENT

The Federal Military Government governs through a Supreme Military Council, responsible for the maintenance of law and order, defence, and security of the State, and a Federal Executive Council.

FEDERAL MILITARY GOVERNMENT OF NIGERIA

The Supreme Military Council

The Head of the Federal Military Government, Commander in Chief of the Armed Forces
and President of the Council:
Major-General Y. Gowon
Chief of Naval Staff and Vice-President of the Council: Rear-Admiral J. E. A. Wey
The Head of the Nigerian Army: Major-General Y. Gowon
The Head of the Nigerian Air Force: Colonel E. E. Ikwue
Chief of Staff of the Armed Forces: Brigadier Ekpo
Chief of Staff of the Nigerian Army: Brigadier Hassan Usman Katsina
Inspector-General of Police: Alhaji Kam Selem, Brigadier D. A. Ejoor
Deputy Chief of Naval Staff and NOIC Lagos: Commodore Nelson B. Soroh
Commandant, Nigerian Defence Academy: Major-General R. A. Adebayo

Military Governor of:

Lagos State	Colonel M. O. Johnson
Western State	Colonel C. C. Rotimi
Kwara State	Lt-Col. D. L. Bamigboye
North Western State	Mallam Usman Faruk
North Central State	Lt-Col. Abba Kyari
Kano State	Alahji Audu Bako
North Eastern State	Lt-Col. Musa Usman (NAF)
Benu-Plateau State	Mr J. D. Gomwalk
South Eastern State	Col. J. J. Esuene (NAF)
East Central State	Mr A. Ukpabi Asika (Administrator)
Rivers State	Commander A. P. Diete-Spiff (NN)
Mid-Western State	Col. S. O. Ogbemudia

The Federal Executive Council

The Head of the Federal Military Government, Commander in Chief of the Armed Forces
and President of the Council:
Major-General Y. Gowon
The Vice-President of the Council and Commissioner for Finance:
(Vacant)

Chief of Naval Staff and Commissioner for Establishments:
Rear-Admiral J. E. A. Wey
The Head of the Nigerian Air Force: Col. E. E. Ikwue
Chief of Staff of the Armed Forces: Brigadier Ekpo
Chief of Staff of the Nigerian Army: Brigadier Hassan Katsina
Inspector General of the Nigeria Police and Commissioner for Internal Affairs:
Alhaji Kam Selem
Deputy Inspector General of the Nigeria Police: T. A. Fagbola
Attorney-General of the Federation and Commissioner for Justice:
Dr Taslim O. Elias

Commissioners for:
External Affairs	Dr Okoi Arikpo
Works and Housing	Mr Femi Okunnu
Health	Dr J. O. J. Okezie
Economic Development and Reconstruction	Alhaji Shehu Shagari
Agriculture and Natural Resources	Dr J. E. Adetoro
Mines and Power	Dr R. A. B. Dikko
Communications	Alhaji Aminu Kano
Trade and Industry	Alhaji Ali Monguno
Transport	Mr J. S. Tarka
Education	Dr Wenike Briggs
Information and Labour	Chief Anthony Enahoro

JUDICIARY:
Chief Justice: Sir Adetokunbo Ademola, KBE, CFR

Federal Justices (Supreme Court):
G. B. A. Coker	C. O. Madarikan
Sir Ian Lewis	A. Fatayi-Williams
Sir Udo Udoma	G. S. Sowemimo

High Court of Lagos:
Chief Justice: J. I. C. Taylor

Judges (High Court):
S. O. Lambo	B. O. Kazeem
E. A. Caxton-Martins	J. O. Kassim
J. A. Adefarasin	S. D. Adebiyi
O. R. I. George	M. N. Q. Sagoe
B. A. Adedipe	T. S. Gomez

MINISTRIES AND GOVERNMENT DEPARTMENTS

CABINET OFFICE
Secretary to the Federal Military Government: Mr. A. A. Atta.

MINISTRY OF EXTERNAL AFFAIRS
Permanent Secretary: Alhaji Baba Gana

MINISTRY OF DEFENCE
Permanent Secretary: Mallam I. M. Damcida

MINISTRY OF AGRICULTURE AND NATURAL RESOURCES
Permanent Secretary: Dr Bukar Shaib

MINISTRY OF COMMUNICATIONS
Permanent Secretary: Mr S. O. Williams

MINISTRY OF ECONOMIC DEVELOPMENT AND RECONSTRUCTION
Permanent Secretary: Mr I. J. Ebong

MINISTRY OF EDUCATION
Permanent Secretary: Alhaji Ahmed Joda

MINISTRY OF ESTABLISHMENTS
Permanent Secretary: Mr M. A. Tokunboh

MINISTRY OF FINANCE
Permanent Secretary: Mr A. A. Ayida

MINISTRY OF HEALTH
Permanent Secretary: Mr S. I. A. Akenzua

MINISTRY OF INDUSTRIES
Permanent Secretary: Mr A. Liman Ciroma

MINISTRY OF INFORMATION
Permanent Secretary: Alhaji Tatari Ali

MINISTRY OF INTERNAL AFFAIRS
Permanent Secretary: Mr S. B. Awoniyi

MINISTRY OF JUSTICE
Solicitor-General of the Federation and Permanent Secretary: Mr A. A. Adediran

MINISTRY OF LABOUR
Permanent Secretary: Mr S. O. Koku

MINISTRY OF MINES AND POWER	MINISTRY OF WORKS AND HOUSING

MINISTRY OF MINES AND POWER
Permanent Secretary: Mr P. C. Asiodu

MINISTRY OF TRADE
Permanent Secretary: Mr V. Adegoroye

MINISTRY OF TRANSPORT
Permanent Secretary: Mr C. O. Lawson

MINISTRY OF WORKS AND HOUSING
Permanent Secretary: Mr G. A. E. Longe

FEDERAL PUBLIC SERVICE COMMISSION
Chairman: Alhaji Sule Katagum, CBE, OTR

DIPLOMATIC REPRESENTATION

NIGERIAN HIGH COMMISSIONERS IN OTHER COMMONWEALTH COUNTRIES

Britain: Alhaji Sule Dede Kolo; Canada: E. O. Enahoro; The Gambia (resident in Dakar): Alhaji Muhammadu Sani Kontagora; India: J. N. Ukegbu; Pakistan: Alhaji Abdulraham Mora; Ghana: (to be appointed); Sierra Leone: (Acting) J. O. Omolodun; Kenya: Ignatius Olisemeka; Uganda: E. Etuk; Tanzania (Diplomatic relations broken off on 13th April 1968); Zambia: (Diplomatic relations broken off on 20th May 1968).

COMMONWEALTH HIGH COMMISSIONERS IN NIGERIA

Britain: Sir Cyril Pickard, KCMG; Australia: P. N. B. Hutton; Canada: A. S. McGill; Ghana: Major-General N. A. Aferi, DSO; India: A. N. Mehta (designate); Malaysia: T. H. Yogaratnam (Acting); Pakistan: Dr S. M. Koreshi; Sierra Leone: A. Mansaray; Zambia: (Diplomatic relations broken off on 20th May 1968);.

NIGERIAN REPRESENTATION IN NON-COMMONWEALTH COUNTRIES

Algeria (Chargé d'Affaires); Belgium (Ambassador); Brazil (Chargé d'Affaires); Cameroun Republic (Ambassador); Chad (Chargé d'Affaires); Congo (Kinshasa) (Ambassador);Dahomey(Chargé d'Affaires); Equatorial Guinea (Ambassador); Ethiopia (Ambassador); France (Ambassador); Germany (Ambassador); Guinea (Ambassador); Italy (Ambassador); Ivory Coast (relations broken off on 15th May 1968); Japan (Ambassador); Liberia (Ambassador); Mali (Chargé d'Affaires); Morocco (Chargé d'Affaires); Netherlands (Ambassador); Niger (Chargé d'Affaires); Republic of Ireland (Ambassador) (resident in London); Poland (Chargé d'Affaires); Saudi Arabia (Ambassador) (resident in Khartoum); Senegal (Ambassador); Sudan (Ambassador); Sweden (Chargé d'Affaires); Switzerland (Chargé d'Affaires); Togo (Ambassador) (resident in Accra); United Arab Republic (Ambassador); United Nations (Permanent Representative); United States (Ambassador); U.S.S.R. (Ambassador); Warsaw (Chargé d'Affaires).

Nigeria broke off diplomatic relations with Tanzania, Zambia and the Ivory Coast following their recognition of Biafra.

THE STATES

The twelve States were established by decree of 27th May 1967; they are;

Central Eastern State   Aba, Abakaliki, Afikpo Awgu, Awka, Bende, Nsukka, Okigwe, Onitsha, Orlu, Owerri and Udi divisions.

Lagos State   The Federal Territory and Badagry, Epe and Ikeja divisions.

Rivers State   Ahoada, Brass, Degema, Ogoni and Port Harcourt divisions.

Western State   Egba, Egbado, Ekiti, Ibadan, Ife, Ijebu, Ijebu Remo, Ilesha, Okitipupa, Ondo, Oshun, Owo and Oyo divisions.

South Eastern State   Ogoja, Obudu, Obubra, Ikom, Abak, Calabar, Eket, Nyong, Ikot-Ekpene, Opobo and Uyo divisions.

Kwara State   Ilorin, Lafiagi-Pategi, Borgu, Igala, Igbirra, Kabba and Kwara, Koton-Karfi divisions.

Mid-Western State   Aboh, Afenmai, Akoko-Edo, Asaba, Benin, Ishan, Isoko, Urhobo, Warri and Western Ijaw divisions.

North Central State   Katsina, Jema'a, Kaduna Capital Territory and Zaria divisions.

Benue-Plateau State Akwanga, (Southern) Idoma, Lafia, Nasarawa, Tiv, Wukari, Jos, Lowland (Shendam) and Pankshin divisions.

North-Western State Argungu, Gwandu, Sokoto, Abuja, Bida, Kontagora and Minna divisions.

North-Eastern State Bedde, Biu, Bornu, Dikwa, Potiskum, Adamawa, Muri, Numan, Sardauna (Northern), Sardauna (Southern), Bauchi, Gombe and Katagum divisions.

Kano State Kano and Northern divisions.

Each state has its own Military Governor and (almost entirely) civilian Executive Council. Each state has its own civil service and its own capital and receives a defined individual share of the Federal Revenue. The Military Governors are members of the Supreme Military Council and each State has its own civilian representative on the Federal Executive Council.

NIGERIAN TITLES

NORTHERN STATES

Note: The possessive is formed by adding 'n' to the end of the title, *e.g.* Galadiman Pategi or Galadima of Pategi (although Dallater becomes Dallatun, and Wambai becomes Wamban).

Alhaji	One who has performed the pilgrimage to Mecca.
Alkali	Moslem Judge.
Atta(h)	Chief.
Ciroma	Eldest son of an Emir.
Dallater	District Head.
Galadima	District Head.
Kadi	Chief Moslem Judge.
Ma'ajin	Treasurer.
Magajin Garin	District Head
Magatakarda	Chief Scribe.
Mai	Kanuri title for Emir or Administrative Head. Equivalent to Hausa 'Sarki'.
Makama	District Head.
Mallam	Moslem scholar. In normal use equivalent to 'Mr'.
Sardauna	Chief District Head
Sarki	Title for an Emir or District Head. Nearest English equivalent 'Governor', *e.g.* Sarkin Fadan Zazzau—Governor of Internal Domestic Affairs, Zazzau; and Sarkin Fillanin Ja'idanawa—Governor of Ja'idanawa (a sect of Fillanin).
Shehu	Title accorded to a very learned man.
Shettima	Leader of Moslem scholars. Equivalent to an Honorary Doctorate.
Tafida	District Head.
Turaki	District Head
Wali	Legal Adviser.
Wambai	District Head.
Waziri	Vizier or Chief Minister, *e.g.* Wazirin Ayyukan Katsina—Chief Minister of Works, Katsina.
Zanna	Equivalent to English title 'Lord' (Kanuri).

WESTERN STATE AND MID-WESTERN STATE

There are numerous individual titles in Western and Mid-Western Nigeria, *e.g.* Oni, Alake, Olubadan, Ataoja and Olu. The title is normally prefixed to the name of a district, in which case the titles mentioned above become Oni of Ife, Alake of Abeokuta, Olubadan of Ibadan, Ataoja of Oshogbo and Olu of Warri. When not so prefixed, the word 'Oba' meaning 'Ruler' of a district may be used in place of the title, *e.g.* 'Oba of Lagos' and 'Oba of Benin'. The titles may further be preceded by the personal names of the holders of the titles in the same manner as the names of monarchs of England and other European countries, *e.g.* His Highness Aderemi II, the Oni of Ife; His Highness Gbadebo II, the Alake of Abeokuta, or His Highness Akenzua II, the Oba of Benin. In recent times the words 'His Highness' are most often replaced in Western Nigeria by the Yoruba equivalent 'Oba Alaiyeluwa'.

NIGERIAN STATE ORDERS, DECORATIONS AND MEDALS

GCON	Grand Commander of the Order of the Niger
CON	Commander of the Order of the Niger
OON	Officer of the Order of the Niger
MON	Member of the Order of the Niger
GCFR	Grand Commander of the Order of the Federal Republic
CFR	Commander of the Order of the Federal Republic
OFR	Officer of the Order of the Federal Republic
MFR	Member of the Order of the Federal Republic

PAKISTAN

THE Islamic Republic of Pakistan consists of two physically separate wings, East and West, on opposite sides of the Indian sub-continent and more than 1,000 miles apart. West Pakistan comprises the provinces of Sind, North West Frontier Province (NWFP), Baluchistan and Punjab (West Punjab of undivided India). The former Princely States of Swat, Dir and Chitral form part of the NWFP, Bahawalpur of Punjab and Kalat of Baluchistan. The territory of the official capital, Islamabad, as well as some of the tribal areas, falls under the direct jurisdiction of the central government, The commercial capital, Karachi, is now part of Sind. East Pakistan, much smaller in area and much more densely populated than West Pakistan, comprises the former province of East Bengal together with the Sylhet District of Assam. The total area of Pakistan is 365,529 square miles. In West Pakistan the mountain ranges lie on a north-east south-west axis. In the extreme north-east are the Chitral mountains, part of the Hindu Kush range, in which is located Pakistan's highest mountain Tirich Mir (25,230 feet above sea level). The average height of the Chitral mountains and the Sulaiman range which adjoins, running to South Waziristan, is about 14,000 feet. From South Waziristan the Kirthar range runs south-west to the Mekran range (average height 6,000 feet).

The five main rivers of West Pakistan are the Indus, the Jhelum, the Chenab, the Ravi and the Sutlej. It was from these five rivers (*panjab*) that the Punjab took its name. Most of the province of East Pakistan consists of an alluvial plain, forming part of the Gangetic delta. It is crossed by a network of navigable rivers, including the eastern arms of the Ganges, the Jamuna (or Bramaputra) and the Meghna, flowing into the Bay of Bengal.

West Pakistan has an arid and semi-arid climate with three distinct seasons. Winter lasts from November to February, summer from March to June and the monsoon period July to September. The climate is more extreme inland than on the coast. The inland plains are hot in summer and cool or cold in winter: in January and February the night temperature may drop to freezing point, while in the summer maximum temperatures range between 32°C (89·6°F) and 49°C (120°F). The annual rainfall varies in different regions from about 4 inches to 40 inches, most of it falling in July, August and September. The southern areas are arid and depend on irrigation from rivers and canals.

East Pakistan has a tropical monsoon climate, hot and extremely humid during the summer and mild and dry during the short winter. The rainfall is heavy, ranging from 50 inches to 135 inches in different districts, and the bulk of

An outline of the history and constitutional development of the Indian sub-continent prior to August 1947 may be found in the *Commonwealth Office Year Book*, 1967.

it falls during the monsoon season (from June to September). The mean temperature during the winter (November to February) is about 20°C (68°F) and during the hot season 30°C (86°F).

The total population, according to the 1961 census, was 93,721,000 of whom 42,881,000 lived in West Pakistan and 50,840,235 in East Pakistan. 1961 census figures for the principal towns were Rawalpindi 340,175, Karachi 1,912,598, Lahore 1,296,477, Dacca 556,712, Hyderabad 434,537, Lyallpur 425,248, Chittagong 364,205. The estimated present population of the country (1971) is 132 millions. West Pakistan 60 million; East Pakistan 72 million.

Until 1960 the capital of Pakistan was Karachi. It was then announced that Rawalpindi was to be the principal seat of the Central Government of Pakistan until a new capital had been built at Islamabad, a few miles north of Rawalpindi. This decision was reaffirmed in the 1962 Constitution which also declared that Dacca was to be the second capital and principal seat of the National Assembly. The President lives at Rawalpindi; all the main offices of the Central Government and most of the Diplomatic Corps are now in Islamabad. The Assembly used to meet alternately at Dacca and Rawalpindi. Islamabad had a population of 30,000 in 1968, but this is increasing steadily.

The national languages of Pakistan are Bengali and Urdu, but the English language may be used for official and other purposes until arrangements for its replacement are made. The question of the replacement of the English language for official purposes is under consideration. Various regional languages are in use in West Pakistan, the main ones being Punjabi, Pushtu, Sindhi and Baluchi. Other languages, such as Gujarati, are also used by Pakistanis who used to live in India.

About 90 per cent of the population of Pakistan are Muslims. The majority of the remaining 10 per cent are Hindus, most of whom live in East Pakistan. There are smaller communities of Christians and Buddhists in both wings of the country, and a few Parsis.

National Day: Pakistan Day, 23rd March.

EDUCATION

Primary education (from 6–11) is free but not yet universal; 45 per cent of the children eligible were estimated to be at school in 1965. Enrolment in secondary schools is over $2\frac{1}{2}$ millions (1967). There are twelve universities with a 1966-7 enrolment of 24,409, three specialise in agriculture and two in engineering. But to this total should be added the 300,000 students in the degree-granting general arts and science colleges which are affiliated to universities and sometimes on the same campus. Literacy is estimated at 19 per cent of the whole population and 29 per cent of the male population.

TRANSPORT AND COMMUNICATIONS

Principal seaports, with total import and export tonnages for 1968/69 in millions, are Karachi 8·4; Chittagong 4·5; Chalna 2·2. The principal shipping line is the National Shipping Corporation.

The principal airports with runway lengths in feet are: Karachi (10,500 and 7,500); Lahore (7,500 and 5,040); Islamabad (9,700 at present but capable of extension to 12,000); Dacca (9,000); Chittagong (6,000 and 5,500), Quetta (12,000) and Peshawar (9,000). The national airline is Pakistan International

Airways, which provides all domestic services and operates a substantial network of international services.

There are about 26,600 miles of roads in Pakistan (22,700 in West Pakistan and 3,900 in East Pakistan). Out of this total about 12,700 miles are metalled (1969); 10,300 in West Pakistan and 2,400 in East Pakistan.

There are 10,204 miles of railway track in Pakistan: 7,604 in West Pakistan and 2,600 in East Pakistan. The main gauge is 5 ft. 6 in. but there are also about 2,036 miles of metre gauge (3 ft. 3¾ in.) and 475 miles of narrow gauge (2 ft. 6 in.). Radio Pakistan, under the control of the Central Government, provides the sole national broadcasting service. A television service was introduced in Lahore and Dacca in 1965, and in Rawalpindi and Karachi in 1967.

THE ECONOMY

The economy of Pakistan is regulated in accordance with a series of Five Year Plans, the fourth of which commenced in July 1970. A main objective of these Plans, the attainment of food grain self-sufficiency, has now been largely achieved through the use of improved strains of wheat and rice, increased fertiliser inputs and the extension of the irrigation system. Overall economic growth rates achieved in recent years are, at 1959/60 constant prices: 1965/66 4·6 per cent, 1966/67 5·0 per cent, 1967/68 7·5 per cent, 1968/69 5·7 per cent and 1969/70 5·8 per cent. The objectives of the Fourth Plan are to continue economic growth at a projected rate of at least 6·5 per cent per annum with special emphasis on reducing the disparity between the East and West Wings, and also to achieve a better balance between economic and social objectives, notably by increasing educational facilities and a wider distribution of wealth and income.

Disbursements of aid to Pakistan in 1969/70 are estimated to be US$550 million of which $423 million were provided by the World Bank-sponsored Pakistan Consortium, and about $127 million from other sources. Total foreign assistance over the Third Plan period amounted to approximately $2,830 million. Pakistan's foreign trade in 1969/70 showed a deficit of visibles of Rs.1,761 million, with imports totalling Rs.5,098 million and exports Rs.3,337 million. (Official exchange rate: Rs.11.43=£1). Main exports were raw jute (Rs. 762·4 million), jute manufactures (Rs.516·6 million); raw cotton (Rs.224·6 million); cotton twist yarn and thread (Rs.280·1 million) and cotton fabrics (Rs.269·7 million). In 1969/70 the United States was Pakistan's principal trading partner, taking 11·4 per cent of Pakistan's exports and supplying nearly 26·8 per cent of her imports. The United Kingdom provided the second largest market for Pakistan's exports (11·3 per cent) and supplied nearly 11·4 per cent of her imports. Japan and Hong Kong were Pakistan's third and fourth largest markets respectively.

The Central Government Budget for 1970/71 provided for revenue expenditure of Rs.5,572 million and development expenditure of Rs.7,270 million. The total is the largest in the country's history and budgeted revenue surplus for the year, at Rs.1,589 million, is greater than the entire revenue for 1954/55. The principal sources of Central Government revenue from taxation will be Customs 21 per cent, Internal Excise 31 per cent and Income and Corporation taxes 12·6 per cent. Further measures to augment revenue inflows were announced in early 1971. The Development Budget will be provided from foreign development credits (30 per cent) and loans and grants from internal resources (52 per cent). Principal items of expenditure from the Revenue Budget are Defence 54 per cent, Civil Administration 13 per cent, Grants to Provincial Governments 6 per cent and interest payments 20 per cent of total reserve.

Particular attention has been paid to power and irrigation. In West Pakistan the coming into service of the hydro-electric installations at the Mangla Dam on the Jhelum River (one of the Indus Basin Works) and the completion of the thermal power stations at Lyallpur and Multan, will provide sufficient capacity into the early 1970s. Thereafter they will be supplemented by the Tarbela Dam on the Upper Indus, now under construction and due to be completed in 1975, and by the Canadian-financed nuclear power station at Karachi. In East Pakistan installed power generating capacity was over 300 megawatts in 1968, being provided by thermal power stations supplemented by gas turbine units. Many large projects are underway to provide flood protection, irrigation and drainage.

The high cumulative growth of G.N.P. is not reflected by a corresponding increase in per caput income because of the population increase, current estimates of which vary between 2·7% and 3·3% per annum. The Government is vigorously supporting a family planning programme.

CONSTITUTIONAL DEVELOPMENT FROM 1947

The Indian Independence Act of 1947 provided that the Government of India Act of 1935 should remain in force in the two new Dominions and empowered the Governor-General of each Dominion to modify the Act in accordance with its needs. Such modifications were made for Pakistan by the Pakistan (Provisional Constitution) Order of 1947, and the Government of India Act thus modified and as subsequently amended remained the Constitution of Pakistan until 23rd March 1956.

After partition, the Constituent Assembly, which was composed of those members of the pre-partition Constituent Assembly of India who had been elected from provinces which acceded to Pakistan, formed committees to submit recommendations on various aspects of the desired Constitution. Work was slow, partly because of the general difficulties which faced Pakistan after independence and partly because the Constituent Assembly had also to discharge legislative functions. In 1954 the Basic Principles Committee finally submitted a lengthy report setting out in great detail the main terms of the Constitution. The Government hoped that they would be able to introduce and pass the Bill giving effect to these proposals by the end of that year. In October 1954, however, it became clear that there was fundamental disagreement in the country and amongst politicians on many of the provisions of the proposed Constitution and the Governor-General issued a proclamation dissolving the Constituent Assembly on the grounds that it had lost the confidence of the people.

At the request of the Governor-General, the Prime Minister, Mr Mohammed Ali, formed a new administration under which indirect elections were held in June 1955 for a new Constituent Assembly. Seventy-two members were returned by the provincial legislatures of East Bengal, the Punjab, the North West Frontier Province and Sind, and from representative bodies in Baluchistan and Karachi; to these were later added eight members representing the States and the tribal areas. These elections were delayed by protracted litigation on the Governor-General's power to dissolve the former Constituent Assembly. The issue was finally settled in the Governor-General's favour by the Federal Court, and the new Constituent Assembly met in July 1955. It immediately became apparent that the Prime Minister could not command a majority in the new Assembly and a Cabinet reshuffle in August 1955 placed Chaudhri Mohamad Ali at the head of a Coalition Government committed to introducing a Constitution as quickly as possible.

Certain preliminary measures were necessary before a Constitution could be introduced, chief among which was a Bill to amalgamate the provinces of West Pakistan into a single unit, both on grounds of administrative efficiency and in order to achieve strict parity with East Pakistan. The Establishment of West Pakistan Act (*see* page 348) came into force on 14th October 1955, and, after several drafts had been considered and after protracted and difficult discussion within the Coalition Party, the new Constitution was finally presented to the Constituent Assembly in January 1956. A lengthy debate, involving many late sittings and 'guillotine' threats from the Government, ensued and the Constitution finally received the Governor-General's assent on 2nd March 1956. On 23rd March 1956 the Islamic Republic of Pakistan came into being, the Governor-General was elected the first President by the Constituent Assembly and the Constituent Assembly became the National Assembly empowered to carry on until the first elections under the new Constitution. A summary of the provisions of the Constitution of 1956 can be found in pages 172 to 174 of *The Commonwealth Relations Office List*, 1958.

PROCLAMATION OF MARTIAL LAW

On 7th October 1958 Martial Law was proclaimed, the Constitution abrogated, the Central and Provincial Governments dismissed, the National Parliament and Provincial Assemblies dissolved, political parties abolished, and General Mohammad Ayub Khan, Commander-in-Chief, Pakistan Army, appointed Chief Martial Law Administrator with command of all the armed forces of Pakistan. On 27th October 1958 General Mohammad Ayub Khan assumed the Presidency.

BASIC DEMOCRACIES

The Basic Democracies Order, promulgated on 27th October 1959, together with the Municipal Administration Ordinance, promulgated on 11th April 1960, provided the legal basis for a new system of local self-government. The 'basic democracies' were the Union Councils in rural areas and the Union Committees and Town Committees in urban areas. These were the basic institutions of a system of Councils leading up to the higher-level administrative units at the *Tehsil*, *Thana* sub-division or Municipality, and above them at the District and Division.

By the Presidential (Election and Constitution) Order promulgated on 13th January 1960 it was provided that the 80,000 elected members of the basic democracies should declare by vote in a secret ballot whether or not they had confidence in President Mohammad Ayub Khan. The Order added that in the event of a majority favourable to the President he should be deemed thereby both to have been given authority to proceed with the making of a Constitution and also to have been elected President of Pakistan to hold office thenceforward and for the first term of office of the President under that Constitution.

The Presidential ballot was accordingly held on 14th February 1960 when over 95·6 per cent of the total number of votes cast were affirmative.

Field-Marshal Mohammad Ayub Khan (as he had become on 27th October 1959) was therefore sworn in as the first elected President of Pakistan on 17th February 1960.

Following the ceremony, the President announced the appointment of a Constitution Commission. Its report, submitted on 6th May 1961, was considered by a Committee of the Cabinet, and following a series of deliberations at cabinet level, President Ayub promulgated a new Constitution for Pakistan on 1st March 1962.

The main provisions of the 1962 Constitution to which there had been eight amendments (to March 1969) are summarized on pages 315-318 of *A Year Book of the Commonwealth* 1969.

Elections to the National and to the Provincial Assemblies were held in April and May 1962 and the new National Assembly met for the first time on 8th June, when Martial Law was withdrawn.

The first general election since the introduction of the 1962 Constitution took place between November 1964 and May 1965. It comprised four separate elections. The Electoral College was elected in November 1964 and this was followed by the Presidential election in January 1965, when President Ayub Khan was re-elected to fill the presidential office for a further five years from 23rd March 1965. The National and Provincial Assemblies elections were held in March and May and the first session of the National Assembly was inaugurated by the President on 12th June 1965. Provision was made for the Electoral College to be expanded to 120,000 members by the Electoral College (Amendment) Act, 1967. President Yahya Khan retained the structure of Basic Democracies, but renamed it Local Government.

INDO-PAKISTAN HOSTILITIES, 1965

A dispute over the ownership of a part of the Rann of Kutch resulted in a minor outbreak of hostilities between Pakistan and India on 4th April 1965. Following the intervention of the British Prime Minister, a *de facto* cease-fire came into effect on 30th April 1965, and was confirmed under an agreement signed on 30th June 1965. The agreement also provided for a withdrawal of forces and the appointment of a tribunal for the settlement of the dispute. This international tribunal reported in February 1968. Its conclusions, that 10 per cent of the area in dispute should go to Pakistan and the rest to India, were accepted by both India and Pakistan. Demarcation of this area has now been completed.

A more serious conflict between the two countries occurred in August/September 1965, when the armed forces of Pakistan and India were heavily engaged. After three United Nations Security Council Resolutions calling for a cease-fire and withdrawal, the two countries agreed to a cease-fire on 22nd September. Withdrawals did not follow until the President of Pakistan and the Prime Minister of India had signed an Agreement at Tashkent, U.S.S.R., on 10th January 1966.

It was agreed at Tashkent to hold further talks between the two countries about ways of resolving the conflict. The first such ministerial meeting was held in Rawalpindi in March 1966, but agreement has not yet been reached to hold a further meeting. Talks between officials have, however, been held to discuss such technical subjects as telecommunications and the Farakka Barrage project on the Ganges.

M

POLITICAL AND CONSTITUTIONAL DEVELOPMENTS 1968-71

Several months of disturbances of an increasingly political nature, beginning with students' demonstrations in Rawalpindi in November 1968, led President Ayub to make, in February 1969, an offer of talks on constitutional changes to the opposition politicians. After certain relaxations had been made by the Government, such as the ending of the State of Emergency introduced in September 1965, talks were held in March 1969, but led only to agreement on a parliamentary system of government with elections to be held on adult franchise. Other questions, e.g. of relative regional powers, remained undecided. Faced with continuing disturbance in industry and the countryside, President Ayub, who had in February announced his decision not to stand for re-election in 1969–70, resigned on 25th March 1969 and handed over to the Commander-in-Chief of the Army, General Yahya Khan. General Yahya immediately declared the country under Martial Law with himself as Chief Martial Law Administrator, abrogated the 1962 Constitution, and dissolved the three Assemblies. The two Governors and all Ministers ceased to hold office. General Yahya assumed the office of President on 31st March 1969 with the declared aims of improving the standards of administration and creating a peaceful and settled atmosphere in which elections could be held on adult franchise to a parliament. He appointed a Chief Election Commissioner to draw up electoral rolls and a Council of Ministers.

In a broadcast to the nation on 28th November 1969, President Yahya discussed the formation of a new constitution and the progress of Pakistan to democratic government. He said that there was no disagreement in the country on certain issues such as the need for a parliamentary federal form of government, for direct adult franchise, for safeguarding the rights of citizens and the independence of the judiciary, and for a constitution of Islamic character which would preserve the ideology on which Pakistan was created. In the light of his soundings of public opinion the President had decided that there was a general desire to revert to a system of separate provinces instead of the arrangement of One Unit in West Pakistan and also a desire that elections should be based on the principle of one man one vote. Other aspects of the constitution, in particular, the relationship between the Centre and the Provinces, would be decided by a Constituent Assembly to be elected on 5th October 1970. If the Assembly failed to complete this task in 120 days it would stand dissolved and the nation would go to the polls again. Meanwhile Martial Law would remain supreme and work would continue on electoral rolls and the delimitation of constituencies.

On 1st January 1970 normal political activity was permitted again within the standards of conduct laid down in Martial Law Regulation 60.

In a broadcast to the nation on 28th March 1970, President Yahya stressed that progress must be orderly. West Pakistan would revert as closely as possible to the pre-One Unit position, and the new provincial Administrations would start operating by 1st July 1970. Elections to all Provincial Assemblies would be held not later than 22nd October 1970, but the Assemblies would not function until after Presidential authentication of the constitution. The Legal Framework Order published on 30th March gave the main base for the operation of the National Assembly. Seats, including some reserved for women, were allocated to Provinces on the basis of population, thus:

	General	Women
East Pakistan	162	7
Punjab	82	3
Sind	27	1
Baluchistan	4	1
North-West Frontier Province	18 ⎫	
Centrally Administered	⎬	1
Tribal Areas	7 ⎭	
Totals	300	13

The National Assembly would decide its own voting procedures. The Order also gave five basic principles for the constitution—Islamic ideology, integrity of Pakistan, democracy, maximum autonomy for Provinces while retaining adequate powers for the Centre, removal of disparity between different regions.

The President's announcements about the break up of One Unit in West Pakistan were put into effect by the Province of West Pakistan (Dissolution) Order 1970 published on 1st April.

The elections to the National and Provincial Assemblies, originally due to be held on 5th and 22nd October 1970, were postponed until 7th and 17th December on account of serious floods in East Pakistan at the beginning of August. In the event, a far more serious natural catastrophe took place there on 12th and 13th November when a cyclone caused immense flood damage and loss of life. Despite this, the elections were not postponed a second time but proceeded on schedule except in the worst affected areas where pollling was held in January 1971. The result of the elections was a large majority in East Pakistan for the Awami League, led by Sheikh Mujibur Rahman (which won 160 out of 300 "general" seats in the National Assembly) and a narrower majority in West Pakistan for the Pakistan People's Party under Mr Z. A. Bhutto (which won 81 of the 138 National Assembly "general" seats available in that wing). Elections for 13 National Assembly seats reserved for women were never held.

To allow time for the leaders of the two major parties to reach prior agreement on the outline of the future constitution the President deferred summoning the National Assembly until 13th February, when he announced that its opening session would take place in Dacca on 3rd March. Disagreement however persisted between Sheikh Mujib and Mr Bhutto and the latter was led in February to insist that failing the receipt from Sheikh Mujib of assurances that his point of view would be heard and taken into account when framing the constitution neither he nor his party would attend the Assembly. And on 1st March the President announced that the National Assembly would be postponed *sine die*. He appointed the four governors of the West Pakistan Provinces as Martial Law Administrators in their areas and Lt. Gen. Yaqub Khan, Martial Law Admin-East Pakistan, to assume additional civil administration duties in place of the former governor, Vice-Admiral Ahsan.

On the announcement of the postponement of the National Assembly, Sheikh Mujib declared a hartal (strike) and non-cooperation movement in East Pakistan which was implemented on 2nd March and continued, though with some relaxation, for the next three weeks. During this time, the Awami League in effect assumed administrative control of East Pakistan. On 3rd March the

President invited Sheikh Mujib and 11 other leaders of parliamentary parties to meet in Dacca on 10th March: Mujib refused.

On 6th March President Yahya broadcast to he Nation announcing that the National Assembly would be convened in Dacca on 25th March and appealing to the party leaders to sink their differences in the interests of national unity. He said that he would himself go to Dacca in an attempt to facilitate agreement. Mr Bhutto then stated that he would attend the Assembly on 25th March and was also prepared to fly to Dacca for meetings with Sheikh Mujib. The latter, however, announced in a speech on 7th March that he would only attend the Assembly on four conditions: the withdrawal of Martial Law, the return of troops in East Pakistan to their barracks, the establishment of an official enquiry into the shooting of a number of civilians in East Pakistan on 2nd March and the transfer of power to elected representatives.

President Yahya flew to Dacca on 15th March and engaged in consultations with Sheikh Mujib and later with Mr Bhutto, which continued until 22nd March when it appeared that there was good hope of an agreement. In a broadcast to the Nation on 23rd March (Pakistan Day) President Yahya said that the stage was set for the elected representatives to work together for the common goal. But this hope of agreement proved illusory.

On the night of 25th/26th March the army arrested Sheikh Mujib as a traitor and reassumed control of Dacca, and subsequently of other major cities in East Pakistan, at the cost of considerable loss of life. In a broadcast on 26th March, the President announced a ban on political activities throughout the country, a ban on the Awami League as a political party, and complete press censorship. He reiterated that his main aim remained the transfer of power to the elected representatives of the people and that as soon as the situation permitted he would take fresh steps towards the achievement of this object.

HISTORICAL LIST OF HEADS OF STATE

GOVERNORS-GENERAL
(Dominion of Pakistan)

Quaid-i-Azam Mohammed Ali Jinnah, 15th August 1947 to 11th September 1948
Khwaja Nazimuddin, 14th September 1948 to 17th October 1951
Ghulam Mohammad, 19th October 1951 to 5th October 1955
Major-General Iskander Mirza, 6th October 1955 to 22nd March 1956

PRESIDENTS
(Republic of Pakistan)

Major-General Iskander Mirza, 23rd March 1956 to 27th October 1958
General (later Field-Marshal) Mohammad Ayub Khan, NPk, HJ, 27th October 1958 to 8th June 1962
Field-Marshal Mohammad Ayub Khan, NPk, HJ, 8th June 1962 to 23rd March 1965
Field-Marshal Mohammad Ayub Khan, NPk, HJ, from 23rd March 1965 to 25th March 1969
General Agha Muhammad Yahya Khan, HPk, HJ from 31st March 1969 (with retroactive effect from 25th March 1969)

HISTORICAL LIST OF MINISTRIES

Quaid-i-Millat Liaqat Ali Khan, 15th August 1947 to 16th October 1951
Khwaja Nazimuddin, 17th October 1951 to 17th April 1953
Mohammed Ali (Bogra), 17th April 1953 to 10th August 1955
Chaudhri Mohamad Ali, 11th August 1955 to 12th September 1956
H. S. Suhrawardy, 12th September 1956 to 18th October 1957
I. I. Chundrigar, 18th October 1957 to 16th December 1957
Malik Firoz Khan Noon, 16th December 1957 to 7th October 1958

GOVERNMENT

President, Chief Martial Law Administration, Supreme Commander-in-Chief, and Chairman of the Martial Law Council of Administrators:
General Agha Mohammad Yahya Khan, H Pk, H J

COUNCIL OF ADMINISTRATION
(Deputy Chief Martial Law Administrators)
Lieutenant-General Abdul Hamid Khan, HQA, SPk
Vice-Admiral Muzaffar Hasan, HQA, SK
Air Marshal A. Rahim Khan, HQA, SPk, SBT

JUDICIARY
Chief Justice, Supreme Court: Hamood-ur-Rahman
Chief Justice, East Pakistan High Court: B. A. Siddiky
Chief Justice, West Pakistan High Court: Qadar-ud-Din Ahmed

ARMED FORCES
Commander-in-Chief, Pakistan Army: General A. M. Yahya Khan, HPk, HJ
Commander-in-Chief, Pakistan Navy: Vice-Admiral Muzaffar Hasan, HQA, SK
Commander-in-Chie f, Pakistan Air Force: Air Marshal A. Rahim Khan, HQA, SPk, SBT

MINISTRIES AND GOVERNMENT DEPARTMENTS

PRESIDENT'S SECRETARIAT (PUBLIC)
Principal Staff Officer to the President: Lieutenant-General S. G. M. M. Peerzada, SQA

PRESIDENT'S SECRETARIAT (PERSONAL)
Military Secretary to the President: Major-General Mohammad Ishaq
Economic Adviser to the President: M. M. Ahmad, HQA, SPk, CSP, CAPS

CABINET SECRETARIAT
(including Establishment Division)
Secretary: Ghulam Ishaq Khan, HQA, SPK, CSP

COMMERCE
Secretary: V. A. Jaffery, SQA, CSP

COMMUNICATIONS
Minister: Dr G. W. Choudhury
Secretary: Ali Hasan, SQA, TPk, CSP

DEFENCE
Secretary: S. Ghiasuddin Ahmed, HQA, SPk, SQA, CSP

ECONOMIC CO-ORDINATION AND EXTERNAL ASSISTANCE DIVISION
Secretary: S. S. Iqbal Hussain, SQA, PMAS

EDUCATION AND SCIENTIFIC RESEARCH
Secretary: Dr Z. A. Hashmi, SQA
Establishment Division Secretary: Vagar Ahmed, SP k, SQA, PA & AS

FINANCE
Secretary: A. G. N. Kazi, SP k, SK, CSP

FOOD, AGRICULTURE AND WORKS
Secretary: A. K. M. Ahsan, TQA, CSP

FOREIGN AFFAIRS
Secretary: S. M. Khan, SPk, SQA, PFS
Additional Secretary: Mumtaz A. Alvie, PFS

HEALTH, LABOUR, SOCIAL WELFARE AND FAMILY PLANNING
Secretary: Mian Riazuddin Ahmad, CSP

HOME, KASHMIR AFFAIRS AND STATES AND FRONTIER REGIONS
Secretary: S. A. Chaudhury

INDUSTRIES AND NATURAL RESOURCES
Secretary: Qamarul Islam, SPk, SQA, CSP

INFORMATION AND BROADCASTING
Secretary: Roedad Khan, SQA, TPk, CSP

LAW AND PARLIAMENTARY AFFAIRS
Secretary: Justice Mohammed Gul, SK
Attorney-General: Syed Sharifuddin Pirzada,

PLANNING DIVISION
Deputy Chairman: M. H. Sufi, SPk, SQA, CSP
Secretary: A. Rab, SQA, EPCS

DIPLOMATIC REPRESENTATION

PAKISTAN HIGH COMMISSIONERS IN OTHER
COMMONWEALTH COUNTRIES

Australia: M. Aslam Malik; Britain: Solman A. Ali, SQA; Canada: M. S. Sheikh; Ceylon: A. A. Sheikh; Cyprus: M. R. Ahmed (resident in Beirut); Gambia: Mohd. Shahryar Khan (resident in Dakar); Ghana: S. A. Moid; Guyana: (resident in Ottawa); Hong Kong: Ahmad Ali Khan (Trade Commissioner); India: Sajjad Hyder, SQA; Jamaica: (resident in Washington); Kenya: Air Vice-Marshal Mohammed Khyber Khan SQA; Malaysia : S Irtiza Hussain; Malta: Hamid Nawaz Khan (resident in Rome); Mauritius: M. Anwar Khan (Acting High Commissioner); New Zealand: (resident in Canberra); Nigeria: Dr S. M. Koreshi; Sierra Leone: (resident in Accra); Singapore: H. Imam (resident in Rangoon); Tanzania: M. R. Ahmad; Trinidad and Tobago: (resident in Ottawa); Uganda: (resident in Nairobi).

COMMONWEALTH HIGH COMMISSIONERS
IN PAKISTAN

Australia: F. H. Stuart; Britain: J. L. Pumphrey, CMG; Canada: C. J. Small; Ceylon: Faisal Juraid, OBE; Ghana:

Maj-Gen. C. C. Bruce, CBE; India: B. K Acharya; Malaysia: Mohammed Sopieebin Shaikh Ibrahim; Mauritius: Ameer Kasanally; Nigeria: H. D. Kolo (Acting).

PAKISTAN REPRESENTATION IN
NON-COMMONWEALTH COUNTRIES

Afghanistan; Albania*; Algeria; Argentina; Austria; Belgium; Bolivia*; Brazil; Bulgaria; Burma; Cambodia*; Cameroon*; Chad*; Chile*; China; Cuba*; Czechoslovakia; Dahomey*; Denmark*; Ethiopia*; Finland*; France; Gambia*; Germany; Greece*; Guinea*; Holy See*; Hungary*; Indonesia; Iran; Iraq; Irish Republic*; Italy; Ivory Coast*; Japan; Jordan; Kuwait; Laos*; Lebanon; Liberia*; Libya; Luxembourg*; Malagasy Republic*; Maldive Islands*; Mali*; Mexico*; Mongolia*; Morocco; Nepal; Netherlands; Niger*; Norway*; Panama*; Paraguay*; Philippines; Poland (Chargé d'Affaires); Portugal; Romania; Saudi Arabia; Senegal; Somalia*; Southern Yemen; Spain; Sudan; Sweden; Switzerland; Syria; Thailand; Togo*; Tunisia; Turkey; U.S.S.R.; U.A.R.; United Nations; U.S.A.; Upper Volta*; Uruguay*; Venezuela*; Yemen*; Yugoslavia.

PROVINCIAL ADMINISTRATION

WEST PAKISTAN

The unification of the Province of Sind, the western part of the former Province of the Punjab, the North West Frontier Province (NWFP), the Chief Commissioner's Province of Baluchistan, and the former Princely States of Kalat, Makran, Las Bela, Kharan, Bahawalpur, Khairpur, Chitral, Dir, Swat, and Amb was effected by the Establishment of West Pakistan Act, 1955, which came into force on 14th October 1955. Karachi was merged with West Pakistan in July 1961. However, the West Pakistan Dissolution Order of 1st April 1970 announced that West Pakistan was to be divided into the four provinces of Punjab (including Bahawalpur), Sind (including Karachi), NWFP, Baluchistan and the two centrally-administered areas of Islamabad Capital Territory and the Tribal Areas. The new Provincial administration became operative on 1st July 1970.

The area of West Pakistan is 310,403 square miles and the population 42,881,000 (1961 census). The former provincial capital was Lahore.

The Provinces are divided into divisions as follows:

Pun·ab (capital, Lahore): Rawalpindi, Lahore, Sargodha, Multan, Bahawalpur.

North West Frontier Province (capital, Peshawar): Peshawar, Malakand, Dera, Ismail Khan.

Sind (capital, Karachi): Karachi, Hyderabad, Khairpur.

Baluchistan (capital, Quetta): Quetta, Kalat.

Of these divisions, Peshawar, Dera Ismail Khan and Quetta are responsible for the Tribal Agencies adjoining them.

---

* Non-resident representation.

Senior appointments in the West Pakistan Provincial Governments:

Punjab

Governor: Lieutenant-General Atiqur Rahman, HQA, SPk, MC
Chief Secretary: S. Afzal Agha, SQA, CSP

Sind

Governor: Lieutenant-General Rakhman Gul, SQA, SK, MC
Chief Secretary: S. Manzoor Ilahi, SQA, CSP

North-West Frontier Province

Governor: Lieutenant-General Khawaja Mohammed Azhar Khan, SQA
Chief Secretary: Ejaz Ahmed Naik, TPK, CSP

Baluchistan

Governor: Lieutenant-General Riaz Hussain, SK
Chief Secretary: Rifat Pasha Sheikh, SQA, CSP

EAST PAKISTAN

This comprises the Eastern part of the former Province of Bengal, together with Sylhet District, formerly part of Assam. The area is 55,126 square miles and the population 50,840,235 (1961 census). The provincial capital is Dacca.

The various districts of the Province are grouped into four Divisions with headquarters at Dacca, Chittagong, Rajshahi and Khulna.

Under the Martial Law Administration East Pakistan is Zone "B".

Governor: Lieutenant General Tikka Khan ,SPk
Chief Secretary: S. M. Shafiul, SQA, CSP

HONORIFIC TITLES IN USE IN PAKISTAN

The best known of the titles specifically bestowed on individuals are Quaid-i-Azam, 'The Great Leader' (bestowed on Mr Mohammed Ali Jinnah), and Quaid-i-Millat, 'The Leader of the Nation' (bestowed on Mr Liaqat Ali Khan).

The honorific titles in use in Pakistan are not in all cases capable of accurate rendering into English by way of translation or equivalence, but may be classed in various groups. Thus among prefixes Amir, Jan, Mehtar, Mir, Nawab and Wali are titles of nobility borne by territorial rulers; Chaudhury, Khan, Malik, Mian, Mir and Sardar denote a tribal chieftain or a landowner; Nawabzada and Khanzada indicate sons of rulers; Imam, Kazi, Maulana, Maulvi, Molla (Mullah) and Mufti indicate a religious leader, while Khwaja, Pir and Pir denote descent from a saint, and Sayyid or Syed descent from the Prophet. Al-Haj or Haji indicates one who has made the pilgrimage to Mecca, Shaikh or Sheikh was originally an indication of a leader, perhaps of Arab descent, but has now generally become part of the name and has no special significance. The suffix Khan has also become part of the name, but usually indicates Pathan descent.

Mr and Begum are used for Mr and Mrs respectively but it is incorrect to use Mr where an honorific of any kind prefixes the name.

PAKISTAN CIVIL AWARDS

Pakistan Civil Awards consist of five Orders: The Order of Pakistan (Pk), for services of the highest distinction to the State; The Order of Shujaat (St), for acts of the greatest heroism and most conspicuous courage in circumstances of extreme danger; The Order of Imtiaz (I), for conspicuously distinguished services in literature, art, sports or science; The Order of Quaid-i-Azam (QA), for special merit or for eminent service in the civil, military, or any other field of national activity; The Order of Khidmat (K), for meritorious service.

The Orders have four descending Classes, *viz:* Nishan (N), Hilal (H), Sitara (S) and Tamgha (T). The Order of Pakistan, First Class, is, for example, Nishan-i-Pakistan (NPk) and the Order of Khidmat, Third Class, is Sitara-i-Khidmat (SK), the Class preceding the title of the Order and being followed by -i-. The -i- is, however, omitted in the abbreviated forms.

ARMED FORCES AWARDS

Awards for the Armed Forces are in order of seniority: Nishan-i-Haider (NH) for acts of the greatest heroism; Hilal-i-Juraat (HJ); Sitara-i-Juraat (SJ); Tamgha-i-Juraat (TJ); Tamgha-i-Basalat (TIB); Tamgha-i-Khidmat (TK); Tamgha-i-Difa'd (TD).

SIERRA LEONE

SIERRA LEONE lies on the west coast of Africa between 6° 55′ and 10° N. latitude and 10° 16′ and 13° 18′ W. longitude. Its 210-mile sea coast extends from the border of Guinea to the border of Liberia, these two countries enclosing Sierra Leone inland. The total area of Sierra Leone is 27,925 square miles. Sierra Leone is the only West African country with a hilly coastline and the name is a derivation of the Portuguese for 'Lion Mountain'. It was given to this part of the coast by Pedro de Cintra in about 1462, when lions may have been common, though there are none there now. De Cintra's expedition was one of the last great Portuguese voyages of discovery carried out under the direct influence and authority of Don Henry (Henry the Navigator) who died the following year.

The highest mountains are inland and include Bintimani (also known as Loma Mansa) in the Loma mountain range near the Guinea border to the north-east, 6,390 feet, and Sankan-Biriwa, 6,080 feet. The main estuaries navigable by ocean vessels are the Sierra Leone river and the Sherbro river, while small craft can travel certain distances on the Great and Little Scarcies, Bangru, Jong, Sewa, Waanje and Moa rivers. The source of the Niger which runs into the sea at Port Harcourt, Nigeria, is just within the north-eastern boundary.

There are two distinct seasons: the dry season from October to May and the rainy season for the rest of the year. The heaviest rainfall is on the coast from July to September. The annual rainfall ranges from 75 inches to more than 130 inches, with 250 inches at Guma Valley, 10 miles south of the capital, Freetown. The mean temperature is 80°F with little variation. At the beginning of the dry season the country experiences the *harmattan*, a dry, sand-laden wind from the Sahara.

The last census, in 1963, showed a population of 2,183,000 of whom 195,000 lived in the Freetown peninsula.

The official language is English while the main languages in the Provinces are Mende, Temne and Krio (or Creole). There are, however, at least thirteen tribes living in Sierra Leone, each of which has its own language.

The University of Sierra Leone was created in 1967. It consists of two constituent Colleges—Fourah Bay College, the oldest institution of higher education in West Africa, and Njala University College. The Milton Margai Teachers College near Freetown caters for secondary school teachers, and there are eight primary teacher training colleges situated throughout the country.

In the Western Province there are 25 secondary schools, while the other areas of Sierra Leone now have a further 66 secondary schools. 1,023 primary schools are now operating throughout the country. The literacy percentages are given as 38 per cent for the Western Province and 7·7 per cent for the whole country. The main religions are Christianity and Islam.

Outside the Freetown peninsula, which is officially known as the Western Area, the country is divided into the Southern, Eastern and Northern Provinces, and the provinces are further divided into twelve Districts. The Southern Province includes the Districts of Bo, Bonthe, Moyamba and Pujehun, with headquarters of the administration located at Bo. The Eastern Province includes the Districts of Kenema, Kailahun and Kono, with provincial headquarters at Kenema. The Northern Province comprises the Districts of Bombali, Kambia, Koinadugu, Port Loko and Tonkolili and the headquarters of the provincial administration are at Makeni.

In each of the three Provincial Headquarters towns a Resident Minister represents the Central Government. The Resident Ministers also have a seat each in the Cabinet where they represent the interests of the Provinces. The day to day administration of the Provinces is in the hands of Provincial Secretaries and the Districts are administered by District Officers. There are 147 Chiefdoms in Sierra Leone and in each of these the Chiefdom Councillors elect a Paramount Chief. District Officers are Chairmen of the Committees of Management appointed to perform the duties of the former District Councils.

Sierra Leone has three ports—Freetown, Bonthe and Pepel. The most important of these is Freetown, which is one of the largest natural harbours in the world with extensive deep water near the shore. Sierra Leone Ports Authority handled 542,356 tons of cargo and produce and 458,567 tons of oil and fuel during 1970. In the same year a total of 4,895 passengers passed through the port of Freetown which was visited by 1,326 ships. Work started in 1966 on a major extension of the deep water Queen Elizabeth II Quay, which could berth only two ships, and the project was completed towards the end of 1969 at a total cost of £7 million. Berthing facilities for an additional four ships are now available alongside. Freetown is the only port for imports and it also exports agricultural produce. Bonthe exports piassava, coffee, bauxite, and rutile whilst Pepel is the iron ore exporting port.

Lungi international airport is on the northern bank of the Sierra Leone River opposite Freetown. Passengers are taken by ferry and bus to the airport (travelling time approximately $1\frac{1}{2}$ to 2 hours). The extension of the runway to 10,500 feet was completed in May 1967 and the development to International Standard 'A' was completed early in 1968. The work was financed partly by a loan of £1 million from the British Government. There are small airfields at Hastings, Bo, Kenema, Yengema, Tongo, Bonthe and Gbangbatok. Internal air services are operated by Sierra Leone Airways.

The railway mileage is 368 which includes 57 miles of track privately owned by the Sierra Leone Development Company and used for transporting iron ore from the mines at Marampa to the port of Pepel. Except for this 57 miles the gauge is 2 ft. 6 ins. The Government has accepted the recommendation of a firm of consultants commissioned by the World Bank and the Sierra Leone Railway is being phased out. A team from Crown Agents has arrived in Freetown to assist with the phasing out operation. With financial assistance from Britain, the Federal Republic of Germany and the World Bank, a parallel development of the road network is being carried out. Britain has already made available a loan of up to £1·8 million for the Taiama/Bo section and work has commenced under the supervision of a Crown Agents team. The Federal Republic of Germany is providing a loan of £1·5 million for the Lunsar/Makeni section and construction is under way. It is expected that the World Bank will assist financially with the Bo/Kenema section and international tenders have been called. There are 4,000 miles of road of which 400 miles are surfaced.

Radio Sierra Leone in Freetown serves the whole country although reception conditions vary widely. Sierra Leone Television services can be received within Freetown area only. The Government has accepted the report of a Committee of Broadcasting Consultants which made a comprehensive study of radio and television during 1969. Tenders are being considered for the re-equipment and rehabilitation project and a decision on the award of the contract is expected shortly.

The Sierra Leone economy depends very largely on the export of minerals, in particular diamonds and iron ore. Diamonds are mined by the National Diamond Mining Company (Sierra Leone) Ltd., (Diminco), in which the Government has a 51 per cent shareholding. The balance of shares are held by Consolidated African Selection Trust Limited. Diminco has concessions in the Yengema and Kono districts. Outside these concessions individual Sierra Leone diggers are licensed under the alluvial diamond mining scheme. Purchases of diamonds by the Government Diamond Office during 1970 were valued at £13·1 million as compared with £16·9 million in 1969. Exports of diamonds in 1970 totalled £25·5 million compared with £31 million in 1969. Iron ore is mined by the Sierra Leone Development Company (whose shares are held mainly by William Baird & Company of Glasgow) at Marampa; exports of iron ore and concentrates in 1970 were valued at £5·3 million compared with £5 million in 1969. The production of bauxite by Sierra Leone Ore and Metal Company Limited commenced in 1963 and exports of bauxite in 1970 were valued at £0·8 million compared with £0·7 million in 1969. A comparatively new development is the mining of rutile and the deposits are reported to be the largest in the world. Production started in 1967 by Sherbro Minerals Limited, a USA/British venture, and the first shipment was made in June of that year. Exports of rutile in 1970 reached a value of £1 million compared with £0·5 million in 1969. In April 1971, Sherbro announced its decision to suspend operations due to continuing financial losses and Receivers have been appointed. It is hoped that another company will acquire the concession and assets. In December 1969 the Government announced its intention to acquire a majority shareholding in all mining companies operating in Sierra Leone but, so far, negotiations have been held and concluded only in the diamond sector.

In 1970 total imports (£48·5 million) exceeded exports (£41·6 million) by £6·9 million. Diamonds and iron ore together provided about 75 per cent of the country's export earnings. Agricultural exports including palm kernels, coffee, cocoa, ginger, kola nuts and piassava, amounted to £7·8 million in 1970. The main imports are machinery and plant, vehicles, electrical equipment, food stuffs and mineral fuels. There are no exchange control regulations in force. The smallness of the market limits the potential for manufacturing in Sierra Leone. The estimated annual per capita income is about £50. Rice, fish and cassava are the staple foods of the population and, at present, a proportion of the total rice consumption has to be imported. The Government has declared its intention of stepping up agricultural development and a number of British tractors have been imported for use by small farmers.

In the Government's 1970/71 Budget the development and recurrent estimates were presented together. Current revenue was estimated at £25·5 million and current expenditure at £23·15 million. Development expenditure was estimated at £6·6 million; the overall deficit was estimated at £1·5 million.

Among the national projects not mentioned elsewhere is the King Tom Power Station in Freetown for which the World Bank lent the Government $3·9 million in 1968. The Guma Valley Water Scheme including the Guma Valley Dam (officially opened in 1967) which has a capacity of 4,800 million gallons was supported by a Commonwealth Development Corporation loan of £2 million in 1963. The African Development Bank have agreed to provide a further loan of £625,000 to extend the reservoir capacity and to duplicate the pipeline to Freetown. In 1963 another British loan was made in respect of the erection of a 2·4 megawatt hydro-electric station which came into operation in 1967.

I National Oil Refinery was completed in February 1969. It was built by a Japanese company and financed from an Israeli source. It is now on stream and is operated by the Government together with a consortium of five overseas oil companies and managed mainly by British expatriate staff seconded from BP Ltd. The refinery has a capacity of 10,000 barrels per day which can more than cope with Sierra Leone's requirements. The Memorandum and Articles of Association were signed in April 1970 but the final agreement has not yet been ratified by Parliament.

At the end of December 1969, the International Development Association announced a loan of 3 million US dollars to assist the Sierra Leone Government in financing the extension of certain educational institutions. The Canadian International Development Agency is to provide equipment for these institutions to the value of 650,000 US dollars. The duration of the project will be three years and a Project Unit is in operation.

Sierra Leone's National Day, Independence Day, is celebrated on 27th April.

HISTORY

Before Independence, Sierra Leone consisted of the Colony, which was broadly identical with the peninsula on which Freetown stands, and the Protectorate on the mainland.

The history of modern Sierra Leone dates from 1787 when Granville Sharp and other British abolitionists, acting on a scheme proposed by Dr Henry Smeatham, purchased from a local chief named Naimbana a strip of land on the peninsula and settled on it 400 freed slaves. In 1791 a Royal Charter was granted to a Sierra Leone company, of which both Sharp and William Wilberforce were directors, and, despite difficulties with local tribesmen and with the French, more settlers were introduced, many being freed slaves from Jamaica and Nova Scotia. In 1800 the peninsula was granted to the chartered company by letters patent; and the court of directors was empowered to appoint a Governor and Council, the former having powers to make laws. In 1807, when Britain outlawed slave trading, a naval station was established at Freetown, and slaves freed in operations by the ships stationed there were brought back to the settlement. Finally in 1808 Freetown became a colony, and the jurisdiction of the company was assumed by the Crown. From 1816 to 1843 The Gambia was governed from Sierra Leone; and the Gold Coast was a dependency from 1843 to 1850.

In 1862 a large tract of coastal area including Sherbro Island was added to the colony, and as the century progressed treaties were made with neighbouring Chiefs to protect the trade of the colony with the hinterland, and British influence was thus extended. To define the geographical extent of this influence, an agreement on boundaries was made with Liberia in 1885 and with France in 1895; and in 1896 a protectorate was declared over the territories so defined. Although British law and taxation procedure were introduced, the people of the protectorate still continued to be administered indirectly through their own rulers.

CONSTITUTIONAL DEVELOPMENT UNTIL INDEPENDENCE IN 1961
Until 1863 the Government of Sierra Leone consisted of a Governor and an Advisory Council comprising *ex officio* members and one or two appointed members.

In 1863 an Executive Council and Legislative Council were created. In 1866 Sierra Leone was joined with The Gambia, the Gold Coast and Lagos to form the West Africa Settlements with a Governor in Chief in Freetown. In 1874 Lagos and the Gold Coast jointly became a separate colony and The Gambia was separated as a colony from Sierra Leone in 1888.

In 1924, by Order in Council dated 16th January, a new and considerably enlarged Legislative Council was set up providing for elected members, and also providing for direct representation of Protectorate interests for the first time.

An Order in Council in 1951 provided for a Legislative Council of thirty-two members, consisting of seven *ex officio* members, seven members elected from the Colony districts, twelve members elected from the Protectorate District Councils, two members elected from the Protectorate Assembly and two members nominated by the Governor, together with the Governor as President and a Vice-President. Provision was made by Royal Instruction for an Executive Council of four *ex officio* members and not less than four unofficial members appointed from among the elected members of the Legislative Council.

In 1953 a Ministerial system was introduced and in the next year the title of Chief Minister was accorded to the leader of the majority party in the Legislative Council.

Under a new constitution in 1956 the Legislative Council became the House of Representatives and was enlarged to consist of a Speaker, four *ex officio* members, fifty-one elected members and two nominated members (the last had no voting powers). In the General Election of 1957 virtually all adult males and all adult female taxpayers or property owners were eligible to vote. The Constitution was further altered in 1958 by the exclusion of *ex officio* members from the Executive Council and House of Representatives. The new Executive Council included eleven Ministers appointed from among the elected members of the House of Representatives. Dr (later Sir Milton) Margai, who had been Chief Minister under the previous constitutional arrangements, was appointed Prime Minister.

At the Constitutional Conference held in London from 20th April to 4th May 1960 the constitutional changes necessary before Sierra Leone became independent were agreed. Sierra Leone attained complete independence as a fully self-governing Member of the Commonwealth with Her Majesty The Queen as Sovereign on 27th April 1961.

CONSTITUTIONAL DEVELOPMENT FROM INDEPENDENCE TO MARCH 1967
The Constitution of Sierra Leone, contained in the Sierra Leone (Constitution) Order in Council 1961, included provision for a Governor-General appointed by Her Majesty The Queen and for a House of Representatives consisting of not less than sixty members with a Speaker elected by the members from among their own number or from persons who were qualified to become members. For an interim period until a new House of Representatives was elected the House as established by the previous Constitution remained the legislative body.

To qualify for election to the House of Representatives a person had to be a citizen of Sierra Leone, had to have attained the age of twenty-five and had to speak English well enough to be able to take an active part in the proceedings of the House. Provision was made for the establishment of an Electoral Commission of a chairman and up to four members.

Provision was made for questions coming before the House of Representatives to be determined by a majority vote of the members present and voting, except in the case of certain constitutional amendments which required a two-thirds majority of all members in two successive sessions of the House, one before and the other following a dissolution. Finance Bills could only be introduced by a Minister of the Government. The House had a normal life of five years, unless sooner dissolved, and had to meet at least once a year.

Executive responsibility rested with a Cabinet of Ministers drawn from among the members of the House of Representatives. The Cabinet was presided over by a Prime Minister appointed by the Governor-General as the person likely to command the support of a majority of the members of the House. Other Ministers were appointed on the advice of the Prime Minister.

THE NATIONAL REFORMATION COUNCIL

Following a general election on 17th March 1967 the two main political parties (Sierra Leone People's Party and All People's Congress) obtained an almost equal number of seats. On 21st March, after general uncertainty about the exact result, the Governor-General appointed Mr Siaka Stevens, Leader of the A.P.C., as Prime Minister and invited him to form a government. Mr Stevens went the same day to State House, where he was detained shortly after being sworn in. That evening Brigadier Lansana, the Army Commander, broadcast a statement to the effect that, since the elections of Paramount Chiefs were only then taking place and no Party had won a majority of all 78 Chiefly and ordinary seats, the All People's Congress was attempting to seize power by force. Brigadier Lansana announced that he had, therefore, decided to protect the Constitution and to place the country under martial law.

On 23rd March, Major Charles Blake announced in a broadcast statement that he and a number of other army officers, with the Commissioner and an Assistant Commissioner of Police, had established a National Reformation Council, that the Army and Police were in complete control and that the Constitution was suspended. He explained that he and his colleagues had come to the conclusion that Brigadier Lansana was not trying to bring about a national government but to impose Sir Albert Margai as Prime Minister. To prevent this they had divested Brigadier Lansana of control and arrested him, and had also taken into custody Sir Albert Margai and Mr Siaka Stevens. The Governor-General was under house arrest and all political parties were dissolved.

On 25th March 1967 a proclamation was issued which formally established the National Reformation Council, constituted as follows:—Chairman; Deputy Chairman; and not more than six other members. Under the Proclamation all the provisions of the Constitution of Sierra Leone, 1961 (which came into operation on 27th April 1961) which are inconsistent or in conflict with the proclamation or any law under it were deemed to have been suspended with effect from 23rd March 1967.

Under the proclamation the House of Representatives was dissolved, all political parties were dissolved and membership of political parties was prohibited. In addition, any reference to Governor-General, Prime Minister, Minister or Cabinet in the 1961 Constitution was to be construed as a reference to the National Reformation Council. Government Ministries were subsequently reorganised into nine Departments and members of the National Reformation Council given responsibilities for them.

On 27th April 1967 the National Reformation Council issued an amendment to the Proclamation to the effect that all Laws which had been passed since then and thenceforth should be referred to as Decrees.

On 13th May the National Reformation Council issued a Decree, effective from 25th March, giving them power to appoint an Advisory Council consisting of not less than ten members. Their terms of reference were (1) to work out ways and means of calming down political feelings and bringing about national unity, free of tribalism and separatist agitation; (2) to work out steps leading to a peaceful return to civilian rule after a general election; (3) to work out a Constitution designed to incorporate the results of (1) above and to obviate all the underlying causes of the previous conflicts and corruption; (4) to advise on all matters referred to it by the National Reformation Council; and (5) to advise on any other matter which is in the general interest of the nation.

RETURN TO CIVILIAN RULE

On 22nd May 1967 the National Reformation Council established a Commission of Enquiry, under the chairmanship of Mr Justice Dove-Edwin, to enquire into the conduct of the last General Election and also, *inter alia*, into the election results. The Commission's report, which was submitted in September 1967, included a specific statement that the All People's Congress had won the election on their own merit and that the Governor-General was manifestly right in appointing Mr Siaka Stevens as Prime Minister. The National Reformation Council did not accept the report *in toto* but stated that the report confirmed their view that the elections were rigged and corrupt. Subsequently, in November 1967, the National Reformation Council affirmed that it agreed in principle to hand over to civilian government in the shortest possible time and announced that a Civilian Rule Committee—representing all sections of the community—would be appointed to advise on the method and procedure of handling over to civilian government. The Committee finally began its sessions in February 1968 with instructions to advise on the necessity for a fresh General Election; and, if this was not necessary, the method by which a National Government could be formed.

The Committee reported in March 1968 but, before its recommendations were published the National Reformation Council itself was overthrown by an uprising of other ranks of the army and police on the night of 17/18th April. Nearly all army and police officers were placed in detention and an Anti-Corruption Revolutionary Movement was formed of Warrant Officers, NCOs and junior police officers pledged to restore civilian rule immediately. They also set up a National Interim Council charged with the specific task of ensuring how this might be done in the shortest possible time and the Chief Justice, Mr Tejan-Sie, was sworn in as Acting Governor-General. Mr Tejan-Sie immediately invited all successful candidates at the last (March 1967) General Election to meet for consultations. These consultations led to an agreement to form a National Government under the leadership of Mr Siaka Stevens, who had been appointed Prime Minister in March 1967 but was prevented from holding office by the coup.

Mr Stevens proceeded to form a Government consisting of 18 Ministers, 9 of whom (including himself) were members of the All People's Congress and 4 from the other major political party, Sierra Leone People's Party. The remaining offices were filled by Independents and Paramount Chiefs.

The House of Representatives met on Wednesday, 5th June 1968, to enable members to take the oath and to elect a Speaker. Parliament was formally opened on 26th June 1968.

On 11th April 1969 certain Cabinet changes were made providing a total of 20 Ministers of whom 16 were drawn from the A.P.C. The remaining places were filled by two Independents and two Paramount Chiefs. Further Ministerial changes were made on 12th May 1970.

On 11th September 1970 two senior Cabinet Ministers resigned from the Government. Following disturbances in the provinces a State of Emergency was declared on 14th September. On 15th September a reshuffled Cabinet was announced. A group of leading opposition personalities, including the two former Ministers mentioned above, formed a new political party called the United Democratic Party (UDP) on 19th September. The UDP was banned under the Emergency Regulations on 8th October and its leaders were detained. Most of them were released by the early part of 1971 but the State of Emergency, continued.

On 23rd March 1971 two attempts were made to kill the Prime Minister and the Force Commander, Brigadier Bangura, broadcast that the army had taken control of the situation. He had little support within the army and the coup quickly collapsed. On 28th March the Prime Minister signed a defence agreement with Guinea.

The Governor-General, Sir Banja Tejan-Sie, was relieved of his office and departed on leave with effect from 5th April 1971.

On 19th April 1971 Sierra Leone became a Republic under a Constitution which provided for a Ceremonial President and the Acting Governor-General, Mr Christopher Cole, was sworn in as President. On 21st April the Constitution was amended to provide for an Executive President and the Prime Minister, Dr Siaka Stevens, was sworn in as President.

HISTORICAL LIST

GOVERNORS GENERAL

Sir Maurice Dorman, GCMG, GCVO, 27th April 1961 to 5th May 1962
H. J. Lightfoot, CMG, JP (later Sir Henry Lightfoot Boston, GCMG) 5th May to 11th July 1962 (acting)
Sir Henry Lightfoot Boston, GCMG, JP, from 11th July 1962 to May 1967
Siaka P. Stevens as Prime Minister 26th April 1968 to 21st April 1971; as President from 21st April 1971.

CABINET

President (with responsibility for Defence): Hon. Dr Siaka P. Stevens
Vice-President and Prime Minister: Hon. S. I. Koroma
Minister of Finance: Hon. C. A. Kamara-Taylor
Minister of External Affairs: Hon. S. A. J. Pratt
Attorney-General: Hon. L. A. M. Brewah
Minister of Lands and Mines: Hon. S. W. Gandi Capio
Minister of Interior: Hon. S. D. Kawusu-Conteh
Minister of Trade and Industry: Hon. S. A. Fofana

Minister of Agriculture and Natural Resources: Hon. A. G. Sembu Forna
Minister of Works: Hon. D. F. Shears
Minister of Information and Broadcasting: Hon. K. A. Daramy
Minister of Health: Hon. C. P. Foray
Minister of Education: Hon. J. Barthes-Wilson
Minister of Transport and Communications: Hon. E. J. Kargbo
Minister of Social Welfare: Hon. S. A. T. Koroma
Minister of Development: Hon. A. K. Khazali
Minister of Housing and Country Planning: Hon. M. O. Cole
Minister of Labour: Hon. F. B. Turay
Ministers of State:
Hon. P. C. Bai Koblo Pathbana, CBE
Hon. P. C. A. J. Kaikai, MBE
Hon. J. C. O. Hadson-Taylor
Resident Minister, Eastern Province: Hon. F. S. Anthony
Resident Minister, Northern Province: Hon. Bangali Mansaray
Resident Minister, Southern Province: Hon. G. G. Lamin

DEPUTY MINISTERS

Deputy Minister, President's Office and Ministry of Defence: Hon. K. C. Gbamanja
Deputy Minister, Ministry of Finance: Hon. D. Kelfala
Deputy Minister, Ministry of Education: Hon. L. P. Allen
Deputy Minister, Ministry of Interior: Hon. A. B. M. Janneh
Deputy Minister, Ministry of Works: Hon. A. B. Kamara
Deputy Minister, Ministry of Transport and Communications:
Hon. Formeh Kamara

HOUSE OF REPRESENTATIVES
Speaker: The Hon. Sir Emile F. Luke, KBE
Deputy Speaker: The Hon. S. B. Koroma
Clerk, House of Representatives: J. Davies

CHIEF JUSTICE
The Hon. Mr. Justice C. O. E. Cole, CMG, OBE

JUSTICES OF THE SUPREME COURT
The Hon. Justice Sir Samuel Bankole-Jones Kt
The Hon. Mr Justice J. B. Marcus-Jones, CBE
The Hon. Mr Justice G. F. Dove-Edwin, CBE
The Hon. Mr Justice H. W. Tambiah, QC
The Hon. Mr Justice S. C. W. Betts

JUSTICES OF THE APPEAL COURT
The Hon. Mr Justice N. E. Browne-Marke
The Hon. Mr Justice C. A. Harding
The Hon. Mr Justice S. J. Forster, CBE
The Hon. Mr Justice P. R. Davies, MBE

JUSTICES OF THE HIGH COURT
The Hon. Mr Justice O. B. R. Tejan
The Hon. Mr Justice Rowland E. A. Harding
The Hon. Mr Justice D. M. A. Macaulay
The Hon. Mrs Justice Agnes Macaulay
The Hon. Mr Justice Ken Omotayo During
The Hon. Justice S. Beccles Davies
The Hon. Mr Justice E. Livesey Luke
The Hon. Mr Justice S. C. Warne

DIPLOMATIC REPRESENTATION

SIERRA LEONE REPRESENTATIVES IN COMMONWEALTH COUNTRIES
Britain: H. M. Lynch-Shyllon (Acting High Commissioner); Ghana: L. K. Randall (High Commissioner); Nigeria: A. B. Mansaray (Acting High Commissioner).

COMMONWEALTH REPRESENTATIVES IN SIERRA LEONE
Britain: S. J. L. Olver, CMG, MBE (High Commissioner); Canada: A. McGill (High Commissioner) (resident) in Lagos); Ghana: E. B. Awoonor-Williams (High Commissioner); Nigeria: J. Tanku Yusuf (High Commissioner); Gambia: S. J. O. Sarr (High Commissioner) (resident in Dakar); Botswana: C. D. Malapo (High Commissioner) (resident in Nairobi); Tanzania: R. Salim (High Commissioner) (resident in Conakry); Zambia: S. G. Mwale (High Commissioner) (resident in Abidjan).

SIERRA LEONE REPRESENTATION IN
NON-COMMONWEALTH COUNTRIES
Germany: D. Luke (Ambassador); Guinea:
Sorsoh Conteh (Ambassador); Liberia:
R. E. Kelfa-Coker (Ambassador); U.A.R.:
Alhaji Gibril Sesay (Chargé d'Affaires UN:
Dr Davidson, E. H. Nicol (Permanent Repre-
sentative); U.S.A.: Collins O. Bright (Chargé
d'Affaires); U.S.S.R.: Professor E. W.
Blyden (Ambassador); Ethiopia: P. Palmer
(Ambassador); O.A.U.: P. Palmer (Am-
bassador); France: Belgium: Italy: Nether-
lands: Luxembourg: E.E.C.: D. Luke
(Ambassador) (resident in Bonn).

SINGAPORE

SINGAPORE is an island to the south of the Malay Peninsula, from which it is separated by a narrow channel crossed by a causeway three-quarters of a mile long. Included within its boundaries are a number of smaller islands. A few miles to the south are islands belonging to Indonesia. Singapore is situated just north of the equator, its central point being about 1° 20′ N. latitude and 103° 40′ E. longitude. The area is 224·5 square miles, and the highest point, Bukit Timah, is 581 feet above sea level. The name is derived from the Sanskrit 'Singa pura', or 'City of the Lion'.

The climate of Singapore is similar to that of West Malaysia, being hot and humid with no clearly defined seasons. Rainfall averages 91 inches a year, and the average daytime maximum temperature is 87° dropping to an average minimum of 75° at night.

A full census was held in June 1970 when the total population of the Republic was 2,074,507. Racial groups comprised:

Chinese	1,579,866
Malays	311,379
Indians	145,169
Other races (Europeans, Eurasians, etc.) ..	38,093

The birth rate in 1970 was 22·1 per thousand and the death rate 5·2 per thousand.

At least eight different Chinese dialects are used. However, many Chinese speak Mandarin in addition to their own dialect and many speak English and Malay. The Chinese written language is common to all Chinese. The principal Indian language is Tamil, but many others are spoken. Malay and English are also commonly used, and Malay, Mandarin, Tamil and English are official languages.

Primary education is free and universal. The literacy rate (1957) was 52·3 per cent but this has risen considerably since then.

The main religions are Buddhism, Taoism, Islam, Hinduism and Christianity. Many Chinese follow the Confucian system of ethics.

Singapore's traditional means of livelihood is its entrepôt trade, including the processing of primary produce from neighbouring countries, but since 1961, as a result of various official incentive schemes, a large number of new factories have been set up. Singapore is one of the largest ports in world, with deep water wharves and ship repairing facilities. Ships also anchor in the roads and unload into lighters which bring the cargo ashore, usually into the Singapore River. the total cargo handled in 1969 was 37·9 million tons. The airport is at Paya Lebar, 6½ miles from the centre of the city with a runway of 11,000 feet. Malaysia

Singapore Airlines Ltd is the joint national airline of both Singapore and Malaysia. There are 16 miles of metre gauge railway, the railway crossing the Straits of Johore by the causeway and forming a part of the Malaysian system. In addition, eight miles of railway were completed in November 1965 to connect with the new industrial area at Jurong. There are 1,199 miles of roads, 809 miles of which are paved.

Radio Singapore, owned and operated by the Singapore Government, broadcasts programmes in Chinese, English, Malay and Tamil and provides facilities for commercial advertising. Approximately 90 per cent of all households possess a radio set. In addition, Rediffusion Ltd, a private commercial enterprise, operate a wired radio service, providing advertising facilities in Mandarin, Malay and English. There are approximately 61,000 Rediffusion subscribers. Government-owned television, introduced in 1963, operates on two channels, programmes being in Chinese, Malay, Tamil and English, as with radio. Approximately 1·3 million people are believed to watch regularly. Television also offers facilities for commercial advertising. Educational T.V. operated by the Ministry of Education and using T.V. Singapura's facilities was started in 1967. This is directed at secondary schools. T.V. Malaysia is also received in Singapore.

In his Budget Speech on 8th March 1971, the Minister of Finance indicated that estimated government expenditure for the year 1st April 1971–31st March 1972 was S$1,306·8 million (25·5 per cent higher than 1970). Estimated revenue was S$1,307·2 million (10·6 per cent higher than the actual 1970 revenue). Defence expenditure accounted for 37 per cent of the Budget. The Minister explained that the rapid growth of Singapore's economy and higher earnings were mainly responsible for an increase of S$125·3 million or 10·6 per cent in the actual revenue of S$1,181·9 over the previous year. The Development Estimates for 1971/72 provide for expenditure of an additional S$364·4 million for Government development projects and loans to statutory authorities and Government-owned companies.

Having a limited land space and no natural resources Singapore's prosperity was built up on entrepôt trade with the Port of Singapore, one of the largest in the world in terms of annual tonnage, as the keystone of the economy. To broaden the base of the economy and provide for more rapid growth an industrialisation progrmme was launched in 1960 which has since been accelerated in view of the decision to withdraw British forces by the end of 1971. Singapore actively encourages foreign private investors by offering tax and other incentives and free repatriation of profits and capital. As a result of active promotional steps by the Government the manufacturing sector has achieved an impressive growth in recent years. In 1969 output reached in value S$2,636 million (of which gross local value added was S$782 million) as compared with S$1,086 million (local value added S$348 million) in 1965. One of the main factors responsible for industrial growth has been the provision of generous fiscal and other incentives. Although several industrial estates have been established the Jurong Industrial Complex with an estimated area of 12,000 acres, some 236 factories in production and another 100 planned or under construction is the largest industrial estate in South East Asia.

Apart from the expansion of the manufacturing industry other growth sectors of the economy are shipbuilding/repairing and tourism. Business in shipbuilding and repairing earned about S$140 million in 1969 and this figure was estimated to have reached S$200 million by the end of 1970 with ship repairing accounting for 80 per cent of the total. Although still comparatively small, tourism is one of the fastest growing sectors of the economy. Since 1968 some 25 new hotels have either been completed or are in course of construction. In the first 6 months of 1970, 268,800 visitors came to Singapore by air and by sea—mainly from the USA, Britain, Australia, Indonesia, Malaysia and Japan. This represented an increase of 32 per cent over the corresponding period of 1969. In addition, because of its location and its high reputation for efficient communications and financial facilities, Singapore is becoming the region's biggest logistical and supply centre for the off-shore oil exploration activites in South East Asia. It is being called upon to provide a wide variety of goods and supporting services.

Singapore's external trade in 1970, including trade with West Malaysia, rose to an all-time record. Provisional figures show that trade, excluding trade with Indonesia, rose in 1970 to S$12,290 million, an increase of S$1,305 million over 1969. Imports were worth S$7,534 million (S$6,244 million in 1969) and exports were S$4,756 (S$4,741 million in 1969).

The Special Aid programme of £50 million provided to help the Singapore Government overcome the economic effects of the British military withdrawal is well under way. By the end of 1970/71 £25 million had been disbursed. The main projects in the economic sphere are the establishment of a wide-ranging technical education programme, substantial contributions to infrastructural projects such as roads and factories, the improvement of dockyard facilities and the provision of a wide range of British manufactured goods. Special Aid funds have also been used for defence projects.

Singapore's National Day is 9th August.

HISTORY

The history of Singapore prior to 1948 is outlined in the history of Malaysia. Singapore's rapid development from the time of Sir Stamford Raffles was due in part to the farsightedness of Raffles himself in choosing an island lying, with its magnificent natural harbour, not only on the trade routes to the Far East but also placed so as to be the natural trading centre for all the surrounding territories. Over the years Singapore flourished as a free port, living on its trade, its docking facilities and its processing of imported raw materials. It was not until 1921, with the emergence of Japan as the third naval power in the world, that a decision was made to construct there, in the channel between the island and the State of Johore, a first-class naval base with graving and floating docks to take the largest ships afloat. This base was completed in 1938. The defences of the island were however designed for resistance to attack by sea and in February 1942 it fell to a Japanese land attack down the Malay Peninsula and across the Johore Strait. On the liberation of Singapore in 1945, the island was detached from the other Straits Settlements and established as a separate Colony in 1946. At the same time Labuan was detached from Singapore and became part of the Colony of North Borneo; and the Cocos (Keeling) Islands (which were never occupied by the Japanese) and Christmas Island were transferred to Australia in 1955 and 1958 respectively. The Colony remained a free port and still continued to handle much of the trade of Malaya and to a lesser extent that of Indonesia. At the same time local industries were developed. A new constitution conferring full internal self-government and the title 'State of Singapore' was introduced in 1959, Singapore became a State of Malaysia on 16th September

1963. On 9th August 1965, it was separated from Malaysia and became an independent sovereign state.

CONSTITUTIONAL DEVELOPMENT

After the end of the war with Japan, a short period of military administration was followed by the restoration of civil government on 1st April 1946. By Order in Council of 27th March 1946 Singapore was established as a separate Colony and a provisional Advisory Council was created pending the establishment of fully representative Executive and Legislative Councils.

The Advisory Council met for the first time on 11th April 1946 and set up a Committee to make recommendations as to the form of the Legislative Council. As a result of their recommendations, a partly elected Council met on 1st April 1948, with six Members elected from territorial constituencies. For the elections in 1951 the number of elected Members was increased to nine. In 1953 a Commission under the chairmanship of Sir George Rendel was set up to advise on a new constitution; and by Order in Council which came into force on 8th February 1955 Singapore was given a large measure of internal self-government. A Council of Ministers was formed, responsible collectively to a Legislative Assembly of thirty-two Members, of whom twenty-five were elected from single-member constituencies, three were *ex officio* Members and four were Nominated Unofficial Members. The Governor ceased to preside over the Assembly and was replaced by a Speaker. There was a Council of Ministers consisting of the Governor, three *ex officio* Members and seven Ministers appointed from among the elected and nominated Members of the Assembly. Mr David Marshall became Singapore's first Chief Minister, but was succeeded by Mr Lim Yew Hock in the following year.

In 1957, after discussions in Singapore and London, an Agreement was signed in London providing for the constitution of a State of Singapore with full internal self-government and the creation of a Singapore citizenship. The new constitution provided for a Head of State to be known as the Yang di-Pertuan Negara, a Cabinet presided over by a Prime Minister, and a fully elective Legislative Assembly of fifty-one Members with a Speaker and Deputy Speaker. On the coming into force of this Constitution in 1959 the Governor, Sir William Goode, became the first Yang di-Pertuan Negara of the State of Singapore and the first United Kingdom Commissioner; but he relinquished the former post six months later, Enche Yusof bin Ishak being appointed in his place. The first Prime Minister was Mr Lee Kuan Yew. One of the first acts of the new Government was to abolish the Singapore Municipal Council and to assume its functions. The United Kingdom Commissioner remained responsible for Defence and External Affairs but certain responsibilities in respect of the latter were delegated to the Government of Singapore. The Singapore Government was responsible for internal security subject to the oversight of an Internal Security Council consisting of three British Representatives, three Singapore representatives and one representative of the Federation of Malaya.

On Singapore's entry into Malaysia the Internal Security Council ceased to exist, internal security becoming the responsibility of the Malaysian Government. The office of United Kingdom Commissioner was also abolished, the senior British representative being the Deputy High Commissioner who was responsible to the British High Commissioner in Kuala Lumpur. After the separation from Malaysia, a British High Commissioner was appointed to Singapore.

On 7th August 1965 the Prime Ministers of Malaysia and Singapore concluded an agreement on the separation of Singapore from Malaysia as an independent sovereign state from 9th August. The Malaysian Government agreed to enact constitutional instruments to give effect to the separation. On 9th August the Malaysian Parliament passed the Constitution of Malaysia (Singapore Amendment) Act, 1965, providing for Singapore to become independent on that date and Singapore became a Member of the Commonwealth. By legislation passed in December 1965, with retrospective effect to 9th August, the island became a Republic, the Yang di-Pertuan Negara was re-styled President and the Legislative Assembly renamed Parliament. Singapore established a Presidential Council by legislation passed in December 1969. The 21-member Council, chaired by the Chief Justice, exists to examine legislation to see whether it contains elements which differentiate between racial or religious communities or contains provisions inconsistent with the fundamental liberties of Singapore citizens, and to report and advise the Government thereon.

HISTORICAL LIST OF MINISTRIES

Lee Kuan Yew, from 3rd June 1959

GOVERNMENT

Following a General Election on 13th April 1968 the Government (People's Action Party) hold all 58 seats in the new Parliament. Of the 58 constituencies only seven were actually contested at the Election, the remaining PAP members being returned unopposed. In those constituencies where voting took place, there was a 91·7 per cent poll, with some 77·6 per cent of the votes cast for PAP candidates and 11·8 per cent for opposition candidates. By-elections took place in five constituencies in 1970, with the PAP retaining all 58 seats in Parliament: three PAP candidates were returned unopposed on nomination day and the other two PAP candidates obtained a majority on polling day.

HEAD OF STATE

The President: Dr Benjamin Henry Sheares

CABINET

Prime Minister: Mr Lee Kuan Yew
Minister for Science and Technology: Dr Toh Chin Chye
Minister for Defence: Dr Goh Keng Swee
Minister for Foreign Affairs and Labour: Mr S. Rajaratnam
Minister for Home Affairs: Mr Ong Pang Boon
Minister for Communications: Mr Yong Nyuk Lin
Minister for Education: Mr Lim Kim San
Minister for Culture: Mr Jek Yeun Thong
Minister for Social Affairs: Enche Othman bin Wok
Minister for Law and National Development: Mr E. W. Barker
Minister for Health: Mr Chua Sian Chin
Minister for Finance: Mr Hon Sui Sen

PARLIAMENT

Speaker: Yeoh Ghim Seng
Clerk to the Parliament: A. Lopez

THE JUDICIARY
THE HIGH COURT OF SINGAPORE

Chief Justice of the High Court in Singapore: The Hon. Mr Justice Wee Chong Jin

Judges:

The Hon. Mr Justice Tan Ah Tah	The Hon. Mr Justice T. Kulasekaram
The Hon. Mr Justice F. A. Chua	The Hon. Mr Justice Choor Singh
The Hon. Mr Justice A. V. Winslow	The Hon. Mr Justice Denis de Cotta

Registrar of the High Court in Singapore: Eu Cheow Chye

MINISTRIES AND GOVERNMENT DEPARTMENTS

PRIME MINISTER'S OFFICE

Secretary to the Cabinet: Wong Chooi Sen
Commissioner, Bases Economic Conversion Department: K. R. Chandra

MINISTRY OF FINANCE

Permanent Secretary (Treasury): Lee Keng Tuan (acting)
Permanent Secretary (Economic Development): George E. Bogaars
Chairman, Economic Development Board: I. F. Tang
Director of Audit: Chee Keng Soon (acting)

MINISTRY OF FOREIGN AFFAIRS

Permanent Secretary for Foreign Affaris: S. T. Stewart

MINISTRY OF LABOUR

Permanent Secretary and Commissioner for Labour: Kwa Soon Chuan

MINISTRY OF EDUCATION

Permanent Secretary and Director of Education: Kwan Sai Kheong

MINISTRY OF LAW AND NATIONAL DEVELOPMENT

Permanent Secretary (Law): T. Chelliah (acting)
Permanent Secretary (National Development): Tan Chok Kian
Attorney-General: Tan Boon Teik
Chairman, Housing and Development Board: M. Coomaraswamy (acting)
Director of Public Works: Hiew Siew Nam (acting)

MINISTRY OF COMMUNICATIONS

Permanent Secretary: Ngiam Tong Dow (acting)
Director of Marine: Capt Goh Choo Seng
Director of Civil Aviation: Cheong Pak Chow
Director of Telecommunications: Goh Seng Kim
Postmaster General: M. Bala Subramanion
Chairman, Port of Singapore Authority: Howe Yoon Chong

MINISTRY OF DEFENCE

Permanent Secretary: Pang Tee Pow
Permanent Secretary (additional): J.A.Y.M. Pillay

MINISTRY OF HOME AFFAIRS

Permanent Secretary: Tay Seow Huah
Controller of Immigration: Wong Lee Moong (acting)
Commissioner of Police: Cheam Kim Seang

MINISTRY OF CULTURE

Permanent Secretary: Lim Phai Soon (acting)

MINISTRY OF SOCIAL AFFAIRS

Permanent Secretary: Otham Bin Omar (acting)

MINISTRY OF HEALTH

Permanent Secretary (Health) and Director of Medical Services: Dr Ho Guan Lim
Permanent Secretary (Special Duties): Tan Teck Khim

PUBLIC SERVICES COMMISSION

Chairman: Dr Phay Seng Whatt

DIPLOMATIC REPRESENTATION

SINGAPORE REPRESENTATIVES IN OTHER COMMONWEALTH COUNTRIES

Britain: Lee Yong Leng (High Commissioner); Australia: P. S. Raman (High Commisstioner); New Zealand: K. M. Byrne (High Commissioner); Malaysia: M. Baker (High Commissioner); India: P. Coomaraswamy (High Commissioner).

COMMONWEALTH HIGH COMMISSIONERS IN SINGAPORE

Britain: Samuel Falle, CMG DSC; Australia:

N. F. Parkinson; Canada: J. G. Hadwen (resident in Kuala Lumpur); New Zealand: H. H. Francis; India: Prem Bhatia; Pakistan: Zahir M. Farooqi; Malaysia: Abdullah bin Ali.

SINGAPORE REPRESENTATION IN NON-COMMONWEALTH COUNTRIES

Cambodia: (Ambassador); Thailand: (Ambassador); U.A.R.: (Ambassador); U.S.A.: (Ambassador); Japan: (Ambassador); Indoniesa: (Ambassador).

SWAZILAND

SWAZILAND takes its name from the Swazi tribe, a composite people of various clan origins who have existed as a distinct tribe only since the beginning of the nineteenth century. The country lies to the east of the Transvaal Province of the Republic of South Africa, which bounds it on the north, west and south. On the east it borders Mozambique and the South African province of Natal. Most of the country is between latitudes 26° and 27° S. and longitudes 31° and 32° E. The area is 6,705 square miles.

Swaziland has four well-defined topographic regions. These extend longitudinally north and south throughout the country in roughly parallel belts. The Highveld (westernmost), Middleveld and Lowveld are of more or less equal breadth and the Lubombo is a narrower strip along the eastern border. The Highveld is a north-eastward continuation of the Natal Drakensberg. The average elevation is 3,500 to 4,500 feet, with the highest altitudes at the summits of Emlembe (6,100 feet) and Ngwenya (6,000 feet). The area is 2,000 square miles. The Middleveld is rolling tall grass country of an average altitude of 2,000 to 2,500 feet. Its area is 1,900 square miles. The Lowveld or Bushveld is a gently undulating lowland but seldom a true plain. Isolated knolls and ridges rise above the general level of 500 to 1,000 feet to more than 2,300 feet. It covers some 2,200 square miles. The Lumbombo is an impressive escarpment which rises along the whole length of the eastern Lowveld, terminating it seaward and interrupted only by the gorges of the Ingwavuma, Usutu and Mbuluzi Rivers.

In their journey to the sea Swaziland's major rivers traverse all four regions. The mean discharge where the rivers leave the country would be about two million gallons a minute if no water was taken from them. However, the Lowveld and Middleveld increasingly draw on their reaches of river for supplies of irrigation water. Nearly all Highveld streams are perennial. In contrast, the water courses of the Lowveld, other than the trunk rivers, are only filled after heavy rainstorms and at other times are dry channels or wadis. From the Highveld, the Lomati, Komati, Mbuluzi, Usushwane (or Little Usutu), Usutu (or Great Usutu), Ngwempisi, and Mkhondo (or Assegai), fed by countless minor streams, flow in a generally eastward direction towards the Indian Ocean. None of the rivers is navigable in the true sense of the word.

The Highveld region has a humid near-temperate climate, with 40 to 90 inches mean annual rainfall, while the Middleveld and Lubombo are sub-tropical and less humid (30 to 45 inches). The Lowveld is near-tropical but drier, receiving 20 to 35 inches of rain in an average year. Most of the rain falls in the summer— from October to March. The winter period, April to September, is comparatively dry throughout the country. The mean annual temperature on the Highveld is just over 16°C (60°F), and in the Lowveld it is about 22°C (72°F). Seasonal and daily ranges of temperature are greatest in the Lowveld and least on the Lubombo and Highveld. There is a low incidence of frost, but it can be expected for a few days in most years on much of the Highveld and Middleveld and in valley bottoms throughout the country.

Population censuses take place at intervals of 10 years. The last census was held in May 1966, when a *de jure* population figure of 395,138 was arrived at. The 1970 estimate is about 450,000 including those temporarily absent from the country. Nearly 90 per cent of the population is Swazi, the remainder being

Africans from other countries, Europeans, and people of mixed race. The Swazi language, siSwati, is the main language spoken. English is the official language but there are statutory provisions under which siSwati can be used in Court proceedings.

In 1962 it was estimated that there were 73,400 Christians in Swaziland, and about 51,600 adults holding traditional beliefs.

About 43 per cent of adult Africans hold indigenous beliefs. Almost all the rest of the adult population are Christians.

In 1966 the birth rate was estimated to be 48 per thousand of the total population and the death rate about 22 per thousand; the population is increasing at the rate of about 2·8 per cent per year.

Government provides curative and preventive medical services, aided in the curative field by the missions, certain industrial concerns, and by private practitioners. Tuberculosis, especially pulmonary tuberculosis, is one of the main health problems and is being actively tackled by the National T.B. Control Centre, which is based in Manzini. Malnutrition is still a major cause of morbidity and mortality in children. This condition, together with gastro-enteritis, is the principal cause of death in young children. Skim milk powder, received from the United States through UNICEF, is distributed to the under-five-year-olds at maternity and child welfare centres to help reduce protein deficiency. Typhoid and para-typhoid fevers are prevalent and are likely to remain so until rural hygiene can be undertaken on a larger scale. Malaria, while still present, has been controlled and does not present a serious public health problem. The incidence of bilharzia is increasing slightly and the position will not improve until a relatively cheap and efficient molluscicide and a cheap therapeutic agent are discovered. Immunisation against enteric fever, diphtheria, whooping cough, tetanus, poliomyelitis, and smallpox is offered at all hospitals and health offices. The number of beds at hospitals in 1970 was: Government hospitals 1,038, subsidised mission hospitals 356; Industry and Private hospitals 93.

Swaziland is divided into four districts—Manzini, Lubombo, Shiselweni and Hhohho. Figures obtained from the 1966 census give the district populations as: Manzini, 101,277; Lubombo, 81,800; Shiselweni, 95,735; and Hhohho, 95,759. These figures exclude some 20,500 people who were absent from Swaziland during the census, most of them working in South Africa. Mbabane, situated in the Highveld, is the capital of Swaziland and administrative headquarters of the Hhohho district. It has a population of 13,800.

The Christian festivals are observed as Public holidays in Swaziland, including Easter Saturday, Easter Monday and Ascension Day. New Year's Day is also celebrated. Other Public holidays are National Flag Day (25th April), Commonwealth Day (second Monday in June), the King's Birthday (22nd July), Umhlanga (Reed Dance) Day (variable Mondays in July and August), Somhlolo Day (Independence Day) (6th September), and Newala Day (to be appointed each year).

The following table shows the estimated number of wage employees, according to origin and industry in 1969, as in the 1970 Statistical Bulletin of the Swaziland Government:

Industry Group	Total 1968	Total 1969	Swazi-land citizens	African non-citizens	European non-citizens
			Distribution by Citizenship 1969		
11 Agriculture and Livestock	13,730	14,884	12,574	2,060	250
12 Forestry and Logging	3,060	2,647	2,494	67	86
2 Mining and Quarrying	2,670	2,720	2,150	374	196
3 Manufacturing	4,690	5,119	4,176	433	510
31 Manufacturing of Food and Drink	2,140	2,188	1,652	319	217
33 Manufacturing of Wood and Wood Products	2,190	2,235	1,937	84	214
3x Other Manufacturing	360	696	587	30	79
4 Electricity and Water Supply	450	498	480	3	15
5 Construction	4,480	2,823	2,516	96	211
6 Distributive Trades	2,910	3,477	3,012	137	328
61 Wholesale Trade	430	606	504	17	85
62 Retail Trade	1,880	1,904	1,650	65	189
63 Hotels and Restaurants	600	967	858	55	54
71 Transport and Storage	1,620	1,674	1,443	64	167
72 Communication	410	364	330	—	34
8 Financial and Business Services	580	501	300	28	173
91 Public Administration	2,570	3,061	2,823	41	197
931 Education Services	2,280	2,697	2,319	105	273
933 Medical and Veterinary Services	1,060	1,208	1,152	18	38
95 Personal and Household Services	6,790	6,731	6,405	282	44
9x Other Services	320	237	203	9	25
Total	47,620	48,641	42,377	3,717	2,547
Males	36,590	39,247	33,795	3,466	1,986
Females	11,030	9,394	8,582	251	561

Source: Department of Statistics.

(1) All private firms regardless of number of employees are included.

(2) All Government employees included, except employees of the Swazi National Administration.

(3) Classification is based upon International Standard Industrial Classification List.

The traditional migration of Swazi labour to South Africa has diminished over the years but is still considerable. In 1960, 43 per cent of the male and 36 per cent of the female rural working population were employed outside Swaziland. Most of the Swazi who migrate in search of employment are recruited for work in the gold mines. Such recruitment is controlled under the Employment Proclamation, 1962. At the end of 1969 there were 9 registered trade unions. Some of the unions were, however, inactive.

Maize is the staple crop but cotton is the most significant dryland cash crop. In 1966/67 maize was grown on some 230,000 acres. Other important dryland crops are sorghum, tobacco and pineapples. Sugar is the most important irrigated crop. Citrus and rice are the other main crops grown under irrigation. With the exception of maize, and sorghum, all major crops are grown for export. In 1970, Swaziland had 568,369 head of cattle, 259,047 goats, 34,749 sheep, 2,300 horses, 14,704 donkeys, 359,043 poultry and 11,460 pigs. Some 48,130 cattle were slaughtered during 1969 and 4,641 were exported live. In 1968 there were 174,400 acres of established pine forest, 17,700 acres of eucalyptus and 23,000 acres of wattle. The exploitation of timber resources is now playing an important role in the economy of the country.

Asbestos and iron ore are the country's two most important minerals and iron ore is Swaziland's main export. Asbestos is produced at the Havelock Mine, near Pigg's Peak, while the Ngwenya mine, near Mbabane, is working a rich iron ore deposit. Both the Ngwenya mine and the country's only colliery, at Mpaka, started production in 1964. Swaziland's manufacturing industries are mainly concerned with the processing of agricultural, livestock and forestry products. The Usutu Pulp Company's mill at Bunya has an annual output of some 100,000 short tons of unbleached sulphate pulp, while the sugar mills at Big Bend and Mhlume produce about 170,000 short tons of sugar each year. The Swaziland Cotona cotton ginnery processes a significant proportion of the 6,000 tons of high quality cotton grown in the country each year, and the Swaziland Meat Corporation's abattoir and cannery at Matsapa processes meat for both local and export markets. Messrs Peak Timbers and Swaziland Plantations in the north of the country are producing a variety of building timber requirements from about 80,000 acres of planted pine. The sole fruit processing factory in the country, at Malkerns, processes mainly pineapple and grapefruit. Maize grown in Swaziland is milled in Manzini by the Swaziland Milling Company, which also has a rice drying plant. Butter is produced in Manzini and there is a small milk processing plant in Mbabane.

The table below lists the principal exports, with their values, for the years 1966, 1967, 1968 and 1969 (provisional) with certain of the 1970 provisional figures:

	1966 R('000)	1967 R('000)	1968 R('000)	1969 R('000) Provisional	1970 R('000) Provisional
Foodstuffs and Tobacco					
Live animals chiefly for food	747·1	595·8	281·5	377·6	
Butter and Butterfats	74·9	93·5	82·3	44·9	
Meat and meat products	1,254·0	1,871·6	2,270·5	1,275·1	
Rice	709·5	652·6	724·2	896·6	
Citrus fruits	1,166·0	1,398·9	1,776·3	3,510·9	
Canned fruits	380·2	673·6	673·0	773·9	
Sugar	10,216·3	9,547·1	7,779·9	10,478·7	11,777·4
Molasses	347·4	508·4	472·3	458·2	

	1966 R('000)	1967 R('000)	1968 R('000)	1969 R('000) Provisional	1970 R('000) Provisional
Foodstuffs and Tobacco					
Other vegetable foodstuffs	144·5	180·0	150·0	150·0	
Tobacco (raw)	42·6	33·7	35·5	50·6	
Raw Materials					
Asbestos	4,986·8	5,858·0	6,045·7	6,228·5	5,239·5
Gold	7·7	—	—	—	—
Iron Ore	10,333·0	11,320·8	11,828·4	9,617·9	11,041·2
Coal	37·7	64·3	94·7	161·2	
Other minerals	19·2	28·0	37·9	30·9	
Hides and skins	167·7	110·8	121·6	117·3	
Forest products	8,150·9	6,880·2	8,475·4	9,255·9	
Seed cotton (raw)	451·7	934·4	695·9	412·5	
Cotton lint	801·9	763·4	453·1	549·1	
Cotton seed	133·7	94·6	67·8	99·8	
Wool and Mohair	3·9	2·8	2·0	1·1	
Blood and carcase meal	15·4	12·1	37·7	27·0	
TOTAL	40,921·1	41,624·6	42,105·7	44,517·7	

The value of imports in 1966 was R25,685,000, in 1967, R35,027,000, in 1968, R34,104,500 and in 1969, R37,355,000.

At the end of 1970 there were 28 established co-operative organisations in Swaziland. The two main co-operatives are the Swaziland Tobacco Co-operative Co. Ltd, which has offices, store and factory at Nhlangano, and markets all tobacco produced in the country; the Swaziland Co-operative Rice Co. Ltd, which is managed by the Swaziland Milling Company and markets the rice grown by members in the Malkerns Valley area. The remaining 26 co-operatives are mainly farmers' co-ops and Credit Unions. Sugar is marketed through the Swaziland Sugar Association.

The main airport, Matsapa, five miles from the town of Manzini, has a 4,800 feet runway. Swaziland's railway, which has a 3 feet 6 inches gauge, and which is for goods traffic only, runs from Kadake, near the Ngwenya iron ore mine on the western border, through the middle of the country to Goba, on the eastern border, where it connects with the Mozambique railway to the port of Lourenço Marques. The railway and the Ngwenya mine were officially opened on 5th November 1964. A spur line connecting the Matsapa Industrial Estate to the main line was completed in mid-1965. The total route miles open to traffic is 139·5. The trans-territorial highway from Oshoek, on the Transvaal border, to Lomahasha on the Mozambique border is tarred for about 70 miles, the remaining 40 miles being of high-class gravel. Thirty miles of tarred road link Mhlambanyeti and Bunya with the trans-territorial highway. Most other roads in the country have good gravel surfaces. The only airline in Swaziland is Swazi Air Ltd, a subsidiary of a South African airline. There are flights three times a week to and from Johannesburg and twice weekly to Durban, in South Africa, and to Lourenço Marques in Mozambique.

A Government-operated broadcasting station transmits programmes in siSwati and English for three hours each morning, two hours at lunchtime and five hours each evening. Programmes for schools are broadcast for almost four hours each school day. There is a 10 kW transmitter in Mbabane along with a 100W F.M. transmitter and also a 20W F.M. transmitter in Manzini (both F.M. transmitters are on loan from the South African Broadcasting Corporation). The station opened in April 1966.

Under its post-Independence Development Plan for 1969-72 the Government proposes to undertake projects involving a total of about R18m. The British Government have agreed to make available over the three years 1970/71–1972/73 a total amount of £6,395,000. This includes an amount of £250,000 as a contribution to the Swaziland Government's general revenue balance. The remainder will take the form of development aid to be spent on projects jointly agreed by the Swaziland and British Governments. The main objectives are to raise living standards by generating increased industrial and agricultural development in both the public and private sectors and to improve educational levels to enable the Swazi people to play their rightful role in the affairs of their country.

Since 1910, Swaziland (with Botswana and Lesotho) has been in a customs and currency union with the Republic of South Africa. The original Customs Union Agreement was renegotiated in 1969 and the revised agreement came into force on 1st March 1970. In addition to changing the formula for the distribution of the pool of customs, excise, addition duties and sales tax the new Agreement deals with other matters of commercial importance to the four signatory governments. The new formula is no longer a fixed percentage (as it was under the 1910 Agreement) but fluctuates according to the actual value of imports into each of the four countries. In the case of Swaziland, the immediate consequences of the new Agreement have been very favourable: customs and excise receipts have now displaced income tax as the main source of Government revenue and, as a result, the need for budgetary grant-in-aid from Britain disappeared entirely in the 1969/70 financial year. In 1969/70 revenue under the new Agreement amounted to R7,536,000 and is expected to have totalled R6,700,000 in 1970/71 and to total R8,488,000 in 1971/72. The comparable figures for income tax—the second largest source of revenue—are R4,030,000 in 1970/71 and estimated for 1971/72 R4,187,000. Income tax is payable by all persons with incomes exceeding R600 p.a. (unmarried) and R1,200 p.a. (married) and is collected on the P.A.Y.E. system. Personal income tax contributes only a small amount to the total, however, and the major source is industry and commerce, especially mining. Non-residents are liable to a withholding tax of 50 per cent on dividends and $7\frac{1}{2}$ per cent on other interest. The minimum on other interest is $7\frac{1}{2}$ per cent. In 1969, a single graded tax ranging from R4,20 for incomes up to R300 to R18 for incomes over R600 and payable by persons over 18 years of age, was introduced to replace the former poll tax, Swazi tax and the Swazi national levy. Licensing exists for many trades and death duties are also levied. A double taxation agreement with Britain was signed in 1968.

Government revenue in 1971/72 for all sources is expected to amount to R17,241,026 and expenditure to R16,505,459.

Primary education is not yet universal. There are no tuition fees but pupils pay a nominal sum to the school fund and also pay for their books. In 1970 the primary school enrolment was 69,055. The enrolment in secondary classes was 8,027 in 1970. There are two teacher training colleges, an Industrial Training

Institute and a Staff Training Institute. The Swaziland Agricultural College and University Centre at Luyengo is associated with the University of Botswana, Lesotho and Swaziland (UBLS) and offers a 2-year University diploma course in Agriculture as well as shorter certificate courses. As from July 1971, UBLS will be undertaking teaching for Part I of many of their courses in Swaziland. In July 1972 the University will move into a new university complex financed by Britain, Canada and the United States on land provided by the King at Kwaluseni. The 1966 census revealed that 68·7 per cent of the men and 72·5 per cent of the women had had less than four effective years of schooling but the situation is improving rapidly and in the younger age groups the comparable figure is probably less than 50 per cent. There are no public libraries, but clubs and associations run small libraries in the main centres. A Swaziland National Library Service, has been established in Manzini, with the assistance of the British Council.

HISTORY

Swaziland remained nominally independent until 1890. From 1890 to 1894 the United Kingdom and the Transvaal (South African Republic) Governments established a species of condominium which was replaced in 1894 by an arrangement under which South Africa was given powers of protection and administration without actual incorporation. After the Anglo-Boer War, the administration of Swaziland was transferred to the Governor of the Transvaal, who was also the High Commissioner of South Africa, but in 1907 responsibility for Swaziland was transferred from the Governor to the High Commissioner for South Africa. Swaziland therefore remained under the control of the United Kingdom when the Transvaal became a province of the Union of South Africa in 1910. Swaziland became an independent Member of the Commonwealth on 6th September 1968.

CONSTITUTIONAL DEVELOPMENT

In May 1963 the Secretary of State for the Colonies published a White Paper (Cmnd 2052) outlining a constitution for Swaziland. This constitution was established by the Swaziland Order in Council 1963, which was made on 20th December. Under this constitution, Swaziland was administered by Her Majesty's Commissioner, a post equivalent to that of Governor. The Commissioner assented to legislation and was directly responsible to the Secretary of State. The constitution made provision for an Executive Council of eight members (four official and four unofficial) and a Legislative Council of four official members, 24 elected members and up to three members nominated by Her Majesty's Commissioner. In August 1965 the number of unofficial members in the Executive Council was increased from four to six and in October 1966, to seven.

Of the 24 elected Legislative Council members, eight were Swazi or Eurafricans certified by the Ngwenyama (the Paramount Chief) in Council as having been elected in accordance with Swazi traditional methods; eight were Europeans or Eurafricans, of whom four were elected by voters registered on a 'European Roll' and four elected by voters registered on a 'National Roll'; and eight were persons of any race elected by voters registered on the National Roll. Election on the national roll was virtually by universal adult suffrage.

The country was divided into four national roll constituencies to correspond with the four administrative districts. Each constituency returned three members, one of whom must be European or Eurafrican. The European roll constituency was the whole of Swaziland.

The elections for the first Legislative Council took place in June 1964. The Imbokodvo National Movement won 10 national roll seats and the United Swaziland Association gained two national roll seats and the four European roll seats. Five other political parties contested the elections but failed to win a seat. Her Majesty's Commissioner nominated one person to the Legislative Council.

In August 1965 a local committee was set up to review the constitution and make detailed recommendations on the form of a new one to the Secretary of State for the Colonies. The committee comprised 12 unofficial members chosen from the membership of the Legislative Council, and two officials. The Queen's Commissioner was chairman. The committee's proposals on a constitution which would give the country internal self-government were sent to the Secretary of State in March 1966. The British Government had informed the committee that it proposed to grant Swaziland internal self-government and was willing, subject to the approval of Her Majesty The Queen, to change the territory's status to that of a Protected State with the Ngwenyama recognised as King and Head of State. Britain's protection would continue until Swaziland attained independence not later than the end of 1969.

CONSTITUTION

Following further discussions with the Swaziland Government, the Secretary of State for the Colonies published a White Paper (Cmnd 3119) in October 1966 containing a draft of the proposed Agreement which would turn Swaziland into a Protected State and an outline of the proposed internal self-government constitution. This constitution was contained in a schedule to the Swaziland Constitution Order 1967, made on 22nd February 1967. The constitution, which came into operation on 25th April 1967, provided that:

(i) The Ngwenyama was recognised as King of Swaziland and Head of State.

(ii) Her Majesty's Commissioner, who was also the representative of Her Majesty's Government in Swaziland, retained responsibility for external affairs, defence and internal security and also certain responsiblility in the fields of finance and the public service; and there was a Consultative Council consisting of local representatives of Her Majesty's Government and of the Swaziland Government, for consultation on the exercise of these responsibilities.

(iii) There was a Parliament comprising a House of Assembly (consisting of a Speaker, 24 members elected by adult suffrage in 8 three-member constituencies, 6 members appointed by the King, and the Attorney-General (who had no vote) and a Senate (consisting of 6 members elected by the members of the House of Assembly and 6 members appointed by the King).

(iv) Subject to the powers of Her Majesty's Commissioner referred to in (ii) above, executive authority was vested in the King and exercised through a Cabinet consisting of a Prime Minister, a Deputy Prime Minister and up to six other Ministers; the Attorney-General normally attended Cabinet meetings in an advisory capacity.

(v) There was a Public Service Commission and a Judicial Service Commission, which became executive on 1st April 1968.

(vi)   The constitution provided for citizenship of Swaziland, which until independence had a purely local significance.

(vii)   Her Majesty retained general power to amend the constitution but it was open to the Swaziland Government to request amendments provided that certain specified procedures had been carried out.

(viii)   All minerals were vested in the Ngwenyama in trust for the Swazi nation, and the right to make grants in respect of minerals was vested in the King, who in exercising the power to make such grants acted in accordance with the advice of the Cabinet, but before giving its advice the Cabinet was required to consult a committee appointed by the King after consultation with the Swazi National Council.

The Agreement whereby Swaziland became a Protected State was signed by the Queen's Commissioner and the Ngwenyama on 24th April 1967 and came into force on 25th April.

In September 1967 the House of Assembly and the Senate approved motions authorising the Swaziland Government to ask Her Majesty's Government to grant Swaziland independence on 6th September 1968. Two months later Britain announced that she agreed to this request.

The 1967 Constitution was designed to take the country into independence with only a few alterations, and these were agreed by both Her Majesty's Government and the Swaziland Government at an independence conference held in Marlborough House, London, in February 1968. The present Constitution is contained in a schedule to the Swaziland Independence Order, 1968 which was made on 26th August 1968 and came into operation immediately before Independence on 6th September 1968. The major difference in the Independence Constitution compared with the 1967 Constitution apart from the abolition of the office and powers of Her Majesty's Commissioner; the abolition of the power of Her Majesty to amend the Constitution; and the lifting of the restriction on the number of Cabinet Ministers; is the provision regarding the control of minerals. Under the Independence Constitution, minerals and mineral oils are vested in the Ngwenyama, who is advised by a Minerals Committee (instead of the Cabinet) appointed by him after consultation with the Swazi National Council.

LAND POLICY

The complex pattern of land ownership in Swaziland is largely the result of historical events which occurred before the establishment of the British Administration in 1902. Between the years 1875 and 1889 the Swazi ruler Mbandzeni granted numerous concessions to Europeans which included grants and leases of land for grazing and agricultural purposes. The concessions covered almost the whole extent of the Territory and many of the deeds contained clauses which reserved to the Ngwenyama his sovereign rights and forbade the concessionaires from interfering with the rights of the Swazi living within the area of the concessions. In terms of the Swaziland Convention of 1890, a Chief Court was established to undertake an enquiry into the validity of disputed concessions. It did, in fact, examine the initial validity of the majority of concessions and its decisions were adhered to by the British Administration. The Swaziland Administration Proclamation (No. 3 of 1904) provided for the establishment of a commission which was, *inter alia*, required to examine each land and grazing concession and cause their boundaries to be defined and surveyed. On the completion of the commission's work, a Special Commissioner was appointed in terms of the Swaziland Concessions Partition Proclamation (No. 28 of 1907) to set aside areas for the sole and exclusive use and occupation of the Swazi. He was empowered to expropriate one third of the area of each concession without compensation, but should more than this be required, compensation was payable. The remaining concessions were freed from any rights of use and occupation possessed by the Swazi, and the owners of concessions who held title to the ownership of the land or leases of not less than 99 years' duration, with or without rights of renewal, were granted freehold title. The reversionary rights to land and mineral concessions were vested in the Crown in terms of the Swaziland Crown Lands and Minerals Order in Council of 1908 as amended by a subsequent Order in Council in 1910. Following the partition of the Territory, further legislation was passed to secure the rights of the Swazi in the areas that had been set aside for them (Proclamation No. 39 of 1910), also to define the conditions under which the Crown could sell, lease or otherwise dispose of Crown Land (Proclamation No. 13 of 1911). Proclamation No. 2 of 1915 made provision for securing for the benefit of the Swazi any land acquired on behalf of the Swazi Nation.

Abortive efforts were made by the Swazi in 1922 and 1923 to set aside the Partition Proclamation of 1907; but a petition to King George VI in 1941 was more successful and resulted in the introduction of the Swazi Land Settlement Scheme (see below). The land question was raised at the independence conference in 1968 and at subsequent post-independence talks in November/December 1968, the British Government stated their willingness to examine the matter on strictly economic grounds. This offer was accepted by the Swaziland Government and a working party under the independent chairmanship of Mr R. E. T. Hobbs and consisting of two nominees each of the British and Swaziland Governments was appointed. The Working Party presented its Report ("The Hobbs Report") on 14th March 1969, and its conclusions were accepted in principle by both Governments. On 22nd April 1970, the Minister of Finance in Swaziland was able to announce that a substantial part of British development aid to the agricultural sector would be earmarked for a land purchase and development programme "aimed at restoring a considerable acreage to Swazi ownership".

At the end of 1967, some 56 per cent of the total area of the Territory, which covers 4,290,944 acres, was reserved for occupation by the Swazi. This comprised Swazi Area, land purchased by the Swazi Nation and Swazi Land Settlement areas. Swazi Area, which was set aside by the Concessions Partition Commissioner for occupation by the Swazi in 1910, is vested in the Ngwenyama as Swazi Nation Land in trust for the Swazi Nation. It is scattered throughout the Territory in blocks of varying size and covers 1,639,687 acres or 38·2 per cent of the total area of the country. The purchase of land by the Swazi Nation started initially as a reaction to the partition of the Territory. The Swazi were encouraged by the Chief Regent to go to the Transvaal in order to earn money with which to purchase land from European holders. Purchases continued to be made with monies raised locally by collections or levies until the start of the Lifa Fund in 1946. The purposes of this fund were to reduce overstocking and to purchase additional land. Under an order made by the Ngwenyama in Libandla (Council), cattle were culled from the herds of those Swazi who owned more than 10 head. The animals thus acquired were auctioned and a levy on the proceeds credited to the Lifa Fund. By the end of 1964, the area of land purchased in this way amounted to some 268,000 acres. The Lifa Fund was wound up in 1968.

Swazi Land Settlement areas, which consist of farms purchased from European owners and Crown Land set aside for the purpose by Government, were defined in 1946 and are generally contiguous with the existing Swazi areas. This land, some 316,700 acres in extent, is now vested in the Ngwenyama as Swazi Nation Land in trust for the Swazi Nation.

Land owned by individual Africans, missions, Europeans, Eurafricans and others covers about 44 per cent of the total area of the Territory. Of this privately-owned land, less than 10 per cent now consists of land concessions, held in perpetuity or on leases of more than 99 years' duration. In order to avoid the complications which have persisted because of differing forms of title, the owners of these concessions have been requested to exercise their option under the provision of Proclamation No. 28 of 1907 and convert their title to freehold. Farms which are purchased by individual Africans are registered in their own names. The area owned by individual Swazis totals 23,700 acres. Missions own 21,100 acres and the extent of farms owned by Europeans, Eurafricans and others or of land situated in proclamation townships, is 1,873,400 acres. The remaining area of the Territory comprises Government-owned land some 101,900 acres in extent and this, excluding land required for public purposes (schools, police posts, townships, etc.), is being transferred to the Ngwenyama as Swazi Nation Land in trust for the Swazi Nation.

On Swazi Area a system of communal land ownership is practised. One of the most important rights exercised by the chiefs is the allocation of residential and ploughing land. The Ngwenyama is recognised as having overall control of Swazi Area but in practice he defers to local chiefs in all matters of rights of occupancy, except in areas which, by tradition, belong to the Swazi ruling house. An individual obtains rights to use and occupy land from the chief of an area. Such rights once granted are firm and can only be extinguished by the individual concerned relinquishing them or by his being arraigned before a chief for a misdemeanour, such as witchcraft or adultery, sufficiently serious to justify banishment. An appeal against such an order would lie to the Ngwenyama. As might be expected, however, from a contact of over 50 years with European systems of land tenure and an increasing scarcity of the land, the traditional system of land ownership is gradually acquiring a more clearly defined individual emphasis in many areas.

The principles of the Roman-Dutch law of land ownership, which apply to land owned in freehold, embody the Roman Law conception of absolute ownership of land in contradistinction to the English law of tenure which, in theory, holds that all land is held by the Crown. Freeholders and, if their concessions do not prohibit this, concessionaires occasionally grant occupation or grazing leases, and, in a few instances, land is farmed on a crop share basis. Outside urban areas, some freehold and concession land is subject to the payment of quitrent, generally of a small amount. Townships stands are subject to a fixed quitrent of one rand per annum.

GOVERNMENT

Elections to fill the 24 elected seats in the House of Assembly took place on 19th and 20th April 1967; they were contested by four parties, but all the seats were won by the Imbokodvo National Movement.

HEAD OF STATE
His Majesty King Sobhuza, II, KBE

CABINET
Prime Minister and Minister of Foreign Affairs: Prince Makhosini Dlamini
Deputy Prime Minister: Z. A. Khumalo
Minister of Finance: Leo Lovell
Minister of Commerce, Industry and Mines: Simon S. Nxumalo
Minister of Local Administration: Prince Mfanasibili Dlamini
Minister of Works, Power and Communications: J. M. B. Sukati, BEM
Minister of Health and Education: Dr A. M. Nxumalo
Minister of Agriculture: A. K. Hlope
Minister of Justice: P. L. Dlamini, OBE

HOUSE OF ASSEMBLY
The Speaker: Ian B. Aers. OBE
The Attorney-General
24 Elected Members
6 Members appointed by the King

SENATE
The President: Sir John Houlton, CSI, CIE
Deputy President: Chief J. M. Mamba
6 Members elected by members of the House of Assembly
6 Members appointed by the King

A great deal of the structure of the traditional Swazi political system has been retained in the modern pattern of the Swazi National Administration. The Ngwenyama is a constitutional ruler who is advised by his kinsmen and chosen councillors and cannot initiate action without the approval of two formally constituted councils. The smaller of these, the Liqoqo, comprises the more important of the Ngwenyama's agnatic kin and a number of chosen advisers. It meets once a week to deal with national matters which are usually channelled to it by a standing committee of the larger council, the Libandla. The Libandla embraces every adult male in the Swazi Nation. It usually meets once a year and it is recognised as the final body from which approval for any contemplated act of legislation should be obtained. Day-to-day contact between the Government and the main council is maintained through the standing committee of the council. To this traditional ruling system has been appended the Swazi National Treasury, with a revenue in the region of R240,000 per year, and formally constituted Swazi Courts from which appeal ultimately lies to the High Court of Swaziland.

From the central institutions of the Swazi National Administration, responsibility devolves upon the chiefs and their ndunas.

GOVERNMENT DEPARTMENTS

PRIME MINISTER'S OFFICE

Cabinet Office

Secretary to the Cabinet and Head of the Civil Service: C. M. E. Dlamini

Department of Foreign Affairs
Minister of State: The Hon. H. K. Dlamini
Permanent Secretary: N. D. Ntiwane.

Establishment & Training Division
Minister of State: The Hon. E. S. Dhladhla
Permanent Secretary: J. S. F. Magagula

DEPUTY PRIME MINISTER'S OFFICE
Assistant Minister: The Hon. Prince Masitsela Dlamini
Permanent Secretary: S. Z. S. Dlamini.

Labour Division
Labour Commissioner: D. E. Motha

Prisons Department
Director of Prisons: R. L. Mkhatshwa

Immigration Department
Chief Immigration Officer: H. K. Dlamini

Swaziland Broadcasting Service
Principal Broadcasting and Information Officer: D. Nkosi

Registrar-General's Office
Registrar-General: E. Kumalo

MINISTRY OF AGRICULTURE
Permanent Secretary: S. J. S. Sibanyoni
Agricultural Officer: G. M. Maina (Acting)

MINISTRY OF EDUCATION
Permanent Secretary: J. L. F. Simelane
Chief Education Officer: L. Sithebe

MINISTRY OF FINANCE
Permanent Secretary: J. Nxumalo
Accountant-General: M. O. Udeariry
Collector of Income Tax: B. B. Ockei

MINISTRY OF COMMERCE, INDUSTRY AND MINES
Permanent Secretary: T. Zwane
Director of Geological Survey and Mines: Dr. J. Bennett

MINISTRY OF HEALTH
Permanent Secretary, Dr Friedman, MBE
Director of Medical Services: Dr J. M. L. Klopper, OBE

MINISTRY OF LOCAL ADMINISTRATION
Assistant Minister: The Hon. B. A. Dlamini
Permanent Secretary: A. A. Zwane

MINISTRY OF WORKS, POWER AND COMMUNICATIONS
Permanent Secretary: A. R. V. Khozo
Director of Public Works: J. S. Russell

Department of Posts and Telecommunications
Director: R. Kirkwood, CBE

AUDIT DEPARTMENT
Director of Audit: I. D. Spicer

JUDICIARY
Chief Justice: Sir Philip Ernest Housden Pike
Registrar of the High Court: B Barnard (Acting)

LAW OFFICE
Attorney-General: W. A. Ramsden, QC

SWAZILAND POLICE FORCE
Commissioner of Police: V. Smithyman

PUBLIC SERVICE COMMISSION
Chairman: G. L. Oscroft

UNITED REPUBLIC OF TANZANIA

THE United Republic of Tanzania was formed on 26th April 1964 by the union of that part of the East African mainland known as Tanganyika, which included Mafia and a number of other small off-shore islands, and Zanzibar, which included not only the island of Zanzibar itself but also the islands of Pemba and Latham. The name Tanzania was adopted on 29th October 1964. The total area of the country is 363,708 square miles.

The area of the mainland (Tanganyika) is approximately 362,700 square miles, including some 20,000 square miles of inland water. It is bounded on the east by the Indian Ocean, on the north by Kenya, Lake Victoria and Uganda; on the west by Rwanda, Burundi, Lake Tanganyika (across which is the Congo); and on the south by Zambia, Malawi, Lake Malawi and Mozambique.

The mainland contains the two extremes of topographical relief of the whole continent of Africa: Kilimanjaro, with a permanent ice-cap rising to 19,340 feet above sea level, and the deep trough-like depression filled by Lake Tanganyika, the world's second deepest lake. Mount Meru, 50 miles west of Kilimanjaro, rises to 14,974 feet. The Mbulu Range of mountains (highest point Mount Hanang, 11,215 feet) lies 150 miles S.W. of Mount Kilimanjaro, and the Mbeya Range (highest point Mount Rungwe, 9,713 feet) lies to the north of Lake Malawi. The Kipengere Range (highest peak 9,715 feet) and the Livingstone Mountains (9,600 feet) and other large mountains are just north of the Mbulu Range and include Loolmalasin (11,969 feet) and the still active volcano Oldonyo Lengeri.

The main rivers are the Pangani or Ruvu, the Wani, the Ruvu (Kingoni), the Rufiji, the Great Ruaha, the Matandu, the Mbwemkuru, the Lukuledi and the Ruvuma, which drain the central plateau and flow into the Indian Ocean; and the Mori, Mara and Kegera, the Malagarasi, the Songwe and Ruhuhu which feed the great lakes.

The climate is very varied and not typically tropical; rainfall can be anything between 14·3 inches to 123·4 inches a year. There are three climatic zones: the hot and humid coastal area; the drier central plateau with a great deal of seasonal variations of temperature; and the semi-temperate mountain areas.

Zanzibar consists of Zanzibar Island, Pemba Island and Latham Island. Zanzibar Island is situated in the Indian Ocean in latitude 6° S. and longitude 39° E. It is separated (22½ miles) from the mainland by the Zanzibar Channel and is the largest island off the coast of East Africa, being fifty-three miles long and twenty-four miles wide, with a total area of 640 square miles. The eastern and central parts, comprising two-thirds of the island, consist of low-lying coral country covered by bush and grass plains, largely uninhabited except for fishing settlements on the east coast. The western side of the island is fertile and densely populated, with several ridges rising to over 200 feet above sea level; the highest ridge, the Masingini Ridge, is 390 feet above sea level. In this area coconuts and to a lesser extent cloves are extensively grown. The island of Pemba lies twenty-five miles to the north-east, in latitude 5° S. and longitude 39° E. It is forty-two miles long and about fourteen miles wide, with an area of 380 square miles. The west and centre of the island consists of a flat-topped ridge about six miles wide, deeply intersected by streams. The coastline is deeply indented especially in the west and the inlets are mostly filled with mangrove swamps. Apart from the narrow belt of coral country in the east the island is fertile and densely populated, clove growing being the major industry. Pemba provides about 83 per cent of Zanzibar's cloves, the total exports of which in 1969 were valued at £9m. sterling. Forty miles to the south-east of Zanzibar is Latham Island, which is no more than an outcrop of calcareous beach rock 300 yards long by 170 yards wide. It is principally notable as the breeding ground for booby, tern and green turtle.

Mafia Island is situated 80 miles south of Dar-es-Salaam and has excellent deep-sea fishing grounds. East African Airways run scheduled flights to the island and small aircraft land visitors on the Fishing Club's own airstrip.

The climate of Zanzibar is tropical, tempered throughout the year with constant sea breezes except during the rainy seasons. The heavy rains fall in April and May with lesser rains in November and December. The mean maximum and minimum temperatures for Zanzibar town are 84·4°F and 76·6°F respectively and for Wete, in Pemba, 86·3°F and 76·1°F. The annual rainfall for Zanzibar town averages 61·9 inches and for Wete 76·9 inches.

At the last census in August 1967 the total population was 12,311,911 of whom 11,957,176 lived on the mainland and 480,000 in Zanzibar. The estimated annual growth rate is at present 2·6 per cent. It is expected that the rate will be higher after 1975 and the population is expected to reach the 17·9 million mark in 1980.

There are some 120 tribes on the mainland, none of which exceed 10 per cent of the population. Tne largest is the Sukuma tribe and others include the Nyamwezi; Ha; Makondi; Gogo, Haya; Masai and Chagga. Swahili is the principal language and with English, the official language. The main religions are Islam and Christianity of many denominations.

For administrative purposes the mainland is divided into 17 regions under Regional Commissioners, namely Arusha, Coast, Dodoma, Kigoma, Kilimanjaro, Mara, Morogoro, Mtwara, Mwanza, Ruvuma, Shinyanga, Iringa, Mbeye, Tabora, Tanga, Singida and West Lake. The regions are further divided into Districts under Area Commissioners.

The capital of Tanzania, Dar-es-Salaam, had a 1967 population of 272,821. Other leading towns include, Zanzibar (68,490), Tanga (61,058), Mwanza (34,864), Arusha (32,452), (Administrative Centre of the East African Community), Moshi (26,864), Morogoro (25,262), Dodoma (23,559), Iringa (21,746), Kigoma (21,369) and Mtwara (20,413).

Dar-es-Salaam is the principal port and handled 2·2 million deadweight tons of cargo in 1969. Major extensions to port facilities are in progress. Other ports include Tanga, Mtwara, Zanzibar and Wete together with Mwanza, Musoma and Bukoba on Lake Victoria and Kigoma on Lake Tanganyika. Coastal shipping services connect the mainland and Zanzibar and Lake services are operated on Lake Victoria, Lake Tanganyika and Lake Malawi with neighbouring countries.

The principal international airport is Dar-es-Salaam (runway 2,400 metres). Other airports include Zanzibar, Arusha, Mwanza and Tanga. Frequent air services are operated by East African Airways and there are a number of air charter firms. A new international airport is being built between Arusha and Moshi to take 'Jumbo Jets'.

The railway system is part of East African railways and consists of over 1,600 miles of metre gauge track. A new railway linking Dar-es-Salaam with Zambia (The Tanzam Railway) is under construction, There are over 19,200 kilometres of roads of which over 2,500 kilometres are bitumenized. Road links with Zambia, Rwanda, Burundi and Kenya are being modernised in a major development programme. An oil pipeline 1,700 kilometres long supplies oil products from a refinery in Dar-es-Salaam to Zambia. Radio Services are operated by Radio Tanzania in Dar-es-Salaam and Zanzibar.

The economy of Tanzania has grown considerably since Independence. Gross domestic product (GDP) increased from £384 million sterling in 1966 to £433 million in 1970 (at 1966 prices) of which the monetary sector in 1969 accounted for 71·2 per cent. 40·3 per cent of GDP was agricultural in 1969 and 7·6 per cent manufacturing, but the latter grew by 10·8 per cent in 1968-69. Tourism is now growing at about 30 per cent annually. Overall economic and development policy is governed by the 1969-74 Development Plan and by the precepts of the 1967 Arusha Declaration in emphasising self-reliance and the equitable distribution of economic resources.

Tanzania is a member of the East African Community and shares common services with Kenya and Uganda. In 1970 total exports and re-exports were £99·4 million and total imports £113·2 million. 22 per cent of exports went to Britain and 30 per cent to the rest of the sterling area. 21 per cent of imports came from Britain, 25 per cent from EEC and 17 per cent from Kenya and Uganda. Leading exports were coffee, cotton, diamonds, sisal, cloves, cashew nuts and petroleum products. Leading imports were manufactured goods, machinery and transport equipment.

Forecast recurrent revenue for 1970-71 is £96·5 million, recurrent expenditure £96·3 million and development expenditure £55·5 million.

Tanzania's National Days are:—

12th January (Anniversary of the Zanzibar Revolution in 1964);

26th April, Union Day (Anniversary of the Union of Tanganyika and Zanzibar in 1964);

7th July, Saba Saba Day (Anniversary of the founding of TANU in 1954); and

9th December, Jamhuri Day (Anniversary of Tanganyika's independence in 1961 and of the formation of the Republic in 1962).

HISTORY

It is known that the East African coast had trade connections with Arabia and India before the beginning of the Christian era.

In the first century A.D. the coast, including Zanzibar, was, and had long been, under the control of the ruler of south-western Arabia; the geography and products of the area were known to the Greeks of Alexandria and the most southerly market-town known to the ancients, Rhapta, must have been situated somewhere on the coast within a hundred miles of Dar-es-Salaam. From the eleventh century onwards the Sultanate of Kilwa came into prominence, attaining its greatest prosperity in the fourteenth and fifteenth centuries when its rulers controlled the trade of a long stretch of the coast, extending down to Sofala, near the present Beira in Mozambique.

In 1498 the arrival of Vasco da Gama off the coast of East Africa heralded a period of Portuguese predominance over the coasts and waters of East Africa. Though very few of the Portuguese settled in the country, the civilisation of the coastal towns suffered a severe decline. Towards the end of the sixteenth century, however, the Portuguese began to give way to the Turks and Arabs, notably the Imams of Oman. But Arab influence declined during the eighteenth century and the allegiance to Muscat became more and more shadowy until 1832 when the fifth ruler of the Albusaidi dynasty, Seyyid Said, moved his capital from Muscat to Zanzibar. The second period of Arab domination was the great period of the slave trade. Bagamoyo, Sadani and Pangani on the Tanganyika coast were the usual points of departure and Tabora the most important inland centre. After Seyyid Said's death in 1856 his territories were divided between his two elder sons, and Zanzibar, with the adjacent coast, became an independent sultanate.

The country later known as Tanganyika came under German influence largely through the initiative of Dr Karl Peters, who in 1884 journeyed into the interior and in six weeks concluded twelve treaties with chiefs, whose chiefdoms were then declared to be German territory. In 1885 the land which Peters had acquired, including 60,000 square miles of territory over which the Sultan of Zanzibar claimed suzerainty, was placed under the protection of the Imperial German Government. A ten-mile belt along the coast was regarded as belonging to Zanzibar but in 1888 Germany acquired the right of collecting duties on the coast and in 1890 took over the coastal strip on payment of £200,000 to the Sultan of Zanzibar. Later the same year the supremacy of British interests in Zanzibar and Pemba was recognised by France and Germany and on 4th November the islands were proclaimed a British Protectorate, Zanzibar affairs being handled by the Foreign Office. In 1891 a constitutional government was established in Zanzibar and the Sultan appointed a British subject, Lloyd Mathews, as his First Minister. The British Representative at that time was the Consul-General, Sir Gerald Portal.

Soon after the outbreak of the 1914-18 War clashes took place between British and German forces on the northern frontier of Tanganyika, but the main campaign to occupy the country did not begin until 1916. By the end of that year all the country north of the Central Railway was occupied by British or Belgian forces and a provisional Civil Administration was established for that area on the 1st January 1917. In November 1917 the German forces were driven across the Ruvuma River into Portuguese East Africa and the occupation of the whole of the territory was then completed.

By Article 119 of the Treaty of Peace with Germany, signed at Versailles on the 28th June 1919, Germany renounced in favour of the Principal Allied and Associated Powers all her rights over her overseas possessions, including her East African colony. The Principal Allied and Associated Powers agreed that His Britannic Majesty should exercise a mandate to administer this former German colony, except for the areas of Ruanda and Urundi for which the mandate was given to the Belgian Government. The administration of Tanganyika continued to be carried out under the terms of the mandate until its transfer to the Trusteeship System under the Charter of the United Nations by the Trusteeship Agreement of 13th December 1946.

TANGANYIKA
CONSTITUTIONAL DEVELOPMENT

The Legislative Council was first constituted by the Tanganyika (Legislative Council) Order in Council, 1926, and consisted of the Governor as President, 13 Official members and not more than ten Unofficial members. The full quota of Unofficials was not filled until 1935, when seven Europeans and three Asians were nominated. In the same year changes were made in the Official membership and a further revision took place two years later.

In 1945 the Legislative Council was enlarged to consist of the Governor as President, 15 Official and not more than 14 Unofficial members. As a result of these changes the 14 Unofficial Members included, from 1948 onwards, four Africans (two appointed in 1945, a third in 1947 and a fourth in 1948) and three Asians. In 1949 the Governor appointed a Committee including African, Asian and European representatives to review the country's constitutional structure. Its report was published in 1951 and recommended equal representation of the territory's three main races in the unofficial membership of an enlarged Legislative Council with the retention of an official majority. After further examination the recommendations were put into effect in 1955. The new Council was presided over by a Speaker and had 31 Official members and 30 Unofficials (comprising ten Africans, ten Asians and ten Europeans).

From 1948 onwards the Executive Council, which assisted the Governor in an advisory capacity, was remodelled on the 'Member' system, whereby groups of Government Departments were the responsibility of certain individual members of the Executive Council. By the end of 1954 the Executive Council consisted of the Governor as President, three *ex officio* members, five nominated Official members and six Unofficial members (of whom two were Europeans, two Asians and two Africans). In 1957 the Official members of the Executive Council were redesignated as Ministers and at the same time six Assistant Ministers (four Africans, one European and one Asian) were appointed. The Assistant Ministers became *ex officio* members of the Legislative Council with the duty of speaking for the departments assigned to them but they were not, however, members of the Executive Council although they might attend meetings and take part in discussions when matters affecting their departments came before it.

The first General Election in Tanganyika was held in 1958-59 in two phases, because of the administrative and other problems involved in holding this first series of elections in such a vast country.

After the elections the Governor announced that it was proposed to set up a Council of Ministers in which Unofficials, including Africans, would for the first time be appointed to Ministerial office. The new Council which took office in July 1959 had 12 Ministers, five of whom were elected Unofficials (three African, one Asian and one European), and it advised the Governor on constitutional and legislative matters. The Executive Council was still in existence but only advised the Governor on a limited range of subjects.

The Governor announced in December 1959 that there would be new elections followed by important constitutional changes.

The second General Election, which brought in an elected majority in both the executive and the legislative spheres, was held in August 1960. The elected side of the Legislature comprised 71 seats and of this figure 50 seats were open to contest by all races and 21 reserved for minority communities, 11 Asians and 10 Europeans. Although there were 71 seats in fact there were only 13 contests in 11 constituencies because 58 candidates, 17 of whom were former members of Legislative Council, were returned unopposed.

Only two Parties contested the election, the Tanganyika African National Union and the African National Congress. There were, however, a number of independent candidates.

The election resulted in an overwhelming victory for the Tanganyika African National Union under the leadership of Mr Julius Nyerere, which obtained 70 of the 71 elected seats. The single successful non-TANU candidate stood as an Independent.

On the new government taking office certain changes took place in the constitutional framework of the executive, the principal of which was the abolition of the office of Chief Secretary and the creation of the new office of Deputy Governor, who was a member of the Council of Ministers but not of the Legislative Council. With this change came the abolition of the Executive Council and the introduction of the office of Chief Minister.

After the Constitutional Conference held in Dar-es-Salaam in March 1961, under the chairmanship of the Secretary of State for the Colonies, the British Government announced that it had agreed to grant internal self-government to Tanganyika from 1st May 1961 and full independence from 28th December 1961. The latter was later altered to 9th December 1961.

During the period 1st May to 9th December 1961 the Governor continued to be responsible for Defence and External Affairs. On 1st May 1961 Mr Nyerere, formerly Chief Minister, became the country's first Prime Minister, at the head of a Cabinet of 12. On the same day the Legislative Council was re-named the National Assembly, its composition remaining unchanged. The post of Deputy Governor was abolished from 1st July 1961.

In June 1961 the Tanganyika National Assembly unanimously passed a motion asking other member governments of the Commonwealth to join with the British Government in supporting Tanganyika's desire to become a Member of the Commonwealth. All Commonwealth Governments agreed to this and Tanganyika became a Member of the Commonwealth on achieving independence on the 9th December 1961. At the same time the Trusteeship Agreement was terminated by the United Nations.

On 15th February 1962 the Tanganyika National Assembly unanimously adopted a government motion that the Constitution be amended to provide for Tanganyika to become a Republic within the Commonwealth. At the Meeting of Commonwealth Prime Ministers held in London on 10th September 1962 the Prime Minister of Tanganyika was informed by the Heads of Delegations of the other member countries of the Commonwealth that the present relations between their countries and Tanganyika would remain unaffected by this constitutional change and that they would be happy to recognise Tanganyika's continued membership of the Commonwealth.

The Republic of Tanganyika was inaugurated on the 9th December 1962. Its Constitution provided for a President who was executive Head of State and Commander-in-Chief of the Armed Forces; he was empowered to appoint a Vice-President and Ministers of his Cabinet, though he was not bound to act on their advice. The first President, Dr Nyerere, was directly elected by universal suffrage. The Constitution provided for the election of subsequent Presidents by the National Assembly at five-yearly intervals or on the dissolution of Parliament.

ZANZIBAR

CONSTITUTIONAL DEVELOPMENT

On 1st July 1913 the control of Zanzibar passed from the Foreign Office to the Colonial Office, and by a Zanzibar Order in Council of 1914 the offices of British Consul-General and the Sultan's First Minister were merged in the newly-created post of British Resident, who was appointed, subject to the control of the Governor of the British East Africa Protectorate, as High Commissioner. A Protectorate Council was constituted as an advisory body with the Sultan as President and the British Resident as Vice-President. In 1925 the office of High Commissioner was abolished and the British Resident was made directly responsible to the Colonial Office. Executive and Legislative Councils were constituted in 1926 in place of the old advisory Protectorate Council. In 1960, following recommendations made by Sir Hilary Blood who had been appointed Constitutional Commissioner, a degree of responsible government was granted. Elected Ministers, one of whom was Chief Minister, formed the majority in the Executive Council, and in the Legislative Council there was a large elected majority.

In 1962 the franchise was extended to provide for universal adult suffrage, and a Delimitation Commission recommended an increase in the number of elected members in the Legislative Council. On 24th June 1963 internal self-government was introduced. After a General Election in July a Government was formed from a coalition between the Zanzibar Nationalist Party and the Zanzibar and Pemba People's Party, which had won a majority of seats (though not of votes) over the Afro-Shirazi Party headed by Sheikh Abeid Amani Karume. At the Independence Conference held in London in September 1963 arrangements were agreed for the final transfer of power, and Zanzibar attained full sovereign independence on 10th December 1963 under the Sultan as Head of State.

Establishment of The People's Republic of Zanzibar

On 12th January 1964 the Sultan's Government was overthrown by a sudden internal uprising. Zanzibar was proclaimed a People's Republic, with Mr Karume as President. The former constitution was abrogated, but other existing laws continued in force. A Revolutionary Council of 32 members was declared the Supreme Authority in the Republic. A Cabinet of Ministers was appointed to exercise executive power on behalf of, and with the advice of, the Revolutionary Council. Under a Presidential Decree made in February 1964 the Revolutionary Council was to enact constitutional Decrees which were to form the basic law of the Republic, and a Constituent Assembly was to be convened to consider these basic provisions which, after having received the Assembly's assent, were to be the Constitution of Zanzibar. A further Presidential Decree of 11th May 1965 established the Afro-Shirazi Party as the sole party and supreme authority in Zanzibar.

UNION OF TANGANYIKA AND ZANZIBAR

After meetings between President Nyerere and President Karume it was decided that Tanganyika and Zanzibar should form one Sovereign State. Articles of Union were signed on 22nd April 1964 and on 25th April 1964 legislation ratifying these Articles was enacted by both the Tanganyika Parliament and the Revolutionary Council of Zanzibar. By this legislation the United Republic of Tanganyika and Zanzibar was created as a single sovereign state, as from 26th April 1964, under President Nyerere. President Karume was declared 1st Vice-President of the United Republic, while retaining the style of President of Zanzibar as head of the separate Legislature and Executive for Zanzibar. There were 18 members from Zanzibar in the National Assembly of the United Republic and some of these became Ministers and Parliamentary Secretaries in the United Republic Government.

The legislation provided for an interim constitution which laid down that the United Republic should be governed in accordance with the provisions of the existing Tanganyika Constitution suitably modified to provide for a separate Legislature and Executive in Zanzibar with exclusive authority over matters other than reserved matters. Reserved matters were: external affairs; defence; police; emergency powers; citizenship; immigration; external trade and borrowing; The Public Service of the United Republic; income tax, corporation tax, customs and excise duties; harbours, civil aviation, posts and telegraphs.

The main subjects which remained within the competence of the Zanzibar Government and for which there were separate ministries or departments included agriculture and fisheries; education and national culture; health and social insurance; information and broadcasting; labour; prisons; roads, power, works and justice.

The United Republic of Tanganyika and Zanzibar became the United Republic of Tanzania on 29th October 1964.

On 5th July 1965 the National Assembly passed the Interim Constitution Act which formerly declared Tanzania to be a one-party state. A revised TANU constitution formed the first schedule of the Act, which looked forward to the union of TANU and the Afro-Shirazi party.

By the Interim Constitution Act the National Assembly was enlarged and consisted of 107 members elected from the Mainland, 15 elected by the Assembly itself, 17 Regional Commissioners from the Mainland and 3 from Zanzibar, up to 32 members of the Zanzibar Revolutionary Council, up to 10 Mainland residents chosen by the President and up to 20 Zanzibar residents similarly chosen. Zanzibar appointments require the approval of the President of Zanzibar. The number of constituencies was increased to 120 for the 1970 General Elections.

HISTORICAL LIST

TANGANYIKA
GOVERNOR-GENERAL
Sir Richard Turnbull, K CMG (later G CMG), 9th December 1961 to 8th December 1962

MINISTRIES
Mwalimu Julius K. Nyerere, 9th December 1961 to 22nd January 1962
Rashidi Kawawa, 22nd January 1962 to 8th December 1962

PRESIDENT OF THE REPUBLIC OF TANGANYIKA
Mwalimu Julius K. Nyerere, 9th December 1962 to 25th April 1964

ZANZIBAR
SULTAN
His Highness Seyyid Jamshid bin Abdulla, 10th December 1963 to 11th January 1964

MINISTRY
Sheikh Mohammed Shamte Hamedi, M BE, 10th December 1963 to 18th January 1964

PRESIDENT OF PEOPLE'S REPUBLIC OF ZANZIBAR
Sheikh Abeid Amani Karume, 12th January 1964 to 25th April 1964

UNITED REPUBLIC OF TANGANYIKA AND ZANZIBAR
PRESIDENT
Mwalimu Julius K. Nyerere, from 26th April 1964

FIRST VICE-PRESIDENT
Sheikh Abeid Amani Karume, from 26th April 1964

SECOND VICE-PRESIDENT
R. M. Kawawa, from 26th April 1964

GOVERNMENT

Before the dissolution of Parliament on 10th July 1965 all the 71 Mainland seats were held by the TANU party and all the 18 Zanzibar seats by the Afro-Shirazi party. At the Mainland elections in September 1965 a total of 700 nominations were received by the District Conferences for the 107 seats and these were reduced to 208 by the National Executive Conference of TANU after the District Conferences had examined and voted on the candidates. Only two candidates were allowed to stand in each constituency, there being 101 contested seats and 6 uncontested. All candidates were required to be party members.

The elections were notable for the fact that many of the previous members of Parliament lost their seats.

At the Presidential elections, which took place at the same time, there was only one candidate for the office of President. Electors were asked to vote for or against and President Nyerere was re-elected by an overwhelming majority.

PRESIDENT AND MINISTERS

President of the United Republic of Tanzania, Commander in Chief of the Armed Forces, Minister of Foreign Affairs and Minister for Regional Administration and Rural Development:
His Excellency Mwalimu Julius K. Nyerere
First Vice-President and President of Zanzibar: Hon. Sheikh Abeid A. Karume
Second Vice-President: Hon. Rashidi M. Kawawa
Minister of Agriculture and Co-operatives: Hon. Derek N. M. Bryceson
Minister of Finance: Hon. Amir H. Jamal
Minister of Economic Affairs and Development Planning: Hon, Abdulrahman M. Babu
Minister of Commerce and Industry: Hon. Paul Bomani
Minister of Communications, Transport and Labour: Hon. Job M. Lusinde
Minister of National Education: Hon. Chediel Y. Mgonja
Minister of Lands, Housing and Urban Development: Hon. John A. Mhaville
Minister of Home Affairs: Hon. Saidi A. Maswanya
Minister of Information and Broadcasting: Hon. Jacob D. Namfua
Minister of Health and Social Welfare: Hon. L. Nangwanda Sijaona
Minister of Natural Resources and Tourism: Hon. Hasnu Makame
Minister of Water Development and Power: Hon. Dr Wilbert K. Chagula
Minister of State (Foreign Affairs): Hon. Isael Elinawinga
Minister of State (Regional Administration and Rural Development): Hon. Peter A. Kisumo
Minister of State (President's Office): Hon. Sheikh A. H. Mwingi
Minister of State (2nd Vice-President's Office): Hon. Edward M. Sokoine

PARLIAMENTARY SECRETARIES

Office of the Second Vice-President: (vacant)
Ministry of Agriculture and Co-operatives: Hon. P. S. Qorro
Ministry of Communications, Transport and Labour: (Vacant)
Ministry of Health and Social Welfare: Hon. Miss L. S. Lameck

MINISTRIES AND GOVERNMENT DEPARTMENTS

PRESIDENT'S OFFICE AND CABINET SECRETARIAT
Principal Secretary: D. A. Nkembo
Chairman, Permanent Commission of Enquiry: Hon. Mr Justice M. P. K. Kimicha
Principal Secretary (Establishments): D. A. Mwakosya
Private Secretary: J. W. Butiku
Press Secretary: P. A. Sozigwa

MINISTRY OF REGIONAL ADMINISTRATION AND RURAL DEVELOPMENT
Principal Secretary: A. Mushi

MINISTRY OF FOREIGN AFFAIRS
Principal Secretary: D. N. M. Mloka

OFFICE OF THE SECOND VICE-PRESIDENT
Principal Secretary: B. Mulokozi
Chief of Defence Forces: Brigadier M. S. H. Sarakikya
Attorney-General: Hon. M. D. Bomani

MINISTRY OF AGRICULTURE AND CO-OPERATIVES
Principal Secretary: T. Apiyo

MINISTRY OF FINANCE
Principal Secretary to the Treasury: C. D. Msuya

MINISTRY OF ECONOMIC AFFAIRS AND DEVELOPMENT PLANNING
Principal Secretary: E. A. Mulokozi

MINISTRY OF COMMERCE AND INDUSTRY
Principal Secretary: O. M. Katikaza

MINISTRY OF COMMUNICATIONS, TRANSPORT AND LABOUR
Principal Secretary: I. M. Kaduma

MINISTRY OF NATIONAL EDUCATION
Principal Secretary: J. D. Mganga

MINISTRY OF LANDS, HOUSING AND URBAN DEVELOPMENT
Principal Secretary: E. P. Mwaluko

MINISTRY OF HOME AFFAIRS
Principal Secretary: J. P. Singano
Inspector-General of Police: H. Aziz

MINISTRY OF INFORMATION
AND BROADCASTING
Principal Secretary (Acting): J. Sepeku

MINISTRY OF HEALTH
AND SOCIAL WELFARE
Principal Secretary: B. J. Maggid

MINISTRY OF NATURAL
RESOURCES AND TOURISM
Principal Secretary: G. J. Kileo

MINISTRY OF WATER
DEVELOPMENT AND POWER
Principal Secretary: F. K. Lwegarulik

SPEAKER'S OFFICE
Speaker; Chairman of Electoral Commission: Chief Adam Sapi Mkwawa, OBE
Clerk of National Assembly and Director of Elections: Y. Osman

CIVIL AND LOCAL GOVERNMENT SERVICE
COMMISSIONS
Chairman: Chief P. I. Marealle, MBE

JUDICIARY
Chief Justice: The Hon. Mr Justice A. Saidi

Judges:

The Hon. Mr Justice M. C. E. P. Biron
The Hon. Mr Justice C. E. Bramble
The Hon. Mr Justice L. M. Makame
The Hon. Mr Justice Onyinke

The Hon. Mr Justice N. S. Mnzavas
The Hon. Mr Justice Z. N. El Kindy
The Hon. Mr Justice P. H. Kisanga
The Hon. Mr Justice M. H. A. Kwikima

REGIONAL COMMISSIONERS

Arusha Region — A. W. Mwakang'ata
Coast Region (H.Q. Dar-es-Salaam) — K. Ngombale-Mwiru
Dodoma Region — J. W. Kihampa
Iringa Region — Dr W. Klerru
Kigoma Region — P. J. Ndobho
Kilimanjaro Region (H.Q. Moshi) — L. A. Sazia
Lindi Region — Vacant
Mara Region (H.Q. Musoma) — A. L. S. Mhina
Mbeya Region — P. S. Siyovelwa
Morogoro Region — A. Lyander
Mtwara Region — J. B. Mwakangale
Mwanza Region — O. A. Muhaji
Ruvuma Region (H.Q. Songea) — H. M. Makwaia
Shinyanga Region — M. M. Songambele
Singida Region — C. M. Kapilima
Tabora Region — J. D. Njau
Tanga Region — J. W. L. Makinda
West Lake Region (H.Q. Bukoba) — S. S. Shemsanga

ZANZIBAR

CABINET

President of Zanzibar and Minister for Finance: Hon. Sheikh Abeid A. Karume
Minister of State, First Vice-President's Office: Hon. Aboud Jumbe
Minister of Trade and Industry: Hon. Sheikh Thabit Kombo
Minister for Health: Hon. Ali Sultan Issa
Minister for Education: Hon. Hassan Nassar Moyo
Minister for Agriculture: Hon. Rashid Abdulla
Minister for Communications, Power and Works: Hon. Hamdan Muhiddin
Parliamentary Secretary for Foreign Affairs: Hon. Tawakali Khamis
Attorney-General: Hon. Wolfgang Dourado

DIPLOMATIC REPRESENTATION

TANZANIAN HIGH COMMISSIONERS
ABROAD
Britain: G. N. Nhigula; Canada: Abbas K. Sykes; India: S. Chale; Zambia: C. P. Ngaiza.

TANZANIAN AMBASSADORS ABROAD
China: R. S. Wamburu; Congo (Kinshasa):

C. A. Kellaghe; Ethiopia: F. Rutakyamirwa; France: A. Faraji; Germany: A. B. Nyakyi; Guinea: S. S. Rashid; Japan: G. B. Rusimbi; Netherlands: I. A. Wakil; Sweden: Chief M. M. Lukumbazya; U.A.R.: Vacant. U.S.A.: G. Rutabanzibwa; U.S.S.R.: R. Lukindo; United Nations: S. A. Salim.

TONGA

THE Kingdom of Tonga comprises a group of islands situated in the south-west Pacific between latitudes 15° and 23° 30' S. and longitudes 173° and 177° W. The group, known as the Tonga or Friendly Islands, is divided into three main sub-groups: Vava'u, Ha'apai and Tongatapu. The total estimated area, including inland waters, is 270 square miles. Tongatapu, the largest island, has an area of 99·2 square miles. The islands on the eastern side are of coral formation, those on the west are volcanic. There are active volcanoes on four of the islands.

The climate is healthy, though hot and humid from January to March with temperatures of 32°C (90°F); during the rest of the year it is pleasantly cool with temperatures as low as 11°C (52°F) on Tongatapu. The mean annual temperature is 23°C (73°F); the mean annual rainfall is 70 inches on Tongatapu and 110 inches on Vava'u.

The population, as recorded in the 1966 census, numbered 77,429, of whom 76,121 were Tongans.

The administrative capital is Nuku'alofa on Tongatapu, the population of which was 15,545 in the 1966 census.

In 1969 there were 184 primary schools (83 state schools and the remainder run by Missions); post-primary education is provided by three Government and 58 Mission schools. Total estimated expenditure on education in 1969 amounted to T$1,319,426.

The Government of Tonga Medical Department operates three public hospitals and a number of dispensaries. A new modern Government hospital is under construction and is being financed mainly from British development funds. Estimated Government expenditure on medical services (exclusive of buildings and building maintenance) was T$319,621 in 1969.

There is a good regional airport on the island of Tongatapu, situated about 13 miles from Nuku'alofa, and there are limited seaplane facilities at Nuku'alofa and Vava'u harbour. Fiji Airways Limited operate a four times a week schedule between Fiji and Tongatapu and in conjunction with Polynesian Airlines twice a week service from Western Samoa.

There are approximately 105 miles of metalled road in Tongatapu and 35 miles in Vava'u suitable for motor traffic. There are some 58·5 miles of unsealed roads which can only be used by motor traffic in dry weather.

The chief ports, which are also ports of entry, are Nuku'alofa and Neaifu on Vava'u. 123 vessels, exclusive of warships and yachts, entered the country during the year 1969. A regular monthly passenger and cargo service from New Zealand via Fiji is maintained by the Union Steam Ship Company of New Zealand. Regular cargo services are also operated by vessels of the Bank Line and the Union Steam Ship Company. The Tonga Shipping Agency has been set up under the joint control of the Government and the Tonga Copra Board. It maintains internal services between islands of the group and a passenger and cargo service with Fiji and other adjacent islands as well as Australia.

Broadcasting is administered by the Tonga Broadcasting Commission. The studios are situated at Nuku'alofa and the transmitter at Fongoloa, about one mile away. The station (ZCO), known as 'The Call of the Friendly Islands', was opened by the late Queen Salote Tupou on 4th July 1961. The station broadcasts for seven hours daily from Monday to Friday, for six and half hours on

Saturdays and a minimum of two hours on Sundays, in English and Tongan. Transmissions are on medium wave on a frequency of 1,020 kc/s, and can also be heard in New Zealand, Fiji, Norfolk Island, Samoa and Niue. The station broadcasts Samoan and Fijian sessions as well. Commercial advertising is accepted in English and Tongan. The output of the station consists of locally originated programmes including traditional Tongan music and spoken word, news bulletins and weather forecasts.

Tonga is essentially an agricultural country, and, in general, a land of peasant proprietors. Only a very small proportion of the population seeks employment in the Government services or in commerce.

The main crops are coconuts, bananas, kumalas, yams, taro, cassava, groundnuts, maize, watermelons and pineapples.

There is an abundance of fish in the waters of the group which provides a staple fish diet for the inhabitants.

Livestock numbers in 1968 were as follows: horses 8,035, cattle 2,217; goats 4,039; pigs 32,018; poultry 141,891.

Limited areas of forest land are found in the islands of 'Eua and Vava'u, but timber is not exported.

The manufacturing industries in Tonga are the production of desiccated coconut, coir and tobacco goods, which only began quite recently.

PRINCIPAL EXPORTS BY QUANTITY AND VALUE

		1965	1966	1967	1968	1969
Copra	tons	6,931	12,441	10,650	8,089	13,354
	T$	1,151,718	1,984,434	1,709,944	1,430,880	2,103,685
Bananas	cases	315,686	455,468	609,888	535,898	210,374
	T$	941,222	1,337,554	1,612,458	1,738,679	683,640

The chief imports are textiles, flour, preserved meats, sugar, hardware, soap petrol, kerosene, spirits, beer and wines, tobacco and cigarettes.

The Tonga Copra Board and the Tonga Produce Board, established under the provisions of the Agriculture Organisation Act, 1940, both of which are non-profit-making concerns, are charged with purchase, sale and marketing in the interests of the producers.

In 1968 traces of oil were found off 'Eua, but it will be some time before it can be established whether any deposit of commercial value exists.

Revenue and expenditure during the years 1964-69 were:

	Revenue	*Expenditure*
	T$	T$
1964–65	1,742,520	1,616,640
1965–66	1,968,180	1,872,356
1966–67	2,125,751	1,798,064
1967–68	2,618,200	1,930,935
1968–69	2,608,376	2,182,524

About 50 per cent of revenue accrues from customs duty. The main heads of expenditure are public works, medical services, education and agriculture. The financial year begins on 1st July. There is no Public Debt and the surplus funds account stood at T$2,454,900 on the 30th June 1969.

An annual rent of 8s. a year is payable in respect of the allotments of land to which all male Tongans are entitled (*see below*: Land Policy). In addition there is an annual tax of 32 shillings, for which free education, medical, hospital and dental treatment are provided. Indirect taxation includes import duties (general tariff 50 per cent *ad valorem*, British preferential tariff 33⅓ per cent *ad valorem*) and a port and customs service tax on imports of 5 per cent. There is also an export duty on copra of 10 per cent of the f.o.b. value at date of export.

HISTORY

During the first half of the nineteenth century civil wars were rife in the islands. They were finally checked during the reign of King George Tupou I (1845–93) who had by conquest gathered all power in his own hands.

Wesleyan missionaries landed on Tonga in 1826 and by the middle of the century practically all the chiefs and people had been converted to Christianity. Not until the last decade of the century, however, were questions regarding freedom of worship and the relationship of Church and State peaceably settled. In 1900, by a Treaty of Friendship and Protection, Tonga became a British Protected State. There have been three subsequent revisions of the Treaty reflecting the changes which have occurred during the 20th century. Under the latest, by an exchange of letters on the 19th May 1970, it was agreed that the United Kingdom Government should, as from the 4th June 1970, cease to have any responsibility for the external relations of the Kingdom of Tonga. The provisions of Articles II, III, IV and V of the 1968 Revised Treaty accordingly ceased to have effect. At the same time Tonga became a full member of the Commonwealth and accepted The Queen as a symbol of the free association of independent member nations and as such The Head of the Commonwealth. The British High Commissioner in New Zealand was appointed concurrently United Kingdom High Commissioner (non-resident) in Tonga, while the former resident post of Commissioner and Consul became Deputy High Commissioner.

CONSTITUTION

The present constitution is based, with relatively little amendment, on that granted in 1875 by King George Tupou I. It provides for a Government consisting of the Sovereign (at present King Taufa'ahau Tupou IV, GCVO, KCMG, KBE) a Privy Council and Cabinet, a Legislative Assembly and a Judiciary. The Legislative Assembly consists of the Premier and Ministers of the Crown (including the Governors of Vava'u and Ha'apai), seven representatives of the nobles elected by their peers, and seven representatives of the people elected by popular franchise, every male Tongan of 21 years of age who pays taxes and can read and write and every female Tongan of 21 years of age who can read and write, being qualified to vote. In 1960 for the first time women were included, and held a vote, in the election of Legislative Assembly members. Several women also stood for election but were defeated at the polls. Elections are held every three years. The President of the Legislative Assembly is the Speaker, appointed by the Sovereign. The courts consist of a Supreme Court, a Magistrate's Court and a Land Court.

LAND POLICY

Every male Tongan on reaching the taxable age of 16 years is entitled to 8¼ acres of land for cultivation in addition to a small village allotment for his dwelling. Land may not be leased to non-Tongans without the consent of the Government. Immigrant settlement is not encouraged owing to the increasing shortage of land available.

GOVERNMENT

Premier, Minister of Foreign Affairs and Minister of Agriculture:
H.R.H. Prince Fatafehi Tu'ipelehake, CBE
Deputy Premier and Minister of Finance: Hon. Mahe U. Tupouniua
Minister of Lands: Hon. Laufilitonga Tuita
Minister of Police: Hon. 'Akau'ola
Minister of Education and Works: Hon. S. Langi Kavaliku
Minister of Health: Hon. Dr S. Tapa
Governor of Vava'u: Hon. Ma'afu Tupou
Governor of Ha'apai: Ve'ehala

DIPLOMATIC REPRESENTATION

COMMONWEALTH REPRESENTATIVES IN TONGA

British High Commissioner (non-resident): Sir Arthur Galsworthy, KCMG; Deputy British High Commissioner (resident): H. A. Arthington-Davy, OBE.

TONGA REPRESENTATIVES IN OTHER COMMONWEALTH COUNTRIES

High Commissioner in the United Kingdom: Baron Vaea (also accredited to Belgium and France).

OTHER COUNTRIES WITH REPRESENTATIVES ACCREDITED TO TONGA

New Zealand (High Commissioner resident in Apia); India (High Commissioner resident in Suva); Australia (High Commissioner resident in Suva); South Korea (Ambassador resident in Canberra); Canada (High Commissioner) (resident in Wellington).

READING LIST

LEDYARD, Patricia. Friendly Island. *Peter Davies*, 1956.

LUKE, Sir Harry. Queen Salote and Her Kingdom. *Putnam*, 1954.

MACQUARRIE, H. Friendly Queen. *Heinemann*, 1955,

NEILL, J. S. Ten Years in Tonga. *Hutchinson*, 1955.

ROSENDAL, J. The Happy Lagoons: the world of Queen Salote. *Jarrold*, 1961

BAIN, K. R. The Friendly Islanders. *Hodder and Stoughton*, 1967.

SNOW, P. A. A Bibliography of Fiji, Tonga and Rotuma. *University of Miami Press*.

TRINIDAD AND TOBAGO

THE islands of Trinidad and Tobago lie between latitudes 10° and 11° N. and longitudes 61° and 62° W. The area of the two islands is 1,980 square miles (Trinidad 1,864 and Tobago 116). Trinidad is traversed by two mountain ranges, the northern and southern ranges, running roughly east and west, and a third, the central range, running diagonally across the island. Between the northern and central ranges the land is flat and well-watered; south of the central range it is undulating and the water supply poor. Apart from small areas in the northern range, of which the main peaks are Cerro del Aripo (3,083 feet) and El Tucuche (3,072 feet), and in the central range, of which Mount Tamana (1,009 feet) is the principal peak, all the land is below 1,000 feet.

The rivers though numerous are unimportant. A main ridge of hills, eighteen miles in length, extends nearly two-thirds of the length of Tobago from its north-eastern extremity. The highest point is 1,890 feet. About 300,000 acres or 22 per cent of the two islands is forest. The climate is tropical. The temperature varies between 64°F and 92°F with mean night and day temperatures of 74°F and 82°F respectively. The coolest months are from December to April. Rainfall is heaviest in June (11·4 inches). There is a dry season from January to mid-May and a wet season from June to December, with a short break in September.

The population of Trinidad and Tobago at the census of April 1960 was 827,957. The populations of the principal towns were: Port of Spain, the capital, 93,954; San Fernando 38,830; Arima 10,982. The main population divisions were: Negro 358,588 (43·5 per cent); East Indian 301,946 (36·5 per cent); Mixed and Others 143,344 (13 per cent); White 15,718 (1·9 per cent); Chinese 8,361 (1·2 per cent). The estimated population in 1970 was 1,100,000. The birth rate, based on 1962 figures, is 38·1 per 1,000 and the death rate 7·5 per 1,000. The main religions are Roman Catholicism 36 per cent; Hinduism 23 per cent; Protestantism 21 per cent and Islam 6 per cent.

Primary education is free and universal, while free secondary education is available by competitive examination at the age of 11 years. The literacy percentage, at the 1960 census, was 89.

The principal seaports are: Port of Spain, the main seaport; Scarborough in Tobago, a deep water harbour; Chaguaramas, transfer stations for handling the transhipment of bauxite from the Guianas for Canada and the United States of America; Pointe-à-Pierre and Point Fortin, oil terminals; Brighton, an asphalt and oil loading point; and Point Lisas, a fertiliser wharf, which also provides bulk loading facilities for sugar.

The principal local shipping line is West Indies Shipping Service, jointly owned by Trinidad and Tobago, Jamaica, Barbados and the Windward and Leeward Islands.

The customs airport of Trinidad is Piarco (runway length 9,500 feet), which is located sixteen miles south-east of Port of Spain. The airline is British West Indian Airways Ltd.

The Trinidad Government Railway has been phased out. Road passenger services, which serve all parts of the country, are operated by the Public Transport Service Corporation. Total road mileage is approximately 1,440 miles.

Radio transmissions in Trinidad and Tobago come from Radio Trinidad, which is under the control of Rediffusion Limited, and Radio 610, formerly Radio Guardian, which was taken over by the Government in 1969. Trinidad and Tobago Television is also Government-owned, having been taken over at the same time as Radio Guardian.

Trinidad's economy is based mainly on oil and sugar and more recently on a growth of a range of manufacturing industries, including the manufacture of cement, chemicals, fertilisers, motor vehicle assembly and household electrical appliances. Although the sugar industry remains the largest employer, oil in fact dominates the local scene. Refining capacity (which includes the largest refinery in the Commonwealth) is about 376,000 barrels a day, of which approximately one-third is refined from local crude oil production, crude being obtained from both land and off-shore deposits. Tobago is essentially agricultural with a small but growing tourist industry.

Total exports in 1969 were TT$949 million, which included the following:—

	TT$ Millions
Mineral fuels and petroleum products	732
Sugar and sugar preparations	52
Ammonium compounds	38
Tar oils	32
Coffee and cocoa beans	10
Fertiliser	13

Total imports in 1969 were TT$965 million, of which the biggest single import was crude oil, TTS496 million. The balance of imports came from many countries, the principal sources being Britain, the U.S.A. and Canada.

The 1970 estimate of Government revenue was TT$346 million and of expenditure was TT$375 million. The third Five-Year Plan 1969–1973 envisages a total net investment of TT$907 million during the period.

The following have their headquarters in Trinidad: Citrus Research Unit (shared by British Honduras, Jamaica, Dominica and Trinidad and Tobago); Regional Research Centre (Agricultural and Soils Research); Regional Virus Laboratory; Seismic Research Unit; Standing Advisory Committee for Medical Research in the Caribbean. The following Commonwealth Regional Organisations also exist in Trinidad: The Regional Shipping Council, West Indies Shipping Service; the Commonwealth Institute of Biological Control (*see Part VIII*, Commonwealth Agricultural Bureaux); the Caribbean Meteorological Organisation.

Trinidad joined O.A.S. on 23rd February 1967 and C.A.R.I.F.T.A. on 1st May 1968.

Trinidad and Tobago's National Day is Independence Day, 31st August, which commemorates the achievement of independence on 31st August 1962.

TRINIDAD

The aboriginal name for the island was Iere (Land of the Humming Bird). Columbus landed there on his third voyage in 1498 and, taking possession on behalf of the Crown of Spain, named the island Trinidad.

No Governor was appointed by the King of Spain until 1532 and even then, and for many years afterwards, the Spanish colonists had the greatest difficulty in maintaining a footing on the island. In 1595 Sir Walter Raleigh destroyed the newly-founded town of St Joseph. In 1640 it was raided by the Dutch, and in 1677 and 1690 by the French.

Towards the end of the seventeenth and the beginning of the eighteenth centuries, cocoa was largely and successfully cultivated, but in 1725 a blight fell upon the plantations. Thereafter Trinidad made scarcely any progress until 1783 when, in consequence of representations made to the Court of Madrid as to its exceptional fertility, a royal proclamation was issued by which extraordinary advantages were offered to Roman Catholics of all nations friendly with Spain to settle there. The consequence of the proclamation was a large influx of population, soon augmented by many French families driven from Santo Domingo and elsewhere by the events of the French Revolution and to this cause is to be traced the large French element in a colony which never belonged to France.

In 1797, during the Revolutionary War, a British expedition sailed from Martinique for the reduction of Trinidad. The expedition resulted in the surrender of the island to His Majesty's Forces. In 1802 Trinidad was ceded to the British Crown by the Treaty of Amiens.

Emancipation of slaves in 1834 and the adoption of free trade by Britain in 1846 resulted in far-reaching social and economic changes. To meet the labour shortage immigration was encouraged and between 1845 and 1917 there arrived over 150,000 immigrants from India, China and Madeira. The fall in the price of sugar and the general decline of the sugar industry, which dominated the island's history in the nineteenth century, stimulated the search for substitute crops; by the latter part of the century cocoa had been resuscitated and for a time replaced sugar as the most important industry.

After its cession to Britain in 1802 Trinidad became a Crown Colony. By the terms of the capitulation, the Spanish constitution and laws were maintained and the Governor ruled with the help of a newly-created Council of Advice and the existing Cabildo, a corporate body elected annually by the taxpayers, which combined the functions of a parish vestry, a municipal council, an ecclesiastical council and a council of government. The Council of Advice evolved in 1831 into an Executive Council and a Council of Government, which later became the Legislative Council. In 1840 the Cabildo became the Port of Spain Town Council. By the middle of the nineteenth century English procedure and legislation had displaced Spanish law.

TOBAGO

Tobago was discovered by Columbus in 1498, at which time it was occupied by Caribs. It was visited in 1596 and found to be uninhabited. The island remained unoccupied until 1632 when 300 Zealanders were sent out by a Company of Dutch merchants who styled it New Walcheren. After a residence of about two years these settlers were all killed or expelled by the Indians and Spaniards from Trinidad. In 1641 James, Duke of Courland, obtained a grant of the island from Charles I and in 1642 two vessels arrived with a number of Courlanders who settled on the north side. These were followed by further Dutch colonists in 1654 who, having effected a compromise with the Courlanders, established themselves on the southern coast; but in 1658 the Courlanders were overpowered by the Dutch, who remained in possession of the island until 1662 when the Dutch company resigned their right to it. In this year Cornelius Lampsius procured Letters Patent from Louis XIV creating him the Baron of Tobago and proprietor of the island under the crown of France.

In 1664 the grant of Tobago to the Duke of Courland was renewed by Charles II. The Dutch refused to recognise the Duke's title but in 1667 they themselves were compelled by the French to evacuate the island. Louis XIV restored the island to the Duke of Courland who, in 1681, made over his title to a company of London merchants. In 1748, by the Treaty of Aix-la-Chapelle, Tobago was declared neutral; the subjects of all European Powers were at liberty to form settlements or carry on commerce but not to place garrisons upon it. At the peace of 1763, by the Treaty of Paris, Tobago was ceded by France to England in perpetuity.

In 1781 Tobago was captured by the French after a gallant defence by the colonists. In 1783 it was surrendered by treaty to the French Crown. On 15th April 1793 it was captured by British Forces under Admiral Lefrey and General

Cuyler. It was once more restored to the French by the Treaty of Amiens in 1802 and again re-conquered in 1803. In 1814 it was ceded in perpetuity to the British Crown.

Tobago continued to keep its old institutions, its House of Assembly, its Legislative Council, its Privy Council and its numerous Law Courts until 1874, when the House of Assembly was abolished and a one-Chamber Legislative Council formed. The abolition of slavery, the great storm of 1847 when most of the sugar works were damaged, the introduction of beet sugar in Europe, the lack of capital and many other factors had by this time resulted in a depressed state of trade. Tobago became a Crown Colony in 1877 at the request of the Legislative Council following the disastrous Belmanna riots. The Government was then administered by a resident administrator, subordinate to the Governor-in-Chief of the Windward Islands at Grenada, and a Legislative Council was established by an Order in Council on 7th February 1877, to consist of not less than three persons designated by Her Majesty The Queen.

The fall in the price of sugar gave the final blow to Tobago's status as a separate colonial unit, and in 1888 Tobago was amalgamated with Trinidad.

TRINIDAD AND TOBAGO

By Order in Council dated 17th November 1888 Tobago was amalgamated with Trinidad, the name of the new Colony being Trinidad and Tobago. The latter island was then administered by a Commissioner appointed by the Governor of the United Colony, who was *ex officio* a member of the Legislative Council. One unofficial member of Council represented Tobago. The Commissioner was assisted by a financial board of five members, two nominated by the Governor, and three elected. The revenue, expenditure and debt of the islands remained distinct, but there was a freedom of commercial intercourse between them and the laws of Trinidad were, with some specified exceptions, the laws of both.

By an Order in Council of 20th October 1898 the Order in Council of November 1888 was almost entirely revoked and it was provided that the Island of Tobago should become a Ward of the United Colony of Trinidad and Tobago; that the revenue, expenditure and debt of Tobago should be merged with those of the United Colony; that the debt due from Tobago to Trinidad should be cancelled; that (with some specified exceptions) the laws of Trinidad should operate in Tobago, and those of Tobago cease to operate so far as they conflicted with the laws of Trinidad; that all future Ordinances of the Legislature of the Colony should extend to Tobago, with the proviso that the Legislature should be able to enact special and local ordinances and regulations applicable to Tobago as distinguished from the rest of the Colony. This Order in Council was brought into effect on 1st January 1899 by a Proclamation of the Governor. The post of Commissioner for the island of Tobago then ceased to exist and the post of Warden was created instead.

In 1924 the elective principle was introduced for the formation of the Legislative Council. Adult suffrage and further steps towards self-government and independence then followed (*see* Constitutional Development *below*).

The discovery of oil in the south of Trinidad and its exploitation after 1910 made it the most important industry but agriculture continued to play a major role. In 1931 sugar regained its lead over cocoa as the most important agricultural industry and today oil, sugar (with its by-products, molasses and rum), cocoa, asphalt, chemicals, coffee and fertilisers constitute the main exports. There has been a steady expansion of the manufacturing industry since 1950, assisted by pioneer aid legislation.

CONSTITUTIONAL DEVELOPMENT

The 1924 Constitution of Trinidad and Tobago, which was contained in the Trinidad and Tobago (Legislative Council) Order in Council 1924 (subsequently amended by Orders of 1928, 1941, 1942 and 1945) provided for twelve official, six nominated unofficial and seven elected members. The 1941 Order in Council made the Constitution more liberal by eliminating nine nominated official members and increasing the elected members to nine. During this period, the Executive Council, the composition of which was controlled by Royal Instructions passed in 1924 and 1941, consisted of three *ex officio* members and such other persons as the Governor might appoint, usually one nominated and four elected members.

The 1945 amending Order in Council brought into effect universal adult suffrage and reduced the qualifications for election as a member of the Legislative Council. In February 1947, following a resolution moved by one of the elected members of the Legislative Council, a Committee was appointed to consider the reform of the Constitution; its report, and subsequent discussions, led to the introduction of the Constitution of 1950.

The Constitution of 1950, subsequently amended in 1956 and 1959, provided for a unicameral legislature (Legislative Council) with an elected majority, the composition being three *ex officio* members, five nominated members and eighteen elected members, presided over by a Speaker, with neither an original nor a casting vote, appointed by the Governor from outside the Council. Other provisions were: an executive Council, which was the chief instrument of policy, comprising three *ex officio* members, one nominated member and five elected members elected by the Legislative Council; a quasi-ministerial system in which members of the Executive Council were associated with the administrative work of Government Departments; reserve powers of the Governor to be exercisable with the consent of the Executive Council, but in the event of their refusing to give such consent, with the approval of the Secretary of State; a Public Service Commission.

After further changes introduced by Orders in Council in 1956, 1958 and 1959, the Constitution in 1959 provided for a Legislative Council consisting of a Speaker elected by the members; two *ex officio* members (the Chief Secretary and the Attorney-General), five members nominated by the Governor and twenty-four elected members. The Cabinet consisted of nine Ministers including the Premier, who were elected members of the Legislative Council, and two *ex officio* members (the Chief Secretary and the Attorney-General), neither of whom was entitled to vote. The Governor did not normally preside at Cabinet meetings, but had the power to call special meetings of the Cabinet and, if he did so, to preside over them. With certain exceptions, the Governor had to consult with the Cabinet in the exercise of his powers and act in accordance with its advice. At this stage, the Constitution also contained provisions for the establishment of a Judicial and Legal Service Commission and a Police Service Commission, as well as a Public Service Commission. The Governor was bound to accept the recommendations of these Commissions on appointments and promotions, except in respect of a few special posts.

In elections held on 24th September 1956, under the 1950 Constitution, as amended, the People's National Movement (P.N.M.) gained thirteen seats and formed a Government under the leadership of Dr Eric Williams. The People's Democratic Party (now the Democratic Labour Party—D.L.P.) gained five seats; the Home Rule Party two seats; the Trinidad Labour Party two seats and Independents two seats.

After further Constitutional discussions held in London in November 1959 and June 1960, the Secretary of State for the Colonies announced agreement on a new Constitution providing for full internal self-government with a bicameral legislature consisting of a nominated Senate and an elected House of Representatives. This new Constitution was brought fully into operation following the General Election held on 4th December 1961, at which the P.N.M. was again returned to power, winning twenty of the seats in the House of Representatives and polling 58 per cent of the total votes cast. The D.L.P. won the remaining ten seats polling 39·7 per cent of the total votes cast. The 1960 Constitution provided that of the twenty-one nominated members of the Senate, twelve should be appointed on the advice of the Premier, two on the advice of the Leader of the Opposition and seven by the Governor in his discretion to represent special interests. The Cabinet was to consist of the Premier (as the Chief Minister was now called) and not more than eleven other Ministers (of whom one would be the Attorney-General). There was a wholly-elected House of Representatives of 30 members which was later increased to 36 members. The People's National Movement was again returned at the General Election held on 7th November 1966, winning 24 of the 36 seats in the Lower House and polling 52 per cent of the votes cast. The Democatic Labour Party, which won the remaining 12 seats and polled 34 per cent of the votes cast, again formed the Opposition.

In 1958 the Federation of the West Indies was formed with a membership consisting of Trinidad and Tobago, Jamaica, Barbados and the Leeward and Windward Islands. Agreement had been reached in principle on a Constitution under which the Federation would proceed to Independence on 31st May 1962; but in September 1961 the Jamaican Government held a referendum on the question of membership of the Federation which resulted in a vote in favour of withdrawal. The British and the Jamaican Governments subsequently agreed that Jamaica would withdraw from the Federation and would proceed to Independence on its own. As a consequence, on 14th January 1962, the General Council of the People's National Movement unanimously approved a resolution that Trinidad and Tobago should also proceed forthwith to independence without prejudice to the possibility of the territory's future association in a unitary state with other territories in the East Caribbean. The resolution also requested the Government to take the initiative in proposing the maximum possible measure of collaboration between the former members of the Federation of the West Indies regarding common services, and to declare their willingness to take part in and work for a Caribbean economic community. This resolution was endorsed at a special convention of the party held towards the end of January and the Government accepted the terms of the resolution as their policy in this matter. In April the Secretary of State for the Colonies, in reply to a despatch from the Governor, agreed that Trinidad and Tobago should become independent as early as practicable in 1962, and proposed that, provided the necessary steps could be taken in time, an independence conference should be held in London towards the end of May to agree upon a constitution and the date of independence.

Meanwhile, in February, the Government of Trinidad and Tobago had published the first draft of an independence constitution: this was distributed widely in the territory, and organisations and the general public were invited to submit written comments on it by 31st March. Over 160 memoranda were received, and from 25th to 27th April the Government held meetings with those who had submitted memoranda, at which the draft constitution was considered. The draft constitution, as amended in the light of these consultations, was considered by a Joint Select Committee of the Senate and House of Representatives, after which it was debated and, on 11th May, approved by a majority of 16 to 9 in the House of Representatives.

The revised draft of the independence constitution, as approved by the Legislature, formed the basic document at the Trinidad and Tobago Independence Conference held in London between 28th May and 8th June 1962. At this Conference, at which the Trinidad and Tobago delegation unanimously expressed the wish that an independent Trinidad and Tobago should be accepted as a Member of the Commonwealth and stated that it was the firm wish of the people of Trinidad and Tobago to continue after Independence in their allegiance to Her Majesty The Queen, it was agreed that Trinidad and Tobago should become independent on the 31st August 1962.

CONSTITUTION

The Constitution of Trinidad and Tobago is contained in the Trinidad and Tobago (Constitution) Order in Council 1962 (S.I. 1962 No. 1875). It provides for a Governor-General, appointed by Her Majesty The Queen on the advice of the Prime Minister, and for a bicameral Legislature. The Senate (Upper House) consists of 24 Senators, 13 of whom are appointed on the advice of the Prime Minister, 4 on the advice of the Leader of the Opposition and 7 on the advice of the Prime Minister after consultation with those religious, economic and social organisations from which the Prime Minister considers that such Senators should be selected. In 1966 the Electoral Boundaries Commission recommended that the number of seats in the House of Representatives (Lower House) be increased from 30 to 36. This proposal was adopted and the General Election of November 1966 was fought in 36 constituencies. There is universal adult suffrage.

The normal life of Parliament is 5 years. The Cabinet consists of the Prime Minister, who must be a member of the House of Representatives, and such other ministers as the Governor-General, acting on the advice of the Prime Minister, appoints from among the senators and members of the House of Representatives. The Attorney-General must be a member of the Cabinet. The Governor-General appoints as Leader of the Opposition the member of the House of Representatives who, in his judgement, is the Leader in the House of the party commanding the support of the largest number of members of the House in opposition to the Government.

The principal provisions of the Constitution are entrenched and, of these, the most important are specially entrenched. The ordinary entrenched provisions can only be amended by a vote of two-thirds of all the members of both Houses; these include the provisions relating to human rights and freedoms, prorogation of Parliament, appointment, etc., of judicial officers, the various Service Commissions and the office and functions of the Auditor-General. Specially entrenched provisions can only be altered by a vote of three-quarters of all the members of the House of Representatives and two-thirds of the Senate. The specially entrenched provisions included among other things those concerning the office of the Governor-General, the establishment of Parliament and the composition of the two Houses, general elections and the appointment of Senators, the establishment of boundaries and election commissions and matters affecting the Judiciary.

There is a Supreme Court of Judicature, consisting of a High Court and a Court of Appeal, and in certain cases a further appeal lies to the Judicial Committee of Her Majesty's Privy Council. The Chief Justice is appointed by the Governor-General acting on the advice of the Prime Minister. Puisne Judges are appointed by the Governor-General acting in accordance with the advice of the Judicial and Legal Service Commissions.

The Constitution also contains provisions relating to citizenship; an amendment to the Constitution in 1965 provided for a limited category of dual nationality.

GOVERNMENT

At the general election in May 1971 the People's National Movement won all 36 seats in the House of Representatives.

GOVERNOR-GENERAL
His Excellency Sir Solomon Hochoy, TC, GCMG, GCVO, OBE

MINISTRIES AND GOVERNMENT DEPARTMENTS

MINISTRY
Prime Minister: Dr The Rt Hon. Eric Williams, MP, CH
Minister of External Affairs and Minister of West Indian Affairs:
The Hon. K. Mohammed, MP
Minister of Public Utilities and Minister of Housing: Senator The Hon. D. P. Pierre
Minister of Agriculture, Lands and Fisheries: The Hon. L. M. Robinson, MP
Minister of Works: The Hon. V. L. Campbell, MP
Minister of National Security: The Hon. B. L. B. Pitt, MP
Minister of Health and Minister of Local Government: Senator The Hon. F. C. Prevatt
Minister of Labour, Social Security and Co-operatives: The Hon. E. E. Mahabir, MP
Attorney General and Minister for Legal Affairs: The Hon. K. T. Hudson-Phillips, QC, MP
Minister of Finance and Minister of Planning and Development:
The Hon. G. M. Chambers, MP
Minister of Education and Culture: The Hon. C. Gomes, MP
Minister of Petroleum and Mines and Minister of Industry and Commerce:
The Hon. O. R. Padmore, MP
Minister for Tobago Affairs: The Hon. W. Winchester, MP

MINISTERS OF STATE
Ministry of the Prime Minister: The Hon. Dr C. Joseph, MP
Ministry of Local Government: The Hon. S. S. Mohammed, MP
Ministry of Finance: The Hon. B. M. Barrow, MP
Ministry for Legal Affairs: The Hon. H. O. N. McLean, MP

PARLIAMENTARY SECRETARIES
Ministry of Works: The Hon. W. Hinds, MP
For Better Village Programme and Special Works Projects:
The Hon. Mrs M. Donawa-McDavidson
Ministry of Agriculture, Lands and Fisheries: The Hon. A. Ali, MP
Ministry of Petroleum and Mines: The Hon. P. Manning, MP
Ministry of Public Utilities: The Hon. T. K. Ali, MP
Ministry of Planning and Development: The Hon. J. R. F. Richardson, MP
For Youth Affairs and Sport: The Hon. S. Charles, MP
Ministry of Labour, Social Security and Co-operatives:
Senator The Hon. J. C. Daniel, Senator The Hon. Miss Ruby Felix

SENATE
President of the Senate: Senator Dr Wahid Ali
Clerk of the Senate: J. E. Carter

HOUSE OF REPRESENTATIVES
Speaker: The Hon. A. Thomasos
Clerk: G. R. Latour

LEADER OF THE OPPOSITION IN THE HOUSE OF REPRESENTATIVES
(Vacant)

JUDICIARY
Court of Appeal
Acting Chief Justice and President of the Court of Appeal: The Hon. Mr Justice C. E. Phillips
Mr. Justice H. A. Fraser
Mr Justice K. de la Bastide
Mr Justice P. T. Georges

INDUSTRIAL COURT
President: Mr Justice I. E. Hyatali
Vice-President: Mr Justice J. A. M. Braithwaite

HIGH COURT
Judges:

Mr Justice J. A. Braithwaite
Mr Justice M. A. Corbin
Mr Justice C. E. Achong
Mr Justice Evan Rees
Mr Justice K. McMillan

Mr Justice R. Narine
Mr Justice G. M. Scott
Mr Justice N. Hassanali
Mr Justice D. Malone
Mr Justice G. Des Iles

Registrar and Marshal: G. R. Benny
Chief Magistrate: W. Bruno

CENTRAL BANK OF TRINIDAD AND TOBAGO
Governor: Mr Victor Bruce

MINISTRIES AND GOVERNMENT DEPARTMENTS

PRIME MINISTER'S OFFICE
Permanent Secretary to the Cabinet and Head of the Civil Service: D. Alleyne
Economic Adviser: (vacant)

MINISTRY OF NATIONAL SECURITY
Permanent Secretary: E. H. Nunez

MINISTRY OF HEALTH
Acting Permanent Secretary: J. L. Nunez

MINISTRY OF AGRICULTURE,
LANDS AND FISHERIES
Permanent Secretary: F. Barsotti

MINISTRY OF HOUSING
Permanent Secretary: U. L. Pierre

MINISTRY OF INDUSTRY, COMMERCE,
PETROLEUM AND MINES
Permanent Secretary: E. A. Braithwaite
(Industry and Commerce)
Acting Permanent Secretary: O. Fernandez
(Petroleum and Mines)

MINISTRY OF WORKS
Permanent Secretary: G. Phillip

MINISTRY OF PUBLIC UTILITIES
Permanent Secretary: J. H. Herrera

MINISTRY OF EXTERNAL AFFAIRS
Acting Permanent Secretary: V. C. McIntyre

ATTORNEY GENERAL AND MINISTRY OF
LEGAL AFFAIRS
Legal Secretary: Miss A. Bourne

MINISTRY OF WEST INDIAN AFFAIRS
Permanent Secretary: L. C. Nanton

MINISTRY OF LABOUR AND
SOCIAL SECURITY
Permanent Secretary: L. P. E. Ramchand

MINISTRY OF FINANCE
Permanent Secretary: F. Rampersad

MINISTRY OF LOCAL GOVERNMENT
Permanent Secretary: I. Rampersad

MINISTRY OF EDUCATION AND CULTURE
Acting Permanent Secretary: H. Leacock

MINISTRY OF PLANNING AND DEVELOPMENT
Permanent Secretary: E. Moore

TOBAGO AFFAIRS
Permanent Secretary: J. F. Belle

SERVICE COMMISSIONS
Chairman, Public Service Commission: Sir
  Werner J. Boos, CBE
Chairman, Police Service Commission: Sir
  Werner J. Boos, CBE
Chairman, Judicial and Legal Service Com-
  mission: Mr Justice A. H. McShine
Chairman, Electoral Boundaries Commis-
  sion and Elections Commission: Sir Alan
  Reece, CMG

DIPLOMATIC REPRESENTATION

TRINIDAD AND TOBAGO REPRESENTATIVES
IN OTHER COMMONWEALTH COUNTRIES
Britain: Dr P. V. J. Solomon (High Com-
missioner); Canada: Matthew Ramcharan
(High Commissioner); Ceylon; India; Singa-
pore: A. Sinanan (resident in Delhi);
Jamaica: A. Sabga-Aboud; Guyana: E. A.
Murray; Bardados and West Indies Asso-
ciated States: Mrs V. Crichlow

COMMONWEALTH HIGH COMMISSIONERS
IN TRINIDAD AND TOBAGO
Britain: R. C. C. Hunt, CMG; Canada: G. E.
Rau; India: L. N. Ray; Jamaica: I. S. de
Souza, OBE; Pakistan: M. S. Shaikh (resident
in Ottawa)

TRINIDAD AND TOBAGO REPRESENTATION
IN NON-COMMONWEALTH COUNTRIES
Argentina: M. Ramcharan (resident in
Ottawa); Brazil: G. Montano; Ethiopia:
Mrs I. U. Teshea; Austria; Belgium;
European Economic Community; France;
Federal Republic of Germany; Finland;
Italy; Luxembourg: Netherlands; Norway;
Sweden; Switzerland; Dr P. V. J. Solomon
(resident in London); Japan: A. Sinanan
(resident in Delhi); United Nations: E.
Seignoret (Permanent Representative);
United States: Sir Ellis Clarke, CMG (also
Ambassador to Mexico); Venezuela: S.
Lutchman (also Ambassador to Colombia);
Geneva: C. Archibald (Permanent Represen-
tative)

UGANDA

U GANDA is near the centre of the continent of Africa. It is bounded on the
east by Kenya, on the south by Tanzania and Rwanda, on the west by
the Congo and on the north by the Sudan. The distance from north to
south of the country is about 400 miles and from east to west about 350 miles.
  The total area is 91,076 square miles, of which 16,364 square miles are open
water. This area of open water consists of parts of Lakes Victoria, Albert and
Edward and all of Lakes George and Kyoga. From Lake Victoria at Jinja the
Nile begins its 3,800 miles journey to the Mediterranean.
  Lake Victoria is 3,720 feet above sea level: in the north at the Sudan frontier
the altitude is only 2,000 feet. The ground rises towards Mount Elgon (14,178
feet) in the east and towards the Ruwenzori Mountains in the west. The highest
peak of the snow-capped Ruwenzori range is 16,794 feet, the third highest
mountain in Africa. Uganda has thus great variety of landscape and vegetation.
There are hot, dry deserts in the north-east, luxurious rain forests in the west
and south-east, the remainder being mostly tree-savannah with extensive
sluggish swamps. Wildlife is varied and abundant.
  Over most of the country the weather is that of a perpetual summer, with hot
sunshine, cool breezes and showers of rain. Temperature ranges at Entebbe are
about 17·5°C (62°–64°F) minimum and 26°–27°C (77°–81°F) maximum. The
mean annual rainfall at Entebbe is 63·44 inches.

The principal towns are Kampala, the capital (population including suburbs 331,889), Jinja (population 47,298) and Mbale (population 23,539).

At the 1959 census the population was 6,536,616, of whom 6,449,558 were Africans (approximately 680,000 of whom were not of Uganda origin), 10,866 Europeans and 76,192 persons of other race (mostly originating from the Indian sub-continent). This represented an average rate of increase of approximately 2·5 per cent per annum since the previous census. In 1961 the population was estimated to number some 6,845,000 of whom 6,751,000 were Africans, 11,600 Europeans, and the remainder mostly Asians. In mid-1965 it was estimated that the population was 7,551,000. The provisional 1969 census results show a population of 9,526,237, an increase of 47 per cent since the 1959 census. The analysis of the African population by tribes showed the Baganda to be the largest (just over one million), followed by the Iteso, Banyankore and Basoga with about half a million members each. Twenty-four other tribes showed totals in excess of 10,000 each. 24 languages in various groups (Bantu, Nilotic and Hamitic) are spoken but English is the official language. No statistics are available giving information about the main religions but it is believed that one-third of the people are Roman Catholic, one-third Protestant, one-sixth Muslim and a sixth not conforming to any organised religion.

In 1968 Uganda had 2,671 grant-aided primary schools with an enrolment of 632,132 children while 31,637 students were enrolled in secondary schools, 2,067 students at Technical Schools and 4,292 at Teacher Training Colleges. Makerere University College, opened as a technical school in 1921, achieved its status as a constituent college of the University of East Africa in 1963. On 1st July 1970, Makerere became a separate national University as Makerere University, Kampala. First degree courses are offered at Makerere in Agriculture, Arts and Social Science, Education, Medicine, Science, Fine Art and Technology; and except for Science, post graduate diplomas are also offered in these faculties. Total enrolment at Makerere for 1969/70 was 2,211. In 1970, 1,865 Ugandans were enrolled in Universities and institutions of higher education abroad (1,002 in Britain).

Having no sea coast, Uganda is dependent principally upon the railway line to Mombasa, Kenya, for her imports and exports, and in 1969 more than 562,000 tons of goods were carried from Mombasa to destinations in Uganda. There are nearly 700 miles of mainline railways in Uganda between Tororo and Kasese and Tororo and Pakwach. With the erection of a bridge over the Nile it is planned to extend the railway to Arua. There are 15,000 miles of roads of all sorts, of which just over 1,000 miles are bitumenised main highways.

Uganda's international airport is situated at Entebbe, twenty-one miles from Kampala. The runway is 9,900 feet in length. There are also landing grounds at Tororo, Jinja, Soroti, Gulu, Arua, Kasese, Murchison Falls and Mbarara from which internal services are operated by the East African Airways Corporation.

Radio Uganda and Uganda Television are both controlled by the Ministry of Information and Broadcasting.

Uganda's exports and re-exports in 1969 amounted to Shs.1,602m. of which exports to neighbouring Kenya and Tanzania accounted for Shs.190m. Main overseas export earners were: coffee (Shs.779·9m.); cotton (Shs.250·9m.); copper (Shs.120·3m.); tea (Shs.9·3m.); animal feeding stuffs (Shs.42·1m.); hides and skins (Shs.26·7m.).

Britain's purchases from Uganda in 1969 were Shs.315·8m. (22·6 per cent).

Goods to the value of Shs.910m. were imported by Uganda from overseas in 1969. Imports from Kenya and Tanzania in the same period were Shs.343m. Britain (Shs.312m.) was Uganda's largest overseas supplier.

In 1970/71 a recurrent revenue of Uganda Shs.1,170m., including Shs.28m. from new taxation proposals, is expected with an expenditure of Shs.1,121m. Development resources are expected to amount to Shs.414·2m., of which Shs.135·4m. is expected to come from external or tied sources, Shs.199·9m. from internal loan finance and the remainder from development revenue and the recurrent budget surplus. The net gap in budget finances will be Shs.97·7m., to be met from local short term borrowing.

Uganda's Independence Day is 9th October.

HISTORY

Archaeological evidence points to human occupation of the area which is now Uganda from the earliest times. The pursuit of agriculture may have originated in the first millenium B.C., probably coincidentally with Bantu settlement. For a time the earlier stone-age inhabitants and the agriculturalists continued to exist side by side, the former being gradually absorbed. The working of iron was learned perhaps a thousand years ago.

The fertility of the south and west of the country favoured the development of political institutions, and in those areas there grew up a number of highly coherent, centrally controlled units. Up to the nineteenth century the most powerful of these was Bunyoro, but in that century Buganda took the lead. In the north, different conditions had favoured the development of small tribal organisations.

During the nineteenth century, the first British traders, explorers and missionaries reached Uganda. Speke and Grant penetrated from the east coast of Africa in 1862; Baker from the north in 1864. In the 1870s there were unsuccessful attempts by Egypt to obtain control. In the late 1870s the first missionaries reached Buganda.

In 1888 British interests in East Africa were assigned by Royal Charter to the Imperial British East Africa Company, and in 1890 Captain (later Lord) Lugard was sent to represent the Company in Uganda. He concluded a treaty with the Kabaka of Buganda and established the Company's influence.

The cost of the Company's operations was, however, prohibitive, and in 1893 an Imperial Commissioner, Sir Gerald Portal, assumed the obligations and rights of the Company on behalf of the British Government. Buganda was formally declared a Protectorate in 1894; Bunyoro, Tororo, Ankole and Busoga followed in 1896. New agreements were negotiated with Buganda, Toro and Ankole in 1900 and 1901.

The basic pattern of Uganda's economic development was laid down before the First World War, in spite of the Administration's pre-occupation with the suppression of an outbreak of sleeping sickness which devastated the country. Cotton growing by peasant farmers, introduced in 1904, flourished, and the development of this sector of the economy stimulated the growth of transport and communications. The construction of a network of all-weather roads was begun, and a connection with the coast was obtained by a shipping service across Lake Victoria to Kisumu in Kenya, which was linked to Mombasa by rail in 1901. In 1913 the Busoga Railway was completed, and this, with the system of waterways radiating from the Nile basin, helped the development of the area of fine cotton-growing soil in the eastern part of the country.

The 1914-18 War made considerable demands on manpower, and checked Uganda's economic progress, especially in the context of world depression in the early 1920s. Coffee was developed as an alternative cash crop, and the first sugar refinery was opened in 1924. By 1928 the railway from the coast had been extended as far as Jinja, and the completion of a bridge over the Nile in 1931 finally linked Kampala with the Indian Ocean.

Under British administration land policy prohibited acquisition by non-Africans of freehold title to land. As a result European settlement did not become a feature of Uganda's development; and in Buganda, where title to land was held almost exclusively by Africans, indiscriminate purchase and exploitation by non-Africans was eliminated. This was an important factor in the development of harmonious race relations in Uganda.

The war of 1939-45 also made great demands on Uganda's resources and the emphasis of Government policy in the immediate post-war period was upon economic rehabilitation and development, a programme which was greatly helped by the high prices obtainable for cotton and coffee.

CONSTITUTIONAL DEVELOPMENT

The Uganda Order in Council 1902 made provision for the government of the protectorate, and control was passed from the Foreign Office to the Colonial Office in 1905. By 1914 a series of boundary commissions had established the country's boundaries which remained unchanged until the present day except for the transfer of Rudolph Province to Kenya in 1926. In 1921 Executive and Legislative Councils were created, and the latter was expanded in 1953 to make it more representative. The Legislative Council was further increased in 1955, half the membership then being African. At the same time a ministerial system was introduced, a number of the ministers being non-officials. In 1958 direct elections of African Representative Members to the Legislative Council were held in a number of Districts. Buganda, however, did not take part and was consequently not represented in the new Council. The year 1960 saw further constitutional advance, with the general objects of broadening the composition of the Legislative Council and restricting its membership almost entirely to elected members, and of converting the Governor's Executive Council into a Council of Ministers. A Commission under Lord Munster considered the relationships between the Kingdoms and the Central Government.

A general election under the new arrangements was held in March 1961 and resulted in a majority for the Democratic Party, led by Mr Benedicto Kiwanuka, who became Chief Minister. Following a constitutional conference in London later the same year Uganda attained internal self-government in March 1962 and Mr Kiwanuka became the first Prime Minister.

The new Constitution provided for a Legislature of a single Chamber, styled the National Assembly, consisting of a Speaker, 82 Elected Members and 9 Specially Elected Members. Of the Elected Members, 21 were elected within Buganda (excluding the Municipality of Kampala) and the Buganda Lukiiko (Legislative Assembly) had the power to declare before each General Election that these Members should be elected by the Lukiiko itself. The executive power was to be exercised on behalf of Her Majesty by the Governor but, except in regard to certain reserved functions, he could assign responsibilities to Ministers and was normally required to act on the advice of the Cabinet which was collectively responsible to the National Assembly. Buganda's relationship with Uganda was defined as a federal one.

A general election held in April 1962 resulted in a majority for the Uganda People's Congress, supported until 24th August 1964 by the Kabaka Yekka, a Buganda political organisation. Mr Milton Obote, leader of the U.P.C. became Prime Minister.

At the opening of the new Parliament the Governor announced that his Ministers desired that Her Majesty should be Queen of independent Uganda and that Uganda would seek membership of the Commonwealth.

Following a further Constitutional Conference in London in June 1962 Uganda became an independent sovereign country and a Member of the Commonwealth on the 9th October 1962.

In 1963 the Uganda Parliament amended the Constitution so that from 9th October 1963 (the anniversary of Independence) Her Majesty The Queen would no longer be the Head of State of Uganda and instead Uganda would be a sovereign independent country with a citizen of Uganda as Head of State, to be known as 'President of Uganda'. The first holder of this office was the Kabaka of Buganda, Sir Edward Mutesa. At the same time Uganda expressed a desire to continue as a Member of the Commonwealth of which the Queen is the Head.

On 24th February 1966, the Prime Minister, the Hon. Dr A. M. Obote, MP, announced that the Constitution had been suspended, except for certain specified subjects. On 2nd March 1966 it was announced that Dr Obote acting with the advice and consent of the Cabinet had declared that the executive authority of Uganda should vest in the Prime Minister (instead of the President) and that the duties, powers and other functions performed or exercisable by the President or Vice-President should vest in the Prime Minister. On 15th April in the National Assembly, Dr Obote announced the abrogation of the 1962 Constitution and moved a motion for the introduction of a new Constitution which was adopted by 55 votes to 4. Dr Obote was then sworn in as President.

Under the 1966 Constitution, the President was both Head of State and Head of the Executive, advised by a Cabinet of Ministers of which he was a member. The National Assembly consisted of 82 elected members, all directly elected, including 21 from Buganda (exclusive of Kampala) and nine specially elected members. Parliament was to continue for five years unless sooner dissolved by the President, acting on the advice of the Cabinet.

In June 1967 the National Assembly resolved itself into a Constituent Assembly to consider proposals submitted to it by the Government for the amendment of the 1966 constitution. After due consideration the proposals, as modified following debate, were adopted, and a new Constitution under which Uganda became a Republic was proclaimed on 8th September 1967. The main changes from the previous constitution were the abolition of the old kingdoms and the dissolution of Buganda into four districts for administrative purposes; and provision for specially elected members in number related to the strength of the party having greatest numerical strength in the National Assembly in order to give that party a majority of not more than ten. The number of elected members remained at 82. The powers of the President were defined and the rights and freedoms of the individual prescribed. It was decided that subject to the provisions of the Constitution for dissolution, the life of the Parliament should be five years from the introduction of the preceding constitution, *viz.* 15th April 1966.

On 25th January 1971 the Commander of the Armed Forces, Major-General Idi Amin mounted a successful *coup d'état* against Dr Obote. A military government was set up headed by General Amin as President and consisting of a cabinet of ministers nearly all of whom are civilians. Parliament was dissolved and those Sections of the 1967 Constitution dealing with executive and legislative powers suspended. The President rules by decree, advised by his cabinet. Otherwise the provisions of the 1967 Constitution remain in force. Free elections and a return to civilian rule have been promised.

HISTORICAL LIST
PRESIDENTS
Sir Edward Mutesa, 9th October 1963 to 24th February 1966
Dr A. Milton Obote, from 15th April 1966 to 25th January 1971
General Idi Amin Dada, from 20th February 1971

PRIME MINISTER
Dr A. Milton Obote, MP, from 9th October 1962 to 15th April 1966

GOVERNMENT

PRESIDENT
His Excellency General Idi Amin Dada

MINISTERS
Minister of Foreign Affairs: Hon. Wanume Kibedi
Minister of Internal Affairs: Hon. Lt.-Col. Eat Obitre Gama
Minister of Finance: E. B. Wakhweya
Minister of Defence: Hon. A. C. K. Oboth Ofumbi
Minister of Commerce, Industry and Tourism: Hon. W. Lutara
Minister of Agriculture, Forestry and Cooperatives: Hon. F. L. Okwaare
Minister of Planning and Economic Development: Hon. A. K. Kironde
Minister of Mineral and Water Resources: Hon. E. W. Oryema
Minister of Education: Hon. A. Mayanja
Minister of Health: Hon. Dr J. H. Gesa
Minister of Culture and Community Development: Hon. Y. Engur
Minister of Works, Communications and Housing: Hon. J. M. N. Zikusoka
Minister of Information and Broadcasting: Hon. W. Naburi
Minister of Labour: Hon. J. M. Byagagaire
Minister of Public Service and Local Administrations: Hon. V. A. Ovonji
Minister of Animal Industry, Game and Fisheries: Hon. Professor W. B. Banage
Attorney-General: Hon. P. J. Nkambo-Mugerwa

NATIONAL ASSEMBLY
Speaker: Hon. Narendra Patel, MP
Deputy Speaker: Hon. A. N. Name, MP
Clerk to the National Assembly: E. T. A. Ochwo

JUDICIARY
Chief Justice: Sir Dermot Sheridan, CMG

Puisne Judges:

D. J. Jones	A. R. F. Dickson
K. T. Fuad	P. V. Phadke
L. P. Saldhana	S. Musoke
E. E. Youds	S. W. W. Wambuzi
R. E. G. Russell	A. W. K. Mukasa
J. W. Mead	E. A. Oteng
W. H. Goudie	

Chief Registrar:
S. K. Kulubya

MINISTRIES AND GOVERNMENT DEPARTMENTS

PRESIDENT'S OFFICE
Permanent Secretary and Secretary to the Cabinet: Z. H. K. Bigirwenkya
Principal Private Secretary to the President: J. E. Ekochu
Secretary for Administration: Y. H. Wacha-Olwol
Secretary for Research: W. Okwenje
Secretary for Economic and East African Affairs: A. M. Sibo

MINISTRY OF FOREIGN AFFAIRS
Permanent Secretary: S. E. C. Baingana

ATTORNEY-GENERAL'S CHAMBERS
Solicitor-General: A. Lule (Acting)

MINISTRY OF DEFENCE
Permanent Secretary: N. Rubanga
Commander-in-Chief of the Armed Forces: General Idi Amin Dada

MINISTRY OF INTERNAL AFFAIRS
Acting Permanent Secretary: S. E. Etoorie
Inspector-General of Police: Vacant
Commissioner of Prisons: L. Kigonya
Principal Immigration Officer: A. J. Karagaba

MINISTRY OF FINANCE
Secretary to the Treasury: J. Geria

MINISTRY OF COMMERCE AND INDUSTRY AND TOURISM
Permanent Secretary: A. K. K. Mubanda

MINISTRY OF AGRICULTURE, FORESTRY AND CO-OPERATIVES
Permanent Secretary: J. S. Laker
Commissioner for Agriculture: H. R. Berunga
Chief Conservator of Forests: M. L. Rukuba
Commissioner for Co-operatives: P. Kwebiha

MINISTRY OF ANIMAL INDUSTRY, GAME AND FISHERIES
Permanent Secretary: H. S. K. Nsubuga
Commissioner of Veterinary Services and Animal Industry: J. H. Kagoda
Chief Tsetse Officer: W. R. Wooff
Chief Game Warden: S. Ruhweza
Chief Fisheries Officer: S. N. Semakula

MINISTRY OF MINERAL AND WATER RESOURCES
Permanent Secretary: S. L. Okec
Commissioner of Lands and Surveys: G. W. Bakinbinga
Commissioner of Geological Surveys and Mines Department: C. E. Tamale-Ssali
Commissioner of Water Development: D. A. Kabega

MINISTRY OF PUBLIC SERVICES AND LOCAL ADMINISTRATIONS
Permanent Secretary: S. E. Egweu

MINISTRY OF EDUCATION
Permanent Secretary: W. W. Rwetsiba
Chief Education Officer: E. K. K. Sempebwa
Chief Inspector of Schools: J. M. Aryada

MINISTRY OF HEALTH
Permanent Secretary/Chief Medical Officer: Y. B. Semambo

MINISTRY OF CULTURE AND COMMUNITY DEVELOPMENT
Permanent Secretary: A. B. Adimola

MINISTRY OF WORKS, COMMUNICATIONS AND HOUSING
Permanent Secretary: G. N. Karugonjo (Acting)

MINISTRY OF INFORMATION AND BROADCASTING
Permanent Secretary: M. Emojong

MINISTRY OF LABOUR
Permanent Secretary, Labour Commissioner and Registrar of Trade Unions: L. Katagyira

MINISTRY OF PLANNING AND ECONOMIC DEVELOPMENT
Permanent Secretary: K. Kabanda

OFFICE OF THE CONTROLLER AND AUDITOR-GENERAL
Controller and Auditor-General: G. A. Kabiswa

OFFICE OF THE PUBLIC SERVICE COMMISSION
Chairman: H. E. Abdula-Anyuru
Deputy Chairman: M. T. Katuramu
Second Deputy Chairman: J. E. I. Ogaino

CHAIRMEN OF PARASTATAL BODIES
Coffee Marketing Board: G. W. Gowa (acting).
Lint Marketing Board: C. H. M. Barlow
National Trading Corporation: E. M. F. Kate (acting)
Produce Marketing Board: M. S. Kiingi
Uganda Development Corporation: S. Nyanzi
Uganda Electricity Board: E. Kironde
GOVERNOR OF TOE BANK OF UGANDA: J. M. Mubiru

O

DIPLOMATIC REPRESENTATION

UGANDA HIGH COMMISSIONERS IN OTHER COMMONWEALTH COUNTRIES

Britain: Lt.-Col. S. E. Lukakamwa; India: Major M. E. Ombia; Ghana: Brig. S. O. Opolot; Uganda also has diplomatic representation in Ethiopia, France, the Federal Republic of Germany, the United Arab Republic, the United States of America, the U.S.S.R., and at the United Nations.

COMMONWEALTH HIGH COMMISSIONERS IN UGANDA

Britain: R. M. K. Slater, CMG; Canada: J. M. Cook (resident in Nairobi); Australia: K. Rogers (resident in Nairobi); India: D. Deva; Pakistan: R. R. Noore (resident in Nairobi); Ghana: A. E. K. Fori-Atta; Nigeria: M. J. Etuk; Zambia:Dr D. K. Konoso (acting) (resident in Nairobi).

THE UNITED KINGDOM OF GREAT BRITAIN AND NORTHERN IRELAND

As a result of the elections held on 18th June, 1970, the Conservative Party who had been in opposition since October 1964, were returned to power. The state of the parties was as follows:

Conservatives 330, Labour 287, Liberals 6, Others 7.

At subsequent by-elections the Conservative Party lost one seat to the Labour Party. At the time of going to press (September 1971) there were three by-elections pending.

HER MAJESTY'S GOVERNMENT

THE CABINET

Prime Minister and First Lord of the Treasury and Minister for the Civil Service: The Rt Hon. Edward Heath, MP

Secretary of State for the Home Department: The Rt Hon. Reginald Maudling, MP

Secretary of State for Foreign and Commonwealth Affairs: The Rt Hon. Sir Alec Douglas-Home, MP

Lord Chancellor: The Rt Hon. Lord Hailsham of St Marylebone

Chancellor of the Exchequer: The Rt Hon. Anthony Barber, MP

Lord President of the Council: The Rt Hon. William Whitelaw, MP

Secretary of State for Defence and Minister of Aviation Supply: The Rt Hon. Lord Carrington

Secretary of State for Social Services: The Rt Hon. Sir Keith Joseph, MP

Chancellor of the Duchy of Lancaster: The Rt Hon. Geoffrey Rippon, QC, MP

Secretary of State for Employment: The Rt Hon. Robert Carr, MP

Secretary of State for Education and Science: The Rt Hon. Margaret Thatcher, MP

Secretary of State for Scotland: The Rt Hon. Gordon Campbell, MP

Lord Privy Seal: The Rt Hon. The Earl Jellicoe

Secretary of State for the Environment: The Rt Hon. Peter Walker, MP

Secretary of State for Wales: The Rt Hon. Peter Thomas, QC, MP

Minister of Agriculture, Fisheries and Food: The Rt Hon. James Prior, MP

Secretary of State for Trade and Industry and President of the Board of Trade: The Rt Hon. John Davies, MP

MINISTERS NOT IN THE CABINET

Minister of Posts and Telecommunications: The Rt Hon. Christopher Chataway, MP

Paymaster-General: The Rt Hon. The Viscount Eccles

Minister of Trade: The Rt Hon. Michael Noble, MP

Minister for Aerospace: The Rt Hon. Frederick Corfield, MP

Minister for Overseas Development: The Rt Hon. Richard Wood, MP

Minister for Housing and Construction: The Rt Hon. Julian Amery, MP

Minister for Transport Industries: The Rt Hon. John Peyton, MP

Minister for Local Government and Development: Mr Graham Page, MP

Minister for Industry: Sir John Eden, MP

Minister of State, Home Office: Mr Richard Sharples, MP

Minister of State, Home Office: Lord Windlesham
Minister of State for Foreign and Commonwealth Affairs:
The Rt Hon. Joseph Godber, MP
Chief Secretary, Treasury: Mr Maurice Macmillan, MP
Parliamentary Secretary, Treasury (Chief Whip): The Rt Hon. Francis Pym, MP
Financial Secretary, Treasury: Mr Patrick Jenkin, MP
Minister of State, Treasury: Mr Terence Higgins, MP
Minister of State for Defence: Lord Balniel, MP
Minister of State for Defence Procurement: Mr Ian Gilmour, MP
Minister of State, Department of Health and Social Security: Lord Aberdare
Minister of State, Department of Employment: Mr Paul Bryan, MP
Minister of State, Scottish Office: Lady Tweedsmuir
Minister of State, Welsh Office: Mr David Gibson-Watt, MP
Minister without Portfolio: The Rt Hon. The Lord Drumalbyn

LAW OFFICERS

Attorney-General: The Rt Hon. Sir Peter Rawlinson, QC, MP
Lord Advocate: The Rt Hon. Norman Wylie, QC, MP
Solicitor-General: Sir Geoffrey Howe, QC, MP
Solicitor-General for Scotland: Mr David Brand, QC

DEPARTMENTS OF STATE AND MINISTERS

AGRICULTURE, FISHERIES AND FOOD

Minister: Mr James Prior, MP
Parliamentary Secretary: Mr Anthony Stodart, MP

CIVIL SERVICE

Minister: The Prime Minister
Lord Privy Seal: Earl Jellicoe, DSO, MC
Parliamentary Secretary: Mr David Howell, MP

DEFENCE

Secretary of State and Minister of Aviation Supply: Lord Carrington, KCMG, MC
Minister of State: Lord Balniel, MP
Minister of State for Defence Procurement: Mr Ian Gilmour, MP
Parliamentary Under Secretary of State for the Royal Navy: Mr Peter Kirk, MP
Parliamentary Under Secretary of State for the RAF: Mr Anthony Lambton, MP

EDUCATION AND SCIENCE

Secretary of State: Mrs Margaret Thatcher, MP
Paymaster General (with responsibility for the Arts): Viscount Eccles, KCVO
Parliamentary Under Secretaries of State: Mr William Van Straubenze, MBE, MP; Lord
Belstead

EMPLOYMENT

Secretary of State: Mr Robert Carr, MP
Minister of State: Mr Paul Bryan, MP
Parliamentary Secretary of State: Mr Dudley Smith, MP

ENVIRONMENT

Secretary of State: Mr Peter Walker, MBE, MP
Minister for Local Government and Development: Mr Graham Page, MBE, MP
Parliamentary Under Secretaries of State: Mr Michael Heseltin, MP; The Rev. Lord
Sandford, DSC
Minister for Housing and Construction: Mr Julian Amery, MP
Parliamentary Under Secretary of State: Mr Paul Channon, MP
Minister for Transport Industries: Mr John Peyton, MP
Parliamentary Under Secretary of State: Mr Eldon Griffiths, MP

FOREIGN AND COMMONWEALTH OFFICE

Secretary of State: Sir Alec Douglas-Home, KT, MP
Chancellor of the Duchy of Lancaster: Mr Geoffrey Rippon, QC, MP
Minister of Overseas Development: Mr Richard Wood, MP
Minister of State: Mr Joseph Godber, MP
Parliamentary Under Secretaries of State: The Marquess of Lothian; Mr Anthony Royle, MP;
Mr Anthony Kershaw, MC, MP

HEALTH AND SECURITY

Secretary of State for Social Services: Sir Keith Joseph, BT, MP
Minister of State: Lord Aberdare, DL
Parliamentary Secretaries: Mr M. Alsion, MP (Health): Mr P. Dean, MP (Social Security)

HOME DEPARTMENT

Secretary of State: Mr Reginald Maudling, MP
Ministers of State: Mr Richard Sharples, OBE, MC, MP; Lord Windlesham
Parliamentary Under Secretary of State: Mr Mark Carlisle, MP

LAW OFFICERS

Attorney-General: Sir Peter Rawlinson, QC, MP
Solicitor-General: Sir Geoffry Howe, QC, MP
Lord Advocate: Mr Norman Wylie, VRD, QC, MP
Solicitor-General for Scotland: Mr David Brand, QC

LORD CHANCELLOR

Lord Hailsham of St Marylebone

LORD PRIVY SEAL

Earl Jellicoe, DSO, MC

PAYMASTER-GENERAL

Viscount Eccles, KCVO

POSTS AND TELECOMMUNICATIONS

Minister: Mr Christopher Chataway, MP

PRIVY COUNCIL

Lord President of the Council: Mr William Whitelaw, MC, MP

SCOTTISH OFFICE

Secretary of State: Mr Gordon Campbell, MC, MP
Minister of State: Lady Tweedsmuir
Parliamentary Under Secretaries of State: Mr Alick L. Buchanan-Smith, MP (Home Affairs
    and Agriculture); Mr Hector Monro, MP (Health and Education); Mr George Younger
    TD, MP (Development)

TRADE AND INDUSTRY

Secretary of State and President of the Board of Trade: Mr John Davies, MBE, MP
Minister for Trade: Mr Michael Noble, MP
Minister for Industry: Sir John Eden, BT, MP
Minister for Aerospace: Mr Frederick Corfield, MP
Parliamentary Under Secretaries of State: Mr Anthony Grant, MP (Trade); Hon. Nicholas,
    Ridley, MP (Industry); Mr David Price, MP (Aerospace)

TREASURY

Prime Minister and First Lord of the Treasury: Mr Edward Heath, MBE, MP
Chancellor of the Exchequer: Mr Anthony Barber, TD, MP
Chief Secretary: Mr Maurice Macmillan, MP
Lords Commissioners: Mr B. Weatherill, MP; Mr W. Clegg, MP; Mr V. Goodhew, MP;
    Mr P. Hawkins, TD, JP, MP
Parliamentary Secretary: Mr Francis Pym, MC, MP
Financial Secretary: Mr Patrick Jenkin, MP
Minister of State: Mr Terence Higgins, MP
Assistant Whips: Mr Tim Fortescue, MP; Mr Keith Speed, RD, MP; Mr Hugh Rossi, MP

WALES

Secretary of State: Mr Peter Thomas, QC, MP
Minister of State: Mr David Gibson-Watt, MC, MP

HER MAJESTY'S HOUSEHOLD

Lord Chamberlain: The Lord Cobbold, KG, GCVO
Lord Steward: The Viscount Cobham, KG, GCMG, TD
Master of the Horse: The Duke of Beaufort, KG, GCVO
Lords in Waiting: Lord Nugent, KCVO; Earl of Westmorland, KCVO; Lord Hamilton of Dalziel, MC; Lord Denham; Earl Ferrers; Lord Mowbray Seagrave and Stourton.
Captain of the Gentlemen-At-Arms: Earl St Aldwyn, KBE, TD
Captain, Yeoman of the Guard: Viscount Goschen, OBE
Treasurer of the Household: Mr Humphrey Atkins, MP
Comptroller of the Household: Mr Reginald Eyre, MP
Vice-Chamberlain of the Household: Mr Jasper More, MP

HOUSE OF COMMONS

Speaker: The Rt Hon. Mr Selwyn Lloyd, QC, MP
Chairman of Ways and Means: Wing Commander Sir Robert Grant-Ferris, MP
Deputy Chairman of Ways and Means: Miss Margaret Betty Harvie Anderson, OBE, TD, MP
Clerk of the House of Commons: Sir Barnett Cocks, KCB, OBE
Serjeant at Arms: Rear-Admiral A. H. C. Gordon Lennox, CB, DSO

LEADER OF THE OPPOSITION

The Rt Hon. Harold Wilson, OBE, MP

HOUSE OF LORDS

Speaker: The Rt Hon. The Lord Hailsham of St Marylebone
Lord Chairman of Committees: The Rt Hon. Earl of Listowel, GCMG
Clerk of the Parliaments: Sir David Stephens, KCB, CVO

NORTHERN IRELAND

Northern Ireland has a total area of 5,462 sq. miles (land 5,206 sq. miles; inland water and tideways 256 sq. miles) with a density of population of 283 persons per sq. mile in 1966 when the Census showed a total population of 1,484,775 (males 723,884; females 760,891) an increase of 59,733 or 4·2 per cent over the total at the Census of 1961. Under the Government of Ireland Act 1920, a separate Parliament and Executive Government were established for Northern Ireland. Under the Constitution certain legislative and fiscal powers are reserved to the Parliament of the United Kingdom. The Northern Ireland Parliament consists of a House of Commons of 52 elected members and a Senate of one ex-officio Senator and 24 Senators elected by the members of the House of Commons on the proportional representation system. The state of the parties in April 1971 was—Unionists 35, Social Democratic and Labour 6, Nationalists 4, Protestant Unionists 2, Independent Uionists 2, Northern Ireland Labour 1, Republican Labour 1, Independent 1. Under the Act of 1920 Northern Ireland returns 12 members to the House of Commons at Westminster. The Executive power is vested in the Governor on behalf of Her Majesty The Queen; he holds office for 6 years.

Governor: His Excellency the Lord Grey of Naunton, GCMG, KCVO, OBE
(appointed 3rd December 1968 (Government House, Hillsborough, Northern Ireland))

MEMBERS OF THE CABINET

Prime Minister and Minister of Home Affairs: Rt Hon. A. B. D. Faulkner, MP
Minister in the Senate: Senator Rt Hon. J. L. O. Andrews
Minister of Finance: Rt Hon. H. V. Kirk, MP
Minister of Health and Social Services: Rt Hon. W. K. Fitzsimmons, MP
Minister of Education: Capt. Rt Hon. W. J. Long, MP
Minister of Agriculture: Rt Hon. H. W. West, MP
Minister of Commerce: Rt Hon. R. J. Bailie, MP
Minister of Development: Rt Hon. R. H. Bradford, MP
Minister of Community Relations: (Vacant)

Leader of the House of Commons and Minister of State, Ministry of Development:
Rt Hon. N. O. Minford, MP
Minister of State, Ministry of Home Affairs: Rt Hon. J. D. Taylor, MP
Minister of State, Ministry of Finance and Chief Whip:
Capt. Rt Hon. J. W. Brooke, MP

THE CHANNEL ISLANDS AND THE ISLE OF MAN

The Channel Islands and the Isle of Man are dependencies of the Crown and do not form part of the United Kingdom. They have their own legislative assemblies and legal and administrative systems, their laws depending for their validity on Orders made by the Queen in Council. Her Majesty's Government is responsible for the defence and international relations of the Islands and the Crown is ultimately responsible for their good government.

The Channel Islands consist of two Bailiwicks, Jersey constituting one and the other comprising Guernsey and the adjacent islets of Herm and Jethou, together with Alderney and Sark, the two latter having their own legislative assemblies. The Sovereign is represented in each Bailiwick by a Lieutenant Governor, who is the official channel of communication between Her Majesty's Government in the United Kingdom and the insular administrations. In Jersey and Guernsey, the Bailiff, who is appointed by the Crown, presides over the Royal Court and the representative assembly (the States) and is the head of the Island administration.

The Queen is similarly represented by a Lieutenant Governor in the Isle of Man, where the legislative assembly is the Court of Tynwald, which comprises the Legislative Council and the House of Keys. The Lieutenant Governor presides in Tynwald and in the Legislative Council and the Speaker in the House of Keys. The Executive Council, to which appointments are made from Tynwald, is presided over by the Lieutenant Governor.

BAILIWICK OF JERSEY

Lieutenant Governor and Commander in Chief:
His Excellency Air Chief Marshal Sir John Davis, GCB, OBE
Bailiff: Sir Robert Le Masurier, DSC
Deputy Bailiff: H. F. C. Ereaut
H.M. Attorney-General: P. L. Crill
H.M. Solicitor-General: V. A. Tomes
Greffier of the States: E. J. M. Potter
Finance and Economics Committee: Senator C. Le Marquand
Defence Committee: Senator W. H. Krichefski, OBE
Harbours and Airport Committee: Deputy J. W. Ellis
Public Works Committee: Senator L. H. White
Education Committee: Deputy R. R. Jeune
Public Health Committee: Senator Mrs G. C. Huelin, MBE
Committee of Agriculture: Deputy J. R. C. Riley
Tourism Committee: Senator C. S. Dupré
Social Security Committee: Deputy M. L. Thomas
Island Development Committee: Deputy P. M. de Veulle
Housing Committee: Deputy A. C. Querée
Sewerage Board: Senator C. G. Farley
Telephones Committee: Deputy C. P. Tanguy
Legislation Committee: Senator R. Vibert

BAILIWICK OF GUERNSEY

Lieutenant Governor and Commander in Chief:
His Excellency Vice-Admiral Sir Charles Mills, KCB, CBE, DSC

GUERNSEY

Bailiff: Sir William Arnold, CBE
Deputy Bailiff: J. H. Loveridge, CBE
HM Procureur (Attorney-General): E. P. Shanks, QC
HM Comptroller (Solicitor-General): C. K. Frossard
HM Greffier: R. H. Videlo

ALDERNEY

President of the States: G. W. Baron
Chairman of the Court: Jurat M. St J. Packe

SARK

Dame de Serk: Dame Sibyl Hathaway, DBE
Seneschal: B. G. Jones

ISLE OF MAN

Lieutenant Governor: His Excellency Sir Peter H. G. Stallard, KCMG, CVO, MBE
Government Secretary: W. B. Kennaugh

CHAIRMEN OF GOVERNMENT BOARDS

Agriculture and Fisheries: E. N. Crowe, MLC
Airports: Lt. Cdr. C. L. P. Vereker, MHK
Assessment: H. H. Radcliffe, MLC
Civil Defence: T. A. Corkish, MHK
Civil Service: Edward Callister, MHK
Education: G. V. H. Kneale, MHK
Forestry, Mines and Lands: Lt. Col. P. A. Spittall, MHK
Harbours and Government Property: Wing Cdr. Roy MacDonald, MHK
Health Services: J. R. Creer, MHK
Highway and Transport: R. E. S. Kerruish, MLC
Local Government: P. Radcliffe, MHK
Police: C. C. Burke, MHK
Social Security: J. C. Nivison, MLC
Tourism: W. E. Quayle, MLC
Water: A. H. Simcocks, MHK

LEGISLATIVE COUNCIL

President: the Lieutenant Governor
Clerk: W. B. Kennaugh

HOUSE OF KEYS

Speaker: Hon. H. C. Kerruish, OBE
Secretary: T. E. Kermeen

JUSTICE

First Deemster and Clerk of the Rolls: His Honour G. E. Moore
Second Deemster: His Honour R. K. Eason, LLB
H. M. Attorney-General: D. D. Lay, TD

WESTERN SAMOA

WESTERN Samoa lies in central Polynesia in the South West Pacific Ocean between latitudes 13° and 15° south and longitudes 171° and 173° west. The Samoan group lies 2,600 miles south-west of Hawaii, 2,700 miles from Sydney, 1,800 miles north-east of New Zealand. The islands are formed mainly of volcanic rock and coral reefs surround much of Western Samoa's coastline. Fresh water is plentiful in rivers and lakes. More than half of the total land in Upolu which is suitable for cultivation is around the three- to four-mile limit inland from the coast where most of the population is also settled. It is estimated that an area of 270 square miles is under cultivation.

Nine islands make up Western Samoa and the total land area is some 1,090 square miles. Of this area, some 660 square miles form the island of Savai'i and 430 square miles the island of Upolu. The other islands are Apolima, Manono, Fanuatapu, Namua, Nuutele, Nuulua and Nuusafee. The climate is tropical ranging normally from 72° to 86°F. The cooler months are from May to November when the fresh trade winds blow and the rainy season extends from December to April. The rainfall is uneven in territorial distribution and the northern coast of Upolu normally receives less than the southern and the western less than the eastern coast. The annual figures for rainfall are 112 inches for the northern coast and 110 inches for the western end. An analogous distribution occurs on Savai'i. Hurricanes are not unknown in Western Samoa, very bad ones occurring in 1889, 1966 and again in 1968, causing great damage to property and crops.

The Samoans are a Polynesian people akin to the Maori of New Zealand and the Tongans. Since 1960 people residing in Western Samoa are classed either as Western Samoan citizens or as foreigners; citizens travel on Western Samoan passports. The pre-requisite for Samoan citizenship is to be born in the country or to have seven years residence. Other racial groups in Samoa include Euronesians, other Pacific Islanders, Chinese and Europeans.

At the census of November 1966, the population was 131,377. This was an increase of 16,950 or about 15 per cent over the preceding 5-year period. There has been a steady increase in Samoan population from 33,478 in 1906 when the first census was taken, and it is now estimated to exceed 140,000. The main island of Upolu has the largest population of some 95,344 while Savai'i has 36,238. The population of Apia, the capital, on the island of Upolu, is 25,000.

In 1936 Samoan births were recorded at 2,124 and deaths at 618, while in 1965 there were 4,115 births and 702 deaths. In 1969 there were 652 deaths (593 in 1968) and 4,330 births (3,799 in 1968). The rate of population increase between 1966 and 1969 is 11 per cent. The growth of population from 1931 to 1945 averaged 2·5 per cent per year. This increased between 1945 and 1951 to 3·7 per cent and estimates for 1966 indicated a 3·3 per cent annual rate of increase.

The Samoans are Christian by religion and have assimilated religious observances into the pattern of village life. Among the Christian missions which have established themselves in Western Samoa are the Congregational, the Roman Catholic, the Methodist, the Latter Day Saints and the Seventh Day Adventists.

The main languages spoken in Samoa are Samoan and English.

THE ECONOMY

The Western Samoan $ (tala) replaced the £ Samoan in July 1967.

Land tenure in Samoa is of considerable importance. Since 1961 all land in Western Samoa has been held as:—

   (i) customary land held from the State in accordance with Samoan custom;

   (ii) freehold land which is held from the State of Western Samoa in fee simple; and

   (iii) public land (formerly Crown Land) being land that is free from customary title and from any estate in fee simple.

Of the 1,090 square miles that make up the land of Western Samoa some 80·5 per cent is 'customary land' controlled by the matai or chiefs and held in accordance with Samoan custom and usage. The matai is in effect the trustee of the extended family group. The control of the land does not necessarily pass from the chief to his son as there is an election of a new matai when the former matai dies. Customary land can be leased but not purchased. At independence, of a total 725,000 acres in the islands of Western Samoa, 32,000 acres were Trust Estate land, 561,062 acres were indigenous land and 26,953 acres were freehold land. The remainder was crown land, now called public land.

Agriculture has formed the basis for Western Samoa's economy and seems likely to continue to play a most important role. Agriculture has largely been of a subsistence type with little money income accruing to the average Samoan planter. The land and the sea have provided food and the means for shelter for the Samoans and until recently there has been little intensive agriculture.

The three major crops are coconuts (copra), cocoa and bananas. It is estimated that some 55,000 acres are planted in coconuts, 18,000 acres in cocoa and 17,000 in bananas. All copra is marketed through the Copra Board and the average annual production for export is 15,000 tons. Efforts have been made in recent years to eradicate plant diseases and pests and so to increase production. Western Samoan cocoa has a flavour variety of very high quality, and is eagerly sought after for blending. Some 5,000 tons of cocoa was exported in 1962 but the hurricane of 1966 had an adverse effect on the cocoa group and only 2,725 tons were exported in that year. Production of bananas, the third major crop, has fluctuated. In 1962 some 660,935 cases were exported but since then there has been a steady decline due to adverse conditions and the effect of hurricanes, and in 1966 only 61,903 cases were exported. Production which was further set back by the 1968 hurricane has now returned to higher levels. A total of 216,759 cases was exported in 1969 and 200,579 in 1970. Other agricultural exports include coffee, timber, taro and other tropical fruits and seeds.

The estimated figures for livestock as at 1966 were: 2,600 horses, 20,000 cattle, including a small number of dairy cattle, 40,000 pigs and 500,000 poultry. Cattle are used for fresh beef for local consumption and provide hides for export. There is a dairy located near Apia.

As far as fisheries are concerned, marine products are gathered by the Samoans mainly for personal consumption and commercial fishing is not yet of any significance. Efforts are, however, being made to develop marine resources generally.

As a result of Government encouragement under the Enterprises Incentives Act a number of small industries have been established in recent years. These include two saw mills, an ice cream and a soft drinks factory, two biscuit factories, a soap factory, fruit cannaries, two garment factories, a footwear factory, four hotels and other small enterprises, which are mainly designed to

o*

supply the local market. A food processing laboratory has been set up with the basic equipment supplied by Australia. Large scale exploitation of forest resources on the island of Savai'i has begun. It is expected that fifteen million board feet of indigenous hard woods will be exported each year.

Western Samoa's approach to tourism reflects its concern to preserve the Samoan way of life. The economic benefits of tourism are, however, recognised and a policy of positive development is now being pursued. Expansion of hotel facilities is being undertaken together with the upgrading of Western Samoa's airport and roads. The number of tourists visiting Western Samoa has increased steadily over recent years.

The pattern of Western Samoa's exports reflects the situation in a country where, with very little secondary industry, the main emphasis is on agriculture. Total exports in 1969 were worth some WS$4,630,000. In that year, the largest income earner was cocoa with about 40 per cent of total exports; the second most important crop was copra amounting to some 35 per cent of the total and the export of bananas was third with some 15 per cent of total exports. Among the remaining exports were sales of taro to New Zealand, processed foods to American Samoa and some re-exports. The most important purchasing countries are New Zealand, the Netherlands, Britain, West Germany, Australia and Japan.

An analysis of Western Samoa's imports shows a concentration of foodstuffs, most of which are imported from New Zealand and Australia. Other imports include alcoholic beverages, tobacco, textiles, machinery and tools, transport equipment, fuel and lubricants, chemicals and other manufactured goods. The total value of imports in 1969 was WS$7,373,670.

The Western Samoan Budget for 1970 was as follows:—

Capital	591,157
Maintenance	5,343,100
Developments	540,465
Statutory Expenditure	365,930
	WS$6,840,650

There are some 477 miles of roads in Western Samoa of which 80 miles are surfaced. As far as shipping services are concerned, a regular fortnightly service operates to New Zealand via Fiji, Tonga and Niue. A daily service links Apia and Pago Pago in American Samoa. There are also shipping connections with Australia, direct line services with Britain and Europe approximately once every six weeks, with Japan every three months, and with the Pacific coast of America once a month. Air New Zealand serves American Samoa and there are daily air services from Apia operated by Polynesian Airlines to Pago Pago which connect with a service to Fiji, New Zealand, America and Australia. There is a twice weekly service to Fiji and Tonga. There are also inter-island daily air services between Upolu and Savai'i operated by Air Samoa and Samoa Aviation. A deep water wharf at Apia was opened in April 1966. A second port for ocean-going vessels at Asau on the island of Savai'i is near completion.

The problems of economic development in Western Samoa differ little from those experienced in other developing countries. Broadly stated, the difficulty is to sustain a policy of rational economic growth against the background of a rapidly increasing population, limited agricultural exports and the relatively wide fluctuations in the prices paid on the international market for these products. Special circumstances in Western Samoa, however, tend to sharpen and accentuate the effects of these difficulties. These include geographical isolation, an absence of mineral resources, the lack of nearby markets and of a large domestic market, and the low level of productive efficiency in the agricultural sector of the economy.

New Zealand in particular has sought to assist in the economic development of the country as has the UN Development Programme, which undertook an economic survey in 1962 in order to find the practical bases for a development programme. In September 1964, an Economic Development Board was established by the Cabinet and in October 1965, an Economic Development Act was passed establishing a Department of Economic Development. Two other Acts in 1965 established two additional development organisations. One was the Enterprises Incentives Act to encourage the establishment of manufacturing, fisheries and tourism and incentives which are offered include tax concessions and duty-free import of building materials, equipment, etc. The other Act set up a Handicrafts Industry Development Corporation to encourage the manufacture of local handicrafts. On the recommendations of the Economic Development Board in 1965, the Cabinet approved a 5-year Development Programme from 1965 to 1970. The total cost involved was £957,467 and included development in agriculture, tourism, secondary industries, public works, health and education, trade development and telecommunications. Although the development plan for agriculture was devoted mainly towards increasing the yield of the three main crops, there was also some provision for diversification into other small crops and stock production. A second 5-year plan has been produced for the period 1971 to 1975.

New Zealand provides technical and capital assistance to Western Samoa in a number of fields including health, education, civil aviation, meteorological services and harbour development. Substantial technical assistance is also provided under various programmes of the United Nations. The UNDP, whose regional headquarters for the Pacific are located in Apia, provides a number of experts in various fields including economic development, engineering, forestry, statistics and planning. A number of Commonwealth countries assist Western Samoa by making available teachers and training awards for Western Samoan students. Australia in addition provides expert personnel, machinery and equipment. Expert personnel are also supplied by the United Kingdom. The New Zealand Volunteer Service Abroad and the United States Peace Corps have a number of volunteers serving in Western Samoa.

THE SOCIAL SERVICES

Samoa is fortunate in that most of the worst tropical diseases are unknown in the islands. There is a Department of Health and there are fourteen health districts with Medical Officers responsible for health activities in each district. The Apia General Hospital, with 310 beds, is the main hospital in the country. There are programmes for assisting in tuberculosis control, filariasis and yaws. The cost of health services in the country was WS$700,615 in 1969, and WS$878,374 in 1970.

Samoa participates in the South Pacific Health Service, a regional organisation with its headquarters and Director-General at Suva in Fiji; through this the country is involved in the regional planning in the area. For both training and treatment the universities and teaching hospitals in New Zealand play an important role for the whole region.

Education in Western Samoa is a Government responsibility carried out through a Department of Education, but several missions also operate schools. The education system is divided into three divisions: primary, intermediate and secondary, and all are based on the New Zealand system. Up to 1971 there were 159 primary, 39 intermediate and 15 secondary schools in the country with a total school population of over 34,000. There are also a Trades' Training Institute, Teachers' Training College and a college for tropical agriculture in Western Samoa. Western Samoa has joined other Governments in the area in establishing the regional University of the South Pacific and a Samoan is currently serving as pro-Chancellor.

Labour matters in Western Samoa are governed by a Labour Ordinance and Workers' Compensation Act passed in 1960. There are probably 10,000 people in the country who could be classed as wage earners and at least half of them are employed by the Government or the Trust Estates Corporation. It is calculated that another 17,000 are employed in village agriculture. There are no trade unions and the Government works on the basis of a 40-hour week which is generally followed by private enterprise. There is a substantial annual migration to New Zealand. Some thousands have migrated in this way on a permanent or semi-permanent basis.

HISTORY

Little is known of Samoan history before the 13th century but some archaeological evidence indicates that Samoa could have been settled as far back as 1000 B.C. After 1250, genealogies of important titles, legends and charts provide a reasonably clear outline of the main events of Samoa's political history. Fijian nobles feature in many Samoan legends, indicating connection with and knowledge of Fijian peoples and customs. This applies also to the Tongans. Throughout this early period there was intermittent contact both friendly and hostile between the three groups of islands.

The first European contact with Samoa came in 1722 with a visit by the Dutch navigator, Jacob Roggeveen. In 1830, the missionary John Williams, landed in Savai'i and Samoan society has been in contact with the Western world from that time onwards. But it has largely retained its traditional organisation, modifying and adapting intrusive elements to suit its needs.

Towards the end of the 19th century, Germany, Britain and America obtained privileges in Western Samoa for themselves and their nationals. Rivalry between these three powers reached a climax in 1889 when a special commission was set up to solve the three-way power struggle. This Commission divided the group between Germany and the USA: Germany taking Savai'i, Upolu and the adjacent smaller islands (Western Samoa) and America taking Tutuila and adjacent small islands (American Samoa). Britain, having rights in other Pacific Islands, withdrew. Germany administered Western Samoa until 1914 when New Zealand military forces occupied it. In 1919, New Zealand was granted a League of Nations Mandate for Samoa. Shortly after the end of the Pacific War in 1946, Western Samoa was made a UN Trust Territory with New Zealand as the administering power. The Samoan people requested independence but were not granted it at that stage.

CONSTITUTIONAL DEVELOPMENT

From 1947 to 1961 there was a series of constitutional advances which brought Samoa from a dependent status to self-government and independence. In 1947 a Legislative Assembly was established. In March 1953, New Zealand proposed to quicken the pace of political and economic development and in 1954 a Constitutional Convention, representing all sections of Samoan society, met to study proposals for political development. Its recommendations were in the main adopted by the New Zealand Government and these set the pattern for evolution towards constitutional government. From this time members of the Legislative Assembly assumed an increasingly greater role in the conduct of Government affairs culminating in the appointment of the Hon. E. F. Paul as Leader of Government business in 1959. In January 1959, a Working Committee on self-government was established and empowered to work out a draft constitution. Cabinet Government was inaugurated in October 1959 and the Honourable Fiame Mata'afa became the first Prime Minister. In August 1960, a Constitutional Convention met and formally adopted the Constitution. This was an instrument combining the cherished elements of traditional Samoan society and the needs of a modern state. A plebiscite was held in May 1961 under the auspices of the United Nations and an overwhelming majority of the Samoan people voted for independence on the basis of the Constitution. In October 1961, the UN General Assembly at the request of New Zealand and on the claim of Western Samoa to independence, voted unanimously to end the Trusteeship Agreement. The New Zealand Parliament then passed the Independence (State of Western Samoa) Act, formally ending New Zealand's powers over the country.

FOREIGN RELATIONS

Western Samoa is an independent and sovereign state; under a Treaty of Friendship between Western Samoa and New Zealand signed eight months after Western Samoa became independent, New Zealand agreed to assist in the independent state's foreign relations 'in such a manner as will in no way impair the rights of the Government of Western Samoa to formulate its own foreign policies'. In other words, the New Zealand Government merely acts as the agent of the Western Samoan Government when requested to do so. Western Samoa has chosen not to seek admission to the UN but has nevertheless joined ECAFE, WHO, ADB and the South Pacific Commission. Following consultation with Commonwealth governments, it was agreed that pending a decision by the Western Samoan Government on whether to seek membership, Western Samoa would be treated for most purposes as if it were a member of the Commonwealth.

The Western Samoan Government decided in 1970 to seek membership and following consultations with Commonwealth Governments became a full member of the Commonwealth in August 1970.

THE GOVERNMENT

Western Samoa has a strong, stable and democratic, system of parliamentary government which is a blend of Polynesian and British practices. The Constitution which came into force on 1 January 1962, provides for a Head of State to be elected by the Legislative Assembly for a term of five years. In the first instance, however, it was decided that two of the four Paramount chiefs should jointly hold the office of Head of State for life. On 5 April 1963, one of the Paramount Chiefs died and in accordance with the provisions of the constitution, Malietoa Tanumafili II became the holder of the office of Head of State for life. The Head of State, whose functions are analogous to those of a constitutional monarch, appoints the Prime Minister who has the support of a majority of the elected members of the Assembly and is himself an elected member. Executive government is carried out by the Cabinet consisting of a Prime Minister and eight other Ministers, selected by the Prime Minister. All legislation passed by the Legislative Assembly must have the assent of the Head of State before it becomes law. The Head of State also has other powers such as the granting of pardons and reprieves or suspending sentences.

The Legislative Assembly is composed of the Speaker and forty-six members. Forty-five members of Parliament are elected in the traditional Samoan manner by holders of matai titles of whom there are about 9,500 on the rolls. Two members represent those of the population who are registered on the individual voters' roll. Election of these two members is by universal adult suffrage.

General elections are held every three years, the last being held on 25 February 1970. Only Western Samoan citizens may stand for elections or vote in them.

The Parliament elected in 1970 selected Tupua Tamasese Lealofi IV as Prime Minister and he was duly appointed Western Samoa's second Prime Minister since independence in 1962.

There are no formally established political parties and as a consequence parliamentary candidates generally campaign as individual candidates. The voting system allows the Samoan social structure to function in the traditional manner. This structure has as its basis the 'aiga' (extended family) unit headed by a matai who speaks for the entire 'aiga'. The plebiscite on the Constitution held in May 1961 resulted in clear acceptance of matai suffrage.

The Constitution also provides for a Council of Deputies to consist of not more than three persons. The function of the Council is to act in place of the Head of State if a vacancy exists in that office or the holder of that office is incapacitated or absent from the country.

Local government is based on the matai system through meetings of family heads in the village.

The Constitution provides for a Public Service Commission which determines salaries and other conditions of service in the Western Samoan Public Service.

HISTORICAL LIST OF MINISTRIES
Fiamé Mata'afa Faumuina Mulinu'u II, 1962 to 1970
Tupua Tamasese Lealofi IV, from 1970

HEAD OF STATE
His Highness Malietoa Tanumafili II

CABINET
Prime Minister and Minister of External Affairs, Immigration, Labour, Police: Hon. Tupua Tamasese Lealofi IV
Minister of Justice and Minister in charge of Land and Titles matters and Central Registry: Hon. Amoa Tausilia
Minister of Finance, Economic Development and Customs: Hon. Tofa Siaosi
Minister of Education: Hon. Tuala Paulo
Minister of Works, Transport, Marine and Civil Aviation: Hon. Tupuola Efi
Minister of Post Office, Radio and Broadcasting: Hon. Fuimaono Moasope
Minister of Agriculture: Hon. Asi Tuiataga Laaulépóná
Minister of Health: Hon. Va'ai Kolone
Minister of Lands and Land Registry: Hon. Polataivao Fogi

LEGISLATIVE ASSEMBLY

Speaker: Hon. Magele Ate
Clerk: G. A. Fepulea'i

JUDICIARY

SUPREME COURT OF WESTERN SAMOA
Chief Justice: B. C. Spring

LAND AND TITLES COURT

President: Chief Justice B. C. Spring
Vice-President: Meleisea Folitau

GOVERNMENT DEPARTMENTS

PRIME MINISTER'S DEPARTMENT
Secretary to Government (acting): K. L. Enari

TREASURY DEPARTMENT
Financial Secretary: A. J. Wendt

HEALTH DEPARTMENT
Director: J. C. Thieme

EDUCATION DEPARTMENT
Director: Dr F. M. Larkin

AGRICULTURE DEPARTMENT
Director: W. F. Meredith

CUSTOMS DEPARTMENT
Collector: V. F. Brebner

INLAND REVENUE DEPARTMENT
Commissioner: R. E. Meredith

PUBLIC WORKS DEPARTMENT
Director: L. McQuitty

JUSTICE DEPARTMENT
Secretary: F. J. Thomsen

ECONOMIC DEVELOPMENT DEPARTMENT
Director: H. E. Kruse

POLICE DEPARTMENT
Commissioner: Lavea Unasa Lio

LANDS AND SURVEY DEPARTMENT
Director: A. P. Hunter

POST OFFICE AND RADIO DEPARTMENT
Director: E. D. Williams

BROADCASTING DEPARTMENT
Director: J. W. Moore

ATTORNEY-GENERAL'S OFFICE
Attorney-General: I. Hay

OFFICE OF THE PUBLIC TRUSTEES
Public Trustee: S. Apa

PUBLIC SERVICE COMMISSION
Chairman: Lauofo Meti

DIPLOMATIC REPRESENTATION

COMMONWEALTH HIGH COMMISSIONERS
IN WESTERN SAMOA
New Zealand: W. G. Thorp; Australia:
Rowen F. Osborn; (resident in Suva)
Britain: Sir Arthur Galsworthy (resident in Wellington).

ZAMBIA

ZAMBIA lies between latitudes 8° and 18° S., and longitudes 22° and 34° E. The country is land-locked and its neighbours are Angola on the west, South-West Africa (via the Caprivi Strip), the Republic of Botswana and Rhodesia on the south, Mozambique and Malawi on the south-east and east, the United Republic of Tanzania on the north-east and the Congo on the north and north-west. The name Zambia is derived from Zambesi, the river which flows through the country and provides the boundary with Rhodesia.

The area of Zambia is 290,600 square miles, which is well over five times the size of England. It consists mostly of a high plateau from 3,500 to 4,500 feet above sea level except where occasional mountains rise to over 7,000 feet, or where the plateau is deeply entrenched by the Zambesi River and its tributaries, the Kafue and the Luangwa Rivers, or by the Luapula River, which forms part of the headwaters of the River Congo, in the north-west. The Mafinga Mountains, the highest in the country, form part of the great escarpment running down the eastern edge of the Luangwa River valley, with peaks rising to just over 7,000 feet. There are three great lakes: Lake Mweru on the northern boundary with the Congo; Lake Tanganyika on the north-western boundary with Tanganyika; Lake Bangweulu and its swamps, in the northern district, covering an area of approximately 3,800 square miles. Along the southern border stretches Lake Kariba, at present the world's largest man-made lake.

There are three seasons: a cool dry season from May to August, a hot dry season from September to November, and a wet season from December to April. In the hot season day temperatures may vary from 27-38°C (80-100°F), but at night there is a very distinct drop in the temperature and at times frost occurs in some areas. The rainfall range is 30-50 inches a year.

The last official census of the population was held in 1969 when they numbered 4,054,000 (as compared to 3,490,000 on 30th June 1963). Of this approximately 43,500 are Europeans and 10,000 are Asians. There are 73 tribes of which the largest are: Bemba, Ngoni, Chewa, Bisa, Lozi, Tonga, Luvale, Lenje, Ila, Senga, Lala, Lunda. English is widely spoken throughout the territory and is the official language. There are six main vernacular languages, viz., Nyanja, Bemba, Tonga, Lozi, Lunda and Luvale. Primary education is free and is not yet universal. About 85 per cent of the children in the age groups concerned attend primary school, and of these, about 25 per cent to 30 per cent go on to take the five-year course in secondary schools. The University of Zambia was established in 1965 and the first students were admitted in March 1966. In 1968 there were 948 students. Christianity is the main religion.

For administrative purposes, Zambia is divided into eight provinces, Central, Copperbelt, Eastern, Luapula, Northern, North-Western, Southern and Western.

The populations of Lusaka, the capital, and other main centres in 1970 were as follows:

Lusaka		353,975
Kabwe (formerly Broken Hill)		85,437
Kitwe	⎫	199,798
Ndola	⎪	159,786
Mufulira	⎪	107,802
Luanshya	⎬ Copperbelt	96,282
Chingola	⎪	103,292
Chililabombwe (formerly Bancroft)	⎪	44,862
Kalulushi	⎭	32,272
Livingstone		49,063

Zambia Railways was established in 1967 and took over the former North West Region of Rhodesia Railways. The gauge is three feet six inches, and the main line runs from Livingstone via Lusaka to the Copperbelt where it links with the B.C.K. (Congo). The main roads from Livingstone and Salisbury to Lusaka and on to the Copperbelt are tarmac. The Great East Road to Malawi, and the Great

North Road to Tanzania are now also tarmac. The principal airports are at Lusaka and Livingstone, with runway lengths of 13,000 and 7,500 feet respectively. A third principal airport is at Ndola where a new runway (length 8,240 feet by March 1972) is being constructed to replace the present runway which measures 4,000 feet. In addition there are 12 secondary airports, 31 minor airports and 34 privately owned and operated airstrips. The main airlines are Zambia Airways (operated by Alitalia), East African Airways, BOAC, Caledonian and BUA. The Zambia Broadcasting Services and Zambia Television are government-run; Zambia Television covers Lusaka and the Copperbelt.

Copper mining is the economic mainstay of Zambia, and provides about 95 per cent of Zambia's export earnings, 60 per cent of Government revenue and 50 per cent of the gross domestic product. In 1970 a total of 611,112 tons of copper were produced, valued at K648·5 million. The total production of minerals was valued at K673·5 million, with production as follows:—

				Long tons	*Kwacha**
All Minerals ..	..	..	..	—	673,509,850
Copper	..	..	..	611,112	648,507,510
Zinc ..	..	..	..	52,612	10,304,271
Lead ..	..	..	..	26,777	5,159,730
Cobalt	..	..	..	4,523,445 (Lbs)	4,523,445
Other ..	..	..	..	—	5,014,894

The main crops are cassava, maize, tobacco and groundnuts. Small quantities of cotton, rice, pulses, citrus, potatoes, tropical fruits, vegetables, wheat and beeswax are also produced.

For the twelve months ending December 1971, Government revenue is estimated at K346 million, recurrent expenditure at K329 million and capital expenditure at K173 million.

The National Day is 24th October, Independence Day.

HISTORY

The early history of Zambia is fragmentary, being based on tribal oral tradition and on accounts of early European explorers such as Dr Lacerda who led an expedition to Lake Mweru in 1798, and Livingstone who travelled from Bechuanaland through Barotseland to Luanda in 1853 and returned to Mozambique in 1855.

During the early part of the nineteenth century the country was invaded by Arabs, who established a slave trade on a route via Lake Malawi to the east coast. This flourished until 1893 when British forces put a stop to it. The territory was also invaded by the Ngoni branch of the Zulus and by the Makololo, migrating from Basutoland, who established themselves as the dominant tribe in Barotseland and neighbouring districts until they were defeated by the indigenous Lozi, under their leader Chief Lewanika. Meanwhile British influence had been spreading north from the Cape, and the Africa Order in Council in 1889 included the area of Northern Rhodesia as one that was subject to Her Majesty's protection. But administration, when it came to Northern Rhodesia, was administration not by the Colonial Government in the Cape but by the British South African Company which had in 1889 received a Royal Charter which empowered it to

---

* The £ Zambian did not follow the £ sterling, with which it was previously at par, into devaluation in November 1967 but the Zambiam currency was decimalised on 16th January 1968—the main unit, the Kwacha, is worth 58 new pence.

exercise complete administrative and legislative control over Southern Rhodesia and northern Bechuanaland, subject to a requirement that it must pay attention to the wishes of the British High Commissioner in Cape Town. From 1889 onwards the British South Africa Company extended its activities to Northern Rhodesia and within a few years had stamped out the Arab slave-trading in the territory.

The Barotseland-North Western Rhodesia Order in Council dated 28th November 1899 provided for the administration of the western half of Northern Rhodesia by the British South Africa Company under an Administrator nominated by the Company and appointed by the British High Commissioner in South Africa. A similar Order, The North-Eastern Rhodesia Order in Council dated 29th January 1900, provided for the administration of the eastern half of Northern Rhodesia by an Administrator nominated by the Company and appointed by the Consul-General and Commissioner for the British Central Africa Protectorate. Both these orders were revoked in 1911 by the Northern Rhodesia Protectorate Order in Council (S.I. 438) by which the two territories were combined to form the Protectorate of Northern Rhodesia, under the control of the British High Commissioner in South Africa. The British South Africa Company, however, continued to exercise administrative and legislative control. The Company was empowered to administer the country in accordance with its Charter and the Order in Council. The Secretary of State reserved the right to appoint a Resident Commissioner who would report to the British High Commissioner in South Africa on any proclamations issued by the Administrator nominated by the Company. The High Commissioner was empowered to alter or repeal any proclamation for the administration of justice and the raising of revenue and generally to provide for the peace, order and good government of the territory.

In July 1923 a settlement was arranged of the various outstanding problems relating to the Company's position in Northern Rhodesia. The Company surrendered its buildings and assets and its land and monopoly rights, other than mineral rights, but retained freehold land in north-eastern Northern Rhodesia. In return the Company received a cash payment on 1st October 1923 from the British Government.

CONSTITUTIONAL DEVELOPMENT

The office of Governor of Northern Rhodesia was created in 1924 by the Northern Rhodesia Order in Council dated 20th February 1924, and Executive and Legislative Councils were established. On this date the High Commissioner in Cape Town ceased to have any jurisdiction in Northern Rhodesia. Until 1935 the capital was at Livingstone but in that year it was moved to Lusaka.

The first Executive Council consisted of the Governor as President, the Chief Secretary, the Attorney-General, the Treasurer, the Secretary for Native Affairs and the Principal Medical Officer. The Legislative Council was composed of the Governor, as President, members of the Executive Council *ex officio*, four nominated members, and five unofficial members who were to be nominated until such time as provision could be made for election. The first elected members took their seats in 1926. In 1938 an unofficial member, nominated by the Governor to represent African interests, was appointed to the Council. The number of unofficial members was increased to seven in 1929 and to nine in 1938.

In 1945 the number of unofficial members was increased from nine to thirteen, of whom eight were elected and five nominated by the Governor. Of the nominated members three were nominated to represent African interests.

In 1948 further changes took place. The Executive Council was composed of the Governor, as President, the Chief Secretary, the Financial Secretary, the Secretary for Native Affairs, the Administrative Secretary, the Economic Secretary, the Director of Development, four unofficial members, of whom three were elected members of the Legislative Council and one a nominated member of the Legislative Council representing African interests. In the Legislative Council a Speaker was appointed to replace the Governor. In addition there were nine official members and fourteen unofficial members (consisting of ten elected European members, two European members to represent African interests and two African members).

As a result of a series of conferences held in 1951, 1952 and 1953 to consider the closer association of Northern Rhodesia, Southern Rhodesia and Nyasaland, a draft Federal scheme was prepared setting out the details for the Constitution of the Federation of Rhodesia and Nyasaland. Whether or not to participate in this was the subject of a referendum in Southern Rhodesia in April 1953 and in the same month the proposals were approved by the Legislative Councils of Northern Rhodesia and Nyasaland. The appropriate Order in Council received Royal Assent on 14th July 1953 and the Federation of Rhodesia and Nyasaland came into existence on 3rd September 1953. The Constitution Order in Council defined the functions and responsibilities of the Federal and Territorial legislatures.

In December 1953 the composition of the Northern Rhodesia Legislative Council consisted of a Speaker and twenty-six members, comprising eight officials and eighteen unofficials. Four of the officials were *ex officio* and the eighteen unofficials consisted of twelve elected members, four African members (appointed by the Governor on the advice of the African Representative Council), and two members nominated to represent African interests. The Executive Council consisted of the four *ex officio* official members of the Legislative Council, three elected members and one of the nominated unofficial members of the Legislative Council, presided over by the Governor.

In 1959 the elected membership of the Legislative Council was increased to provide a majority of 22 out of 30 seats. At the same time an unofficial majority was introduced in the Executive Council and the number of officials was reduced.

Under the Constitution which came into force on 11th September 1962, the Executive Council comprised ten Ministers of whom four were *ex officio* members. The Legislative Council consisted of a Speaker, forty-five elected members, six official members, including the four *ex officio* Ministers and one or two unofficial members nominated by the Governor.

As a result of the dissolution of the Federation of Rhodesia and Nyasaland, on 31st December 1963, the territorial Government of Northern Rhodesia re-assumed the functions which were transferred to Federal responsibility by the Federation of Rhodesia and Nyasaland Constitution Order in Council of 1953.

A new Constitution giving the country internal self-government came into effect in January 1964. The final form of Northern Rhodesia's independence constitution was settled at a conference held in London in May 1964. Northern Rhodesia, under the name of the Republic of Zambia, became independent and a Member of the Commonwealth on 24th October 1964.

CONSTITUTION

Under the Independence Constitution the head of state of Zambia is the President who is also commander-in-chief of the armed forces. The President is elected by the electorate at the time of any general election. The Vice-President is also leader of the House in Parliament. The Vice-President, Ministers and Ministers of State are appointed by the President from amongst the members of the National Assembly.

The Cabinet, subject to the powers of the President as head of state, is responsible for government policy and for advising the President on all matters referred to it.

The legislative powers of the Republic are vested in Parliament consisting of the President and a National Assembly of 105 members elected from single member constituencies. The President has also powers to nominate up to five persons as special members to the National Assembly in the public interest.

The franchise is based on universal suffrage for all persons aged 18 years and over who are citizens of Zambia. There is provision for an Electoral Commission to prescribe and review the delimitation of constituency boundaries.

Under the constitution no bill may become law until it has been passed by the National Assembly and given the President's assent. Parliament has power to alter the constitution only if the proposed amendment has the support of two-thirds of all the members at the second and third readings of the Bill.

The House of Chiefs may consider and discuss Bills and other matters referred to it by the President and may submit resolutions on any such Bill or other matter to the President.

The Constitution contains a Bill of Rights, setting out the fundamental rights and freedoms of the individual and providing protection from discrimination on grounds of race.

On 17th June 1969 a national Referendum was held to decide whether those entrenched clauses of the Constitution (including the sections on the Bill of Rights and on the Judiciary) which required the approval of a Referendum before they could be amended should, like the rest of the Constitution, be capable of amendment by a simple two-thirds majority of Parliament. The Referendum was approved by 57 per cent of the registered electorate, thus giving the Government the powers which they sought.

There is a High Court and a Court of Appeal; and a Judicial Service Commission to deal with the appointment, discipline and removal from office of the magistracy and to advise the President on the appointment of puisne judges.

There is a Public Service Commission consisting of a Chairman and from three to six members appointed by the President.

THE GOVERNMENT

After the General Election held in December 1968 the composition of the political parties in the National Assembly was: United National Independence Party 86 seats, African National Congress 23 seats, and Independent 1 seat. The United National Independence Party seats include those of five members nominated by the President. However, African National Congress seats now total 17 as a result of resignations and expulsions from the party in the past two years. By-elections are still pending in five of the constituencies affected. The sixth M.P. resigned from ANC to join UNIP but has not as yet been accepted into that party. (President Kaunda had announced on 14th August 1968 that he had banned Zambia's other former opposition party, the United Party, because it constituted a threat to the security of the State).

President of the Republic of Zambia: His Excellency Dr K. D. Kaunda

THE CABINET

Vice-President: Hon. M. M. Chona, MP
Minister of Provincial and Local Government and Cultural Affairs:
Hon. S. M. Kapwepwe, MP
Minister of Rural Development: Hon. R. Kamanga, MP
Minister of Finance: Hon. J. M. Mwanakatwe, MP
Minister of Defence: Hon. A. G. Zulu, MP
Minister of Foreign Affairs: Hon. E. K. H. Mudenda, MP
Minister of Mines and Mining Developments: Hon. H. Mulemba, MP
Minister of Education: Hon. W. P Nyirenda, MP
Minister of Labour and Social Services: Hon. W. Chakulya, MP
Minister of Power, Transport and Works: Hon. H. D. Banda, MP
Minister of Information, Broadcasting and Tourism: Hon. S. Wina, MP
Minister of Lands and Natural Resources: Hon. S. Kalulu, MP
Minister of Trade and Industry: Hon. A. J. Soko, MP
Minister of Home Affairs: Hon. L. Changufu, MP
Minister of Legal Affairs and Attorney-General: Hon. F. Chuula, MP
Secretary-General to the Government: Hon. A. M. Milner, MP
Minister of Health: Hon. P. W. Matoka, MP

CABINET MINISTERS FOR

Western Province: Hon. J. B. A. Siyomunji, MP
Copperbelt Province: Hon. A. Shapi, MP
Eastern Province: Hon. W. Nkanza, MP
Luapulu Province: Hon. R. Makasa, MP
Northern Province: Hon. S. C. Mbilishi, MP
North-Western Province: Hon. H. Shamabanse, MP
Southern Province: Hon. A. Mutemba, MP
Central Province: Hon. W. Chakulya, MP

MINISTERS OF STATE

UNIP Headquarters: Hon. A. B. Chikwanda, MP; Hon. A. Simbule, MP;
Hon. S. Soko, MP; Hon. F. Bulawayo, MP; Mrs. T. Kankasa, MP; F. Liboma, MP
Eastern Province: Hon. J. C. Sinyangwe, MP
North-Western Province: Hon. J. Mambwe, MP
Northern Province: Hon. P. K. Kasutu, MP
Western Province: Hon. F. Liboma, MP
Luapulu Province:
Central Province: Hon. H. Mwale, MP
Southern Province: Hon. J. C. C. P. Ngoma, MP
Copperbelt Province: Hon. F. Bulawayo, MP, B. Kapula, MP
Office of the Vice-President:
Hon. U. G. Mwila, MP (Guidance); Hon. K. H. Nkwabilo (Development)
Foreign Affairs: Hon. T. Kankasa, MP
Technical Education: Hon. C. H. Thornicroft, MP
Home Affairs: Hon. C. Mwananshiku, MP
Education: Hon. P. N. Kapika, MP
Rural Development: Hon. V. Ngandu, MP; Hon. O. T. N. Vibetti, MP
Finance: (vacant)
Information, Broadcasting and Tourism: Hon. A. S. Masiye, MP
Labour and Social Services:
Hon. M. J. Chapoloko, MP (Health); (vacant) (Labour)
Provincial and Local Government and Cultural Affairs:
Hon. M. J. Banda, MP; Hon. N. Tembo, MP
Power, Transport and Works: Hon. N. S. Mulenga, MP; Hon. J. Monga, MP
Lands and Natural Resources: Hon. W. K. Sikalumbi, MP
Trade and Industry: Hon. S. Tembo, MP

THE NATIONAL ASSEMBLY
Speaker: The Hon. R. M. Nabulyato
Deputy Speaker: Hon. P. B. Muwowo, MP

LEADER OF ANC
H. Nkumbula, MP

JUDICIARY
Chief Justice: B. Doyle
Judge President of Court of Appeal: T. Pickett
Justices of Appeal: S. W. Magnus; B. T. Gardner

Puisne Judges:

G. Muwo
J. J. Hughes
W. S. Bruce-Lule

F. M. Chomba
L. S. Baron

Registrar of the High Court: B. Cullinan

MINISTRIES AND GOVERNMENT DEPARTMENTS

PRESIDENTIAL AND CABINET OFFICES
Permanent Secretaries: M. C. Chona
(Special Assistant for Political Affairs);
A. Phiri (Acting) (Establishments); S. Zulu
(Solicitor-General); H. D. Ngwane
(Principal Private Secretary).

OFFICE OF THE VICE-PRESIDENT
Permanent Secretary: Dr H. S. Meebelo

MINISTRY OF FINANCE
Permanent Secretary: E. G. Kasonde

MINISTRY OF DEFENCE
Permanent Secretary: D. Bowa

MINISTRY OF PROVINCIAL AND
LOCAL GOVERNMENT AND
CULTURAL AFFAIRS
Permanent Secretary: F. Nchoma

MINISTRY OF LANDS AND
NATURAL RESOURCES
Permanent Secretary: P. Banda

MINISTRY OF TRADE AND INDUSTRY
Permanent Secretary: E. B. Mbozi

MINISTRY OF RURAL DEVELOPMENT
Permanent Secretary: I. E. L. Wilima

MINISTRY OF HOME AFFAIRS
Permanent Secretary: J. Mulwanda

MINISTRY OF INFORMATION, BROADCASTING
AND TOURISM
Permanent Secretary: J. C. Milimo-
Punabantu

MINISTRY OF MINES AND
MINING DEVELOPMENT
Permanent Secretary: K. Nyalugwe

MINISTRY OF FOREIGN AFFAIRS
Permanent Secretary: E. G. Sampa

MINISTRY OF LABOUR AND
SOCIAL SERVICES
Permanent Secretaries: J. B. Nyirongo
(Labour); M. M. Nalumango (Health)

MINISTRY OF EDUCATION
Permanent Secretary: V. Lavu

MINISTRY OF POWER, TRANSPORT AND
WORKS
Permanent Secretaries: P. J. Chisanga
(Transport); P. Siwo (Power and Works)

WESTERN PROVINCE
Permanent Secretary: A. U. Mwale (Acting)

COPPERBELT PROVINCE
Permanent Secretary: N. Muttendango

CENTRAL PROVINCE
Permanent Secretary: W. K. Mayondi

EASTERN PROVINCE
Permanent Secretary: J. A. Sakala

LUAPALA PROVINCE
Permanent Secretary: D. R. Chilao

NORTHERN PROVINCE
Permanent Secretary: P. K. Banda

NORTH-WESTERN PROVINCE
Permanent Secretary: B. Monze

SOUTHERN PROVINCE
Permanent Secretary: G. I. Yeta

DIPLOMATIC REPRESENTATION

ZAMBIA REPRESENTATIVES IN OTHER COMMONWEALTH COUNTRIES

Botswana: M. Sokoni (High Commissioner) (also accredited to Lesotho and Swaziland); Britain: Hon. A. Phiri (High Commissioner) (also accredited to the Holy See); Kenya: A. N. Kalyati (High Commissioner); Tanzania: C. S. Mukando (High Commissioner) (also accredited to Burundi); Malawi: R. K. Chinambu (Acting High Commissioner).

COMMONWEALTH HIGH COMMISSIONERS IN ZAMBIA

Botswana: P. P. Makepe; Britain: J. S. R. Duncan, CMG, MBE; Canada: J. Irwin (resident in Dar-es-Salaam); India: B. M. Dutt (Acting High Commissioner); Kenya: L. P. Odero.

ZAMBIA REPRESENTATIVES IN NON-COMMONWEALTH COUNTRIES

Congo (Lubumbashi): A. W. Mbewe (Consul General); Congo (Kinshasa): A. Chalikulima (Ambassador) (also accredited to Congo (Brazzaville); Ethiopia: The Hon. P. Chanda, MP (Ambassador); Ivory Coast: S. G. Mwale (Ambassador) (also accredited to Guinea, Sierra Leone, The Gambia and Mauritania); United Arab Republic: Hon. M. Ngalande, MP (Ambassador); United States: Hon. A. B. Mutemba, MP (Ambassador); United Nations: V. J. Mwaanga (Permanent Representative) (also accredited to Jamaica, Trinidad and Tobago, Barbados and Guyana); U.S.S.R.: P. J. F. Lusaka (Ambassador) (also accredited to Romania and Yugoslavia); Federal Republic of Germany: Hon. M. Nkama (Ambassador) (also accredited to France); People's Republic of China: Hon. J. K. Chivunga MP (Ambassador) (also accredited to the, Democratic People's Republic of Korea (North Korea)).

DIPLOMATIC REPRESENTATION

PART V
COUNTRIES OF THE COMMONWEALTH FOR WHOSE EXTERNAL AFFAIRS BRITAIN IS RESPONSIBLE

ANTIGUA

ANTIGUA lies in the northern group of the Leeward Islands chain in the East Caribbean, longitude 61° 8′ W., latitude 17° 1′ N. It is approximately 40 miles north of Guadeloupe. The territory consists of the islands of Antigua and its dependencies Barbuda and Redonda, the last named being an uninhabited rocky islet about half a square mile in area.

The area of Antigua is 108 square miles and the dependency of Barbuda 62 square miles. Barbuda lies 25 miles to the north, Redonda 25 miles to the south-west of the main island.

The western part of the island of Antigua is composed entirely of volcanic rocks (highest point Boggy Peak, 1,330 feet). The eastern and northern parts are of limestone, less than 500 feet above sea level, and a central plain stretches diagonally across the island.

The absence of high hills and forest distinguishes Antigua from the rest of the Leeward group. There are no rivers and few springs in the islands, so they are frequently subject to droughts, although the mean annual rainfall is between 43 and 45 inches. The climate is drier than that of most of the West Indies and is delightful from the end of November to the beginning of May, when the north-east trade winds begin to fail. The hot season then sets in, during which the weather is generally rainy. The shade temperature seldom exceeds 90°F. Barbuda is very flat, with a large lagoon on the west side.

The population at the 1960 census was 54,304. St John's, the capital, then had a population of about 21,600.

There is one hospital with 225 beds, three health centres and 17 dispensaries which are staffed by the District Medical Officers. In 1969, 27,526 patients were treated at the Hospital.

The main forms of taxation are import duties, income tax, excise and consumption taxes. The rates of individual income tax range from $2\frac{1}{2}$ cents to 55 cents (on chargeable income of $30,000) per dollar of chargeable income. Company tax is 40 per cent of chargeable income.

Provision has been made for double taxation relief with the United Kingdom, Canada, New Zealand, Sweden, Denmark, Norway and the U.S.A., and consideration is being given to extending the arrangements to other countries.

Public Finance figures are as follows:—

			Revenue $WI	Expenditure $WI
1965	..	..	9,160,141	9,116,500
1966	..	..	11,570,582	10,311,533
1967	..	..	17,939,229	17,924,375

HISTORY

Antigua was discovered by Christopher Columbus in the year 1493 on his second voyage to the West Indies. He named it after a church, Santa Maria de la Antigua, in Seville. The Spaniards attempted to settle in the island in 1520 but they found it too dry. The French under d'Esnambuc made an abortive

433

attempt at settlement in 1629, but abandoned it in favour of the richer soil of St Kitts. Antigua was eventually colonised in the year 1632 by Sir Thomas Warner. In the early years the settlers suffered much from raids by the Caribs.

At that time the chief crop was tobacco but in the second half of the seventeenth century it was found that sugar was more profitable. This required heavy labour. At first, the defeated armies in the English Civil War were sent to work on the plantations in the West Indies, but when these were found to give indifferent results in the tropical climate the trade in slaves from Africa began and it was at its height throughout the eighteenth century. The operation of sugar estates became extremely profitable and the wars between the English and French were much concerned with the possession of the sugar islands. Antigua was the only British island to possess a good harbour and English Harbour was the dockyard for the British West Indies throughout the period. Though on one occasion the French made a successful landing on Antigua, the island never passed out of British hands and shows no trace of French influence.

Antigua emancipated its slaves in 1834, four years before the general emancipation in British territories. This led at first to some difficulty in obtaining labour for the sugar estates. A disastrous fire in 1841, an earthquake which destroyed the Cathedral in St John's in 1843, and a hurricane which did £100,000 damage in 1847 were serious economic blows. There have since been several periods of relative prosperity and depression according to the price of sugar.

The Naval Dockyard at English Harbour was closed in 1854, and re-opened in November 1961 as a restored historic monument and yachting centre. In 1968 a deep-water harbour was opened.

CONSTITUTION

Following decisions taken at a conference in London in February and March 1966, subsequently endorsed by a resolution of the Legislative Council, provision was made in the West Indies Act 1967 under which Antigua assumed a status of association with the United Kingdom on 27th February 1967. The association is a free and voluntary one, terminable by either country at any time. Antigua is fully self-governing in all its internal affairs. The United Kingdom is responsible for defence and external affairs. Agreement has been reached on close consultation over the discharge of these responsibilities and on the delegation of executive authority in a wide field of external relations. The British Government conduct their affairs with Antigua and the rest of the West Indies Associated States through the British Government Representative, whose headquarters are at Castries, St Lucia.

Under the Constitution the Governor is Her Majesty's Representative. Except where otherwise provided the Governor is required to act in accordance with the advice of the Cabinet or a Minister acting under the general authority of the Cabinet.

The Cabinet is collectively responsible to Parliament for the government of Antigua. The Cabinet consists of the Premier, and other Ministers and the Attorney-General whether or not he is a Minister. The Governor appoints as Premier the member of the House of Representatives who appears to him best able to command a majority in that House. The other Ministers are appointed on the advice of the Premier; at least one of them must be a Senator. There is provision for the appointment of Parliamentary Secretaries from either House.

Parliament consists of Her Majesty, a Senate and a House of Representatives. The ten Senators are appointed, seven in accordance with the advice of the Premier and three after consultation with the Premier. From among its members who are not Ministers or Parliamentary Secretaries the Senate elects a President. The House of Representatives consists of the Speaker, Members elected under universal adult suffrage in not less than ten single-member constituencies, of whom one may be the Speaker, and, so long as the office of Attorney-General remains an office in the public service, the Attorney-General. Traditionally the House of Representatives includes the Speaker and ten elected Members of the former Legislative Council, and the Attorney-General; and now includes four additional Members.

Parliament may make laws for the peace, order and good government of Antigua. The Constitution contains safeguards for fundamental rights and freedoms. Special provisions relate to a Bill to alter the Constitution or the law establishing the West Indies Associated States Supreme Court or the law relating to appeals to the Privy Council.

A Puisne Judge of the West Indies Associated States Supreme Court, (*q.v.*), established by Order in Council, is resident in Antigua.

The appointment, dismissal and disciplinary control of public officers is, with certain exceptions, vested in the Public Service and Police Service Commissions. Disciplinary cases may be reviewed at the request of the officer concerned under regulations to be made by the Governor.

GOVERNOR
His Excellency Sir Wilfred E. Jacobs, OBE, QC

CABINET
Premier and Minister of Finance and Planning: Hon. G. A. Walter
Minister of Agriculture, Lands and Fisheries: Hon. R. V. L. Hall
Minister of Public Works and Housing: Hon. S. U. Prince
Minister of Home Affairs and Labour: Hon. D. A. S. Halstead
Minister of Education, Health and Culture: Hon. B. A. Peters, BA, Dip. Ed
Minister of Public Utilities and Communications: Hon. G. O. A. Watt
Minister of Trade, Industry and Commerce: Hon. S. A. Walter, BSC
Attorney-General: Harold Harney

Parliamentary Secretaries:
Parliamentary Secretary to the Premier: Hon. C. E. Francis, LLB
Parliamentary Secretary to the Premier and Cabinet Secretary: Hon. G. D. Scotland, BA
Parliamentary Secretary to the Minister of Health, Education and Culture:
Hon. V. E. McKay

BRITISH GOVERNMENT REPRESENTATIVE
J. E. Marnham, CMG, MC, TD
(resident in Castries, St Lucia)

DEPUTY BRITISH GOVERNMENT REPRESENTATIVE
J. H. Reiss
(resident in St. John, Antigua)

BRUNEI

THE State of Brunei is situated on the north-west coast of Borneo and lies between latitudes 4° 2′ and 5° 3′ North and longitudes 114° 4′ and 115° 22′ East. It has an area of 2,226 square miles, and has a coast line of approximately one hundred miles. The country consists of two separate enclaves, each surrounded on the landward side by Sarawak. There is a narrow coastal plain intersected by several rivers descending from the hilly hinterland.

The climate is tropical and is characterised by a uniform temperature throughout the year, a high humidity and heavy rainfall, varying from 100 inches a year at the coast to over 200 inches in certain parts of the interior. In 1970 the estimated population was 142,800, consisting in the main of Malays (52 per cent), other indigenous peoples (15 per cent) and Chinese (28 per cent). The principal towns are Bandar Seri Begawan, the capital (estimated population 22,200), Seria and Kuala Belait. Bandar Seri Begawan and Kuala Belait are the two ports.

Brunei's income is derived almost entirely from royalties on the sale of crude oil from Shell's Seria oilfields, which produced 6,011,000 tons in 1969. Other exports include natural gas, rubber and timber. The favourable trade balance in 1967 was B$110,601,389, in 1968 B$71,689,356 and in 1969 B$48,104,597*. The main crops are rice, rubber and sago.

Brunei is a Sultanate and the present Ruler, the twenty-ninth of his line, succeeded to the throne on 4th October 1967 following the abdication of his father. The constitution promulgated on 29th September 1959 provided for a Privy Council, a Council of Ministers and a Legislative Council. A Mentri Besar (Chief Minister) appointed by the Sultan is responsible to him for the exercise of executive authority.

Relations with Britain. In 1847 the Sultan entered into a Treaty with Britain for the furtherance of commercial relations and for the suppression of piracy. By a further Treaty in 1888 Brunei was placed under British protection, and the Sultan agreed that the foreign relations of the State should be conducted by Her Majesty's Government. In 1905 a supplementary agreement was entered into whereby the Sultan undertook to accept a British officer, to be styled a Resident, who should be the agent and representative of the British Government under the High Commissioner for the Malay States. The Governor of Sarawak was High Commissioner for Brunei from 1948 until 1959.

On 29th September 1959 a further agreement was concluded between Her Majesty The Queen and His Highness the Sultan replacing the 1905-06 Agreement, under which the British Government continued to be responsible for the defence and external affairs of the State. The Agreement provided for the appointment of a High Commissioner, styled as 'Her Majesty's High Commissioner in the State of Brunei.'

At talks in London in April/May 1971 the Sultan and the British Government agreed the text of an agreement amending the 1959 Agreement which was to be signed later in the year. Under the 1959 Agreement as amended the British Government would continue to be responsible for the external affairs of the State, and would cooperate in the arrangements for its defence.

---

*B$ 7·3469 = £1

HEAD OF STATE

Duli Yang Maha Mulia Paduka Seri Baginda Sultan dan Yang Di-Pertuan Hassanal Bolkiah Mu'izzaddin Waddaulah, DK, DPKG, DPKT, PSPNB, PSNB, PSLJ, SPMB, PANB, CMG, DK (Kelantan), DK (Johore)

PRIVY COUNCIL

President: His Highness the Sultan

Members:

Duli Yang Teramat Mulia Paduka Seri Begawan Sultan Sir Muda 'Omar 'Ali Saifuddin ibni Al-Marhum Sultan Muhammad Jamalul 'Alam, DK, KCMG, Brunei

Yang Teramat Mulia Seri Paduka Duli Pengiran Perdana Wazir Sahibol Himmah Wal-Waqar Muda Mohamed Bolkiah ibni Duli Yang Teramat Mulia Paduka Seri Begawan Sultan Sir Muda 'Omar 'Ali Saifuddin, DK, PHBS, Brunei

Yang Teramat Mulia Seri Paduka Duli Pengiran Bendahara Seri Maharaja Permai Suara Muda Haji Hashim ibni Al-Marhum Duli Pengiran Bendahara Anak 'Abdul Rahman, DK, SPMB, POAS, Brunei

Yang Teramat Mulia Seri Paduka Duli Pengiran Pemancha Sahibol Rae' Walmashuarah Muda Haji Mohamed 'Alam ibni Al-Marhum Duli Pengiran Bendahara Anak 'Abdul Rahman, DK, SPMB, DSNB, POAS, OBE, Brunei

Yang Amat Mulia Pengiran Setia Negara, Pengiran Haji Mohd. Yusuf bin Pengiran Haji 'Abdul Rahim, DK, SPMB, DSNB, CBE, POAS, PHBS, Mentri Besar, Brunei

Yang Berhormat Pehin Orang Kaya Laila Setia Bakti Di-Raja, Dato Utama Uwang Isa bin Pehin Datu Perdana Menteri Awang Haji Ibrahim, DK, SPMB, DSNB, OBE, PHBS, Timbalan Mentri Besar, Brunei

Yang Amat Mulia Pengiran Maharaja Anakda, Pengiran Haji Ahmad ibni Al-Marhum Duli Pengiran Bendahara Anak Haji Mohd. Yassin, DPMB, Brunei

Yang Berhormat Pehin Orang Kaya Shahbandar Dato Setia Awang Haji Ahmad bin Daud, DSNB, POAS, MBE, Brunei

Yang Amat Mulia Pengiran Paduka Tuan Sahibol Karib, Pengiran Haji Abu Bakar ibni Al-Marhum Duli Pengiran Pemancha Anak Mohd. Saleh, DSNB, POAS, Brunei

Yang Amat Mulia Pengiran Jaya Negara, Pengiran Haji Abu Bakar bin Pengiran 'Umar, DK, DSNB, POAS, PHBS, MBE, Brunei

Yang Berhormat Pehin Jawatan Dalam Dato Setia Awang Haji Mohamed Noor bin Pehin Orang Kaya Laksamana Awang Haji 'Abdul Razak, DSNB, POAS, Brunei

Yang Berhormat Pehin Orang Kaya Amar Di-Raja Dato Utama Awang Haji Mohd. Jamil bin Begawan Pehin Udana Khatib Awang Haji 'Umar, DK, DSLJ, DPMB, PHBS, POAS, Brunei

Yang Amat Mulia Pengiran Perdana Cheteria Laila Di-Raja Sahibon Nabalah, Pengiran Anak Haji Khamis ibni Al-Marhum Kebawah Duli Sultan Hashim, DK, DPMB, POAS, Brunei

Yang Amat Mulia Pengiran Shahbandar Sahibol Bandar, Pengiran Haji Mohamed bin Pengiran Piut, DK, SPMB, DSNB, PANB, POAS, MBE, Brunei

Yang Berhormat Pehin Orang Kaya Di-Gadong Dato Utama Awang Haji Mohamed Yusof bin Pehin Jawatan Dalam Awang Haji Mohamed Hussein, DK, PSNB, DPMB, POAS, Brunei

Yang Berhormat Begawan Pehin Udana Khatib Dato Seri Paduka Awang Haji 'Umar bin Awang Rendah, SPMB, DSNB, PHBS, Brunei

Yang Berhormat Pehin Orang Kaya Laksamana Dato Utama Awang Haji 'Abdul Rahman bin Pehin Orang Kaya Shahbandar Awang Haji Mohamed Tana, DK, SPMB, DSLJ, PSB, POAS, PHBS, Brunei

Yang Berhormat Pehin Jawatan Luar Pekerma Raja, Dato Utama Awang Haji Mohamed Taha bin Pehin Ratna Di-Raja Awang Hussein, DK, SPMB, DSNB, POAS, Brunei

Yang Berhormat Pehin Datu Temenggong, Awang Lim Cheng Choo, SNB, SMB, POAS, Brunei

Yang Amat Mulia Pengiran Kerma Negara, Pengiran Anak 'Abdul Wahab bin Pengiran Sabtu Kemaluddin, DSNB, SMB, PHBS, Brunei

Yang Amat Mulia Pengiran Penggawa Laila Bentara Istiadat Di-Raja Dalam Istana, Pengiran Haji Mohtar Puteh bin Pengiran Haji Rajid, DK, DSNB, DPMB, PNB, PHBS, Brunei

Yang Amat Mulia Pengiran Sanggamara Di-Raja, Pengiran Anak Chuchu ibni Al-Marhum Pengiran Muda Mohd. Saleh, DK, SLJ, PHBS, Brunei

Yang Amat Mulia Pengiran Maharaja Lela Sahibol Kahar, Pengiran Anak Mohd. Yusof ibni Duli Pengiran Pemancha Muda Haji Mohamed 'Alam, DK, SNB, Brunei

Yang Amat Mulia Pengiran Setia Raja, Pengiran Jaya bin Pengiran Haji Rajid, DK, DHPNB, PHBS, Brunei

Yang Amat Mulia Pengiran Setia Jaya, Pengiran Haji 'Abdul Momin bin Pengiran Othman, DK, DSNB, SLJ, PSB, POAS, PHBS, Brunei

Yang Berhormat Pehin Orang Kaya Ratna Di-Raja, Dato Utama Awang Haji Mohd. Zain bin Haji Serudin, DK, DSLJ, PHBS, Brunei

Yang Berhormat Pehin Datu Saudagar Derma Laila, Dato Setia Awang R. T. Lloyd Dolbey, DSNB, DSLJ, POAS, Brunei

Yang Berhormat Pehin Datu Derma Setia, Dato Setia Awang P. A. Coates, DSNB, DSLJ, DPMB, Brunei
Yang Amat Mulia Pengiran Maharaja Setia Laila Di-Raja Sahibol Irshad, Pengiran Anak Haji 'Abdul 'Aziz bin Pengiran Jaya Negara Pengiran Haji Abu Baker, DK, Brunei
Yang Amat Mulia Pengiran Kerma Indera, Pengiran Anak Tajuddin bin Pengiran Haji 'Abdul Momin, DSLJ, Brunei
Yang Berhormat Pehin Orang Kaya Laila Kanun Di-Raja, Dato Utama Awang Idris Talog Davies, DK, SPMB, DSNB, CBE, PHBS, AK, PJK, Peguam Negara, Brunei
Yang Berhormat Pehin Orang Kaya Khazanah Negara Laila Di-Raja, Dato Utama Awang John Lee, DK, SPMB, DSNB, CBE, PHBS, Pegawai Kewangan Negara, Brunei
Yang Berhormat Pehin Orang Kaya Tabib Laila Di-Raja, Dato Seri Paduka Dr P . I. Franks, SPMB, DSNB, DSLJ, PHBS, POAS, PIS (Johor), Brunei
Yang Amat Mulia Pengiran Dipa Negara, Pengiran Momin bin Pengiran Haji Ismail, DPMB, POAS, PJK, Setiausaha Kerajaan, Brunei

COUNCIL OF MINISTERS
President: His Highness the Sultan

Members:
His Excellency the High Commissioner

Ex-officio members viz:
Yang Teramat Mulia Seri Paduka Duli Pengiran Perdana Wazir
Mentri Besar
Deputy Mentri Besar
State Secretary
Attorney-General
State Financial Officer
Religious Adviser

4 other Members

LEGISLATIVE COUNCIL
Speaker: (vacant)

Members:
Ex-officio members:
Mentri Besar
Deputy Mentri Besar
State Secretary
Attorney-General
State Financial Officer
Religious Adviser

10 Nominated Members
5 Official Members

CIVIL ESTABLISHMENT
HIGH COMMISSIONER: A. R. Adair, CVO, MBE

Mentri Besar: Y. A. M. Pengiran Setia Negara Pengiran Haji Mohd. Yusuf bin Pengiran Haji 'Abdul Rahim, DK, SPMB, DSNB, CBE, POAS, PHBS

Deputy Mentri Besar: Y. B. Penin Orang Kaya Laila Setia Bakti Di-Raja Dato Utama Awang Isa bin Pehin Datu Perdana Mentri Dato Seri Utama Awang Haji Ibrahim, DK, SPMB, DSNB, OBE, PHBS

State Secretary: Y. A. M. Pengiran Dipa Negara Pengiran Momin bin Pengiran Haji Ismail, DPMB, POAS, PJK

Attorney-General: Y. B. Pehin Orang Kaya Laila Kanun Di-Raja Dato Utama Awang Idria Talog Davies, DK, SPMB, DSNB, CBE, PHBS, AK, PJK

State Financial Officer: Y. B. Pehin Orang Kaya Khazanah Negara Laila Di-Raja,

Dato Utama Awang John Lee, DK, SPMB, DSNB, CBE, PHBS

Director of Public Works: Dato Paduka Awang R. Waddell, DPMB, OBE, SMS, JMN, PJK

Director of Education: Dato Laila Jasa Awang M. MacInnes, DSLJ, DPMB

Director of Medical Services: Pehin Orang Kaya Laila Tabib Di-Raja Dato Setia P. I. Franks, DSNB, DSLJ, DPMB, POAS

Commissioner of Police: Dato Laila Jasa Awang J. R. H. Burns, CBE, DSNB, DSLJ

Director of Agriculture: Awang K. G. Malet

Commissioner of Labour: Awang Mohd. Ali bin Awang Besar, SMB (Acting)

State Religious Affairs Officer: Y. B. Pehin Orang Kaya Ratna Di-Raja, Dato Utama Awang Haji Mohd. Zain bin Haji Serudin, DK, DSLJ, PHBS, Brunei

Chief 'Adat Istiadat Officer: Duli Yang Teramat Mulia Seri Paduka Pengiran Pemancha Sahibul Rae' Walmashuarah Muda Haji Mohd. 'Alam ibni Al-Marhum Duli Pengiran Bendahara Anak Abdul Rahman, DK, SPMB, DSNB, POAS, OBE

Controller of Telecommunications: Awang C. E. B. Parrott, PANB, MBE

Welfare Commissioner: Pehin Orang Kaya Laila Wangsa Awang Salleh bin Haji Masri, SLJ

Director of Broadcasting and Information: Awang G. V. de Freitas, SLJ, POAS

Controller of State Pensions: Pehin Orang Kaya Khazanah Negara Laila Di-Raja Dato Utama Awang John Lee, DK, CBE, DSNB

Surveyor General: Awang N. C. Peat, SNB

Commissioner of Development: Awang J. L. Firth, SMB

Controller of Customs and Excise: Awang Osman Chua Kong Soon, SMB

Commissioner of Lands: Awang B. C. Cartland, SMB

Controller of Government Stores: Awang A. S. Newn, PJK

Director of Marine: Awang J. Turner, SMB

Postmaster General: Pengiran Bahar bin Pengiran Shahbandar Anak Hashim

Superintendent of Prisons: Pengiran Hidup bin Pengiran Hashim, SNB

Controller of Fire Services: Awang E. C. G. Simpson

Controller of Land Transport: Dato Pudaka Awang Abdul Ghani bin Jamil, DPMB, POAS

Auditor General: Awang G. T. Hambly, SLJ

Controller of Civil Aviation: Dato Laila Jasa Awang W. I. Glass, DSLJ, DPMB, PANB

Conservator of Forests: Awang I. P. Tamworth

Chief Electrical Engineer: Awang T. P. Brown

Clerk of Council: vacant

Controller of Immigration: Awang T. P. Forde

Stipendiary Magistrate: Awang Charlie Foo Chee Tung SLJ

Establishment Officer: Dato Laila Jasa Awang W. I. Glass, DSLJ, DPMB, PANB

Commander Royal Brunei Malay Regiment: Col. J. J. H. Simpson

Chief Justice: Sir Ivo Charles Clyaton Rigby

Curator of Museum: P. M. Sharifuddin, PSB

Director of Language and Literature Bureau: Pehin Orang Kaya Amar Di-Raja Dato Utama (Dr) Awang Haji Mohd. Jamil Al-Sufri bin Begawan Pehin Udana Khatib Dato Seri Paduka Awang Haji Umar, DK, DSLJ, DPMB, POAS

Resettlement Officer: Y. A. M. Pengiran Indera Mahkota Pengiran Muda Kamaluddin ibni Al-Marhum Duli Pengiran Bendahara Anak Mohamed Yassin Al-haj, SPMB, DSLJ, POAS, PHBS

State Fisheries Officer: Dr E. Birkenmeier

State Geologist: Awang R. B. Tate

Supervisor of Elections: Dato Paduka Awang Matnoor McAfee, SMB, POAS

District Officer Brunei and Muara: Pengiran Dato Paduka Haji Abdul Rahman bin Pengiran Haji Abdul Rahim, DPMB, PNB

District Officer, Belait: Awang Haji Ali Khan bin Abdul Khan, SNB

District Officer, Tutong: Pengiran Othman bin Pengiran Anak Mohd. Salleh, SMB, POAS

District Officer, Temburong: Awang Salleh bin Hidup

A detailed list of Brunei titles, orders and decorations may be found in the *Commonwealth Relations Office Year Book* 1966. The following Orders are additional to those shown in the Order of Precedence: PSLJ—Paduka Seri Laila Jasa (The Order of Laila Jasa, 1st Class), which precedes the SPMB; DSLJ—Dato Seri Laila Jasa (The Order of Laila Jasa, 2nd Class), which precedes DPMB; SLJ—Seri Laila Jasa (The Order of Laila Jasa, 3rd Class), which precedes SMB. The PSNB (Paduka Setia Negara Brunei) was incorrectly described as The Most Honourable Order of the Crown of Brunei, 1st Class and should have been described as The Most Blessed Order of Setia Negara Brunei, 1st Class. In the 2nd, 3rd and 4th Classes of the Order and also for the PSPNB the word 'Setia' should be substituted for the word 'Stia', which is an abbreviation.

DOMINICA

DOMINICA lies in the Windward Islands group between the French islands of Guadeloupe, to the north, and Martinique, to the south, near to the intersection of the parallels 15° N. and 61° W.

The island is 29 miles long and 16 miles wide, with an area of 289·8 square miles. It is roughly rectangular in shape with rounded projections at each end and is very mountainous, picturesque and well-watered. A central ridge with lateral spurs runs from Cape Melville in the north to terminate in cliffs in the extreme south, where is found the largest concentration of high land. Morne Diablotin (4,747 feet) in the north is the highest point.

P

During the cool months of the year—December to March—the climate is particularly pleasant. The dry season lasts from about February to May; June to October are generally the wettest months and the period during which hurricanes occur. The annual temperature ranges from 78°F to 90°F in the hottest month —generally July. The rainfall is heavy, especially in the mountainous areas, where the average figure is 250 inches as compared with 70 inches along the coast. There are numerous rivers but none is navigable.

The last census, taken in April 1970, gave the population as 70,302. Roseau, the capital, has a population of about 16,800.

The population is composed of people of African descent, people of mixed descent, Europeans, Syrians and Caribs, the last three groups in small numbers. English, the official language, is very widely spoken and almost universally understood but a French *patois* persists as the medium of conversation among the masses. Religious adherence is predominantly Roman Catholic but the Church of England and the Methodist Church have also been long established.

There are six Government hospitals including two cottage hospitals, a leper sanatorium and a mental hospital with a total of 316 beds. The main hospital, the Princess Margaret, in Roseau, includes a 40-bed wing for the care of patients suffering from chest conditions. Regular general medical care clinics are held throughout the year by district medical officers at 27 dispensaries, cottage hospitals and health centres distributed all over the island. A maternity, child hygiene and school health service, with headquarters in Roseau, is operated under the direction of the Chief Medical Officer. For the co-ordination of the District Health Services and improvement in Public Health Services a Medical Officer of Health and a Superintendent of Public Health Nurses have been appointed. Powdered skimmed milk donated by UNICEF as well as vitamins and other food supplements are distributed at maternity and school clinics. The most prevalent diseases on the island are gastro-enteritis, deficiency diseases, tuberculosis and helminthiasis.

Agriculture is the principal occupation, but road and building construction, secondary industries, transport and commerce absorb a large number of the working population. No statistics of occupations are available. The estimated labour force in 1965 was 24,249, of whom 13,743 were males and 10,506 females. Of these all but 549 males and 315 females were employed and the working population was estimated at 23,386. There are six registered trade unions.

The main crops are bananas, limes, coconuts, grape-fruit, oranges, cocoa, vanilla, mangoes, avocado pears and various ground provisions for domestic use. The main products are raw and sweetened lime juice, lime oil, copra and rum. The livestock population based on the 1961 census consists of about 3,109 head of cattle, 6,976 pigs, 2,533 sheep and 4,602 goats.

Forest resources in merchantable timber are considerable. According to a Canadian-sponsored survey carried out in 1962 there are over 470 million board feet of gommier, the dominant of three merchantable species. Timber production is on the increase since the establishment of a saw mill. A small export trade in timber is developing.

There is a Government-controlled fisheries scheme which in its present form provides, as one of its main features, interest loans to fishermen through a co-operative to purchase outboard motors and fishing boats.

The only mineral so far found on the island is pumice, a light-weight concrete aggregate of volcanic origin used chiefly for building purposes. It is at present mined under licence by a group of American investors.

The principal manufactures are cigarettes, cigars, handcrafts and canned citrus juices, some of each of which are exported. Also produced are quantities of edible oils, laundry and toilet soaps, coconut meal and crude oil.

There were 19 registered Credit Unions at the end of 1965, with a membership of 8,083 and a share capital of $933,584*. There were also four marketing co-operatives (lime, grapefruit, oranges and copra) with a membership of well over 200.

Roseau is the principal port but the banana boats of Geest Industries Ltd, the marketing company, call regularly at Portsmouth, the second town, to collect the bananas of the northern district.

The Melville Hall Airport is situated in the north-east of the island approximately 34 miles from Roseau. Airmail, freight and passenger services are provided by the Leeward Islands Air Transport (LIAT) which operates a daily schedule between Antigua and Barbados by Avro 748 planes carrying 48 passengers.

The following steamship services call at Dominica: the West Indies Shipping Service, Harrison Line, Saguenay Shipping Ltd, Compagnie Génerale Transatlantique Ltd, Royal Netherlands Steamship Ltd, Geest Lines. Lamport and Holt Line Ltd, Grimaldi Siosa Lines, Booth American Shipping Corporation, and the Linea 'C' Line. In addition there are about 80 small sailing craft and seven West Indian-owned motor vessels, ranging between 23 tons and 130 tons, which connect Dominica with the other islands of the Eastern Caribbean.

At the end of 1969 there were 182·5 miles of first-class bituminous roads, 190·75 miles of second class, and some 373 miles of unoiled roads and pedestrian tracks. There were 2,720 registered motor vehicles in 1969.

The territory was allocated £2,719,120 ($13,051,776) to March 1959 under the Colonial Development & Welfare Acts 1945 and 1959. Under the 1963 and 1966 Acts, further allocations of £350,000 ($1,680,000), £300,919 ($1,444,411·20) and £1,026,000 ($4,924,800) were granted making a total accumulated allocation from Colonial Development & Welfare Funds of £4,396,039 ($21,100,987·20).

The main heads of taxation are income tax and customs and excise duties. In the case of individuals income tax ranges from 4 cents for every dollar of the first $500 of chargeable personal income to 50 cents for every dollar over $10,000; companies are charged at the rate of 40 per cent on every dollar of chargeable income. Customs duties on goods imported into the territory are generally specific in regard to foodstuffs and *ad valorem* on other commodities. The rate of *ad valorem* duty varies between 5 per cent and 30 per cent preferential, and 8 per cent and 40 per cent general. Most *ad valorem* goods are chargeable at 20 per cent and 30 per cent preferential and general respectively. Export duty, at varying rates is payable on the principal agricultural products. Excise duty is payable on rum, cigarettes, cigars and tobacco. Other forms of taxation are estate duty and stamp duty. There is provision for double income tax relief in respect of Britain, Canada, the United States, Sweden, Denmark and Norway.

The estimated revenue for 1970 was $11,911,135.

In 1970 there were 58 elementary schools providing primary and post-primary education, with a total enrolment of 20,476 pupils, and four secondary (grammar) schools, two for boys and two for girls with a total enrolment of 1,738 pupils.

---

* $4·80 = £1.

One of the boys' secondary schools (the Dominica Grammar School) to which a technical wing is attached, is wholly maintained by the Government. Primary education is free. Attendance is compulsory wherever adequate school facilities exist. So far 19 areas have been declared compulsory attendance areas. There are also 26 subsidised private infant schools for children of pre-school age. Secondary education is provided up to University-admission level. The secondary schools prepare pupils for the Cambridge G.C.E. examination, on the results of which an annual Government Scholarship is awarded. An increasing number of opportunities for higher education by way of scholarships, bursaries and training courses have been made available in recent years mainly by the United Kingdom, Canada and the University of the West Indies.

There is one central free library in Roseau, with branches at Portsmouth, the second town, in the north of the island and Grand Bay in the south. The service has been extended to other rural districts by means of a Mobile Library Service. There are three commercial cinemas, the Carib and the Arawak in Roseau and the Arbedee in Portsmouth.

The Dominica broadcasting station is a branch of the Windward Islands Government's jointly-owned broadcasting station in Grenada. A national radio station is being set up and should be operating shortly.

HISTORY

Dominica was discovered by Columbus on Sunday (*dies dominica*) 3rd November 1493. It was then a stronghold of the Caribs, who had arrived in the Antilles from the mainland of South America and were in course of driving out the less warlike Arawaks. The Spanish made no attempt to establish settlements on the island either then or later, probably because of the strength of the Caribs and the forbidding terrain.

English associations with Dominica did not begin until 1627, when it was included in a grant of sundry islands in the Caribbean made to the Earl of Carlisle; several attempts to take possession, however, proved abortive.

Under the treaty of Aix-la-Chapelle, 1748, Great Britain and France agreed to treat the island as neutral ground and to leave it to the Caribs. Nevertheless, French planters continued to settle and establish plantations and Dominica came to be regarded as a *de facto* French colony. In 1759 the English captured it from the French and the conquest was acknowledged in the ninth article of the Peace of Paris 1763. The French settlers were generously secured in their possessions on condition of taking the oath of allegiance and paying a small quit rent. In 1775, by Royal Proclamation, a House of Representatives was established.

In 1778, the French in Martinique, attracted by the fertility of Dominica and encouraged by some of their countrymen on the island, launched a military and naval assault under the Marquis de Bouillé. They captured Dominica on 7th September after an obstinate resistance. Marquis Duchilleau, a cruel and tyrannical officer, was appointed Governor. Trade failed and great distress followed.

In 1783 the island was again restored to the English and Sir John Ord, Bart. was appointed Governor.

In 1795 another invasion of the island was attempted by Victor Hugues, the French Republican leader who had previously forced the British troops to evacuate Guadeloupe. The brave and well-directed resistance of the inhabitants, under the command of Governor Hamilton, forced part of the enemy to flee, and the rest to surrender.

In 1805 the French again landed at each flank of Roseau. The regular troops and the militia fought gallantly, but unfortunately the capital was set on fire accidently and was obliged to capitulate, paying the enemy £12,000 to quit; whilst the Governor, Sir George Prévost, and the troops (regular and militia) proceeded across the island to the superior position of Prince Rupert, near the town of Portsmouth. The French withdrew and made no further attempt to capture the island.

In 1833 the island was, with Antigua and the other Leeward islands, formed into a general government, under a governor-in-chief, resident at Antigua.

In 1871 Dominica and other British islands to the north were formed into the federation of the Leeward Islands Colony to which Dominica remained attached until 1939. In 1940 the island became a unit of the Windward Islands group. In January 1960 the post of Governor of the Windward Islands was abolished and the Windwards Group was dissolved as an administrative unit.

CONSTITUTION

Following decisions taken at a conference in London in April and May 1966, subsequently endorsed by a resolution of the Legislative Council, provision was made in the West Indies Act, 1967, under which Dominica assumed a status of association with the United Kingdom on 1st March 1967. The association is a free and voluntary one, terminable by either country at any time. Dominica is fully self-governing in all its internal affairs. The United Kingdom is responsible for defence and external affairs. Agreement has been reached on close consultation over the discharge of these responsibilitiies and on the delegation of executive authority in a wide field of external relations. The British Government conduct their affairs with Dominica and the rest of the West Indies Associated States through the British Government Representative, whose headquarters are at Castries, St Lucia.

Under the Constitution the Governor is Her Majesty's Representative. Except where otherwise provided the Governor is required to act in accordance with the advice of the Cabinet or a Minister acting under the general authority of the Cabinet.

The Cabinet is collectively responsible to Parliament for the government of Dominica. The Cabinet consists of the Premier, the other Ministers and at any time when his office is a public office, the Attorney-General *ex-officio*. The Governor appoints as Premier a member of the House of Assembly who appears to him likely to command a majority in that House. Other Ministers not exceeding five, are appointed on the advice of the Premier. There is provision for the appointment of Parliamentary Secretaries not exceeding three.

Parliament consists of Her Majesty and a House of Assembly. The House of Assembly consists of a Speaker, members, for the present eleven, elected by universal adult suffrage in single member constituencies (one of whom may be the Speaker), three nominated members and, at any time when his office is a public office, the Attorney-General *ex-officio*. Transitionally, the Speaker and other members of the Legislative Council became the Speaker and members of the first House of Assembly.

Parliament may make laws for the peace, order and good government of Dominica. The Constitution contains safeguards for fundamental rights and freedoms. Special provisions relate to a Bill to alter the Constitution or the law establishing the West Indies Associated States Supreme Court or the law relating to appeals to the Privy Council.

A puisne Judge of the West Indies Associated States Supreme Court (*q.v.*), established by Order in Council, is resident in Dominica.

The appointment, dismissal and disciplinary control of public officers is, with certain exceptions, vested in the Public Service and Police Service Commissions, the members of which are appointed by the Governor in accordance with the advice of the Premier, one from amongst persons selected by the appropriate representative body. There is provision for appeal in disciplinary cases to a Public Service Board of Appeal.

LAND POLICY

The freehold system remains the predominant form of land tenure. Alienated Crown Lands have been sold to residents without any preconditions since 1962. Aliens must first obtain a licence from the Government, to which certain conditions are attached, before being able to purchase lands in the territory. The leasehold system still exists on estate lands and the relations between landlords and tenants are governed by the Agricultural Small Tenancy Ordinance, 1953 (Cap. 74). The Crown occupies approximately 50 per cent of the total land area.

GOVERNOR
His Excellency Sir Louis Cools-Lartigue, OBE

CABINET
Premier: Hon. E. O. LeBlanc
Deputy Premier and Minister of Finance, Trade and Industry: Hon. R. O. P. Armour
Minister for Communications and Works: Hon. P. R. John
Minister for Education and Health: Hon. H. L. Christian
Minister for Agriculture, Lands and Cooperatives: Hon. Thomas Etienne
Minister for Home Affairs: Hon. E. A. Leslie
Attorney-General: Hon. L. I. Austin, OBE

Secretary to the Cabinet: C. A. Seignoret, OBE
Financial Secretary: C. A. Sorhaindo, OBE
Permanent Secretary, Ministry of Agriculture, Lands and Cooperatives:
J. J. Robinson
Permanent Secretary, Ministry of Education and Health: M. C. Docrove
Permanent Secretary, Ministry of Home Affairs: A. C. B. Watty
Permanent Secretary, Ministry of Communications and Works: P. R. John
Permanent Secretary, Ministry of Finance, Trade and Industry: J. Barzey
Secretary, Planning and Development: N. E. Watty
Chief Establishment Officer: V. L. Shaw
Deputy Financial Secretary: A. B. A. Lazare

BRITISH GOVERNMENT REPRESENTATIVE
J. E. Marnham, CMG, MC, TD
(Resident in Castries, St. Lucia)

GRENADA

MOST southerly of the Windward Islands, Grenada lies approximately 90 miles north of Trinidad and 68 miles south-south-west of St Vincent. The island is about 21 miles in length and 12 miles in breadth at its extremes and has an area of 120 square miles. Between it and St Vincent lie the islets known as the Grenadines, some of which are included in the territory of St Vincent and some in that of Grenada. The largest of the latter is Carriacou, 13 square miles in area.

Grenada is mountainous and very picturesque, its ridges of hills covered with thick forest and brushwood. The mountains are chiefly volcanic, running off in spurs from a central backbone range which extends along the entire length of the island. The highest peak is Mount St Catherine, 2,756 feet. The terrain slopes gradually to the east and south-east coast.

The island contains a number of mineral and other springs and is well watered by quick-flowing streams. A small lake, the Grand Etang, lies at a height of 1,740 feet above sea level in an old crater near the summit of a mountain and is one of the most remarkable features of the island.

The climate is good with a dry season which extends from January to May and a wet season which occupies the rest of the year. During the dry season when the trade winds prevail the climate is especially agreeable, the temperature falling as low as 65°F at night. During the wet season, when the temperature rises to as high as 90°F on the low lands, there is little variation between night and day. Although this season is oppressive, it is not unhealthy. The rainfall varies considerably, the average for the coastal districts being about 60 inches and in the mountainous interior as much as 150 to 200 inches. The average for Carriacou is about 50 inches.

The population in the 1970 census was 94,821 with a birth rate of 2,649. The number of deaths in 1969 was 772 of which 108 were infants under one year. The majority of the population are of African and mixed descent. There is a small European population, a number of Indians and a small community of the descendants of early European settlers. The people are predominantly Roman Catholic, although there is a substantial Anglican minority. English is universally spoken, but a French *patois* survives in some of the villages among the old peasants. St George's, the principal town, lies in the south-west of the island and has a fine natural harbour. The town of St George's has an estimated population of 8,866. The other towns are Gouyave, Victoria, Grenville, Sauteurs, and Hillsborough in Carriacou.

Located in St George's and operated by the health Services are the General Hospital (240 beds), mental and isolation hospitals, a sanatorium and homes for handicapped children, the chronically sick and the aged. At St Andrew's the Princess Alice Hospital provides 40 beds as does the Princess Royal Hospital at Carriacou. There are three main health centres at St Georges', Gouyave and St David's. Maternity and child welfare work is carried out at 30 district medical visiting stations, each of which is in the charge of a nurse-midwife and is visited by one of the territory's eleven Medical Officers, who hold clinics.

The insect control programme, launched in 1953, has completely eradicated malaria in the island. In 1956 *aedes aegypti* (the yellow fever mosquito) was eradicated in the island, but in Carriacou it developed a resistance to DDT. As a result the World Health Organisation was asked to carry out a survey, and a new plan for the eradication of these insects was implemented in 1964. There was a recent reinfestation on the mainland. Following susceptibility studies suitable insecticides have been selected and a programme prepared with the assistance of PAHO for the eradication of the *aedes aegypti* Mosquito began in June 1970.

The WHO-UNICEF programme for the improvement of sanitation is making good progress.

Although school attendance is not compulsory, a total of 28,402 was receiving primary education at 11 Government and 45 denominational schools on 31st December 1966. The territory has one Government, eight aided and two private secondary schools which had a total roll of 2,703 pupils at the end of 1966. All secondary schools teach up to G.C.E. 'O' level standard. A Technical Training Centre has been established as an integral part of the Grenada Boys' Secondary School and a Commercial and Domestic Arts Institute has been built. The Island has five housecraft centres and four handicraft centres. There is a free public library in St George's and branch libraries in three of the six Parishes and the Dependency of Carriacou.

Among other awards the Government grants two biennial island scholarships, a Grenada Scholarship and an Agricultural Scholarship, tenable at the University of the West Indies or in the case of the Grenada Scholarship at any other recognised University within the Commonwealth if the candidates wish to study a subject which is not available at the University of the West Indies. There is a Teachers' Training College.

The well-sheltered natural harbour of St George's is the territory's chief port. The inner harbour possesses an 800 feet long pier with a minimum depth of 30 feet alongside. The eastern side of the pier can accommodate two ocean-going vessels with a length of 400-500 feet, whilst the western side provides berths for small craft. The portion of the harbour known as the Lagoon affords ideal facilities for repairs and careenage. Several international shipping lines provide regular cargo services from British, European, Canadian and U.S. ports. The ships of Geest Industries carry a limited number of passengers to Britain, but passengers for Canada and the U.S.A. have to travel *via* Trinidad or Barbados.

Passenger and cargo services between the territory and neighbouring islands are provided by ships of the West Indies Shipping Company, together with numerous small motor vessels and auxiliary powered schooners.

Pearls Airport is located at the north-eastern corner of the island and can accommodate Viscount aircraft. British West Indian Airways Ltd. operate daily schedules from Pearls to other parts of the Caribbean. The schedules vary with the seasons and are adjusted to ensure regular connections with major world airlines at Trinidad and Barbados. A small airstrip is planned for early construction in Carriacou.

The island has a good network of approximately 566 miles of roads, which are divided into four classes according to the standard of construction. Grenada is crossed by two first-class roads and a further first-class road runs completely round the island. About 356 miles have an oiled surface and in recent years a programme of widening surfaces and improving corners has been carried out. There are no railways in the territory. Cable and Wireless (West Indies) Ltd. operate on behalf of the Government an automatic telephone network covering the whole island and in addition provide cable and radio-telephone facilities with most parts of the world.

The Windward Islands Broadcasting Service has its headquarters at St George's and has made considerable advances in the scope of its programmes and technical efficiency since its inauguration in 1955. The capital outlay and initial running costs were provided from Colonial Development and Welfare Funds, but since 1959 the service has been maintained by the four Windward Islands Governments. There is a medium-wave relay station on each island of the Windwards group for local programmes, whilst short-wave transmissions reach a wide audience in the eastern Caribbean.

All towns on the island and many villages are served by a piped water supply. The island's electricity is generated and distributed by Grenada Electricity Service Ltd., a company formed in 1961 between the Government and the Commonwealth Development Corporation.

In 1960 the labour force numbered 25,170 with over 9,300 employed in agriculture, forestry and hunting. The total acreage of Grenada is 76,548 and the major crops are cocoa, nutmegs, mace, limes and bananas. A wide variety of fine quality tropical fruits is available and efforts are being made to increase production of pigeon peas, yams, pumpkins and green and yellow vegetables for local consumption. The total acreage of Carriacou is 8,467, and lime oil and cotton are the main exports, although production of the latter has shown a marked decrease in recent years. Although livestock production is an important part of the territory's economy, local requirements of meat and milk are not met and animal rearing remains largely a peasant undertaking, with few large operators. The Livestock Division of the Department of Agriculture operate an artificial insemination service for cattle. The livestock population is estimated at: cattle 6,100; horses 1,500; sheep and goats 7,000. The poultry population numbers 90,000 and meets much of the local demand.

There are approximately 1,700 fishermen and fishing is practised on all coasts. Although a variety of boats is used the traditional methods predominate and are by seine, trolling, banking and drifting with hand lines. In 1965 the estimated catch was 2,943,967 pounds.

The territory has few manufacturing industries and they employ only 2,600 people out of the total labour force. The Grenada Sugar Factory Ltd., produces unrefined sugar for local consumption, but supplies are inadequate to meet the island's requirements. In addition, this factory, together with a number of estates, supplies the local demand for uncured rum. There is a copra mill which produces soap and edible fats, a modern cigarette factory, a lime oil factory, a brewery and in Carriacou a government-owned cotton ginnery. There are seventeen registered trade unions and numerous marketing co-operatives.

The Government owns approximately 75 per cent of Grenada's estimated 10,000 acres of rain forest. The Government reserves are located chiefly in the water catchment area in the Central highlands and exploitation is confined to not more than 50 acres annually. Since 1957, approximately 510 acres of Government forest lands have been reafforested with Blue Mahoe, Teak and Honduras Mahogany. Pinus Caribara var. Hondurensis is undergoing intensive research with good promise. A road construction project was incorporated into the scheme but was suspended due to unavailability of funds.

One forester attended the Overseas Foresters' Six Months Training Course run by the Forestry Commission, U.K., during February to July 1969.

P*

Principal domestic exports by quantity and value for 1966 are as follows:—

Commodity	Unit	Britain	Canada	U.S.A.	Total to all countries
Bananas	Lbs.	45,450,948	—	—	45,450,948
	Stems	1,690,555	—	—	1,690,555
	Value $WI	2,578,740	—	—	2,578,740

Principal domestic exports by quantity and value for 1968 are as follows:—

Commodity	Unit		Britain	Canada	U.S.A.	Total to all countries
Cocoa beans	Lbs.		2,991,800	80,000	—	3,930,945
	Value	$WI	1,772,497	46,545	—	2,312,899
Mace	Lbs.		209,690	32,980	13,450	362,254
	Value	$WI	436,293	73,228	29,312	721,644
Nutmegs	Lbs.		335,600	154,600	545,310	2,964,176
	Value	$WI	218,992	142,022	437,430	2,548,599

Imports in 1968 were:

		Value
Food	$WI	7,468,513
Beverages and tobacco	$WI	751,551
Crude materials, inedible (except fuels)	$WI	1,160,321
Minerals, fuels, lubricants and related materials	$WI	1,066,425
Animal and vegetable oils and fats	$WI	235,939
Chemicals	$WI	2,884,439
Manufactured goods classified chiefly by materials	$WI	5,400,570
Machinery and transport equipment	$WI	3,336,951
Miscellaneous manufactured articles	$WI	4,025,695
Miscellaneous transactions and commodities, e.g., parcel post, live animals not food	$WI	15,692
Total ..	$WI	26,346,096

Forms of direct taxation include income tax, estate duties and property tax. Income tax is based on a graduated scale, varying from 5 cents to 65 cents in the $ for individuals (on chargeable income for the year immediately preceding the year of assessment). Companies pay at the rate of 40 per cent. There is a land tax of 25 cents per acre and house tax is levied on a sliding scale varying from $1·20 per house of rental value between $24·00 and $28·80 per annum, and at 8% in the case of houses with rental value over $144·00 per annum. Other forms of taxation include import, export and excise duties and motor vehicle tax.

In 1968 the territory's provisional revenue figures were as follows:—

Local Revenue	..	$10,595,720
Grant-in-Aid	..	1,853,557
C.D. & W. ..	..	1,852,550
Other and Loans	..	1,841,082
Total ..	..	$16,142,909

In 1966 total Revenue amounted to $12,071,410, made up as follows:—

Local Revenue	..	$8,569,328
Grant-in-Aid	..	1,857,080
C.D. & W. ..	..	822,549
Other and Loans	..	822,453
Total ..	..	$12,071,410

The Grenada Five Year Development Plan for 1967-71 ensivages an expenditure of $WI 45·6 million, of which almost a third will be allocated to agriculture. In 1965 the estimated income from tourists was $WI 3,373,152 and efforts are being made to attract external investment for the development of the tourist industry.

HISTORY

Discovered by Christopher Columbus on 15th August 1498, the island now known as Grenada was given the name of Conception. In 1609 a company of London merchants attempted to form a settlement, but were so harassed by the Caribs that they were compelled to abandon the attempt. In 1650 Du Parquet, Governor of Martinique, purchased the island from a French company and established a settlement at St George's. Finding the venture did not pay, Du Parquet sold the island in 1657 to the Comte de Cerrillac and in 1674 it was annexed to France, the proprietors receiving compensation for their claims.

Invested by the British under Commodore Swanton in 1762, the island surrendered and was formally ceded to the British Crown by the Treaty of Paris on 10th February 1763. Sixteen years later it was retaken by the French under the Comte D'Estaing, only to be restored to Great Britain by the Treaty of Versailles in 1783. In 1795-6 it was the scene of a rebellion against the British rule by a French colonist. The Lieutenant-Governor and 47 other British subjects were massacred by the rebels. Sir Ralph Abercromby suppressed the uprising in June 1796 and the ringleaders were executed.

Grenada joined the Federation of the West Indies as an independent member on its formation on 3rd January 1958, and remained a member until its dissolution following an Order in Council dated 23rd May 1962.

CONSTITUTION

Following decisions taken at a Conference in London in April and May 1966, subsequently endorsed by a Resolution of the Legislative Council, provision was made in the West Indies Act, 1967, under which Grenada assumed a status of association with the United Kingdom on 3rd March 1967. The association is a free and voluntary one, terminable by either country at any time. Grenada is fully self-governing in all its internal affairs. The United Kingdom is responsible for defence and external affairs. Agreement has been reached on close consultation over the discharge of these responsibilities and on the delegation of executive authority in a wide field of external relations. The British Government conduct their affairs with Grenada and the rest of the West Indies Associated States through the British Government Representative, whose headquarters are at Castries, St Lucia.

Under the Constitution the Governor is Her Majesty's Representative. Except where otherwise provided the Governor is required to act in accordance with the advice of the Cabinet or a Minister acting under the general authority of the Cabinet.

The Cabinet is collectively responsible to the Legislature for the government of Grenada. The Cabinet consists of the Premier, the other Ministers and, at any time when his office is a public office, the Attorney-General. The Governor appoints as Premier a member of the House of Representatives who appears to him likely to command a majority in that House. The other Ministers are appointed on the advice of the Premier from among the Senators and members of the House of Representatives. There is provision for the appointment of Parliamentary Secretaries from either House.

The Legislature consists of Her Majesty, a Senate and a House of Representatives. The nine Senators are appointed by the Governor, five on the advice of the Premier, two on the advice of the Leader of the Opposition and two on the advice of the Premier after he has consulted interests which he considers Senators should be selected to represent. The Senate elects a President from among those of its members who are not Ministers or Parliamentary Secretaries. The House of Representatives consists of the Speaker and members (at present ten) elected in single member constituencies under universal adult suffrage, one of whom may be the Speaker. Transitionally the two nominated members of the Legislative Council became Senators and the Speaker and elected members became members of the House of Representatives.

Parliament may make laws for the peace, order and good government of Grenada. The Constitution contains safeguards for fundamental rights and freedoms. Special provisions relate to a Bill to alter the Constitution or the law establishing the West Indies Associated States Supreme Court or the law relating to appeals to the Privy Council.

The headquarters of the West Indies Associated States Supreme Court (*q.v.*), established by Order in Council, is in Grenada.

The appointment, dismissal and disciplinary control of public officers is, with certain exceptions, vested in the Public Service Commission, the Chairman and the four members of which are appointed by the Governor on the advice of the Premier—in the case of two members after the Premier has consulted the appropriate representative body. There is provision for appeals to a Public Service Board of Appeal.

LAND POLICY

All persons who are not British Commonwealth citizens wishing to own land or take shares in locally registered companies are required by law to obtain a licence. Before such licence is granted, however, each applicant must satisfy the Government as to his or her background, financial standing and general suitability. The Government imposes certain restrictions to protect the agricultural potential of the territory and to achieve balanced development.

The Government Land Settlement Policy is aimed at providing peasants with agricultural land ranging from two to five acres. Twenty settlements in Grenada and Carriacou have been established, the majority of which are freehold. Thirteen housing settlements have also been established to provide quarter acre lots for peasants evicted from estate lands.

ST CHRISTOPHER, NEVIS AND ANGUILLA

THE three islands of St Christopher (St Kitts), Nevis and Anguilla, lie in the northern part of the Leeward group of the Lesser Antilles in the Eastern Caribbean. They were united by Federal Act in 1882 and became an independent state in association with Britain on 27th February 1967.

St Kitts and Nevis are separated by a channel some two miles in width. Anguilla is approximately 65 miles N.N.W. of St Kitts and nine miles from its nearest neighbour St Maarten (St Martin)*.

St Kitts (17° 20′ N., 62° 48′ W.) is roughly oval in shape, with a narrow neck of land extending like a handle from the south-eastern end. The total length of the island is 23 miles and its area is 65 square miles. The central part of the main body consists of a rugged mountain range, whose highest point is Mount Misery (3,792 feet). A branch of the range encloses a spacious and fertile valley, on the seaboard of which lies the capital, Basseterre, with a population of about 16,000. This valley and the circle of land formed by the skirts and lower slopes of the mountains constitutes most of the arable and cultivated portion of the island. The higher slopes are covered with short grass, affording excellent pasturage, and the summits of the range are crowned with dense forest. St Kitts is of volcanic formation and most of the beaches are of black volcanic sand but

---

* The southern part of this island belongs to the Netherlands Antilles, the northern part to France.

the best, fringing the peninsula (known as the Salt Ponds) which reaches out towards Nevis, are golden.

Nevis (17° 10′ N., 62° 35′ W.) has an area of 36 square miles. Like St Kitts, it was discovered by Columbus in 1493. It was first colonised by English settlers from St Kitts in 1628. The island's dominant central peak, its tip usually encircled by clouds, rises gradually in an almost perfect cone to 3,232 feet, giving Nevis a spectacularly beautiful appearance from the sea. There are long stretches of golden sandy beaches. Most of the inhabitants are peasant farmers. As on St Kitts, the main crops are sugar cane, sea island cotton, vegetables and coconuts, but whereas the soil of St Kitts (except in the mountains) is light and porous that of Nevis is stiff clay studded with volcanic boulders. The only township, Charlestown, has a population of about 2,500.

Anguilla (18° 12′ N., 63° 05′ W.) is a flat, coralline island, rather less than 16 miles in length and about three and half miles across at its widest point. Its area is about 35 square miles and its highest point is only 213 feet above sea level. The island is covered with low scrub and fringed with some of the finest white coral-sand beaches in the Caribbean. Apart from sheep and goats, its chief product is salt. Sea island cotton and other crops are grown in bottoms of rich soil scattered across the island. Wells said to have been dug by the Caribs are still in use. The sea off Anguilla is remarkably clear and fish can be seen entering the bays. At many points the reef is close inshore, affording perfect conditions for diving and snorkling.

The climate of St Christopher-Nevis-Anguilla is pleasant and healthy. The islands lie in the path of the north-east trade winds and there is a steady cooling breeze throughout the year. The highest temperature recorded in this century is 92°F and the lowest 62°F. Humidity is low and there is no rainy season. Average annual rainfall on St Kitts is about 55 inches. Tropical diseases are virtually non-existent.

The last census held in the territory was in 1970. The total population in St Kitts and Nevis was then found to be 45,457 (St Kitts 34,227; Nevis 11,230). It was not possible for Anguilla to be included in the census, but the average population there is about 5,500. The majority of the population are African or mixed descent.

In 1970 there were approximately 3,750 men and women employed on sugar estates in the territory and 850 men and women at the St Kitts (Basseterre) Sugar Factory. The Civil Service comprised 1,721 men and women employed on a pensionable basis and approximately 1,700 were employed by Government Departments on a non-pensionable basis. There were 325 water front workers, 220 men and women at the Frigate Bay Development, 290 men and women at the Curtis Mathes Factory for the production of television spare parts, and approximately 3,500 men and women employed in building and construction, commerce, Hotels, Aerated Beverage Plants, the Beer and Malt Factory and domestic service.

Government revenue and expenditure for 1970 (from all sources) were estimated at E.C. $26,251,343 and E.C. $27,118,290 respectively.

There are 30 Government Primary, one Senior and two Secondary Schools in St. Kitts and Nevis with an enrolment of 14,826 pupils and employing 445 teachers. Primary education is compulsory for all children between the ages of 6 and 14. Pupils may remain at school until the age of 16 at Senior Schools or in the senior departments of all-age Primary Schools.

Approximately 80 per cent of the arable land in St Kitts is divided into 35 large sugar estates which employ most of the agricultural labour on the island. As employment on the estates is seasonal and there are few alternative jobs, there is considerable under-employment from August to January. Small farming in St Kitts serves as a supplement to employment on the estates. Agriculture in Nevis is almost exclusively on a peasant small-holding basis and more than half the small farms in the territory are on this island. There are, however, five large coconut estates and some privately-owned livestock farms. The main crops are cotton, sugar cane and vegetables, with sugar cane very much on the decline. Farming in Anguilla follows a similar pattern to that of Nevis, though livestock raising is more prevalent and fishing plays a major part in the economy.

Sugar, mainly from St. Kitts, represents about 80 per cent of exports from the territory, In 1963 the St. Kitts factory produced 39,566 tons of sugar, in 1964 the yield was 43,629 tons, in 1965 the yield was 38,921 tons, in 1966 the yield was 38,730 tons, in 1967 the yield was 39,195 tons, in 1968 the yield was 35,390 ton in 1969 the yield was 36,001 tons and in 1970 the yield was 27,163 tons, the lowest in more than ten years.

The total area under sugar cane in St. Kitts in 1970 was about 12,000 acres, of which 9,704 were harvested. The average yield of cane per acre was 33.56 tons. The yield of sugar per acre from cane grown on estates in St. Kitts was 2.8 tons.

In 1969/70 Nevis had 50 acres under cotton. Total production of clean lint was 5,422 lbs.

Airports in the territory are: Golden Rock, St Kitts, runway length 5,200 feet, about 1·5 miles from Basseterre; Newcastle airfield, Nevis, runway length 2,700 feet, 7·5 miles from Charlestown; the Wall Blake airfield, Anguilla, runway length 2,800 feet.

There is a narrow-gauge light railway in St Kitts, owned and operated by the St Kitts (Basseterre) Sugar Factory Ltd. It is 36 miles long and is used to transport cane from the fields to the factory and sugar from the factory to the wharf.

St Kitts has approximately 60 miles of road, Nevis 63 miles and Anguilla 35 miles.

In recent years efforts have been made to diversify the economy and encourage the development of tourism.

HISTORY

St Christopher, discovered by Columbus on his second voyage in 1493, was the first island in the West Indies to be colonised by the English, when Sir Thomas Warner took settlers there in 1623. In 1624 the French, under d'Esnambuc, also colonised part of the island.

Intermittent warfare between the French and British settlers during the seventeenth century ravaged the economy of the island. It was, however, ceded to Britain by the Treaty of Utrecht in 1713. The last fighting on the island took place in 1782 when the French captured Brimstone Hill after a memorable siege and once more took possession of St Christopher. The island was finally restored to Britain by the Treaty of Versailles in 1783.

Nevis, also sighted by Columbus on his second voyage, was settled by the English in 1628 and soon became one of the most prosperous of the Antilles. Although it suffered from French and Spanish attacks in the seventeenth and eighteenth centuries, it maintained a sound economic position until the middle of the nineteenth century.

Anguilla, too was probably first sighted by Columbus. The island remained continuously British after its colonisation in 1650 but was subject in its early days to severe depredations by pirates.

CONSTITUTION

Following decisions taken at a conference in London in May 1966, subsequently endorsed by a resolution of the Legislative Council, provision was made in the West Indies Act 1967, under which St Kitts, Nevis and Anguilla assumed a status of association with the United Kingdom on 27th February 1967. The association is a free and voluntary one, terminable by either country at any time. The State is fully self-governing in all its internal affairs. The United Kingdom is responsible for defence and external affairs. Agreement has been reached on close consultation over the discharge of these responsibilities and on the delegation of executive authority in a wide field of external relations. The British Government conduct their affairs with the State and the rest of the West Indies Associated States through the British Government Representative, whose headquarters are at Castries, St Lucia. On 19th March 1969, H.M. Commissioner was installed on the island of Anguilla under the Anguilla (Temporary Provision) Order in Council, 1969. Additional powers were conferred upon H.M. Commissioner by the Anguilla (Administration) Order in Council which was made on 28th July 1971 under the provisions of the Anguilla Act 1971.

Under the Constitution the Governor is Her Majesty's Representative. Except where otherwise provided the Governor is required to act in accordance with the advice of the Cabinet or a Minister acting under the general authority of the Cabinet.

The Cabinet is collectively responsible to the Legislature for the government of the State. The Cabinet consists of the Premier, the other Ministers and at any time when his office is a public office, the Attorney-General *ex officio*. The Governor appoints as Premier a member of the House of Assembly who appears to him likely to command a majority in that House. The other Ministers are appointed from among the members of the House on the advice of the Premier. There is provision for the appointment of Parliamentary Secretaries.

The Legislature consists of Her Majesty and a House of Assembly. The House of Assembly consists of a Speaker; members (for the present, ten) elected in single member constituencies under universal adult suffrage, one of whom may be the Speaker; and three nominated members or, if a nominated member is Attorney-General, four. Transitionally the first House of Assembly includes the Speaker and elected members of the former Legislative Council.

The Legislature may make laws for the peace, order and good government of the State. The Constitution contains safeguards for fundamental rights and freedoms. Special provisions relate to a Bill to alter the Constitution or the law establishing the West Indies Associated States Supreme Court or the law relating to appeals to the Privy Council.

A Puisne Judge of the West Indies Associated States Supreme Court (*q.v.*) is resident in St Kitts.

The appointment, dismissal and disciplinary control of public officers is, with certain exceptions, vested in the Public Service and Police Service Commissions. There is provision for appeals to the Public Service Board of Appeal.

LAND POLICY

Aliens cannot own land except under licence from the Government.

GOVERNOR
His Excellency Mr M. P. Allen, OBE (Acting)

MINISTRY
Premier: The Hon. Robert L. Bradshaw, JP
Deputy Premier, Minister of Finance, Trade, Development and Tourism:
The Hon. C. A. Paul Southwell, JP
Minister of Education, Health and Welfare: The Hon. F. C. Bryant, JP
Minister of Agriculture and Labour: The Hon. L. E. St John Payne
Minister of Communications, Works and Transport: Hon. C. I. de Grasse
Minister without Portfolio: The Hon. J. N. France
Attorney-General: The Hon. Lee L. Moore, LLM
Director of Public Prosecutions: H.M. Squires

Cabinet and External Affairs Secretary: Ira Walwyn, OBE
Deputy Premiers Permanent Secretary: J. E. D. Osbourne (Acting)
Permanent Secretary, Communications: Byron Cox

BRITISH GOVERNMENT REPRESENTATIVE
J. E. Marnham, CMG, MC, TD
(resident in Castries, St Lucia)

H.M. COMMISSIONER, ANGUILLA
A. C. Watson

ST LUCIA

ST LUCIA, in the Windward Island group, lies 24 miles to the south of Martinique and 21 miles north-east of St Vincent, latitude 13° 54′ N., longitude 60° 59′ W. The island is pear-shaped and measures 27 miles by 14 miles. Its circumference is 150 miles and its area about 238 square miles.

The island is mountainous, with magnificent scenery. The highest peak is Mt Gimie (3,145 feet); the most spectacular are the Gros Piton (2,619 feet) and the Petit Piton (2,461 feet) which are old volcanic forest-clad cones rising sheer out of the sea near the town of Soufrière on the leeward coast. A few miles away in an ancient crater are hot, sulphurous springs. The mountains are intersected by numerous short rivers. In places, these rivers debouch into broad, fertile and well cultivated valleys. The scenery is of outstanding beauty, even when compared with other Caribbean islands, and in the neighbourhood of the Pitons it has the less common element of grandeur.

There is a dry season roughly from January to April, and a rainy season from May to August, with an Indian summer in September-October. Towards the end of the year it is usually wet. The island lies in latitudes where the north-east trade winds are an almost constant influence. The mean annual temperature is about 80°F. Rainfall varies (according to altitude) in different parts of the island from 60 inches to 138 inches.

The population of St Lucia, according to the 1970 census, was 101,000. The population of the capital, Castries, is about 45,000.

There are eight secondary schools with about 2,355 students, and some 71 primary and infant schools. The number of children in these schools is about

28,000. Adult education is provided by the Extra Mural Department of the University of the West Indies and by organised voluntary groups. Community education centres provide facilities whereby the people of the area can meet to discuss matters of common interest and to take part in recreational activities.

Medical services are provided by seven district medical officers and three specialists based at Victoria Hospital, Castries, where there are also two resident medical officers. Available beds are 233 general (including obstetrics), 50 tuberculosis, 140 mental and 120 geriatric. There are 22 health centres.

There are two airfields—Vigie Airport and Hewanorra International Airport (formerly Beane Field)—owned and operated by the Government of St Lucia for scheduled and charter service. The airstrip at Hewanorra, which is located in the Vieux Fort District, was recently lengthened from 5,000 feet to 9,000 feet. Air services with other territories are maintained by British West Indian Airways (BWIA) and Leeward Islands Air Transport (LIAT), Caribbean Atlantic Airlines (CARIBAIR) and Dutch Antillean Airlines (ALM). LIAT is owned by the Trinidad Government and is a subsidiary of BWIA.

There are about 500 miles of roads.

The island is served by the following shipping lines: Harrison Lines—cargo vessels; Geest Industries—cargo and passenger vessels; French Lines—passenger vessels. During 1969, 578 vessels called at St Lucia. Gross tonnage handled was 2,835,646.

Radio Caribbean International St Lucia, a commercial radio station with a power output of 10,000 watts, broadcasts daily in French and English, and there is a sub-station of the Windward Islands Broadcasting Service, which recently acquired a 10 kilowatt transmitter. A commercial television service is also in operation.

The main crops are bananas, coconuts, cocoa, fruit, nutmegs, mace, root crops, such as cassava and yams, and citrus fruits. There is a fair amount of fishing, but the supply of fish does not meet the demand.

The principal manufactures are rum, citrus products, coconut products (copra and edible oils, soap), cigarettes and mineral waters.

Principal Exports by Value

			1967	1969
Copra ..	..	$000	1,062	1,236
Coconuts	..	$000	0·2	18
Coconut oil (unrefined)		$000	662	701
Cocoa ..	..	$000	89	162
Bananas ..	..	$000	9,002	10,800
Nutmeg ..	..	$000	24	11
Fresh fruit	..	$000	90	35
(oranges, plantains, mangoes, avocadoes, pineapples).				

In 1970, 34 per cent of total imports came from the United Kingdom, 35 per cent from other Commonwealth countries and 31 per cent from foreign countries. In 1970, 75 per cent of the island's exports were to Great Britain.

The main form of direct taxation is income tax, the rates of which vary from

12c. in every $4.80 of the first $480.00, to $3.12 in every $4.80 above $24,000. Companies pay $1.92 in every $4.80 on their chargeable income.

Revenue for 1969 (estimated) was $12·1 m. mainly derived from customs and excise duties.

The economy is now being diversified and tourism developed.

HISTORY

Neither the date of discovery nor the discoverer of St Lucia is known, for according to the evidence of Columbus's voyage, he appears to have missed the island. As early as 1605, 67 Englishmen *en route* to Guiana, touched at St Lucia and made an unsuccessful effort to settle. The island at the time was peopled by Caribs and continued in their possession till 1635, when it was granted by the King of France to MM. de L'Olive and Duplessis. In 1638 the first recorded settlement was made by English from Bermuda and St Kitts but the colonists were murdered by the Caribs about three years later.

In 1642 the King of France, still claiming a right of sovereignty over the island, ceded it to the French West India Company, who in 1650 sold it to MM. Honel and Du Parquet. After repeated attempts by the Caribs to expel the French, the latter concluded a treaty of peace with them in 1660.

In 1664 Thomas Warner, son of the Governor of St Kitts, made a descent on St Lucia. The English continued in possession till the Peace of Breda in 1667, when the island was restored to the French. In 1674 it was re-annexed to the Crown of France, and made a dependency of Martinique.

After the Peace of Utrecht, in 1713, the rival pretensions of England and France to the possession of St Lucia resulted in open hostility. In 1718 the Regent, d'Orleans, made a grant of the island to Marshal d'Estrées, and in 1722, the King of England made a grant of it to the Duke of Montague. In the following year, however, a body of troops, despatched to St Lucia by the Governor of Martinique, compelled the English settlers to evacuate the island and it was declared neutral.

In 1743 the French took advantage of the declaration of war to resume possession of St Lucia, which they retained till the Treaty of Aix-la-Chapelle in 1748, when it was again declared neutral. In 1756, on the renewal of hostilities, the French put the island in a state of defence; but in 1762 it surrendered to the joint operations of Admiral Rodney and General Monckton. In the following year, by the Treaty of Paris, it was assigned to the French, who continued in peaceable possession till 1778, when effective measures were taken by the British for its conquest, but by the Peace of Versailles, St Lucia was once more restored to France.

In 1793, on the declaration of war against revolutionary France, the West Indies became the scene of a series of naval and military operations which resulted in the surrender of St Lucia to the British on 4th April 1794. In 1796 the British Government despatched to the relief of their West Indian possessions a body of troops, 12,000 strong, under the command of Sir Ralph Abercromby, supported by a squadron under Admiral Sir Hugh Christian. On 26th April these forces appeared off St Lucia, and after an obstinate and sanguinary contest, which lasted till 26th May, the Republican party, which had been aided by Victor Hugues and his guerilla band, laid down their arms and surrendered as prisoners of war. The British retained possession of St Lucia till 1802, when it was restored to France by the Treaty of Amiens; but on the renewal of hostilities it surrendered by capitulation to General Grinfield on 22nd June 1803, and was finally ceded to Britain in 1814 by the Treaty of Paris.

CONSTITUTION

Following decisions taken at a Conference in London in April and May 1966, subsequently endorsed by a resolution of the Legislative Council, provision was made in the West Indies Act, 1967, under which St Lucia assumed a status of association with the United Kingdom on 1st March 1967. The association is a free and voluntary one, terminable by either country at any time. St Lucia is fully self-governing in all its internal affairs. The United Kingdom is responsible for defence and external affairs. Agreement has been reached on close consultation over the discharge of these responsibilities and on the delegation of executive authority in a wide field of external relations. The British Government conduct their affairs with St Lucia and the rest of the West Indies Associated States through the British Government Representative, whose headquarters are at Castries.

Under the Constitution the Governor is Her Majesty's Representative. Except where otherwise provided the Governor is required to act in accordance with the advice of the Cabinet or a Minister acting under the general authority of the Cabinet.

The Cabinet is collectively responsible to the Legislature for the government of St Lucia. The Cabinet consists of the Premier and other Ministers and, so long as his office is a public office, the Attorney-General *ex officio*. The Governor appoints as Premier a member of the House of Assembly who appears to him likely to command a majority in that House. Other Ministers are appointed on the advice of the Premier. There is provision for the appointment of Parliamentary Secretaries.

The Legislature consists of Her Majesty and a House of Assembly. (There is provision for a Senate if the House of Assembly should resolve in favour of establishing it.) The House of Assembly consists of a Speaker; members (for the present ten) elected in single member constituencies under universal adult suffrage (one of whom may be the Speaker); three nominated members appointed by the Governor, two on the advice of the Premier and one in his own deliberate judgment; and, so long as his office is a public office, the Attorney-General *ex officio*.

The Constitution contains safeguards for fundamental rights and freedoms. Special provisions relate to a Bill to alter the Constitution or the law establishing the West Indies Associated States Supreme Court or the law relating to appeals to the Privy Council.

A Puisne Judge of the West Indies Associated States Supreme Court (*q.v.*) established by Order in Council, is resident in St Lucia.

The appointment, dismissal and disciplinary control of public officers is, with certain exceptions, vested in the Public Service Commission, appointed by the Governor in accordance with the advice of the Premier. There is provision for appeals to the Public Service Board of Appeal.

GOVERNOR
His Excellency Sir Frederick Clarke

MINISTRY

Premier and Minister of Finance, Planning and Development:
The Hon. John G. M. Compton
Minister of Education and Health: The Hon. Hunter J. Francois
Minister of Trade, Industry, Agriculture and Tourism: The Hon. George W. Mallet
Minister of Housing, Community Development, Social Affairs and Labour:
The Hon. J. M. D. Bousquet
Minister of Communications and Works: The Hon. J. R. A. Bousquet
Parliamentary Secretary to the Premier: The Hon. Dr V. Monrose
Attorney-General: The Hon. J. D. B. Renwick, QC

Cabinet Secretary: Dr Graham Louisy, MBE
Labour Commissioner and Acting Secretary for External Affairs: Martin C. Elwin
Permanent Secretary Ministry of Health: C. C. K. Wooding
Permanent Secretary Ministry of Education: G. Theophilus
Permanent Secretary Ministry of Housing, Community Development,
Social Affairs and Labour: S. James
Acting Permanent Secretary Trade, Industry, Agriculture and Tourism and Veterinary Officer:
Acting Permanent Secretary Communications and Works: F. Louisy
Acting Permanent Secretary Establishments: J. Ferdinand
Permanent Secretary Development Planning and Statistics: Charles Cadet
Financial Secretary: George Girard
Director of Audit: George Noon

BRITISH GOVERNMENT REPRESENTATIVE
J. E. Marnham, CMG, MC, TD

ST VINCENT

THE island of St Vincent was discovered by Christopher Columbus on 22nd January, 1498 (St Vincent's Day). The territory includes the northern Grenadines, some of the larger islands are: Bequia, Canouan, Mayreau, Mustique, Isle D'Quatre and Union Island. The island lies between latitudes 13° 6′ and 14° 35′ N. and longitudes 61° 6′ and 61° 20′ W. at a distance of 21 miles to the south-west of St Lucia and 100 miles west of Barbados. Including the Grenadines the territory comprises 150·3 square miles. (Total area of 96,000 acres).

The main island St Vincent is 18 miles by 11 miles at its extremities and has an area of 133 square miles (85,120 acres) of which 39,800 acres are forested.

The most striking natural feature of St Vincent is the Soufrière, or volcano, situated at the northernmost extremity of the island and rising to 4,048 feet above sea level. After a violent eruption in 1812, it remained dormant for a period of ninety years and then broke into violent eruption again on 7th May 1902, when the entire northern half of the island was devastated and nearly 2,000 lives were lost. The eruption synchronised with that of Mont Pélée in Martinique which destroyed the town of St Pierre. The Soufrière was intermittently active throughout 1902 and there was a further eruption in 1903. Since then it has been inactive.

The whole island is of volcanic origin. A backbone of densely wooded and almost impassable mountains traverses it from the Soufrière at its northern end to Mount St Andrew (2,500 feet) dominating the Kingstown valley in the south. The range sends off spurs on each side, cutting up the island into a series of valleys trending east and west from the central range to the coast. There is a somewhat level tract called the Carib Country at the north-east of the island between the Soufrière and the sea. The second highest point in the range is Richmond Peak (3,539 feet). The streams are numerous but, except after heavy rains, small. None of them is navigable.

, Average temperatures range from 18-32°C (64-90°F) and the maximum rarely exceeds 93°F in the shade. At Kingstown station (60 feet above sea level) the mean temperature in 1967 was 82·8°F and the total rainfall 109·51 inches. From January to May there is a pronounced dry season. From May or June the rains start in earnest and continue to the end of the year. Annual rainfall ranges from 60 inches in the extreme south to 150 inches in the interior of the island.

The last census was in 1970. The population was then 89,632. The great majority of the population are of Negro stock or mixed race; there are minorities of East Indians, Europeans and Caribs.

English is the only language in general use. The main religious denominations are Methodist, Anglican and Roman Catholic.

Declining mortality among children under the age of two is largely responsible for a concomitant fall in the crude death rate which was 9·28 per thousand in 1966. Health measures and health education are mainly directed to the control of infantile malnutrition and gastro-enteritis. Insect-borne diseases are not prevalent.

There are 31 dispensaries. Some 340 hospital beds are maintained by the Government, and in 1967 in-patients numbered 5,307. Total expenditure on Government medical and health services in 1970 was EC$1,623,733.

The island is divided into five parishes, Charlotte, St George, St Andrew, St David and St Patrick. The nine political divisions are South Leeward, North Leeward, Kingstown, East St George, West St George, South Windward, Central Windward, North Windward and the Grenadines.

Kingstown, the capital, has a population of 23,645 including the suburbs. The other principal towns are Georgetown, Calliaqua, Layou, Barrouallie and Chateaubelair. The working population is estimated to be 32,000, about 50 per cent of whom are engaged in agriculture, forestry and fishing.

The main crops in order of importance are bananas, arrowroot, copra and coconuts, sweet potatoes, nutmegs and mace, starchy food crops (yams, tannias and eddoes), peanuts, cocoa and cassava.

A rough estimate of the livestock population is: cattle 7,500; goats, 4,500; sheep 5,500; asses 1,000; horses and mules 60; pigs 6,000; poultry 100,000 (all types).

Sales of timber on Crown Lands are restricted to a minimum so as to avoid excessive exploitation at the expense of soil and water conservation.

Extensive in-shore fishing is carried on, but little off-shore. Recorded fish landings for 1970 amounted to 632,649 pounds, valued at EC$218,862. This figure represents about 60 per cent of total landings, as much fish is sold outside established fish markets. An ice making and cold storage plant has been installed in the Kingstown Market and commenced operations in 1969. The Marketing Board took over the marketing of fish in Kingstown in 1969.

An F.A.O.-sponsored regional investigational and training scheme for the Caribbean area is expected to bring improvements to fishing. Barbados is the headquarters for the operation of the scheme.

Industry is based mainly on agriculture. There is a modern arrowroot factory and four privately owned mills operating for processing arrowroot and cassava. Due to the slump in the arrowroot market many private mills have ceased operations. Two privately-owned plants for processing copra were in operation during 1968. There is a small cigarette factory, which in 1969 produced 1,760,000 packets of (10) cigarettes. All tobacco is imported. Other small industries include a rum distillery based on molasses imported from St Kitts, two plants producing aerated drinks, two tyre recapping plants and several furniture-making concerns.

Exports include bananas, arrowroot, coconuts, and various root crops and spices. The main imports are foodstuffs, cotton piecegoods, cement, timber, motor spirit, fertilisers and motor vehicles.

At the end of 1969 there were 18 registered co-operative societies.

A statutory Marketing Board mainly handles sweet potatoes but a substantial trade has also been built up in other starchy roots, mainly with the United Kingdom, the United States of America and Trinidad. The board assists in the marketing of pasteurised milk.

Apart from agriculture, tourism is the main field in which the economy expanded in 1969. The number of short-stay visitors arriving in the territory in 1970 was 17,586, as compared with 15,569 in 1969. It has been estimated that tourism brought over $5·5 million to the island in 1970, as compared with $4·6 million in 1969.

The principal port is Kingstown.

The airstrip is located at Arnos Vale, 1½ miles south-east of the capital—Kingstown. The runway is 4,650 feet long by 150 feet wide, lying in a strip 500 feet wide. Scheduled daily services are operated by Leeward Islands Air Transport using AVRO-748's and D. H. Twin Otters. There are also two airstrips in the Grenadines, Prune Island and Mustique, the first of which is presently licensed and the other expected to be so shortly. The present schedules and services provide daily flights to all Caribbean Islands stretching from Puerto Rico to Trinidad, and same day connections are possible to Europe and North America.

There are 170 miles of all-weather roads, 200 miles of rough motorable, and 204 miles of tracks and by-ways. 7 miles of all-weather roads were constructed during 1969.

The main shipping lines calling at St Vincent are the Royal Netherlands Steamship Co., Booth American Shipping Co., Harrison Line, Atlantic Line, West India Shipping Co., Saguenay Shipping, the Geest Line, Fratelli Grimaldi and Canadian Pacific, James Nourse Line, and Blue Ribbon Line.

Cable and Wireless (W.I.) Ltd., who provide International Telephones, Telegraph and Telex service, brought into operation an automatic telephone system in Kingstown and Calliaqua on 1st February 1969. This system now extends over the whole island and to the Grenadines.

There is a broadcasting sub-station on St Vincent which relays the programmes of the main WIBS station in St George's, Grenada, but time is allowed for local programmes usually of 15 minutes each. Time for important *ad hoc* local programmes is allocated as required. Television reception of the Trinidad and Barbados programmes is possible in some localities.

The 1966-70 Development Plan provides for a capital expenditure of $41·2m. and recurrent expenditure of $6·3m. It is emphasised that tourism is the sector with the greatest growth potential in the future and accordingly investment is devoted to the development of the infrastructure, especially in the Grenadines.

Expenditure in agriculture is aimed at both the diversification and increase in yields of agricultural products. An Agricultural and Co-operative Bank to facilitate credit to farmers commenced operation on 15th February 1969. While it is recognised that the economy will still remain largely dependent on agriculture in the foreseeable future, provision has been made for establishing light industries to utilise local produce through the formation of a Development Corporation.

A graduated income tax is imposed on individuals, ranging from 3 cents to 65 cents on every dollar of chargeable income. The present scale of allowances is a 10 per cent reduction of earned income up to a maximum of $500, personal allowance for a single man of $600 and for a married man of $1,000, for each child $200, for a widower or widow a housekeeper allowance of $125 and a similar allowance for a dependent relative. There is also relief for life assurance. A simplified non-cumulative PAYE system is in operation for employees. Companies pay at a flat rate of 40 per cent.

TRADE—1969 $E.C.

Estimated Total Imports	..	..	..	..	$18,467,693
Estimated Total Visible Exports	..	..	..		$7,151,958
Main Countries					*Exports to—*
United Kingdom	..	..	..	..	$4,598,013
North America	..	..	..	..	$559,850

PRINCIPAL DOMESTIC EXPORTS

Commodity				Unit	Quantity	Value EC$
Bananas	..	..	..	lbs	59,072,189	4,211,035
Arrowroot	..	..	..	lbs	4,682,032	1,070,728
Copra	..	..	..	100 lbs	5,050	91,190
Coconuts	..	..	..	No	1,797,961	69,190
Sweet Potatoes	..	..	..	lbs	5,383,149	152,779
Tannias	..	..	..	lbs	1,013,615	59,943
Yams ..	..	..	..	lbs	1,124,148	56,943
Nutmegs	..	..	..	lbs	212,618	154,175
Mace ..	..	..	..	lbs	38,546	57,620

Primary education is free (except in the case of the Kingstown Preparatory School) but not compulsory. Secondary education is offered in two Government Secondary Schools—one for boys and one for girls—and in seven Assisted Secondary Schools and two unaided Secondary Schools. These are fee-paying schools, but Government's contribution to the expenses of the two Government Schools far exceeds the amount of fees collected. There are several primary schools which are conducted under private ownership but their number is not known. The literacy rate is estimated to be 85 per cent.

HISTORY

St Vincent was included in a patent given by Charles I to the Earl of Carlisle in 1627. In 1660 England and France agreed that the island should be neutral, but in 1672 Charles II granted it to Lord Willoughby. In 1673 the first people of African origin arrived, a party of slaves shipwrecked in the Grenadines who eventually reached St Vincent and intermarried with the Carib inhabitants. Later, French settlements were made along the leeward coast including the site of the present capital. By the Treaty of Aix-la-Chapelle, St Vincent was declared neutral but was captured by the British in 1762. After the conclusion of peace in 1763, European settlers began to arrive. During the American War of Independence, France declared war on Britain and St Vincent fell into the hands of the French in 1779. With the signing of the Treaty of Versailles in 1783 it was restored to Britain. In March 1795 the Caribs, aided by the French residents, threatened to master the whole island, but they were finally subdued in June 1796 when Sir Ralph Abercromby arrived with further reinforcements. During this outbreak the Carib leader Chatoyer was killed in single combat with Major Alexander Leith. The majority of the Caribs were deported to the island of Rattan in the Bay of Honduras and peace was restored.

In 1812 the Soufrière erupted and devastated the greater part of the island. In 1848 due to the shortage of local labour, Portuguese were imported in fairly large numbers from Madeira to work on the sugar estates, and a little over a decade later East Indians arrived for the same purpose. Both the Portuguese and the East Indians are now respected members of the island community.

In the second half of the nineteenth century the price of sugar fell and a serious depression set in which lasted until the end of the century. Before prosperity returned, the island suffered a great calamity in the hurricane of 1898 which killed about 300 people and damaged a large number of buildings. This was followed in 1902 by the disastrous volcanic eruption mentioned at the beginning of this chapter.

In 1951 universal adult suffrage was granted, and in 1956 elected members were given a majority in the Executive Council and elected Ministers took office for the first time.

CONSTITUTION

Following decisions taken at a conference in London in April and May 1966, subsequently endorsed by a resolution in the Legislative Council, and further discussions in London in January and February, 1967, provision was made in the West Indies Act 1967 under which St. Vincent could assume a status of association with the United Kingdom. The appointed day was intended to be not later than 1st June 1967, but due to political problems within St Vincent this date was delayed.

A further Constitutional Conference was held in London in June 1969 to reach final decisions on the Constitution. As a result, St Vincent became an Associated State on 27th October 1969.

The association is a free and voluntary one, terminable by either country at any time. An Associated State is fully self-governing in all its internal affairs. The United Kingdom is responsible for defence and external affairs. By agreement there is close consultation over the discharge of these responsibilities and delegation of executive authority in a wide field of external relations. The British Government conduct their affairs with all the West Indies Associated States through the British Government Representative who has his headquarters in Castries, St Lucia, or through his deputies in Antigua and St Vincent.

It was agreed that as an Associated State St Vincent would have a new Constitution under which there is a Governor who is Her Majesty's Representative. Except where otherwise provided the Governor is required to act in accordance with advice of the Cabinet or a Minister acting under the general authority of the Cabinet.

The Cabinet is collectively responsible to the Legislature for the government of St Vincent. It consists of the Premier, the other Ministers and, at any time when his office is a public office, the Attorney-General *ex officio*. The Governor is required to appoint as Premier a member of the House of Assembly who appears to him best able to command a majority in that House. The other Ministers are appointed on the advice of the Premier.

The Legislature consists of Her Majesty and a House of Assembly. The House of Assembly consists of a Speaker; members, at the moment nine but after the first general election thirteen, elected in single member constituencies under universal adult suffrage, one of whom can be the Speaker; three nominated members appointed by the Governor, two on the advice of the Premier and one on the advice of the Leader of the Opposition; and, so long as his office is a public office, the Attorney-General *ex officio*.

Under the constitution the St Vincent Legislature may make laws for the peace, order and good government of the territory. The Constitution contains safeguards for fundamental rights and freedoms. There are special provisions relating to a Bill to alter the Constitution or the law establishing the West Indies Associated States Supreme Court or the law relating to appeals to the Privy Council.

The West Indies Associated States Supreme Court (*q.v.*), was established by Order in Council, to serve all the six territories which were intended to become Associated States, and Montserrat and the Virgin Islands.

LAND POLICY

All land, other than Crown Land, is freehold. Individual ownership is recognised, but aliens may purchase land only with the approval of the Government.

GOVERNMENT

GOVERNOR
His Excellency Sir Rupert Godfrey John, BA, DipEd

MINISTRY
Hon. R. M. Cato, Premier and Minister of Finance
Hon. L. C. Latham, Minister for Communications, Works and Labour
Hon. H. K. Tannis, Minister for Education and Health
Hon. J. F. Mitchell, Minister for Agriculture, Trade and Tourism
Hon. R. F. Marksman, Minister for Housing, Local Government and Community Development
Hon. S. E. Slater, Minister of Home Affairs
Hon. A. T. Warner, Attorney-General

HOUSE OF ASSEMBLY
C. St C. Dacon, Speaker
R. M. Cato, Member for East St George, Premier
S. E. Slater, Member for North Leeward
R. F. Marksman, Member for West St George
J. F. Mitchell, Member for the Grenadines
L. C. Latham, Member for South Windward
H. K. Tannis, Member for Kingstown
A. T. Warner Attorney-General
E. T. Joshua, Member for Central Windward
Mrs I. I. Joshua, Member for North Windward
J. L. Eustace, Member for South Leeward
J. A. Ferdinand, Nominated Member
E. A. C. Hughes, OBE, Nominated Member and Deputy Speaker
Clerk: O. Cuffy

CIVIL ESTABLISHMENT

Financial Secretary: C. A. Jacobs, M B E

Permanent Secretary, Premier's Office: F. G. Thomas

Permanent Secretary, Ministry of Agriculture, Trade and Tourism: O. E. Leigertwood

Permanent Secretary, Ministry of Communications, Works and Labour: M. V. Williams

Permanent Secretary, Ministry of Education and Health: T. V. Keane

Permanent Secretary, Ministry of Home Affairs: T. M. Velox

Director, Economic Planning Unit: W. F. Dear

Commissioner of Police: R. M. Thomas

Senior Medical Officer: K. W. Fenwick

Chief Personnel Officer: J. A. Pompey

Senior Surgeon: Dr S. D. Gun Munro, M B E

Chief Technical Officer: A. W. Dalrymple

Chief Agricultural Officer: H. S. McConnie, M B E

Chief Education Officer: C. D. Hercules

Veterinary Officer: Dr I. A. E. Kirby

Accountant General: A. J. Da Silva

Director of Audit: H. H. Hamlet, M B E

Chief Surveyor: C. E. R. Williams

Comptroller, Inland Revenue: N. R. Cummings

Comptroller of Customs and Excise: S. Joshua

Labour Commissioner: E. H. N. LaBorde

Port Officer: L. Fraser

Statistical Officer: T. A. Browne

Manager, Central Water Authority: S. Branch

Manager, Airport: J. V. Velox

Government Information Officer: C. G. O. King

District Officer, Southern Grenadines: A. W. Lewis

Postmaster: M. Scott

Superintendent of Prisons: F. O. Mason

JUDICIARY

Puisne Judge, St Vincent Circuit: N. Peterkin

Magistrates: C. E. A. Rawle; C. Dougan

Registrar, Supreme Court: A. T. Woods

READING LIST

ASPINALL, Sir A. Pocket Guide to the West Indies, *Methuen*, 1960.

BURNS, Sir A. History of the British West Indies, *Allen and Unwin*, 1954.

DUNCAN, E. A brief history of St Vincent with studies of citizenship. Third Edition, Kingstown, St Vincent, 1963.

SOUTHERN RHODESIA

THE country takes its name from Cecil John Rhodes (1853-1902) on whose initiative it was opened up for European settlement and development. Since the independence of Northern Rhodesia as the Republic of Zambia on the 24th October 1964 it has become the generally accepted practice to refer to the country as 'Rhodesia' and this title is therefore employed here, except where the use of Southern Rhodesia is appropriate in referring to past constitutional development. The legal name remains Southern Rhodesia.

Rhodesia extends from the Zambesi River (latitude 15° 50′ S.) to the Limpopo River (latitude 22° 25′ S.) and from Botswana in longitude 25° 14′ E. to Mozambique in longitude 33° 4′ E. Entirely land-locked, its neighbours are Zambia on the north and north-west, Botswana on the south-west, the Republic of South Africa on the south, and Mozambique on the east and north-east. Part of the boundary to the north with Zambia runs through Lake Kariba which was formed by the damming of the Zambesi in the Kariba Gorge. This was completed in 1959. The Lake is 175 miles long, up to 20 miles wide, and covers 2,000 square miles.

The area of Rhodesia is 150,820 square miles, which is about three times the size of England. Although Rhodesia lies within the tropics the climate is not typically tropical owing to the elevation of much of the country particularly in the High Veld areas where the majority of the population lives. Of the total area 21 per cent lies over 4,000 feet above sea-level. Temperatures range from a mean minimum of 40°F to a mean maximum of 85°F on the central plateau. The central plateau, known as the High Veld, traverses the country in a north-easterly direction until it links up with a narrow belt of mountainous country striking north and south along the eastern border. There are two important offshoots from the main plateau to the north-west and north of Salisbury. On either side of the main plateau is the Middle Veld which lies between 4,000 and 2,000 feet above sea-level. The Low Veld region, below 2,000 feet, is found along a narrow strip in the Zambesi valley and in a broader tract in the basin of the Limpopo and Sabi Rivers. The lowest point is 660 feet above sea-level where the Limpopo River leaves the country. The greatest rainfall occurs in the mountainous country along the eastern border where considerable areas have an annual mean of over 48 inches. In the centre of the country annual rainfall varies from a mean of 33 inches in the Salisbury area to a mean of 24 inches in the Bulawayo area.

The highlands are in two main portions. The northern portion is generally about 6,000 feet high, rising at the highest point to 8,517 feet above sea-level. The southern portion forms the Vumba Mountains, the Chimanimani Range, which has peaks rising to a height of over 8,000 feet, and the Melsetter Uplands. Between them is the Umtali gap through which run the road and railway to Beira, the nearest outlet to the sea.

In June 1970 the total population was estimated to be 5,310,000, comprising 5,050,000 Africans, 239,000 Europeans, 16,100 persons of mixed race and 9,200 Asians. (The accuracy of these figures cannot be determined). The African population is composed mainly of the Mashona and Matabele and their related tribes. No reliable figures are available of the breakdown into tribes but there is no doubt that in the country as a whole the Mashona and their related tribes are in the majority. The official language is English but Shona and Sindebele are important vernaculars. Numerous Christian missions of various denominations including Anglican, Roman Catholic and non-Conformist are active throughout the country, but the majority of Africans are still non-Christian, adhering to tribal, animistic and other beliefs. There are small Muslim, Hindu and Jewish communities.

The capital of Rhodesia is the city of Salisbury. Since its foundation in 1890, the city has become the centre of a large urban complex which now extends over an area of 184 square miles and the population in June 1970 was estimated to be 423,000 of which 102,100 were Europeans. Salisbury and Bulawayo, the second largest city and the railway centre, possess the two largest concentrations of secondary industry in Rhodesia.

The other areas of greatest industrial development are situated in the Midlands (Gwelo, Que Que and Gatooma) and at Umtali, near the border with Mozambique.

Salisbury Airport, eight miles by road from the city, is the centre of Rhodesia's internal and external civil air communications. The other principal civil airport in Rhodesia, Woodvale Airport, is 10 miles from the city of Bulawayo.

The total mileage of roads open to traffic at the end of 1964, excluding those falling under the responsibility of local authorities, was 43,382 of which 2,517 were of bitumen standard. All the main centres of population are also served by Rhodesia Railways, which are connected with, and operate in conjunction with, the South African, Mozambique and Angola railways. Rhodesia has 2,706 miles of 3ft 6 in. gauge railway line.

The Rhodesia Broadcasting Corporation broadcasts from Salisbury and Bulawayo using short and medium wave transmitters which, with the help of booster and satellite stations, provide country-wide coverage. Television is at present available in the Salisbury and Bulawayo areas only.

The last detailed economic statistics to be published were those for the year ending December 1965. In that year the Rhodesian Gross Domestic Product was £R352·1 million of which agriculture made up £R66·7m. (19·2 per cent) and the manufacturing industry £R66·6m. The régime claim that in 1969 the GDP was £R446·2 million of which agriculture made up £R81·9m (18·1 per cent) and the manufacturing industry £R84·7m. Although the GDP in 1969 has increased in money terms the real *per capita* income when price increases and the increase in population are taken into account is still only at the same level as in 1959.

In agriculture, the main crops were, until 1965, tobacco, sugar, maize and cotton. Since 1965 however, tobacco production has had to be cut back by over 60 per cent because of sanctions.

Rhodesia also produces a wide variety of minerals, notably asbestos, gold, chrome and copper. Total mineral production in 1968 was valued at £R33·7m. Other minerals produced in Rhodesia include coal, lithium, nickel and iron ore.

On 12th November 1965, immediately following the illegal declaration of independence, the Security Council passed a Resolution (No. 216) condemning the unilateral declaration of independence and calling upon all States not to recognise the illegal regime and to refrain from rendering any assistance to it. On 20th November 1965 the Security Council passed Resolution No. 217, which, *inter alia*, called on all States to do their utmost to break all economic relations with Southern Rhodesia, and included an embargo on oil and petroleum products. A large number of countries thereupon severed all trading links with Rhodesia and others placed a partial embargo on trade with Rhodesia. The United Kingdom applied a wide variety of economic and other sanctions to Rhodesia and by February 1966 had cut off virtually all trade with Rhodesia. The effect of these international sanctions (which were still voluntary) was to reduce Rhodesia's exports from £142·5m. in 1965 to an annual rate of around £R100m., thereby causing a reduction in Rhodesia's imports of about one third.

On 9th April 1966, following an attempt to supply petroleum to Rhodesia in defiance of Resolution No. 217, the Security Council passed another Resolution (No. 221) which called upon the United Kingdom to prevent, by the use of force if necessary, the arrival at Beira of vessels reasonably believed to be carrying oil destined for Rhodesia. The Resolution and the subsequent patrolling of the Mozambique Channel have effectively prevented the illegal regime from obtaining supplies of crude oil to operate their refineries.

On 16th December 1966, the Security Council adopted a resolution (No. 232) on selective mandatory sanctions against Rhodesia.

The Security Council adopted a further resolution (No. 253) on 29th May 1968, which, *inter alia*, imposed comprehensive mandatory economic sanctions against Rhodesia covering virtually all trade.

On 18th March 1970, the Security Council adopted another resolution (No. 277), which, *inter alia*, called for the severance of all diplomatic, consular, trade and other relations with the illegal régime and the interruption of existing means of transportation to and from Rhodesia.

The provisions of previous resolutions were reaffirmed by Security Council resolution (No. 288), which was passed on 17th November 1970.

HISTORY

It is thought that Rhodesia was first settled by peoples of Bantu stock (a linguistic classification) between 1,000 and 1,500 years ago, during a great southward migration which also led to the Bantu colonisation of Natal. These immigrants, who are believed to have been the ancestors of the tribes now collectively known as the Mashona, found the country inhabited by the so-called Bushmen, the last representatives of a succession of Stone Age cultures of which remains have been discovered 500,000 years old. The Bushmen, hunting peoples who possessed a highly developed artistic sense, were gradually displaced by the Bantu agriculturalists and have now almost disappeared from Rhodesia.

The second great movement of Bantu peoples into Rhodesia occurred in 1830, when off-shoots of the Bantu who had reached Natal, and who had by then combined to form the Zulu nation, moved northwards. The most important of these were the Matabele, under Mzilikazi, who eventually settled in the south-west of the country, in the area now known as Matabeleland.

As a result of their attempts in the sixteenth century to open up south central Africa from the east coast of Africa, the Portuguese were the first Europeans to explore what is now Rhodesia. In 1514 Antonio Fernandez reached the region of Que Que, and nearly half a century later the Jesuit priest Gonzalo da Silveira reached Mount Fura, where he was murdered after visiting and baptising the so-called Emperor Monomatapa (actually paramount chief of the Makaranga). In 1569 Francesco Barreto led a large military expedition into the interior with the primary object of exploiting the reputed goldfields. The expedition failed and Barreto died at Sena on the Zambesi River.

For some three hundred years there was no further European contact with the hinterland until the coming of the great missionary-explorers, the hunters, traders and gold-seekers, who between them opened up much of Africa to European influence. David Livingstone first sighted the Zambesi river in 1851 and reached the Victoria Falls in 1855. In 1857 the missionary, Robert Moffat, visited Mzilikazi in Matabeleland, and this led to the establishment in 1861 of the first mission to the Matabele by the London Missionary Society. A second mission was established in 1875 at Hope Fountain.

In 1887 Cecil Rhodes was instrumental in the despatch of J. S. Moffat to Matabeleland to safeguard British interests. On 11th February 1888 Lobengula, son and successor to Mzilikazi, signed a treaty pledging not to cede territory without leave of the British High Commissioner at the Cape. Later in the same year, on 30th October, Lobengula granted the Rudd Concession over the minerals in his kingdom. This led to the formation of the British South Africa Company which was granted a Royal Charter on 29th October 1889 for the purpose of promoting trade, commerce, civilisation and good government in the region of Southern Africa lying immediately to the north of British Bechuanaland (now Botswana), and to the north and west of the then South African Republic, and to the west of the Portuguese Dominions. The Pioneer Column and its escort of police set out from Bechuanaland in 1890 and after skirting Matabeleland reached the present site of Salisbury on 12th September 1890, without bloodshed or incident. The Anglo-Portuguese Agreement of 1891, which was finally confirmed by Signor Vigliani's award in 1897, settled the boundary disputes with the Portuguese on the eastern border.

The Mashona at first accepted the arrival of the Europeans but the Matabele resented the restrictions which this placed on their use of Mashona territory. In 1893 a Matabele raid led to the Matabele War which terminated the next year in the destruction of the Matabele power and the flight of Lobengula from Bulawayo. Matabeleland then came under the Chartered Company's civil administration.

Originally, the territories under the Company's administration were known as Zambesia, but on the 3rd May 1895 they were formally named 'Rhodesia' by proclamation.

The second Matabele War broke out in 1896, due partly to the effects of drought and cattle disease and partly to resentment at the defeat in 1893. The War ended in August 1896 when Cecil Rhodes and a small party met the Matabele leaders in the Matopos Hills near Bulawayo and arranged a settlement. A series of wars with the Mashona dragged on until 1897 when peace was finally restored.

CONSTITUTIONAL DEVELOPMENT

The territory was administered by the British South Africa Company from the commencement of European colonisation in 1890 until the grant of responsible government in 1923. The Charter granted to the Company provided that it was subject to review, and possible termination, after twenty-five years from the date of the grant, and every period of ten years thereafter. From the early years of the occupation the settlers had consistently criticised the Administration and at various times had demanded self-government. Their demands for increased representation on the Legislative Council, which consisted of elected members (settlers) and official members (heads of departments), resulted in concessions being made from time to time, so that in 1903 there were seven of each, and four years later the number of official members was reduced by two to give the settlers a majority. When the first period of twenty-five years of Charter rule expired in 1914, the Council, on which the settlers had a majority, requested that the Charter be continued for a further ten years, but in 1920 the Council passed a resolution requesting the establishment of responsible government 'forthwith'. The issue was put to the electorate as one of two choices, responsible government or entry into the Union of South Africa as the fifth province, and at a referendum in 1922 8,744 votes were cast for self-government and 5,989 for the alternative.

After the 1922 referendum Southern Rhodesia was formally annexed to His Majesty's dominions as a Colony on 12th September 1923; under the Southern Rhodesia Constitution Letters Patent, 1923, issued on the 1st October 1923, the Colony was granted full self-government with the exception that legislation affecting African interests, the Rhodesia Railways and certain other matters were reserved to the Secretary of State. Except for those concerning differential legislation affecting the African population, these reservations fell away in time so far as internal affairs were concerned. The British Government conducted formal international relations on behalf of Southern Rhodesia:

Commonwealth relations, trade relations, and relations with Colonial territories in Africa were mainly conducted by the Southern Rhodesian Government direct.

As a result of a series of conferences held in 1951, 1952 and 1953 on the closer association with Southern Rhodesia, Northern Rhodesia (now Zambia) and Nyasaland (now Malawi), a draft Federal Scheme was prepared setting out the details of the Constitution of a Federation of Rhodesia and Nyasaland. This was the subject of a referendum in Southern Rhodesia in April 1953, when it was approved by 25,570 votes to 14,279. In the same month the proposals were approved in the Legislative Councils of Northern Rhodesia and Nyasaland. The Federation subsequently came into existence on the 3rd September 1953 when certain powers hitherto exercised by the Southern Rhodesian Government were transferred to the Federal Government, though the actual process of transfer took some months to complete. The most important powers transferred in this way were defence, the regulation of commerce and industry, immigration, health, European education and European agriculture. The main functions which continued to be exercised by the Territorial Government were African administration, education and agriculture, local government and housing, police and internal security, industrial relations, land, roads, mining and irrigation.

In 1959 the Southern Rhodesian Government proposed to the British Government that the Constitution of Southern Rhodesia should be revised, with a view to transferring to Southern Rhodesia the exercise of the powers vested in the British Government. After consultations between the two Governments a Constitutional Conference was convened in London in December 1960, under the Chairmanship of the Secretary of State for Commonwealth Relations. The conference adjourned after procedural meetings and resumed in Salisbury from 30th January 1961 to 7th February 1961.

Proposals for a new Constitution, based on the conclusions of the Constitutional Conference, were published in June 1961 in two White Papers (Cmnd. 1399 and 1400). At a referendum of the Southern Rhodesia electorate held in July 1961, the proposals were approved by 42,004 votes in favour to 21,846 votes against. In November 1961 Parliament at Westminster passed the Southern Rhodesia (Constitution) Act, which authorised Her Majesty to grant a new Constitution to Southern Rhodesia by Order in Council. The new Constitution was brought into force by the Southern Rhodesia Government in November 1962.

The Federation of Rhodesia and Nyasaland was dissolved on the 31st December 1963. The Southern Rhodesian Government on 1st January 1964 resumed the powers which had been transferred to the Federal Government in 1953.

On 11th November 1965 the Rhodesian Prime Minister Mr Ian Smith and his ministerial colleagues purported to declare Rhodesia independent. In the face of this illegal action, the Queen, acting through her representative the Governor, dismissed them from office and the British Parliament passed the Southern Rhodesia Act 1965 (see below).

The approach of the British Government towards the problem of granting independence to Rhodesia has throughout been governed by certain basic requirements. These have been formulated as five principles:

(1) The principle and intention of unimpeded progress to majority rule, already enshrined in the 1961 Constitution, would have to be maintained and guaranteed.

(2) There would also have to be guarantees against retrogressive amendment of the Constitution.

(3) There would have to be immediate improvement in the political status of the African population.

(4) There would have to be progress towards ending racial discrimination.

(5) The British Government would need to be satisfied that any basis proposed for independence was acceptable to the people of Rhodesia as a whole.

Successive British Governments have made clear their desire for a just and honourable settlement on the basis of these principles. The British Prime Minister explored the possibilities of arriving at such a settlement in meetings with Mr Smith on board HMS *Tiger* in December 1966 and HMS *Fearless* in October 1968. This was followed in November by a visit to Salisbury by a British Minister, but shortly afterwards the ensuing correspondence was broken off.

On 20th June 1969, a referendum was held among those inscribed on the A and B rolls. Voters were invited to give their approval to certain constitutional proposals which had previously been published in outline and to the adoption of a republican form of government. There was an 80% poll of which 82% voted in favour of a republican form of government while 73% favoured amendment of the Constitution on the lines proposed. On 24th June 1969, the Foreign and Commonwealth Secretary announced to the House of Commons that the Governor, with the full agreement of Her Majesty's Government in the United Kingdom, had sought The Queen's permission to resign and that this had been granted. In addition, he announced the withdrawal of the British Residual Mission from Salisbury and the closing of Rhodesia House in London, both of which took effect on 14th July 1969. At the time of this announcement, British Ministers also stated publicly that the Government was ready to resume links with Rhodesia as soon as there were people there with effective support and who shared the British principles.

On 2nd March 1970 Parliament in Rhodesia was dissolved and the republican constitution which the illegal régime had purported to enact was brought into force. The then Foreign and Commonwealth Secretary told the House of Commons that this further illegal act in no way affected the constitutional position: Rhodesia remained part of Her Majesty's dominions.

In November 1970 the Foreign and Commonwealth Secretary announced that an exploratory message had been sent to Mr Smith in an effort to establish whether or not a basis for negotiations within the Five Principles could be found.

CONSTITUTION

The Constitution of Rhodesia is contained in the Southern Rhodesia (Constitution) Order in Council 1961 (S.I. 1961 No. 2314), which must be read in conjunction with the Southern Rhodesia Act 1965 (Chapter 76) and the Southern Rhodesia Constitution Order 1965 (S.I. 1965 No. 1952).

The 1961 Constitution eliminates most of the reserved powers of the British Government for the disallowance of laws passed by the Legislative Assembly. It contains a number of safeguards for the rights of individuals and of communities such as the Declaration of Rights and provision for a Constitutional Council. Certain basic provisions are specifically entrenched. They include provisions relating to the franchise, the Declaration of Rights, and Constitu-

Q

tional Council, appeal to the Privy Council and certain matters concerning Tribal Trust Land. The effect of such entrenchment is to make it impossible to amend the basic provisions without either the agreement of a majority of votes in each of the four principal racial communities voting separately in a referendum or alternatively the approval of the British Government.

The Legislative Assembly consists of sixty-five members of whom fifty are returned predominantly by 'A' Roll voters in constituencies and fifteen predominantly by 'B' Roll voters in electoral districts.

Following the illegal declaration of independence the British Government passed the Southern Rhodesia Act 1965 which declares that Southern Rhodesia continues to be part of Her Majesty's dominions and that the Government and Parliament of the United Kingdom continue to have responsibility and jurisdiction for and in respect of it. The Act empowers Her Majesty by Order in Council to make such provision in relation to Rhodesia or persons or things in any way belonging to or connected with Rhodesia as appear to her to be necessary or expedient in consequence of any constitutional action undertaken therein. The Southern Rhodesia Constitution Order 1965 which was made under this Act, declares that any Constitution which the illegal régime may purport to promulgate is void and of no effect. The Order also prohibits the Legislative Assembly from making laws or transacting any other business and declares any proceedings in defiance of this prohibition void and of no effect. It also suspends the Ministerial system and empowers a Secretary of State to exercise the executive authority of Rhodesia on Her Majesty's behalf.

MINISTRIES

Sir Charles P. Coghlan, KCMG, 1st October 1923 to 1st September 1927
H. U. Moffat, CMG, 2nd September 1927 to 5th July 1933
G. Mitchell, 6th July to 11th September 1933
Sir Godfrey Huggins, PC, CH, KCMG (later 1st Viscount Malvern), 12th September 1933 to 7th September, 1953
R. S. Garfield Todd, 7th September 1953 to 17th February 1958
Sir Edgar Whitehead, KCMG, OBE, 18th February 1958 to 16th December 1962
W. J. Field, CMG, MBE, 17th December 1962 to 13th April 1964
I. D. Smith, from 13th April 1964 to 11th November 1965

PART VI

DEPENDENT TERRITORIES OF COMMONWEALTH COUNTRIES

COMMONWEALTH OF THE BAHAMA ISLANDS

THE Commonwealth of The Bahama Islands comprise an archipelago of about 700 islands and more than 2,000 rocks and cays, lying between latitudes 20° 55′ and 27° 25′ N. and longitudes 72° 35′ and 50° 5′ W.; the total land surface area of the islands is 5,380 square miles. The group is separated from Florida on the west by the Straits of Florida and on the south from Cuba by the Old Bahama and Nicholas Channels. About 30 of the islands are inhabited and the more important of these include Abaco, Acklins and Crooked Island, Andros, the Berry and Bimini Islands, Cat, Cay Sal and Cay Lobos, Eleuthera, Exuma, Grand Bahama, Long Island, Mayaguana, New Providence, Ragged Island, Rum Cay and San Salvador. Andros is the largest in size, but New Providence upon which the capital, Nassau, is situated, is the most important.

The Bahamas lie on a submarine shelf which rises steeply in the east from depths of over 2,000 fathoms, and in the west forms the shallow seas of the Great Bahama Bank. Most of the islands are located on the eastern edge of this shelf and since the seas are coral-bearing the coasts tend to be complex. The islands are composed of corraline limestone and are usually long and narrow, each rising from the shore to a low ridge, beyond which lie lagoons and swamps. The highest point, in Cat Island, is 206 feet above sea level, but Grand Bahama barely reaches 40 feet. Since the rock is permeable there are no streams and the water supply has to be derived either from shallow wells or from rainwater collected in catchments and cisterns. The shallow soils found in small pockets in the limestone rock afford limited cultivation and suit a variety of sub-tropical vegetables and fruit.

The warm waters of the Gulf Stream render the winter climate of the Bahamas agreeably mild and frosts are never experienced. Temperatures during this season average 21°C (70°F), and summer temperatures, although modified by the sea, vary between 27° and 32°C (80° and 90°F). Most of the rain falls in May, June, September and October and thunderstorms are frequent during the summer months. The total rainfall is comparatively slight, averaging 44 inches per annum, but it varies between the islands from 30 to 60 inches.

Censuses are taken every ten years and the population at the last census (April 1970) was 168,812. The population is very unevenly distributed, with 60 per cent of this population (101,503) residing in New Providence; the average population density of the islands is only 31 persons per square mile. Abaco, Andros, Eleuthera, Exuma and Cays, Harbour Island and Spanish Wells, Long Island all have more than 3,200 inhabitants. On 31st December 1970 the population of the Bahamas was estimated to be 174,365. The birth-rate in 1969 was 26.80 per 1,000 and the death-rate 6.83 per 1,000. Religion is predominantly Christian, the main denominations being Baptist, Anglican and Roman Catholic. English is the official and spoken language.

The climate of the islands is healthy and tropical diseases are absent. Preventive needs are met by child welfare and ante-natal clinics. Immunisation against smallpox, diphtheria, pertussis, tetanus and poliomyelitis is given at these clinics, and is a requirement for primary school entry. The public health department also has health inspectors to advise on hygiene and sanitation. Curative needs are met by Princess Margaret Hospital on New Providence Island which has 457 beds, full supporting services and full-time consultant specialists in medicine, surgery, anaesthesia, paediatrics, chest diseases, pathology, radiology, obstetrics, gynaecology and ophthalmology. Serious cases from the Out- Islands are brought into this hospital by air. A mental hospital and rehabilitation unit of 230 beds, and a geriatric hospital of 140 beds are also situated on New Providence. Altogether there are 8 medical officers on the Out-Islands and 49 clinics where there is not a resident doctor; doctors from New Providence visit the clinics regularly on a Flying Doctor Service. On five Out-Islands there are government run cottage hospitals, and on Grand Bahama there is a hospital which has recently been transferred to Government control.

Under the Bahamas Education Act of 1968, education is compulsory and free between the ages of 5 and 14. There are 141 secondary schools or secondary sections of all-age rural schools, a teacher-training college and two technical schools. There is a Department of Extra-mural Studies of the University of the West Indies in Nassau. More than 400 Government scholarships for higher education overseas are awarded annually. There is one reformatory school for boys under the Industrial School Act and one for girls. Literacy is estimated to be 90 per cent. There are 5 public libraries in Nassau and 34 village libraries on the Out-Islands.

The main seaports are Freeport (Grand Bahama Island), Matthew Town (Inagua Island) and Nassau (New Providence); the net tonnage figure for ships entering the Bahamas in 1968 was 6,229,171 and 10,677,536 in 1969; the tonnage of vessels cleared was, 1968 6,260,813 and 1969 7,041,903. The country is served by Saguenay Shipping Ltd, the Royal Mail Line, the Pacific Steam Navigation Company, the Royal Netherlands Line and the United Fruit Steamship Company.

The principal airports in the Bahamas are situated at Nassau, 12 miles from the town (runway 11,000 feet) and Freeport, Grand Bahama (runway 8,300 feet) from which international services are operated; and at West End, Grand Bahama (runway 8,000 feet) and Rock Sound, Eleuthera. There are 55 smaller airports and landing strips designed to facilitate services between the Out-Islands. This service is operated by Flamingo Airlines and Out-Island Airways. There are 250 miles of roads on New Providence maintained by the Ministry of Works, 125 miles of asphalt roads on Eleuthera, and 130 on Grand Bahama. Roads are under construction on Andros Island and on most of the smaller islands where previously only rough tracks existed. At present there is a total of 550 miles of paved roads in other Out-Islands. There is a considerable mileage of privately owned and maintained roads, mainly on New Providence. There are no railways in the territory.

The Government-owned broadcasting station, operated by the Bahamas Broadcasting and Television Commission, is located in Nassau. The power of its transmitter is 10 kW, frequency 1,540 kc/s and call sign ZNS. Commercial operation began in 1950, althongh a broadcasting station has existed since 1936. The Commission took over in 1957. In 1962 a second channel opened transmission on a frequency of 1,240 kc/s with a power of 1,000 watts, serving the island of New Providence only. However, it can be heard in some of the nearer

Out-Islands. There is no direct television but a re-diffusion service from Florida is operated by Greater Freeport Services Ltd on Grand Bahama. New Providence viewers are able to receive television direct from Florida.

The principal crops include fresh vegetables, tomatoes, pineapples, bananas, citrus fruits, avocados, mangos, egg-plant, squash and sisal. The quality of local stocks of pigs and sheep is being improved by the importation of pure-bred animals, and the Government is encouraging the establishment of beef and dairy herds. The latest estimated livestock figures are those for 1966 which show: sheep 22,900; goats 14,100; pigs 10,700; cattle 3,400; horses 3,600; poultry 650,000.

Total exports for the preceding years are as follows:

1968 $B	1969 $B	1970 $B
51,781,802	54,325,928	89,602,498

Of these the principal exports were:

	1969 $B	1970 $B
Oil	N.A.	28,749,268
Cement	N.A.	11,100,404
Hormones	—	4,499,086
Pulpwood	1,653,974	3,541,777
Salt	1,982,342	2,847,089
Rum	3,523,827	2,675,545
Crawfish	677,211	461,574

There are four canning plants in the Bahamas, mainly engaged in canning tomatoes and pineapple. Most of the output is consumed locally. The exploitation of forest products is confined to the yellow pine* forests on Andros and Abaco. Straw products are manufactured as cottage industries and the raw material for this work is chiefly obtained from palm fronds and sisal fibre.

Electricity production in recent years was (million kWh): 1963, 113; 1964, 123; 1965, 137; 1966, 155; 1967, 175; 1968, 215.

Nearly all the territory's requirements are imported and include provisions, hardware, fresh beef, furniture, lumber, clothing, motor vehicles and fuel oil. The c.i.f. value of imports in previous years are as follows:

	$B million
1968	180
1969	302
1970	337

The increase between 1968 and 1969 is due in part to the inclusion of statistics of duty free imports at Freeport for the first time.

Apart from a tax on real property of 0·5 per cent of the assessed market value of the land and structure there is no direct taxation. Government revenue is derived chiefly from import duties, casino tax, airport departure tax, stamp duties, vehicle tax and from fees of various sorts. Revenue which has risen progressively over the years showed signs of levelling off in 1970 though at $91 million it was the highest ever achieved. Expenditure on revenue account was $97

---

* *pinus caribaea.*

million.Revenue on Capital account was $16·75 million and expenditure was $20·5 million.

Tourism continues to be the main industry of the Bahamas and has expanded greatly in recent years, as the following figures show:

		No. of visitors
1949	..	32,000
1965	..	720,000
1966	..	822,317
1967	..	915,273
1968	..	1,072,213
1969	..	1,332,396

The second main industry is banking and the management of finance on an international scale in which Eurodollar and trust business is an important part. The Bahamas is a tax haven and thus attracts much offshore business. In 1970 there were 282 registered banks in operation. The Bahamian dollar was revalued in January 1970 to 2·40 to the £ sterling, the same as the official rate for the U.S. dollar.

Agricultural production is on only a modest scale. There are Tomato Growers' Associations on Eleuthera and Cat Islands and active Farmers' Associations are situated throughout the Bahamas; these are assisted by the Ministry of Agriculture, which advances seed and fertilizer for the crops. The Produce Exchange in Nassau assists the farmers in the disposal of their produce in order to avoid glutting the market and depressing prices unnecessarily.

Other important developments include the establishment of a substantial oil refinery at Freeport, Grand Bahama which came into production during 1970 and has a capacity of 250,000 barrels a day. Aragonite mining has also commenced on Ocean Cay where an artificial island is being created by this $15 million project. Substantial land sales continue in many islands for the erection of holiday and residential homes and for the creation of tourist facilities on a considerable scale.

HISTORY

San Salvador, so called by Columbus, or Watling's Island, the Amerindian name being Guanahani, one of the islands composing the Bahama chain, was the first land discovered by him on his voyage in 1492. A few years later all the Carib inhabitants were transported to work in the Cuba mines. It does not appear that the Spaniards had any settlements on any of the islands of this group at any time. Early in the 17th century the islands were well known to the settlers of Bermuda and the Carolinas. They were included in the Royal Grant of Sir Robert Heath, the Attorney-General of England, of the 30th October 1629. By 1640 the islands had become a well-known place of resort by the inhabitants of Bermuda, and on the 9th July 1647 the Company of Eleutherian Adventurers was formed in London for the purpose of making an organised attempt at a systematic colonisation and development of the islands. William Sayle, a former Governor of Bermuda, was the moving spirit of this venture, and associated with him were a number of influential city merchants and Members of Parliament. On the 31st August 1649, on the petition of Sayle and others, Parliament passed 'An Act for the Adventurers for the Eleutherian Islands' which constituted Sayle and his associates the 'Proprietors of the Islands'. Notwithstanding the Royal Grant to Heath in 1629 and the Cromwellian Act of 1649, Charles II, on 1st November 1670, granted the islands to six of the Lords Proprietors of Carolina, namely, the Duke of Albermarle, the Earl of Craven, Lord Berkley, Lord Ashley, Sir George Carteret and Sir Peter Colleton. Before the Royal Grant of 1670 the inhabitants of the islands had organised the settlement, instituted a form of government which included an elective House of Assembly, and chosen Captain John Wentworth as their Governor. Wentworth applied to and received commissions from the Governors of Jamaica. The Lords Proprietors appointed Hugh Wentworth as their first Governor on 24th April 1671, but he did not take up the appointment. They then confirmed in office John Wentworth, the popularly elected Governor, on the 26th December 1671. A regular system of government was established including a parliament, the lower house of which was elective, and this was continued with several breaks until the civil and military government of the islands was resumed by the Crown on the surrender of their rights by the Lords Proprietors on the 28th October 1717. Thirteen Proprietary Governors were appointed between 1671 and 1715. The settlement on New Providence was sacked by the Spaniards on several occasions between 1680 and 1684. In 1684 nearly all the inhabitants were driven away, and it was not until 1688 that the settlement was re-formed by their return, principally from Jamaica, under the leadership of Thomas Bridges. Bridges was recognised as Governor by the Lords Proprietors on the 12th July 1688, and the settlement had reached some importance when it was practically annihilated by the French and Spaniards in 1703. However, a year or so after this the dispersed inhabitants returned to New Providence and another Proprietary Governor was appointed in 1707. But the islands became a regular rendezvous for pirates, and this finally determined the Crown to resume the civil and military government of the place, thus acceding to the numerous petitions which the inhabitants had been making for several years and also carrying out the express wishes of Parliament. Since 1717 there has been a continuous line of Royal Governors. The islands were surrendered to a fleet of the American rebels in 1776 and again to the Spaniards in 1781, but they had been re-taken by a British force under Colonel Deveaux before the conclusion of the war in 1783, when British possession was confirmed.

A significant event in Bahamian history was the influx of Loyalists who had asked to remain under British rule after the Treaty of Versailles. In 1783-84, when the islands' population was 4,058, the Loyalists started to arrive with their families and slaves. By 1789 the population had risen to more than 11,000. The names of some 630 Loyalist families are to be found widely distributed throughout all sections of the community today. The Loyalists received substantial assistance from England, and on the 19th March 1787 the Lords Proprietors surrendered all their proprietary rights to the King for the sum of £12,000, provided by Parliament.

The final abolition of slavery in 1838 caused an economic and social change in the Bahamas. The outbreak of civil war in the United States led to a period of considerable prosperity: between the years 1861 and 1865 they became a depot for vessels running the blockade imposed against the Confederate States.

Q*

However, the boom years were followed by a period of slump during which occurred one of the worst hurricanes in the islands' history. The hurricane struck New Providence on 1st October 1866, causing widespread damage. In the latter part of the nineteenth century efforts were made to exploit a number of commercial products, such as sisal, conch shells for cameo brooch-making, and pineapples. The sponge industry was also established and at its height in 1901 employed nearly 6,000 men or roughly one-third of the available labour force. The early 1900s were nonetheless lean years and it was not until 1920, when Nassau became an entrepôt for the American bootlegging trade that some degree of prosperity returned, and remained until the end of the prohibition era. In 1939 the sponge industry collapsed as the result of a fungus disease and the islands' fortunes again appeared to be on a downward trend but since World War II the country has experienced phenomenal growth, based almost entirely on the success of the tourist industry and more recently on the banking industry. Taxation advantages, economic and political stability have encouraged foreign investments; and millions of pounds have poured into the Bahamas during the last two decades.

Up to 1964, representative but not responsible government existed in the Bahamas. The executive government was in the hands of a Governor, appointed by the Crown, who had the power of veto and was advised by an Executive Council of not more than nine members of whom six were unofficials. Various executive powers and the right to enact certain subsidiary legislation were vested by law in the Governor in Council. A Legislative Council had been created as a separate Council by Royal Letters Patent in 1841; and in 1963 it consisted of eleven members nominated by the Crown, of whom nine were unofficials.

The Turks and Caicos Islands (*q.v.*) which are a geographical part of the Bahamas chain and which had often in their early history been claimed both by Bermuda and the Bahamas, were separated from the Bahamas in 1848.

CONSTITUTIONAL DEVELOPMENT

At the Constitutional Conference held in 1963, constitutional changes were agreed. These were embodied in a written constitution which came into effect early in 1964, giving the territory internal selfgovernment. The bi-cameral Legislature was reconstituted to consist of an Upper House called the Senate and a Lower House called the House of Assembly. The Senate then consisted of fifteen members of whom eight were appointed by the Governor after consultation with the Premier and such other persons as he may in his discretion have decided to consult, five by the Governor on the advice of the Premier, and two by the Governor on the advice of the Leader of the Opposition. Following the general election of January 1967 the House of Assembly consisted of 38 members elected under universal adult franchise, 21 representing Out Island constituencies and 17 from New Providence. The Cabinet consisted of a Premier and not less than eight other Ministers. The Governor appointed as Premier the person who appeared to him to be best able to command a majority in the House of Assembly. The remaining Ministers were appointed by the Governor on the advice of the Premier. The Premier and his Ministers were members of the Progressive Liberal Party. The United Bahamian Party was recognised as the official opposition.

In December 1967 a seven-man committee was appointed to make recommendations for constitutional advance to full internal self-government. Subsequently the death of a Member of the House of Assembly necessitated a General Election at which on 10th April 1968 the Progressive Liberal Party won 29 seats and the United Bahamian Party won seven seats. One representative of the Labour Party and one Independent (the Speaker of the House) were returned as before.

Formal proposals on constitutional advance together with the comments of the Opposition parties were forwarded to London later in the year and these were the basic documents for a Constitutional Conference held in September, 1968. The proposals agreed at this Conference were incorporated in the Bahama Islands (Constitution) Order 1969 which came into operation on 10th May of that year. There have been no amendments to this constitution.

The Constitution provides that the territory should have an advanced measure of self-government, be called the Commonwealth of the Bahama Islands and that there shall be a Prime Minister appointed by the Governor from amongst the Representatives. The Governor is appointed by the British Government and he is assisted by a Deputy Governor whom he appoints.

The Cabinet consists of the Prime Minister and not less than 8 other Ministers, one of whom shall be the Minister of Finance appointed on the advice of the Prime Minister. The Cabinet has the general direction and control of the government and is collectively responsible therefore to the legislature.

The Senate consists of 16 members, 9 of whom are appointed by the Governor on the advice of the Prime Minister, 4 on the advice of the Leader of the Opposition and 3 after consultation with the Prime Minister and such other persons as the Governor in his discretion may decide to consult. The period for which the Senate may delay non-money bills and taxation bills is 9 months.

The House of Assembly has a membership of 38 elected Representatives known as Members of Parliament.

The Governor retains ultimate responsibility for the Royal Bahamas Police Force and for internal security: he is required to entrust immediate responsibility for these matters to a Minister designated on the advice of the Prime Minister. This Minister is required to keep the Governor and the Security Council informed on all important matters of policy within the field of entrusted responsibility.

There is a Security Council appointed by the Governor of which he is the Chairman. Other members are the Prime Minister, another Minister and such other persons as the Governor may appoint after consulting the Prime Minister. The Council discusses matters of policy relating to external affairs, defence, the police and internal security, considers matters relating to the police and internal security, and advises the Governor on the discharge of his ultimate responsibility for the police and internal security. In the discharge of the responsibility he is not obliged to accept the advice of the Council, and may, at his discretion act on his own account and give to the Commissioner of Police such instructions as he might think fit.

The Governor is responsible for defence and external affairs but is required to consult Ministers through the Security Council on matters which might involve the political, economic or financial interests of the territory. The British Government has delegated to the Government of the Bahamas authority to negotiate and conclude trade agreements with other countries or the United

States of purely local concern, or relating to technical assistance or emigration

During 1970 the Progressive Liberal Party split and eight of its supporters later created a new party and were recognised by the Governor as the Opposition in place of the United Bahamian Party.

The next General Election must be held on or before the 10th April, 1973. Under the Representation of the Peoples Act, 1969, all persons over the age of 18 years, of Bahamian status and not subject to the usual disqualifications are entitled to apply for registration as voters.

LAND POLICY

The Status of Aliens Act (Cap. 237) empowers an alien to acquire and hold property within the Commonwealth of the Bahama Islands.

GOVERNMENT

CABINET

Prime Minister: The Hon. Lynden O. Pindling, MP
Deputy Prime Minister and Minister of Home Affairs: The Hon. Arthur D. Hanna. MP
Minister of Finance: The Hon. Carlton E. Francis, MP
Minister of Works: The Hon. Livingston N. Coakley, MP
Minister of Education and Culture: The Hon. Carlton E. Francis, MP
Minister of Health: The Hon. Clement T. Maynard, MP
Minister of Tourism and Telecommunications: The Hon. Clement T. Maynard, MP
Minister of Agriculture and Fisheries, Labour and Welfare: The Hon. Milo B. Butler, MP
Minister of Development: The Hon. Jeffrey M. Thompson, MP
Minister of Transport: Dr. The Hon. Doris L. Johnson, MP
Minister of State: The Hon. C. Darling, MP

SENATE

President: The Hon. L. J. Knowles, CBE
Vice President: The Hon. K. G. L. Isaacs CBE, QC
and 15 other nominated members

HOUSE OF ASSEMBLY

Speaker: The Hon. A. R. Braynen, MP
Deputy Speaker: The Hon. Arlington Butler, MP
and 36 other elected members

CIVIL ESTABLISHMENT

Governor and Commander-in-Chief: The Rt. Hon. Lord Thurlow, KCMG
Deputy Governor: L. M. Davies, CMG, OBE
A.D.C.: Col. J. Chapman, CVO, OBE.

Secretary to the Cabinet: R. E. Bain
Financial Secretary, Ministry of Finance: R. L. Wood
Chairman, Public Service Commissioner: J. H. Bamforth
Permanent Secretary, Ministry of External Affairs: (Vacant)
Permanent Secretary, Local Government Division: C. P. Erskine-Lindop
Permanent Secretary, Ministry of Home Affairs: B. B. Bethel
Permanent Secretary, Ministry of Agriculture and Fisheries: O. S. Russell
Permanent Secretary, Ministry of Labour and Welfare: C. A. P. Smith
Permanent Secretary, Ministry of Development: Mrs J. Bethel
Permanent Secretary, Ministry of Education and Culture: H. Sands
Permanent Secretary, Ministry of Health: H. Munnings

Permanent Secretary, Ministry of Transport: H. H. Thompson
Permanent Secretary, Ministry of Works: A. K. Wright, MC
Permanent Secretary, Ministry of Tourism and Telecommunications: E. A. Thompson
Director of Agriculture: C. E. M. Smith
Director of Agriculture: C. W. Lynn, CBE
Auditor: K. H. E. Albury
Director of Lands and Surveys: R. E. A. Sweetnam
Director of Education: Lewis Morgan (acting)
Director of Statistics: J. E. Tertullien
Director of Immigration: (vacant)
Director of Civil Aviation: D. A. F. Ingraham
Superintendent of Prisons: C. E. Albury

Law Officers:
Attorney-General: G. D. M. Collett
Solicitor-General: Langton Hilton
Chief Medical Officer: (Vacant)
Director of Tourism: S. N. Chib
Chief Out-Island Commissioner: V. A. Knowles, BEM
Port Director: Leon Flowers (acting)
Commissioner of Police (and Provost Marshal): (vacant)

Postmaster: C. Saunders
Director of Public Works: C. Cooper
Registrar-General: B. W. Prescod
Controller of Road Traffic: R. V. E. Wood
Treasurer: O. M. Watson
Comptroller of Customs: (vacant)
Manager, Bahamas Money Authority: T. B. Donaldson
Parliamentary Registrar: A. A. Dean

JUDICIARY

Justices of the Court of Appeal:
Sir Paget Bourke: Sir Clyde Archer; Sir Michael Hogan CMG, QC
Chief Justice: Sir Gordon W. G. Bryce, CBE, TD
Puisne Judges: H. C. Smith; J. A. Smith, CBE, TD
Chief Magistrate: K. H. J. Ireland
Registrar: M. J. Tompson OBE

READING LIST

BRUCE, P. H. Bahamian Interlude. Reprinted from the Memories of Bruce, 1782. *London, Culmer,* 1949.

CARTWRIGHT, W. W. Pocket Guide to Nassau, *Nassau,* 1951.

CRATON, M. A. A. History of the Bahamas. *London, Collins,* 1962.

DOWSON, W. A. Mission to the West India Islands: Dawson's Journal for 1810-17. *Nassau, Deans Peggs Research Fund,* 1960.

FARQUHARSON, J. A. Relic of Slavery: Farquharson's Journal for 1831-32. *Nassau, Deans Peggs Research Fund,* 1957.

HANNAU, H. W. Nassau in the Bahamas. *Munich, W. Andermann Verlag,* 1962.

MALCOLM, Harcourt. Historical Documents relating to the Bahama Islands. *Nassau,* 1910.

MANWARING, G. E. Woodes Rogers, Privateer and Governor. *Nassau, Deans Peggs Research Fund,* 1957.

OLDMIXON, J. History of the Isle of Providence. First published in The British Empire in America, 1741. *London, Culmer,* 1949.

PEGGS, A. Deans. A Short History of the Bahamas. *Nassau,* 1959.

RICHARDSON, J. Henry. Review of Bahamian Economic Conditions and Post-War Problems. *Nassau,* 1944.

THOMPSON, T. A. Short Geography of the Bahamas. *Nassau,* 1944.

WAKEFIELD, A. J. Report on Agricultural Development in the Bahamas. *Nassau,* 1942.

Bahamas Handbook and Businessmen's Annual, edited by E. Dupuch and S. J. Perfetti. 5th ed. *Nassau, E. Dupuch,* 1968-69.

Bahma Islands Report, Government Information Services, 1968-69.

BERMUDA

THE Bermudas or Somers Islands derived their names from the Spanish seaman Juan Bermudez, who sighted the group before 1515, but no settlement was made until 1609, when Sir George Somers, who was shipwrecked on his way to Virginia, colonised the islands. Bermuda is situated in the Western Atlantic Ocean about 570 miles east of Cape Hatteras, North Carolina, 32° 18′ N. latitude, 64° 46′ W. longitude. Until 1940 it had an area of 19·34 square miles. As a result of work done by the United States authorities since 1940 to unite and extend some of the islands with materials dredged from the sea, their total area is now 20·59 square miles, of which 2·30 square miles are leased to the Government of the United States for naval and military bases, leaving 18·29 square miles available to the civil population. The United States bases include a large airfield which is used by both military and commercial traffic.

The Bermudas consist of about 150 islands and islets, roughly in the form of a fishhook, along the southern rim of the oval plateau summit, about 22 miles from east to west and 14 miles from north to south, of a steep submarine volcanic mountain which is reputed to be between 14,000 and 15,000 feet in height. The ten principal islands are connected by bridges and form a chain about 22 miles long between its north-east and south-west extremities. These islands vary in width but the main island, which is about 14 miles long, has an average width of about one mile; it contains about 9,000 acres of land, the highest point being only 259·4 feet above the sea. All the other islands and the areas reclaimed for the United States Bases aggregate about 4,240 acres. There are no rivers or lakes.

The City of Hamilton, the capital since 1815, with a population estimated at about 2,500, is situated on the main island. The town of St George on the island of St George was formerly the capital. Its population is estimated at about 2,000.

The climate is generally mild and humid with a mean annual temperature of 70°F and average annual maximum and minimum temperatures of 90°F and 47°F respectively. The coldest and hottest months are February and August. The average annual rainfall is 58·1 inches.

Bermuda's last census held in 1970, revealed a resident civil population of 53,000. All the statistics resulting from the census will not be tabulated before late 1971. The official language is English.

During 1970, 1,061 births were recorded, representing a birth-rate of 20·44 per 1,000. For the first time in 10 years an increase in the birth rate has been recorded. The death-rate in 1970 was 7·42 per 1,000. The Department of Health and Welfare is responsible for providing medical services and facilities. These include baby and pre-school clinics, and medical and dental services for school children. There are four hospitals: King Edward VII Memorial (general hospital) (230 beds); St Brendan's (mental hospital) (240 beds); Prospect and Lefroy House (geriatric hospitals).

At the end of 1970 the total number of persons employed, excluding US citizens at the American bases, totalled 24,700. The principal occupations were: domestic, private and hotels 3,338; office clerks, etc. 4,337; shop assistants 2,021; labourers 1,147; masons 700; wood-workers 558; teachers 710; truck drivers 1,011; telecommunications 427.

There are eight registered trade unions: Bermuda Industrial Union, membership 3,494; Amalgamated Bermuda Union of Teachers (374); Bermuda Employers Council (119); Bermuda Civil Service Association (393); Electricity Supply Trade Union (148); Bermuda Federation of Variety Artists (314); the Union of Government Industrial Employees (89); Hotel Employers of Bermuda (25).

The area of arable land, always small, is steadily diminishing owing to encroachment by building development. Of 740 acres now remaining some 300 acres are utilised for vegetable crops, 220 for fruit and 50 for flowers. The climate permits double cropping for most vegetables and four crops a year for beans. The value of the 1970 vegetable crop was $687,760. Bananas valued at $222,410 and citrus fruits valued at $72,000 were produced. Cut flowers valued at $19,227 were exported.

Dairy farming is the most important branch of agriculture. The quantity and value of produce was: eggs 1,354,600 dozen, $1,307,508; milk 479,694 gallons, $479,694; poultry 86,440 lb, $20,736; pork 209,400 lb, $50,156; beef 200,000 lb, $50,000.

A major undertaking of the Department of Agriculture and Fisheries since 1949 has been re-afforestation. Work started as a result of losing 80 per cent of the native cedar trees through a severe infestation of the juniper scale. Clearance of the dead areas and planting of the cleared areas began in 1952.

Research is being conducted at the Government Aquarium into the development potential of deep sea fishing. The rocky sea bed makes trawling impracticable and most fish are caught by pots, hand-lines and seines. In 1970 the estimated catch was 140,000 lb. of spiny lobsters and 1,450,000 lb of fish (dressed weight), value $720,000. Commercial fishing boats are available for hire. The principal game-fish are marlin, tuna, dolphin, wahoo, bonito, amberjack and barracuda.

The principal imports and exports by value are shown in the table on page 486.

The tourist industry in 1970 continued to provide Bermuda's major source of revenue. The trade is maintaining a satisfactory growth rate:

	1967	1968	1969	1970
Regular visitors (living ashore) ..	237,163	167,442	280,987	302,776
Cruise passengers (living aboard ship)	44,004	63,937	89,933	86,138
TOTALS	281,167	331,379	370,920	388,914

The tourist industry had an estimated value to Bermuda of £14,477,000 in 1966, £18,420,000 in 1967, £26,117,953 in 1968, £27,500,000 in 1969 and £30,400,000 in 1970.

The pattern of tourist origins remained steady with 84 per cent from the USA, 10 per cent from Canada and 3 per cent from the United Kingdom.

Expansion of tourist facilities included an increase in the number of hotel beds from 5,655 in 1967 to 7,440 in 1971.

The promotion of tourism is the responsibility of the Bermuda Department of Tourism and Trade Development which has its head office in Hamilton and branch offices in London, New York, Chicago and Toronto.

Bermuda has two ports, Hamilton, the present capital, centrally situated on a deep-water landlocked harbour and including the former Royal Navy dockyard and basin, situated at the western end of the island in Sandys Parish, and St

Principal Imports

Commodity	1968 Quantity	1968 Value £	1969 Quantity	1969 Value £	1970 Quantity	1970 Value B$
Beef, fresh	1,717 tons	1,153,846	1,745 tons	1,449,811	2,063,617 lbs.	2,571,621·09
Poultry and Game	1,015 tons	366,084	1,112 tons	406,126	1,073,900 lbs.	855,794·39
Butter	408 tons	95,434	423 tons	91,523	397,366 lbs.	180,481·19
Milk, evaporated and tinned	84,455 cases	135,732	65,757 cases	128,765	132,951 lbs.	144,366·44
Flour	2,415 tons	138,397	2,373 tons	147,274	1,613,252 lbs.	186,836·83
Sugar	2,552 tons	79,495	1,794 tons	89,354	1,066,804 lbs.	154,190·83
Malt liquor	808,930 gal.	410,879	839,961 gal.	483,360	368,105 gal.	730,746·20
Whiskey	98,705 gal.	284,350	116,764 gal.	336,213	95,772 gal.	481,610·51
Tobacco		336,042		299,474	474,054 lbs.	685,274·73
Lumber	4,440,000 feet	271,260	5,333 feet	368,753	1,598,106 B.feet	1,030,776·92
Footwear, leather	13,891 cases	492,884	33,753 cases	468,128	159,963 pairs	1,347,724·05
Cotton clothing	53,971 pkgs	1,124,026	48,392 pkgs	1,440,096	165,512 c/s lbs.	1,726,921·42
Woollen clothing	12,817 pkgs	962,101	11,807 pkgs	1,053,479	130,999 c/s lbs.	2,231,493·64
Rayon clothing	1,154 pkgs	88,424	1,047 pkgs	101,783	459,961 c/s lbs.	4,447,658·93
Hardware	62,102 cases	520,816	41,632 cases	631,779	6,517 c/s	1,989,316·74
Furniture	32,492 cases	777,127	40,188 cases	1,107,799	1,611,734 c/s lbs.	1,329,624·15
Electrical supplies	83,689 cases	1,516,002	60,836 cases	2,135,889	16,458 c/s	1,647,862·59
Motor vehicles (passenger)	1,607 No.	727,169	2,392 No.	1,047,111	26,266 No.	622,751·49
Petrol	4,931,530 gal.	229,123	7,890,708 gal.	392,069	3,179,312 gal.	921,291·22
Diesel oil	42,758 tons	365,965	24,469 tons	196,176	3,266,679 tons	

Principal Domestic Exports

Commodity	1968 Quantity	1968 Value £	1969 Quantity	1969 Value £	1970 Quantity	1970 Value B$
Concentrated essences	8,006 pkgs	450,855	3,427 pkgs	991,629	4,602 pkgs	667,359·92
Flowers cut	1,953 pkgs	9,608	1,364 pkgs	7,168	1,705 crates	19,227·42
Pharmaceutical	90 pkgs	32,609	—	8,280	— pkgs	1,718·90
Beauty preparing	9 pkgs	58,866	348 pkgs	73,001	72 pkgs	216,238·14

George, the former capital, also situated on a deep-water landlocked harbour at the east end of the islands and including an oil dock at Murray's Anchorage on the north shore of St George's Parish. Three large, two-storey, covered wharves and one open wharf extend along the Hamilton waterfront. The three covered wharves accommodate ocean-going vessels drawing not more than 26·5 feet; the two eastern ones have a combined water frontage of 1,100 feet and the western one has a water frontage of 455 feet. The open wharf, which is between them, is 150 feet long with a depth of 24 feet of water alongside. At the eastern end of the port installations there is an area of some two acres which is used as a container park. There is also offshore anchorage in the harbour for three ocean-going vessels. The fuelling depot of the Royal Navy is now managed on behalf of the Admiralty by the Shell Company of Bermuda, Limited, and is sometimes used to bunker commercial vessels. Because of the depth of water and the crane facilities in the former dockyard it is occasionally used by commercial vessels to load or unload heavy cargoes, or by the Ports Authority for repairs. In St George there are two wharves: Penno's which is 1,200 feet long with a depth of 32 feet of water alongside, and Ordance Island which is 350 feet long with 24 feet of water alongside. There is also offshore anchorage in the harbour for ocean-going vessels. The oil dock at Murray's Anchorage is operated by Esso Standard Oil, S.A., and has a depth of 33 feet of water alongside. The berthing arrangements and supervision of shipping in the harbours is the responsibility of the Department of Marine and Ports Services. The construction and maintenance of harbour buildings, wharves, etc., and dredging within the harbours, are the responsibilities of the Corporations of Hamilton and St George.

Direct or indirect seaborne passenger and cargo services are maintained with varying frequency and regularity with all parts of the world by the following shipping lines: Bermuda Shipping Company, Booth-Import, Furness-Withy, Independent Gulf, Isbrandsten, Manz, Pacific Steam Navigation, Royal Mail, Saguenay and Cunard.

The only airfield is at the United States Naval Air Station, which was originally constructed during the last war solely for military purposes. In 1948 this base, known as Kindley Field, was opened to civil aircraft in accordance with the provisions of a treaty agreement between the Governments of the United States of America and the United Kingdom. The base itself is leased to the United States Government for 99 years. Civil aircraft are handled in a sub-leased area at the western end of the airfield which has been extended to accommodate 'Jumbo Jets'. Both military and civil aircraft use the same runways and technical facilities of air traffic control, communications, weather and navigation aids. The airlines serving Bermuda are B.O.A.C., Pan American, Eastern, Northeast Airlines, Air Canada and Qantas.

There are 132 miles of central and local Government roads, most of which are surfaced; they include 3·55 miles reserved for cyclists and pedestrians. There are also many surfaced 'estate roads' and unsurfaced private roads.

Prior to 1946 there was little broadcasting in Bermuda and local listeners relied principally on broadcasts from North America and England. In 1943 the Bermuda Broadcasting Company was formed and in 1946 started commercial broadcasting with the call-sign ZBM on 1,240 kc/s with a power output of 250 watts. In 1953 a second station ZBM-2 was opened and in 1962 power on both stations was increased to 1,000 watts and an FM station, ZBM-FM, was inaugurated. 1962 also saw the formation of a second commercial broadcasting company, Capital Broadcasting, using the call-sign ZFB, which operates with 1,000 watts power. All stations broadcast 24 hours a day except for the FM station which operates from 0700-2200 hours daily. In 1968 ZBM-FM inaugurated stereophonic transmission.

Bermuda's first commercial television station ZBM-TV began operations in January 1958, and now operates for approximately nine hours daily. In August 1964 the Bermuda Government granted to Atlantic Broadcasting Co. Ltd a licence to establish and operate a second commercial television channel. This station, ZFB-TV, began broadcasting in August 1965 and now operates for approximately nine hours daily.

Income tax and estate duty are not levied in Bermuda but legislative approval was given in 1967 for the introduction of a property tax. This tax is similar to the rates levied by local authorities in the United Kingdom. Revenue is mainly derived from customs duties and 1970 these duties accounted for $18,116,125 of the Government's total revenue of $36,808,215. Miscellaneous stamp duties accounted for $2,086,724. Company taxes realised $1,123,926, vehicle licences $1,656,229 and omnibus services $1,067,278. The new land tax for 1970 realised $1,660,605. In accordance with the provisions of the Exempted Undertakings Tax Protection Act 1966, foreign companies can be granted freedom from liability for present or future taxes computed on profits or income or capital assets, gains and appreciation. Undertakings operating in the Bermuda freeport also obtain customs tariff concessions.

Retail price indices for the period 1960-1970 for working class families (January 1961 = 100) were:

1960 Average		..	—
1961	„	..	—
1962	„	..	101
1963	„	..	102
1964	„	..	104
1965	„	..	105
1966	„	..	107
1967	„	..	111
1968	„	..	123·1
1969	„	..	128·6
October 1970	„	..	140·4

Government expenditure in 1970 was $34,023,246 and the Public Debt at 31st December 1970 was $5,205,600.

The general administration of education is vested by law in the Member of the Executive Council responsible for education, who is assisted by a Parliamentary Secretary and an Advisory Board. Primary education was provided free for the first time in 1949 for children over 7 and under 13 years of age. Attendance between those ages had long been compulsory and continued until 1965 when it was extended to 5 to 15 years. In 1969 the leaving age was raised to 16. There are 42 Aided and Maintained schools providing free education, and 3 private schools at which fees are charged. The management of 35 of the schools is carried on by the Department of Education, that of the remainder being vested in local governing bodies. Secondary education is provided at six of the schools under the administration of the Board of Education and at five other schools. A sixth form centre has been established to prepare students for advanced level G.C.E. examinations. The entrance qualification is five or more G.C.E. passes at the ordinary level or their equivalent. Technical training, including technical high school and trades training courses, is provided at the Technical Institute, while the four new secondary schools include training of a practical nature (woodwork, metalwork, domestic science and shorthand-typewriting) in their syllabuses. There is a training school for delinquent boys and another for delinquent girls up to the age of 17. There is also a free school for handicapped children and four special schools for educationally sub-normal children.

Higher education is not available in Bermuda, but one Rhodes Scholarship and six others tenable at universities abroad may be awarded annually. There are also a number of scholarships offered by the Department of Education to enable prospective teachers to take training courses abroad. Government expenditure on education in 1970 was $6,747,152.

The Member of the Executive Council responsible for education is also responsible for the Libraries Department. This is a subscription library which was opened in 1839. In 1969 the total book stock was 87,279 volumes and there were 5,471 registered borrowers. Weekly Radio Book broadcasts and programmes of classical music are presented by staff members.

HISTORY

According to the Spanish navigator and historian Ferdinand d'Oviedo, who sailed close to the islands in 1515, they were discovered by Juan Bermudez. A 17th century French cartographer gives the date of their discovery as 1503 and there is evidence that the islands were known as 'La Bermuda' by 1510. The Spaniards do not appear to have taken any steps to form a settlement and the islands were still entirely uninhabited when in 1609 Admiral Sir George Somer's ship *The Sea Venture* was wrecked upon one of the reefs while carrying a party of colonists to Virginia. Reports of the beauty and fertility of the land caused the Virginia Company to seek an extension of their charter so as to include the islands within their dominion. This was granted by King James I in 1612 and the first emigrants went out in that year. Shortly afterwards the Virginia Company sold the islands for £2,000 to a new body of adventurers called 'The Governor and Company of the City of London for the Plantation of the Somers Islands', and for a considerable time afterwards the islands bore that name. In 1684 the charter of the Bermuda Company of London was annulled and government passed to the Crown.

As in the West Indies, slavery was permitted from the colony's earliest days, but following William Wilberforce's crusade in England it was abolished absolutely in Bermuda in 1834.

Later in the nineteenth century, following the inauguration of steamship services, Bermuda, in addition to enjoying a profitable agricultural export trade in vegetables, gradually became noted for its climate and charm. Slowly the tourist trade grew, many visitors coming annually to escape the rigorous North American winters and, as larger and faster ships were built and hotels erected, it finally became the colony's most important business. Since the Second World War, the tourist season has become virtually year-round, with the greatest influx of visitors coming during the long summer season.

The year 1959 was the 350th anniversary of the settlement of Bermuda. Throughout the year a comprehensive programme of functions and celebrations was carried out, and a special Crown piece was issued by the Royal Mint. His

Royal Highness Prince Philip, Duke of Edinburgh, paid a flying visit in April 1959.

The Parliamentary Election Act, passed in December 1962, marked an important step in the political evolution in Bermuda. Throughout its history, members of the House of Assembly had been elected by the privileged few who could meet a freehold voting qualification (5,500 in 1962). The new act enfranchised everyone over the age of 25, thus creating a potential electorate of 22,000, while retaining for property-owners the privilege of an extra vote.

Bermuda's first political party, the Progressive Labour Party, was formed shortly before the elections held in May 1963 but the majority of seats was won by independent candidates. In the following year however most of the independent members formed a second party, the United Bermuda Party.

In November 1963 the Legislature appointed a Joint Select Committee to consider constitutional change. In an interim report the Committee recommended the abolition of the additional Property Vote and reduction of the voting age from twenty-five to twenty-one years. These changes became law early in 1966.

In its second report, published in November 1965 the Joint Select Committee made detailed recommendations for constitutional change. This report was accepted by the Legislature and subsequently a Constitutional Conference was convened in London in November 1966. In addition to the Governor and the Attorney-General, a representative delegation consisting of eighteen members of the Legislature attended. A new Constitution providing responsible internal self-government came into force on 8th June, 1968, following a General Election on 22nd May, which resulted in the United Bermuda Party winning 30 seats in the House of Assembly and the Progressive Labour Party became the official opposition holding the other ten seats. The election campaign was marred by an outbreak, during April, of two days of civil disorder, which resulted in few casualties but over £400,000 in property damage due mainly to arson.

His Royal Highness the Prince of Wales visited Bermuda from 20 October to 22 October in connection with the 350th Anniversary of Bermuda's Parliament.

CONSTITUTION

Following the constitutional conference held in London in November 1966, a new written constitution was introduced on 8th June 1968 providing a responsible form of government.

The House of Assembly adopted the report of a Boundaries Commission that the general election, held on 22nd May 1968, should result in 20 constituencies each sending two members to parliament under full universal adult suffrage.

Under the new constitution the Executive Council is drawn from the Legislature, to which it is responsible, and the Governor is normally bound to act on the advice of the Executive Council except in relation to external affairs, defence, internal security and the police, for which subjects he retains special responsibility.

The Governor appoints as Government Leader the member of the House of Assembly whom he thinks best able to command the confidence of a majority of members, and other appointments to Executive Council and the allocation of portfolios and the appointment of Parliamentary Secretaries are made on the advice of the Government Leader.

The Legislative Council, which has power to delay legislation and to introduce and amend Bills other than Money Bills, consists of eleven members. Five are appointed by the Governor in his discretion, four on the advice of the Government Leader and two members on the advice of the Opposition Leader.

There are an independent Judiciary and a Public Service Commission for Bermuda.

LAND POLICY

The Government has exercised control of development, in some form or other, for a considerable time.

In May 1962 it was decided to review town and country development in the light of a report submitted by a commission appointed in 1944 to survey housing in the Colony, and to make recommendations for the future control and development of buildings and land. Following the review in 1962, funds were provided and arrangements made for Mr H. Thornley Dyer, FRIBA, AMTPI, Town Planning Adviser for the Kenya Government from 1945-62, to come to Bermuda for six months to prepare a development plan for Bermuda. As a result of Mr Dyer's report a Bill was forwarded to the Legislature early in 1965 and became operative on 3rd August 1965. There is a Department of Planning for the orderly development of land and for the preservation and improvement of amenities, including the acquisition of land, compensation, appeals etc. The Development and Planning Act (1965) provides a comprehensive code for the control of development having due regard to private interests where they conflict with the public need. Final development plans, based on Mr Dyer's recommendations and drafted for Legislative approval, were approved by the legislature at the end of 1968.

GOVERNMENT

THE EXECUTIVE COUNCIL

H.E. The Governor and Commander-in-Chief
Government Leader: Hon. Sir Henry Tucker, CBE, JP, MCP
Member for Immigration and Labour: Hon. Sir Edward Richards, Kt, CBE, JP, MCP
Member for Finance: Hon. John H. Sharpe, JP, MCP
Member for Education: Dr the Hon. E. S. D. Ratteray, JP
Member for Trade and Tourism: Hon. David E. Wilkinson, JP, MCP
Member for Agriculture and Works: Hon. John M. S. Patton, GC, JP, MCP
Member for Health and Welfare: Hon. Mrs McPhee, JP, MCP
Member for Ports and Civil Aviation: Hon. James E. Pearman, CBE, JP, MCP
Member for Planning: Hon. C. Vail Zuill, CBE, JP, MCP
Member for Transport: Hon. F. John Barritt, JP, MCP
Member for Government Organisation: Hon. John R. Plowman, OBE, JP
Member without Portfolio, particularly concerned with Youth Activities:
Hon. Lancelot Swan, JP, MCP

Secretary to Executive Council: W. W. Wallace, OBE, DSC
N.B. All Members of Executive Council are ex-officio J.P.'s

THE LEGISLATIVE COUNCIL

Hon. George O. Ratteray, CBE (President)
Hon. Arnold A. Francis (Vice-President)
Hon. John R. Plowman, OBE
Hon. E. Harley Barnes
Hon. Richard M. Gorham, DFC
Hon. E. Stanley Ratteray
Hon. Hugh E. Richardson
Hon. Arthur D. O. Hodgson
Hon. Gilbert A. Cooper, CBE, ED, JP
Hon. Sir Baynard Dill, CBE
Hon. Norman R. Roberts, JP
Clerk: A. D. Eve

His Honour the Speaker: Lieut.-Col. The Hon. J. C. Astwood, CBE, ED, MCP

Deputy Speaker: E. W. P. Vesey, MCP
40 Elected Members
Clerk: S. C. Tatem

Sergeant-at-Arms: T. S. Weldon
(Members of the House of Assembly are designated MCP)

LOCAL GOVERNMENT

There are two municipalities—The City of Hamilton (incorporated 1793 and made a city by act of legislation in 1897) which is governed by a corporation: and the town of St George (incorporated 1797) one of the oldest settlements in the Western Hemisphere and the capital of Bermuda until 1815. Charges for dock facilities and water are the Hamilton corporation's main source of revenue but both governing bodies derive revenue from rents and municipal taxes.

HAMILTON
Mayor: The Worshipful G. A. Cooper, CBE, ED, JP
Secretary: H. A. Leseur

ST GEORGE'S:
Mayor: The Worshipful N. R. Roberts, JP
Secretary: R. J. Pitcher

Parish vestries are elected annually for the administration of general parochial affairs of the Poor Law by the parishes of St George's, Hamilton, Smith's, Devonshire, Pembroke, Paget, Warwick, Southampton and Sandys. These vestries have authority to levy taxes and manage local affairs. They derive revenue from the collection of rates and from fees for liquor licences. The systems of law applicable in Bermuda are the common law, the doctrines of equity and all English Acts of general application which were in force on the 11th July 1612. These systems are subject to Acts passed in Bermuda since that date in any way altering, modifying or amending those laws or doctrines. The Public Acts and Statutory Instruments made thereunder were reprinted in 1964/5 and are now available in six loose-leaf volumes with a further volume containing tables and indices. There exists also an edition of private acts in two volumes.

CIVIL ESTABLISHMENT

GOVERNOR AND COMMANDER-IN-CHIEF: The Rt Hon. Lord Martonmere, PC, KCMG

Aide-de-Camp: Captain Sir Robert Green-Price

Chief Secretary: I. A. C. Kinnear
Secretary to Executive Council: W. W. Wallace, OBE, DSC
Financial Secretary: C. W. Kempe, OBE
Permanent Secretary (Education): S. Gascoigne
Permanent Secretary (Health and Welfare): J. B. Nichoson, OBE
Permanent Secretary (Labour and Immigration)/Labour Relations Officer: W. Perston
Collector of Customs: R. L. Gauntlett, OBE
Auditor: D. H. Owen

Director of Agriculture and Fisheries: G. R. Groves, OBE
Director of Civil Aviation: Wing Commander E. M. Ware, OBE, DFC
Director of Education: D. J. Williams
Chief Medical Officer: S. M. Frazer, OBE
Chief Immigration Officer: C. E. Thompson
Law Officers: Attorney-General: J. C. Summerfield, CBE, QC; Solicitor-General: A. W. Sedgwick
Director of Marine and Ports Services: E. J. C. Bennett

Registrar of the Supreme Court: J. L. Barrington-Jones, JP
Registrar-General: Mrs R. E. M. James, MBE
Director of Planning: M. I. Montague-Smith
Commissioner of Police: George Duckett, CBE
Postmaster: S. B. Corbett
Director, Public Transportation: J. B. Watlington
Director of Public Works: J. Smith
Director, Department of Tourism and Trade Development: W. J. Williams, OBE, MVO

JUDICIARY

Court of Appeal:
President: Sir Paget Bourke, SC
Members: Sir Clyde Archer
Sir Michael Joseph Hogan, CMG, QC
Chief Justice: Sir Myles Abbott
Puisne Judge: H. Barcilon
Senior Magistrate: R. H. Lownie
Magistrate: Richmond Smith

READING LIST

General

DYER, H. THORNLEY. The next twenty years; a report on the development plan for Bermuda, prepared by the Government of Bermuda. *Hamilton, Bermuda Press*, 1963.

HEYL, EDITH STOWE GODFREY. Bermuda's Early Days. Bermuda Department of Education, 1959. An account of Bermuda's early days of adventure and colonisation from 1511 to 1684.

HUMPHREYS, JOHN S. Bermuda Houses. *Boston, Marshall Jones*, 1923. The best era in local architecture is typified in the excellent illustrations and house plans contained in this book.

KENNEDY, SISTER JEAN DE CHANTAL. Biography of a Colonial Town. *Bermuda Book Store*, 1961. A history of Hamilton.

KERR, WILFRED BRENTON. Bermuda and the American Revolution. *Princeton University Press*, 1963. An instructive account of its subject.

LEFROY, J. H. Memorials of the Discovery and Early Settlement of the Bermudas or Somers Islands, 1515–1687, 2 vols. London. *Longmans Green*, 1877 and 1879. The standard work on Bermuda's history.

LUDINGTON, M. H. Post Office, Postal Markings and Adhesive Stamps of Bermuda. *London, Lowe*, 1962.

STRODE, HUDSON. Story of Bermuda. *New York, Smith*, 1932 and 1946. Contains outstanding photographs of different aspects of local life.

TUCKER, TERRY. Bermuda's Story. rev. ed. *Hamilton, Bermuda Book Store*, 1967. A simplified history, 1609–1966, commissioned by the Department of Education and first published by them in 1959.

WHITNEY, CHRISTINE M. The Bermuda Garden. *The Garden Club of Bermuda*, 1955. A comprehensive and beautifully illustrated book on gardening in Bermuda.

WILKINSON, HENRY C. The adventurers of Bermuda: a history of the island from its discovery until the dissolution of the Somers Island Company in 1684. *London, Oxford University Press*, 1958.

WILKINSON, HENRY C. Bermuda in the Old Empire, 1684–1784. *London, Oxford University Press*, 1950. (Both Dr Wilkinson's volumes contain useful bibliographies on the early history of Bermuda).

WILLOCK, ROGER. Bulwark of Empire: Bermuda's Fortified Naval Base, 1860–1920. *Princeton, privately printed*, 1962.

Guides and Manuals

BELL, EUPHEMIA YOUNG. Beautiful Bermuda. 10th edition, revised and enlarged by S. E. Bell and William A. Bell, New York and Bermuda. *Beautiful Bermuda Publishing Co.*, 1947. A comprehensive handbook, first published in 1902.

FODOR, EUGENE, ed. Fodor's Guide to the Caribbean, Bahamas and Bermuda. *London, Newman Neame Ltd.* Annual.

Biography

NORWOOD, RICHARD. Journal of Richard Norwood. *New York.* Scholar's Facsimiles and Reprints, 1945. A diary kept by the famous surveyor which gives a vivid picture of life in the islands during the seventeenth century.

Natural History

BEEBE, C. W. Nonsuch: Land of Water. *New York, Brewer Warren and Putnam,* 1932.

BEEBE, C. W. Field Book of the Shore Fishes of Bermuda. *New York, G. P. Putnam's Sons*, 1933.

Birds of the Bermudas. *Hamilton Book Stores*, n.d.

COX, WILLIAM N. Bermuda's Beginning. *London, C. Tinling and Co., Ltd.*, 1959. A booklet for the layman on the geological aspects of Bermuda.

VERRILL, ADDISON E. Bermuda Islands; an account of their scenery, productions, physiography, natural history and geology, with sketches of their discovery and early history and the change in their flora and fauna due to man. *New Haven, Conn., Addison E. Verrill,* 1902.

WATSON, JAMES WREFORD. A geography of Bermuda. *London, Collins*, 1965.

WINGATE, DAVID B. ed. A checklist of the birds, mammals, reptiles and amphibians of Bermuda, compiled by a committee of the Bermuda Audubon Society, Hamilton. *Bermuda Audubon Society*, 1959.

Periodicals

Bermuda Department of Agriculture and Fisheries. Monthly bulletin since January, 1925.

The Bermudan Churchman. *Church of England, Bermuda.* Jan. 1956—monthly. Formerly published as the Diocesan Magazine.

The Bermuda Historical Quarterly, 1944.

Bermudian Magazine. *Hamilton, Bermudian Publishing Co. Ltd.* 1930—monthly.

Newspapers

Bermuda Sun Weekly, 1964—
Mid-Ocean News, 1911—Weekly.
Recorder, 1938—Weekly.
Royal Gazette, 1784—Daily.

Reports

Bermuda Annual Report 1969. HMSO London 1971 SBN11 580059X.

Some of the books listed above are out of print but are available for reference in the Bermuda Library, Hamilton, Bermuda, and possibly also in other reference libraries abroad.

BRITISH ANTARCTIC TERRITORY

THE British Antarctic Territory was designated by an Order-in-Council which came into force on the 3rd March 1962, and with the exception of the island of South Georgia and the South Sandwich Islands, consists of the area previously known as the Falkland Islands Dependencies. The territory lies between longitudes 20° and 80°W. south of latitude 60°S. Within these bounds lie the South Orkneys, the South Shetlands and the Antarctic Peninsula, together with all adjacent islands and the land mass extending to the South Pole.

The majority of the islands in the territory are wild and rugged with many glaciers. The Antarctic Peninsula is mountainous, the highest peak being Mount Andrew Jackson (about 11,000 feet). There is a snow-covered plateau which extends along the peninsula but declines from 7,000 feet in the south to about 4,000 feet in the north. The main continental area is covered by ice and fringed by floating ice shelves, generally about 800 feet thick. The territory has a rigorous polar climate.

The British population of the territory consists solely of male scientists and technicians who man the British Antarctic Survey scientific stations. During the winter of 1971 the total number was 74. In the summer months when relief personnel arrive, together with summer field workers, this figure may almost double. The exact number of other nationals working in the area is not known. There are no towns in the territory and scientific and field stations are situated on various islands and parts of the mainland.

The Antarctic bases are relieved, resupplied and restaffed between November and May each year, by the Survey's Royal Research Ships *Bransfield* and *John Biscoe*. Two light aircraft, which are wintered in Canada, assist with the annual relief and provide support for field parties. One base, Fossil Bluff is supplied entirely by air from Adelaide Island.

In addition to normal radio communication, teleprinters link four of the bases to administrative offices in the Falkland Islands and London.

Until the year ended 30th June 1962 British Antarctic Territory finances were embodied in those of the Falkland Islands Dependencies. From 1st April 1967 responsibility for the British Antarctic Survey was transferred from the Commonwealth Office to the Ministry of Education and Science. The Survey and the territory were separately financed from 1st July 1967. The following table shows revenue and expenditure for the years 1968-71.

	Revenue	*Expenditure*
1969-70 British Antarctic Survey—	£68,404	£1,953,923
British Antarctic Territory—	£31,447	£11,052
1970-71 British Antarctic Survey—	£38,857	1,816,564 (estimated)
British Antarctic Territory—	£41,710	£69,357 (estimated)
1971-72 British Antarctic Survey—	£66,000	£1,355,800 (estimated)
British Antarctic Territory—	£39,910	£45,190 (estimated)

HISTORY

The main island group of the South Shetlands was discovered and taken possession of by Captain W. Smith in 1819, whilst the South Orkney Islands owe their discovery to Captain G. Powell in 1821.

The Antarctic Peninsula was discovered in 1820 by Edward Bransfield, R.N., and taken into the possession of Great Britain by John Biscoe in 1832. The penetration of what is now known as the Weddell Sea and the final discovery of the continental land masses to the south and east of the Antarctic Peninsula can be attributed to many great explorers—Cook, Weddell, Ross and Bruce to name but a few. Many of the islands within the territory were used as temporary bases for the early sealing and whaling expeditions, but at Deception Island of the South Shetlands Islands a more permanent and more active whaling station was in operation from 1906 to 1931. During this time a magistrate was in permanent residence for the summer months.

In the 1943-44 season, under the code name of 'Operation Tabarin', the first of what are now known as the British Antarctic Survey bases were established at Deception Island and Port Lockroy. Since then the number of occupied stations has at times been as many as 12 but in recent years the number has been 6, most stations being somewhat larger. In December 1967 Deception Island was temporarily evacuated because of a volcanic eruption. A second eruption in February 1969 partially destroyed the station, which has now been abandoned.

The locations of the occupied stations are:

Signy Island—South Orkney Islands 60° 43′ S., 45° 36′ W.

Argentine Islands (Galindez Island)—West coast of Graham Land 65° 15′ S., 64° 16′ W.

Adelaide Island—West coast of Graham Land 67° 46′ S., 68° 54′ W.

Stonington Island—Marguerite Bay 68° 11′ S., 67° 00′ W.

Fossil Bluff—George VI Sound 71° 20′ S., 68° 17′ W.

Halley Bay—Caird Coast 75° 30′ S., 26° 39′ W.

A station is also maintained by the Survey at King Edward Point, South Georgia (51° 17′ S., 36° 30′ W.) in the Falkland Islands Dependencies (*q.v.*).

Other bases which have been established, but are at present unoccupied, are:

Cape Geddes, Laurie Island, South Orkney Islands.

Admiralty Bay, King George Island, South Shetland Islands.

View Point, Duse Bay.

Deception Island, South Shetland Islands.

Hope Bay, Trinity Peninsula.

Danco Coast, Graham Land.

Anvers Island, Palmer Archipelago (now used as a summer air facility).

Port Lockroy, Wiencke Island, Palmer Archipelago.

Prospect Point, Graham Coast.

Detaille Island, Loubet Coast, Graham Land.

Horseshoe Island, Marguerite Bay.

The territory is administered by the High Commissioner, resident in Stanley, Falkland Islands.

A Court of Appeal was set up on the 1st July 1965 for the purpose of hearing and determining appeals from the courts of the territory.

HIGH COMMISSIONERS

1962 Sir Edwin Arrowsmith, KCMG
1964 Sir Cosmo Haskard, KCMG, MBE
1971 Mr E. G. Lewis, OBE

DIRECTOR, BRITISH ANTARCTIC SURVEY
Sir Vivian Fuchs

READING LIST

CHRISTIE, E. W. H. The Antarctic Problem. *Allen & Unwin*, 1951.

COLEMAN-COOKE, J. Discovery II in the Antarctic. *Odhams Press*, 1963.

KING, H. G. R. The Antarctic. *Blandford Press, Ltd.*, 1969.

PRIESTLEY, R. E. *et al.*, Eds.. Antarctic Research: A Review of British Scientific Achievement in Antarctica. Foreword by H.R.H. The Duke of Edinburgh. *Butterworth*, 1964.

BRITISH HONDURAS

B RITISH HONDURAS is situated on the east coast of Central America bounded on the north and part of the west by Mexico and by Guatemala on the remainder of the west and south. In length the country extends 174 miles from the Rio Hondo in the north to the Sarstoon River in the south. In breadth the widest part (Belize City to Benque Viejo del Carmen) is 68 miles Its land area is about 8,866 square miles which includes a number of islets (known as cayes) lying off the coast.

The coastline is for the most part flat and swampy but the country rises gradually towards the interior. The Maya Mountains and the Cockscombs, which reach a height of 3,800 feet (Victoria Peak), form the backbone of the southern half of the territory. All the Western (Cayo) District is hilly and includes the Mountain Pine Ridge most of which lies between 1,000 and 2,000 feet above sea level but rises in parts to around 3,000 feet. The northern districts are also hilly except towards the coast but contain considerable areas of low tableland. There are seventeen principal rivers, of which the Belize River is the most important. None is navigable by vessels over five feet draught and few for any distance.

The coastal waters are shallow for 10-20 miles to the east. This shallow sea is dotted with cayes and is bounded by a coral encrusted reef second only in size to the great barrier reef off the eastern coast of Australia. Three separate reef areas lie still further to the east and the most easterly islet is more than 60 miles to the east of Belize City.

The climate is sub-tropical and on the whole agreeable. In the largest city, Belize City, the temperature averages 75°F from November to January and 81°F from May to September. The mean annual temperature is 79°F. Day temperatures often reach 90°F-96°F and night temperatures may very occasionally fall to the fifties. Most of the year the heat and humidity are tempered by sea breezes. This description applies with small variation along the whole coastal area. Inland, the day temperatures during the dry season tend to be higher, but drop considerably at night. Rainfall increases from north to south:

	Annual average inches
Corozal (north)	51
Belize City (central)	63
San Ignacio (western central)	52
Stann Creek (upper south)	147
Toledo (south)	175

There are two dry seasons, the main one from March to May and the other in August and September (called the Maugre Season).

British Honduras has been struck from time to time by hurricanes. In recent years: a hurricane struck Belize City on 10th September 1931, causing heavy loss of life and property; on 27th September 1955 hurricane 'Janet' struck the northern part of the country completely destroying the town of Corozal and damaging dozens of villages in the Corozal and Orange Walk Districts; on 15th July 1960 hurricane 'Abby' struck the area of the Sittee River, south of Stann Creek, causing some damage to crops and dwellings; on 24th July 1961 hurricane 'Anna' wrought fairly extensive damage to crops and houses in the villages of Seine Bight and Placentia and Sittee River and almost completely destroyed banana plantations at Waha Leaf in the Stann Creek District; on 31st October 1961 hurricane 'Hattie' caused 262 deaths and most serious damage to Belize City; Stann Creek Town and other parts of the country.

The population at 7th April 1970 (provisional census figures) was 119,863. The final figures are to be released at the end of 1971. In 1966 the birth rate was 43·6 per 1,000 population; the death rate 6·9 per 1,000. The infant death rate per 1,000 live births was 50. The main racial groups are: Creoles, Mestizos (Maya/Spanish), and Caribs. There are also a number of persons of East Indian and Spanish descent. The races are, however, now heavily inter-mixed and a great many persons would have considerable difficulty in deciding to which group they belong. There are 3,300 Mennonites.

The great majority of the population belong to one or other of the Christian churches. About 60 per cent are Roman Catholics and 40 per cent Protestants. In addition to a large contribution in the field of education a few of the denominations, notably the Roman Catholics and Nazarenes, operate health clinics, and many provide social and family welfare services.

Until 1st August 1970, Belize City was the capital, where one third of the country's population live (39,332). The new capital of the country is Belmopan, situated at Roaring Creek, some fifty miles inland on the Western Highway. It had a population of nearly 2,000 by end of March 1971.

English is the official language. In certain areas, for instance in Corozal, Orange Walk and Cayo Districts, the mother tongue of the people is Spanish and in the southern districts, Stann Creek and Toledo, there are ethnic groups whose first language is Carib or Maya. But everywhere English is, from the beginning, the medium of instruction in schools. A start has now been made in introducing the teaching of Spanish in primary schools and bilingualism is the objective. In addition to English, nearly everyone speaks a dialect known as 'creole'. It is the most popular vernacular of the country.

Education is compulsory from the age of six to 14. Primary school education is provided by 160 schools run almost entirely by the churches with a Government subsidy. In 1968, 28,257 pupils were enrolled free of cost, in Government and Government-assisted schools, with about 1,000 more pupils enrolled in private schools. Secondary education is provided by 17 schools with a total of 2,642 pupils. All these, with the exception of the Belize Technical College, a Government institution, are church schools and school fees are charged, but the Government provides more than 317 students with scholarships. A Junior College run by Government was opened in January 1969. It has an enrolment of over 300. No fee is charged. There is a Teachers' Training College (the Belize Teachers' College) in Belize City where about 115 teachers pursue various courses. Four Church Secondary Schools now offer a two-year post-high school course. The students sit advanced level G.C.E. examinations. There is no university and students must go abroad for further study, scholarships being awarded to the University of the West Indies and other universities in Britain, Canada and the U.S.A. Expenditure on education in 1971 was 20·2 per cent of the national revenue, or $2,920,986 BH*. Only about 5 per cent of the population over the age of 10 years are illiterate. In addition $717,630 was spent on capital projects. A comprehensive secondary school and two primary schools are operating in Belmopan, the new capital.

The Baron Bliss Institute which was opened in May 1954 is maintained and operated by the Government for the encouragement of cultural activities. The National Library Service, the headquarters of which are housed in a section of the institute, has established 74 service points all over the country. There is a British Council library in Belize City.

The Government operates a radio broadcasting service (Radio Belize). Programmes are in English and Spanish. It is semi-commercial.

The country is relatively free from endemic diseases. Malaria, which was most prevalent, is no longer a problem owing to an intense programme of malaria eradication. The main general hospital with 162 beds is in Belize City. A new hospital with 40 beds was opened in Punta Gorda in the Toledo District in 1965 and there are small hospitals in all the other districts. There is also a 21-bed private hospital in Belize City. There are some twenty Government and Mission rural dispensaries. An infirmary and a mental hospital are maintained by the Government in Belize City and there is a temporary tuberculosis sanatorium some 18 miles outside the city. Expenditure on medical and health services in 1968 amounted to $1,332,300 B.H. plus $225,000 on capital projects. The new capital, Belmopan, has a hospital of 40 beds.

The Belize City International Airport is ten miles north-west of Belize City. It is the principal airport of the territory and international air services are operated by *Transportes Aeros Centro Americanos, S.A.* (T.A.C.A. International Airlines), *Servicio Aereo de Honduras S.A.* (S.A.H.S.A.), and *Transportes Aereo Nationales, S.A.* (T.A.N. Airlines), to and from all parts of Central America and to Miami and New Orleans in the United States. The runway has been resurfaced and lengthened to 6,300 feet. On completion in September 1968 it was upgraded to a category 'C' airport able to accommodate all types of short range and some medium range jet aircraft. A regular service of BAC 111 jets was introduced in December 1966 by TACA.

* B.H. $4=£1 *sterling*.

Belize City is the principal port. Regular cargo services are maintained by ships of the United Fruit Company with New Orleans and New York; T. & J. Harrison Ltd with the United Kingdom; Royal Netherlands Lines with Europe, and the K-Line with Japan and 12 other minor lines. The port deals with some 1,259,109 tons of cargo annually (including Stann Creek, the next busiest port.) A study has just been completed by the Overseas Development Administration for a deep water port for which finance is being sought.

There are 390 miles of all-weather, main and feeder roads, 177 miles of cart roads and bush trails, and a further 890 miles of dry weather roads, including forest roads, maintained by the Government. There are no railways.

Approximately 42 per cent of the working population is engaged in agriculture, of which about a third are working on their own account. The estimated numbers engaged in the principal wage-earning occupations at the end of 1967 were: services 4,268; agriculture, forestry and fishing, 4,800; manufacturing, 2,743; construction, 1,316; trade and commerce, 1,502; transport, 589; others, 354.

Indian corn (maize), beans and peas, rice, sugar, cassava and yams are the principal food crops. Cattle, pigs and poultry are raised throughout the country. The main export crops are citrus fruits, processed citrus and sugar-cane, cucumber and tomatoes. Sugar in the form of raw sugar and molasses is the main export and with the development projected it is anticipated that production will eventually be raised to some 150,000 tons annually in the longer term. Production in 1969/70 amounted to 66,793 tons and 3,864,138 gallons of molasses. Timber is also a main export. Lobster and scale fish and conch export has passed the one million dollar mark.

Citrus exports during the period 1962-68 are shown in the following table:

| | Grapefruit '000 lbs.— | | | | Oranges '000 lbs.— | | | |
Year	Fresh Fruits	Seg- ments	Juice	Concen- trate	Fresh Fruits	Juice	Concen- trate	Value (£m.)
1962 ..	9	2,834	426	17	182	6,539	170	2·87
1963 ..	2,429	5,300	1,525	68	2,111	7,999	54	4·87
1964 ..	2,532	1,138	1,372	250	225	15,962	6,055	5·66
1965 ..	11	4,722	973	402	533	13,369	6,391	4·80
1966 ..	100	7,602	1,832	282	578	8,295	7,004	1·16
1967 ..	—	7,072	569	56.5	546·5	6,158	4,911	1·12
1968 ..	12	6,978	1,880	47	640	9,607	4,399	1.06

In 1968 the total value of domestic exports was $20,005,153 BH. Goods to the value of $44,200,780 BH were imported and goods valued at $5,189,202 BH were re-exported.

British Honduras imports all its capital equipment and most of its consumer goods. The trade gap of $16·48m. B.H. was financed in the main by foreign investment capital, British development aid funds and remittances from abroad.

The provisional figure for Government recurrent revenue in 1971 was $17,504,871 BH and for recurrent expenditure it was $16,107,850 BH. The corresponding figures for capital revenue and capital expenditure were $13,025,980 BH and $13,025,980 BH respectively. There was no grant-in-aid for 1970 and the balance of the budget was made up almost entirely by grants from Britain under C. D. & W. which totalled $9,874,442 BH and loans raised locally which totalled $180,000 BH. Most of the capital expenditure is being used on the construction of the new capital.

During 1963 Government published a Development Plan for the period 1964 to 1970 based largely on the report of a United Nations economic survey mission that year. The plan which is confined largely to planned expenditure in the Public Sector, envisaged a total expenditure of just under $53m. B.H. including communications $15·3m. B.H., housing $11·1m. B.H., education $8·6m. B.H., public health and sanitation $6·4m. B.H., agriculture $5·9m. B.H., and training $1·1m. B.H.

The plan recognised the general shift of the main economic base from forestry to agriculture since the early 1950's. Main sources of finance envisaged in the plan were grants $31·5m. B.H. and loans $21·48m. B.H. Funds were not forth-coming from these sources as expected and as a result many of the targets have not been achieved.

The Development Plan has been revised on the basis of changed circum-stances since 1963 and in the light of the report of the Tripartite Economic Survey Mission in 1966 which was sponsored by the Governments of the United Kingdom, the United States of America and Canada. A new five-year plan is being prepared and will be published in mid-1971.

HISTORY

Little is known of the early history of the area which is now British Honduras but the numerous ruins throughout the territory indicate that for hundreds of years it was heavily populated by Maya Indians. The Maya civilisation appears to have reached its apogee about the 8th century. It then collapsed and many of the people migrated.

In 1502 Columbus discovered and named the Bay of Honduras though he did not actually visit that part of the coast which later became British Honduras. The present settlement was established in 1638 but British sea rovers frequented the bay long before that and there is some evidence that a settlement was formed in or about 1603. From then on the coast was visited by buccaneers and log-wood cutters, logwood being in great demand in Europe for the manufacture of dyes. The British settlement of 1638 (known as the Bay Settlement), aug-mented intermittently by sea rovers and particularly disbanded British sailors and soldiers after the capture of Jamaica in 1665, had a troubled history during the next 150 years. It was subjected to repeated attacks from neighbouring Spanish settlements, for Spain, with papal sanction, claimed sovereignty over the whole of the New World except the regions of South America assigned to Portugal.

By the Treaty of Madrid of 1670 Spain accorded recognition to the *de facto* British possessions in the Caribbean area but did not accept Britain's contention that the terms of the treaty included the Bay Settlement and Spanish attacks on the settlers continued. During the 18th century the status of the logwood cutters remained an issue between the two powers and it was not until 1763 under the Treaty of Paris that Spain, while retaining sovereignty over Belize, conceded to the British settlers the right to engage in the logwood industry. This was re-affirmed by the Treaty of Versailles in 1783 and by a further treaty of 1786—the Convention of London—the area of the logwood concession was extended while Britain gave up her claim to the Mosquito Coast further south on the mainland of Central America. Despite these concessions, the Spaniards con-tinued their attacks, while the settlers protested that the extended limits of the logwood concession were insufficient. Two years after the outbreak of war between England and Spain in 1796, a strong Spanish attack was launched in a naval engagement off St. George's Caye. The Baymen, although badly under-armed and heavily outnumbered, resisted and after several days of skirmishing the forces met in a sea battle off St. George's Caye. Supported by H.M. sloop *Merlin* the Baymen fought with such determination that the Spaniards were forced to retreat. This was their last attempt to dislodge the Baymen by force of arms. British *de facto* control over the area gradually increased as Spanish power over the West Indies and Central America declined, and in 1862 British Honduras was recognised by Britain as a British Colony.

Until 1786 the Baymen governed themselves. In that year, after many petitions, Britain appointed and sent out a Superintendent, but the office was allowed to lapse in 1791. In 1797 Colonel Thomas Barrow was appointed Superintendent and also was given the title of Commander-in-Chief (held by the Governors of the Colony ever since) to enable him to organise a defence against the obviously impending Spanish attack. Thereafter the office of Superintendent continued until 1862 when it was replaced by that of a Lieutenant-Governor under the Governor of Jamaica and the settlement raised to the status of a Colony; the Baymen resented being subordinated to Jamaica and in 1884 the Colony was detached and a Governor was appointed.

CONSTITUTIONAL DEVELOPMENT

From a very early date the settlers achieved a primitive form of democratic government by Public Meeting, at which all settlers were eligible to vote and voice their opinions. Each year the Public Meeting elected members of the community to be unpaid magistrates empowered to make laws, levy taxes, dispense justice and carry out many other duties.

In 1765 Admiral Sir William Burnaby, who had been sent to the territory to enquire into the fulfilment of treaty obligations by Spain, codified the laws and granted, in the King's name, a constitution founded on the then existing form of government. In 1786, in the face of opposition from the settlers, the first Superintendent abolished this system of government by elected magistrates. In 1790 however, with further changes in relations with Spain, the Burnaby Code was restored in its entirety and started functioning after the Superintendent left the settlement in 1791. It continued to be enforced without material change until about 1825 when the Public Meeting's privilege of choosing subjects for discussion was curtailed. Seven years later the annual election of the magistracy by the Public Meeting was superseded in favour of appointment by the Superintendent; and in 1840 the whole of what remained of the Burnaby Code was replaced by the law of England. An Executive Council was then created and in 1853 the Public Meeting, which had become something of a closed oligarchy, was finally displaced by a Legislative Assembly of 18 elected and three nominated members, with the Superintendent as chairman.

The quality of the members of the Legislative Assembly deteriorated during the nineteenth century and by 1870 it was realised that the old system had become unworkable and unrepresentative of the people as a whole. In 1871 the elected Legislative Assembly was replaced by a nominated Legislative Council with an official majority and the Lieutenant-Governor as President. An attempt to re-introduce elected members in 1890 was turned down but in 1892 an un-official majority was created in the Legislative Council, and this constitution, with only minor modifications, continued until 1935 when the elective principle was once again introduced.

Following a disastrous hurricane in 1931, British Honduras became dependent on financial aid from Britain and found it necessary to raise a reconstruction loan. The British Government would only guarantee this on condition that reserve powers for the Governor were incorporated into the constitution. This was done by the British Honduras Constitution Ordinance of 1935 under which the Legislative Council was reconstituted to compose five official and seven unofficial members, with the Governor as President with casting vote and reserve powers. Of the seven unofficial members, two were nominated by the Governor and five elected by secret ballot of the registered voters from four constituencies. Men and women, without distinction of race, colour or creed, were entitled to vote subject to a small income qualification or a small property qualification and to being sufficiently literate to write the date and to sign their name on an application form. Amendments were made to this Ordinance in 1938 when the number of elected members on the Legislative Council was increased by one, owing to the formation of a fifth constituency. In 1945 the constitution was again amended when the proportion of unofficial members was considerably increased. The executive government devolved on the Governor and an Executive Council, composed of three *ex-officio* members (The Colonial Secretary, the Attorney. General and the Financial Secretary) and four nominated unofficial members, The Legislative Council was reconstituted to consist of the Governor as President- the same three *ex-officio* members and ten unofficial members, of whom four were nominated by the Governor and six were elected from the constituencies.

In 1954 the Legislative Council was replaced by a Legislative Assembly composed of nine elected members, three *ex-officio* members and a Speaker and three unofficial members nominated by the Governor. The status of the Executive Council was changed to that of chief instrument of policy and it was composed of the Governor, as Chairman, three *ex-officio* members and six members of the Legislative Assembly. The latter were elected by the Assembly but included not less than two of the nominated unofficial members of that body. Universal adult suffrage was also introduced in 1954, and the first general election under the new Constitution was held on 28th April 1954. The only fully organised party, the People's United Party, gained eight of the nine elected seats. The principle of Steering Members, appointed by the Governor from among the unofficial members of the Executive Council as the first step towards full ministerial status, was adopted in 1955. At the general elections which took place on the 20th March 1957 the People's United Party gained all nine of the elected seats.

In February 1960 a conference was convened in London to consider proposals for further development of the Constitution of British Honduras. The conference decided to adopt a ministerial form of government based on a revised Legislative Assembly and Executive Council. This revised constitution was introduced in March 1961 following a general election. The new Legislative Assembly, presided over by a Speaker, consisted of 18 members elected by the general public, five nominated members and two *ex-officio* members (the Chief Secretary (formerly known as Colonial Secretary) and the Attorney-General). The normal life of the Assembly was four years. The revised Executive Council under the chairmanship of the Governor, consisted of two *ex-officio* members (the Chief Secretary, responsible, *inter alia*, for defence, security and external

R

affairs, and the Attorney-General) and six unofficial members holding various departmental portfolios as Ministers, of whom at least one was a nominated member of the Legislative Assembly. The leader of the political party obtaining a majority at a general election for the Legislative Assembly seats was appointed First Minister and the remaining five unofficial members of the Executive Council were elected by the unofficial members of the Legislative Assembly from among their own number. The Governor appointed the five nominated members of the Legislative Assembly, after consultation with the First Minister in respect of two seats and after consultation with the leader of the minority party in respect of one seat, the remaining two seats being filled by the Governor after consultation with the leaders of both the majority and minority parties.

At the general election held in March 1961, the People's United Party, led by Mr George Price, won all the 18 elected seats in the Legislative Assembly. Mr Price was thereupon appointed First Minister.

PRESENT CONSTITUTION

At a Constitutional Conference held in London in July 1963 a Ministerial system of internal self-government with a two-chamber legislature was agreed. Under this new Constitution introduced on 6th January 1964, the Governor has special responsibilities for defence, external affairs, internal security and the safeguarding of the terms and conditions of service of public officers. Further, for so long as the Government of British Honduras continued to receive money from the United Kingdom Government in the form of Grant-in-Aid of the current revenues, the Governor would have a special responsibility for maintaining or securing the financial and economic stability of British Honduras and for ensuring that any condition attached to any financial grant or loan made by Her Majesty's Government was complied with. This latter responsibility came to an end on the 31st December 1966 when the Grant-in-Aid ceased.

The Executive Council has been replaced by a Cabinet consisting of a Premier and other Ministers. Ministers are appointed by the Governor on the advice of the Premier. The Governor appoints as Premier the person who appears to him to be likely to command the support of the majority party in the House of Representatives.

The bi-cameral legislature is known as the National Assembly and comprises a House of Representatives and a Senate. The House of Representatives consists of 18 members elected under the system of universal adult suffrage. The Speaker may be elected by the House from among its own number or from outside the House but the Deputy Speaker is elected by the House from amongst its own number. The Senate consists of eight members appointed by the Governor. Five are appointed on the advice of the Premier, two on the advice of the Leader of the Opposition and one after consulting such persons as the Governor considers appropriate. The President may be elected by the Senate from amongst its own number, or from outside the Senate, but the Vice-President is elected by the Senate from amongst its own number.

LAND POLICY

The alienation of Crown land is carefully controlled to prevent, as far as possible, the acquisition of such land for purely speculative, non-productive purposes. No racial discrimination is exercised. During 1953 and 1954 a land use survey was carried out. A land policy, based on the findings and recommendations of the Survey Team, has been formulated and was published by Government in 1958. In order to encourage the economic development of the country a tax on undeveloped rural land was introduced in January 1966. In 1971 land tax was doubled on holdings over 60 acres. The normal land tax was considered by a special fiscal committee to be extremely low.

GOVERNMENT

At the 1963 Constitutional Conference it was agreed that the next general election should be held when it became due in the ordinary course, *i.e.* not later than March 1965. As the members of the legislature at that time were elected on the basis of the 1961 constitution, the conference agreed that the alterations in the legislature should not take place until after the next General Election, except that the two official seats in the legislature should be abolished when the new Constitution was introduced. The Constitution was introduced on 6th January 1964 and at the election held on 1st March 1965 the People's United Party (PUP) secured 16 seats and the National Independence Party (NIP) two seats. The House of Representatives elected a Speaker from outside the House. In the Senate a President was elected outside the Senate. The second election under the 1963 Self Government Constitution was held on 1st December 1969. The People's United Party won 17 out of 18 seats under the leadership of Premier George Price.

GOVERNORS SINCE 1884

1884	Sir R. T. Goldsworthy, KCMG	1932	Sir H. B. Kittermaster, KCMG, KBE
1891	Sir C. A. Moloney, KCMG	1934	Sir Alan Burns, GCMG
1897	Colonel Sir David Wilson, KCMG	1940	Sir John Adams Hunter, KCMG
1904	Sir Bickham Sweet-Escott, KCMG	1947	Sir E. G. Hawkesworth, KCMG, MC
1906	Colonel Sir E. J. E. Swayne, KCMG, CB	1948	Sir Ronald Garvey, KCMG, MBE
1913	Sir Wilfred Collet, KCMG	1952	Sir Patrick Renison, KCMG
1918	W. Hart Bennett, CMG	1955	Sir Colin Thornley, KCMG, CVO
1919	Sir Eyre Hutson, KCMG	1961	Sir Peter Stallard, KCMG, CVO, MBE
1925	Major Sir J. A. Burdon, KBE, CMG	1966	Sir John Paul, GCMG, OBE, MC

GOVERNOR AND COMMANDER-IN-CHIEF:
His Excellency Sir John Paul, GCMG, OBE, MC

THE CABINET
Premier and Minister of Finance and Development: The Hon. George Price
Minister of Trade and Industry: The Hon. A. A. Hunter
Minister of Home Affairs and Health: The Hon. C. L. B. Rogers
Minister of Education, Housing and Labour: The Hon. S. Perdomo
Minister of Power and Communications: The Hon. A. Arthurs
Minister of Local Government, Community and Social Development:
The Hon. L. S. Sylvestre
Minister of Agriculture, Lands and Cooperatives: The Hon. F. H. Hunter
Minister without Portfolio: The Hon. J. Gray (Leader in the Senate)
The Attorney-General and Minister of Public Works: The Hon. V. H. Courteney
Secretary to the Cabinet: A. V. Campbell

PARLIAMENTARY SECRETARIES
Education, Housing and Labour: The Hon. F. Marin
Communications: The Hon. E. Urbina
Agriculture, Lands and Cooperatives: The Hon. D. L. Mckoy

LEADER OF THE OPPOSITION
Hon. P. S. W. Goldson

HOUSE OF REPRESENTATIVES
Speaker: The Hon. W. H. Courtenay, OBE
Deputy Speaker: The Hon. Guadalupe Pech
Clerk of the National Assembly: S. E. Hulse, MBE

THE SENATE

President: Ewart William Francis, OBE
Vice-President: J. N. Meighan, MBE

Leader of Government Business: J. Gray

CIVIL ESTABLISHMENT

Governor and Commander-in-Chief: His Excellency Sir John Paul, GCMG, OBE, MC
Permanent Secretary, External Affairs: M. W. Atkinson, MBE

PUBLIC SERVICE COMMISSION

D. N. F. Fairweather, OBE, ED (Chairman); A. S. Burns, OBE, JP; A. S. Pinks, JP;
Miss K. M. Usher, JP; R. G. Hulse, JP

OFFICE OF THE SERVICE COMMISSION AND ESTABLISHMENT
Permanent Secretary: W. J. Hoy, MBE

MINISTRY OF FINANCE AND ECONOMIC DEVELOPMENT

Financial Secretary: R. A. Fonseca, CMG
(who acts as Governor when H.E. is out of the country)
Head of Planning Unit: G. Graham
Accountant General: H. E. Cain, MBE
Commissioner of Income Tax: T. C. Vernon
Comptroller of Income Tax: J. J. Robateau

MINISTRY OF TRADE AND INDUSTRY

Permanent Secretary: R. A. Fuller
Chief Forest Officer: L. Lindo
Archaeologist: P. Schmit
Secretary of Tourist Board: R. I. Clark
Secretary of Sugar Industry: S. Pinto
Fisheries Officer: G. Rosado
Price Control Officer: W. Longsworth

MINISTRY OF HOME AFFAIRS AND HEALTH

Permanent Secretary: J. L. Castillo
Permanent Secretary, Establishment: W. J. Hoy, MBE
Chief Medical Officer: N. L. Mason-Browne
Commissioner of Police: A. S. Adolphus
Chief Information Officer: R. I. Castillo
Chief Broadcasting Officer: E. W. Waight
Government Printer: W. T. Middleton

MINISTRY OF EDUCATION, HOUSING AND LABOUR

Permanent Secretary: M. Hulse
Chief Education Officer: E. P. Yorke, MBE
Housing Officer: L. F. J. Longsworth
Commissioner of Labour: K. Dunn

MINISTRY OF POWER AND COMMUNICATIONS

Permanent Secretary: S. E. Smith
Chief Civil Aviation Officer: L. C. Balderamos, MBE
Postmaster-General: C. B. Hyde
Water Authority: E. Meighan
Electricity Board: E. Robinson

MINISTRY OF LOCAL GOVERNMENT, COMMUNITY AND SOCIAL DEVELOPMENT

Permanent Secretary: H. McCain
Social Development Officer: Mrs E. Middleton
Superintendent of Prisons: S. P. S. Campbell

MINISTRY OF AGRICULTURE AND LANDS AND COOPERATIVES

Permanent Secretary: (vacant)
Chief Agriculture Officer: E. W. King
Marketing Officer (Domestic): H. Usher
Surveyor General: K. L. Gibson
Registrar of Cooperatives: C. M. Woods

JUDICIARY

Chief Justice: Sir Clifford De L. Inniss, QC

MAGISTRATES—BELIZE CITY

Magistrate: (vacant)
Assistant Magistrate: A. B. Balderamos
Assistant Magistrate: (vacant)
Travelling Magistrate: (vacant)

REGISTRAR OF SUPREME COURT AND REGISTRAR-GENERAL:

(Vacant)

THE JUDICIAL COMMISSION

Sir Clifford De L. Inniss, QC (Chief Justice)
Puisne Judge: C. A. B. Ross
D. N. A. Fairweather, OBE, ED

ATTORNEY-GENERAL'S OFFICE

Director of Public Prosecutions: A. L. Staine
Solicitor-General: A. Corrigan
Crown Counsel: E. M. Johnson
Chief Engineer: J. Flowers

AUDIT

Principal Auditor: B. Malher

MAIN TOWNS

Mayors:
Belize City: W. Coffin
Corozal Town: Hugh Rodney Moguel
Orange Walk Town: I. Vega
San Ignacio: E. Luna
Stann Creek Town: C. Nolberto
Benque Viejo del Carmen: Chairman, N. Luna
Monkey River Town: Chairman, S. Ramclam
Punta Gorda: A. Vernon

DISTRICT OFFICERS

(*Court Magistrates*)
Cayo: E. Fairweather
Corozal: R. Ramirez
Orange Walk: D. K. Barrow (Acting)
Stann Creek: H. Tillett
Toledo: S. Goff (Acting)

READING LIST

ANDERSON, A. H. Brief Sketch of British Honduras—Past, Present and Future. 7th Edition. *British Honduras Printing Company*, 1958.

ASPINALL, Sir A. The Pocket Guide to the West Indies. *Methuen*, 1960.

BLOOMFIELD, L. M. The British Honduras-Guatemala Dispute. *The Carswell Company Ltd*, Toronto, Canada, 1953.

CARR, D. and THORPE, J. From the Cam to the Cays. *Putnam*, 1961.

GANN, THOMAS. Mystery Cities. *Duckworth*, 1925.

GANN, THOMAS. Ancient Cities and Modern Tribes. *Duckworth*, 1926.

GAUDET, WILLIAM. A New Look at Belize. *Government Information Services, Belmopan.*

GIBBS, ARCHIBALD ROBERTSON. British Honduras. An Historical and Descriptive Account of the Colony from its Settlement, 1670. *Sampson Low*, 1833.

GREGG, A. ROBERT. British Honduras. *Corona Library*, 1968.

JOYCE, T. A. Report on the Investigations at Lubantuum, British Honduras. London. *Royal Anthropological Institute*, 1926.

PENDERGAST, Dr DAVID. Altun Ha. *Government of Belize*, 1969.

SHERLOCK, PHILIP. History of Belize, *Education Department, Belize City*, 1969.

SWAN, M. British Honduras. *Phoenix House*, 1957.

WADDELL, D. A. G. British Honduras; A Historical and Contemporary Survey. *O.U.P.*, 1961.

BRITISH INDIAN OCEAN TERRITORY

THE British Indian Ocean Territory consists of the Chagos Archipelago and the islands of Desroches, Farquhar and Aldabra. The headquarters of the territory is at Victoria on the island of Mahé in Seychelles. This island, which does not form part of the territory, lies some 1,000 miles east of Mombasa.

The Chagos Archipelago is composed of six main groups of islands situated on a large shoal area, the Great Chagos Bank, the whole covering some 21,000 square miles of ocean. Diego Garcia, the largest and most southerly of the Chagos islands is 1,100 miles east of Mahé and consists of a V-shaped sand cay some 15 miles long with a maximum width of 7 miles. The arms approach at the top of the V almost enclosing the large, deep lagoon. The permanent land area is about 17 square miles. The other main island groups of the archipelago are Peros Banhos and Salomon both of which consist of small sand cays lying on large, roughly circular atolls. In the case of Peros Banhos there are 29 islands with a total land area of 4 square miles and in Salomon there are 11 islands with a land area of 2 square miles.

Copra is produced on Peros Bannos and Salomon, with an annual output of about 550 tons. Most of the other islands of the archipelago were formerly coconut plantations but they are now uninhabited except for large flocks of sea birds.

Desroches is a small sand cay 3¼ miles long and varying in width from a quarter to three-quarters of a mile with an area of 800 acres. It is 120 miles south-west of Mahé and is situated on the southern edge of an almost circular atoll 12 miles in diameter. The whole island is given over to coconut production and gives an average of 200 tons of copra a year.

Farquhar, some 430 miles south-west of Mahé is an atoll 10 miles by 5 miles in extent. The principal islands occur on the northern and eastern sides of the atoll but there is also a small group of islands on the north-western rim. The total land area is some three square miles, all the suitable parts of which have been planted with coconuts. Some maize is also grown. Farquhar is the only island in the territory which is in the cyclone belt and considerable damage was done to the island by cyclones in 1930, 1954 and 1966. The present production of the island is about 250 tons of copra a year. There are large colonies of sea birds on the islands.

Aldabra, the largest of the islands in the Territory, is a raised reef atoll nineteen miles in length and up to $7\frac{1}{4}$ miles in width with a land area of about 60 square miles. The land rim of the atoll is almost continuous being broken only by four narrow passages, the large but shallow lagoon containing many small islets and mud banks. On the seaward side the island is fringed by low cliffs rising to some 15 feet. On the southern side of the island there are stable sand dunes rising to 50 feet in some places. Inside the lagoon the perimeter is indented with innumerable small creeks and there are large areas of mangrove in the intertidal areas.

The land surface of Aldabra is composed of limestone either of the champignon or pavè type. In the former type, which is the more common, the limestone has been eroded into a maze of jagged pinnacles, pits and crevices and is covered with dense scrub. The pavè consists of slabs of limestone with vegetation growing in the hollows.

Aldabra has an interesting flora and fauna including some rare and unique species. With the exception of the Galapagos it is the only remaining place where the giant tortoise is found in its natural state. The bird life is very rich including large colonies of frigate birds, some flamingos and a species of flightless rail thought to be unique to the island. It is also one of the breeding grounds of the sacred ibis.

The comparatively undisturbed state of the eco-system of Aldabra has aroused considerable scientific interest in recent years and the Royal Society, which has acquired the lease of the island, has established a research station there.

The islands of the Territory are all owned by the Crown and there is no permanent population on any of them, the inhabitants being mainly labourers employed on contract. This transient population varies considerably from time to time depending on the work being undertaken on the plantations; at the last census they numbered 550.

The islands have a typical tropical maritime climate. The average temperature in Diego Garcia, the only island for which accurate records exist, is 81°F, the average maximum and minimum temperatures being 84°F and 77°F. Rainfall in the Chagos archipelago is between 90 and 100 inches a year and between 40 and 60 inches in the other islands. There have been occasional outbreaks of malaria on Aldabra but apart from this the territory has few of the diseases normally associated with tropical climates.

The British Indian Ocean Territory was established by an Order in Council on 8th November 1965 which provided for the appointment of a Commissioner who is responsible for the administration of the Territory. Before this date the islands of the Chagos archipelago were administered by the Government of Mauritius and the other islands by the Seychelles Government. The legislation in force in the individual islands at the time of the establishment of the Territory has remained in force except where it has been modified by laws made under the Order in Council. The history of the islands before the creation of the Territory is given in the sections on Mauritius and Seychelles.

The currency is the Seychelles and Mauritius rupees both of which are tied to sterling at the rate of 7½p to one rupee. A definitive issue of B.I.O.T. stamps was made in January 1968 to replace the Seychelles and Mauritius stamps formerly used in the Territory. This consisted of Seychelles stamps overprinted B.I.O.T. and was replaced in October 1968 by a thematic series showing fishes of the Indian Ocean.

There are no air communications. The islands are served by a B.I.O.T.-owned cargo/passenger boat which visits them approximately every three months. Small schooners from Seychelles pay occasional visits.

Commissioner: Sir Bruce Greatbatch, CMG, CVO, MBE
Administrator: J. R. Todd

BRITISH VIRGIN ISLANDS

THE Virgin Islands are situated approximately 50 miles east of Puerto Rico and straddle latitude 18° 25′ N and longitude 64° 30′ W. The territory covers an area of 59 square miles and consists of 36 islands, the largest being Tortola (21 square miles), Anegada (15 square miles), Virgin Gorda (8¼ square miles) and Jost Van Dyke (3½ square miles). With the exception of Anegada, the islands represent a projection of Puerto Rico and the United States Virgin Islands archipelago. Anegada, a flat coral feature consisting entirely of limestone, is the northernmost of the islands in the Atlantic and is surrounded by dangerous reefs. The other islands are hilly. Virgin Gorda rises to a central peak 1,370 feet high whilst Sage Mountain on Tortola reaches a height of 1,780 feet. There are no rivers and the vegetation is mostly light bush.

The islands lie within the Trade Wind belt and possess a pleasant and healthy sub-tropical climate. The average temperature in Winter ranges from 71°-82°F and in Summer from 78°-88°F although the summer heat is tempered by sea breezes and there is usually a drop of 10°F at night. The average rainfall is 50 inches. Excellent beaches for bathing and swimming are to be found on all the major islands and there are very good facilities for yachting, diving, fishing and hunting. There are some fifteen hotels and several guest houses, about half of which are in Road Town, Tortola, and the remainder scattered over the other islands. Charter boat services are available on Tortola and Virgin Gorda.

The 1970 census gave a population figure of 10,484. The principal town and port is Road Town on Tortola which has a population of 2,183. The great majority of the people are of Negro stock. English is the main and official language. The Methodists are the largest religious denomination, followed by the Church of God; the Anglican, Baptist, Adventist and Roman Catholic Churches are also represented in the territory.

Medical services are mainly provided by the Government and the general health of the population is good. There is a 35-bed cottage hospital on Tortola and in 1971 total estimated expenditure on the medical services was estimated at US$459,117.

Primary education is free and universal and the illiteracy rate is virtually non-existent. All 14 primary schools and one secondary school are directly maintained by the Government. There are also three private schools. In 1969 a total of 2,900 pupils were enrolled in all schools. Secondary schools provide education to G.C.E. Ordinary level standard and several scholarships tenable at universities in the U.S.A., Canada and in Puerto Rico and the University of the West Indies are awarded. There is a library at Road Town and library deposit stations in the out-islands.

There are four direct steamship services, one from the United Kingdom, one from Holland and two from the United States. Launches and a new hydrofoil maintain a daily passenger and mail service with St Thomas (United States Virgin Islands). An external telephone service links Tortola with Bermuda and the rest of the world, and cable communications also exist to all parts of the world. There are airports suitable for small aircraft on Beef Island, Virgin Gorda, and Anegada. The main airport at Beef Island has been recently extended by the Royal Engineers and it now accommodates aircraft as large as the AVro 748 carrying 50 passengers. Two scheduled air services operated by PRINAIR and LIAT provide direct daily communication with Puerto Rico and the Eastern Caribbean. The territory possesses approximately 40 miles of roads, but no railways. Although the territory is not served by a television network, a radio broadcasting station is located at Baugher's Bay, Tortola, and its transmissions reach the United States Virgin Islands and the northern Leeward Islands. A television licence has been issued to a private company and TV broadcasts will commence in due course.

The main crops are bananas, vegetables and coconuts, although livestock and fish are most important exports. In 1969 exports of livestock were valued at US$7,615, whilst the other principal exports were fish, including turtles and shellfish, US$30,603; fruit US$6,572; and vegetables US$877. Exports are almost entirely confined to the United States Virgin Islands and the French islands of Guadeloupe and Martinique. Industry is extremely limited and consists of a rum distillery on Tortola, 15 plants making hollow concrete blocks, a mineral water factory, and three stone-crushing plants and one paint factory opened in 1969. Two printeries are in operation and a joinery works has been built. A bulk cement bagging plant is expected to be in operation in 1971. The chief imports are timber, foodstuffs, machinery, motor cars and alcoholic beverages.

The income tax law has been amended to provide generous family allowances of up to $7,000 with medical and schooling deductions of up to $2,000 and $1,000 respectively. Taxable income bears income tax at a flat 12%. Gross income is taxed at 3% under a separate law. Companies pay a flat rate of 12 cents in the Dollar.

In 1970 recurrent Government revenue was U.S. $3·147 million and Expenditure U.S. $3·450 million. The estimated figures for 1971 are U.S. $3·516 million and U.S. $4·032 million respectively.

The six-year development plan for 1966-71 envisages a total expenditure of almost US$18 million of which US$5·6 million would be in the public sectors:

of the latter, nearly half is allocated to communications including the extension and improvement of the airport at Beef Island and improvement of the territory's road system and port facilities.

HISTORY

The Virgin Islands were discovered in 1493 by Christopher Columbus who named them Las Virgenes in honour of St Ursula and her companions. In the early years of European settlement in the West Indies, the group appears to have been a haunt of buccaneers and pirates.

In 1672 the Governor of the Leeward Islands, Colonel Stapleton, formally annexed the island of Tortola, demolished the fort and forced the inhabitants to move to St Kitts. In 1680 a few planters moved with their families from Anguilla in the Leewards to Virgin Gorda, starting a stream which by 1717 had raised the European population of that island to 317 and that of Tortola to 159. In 1773, on their second petition, the planters were granted civil government and constitutional courts with a completely elected House of Assembly (12 members) and a partly elected and partly nominated Legislative Council or 'Board' which met for the first time on 1st February 1774.

The islands became part of the Colony of the Leeward Islands in 1872 and continued as such with various constitutions until 1st July 1956 when the Leeward Islands were defederated and the presidencies of Antigua, St Kitts, Montserrat and the Virgin Islands became separate colonies. The island continued to be administered by the Governor of the Leeward Islands until January 1960 when this office was abolished and the Administrator of the Virgin Islands became directly responsible to the Colonial Office. In August 1971, by Order in Council, the title of Administrator was changed to Governor. The territory did not, unlike the other former Leeward Islands, become part of the West Indies Federation which was dissolved in 1962.

CONSTITUTION

The new constitution, which came into effect in April 1967, provides for the first time for a ministerial system. The Governor remains responsible for defence and internal security, external affairs, the civil service, the administration of the courts and finance, and continues to have reserved legislative powers necessary in the exercise of his special responsibilities, but on other matters is normally bound to act in accordance with the advice of the Executive Council. The Executive Council is comprised of the Governor as Chairman, two *ex-officio* members (the Attorney-General and Financial Secretary), the Chief Minister appointed by the Governor as the elected member who appears best able to command a majority and has two other ministers ppointed by the Governor on the advice of the Chief Minister. The Legislative Council consists of a Speaker chosen from outside the Council, two *ex-officio* members (the Attorney-General and Financial Secretary), one nominated member appointed by the Governor after consultation with the Chief Minister and seven elected members returned from seven one-member electoral districts.

Justice was formerly administered in the territory by the Supreme Court of the Windward and Leeward Islands, the Court of Summary Jurisdiction and the Magistrate's Court and a Puisne Judge of the Supreme Court visited the islands twice a year. With the replacement of the Supreme Court by the West Indies Associated States Supreme Court arrangements have been made for this Court to serve the Virgin Islands.

R*

LAND POLICY

British subjects who are not Virgin Islanders and all aliens are required to obtain a licence before they may acquire land. Applications are however readily granted, usually on condition that the applicant undertakes appropriate development within a certain period.

Most of the land is in private ownership but Crown lands are estimated at 15,121 acres and are normally leased for a period not exceeding 99 years. Rental is based either on tender or on 5 per cent of the unimproved value of the land which is reviewed at intervals of 10 years.

GOVERNMENT

A General Election was held on 2nd June 1971. The Democratic Party secured three seats, the Virgin Islands Party two seats, the United Party one seat and there was one independent elected.

Governor: D. G. Cudmore, OBE

EXECUTIVE COUNCIL
The Governor (Chairman)
Attorney-General (*ex-Officio*) Hon. N. Jacobs
Financial Secretary
(*ex-officio*): Hon. C. B. Romney, MA
Chief Minister: Hon. Willard Wheatley, MBE
Minister for Natural Resources:
Dr. the Hon. Q. W. Osborne
Minister for Communications, Works and Industry: Hon. Oliver Cills

LEGISLATIVE COUNCIL
Speaker: Hon. H. R. Penn, OBE
Attorney-General (*ex-officio*)
Financial Secretary (*ex-officio*)
Nominated Member: Hon. I. Dawson
Elected Members: Hon. Willard Wheatley, MBE; Dr. the Hon. Q. W. Osborne;
Hon. O. Cills; Hon. A. A. Henley; Hon. H. L. Stoutt; Hon. R. George;
Hon. Conrad Maduro.

CIVIL ESTABLISHMENT

Governor: D. G. Cudmore, OBE
Financial Secretary: C. B. Romney, MA
Chief Secretary: A. E. Penn
Administrative Secretaries: G. E. U. Dawson; A. U. Anthony; S. Gordon; A. O. Shirley

LEGAL
Attorney-General: N. Jacobs
Legal Assistant: E. A. C. Hewlett

JUDICIAL
Magistrate: K. McAllister
Registrar: Miss P. Beaubrun

MEDICAL AND HEALTH
Chief Medical Officer: P. Smith
Surgeon: R. E. Tattersall
Medical Officer: R. R. Thomas
Dental Officer: K. P. Adamson

PUBLIC WORKS DEPARTMENT
Chief Engineer, P.W.D.: J. L. Steven

ELECTRICITY DEPARTMENT
Chief Electrical Engineer: D. G. Pritchard

AUDIT
Senior Auditor: R. Hudson

AGRICULTURE
Superintendent of Agriculture: (vacant)

TREASURY AND CUSTOMS
Accountant General: A. O. Shirley, MBE
Comptroller of Customs: A. A. de Castro

EDUCATION
Chief Education Officer: J. Clough
Supervisor Primary Schools: Miss E. L. Scatliffe
Principal, V. I. High School: C. E. Wallace
Librarian: Miss V. Penn

POLICE AND PRISON
Chief of Police: B. E. Graves

READING LIST

British Virgin Islands Reports for 1961-62, 1963-64 and 1965-69.

Report of the Development Advisory Committee for the period 1966-71 (obtainable from the Administrator's Office, British Virgin Islands).

EGGLESTON, GEORGE T. Virgin Islands. Princeton. *D. Van Nostrand*, 1959.

PHILLIPS, William T. A. Report on the British Virgin Islands with Recommendations for Accelerating Economic and Social Development.

O'LOUGHLIN, Dr Carleen. A Survey of the Economic Potential, Fiscal Structure and Capital Requirements of the British Virgin Islands 1962.

SUCKLING, GEORGE. An Historical Account of the Virgin Islands. *Benjamin White*, 1780.

Report of the Fiscal Review Committee 1967-68.

Triennial Report, 1966-1967-1968 (Now in progress).

DOOKHAN, ISAAC: A History of the British Virgin Islands, 1968.

CAYMAN ISLANDS

T HE Cayman Islands consist of Grand Cayman, Cayman Brac and Little Cayman and they lie in the Caribbean Sea between latitudes 19° 15′ and 19° 45′ North and longitudes 79° 44′ and 81° 27′ West. Their total area is about 100 square miles.

All the islands are low lying and do not reach a height of more than 60 feet above sea level except in Cayman Brac where the eastern end rises to 140 feet. The principal island—Grand Cayman—is about 180 miles west-north-west of Jamaica, it is about 22 miles in length with a breadth varying from 4 to 8 miles: very low lying, it is difficult to sight from the sea. Most of the west end of the island is taken up by North Sound, a shallow bay, 36 square miles in area, protected by a reef. North Sound provides a safe haven for small craft and a convenient area for turtle 'crawls' (corrals). Little Cayman has a similar geographical formation to Grand Cayman. Cayman Brac is distinguished from the other islands by a massive central limestone bluff. The coasts are for the most part rock-bound, protected by coral reefs enclosing a few fair harbours. Grand Cayman has a magnificent seven-mile beach. There are no rivers in any of the islands. There are quite a few species of birds found, none of which appear to be indigenous to the Caymans.

Grand Cayman is divided into six districts: George Town with a population of 3,975, West Bay with a population of 2,725, Prospect (the population figure is included with George Town), Bodden Town with a population of 980 and North Side and East End with populations of 515 and 737 respectively. Cayman Brac is divided into four districts, Stake Bay, West End, Creek and Spot Bay. The total population of these is 1,297. Little Cayman is divided into two districts, South Town with a population of 20 and Jacksons which has no inhabitants. An estimated 700 men are at sea at any one time.

The Caymans are cool from November to March, the prevailing winds being from the north and temperatures range from 65° to 75°F but have dropped to

54°F. From May to October the range of temperature is some 10° higher and has risen to 91°. At certain periods mosquitoes abound but are decreasing through the effort of the Mosquito Research and Control Unit set up in late 1965. The rainfall at George Town averages 56 inches a year. The hurricane season lasts from July to November and the islands have occasionally been hit, e.g. 1876, 1903, 1909, 1917, 1932 and 1944. In October 1952 they narrowly escaped severe damage, catching the edge of a hurricane whose centre passed only 40 miles to the West of Grand Cayman. 'Camille' in 1969 and 'Celia' in 1970 both spawned near to the islands but caused little local damage.

The last population census in the Cayman Islands was carried out in 1970 and gave the following figures: Grand Cayman 8,932; Cayman Brac 1,297; Little Cayman 20. In 1970 313 births and 60 deaths were registered. Since 1891 a census has been taken six times at intervals which varied from 9 to 20 years.

The official and spoken language of the Cayman Islands is English; the currency is Jamaican Decimal Currency introduced on 8th September 1969. A local currency issue to replace the Jamaican currency is proposed to be introduced in 1972.

Education is compulsory for children between the ages of five and fifteen. It is provided free in nine Government primary schools and there are five church-sponsored primary schools in which fees are charged.

There are two Government secondary schools (one comprehensive and one Junior High) and two private secondary schools. Enrolment in all schools in 1970 was 2,583, of whom 717 were receiving post-primary education. Recurrent expenditure in 1970 was J$235,786.

The Medical Department consists of a Government hospital and dental clinic in George Town and six district clinics. Four of these are in outlying districts of Grand Cayman and two in Cayman Brac. Expenditure on medical and health services during 1970 was J$100,318. The hospital has accommodation for 36 patients. The Government Medical Officers now number four and a fifth is expected to join the staff in 1971. All these doctors were appointed direct by the Grand Cayman Government on recommendation from the Overseas Development Administration in Great Britain. A District Medical Officer, to whom a retainer from public funds is paid to assist the Government Medical Officers has been in practice in Grand Cayman since 1957. In George Town there is a dentist engaged in private practice. Tropical diseases are virtually absent from the Caymans.

Tourism is now the main economy and chief industry of the island, the catching and exporting of turtle and the making and exporting of thatch rope both having totally ceased during 1970. Some of the inhabitants engage in other fishing pursuits and in agriculture, but the main source of income is from seamen. Caymanians, who are first-class seamen, readily find employment with overseas shipping companies. Remittances to their families enable a higher standard of living to be maintained than the resources of the islands could justify. Despite the incentives offered by the Pioneer Industries (Encouragement) Law 1950 very few light industries have been established in the islands. Trade union legislation is in existence and three unions, the Global Seaman's Union, the Cayman Islands Taxi-Cab Association and the Cayman Airlines Association have been registered. The Cayman Islands Chamber of Commerce was set up in 1965 in Grand Cayman.

The Caymans are not self-supporting in foodstuffs. The production of food crops and cattle raising are restricted by the nature of the limestone soil. Import figures for 1965–70 and particulars of the principal domestic exports are given below:

	TOTAL IMPORTS £	DOMESTIC EXPORTS £
1965	1,157,157	21,438
1966	1,490,914	23,716
1967	1,711,108	23,790
1968	2,675,706	8,123
1969	2,923,492	4,377
1970	7,766,578	8,128—Dried Turtle meat only

PRINCIPAL DOMESTIC EXPORTS BY QUANTITY AND VALUE

		1965	1966	1967	1968	1969	1970
Turtles	No.	400	400	—	—	—	—
	£	2,240	2,240	—	—	—	—
Turtle Skins	lb.	260	3,874	500	4,217	2,412	—
	£	120	3,415	240	3,453	2,206—J$4,412	—
Rope	'000 fathoms	744	576	395	183	127	—
	£	8,865	7,954	5,330	2,597	1,851—J$3,702	—
Turtle Shell	lb.	2,717	2,476	2,199	758	320	387
	£	4,412	3,551	3,300	758	320—J$640	387—J$703

The trade of the Cayman Islands is mainly with the United States and Jamaica. George Town is a port of registry with a total of 21,366 gross tons on the register at the end of 1970. During that year 303 ships arrived in the port. The islands are not served by a steamship line, but a motor vessel service is maintained between Kingston, Tampa (Florida) and all three islands. There is also more or less regular communication with Central American ports by sailing and motor vessels.

Owen Roberts airfield in Grand Cayman is used by *Lineas Aereas Costarricenses, S.A.* and Cayman Airways Ltd. There are regular air services between Grand Cayman and Kingston, Miami and San José (Costa Rica). A 3,250 ft airstrip has been constructed in Cayman Brac and a regular service by small aircraft is in operation. A private airstrip has also been constructed on Little Cayman capable of taking light aircraft.

Motorable roads connect all districts in Grand Cayman and Cayman Brac; there is a motorable track in Little Cayman.

In 1967 Cable and Wireless (W.I.) Ltd opened an overseas telephone link, using the Tropospheric Scatter System. The islands now have an excellent internal and overseas telephone service. The Government wireless stations at George Town, Grand Cayman, and Stake Bay, Cayman Brac have been closed.

The Caymans had an allocation of approximately J$600,000 for the period

1st April 1970 to 31st March 1971 under the 1970 Development Aid Programme. In 1969 and 1970 five primary schools were constructed from aid funds and one from local revenue; new buildings are underway at the comprehensive school; five houses and two blocks of apartments have been built to house expatriate staff; and a major road programme in the Eastern districts has made good progress. Projects planned for 1971 are a new Court House and a Legislative Building, Airport improvements, new harbour facilities in Grand Cayman and Cayman Brac and extensive major road works.

In recent years 15 hotels catering for tourists have been opened on Grand Cayman and one on Cayman Brac, and improved communications have greatly increased the tourist trade.

Government revenue in 1970 was J$2,643,534 and expenditure was J$2,320,224. There is no income tax, companies tax, estate or excise duty. The principal source of government revenue is from import duties and the sale of postage stamps.

A poll tax of J$2·00 per adult male between the ages of 18 and 60 is collected annually. An *ad valorem* Customs duty of 20 per cent is levied on most imported commodities, with specific duties on alcoholic liquors and tobacco. There is a preferential tariff on certain Commonwealth goods.

Stamp duties are payable on receipts and specified instruments and documents. The rate varies from 3 cents on every J$100 for receipts to five per cent on conveyances.

HISTORY

Cayman Brac and Little Cayman were sighted by Christopher Columbus on 10th May 1503 during his last voyage to the West Indies, though the islands are shown in approximately their correct position on maps published prior to this date. The Spaniards first called the group Las Tortugas because of the large numbers of turtles they saw in the surrounding waters, but by 1530 they were generally referred to as the Caimanas or Caymanes*. The Caymans were frequently visited by Spanish, English and French ships for revictualling but none of the powers laid claim to the islands or attempted to settle them until 1670, when Jamaica was ceded to the British Crown by the Treaty of Madrid and the Caymans similarly came under British rule. They were subsequently colonised mainly from Jamaica, though some English and Scottish seamen shipwrecked on the Cuban coast also made their way to the islands, which, owing to their remoteness were for long a favourite refuge for fugitives of one kind or another.

By the end of the 18th century the ruthless exploitation of turtles had so far reduced their numbers that their virtual extermination in Cayman waters

---

* Cayman derives from a Carib word covering crocodilians in general and there is sufficient evidence that the islands were so named by the Spaniards because of the large numbers of crocodiles (almost certainly the largely-marine *crocodylus acutus*) they found on shore. Dampier (*Voyages and Discoveries*, 1676) reported many crocodiles on Grand Cayman, which he carefully distinguished from alligators he had encountered elsewhere during his travels, noting that 'both kinds are called Caymanes by the Spaniards; therefore probably they reckon them for the same'. Incorrect identification probably accounts for later reports of 'alligators' on the islands (e.g. by Dr Hirst in 1910 and by observers during a hurricane in the 1930's). According to Dampier both crocodiles and alligators were commonly used as a source of fresh meat. Slaughter by ships' crews would account for the subsequent disappearance of crocodiles from the islands, which offered only limited areas of suitable cover. Specimens of *crocodylus acutus* have been taken on Little Cayman at least as recently as 1939 (*vide* Chapman Grant, *The Herpetology of the Cayman Islands*, Institute of Jamaica, 1940).

became inevitable, and the Caymanians, who had few other resources, were obliged to go further afield in search of new turtling grounds. They first turned to the uninhabited cays off Cuba but by 1839 their operations had been extended to the Nicaraguan and Hondurean coasts (*vide* Thomas Young: *Narrative of a Residence on the Mosquito Shore, During the Years* 1839, 1840 *and* 1841). This source of supply ceased in 1967 when all permits to fish in territorial waters were withdrawn by the Nicaraguan Government.

The islands of Cayman Brac and Little Cayman were permanently settled only in 1833, when several families from Grand Cayman established themselves on Cayman Brac. They lived in isolation until 1850, when, then numbering 36, they built themselves a boat. As late as 1877 there was no administrative connection between Grand Cayman and the two lesser islands. In 1877 a Justice of the Peace was appointed in Cayman Brac but not until 1887 were any more formal links established.

The islands were favourably located for trade with passing shipping in the days of sail, and Caymanians achieved a considerable reputation as builders of small schooners; but as the 19th century advanced the islands became more and more cut off from the outside world, a state of affairs which lasted effectively until the 1940s and the era of air transportation. The result was extensive emigration to Nicaragua and the settlement of the Bay Islands (at one time British but now part of Honduras) and later emigration to Florida.

CONSTITUTION

When Jamaica achieved independence on 6th August 1962, the office of Governor of Jamaica, and consequently also of Governor of the Cayman Islands, disappeared. The 1959 Constitution was accordingly amended by Order in Council to provide for the assumption by the Administrator of most of the powers and responsibilities formerly exercised by the Governor. The Executive Council consists of two official and three unofficial members, with the Administrator presiding. The Legislative Assembly consists of the Administrator as President, two or three official members appointed by the Administrator, two or three nominated non-official members appointed by the Administrator and twelve members elected on a constituency basis by universal adult suffrage. The appointments of the official and nominated members to the Legislative Assembly are made in pursuance of instructions given to the Administrator by Her Majesty through a Secretary of State. The Assembly elects a Deputy President who presides in the absence of the Administrator. It also elects two of the three unofficial members of the Executive Council. During 1962, the 'Membership' system of Government was introduced, under which the three unofficial members of the Executive Council assume a special interest in a range of subjects and advise the Government in the subjects with which they are associated.

On the 6th August 1962, all Acts, Ordinances, rules, regulations, orders, and other instruments made under or having effect by virtue of the 1959 Order in Council had effect as if they had been made under or by virtue of the 1962 Order, e.g., the Jamaica Laws which had been applied to the Cayman Islands became in effect Laws of the Cayman Islands.

LAND POLICY

There is no restriction on alienation to non-natives.

EXECUTIVE COUNCIL
The Administrator,
D. V. Watler, OBE, JP (Deputy Administrator)
G. E. Waddington, QC (Attorney-General)
E. E. Kirkconnell
B. O. Ebanks, Jr
W. W. Conolly, JP

LEGISLATIVE ASSEMBLY
President: The Administrator
Appointed Members: 2-3 official; 2-3 nominated
Elected Members: 12 representing six electoral districts and elected triennially

CIVIL ESTABLISHMENT

Adminstrator (also Registrar General): A. C. E. Long, CMG, CBE

Deputy Administrator: D. V. Watler, OBE, JP

Senior Administrative Officers: D. H. Foster, MBE, JP; H. M. McCoy, BEM

Administrative Officers: W. L. Bodden; V. L. Jackson

District Commissioner, Postmaster and Collector of Customs, Lesser Islands: Guy A. Banks

Financial Secretary: V. G. Johnson, OBE

Attorney-General: G. E. Waddington, QC

Stipendiary Magistrate: G. J. Horsfall, CBE

Registrar/Magistrate: J. H. B. Tyson

Chief of Police: R. F. Pocock

Chief Agricultural Officer: C. D. Hutchings, BSc DipAg

Director of Mosquito Research and Control Unit: M. E. C. Giglioli, PhD

Chief Education Officer: Mrs I. Conolly

Chief Medical Officer: Dr V. Billington, MB, MRCS, LRCP

Dental Officer: J. F. Devine, LDS, RFPS

Director of Civil Aviation: F. L. Chadwick, OBE

Chief Engineer: S. G. Cook

Postmaster, Grand Cayman: Mrs H. D. E. Glidden-Borden (Acting)

Chief Customs Officer: C. V. Thompson, ISO

READING LIST

BILLMYER, J. H. S. The Cayman Islands. *Geographical Review*, Vol. 36, No. 1, 1946.

CARR, A. The Windward Road. *Robert Hale*, 1957.

DOUGLAS, A. J. A. The Cayman Islands, *Geographical Journal*, Vol. 95, No. 2, February 1940.

HIRST, G. S. S. Notes on the History of the Cayman Islands. Jamaica, 1910.

WILLIAMS, Neville. A History of the Cayman Islands. 1970.

FALKLAND ISLANDS AND DEPENDENCIES

THE Falkland Islands are situated in the South Atlantic and lie some 480 miles north-east of Cape Horn. The numerous islands of which they are composed cover 4,700 square miles. The Dependencies now consist only of South Georgia, 800 miles east-south-east of the Falklands, and the South Sandwich Group, some 470 miles south-east of South Georgia. Those territories south of latitude 60° S. which were formerly part of the Falkland Islands Dependencies, namely the South Orkney Islands, the South Shetland Islands, and the Antarctic Peninsula together with the sector of the Antarctic continent lying between longitudes 20° W. and 80° W. were constituted a separate territory on 3rd March 1962 under the name of the British Antarctic Territory. There are two large islands, the East and West Falklands, and numerous smaller islands. The coastline is deeply indented and affords several good anchorages. The relief, except in Lafonia, is hilly and the maximum height above sea-level is in East Falkland where Mount Usborne rises to 2,312 feet. There are no large inland waters. Peculiar to the treeless, moorland scenery are the 'stone runs', long 'rivers' of angular, quartzite boulders. The island of South Georgia in the Dependencies is a mass of high mountains which are covered with deep snow where they are not too precipitous, and the valleys between are filled with glaciers which in many cases descend to the sea.

The islands are in the same latitude south as London is north but apart from hours of sunshine, which are similar, there are marked climatic differences. The main feature of the Falklands' weather is the strong winds, which occur particularly in the spring. Climatic figures for Stanley are:

Mean annual temperature	42°F
Mean annual wind speed	17 knots
Mean annual rainfall	25 inches
Annual maximum temperature around	70°F
Annual minimum temperature around	22°F

The Dependencies have a rigorous climate of Antarctic character.

On 31st December 1970 the population, excluding the Dependencies, was 2,045, there being rather more males than females. All were of European descent and most were British. The population of the Dependencies on 31st December 1970 was 21.

Stanley, the capital (population 1,074 at 1962 census), is the only town. In the Camp (the countryside other than Stanley) the largest settlement is at Goose Green on East Falkland where there are some 100 residents.

There are three churches in Stanley, the Cathedral of the Anglican diocese of the Falkland Islands and Eastern South America, St Mary's Roman Catholic Church and the United Free Church.

In 1970 there were 383 children receiving education. There is no secondary or higher education but arrangements exist for secondary education in the United Kingdom and elsewhere. In Stanley the Government schools cater adequately for children between the ages of five and fifteen though a number stay until their sixteenth year, and in some subjects reach General Certificate of Education standard. Outside Stanley, education is carried on either in settlement schools, some of which are very small, or by itinerant teachers. A boarding school opened in 1956 at Darwin on East Falkland can accommodate 42 boarders and caters for as many day pupils as there are in the two nearby settlements. Attendance at school is compulsory in Stanley, and in the Camp, where there are boarding or settlement schools and where itinerant teachers call. In 1970, 9 travelling teachers were employed among the 111 children outside Stanley, Darwin and settlement schools. Education is free except at Darwin Boarding School where a boarding fee of £12 a year is levied in respect of the first child of each family, and a £9 a year in respect of second and subsequent children.

A competitive overseas scholarship examination is held each year, successful candidates being granted places at boarding grammar schools in Dorset or at the British Schools, Montevideo, Uruguay. Total approved expenditure upon education for 1970/71 was £67,194.

There is a lending library in Stanley operated by the town council with a postal service designed to bring library facilities to residents outside Stanley.

The Government has one hospital, situated in Stanley. It is modern and well-equipped, and has 27 beds for the treatment of medical, surgical, obstetric and geriatric cases. The Government medical department employs a senior medical officer, three medical officers (one of whom is in Stanley, one at Darwin in Lafonia and the third at Fox Bay, on West Falkland), two dental surgeons, a dental technician, a matron, three nursing sisters and up to six staff nurses.

The Government air service is used for medical transport to and from Stanley. The m.v. *Forrest* is also at the disposal of the Medical Department for use when the weather does not permit the use of the aircraft. Total approved expenditure on the medical department in 1970/71 was £53,330.

The Government operates a broadcasting station at Stanley on 536 and 3,958 kc/s, with a power of 5kW and 500 watts respectively. In 1970 there were 705 radio licence holders; the Government also operates a wired broadcasting service in Stanley which in 1970 had 387 subscribers. There is also a Government wireless station on West Falkland to which most of the farms are linked by telephone. East Falkland has telephone facilities similar to those on the West. The Government operates international and inter-island radio-telephone services.

Transport communication between the islands and the mainland of South America is maintained by the Falkland Islands Company's vessel, R.M.S. *Darwin*, which runs a mail and passenger service 12 times a year to Montevideo. Internal transport communications are mantained by sea with the Government-owned *Forrest*, the *Darwin* and a few small private vessels. There is also a small Government-owned air service. Travellers also use horses or Land Rovers when moving between neighbouring settlements. The British Antarctic Survey Royal Research vessels call at South Georgia in the Dependencies during the southern summer. There are no roads except in Stanley, although unsurfaced tracks connect most settlements on the main East and West Islands and travel is possible by means of Land Rover or motor-cycles, depending on weather conditions. There is no inland waterway or rail service.

Agriculture is limited to a very small acreage of oats grown for hay, while householders in Stanley and the Camp grow their own vegetables. There are no minerals and no manufacturing industries of note. The East and West Falklands are given over almost completely to sheep farming and the principal product is wool.

Principal Domestic Exports by value:

	1938	1968	1969	1970
Wool (£'000)	163	811	878	772 (est.)
Hides and Skins (£'000) ..	19	29	28	28 (est.) (skins only)

The chief imports are provisions, alcoholic beverages, timber, clothing and hardware.

Direct taxation is in the form of income tax, individuals paying a graduated tax ranging from 5p in every £ of the first £100 of taxable income to 35p in every £ exceeding £10,000. Companies pay a flat rate of 35p in the £. A profits tax, levied at 20p in the £ for incorporated bodies and 15p for unincorporated bodies is payable in addition to income tax but is subject to a rebate or investment allowance of up to 50 per cent. Arrangements have been concluded with the United Kingdom, Switzerland, Canada, Sweden, Denmark, Norway and the United States of America for the avoidance of double taxation. There is no general customs tariff and import duties are confined to spirits, beer, tobacco and matches.

Public Finance tables are as follows:

Falkland Islands

		Revenue	Ordinary Expenditure	Capital Expenditure financed from	
				Colony Sources	C.D. & W. Sources
		£	£	£	£
1963-64	..	286,000	316,500	33,500	500
1964-65	..	406,500	342,000	37,500	7,500
1965-66	..	410,000	365,500	12,500	5,500
1966-67	..	380,000	392,000	86,000	33,000
1967-68	..	474,000	419,000	51,000	60,000
1968-69	..	407,000	465,000	16,000	5,000
1969-70	..	395,000	464,000	25,000	21,000
1970-71†	..	489,000	476,000	1,000	50,000
					(UK Funds)

† Estimated.

Dependencies

		Revenue		Expenditure	
		Excluding grant from H.M.G.	Grant from H.M.G.	Ordinary	Special
		£	£	£	£
1962-63	..	49,000	100,000	64,000	187,000
1963-64	..	138,500	5,000	78,500	30,000
1964-65	..	57,000	1,950 (CDW)	61,500	15,000
1965-66	..	19,000	14,500	57,000	6,000
1966-67	..	10,000	43,000	53,000	1,000
1967-68	..	8,000	40,000	49,000	Nil.
1968-69	..	15,000	35,000	40,000	Nil.
1969-70	..	21,000	1,000	20,000	Nil.
1970-71†	..	19,000	Nil.	6,000	Nil.

† Estimated.

HISTORY

The Falklands are said to have been discovered by Davis in 1592 and may have been sighted by Hawkins in 1594. On the other hand it is claimed by some historians that Vespucci sighted the Falklands in 1502. In 1764 de Bougainville established a small French settlement at Port Louis in the East Falkland which was handed over to Spain in 1767 on the payment of a sum said to have amounted to £24,000. In 1765 Captain Byron took possession of the West Falkland and left a small garrison at Port Egmont on Saunders Island, whence it was driven out by the Spaniards in 1770. This action on the part of Spain brought that country and Britain to the verge of war. The Spaniards restored the settlement to the British in 1771, but it was abandoned in 1774. The Spaniards also abandoned their settlement at Soledad (Port Louis) in the early nineteenth century.

In 1828 the Buenos Aires Government established a settlement at Soledad which was destroyed in 1831 by the U.S. warship *Lexington* as a reprisal for interference with American sealers.

In 1833 the occupation of the islands was resumed by the British Government. In 1841 a civil Lieutenant-Governor was appointed, who took over the following year from the naval officer then in charge of the islands. In 1843 an Act of Parliament placed the civil administration on a permanent footing and the Lieutenant-Governor's title was changed to Governor. In 1844, following a decision taken the previous year, the seat of government was removed from Port Louis to Port William, where the settlement was named Stanley.

A grant-in-aid was approved in 1841 and continued until 1880. A grant-in-aid for a mail service continued until 1884-85, since when the territory has been self-supporting. The development of the islands has been closely linked with the growth of the Falkland Islands Company, the largest landowner and trading company, formed in 1851.

Of the Dependencies, South Georgia was probably discovered by the London merchant de la Roche in 1675 and formally annexed in 1775 by Captain Cook, who in the same year discovered and took possession of the South Sandwich group.

In 1969, a British Antarctic Survey was been set up at King Edward Point, South Georgia, where there has been a Government Station since 1909. It was manned in 1971 by a wintering party of 13. The Base Commander is responsible for the local administration of the Island.

LAND POLICY

All the land in the Colony is held freehold and mostly by a very few large farms. Certain areas are Crown reserves.

CONSTITUTION

The Government is administered by a Governor aided by an Executive Council which is composed of two *ex-officio* members, two unofficial members appointed by the Governor and two elected members of the Legislative Council elected by that Council's elected and independent members, and a Legislative Council composed of two *ex-officio* members, two nominated independent members and four elected members. There is a town council for Stanley. A Court of Appeal was set up on 1st July 1965, to hear and determine appeals from the courts of the Falkland Islands and the Dependencies.

HISTORICAL LIST OF GOVERNORS
(From 1833 to 1842 the Settlement was in charge of a serving naval officer.)

1842	Lieut. R. C. Moody	1915	Sir W. D. Young, KBE, CMG
1848	George Rennie	1920	Sir John Middleton, KBE, CMG
1855	Captain T. E. L. Moore, RN	1927	Sir Arnold Hodson, KCMG
1862	Captain J. G. McKenzie, RN	1931	Sir James O'Grady, KCMG
1866	W. C. F. Robinson	1935	Sir Herbert Henniker-Heaton, KCMG
1870	Col. G. A. K. D'Arcy	1941	Sir Allan Cardinall, KBE, CMG
1876	T. F. Callaghan, CMG	1946	Sir Miles Clifford, KBE, CMG, ED
1880	Thomas Kerr, CMG	1954	Sir Rayner Arthur, KCMG, CVO
1891	Sir R. T. Goldsworthy, KCMG	1957	Sir Edwin Arrowsmith, KCMG
1897	Sir Wm. Grey-Wilson, KCMG, KBE	1964	Sir Cosmo Haskard, KCMG, MBE
1904	Sir W. L. Allardyce, KCMG	1970	E. G. Lewis, OBE

EXECUTIVE COUNCIL
The Governor
The Colonial Secretary
The Colonial Treasurer
A. G. Barton, CBE, JP
S. Miller, JP
R. V. Goss, OBE, ED
R. M. Pitaluga
Clerk: H. L. Bound, MBE, JP

LEGISLATIVE COUNCIL
The Governor (*President*)(*ex-officio*)
The Colonial Secretary (*ex-officio*)
The Colonial Treasurer (*ex-officio*)
R. V. Goss, OBE, ED
S. Miller, JP
Mrs N. King
R. M. Pitaluga
W. H. Clement, JP
R. W. Hills
Clerk: H. L. Bound, MBE, JP

CIVIL ESTABLISHMENT

GOVERNOR AND COMMANDER-IN-CHIEF: Mr E. G. Lewis, OBE

—

Colonial Secretary: J. A. Jones, OBE
Colonial Treasurer: L. C. Gleadell, OBE, JP
Auditor: (Vacant)
Inspector of Police: T. J. Peck
Collector of Customs and Harbour Master: H. T. Luxton.

Registrar-General: H. Bennett, JP
Senior Medical Officer: Dr J. H. Ashmore, JP
Superintendent of Education: D. J. Draycott
Superintendent, Posts and Telecommunications: J. Bound, ED, JP
Superintendent of Works: T. W. Royans
Director of Civil Aviation: J. Kerr, MBE
Superintendent, Power and Electrical: E. C. Gutteridge, JP

READING LIST

CAWKELL, M. B. R., MALING, D. H. and CAWKELL, E. M. The Falkland Islands. *Macmillan*, 1960.

FISHER, Margery and FISHER, J. Shackleton. *Barrie*, 1957.

LANSING, A. Shackleton's Valiant Voyage. *University of London Press*, 1963.

SUTTON, G. Glacier Isle: the official account of the British South Georgia Expedition 1954-55. *Chatto and Windus*, 1957.

Falkland Islands Journals 1967-70.

Falkland Islands & Dependencies Report for 1968 & 1969 HMSO 1971.

GIBRALTAR

GIBRALTAR is a narrow peninsula running southwards from the south-west coast of Spain to which it is connected by a sandy isthmus about one mile long and half a mile wide. The name derives from the Arabic *jabal Tariq* (Tariq's mountain), after the Berber leader Tariq ibn Ziyad, who landed at or near Gibraltar in A.D. 711. The territory consists of a long, high mountain known as the Rock and a sandy plain to the north of it, raised only a few feet above sea level, called the North Front. The total area of the territory is two and a quarter square miles. Five miles across the bay to the west lies the Spanish port of Algeciras and 20 miles across the Straits, to the south, is Africa. The Mediterranean lies to the east. The distance to Britain is approximately 1,400 miles by sea.

The top of the Rock is a sharp, knife-edge ridge extending for about a mile and a half from the north escarpment, which is completely inaccessible, and then sloping gradually to the south for about a mile, to terminate at the southern extremity, Europa Point, in perpendicular cliffs about a hundred feet high. Its greatest elevation is 1,396 feet. The whole upper length of the eastern face is inaccessible and the steep upper half of the western slopes is uninhabited.

The two main sources of water supplies in Gibraltar are the wells on the sandy plain to the north, and a 225,000g.p.d. distiller commissioned in 1969. Rainwater is collected on the water catchments on the east side of the rock face, and led into reservoirs hollowed out inside the Rock.

The climate of Gibraltar is temperate. During the winter months the prevailing wind is from the west, often north-west and occasionally south-west. Snow or frost is extremely rare. The mean minimum and maximum temperatures during this period are 12°C (54°F) and 18°C (65°F) respectively.

In summer a warm breeze laden with moisture, known as the "Levanter", strikes the eastern face of the Rock, condenses in the sky above and causes a cloud pall to hang over the city and bay. During this period the climate is humid and relaxing. The minimum and maximum temperatures in the summer are 13°C (55°F) and 29°C (85°F) respectively. The rainy season is spread over the period September to May; the average annual rainfall is 35 inches.

The population of Gibraltar is European, of British, Genoese, Portuguese and Maltese extraction. During the long period of British possession of the Rock it has grown into a prosperous and homogeneous community with strong links with Britain.

The first post-war census, taken in 1951, showed a total civilian population of 22,848, which had increased to 24,075 by 1961. The next census, which was due to have been taken in 1971, was brought forward to 1970 and revealed a population of 26,833. These figures exclude visitors and transients, but do include families of service personnel. The increase in population between 1961 and 1970 is largely accounted for by the fact that the 1970 census figure includes Moroccan temporary residents, who—since 1969—have replaced some of the Spanish frontier labour force, which in 1961 were not included in the census, because of their living in Spain and coming daily to work in Gibraltar. The official language is English, though the population is bilingual in English and Spanish.

The main religious denominations are Roman Catholic, who make up 78 per cent of the population, Church of England and Jewish. The Church of England and Jewish communities represent 8 per cent and 2½ per cent respectively. There are small communities of other religious denominations. There are also some 2,000 Moslems (about 8 per cent) who are temporarily resident in Gibraltar for purposes of employment.

There were 573 births and 268 deaths in 1970.

Total expenditure on medical and public health services in 1970 was £442,686. The number of beds available in hospitals was 242 and there were 3,762 inpatient admissions during the year.

Almost half the male wage-earners in Gibraltar are employed in one or other of the United Kingdom Departments (i.e. Ministry of Defence and the Department of the Environment) or the Gibraltar Government. In the private sector the main sources of employment are the construction industry, hotel and catering services and retail distribution. A substantial number of clerical workers are also employed in shipping offices and trading agencies.

There are a number of small industrial concerns such as coffee roasting and blending, meat canning, assembling of watches, and the manufacture of mineral water and various items of clothing for local needs and export.

RETAIL PRICE INDICES
Working Class
January 1954 = 100

1960 Averages	..	118
1961 „	..	119
1962 „	..	122
1963 „	..	129
1964 „	..	132
1965 „	..	137
1966* „	..	101
1967 „	..	104
1968 „	..	110
1969 „	..	116
1970 „	..	126

* A new index was introduced as from January 1966.

The value of all imports during 1970 was £10,315,751 of which about £2·8 million was in respect of foodstuffs. 57 per cent came from the United Kingdom, which is by far the leading supplier of goods to Gibraltar.

			IMPORTS £m.	EXPORTS £m.
1963	..	..	13·1	2·65
1964	..	..	13·2	2·71
1965	..	..	9·2	3·1
1966	..	..	9·2	2·8
1967	..	..	9·6	2·6
1968	..	..	10·2	2·4
1969	..	..	10·0	2·1
1970	..	..	10·2	3·1

At the end of 1970 the total insured labour force was 9,586. This includes 3,198 aliens. There are 16 registered trade unions and 11 employers' associations.

The Port of Gibraltar offers 5,500 feet of alongside and protected berths to merchant shipping for passenger and cargo handling, bunkering, taking on supplies and for repairs. An additional 3,000 feet of alongside berths is available on a restricted basis for bunkering and for repairs. It also has a general purpose anchorage, the Commercial Anchorage, which is used by just over 50 per cent of the deepsea vessels calling at Gibraltar. A fully equipped Yacht Marina offers well protected berths for yachts and provides many auxiliary facilities.

There is a commercial ship repair yard and foundry capable of all types of repairs to hulls and marine engines. Another firm specialises in the underwater cleaning of ships' hulls and various underwater hull repairs. H.M. Dockyard drydock, slipway and repair facilities are available on application and subject to service requirements. No. 1 drydock is 904·8 feet in length (caisson in outer stop'), 122·7 feet in breadth at entrance and the sill is 36·5 feet below chart datum. A quick and efficient oil bunkering service is provided on a 24-hour basis at alongside and anchorage berths.

A total of 2,368 merchant ships of 10,171,848 net registered tons including R.F.A.'s. entered the Port of Gibraltar during 1970. Of these 1,765 were deep-sea ships amounting to 9,922,962 n.r.t. including 89 cruise ships. Additionally, 1,130 yachts amounting to 34,923 n.r.t. called at the Port.

66,002 passengers disembarked, there were an additional 59,478 sightseeing passengers and 37,433 passengers embarked from Gibraltar during the year (by sea). The number of passengers embarked and disembarked includes 26,859 day excursionists.

Gibraltar Airport is situated at North Front in the area adjoining the frontier with Spain and approximately 1 mile from the centre of Town. The runway is 2,000 yards long. Air Traffic Control, meteorological facilities and the maintenance and operation of Gibraltar Airport are the responsibility of the R.A.F. who have an agreement with Gibraltar Airways for the handling by the latter of all civil aircraft.

There are regular air services operated by British European Airways and Caledonian/BUA direct from London to Gibraltar. BEA also operate a once-weekly service to and from Madrid and commenced a winter through service to Marrakesh in November 1970. Gibraltar Airways, a BEA Associate Company, provides twice-daily services between Gibraltar and Tangier. During 1970 there was a total of 1,272 commercial flights. The main operators were BEA, Gibair and BUA.

Bland Line operate a passenger and car ferry between Gibraltar and Tangier giving 5 services per week in winter and 8 services per week in summer.

There are no railways in Gibraltar. The total mileage of roads is 25¾. The length of road open to traffic in the City is 8 miles, in the South District 6½ miles and in the area of North Front and Catalan Bay 5½ miles, in the Port 1½, on the Upper Rock 3½, and in tunnels ¾ miles. There are also some 4½ miles of pedestrian way, making up a total of 30 miles. The motor roads are in good condition and suitable for vehicular traffic. A number of bus services maintain communication between all parts of the City and North and South districts.

The Gibraltar Broadcasting Corporation, formed late in 1963, is responsible for radio and television broadcasting with Thomson Television International as the managing agents. In 1958 Radio Gibraltar was inaugurated with two ·5 Kilowatt transmitters operating on a frequency of 1,484 Kc/s, 202·2 metres. A third transmitter operating on 1 kilowatt was installed in 1961. G.B.C.-Radio (Radio Gibraltar) broadcasts in English and Spanish for 16 hours daily, an average of 5 hours weekly being devoted to commercial broadcasting. In addition to live and locally recorded programmes, use is made of B.B.C. transcriptions and relays. At the end of 1970, 3,514 radio receiving licences were held by radio owners. G.B.C.-T.V. operates for 4½ hours daily in English. The station operates on frequency allocations of E6 182.25–187, 75–7,000 MK/s link. There were 6,869 licensed T.V. sets at the end of 1970.

The expenditure on new housing amounted to £741,330 of which £341,330 was met from grants and the remainder from local funds. A total of 368 flats were under construction during 1970. Two blocks, comprising 110 flats, were due for completion during 1971 while the remainder, comprising the Glacis Scheme, were due to be completed between the end of 1971 and mid 1972.

In the private sector, construction was confined to enlarging existing buildings and alterations to internal layouts mainly to improve sanitary facilities. Developments completed in 1970 were extensions to the Caleta Palace Hotel and the Rock Hotel, contributing largely to the 21 per cent increase in the number of beds available to tourists.

Assistance towards the cost of financing these and other developments has been forthcoming from the Gibraltar Government Programme assistance for hotel development. In addition, all these projects will qualify under the Development Aid Ordinance for relief from income tax and rates.

In December 1969 the British Government agreed to provide financial and technical assistance to Gibraltar in support of the current development programme (1970-73), totalling some £4·1 million (excluding the cost of technical assistance). Included in this programme are schemes for housing and tourist development, and educational, medical and public health projects.

The British Government have subsequently undertaken to provide further aid amounting to £5·15 million in support of the next development programme for the years 1973-76. This will be largely utilised for the construction of a housing estate comprising 650 dwellings and connected amenities.

Taxation is mainly indirect but income tax was introduced in 1953. The main heads of taxation and the yields in 1970 were: Customs, £1,208,711; Estate Duties, £62,411; Stamp Duties, £14,030; Licences, £74,408; Income Tax, £520,416. In addition the Gibraltar Government Lottery yielded a profit of £116,352. The standard rate of income tax is 37½p in the £ (four-fifths of which is applicable to taxpayers other than companies or individuals). The rates applicable to individuals resident in Gibraltar range from 5p to 30p in the £.

COMMERCIAL BANKS

| | | LIABILITIES (£m.) | | | ASSETS (£m.) | |
| | | Balances due to Banks | | | Loans and | Balances due from Banks | |
	Deposits	abroad	Other		Advances	abroad	Other
1964	7·1	—	0·7		1·4	4·4	2·0
1965	6·4	—	0·6		1·5	4·0	1·5
1966	6·7	—	0·6		1·8	3·7	1·8
1967	7·5	0·1	0·7		2·5	3·9	1·9
1968	8·2	0·3	0·6		2·4	4·2	2·5
1969	8·7	0·8	1·0		5·1	2·1	3·3
1970	10·4	1·3	1·2		5·5	4·0	3·4

Under the Development Aid Ordinance, including schemes of mechanisation, profits accruing from capital invested on approved schemes of development are granted relief from income tax to the extent of the amount of capital invested in the scheme.

With the introduction of the 1970 budget a new 10 per cent *ad valorem* import duty was imposed on all items which had previously been duty free, with a few exceptions such as foodstuffs, drugs and medical preparations and certain basic building materials. Preferential rates of duty apply to certain imports of Commonwealth origin, while alcoholic beverages imported in bulk attract reduced rates. A drawback is allowed on certain goods warehoused in a Government store and subsequently exported from Gibraltar and on clothing materials used in the local manufactures of garments for export.

Stamp Duties are chargeable under the Stamp Duties Ordinance, the provisions of which follow closely the Stamp Act, 1891, the rates being the same as those in force in Britain. The bulk of the revenue from stamp duties in Gibraltar is derived from transactions in real property.

Estate Duty is levied on a sliding scale ranging from 1 per cent on an estate valued at between £2,000 and £3,000 to 20 per cent on an estate exceeding £100,000 in value. Estates the value of which do not exceed £2,000 are exempt.

Revenue for 1969 totalled £2,635,871. Customs accounted for £956,502 and licences and internal revenue for £571,978. Expenditure in 1969 amounted to £2,467,004 of which the main heads of expenditure were Social Services, £962,004; Public Works, £252,479; Justice, Law and Order, £206,057.

Education in Gibraltar is free and universal and the medium of instruction in the schools is English. Education is compulsory between the ages of five and fifteen and scholarships are made available for universities, teacher training and other higher education in Britain. There are ten Government primary schools and two private schools and two Services schools. At the end of the year there were 2,044 pupils enrolled in Government schools and 1,338 in private schools and Services schools, making a total of 3,382. Secondary education is provided by two selective schools, one for boys and one for girls and four non-selective schools. The age of transfer is 11+.

On 31st December 1970, there were 625 pupils in selective schools (319 boys, 306 girls) and 1,109 pupils in non-selective schools (575 boys, 534 girls) and 51 girls in the commercial school. The schools prepare candidates for the G.C.E. papers of the Cambridge Local Syndicate and Royal Society of Arts examinations. Government recurrent expenditure on education in 1970 amounted to £297,100. The number of children at school was 5,217 including 50 in technical and vocational schools.

A lending library is maintained by Government in the cultural centre—John Mackintosh Hall—to which the British Council also make a contribution. At the Gibraltar Garrison Library, established in 1739, an extensive reference section and lending library are available to members. The Museum contains exhibits of historical interest connected with Gibraltar.

HISTORY AND CONSTITUTION

Gibraltar was possessed successively by the Phoenicians, Carthaginians, Romans and Visigoths, but remained uninhabited till the Mohammedan invasion of Spain. It was held alternately by Moors and Spaniards until 1704, when during the war of the Spanish succession it was captured by the British forces under Admiral Sir George Rooke and ceded to Great Britain by the Treaty of Utrecht in 1713. The cession was renewed by the Treaty of Versailles in 1783. Many attempts have been made to take Gibraltar, especially during the great siege in 1779–83, when General Eliott (afterwards Lord Heathfield) defended it against the united forces of Spain and France, but all have been unsuccessful and it has remained in British hands since its capture in 1704.

On 10th September 1967 Her Majesty's Government held a referendum in Gibraltar in which they invited the Gibraltarians to state which of the following courses would better serve their interests:—

A. To pass under Spanish sovereignty in accordance with the terms proposed by the Spanish Government to the Government of the United Kingdom on 18th May 1966; or

B. Voluntarily to retain their link with the United Kingdom, with democratic local institutions and with the United Kingdom retaining its present responsibilities.

The result of the referendum was as follows:

Total votes cast	12,237
Votes cast for alternative A	44
Votes cast for alternative B	12,138
Invalid votes	55

Under the Gibraltar Constitution Order in Council 1964, there was a Gibraltar Council, a Council of Ministers, and a Legislative Council consisting of a speaker appointed by the Governor, 11 elected members and two *ex-officio* members, the Attorney-General and the Financial Secretary. At Constitutional talks held in Gibraltar in July 1968, agreement was reached with local leaders on the lines of certain constitutional changes. These were incorporated in the new 1969 Constitution which is contained in the Gibraltar Constitution Order 1969, and which came into effect on 11th August, 1969. This replaced the Legislative Council by a House of Assembly consisting of a Speaker, 15 elected members, the Attorney-General and the Financial & Development Secretary and formalised the devolution of responsibility for certain defined domestic matters to Ministers appointed from among the elected members of the Assembly. It also made provision for the abolition of the City Council, which dealt with municipal affairs and public utilities. The Governor retains direct responsibility for matters relating to defence, external affairs and internal security. He has the power to intervene in the conduct of domestic affairs in support of this responsibility; and has certain powers of intervention in the interests of maintaining financial and economic stability.

Executive authority is exercised by the Governor, who is also Commander in Chief. In the exercise of his functions relating to matters not dealt with by Ministers, the Governor, whilst retaining the usual reserved powers, normally acts in accordance with the advice of the Gibraltar Council (which consists of the Chief Minister, the Deputy Fortress Commander, the Deputy Governor, the Attorney-General, the Financial Secretary and four other Ministers). The elected members of the Gibraltar Council are appointed by the Governor after consultation with the Chief Minister. There is a Council of Ministers composed of all the Ministers and presided over by the Chief Minister.

The preamble to the Order in Council (to which the new Constitution is an annex) contains the following:

"Whereas Gibraltar is part of Her Majesty's dominions and Her Majesty's Government have given assurance to the people of Gibraltar that Gibraltar will remain part of Her Majesty's dominions unless and until an Act of Parliament otherwise provides, and furthermore, that Her Majesty's Government will never enter into arrangements under which the people of Gibraltar would pass under the sovereignty of another state against their freely and democratically expressed wishes."

The Constitution also contains a Chapter providing for the protection of fundamental rights and freedoms on the lines of similar Chapters in the constitutions of various other territories within the Commonwealth.

Governors of Gibraltar since the Great Siege of 1779–1783

1776	Lt.-Gen. Sir G. A. Eliott, KCB (later Baron Heathfield of Gibraltar)	1891	General Sir L. Nicholson, KCB
1784	Major-Gen. C. O'Hara	1893	General Sir R. Biddulph, GCB, GCMG
1791	Lt.-Gen. Sir R. Boyd	1900	Field Marshal Sir G. S. White, VC, GCB, OM, GCSI, GCMG, GCIE, GCVO
1794	General Sir H. Clinton, KCB (*Lieut.-Governor*)		
1794	General Rainsford	1905	General Sir F. W. E. F. Forestier-Walker, GCMG, KCB
1795	General C. O'Hara	1910	General Sir Archibald Hunter, GCB, GCVO, DSO
1801	Major-Gen. Sir T. Trigge, KB (*Lieut.-Governor*)		
1802	H.R.H. the Duke of Kent, KG	1913	Lt.-Gen. Sir H. S. G. Miles, GCB, GCMG, GBE, CVO
1802	Major-Gen. Barnett	1918	General Sir Horace Smith-Dorrien, GCB, GCMG, DSO
1804	Lt.-Gen. The Hon. R. E. Fox		
1806	Lt.-Gen. Sir H. Dalrymple, KCB	1923	General Sir Charles Monro, Bt, GCB, GCMG, GCSI
1806	Major-Gen. Drummond	1928	General Sir Alexander Godley, GCB, KCMG
1809	General Sir J. Cradock, KCB	1933	General Sir Charles Harington, GCB, GBE, DSO
1810	Lt.-Gen. Sir C. Campbell, KCB		
1814	Lt.-Gen. Sir G. Don, GCB	1938	General Sir Edmund (afterwards Field Marshal, Lord) Ironside, GCB, CMG, DSO
1814	Major-Gen. Smith		
1820	General J. Pitt, Earl of Chatham, KG	1939	Lt.-Gen. Sir Clive Liddell, KCB, CMG, CBE, DSO
1831	General Sir W. Houston, Bt., GCB, GCH (*Lieut.-Governor*)	1941	General (afterwards Field Marshal) the Viscount Gort, VC, GCB, CBE, DSO, MVO, MC
1835	Major-Gen. Sir A. Woodford, GCB GCMG		
1842	General Sir R. T. Wilson	1942	Lt.-Gen. Sir Noel Mason-MacFarlane, KCB, DSO, MC
1848	Major-Gen. Sir R. W. Gardiner, KCB KCH	1944	Lt.-Gen. Sir Ralph Eastwood, KCB, DSO, MC
1855	Lt.-Gen. Sir J. Fergusson, GCB	1947	General Sir Kenneth Anderson, KCB, MC
1859	Lt.-Gen. Sir W. J. Codrington, KCB		
1865	Lt.-Gen. Sir R. (later Lord) Airey, GCB	1952	General Sir Gordon MacMillan, KCB, KCVO, CBE, DSO, MC
1870	General Sir W. F. Williams of Kars, Bt., GCB	1955	Lt.-Gen. Sir Harold Redman, KCB, CBE
1876	General Lord Napier of Magdala, GCB, GCSI	1958	General Sir Charles Keightley, GCB, GBE, DSO
1883	General Sir J. M. Adye, GCB	1962	General Sir Dudley Ward, GCB, KBE, DSO
1886	General Sir A. E. Hardinge, KCB, CIE	1965	General Sir Gerald W. Lathbury, GCB, DSO, MBE
1890	General Sir Leicester Smyth, KCB, KCMG	1969	Admiral of the Fleet Sir Varyl Begg, GCB, DSO, DSC

The 1802–1814 entries (Barnett through Smith) are bracketed as *Lieut.-Governors.*

Gibraltar Council

The Governor

Ex-officio Members

The Deputy Fortress Commander
The Deputy Governor
The Attorney-General
The Financial and Development Secretary

Elected Members
Major R. J. Peliza
M. Xiberras
Major A. Gache
J. Caruana
W. M. Isola

COUNCIL OF MINISTERS

Major R. J. Peliza (Chief Minister)
M. Xiberras (Minister for Labour and Social Security)
J. Caruana (Minister for Public Works and Housing)
Major A. Gache (Minister for Information, Port, Trade and Industry)
W. M. Isola (Minister for Tourism and Municipal Services)
L. Devincenzi (Minister for Education and Recreation)
Miss C. Anes (Minister for Medical and Health Services)

HOUSE OF ASSEMBLY
The Speaker: A. J. Vasquez

The Attorney-General
The Financial and Development Secretary
15 Elected Members
Clerk of the Council: Joseph L. Ballantine

CIVIL ESTABLISHMENT

GOVERNOR AND COMMANDER-IN-CHIEF
Admiral of the Fleet Sir Varyl Begg, GCB, DSO, DSC
Military Assistant:
Brigadier (Retd.) S. C. Chambers, CBE
Aide-de-Camp: Captain R. H. Stopford, The Black Watch

Deputy Governor: E. H. Davis, CMG, OBE
Attorney-General: R. H. Hickling, CMG
Financial and Development Secretary: A. Mackay, CMG
Administrative Secretary: J. L. Pitaluga, MBE
Accountant-General: J. H. Romero
Deputy Commissioner of Income Tax: J. De la Paz
Director of Audits: J. A. Frost
Chief Education Officer: (vacant)
Director of Labour and Social Security: C. J. Gareze
Director of Public Works: J. Martin, OBE
Commissioner of Lands and Works: J. W. Coelho

Director of Medical and Health Services: Dr D. Bacarese-Hamilton
Hospital Administrator: Surgeon Captain E. H. Murchison, OBE
Commissioner of Police: J. B. O. Bird, MBE, QPM
Deputy Commissioner of Police: F. Llambias, MBE, QPM
Captain of the Port and Shipping Master: R. L. Rickard, OBE
Postmaster: J. A. Giraldi
Superintendent of Prison: F. Massetti
Director of Tourism: J. E. A. Vaughan, MBE
Chief Planning Officer: H. Kendall, OBE

JUDICIARY
Chief Justice: Sir Edgar Unsworth, CMG
Judge of the Court of First Instance, Stipendiary Magistrate,
Coroner and Public Trustee: J. E. Alcantara
Registrar, Supreme Court: F. E. Pizzarello

READING LIST

ANDREWS, A. Proud Fortress: the fighting story of Gibraltar. *Evans*, 1958.

CONN, S. Gibraltar in British Diplomacy in the Eighteenth Century. *Oxford University Press*, 1942.

DRINKWATER, Col. J. A History of the Siege of Gibraltar 1779–1783. New Edition. London, 1905.

GARRATT, G. T. Gibraltar and the Mediterranean. *Cape*, London, 1939.

HOWES, Dr H. W. The Story of Gibraltar. *Philip & Tacey*, 1946.

HOWES, Dr H. W. The Gibraltarian. *City Press*, Colombo, 1951.

KENYON, E. R. Gibraltar Under Moor, Spaniard and Briton. *Methuen*, 1938.

McGuffie, T. H. The Siege of Gibraltar. *Batsford*, 1965.

Russell, J. Gibraltar Besieged 1779–1783. *Heinemann*, 1965.

HMSO London, (Miscellaneous No. 12) (1965)—Gibraltar, Recent Differences with Spain (Cmnd 2632), April 1965.

HMSO London (Miscellaneous No. 13) (1966)—Gibraltar, Talks with Spain (Cmnd 3131), May, October, 1966.

HMSO London (Miscellaneous No. 6) (1967)—Further Documents on Gibraltar (Cmnd 3325), October 1966–June 1967.

HONG KONG

H ONG KONG was founded as a British trading depot in 1841, the cession of the Island to Great Britain being confirmed by the Treaty of Nanking in 1842. The area on which the main urban part of Kowloon now stands, together with Stonecutters Island in the harbour, Ap Lei Chau and Green Island, was ceded by the Convention of Peking in 1860; and in 1898 the New Territories, whch consist of the rural area north of Kowloon and the islands around Hong Kong, were leased to Great Britain for 99 years. Hong Kong was occupied by the Japanese from 1941 to 1945, and in the following four years made a remarkably rapid recovery.

The territory consists of the island of Hong Kong and a portion of the mainland to the North, together with 235 adjacent islands ranging from Lantao with an area of about 58 square miles, to uninhabited rocky islets. A peninsula, on which Kowloon stands, juts southward from the mainland towards Victoria on Hong Kong island. Between these two lies the harbour, one of the finest natural ports in the world. Much of the built-up area surrounding the harbour has been reclaimed or levelled.

Hong Kong lies on the south-east coast of China, adjoining the province of Kwangtung. It is just inside the tropics, less then 100 miles south of the tropic of Cancer, and lies between latitudes 22° 9′ and 22° 37′ N. and longitudes 113° 52′ and 114° 30′ E.

The area of land is approximately 398½ square miles (Hong Kong Island 29 square miles, Kowloon 3½ square miles, Stonecutters Island ¼ square mile, New Territories (leased) 365¾ square miles). It includes all islands within a rectangular area of some 738 square miles, containing the leased and ceded territory. British waters are bounded on the north by the shores of Deep Bay and Mirs Bay, between which lies the land frontier with China.

The overwhelming majority of the population lives on Hong Kong Island or in Kowloon. The capital is Victoria, on Hong Kong Island. The principal centres of population in the New Territories are Tsuen Wan, which has grown over the past 20 years into an important industrial centre with large textile, enamel and rubber factories, iron works, etc.; Cheung Chau, a small but densely populated island, important as a market and fishing centre; Yuen Long, a mainland market town; Tai O, a fishing and market centre on Lantao Island; Tai Po and Shek Wu Hui, both mainland market towns; and Peng Chau, an island fishing port, with some industries. The success of the planned development of Tseun Wan into an industrial satellite has led to the formulation of similar proposals for Castle Peak and Sha Tin. Site preparation for these areas is now well advanced.

The greater part of the territory consists of steep, unproductive hillside, in some parts covered with dense scrub. The erosion which resulted from indiscriminate felling of trees during the Japanese wartime occupation has been extensively repaired under a vigorous programme of afforestation. Cultivation is confined mainly to the narrow valleys. The coastline is sharply indented. A steep range of hills divides Kowloon from the New Territories to the North, in the centre of which is the highest mountain—Tai Mo Shan, 3,140 feet; Lantao Peak is 3,061 feet and Victoria Peak on Hong Kong Island 1,809 feet high.

The climate is sub-tropical and governed by monsoons, the winter being cool and dry, the summer hot and humid. The mean monthly temperature varies from 15°C (59°F) in February to 28°C (82°F) in July. The actual temperature rarely rises above 35°C (95°F) or falls below 4°C (40°F). The average annual rainfall is 2,168·8 mm. (85·39 in.), three-quarters of which falls between May and September. The mean relative humidity exceeds 80 per cent during the summer but in early winter sometimes falls as low as 20 per cent. The temperature range is 0°-36°C (32°F-97°F) and the annual rainfall range is 901·1-3,040·7 mm. (35·48-119·71 in.). The Royal Observatory provides all meteorological information in Hong Kong and also forms part of a worldwide network of meteorological services.

Censuses are normally taken every ten years but there was a long gap between the census of 1931 and that of 1961 when the population was 3,133,131. A by-census was taken in August 1966 and the total population was 3,716,400. The 1971 census showed that the population had increased to 3,950,802. The registered numbers of live births and deaths for the year 1970 were 77,465 and 20,763 respectively. No division by 'race' or 'tribe' is possible, but about 98½ per cent speak a Chinese language or have traditional connections with China, though 57 per cent are British subjects by virtue of birth in Hong Kong. 81 per cent of the population speak Cantonese as their usual language, but there are substantial minorities speaking Hakka, Hoklo and Sze Yap and smaller groups who speak English (the official language of the territory), Shanghai, Kuo Yu, Portuguese and Malay. Most of the younger members of these minority groups also speak Cantonese.

A brief account of religious practices in Hong Kong must embrace such diverse subjects as traditional Chinese beliefs, Taoism, the religious aspects of Confucian teaching, Buddhism, Islam, Hinduism and a kaleidoscope of Christian sects. In seeking one idiom to express all this it is easy to be misled by the entirely different appearances of religious observance, particularly between the traditional Chinese practices and those of the Christian churches, and even to assume a relative lack of religion in Chinese life. It is true that Hong Kong's business centre may not have as many temples as there are Wren churches in the City of London, but there are likely to be at least as many signs of religion in the average Chinese home, or business, as in its Western counterpart. Almost every Chinese shop has its 'God Shelf' and many homes their ancestral shrines. Whether the devotion before such symbols is intense or perfunctory there is an unmistakably religious element in Chinese culture. It may find expression in traditional ancestral ceremonies encouraged by Confucius or through a wide variety of Taoist rituals. There has been a notable revival of Buddhism and Taoism in recent years mainly due to the immigration of Buddhists from China. Buddhism appears to have more followers in Hong Kong, but both maintain a strong hold among the older Chinese and are far from dying out among the younger people. The Hong Kong Buddhist Association is their main organisation, although a Taoist Association has now also been formed.

The fact that Chinese may follow one or the other of these ways, or may combine them without any feeling of incongruity, has often meant that Christianity with its exclusive claims has been politely ignored in the Chinese world; but it is nevertheless rooted deeply and growing rapidly in Hong Kong. Its roots go back indeed to the earliest days of the territory. St John's Cathedral was founded in 1842, and established as a Cathedral by Letters Patent from Queen Victoria in 1850. A representative of the London Missionary Society arrived at about the same time. St Andrew's Church celebrated its Diamond Jubilee in 1966. It is estimated there are now 261 churches and chapels in the territory.

The major world denominations are represented in Hong Kong in the Adventists, Anglicans, Baptists, Lutherans, Methodists, and Pentecostals, etc., while Congregational and Presbyterian effort contributed to the Church of Christ in China. Most of these engage in educational work to some extent.

The first Roman Catholic priests to arrive in Hong Kong were chaplains serving the spiritual needs of British soldiers of the Catholic faith. On 23rd April 1841, Pope Gregory XVI established the Apostolic Prefecture of Hong Kong with Mgr Theodore Joset as the first prefect. Since the Second World War the Catholic Church has notably expanded its educational and social activities. There are at present 259 Catholic primary and secondary schools with an aggregate enrolment of 224,151 pupils.

Hong Kong's Jewish community worships at a synagogue in Robinson Road constructed in 1901 on land given by Mr Joseph Sassoon and his family. Mr Sassoon built the synagogue in memory of his mother Leah and it is therefore known as the Synagogue 'Ohel Leah'. The Jewish Recreation Club and the residential rabbi's apartments are on the same site. There are about 500 people in the congregation and they belong to families who originally came from Britain, China, India, Eastern and Western Europe, and the United States, as well as people born in Hong Kong.

There are about 8,000 followers of Islam in Hong Kong, most of them Chinese who have immigrated during the past two decades. The other members of the Muslim community are mainly Pakistanis, Malaysians, Persians and people from neighbouring regions. They gather for prayer at the Shelley Street Mosque on Hong Kong Island and at the Nathan Road Mosque in Kowloon.

The Health division of the Medical and Health Department undertakes the control of anti-epidemic measures, the care of expectant and parturient mothers, infant welfare work and preventive measures against disease in schools. It is also responsible for port and airport health work, social hygiene, industrial health, tuberculosis control and a B.C.G. campaign, food and drug control, public health propaganda and pathological, chemical and biochemical laboratory work.

The general state of health is good. The crude birth rate in 1970 was 18·9 per 1,000 population and the crude death rate was 5·1 per 1,000 population. Infant mortality rate was 19·6 per 1,000 live births and the maternal mortality rate was 0·19 per 1,000 total births.

The Government maintains and operates sixteen general and special hospitals and provides financial assistance to seventeen other hospitals run by voluntary organisations. In addition, there are eleven private hospitals which do not receive financial help from the Government. At the end of 1970 the number of beds in the three groups of hospitals including maternity beds was 6,299, 7,533 and 1,806 respectively giving a total of 15,638 beds.

In patients treated in all hospitals during 1970 totalled 323,853 and out-patient attendances at Government and Government-aided institutions totalled 9,262,368. There are large numbers of dispensaries and clinics in both urban and rural areas and the more remote places are served by mobile dispensaries, 'floating clinics' and a 'flying doctor' service.

Government expenditure on these services during the year 1970/71 was approximately $234·6 million, compared with $205·9 million in the previous year, excluding capital expenditure on medical projects under Public Works Non-recurrent head.

Cholera has not appeared since notification of the last case in October 1969. While tuberculosis remains the major public health problem in Hong Kong, deaths from cancer, diseases of the heart, cerebrovascular lesions and pneumonia are the leading causes of death. The other major infectious diseases, particularly diphtheria and poliomyelitis, remained at a low incidence due to continuing innoculation campaigns. Since December 1967, measles vaccine has been offered to children under four years of age.

Before the war most of the urban population was engaged in commerce but, since 1948, there has been a significant growth in industry. In 1970 there were 589,505 employees in 17,239 registered and recorded factories and industrial undertakings.

The general employment pattern in the 1966 by-census showed that about 47 per cent of the working population was engaged in construction, manufacturing, mining, quarrying and the utilities, about 24 per cent in various services, 17 per cent in commerce, seven per cent in communications and five per cent in agriculture, forestry and fishing. Based on this pattern, the estimated employment figures at the end of 1970 were: manufacture 613,620; services 375,440; commerce 259,690; construction 96,000; farming and fishing 81,300; communications 106,600; public utilities 15,210; mining and quarrying 4,670.

On 31st December 1970 there were 265 registered workers' unions with a declared membership of 176,598; 50 employers' associations with a declared membership of 5,283 and 12 mixed unions with a declared membership of 6,583.

Since the end of the last war, the pattern of agricultural production has largely changed from a subsistence economy based on rice to the intensive cultivation of vegetables, poultry and pigs. Sold through wholesale markets during 1970 were 62,413 metric tons of locally produced vegetables, valued at HK$54,072,619, and 77,944 metric tons of fish valued at HK$136,773,261. Local pig and poultry production is valued at HK$32 million and HK$176·3 million per annum respectively.

CONSUMER PRICE INDEX

Urban households spending less than HK$2,000 per month
September 1963–August 1964=100

1965 Average	..	102·0
1966 „	..	104·7
1967 „	..	111·2
1968 „	..	114·0
1969 „	..	119·0
1970 „	..	126·0

S

Small tonnages of iron ore, wolframite, graphite, kaolin, feldspar and quartz are mined. Of these, the feldspar and quartz and about 20 per cent of the kaolin are consumed by local light industries, the remainder being exported. The total value of minerals exported is about 7 million dollars annually.

Hong Kong, which lies on the main sea and air routes of the Far East, is now established as an industrial territory with an economy based on exports rather than on entrepôt trade. Although entrepôt trade is still significant, accounting for 19 per cent of total exports, it has declined from its traditional supremacy as a result of political changes in China, of the Korean war and of the restrictions on trade with China. The following table shows the overseas trade of Hong Kong for the last three years:

	1968 HK$ million	1969 HK$ million	1970 HK$ million
Imports	12,472	14,893	17,607
Exports	8,428	10,518	12,347
Re-exports	2,142	2,679	2,892

Domestic Exports
1970 total value HK$12,347 million

	per cent of all exports in 1970
Clothing	35
Miscellaneous manufactured articles, n.e.s.	25
Electrical machinery	10
Textile yarn, fabrics and made-up articles	10
Manufactures of metal, n.e.s.	3
Footwear	2

	1970 HK$ million	1969 HK$ million	per cent increase or decrease
Clothing	4,337	3,828	+ 13
Jackets, jumpers, sweaters, cardigans and pullovers, knitted	761	745	+ 2
Slacks, shorts, jeans, trousers, overalls and pinafores, other than knitted	589	553	+ 7
Shirts other than knitted	539	463	+ 16
Suits, jackets, uniforms and overcoats, other than knitted	293	272	+ 8
Other garments, knitted	267	273	− 2
Gloves and mittens of all materials	238	192	+ 24
Shirts, knitted	197	174	+ 13
Blouses and jumpers, other than knitted, not embroidered	169	104	+ 62
Underwear and nightwear, other than knitted	160	164	− 2

	1970 HK$ million	1969 HK$ million	per cent increase or decrease
Clothing continued			
Skirts, dresses, frocks, gowns and house-coats, other than knitted	150	158	— 5
Underwear and nightwear, knitted	127	103	+ 23
Outer garments, other than knitted	108	127	— 15
Miscellaneous manufactured articles, n.e.s. ..	3,142	2,495	+ 26
Wigs, false beards, hair pads, etc.	937	647	+ 45
Plastic toys and dolls	872	771	+ 13
Artificial flowers, foliage or fruit (plastic) ..	416	366	+ 14
Toys and dolls (not plastic)	173	110	+ 57
Plastic coated rattan articles (not furniture) ..	90	100	— 10
Metal watch bands	78	58	+ 26
Electrical machinery	1,293	1,058	+ 22
Transistorised radio receiving sets	549	472	+ 16
Transistors and thermionic and electronic tubes and valves	259	232	+ 12
Textile yarns, fabrics and made-up articles ..	1,277	1,126	+ 13
Cotton grey sheeting	136	114	+ 20
Cotton towels, not dish towels, not embroidered	103	104	— 1
Cotton yarn	101	88	+ 15
Cotton canvas and ducks, grey	64	62	+ 4
Cotton grey twill and sateen	61	45	+ 35
Cotton grey drills	56	59	— 5
Cotton flannels, other than grey	55	48	+ 13
Manufactures of metal, n.e.s.	345	292	+ 18
Domestic utensils of other metals	73	59	+ 24
Locks, padlocks and keys and key chains ..	61	49	+ 25
Domestic utensils of iron and steel, enamelled	32	44	— 26
Footwear	302	295	+ 2
Footwear of textile materials with rubber soles	122	133	— 8
Plastic footwear	73	62	+ 17
Other			
Handbags, wallets, purses and similar articles	124	103	+ 21
Watches, complete	90	81	+ 11
Electric torches	68	65	+ 5
Prawns and shrimps, fresh or frozen	64	78	— 18

Imports in 1970 were valued at HK$17,607 million, of which about 17 per cent was accounted for by foodstuffs. The largest supplier was Japan ($4,188 million), followed by China ($2,830 million), U.S.A. ($2,317 million), U.K. ($1,517 million) and Taiwan ($820 million). The principal import items were live animals, rice, fish and fruit, cotton, crude vegetable materials, plastic materials, textile yarns and fabrics, base metals, machinery and transport equipment, apparatus and appliances.

The value of domestic exports was HK$12,347 million, of which 45 per cent was accounted for by garment and textile products. The leading overseas customers were U.S.A. ($5,190 million), U.K. ($1,481 million), the Federal Republic of Germany ($985 million), Japan ($492 million), Canada ($389 million), and Australia ($359 million). The most important items of domestic manufacture entering the exports trade were clothing, cotton piece goods, toys and games, artificial flowers, footwear, transistor radios, cotton yarn, rattan articles, wigs and false beards, electric torches and enamel ware.

The value of re-exports totalled $2,892 million and the main re-export markets were Japan ($584 million), Singapore ($337 million), U.S.A. ($244 million), Indonesia ($202 million) and Taiwan ($154 million). The principal commodities in the re-export trade were diamonds and jewellery, textiles, medicinal and pharmaceutical products, fruits and vegetables, crude vegetable materials, watches and clocks.

The value of imports, exports and re-exports by main groups for 1960 and 1970 are shown below.

	1960			1970		
	Imports	Exports	Re-exports	Imports	Exports	Re-exports
Commodity	HK$ '000	HK$ '000	HK$ '000	HK$ '000	HK$ '000	HK$ '000
Food, beverages and tobacco	1,468,556	143,447	192,853	3,379,375	243,060	332,072
Crude materials ..	687,462	137,911	171,798	1,328,075	233,222	170,015
Mineral fuels and lubricants ..	197,571	6	5,759	515,126	—	42,146
Animal and vegetable oils and fats ..	64,889	3,600	16,561	99,462	4,299	9,170
Chemicals and chemical products ..	465,903	51,092	130,046	1,422,801	104,109	492,678
Manufactured goods classified by materials ..	1,932,050	769,546	380,489	5,824,848	1,845,540	1,196,220
Machinery and transport equipment..	598,838	76,800	66,151	2,897,029	1,454,723	276,724
Miscellaneous manufactured articles ..	427,360	1,672,761	105,705	2,110,883	8,433,454	358,264
Miscellaneous transactions	21,064	12,086	1,095	29,116	28,095	14,280
Merchandise Total ..	5,863,694	2,867,249	1,070,456	17,606,715	12,346,502	2,891,569
Gold and specie ..	292,759	202	316,822	306,724	—	192,438
Grand Total ..	6,156,453	2,867,451	1,387,278	17,913,438	12,346,502	3,084,007

Direction of Merchandise Trade by percentage

	1960	1970
Imports from		
Japan	16	24
China	20	16
U.S.A.	12	13
United Kingdom	11	9
Exports to		
U.S.A.	26	42
United Kingdom	20	12
Federal Republic of Germany	4	8
Japan	4	4
Re-exports to		
Japan	12	20
Indonesia	7	7
Singapore	18	12
U.S.A.	3	8
Taiwan	6	5

Hong Kong is now also established as one of the main tourist centres in the Far East, and numbers of visitors during 1968, 1969 and 1970 were 618,410, 765,213 and 927,256 respectively.

Hong Kong Banking Statistics

LIABILITIES (£m.)   ASSETS (£m.)

	Deposits	Balances due to Banks abroad	Other	Loans and Advances	Balances due from Banks abroad	Other
31.12.1962	269·4	18·9	192·2	178·0	105·5	197·0
31.12.1963	339·0	25·6	234·6	227·6	129·4	242·2
31.12.1964	405·7	36·2	205·8	288·2	109·1	250·4
31.12.1965	453·2	52·2	248·7	314·8	182·0	257·3
31.12.1966	525·3	62·1	276·7	336·2	238·4	289·5
31.12.1967	561·1	82·4	335·1	367·3	243·0	368·3
31.12.1968	712·5	97·3	359·6	415·0	360·0	394·4
31.12.1969	844·0	126·7	387·8	541·1	392·7	424·7
31.12.1970	1,027·8	152·1	458·0	664·6	487·9	485·4

There are 31 vegetable marketing co-operative societies with a membership of 8,719. These societies have formed a Federation of Vegetable Marketing Co-operative Societies. In addition, four salaried workers' thrift and loan societies, nine consumers' societies, one fish pond society, 234 housing societies, 12 agricultural credit societies, seven thrift and loan societies, 23 better living societies, two apartment owners' societies and 35 pig raising societies have been formed. Many of the last named have also federated and formed a Federation of Pig Raising Societies. Fishermen are becoming more aware of the benefits of co-operation and there are 62 fishermen's credit societies and two fishermen's credit and housing societies. Fifty-four fishermen's co-operative societies have formed themselves into four Federations. The total number of members of co-operative societies is 22,930. Seven wholesale fish markets are operated by the Fish Marketing Organisation. This Organisation also operates schools for fishermen's children and provides education for some 4,000 students.

Some 7,147 ocean-going vessels entered and cleared Hong Kong harbour during 1970, their net registered tonnage being 23,008,320; more than 24,200 passengers landed or embarked by sea during the same period. Frequent ferry services cross the harbour and link the principal islands.

Hong Kong International Airport, Kai Tak, is situated on the mainland portion of the territory on the north shore of Kowloon Bay. It is some 3 miles from the centre of Kowloon, and has a modern runway 8,350 feet long, which is to be extended to 11,130 feet. Twenty-eight international airlines operate regular services to and from Hong Kong.

There is a railway 36 kilometres long connecting Kowloon with the Chinese frontier, but there has been no through passenger traffic since October 1949. Through goods traffic is conveyed in Chinese section wagons. Total goods carried during 1970 amounted to 859,998 metric tons and 10,318,789 passengers were carried.

There are 606 miles of road in the territory maintained by the government. A total of $48 million was spent on major road projects and $11·6 million on road improvements and maintenance during 1970.

Radio Hong Kong is the Government-owned broadcasting service. It transmits programmes on medium wave (20kW) and VHF/FM (50 kW ERP) from two separate stations, in English and four Chinese dialects. There are an estimated 1·5 million radio receivers in use. Receiving licences are not required for radio receivers. Rediffusion (Hong Kong) Ltd operate a commercial wired broadcasting service with programmes in English and Chinese. The organisation is required to relay a certain proportion of programmes from Radio Hong Kong and/or the BBC. At the end of 1970 there were 40,000 loud speakers connected to the service. Rediffusion Ltd also operates a commercial wired television service. The Hong Kong Commercial Broadcasting Company Ltd transmits commercial radio programmes on medium wave (10 kW) in English and Chinese. Hong Kong Television Broadcasts Ltd transmits commercial television programmes on the UHF 625 line PAL colour system, channels 21 and 25, in English and Chinese, video power 10 kW ERP, audio power 2 kW ERP. The annual fee for a television receiving licence is HK $36. Television Broadcasts Ltd is required to permit the Government to use its transmitting facilities for public affairs programmes up to a maximum of one hour daily, and for educational programmes for schools up to a maximum of sixteen hours per week. Public affairs programmes will be produced by a television production unit of Radio Hong Kong, and educational television programmes by a production unit of the Education Department; both units are scheduled to begin operations in 1971. There are now more than two million television viewers, watching some 310 hours of television a week.

Shipping lines serving Hong Kong include: American President Lines Ltd; The Bank Line (China) Ltd; The Ben Line Steamers Ltd; Butterfield & Swire (Hong Kong) Ltd; Compagnie des Messageries Maritimes; Compagnie Maritime des Chargeurs Réunis; Dodwell & Co., Ltd; The East Asiatic Co., Ltd; Far East Enterprising Co. (Hong Kong), Ltd; Gilman & Co., Ltd Shipping

Department; Hong Kong & Eastern Shipping Co., Ltd; Jardine Matheson & Co., Ltd; Jebsen & Co.,; Mackinnon Mackenzie & Co. of Hong Kong Ltd; Mitsui O.S.K. Lines Ltd; Nippon Yusen Kaisha Ltd; Royal Interocean Lines; C. F. Sharp & Company, S.A.; Shun Cheong Steam Navigation Co., Ltd; Thoresen & Co., Ltd; United States Lines Co.; Wallem & Co., Ltd; World-Wide (Shipping) Ltd.

The tremendous growth of population and industry since the end of World War II has created a demand for land and many major reclamations and land formation projects have been carried out. Since 1945, over 1,900 acres have been reclaimed from the sea. These include 680 acres on the east side of Kowloon Bay on part of which the industrial suburb of Kwun Tong is now well established. At Tsuen Wan and Kwai Chung in the New Territories, 370 acres have been reclaimed for development and much of the land formation has already been carried out for new towns at Castle Peak and Sha Tin.

The rapid post-war growth of population in Hong Kong has led to a massive programme of public housing. In addition to resettlement and low cost housing built by the Government there are a number of agencies which build housing, subsidised by the Government. The two most important of these are the Hong Kong Housing Authority and the Hong Kong Housing Society. At 31st December 1970, 1,339,665 people were housed in resettlement and Government low cost housing estates and a further 321,457 in Housing Authority and Housing Society Estates, representing about 43 per cent of the Colony's population.

At the end of 1970 there was in the urban areas of Hong Kong Island, Kowloon and New Kowloon a total of about 280,800 private dwelling units i.e. tenement floors, large and small flats, houses and low cost units. The growth in both Government and private accommodation in recent years has been considerable.

Due to the increase in water demand, which was 6·1 per cent higher in 1970 than in 1969, and to the absence of perennial streams and shortage of good reservoir sites, the provision of adequate resources has always been a problem. In the past restrictions on the hours of supply have been the rule rather than the exception. With the completion of Shek Pik Reservoir at the end of 1963 and the purchase of substantial quantities from China a full supply was possible for over two years, but with the drought conditions from August 1966 to July 1967, and failure to negotiate the purchase of additional supplies from China, severe restrictions had again to be imposed. These restrictions were lifted on the completion of the conversion of the sea inlet of Plover Cove to a fresh water lake in October 1967. With the availability of water from Plover Cove and an annual purchase of 15,000 million gallons from China, the resources are sufficient to meet demand, even allowing for drought conditions. The 24-hour demand, excluding flushing water which is largely provided from independent wells and sea water from a public supply system, averaged 160 million gallons per day during 1970.

Three projects are now being developed to further increase supplies. The first involves the raising of the Plover Cove spillway and dams by 12 feet, bringing the reservoir's total storage capacity up to 50,000 million gallons, The second envisages a high-output desalting plant for utilising sea water. The third, and largest, is a plan for draining and damming the sea channel between High Island and the Sai Kung peninsula to develop a reservoir storing 60,000 million gallons.

The different sources of Government revenue are:

(1) *Earnings and Profits Tax.*—This tax, introduced for the first time in 1947 by the Inland Revenue Ordinance, is a substitute for the more orthodox type of income tax. Instead of one comprehensive tax there are four separate taxes: profits tax (subdivided into corporation profits tax and business profits tax); salaries tax; interest tax and property tax.

The standard rate is 15 per cent and this rate is applied in full in the case of profits tax and interest tax, business profits tax being subject to a limitation that the amount of tax shall not be greater than half the sum by which the profits exceed $7,000. Salaries tax is levied on net income from employment after deducting a personal allowance of $7,000, an allowance for a wife of $7,000 and allowances for up to nine children. The rates of salaries tax charged with effect from 1st April 1966 vary from 2¾ per cent on the first $5,000 of chargeable income to 30 per cent or double the standard rate on chargeable income exceeding $45,000. There is, however, a provision whereby the maximum charge for salaries tax shall not exceed the amount of the standard rate on the total assessable income before deduction of allowances. Property tax is charged on the net rateable value of all land and buildings situated in Hong Kong with the exception of properties in the New Territories. The rate of tax is one-half of the standard rate if the rent receivable is in fact controlled by the 1941 rentals but is at the full standard rate on all other properties. However, property wholly occupied by the owner exclusively for residential purposes is free from property tax.

Under all four taxes the charge is limited to profits or income arising in or derived from the territory. As an alternative to these separate taxes, a resident of Hong Kong may elect to be personally assessed on his total Hong Kong income. A single assessment is then made allowing similar allowances and charging similar rates of tax, as is the case under salaries tax. A set-off is then allowed for any amounts already paid under the four separate taxes.

(2) *Estate Duty.*—Estate Duty is levied on conventional lines at rates varying between 5 per cent in the case of estates valued between $200,000 and $300,000, and 20 per cent in the case of estates valued at over $2 million.

(3) *Other Sources of Revenue.*—Other sources of revenue are rates, stamp duties, entertainments tax, betting tax, business registration fees and hotel accommodation tax. Excise duties are also payable on tobacco, hydro-carbon oils, liquor and table waters.

The following table shows Government revenue and expenditure from 1965 to 1970:

	Revenue HK$	Expenditure HK$
1965–66	1,631,701,213	1,769,130,468
1966–67	1,817,761,552	1,806,066,602
1967–68	1,899,527,499	1,766,022,040
1968–69	2,081,118,425	1,872,974,955
1969–70	2,480,657,388	2,032,183,388
1970–71*	2,584,204,000	2,393,081,220

*(provisional)

Note: The value of the Hong Kong dollar is HK$1 =seven new pence.

For the school year 1970–71, as at September 1970, there were 765,397 children enrolled in primary schools. Primary education is not compulsory and standard fees are charged in government and aided primary schools, although they vary according to whether the school is in an urban or a rural district. New primary places provided during the year totalled 37,443. As at September 1970, the number of pupils receiving secondary education of one form or other totalled 279,318. Day school pupils accounted for 235,406 of these. During the year, 12,181 places were provided in new secondary school buildings.

The City Hall, a modern complex of well-equipped buildings, provides separate facilities for exhibitions, lectures, meetings and the presentation of concerts, plays and other shows both by local performers and by artistes of international repute. Since its opening in 1962 the facilities of the City Hall—in particular its two main auditoria—have been in constant and heavy use. The City Museum and Art Gallery in the City Hall houses and exhibits the Hong Kong Government's Collections of historical paintings, archaeology and antiquities, all relating to Hong Kong and China. In addition, there are regular and frequent temporary exhibitions of Chinese and Western art. The Fung Ping Shan Museum of Chinese antiquities, the teaching museum of the University of Hong Kong, is also open to the public.

The principal public library service is provided by two Urban Council Public Libraries—one in the City Hall on the Island and the other in Kowloon. Additional branch libraries are planned. There are also two British Council libraries and a number of small libraries run by the Social Welfare Department.

HISTORY

The history of the Hong Kong community begins with the arrival of the Portuguese on the China coast in 1513, and the problems they faced in trying to establish commercial relations with China, where the main current of authoritative opinion was traditionally not interested in foreign trade.

By dint of persistence the Portuguese were allowed to establish themselves at Macao in 1557, but when the British and Dutch reached the Far East in the first decade of the 17th century they found their way blocked by Chinese refusal to deal with any Europeans other than the Portuguese. Beginning with the Weddell expedition in 1635, a number of British attempts were made to open trade with Canton, Amoy, and other Chinese ports; but it was not until 1700 that regular British trade with China began, as a result of a change in Chinese policy permitting trade with countries that did not acknowledge China as suzerain.

From then on, European trade with China developed steadily, with the British as the principal European nation concerned. From about 1705 the East India Company had a house in Canton, but Europeans were obliged to quit the city during the off-season. Other European companies and individual traders soon solved this problem by renting houses in Macao, a practice which, though strictly against Portuguese law, was tolerated. In 1773 the East India Company also established themselves permanently in Macao, the company's officers proceeding to Canton for each trading season.

Trade with the Chinese was conducted through a Chinese monopoly guild, charging prices far in excess of market values, and itself subject to ruthless extortion by corrupt officials. British diplomatic missions in 1793 and 1816 failed to obtain better treatment of British merchants in China, or a better basis for international trade; little change might have been expected had not the East Indian Company's charter been abolished, in India in 1813 and in China in 1833.

s*

The China trade then fell firmly into the hands of independent merchants, who previously had only limited chances of showing their capability.

The British led the way in demanding that the Chinese Government provide Europeans with a port, where they could be free to trade with whom they wished, under their own laws. Finally, on the long-term issue of proper treatment for foreign traders, and on the more immediate issue of the import of opium into China, war between Great Britain and China broke out (1839-42). In the course of this, the Emperor's negotiator provisionally offered the island of Hong Kong as a trading depot. This offer was immediately accepted and the island occupied in January 1841. The cession of Hong Kong to the British Crown was confirmed by the Treaty of Nanking, 1842. From the start, Hong Kong was declared a free port, open to all comers, and thus it has grown into one of the world's greatest international trading centres.

In 1860, by the Convention of Peking, Kowloon and Stonecutters Island were ceded to the Crown; and in 1898, by another Convention of Peking, the area known as the New Territories was leased to Great Britain for 99 years, thus bringing Hong Kong to its present size.

Prior to 1841 there was no recognised name for the island of Hong Kong. The anchorage at Aberdeen was known to sailors as Heung Kong and the Chinese characters representing the name may be translated as 'Fragrant Streams' or 'Fragrant Harbour'. Kowloon is the anglicised form of the Chinese Kau Lung (nine dragons). This name is derived from the ridge of nine hills which form a rampart along the northern side of the harbour and seem to guard the approach to China.

CONSTITUTION

The principal features of the constitution are prescribed in Letters Patent passed under the Great Seal of the United Kingdom, which provide for a Governor, an Executive Council, and a Legislative Council. Royal Instructions to the Governor, supplemented by further Instructions from the Sovereign to the Governor, prescribe the membership of the Executive and Legislative Councils.

LAND POLICY

All land is owned by the Crown. In the early days of the colony, Crown leases were granted for 75, 99 or 999 years. Nowadays, except in the New Territories, they are granted for 75 years, usually renewable for a further 75 years at a reassessed Crown rent. Crown leases for New Territories lands are now normally granted for a period of 99 years, less three days, from 1st July 1898. The Government's basic policy is to sell leases to the highest bidder at public auction. Land for special housing projects, for public utilities, schools, clinics, religious and approved charitable purposes is usually granted by private treaty.

GOVERNMENT

The Executive Council, which is presided over by the Governor, consists of five *ex officio* and one nominated official member, and eight nominated unofficial members. The *ex officio* members are the Commander British Forces, the Colonial Secretary, the Attorney-General, the Secretary for Home Affairs, and the Financial Secretary. The eight unofficials at present include five local members.

The main function of the Executive Council is to advise the Governor, who must consult its members on all important matters. The responsibility for deciding which questions should come before the Council and for taking action afterwards rests with the Governor, who is required to report his reasons fully to the Secretary of State if he acts in opposition to the advice given by members. The Governor in Council (i.e. the Governor in the Executive Council) is also given power under numerous ordinances to make subsidiary legislation by way of rules, regulations and orders. A further function of the Council is to consider appeals and petitions under certain ordinances.

With the exception of the Commander British Forces, the *ex officio* members of the Executive Council serve also on the Legislative Council, of which the Governor is both a member and the President. In addition, there are eight nominated official members, making a total official membership of thirteen. There is an equal number of unofficial members, nominated by the Governor. At present they include eleven Chinese members, one of them a woman.

The laws of Hong Kong are enacted by the Governor with the advice and consent of the Legislative Council, which controls finance and expenditure through its Finance Committee, on which three officials and all the unofficial members sit. Procedure in the Legislative Council is based on that of the House of Commons.

LIST OF GOVERNORS

1843	The Rt. Hon. Sir Henry Pottinger, BT, GCB
1844	Sir John F. Davis, BT, KCB
1848	Sir George Bonham, BT, KCB
1854	Sir John Bowring
1859	The Rt Hon. Sir Hercules Robinson (later Lord Rosmead), GCMG
1866	Sir Richard MacDonnell, KCMG, CB
1872	Sir Arthur Kennedy, KCMG, CB
1877	Sir John Pope Hennessy, KCMG
1883	The Rt. Hon. Sir George Ferguson Bowen, GCMG
1887	Sir William Des Voeux, GCMG
1891	Sir William Robinson, GCMG
1898	Sir Henry Arthur Blake, GCMG
1903	Lt.-Col. Sir Matthew Nathan, KCMG
1907	The Rt. Hon. Sir Frederick (later Lord) Lugard, GCMG, CB, DSO
1912	Sir Francis Henry May, GCMG
1919	Sir Reginald Stubbs, GCMG
1925	Sir Cecil Clementi, GCMG
1930	Sir William Peel, KCMG, KBE
1935	Sir Andrew Caldecott, KCMG, CBE
1937	Sir Geoffrey Northcote, KCMG
1941	Sir Mark Young, GCMG
1947	Sir Alexander Grantham, GCMG
1958	Sir Robert Black, GCMG, OBE
1964	Sir David Trench, GCMG, MC

EXECUTIVE COUNCIL
(Presided over by the Governor)
The Commander, British Forces (*ex-officio*)
The Colonial Secretary (*ex-officio*)
The Attorney-General (*ex-officio*)
The Secretary for Home Affairs (*ex-officio*)
The Financial Secretary (*ex-officio*)
Appointed Official Member: G. T. Rowe (Director of Social Welfare)

Nominated Unofficial Members:

Sir Albert Rodrigues, CBE, ED
Sir Cho-yiu Kwan, CBE
J. D. Clague, CBE, MC, QPM, TD
Sir Kenneth Ping-fan Fung, CBE

S. S. Gordon, CBE
Kan Yuet-keung, CBE
J. A. H. Saunders, CBE, DSO, MC
Tang Ping-yuan, CBE

Clerk of Councils: R. W. Primrose, MBE

LEGISLATIVE COUNCIL

The Governor (*President*) (*ex-officio*)
The Colonial Secretary (*ex-officio*)
The Attorney-General (*ex-officio*)
The Secretary for Home Affairs (*ex-officio*)
The Financial Secretary (*ex-officio*)

8 Appointed Official Members:

R. M. Hetherington, DFC (Commissioner of Labour)
D. R. W. Alexander, MBE (Director of Urban Services)
J. J. Robson (Director of Public Works)
D. C. Bray (District Commissioner, New Territories)

J. Canning (Director of Education)
Dr G. H. Choa (Director of Medical and Health Services)
Paul Tsui Ka-Cheung, OBE (Commissioner for Resettlement)
J. Cater, MBE (Director of Commerce and Industry)

13 Nominated Unofficial Members:

Kan Yuet-keung, CBE
Woo Pak-cheun, OBE
Szeto Wai, OBE
Wilfred Wong Sien-bing, OBE
Mrs Ellen Li Shu-pui, OBE
Wilson Wang Tze-sam
H. J. C. Browne

Dr Chung Sze-yuen, OBE
Lee Quo-wei, OBE
Oswald V. Cheung, QC
G. M. B. Salmon
Ann Tse-kai, OBE
Lo Kwee-seong

Clerk of the Legislative Council: R. J. Frampton

CIVIL ESTABLISHMENT

GOVERNOR AND COMMANDER-IN-CHIEF
Sir Crawford Murray MacLehose, KCMG, MBE

Colonial Secretary: Sir Hugh Norman-Walker, KCMG, OBE
Financial Secretary: Sir John Cowperthwaite, KBE, CMG
Secretary for Home Affairs: D. R. Holmes, CMG, CBE, MC, ED
Deputy Colonial Secretary: M. D. A. Clinton, GM
Deputy Economic Secretary: D. H. Jordan, MBE
Deputy Financial Secretary: C. P. Haddon-Cave
Establishment Secretary: S. T. Kidd
Principal Assistant Colonial Secretary (E): J. N. Henderson
Defence Secretary: G. P. Lloyd, CMG
Principal Assistant Colonial Secretary (General): H. M. A. Bristow
Principal Assistant, Colonial Secretary (Social): J. M. Rowlands
Principal Assistant, Colonial Secretary (Lands): D. Akers-Jones
Political Adviser: A. F. Maddocks
Accountant General: D. Blye
Director of Agriculture and Fisheries: E. H. Nichols
Director of Audit: P. T. Warr
Commissioner of Census and Statistics: K. W. J. Topley
Director of Broadcasting: D. E. Brooks
Director of Civil Aviation: T. R. Thomson,
Director of Commerce and Industry: J. Cater, MBE
Director of Education: J. Canning
Director of Fire Services: A. E. H. Wood
Commissioner for Housing: D. Liao Poon-huai

Director of Immigration: W. W. E. Collard
Commissioner of Inland Revenue: A. D. Duffy, OBE
Commissioner of Labour: R. M. Hetherington, DFC
Administrative Commission for the Government of Hong Kong in London: A. M. J. Wright, CMG
Law Officers:
Attorney-General: D. T. E. Roberts, CBE, QC
Solicitor-General: G. R. Sneath, QC
Director of Marine: K. Milburn, OBE
Director of Medical and Health Services: Dr G. H. Choa
District Commissioner, New Territories: D. C. Bray
Commissioner of Police: C. P. Sutcliffe, OBE, QPM
Postmaster-General: M. Addi
Government Printer: J. R. Lee
Commissioner of Prisons: G. R. Pickett
Director of Information Services: N. J. V. Watt, OBE
Director of Public Works: J. J. Robson
Director of Lands and Surveys: P. C. Clarke
Director of Water Supplies: A. S. Robertson
Director of Engineering Development: G. J. Skelt
Director of Building Development: P. V. Shawe
General Manager, Kowloon-Canton Railway: Lam Po-hon, ISO
Commissioner of Rating and Valuation: N. Cooke
Registrar-General: W. Hume
Commissioner for Resettlement: Paul Tsui Ka-Cheung, OBE

Director of Royal Observatory: G. J. Bell
Director of Social Welfare: G. T. Rowe
Controller of Government Supplies: F. J.
Young
Commissioner of Transport: A. J. Shephard
Director of Urban Services: D. R. W.
Alexander, MBE

Chairman, Public Services Commission:
Sir Charles Hartwell, CMG

* * * * *

JUDICIARY

Chief Justice: Sir Ivo Rigby
Senior Puisne Judge: A. D. Scholes
Puisne Judges: W. A. Blair-Kerr; G. G. Briggs; A. A. Huggins; R. H. Mills-Owen;
A. M. McMullin; W. F. Pickering
Registrar, Supreme Court: E. S. Haydon

READING LIST

History: Pre-1841

BALFOUR, S. F. Hong Kong Before the British. *Shanghai*, 1941.

LO, HSIANG-LIN. Hong Kong and its External Communications before 1842:
The History of Hong Kong Prior to British Arrival. *Hong Kong*, 1963.

History: Colonial Period

ENDACOTT, G. B. A History of Hong Kong. *O.U.P.*, 1958.

KIRBY, S. W. The War against Japan: Official History of the Second World
War (3 vols.). *H.M.S.O., London*, 1957–61.

HO, S. DZU-FANG. A Hundred Years of Hong Kong. *Ann Arbour, Michigan*,
1952.

STOKES, G. Hong Kong in History. *Hong Kong Government Press*, 1965.

Social Organisation

BAKER, H. Aspects of Social Organisation in the New Territories. *Hong
Kong Branch of Royal Asiatic Society*, 1964.

TOPLEY, M. Some Traditional Chinese Ideas and Conceptions in the Hong
Kong Social Life Today. *Hong Kong Branch of Royal Asiatic Society*,
1964.

Government and Administration

ENDACOTT, G. B. Government and People in Hong Kong. *Hong Kong
Government Press*, 1964.

HSEUH, S. S. Government and Administration in Hong Kong. *Hong Kong
University Press*, 1962.

Economy

SZCZEPANIK, E. F. The Gaqins of Entrepôt Trade. *Hong Kong*. 1954.

PENNELL, W. V. History of the Hong Kong General Chamber of Commerce.
Hong Kong, 1961.

General

Hong Kong Annual Report, 1970. *Hong Kong Government Press*, 1970. and
available from *H.M.S.O.*, (*SBN* 580061 1).

MONTSERRAT

MONTSERRAT was discovered by Christopher Columbus in 1493. It is part of the Leeward Islands group of the Lesser Antilles in the Eastern Caribbean, latitude 16° 45′ N., longitude 62° 10′ W., and has an area of 39·5 square miles. It is entirely volcanic, very mountainous and comprises three main mountain ranges, Silver Hills in the north (1,323 feet), Centre Hills (2,429 feet) and Soufrière Hills with Chance Peak, (3,000 feet) in the south. The coastline is rugged and offers no all weather harbour although there are several anchorages in the lee of the island sheltered from the prevailing trade winds. There are seven active *soufrières* in Montserrat. Montserrat together with most West Indian islands has a seismographic recording station.

There is no well defined rainy season in Montserrat. Normally the first six months of the year are drier than the last six months, a 50-year average showing 23·55 inches for January to June and 39·74 inches for July to December. The rainfall in 1970 at the Grove Agricultural Station was 70·02 inches against the 50-year average of 63·29 inches. The coolest time of the year when temperatures have been as low as 15·5°C (60°F) is between the months of December and March. The hottest time of the year is between June and November which is also the hurricane season. The average mean minimum temperature is 23°C (73·5°F) and the mean maximum temperature is 30°C (86·5°F).

A complete census was held in April 1970. Preliminary figures indicate a population of 12,300 which shows a negligible increase over the 1960 Census due to large scale emigration in the early sixties. During 1970, 302 births and 121 deaths were registered.

Plymouth, the capital and suburbs had a population of 1,911 at the 1960 census. It is now estimated to have population of 3,000.

The language is English but traces of an Irish brogue can be found in parts of the island. Anglican, Methodist and Roman Catholic are the main religious denominations but in recent years Seventh Day Adventist and Pentecostal persuasions have assumed an increasing importance.

The Montserrat Government maintains a 60-bed hospital. The average daily occupancy of beds in 1970 was 28. During the same year there were 1,048 admissions and 235 maternity cases, and 120 major and 399 minor operations were carried out. The Government provides free dental treatment for expectant and nursing mothers, school children and old people. The Government also operates three health centres and eight dispensaries in the country districts, an infirmary and a cleansing service. There is a family planning association and an old people's welfare association in the island. Infant mortality rates per 1,000 live births were:—

	1970	1969	1968	1967
Under one month	(5) 16·6	(4) 15·2	(9) 28·0	(9) 24·8
0–1 year	(13) 43·0	(10) 37·9	(14) 43·5	(17) 46·8

Tourism and the construction and engineering industries have now overtaken agriculture as the principal sector of the economy. Ten years ago agriculture contributed 41 per cent to the GDP whilst in 1970 it has diminished to 16 per cent. The GDP itself has increased from $3,544,000 to $11,847,000 or on a per capita basis from $295 to $987 approximately. Montserrat's tourism is closely inter-related to real estate construction around the Belham River Valley Golf

Course and Foxes Bay and its attraction is one for retirement or second homes rather than a recreational centre.

Cotton is still the most important cash crop but its importance is dwindling rapidly and is likely to be overtaken by livestock production and market gardening in 1971. The future of agriculture is dependent upon the newly established Land Settlement Board and the proposed Agricultural/and Marketing Corporation becoming effective with Caribbean Development Bank and British Development Division assistance. The proposed re-establishment of the lime industry in conjunction with CDC is also a most important agricultural project.

The estimated distribution of employment in December 1967 was as follows; an up-to-date distribution will be available when the census information has been processed.

Private Undertakings

Occupation	Males	Females	Totals
Seamen and waterfront workers	85	—	85
Agriculture	847	715	1,562
Construction	460	—	460
Retail distribution and other minor industries	350	450	800
Totals	1,742	1,165	2,907

Government Undertakings

Occupation	Males	Females	Totals
Public Works Department	198	—	198
Health Department	37	27	64
Agricultural Department	38	6	44
Electricity	31	1	32
Totals	304	34	338

The cotton crop for 1967-68 and 1968-69 totalled 269 and 270 bales from 690 and 512 acres respectively. The 1969-70 crop of 280 acres yielded over 90 bales. The 1970/71 crop of 240 acres is expected to yield 50 bales approximately. The future of cotton now greatly depends upon the successful application of mechanical harvesting in some of the other Caribbean territories. The problem is not to break the extra long staples which give West Indies Sea Island Cotton its distinctive quality. Mechanisation is probably impossible in Montserrat due to the hilly terrain.

Great efforts are now being made to redevelop the agricultural industry. Potential markets for Montserrat produce are now being explored right from Canada through the entire Caribbean and in Europe. As a result of this work very considerable markets are being found for Montserrat produce. There is a large local market for a wide range of vegetables, together with a lot of scope in the main tourist areas of the Caribbean. Exports to both Canada and the United Kingdom are expected to develop during 1971.

Experimental work is currently proceeding in tomatoes, cucumbers, capsicums, melons, and egg plants and it is hoped to greatly extend this work in the near future. It is planned to encourage the expansion of both market garden production and specialised production. Montserrat is beginning to become known as a supplier of hot pepper and tamarind products.

The estimated livestock population in 1970 was: cattle 6,500; pigs 3,500; sheep and goats 6,000; poultry 10,000. The island is now self-supporting in eggs.

The use of available land on the island in 1967 is shown in the tables below. Since then the area of land farmed has decreased.

Land in agricultural use:

Field Crops	2,272 acres	
Grassland	3,195 ,,	
Tree crops	300 ,,	
	5,767 ,,	5,767

Land not available for agriculture:

Urban area and real estate	2,393 ,,	
Natural forest	2,416 ,,	
Planned reafforestation	754 ,,	
Other land, ghauts and cliffs	2,458 ,,	
	8,021 ,,	8,021

Land available for agricultural development:

Immediate agricultural and grazing development	8,795 ,,	
Available after major rehabilitation	2,697 ,,	
	11,492 ,,	11,492
Total:		25,280 acres

(39·529 square miles)

With the assistance of Freedom From Hunger Campaign and C.D. & W. Grants, a successful fishermen's aid scheme was put into operation during 1966, and continues. By the end of 1970 fishermen were assisted with equipment worth $4,272. The catch for 1970 was 109,818 lbs; some 80,000 less than in 1969. Montserrat continues to support the U.N. Caribbean Fisheries Development Project.

Interest was shown during 1966 in the sulphur deposits to be found in the *soufrières* on the island and the Government enacted legislation vesting in the Crown all minerals in the Colony and providing control by the Government of prospecting for and mining minerals. This interest has not resulted in any mining venture.

The Government operates a cotton ginnery, and the seed which used to be processed into oil is now sent to Antigua. The Government also runs a cement block making machine. Private enterprises operate two cement block making machines, a rum distillery, two soft drink factories, a glass-fibre panel and tile factory, a liqueur distillery, a printing works, two furniture factories, a lime juice concentrate plant, a bay rum factory, quarry operations, watch and clock assembly operations, and tyre recapping operations.

Values of the main domestic exports for the last four years were:

	1967	1968	1969	1970
Cotton Lint	†	$74,933	$75,696	$192,956
Cotton Seed	—	—	—	$4,785
Bananas	$5,200	$855	$1,255	$843
Tomatoes	$5,709	$5,088	$9,264	$14,240
Cucumbers	—	—	—	—
Vegetables	N.A.	$23,220	$12,524	$10,500
Fresh Limes	$8,144	$3,552	$398	$8,451
Lime Juice	$5,015	$11,710	NONE	NONE
Hot Peppers	—	—	$1,845	$9,894
Mangoes	$2,308	$2,280	$1,200	$12,546
Tamarinds	—	—	—	$5,956
Fruits	—	—	—	$2,176
Eggs	—	—	—	$1,089
Bay Oil and Bay Rum	—	—	—	$6,302
Rum Punch	—	—	—	$2,375

Imports for the years 1962 and 1967 were:

	Value		
	(*East Caribbean dollars*)		
	1962	1967	1970
Food and beverages	$792,228	$1,813,961	(No
Cement	$72,712	$224,952	figures
Manufactured goods less cement	$340,793	$1,238,697	avail-
Passenger cars	$163,482	$287,899	able due to
Machinery and transport equipment excluding passenger cars	$281,004	$962,634	a change in system)
Fittings and furniture	$71,118	$311,759	
Miscellaneous manufactured articles excluding fittings and furniture	$205,481	$706,894	

†*No exports of cotton lint in 1967, but crop exported in 1968.*

127 bales of the 1968 cotton crop and the whole of the 1969/70 cotton crop were exported early in 1970. The 1970/71 crop at the time of going to press has also been sold.

There are 6 Thrift Credit Unions co-operatives operating in the territory, with a membership of 476.

Plymouth is the only port: 384 steamers, including motor vessels and sailing craft, of a gross registered tonnage of 332,266 tons entered and cleared there in 1970, landing 23,225 tons of cargo and loading 370 tons.

Blackburne Airport is nine miles from Plymouth. A 3,400 feet surfaced runway was opened on 16th August 1967. Leeward Islands Air Transport Service maintains a twice-daily service between Montserrat and Antigua and a five days a week service between Montserrat and Nevis, St Kitts and St Maarten

(Netherlands Antilles). There are 137 miles of roads open for traffic of which 87 miles are all-weather.

Radio Montserrat is a Government-operated station. Radio Antilles, a powerful commercial station, was brought into service in February 1966. It broadcasts in English, Spanish and French. Television can be received from Antigua (Leeward Islands Television Service) *via* a translator station situated on St George's Hill to the East of Plymouth.

Important development projects which have now been completed include: (i) An island-wide electricity expansion scheme costing $1,270,000. There is now an island-wide 11 kV network and three 750 kVA diesel-powered generators have been erected in a new power station; The electricity undertaking is now operated by Montserrat Electricity Supplies (a company jointly owned by C.D.C. and the Montserrat Government); (ii) The lengthening, widening and surfacing of Blackburne runway. This project, which has been satisfactorily completed with C.D. & W. funds, was started in 1966 and was completed 18 months later at a cost of $602,376. Further work on Blackburne with a grant of $250,000 (Canadian) provided a modern air terminal building which was officially opened in July 1969 and funds were provided in 1970 for navigational aids for restricted night flying, air traffic control and a police/immigration/fire station.

Major projects in the planning stage include (i) a new hospital costing over $1·5 million; (ii) the Crown Agents and the British Development Division have recently completed the engineering and economic survey of a deep water harbour, marina and improved warehousing for Plymouth, phase one of which is estimated to cost $1·7 million. An application for this project is presently with the Caribbean Development Bank; (iii) Consulting water engineers have carried out a water design and distribution system with a Canadian grant. Work on the water development construction programme is due to commence in the summer of 1971 with a Canadian grant of $1·8 million (Canadian).

During 1965 income tax rates were reduced with a new maximum of 20 per cent both for corporations and individuals. All property on the island was revalued for the purpose of instituting a new property tax based on the site value of property. The present rate of taxation is 0·9 per cent of market value. There are no estate duties or capital gains taxation.

Increases in Government revenue and expenditure in recent years indicate the growth of Montserrat's economy. The figures below are gross, including grants-in-aid:

	1967	1968	1969	1970
Revenue	$3,562,731	$4,058,454	$4,612,630	$6,466,975
Expenditure	$4,069,478	$4,064,054	$4,491,378	$6,206,719

A Public Accounts Committee has now been formally established.

Primary education is free in the Government and Government-aided Primary Schools throughout the territory. There are two private preparatory schools which are fee paying. In 1970 there were 3,217 children enrolled in the 12 Government, one aided, one unaided, 4 private primary schools, 4 nurseries, one vocational and one Government secondary School. The Secondary school, with an enrolment of 222 in 1970 prepares students up to the Advanced Level of the General Certificate of Education. A 15-classroom Primary School provided by the Canadian Government was constructed in Plymouth. It accommodates

500 pupils. A Junior Secondary School is also under construction with C.D. & W. funds in Salem to serve all the north of the island. Similar schools in Plymouth and Harris are planned. At the moment all students failing to gain entrance to the Secondary School remain at Primary Schools for their whole scholastic career. C.D. & W. funds of £85,000 are also being provided for a Technical and Trade School in Plymouth.

By the end of 1970 the University of the West Indies Extra Mural Centre was completed with funds provided by the Canadian Government, Ford Foundation and the British Government. The centre includes lecture rooms, a library and an open air theatre.

There is a small public library in Plymouth. At the end of 1970 there were 2,220 registered members of whom 990 were juveniles. The book stock comprised 12,755 volumes.

The Government contributes towards the following Regional Organisations:

> West Indies Shipping Service
> British Caribbean Transport Advisory Council
> Regional Research Centre
> Caribbean Seismographic Research
> West Indies Associated States Supreme Court
> Regional Police Training Centre
> University of the West Indies
> University of the West Indies College Hospital
> Carifta and the Regional Secretariat, Commonwealth
>   Caribbean Commission in the United Kingdom for the
>   East Caribbean Governments
> Commission in Canada for the East Caribbean
>   Governments
> Regional Meteorological Service
> Regional Development Agency
> Eastern Caribbean Common Market

HISTORY

Montserrat was discovered in November 1493 by Christopher Columbus, on his second voyage to the New World. The serrated profile of the island reminded him of the locale of the Abbey of Montserrat in the Spanish highlands near Barcelona. Thus the island was named, but never colonised, by Spain.

In 1632 Sir Thomas Warner sent a group of English and Irish from overcrowded St Christopher to settle on Montserrat. Further Irish immigrants arrived during the century from Virginia, driven out because of their religion. They grew tobacco, an important commodity then. Indigo was their second product, then came cotton and later sugar. Through the years the planters were much harrassed by French and Carib Indian raids. The island was stormed and taken by the French in 1664, and again in 1667, but was restored to England in 1668 by the Peace of Breda. In 1671 the Leeward Islands were separated from Barbados and put under the rule of a Captain-General and Commander-in-Chief.

In 1678 Sir William Stapleton, Captain-General and Commander-in-Chief of the Leeward Islands, recorded the population of Montserrat as:

	Men	Women	Children	Total
English	346	175	240	761
Irish	769	410	690	1,869
Scottish	33	6	13	52
Total	1,148	591	943	2,682
Slaves	500	300	292	1,092

The first slaves from Africa arrived in Montserrat in 1644; 14 years later they numbered 1,092, as shown above, and were to reach as many as 9,500 in 1805, at which time the European population had dropped to 1,000.

The French under Cassard with 3,000 men raided Montserrat in 1712. They burned and pillaged to the extent of £203,500 damage, for which a special clause was inserted into the Treaty of Utrecht. The last capture of Montserrat by the French was in 1782, when de Bouillé took most of the Leewards, but it was restored to England in 1783 by the Treaty of Versailles. During the Napoleonic Wars a French fleet under LaGrange attacked the Leewards in 1805 and demanded ransom, of which Montserrat paid £7,500.

On 1st August 1834 slavery was abolished. The planters of Montserrat were paid compensation of £103,556 for 6,401 slaves. Added to the cessation of slavery and the apprentice system, the falling price of sugar in the late 19th century did much to discourage planters, who found it very difficult to run estates profitably; Montserrat's rugged topography and a shortage of capital made it equally difficult to modernise estate agriculture. Between 1890 and 1936 Montserrat's economy had, in addition, to sustain a series of devastating earthquakes and hurricanes. All these factors combined to cause the demise of estate agriculture. In 1857 Joseph Sturge, of Birmingham, England, formed the progenitor of the Montserrat Company Ltd., which bought abandoned estates, planted limes and made Montserrat lime juice famous. This company did much to upgrade the prosperity of the island. They sold plots of land to the peasants, in the conviction that a settled people makes the soundest community. Much of Montserrat today is owned by smallholders. In the 1870s the company also endowed and operated a school for the children of workers, which lasted until 1932. Education had become compulsory in 1892, but not until 1944 did the Government become wholly responsible for primary education, which previously had been provided by church and private schools with the aid of grants from the National Society in England.

The Anglican Church was disestablished in January 1875, and received no more financial aid from the Government. The three main sects were, and still are, Anglican, Roman Catholic and Methodist.

The Leeward Islands Act of 1871 inaugurated the Federal Colony of the Leeward Islands, including the Presidencies of the British Virgins, St Christopher Nevis and Anguilla, Antigua, Montserrat and Dominica. Each Presidency was headed by a Commissioner or Administrator who was responsible to the Governor of the Federal Colony of the Leeward Islands. Since 1960 the Administrator has become Her Majesty's representative in Montserrat. Cabinet government was introduced in Montserrat on the 16th August 1960.

The Federation of the Leeward Islands was abolished on 1st January 1960 to make way for an independent Federation of the West Indies, which had been created on the 3rd January 1958 and which comprised all British West Indian territories including Jamaica and Trinidad and Tobago. This Federation was short-lived as by 1962 Jamaica and Trinidad and Tobago had become independent and the dissolution of the Federation started. From this date an attempt was made to form a smaller federation of the Leeward and Windward Islands and Barbados but this was abandoned in 1966.

Since 1963 real estate development and tourism have done much to aid the island's economy. Her Majesty Queen Elizabeth II visited the territory in February 1966, the first reigning monarch ever to do so.

CONSTITUTION

Following decisions taken at a Constitutional Conference in London in June 1959, a new constitution came into force on 1st January 1960. The Constitution provides for the execution of government through an Administrator who is appointed by Her Majesty The Queen, an Executive Council and a Legislative Council. The Executive Council has the general control and direction of the government of the Territory. It is presided over by the Administrator and there are two *ex-officio* members, the principal law officer (Attorney-General) and the Financial Secretary, and four unofficial members (the Chief Minister, two other Ministers and a Member without Portfolio who, at the discretion of the Administrator, in consultation with the Chief Minister, may be designated a Minister). The three Ministers are appointed from the elected members of the Legislative Council and the other unofficial member is appointed from either the elected or nominated members of the Legislative Council. The Administrator appoints as Chief Minister the member of the Legislative Council who, in his judgement, is most likely to command a majority in the Legislative Council. The other unofficial members of Executive Council are appointed by the Administrator on the advice of the Chief Minister. Ministers are assigned responsibility for any Government business (including financial matters) except criminal proceedings, internal security, the audit of public accounts and the public service.

The Legislative Council is presided over by the Administrator and comprises, besides the Administrator, two official members, seven elected members and one nominated unofficial member. There is a Deputy President elected from within the Council. Elections are by universal adult suffrage.

The appointment, dismissal and disciplinary control of public officers is vested in the Administrator in his discretion, acting after consultation with an advisory Public Service Commission.

LAND POLICY

Under the Landholding Control Ordinance No. 2 of 1970 it is obligatory for all non-Montserratians to obtain a licence from the Government before they obtain any interest in land in the Colony. The Government is not prepared to alienate good agricultural land for real estate development.

GOVERNMENT

At the general election held on 15th December 1970 the Progressive Democratic Party won all seven seats in the Legislature, thus defeating the Labour Party, which had been the Government party since the introduction of the ministerial system in 1960.

Executive Council

The Administrator (*President*): His Honour W. H. Thompson, CBE
Attorney-General: The Hon. B. F. Dias, OBE
Financial Secretary: The Hon. J. Taylor, CMG
Chief Minister, Minister of Finance, and Minister of Communications and Works:
The Hon. P. A. Bramble
Minister of Social Services: The Hon. M. R. Tuitt
Minister of Agriculture, Trade, Lands and Housing: The Hon. J. A. Osborne
Member without Portfolio: The Hon. E. A. Dyer
Secretary to Executive Council: T. E. Ryan, OBE

Legislative Council

President: His Honour the Administrator
Official Members: The Attorney-General; the Financial Secretary
Nominated Member: J. C. Kelsick
Elected Unofficial Members:

Hon. P. A. Bramble (Plymouth District); Hon. M. R. Tuitt (Southern District); Hon. J. A. Osborne (North-western District); Hon. E. A. Dyer (Central District); J. S. Dublin, (Deputy President) (Windward; District W. H. Ryan (Eastern District); J. J. Weekes) (Northern District).

MINISTRIES AND GOVERNMENT DEPARTMENTS

Chief Minister's Office
Permanent Secretary, Secretary to Executive Council: T. E. Ryan, OBE

Ministry of Agriculture and Lands
Permanent Secretary: K. A. Cassell
Director of Agriculture: R. A. Frederick
Veterinary Officer: Dr J. Jackman

Ministry of Social Services
Permanent Secretary: K. W. Lee
Senior Medical Officer: Dr C. D. Wooding
Principal, Secondary School: C. L. Holden
Education Officer: H. A. Fergus
Inspector of Schools: Miss E. White

Ministry of Communications and Works
Permanent Secretary: G. R. E. Cabey
Director of Public Works: I. D. Brown

Ministry of Finance
Financial Secretary: J. Taylor, CMG
Acting Permanent Secretary, Establishment and Finance: J. D. Lewis
Acting Accountant-General and Postmaster: J. T. Skerritt
Comptroller of Inland Revenue: C. L. Thompson

Collector of Customs: A. Jacobs
Postmaster: Mrs U. P. Meade

Attorney-General's Office
Attorney-General: B. F. Dias, OBE
Legal Assistant: D. J. Christian

Magistrate's Office
Magistrate, Registrar and Provost Marshal: J. S. Weekes

Audit
Acting Senior Auditor: S. St A. Meade, OBE

Administration
Administrative Secretary: Miss I. M. Taylor
Chief of Police: H. H. Bisset
Superintendent of Prison: J. H. Greenaway

Public Service Commission
Chairman: R. S. Jordan, OBE
Members: J. E. Wade, OBE; D. R. V. Edwards

Judicial
West Indies Associated States Supreme Court
Puisne Judge (Montserrat Circuit): Hon. Mr Justice Allan Louisey
Magistrate, Registrar and Provost Marshal: J. S. Weekes

Reading List

General

ASPINALL, Sir A. Pocket Guide to the West Indies. *Methuen*, 1954.

ASPINALL, Sir A. A Wayfarer in the West Indies. *West Indies Committee* 1928.

BAKER, E. C. A Guide to Records in the Leeward Islands. *Basil Blackwell* 1965.

BURNS, Sir Alan. History of the British West Indies. *Allen and Unwin*, 1954.

FROUDE, J. A. The English in the West Indies. *Longmans, Green*, 1888.

MESSENGER, John C. The Influence of the Irish in Montserrat. *Caribbean Quarterly, University of the West Indies*.

O'LOUGHLIN, C. The Economy of Montserrat; a national accounts study, *Social and Economic Studies*, Vol. 8, No. 2, 1959.

PARRY, J. H. and SHERLOCK, P. M. A short history of the West Indies. 2nd edition, *Macmillan*, 1963.

STARKEY, O. P. Commercial Geography of Montserrat. *Bloomington, Indiana University*, 1960.

The West Indies and Caribbean Year Book. *Thomas Skinner.*

Montserrat: Official report, 1965-66. *H.M. Stationery Office*, London.

PITCAIRN ISLANDS GROUP

THE small, volcanic island of Pitcairn (1·75 square miles) is situated in the Pacific Ocean (25° 04′ S.; 130° 06′ W.) roughly mid-way between Panama and New Zealand and 1,350 miles east-south-east of Tahiti. It is a rugged island rising to 1,100 feet and even at Bounty Bay, the only landing-place, access from the sea is difficult. The climate is equable. Mean monthly temperatures vary from 19°C (66°F) in August to 24°C (75°F) in February; the average annual rainfall is 80 inches, fairly evenly spread throughout the year. Moderate easterly winds predominate with short east to south-east gales occurring between April and September.

The early history of Pitcairn is uncertain but archaeological remains prove it was inhabited by Polynesians some six hundred years ago, at least for short periods. Modern history began with its discovery by Carteret in 1767, and its occupation by Fletcher Christian and nine of the *Bounty* mutineers, accompanied by twelve Tahitian women and six men, in 1790. Although an American vessel called at the island in 1808 it was not until the visit of H.M.S. *Briton* and H.M.S. *Tagus* in 1814 that the story of the Pitcairn settlement became widely known. The first decade had been marked by jealousies and violence and by 1800 the only adult male survivor was John Adams, who guided and led the small community until his death in 1829. In 1814 the population numbered 40; and by 1831 it had increased to 86 of whom 79 were born on the island. Concern for the future led to evacuation to Tahiti in 1831 but within six months the Pitcairners were back home, less seventeen who had died during the absence. In 1856 the population had reached 194 and the island was again abandoned, a new home having been provided by the British Government on Norfolk Island off the east coast of Australia. By 1864, however, forty-three Pitcairners had found their way back and since then the island has been permanently settled, the population reaching a peak of 233 in 1937. In the last twenty years there has been steady emigration to New Zealand and the population is now less than 100.

Pitcairn is a British settlement under the British Settlements Act 1887, but the islanders count their recognition as a colony from 1838 when Captain Elliott of H.M.S. *Fly* gave them a constitution with universal adult suffrage and a code of law. In 1893 a parliamentary form of government was adopted and in 1898 the island was brought under the jurisdiction of the High Commissioner for the Western Pacific in Suva, which for the next twenty years was exercised through the British Consul in Tahiti. A further change in the constitution in 1904 restored the simpler pattern of 1838 which was retained as the basis for the wider reforms of 1940. In 1952, the Pitcairn Order in Council transferred responsibility for administration to the person of the Governor of Fiji following the separation of the offices of Governor and High Commissioner. Under the provisions of a new

Order adopted on 30 September 1970, Her Majesty appointed Sir Arthur Galsworthy to be Governor of Pitcairn with effect from 10 October 1970. The Local Government Ordinance of 1964 constitutes a Council of ten members of whom four are elected, five are nominated (three by the elected members and two by the Governor) and one is an *ex officio* member, the Island Secretary. The Council is presided over by the Island Magistrate who is elected triennially. All other members hold office for one year. Liaison between the Governor and Council is effected by a Commissioner in the Office of the British High Commission, Auckland.

Land is held under a system of family ownership. based upon the original division of the island by Fletcher Christian and his companions. Alienation to foreigners is not forbidden by law but, as a general rule, the only rights to pass are to their descendants by marriage to a Pitcairn Islander. The control of entry for the purposes of settlement further protects the customary tenure of land.

New Zealand decimal currency, which was introduced on 10th July 1967, is in everyday use. There is no taxation and revenue is mainly derived from the sale of postage stamps. Revenue in 1970/71 was approximately $NZ80,592, and expenditure was approximately $NZ60,263. Development works have largely been concentrated on telecommunications, power supply, improvements to the boat harbour at Bounty Bay and tractors for roadworks and transportation.

Free primary education is provided on the island under the direction of a qualified schoolteacher seconded by the New Zealand Department of Education. Scholarships provided by the Pitcairn Island Government are available for children to receive post primary education or specialist training in other fields in Fiji or elsewhere. A trained nurse, usually the wife of the Pastor, looks after the general health of the community, assisted by surgeons of passing ships when necessary. Government meets two-thirds of transport and hospital costs if a patient has to be transferred to New Zealand. The Islanders have been adherents of the Seventh Day Adventist Church since 1887.

Pitcairn is on the direct shipping line between the Panama Canal and New Zealand and 45 ships called in 1970. Since mid-1968 passenger ships have ceased to call regularly at Pitcairn Island, and sea communications are now maintained by cargo vessels running between New Zealand and Panama which make scheduled calls at approximately bi-monthly intervals in each direction. Shore-to-ship communication is by diesel launch. A telecommunications station maintains contact with the outside world via Fiji.

The community is essentially farming and fishing in character. The fertile soil of the valleys produces a wide variety of tropical and sub-tropical crops which are used for subsistence and money income is earned by the sale of postage stamps and handicrafts. An official Souvenir Agency was established in 1964 and a co-operative store in 1967. A re-afforestation scheme was introduced in 1963 with emphasis on the planting of *miro* trees, which provide the wood used in making handicrafts.

The uninhabited islands of Henderson, lying 105 miles east-north-east of Pitcairn, Oeno, 75 miles north-west, and Ducie 293 miles east, form part of the settlement. The first two islands are visited regularly by the Pitcairn Islanders.

Governor: Sir Arthur Galsworthy, KCMG, (Resident, Wellington, New Zealand)
Commissioner: C. E. Dymond, CBE, (Resident, Auckland, New Zealand)
Island Magistrate and President of Council: P. Young, Adamstown,
Pitcairn Island
Education Officer: R. S. Henry, Adamstown, Pitcairn Island

ST HELENA

(WITH ASCENSION AND TRISTAN DA CUNHA)

S T HELENA lies in the South Atlantic Ocean, latitude 16° S., longitude 50° 45′ W., 700 miles south-east of Ascension and about 1,200 miles from the south-west coast of Africa. It is 10·5 miles long and 6·5 miles broad, covering an area of 47 square miles.

St Helena is rugged and mountainous and of volcanic origin. The highest peak, Mount Actaeon, rises to 2,685 feet. The only inland waters are small streams, few of them now perennial, fed by springs in the central hills. These streams and rain-water are sufficient for domestic water supplies and a few small irrigation schemes.

The cool South Atlantic trade winds blow throughout the year. The climate is mild and varies little, the temperature in Jamestown, on the sea-coast, ranging in summer between 70°F and 85°F, and in winter between 65°F and 75°F. Inland it is some 10°F cooler.

Rainfall figures (in inches) over three years, obtained from stations in the Eastern and Western districts of the country, the higher slopes approaching Jamestown and Jamestown itself, are as follows:

	1967	1968	1969	1970
Hutt's Gate (Eastern)	37·52	33·97	29·87	27·60
Plantation (Western)	41·55	39·53	29·13	25·40
Briars (Higher Slopes)	21·52	22·94	15·93	12·38
Jamestown	9·77	11·87	8·17	7·15

The last census was on 24th July 1966, when the total population was 4,649. The estimated population at 31st December 1970 was 4,952.

According to the last census the division of the population was as follows:

St Helenians	4,470
U.K. citizens	116
Other Commonwealth citizens	16
Others	47

The language of the island has always been English, and the English way of life is firmly established.

The majority of the population belong to the Anglican Communion.

The total number of births during the year 1970 was 167, and the birth rate per 1,000 was 33·65.

The total number of deaths during the year 1970 was 49, and the death rate per 1,000 was 9·87.

St Helena has a very mild climate. There is no industrial pollution of the atmosphere. There are no endemic diseases of note but the population is unusually susceptible to epidemic afflctions and minor ailments, both of which may be attributable to the island's isolation. Infestations with ascaris and enterobius are common but cause little serious illness. Prophylactic measures to eradicate this nuisance have so far proved unsuccessful. It has now been established that leptospirosis is the most common cause of pyrexias of uncertain origin on the island. Research continues with the assistance of the Leptospirosis Reference Laboratory in London. The source is suspected of being mainly in the large rat population which was the subject of an extermination campaign in 1969-70. Fortunately the common varieties of leptospirosis encountered are generally amenable to early treatment and have been responsible for only two deaths in seven years. Progress continues on an island-wide immunisation programme against tetanus.

Increasing numbers of St Helenians are making use of the facilities offered at the infant and child welfare clinics and are obtaining immunisation against diphtheria, tetanus and whooping cough in addition to smallpox.

Three medical officers and a dentist are borne on the territory's establishment; there are no private medical practitioners on the island. A modern hospital of 54 beds provides for the routine and emergency needs of the population. Regular visits by the medical officers and midwife and district nurse to five country clinics supply the out-patient needs of the rural population including the supervision of child welfare and ante-natal care.

Jamestown, the capital, is the only town and has a population of some 1,600.

The principal categories of salaried and wage-earning persons at the end of 1970 were:—

General Labour			
	Full-time	386	
	Casual	109	
	Relief	123	
		——	
			618
Apprentices			90
Skilled			
	Drivers	41	
	Mechanics	17	
	Others	212	
		——	
			270
Professional, Teaching Clerical			320
			———
			1,298

The 1966 census provided the following details:

	Males	*Females*	*Total*
Professional, technical and related workers	41	89	130
Managerial, administrative and clerical workers	88	40	128
Sales workers	23	63	86
Farmers, fishermen, etc.	128	—	128
Workers in transport and communications operations	97	5	102
Craftsmen, production process workers, etc.	241	58	299
Service workers	12	138	150
Security Forces	14	1	15
Not classified	524	—	524
	1,168	394	1,562

At the end of 1970, 494 men were also employed on Ascension: 187 by Messrs Cable and Wireless Limited, 111 by the Department of the Environment, and 196 by the U.S. Base and other interests.

There is only one trade union, the St Helena General Workers' Union, with a membership at the end of 1970 of 1,050.

The main crops are common and sweet potatoes and vegetables. At the end of 1965 the market price of hemp dropped considerably and production ceased in 1966.

The livestock population at the end of 1970 was: horses 19, donkeys 686, cattle 982; sheep 1,260; goats 1,200; pigs 370; poultry 10,856.

Fish of many kinds are plentiful in the waters around St Helena but the catch is usually insufficient to meet the demand. Towards the end of 1965 a licence was granted to a fishing concern in South Africa to develop the island's fish resources, but the company has obtained very poor results.

There is no industry.

The timber resources of the island are so small that all timber for construction purposes has to be imported. There are no minerals of any kind.

There were no exports in 1970.

The main imports in 1969 were: motor vehicles 16,113; fuel oils and motor spirit £57,317; flour £18,902; meat (salted including hams and bacon) £25,715; beer and stout £18,600. Total imports for 1969 were valued at £460,960.

The St Helena Growers' Co-operative Society is the only one on the island. It is both a consumers and a marketing society and provides consumer goods such as seeds, implements, and feeding stuffs to its members, and markets their produce, mainly vegetables, locally, to visiting ships and to Ascension Island. The local market is limited and is soon over-supplied, and this together with the decrease in the number of ships calling over recent years has inhibited the growth of this enterprise.

The only port in St Helena is Jamestown, which is an open roadstead with a good anchorage for ships of any size. Navigation lights are installed on the beacons at Ladder Hill and Munden's Point.

There is no airport or airstrip in St Helena and no railway. The total all-weather road mileage is 46·6. Of this 37·5 miles are bitumen sealed. In addition there are about 18 miles of earth roads used mainly by animal transport and only usable in dry weather by motor vehicles. All roads have steep gradients and sharp curves.

The Union-Castle Mail Steamship Company provides a shipping service to the island. In 1970 there were 14 calls northbound from Cape Town to Southampton and 15 southbound from Britain, by two ships carrying 12 passengers each. No cargo (except a small tonnage of frozen food) is carried by these vessels to or from Ascension or St Helena, but four Clan Line cargo ships northbound and four southbound call each year.

A further allocation of funds has been provided for an extension of the development programme for the period up to March 1971, bringing the total allocation, since the inception of Colonial Development and Welfare assistance in 1947, to £1,226,000.

The Development programme includes agriculture, roads, housing, extension of the electricity distribution system, teacher training, medical services, etc. A survey of water resources has been undertaken and implementation of the recommendations began in 1969/70.

An Income Tax Ordinance came into force on 1st January 1954. The rate for individuals is 1s. 3d. in the £ on the first £1,500 and at the rate of 1s. 9d. in the £ on any excess of £1,500 derived from local sources. In the case of a married person who can prove to the satisfaction of the Commissioner of Income Tax that his wife was living with him or wholly maintained by him during the year immediately preceding the year of assessment there is an abatement of one-third of the tax. A personal tax of £5 per person is also payable by those whose income is above £380 a year and who do not qualify for the payment of Income Tax. Import duties are confined to a very small range of goods. There are also taxes on motor vehicles, shops and entertainments.

Revenue and expenditure for the three years 1968-70 were as follows:

	Revenue £	Expenditure £
1968	514,285	485,497
1969	515,422	547,312
1970	471,537	519,392 (estimated)

Education is compulsory and free for all children between the ages of five and fifteen but power to exempt after the age of fourteen rests with the Education Officer. The standard of work at the Secondary Selective School is increasingly being geared to 'O' Level requirements of the London University General Certificate of Education. The literacy rate is 100 per cent.

There is a free public library in Jamestown financed by the Government and managed by a committee, and a branch library in each country district.

HISTORY

The then uninhabited island of St Helena was discovered on 21st May 1502 by the Portuguese navigator João da Nova Castella, on his homeward voyage from India. He named it in honour of Saint Helena, mother of the Emperor Constantine the Great, whose festival falls on that day in the Eastern Church calendar. The existence of the island appears to have remained unknown to other European nations until 1588 when it was visited by Captain Cavendish on his return from a voyage round the world. Soon afterwards St Helena became a port of call for ships of various nations voyaging between the East Indies and Europe. In 1633 the Dutch formally annexed it but made no attempt to occupy it. In 1659 it was annexed and occupied on behalf of the East India Company but the first official authorisation of the Company's occupation occurs in a charter dated 1661. In January 1673 the Dutch seized the island but were driven out again in May by the English navy. A charter to occupy and govern St Helena was issued by Charles II to the East India Company in December 1673 and it remained under that company until April 1834 when it was brought under the direct government of the Crown by an Act of Parliament of 1833. Napoleon Bonaparte was exiled in St Helena from 1815 until his death in 1821. Longwood House, in which he lived, is an important Napoleonic museum; it is in the custody of the French Republic.

CONSTITUTION

An Order in Council and Royal Instructions of November 1966, which came into force on 1st January 1967, provided for: (1) a Legislative Council consisting of the Governor, two *ex-officio* members (the Government Secretary and the

Treasurer) and twelve elected members; and (2) an Executive Council consisting of the Government Secretary and the Treasurer as *ex-officio* members and the chairmen of the Council Committees (all of whom must be members of the Legislative Council). The Governor presides at meetings of the Executive Council. Under this new constitution, Council Committees, a majority of whose members are members of the Legislative Council, have been appointed by the Governor and charged with executive powers and general oversight of departments of Government. A general election was held in February 1968.

LAND POLICY

Individuals hold land either in fee simple or by lease. Immigrants require a licence to hold land. Crown land may be leased on conditions approved by the Governor. The Government farms approximately half the arable area, and either farms or controls some four-fifths of the grazing areas. Commonage grazing areas are made available by the Government to private stock owners on a *per capita per mensem* basis. There is at present no scheme for land re-settlement and no pressure of demand for additional land. The grazing areas have not sufficient watering points to allow their sub-division into viable smallholdings and the economic nature of arable agriculture is such as not to be attractive to smallholders. It is, therefore, difficult to envisage any change in the present system of land holding.

GOVERNMENT

EXECUTIVE COUNCIL
The Governor (President)
Government Secretary (*ex-officio*)
Treasurer (*ex-officio*)
The Chairmen of the Council Committees

LEGISLATIVE COUNCIL
The Governor (President)
Government Secretary (*ex-officio*)
Treasurer (*ex-officio*)
12 Elected Members
Clerk of Councils: H. G. Richards, MBE

CIVIL ESTABLISHMENT

Governor and Commander-in-Chief: T. Oates CMG, OBE
Government Secretary: I. C. Rose, TD
Treasurer and Collector of Customs: G. O. Whittaker, MBE
Assistant Government Secretary: H. G. Richards, MBE
Agricultural and Forestry Officer: A. S. Leask
Auditor: A. O. Richards
Education Officer: Ralph Billing
Superintendent of Police and Gaol and Registrar, Supreme Court: E. G. Robb
Postmaster: O. N. Duncan
Senior Medical Officer: J. S. Noaks
Medical Officers: C. N. Paine; G. A. Stanton
Matron: Miss G. H. Sim, BEM
Electrical Engineer: E. Clark
Social Welfare Officer: F. M. Ward

JUDICIARY
Chief Justice: W. E. Windham
Magistrate: E. J. Moss, CBE, MC
Justices of the Peace: D. H. Thorpe; J. R. Charlton, MBE; F. I. Gough;
Mrs D. V. Ward

ASCENSION

The small island of Ascension lies in the South Atlantic (7° 56′ S., 14° 22′ W.) 700 miles north-west of St Helena. Its area is 34 square miles and the population at 31st December 1970 was 1,232, of whom 750 were St Helenians.* The island was discovered by the Portuguese on Ascension Day 1501. It was uninhabited until the arrival of Napoleon in St Helena in 1815, when a small British naval garrison was placed there. The island remained under the supervision of the British Admiralty until it was made a dependency of St Helena by Letters Patent in 1922 and came under the control of the Secretary of State for the Colonies.

Ascension is a barren, rocky peak of purely volcanic origin, destitute of vegetation except for about ten acres around the top of the peak (2,870 feet), where Cable and Wireless Limited run a farm producing vegetables and fruit and permitting the maintenance of about 2,000 sheep, and 185 cattle and pigs. The island is famous for green turtles, which land there from December to May to lay their eggs in the sand. It is also a breeding ground of the sooty tern, or wideawake, vast numbers of which settle on the island every eighth month to lay and hatch their eggs. In consequence, Ascension has sometimes been named 'Wideawake Island'. Other wild-life on the island includes feral donkeys, goats and cats, rabbits and partridges. All wild-life except rabbits and cats is protected by law. Shark, barracuda, tuna, bonito and other fish are plentiful in the surrounding ocean.

Cable and Wireless Limited own and operate an important telecommunications station which connects the Dependency with St Helena, Sierra Leone, St Vincent, Rio de Janeiro and Buenos Aires, and through these places, over the Company's system, with all parts of the world.

In 1942 the Government of the United States of America, by arrangement with the British Government, established an air base which became of considerable importance during the 1939-45 war. The United States Government subsequently re-occupied Wideawake Airfield under an agreement with the British Government in connection with the extension of the Long Range Proving Ground for guided missiles centred in Florida.

A British Broadcasting Corporation relay station on the island was opened in 1966.

Administrator: Brigadier H. W. D. McDonald, DSO

TRISTAN DA CUNHA

Tristan da Cunha is a small island in the South Atlantic Ocean, lying about midway between South America and South Africa. It is volcanic in origin and nearly circular in shape, covering an area of 38 square miles and rising in a cone to 6,760 feet. The climate is typically oceanic and temperate. Rainfall averages 66 inches per annum.

Possession was taken of the island in 1816 during Napoleon's residence in St Helena, and a garrison was stationed there. When the garrison was withdrawn, three men, headed by Corporal William Glass, elected to remain and became

---

* *The majority of the remainder being expatriate personnel of Cable and Wireless Limited and the United States base. The population varies from time to time as it is largely determined by the employment offered by these two stations.*

the founders of the present settlement. Because of its position on a main sailing route the colony thrived until the 1880s, but with the replacement of sail by steam, the island ceased to occupy a position on a main shipping route and a period of decline set in. No regular shipping called and the islanders suffered at times from a shortage of food. Nevertheless, attempts to move the inhabitants to South Africa were unsuccessful. The islanders were engaged chiefly in fishing and agricultural pursuits.

The United Society for the Propagation of the Gospel has maintained a missionary teacher on the island since 1922; a number of missionaries had also served on the island prior to this. In 1932 the missionary was officially recognised as Honorary Commissioner and Magistrate.

By Letters Patent dated 12 January 1938 Tristan da Cunha and the neighbouring unsettled islands of Nightingale, Inaccessible and Gough were made dependencies of St Helena, though as a matter of practical convenience the administration of the group continued to be directly supervised by the Colonial office.

In 1942 a meteorological and wireless station was built on the island by a detachment of the South African Defence Force and was manned by the Royal Navy for the remainder of the war. The coming of the Navy re-introduced the islanders to the outside world, for it was a naval chaplain who recognised the possibilities of a crawfish industry on Tristan da Cunha. In 1948 a Cape Town based fishing company was granted a concession to fish the Tristan da Cunha waters. Many of the islanders found employment with the fishing company. In 1950 the office of Administrator was created: the Administrator is also the magistrate. The Island Council received legislative sanction through a Bye-Laws Ordinance enacted in 1952.

On 10th October 1961 a volcanic cone erupted close to the settlement of Edinburgh and it was necessary to evacuate the island. The islanders returned to Tristan da Cunha in 1963, but a few have since re-settled in the United Kingdom. The Administration has been fully re-established and the Island Council re-formed. The population at the end of 1970 was 280.

A new Island Council was elected in November 1969 following the enactment of the Island Council Ordinance, 1969. The Council consists of the Administrator, three appointed members and eight elected members including one woman.

The island is isolated and communications are restricted to a few calls a year by vessels from Capetown and an occasional call by a passing ship. There is no airfield. A wireless station on the island is in daily contact with Capetown. A local broadcasting service was introduced in August 1966. A radiotelephone service was established in 1969.

Electricity was introduced in 1969 to all the islanders' homes.

The island community depend upon fishing for their livelihood. The Company holding the fishing concession has built a new fish-freezing factory and the shore-based fishing industry is being developed following the construction of a harbour. The working population find employment in the Industry and the Departments of the Administration.

The 1969-70 budget is expected to show a small deficit which will be met from reserves. Under Colonial Development and Welfare Acts, grants have been provided for a harbour, for a new hospital (to open in 1971) and a new school and for various minor works projects.

Administrator: J. I. H. Fleming

READING LIST

ST HELENA, ASCENSION AND TRISTAN DA CUNHA

ANONYMOUS. A Description of the Island of St Helena. London, *P. Phillips*, 1805.

AUBRY, Octave. St Helena. London, *Gollancz*, 1937.

BARNES, CAPTAIN JOHN, RN. A Tour through St Helena. London, *J. M. Richardson*, 1817.

BLAKESTON, OSWELL, Isle of St Helena. London, *Sidgwick and Jackson*, 1957.

BROOK, T. H. A History of the Island of St Helena. 2nd edition. *Publishers to the East India Company*, 1824.

DARWIN, CHARLES. The Voyage of a Naturalist Round the World in H.M.S. *Beagle*. London, *Routledge*, 1905.

GOSSE, PHILIP. St Helena, 1502-1938. London, *Cassell*, 1938.

HUGHES, CLEDWYN. Report of an enquiry into conditions on the Island of St Helena. . . (and) observations by the St Helena Government on Mr Hughes' report. 1958. 2 parts.

KORNGOLD, RALPH. The Last Years of Napoleon: his captivity on St Helena. London, *Gollancz*. 1960.

MARTINEAU, Gilbert. Napoleon's St Helena. London, *John Murray*, 1968.

STONEHOUSE, BERNARD. Wideawake Island: the story of the British Ornithologists Union Centenary Expedition to Ascension. London, *Hutchinson*, 1960.

TAYLOR, MARGARET STEWART. St Helena, Ocean Roadhouse. *Robert Hale, London*, 1969.

THOMPSON, J. A. K. Report on a visit to Ascension Island. *St Helena Government Printer*, 1947.

TRISTAN DA CUNHA

BOOY, D. M. Rock of Exile: a narrative of Tristan da Cunha. London, *Dent*, 1957.

CHRISTOPHERSON, ERLING and others. Tristan da Cunha (translated by R. L. Benham). London, *Cassell*, 1940.

CHRISTOPHERSON, ERLING (editor). Results of the Norwegian Scientific Expedition to Tristan da Cunha, 1937-1938. 16 parts. Oslo, *Oslo University Press*, 1940-62..

EARLE, AUGUSTUS. Journal of a Residence in Tristan da Cunha. *O.U.P.*, 1966.

GANE, DOUGLAS M. Tristan da Cunha. London, *Allen and Unwin*, 1932.

SEYCHELLES

THE Seychelles archipelago consists of a scattered group of 40 granitic and 45 coralline islands in the Western Indian Ocean. The islands take their name from the Vicomte Moreau de Séchelles, Controller General of Finance in the reign of Louis XV. The group also includes numerous rocks and small cays. The revised estimate of the land area of Seychelles is 107 square miles.

The largest of the islands is Mahé, named after a former French Governor of Mauritius, which has an area of about 55 square miles and is approximately 17 miles long from north to south. Mahé lies 940 miles due east of Mombasa, 1,750 miles south-east of Bombay, and rather more than 600 miles north of Madagascar. Victoria, the capital of Seychelles and the only port of the archipelago, is on Mahé. It is the only town in Seychelles of any size and has a population of about 14,000.

The granitic islands, which are all of great beauty, rise fairly steeply from the sea and Mahé has a long central ridge which at its highest point, Morne Seychellois, reaches nearly 3,000 feet. Praslin, second largest island in the group is 27 miles from Mahé and the other granitic islands are within a radius of 35 miles. The coral islands are reefs in different stages of formation, rising only a few feet above sea level. For islands so close to the Equator, the climate is tropical but not unpleasant. Maximum shade temperature at sea level averages 29°C (85°F) and during the coolest months, the average minimum temperature drops to 24°C (75°F). At higher levels temperatures are rather lower and the air fresher. There are two seasons, hot from December to May and cooler from June to November while the south-east monsoon is blowing. Rainfall varies over the group; the greater part falls in the hot months during the northwest monsoon and the climate then tends to be humid and somewhat enervating. The mean annual rainfall in Victoria taken over the past 67 years is 93 inches and the mean average temperature 27°C (80°F). All the granitic group lie outside the cyclone belt. High winds and thunderstorms are rare.

The total population of Seychelles on 30th June 1970 was estimated at 52,811. In 1970 there were 1,660 births and 437 deaths. The basis of the school system is a free, non-compulsory, six-year primary school education available to all children between the ages of six and twelve. At the age of twelve those children who do not gain admission to the Secondary Grammar Schools by competition are eligible to go to the Junior Secondary Schools (ages 12–14). At the end of the Junior Secondary course, pupils may apply for places in the vocational and pre-vocational training centres.

Government controls and directs educational policy and is responsible for financing the educational system.

The official language is English and state education at primary and secondary levels is in English. The family language is Creole, a patois of French. In all there are 35 primary schools with an enrolment figure for 1969 of 8,781, of whom 4,424 were boys and 4,357 were girls. In addition there are approximately twenty pre-primary infant and organised kindergarten schools. There are eleven junior secondary and two secondary grammar schools with a total enrolment of 1,062 boys and 1,115 girls. There are four technical and vocational training centres, whose enrolment in 1969 was 229 trainees (181 girls and 48 boys) and one teacher training college.

T

The Seychellois are almost all Roman Catholics (more than 90 per cent of the population); there are small minorities adhering to the Anglican and other sects.

Seychelles has very few of the diseases usually associated with tropical climates. There are no anopheline mosquitos and consequently no malaria. No cases of yellow fever or dengue have ever been reported although there are aedes mosquitos on most of the islands.

Tuberculosis is now under control and there is a decline in the number of notified cases.

The Public Health Service is organised under the Medical Officer of Health and the staff consists of one Chief Health Inspector and seven Health Inspectors. A senior Public Health Sister was appointed at the beginning of 1965 and has thirteen Public Health Nurses in her charge. The main islands are reasonably well provided with hospitals and clinics. Mahé has the main hospital (135 beds) and the Bishop Maradan Sanatorium (82 beds) at Victoria, a small hospital (17 beds) at Anse Royale in the south of the island, and two clinics situated on the west coast. Praslin has a cottage hospital (28 beds) and two clinics; while at La Digue there is a small hospital with 6 beds.

The main diet in the islands is rice, fish and lentils. Meat is eaten occasionally and local vegetables are available.

The Port of Victoria has about one square mile of deep water roadstead for ships of all sizes and an inner harbour of about half that area for small craft. A project to reclaim 56 acres of Victoria harbour, extending the present shoreline of Victoria seawards and establishing a separate and new port area, was approved by the British Government in 1970. Reclamation, using sand and coral cut from the shallow parts of the harbour, began on 1st June 1970. The whole harbour area is protected by a chain of small islands and the number of ocean-going ships which can be accommodated at any one time is four. The new harbour, due to be completed by 1974, will take vessels up to 12,000 tons and of a draught of not more than 32 feet. The number of vessels entered and cleared from Victoria in 1969 was 356. Tonnage handled in 1969 was 11,758 loaded and 66,713 unloaded. An international airport on Mahé was opened in July 1971. Mahé has an extensive road system of which 56 miles are now surfaced. On the island of Praslin the trans-island road from Grand 'Anse to Baie Ste Anne is also surfaced. A five-year plan of further road improvements is now in hand. Technical investigations are in progress with a view to expanding the treated water supply on Mahé. Electricity services are being generally extended on Mahé and a new 5MW power station is being built there.

Radio Seychelles, a Government-owned and equipped broadcasting station, opened in July 1965 and broadcasts in the medium wave band (225.4 metres, 1,331 kilocycles) for four and a half hours daily.

The Seychelles fishing industry is for the most part undeveloped, the local fishermen relying solely on traditional methods and equipment for their livelihood. Fish being a staple food of the islanders, virtually the entire catch goes for local consumption, although a few tons of salted fish are exported every year, mostly to Tanzania.

The main crops for export are coconuts, cinnamon, patchouli and vanilla; tea also is now being produced but so far only for local consumption. The Seychelles Tea Company has some 375 acres of tea planted of which 200 acres has been planted on behalf of the Seychelles Government for allocation in plots of about 5 acres to settlers. In early 1970 the first nine settlers were installed on their plots and others will follow in the future. The tea factory which started production on a small scale in August 1966 is expected to produce 50,000 lbs. of tea in 1970 which will satisfy about three-quarters of total local consumption.

Currency is the Seychelles rupee which is tied to sterling at the rate of 7½p to one rupee.

Total exports in 1970 were valued at Rs.9,487,935. Britain is the most important supplier of imports, and exports go principally to the U.S.A. (cinnamon bark) and India (copra).

Some of the main items imported in 1968 (latest figures available) by quantity and value were: rice, 4,047 tons, Rs.3,993,725 (£299,529); flour, 1,369 tons, Rs.856,521 (£64,239); sugar, 1,611 tons, Rs.795,776 (£59,683); other foodstuffs, Rs.5,071,718 (£380,379); petroleum products, 11,628,065 litres, Rs.4,417,786 (£331,334); cotton fabric, 823,584 yards, Rs.1,972,413 (£147,931); road motor vehicles (including parts) Rs.1,962,277 (£147,171); other articles Rs.14,805,027 (£1,110,377); total imports, Rs.33,875,243 (£2,540,643).

The principal form of direct taxation is income tax. This is chargeable on all earned or investment income arising in or derived from the territory. In addition tax is payable by residents on investment income arising in Seychelles or on earned income remitted thereto, the basis of assessment being income arising in the calendar year preceding the year of assessment.

Rates of tax, after deduction of allowances, are:

4 per cent on first Rs. 1,000 of chargeable income
8 per cent on next Rs. 4,000 of chargeable income
12 per cent on next Rs. 5,000 of chargeable income
18 per cent on next Rs. 5,000 of chargeable income
32 per cent on next Rs. 10,000 of chargeable income
35 per cent on remainder

Companies, partnerships, etc, pay a flat rate of 35 per cent.

Allowances made to resident taxpayers are:

Personal (single):	Rs. 2,250.
Wife (or for alimony):	Rs. 2,000.
Children:	Rs. 800 for the first child; Rs .700 for each child thereafter (maximum Rs. 3,000). Additional allowance of Rs. 3,500 may be claimed for child studying abroad (maximum Rs. 7,000).
Dependent relative:	Rs.750 (limited to one relative).

In addition, allowances may be claimed in respect of life insurance, superannuation, alimony and deduction against plant and machinery owned and operated by the assessee. A land tax of 40 cents per acre is charged.

The principal sources of indirect taxation are customs duties at varying rates. Licensing exists for most trades and professions. There is also a succession duty at a graduated scale.

The territory's recurrent revenue for 1971 (estimated) was £1,858,202 which included £464,650 in Budgetary Aid from the U.K., the total expenditure in 1971 (estimated) was £2,338,894.

HISTORY

There is some evidence to suggest that the Seychelles Islands were known and visited in the Middle Ages by traders from Arabia and the Persian Gulf sailing to and from ports in East Africa with the monsoons; they are clearly associated with the great Portuguese voyages in the Indian Ocean. The Amirantes group was sighted by Vasco da Gama on his second voyage to India in 1502. The first map showing what is thought to be the main group of islands was drawn at about the same time. However, the first well-documented voyage of discovery to the archipelago was made by the English seaman Alexander Sharpeigh. Commissioned by the East Indian Company, Sharpeigh's expedition visited the main granitic group, including Mahé and nearby islands, in 1609, ante-dating the first French visit, with an expedition under Lazare Picault, by almost a century and a half. A circumstantial account of Sharpeigh's voyage is to be found in the *Journal of John Jourdain*, published by the Hakluyt Society.

It was that greatest of all French Governors of Mauritius, the Vicomte Mahé de Labourdonnais, who briefed Picault in 1741 to explore Seychelles. Had Labourdonnais not fallen victim to base intrigues, it is possible, even probable, that he would have turned Mahé into a formidable naval base against Britain at a time when French and British interests were clashing in India. For fifteen years Seychelles remained forgotten and then, on intelligence that the British were seeking uninhabited islands in the Indian Ocean, France decided to annex Mahé and seven other islands of the group. To that end Captain C. N. Morphey was despatched with orders to set up on Mahé a 'Stone of Possession' engraved with the arms of France. He did so at an impressive ceremony at sunrise on 1st November 1756, whereafter he set sail leaving the islands still uninhabited.

By 1763 the French East India Company, owing to mismanagement, had lost most of its possessions in India and disrupted the economy of Mauritius. It was wound up and its remaining assets, including Mauritius and its dependencies, lapsed to the King of France. The transfer was not completed till 1767 when two official Administrators were sent to Mauritius—Jean Dumas in charge of naval and political affairs, and Pierre Poivre in charge of finance and agriculture—to develop the islands and prepare for further hostilities with Britain in the East. Both men soon turned their eyes to Seychelles. Dumas' interests were to find a cheap and reliable source of timber for his naval dockyards, and he despatched an expedition in 1768. Poivre, who had already introduced into Mauritius the cultivation of spices on a considerable scale to offset the Dutch monopoly in the Far East, extended this operation to Seychelles, and a garden was started, as well as a small settlement on St Anne's Island in 1770. Both operations were unsuccessful.

After the first failure, the Administrators of Mauritius repeatedly urged that the King should take over Seychelles. The plan they put forward was to station on Mahé a small garrison and to accept the offer of a number of inhabitants of Mauritius and Réunion to settle there with their slaves. The function of the settlers was to grow food for the garrison and passing ships. Two years later Lieutenant Romainville with 15 soldiers and 12 slaves were sent to set up an Administrative Headquarters on the site around which Victoria was later to arise. Thereafter settlers with parties of slaves began to arrive.

These settlers in the main came of previously well-to-do families who had fled France in face of financial disaster and threatening revolution, or had quit India after the collapse of French supremacy there in 1761. All were faced with the necessity of starting life afresh. Though the official role allotted to them was that of farmers, their primary ambition was to rebuild their shattered fortunes, and they found it quicker and vastly more lucrative to traffic in the island's natural and abundant resources—tortoises and timber. Between 1784 and 1789 alone it was estimated that more than 13,000 giant tortoises had been shipped from Mahé, while many others were slaughtered for home consumption. Damage to the island's magnificent forests had been on much the same scale. Appalled by this devastation, the French authorities in Mauritius sent M. Malavois in 1789 with orders to end it. The colonists were confined to fixed areas and all trading was forbidden. Thereafter their activities were devoted to the raising of crops, and it is to the credit of the colonists that, as long as slavery was permitted to continue, they managed, in addition to feeding themselves and their slaves, to fulfil their intended role as ship chandlers and purveyors to the garrison, even at times producing a surplus of maize, rice and cotton for export. Nevertheless, their ignorance of the nature of tropical soils and their wasteful methods of cultivation (burning tracts of forest land, cropping them until fertility declined and then repeating the operation elsewhere) led to further impoverishment of a soil already poor by nature.

When the French Revolution occurred in 1789, the population of Seychelles numbered 69 persons of French blood, three soldiers of the garrison, 32 coloured persons and 487 slaves. In June 1790 the colonists set up a Permanent Colonial Assembly and a Committee of Administration. They repudiated all links with Mauritius, and invested the Assembly with judicial and other powers of internal self-government, thus anticipating by 113 years the status of Crown Colony granted to Seychelles by Britain in 1903.

Their enthusiasm for the revolution, however, evaporated with the arrival of a Republican Commandant who proclaimed, among other changes, the abolition of slavery without compensation. Almost to a man the colonists boycotted him. He was succeeded by the Chevalier de Quincy, who brought news that the edict concerning slavery had been revoked, and Seychelles once more settled down as a dependency of Mauritius.

For a number of years serious depredations to British shipping in the Indian Ocean had been caused by French privateers. Several of the marauding ships were owned by Seychellois, and it was partly to put an end to such activities that in 1794 a British squadron appeared off Victoria, demanding the unconditional surrender of the island. De Quincy had no forces to repel attack, but nevertheless managed by admirable courage and diplomacy to obtain a deed of capitulation most favourable to the islanders. In 1802 the Peace of Amiens was signed but hostilities broke out again in 1803. With a view to weakening the British hold on India, Napoleon determined to station a strong fleet on the main trade route in the Indian Ocean. To this end, Mauritius was made the naval and military headquarters, Réunion and Madagascar the depots of food and stores, and Seychelles an advanced outpost. Britain's reply was to place a naval blockade on all these islands. In 1804 Seychelles was forced to capitulate for the second time. Again de Quincy's shrewdness served the colonists well, for he obtained a concession whereby ships of Seychelles flying a certain flag could pass through the blockade unmolested. The many ships calling at Mahé for supplies and a virtual monopoly of trade secured by the Seychelles under the terms of the capitulation, brought considerable wealth to the colony. However, with the fall of Mauritius to British forces in 1810, when Britain made it clear that slavery was to be abolished, a number of colonists with their slaves, estimated at nearly half the population, left Seychelles.

During the *pourparlers* to the Treaty of Paris, Britain offered to restore Mauritius and its dependencies to France if that country would renounce all claims to its small remaining possessions in India. France refused and so in 1814 all these islands were formally ceded to Britain. Although all previous undertakings to respect French ownership of property, law and customs were omitted from the treaty, these continued to be honoured in deed. As a further proof of good-will, the Chevalier de Quincy was invited by the British Government to become *Judge de Paix* in Seychelles. He accepted and served with distinction in that office until his death 13 years later.

From the date of its foundation until 1903, Seychelles was regarded as a dependency of Mauritius. A series of Civil Commissioners under the tutelage of Mauritius administered Seychelles from 1811 to 1888, but some degree of separation was effected in 1872 when a Board of Civil Commissioners was appointed with financial autonomy. The powers of this Board under a Chief Civil Commissioner were extended by another Order in Council of 1874. In 1888 the importance of the islands warranted a further change in the constitution, and an Order-in-Council was passed creating an Administrator with a nominated Executive and Legislative Council as from 1889. In 1897 the separation from Mauritius became more marked when the Administrator was endowed with the full powers of Governor. Six years later, by Letters Patent of 31st August 1903, separation was completed and Seychelles became a Crown Colony with a Governor and Executive and Legislative Councils.

CONSTITUTION

A new constitution, which came into force in October 1970, provides for a Council of Ministers (the Executive), with the Governor presiding, consisting of a Chief Minister and up to four other Ministers together with the three ex-officio members.

The Legislative Assembly consists of a Speaker, 15 elected members and the same three ex-officio members of the Council of Ministers.

The Last General Election was held in November 1970.

GOVERNMENT

GOVERNMENT

The Governor: Sir Bruce Greatbatch CMG, CVO, MBE
Aide-de-Camp: N. A. Michel, MBE
Personal Assistant: Miss G. M. Addison, MBE

Deputy Governor: J. R. Todd
Establishment Officer: B. Georges, MBE
Assistant Secretary and Clerk of the Council: O. Hoarau

COUNCIL OF MINISTERS

MINISTERS	EX-OFFICIO MEMBERS
J. R. Mancham (Chief Minister)	J. R. Todd (Deputy Governor)
C. Chetty (Minister of Agriculture, Natural Resources and Marketing)	D. L. Davies, OBE (Attorney-General)
	A. G. Padgett (Financial Secretary)
D. Joubert (Minister of Housing, Labour and Social Services)	
J. Pragassen (Minister of Aviation, Communications and Works)	
R. G. Delorie (Minister without Portfolio)	

LEGISLATIVE ASSEMBLY
Speaker: M. Lousteau-Lalanne
The Deputy Governor
The Attorney-General
The Financial Secretary
15 elected members

SECRETARIES TO GOVERNMENT
P. Wand-Tetley (Office of the Chief Minister)
F. J. R. Williams, (Ministry of Agriculture, Natural Resources and Marketing)
A. C. MacKellar, CMG, (Ministry of Aviation, Communications and Works)
P. J. Heady, (Ministry of Housing, Labour and Social Services)

HEADS OF DEPARTMENTS
Director of Medical Services: P. Hossen
Commissioner of Police: F. G. Fenner
Director of Agriculture: S. M. Savy
Director of Audit: P. Harrison
Director of Education: A. Johns
Director of Public Works: M. B. Grieveson
Director of Civil Aviation: B. F. Sutton
Registrar of Co-operative Societies: J. G. Kent
Public Relations Officer: P. D'Arcy Champney
Statistical Commissioner: A. G. T. Carter
Planning Adviser: D. Komlosy
Port Officer: J. A. Sauvage, OBE

JUDICIARY
Chief Justice: Sir G. L. Souyave, KB, QC
Puisne Judge: A. F. M. A. Sauzier, OBE

TRADE REPRESENTATIVES
East Africa: A. W. Bentley-Buckle, Esq.,
Box 875, Southern House, Kilindini Road, Mombasa, Kenya

READING LIST

BENEDICT, B. People of the Seychelles. *HMSO* 1966.

BRADLEY, J. T. History of the Seychelles Islands. *Port Victoria*, 1936.

LIONNET, G. A Short History of Seychelles. *Seychelles*, 1970.

MOCKFORD, J. Pursuit of an Island. *Staples Press*, 1950.

OMMANNEY, F. D. The Shoals of Capricorn. *Longmans, Green*, 1952.

ROWE, J. W. F. Report on the economy of the Seychelles and its future development. *Government Printer*, Mahé, 1959.

THOMAS, A. Forgotten Eden. *Longmans, Green*, 1968.

TOUSSAINT, A. History of the Indian Ocean. *Routledge and Kegan Paul*, 1966.

TYACK, L. A. M. Mauritius and its dependencies; the Seychelles, treasures of the Indian Ocean. *France Inter Presse*, Lausanne, 1965.

WAUGH, A. Where the Clocks Chime Twice. *Cassell*, 1952.

WEBB, A. W. T. Story of Seychelles. *Seychelles*, 1964.

Seychelles: Proposals for constitutional advance. *Commonwealth Office, HMSO*, 1967.

Seychelles 1970: Report of the Seychelles Constitutional Conference, 9 to 13 March, 1970. *HMSO*, 1970.

Victoria Reclamation Project. *Government Printer*, Mahé, 1970.

TURKS AND CAICOS ISLANDS

T HE Turks and Caicos Islands lie to the south-east of the Bahamas between latitudes 21° and 22° N. and longitudes 71° and 72° 30′ W. The Turks Islands are said to derive their name from a species of cactus (*echinocactus myriostigma*) whose scarlet flowers resemble a Turkish fez. There are a number of theories on how the Caicos Islands got their name, one being that the name is derived from the Spanish name 'Cayos' for cays. The territory is made up of two groups of islands separated by a deep water channel about 22 miles wide known as the Turks Islands passage. The Turks Islands lie to the east of the passage and the Caicos Islands to the west. The Turks Islands consist of two inhabited islands, Grand Turk and Salt Cay, six uninhabited cays and a large number of rocks. The principal islands of the Caicos group are South Caicos, East Caicos, Middle (or Grand) Caicos, North Caicos, Providenciales and West Caicos. Geographically the islands are a part of the Bahamas chain and have the same flat characteristics, there being no land above 250 feet. The total land area is estimated at 166 square miles.

The climate is good. The south-east trade winds blow constantly throughout the year, giving an equable and healthy climate. Rainfall is variable and tends to be higher in the Caicos Islands; on Grand Turk the annual average is about 21 inches. The temperature ranges throughout the year from 60°F to 90°F. Severe hurricanes occurred in 1866, 1873, 1888, 1908, 1926, 1928, 1945 and 1960.

The population at the last census (October 1970) was 5,675. The majority of the population are of African descent. The birth-rate in 1968 was 27·1 per '000 and the death rate 6·3 per '000. Religion is Christian, the main denominations being Baptist, Methodist and Anglican. English is the official and spoken language.

There are 13 Government elementary schools and two Secondary schools on the Islands; education is free. In 1966 a technical wing was set up at the Secondary School. In 1968 there were 1,665 pupils on the rolls. Expenditure on education in 1968 amounted to £48,865. The literacy figure is approximately 96 per cent.

The main seaports are Grand Turk, Salt Cay and Cockburn Harbour on South Caicos. There is an irregular mail and freight service to Jamaica by sea, and ships also call from Holland and Miami. Furness-Withy are continuing a direct shipping service from Great Britain, originally started by the Royal Mail Line in 1968.

Grand Turk island has a number of metalled roads including one from end to end of the island.

There is a regular thrice-weekly air service provided by Air Caicos Limited between Grand Turk, South Caicos and Nassau. Arrangements are in hand to open the Grand Turk United States Air Force airfield for wider use of private planes. There is also a small unmetalled strip for small planes close to the town on Grand Turk.

On South Caicos there is an excellent paved airstrip of 6,000 feet capable of taking planes of considerable size. This strip was paved during the early part of 1968.

There are airstrips on Salt Cay, Providenciales, North Caicos and Middle Caicos. In 1967 Caicos Airways Ltd. established a small internal air service and in 1970 Air Caicos started a twice daily service round the Islands.

South Caicos has a number of minor roads and a road network was provided during 1967 in Providenciales, 1969 in North Caicos and in 1970 in Middle Caicos.

A radio-telephone system connects Grand Turk with Salt Cay and the Caicos Islands as well as providing a service with Jamaica and the United States. There is no broadcasting service but Cable and Wireless (West Indies) Limited broadcast a fifteen-minute daily programme of news and announcements.

Cable and Wireless are putting in, during 1971, automatic telephone exchanges on Grand Turk and South Caicos and radio telephone systems, connecting into these exchanges, on the other inhabited islands.

There is a 20-bed cottage hospital of modern design at Grand Turk, together with a dental clinic. Medical Officers are stationed at Grand Turk and at Cockburn Harbour on South Caicos. There is a clinic at Cockburn Harbour, a maternity clinic in the charge of a midwife at Bottle Creek on North Caicos and a clinic nurse at Salt Cay. Expenditure on medical services in 1970 was £61,000

There is practically no agriculture carried on in Turks Islands and South Caicos, but in the rest of the Caicos Islands corn, beans and other crops are normally grown in sufficient quantity to satisfy local needs. Sisal production ceased in 1968 owing to poor crops and export difficulties. In the past the principal occupation of the population of the Turks Islands group and of South Caicos was the production of salt by solar evaporation. However, because of difficulties in finding markets, the operations on Grand Turk and South Caicos were closed down at the end of 1964. Operations continue on a reduced scale on Salt Cay.

Fisheries have continued to be of great economic importance and crawfish has become the chief export industry of the islands.

In the 1969/70 season 445,438 lobsters were caught and exported, with a return to the fishermen of approximately $180,000. Free diving with the use of a wire noose was the only fishing method practised by the fishermen and was carried out from small power-driven boats and sailing sloops. Efforts are being made to convert the fishermen to the use of traps.

The export of dried conch to Haiti is the second largest export of fisheries products but the industry is declining very rapidly. In 1968, 187,000 dried conch meats were exported, with a return of £597. In conjunction with the export of conch meat 71,000 shells were exported to the United States. These shells are used in the tourist trade.

Other fisheries remain undeveloped.

The main exports in 1969 were: Crawfish £90,000; Salt £6,000. Government revenue in 1969 was £681,593 (including grant-in-aid) and expenditure £683,731. The main head of taxation is Customs import duties (20 per cent preferential and 25 per cent general f.o.b.). There is no direct taxation. Expenditure under the Turks and Caicos Islands Development Plan during the year 1969 was £160,465.

The main imports for the years 1966-69 were:

	1966 £	1967 £	1968 £	1969 £
Food, drink and tobacco ..	233,643	180,792	193,205	242,462
Raw Materials	54,271	33,822	11,847	10,525
Manufactured articles	129,478	138,253	144,308	178,068
Fuel and Lubricants	—	—	69,756	56,800
Unclassified	5,403	3,976	23,677	8,838

T*

HISTORY

The islands were discovered in 1512 by Juan Ponce de Leon while on a voyage from Puerto Rico. At the time of their discovery the islands were apparently uninhabited. The first European occupation was by Bermudians who, beginning at least as early as 1678, came regularly for salt about March, remaining until around November when the salt raking season was over. They sometimes stayed throughout the year.

The Caicos Islands were settled by Loyalist planters from the Southern States of America after the War of Independence. After the abolition of slavery in 1838 the planters left the islands, their former slaves remaining in possession. In the meantime the islands were placed under the Bahamas Government, but in 1848 in answer to a petition from the inhabitants a separate charter was granted divorcing them from the control of the Bahamas; this provided for an elective Legislative Board and a President administering the Government. After a period of severe financial stringency, the Legislative Council in 1873 petitioned Her Majesty that the islands might be annexed to the Colony of Jamaica and from 1874 to July 1959 they were one of its dependencies.

An Order in Council of 1873, which annexed the islands to Jamaica, made provision for the constitution of a Legislative Board for the Turks and Caicos Islands. The Commissioner was *ex-officio* President of the Board, which had full legislative and budgetary powers, but ordinances required the assent of the Governor of Jamaica before becoming law. Laws passed by the Legislature of Jamaica did not apply to the Dependency unless they were made applicable in express terms.

On 20th February 1958 royal assent was given to the Cayman Islands and Turks and Caicos Islands Act, 1958, by which Her Majesty was empowered to make provision by Order-in-Council for the government of the Cayman Islands and Turks and Caicos Islands.

On 25th February 1966 Her Majesty Queen Elizabeth II and His Royal Highness the Duke of Edinburgh in the course of the royal tour of the West Indies visited Grand Turk and South Caicos; this was the first occasion that a reigning monarch had visited the islands.

CONSTITUTIONAL DEVELOPMENT

The Turks and Caicos Islands (Constitution) Order in Council 1959, provided for a new constitution which was brought into operation on 4th July 1959. Under it the office of Governor of the Islands was constituted (the Governor of Jamaica was also Governor of the Islands) and the office of Commissioner replaced by the office of Administrator. The former Legislative Board was replaced by a Legislative Assembly consisting of the Administrator as President, two or three official members appointed by the Governor, two or three nominated non-official members appointed by the Governor and nine members elected on a constituency basis by universal adult suffrage; and an Executive Council was introduced consisting of the Administrator, two official members, one nominated member and two elected members (elected by the nominated and elected members of the Assembly from among the elected members of the Assembly).

On 6th August 1962, when Jamaica attained independence at the wish of the local inhabitants, the Islands became a Crown Colony and the post of Governor was abolished. A new Constitution then came into force, basically the same as that of 1959, but with the powers formerly exercised by the Governor to be exercised by the Administrator.

In 1964 talks were held between representatives of the Government of the United Kingdom, the Bahamas and the Turks and Caicos Islands concerning a closer association between the Bahamas and the Turks and Caicos Islands. As a result of these talks the Turks and Caicos Islands (Constitution) Order in Council 1965 (which came into operation on 5th November 1965) provides that the Governor of the Bahamas shall be also Governor of the Turks and Caicos Islands. The office of Administrator, Turks and Caicos Islands, remains in being.

On 18th June 1969 a new Constitution came into force which provided for an Administrator and a State Council. The State Council consists of a Speaker, three official members, not less than two, nor more than three nominated members and nine elected members. The Council sits in public under its Speaker when dealing with legislation and in private under the Administrator when dealing with executive matters.

LAND POLICY

On Grand Turk and South Caicos Islands much of the land is privately owned, but Crown Land is also available. On the other islands the majority of land is owned by the Crown.

The purchase of private land, which is not controlled in any way, is subject to personal negotiation. A system of registration of land ownership carrying a Government guarantee of the authenticity of title, has been instituted so that title and interests in land are certain and known.

The present policy in respect of Crown Land is not to part with freehold title until an agreed amount of permanent improvement has taken place. Such land will therefore be issued on a conditional purchase lease in the first instance. The conditions are phased over a number of years, usually about five, except in the case of a very large scale development scheme when a longer period would be granted. In any case some progress must be shown within two years. The Government would bind itself to grant freehold title at the end of the period if the agreed development had taken place. If no development takes place within the stipulated period the land would revert automatically to the Crown.

An applicant for Crown Land should give, in some detail, his proposals for development, and the area or areas required, together with details of his financial backing. It is very necessary that all applicants for land or their agents should visit any site proposed before submitting detailed proposals as in some cases only enquiries made locally would reveal whether the site was suitable for development.

STATE COUNCIL
The Speaker
3 Official Members
2 Nominated Members
9 Elected Members

CIVIL ESTABLISHMENT

Administrator: A. G. Mitchell, DFM
Assistant Administrators: Major J. M. E. Wainwright; A. A. Bishop; R. N. Robinson
District Commissioner, Caicos Islands: A. G. Malcolm

Financial Secretary: S. G. Trees
Treasurer and Collector of Customs: A. F. Williams
Postmaster and Controller, Government Savings Bank: C. E. Been
Civil Engineer: (Vacant)

Education Officer: J. H. Prothero
Medical Officer: C. R. Grainger
Officer Commanding Police: V. H. J. Anderson
Magistrate (also acts as Judge of Supreme Court, Registrar of Deeds): H. J. Cridland

Development Officer: Major J. M. E. Wainwright
Land Surveyor: J. Wright
Legal Adviser: (vacant)
Fisheries Officer: J. R. Harland

READING LIST

PUSEY, Rev. J. H. Handbook of the Turks and Caicos Islands. Kingston, *Colonial Publishing Company Ltd*, 1897 (out of print).

TATEM, W. R. Report on the Hurricanes of 1926 and 1928. London, *Waterlow*, for the Commissioner of the Turks and Caicos Islands, 1928.

Turks and Caicos Islands (Constitution) Order-in-Council, 1959. *H.M.S.O.* 1959 (Statutory) Instrument No. 864 of 1959.

Turks and Caicos Islands (Constitution) Order-in-Council, 1962. *H.M.S.O.*, 1962 (Statutory Instrument No. 1649 of 1962).

Turks and Caicos Islands (Constitution) Order-in-Council, 1969, *H.M.S.O.* 1969 (Statutory Instrument No. 736 of 1969).

WESTERN PACIFIC HIGH COMMISSION

(Administrative headquarters: Honiara, British Solomon Islands)

THE office of High Commissioner for the Western Pacific was created by the Western Pacific Order in Council of 1877. The High Commissioner's jurisdiction extends over all islands in the Western Pacific not administered by Australia, New Zealand, Fiji or any other civilised power. By the Pacific Order in Council of 1893 the High Commissioner's jurisdiction is extended to foreigners and (in most cases) to natives residing in British settlements or protectorates within the limits of the Order. Under the New Hebrides Order in Council 1922, the High Commissioner's jurisdiction also extends to the New Hebrides and the Banks and Torres Islands. The expenses of the High Commission are met largely by the British Solomon Islands; but a contribution is paid from United Kingdom funds in respect of expenses of the British Service in the New Hebrides as well as by the Gilbert and Ellice Islands.

The High Court of the Western Pacific was constituted by the Western Pacific (Courts) Order in Council 1961. The Court has jurisdiction in the British Solomon Islands and the Gilbert and Ellice Islands and the Anglo-French Condominium of the New Hebrides. The Court is a superior court of record and has all the jurisdiction which is vested in the High Court of Justice in England subject to the provisions of the Order in Council. Appeals from the decisions of the Court are to the Fiji Court of Appeal.

The Court consists of a Chief Justice, one Puisne Judge and a Senior Magistrate. The Chief Justice lives in the Solomon Islands, and there is a Puisne Judge in the New Hebrides and a Senior Magistrate in the Gilbert and Ellice Islands.

The groups at present under the High Commissioner are:

The British Solomon Islands.
The New Hebrides.
The Gilbert and Ellice Islands (including the Phoenix and Northern Line Islands groups).
The Central and Southern Line Islands.

In 1953 the posts of High Commissioner for the Western Pacific and Governor of Fiji, which had been held conjointly for many years, were separated. The High Commissioner established his headquarters at Honiara and assumed the direct administration of the Protectorate.

CIVIL ESTABLISHMENT

HIGH COMMISSIONER: Sir Michael David Irving Gass, K C M G

SECRETARIAT
Chief Secretary: T. Russell, C B E
Financial Secretary: J. H. Smith, C B E
Deputy Chief Secretary: R. Davies, O B E
Legal Adviser: D. R. Davis
Inspector-General, South Pacific Health Service: C. H. Gurd, C B E
(joint post with other British Pacific Administrations)

JUDICIARY
Chief Justice: Sir Jocelyn Bodilly, V R D
Puisne Judge: J. P. Trainor
Senior Magistrate: T. Van Rees

BRITISH SOLOMON ISLANDS PROTECTORATE

The Solomon Islands were so named by the Spanish navigator Alvaro de Mendana following his discovery of the archipelago in 1568.

The Protectorate consists of a double row of mountainous islands—the South Solomons—situated between the parallels of 5° and 12° 30′ S. and the meridians of 155° and 170° E., and includes the islands of Guadalcanal, Malaita, San Cristobal, New Georgia, Santa Isabel, Choiseul, Mono (or Treasury), Shortlands, Vella Lavella, Ranongga, Gizo, Rendova, Kolombangara, Russell, Florida, and numerous small islands. The total land area is approximately 11,500 square miles. The highest named mountain is Mount Popmanaseu (7,644 feet) on Guadalcanal. There are no navigable rivers.

The climate is equatorial with small seasonal variations defined by the trade winds. The south-east season lasts from April to November when the minimum temperatures are recorded. The highest mean and maximum temperatures and the highest rainfall are, as a rule, recorded in the north-west season from November to April. The mean annual temperature at the capital, Honiara (Guadalcanal) is about 80°F. Annual rainfall varies from 63 to 95 inches.

The first attempt at a census was carried out in 1931 and resulted in an estimated total population figure of 94,066. A sample census in 1969 gave an estimated total of 124,000. The first full census of the Protectorate was held on 1st February 1970. The total population was found to be 160,998 made up of: Melanesians 149,667; Polynesians 6,399; Micronesians 2,362; Europeans 1,280; Chinese 577; others 713.

The largest concentration of population is in the capital, Honiara, where the census gave a total of 11,191 persons, comprising 7,237 males and 3,954 females. This compared with 6,684 in 1965 and 3,548 in 1959. Elsewhere population density varies greatly, from a maximum in Luania on Ontong Java of 633 persons per square mile to a minimum of 2·72 for the 163 people on Vanikovo.

The official language is English in which language all teaching in registered schools is compulsory, but each tribe has its own language and there are numerous dialects. A form of English consisting of an English derived vocabulary based on a typically Melanesian syntax and known as Pidgin is fairly widespread and in some sort serves as a *lingua franca*.

Primary education is largely in the hands of the churches. Government gives aid to scheduled schools in the form of salary subsidies, boarding and equipment grants. In 1970 there were 424 registered schools including 6 secondary schools with altogether 22,312 pupils. There are two teacher training colleges. In January 1969 the marine, agricultural, land survey and clerical schools became integrated with the new Honiara Technical Institute. Overseas scholarships were awarded to 260 students in 1970, for university, medical, higher technical and post-primary studies. 1970 was the third year of the implementation of the White Paper on Educational Development approved in 1967.

The principal endemic diseases are malaria and tuberculosis. The main Government medical institutions are the Central Hospital, Honiara (171 beds), where a School of Nursing is maintained, three District Hospitals, (total 222 beds), three Rural Hospitals (116 beds) and a Leprosarium (88 patients). There are three hospitals (275 beds), including a Leprosarium, operated by the Churches, who also maintain several centres providing a medical service ranging from first-aid treatment to in-patient hospital care.

Following the completion of a malaria eradication pilot project in 1964, a combined Government/WHO pre-eradication programme commenced in January 1965 and continued until the end of 1969, when a full-scale eradication campaign started. This was in accordance with a Malaria Eradication White Paper approved by the Legislative Council in November 1968.

In 1970, 337 new cases of tuberculosis were notified (a reduction of some 9 per cent on 1969) and 33 new cases of leprosy.

In 1970 the total labour force numbered 13,690. Principal occupations were: Government employment (3,525); agriculture, mainly copra production (2,245); forestry (914); construction industry (754); manufacturing (746) and commerce (580).

The main crop of the Solomon Islands is copra. Rice is being grown successfully on the Guadalcanal Plains. Small scale and to some extent experimental production of cocoa, sorghum and spices is carried out. The cattle population in 1970 was 12,000. After copra the main product is timber and there is a small local production of consumer goods such as biscuits and mineral waters. Other industries include the manufacture of plug, cake and twist tobacco, tyre retreading, the export of *béches-de-mer* and rattan furniture production.

Exports of copra and timber over the three-year period 1968-70 were:

	1968	1969	1970
Copra	17,217	23,463	21,050 tons
Timber	4,438,795	7,335,169	7,738,018 cubic ft.

Copra is marketed through the B.S.I.P. Copra Board and timber by the companies holding licences. Small quantities of cocoa, marine shell, scrap metal, crocodile skins and gold are also exported.

The total value of exports in 1970 was \$6,878,197; the value of imports was \$10,045,701.

Two banks are in operation in the Solomons—the Commonwealth Banking Corporation of Australia and the Australia and New Zealand Banking Group Limited.

There are three main ports: Honiara, the principal port, Gizo and Yandina. Other ports are used exclusively for the export of copra and timber and there are numerous landings throughout the islands used by local vessels. Honiara has a deep water berth 235 feet long with a minimum depth of 28 feet alongside, capable of taking vessels up to 650 feet in length. In 1970, 131 overseas vessels discharged or loaded at the port. Yandina has a steel and concrete wharf with 176 feet of face and a minimum depth of 20 feet alongside. Gizo has a jetty with a depth alongside of 9 feet. Sheltered anchorage is available there in 16 fathoms.

Interisland sea transport is provided by private and Government vessels and at the end of 1970 a total of 149 vessels with a gross tonnage of 3,660 were under survey.

Overseas air services are provided twice weekly by Trans-Australia Airlines and by Fiji Airways Limited, four times a week. An internal air service is provided by Solomon Islands Airways Limited operating Baron aircraft.

Principal airports are:

	Runway *(feet)*	Distance from town *(miles)*
Guadalcanal: Honiara (Henderson)	6,100	9
Russell Islands: Yandina	5,800	Nil
New Georgia: Munda	7,000	Nil
Vella Lavella: (Barakoma)	3,600	27
Malaita: Auki (Gwaunaru'u)	3,100	7
San Cristobal: Kirakira	4,000	2
Gizo: (Nusatupe)	3,200	2

There are no railways. The road mileage in 1970 was 166.

The General Post Office, which has a philatelic section, is situated in Honiara and there are four District post offices and four sub-post offices. There are 42 Postal Agencies in outlying areas in operation. Internal and esternal aeradio services are maintained, there is a 24-hour shipping watch and in 1968 a volunteer weather-reporting service was introduced.

The Solomon Islands Broadcasting Service, which is Government owned, broadcasts for 83½ hours a week and includes a commercial advertising service.

From mid-1969 the transmitters in simultaneous use are: VQO 1030 KHz 291m 5,000w; VQO4 3995 KHz 75m 5,000w; VQO7 7235 KHz 42m 5,000w.

The currency is Australian and interchangeable with sterling at £1 Stg. = $A 2·143.

The main sources of internal revenue are import and export duties, income tax and sale of stamps. Important provisions designed to encourage investment in the territory—including in certain circumstances a tax holiday for pioneer industries—are incorporated in the tax law.

The budget is balanced by a grant-in-aid from the United Kingdom. A summary of revenue and expenditure for the years 1965-1970 is given in the following table:

	Local Revenue excluding Grant-in-Aid and Development Funds $	U.K. Aid (Grant-in-Aid and Development Funds) $	Expenditure, excluding contributions to Capital Estimates $
1965 (Actual)	3,639,087	2,509,498	6,086,526
1966 (Actual)	3,982,588	2,742,748	7,062,684
1967 (Actual)	4,421,717	3,302,928	7,725,822
1968 (Actual)	3,858,301	3,644,802	7,711,428
1969 (Actual)	3,912,055	5,209,408	8,751,593
1970 (Revised Estimates)	4,693,780	5,203,331	10,039,393

The following table shows the Retail Price Indices in the territory from 1960-1969:

	Honiara (December 1960=100)		Single Manual worker
	Lower Incomes	Higher Incomes	(Introduced in 1968)
1960 Average ..	100	—	
1961 ,, ..	102	102	
1962 ,, ..	104	104	
1963 ,, ..	108	107	
1964 ,, ..	109	109	
1965 ,, ..	—	111	
1966 ,, ..	110·4	111·8	
1967 ,, ..	114·8	116·2	
1968 ,, ..	119·3	122·1	116·4
1969 ,, ..	128·5	121·4	125·3

The Protectorate's Fifth Development Plan expired on 31st March 1970. An interim programme of capital expenditure was approved for the year 1st April 1970 to 31st March 1971 pending the introduction of the Sixth Development Plan for the period 1971-73. The overall objective of the new Plan, which was adopted by the Governing Council in May 1971, is to lay the basis for substantially reduced dependence on external aid in the present decade. Emphasis is placed on productive investment in the Protectorate's agriculture, forestry and mineral resources, and on the expansion of secondary and tertiary education to meet the manpower needs of localisation.

Total public sector capital expenditure in the Plan period is estimated at $A17,500,000 divided as follows:

	$A million	
Development Sector	10·8	
Natural resources	4·5	(Agriculture 2·8)
Commerce and Industry	1·2	
Economic Infrastructure	5·1	(Roads 2·6)
Social Sector	4·7	
Education	2·6	
Health	1·9	
Administrative Sector	2·0	

HISTORY

The origin of the present Melanesian inhabitants is uncertain.

The era of European discovery opened in 1568 when Mendana sighted land at Santa Isabel. Mendana spent six months exploring in the group before returning to South America. Though he reported evidence of gold he was unable to produce proof and in consequence he lost favour in the Court and his achievements were belittled. Mendana however was convinced of the potential of the islands and partly to impress his countrymen called them the Isles of Solomon, in the hope that they would be connected with the source of King Solomon's wealth. In 1595 Mendana led another expedition to re-discover the archipelago. This time he did not reach the Solomons proper, but discovered the Santa Cruz Group. In Graciosa Bay he founded a short-lived colony which was totally abandoned soon after his death there. Tasman discovered Ontong Java in 1643, but for two centuries the main islands of the group remained lost to the sight of Europeans. It was not until 1767 that Carteret re-discovered what Mendana had seen. Thereafter, European explorers sailed through the Solomon Islands with increasing frequency—Bougainville in 1768, de Surville in 1769, Maurelle in 1781, Shortland in 1788 and d'Entrecasteaux in 1799.

The European explorers had, however, still made no impression on the lives of the indigenous inhabitants. These lived in very small groups, most of them having an anarchical attitude to authority. Gradually, however, here and there, some powerful personality began to assert himself and to gain adherents from other groups of people. Succession and rule were matters of challenge, contest and victory, and life was a pattern of very small communities living in fear of each other; a pattern of internecine warfare, headhunting and cannibalism, lived in such exclusive isolation that even dialects had changed to an extent where adjacent villages had difficulty understanding each other. The pattern remained unaltered until regular visits by Europeans began in the nineteenth century.

The inauguration of sugar plantations in Queensland and Fiji, the arrival of missionaries and traders and the more regular (even if very intermittent) patrols of naval ships began a new era. The overseas plantations needed labour and so the Solomons as well as other island groups, were combed for labour. Some of the recruiters used methods which shocked the outside world and in return provoked reprisals. Massacres of Europeans and natives steadily mounted until Great Britain, in an effort to stem the mounting tide of savagery, declared a Protectorate in 1893 over the Southern Solomons, comprising Guadalcanal, Savo, Malaita, San Cristobal and the New Georgia group. In 1898 and 1899 the islands of the Santa Cruz group were added to the Protectorate, and in 1900 the islands of the Shortland groups, Santa Isabel, Choiseul and Ontong Java were transferred by treaty from Germany to Great Britain.

The copra industry began in 1908, three years after the last worker had been returned from the overseas plantations. The acreage under coconuts continued to expand until the price of copra fell in the early nineteen-twenties. The greater part of the copra produced was in the hands of companies, at least until the Japanese invasion in 1942. The copra industry made a special mark on social life in those parts of the Solomons which provided the labour for the plantations. Young men began to regard it as natural to go away for a couple of years at a time, to earn money and bring back trade goods for their family in the villages, and this became part of family life.

The effect of the spread of Christianity and desire for gainful employment was to check inter-clan warfare and raids on other villages and islands. Missionary societies started schools and began to teach some of the boys various trades; efforts were also made to teach hygiene in the home and child welfare.

The 1914-18 war had no effect on the islands, but in 1942 there came invasion, occupation by the Japanese, counter-attack and battle, air-raids, and finally occupation by United States and Allied forces.

For nearly three years there had been a state of havoc, fear, and uncertainty, and added to this the revelation of material resources such as the Solomon Islanders had never seen before. The loyalty of the islanders was remarkable. Many joined the Defence Force, the combat unit of the Protectorate that took part in active battle, often in the spearhead of the attack where they were employed as guides, or in patrolling behind the enemy lines. They earned military distinction and a number of decorations. In the areas occupied by the enemy, Government headmen carried on, protecting British coast-watchers from capture, rescuing allied airmen shot down behind enemy lines and helping them when the American and British forces landed.

During the war a political movement, known as Marching Rule, started in Malaita, and for over eight years its leaders endeavoured to dominate native affairs in Malaita while their influence spread to other parts of the Protectorate. At the outset the movement preached a policy of improved agriculture, concentration into large villages and non-co-operation with Government and missionary societies. These teachings were coupled with a policy of fostering rumours of an earthly paradise to come, rumours which were earnestly believed and which formed part of the psychological background of the movement.

The year 1952, however, saw a decided lessening of the political tension which had handicapped development and administration during the post-war years. Strenuous efforts to bring about a rapprochement between the Government and the leaders of Marching Rule on Malaita culminated in the formation of a properly organised Council for the whole of Malaita for the first time. The Malaita people, through their representatives on this Council, like the people of other islands, now have a considerable amount of responsibility for the management of their own local affairs. Similar local government councils were established in the years immediately following the war, and the number was gradually increased until in 1966 the whole Protectorate except Tikopia and Anuta was covered by these councils, all the members of which are elected by universal adult suffrage. With the reconstitution of the Honiara Town Council in 1969, a total of twenty-two councils has now been established under the Local Government Ordinance, which was enacted in 1963.

CONSTITUTIONAL DEVELOPMENT

Until 1960 the High Commissioner was assisted by an Advisory Council. In 1960 a Constitution was introduced which provided for the establishment of a Legislative Council and an Executive Council, the members of which were appointed by the High Commissioner.

A revised Constitution was introduced in 1964 providing that the Legislative Council should consist of 3 *ex-officio* members, 8 official members, 8 elected members and 2 nominated members. Seven of the elected members were elected through electoral colleges composed of elected members of the Local Councils in each constituency; in Honiara, election was direct.

The Constitution was revised again in 1967 and from then until its dissolution in March 1970, the Legislative Council consisted of 14 elected members, 3 ex-officio members and 12 public service members. By an Order-in-Council of 24th March 1970 a new Constitution was established in accordance with proposals which were approved by the Legislative Council in June 1969. It provides for an elected majority in a single Governing Council combining legislative and executive functions and exercising executive control through a series of functional committees. A general election under the new Constitution was held from April to June 1970. Direct elections were held in all but one constituency where owing to the difficulty of communications election was by an electoral college. The new Governing Council which consists of 17 elected members, 3 ex-officio members and up to 6 public service members, met for the first time in July 1970.

LAND POLICY

Land policy is concerned with land under public ownership, land owned in accordance with local customary law, and land privately owned in freehold or leasehold.

Public land is administered to ensure a balanced development in town areas and its best economic usage in the rural areas. Large areas of the Guadalcanal Plains have been leased for agricultural development by overseas capital investment. Forest policy is aimed at both the establishment of a permanent forest estate and the economic development of forest resources by private enterprise and was the subject of examination by a Select Committee of the Legislative Council during 1968, culminating in the preparation and approval of a White Paper on Forest Policy. The Forests and Timber Ordinance 1969 which came into effect on 1st October 1970 brought virtually all commercial timber working under licensing control and introduced a new "Timber Levy" tax payable on all timber exported, and on milled timber sold in the country. Simultaneously export duty on timber was revoked.

Land held under customary tenure, which comprises by far the greatest part, may be subject to control of user where valuable natural assets need protection and there is a statutory bar to the acquisition of land so owned other than by the Government or by Solomon Islanders. Registration of land previously held under customary tenure with consequent tenure conversion has begun and will gradually extend through areas subject to economic development where the owners wish it.

All mineral rights in the islands are reserved to the Government. Prospecting and mining are subject to control under modern mining legislation which was revised in 1968. Land privately owned by non-Solomon Islanders is also being brought on to the Land Register under transitional provisions in the land legislation which contain an element of compulsion. Use of such land is subject to the same controls for the protection of valuable natural assets as land under customary ownership.

THE GOVERNING COUNCIL
(as at December 1970)

The High Commissioner for the Western Pacific:
His Excellency Sir Michael David Irving Gass, KCMG

EX-OFFICIO MEMBERS:
T. Russell, CBE (Chief Secretary)
D. R. Davis (Attorney-General)
J. H. Smith, CBE (Financial Secretary)

COMMITTEES OF THE GOVERNING COUNCIL
Communications and Works Committee
*G. Siama (Western District) Chairman
*J. Bryan (East Guadalcanal)
*Dr. C. Ofai (North Malaita)

Dr D. Dawea-Taukalo (Eastern District)
*W. A. Wood (Director of Public Works)

Education and Social Welfare Committee
*W. Betu (Central District) Chairman
J. Fifi'i (Malaita)
S. Kuku (Western District)
S. S. Mamaloni (Eastern District)
A. G. H. House (Director of Education)
B. C. Wilmot (Commissioner of Labour)

Health and Internal Affairs Committee
*M. Kelesi (North-East Malaita) (Chairman)
A. Maeke (Central District)
A. Saru (South Malaita)
P. Salaka (Central District)
*Dr J. D. Macgregor (Director of Medical Services)
*Member of former Legislative Council.

National Resources Committee
*D. N. Kausimae (Malaita) Chairman
*Ven. P. K. Thompson (Malaita)
R. J. Eresi (Western District)
*Ven. E. Kiva (Central District)
G. W. Pugeva (Central District)
*F. M. Spencer (Director of Agriculture)
*J. B. Twomey, OBE (Commissioner of Lands and Surveys)

Finance Committee
J. H. Smith, CBE (Financial Secretary) Chairman
*G. Siama (Chairman. Communications and Works Committee)
*M. Kelesi (Chairman, Health and Internal Affairs Committee)
*W. Betu (Chairman, Education and Social Welfare Committee)
S. S. Mamaloni (Education and Social Welfare Committee)
*D. N. Kausimae (Chairman, Natural Resources Committee)
*Ven. P. K. Thompson (Natural Resources Committee)
B. C. Wilmot (Commissioner of Labour)
*Member of former Legislative Council.

CIVIL ESTABLISHMENT
(as at 31st December 1970)
(For Secretariat see under *Western Pacific High Commission*)

Attorney-General: D. R. Davis
Director of Agriculture: F. M. Spencer
Director of Education: A. G. H. House
Superintendent of Marine: Captain G. Douglas
Director of Medical Services: Dr J. D. Macgregor, OBE
Director of Public Works: W. A. Wood
Solicitor-General: G. P. Nazareth
Establishment Secretary: P. Dale
Accountant-General: R. Pullen
Conservator of Forests: K. W. Trenaman, OBE
Director of Geological Surveys: Dr R. B. Thompson

Commissioner of Lands and Surveys: J. B. Twomey, OBE
Director of Audit: F. Cherry, EM
Superintendent of Civil Aviation: E. E. E. Nielsen
Registrar of Co-operatives: C. N. Colman
Comptroller of Customs and Excise: R. Burrow-Wilkes
Commissioner of Labour: B. C. Wilmot
Chief of Police: B. R. P. Edwards, MBE
Comptroller of Posts and Telecommunications: C. D. Wright

READING LIST

British Solomon Islands Annual Report 1969 *HMSO. London* 1971 SBN11 5800638.

COATES, Austin. Western Pacific Islands. *HMSO*, 1971.

FIRTH, Raymond. Social Change in Tikopia. *Allen & Unwin*, 1959.

FOX, C. E. Lord of the Southern Isles. London, *Mowbray*, 1958.

FOX, C. E. Story of the Solomons. Taroaniara, BSI. *Diocese of Melanesia Press*, 1967.

HORTON, D. C. The Happy Isles—a Diary of the Solomons. London, *Heinemann*, 1965.

LAMBER, S. M. A Doctor in Paradise. London, *Dent*, 1941.

MORRELL, W. P. Britain in the Pacific Islands. *Oxford*, 1960.

SCARR, Deryck. Fragments of Empire: A History of the Western Pacific High Commission 1877-1914. *Australian National University Press*, Canberra, and *C. Hurst and Co.*, London, 1967.

SHARP, A. The Discovery of the Pacific Islands. *Oxford, Clarendon Press*, 1960.

STRUBEN, R. Coral and Colour of Gold. London, *Faber*, 1961.

WHITMORE, T. C. Guide to the Forests of the British Solomon Islands. *Oxford University Press*, 1966.

THE ANGLO-FRENCH CONDOMINIUM OF THE NEW HEBRIDES

The New Hebrides lie in the south-west Pacific between 13° and 21° S. and 166° and 171° E., forming an irregular Y-shaped chain of islands with a total land area of about 5,700 square miles. They were named the New Hebrides in 1774 by Captain Cook. There are in the group some 65 inhabited islands and islets, the larger of which are Espiritu Santo, Malekula, Efate, Ambrym, Tanna, Erromango, Epi, Aoba, Pentecost and Maewo.

The capital of the group is Vila with an urban population of 3,074 and a peri-urban population of 5,034. A second town known as Santo or Luganville, with an urban population of 2,556 and a peri-urban population of 2,682, is situated on the island of Espiritu Santo. (1967 census).

The islands are of coral and volcanic origin with active volcanoes on Tanna, Lopevi and Ambrym. They are almost without exception mountainous, Santo Peak and Tabwemesana on Santo rising to over 6,000 feet. The group is generally well watered. The climate is oceanic tropical and moderated by the south-east trade winds which blow between the months of May and October. During the remainder of the year winds are variable and hurricanes may occur. High humidity occasionally leads to enervating conditions. Temperatures at Vila vary between 16°C (60°F) and 33°C (92°F) and average rainfall ranges from about 90 inches in the south to 150 inches in the north, with a mean figure of 91 inches for Vila.

A general census was carried out in 1967. The total population was 77,988, made up as follows: New Hebrideans 72,243; Other Melanesians 426; Polynesians and Micronesians 1,270; Europeans 1,773; Part-European 1,151; Vietnamese 397; Chinese 252; Others 476. Amongst the non-New Hebridean population there were 3,840 French citizens and 1,631 British subjects. The population at 1st January 1971 was estimated to be 81,000+.

Many languages and dialects are spoken; most belong to the Melanesian family and are related to those of Fiji and New Caledonia. Pidgin English is the *lingua franca*. English and French are the official languages.

The Anglican, Presbyterian and Roman Catholic Churches began missionary work in the New Hebrides in the 19th century. In this century other religious bodies, including the Seventh Day Adventists have become active in various parts of the Group. At present the Presbyterian Church of the New Hebrides has the largest number of adherents with the Anglican and Catholic Churches coming next. All the religious denominations provide educational facilities in co-operation with Government and several of them have made and continue to make important contributions to health services.

Malaria is the most serious endemic disease, and hookworm infections and anaemia are common causes of debility. With WHO assistance the Joint Administration is at present conducting a campaign to control tuberculosis by (a) case finding and (b) B.C.G. vaccination. By the end of 1967 all the population had been vaccinated at least once. Operations are now being extended into maternal and child health and vaccinations against whooping cough, diphtheria and tetanus. The French Government maintains hospitals at Vila and Santo and medical centres at Malekula and Tanna staffed by French army doctors. The British Government maintains rural clinics and dispensaries in the outer islands staffed by Medical Officers (Class III), Medical Assistants, Dressers and Nurses. It also subsidises British Mission Hospitals at Aoba, Vila and Epi, and there is a new British Hospital at Tanna with a British National Service Medical Officer as Superintendent. A new British Base Hospital is to be built to replace the old one in Vila. The Joint Administration Medical Subsidy is shared between the French and British Medical Services. There is also a Condominium Medical Service, mainly concerned with public health and preventive medicine.

Most of the population is employed on plantations and in trading or sub-sistence agriculture. The most important cash crops are copra, cocoa, and coffee. The principal subsistence crops are yam, taro, manioc, sweet potato and bread-fruit. Large numbers of cattle are kept on the plantations and efforts are being made to develop an export trade in meat (frozen and tinned) and to expand the local meat industry. A considerable timber industry, mainly serving Australian plywood factories, has been established in Erromango. In other islands small amounts of timber are felled and milled for local use. At Santo the South Pacific Fishing Company, a British registered concern, operates a plant where tuna and bonito are frozen and prepared for export to the United States, Japan, Europe and elsewhere.

Active measures are being taken towards the development of a tourist industry.

The following are the principal domestic exports by quantity (in metric tons) and value (in Australian dollars):

	1969	1970
Copra (metric tons)	37,015	31,197
$A '000	5,308	4,833
Frozen fish (metric tons)	7,988	9,218
$A '000	3,103	4,666
Manganese (metric tons)	—	28,545
$A '000	—	328
Timber (logs) (metric tons)	12,505	17,013
$A '000	468	664
Canned meat (metric tons)	154	155
$A '000	135	134
Chilled meat (metric tons)	159	287
$A'000	76	152

Values are shown in Australian dollars as this is the *de facto* British currency in the New Hebrides and is now used, parallel with the New Hebridean franc, for all estimating, accounting and statistical purposes in the Condominium.

There are 104 co-operative societies, membership over 5,000 adults, capital investment $A304,812 and a turnover of $A1,213,587 in 1970.

The principal ports of the New Hebrides are Vila and Santo.

The principal airports are Bauer Field (Efate) and Luganville (Santo). Each is situated about three miles from the nearest town (Vila and Santo respectively) and each is 6,000 feet in length. Bauer Field was resurfaced in 1970 to accept jet aircraft. There are 12 smaller airfields on Malekula, Aoba, Pentecost, Epi, Tongoa, Efate, Erromango, Tanna, Futuna and Aneityum.

The New Hebrides possess about 340 miles of roads, 200 of these being seasonal earth motor tracks.

There are two airlines, New Hebrides Airways Ltd. and Hèbridair. They pooled their operations in 1966 to form Air Melanesia, which operates both regular and charter services throughout the Group. External air services are provided by Fiji Airways which operates a service three times a week between Suva, Nandi, Vila, Santo, Honiara and return to Fiji (once a week continuing to Port Moresby from Honiara), and by the French company, Union de Transports Aériens, which provides air communications to and from New Caledonia. Connections can be made with international flights at Nandi and Tontouta (New Caledonia).

Regular shipping services to and from New Caledonia, France and Australia are maintained by Messageries Maritimes. One of its vessels, the *Polynésie*, maintains a regular schedule between Australia, New Caledonia and the New Hebrides, arriving in the territory every three weeks. The Kahlander Line vessel *Sletholm* provides a link between Sydney, Norfolk Island, the New Hebrides and

$A2·143 = £1.

the Solomon Islands every five weeks. Small vessels give a frequent but non-scheduled inter-island service.

In 1966 a broadcasting service known as Radio Vila was established to serve the whole of the Group.

Current development projects, financed from the local development plan, jointly from British development aid funds (formerly Colonial Development and Welfare funds) and their French counterpart F.I.D.E.S., or entirely from British development aid funds, include agricultural development and training, improvement of communications (roads, airports, air and marine navigational aids, radio, deep-water wharf at Vila), provision of launches and ships for administrative touring, geological survey and tellurometer survey. Major expenditure from these sources is on education, for which the British Administration has set up a Teacher Training College. The French Administration provides training for local teachers at an Ecole Normale. A new British Co-educational Secondary School and French *Lycée*, and a number of primary schools have also been established. Both administrations also assist the Voluntary agencies with improvement of their primary schools. A new hospital has recently been built with C.D. & W. funds on Tanna and a new British Base Hospital is under construction to replace the outdated one in Vila. The French Hospital in Vila was entirely renovated in 1969.

The main forms of taxation are import duties (16½ per cent *ad valorem* f.o.b. with certain exceptions), export duties of from 2 per cent to 10 per cent on copra, cocoa, coffee, shell, etc., and trading licences. There is no income tax.

Condominium revenue and expenditure (excluding revenue and expenditure of the British and French National Services) is shown below:

	Revenue $A	Expenditure $A
1969	3,735,475	3,453,458
1970 (rev. est.)	3,849,666	3,644,140

The main sources of revenue are import and export duties estimated at over $A2,157,300 in 1970.

Primary education is not free but only nominal fees are charged. Primary schooling is available for almost all children. Exceptions are the relatively few populated inland areas where changes in patterns of living are taking place for the first time and a desire for education is only now springing up.

Secondary education is available at the British Government Secondary School and the French *Lycée* at Vila. To a limited degree secondary education is available in three British Voluntary Agency post primary schools and at three French Mission Schools.

No statistics on literacy are available but it is fairly widespread amongst persons under 35-40 years. Above 40 years it is often limited to pastors, elders and teachers. Only a small proportion of the population is reasonably literate in English or French. Many New Hebrideans are literate in their own vernacular, although there is practically no secular reading matter in the many vernaculars. New Hebrideans who speak English or French usually also speak Pidgin, though the reverse does not follow.

HISTORY AND CONSTITUTION

The New Hebrides were discovered by the Spanish explorer, de Quiros, in 1606. He was followed by the French navigator, de Bougainville, in 1768, and in 1774 Captain Cook visited and charted the greater part of the chain of islands which comprise the group. Other early visitors were La Perouse who is believed to have passed through in 1788, and d'Entrecasteaux who came in search of La Perouse in 1793. In 1789 the sighting of the Banks Islands was recorded by Captain Bligh in the course of his open-boat voyage to Timor after the mutiny on the *Bounty*. Last century, before any government showed any interest in the New Hebrides, a number of British and French missionaries, planters and traders had established themselves and in 1887, by the Anglo-French Convention of 16th November, the two nations appointed a Joint Naval Commission charged with the protection in the New Hebrides of the lives and properties of the subjects of England and France.

In 1902 Deputy Resident Commissioners were appointed and took up residence in the territory. In February 1906 an Anglo-French conference took place in London. A draft convention was prepared to provide for settlement of land claims and for an arrangement to end the difficulties arising from the absence of jurisdiction over the natives. This was confirmed on 20th October 1906, and an Anglo-French Condominium was established. A Protocol drawn up in London in 1914 to replace the Convention of 1906 was ratified in 1922.

The system of administration is such that the police consists of a British and a French division, education services are national, medical services are joint in the preventive field but national at the hospital level, while the remaining services (agriculture, customs, treasury, pre-audit, personnel, posts and telephones, radio, meteorology, mines, lands registry, survey, local and urban administration, and public works) are joint. The legal system is that Condominium laws apply to all, but in addition national law applies to non-New Hebrideans where no Condominium law exists. Each non-New Hebridean who is not a British subject or a French citizen has to opt to be subject to either the British or the French system of law and courts in the event of prosecution for an offence not provided for under Condominium law.

An Advisory Council was established by Joint Regulation in 1957. It now comprises four official members and 24 private members of whom 10 are nominated by the Resident Commissioners and 14 are elected. Of the nominated members 3 are British, 3 French and 4 New Hebridean; and of the elected members the 3 British and the 3 French members are elected by indirect elections through the electoral machinery of the Chamber of Commerce and the 8 New Hebrideans through electoral colleges. The Council is presided over jointly by the Resident Commissioners.

LAND POLICY

As the New Hebrides is not a territorial possession of either power concerned, there are no Crown lands or their equivalent. The whole of the land area of the Group is held to belong, or to have belonged until alienated, to the natives. The Protocol regulates the acquisition of unregistered land from natives and the registration of land claims. It provides for the creation of inalienable native reserves and for the control of sales of land by natives to non-natives. On the islands of Santo, Malekula, Efate and Epi substantial areas have been alienated. On the other islands little alienation has occurred.

BRITISH NATIONAL ADMINISTRATION
RESIDENT COMMISSIONER: C. H. Allan, CMG, OBE
Assistant Resident Commissioner: M. M. Townsend, OBE, MC
Secretary for Financial Affairs: F. H. Brown
Administrative Officers, Class A: G. Bristow, MBE; K. Woodward, MBE; D. K. H. Dale
Accountant: J. R. Love
Senior Geologist: Dr D. Mallick
Marine Superintendent: Capt. R. Bibby
Senior Medical Officer: R. G. Greenhough
Commandant of Police: D. S. Walford, BEM
Superintendent of Works: R. I. B. Lusk
Information Officer: A. R. Worner

FRENCH NATIONAL ADMINISTRATION
RESIDENT COMMISSIONER: R. Langlois
Chancelier: M. Valy

JOINT SERVICES
Chief Agricultural Officer: B. Thévenin
Registrar of Land Titles: P. Pré
Chief Medical Officer: Médecin-Col. Chassary
Head of Meteorological Department: J. M. Mitchell
Mines Officer: M. Benoit
Ordonnateur/Establishment Officer: P. Viguié
Postmaster: O. Richards
Superintendent of Public Works: P. Garsonnin
Radio Engineer: J. G. Bennett
Treasurer: (Vacant)
Chief Surveyor: L. Page

JUDICIARY
Justice of the High Court and British Judge of Joint Court: J. P. Trainor
French Judge of Joint Court: G. Guésdon

NEW HEBRIDES ADVISORY COUNCIL
JOINT PRESIDENTS
C. H. Allan, CMG, OBE; R. Langlois

OFFICIAL MEMBERS
Condominium Treasurer: (vacant)
Superintendent of Public Works: P. Garsonnin
Assistant Resident Commissioner: M. M. Townsend, OBE, MC
Chancelier: M. Valy

PRIVATE MEMBERS

Nominated (i)	British	The Ven. D. A. Rawcliffe
		R. M. Gubbay
		R. U. Paul
(ii)	French	Father Verlingue
		J. Chauveau
		J. Russet
(iii)	New Hebridean	Mrs. Madeline Kalchichi
		Dr Makau Kalsakau
		Father Gerard Leymang
		Michael Noel
Elected		
(i)	British	G. E. G. Seagoe
		W. Hamlyn-Harris
		J. Burton
(ii)	French	P. Lutgen
		J. Ratard
		P. Delacroix
(iii)	New Hebridean	William Mete
		Iolu Abbil
		George Kalkoa
		Chief Tom Tipoloamata
		Frank Kenneth
		Michael Liliu
		Pastor Titus Path
		Michael Ala

READING LIST

ATTENBOROUGH, D. Quest in Paradise. London, *Lutterworth Press*, 1960.
CHEESMAN. Evelyn. Things Worth While. London. *Hutchinson*, 1957.
COATES, Austin. Western Pacific Islands. *HMSO*. 1970.
DE LA RUE, Aubert. Les Nouvelles-Hébrides. Montreal, 1945.
LARSEN, May and LARSEN, H. Black Sand; New Hebrides, its peoples and places. London, *Oliver and Boyd*, 1961.
LUKE, Sir H. From a South Seas Diary. London, *Nicholson and Watson*, 1946.
MORRELL, W. P. Britain in the Pacific Islands. Oxford, *Clarendon Press*, 1960.
SCARR, Deryck. Fragments of Empire: A History of the Western Pacific High Commission 1877-1914. *Australian National University Press*, Canberra, and *C. Hurst and Co.*, London, 1967.
SIMPSON, Colin. Islands of Men. Sydney, *Angus and Robertson*, 1956.
WILSON, J. S. G. Economic Survey of the New Hebrides. *H.M.S.O.*, 1966.

THE GILBERT AND ELLICE ISLANDS

The Gilbert and Ellice Islands, which also include Ocean Island and the Phoenix and Northern Line Islands, are situated in the South-West Pacific around the point where the International Date Line cuts the Equator. Although the total land area is only 283 square miles it is scattered over more than two million square miles of ocean, and distances between extreme points are enormous. Christmas Island in the east is 2,000 miles from Ocean Island in the west, and the latitude of Washington Island in the north is more than 1,000 miles from the latitude of Niulakita in the south. Furthermore, the islands are remote from large centres of civilisation, and Tarawa, the capital, is about 2,500 miles from Sydney and 1,365 miles from Suva. The scattered nature of the territory and its remoteness cause many difficulties in administration, transport and communications.

The Gilbert and Ellice Islands are atolls composed of coral reefs built on the outer arc of the ridges formed by pressure from the central Pacific against the ancient core of Australia. In most of the atolls the reef encloses a lagoon, on the eastern side of which are long narrow stretches of land varying in length from a few hundred yards to some ten miles, and in width from one or two hundred yards to nearly a mile. The surface of these islands seldom rises more than twelve feet above sea level.

The climate of the central Gilberts, the Phoenix Islands and Ocean Island is of the maritime equatorial type, but that of the islands farther north and south is of tropical type. The mean annual temperature is 27°C (80°F). The trade winds blow throughout the year with a strong easterly component and exercise a moderating influence on the temperature. From October to March there are occasional westerly gales. Rain comes in sharp squalls and is very irregular, giving wide variations in total fall from island to island and year to year. The average is 40 inches a year near the Equator, rising to 120 inches in the extreme north and south.

A census of the population of the islands was held in December 1968. The total population enumerated was 53,517 and comprised 26,404 males and 27,113 females.

The territory lies midway between Polynesia and Micronesia, the people of the Gilbert Islands being Micronesian stock, whilst the people of the Ellice Islands are Polynesians with close connections with Samoa and the Tokelaus to the south and east. The racial groups indicated by the 1968 census were as follows: Micronesians (almost entirely Gilbertese) 44,897; Polynesians (almost entirely Ellice Islanders) 7,465; Europeans 458; Chinese (employed at Ocean Island) 65; Mixed race 566; other races 66.

The land area of the 29 inhabited islands is very small, and although no accurate surveys have been made, it has been estimated that there is an area of 100 square miles in the Gilbert Islands and 10 square miles in the Ellice Islands. With a population estimated to be increasing at a rate to double itself in about 30 years, despite a family-planning campaign, it is not surprising that population pressure is acute. In 1968 the density of population was nearly 0·3 persons per acre.

The people of the territory maintain a reasonable standard of living only by intensive exploitation of the sea and the very limited resources of their infertile atolls, and by sending their young men out to work. A small number find employment on the copra plantations in the Line Islands (Washington, Fanning and Christmas), but the main outlet at present is to the phosphate industry on Ocean Island and Nauru which take approximately 500 and 650 workers respectively, many of them accompanied by their families. There is, already, a surplus of labour available for employment but a critical situation will arise in the late 1970s, when the phosphate which is mined on Ocean Island will be exhausted at the present rate of extraction and the population may well be approaching 68,000 with a density of over 600 to the square mile.

The main languages spoken are Gilbertese, Ellice and English. The official language is English, but on the outer islands away from the headquarters at Tarawa it is seldom used. Practically the entire population is Christian, but whereas the religion of the Ellice Islands is predominantly Protestant, that of the Gilbert Islands is more evenly divided between Protestant and Roman Catholic.

The Medical Department has its headquarters at Bikenibeu, Tarawa, where the Central Hospital (142 beds) is also situated. Another General Hospital (125 beds) is operated at Ocean Island by the British Phosphate Commissioners for their employees. There is a cottage hospital with 20 beds at Funafuti in the Ellice Islands and a small hospital/dispensary with a medical officer or a male medical assistant in charge on all other islands.

The principal endemic diseases are infantile diarrhoea, chicken pox, amoebiasis, bacillary dysentery, filariasis (mostly in the Ellice group), tuberculosis and leprosy. Tuberculosis remains one of the most serious public health problems. Medical expenditure in 1970 including Capital and Aid expenditure amounted to an estimated $A444,590.

The thirty-seven islands of the territory are divided into four districts which are (with their headquarters islands in brackets): Ocean Island, Gilbert Islands (Tarawa), Ellice Islands (Funafuti), and Line Islands (Christmas Island). The Phoenix group is uninhabited. Tarawa is the capital. The main Government Stations are on three separate islets on South Tarawa—Betio (population 4,591), Bairiki (1,300), and Bikenibeu (2,438). Bairiki and Bikenibeu are connected by causeways, but Betio, the port area and scene of the bitter struggle between the United States Marines and the Japanese in 1943, lies two miles west of Bairiki and is served by a scheduled launch service. The headquarters of Government are on Bairiki Islet, where are to be found the Legislative Council building, the Secretariat, Treasury, Legal, Audit, Labour, Information, Broadcasting and Public Works Departments.

The principal occupations for the available labour force of the islands are provided by the open-cast phosphate mining at Ocean Island, work on the copra plantations in the Line Islands, and Government service. Some labour, however, has secured employment overseas, notably in the phosphate workings at Nauru, and with a fishing company and agricultural enterprises in the New Hebrides. The Marine Training School at Tarawa produced 225 seamen who were employed by overseas shipping lines in 1970. Apart from a very small number of skilled or professional expatriates, all workers are Gilbertese and Ellice Islanders to whom, for the most part, work is a profitable way of seeing new islands and of increasing prevailing income levels on their home islands. The bulk of the population is engaged in copra production on a subsistence basis.

During 1970 the British Phosphate Commissioners at Ocean Island employed 608 persons of whom 514 were Gilbert and Ellice Islanders. A further 640 workers from the islands were employed by the Commissioners at Nauru. Estimated numbers in other occupations are: Government service 1,800, and Local Government approximately 200 officials; commerce 736; copra plantations 296. There is only one registered trade union operating at present.

Agriculture is virtually non-existent in the islands due to the poor quality of the soil, which is composed largely of coral sand and rock fragments. The major part of all islands, except Ocean and some of the Phoenix group, is covered with coconut palms which provide the islands with an important source of food and drink, and with copra, which is their only cash crop. In 1970, out of a total production of 7,098 tons of copra, 5,106 tons came from Island producers and 1,992 tons from the Line Islands Plantations. Sea fishing is excellent but on a small scale at present, but a fisheries survey to ascertain whether it will be economic to start a large scale fishing industry was started in 1970. Phosphate of lime is mined at Ocean Island by the British Phosphate Commissioners. Livestock is limited to pigs and poultry. There is little useful timber.

The principal domestic exports are copra, mainly shipped to the United Kingdom, and phosphate (untreated). In 1970, 7,825 tons of copra were exported and the production of phosphate on Ocean Island amounted to 555,100 tons. The values and origins or destinations of imports and exports in 1970 (actual figures) were:

	Imports $A	Exports $A
Britain	454,988	686,741
Australia	2,300,362	4,005,894
New Zealand	132,727	2,595,100
Other countries	1,028,670	10,791
	$A3,916,747	$A7,298,526

Principal imports were:

				$A
Flour	..	..	..	193,834
Rice	..	..	..	200,767
Other foodstuffs		..		944,559
Fuel oils and petrol		..		272,291
Other	..	..	..	2,305,296
				$A3,916,747

Exports of copra and phosphate from 1963-1970 were:

			Copra '000 *tons*	Phosphate '000 *tons*
1963	..	..	6·11	356
1964	..	..	5·32	325
1965	..	..	9·03	361
1966	..	..	8·98	375
1967	..	..	10·84	445
1968	..	..	5·09	523
1969	..	..	7·82	555
1970	..	..	5·74	487

A Copra Board is responsible for all purchases of copra and sales overseas. Internal purchases are made through the agency of the co-operative societies. Most imports and sales or retail goods are handled by a statutory trading organisation, the Wholesale Society and by the co-operatives. The economic life of the indigenous population is based on the co-operative movement. At 31st March 1970 there were 49 co-operative societies (mainly consumer-marketing societies, but including five consumer societies and two secondary societies) having a total membership of 18,992. The volume of private trading is small.

The principal ports are at Betio Islet (Tarawa), and Ocean Island. Small ships of up to 10 feet draught may enter the harbour at Betio, whilst larger vessels drawing up to 28 feet anchor in the lagoon and are serviced by barges. At Ocean Island there is a cantilever through which phosphate is loaded, and barge and boat loading facilities are also provided by the British Phosphate Commissioners. Vessels of up to 30 feet draught can enter the lagoon at Funafuti, while at Christmas Island vessels anchor or lie at buoys outside the lagoon. During 1969 a total of 105 overseas vessels called at ports in the territory. Of this number, 53 (with an estimated tonnage of 353,204 tons) were vessels owned or chartered by the British Phosphate Commissioners at Ocean Island.

There are two airports, located at Tarawa and Funafuti, used for scheduled overseas commercial flights. The airport at Christmas Island is now only used for emergency landings or by military aircraft. The aerodrome at Canton Island has now been closed and all facilities and personnel have been withdrawn. A weekly service from Suva, Fiji, to Tarawa via Nadi and Funafuti is operated with HS 748 aircraft by Fiji Airways Ltd. Air Nauru now operate a fortnightly flight from Nauru to Tarawa using a Falcon jet aircraft. Airfields for an internal service have been completed at Abemama, Tabiteuea and Butaritari in the Gilbert

Islands, and the service, operated by Fiji Airways with a Heron Mark I Aircraft commenced in July 1969.

The Gilbert and Ellice Islands Broadcasting Service (call signs VSZ1 and VSZ2) transmits daily in the medium and shortwave bands from 0615 to 0930 ours GMT, 1200 to 1400 and 1830 to 2000 hours GMT. The morning programmes are devoted mainly to light music, a news relay and record requests. Broadcasts in the evening period are in English, Gilbertese and Ellice.

A development plan for 1970–72 has been approved and includes provision for capital expenditure in excess of \$2,000,000 over the three-year period. The plan will be financed by development aid from the United Kingdom at an anticipated rate of \$750,000 per annum, by assistance from the United Kingdom under the Overseas Service Aid Scheme, from allocations from local revenue or from reserves, by funds provided by international agencies (WHO, UNICEF and UNDP), and by funds provided by technical assistance programmes of the United Kingdom and Australia.

Income tax is levied on chargeable income on a sliding scale rising from $7\frac{1}{2}$ cents per \$2 on the first \$400 to \$1·50 cents per \$2 on income over \$20,000. No super tax is payable. Companies pay $22\frac{1}{2}$ per cent on all chargeable income except for shipping companies and insurance companies, which pay 3·6 cents and 7·2 cents per \$2 respectively. Island Councils have a wide range of rating powers and also levy a landowners tax (based on area and fertility), licence fees and other dues. Import duties, tax on phosphates and export duties on copra are the other main sources of revenue.

In 1970 there were about 14,000 children receiving primary education. Thirty-five primary schools are maintained from Government and local government funds, and 156 are grant-aided and 16 unaided. At Tarawa the Government maintains a co-educational boarding school with an enrolment of 185 boys and 107 girls, and a Teacher's Training College with 29 males and 30 females.

HISTORY

The Gilbertese, who are a Micronesian people, appear to have two separate stories about the origin of their race which, although interwoven by the passage of time and the handing down of verbal traditions, are easily distinguishable. The earlier of the two tells of a creator, Nareau, and a pantheon of gods and goddesses created by him from the void. This tradition appears to have become interwoven with a 'Tree of Life' myth, based upon Samoa, with stories of a cannibal race practising skull-worship on the sacred mountain of Maungatabu. The Tree had its own pantheon of heroes and heroines and they, as well as those of the Nareau creation story, are the sub-deities of Gilbertese traditional beliefs. These stories tell of civil disturbances in Samoa; of the breaking of the 'Tree of Life' and the disposal of its people to the Gilbert Islands; and of their meeting there with a people of similar ancestry. They create the impression that the Gilbertese believe their islands to have been inhabited before their arrival from Nipe by a people holding related traditions. Efforts to trace any substantial reference to the Samoan deity Tangaroa have been unsuccessful. This seems to indicate that the disposal preceded his rise to pre-eminence in Samoan religion, which would place the migration to the Gilbert Islands somewhere between A.D. 1000 and 1300.

The settlement of the Ellice Islands is no better authenticated than that of the Gilberts. The people and the language are both Polynesian, the latter showing

Tonga and Niuean, as well as Samoan, affinities. Tradition speaks of Samoa as the original home but the stories do not appear to have as much detail as those of the Gilberts and it is probable that the islands were settled accidentally by parties drifting westwards from Samoa or adjacent island groups before the south-east trade wind. Curiously enough, some of the heroes of the Gilbertese pantheon appear in Ellice stories and, since Tangaroa receives scant mention, it is just possible that some at least of the Ellice settlers left Samoa at the same time as the Gilbertese and took with them their traditional stories. There are also stories of marauders from the Gilbert Islands and from Tonga.

From the earliest days the Gilbertese have waged a dour fight against starvation. Their islands are infertile coral atolls, periodically ravaged by droughts, and the coconut is the ubiquitous provider, eked out by laboriously-cultivated coarse edible tubers, pandanus, and breadfruit. This simple subsistence agriculture has always been a grim task, one which made land the prize of love and war. But while this struggle went on ashore they were able, in their swift, well-constructed canoes, to fish their lagoons and ocean shores, and their limited navigation served them well enough on their occasional inter-island voyages of depredation. From this background the cautious character of the people grew.

The Ellice people, on islands little touched by drought, where vegetation, though limited, is far more luxuriant than in the Gilberts, show most of the delightful and carefree traits of the Polynesian race. Living on small islands they developed more of a communal spirit than the Gilbertese and, possibly because their populations were small, they appear to have lived a comparatively peaceful existence, except when marauders came to their shores.

The European discovery of the Gilbert and Ellice Islands dates from the 16th century; it is thought that Christmas Island and Nonouti in the Gilbert group were sighted in 1537 by Grijalva's mutinous crew on their disastrous voyage across the Pacific to New Guinea, and it is probable that Mendana discovered Nui and Niuiakita in the Ellice in 1568 and 1595 respectively. Quiros is thought to have discovered Butaritari in the Northern Gilberts in 1606.

After the probable early Spanish sightings, further discovery had to await the latter part of the 18th century and the first quarter of the 19th century. After Captain Byron's visit to Nikunau, in H.M.S. *Dolphin* in 1765, the remaining 24 islands in the group were discovered largely as an unintended result of increasing commercial activity in the Pacific. The last islands to be discovered were, in the Ellice, Niutao and Vaitupu and, in the Gilberts, Onotoa and Beru in 1826.

From the early days of their discovery until about 1870, the waters of the Gilbert Islands were a favourite sperm-whaling ground and the crews of these whalers occasionally deserted and settled ashore. One of the first Europeans to settle in the Gilbert Islands landed about 1837 and the number steadily grew. Trading ships began to visit the islands regularly from 1850 onwards. Although at first trade merely consisted of bartering curios for European luxuries, trade in coconut oil began about 1860 and in ten or twenty years gave way to the sale of copra.

In 1900, by chance, the late Sir Albert Ellis noticed in a Sydney office a sample of rock from German-annexed Nauru and identified it as a piece of valuable phosphate. An expedition was speedily sent by the Pacific Islands Company to the neighbouring Ocean Island to see whether this island also contained the same rock. Although, by agreement with Germany, Ocean Island was at this time within the British sphere of influence, it had not yet been annexed. The representatives of the Pacific Islands Company discovered that the soil of Ocean Island was almost pure phosphate rock and they were able to obtain from the inhabitants a concession to mine it.

Dr Hiram Bingham of the American Board of Foreign Missions landed at Abaiang in 1857 and began to spread Christianity through the Northern Gilbert Islands. The Reverend A. W. Murray of the London Missionary Society, from Samoa, visited the Ellice Islands in May 1865, placing Samoan pastors on the islands; the new faith was universally embraced and all aspects of island life not conforming with the strict tenets of these pastors were cast aside. In 1870 the Society carried Christianity northward and placed Samoan pastors at Arorae, Tamana, Onotoa and Beru. By agreement in 1917, the American Board withdrew from the Colony, handing over the cause of Protestant Christianity to the London Missionary Society. Roman Catholic missionaries landed in the Gilbert Islands in 1888, and Roman Catholicism has now spread to all the Gilberts except the two most southerly, Tamana and Arorae, which are still Protestant strongholds, and to Nanumea and Nui in the Ellice.

In 1892, Captain Davis of H.M.S. *Royalist*, on behalf of Queen Victoria, proclaimed at Abemama a British protectorate in the Gilbert Islands. H.M.S. *Royalist* then visited other Gilbert Islands to raise the flag and Captain Davis was intructed to visit the Ellice Islands to ascertain the wishes of the inhabitants. After the latter had made it clear that they wanted British rule, Captain Gibson of H.M.S. *Curacao* was instructed to proceed to the Ellice Islands and to declare a protectorate. Captain Gibson visited each island where, after a special meeting at which the chief and people of the island had signified their assent, the British flag was hoisted. The headquarters of the Gilbert and Ellice Islands Protectorate was established at Tarawa and district magistrates were assigned to the various islands. A simple code of laws was drawn up based on earlier mission legislation, and the councils of old men were transformed into native courts to administer them. With peace in the groups the people were gathered into orderly villages and an era dawned of simple administration through the Native Governments guided by a very small number of European officers. In 1915, after consultations and at the wish of the Native Governments, the Gilbert and Ellice Islands were annexed by an Order in Council which came into effect on 12th January 1916.

From 1942 to 1943 the Gilbert Islands were occupied by the Japanese. The Administration established a temporary headquarters at Sydney, Australia, which was transferred to Funafuti when United States forces occupied the Ellice group. From there, the Government controlled a war-time administration over the Ellice, Phoenix and Line Islands until, in November 1943, the United States forces drove the Japanese from the Gilberts. Officers of the Administration accompanying the military forces set up headquarters on Tarawa.

LAND POLICY

Since 1917 the sale of land to non-natives has been prohibited and leases may not be taken out without the consent of the Resident Commissioner, or, if the lease is to be for a period in excess of 99 years or for an area exceeding ten acres, without the approval of the High Commissioner. Before 1892 there were, of course, no legal restrictions on alienation and between 1892 and 1917 limited alienation was permitted. Fortunately, in the Gilbert and Ellice groups there was no serious loss of land to the islanders during these periods. An insignificant

U

area now remains alienated. Most of this is owned by Missions and is used for social purposes. Fanning and Washington Islands (in the Line Group) are virtually the only freehold property and are operated as commercial copra plantations by a private company. Christmas Island is owned and worked as a copra plantation by the Government.

CONSTITUTION

The Gilbert and Ellice Islands is one of the territories under the jurisdiction of the High Commissioner for the Western Pacific whose headquarters are at Honiara in the British Solomon Islands Protectorate. In 1915 the High Commissioner was empowered by Order in Council to make ordinances to provide for the administration of Government, provided that such ordinances should not take away or affect any rights secured to Islanders by treaties made on behalf of previous sovereigns, and that in making ordinances he should respect any native laws or customs unless they were injurious to the natives' welfare.

The Resident Commissioner is the High Commissioner's representative in the territory, and has his headquarters at Tarawa, in the Gilbert Islands, where the principal departments of the Administration are located. By an ordinance enacted by the High Commissioner in 1963 an Advisory Council was established whose function was to advise the Resident Commissioner on matters relating to administration. The Advisory Council consisted of the Resident Commissioner as President, the Assistant Resident Commissioner as *ex-officio* Member, not more than four Official Members and not less than eight and not more than twelve Unofficial Members. The Gilbert and Ellice Islands Order in Council 1963 provided for an Executive Council consisting of the Assistant Resident Commissioner as *ex-officio* member, not more than three Official Members and not more than four Unofficial Members.

The Gilbert and Ellice Islands Order 1967 made provision for the government of the territory. It established a Governing Council consisting of the Assistant Resident Commissioner and the Attorney-General, *ex officio*; not more than three appointed members; and five elected members. The Governing Council replaced the Executive Council and has legislative as well as executive functions. The Order also established a House of Representatives consisting of the Assistant Resident Commissioner and the Attorney-General *ex officio*; up to five appointed members and 23 members. The Resident Commissioner presided over both the House and the Council. The elected members of the House and the Council elect from among their own members five members (one of whom was elected as Chief Elected Member) to the Governing Council. The House advised the Governing Council on proposed legislation and other public matters referred to it by the Council or raised by individual members of the House.

In 1970 the next step of constitutional development was approved. The Gilbert and Ellice Islands Order 1970 made new provision for the government of the territory. It established a Legislative Council and Executive Council to replace the House of Representatives and Governing Council. The Legislative Council consists of 3 ex-officio members, 2 public service members and 28 elected members, elected under the principal of universal adult suffrage. The Executive Council comprises the ex-officio and public service members of the Legislative Council, a Leader of Government Business elected by members of the Legislative Council and 4 appointed members of the Legislative Council.

On all sixteen islands of the Gilbert group, and the eight permanently inhabited

Ellice Islands, local governments have been established under the Local Government Ordinance, 1966, which provides the framework for a policy aimed at developing local government authorities able to accept responsibility for and to finance the local services required at island level. These local governments, known as Island Councils, have power, subject to the approval of the Resident Commissioner, to make bye-laws concerning a wide range of subjects, and are charged with the duty of providing services for the general health, security and wellbeing of the inhabitants of the islands.

30 Island Courts have been constituted under the Island Courts Ordinance 1965, by which island magistrates are appointed to the benches of courts subordinate to Magistrates' Courts (Magistrates' Courts Ordinance 1963) but having limited jurisdiction in criminal and civil cases over all races. These courts replace the Native Courts formerly established under the Native Government Ordinance, and form a part of the main judicial system in the Territory.

EXECUTIVE COUNCIL
The Resident Commissioner (*President*)

Ex-officio

Assistant Resident Commissioner; Attorney-General; Financial Secretary

Public Service Members

Hon. R. T. Harberd (Director of Agriculture)
Hon. H. Urquhart (Director of Education)

Elected Members

Hon. Reuben K. Uatioa, MBE (Leader of Government Business)
Hon. Otiuea Tanentoa; Hon. Isakala Paeniu; Hon. Naboua Ratieta;
Hon. Bwebwetake Areieta

LEGISLATIVE COUNCIL
The Resident Commissioner (*President*)

Ex-officio

Assistant Resident Commissioner; Attorney-General; Financial Secretary

Appointed Members

Hon. R. T. Harberd; Hon. H. Urquhart

Elected Members

Hon. Reuben K. Uatioa, MBE (Leader of Government Business)

Hon. Bwebwetake Areieta	Mr Maemae Buatia
Hon. Isakala Paeniu	Mr Paul B. Tokatake
Hon. Naboua Ratieta	Mr Sione Tui Kleis
Hon. Otiuea Tanentoa	Mr Tataua Kauriri
Mr Apinelu Ikapoti	Mr Tebakabo Tebania
Mr Bauro Tiare	Mr Taetoka Tibou
Mr Bauro Tokatake	Mr Tekaai Tekaai
Mr Benjamin Kofe	Mrs Tekarei Russell
Mr Bobo Tauro	Mr Taniera Kauto
Mr Bureua Kamaoto	Mr Toboitabu Bitau
Mr Fataoto Manua	Mr Telavi Faati
Mr Iatiri Awia	Mr Tito Teburoro
Mr Ibeata Tonganibei-a	Mr Tomu Sione
Mr Ioane Kaua	

CIVIL ESTABLISHMENT

Resident Commissioner: Sir John Field, KBE, CMG
Assistant Resident Commissioner: A. J. Hunter
Attorney-General: J. A. Hobbs
Financial Secretary: D. M. Freegard
Senior Assistant Secretaries: H. M. Roemmele, CBE; A. V. Hughes R. Turpin
Administrative Officer, Class A: R. E. N. Smith

Director of Medical Services: A. W. Marr
Director of Public Works: R. Marshall
Director of Education: H. Urquhart
Director of Agriculture: R. T. Harberd
Principal Auditor: P. J. le P. Quantick
Accountant-General: D. L. Hockey
Marine Superintendent: G. W. Sharp

CENTRAL AND SOUTHERN LINE ISLANDS

The five Central and Southern Line Islands do not form part of the Gilbert and Ellice Islands. They consist of Flint, Caroline, Vostock, Malden and Starbuck, and are administered direct by the High Commissioner for the Western Pacific, formerly under Article 6 of the Pacific Order in Council 1893 and more recently in accordance with instructions issued by the Secretary of State in 1903, under Article 4 of the Order in Council.

Flint Island (latitude 11° 26' S., longitude 151° 48' W.) was discovered in 1801. Since 1872 it has been worked intermittently for guano and copra by various British companies under licence issued by the High Commissioner.

Caroline Island (10° S., 150° 14' W.) was discovered in 1795 by Captain W. R. Broughton of H.M. Sloop *Providence* and it has been worked by various British companies since 1846.

Vostock Island (10° 06' S., 152° 23' W.) was discovered by Captain Bellingshausen in 1820 and has been worked sporadically by British companies for guano and copra since 1873. It is now unoccupied and unworked.

Malden Island (4° S., 155° W.) was discovered by Lord Byron, Captain of H.M.S. *Blonde*, in 1825. Its guano deposits were worked by an Australian company from approximately 1860 to 1927. It is now unoccupied and unworked.

Starbuck Island (5° 35' S., 155° 52' W.) was discovered in 1823 by Captain Starbuck, of the whaler *L'Aigle*. It was first worked for guano by a British company during the 1860's. Attempts to plant coconuts on the island failed and since 1920 it has been unoccupied and unworked.

AUSTRALIAN EXTERNAL TERRITORIES

NORFOLK ISLAND

NORFOLK Island, discovered by Captain Cook in 1774, is situated in latitude 29° 3' 30''' S. and longitude 167° 57' 05''' E. Its total area is 8,528 acres, the island being approximately 5 miles long and 3 miles wide. The coast line is 20 miles long and its form that of an irregular ellipse. Norfolk Island is of volcanic origin and its average elevation is in the vicinity of 350 feet with two peaks rising to slightly over 1,000 feet.

The island was first occupied in 1788 by the establishment of a small penal station as a branch settlement of that at Port Jackson, Australia. This existed with one short break until 1855. The descendants of the *Bounty* mutineers, having become too numerous to subsist on Pitcairn Island, were removed thence to Norfolk Island in 1856. The new community numbered 94 males and 100 females and were the descendants of the *Bounty* sailors and Tahitian women. There is no indigenous or native population on Norfolk Island and the inhabitants consist of the descendants of the Pitcairn islanders and settlers from Australia and New Zealand. At 30th June 1967 the estimated population was 1,509.

In 1856 Norfolk Island was created a distinct and separate settlement under the jurisdiction of the State of New South Wales, and in 1896 it was made a dependency of that State. Under the Norfolk Island Act, 1913, it became a Territory of the Commonwealth of Australia. It is administered on behalf of the

Commonwealth Government by an Administrator appointed by the Governor-General of the Commonwealth of Australia. The Governor-General may make ordinances for the peace, order and good government of Norfolk Island. The Norfolk Island Act 1957-1966 provides for the establishment of a Norfolk Island Council which has the function of advising the Administrator on any matter affecting the peace, order and good government of the Territory. The powers of the Council are now provided by the Act. Under the Norfolk Island Council Ordinance 1960-67 the Council is formed of the Administrator as chairman and eight councillors who are elected for terms of two years. The first elections for the Council, reconstituted in 1964, were held on 1st July 1964. Subsequent elections have been held at two-yearly intervals.

There are three regular flights a week from Sydney to the Island.

Administrator: R. Marsh

THE AUSTRALIAN ANTARCTIC TERRITORY

By Order in Council of the 7th February 1933 that part of His Majesty's dominions in the Antarctic Seas which comprised all the islands and territories other than Adélie Terre (which is a French possession occupying an area between 142° and 136° of E. longitude) which are situated south of the 60th parallel of S. latitude and lying between the 160th and 45th meridians of E. longitude was placed under the authority of the Commonwealth of Australia. An Act was passed in June 1933 by the Commonwealth Parliament declaring acceptance of the territory, by the name of the Australian Antarctic Territory, as a territory under the authority of the Commonwealth Government, and the Order in Council was brought into operation on the 24th August 1936, by a Proclamation issued by the Governor-General on that date. The Department of Supply administers the Territory on behalf of the Commonwealth Government and the law operating there is that of the Australian Capital Territory.

The part of Antarctica comprised within the Australian Antarctic Territory is, like the rest of the continent, without permanent inhabitants. Its area is estimated at 2,333,624 square miles of land and 29,251 square miles of ice shelf.

In February 1954 a base, name Mawson, was set up in Mac.Robertson Land for the conduct of meteorological and other research. A second Antarctic base, named Davis, was established in the Vestfold Hills area, some 400 miles east of Mawson in January 1957. Early in 1959 Australia assumed custody of the U.S. base at Wilkes on Budd Coast. A new Australian station is being constructed near Wilkes to replace that built in 1959.

Australia is a party to the Antarctic Treaty which was signed in Washington on 1st December 1959 and entered into force on 23rd June 1961.

HEARD ISLAND AND McDONALD ISLANDS

The Heard Island and McDonald Islands Act 1953-1967 provides for the government of these islands as a Territory of the Commonwealth of Australia. The islands comprise all the islands and rocks lying within the area bounded by the parallels 52° 30′ and 53° South latitude and the meridians 72° and 74° 30′ East longitude. They have been administered by the Commonwealth of Australia since December 1947 when an Australian station was set up on Heard Island. The station has not been manned since March 1955 but Australian expeditions have visited the Territory from time to time since then.

COCOS (KEELING) ISLANDS

The Cocos (Keeling) Islands, two separate groups of atolls comprising some 27 small coral islands with a total area of about 5½ square miles, are situated in the Indian Ocean in latitude 12° 5′ South and longitude 96° 53′ East. They lie some 1,720 miles north-west of Perth and 2,290 miles almost due west of Darwin, whilst Johannesburg is some 3,800 miles distant to the south-west, and Colombo is 1,400 miles to the north-west of the group. The population of the Territory at 30th June 1968 was 622 comprising 140 Europeans and 482 Cocos Islanders.

The main islands of the Territory are West Island (the largest, about 6 miles from north to south) on which is the aerodrome and most of the European community, Home Island, the headquarters of the Clunies Ross Estate and on which the Cocos Islanders reside, Direction Island on which is situated the Cable Station and also the Department of Civil Aviation Marine Base, and Horsburgh Island. North Keeling Island, which forms part of the Territory, lies about 15 miles to the north of the main group and has no inhabitants.

The main group of atolls is low-lying, flat and thickly covered by coconut palms, and surrounds a lagoon which has a harbour in the northern part but which is extremely difficult for navigation.

The climate is equable and pleasant, being usually under the influence of the south-east trade winds for about three-quarters of the year. However, the winds vary at times and meteorological reports from the Territory are particularly valuable to those engaged in forecasting for the eastern Indian Ocean. The temperature varies between 21° and 32°C (70° and 90°F), the rainfall is moderate and there are occasional violent storms.

Qantas Airways and South African Airways operated a regular service between Australia and Johannesburg, via Cocos and Mauritius, until April 1967 when with the introduction of jet aircraft by both airlines on this service flights are now made direct between Perth and Mauritius overflying Cocos. There is a regular service once every two weeks operated by TAA and Ansett ANA aircraft between Perth and Cocos.

The telegraph cable station administered by Overseas Communications Commission (Australia) on Direction Island was closed down in August 1966 since which date communications between Cocos and Australia have been operated by the Administration.

HISTORY

The islands were discovered in 1609 by Captain William Keeling of the East India Company. The islands were uninhabited and remained so until 1826 when the first settlement was established on the main atoll by an Englishman, Alexander Hare, who quitted the islands in about 1831. In the meantime a second settlement was formed on the main atoll by John Clunies Ross, a Scottish seaman and adventurer, who landed with several boat-loads of Malay seamen. In 1857 the islands were annexed to the Crown and formally declared part of the British dominions, and in 1878 responsibility for their supervision was transferred from the Colonial Office to the Government of Ceylon and then, in 1886, to the Government of the Straits Settlements. By indenture in 1886 Queen Victoria granted the land comprised in the islands to John Clunies Ross in perpetuity. The head of the family had semi-official status as resident magistrate and representative of the Government. However, in 1946 when the islands became a dependency of the Colony of

Singapore a Resident Administrator, responsible to the Governor of Singapore, was appointed.

TRANSFER TO THE COMMONWEALTH OF AUSTRALIA

On 23rd November 1955 the Cocos Islands ceased to form part of the Colony of Singapore and were placed under the authority of the Commonwealth. The transfer was effected by an Order in Council made by Her Majesty Queen Elizabeth the Second under the Cocos Islands Act, 1955, of Britain, and by the Cocos (Keeling) Islands Act 1955 of the Commonwealth, whereby the islands were declared to be accepted by the Commonwealth as a Territory under the authority of the Commonwealth, to be known as the Territory of Cocos (Keeling) Islands.

ADMINISTRATION

Responsibility for the administration of the Territory rests with the Minister for External Territories. The first Official Representative was appointed on 23rd November 1955 to take charge of the local administration of the Territory. Under the Official Representative Ordinance 1955-1961 of the Territory, the Official Representative is given such powers and functions in relation to the Territory as are delegated to him by the Minister under the Cocos (Keeling) Islands Act 1955-1966, or are otherwise conferred on him under that Act or by or under any other law of the Territory. The laws of the Colony of Singapore which were in force in the islands immediately before the date of transfer were, with certain exceptions, continued in force by virtue of the Cocos (Keeling) Islands Acts 1955-1966; they may be amended or repealed by ordinances made under the provisions of that Act which empower the Governor-General to make ordinances for the peace, order and good government of the Territory.

Official Representation: P. L. Ryan

CHRISTMAS ISLAND

Christmas Island is an isolated bank in the Indian Ocean, with water 1,000 fathoms deep within three miles of the coast on all sides. It lies in latitude 10° 25' 22" S., longitude 105° 39' 59" E. and is approximately 224 miles south from Java Head, at the south entrance to Sunda Straits, 815 miles from Singapore and 1,630 miles from Fremantle. Christmas Island covers an area of about 52 square miles and consists of a central plateau at 600 to 800 feet, with several prominent rises up to 1,170 feet. The plateau descends to the sea in a series of steep slopes alternating with terraces, the last dropping in a cliff of 200 to 300 feet to a shore terrace, terminating in a sea-cliff of 10 to 150 feet. It is continuous round the island except in a few places, the chief of which is Flying Fish Cove where the shore is formed of coral shingles. The estimated population of Christmas Island at 30th June 1968 was 3,524 consisting of 342 Europeans, 2,056 Chinese, 1,027 Malays and 99 others.

The principal settlement is at Flying Fish Cove which is also the only known anchorage. The main installations of the phosphate industry are located here, together with the European married quarters, and the Chinese and Malay settlements.

The climate is healthy and pleasant. The average yearly rainfall is about 60 inches with a marked summer incidence. The average mean temperature is about 27°C. (80°F.) and does not vary greatly throughout the year.

The only commercial activity carried out is the mining of phosphate. The British Phosphate Commissioners act as managing agents for the Christmas Island Phosphate Commission.

There are three principal phosphate deposits on the island, the largest being that at present worked at South Point. This field is situated on the central plateau and is approximately 12 miles from the drying and shipping plant at Flying Fish Cove. The present output is up to approximately 1 million tons per year.

The Governments of New Zealand and Australia approved proposals by the Commission to develop the Phosphate deposits to an output capacity of 1·6 million tons per year by 1968 and to examine the possibility of still further increasing this output to more than 2·5 million tons per year.

There is little prospect of any economic developments outside the phosphate industry.

Communications with the island are maintained by ships operated by the Phosphate Commission or ships under charter by the Commission. These ships are mainly bulk cargo vessels but there is generally also some passenger accommodation. The ships sail from Singapore.

HISTORY

The first mention of Christmas Island appears in a map published in Holland in 1666, in which it is called Moni Island although it is believed that Captain William Mynors of the East India Company had sighted the island on Christmas Day in 1643 and had named it accordingly.

In June 1888 it was annexed by Captain H. W. May of the H.M.S. *Imperieuse* as part of the British dominions and placed, for administrative purposes, under the supervision of the Government of the Straits Settlements and, following upon this, a small settlement was established at Flying Fish Cove by Mr G. Clunies Ross of Cocos (Keeling) Islands, 530 miles to the west-south-west. In February 1891 Sir John Murray and Mr G. Clunies Ross of Cocos were gsanted a 99-year lease of the island which was transferred to the Christmas Island Phosphate Co. Ltd. in 1897, following the discovery of large deposits of phosphate of lime on the island. In 1900 Christmas Island was incorporated for administrative purposes with the Settlement of Singapore and the laws of Singapore were generally applied to the island.

TRANSFER TO THE COMMONWEALTH OF AUSTRALIA

On the dissolution of the Straits Settlements, Christmas Island was, until 31st December 1957, administered as part of the Colony of Singapore. From that date, by the Christmas Island Order in Council 1957, made by the Queen under the Straits Settlements (Repeal) Act, 1964, and the British Settlement Acts, 1887 and 1945, it was administered as a separate British Crown Colony until 1st October 1958, when it became a Territory of the Commonwealth of Australia. This change in status was initiated by the Christmas Island (Request and Consent) Act 1957 by which the Australian Parliament requested and consented to the enactment by the British Parliament of an Act enabling the Queen to place Christmas Island under the authority of Australia. By the terms of Christmas Island (Transfer to Australia) Order in Council 1958, made under the Christmas Island Act, 1958, of Britain, Christmas Island was placed under the authority of the Commonwealth of Australia and accepted by the Commonwealth under the provisions of the Christmas Island Act 1958 of Australia.

ADMINISTRATION

Responsibility for the administration of the Territory rests with the Minister for External Territories. An Official Representative was first appointed on 1st October 1958 to take charge of the local administration of the Territory. Under the Administration Ordinance 1958-1961 of the Territory, the Official Representative was given such administrative functions as the Minister directed. The laws of the Colony of Singapore which were in force immediately before the date of transfer were continued in force by the Christmas Island Act 1958 of Australia. They may be altered, amended or repealed by ordinances made under the provisions of that Act, which empowers the Governor-General of Australia to make ordinances for the peace, order and good government of the Territory. The first Administrator was appointed on 1st May 1968, to replace the former Official Representative. The Administration Ordinance 1958-1961, has been repealed by the Administration Ordinance 1968, under which an Administrator, appointed by the Governor-General, governs the territory on behalf of the Government of the Commonwealth of Australia. The laws of the Colony of Singapore are continued in force under the Administration Ordinance 1968. In addition, a separate judicial system has been established by ordinance.

Administrator: J. S. White

PAPUA

Papua (formerly called British New Guinea) lies wholly within the tropics. The northernmost point touches 5° S. latitude; its southernmost portion, comprising Toogula and Rossel Islands, lies between 11° S. and 12° S. latitude. It is separated from Australia by Torres Strait. The length of Papua from east to west is upwards of 930 miles; towards either end the breadth from north to south is about 200 miles, but about the centre it is considerably narrower. The territory comprises also the islands of the Trobriand, Woodlark, D'Entrecasteaux and Louisiade groups. The length of the coastline is estimated at 3,664 miles, 1,728 on the mainland and 1,936 on the islands. The total area is 86,100 square miles, of which 83,325 are on the mainland and 2,775 on the islands. The estimated total population of the Territory of Papua at 30th June 1967 was 598,268. The non-indigenous population numbered 14,726. Port Moresby is the capital and administrative centre of the Territory of Papua and New Guinea. It is situated on the hills overlooking an almost land-locked harbour. At the June 1966 census the total population was 42,133, comprising 32,222 indigenous and 9,911 non-indigenous persons.

HISTORY

The Government of Queensland annexed to the British Empire on the 4th April 1883 that portion of New Guinea not claimed by Holland, but this proceeding was not ratified by the Imperial Government. On the Australian colonies agreeing to guarantee £15,000 a year to meet the cost a Protectorate was, however, proclaimed in 1884 over the south-east portion of New Guinea and the adjacent islands, and the territory was annexed to the Crown by the newly-appointed Administrator in 1888. In 1901 the Government of the Commonwealth of Australia agreed to take it over as a territory of the Commonwealth. In 1906 a Proclamation was issued by the Governor-General, under the provisions of the Papua Act 1905, declaring British New Guinea a territory of the Commonwealth, under the name of Papua.

NEW GUINEA

The Trust Territory of New Guinea extends north to south from the Equator to 8° S. latitude, a distance of 400 nautical miles; and west to east from 141° E. longitude (its boundary with West Irian) to 160° E. longitude, a distance of 1,000 nautical miles. The land area of the Territory covers 92,160 square miles and includes that part of the island of New Guinea north of the Papua and east of the West Irian borders, the islands of the Bismarck Archipelago, of which New Britain, New Ireland and Manus are the largest, and the two northernmost islands of the Solomon Group, namely Buka and Bougainville. The estimated total population of the Territory of New Guinea at 30th June 1968 was 1,700,000 including an estimated 23,000 non-indigenes. Rabaul and Lae are important towns. Rabaul and Port Moresby are the busiest ports in the combined Territory of Papua and New Guinea.

HISTORY

On 17th September 1914 the Acting Governor of German New Guinea signed terms of capitulation with the Officer Commanding a naval and military expedition sent from Australia and thereafter the Territory was under military administration until the establishment of civil government on 9th May 1921.

In 1919 it was decided by the Principal Allied and Associated Powers that the Territory of New Guinea, which Germany gave up as one of the terms of peace, should be entrusted under Mandate from the League of Nations to the Government of the Commonwealth. The issuing of the Mandate was, however, delayed, and it was not until 17th December 1920 that its terms were settled, and the Mandate itself did not reach Australia until April 1921.

ADMINISTRATION

The Territory is administered according to the terms of the Trusteeship Agreement approved by the General Assembly of the United Nations on 13th December 1946. Article 5 of the Agreement provided that the Administering Authority (the Commonwealth of Australia) might bring the Territory into a customs, fiscal or administrative union or federation with other dependent territories under its jurisdiction or control and establish common services between the Territory and any or all of these territories if, in its opinion, it would be in the interests of the territory and not inconsistent with the basic objective of the Trusteeship system to do so. The Papua and New Guinea Act was accordingly passed by the Australian Parliament in 1949. (For details of administration see below relating to the Territory of Papua and New Guinea). The development of the Territory is set out in annual reports to the General Assembly of the United Nations.

TERRITORY OF PAPUA AND NEW GUINEA

ADMINISTRATION

After the outbreak of War in the Pacific Ocean, civil administration in Papua and New Guinea was suspended on 11th February 1942, and military control introduced. The Territory of New Guinea came under Japanese occupation in 1942, but the greater part had already been recaptured by Australian and Allied Forces when the Japanese surrendered in August 1945. During the period of military control, matters relating to the former civil administration were dealt with by the Department of External Territories, Canberra. The Minister for External Territories was empowered by National Security Regulations to exercise the powers and functions of the Administrator, officers and authorities of the territories; and the powers of the Supreme Courts of Papua and New Guinea were vested in the Supreme Court of the Australian Capital Territory.

By the provisions of the Papua-New Guinea Provisional Administration Act, 1945, a single Provisional Administration Service was formed to take over from the military authorities in the Territories of Papua and New Guinea. Colonel J. K. Murray was appointed administrator of the combined Territories on 11th October 1945, and the transfer from military to civil control in Papua and that portion of the Territory of New Guinea south of the Markham River was effected on 30th October 1945. The jurisdictions of the Supreme Courts of Papua and New Guinea were then vested in the Supreme Court of the Territory of Papua-New Guinea. As circumstances permitted civil control was extended to other areas until the whole of the Territory of New Guinea came under the control of the Provisional Administration of Papau-New Guinea on 24th June 1946.

The Papua-New Guinea Provisional Administration Act 1945-1946, was repealed by the Papua and New Guinea Act 1949, which approved the placing of the Territory of New Guinea under the International Trusteeship System and provided that the Territories of Papua and of New Guinea should be governed in an administrative union, known as the Territory of Papua and New Guinea.

The Papua and New Guinea Act of 1949-1960 provided for the appointment of an Administrator to administer the government of the Territory on behalf of the Government of the Commonwealth of Australia and for a Legislative Council which, subject to the assent of the Administrator or, in certain cases defined in the Act, the Governor-General, had full legislative power in regard to the peace, order and good government of the Territory. The Council was inaugurated in 1951. In 1961 it consisted of thirty-seven members (including the Administrator) of whom fourteen were officers of the Territory, six were elected by the indigenous population, and six by the non-indigenous population and ten were appointed. All members, except the twelve elected members, were appointed by the Governor-General on the nomination of the Administrator.

The Act also provided for an Administrative Council consisting of the Administrator, three official members of the Legislative Council and three non-official members of the Legislative Council. The Council's functions are to advise the Administrator on any matter he refers to it and other matters as provided by ordinance.

By an amendment of the Papua and New Guinea Act in May 1963 the Legislative Council was replaced by a House of Assembly consisting of sixty-four members, of whom forty-four are elected by the electors of the Territory enrolled on a common roll in single-member constituencies, ten are non-indigenous members elected by the same electors for special electorates comprising one or more of the open electorates and ten are official members. The Administrator's Council was also enlarged by increasing the number of non-official members from three to seven, all of whom must be elected members of the House of Assembly.

A further amendment to the Papua and New Guinea Act in October 1966 abolished the ten special electorates and replaced them with 15 regional electorates. Election as a Member representing a Regional Electorate is based on a minimum educational qualification of the Territory Intermediate Certificate, or equivalent. This provision first applied to the General Election for an enlarged House of Assembly of 94 members, 69 of whom were returned to open electorates by adult franchise, 15 were returned to regional electorates by adult franchise and 10 official members were nominated by the Minister on the Administrator's advice. This election, conducted from 17th February to 10th March 1968, returned 23 of the former M.H.A.'s who stood again, and 61 new members. The proportion of indigenous elected members increased by 10 per cent to its present 77 per cent of all elected members and three indigenous members were returned to the Regional electorates requiring the educational minimum.

In June 1967 the House of Assembly Select Committee on Constitutional Development presented its report which recommended a further advance towards quasi-executive government and was accepted by the Australian Parliament in October 1967. The Papua and New Guinea Act 1968, passed by the Australian Parliament in May 1968, updates the Papua and New Guinea Act 1949-1968, which enables the implementation of the recommendations of the Select Committee, including the new ministerial system and the replacement of the Administrator's Council by the Administrator's Executive Council. These provide for seven Ministerial Members and eight Assistant Ministerial Members both with functions appropriate to a department of the Papua and New Guinea Public Service. The Ministerial Members are leaders of their departments, and represent it in the House of Assembly. The Assistant Ministerial Members assist in representing their departments in the House of Assembly. The Administrator's Executive Council comprises the seven Ministerial Members, three Official Members, the Administrator and, at his discretion, possibly a twelfth Councillor chosen from the elected members who are not holding office as Ministerial Members. A spokesman of the Administrator Executive Council was appointed in 1970 and he was acknowledged as the leader of Government Business in the House.

In March 1971 the Select Committee on Constitutional Development made its final report which recommended that the Territory should take steps during the period 1972-6 to prepare for self-government. The Select Committee favoured a reduction from 10 to 4 in the number of official members in the House of Assembly. They proposed a legislature of 18 Regional Members, 82 members from open electorates, up to 3 nominated members (nominated by the House of Assembly) and 4 official members. The Committee's report was adopted by the House with the exception of the proposal that the Territory's name be changed to Niugini.

The Local Government Ordinance 1963-1967 provides that multi-racial councils may be established and continue in existence councils established under the repealed Native Local Government Councils Ordinance and Regulations. Provision is made for local government councils to be given a wider range of functions of a local nature and to have increased financial powers, including power to levy rates on land. The Ordinance also provided for the appointment of a Local Government Commissioner responsible for administering the Ordinance but in July 1969 the Department of District Administration was absorbed into the Department of the Administrator with headquarters at Konedobu, a suburb of Port Moresby.

Administrator of the Territory of Papua and New Guinea:
L. W. Johnson

MACQUARIE ISLAND

Macquarie Island lies some 1,000 miles to the south-east of Tasmania and has been a dependency of Tasmania since the 19th century. The island is without permanent inhabitants, but a base for meteorological and other research has been maintained there since 1948.

THE ROSS DEPENDENCY (New Zealand)

THE Antarctic territory known as the Ross Dependency was brought within the jurisdiction of the New Zealand Government by Order in Council of 30th July 1923, under the British Settlements Act, 1887. It is defined as 'all the islands and territories between the 160th degree of east longitude and the 150th degree of west longitude which are situated south of the 60th degree of south latitude'. The land area is estimated at 160,000 square miles and permanent shelf ice at 130,000 square miles. There are no permanent inhabitants, but scientific stations are staffed all the year round.

Laws for the Dependency have been made by regulations promulgated by the Governor-General of New Zealand. Administrative powers are vested in the Governor-General of New Zealand, and Administrative Officers (commonly referred to as Administrators) have been appointed from time to time since 1923.

Many famous explorers visited the area during the last century, including Sir James Ross, Captain R.F. Scott, RN, Sir Ernest Shackleton, Roald Amundsen and Richard E. Byrd.

In the 1920s whaling was licensed by the New Zealand Government. Since then, however, the pelagic whaling expeditions have operated on the high seas.

In recent years the territory has been visited by several British and American expeditions. The Dependency is now the scene of greater activity than ever before. Under the auspices of the International Geophysical Year a United States expedition re-activated a scientific station at 'Little America' and constructed an air strip on the bay ice at McMurdo Sound capable of taking heavy aircraft from New Zealand. A joint New Zealand—United States station is being operated at Cape Hallett.

The New Zealand Antarctic Expedition established Scott Base on Ross Island in January 1957. The purpose of the Expedition was twofold: to take part in the Commonwealth Trans-Antarctic Expedition and in the Antarctic Programme of the International Geophysical Year.

In March 1958 the New Zealand Government appointed the Ross Dependency Research Committee to co-ordinate and supervise all New Zealand activity in the Dependency, with particular reference to the scientific and technical programme. A continuing programme of field work and research has since been carried out, including in 1968 the building of a new scientific station near Lake Vanda.

PART VII

REGIONAL ORGANISATIONS

EAST AFRICAN COMMUNITY

FOLLOWING a recommendation of a Parliamentary Commission which visited East Africa in 1924 a Conference of Governors of the British East African territories was held in 1926, to discuss matters of mutual concern. It was decided that a permanent Conference Secretariat should be established at Nairobi and that Conferences should be held when necessary. Subsequently the Joint Select Committee on Closer Union in East Africa recommended that the machinery of the Governors' Conference should be increasingly used for ensuring continuous and effective co-operation and co-ordination in all matters of common interest to the East African territories. The Conference was placed in permanent session, to be convened whenever required, and it was decided that there should be annual meetings of the Governors of Kenya, Tanganyika and Uganda, attended, if desired, by the Governors of Northern Rhodesia and Nyasaland and by the British Resident, Zanzibar.

EAST AFRICA HIGH COMMISSION

The East Africa High Commission replaced the East African Governors' Conference on 1st January 1948. The High Commission, consisting of the Governors of Kenya, Tanganyika and Uganda, was charged with the administration of certain services common to the three territories, e.g. the East African Railways and Harbour Administration, the East African Directorate of Civil Aviation, the East African Posts and Telegraphs Department, the East African Meteorological Department, etc. The East African Central Legislative Assembly was established in 1947, and in 1956 its membership was increased from 24 to 34. The High Commission had power to legislate, with the advice and consent of the Assembly, in respect of inter-territorial common services, and on any matter concerned with the peace, order and good government of the Territories. The establishment of the High Commission involved no change in the constitution or administrative responsibilities of the Governments of the three territories, which remained responsible for basic services such as administration, police, health, education, agriculture, forestry, labour, and housing public works.

EAST AFRICAN COMMON SERVICES ORGANISATION

At the Constitutional Conference in Dar es Salaam in March 1961 the Tanganyika Government expressed the wish to continue participation, after independence, in the common services provided by the East Africa High Commission, in a manner compatible with Tanganyika's independence. Arrangements to this end were worked out in talks, held in London in June 1961 and attended by delegates from Britain, Tanganyika, Kenya and Uganda, and of the East Africa High Commission, and by an observer from Zanzibar. It was agreed that, in the interests of all the Territories concerned, common services should continue to be provided on an East African basis, and that this should be secured, when Tanganyika became independent, by setting up a new organisation called the East African Common Services Organisation. Under the new organisation which came into being on 9th December 1961 Tanganyika, Uganda and Kenya participated as equal partners. Responsibility for the policy of the new Organisation was vested in the East African Common Services Authority which consisted of the Prime Minister of Tanganyika, now the President of Tanzania, the Prime Minister, now the President, of Uganda, and the Prime Minister, now the President, of Kenya.

EAST AFRICAN COMMUNITY

A Treaty for East African Co-operation was signed by the Presidents of the United Republic of Tanzania, the Sovereign State of Uganda and the Republic of Kenya on 6th June 1967. The Treaty came into force on 1st December 1967.

By this Treaty the Governments of Tanzania, Uganda and Kenya established among themselves an East African Community and, as an integral part of such Community, an East African Common Market.

The institutions of the Community are as follows:—

(i) The East African Authority. The Authority consists of the Presidents of Tanzania, Uganda and Kenya who in turn comprise the principal executive authority of the Community.

(ii) The East African Legislative Assembly. This is the Community's legislative body which has the power to pass Bills which require the assent of the Heads of State of Tanzania, Uganda and Kenya. The Treaty provides that members of the Assembly shall be:

> (*a*) the three East African Ministers;
> (*b*) the three Deputy East African Ministers;
> (*c*) twenty-seven appointed members; and
> (*d*) the Chairman of the Assembly, the Secretary-General and the Counsel to the Community.

(iii) The East African Ministers. Tanzania, Uganda and Kenya each nominate a person for appointment by the Authority as an East African Minister. It is the Ministers' responsibility to assist the Authority in the exercise of its executive functions to the extent required by and subject to the directions of the Authority, and to advise the Authority generally in respect of the affairs of the Community. There are also three Deputy Ministers, similarly nominated and appointed.

(iv) The Common Market Council. The responsibilities of the Council are *inter alia* to ensure the functioning and development of the Common Market in accordance with the Treaty and to keep its operations under review. The Council's responsibilities are set out fully in Article 30 of the Treaty.

(v) The Common Market Tribunal. A judicial body established to ensure the observance of law and of the terms of the Treaty in the interpretation and application of so much of the Treaty as appertains to the Common Market.

(vi) The Communications Council. The duties and powers of the Council are set out in Annex XIII to the Treaty. In addition the Council provides a forum for consultation generally on communication matters.

(vii) The Finance Council. The Council's functions are to consult in common on the major financial affairs of the Community, and to consider and approve major financial decisions relating to the services administered by the Community, including their estimates of expenditure and related loan and investment programmes. The Council's functions in respect of the Community do not include the East African Development Bank.

(viii) The Economic Consultative and Planning Council. Its functions are to assist the national planning of the Partner States by consultative means, and to advise the Authority upon the long-term planning of the common services.

(ix) The Research and Social Council. Its functions are to assist, by consultative means, in the co-ordination of the policies of each of the Partner States and the Community regarding research and social matters.

(x) The Court of Appeal for East Africa. The Court of Appeal for Eastern Africa established by the East African Common Services Organisation Agreements 1961 to 1966 is to continue in being under the name of the Court of Appeal for East Africa and is deemed to have been established by the Treaty, notwithstanding the abrogation of those Agreements by the Treaty.

(xi) The East African Industrial Court. The Industrial Court will exercise the powers referred to in Article 84 of the Treaty in accordance with the principles laid down from time to time by the East African Authority.

(xii) The East African Tax Board. This is an advisory body whose membership and functions are set out in Article 88 of the Treaty.

(xiii) The East African Development Bank. The Bank was established under Article 21 of the Treaty, its main objectives being to provide financial and technical assistance to promote the industrial development of the Partner States, and to give priority to industrial development in the relatively less industrially developed Partner States. The Bank's Charter is set out in Annex VI to the Treaty.

Services to be Administered by the Community
1. The secretariat of the Community, including services relating to the Common Market and the Chambers of the Counsel to the Community.
2. The East African Directorate of Civil Aviation.
3. The East African Meteorological Department.
4. The East African Customs and Excise Department.
5. The East African Income Tax Department.
6. The East African Industrial Council.
7. The East African Literature Bureau.
8. The Auditor-General's Department.
9. The East African Community Service Commission.
10. The East African Legislative Assembly.
11. The East African Agriculture and Forestry Research Organisation.
12. The East African Freshwater Fisheries Research Organisation.
13. The East African Marine Fisheries Research Organisation.
14. The East African Trypanosomiasis Research Organisation.
15. The East African Veterinary Research Organisation.
16. The East African Leprosy Research Centre.
17. The East African Institute of Malaria and Vector-Borne Diseases.
18. The East African Institute for Medical Research.
19. The East African Virus Research Organisation.
20. The East African Industrial Research Organisation.
21. The East African Tropical Pesticides Research Institute.
22. The East African Tuberculosis Investigation Centre.
23. Services arising from the operations of the East African Currency Board.

24. Services for the administration of grants or loans made by the government of any country, any organisation or any authority, for the purpose of projects or services agreed between the Authority and the Partner States.

25. Services, including statistical services, for the purposes of co-ordinating the economic activities of the Partner States.

26. Services for the purposes of any body or authority established in pursuance of paragraph 4 of Article 43 of the Treaty.

27. Services for the purposes of the East African Industrial Court established by Article 85 of the Treaty.

Services to be Administered by the Corporations

1. The East African Railways Corporation—services and facilities relating to rail, road and and inland waterways transport and inland waterways ports.

2. The East African Harbours Corporation—harbour services and facilities (other than inland waterways ports).

3. The East African Posts and Telecommunications Corporation—posts, telecommunications and other associated services.

4. The East African Airways Corporation—services and facilities relating to East African and international air transport.

Location of the various Headquarters

(a) the headquarters of the Community at Arusha in Tanzania.

(b) the headquarters of the East African Development Bank at Kampala in Uganda.

(c) the headquarters of the East African Railways Corporation at Nairobi in Kenya.

(d) the headquarters of the East African Harbours Corporation at Dar es Salaam in Tanzania.

(e) the headquarters of the East African Posts and Telecommunications Corporation at Kampala in Uganda.

(f) the headquarters of the East African Airways Corporation at Nairobi in Kenya.

THE EAST AFRICAN COMMON MARKET

The establishment of a Common Market introduced common customs and excise tariffs and the abolition of quantitative restrictions on inter-territorial trade; in certain circumstances a transfer tax may be imposed on some imports from other Partner States in order to protect local industries and there are limited provisions for monetary co-operation.

EAST AFRICAN COMMUNITY RELATIONS WITH THE EUROPEAN ECONOMIC COMMUNITY

On 26th July 1968, in Arusha, Tanzania, the three member states of the EAC signed an Association Agreement with the European Economic Community. The Agreement expired on 31st May 1969 without having come into force, but a sucessor agreement was signed on 24th September 1969. This Agreement is to expire by 31st January 1975 at the latest.

Under the Arusha Agreement exports from the three East African countries to the EEC are admitted duty free, with the exception of three products (coffee, cloves and tinned pineapple) to which duty free quotas are applied. In return the three East African countries give the EEC tariff concessions of 2 to 9 per cent on 54 items. The Agreement also contains provisions governing rights of establishment and provision of services, and the setting up of various institutions, but it makes no provision for aid from the EEC to the East African countries.

REGIONAL INSTITUTIONS IN THE WEST INDIES

THE WEST INDIES ASSOCIATED STATES SUPREME COURT

This Court was established for the six proposed Associated States by Order in Council in February 1967. The Order enabled the Court to have jurisdiction also in Montserrat and the Virgin Islands. The Court consists of a Court of Appeal and a High Court. The Chief Justice is appointed by Her Majesty, and the Justices of Appeal and Puisne Judges on behalf of Her Majesty by the Judicial and Legal Services Commission. The Commission consists of the Chief Justice, one of the Justices of Appeal or Puisne Judges, an ex-Judge appointed with the concurrence of not less than four of the Premiers and the Chairman of two of the Public Services Commissions of the States in rotation. Judges are removable from office only if the Judicial Committee of the Privy Council has advised removal for inability or misbehaviour. The expenses of the Court, after allowing for any contributions from Montserrat and the Virgin Islands, are met by the states in equal shares and are charged on the Consolidated Funds of the respective states by the Order in Council.

Chief Justice: The Hon. Sir Allen Montgomery Lewis, KB, QC

Justices of Appeal:
Mr Justice Keith Lyndell Gordon; Mr Justice Percival Cecil Lewis

High Court Puisne Judges:

Mr Justice Elvin Lloyd St Bernard (Grenada)	Mr Justice Allan F. L. Louisy (Antigua)
Mr Justice Neville Berridge (Dominica & Montserrat)	Mr Justice Neville Peterkin (St Vincent)
Mr Justice Eric Herbert Austin Bishop (St Lucia)	Mr Justice J. D. B. Renwick, QC (Acting)
Mr Justice Eardley Fitzgeorge Glasgow (St Kitts and British Virgin Islands)	

Chief Registrar: E. Wilkinson (resident in Grenada)

INTERIM COMMISSIONER FOR THE WEST INDIES

The office was held from its inception by Sir Stephen Luke, KCMG until October 1968, when Mr Claude Hayes assumed the office. Its few remaining functions relate to pensions in respect of service with the former Government of the Federation of the West Indies and to a small residue of federal assets and liabilities.

THE WEST INDIES (ASSOCIATED STATES) COUNCIL OF MINISTERS

This Council was established on 1st November 1966 in succession to the Regional Council of Ministers. The latter had existed since 1962, having been formed by the Governments of Antigua, Barbados, Dominica, Grenada, Montserrat, St Christopher, Nevis and Anguilla, St Lucia and St Vincent, to consider problems of common interest in connection with the proposal to establish a Federation of those territories. The Regional Council of Ministers was wound up when Barbados proceeded to separate independence in November 1966.

The West Indies (Associated States) Council of Ministers comprises the Premiers of the Associated States and the Chief Minister of Montserrat. The Chairman for the first year was the Premier of Antigua, to be followed for a year at a time by the other members in rotation. The Secretariat is established in St Lucia. The purpose of the Council is to administer such common services and to perform such other functions as may be agreed from time to time.

REGIONAL DEVELOPMENT AGENCY

The Regional Development Agency was formed in 1968 by the Governments represented on the West Indies (Associated States) Council of Ministers and the Government of Barbados. It ceased to exist as a separate organisation on 16th December 1970.

THE CARIBBEAN METEOROLOGICAL SERVICE

The Caribbean Meteorological Service was established in succession to the West Indies Meteorological Service and embraces Antigua, Barbados, British Honduras, British Virgin Islands, Cayman Islands, Dominica, Grenada, Guyana, Jamaica, Monserrat, St Christopher-Nevis-Anguilla, St Lucia, St Vincent and Trinidad and Tobago. Each Government contributes to the cost of a Headquarters Unit based in Trinidad under the direction of the Director-General. Overall responsibility for the Service is vested in the Caribbean Meteorological Council which consists of a representative from each of the participating Governments. The Council meets at least once every year.

There are main meteorological stations at Palisadoes Airport (Jamaica), Piarco Airport (Trinidad) and at Seawell Airport (Barbados). Supplementary stations are at Pearls Airport (Grenada), Arnos Vale (St Vincent) and Stanley Field (British Honduras). A Regional Institute of Tropical Meteorology has been established in Barbados.

THE CARIBBEAN FREE TRADE ASSOCIATION
(CARIFTA)

This Free Trade Area stems from an agreement signed in December 1965 establishing a Free Trade Association between the Governments of Antigua, Barbados, and British Guiana (now Guyana). Proposals for the extension of this Agreement to other Commonwealth Caribbean territories were approved in October 1967 by a meeting of Commonwealth Caribbean Heads of Government in Barbados. The extended Free Trade Association which has resulted from this now comprises the original three signatories, and in addition, in date order of accession, the Governments of Trinidad and Tobago, Dominica, Grenada, St Kitts-Nevis-Anguilla, St Lucia, St Vincent, Jamaica, and Montserrat.

Under the provisions of the Agreement, tariff-free exchange of a wide range of commodities has been introduced. There are, however, reserved commodities to be freed from import duties within a five-year grace period reckoned from 1st May 1968 for the more developed countries and a ten-year period for the less developed members. In addition, the less developed members will have the right of appeal for an extension beyond the ten-year period in cases where it can be established that serious injury would be done to a particular industry.

EASTERN CARIBBEAN COMMON MARKET

This Common Market was set up in June 1968 between the Governments represented on the West Indies (Associated States) Council of Ministers. The Secretariat is now in Antigua.

The objectives of the Common Market are to promote among its Member States the harmonious development of economic activities and expansion by the facilitation of the maximum possible inter-change of goods and services by the progressive elimination of customs duties and quantitative restrictions on the import and export of goods, the establishment of common customs tariffs and commercial and fiscal policies, and the abolition of obstacles to the free movement of persons, services and capital between the Member States.

THE WEST INDIES SHIPPING SERVICE

The West Indies Shipping Corporation Act, 1961, established a Shipping Corporation to operate and maintain a regular shipping service between the territories of the then Federation of the West Indies, using two ships donated by the Canadian Government.

On the break-up of the Federation in 1962 it was agreed that the Service should be continued under the policy direction of a Regional Shipping Council, on which were represented the Governments of Jamaica, Trinidad and Tobago, Barbados and the Leeward and Windward Islands. Guyana has subsequently acceded to membership of this body.

The headquarters of the Shipping Council are in Trinidad.

THE CARIBBEAN DEVELOPMENT BANK

The Bank was formally established in January 1970 with the following members:—

Antigua, Bahamas, Barbados, British Honduras, British Virgin Islands,

Canada, Cayman Islands, Dominica, Grenada, Guyana, Jamaica, Montserrat, St Kitts-Nevis-Anguilla, St Lucia, St Vincent, Trinidad and Tobago, Turks and Caicos Islands, and the United Kingdom.

The purpose of the Bank is to contribute to the harmonious economic growth and development of the member countries in the Caribbean and promote economic cooperation among them, having special and urgent regard to the needs of the less developed members of the region. The Bank has an authorised capital of U.S. $50 m. Membership is open to States and Territories of the region, and non-regional States which are members of the United Nations or any of the specialised agencies or of the International Atomic Energy Agency.

The Bank's headquarters are in Barbados.

SOUTH PACIFIC COMMISSION AND THE SOUTH PACIFIC AIR TRANSPORT COUNCIL

SOUTH PACIFIC COMMISSION

A regional Commission for the South Pacific was established in 1947 (Cmnd 8539) by agreement between the Governments of Australia, France, the Netherlands, New Zealand, the United Kingdom and the United States of America. An amending Agreement signed on 2nd October 1964 provided for the independent State of Western Samoa, and any other territory which becomes independent and was within the Commission's scope immediately before independence, to become a participating member of the Commission if it wishes and is invited to do so by the participating Governments. The Netherlands ceased to be a participating Government on 31st December 1962 and various other changes were made in the Agreement as a result. Nauru became a participating Government in 1969, and Fiji in 1971.

The Commission is a consultative and advisory body to the participating Governments in matters affecting the economic and social development of non-self-governing territories in the South Pacific region, and is able to provide advice, training facilities etc. to these territories and to any which become 'participating Governments' under the amending agreement of 2nd October 1964. The Commission's work is financed mainly by contributions from the participating Governments. Annual sessions of the Commission are held at its headquarters in Noumea, New Caledonia, and are preceded by annual meetings of the South Pacific Conference, comprising territorial delegates, which advises the Commission on the framing of the annual work programme.

The United Kingdom Senior Commissioner is D. Scott, Foreign and Commonwealth Office. Afioga Afoafouvale Misimoa, who was the Secretary-General, died in February 1971, and at the time of going to press a successor had not been appointed.

SOUTH PACIFIC AIR TRANSPORT COUNCIL

The Council is ancillary to the Commonwealth Air Transport Council (*q.v.*) and was established as a result of recommendations of a Civil Aviation Conference held in Wellington in 1946. The Permanent Chairman of the Council is the Australian Minister responsible for Civil Aviation and the Secretariat is in Melbourne, Australia. Britain, Australia, New Zealand and Fiji are members of the Council while the Western Pacific High Commission is represented by Britain. The Constitution provides for associate membership which has been extended to Tonga and Nauru. The Council which normally meets every two years has had twenty meetings since it was formed and has been largely concerned with the development of Nadi (Nandi) airport in Fiji.

PART VIII

COMMITTEES, SOCIETIES AND ORGANISATIONS IN BRITAIN CONCERNED WITH THE COMMONWEALTH

COMMITTEES, SOCIETIES AND ORGANISATIONS IN BRITAIN CONCERNED WITH THE COMMONWEALTH

AFRICAN STUDIES ASSOCIATION OF THE UNITED KINGDOM

c/o Centre of West African Studies, University of Birmingham, P.O. Box 363, Birmingham 15

President: Professor Daryll Forde
Hon. Secretary: Dr R. P. Moss
Members of the Council of the Association:

Mr H. P. White
Mr L. B. Frewer
Mr. C. Fyfe
Dr. J. E. Goldthorpe
Dr A. G. Hopkins
Mrs M. Kettle
Dr. R. F. Montgomery
Professor P. Robson

Mr E. O'Connor
Mr E. W. Ardener
Professor L. C. Beadle
Dr R. C. Bridges
Dr D. Dalby
Professor J. D. Fage
Dr M. E. Humphreys (Polly Hill)

The Association was founded in 1963 with the aim of advancing academic studies relating to Africa by providing facilities for the interchange of information and ideas. It publishes a bulletin three times a year and holds interdisciplinary conferences and symposia. Its members mostly hold teaching or research appointments in universities or other institutions of higher education in the United Kingdom.

ANGLO SIERRA LEONEAN SOCIETY

2 Charterhouse Street, London EC1N 6RX (01-353 1577)

Chief Patron: The Right Hon. Viscount Boyd of Merton, CH
President: Sir George Beresford-Stooke, KCMG
Vice-Presidents: Sir Maurice Dorman, GCMG, GCVO;
The Hon. Mr. Justice G. E. Dove-Edwin; Dr. M. C. F. Easmon, OBE;
Dr W. H. Fitzjohn; The Right Rev. Dr J. L. C. Horstead, CMG, CBE;
Dr. R. E. Kelfa-Caulker; Dr. D. S. H. W. Nicol, CMG;
J. S. Fenton, CMG, OBE; C. P. McConnachie, CBE; J. Johnson, MP
Chairman: D. A. R. Richardson
Hon. Secretary: R. A. Jones

The Anglo Sierra Leonean Society was formed in London in August 1962. Its objects are to foster friendship and understanding between citizens of Great Britain and of Sierra Leone and to assist in the encouragement of cultural, literary and social relations between the two countries. The Society has a Council of mixed members comprising citizens of the United Kingdom and of Sierra Leone.

Membership is open to all citizens of the United Kingdom and Sierra Leone and to any other nationals interested in Sierra Leone.

The Society issues bulletins to members at regular intervals, with news of the activities of the Society, and lectures and film shows are held in the winter months.

In May 1965 a branch of the Society was formed in Freetown.

THE ASSOCIATION OF COMMONWEALTH UNIVERSITIES

36 Gordon Square, London WC1H 0PF (01-387 8572)

Chairman: Dr A. A. Kwapong
Vice-Chairman: Sir Charles Wilson
Hon. Treasurer: Sir Douglas Logan
Secretary-General: Sir Hugh W. Springer
Senior Assistant Secretary: E. E. Temple
Assistant Secretaries: T. Craig; P. B. Hetherington

Almost all Universities and University Colleges of good standing in the Commonwealth are members of this Association, which was founded in 1913 as the Universities Bureau of the British Empire and was named the Association of Universities of the British Commonwealth from 1948 to 1963 when it received a Royal Charter under its present name. There are at present 190 institutions in membership. The Association is a voluntary organisation, financed by the subscriptions of its member institutions; it does not receive any government grant but among the secretariats it provides are those of certain statutory bodies (*e.g.* the Commonwealth Scholarship Commission in the United Kingdom) whose expenditure is reimbursed under contract with the relevant Government departments. Its functions include that of providing liaison between the administrations of the various Universities in Britain and other Commonwealth countries, and the organisation of periodical conferences. Congresses of the Universities of the Commonwealth are held at quinquennial intervals. The tenth Congress was held in Sydney, Australia, in 1968; it was attended by more than 500 members and 156 Commonwealth Universities were represented. The eleventh Congress is planned to take place in Edinburgh in 1973. Since 1948 a number of small conferences of heads of Universities have been held in different parts of the Commonwealth between Congresses, the latest being in 1970 in India. A conference of the executive heads of Commonwealth Universities is being held in Ghana in August-September 1971.

The Association acts as the agent in London of overseas member institutions, particularly in inviting applications and, when requested, reporting on candidates for vacant appointments on their staffs. The Association undertakes certain responsibilities in connection with the Commonwealth Scholarship and Fellowship Plan, particularly by providing the secretariat for the Commonwealth Scholarship Commission in the United Kingdom which selects Commonwealth Scholars, holders of Commonwealth Medical Awards, Commonwealth Academic Staff Fellows and Scholars and Commonwealth Visiting Professors from overseas and places them in, or attaches them to, United Kingdom universities; and makes nominations for scholarships tenable in overseas Commonwealth countries. it also prepares a comprehensive annual report on the working of the Plan in the Commonwealth as a whole. In 1971 the A.C.U. offered the first of its Travelling Fellowships to enable senior administrative officers of Commonwealth Universities to study at first hand the administrative practices of university institutions in any Commonwealth country other than their own.

In general, the Association aims to provide the secretariat for any special operation requested by its member Universities or a group of them. Among the scholarships at present administered are some for non-Commonwealth students. It is in regular contact with national inter-university organisations such as the Association of Universities and Colleges of Canada, the Australian, New Zealand and Nigerian Vice-Chancellors' Committees and the Inter-University Boards of India and Pakistan, as well as with the Inter-University Council for Higher Education Overseas. The staffs of the Committee of Vice-Chancellors and Principals of the Universities of the United Kingdom, whose office is at 29 Tavistock Square, London WC1H 9E2 and of the Universities Central Council on Admissions at Cheltenham, Gloucestershire, are, by formal arrangement, members of the staff of the Association. The Associations' office is open to enquiries on university matters, and the library, containing the calendars, handbooks, prospectuses, etc., of most Commonwealth university institutions, is available for reference purposes. A list of academic visitors to Britain is issued at regular intervals to interested organisations; it includes the names of those known or understood to be in the country at the time and the names of those whose visits are impending. As part of its programme of providing factual information about Universities, and about access to them, the Association publishes annually the *Commonwealth Universities Yearbook* which contains in its 2,000 pages general information about all university institutions in the Commonwealth, including staff directories. Among the Association's other publications are: A Bulletin of Current Documentation *Higher Education in the United Kingdom*, a handbook for overseas students and their advisers, compiled jointly by the A.C.U. and British Council; *Proceedings of the Quinquennial Congresses of Commonwealth Universities;* and *United Kingdom Postgraduate Awards.* Two new handbooks listing sources of financial aid for, respectively, university teachers and postgraduate students who want to teach, study, or undertake research in a Commonwealth country other than their own, are in preparation. The A.C.U. also publishes annually for the U.K. Committee of Vice-Chancellors and Principals *A Compendium of University Entrance Requirements for First Degree Courses in the United Kingdom.* A note on the functions of the Association, an official List of Commonwealth Universities and their addresses, the Annual Report of the Council and a statistical report on overseas students at United Kingdom Universities, are also available as printed leaflets. In 1963 there was published for the Association by the Cambridge University Press *Community of Universities: an Informal Portrait of the Association of Universities of the British Commonwealth* 1913-63.

AUSTRALIAN BRITISH TRADE ASSOCIATION
21 Tothill Street, London, S.W.1 (01–799 7447)
Director (U.K.): C. F. Campbell, MBE
British Council Chairman: W. R. Russell

The Australian British Trade Association was founded in 1910 (as the Australian Association of British Manufacturers and their Representatives) to promote trade between Britain and Australia. Practical assistance on matters connected with exports to Australia is rendered, including specialist services on tariff matters, promotion and public relations, in addition to routine casework service.

The head office is in Canberra, Australia and the Association has branch offices in Melbourne, Sydney, Adelaide, Perth, Brisbane and Hobart.

Membership in the United Kingdom exceeds 300 firms and trade associations and that in Australia is approximately 600.

BRITAIN-NIGERIA ASSOCIATION

Patron: H.R.H. The Prince Philip, Duke of Edinburgh, KG, KT, OM, GBE
President: Sir James Robertson, KT, GCMG, GCVO, KBE
Vice-Presidents:
H. E. Alhaji Sule Dede Kolo, High Commissioner for Nigeria in the United Kingdom
The Rt Hon. Duncan Sandys, MP
The Rt Hon. Arthur Bottomley, OBE, MP
Chairman of the Council: Sir Stafford Foster Sutton, KBE, CMG, QC
Hon. Secretary: J. N. D. Bettley
Hon. Treasurer: Arthur Brown, MBE

The address of the Association is
c/o Barclays Bank DCO, 54 Lombard Street, London E.C.3

The Britain-Nigeria Association is a non-political organisation founded in 1961. Its object is the promotion of friendship and mutual understanding between Britain and Nigeria.

The Association organises regular social and cultural activities which are designed not only to bring Britons and Nigerians together but also to maintain contact with those Britons who have served in Nigeria and wish to keep in touch with Nigeria and each other. All members receive frequent issues of the *Bulletin*, which gives news of the activities of the Association and of its members, together with a summary of the latest news from Nigeria.

Membership is open to all Britons, Nigerians and other nationals interested in Nigeria. The annual subscription is one guinea (30s. where husband and wife join together). Widows and Nigerian students in Britain pay a reduced subscription of 5s. Life membership is available for £10 (£15 for husband and wife). Firms and other bodies with interests in Nigeria are eligible to join the Association as corporate members for a minimum annual subscription of £10.

BRITISH ANTARCTIC SURVEY

(Natural Environment Research Council)
30 Gillingham Street, S.W.1 (01-834 3687-8-9)

Director: Sir Vivian Fuchs
Personnel: W. O. Sloman
Publications Officer: Miss G. E. Todd
Logistics: D. R. Gipps
Accountant: E. M. P. Salmon

The London Office is responsible for the Administration and control of British Antarctic activities, and for publication of the scientific results.

BRITISH ASSOCIATION FOR THE
ADVANCEMENT OF SCIENCE

3 Sanctuary Buildings, 20 Great Smith Street, London S.W.1

(01–799 7657/9)

President 1971/72: Sir Vivian Fuchs
General Treasurer: Sir Eric Mensforth, CBE
General Secretaries:
Professor G. E. Fogg, FRS; Dr H. M. Finniston, FRS; Sir Gordon Cox, KBE, FRS
Secretary: Dr J. A. V. Willis

The British Association, established at York in 1831, is a national institution whose membership is open to all. Its aim is to promote a more general interest in, and understanding of, the concepts, language, methods and applications of science.

The Association pursues this aim in the following ways. First, by the organisation of an Annual Meeting held in a different city in the United Kingdom each year. The Meeting lasts for eight days and is the largest scientific gathering of its kind in the country and the only one which members of the general public can attend on equal terms with scientists. The programme covers the whole field of science (natural, biological and social sciences) with the exception of clinical medicine. Second, the Association arranges all over the country and throughout the year—by means of twenty-three Branch and Area Committees—local programmes of scientific lectures and films. Much of this work is directed at yonug people and in addition to single lectures, major Junior British Association Meetings and Science Fairs (which are designed to exhibit the scientific work of young people in schools) are organised in selected areas each year. Third, the Association's Visual Aids Service arranges film and other programmes to meet the needs of specialised groups (teachers, professional bodies etc.) and advises on sources of visual material. Fourth, the Association arranges conferences and study groups on special problems of national and topical interest. The Association maintains cordial relations with sister Associations for the Advancement of Science in the Commonwealth and in other parts of the world by correspondence, the exchange of delegates at Annual Conferences and the exchange of publications.

The British Association Young Scientists (BAYS) was established in September 1968, aimed to bring young scientists into the membership of the Association; a number of BAYS branches have been set up in various centres all over the country where the young people themselves will be responsible for planning their own programmes of activities.

The Association is a charitable body, run largely by voluntary effort under the direction of an executive Secretary responsible to the Council of the Association.

THE BRITISH ASSOCIATION OF MALAYSIA
AND SINGAPORE

521/524 Grand Buildings, Trafalgar Square,
London W.C.2 (01–930 8631)

President: Sir Dennis White, KBE, CMG
Secretary: W. C. S. Corry, CBE

This Association was founded in 1920 as the successor to the Straits Settlements

W

Association (London), 1867. It has individual and corporate membership of about 2,000. It concerns itself with matters of public interest affecting Malaysia, Singapore and Brunei; provides a link between past and present residents in these territories; interests itself in Malaysian and Singapore students in Britain; publishes a bi-monthly illustrated journal *Malaysia*, and has sponsored the publication of a *Bibliography of Malaya*.

BRITISH ASSOCIATION OF THE EXPERIMENT IN INTERNATIONAL LIVING

"Otesaga", Upper Wyche, Malvern, Worcs. (MALvern 2577)

President: The Earl of Haddo, CBE, KStJ, TD
Vice-Presidents: Professor F. S. Dainton; Mrs K. E. Dodd; J. L. Longland;
Lord Ritchie Calder; Sir R. Birley; Dr D. B. Watt
Secretary: F. J. Elphick

The objects of the organisation are "to promote mutual respect and understanding between people of different nations, races and creeds". Since its beginning, in 1933, the Experiment has aimed to achieve international understanding in a practical way by providing a Homestay with families. An applicant learns about another country's way of life by living it for himself as a member of a family. Careful attention is paid to selection of candidates, and orientation. 80 per cent of applicants are of undergraduate age: members travel in groups of not more than ten plus an older leader.

Currently Britain receives 100 groups and sends 30 groups outbound to 24 countries. These include India, Ceylon, Tanzania, Kenya, Uganda, Canada and Nigeria. Costs are met by the applicant and vary with the distance travelled: most programmes include a travel week or safari, study programme or work project, in company with people of the host country.

BRITISH CARIBBEAN ASSOCIATION

Joint Presidents: The Lord Royle of Pendleton, JP; Nigel Fisher, MC, MP
Joint Chairmen: John Hunt, MP; Dr V. L. Page JP
Joint Deputy Chairmen:
Donald Chapmen; T. L. Harris; Miss Joan Lestor, MP; Councillor Dr D. T. Pitt, JP;
Nicholas Scott, MBE, JP, MP
Hon. Treasurers: A. F. Sievers; T. Cambell
Hon. Secretary:
Leonard Smith, MBE, JP, Booker McConnell Ltd, Bucklersbury House, 83 Cannon Street,
London, EC4N 8EJ (01-248 8051)

The Association was formed in July 1958 with the aim of strengthening friendship and understanding between the peoples of the Caribbean and Britain, and of helping to improve race relations generally.

It has 1,000 members including over 120 Members of Parliament drawn from the three main political parties. Members meetings are held regularly to receive reports on the work of the Association and to make recommendations for constructive action. Contact with the Ministries and Local Authorities concerned is constantly maintained and a *Newsletter* is published twice a year. Social functions are also a popular feature of the Association's activities.

The Association is governed by a Central Council and an Executive Committee composed equally of West Indian and British members.

BRITISH COMMONWEALTH EX-SERVICES LEAGUE

92 New Bond Street, London W.1 (01-629 3106)

Grand President: Admiral of the Fleet The Earl Mountbatten of Burma, KG, PC, GCB, OM, GCSI, GCIE, GCVO, DSO, FRS
Deputy Grand President: General Sir Rodney Moore, GCVO, KCB, CBE, DSO
Honorary Treasurer: K. M. Oliphant
Secretary-General: Air Commodore B. J. R. Roberts

The League was founded in 1921 (as the British Empire Service League) by Field Marshal Earl Haig and Field Marshal Smuts to link together the ex-service organisations of the Commonwealth. The original nine founder-member organisations have now grown to include 40 Commonwealth countries and territories.

In addition to maintaining contact with all its member organisations the League seeks to ensure that no Commonwealth ex-serviceman shall be without help if in need; to further the welfare of ex-servicemen by assisting its member organisations to meet their obligations; and to assist ex-servicemen who migrate within the Commonwealth. It acts as the overseas agent of a number of ex-service charitable organisations in Britain, gives advice and guidance on pension and other technical matters, provides a Commonwealth ex-services information service through a quarterly *Bulletin* issued by headquarters, and undertakes many and varied tasks on behalf of its member organisations.

The League holds triennial conferences to decide its policy and to discuss matters of concern to its members. Between conferences the affairs of the League are controlled by a Council in London on which its members are represented.

THE BRITISH COMMONWEALTH UNION LTD.

60 Buckingham Gate, London S.W.1 (01-834 1647)

President: The Rt Hon. Lord Colyton, PC, CMG
Chairman: John Biggs-Davidson, MP
Board of Management:
C. F. R. Bagnall, CBE
Sir Cyril Black, JP
R. M. Hodges
Air Chief Marshal Sir Hugh Lloyd, GBE, KCB, MC, DFC
Lt.-Colonel E. MacKinnon
V. E. Waldron
Hon. Treasurer: Ronald A. Barter
Director: Dominic Le Foe
Hon. Secretary: Michael Farrow

The British Commonwealth Union, formerly The British Empire Union, was founded in 1915. The name was changed in 1960. It is a non-profit-making company, limited by guarantee.

The objects of the Union are to secure a closer union commercially, politically, socially and otherwise both between Britain and the overseas countries of the Commonwealth and between the Commonwealth and other friendly States. Through the medium of pamphlets, written by experts, it draws attention to specific problems facing Britain and the Commonwealth which often figure in the popular press when the background is unknown to the general public. Its work is extended mainly to those who may not fully appreciate the advantages of unity within the Commonwealth. Many hundreds attend its meetings each week. Interest in schools is stimulated by a national essay competition.

THE BRITISH COUNCIL

65 Davies Street, London W1Y 2AA (01–499 8011)

Chairman: Sir Leslie Rowan, KCB, CVO
Director-General: The Hon. Sir John Henniker, KCMG, CVO, MC
Deputy Director-General: R. A. Phillips, CMG, OBE
Assistant Director-General (Administration): H. P. Croom-Johnson, CMG, CBE
Assistant Director-General (Functional): F. H. Cawson, CBE

The British Council, by the terms of its Royal Charter, exists to promote a wider knowledge of Britain and the English language abroad and to develop closer cultural relations between Britain and other countries.

The Council was founded in 1934. Since the fifties its work has been marked by two main changes: more activity in the developing countries of the Commonwealth and greater attention to the more educational aspects of Council work. As a consequence, help with English teaching became increasingly important. Council officers specialising in this field train teachers and teacher-trainers, advise on the improvement of syllabuses and text-books and conduct "in-service" courses. The Council is directly concerned with the provision of British Tutors for vacation courses for teachers of English, as well as of other subjects, in a number of Commonwealth countries.

Further assistance is supplied by the Aid to Commonwealth English (A.C.E.) scheme, introduced in 1962, under which 80 additional experts, recruited to career service in the Council, are posted to key English teaching posts in Commonwealth countries. Such officers serve in university departments and advanced teacher training institutes, in-service training centres, and centres for curriculum and materials development, and as advisers to ministries of education. Work in English training is reinforced at headquarters by specialist advisory services including an English-Teaching Information Centre which maintains a unique library of over 20,000 volumes.

English teaching also takes place through other media such as television, sound radio and films. Television officers have been trained and are at present working in India and Malta. Working together the Council and the B.B.C. have produced seven series of films for teaching English (including English for Science and English for Business) and for the training of teachers of English. In co-operation with CEDO (Centre for Educational Development Overseas) (q.v.), the Council has expanded its science education work at school level, mainly in Commonwealth Africa and has posted eight Science Education Officers overseas for this purpose. A number of other scientifically-qualified officers are also assisting in this work overseas. In addition, there are currently ten Council officers seconded to posts under the Aid to Commonwealth Teaching of Science (ACTS) scheme; provision has now been made to expand the number of ACTS posts to 30 by the end of 1973.

Other education work takes many forms. The Council assists in the exchange of experts between Britain and India under the Centres of Advanced Study Scheme. It also helps schools overseas in two ways: by recruitment of staff and by grants. Schools so assisted are in India, Pakistan, Cyprus, Canada, Australia, New Zealand, Bermuda, Jamaica, and Tanzania.

The shortage of teachers in Britain inevitably limits the recruitment of British teachers for service overseas. Graduates and school-leavers, through the British Volunteer Programme, in some measure fill the breach. The Council is the 'overseas arm' of Voluntary Service Overseas, the United Nations Association, and the Catholic Institute for International Relations, and as such, is responsible for the care and welfare of the volunteers overseas.

In addition to giving assistance to schools, the Council also assists Universities, training colleges and Ministries of Education in the Commonwealth by recruiting British staff on contract, and by seconding members of its own staff under the Aid to Commonwealth English Scheme.

In addition to providing its own staff for work in the Commonwealth, the Council arranges tours by British specialists and advisers, usually between 100 and 150 a year and mainly in education, medicine, science and technology. Mention must also be made of the Commonwealth University Interchange Scheme, which promotes visits between British and Commonwealth universities by university teachers and research workers and the exchange scheme for young scientists with India.

The Council awards post-graduate scholarships and bursaries to citizens of Commonwealth countries for study in Britain. Many professional visitors from Commonwealth countries are enabled to study aspects of life in Britain under arrangements made by the Council.

In Britain the Council maintains offices or centres in London and elsewhere, mainly in university cities, to provide services for students, professional visitors and others for overseas. The Council meets at port, rail or air termini students of whose arrival in Britain it has been notified. It helps to find permanent accommodation for those students for whose stay in Britain it is responsible or who are recommended to it by High Commissioners or British government departments. The Council is able to give advice about accommodation outside London to other Commonwealth students who seek its aid.

The Council helps Commonwealth students in other ways by arranging social and cultural events, vacation and week-end courses, and visits to places of historical, cultural and industrial interest. Opportunities are also provided for students to find their way into the normal family and community life in Britain.

The Council also provides services for holders of awards given under the Commonwealth Scholarship and Fellowship Plan, the Commonwealth Education Fellowship Scheme, British technical assistance schemes and for those holding Fellowships awarded by United Nations specialised agencies for study in Britain.

The Council's library service operated in 55 countries and in 1970-71 loaned over three million books to Commonwealth members alone. Noteworthy are the multiple-copy collections of students' textbooks, the wide range of periodicals available, children's sections and book-box service. The Council, either alone or in association with others also provides special publications which it has commissioned, speech and music records, films, and educational aids for schools and other institutions. Public Library Development, in which the Council has collaborated with several Commonwealth governments in Africa, has meant provision of capital and for buildings, staff training, initial bookstock and equipment.

Visits of drama companies, orchestras, group and individual performers, and exhibitions of books, periodicals, fine arts and photographs do much to keep the Commonwealth aware of artistic, scientific and technological developments in Britain.

In the dependent territories the Council works in close collaboration with territorial Governments, carrying on educational activities which do not usually fall within the official sphere and thus supplementing the educational and information work of those Governments. In Britain and the Irish Republic the Council is responsible for the welfare of recommended students from the dependent territories.

The British Council has representatives in the following members countries of the Commonwealth: Australia, Canada, Ceylon, Cyprus, Ghana, Guyana, India, Kenya, Lesotho, Malawi, Malaysia, Malta, Mauritius, New Zealand, Nigeria, Pakistan, Sierra Leone, Singapore, Tanzania, Uganda and Zambia. It also has offices in British Honduras and Hong Kong.

THE BRITISH DENTAL ASSOCIATION

64 Wimpole Street, London W1M 8AL (01-935 0875)

Patron: Her Majesty The Queen

Honorary Officers
President: R. G. Swiss, OBE
President-Elect: G. D. Lloyd
Chairman of Representative Board: R. G. Hunt
Chairman of Council: Vacant
Vice-Chairman of Representative Board: W. H. Morrow
Vice-Chairman of Council: R. B. Allen
Honorary Curator: J. A. Donaldson

Administration
Secretary: A. C. L. Mackie, CBE
Assistant Secretaries: S. R. Bragg; R. G. MacLean, TD;
S. H. Richardson
Scottish Secretary: J. Marshall Banks
Editor: J. A. Donaldson
Accountant: W. Donald
Librarian: E. Muriel Spencer
Press Officer: C. J. Stuart

The British Dental Association was founded in 1880 and its principal objects are to promote dental and allied sciences, to maintain the honour and interests of the dental profession and to hold and encourage meetings of members of the Association and of the dental profession generally throughout the world.

The Association maintains close liaison with Dental Associations of the Commonwealth and there is a regular interchange of news and information between these Associations. A conference is held annually to which representatives of affiliated Commonwealth Associations are invited.

The *British Dental Journal*, published twice each month by the Association, circulates widely throughout the Commonwealth.

BRITISH INSTITUTE IN EASTERN AFRICA

Nairobi Office: P.O. Box 7680, Nairobi, Kenya (Nairobi 53330)
London Office: c/o The British Academy, Burlington House, London W.1
(01-734 0457)

President: L. P. Kirwan, CMG
Director: H. N. Chittick

The Institute was founded in 1960 and is supported by a grant from the British Academy. Its object is to promote research into the history and archaeology of East Africa. The Institute is based on Nairobi and is administered by the Director who is responsible to a Governing Council in London. The Institute's research work is carried out by its staff and by Research Students to whom bursaries are awarded from time to time. The results of this research are published in the Institute's annual journal, *Azania*, and in occasional papers and memoirs.

The Institute, though autonomous, has a formal association with the University of Nairobi, involving some supervision by its Staff of students sitting for the advanced degrees of the University, and occasional lecturing.

THE BRITISH INSTITUTE OF INTERNATIONAL AND COMPARATIVE LAW

32 Furnival Street, London E.C.4 (01–405 4051)

Chairman: Rt. Hon. Lord Denning, Master of the Rolls
Chairmen of the Sections of the Advisory Board:
Public International Law: Rt. Hon. Lord Shawcross, QC
Private International Law: Hon. Mr Justice Scarman, OBE
Comparative Law (including Commonwealth and Foreign Law):
The Rt Hon. Lord Cross
Director: Dr K. R. Simmonds
Deputy Director (Commonwealth Law): H. H. Marshall, CMG, QC
Assistant Director (European Law): (Vacant)

The British Institute of International and Comparative Law was founded in 1958 to bring together the Grotius Society and the Society of Comparative Legislation and International Law, to continue and develop their activities and to provide a centre in London for the study of International and Comparative Law.

The Institute is an independent body which receives support from Foundations and is now partly financed by the subscriptions of its members, who are drawn from all countries, including many from Commonwealth countries.

The Council of Management includes special Commonwealth members, who are at present Sir Kenneth Bailey, CBE, QC, of the Department of External Affairs, Canberra, Australia, M. C. Setalvad, formerly Attorney-General of India and D. Park-Jamieson, QC, former President of the Canadian Bar Association.

The Institute is particularly concerned with all aspects of law in the Commonwealth, and this interest is reflected in frequent articles and notes in *The International and Comparative Law Quarterly*, the journal of the Institute. It operates the Commonwealth Legal Advisory Service which is available to Commonwealth countries as a source of information on legal developments in all parts of the Commonwealth; the scheme also envisages, in conjunction with the Overseas Development Administration of the Foreign and Commonwealth Office, the sending of legal experts to territories which request their services. Another aspect of the Institute's interest in the Commonwealth is the Annual Survey of Commonwealth Law, which is produced by the Institute jointly with the Faculty of Law of the University of Oxford. Supplementary to the Commonwealth Legal Advisory Service, the Institute prepares Surveys on legal topics which may be of general interest to all Commonwealth countries. The Institute also organises lectures and conferences on Commonwealth legal themes; it has, for example, been responsible for a series of week-end discussions at Cumberland Lodge, Windsor Great Park, on aspects of West Indian, Indian, Nigerian, East African, Ghanaian, Malaysian, Singapore and Muslim law, confessions in criminal cases, marriage laws and methods of Law Reform, the proceedings of some of which have subsequently appeared as special publications.

THE BRITISH LEPROSY RELIEF ASSOCIATION
50 Fitzroy Street, London W.1 (01–387 7283)

Patron: Her Majesty The Queen
President: The Rt Hon. Viscount Boyd of Merton, CH
Chairman of Executive Committee: Sir George Seel, KCMG
Hon. Treasurer: E. O. Baker
General Secretary: Air Vice-Marshal W. J. Crisham, CB, CBE
Medical Secretary: Dr S. G. Browne, OBE

Lepra, a central authoritative body on leprosy throughout and beyond the Commonwealth, directs all its activities towards attaining its objective—the control and eradication of leprosy.

It supports by grants and trained staff, Government and voluntary organisations engaged in approved anti-leprosy work, with particular emphasis on the early diagnosis, regular treatment, and care of children with leprosy.

Lepra has set up a special Leprosy Control Project at Malawi, endorsed by the World Health Organisation, to demonstrate to countries with a serious leprosy problem, that leprosy can, in fact, be cleared from an endemic area within 10 years, and to show how this can best be done. The Malawi Project, now in its sixth year, is the pattern for Lepra's approach to the problems of leprosy, and its principles and lessons are being studied and applied in other countries, notably in Zambia and Sierra Leone, where projects based on the methods used in the Malawi Control Project have been initiated.

LEPRA promotes research into the causes, treatment and prevention of leprosy, and circulates information on the disease throughout the World.

BRITISH NATIONAL COMMITTEE ON ANTARCTIC RESEARCH
(ROYAL SOCIETY)

6 Carlton House Terrace, London, S.W.1 (01-839 5561)

Chairman: Sir Miles Clifford, KBE, CMG

Since the International Geophysical Year twelve countries have remained actively interested in scientific research in the Antarctic. The Royal Society's British National Committee on Antarctic Research is the United Kingdom committee adhering to the Scientific Committee on Antarctic Research of the International Council of Scientific Unions, which is the international non-governmental organisation responsible for the coordination of the scientific programmes.

BRITISH NATIONAL COMMITTEE ON OCEANIC RESEARCH
(Royal Society)

6 Carlton House Terrace, London S.W.1 (01-839 5561)

Chairman: Sir George Deacon, CBE, FRS

The Royal Society's British National Committee on Oceanic Research is the United Kingdom Committee adhering to the Scientific Committee on Oceanic

Research of the International Council of Scientific Unions. SCOR is an interdisciplinary non-governmental marine science organisation and serves as one of the scientific advisory bodies to the Intergovernmental Oceanographic Commission.

BUREAU OF HYGIENE AND TROPICAL DISEASES

Keppel Street, Gower Street, London WC1E 7HT (01-636 8636)

Director: Dr F. I. C. Apted
Assistant Directors: Dr D. A. Cannon, OBE; Dr S. Caruana, OSTJ
Secretary: A. H. Phipps

The Bureau, established in 1908, is a centre for the collection and general distribution of information with regard to hygiene and tropical diseases. It is maintained by the proceeds of sales of its publications, and by contributions from the British Government and other governments and institutions.

It publishes the *Tropical Diseases Bulletin* and *Abstracts on Hygiene.*

The Bureau is under the general control and direction of an Honorary Managing Committee, appointed by and responsible to the Minister for Overseas Development. The Committee is composed of the following members:

Chairman: The Chief Medical Adviser, Overseas Development Administration
Dr J. M. Liston, CMG

Brigadier Sir John Boyd, OBE, FRS	Dr J. A. B. Gray
Professor L. J. Bruce-Chwatt, OBE	N. Leach, CMG
Dr A. C. E. Cole	Dr T. A. Lloyd Davies
Sir George Godber, KCB	Professor A. B. Semple, CBE
Dr L. G. Goodwin	J. B. Sidebotham, CMG
Dr C. E. Gordon Smith, CB	Dr D. Thomson, CB

Secretary: P. G. Ottewill, GM, AFC (Overseas Development Administration)

CENTRE FOR EDUCATIONAL DEVELOPMENT OVERSEAS

Address:
Tavistock House South, Tavistock Square, London W.C.1 (01-387 0166)

Director-General: J. R. Bunting, CBE
Director of Audio-Visual Aids Division: G. H. Rusbridger, OBE
Director of Broadcasting Division: T. Singleton
Director of Curriculum and Examinations Division: R. W. Morris

The Centre for Educational Development Overseas (CEDO) was established as an independent body by the Minister of Overseas Development on 1st April 1970. Three related organisations which were already in operation formed the nucleus of CEDO. These were the Centre for Educational Television Overseas (CETO), the Centre for Curriculum Renewal and Educational Development Overseas (CREDO) and the Oversea Visual Aids Centre (OVAC).

CEDO helps in establishing and assisting educational centres and systems in developing countries and advises on curriculum renewal, examination and selection methods and the introduction of new educational techniques and media.

Training is arranged in the U.K. and overseas in all aspects of the production and use of educational radio and television, new teaching methods, particularly

w*

those concerned with curriculum changes, and the production and use of educational materials and audio-visual aids.

The collection, collation and dissemination of information on all aspects of educational development is also a central feature of CEDO's activities. Displays of equipment and materials and a reference library are maintained and publications are available.

CENTRE FOR OVERSEAS PEST RESEARCH

College House, Wrights Lane, London W.8 (01-937 8191)

Director: Dr P. T. Haskell

The Centre for Overseas Pest Research—whose parent body is the Overseas Development Administration of the Foreign and Commonwealth Office—came into being in May 1971. It consists of the former Anti-Locust Research Centre, Tropical Pesticides Research Unit, Tropical Pesticides Research Headquarters and Information Unit, and Termite Research Unit—the first three of which had been integral scientific parts of, and the last funded by, the ODA previous to the amalgamation.

Its terms of reference are, substantially:

1. to conduct and foster research and its application for the control of various insect and certain other animal pests affecting overseas, mainly tropical, agriculture and public health. Its focus will be on pest species which are of international significance, either because they migrate between countries (e.g. locusts and weaver birds) or because they are widespread and endemic to several countries or regions (e.g. termites, mosquitoes and other vector species).

2. to promote technical co-operation, by collecting and disseminating information and otherwise assisting overseas governments, regional and international organisations in introducing rational strategies and techniques of pest control.

3. to provide and organise training facilities for students, both in courses and in service.

THE CEYLON ASSOCIATION IN LONDON

2/3 Crosby Square, Bishopsgate, London, E.C.3 (01-588 1812)

President: A. G. Mathewson, OBE
Vice-President: J. Henderson
Director: Capt. A. S. Webb, RN (Retd.)
Secretary: R. J. Barber

The Association was formed on 6th April 1888 and at the inaugural meeting it was decided that its purpose was to be 'the protection and furtherance of the general interests of Ceylon'. It has no Rules or Constitution and membership is open to all who claim to have any interest in, or connection with, Ceylon.

The Association membership includes many banks, shipping companies, brokers and miscellaneous firms, in addition to 100 tea and rubber plantation companies and 14 agency houses who act as secretaries for the plantation companies. There are also over 400 Private Members whose interests are served by the issue of *Quarterly Bulletins* of information and by the organisation of social re-unions.

Its affairs are conducted at monthly meetings of its Council which is representative of all interests. An Annual General Meeting is held in April or May. The Council has no power to enforce compliance with its decisions on members and may be said, therefore, to act in an advisory capacity by means of recommendations.

COMMONWEALTH ADVISORY AERONAUTICAL RESEARCH COUNCIL

Secretariat: National Physical Laboratory, Teddington, Middlesex (01-977 3222)

Chairman: Professor A. D. Young

Executive Delegates:

Britain: Dr J. Seddon
Canada: Dr D. C. MacPhail
Australia: Dr J. Farrands
New Zealand: Mr W. R. Heald
India: (Vacant)

Pakistan: (To be appointed)
Ceylon: (To be appointed)
Ghana: (To be appointed)
Malaysia: (To be appointed)

Secretary: R. W. G. Gandy
Assistant Secretary: Group Captain R. B. Harrison

The Commonwealth Advisory Aeronautical Research Council (C.A.A.R.C.) was formed in 1946. Its objects are to encourage and co-ordinate aeronautical research throughout the Commonwealth, to avoid undesirable duplication of effort, and to ensure that the research programmes of the member countries are, as far as possible, complementary to each other. Membership is open to all countries of the Commonwealth.

The Council, composed of delegates appointed by the Governments of member countries, meets in various countries of the Commonwealth at intervals of not more than three years. Its functions are strictly advisory and, after each meeting, the principal, or 'executive', delegate from each country is responsible for furthering the aims of the Council and steering its recommendations in his own country. The Council selects certain broad subjects or 'fields' in which several Commonwealth countries have an active interest. Each country wishing to collaborate in a particular field appoints a specialist Co-ordinator, usually a man actively engaged in relevant research. He is responsible for keeping himself familiar with the work being done in his own country and for corresponding regularly with his fellow Co-ordinators. Co-ordinators in each field normally meet once between successive Council Meetings to discuss common problems and effective ways in which work may be shared between two or more countries.

Continuity between Council Meetings is provided by a Central Secretariat which meets regularly in London and on which most member countries are represented by appropriate Scientific Liaison Officers. The Central Office of the Council is associated with the Secretariat of the British Aeronautical Research Council. Secretarial and administrative costs of the C.A.A.R.C. are shared by member countries.

THE COMMONWEALTH AGRICULTURAL BUREAUX

Farnham House, Farnham Royal, Slough, SL2 3BN, U.K.

Tel: Farnham Common 2281   Grams: COMAG, SLOUGH

Executive Council

Chairman: Dr V. Armstrong (New Zealand)

Vice-Chairman: E. S. Kapotwe (Zambia)

United Kingdom: (To be appointed)	Jamaica: The Deputy High Commissioner
Canada: J. L. Orr	Trinidad and Tobago: Mrs L. S. Dorset
Australia: Dr E. G. Hallsworth	Uganda: (To be appointed)
India: A. J. Kidwai	Kenya: H.E. The High Commissioner
Pakistan: T. A. Khan	Malawi: W. D. Simfukwe
Ceylon: A. Nesaratnam	The Gambia: O. A. Sallah
Ghana: J. A. Brobbey	Guyana: R. E. Chandisingh
Malaysia: (To be appointed)	Botswana: H.E. The High Commissioner
Nigeria: (To be appointed)	Barbados: The Deputy High Commissioner
Cyprus: (To be appointed)	Mauritius: D. Ramtohul
Sierra Leone: H.E. The High Commissioner	Swaziland: E. E. Kunene
Tanzania: (To be appointed)	Dependent Territories: D. M. Kitching

Commonwealth Scientific Committee (Observer): Dr R. Glen

Secretary: Sir Thomas Scrivenor, CMG

Assistant Secretary: N. G. Jones, DFC

The Commonwealth (Imperial before 1948) Agricultural Bureaux, are governed by an Executive Council consisting of the nominees of the Governments of Britain and other Commonwealth countries. The Irish Republic is associated with the organisation which was set up in 1929 to administer eight bureaux organised to act as clearing-houses of information on research in eight specialised fields of agricultural science and was financed by a common fund provided by the Governments of the Dominions and Colonies. In 1933 the Council was entrusted with the control of the administration and finances of the Imperial (now Commonwealth) Institute of Entomology, originally set up in 1913, and the Imperial (now Commonwealth) Mycological Institute, originally set up in 1920, and of such research activities in Britain as the participating Governments might thereafter agree should be conducted on a co-operative basis. On the recommendations of the British Commonwealth Scientific Conference of 1936, two more Commonwealth Bureaux, for Forestry and Dairy Science were established; and these were followed in 1966 by the Commonwealth Bureau of Agricultural Economics. The Bureau of Helminthology was given Institute status in 1970. The three institutes, in addition to their function of being information services, have important and extensive work connected with identification. The Commonwealth Institute of Biological Control in Trinidad is also under the administration of the Council. It prepares and maintains a catalogue on the parasites and predators of the insects of the world. It also supplies beneficial insects for attacking various pests and takes complete charge of Biological Control Projects for Governments. In collaboration with the Institut für Dokumentationswesen (Frankfurt), the Institute of Food Technologists (Chicago) and the Centrum voor Landbouwpublikaties en Landbouwdocumentatie (Wageningen), the Commonwealth Agricultural Bureaux have established an International Food Information Service which is financed and administered by the four sponsoring organisations. It is based upon a comprehensive abstract journal appearing monthly and publishing over 12,000 abstracts annually. The information in the journal is stored on magnetic tape for retrieval by computer techniques. The annual reports of the Council are submitted to each of the Governments through their several members. In addition to the periodicals listed, each Institute/Bureau publishes occasional publications. These are listed in the Bureaux's printed Publications List. The bodies controlled by the Executive Council are:

COMMONWEALTH INSTITUTE OF ENTOMOLOGY
Identification Service:
c/o British Museum (Natural History), Cromwell Road, London S.W.7
Telephone: 01-589 6323
Publications Office: 56 Queen's Gate, London S.W.7 (01-584 0067)
Director: R. G. Fennah
Periodicals: *Review of Plant Pathology, Series A and Series B, Bulletin of Entomological Research* and *Distribution Maps of Pests.*

COMMONWEALTH MYCOLOGICAL INSTITUTE
Ferry Lane, Kew, Surrey
Telephone: Richmond 4086/7
Director: A. Johnston
Periodicals: *Review of Plant Pathology, Review of Medical and Veterinary Mycology, Distribution Maps of Plant Diseases* and *Commonwealth Phytopathological News.*

COMMONWEALTH INSTITUTE OF BIOLOGICAL CONTROL
Gordon Street, Curepe, Trinidad, W.I.
Director: F. J. Simmonds
Stations: Switzerland: India (Bangalore); Pakistan (Rawalpindi); Uganda (Kawanda). Sub-stations: Ghana, Sabah and South America
Periodical: *Catalogue of the Parasites and Predators of Insect Pests.*

COMMONWEALTH INSTITUTE OF HELMINTHOLOGY
The White House, 103 St. Peter's Street, St. Albans, Herts
Telephone: St. Albans 52126
Director: Sheila M. Willmott
Periodical: *Helminthological Abstracts, Series A and Series B.*

COMMONWEALTH BUREAU OF AGRICULTURAL ECONOMICS
31A St. Giles, Oxford
Telephone: Oxford 59829
Director: J. Owen Jones
Periodical: *World Agricultural Economics and Rural Sociology Abstracts*

COMMONWEALTH BUREAU OF ANIMAL BREADING AND GENETICS
Animal Breeding Research Organisation, The King's Buildings, West Mains Road, Edinburgh EH9 3JX
Telephone: Newington 6901
Director: J. P. Maule
Periodical: *Animal Breeding Abstracts.*

COMMONWEALTH BUREAU OF ANIMAL HEALTH
Central Veterinary Laboratory, New Haw, Weybridge, Surrey
Telephone: Byfleet 42826
Director: M. R. Dhanda
Periodicals: *The Veterinary Bulletin* and *Index Veterinarius.*

COMMONWEALTH BUREAU OF ANIMAL NUTRITION
Rowett Research Institute, Bucksburn, Aberdeen AB2 95B
Telephone: Bucksburn 2162
Director: Miss D. L. Duncan
Periodical: *Nutrition Abstracts and Reviews.*

COMMONWEALTH BUREAU OF DAIRY SCIENCE AND TECHNOLOGY
National Institute for Research in Dairying, Shinfield, Reading, RG2 9AT
Telephone: Reading 883895
Director: E. J. Mann
Periodicals: *Dairy Science Abstracts,* and *Food Science and Technology Abstracts* in collaboration with the Institut für Dokumentationswesen, Frankfurt, and the Institute of Food Technologists, Chicago and Centrum voor Landbouwpublikaties en Landbouwdocumentatie, Wageningen.

COMMONWEALTH FORESTRY BUREAU
Commonwealth Forestry Institute, South Parks Road, Oxford, OX1 3RD
Telephone: Oxford 57185
Director: P. G. Beak
Periodical: *Forestry Abstracts.*

COMMONWEALTH BUREAU OF HORTICULTURE AND PLANTATION CROPS
East Malling Research Station, Nr. Maidstone, Kent
Telephone: West Malling 3033
Director: G. E. Tidbury
Periodical: *Horticultural Abstracts.*

COMMONWEALTH BUREAU OF PASTURES AND FIELD CROPS
Hurley, near Maidenhead, Berks
Telephone: Hurley 363–6
Director: P. J. Boyle
Periodicals: *Field Crop Abstracts* and *Herbage Abstracts.*

COMMONWEALTH BUREAU OF PLANT BREEDING AND GENETICS
Department of Applied Biology and Agricultural Science, Downing Street, Cambridge
Telephone: Cambridge 58381
Director: R. H. Richens
Periodical: *Plant Breeding Abstracts.*

COMMONWEALTH BUREAU OF SOILS
Rothamsted Experimental Station, Harpenden, Herts
Telephone: Harpenden 4671
Director: W. D. Brind
Periodical: *Soils and Fertilizers.*

COMMONWEALTH AIR TRANSPORT COUNCIL

Secretariat: Norman Shaw North Building, Victoria Embankment, London
S.W.1. (01–930 4349)

Member Governments:

Australia	India	Sierra Leone
Barbados	Jamaica	Singapore
Botswana	Kenya	Swaziland
British Overseas Territories	Lesotho	Tanzania
Canada	Malawi	Tonga
Ceylon	Malaysia	Trinidad and Tobago
Cyprus	Malta, G.C.	Uganda
Fiji	Mauritius	United Kingdom
Gambia, The	New Zealand	Zambia
Ghana	Nigeria	
Guyana	Pakistan	

Secretary: Mrs V. A. Purnell

The Commonwealth Air Transport Council, was established in January 1945, as a result of a recommendation approved at the Commonwealth Air Conversations held in Canada in October 1944. The Council keeps under review the progress and development of Commonwealth civil air communications, serves as a medium for the exchange of views and information between Commonwealth countries on civil air transport matters and advises on civil aviation matters referred to it by Commonwealth Governments. The Council last met in 1969. Meetings can be held in any part of the Commonwealth; so far it has been the practice for particular meetings to nominate a working Chairman *ad hoc.* Ancillary to the Council and performing similar functions, but on a regional basis, is the South Pacific Air Transport Council (*see Part VII*).

COMMONWEALTH ASSOCIATION OF ARCHITECTS

66 Portland Place, London W1N 4AD (01-580 5533)

President: J. R. Bhalla, India
Secretary: T. C. Colchester, CMG

Executive Committee:

Max E. Collard, Australia	Kington Loo, Asia
John Lovatt Davies, Canada-Caribbean	N. K. Kaddu, Africa
Professor A. Ling, Europe	

Commonwealth Board of Architectural Education
Chairman: Sir Hugh Wilson
Secretary: T. C. Colchester, CMG

Members:

Professor R. N. Johnson, Australia	F. Foley, Ireland
Professor Owusu Addo, Africa	One vacancy
Zahir-ud-Deen Khwaja Pakistan	

The Commonwealth Association of Architects was formed in 1964 with offices in London and a Secretary. It has 25 constituent member societies covering all the Commonwealth countries where architects are organised in recognised professional institutes. The Association is financed by subscriptions from member societies related to the number of corporate members and from such grants as societies are able to make. Its income from this course is approximately £6,000 and the Association has been also receiving an annual grant of £10,000 from the Commonwealth Foundation primarily for certain education work.

Its Executive Committee is composed of one member from each of the five main regions of the Commonwealth. The purposes of the Association include:

(a) the regular assessment of educational standards in schools of architecture through a Commonwealth Board of Architectural Education which would help member societies with advice, facilitate the recognition of degrees, diplomas and membership examinations and provide an accrediting machinery for professional qualifications thereby assisting the free movement of architects between different countries;

(b) provision of a clearing house of general information and advice concerning architectural practice, management and technique, the recruitment and exchange of teaching staff, for collaboration between architectural schools, the interchange of students, research and teaching methods, training courses for teachers, educational courses and syllabuses, registration requirements, and sources of technical aid;

(c) the drawing up and establishment of a code of professional conduct in consultation with the International Union of Architects and mutual support in professional matters.

The last main Conference of the Association took place in Lagos in March 1969. The next full Conference will be held in Australia in 1971. The 1970 meeting of the Commonwealth Board of Architectural Education was held in Singapore and of the Executive Committee in Edinburgh.

A list of recognised schools of architecture in the Commonwealth was published by the Association in 1968.

Regional Organisation of Member Societies has developed since 1968 and there is considerable activity on a regional basis.

COMMONWEALTH BROADCASTING CONFERENCE

Secretariat: Broadcasting House, London W1A 1AA (01–580 4468 Ext. 5022)

Members:

All India Radio
Australian Broadcasting Commission
British Broadcasting Corporation
Canadian Broadcasting Corporation
Caribbean Broadcasting Corporation
Ceylon Broadcasting Corporation
Cyprus Broadcasting Corporation
Fiji Broadcasting Commission
Ghana Broadcasting Corporation
Guyana Broadcasting Service
Jamaica Broadcasting Corporation
Lesotho National Broadcasting Service
Malawi Broadcasting Corporation
Malta Broadcasting Authority
Mauritius Broadcasting Corporation
New Zealand Broadcasting Corporation
Nigerian Broadcasting Corporation
Radio Botswana
Radio Gambia
Radio and Television Malaysia

Radio Pakistan
Radio and Television Singapore
Radio Tanzania—Dar es Salaam
Radio Uganda and Uganda Television
Sierra Leone Radio and Television
Swaziland Broadcasting Service
Trinidad and Tobago Broadcasting Board
Voice of Kenya
Zambia Broadcasting Services

Associate Members:
Antigua Broadcasting Service
Bahamas Broadcasting and Television Commission
Radio Belize
Radio Hong Kong
Radio Seychelles
Radio ZIZ, St Kitts—Nevis—Anguilla
Solomon Islands Broadcasting Service
Windward Islands Broadcasting Service

Secretary: Alva Clarke

Assistants to Secretary: Miss H. U. Mackenzie; Miss J. D. Farquharson

Established in 1945, the Conference is a standing association of the national public service broadcasting organisations which are responsible for the planning and presentation of the broadcast programmes of independent Commonwealth countries. Holding in common the belief that broadcasting is a public trust, the member organisations are professionally committed to the establishment and extension of national radio and television services as a means of information, education and entertainment. The principal purpose of the Conference is the professional improvement, through collective study and mutual assistance, of the broadcast programmes of the member organisations, and of the technical facilities for their transmission and reception. The intensified and sustained training of professional broadcasting staff, in the fields both of programming and engineering, in support of these ends, is a continuing practical concern of the Conference.

The Seventh Conference met in New Zealand in 1968 and made a particular study of the educational responsibilities of national broadcasting, and considered a report on broadcast training facilities and needs in the Commonwealth. At the Seventh Conference it was agreed to extend membership to include as an associate member, the broadcasting organisation operating a public service of comparable character in any other Commonwealth territory. The Eighth Conference met in Jamaica from 2nd–16th June 1970. The theme was 'Practical Suggestions for Multilateral Co-operation in Broadcasting'. In particular, the Conference took steps for such co-operation to be secured by the grouping of member organisations on regional and other workable bases, and either endorsed or itself originated the proposed operation of such arrangements in the Caribbean, West Africa, and East, Central and Southern African areas.

Effective avenues of mutual co-operation were identified in fields of programme interchange, programme and technical training; in assistance in the maintenance and operation of broadcasting equipment and installations; and where governments of developing countries established the priority they attached to broadcasting, in the mounting of task forces from within the resources of the Conference itself to provide major technical and other professional aid.

It was also decided to disband the Study Group on Training established by the Sixth Conference (Nigeria 1965) and replace it by an *ad hoc* Training Review sub-committee consisting of Engineering and Programme representatives from each of three main geographical zones, to be nominated at each Conference.

COMMONWEALTH COMMITTEE ON MINERAL PROCESSING

Warren Spring Laboratory, Stevenage, Herts. (0438 3388)

Chairman: Dr A. J. Robinson

Members:

Britain	Tanzania
Canada	Jamaica
Australia	Trinidad and Tobago
New Zealand	Uganda
India	Kenya
Pakistan	Malawi
Ceylon	Malta G.C.
Ghana	Zambia
Malaysia	Singapore
Nigeria	Barbados
Sierra Leone	Mauritius

Secretary: A. R. Tron

The Commonwealth Committee on Mineral Processing was formed in 1960 to encourage closer co-operation among those engaged in mineral processing and related activities throughout the Commonwealth.

This Committee promotes collaboration and interchange of information within the Commonwealth through the circulation of research programmes, interesting unpublished reports, details of staff and specialised equipment at mineral processing research establishments in member countries. It also encourages the interchange of staff among the various Commonwealth organisations active in the field of mineral processing.

The Committee publishes annually *Commonwealth Mineral Processing News* which reports the nature and progress of research being carried out in collaborating research organisations in the Commonwealth together with a biennial Directory of Mineral Processing Research Organisations in the Commonwealth.

Membership of C.C.M.P. is open to all member countries of the Commonwealth Scientific Committee.

COMMONWEALTH COMMITTEE ON MINERAL RESOURCES AND GEOLOGY

Africa House, Kingsway, London WC2B 6BD (01–405 7786/7)

Chairman: Dr K. C. Dunham

Members:

Britain	Tanzania
Canada	Jamaica
Australia	Trinidad and Tobago
New Zealand	Uganda
India	Kenya
Pakistan	Malawi
Ceylon	Malta G.C.
Ghana	Zambia
Malaysia	Singapore
Nigeria	Barbados
Sierra Leone	Mauritius

Secretary: R. F. Thyer

A Committee of the British Commonwealth Scientific Official Conference in 1946* recommended that a Commonwealth organisation be established to promote collaboration and the exchange of information in the field of Mineral Resources and Geology. A Specialist Conference in 1948 led to the setting up of permanent machinery in the form of the Commonwealth Committee on Mineral Resources and Geology. A Commonwealth Geological Liaison Office was set up in 1950 under the control of a serving officer of a Commonwealth Geological Survey. This officer acts as Secretary to the Committee and carries out liaison duties for all member countries. His office is housed in the Commonwealth Scientific Liaison Offices.

Membership is open to the member countries of the Commonwealth Scientific Committee.

---

* British Commonwealth Scientific Official Conference, London 1946. Report of Proceedings, Cmd. 6970.

COMMONWEALTH CONSULTATIVE SPACE RESEARCH COMMITTEE

c/o The Royal Society (Executive Secretary: Sir David Martin, CBE),

6 Carlton House Terrace, London S.W.1 (01–839 5561)

Chairman: Sir Harrie Massey, Sec RS

National Correspondents:

Canada: National Research Council
Australia: Commonwealth Scientific and Industrial Research Organisation
New Zealand: Dominion Physical Laboratory
India: National Committee for Space Research

Pakistan: Space and Upper Atmosphere Research Committee
Ghana: Academy of Science
Nigeria: The University of Ibadan
Ceylon: Institute of Scientific and Industrial Research

In August 1960 all Commonwealth countries were invited to send representatives to a meeting arranged by the British National Committee on Space Research with the support of the Commonwealth Scientific Committee; and at that meeting it was decided to form the Commonwealth Consultative Space Research Committee as a permanent scientific committee for the purpose of furthering Commonwealth co-operation in the field of space research. This field may be defined as that in which rocket and satellite vehicles are employed to carry out scientific experiments within and beyond the Earth's atmosphere in the area of research normally covered by astronomy, geophysics, atmospheric physics and geodesy, and includes the investigation into problems relating to the Earth's environment in the solar system.

The Committee is of a consultative nature and its function is to consider and initiate proposals, to work out details of co-operative enterprises and to serve as a centre for the exchange of information. Its chairman is Sir Harrie Massey, Quain Professor of Physics of University College, London, who is also chairman of the British National Committee on Space Research, a committee appointed by the Royal Society. The Committee normally meets when other international meetings bring Commonwealth representatives together at a common centre.

To date, co-operative rocket launchings have been carried out at the Sonmiani range in Pakistan using American rockets carrying British grenade payloads*. A Commonwealth collaborative programme of rocket launchings is being conducted under the sponsorship of the Science Research Council to provide an extensive survey of the upper atmosphere. The programme is intended to cover a wide latitude range and the first campaign of this programme, using small *Skua* rockets containing experiments to obtain scientific data on the D region of the ionosphere, was carried out in early 1970 at the Thumba range in India in association with similar rockets and payloads launched from the South Uist range in the Outer Hebrides. The programme is building up and campaigns using *Petrel* and *Skua* rockets are planned for the winter of 1971/72 at both Thumba and Sonmiani ranges. The proposed experiments will include measurements of electric and magnetic field strengths, and neutral atmosphere phenomena.

---

* The rocket grenade technique enables atmospheric temperature, pressure, density and wind structure up to approximately 100 km to be determined by acoustical and optical ground observations of detonations and gas clouds from grenades ejected from rockets in flight.

COMMONWEALTH CORRESPONDENTS' ASSOCIATION

President: J. C. Essilfie-Conduah (Ghana)
Vice-President: W. G. Matters (Canada)
Hon. Secretary: S. Kabadi (India)
Hon. Treasurer: W. H. Martin (India)

The address of the Hon. Secretary is
2/3 Salisbury Court, London E.C.4 (FLEet Street 2433)

The Commonwealth Correspondents' Association was founded in 1939 to secure recognition and facilities for Commonwealth press representatives in London in the difficulties of war-time conditions. According to its Constitution the Association exists 'to safeguard and promote the rights and interests of its members'.

The Association holds regular monthly meetings and press conferences to bring the members together for the discussion of questions affecting their interests or to hear some prominent guest speaker. The Association's Executive Committee comprises representatives of member-countries of the Commonwealth.

COMMONWEALTH COUNTRIES' LEAGUE

President of Honour: Dame Margery I. Corbett Ashby, DBE
President: Mrs Alice Hemming (Canada)
Vice-Presidents:

Mrs Nesta Patrick (Trinidad and Tobago)	Dame Joan Vickers, DBE, MP
Baroness White	Miss D. D. Solomon
Senator Thérèse Casgrain (Canada)	Mrs Laurel Casinader (Ceylon)
Miss Amy Kane, OBE (New Zealand)	Mrs Priscilla Abwao (Kenya)
Rt Hon. Lakshmi Menon (India) .	Mrs Sugra Visram, MP (Uganda)
Lady Ikramullah (Pakistan)	Princess Nakatindi, MP (Zambia)
Miss Chave Collinson, MA	Mrs Kelfa Caulker (Sierra Leone)
Chief T. Ayo Manuwa, OBE (Nigeria)	Miss Ruby Rich, MBE (Australia)
Mrs G. Adu (Ghana)	Mrs D. Lightbourne, JP (Jamaica)
H.E. Dame Hilda Bynoe, DBE (Grenada)	Mrs T. H. Benjamin

Chairman: Mrs L. Holman
Hon. Treasurer: Miss T. Todd
General Secretary: Mrs G. Davies
The address of the General Secretary is:
62 Corringham Road, London N.W.11 (01-455 7802)

The Commonwealth Countries' League, formerly the British Commonwealth League, was founded in 1925 to co-ordinate in one organisation the work of the Overseas Committee of the International Alliance of Women for Suffrage and Equal Citizenship and the British Dominions Women Citizens' Union. It has affiliations throughout the Commonwealth with which it works closely as well as with individual women of all Commonwealth countries.

The League is non-party, but it recognises the value of political education and the open discussion of current affairs.

The aims of the League are:

To secure equality of liberties, status and opportunities between men and women within the Commonwealth.

(*a*) To link together organisations of women within the Commonwealth in agreement with the objects of the League.

(*b*) To promote the social and political education of women.

(*c*) To increase mutual understanding of common problems.

(*d*) To raise the status of women throughout the Commonwealth.

The work of the League is carried on by means of conferences and social gatherings which provide a meeting-ground for visitors to this country from the Commonwealth. Delegates from national and overseas organisations, meeting at these conferences, have opportunities of hearing leaders of thought and affairs from many parts of the world, thus gaining a wider and more intimate knowledge of the questions which affect the Commonwealth. The League works in close co-operation with other societies with kindred aims; it is represented on their committees; and it takes joint action with them by means of meetings and deputations.

Societies, both British and overseas, with similar aims may become affiliated to the League on payment of one guinea annually. These affiliated societies are entitled to appoint representatives to the Executive Committee of the League.

Individuals who are in agreement with the objects and work of the League are eligible for membership. Annual subscription in Britain, 15/–, Overseas, 10/–.

The Commonwealth Countries' League spends part of its income on entertaining as its guests women of the Commonwealth who are newcomers to this country. We invite them to regular monthly luncheons where they may meet Commonwealth women who are active in the community and hear good speakers from all parts of the Commonwealth.

Further, the League pays the fees of selected girls in Commonwealth Countries where secondary education is not altogether free, so that promising students who could not otherwise afford to do so, may stay at school. A candidate for such sponsorship must be nominated and approved by a representative non-political women's organisation (preferably an affiliate of the C.C.L.), in the girl's own country.

At the same time the League encourages the formation and/or strengthening of such free associations of women in each of the Commonwealth countries, to raise their own status and to work for the good of their families, their community, their country, and the larger family of the Commonwealth.

COMMONWEALTH DEVELOPMENT CORPORATION

33 Hill Street, London W1A 3AR (01–629 8484)

Chairman: Lord Howick of Glendale, GCMG, KCVO
General Manager: Sir William Rendell

The CDC was established by Act of Parliament in 1948 to assist the economic development of dependent territories of the Commonwealth. The original and subsequent Acts setting out the Corporation's functions and responsibilities were consolidated in the Overseas Resources Development Act, 1959.

The Commonwealth Development Act, 1963, restored CDC's full powers of operation in all those Commonwealth countries which had achieved independence since the date of CDC's establishment in 1948 and changed the name from Colonial Development Corporation to Commonwealth Development Corporation. The Overseas Resources Development Act 1969, enacted on 25th July, enables CDC with Ministerial approval to operate in any other country outside the United Kingdom.

The Corporation has powers to undertake either alone, or in association with others, projects for the promotion or expansion of a wide range of enterprises, including agriculture, forestry, fisheries, mining, factories, electricity and water undertakings, transport, housing, hotels, building and engineering.

The 1969 Act increased CDC's long-term borrowing powers from £150m. to £225m. and permits this limit to be further raised by Order to £260m. The ceiling on outstanding advances to the Corporation from U.K. Exchequer funds was also raised to £205m. with provision for further increase by Order to £240m.

At the end of 1970 the corporation had outstanding about £131 million in advances from the Exchequer. It had 189 projects in Africa, the Caribbean and East Asia and the Pacific Islands, with an estimated commitment of some £171·6 million. About half its commitments were for basic developments such as power, water, housing and transport; 19·2 per cent were in agriculture, ranching, forestry and minerals, and 30·5 per cent in factories and industrial and property development companies. Alongside the loans for public utility (infra-structure) purposes, CDC investment is increasingly directed to projects which involve association with, and support of, the people collectively and individually, in the countries in which it operates. These projects include smallholder schemes in agriculture (probably attached to nucleus estates), local development companies for industry and mortgage companies for the prospective house purchaser.

Typical project commitments are: public utility loans: £15 million to Central African Power Corporation (Kariba hydro-electric scheme), £5·4 million to National Electricity Board (Malaysia), £3·7 million to Tana River Development Co. Ltd (Kenya), £2·8 million to Tanzania Electric Supply Co. Ltd, £2·7 million to the East African Power and Lighting Co. Ltd, £2·3 million to Electricity Supply Commission of Malawi and £1·8 million to Guma Valley Water Company (Sierra Leone); industrial investments: £7·1 million in Usutu Pulp Co. Ltd (Swaziland), £1·3 million in Chilanga Cement Ltd (Zambia); agricultural estates: £7·3 million in Swaziland Irrigation Scheme, £5·5 million in BAL Estates Ltd (Sabah); agricultural smallholder schemes: £1·9 million (excluding factories) in Kenya Tea Development Authority, £262,000 in Vuvulane Irrigated Farms (Swaziland); transport: £4·4 million Swaziland Railway; development companies: £2 million in Northern Nigeria Investments Ltd and £1 million in Jurong Town Corporation (Singapore), commitments to development companies in Kenya (£1 million), Uganda (£800,000) and Tanzania (£533,000); house mortgage companies: £8·8 million in Caribbean Housing Finance Corporation Ltd (Jamaica), £2·1 million in Malaysia Barat Building Society Ltd, £2·8 million in Trinidad and Tobago Mortgage Finance Co. Ltd and several million pounds in housing development and mortgage finance companies in Guyana, Barbados and the East Caribbean islands.

COMMONWEALTH DEVELOPMENT FINANCE COMPANY LTD.

1 Union Court, Old Broad Street, London E.C. 2 (01–283 9571)

Chairman: Sir George Bolton, KCMG
Managing Director: B. Berkoff
Secretary: D. A. Wighton

Commonwealth Development Finance Company Limited, (CDFC), is a private enterprise institution. Established in 1953 CDFC is not now necessarily confined to the Commonwealth. It aims to support worthwhile business enterprise wherever this can thrive, especially where CDFC funds and experience can do most good. Its present authorised capital is £30 million, of which £26·3 million has been issued. The issued shares consist of 14·59 million 'A' shares of £1 each (10p paid) and 11·74 million 'B' shares of £1 each (50p paid). The 'A' shares are held by a number of industrial, shipping, mining and banking companies with extensive Commonwealth interests. The 'B' shares are held by the Bank of England and certain Commonwealth and other central banks. The company's paid up capital of £7·3 million is supplemented by extensive borrowings. It has issued £13·5 million debentures and has a substantial borrowing facility with the London clearing banks.

CDFC has seven subsidiaries: CDFC Holdings Ltd, of Toronto, Canada; CDFC Australia Ltd, of Melbourne, CDFC New Guinea Pty Ltd, of Port Moresby; Development Finance International Ltd of Bermuda; and CDFC (Ceylon) Ltd, CFDC (Malaysia) Ltd, and CDFC International Ltd, all of London.

Up to the end of March 1970 CDFC had investments in nearly 100 undertakings. They were spread over a wide range of industry in 27 different countries and had a book value of nearly £27 million. All these commitments were in development projects, mainly those conducted by private enterprise. The company's portfolio covers a wide variety of manufacturing and other productive activities including many kinds of engineering, textiles, cement, fertilisers, pulp and paper, timber, sugar, rubber, tea, processing of agricultural products, and public utilities.

CDFC will provide finance by way of share capital and loans, on a mutually acceptable basis, tailored to the needs of the particular situation.

COMMONWEALTH ECONOMIC CONSULTATIVE COUNCIL

The Commonwealth Trade and Economic Conference held in Montreal in September 1958 agreed to co-ordinate the existing economic consultative machinery of the Commonwealth under the name of the Commonwealth Economic Consultative Council. At the highest level the Council would consist of the Finance and Economic Ministers of the Commonwealth Countries, who would meet together whenever circumstances demanded: the Council would incorporate various channels and bodies through which economic consultation took place and any further bodies that might be set up from time to time on a temporary or permanent basis: meetings at high official level might also be held as necessary to prepare for the meetings of Ministers.

It has become customary for the Council to meet at the level of Finance Ministers each year before the meetings of the International Monetary Fund and the International Bank for Reconstruction and Development, and these meetings are sometimes preceded by meetings of the Council at official level. In 1966 there was also a meeting of the Council at the level of Commonwealth Trade Ministers, preceded by two meetings of the Council at the level of trade officials in order to prepare for the ministerial meeting.

The Council has no permanent headquarters and may meet by arrangement in any Commonwealth country. Its meetings are serviced by the Commonwealth Secretariat.

COMMONWEALTH EDUCATION LIAISON COMMITTEE

Marlborough House, Pall Mall, London S.W.1 (01–839 3411)

Members:

Australia: D. W. Hood
Barbados: F. Brewster
Botswana: B. M. Setshogo
Britain and Dependent Territories: J. Mark
Canada: D. M. Miller
Ceylon: S. Gautamadasa
Cyprus: Dr P. N. Vanezis
Fiji: Mrs A. Dreunamisimisi
The Gambia: O. A. Sallah
Ghana: W. L. Tsitsiwu
Guyana: P. A. Thierens
India: A. J. Kidwai
Jamaica: Mrs H. Y. Turriff
Kenya: P. Mubuta
Lesotho: T. E. Ntlhakana
Malawi: C. M. Mkona
Malaysia: ChangMing Kee
Malta: M. J. Lubrano

Mauritius: L. P. Ramyead
New Zealand: A. C. Doyle
Nigeria: C. C. Uchuno
Pakistan: T. A Khan
Sierra Leone: E. J. Gabbidon
Singapore: Nt Kwee Choo
Swaziland: E. B. Magagula
Tanzania: L. M. Swei
Tonga: D. Tupou
Trinidad and Tobago: C. C. Alleyne
Uganda: J. C. Katuram u
Zambia: S. H. Njelesani

Associated States:
R. A. C. Shillingford

Sir Hugh Springer
Sir Douglas Logan

Members:
Chairman: H. L. Elvin
Secretary: Y. K. Lule

The Commonwealth Education Liaison Committee was set up in 1959 as the result of a recommendation by the First Commonwealth Education Conference held at Oxford in 1959 and was established on a permanent basis by the Second Commonwealth Education Conference at New Delhi in January 1962.

The Committee provides a forum for consideration of matters of principle arising out of the schemes of Commonwealth co-operation in education agreed upon at Commonwealth Education Conferences; and undertakes other functions to supplement normal bilateral arrangements between member Governments and to develop and improve Commonwealth co-operation in education.

The Commonwealth Education Liaison Unit (*see Commonwealth Office Year Book* 1967) which served as the Secretariat of the C.E.L.C. was integrated with the Commonwealth Secretariat on 1st April 1967 to form its Education Division. Integration with the Commonwealth Secretariat had been recommended by the Review Committee on Intra-Commonwealth Organisations and approved by Commonwealth Prime Ministers at their Meeting in London in 1966.

THE COMMONWEALTH ENGINEERING CONFERENCE

Secretariat: The Council of Engineering Institutions, 2 Little Smith Street, London S.W.1

Conference Secretary: Mr M. W. Leonard, BSc(Eng), CEng, FICE, MIMechE

The Institution of Engineers, Australia
The Institution of Engineers, Ceylon
The Institution of Engineers (India)
The New Zealand Institution of Engineers
The Institution of Engineers (Singapore)
The Institution of Engineers, Jamaica
The Ghana Institution of Engineers
The Association of Professional Engineers of Trinidad and Tobago

The Engineering Institute of Canada
The East African Institution of Engineers
The Institution of Engineers, Malaysia
The Institute of Engineers, Pakistan
The Council of Engineering Institutions (U.K.)
The Engineering Institution of Zambia

Associated Institutions:
The Institution of Civil Engineers (U.K.)
The Institution of Electrical Engineers (U.K.)
The Institution of Mechanical Engineers (U.K.)
The Institution of Chemical Engineers (U.K.)
*The Rhodesian Institution of Engineers
The Federation of Societies of Professional
Engineers, South Africa

The Commonwealth Engineering Conference came into being through the initiative of the Councils of three British Engineering Institutions—the Institution of Civil Engineers, the Institution of Mechanical Engineers and the Institution of Electrical Engineers—who, in 1946, sent invitations to the sister Engineering Institutions of the Commonwealth for their Presidents and Secretaries to attend as their guests a meeting in London in the autumn of that year. When the representatives met in London they unanimously supported the view that the bonds between the Engineering Institutions of the Commonwealth, which had been strengthened during the war years, should be consolidated and placed on a more permanent footing; and proposals designed to effect this were agreed by all the participating Councils.

The Conference meets every four years, the last Meeting having taken place in India in November 1969. It is essentially an advisory body. Its Meetings provide an opportunity for the Presidents and Secretaries of the participating Institutions to exchange views on the methods by which the Institutions they represent can best work together to further the aims for which they are severally constituted; and they also enable close personal contacts to be established. It is an International Member of the World Federation of Engineering Organisations.

COMMONWEALTH FORESTRY ASSOCIATION
(*Constituted under Royal Charter in* 1921)

18 Northumberland Avenue, London W.C.2 (01–930 7209)

President: His Grace The Duke of Buccleuch and Queensberry, PC, KT, GCVO
Chairman of Governing Council: Sir Arthur Gosling, KBE, CB
Vice-Chairman of Governing Council: Professor M. V. Laurie, CBE
Editor and Secretary: E. W. March, MA

The objects of the Association are to foster public interest in forestry, secure general recognition of the dependence of timber supply upon forest management, collect and circulate information relating to forestry and the commercial utilisation of forest products, form a centre for all engaged in forestry, and provide a means of communication between all concerned. The Association also seeks to secure general recognition of the beneficial influence of trees and forests in relation to climate and of the need to conserve land and water resources as well as wild life. It welcomes as members all who are interested in forestry and forest industries in the Commonwealth and elsewhere.

The management of the Association is, subject to the control of the general meeting, in the hands of the Governing Council, a body limited to the President, Chairman, Vice-Chairman and to 45 representatives of Britain and other

---

* See Southern Rhodesia chapter in Part V of this Year Book

Members of the Commonwealth. One-third of the members of the Council retire each year, but are eligible for re-election. An Executive Committee of 12 members of the Governing Council is appointed annually, and other committees dealing with technical matters are appointed as occasion requires. Contact is maintained with the various regions of the Commonwealth through local honorary secretaries.

Publications of the Association include the *Commonwealth Forestry Review* (quarterly), the *Commonwealth Forestry Handbook*, and the *British Commonwealth Forestry Terminology*, Parts I and II.

COMMONWEALTH FORESTRY CONFERENCE AND THE STANDING COMMITTEE ON COMMONWEALTH FORESTRY

Office of the Forestry Commission, 25 Savile Row,
London W1X 2AY (01-734 0221)

Standing Committee:
Director-General, Forestry Commission of Great Britain
Director, Commonwealth Forestry Institute, Oxford
Director, Commonwealth Forestry Bureau, Oxford
Director, Forest Products Research Laboratory of the Ministry of Technology,
Princes Risborough
Representative of the Commonwealth Forestry Association
Representative of Ministry of Overseas Development (who also represents Dependent
Territories)
Representative of the Commonwealth Secretariat
Representative of the Government of Northern Ireland
One Representative from each Commonwealth Country
Secretary: Miss M. J. Eden

The Conference meets periodically, usually quinquennially, to discuss questions of forest policy in the Commonwealth and the wider technical aspects of forestry. Owing to the war there was a gap of twelve years between the meeting in South Africa in 1935 and the meeting in Britain in 1947. The ninth Conference was held in New Delhi from 3rd to 27th January 1968.

The functions of the Standing Committee are:

(*i*) To take appropriate follow-up action on all Conference resolutions.

(*ii*) To provide continuity between one Conference and another, including liaison with host countries in pre-Conference planning.

(*iii*) To provide a forum for discussion on any forestry matters of common interest to member Governments which may be brought to the Committee's notice by any member country or organisation; and to that end an inter-Conference meeting could be arranged at the time of the appropriate biennial F.A.O. Conference in Rome.

COMMONWEALTH FORESTRY INSTITUTE,
UNIVERSITY OF OXFORD

Telephone: Oxford 57891

The Commonwealth Forestry Institute building accommodates the University Department of Forestry which carries out teaching, research and advanced study of subjects related to Forestry. The Department is financed by the University of Oxford, with contributions for specific research purposes from Member Governments of the Commonwealth, and from Research Councils and other grant-giving bodies. It provides teaching for undergraduates and graduates (including that for forest officers of the Commonwealth), and supervision of candidates for research degrees such as DPhil, BLitt, etc. Research in the Institute concerns biological, sylvicultural, economic and managerial problems related to forestry and includes pathology and virology and the study of pests and their control. It carries out examination and identification of timbers, identification of trees and the compilation of forest floras and botanical and sylvicultural monographs. It advises on sampling, surveys of resources, experimental methods, computer programming and provides a computer service for Commonwealth Forest Departments. Much, but by no means all the work concerns tropical forestry. In the Institute the departmental library, the forest herbarium and the collection of wood specimens are amongst the most comprehensive in the world and are much used by visiting scholars. The Commonwealth Forestry Bureau, which is also housed in the Institute, is an official abstracting service which produces the quarterly journal "Forestry Abstracts".

COMMONWEALTH FOUNDATION

Marlborough House, Pall Mall, S.W.1 (01-930 3783-5)

Chairman: Robert K. Gardiner
Director: John Chadwick, CMG

At their meeting in 1965 Commonwealth Prime Ministers decided to establish a Commonwealth Foundation to administer a fund for increasing interchanges between Commonwealth organisations in professional fields throughout the Commonwealth. They directed that the British Government should draw up the necessary documents to set up the Trust and to constitute the Foundation as a legal charity.

They also agreed that the Foundation, as an autonomous body, should have the following aims:

(*a*) To encourage and support fuller representation at conferences of professional bodies within the Commonwealth.

(*b*) To assist professional bodies within the Commonwealth to hold more conferences between themselves.

(*c*) To facilitate the exchange of visits among professional people, especially the younger element.

(*d*) To stimulate and increase the flow of professional information exchanged between the organisations concerned.

(*e*) On request to assist with the setting up of national institutions or associations in countries where these do not at present exist.

(*f*) To promote the growth of Commonwealth-wide associations or regional Commonwealth associations in order to reduce the present centralisation in Britain.

(*g*) To consider exceptional requests for help from associations and individuals whose activities lie outside the strictly professional field but fall within the general ambit of the Foundation's operations as outlined above.

To promote these aims Commonwealth Member Governments initially agreed to subscibe pro rata to an annual income of £250,000. Of this sum the British Government undertook to contribute half.

The Heads of Government also agreed that the policy of the Foundation should be directed by a Chairman, who should be a distinguished private citizen of a Commonwealth Member country. The first Chairman to be selected was the Australian Nobel Prize Winner, Sir Macfarlane Burnet, OM. He was succeeded in January 1970 by Mr Robert Gardiner of Ghana, Executive Secretary, Economic Commission for Africa. To fill the post of full-time Director, Commonwealth Governments nominated Mr John Chadwick, formerly of the Foreign and Commonwealth Office. The Director is responsible to a Board of Trustees, each subscribing government having the right to nominate one member to the Board. These nominees, even if officials, are appointed in a peronal capacity. The Commonwealth Secretariat, with which the Foundation works in close liaison, is also represented on the Board of Trustees by the Secretary-General or an officer appointed by him.

The Foundation came into being on 1st March 1966. At an initial meeting of the Trustees in June of that year it was confirmed that dependent territories throughout the Commonwealth would be eligible for assistance and that on achieving independence new member countries would automatically become eligible to join the organisation subject to payment of the appropriate subscription and to the appointment of a Trustee. Twenty-eight Commonwealth Governments currently contribute to the Foundation's income. This, following a decision taken at the Heads of Government Conference in Singapore in January 1971, now stands at £350,000 per annum.

The Commonwealth Foundation is now close on six years old. Its Board meets in plenary session thrice yearly. To assist the Board in handling day to day work, a Sub-committee of five Trustees, empowered to authorise minor grants, has been established. Three Progress Reports, the latest reviewing the period 1966/71 and over a dozen 'Occasional Papers' have been published. In June 1970, the Foundation also issued through Hutchinsons of London 'Professional Organisations in the Commonwealth' (price £4·50), a comprehensive guide to close on 1,200 professional and learned societies. Grants awarded by the Board of Trustees now total upwards of £1½ million. To date, the Director, whose initial appointment has been extended for a further five-year period as from July 1971, has visited all but two of the Commonwealth Member countries and a number of dependent territories.

COMMONWEALTH FRIENDSHIP MOVEMENT

Kingscliffe House, 139-G Marine Parade, Brighton 7, Sussex (Brighton 685211)

President: (Vacant)

Vice-President: The High Commissioners for Canada, Australia, New Zealand, India, Pakistan, Ceylon, Ghana, Nigeria, Sierra Leone and Uganda

Committee:

Geoffrey Johnson Smith	L. Nkurunziza, Uganda
J. H. Bramley	Miss P. Stephens, Nigeria
John Fraser, West Indies	Bernard Hayhoe
M. T. Hyde	D. E. T. Decker, Sierra Leone
A. Melville-Brown	Miss Stella Monk, MBE

Chairman: Geoffrey Johnson Smith
Hon. Treasurer: J. H. Bramley
Director: Miss Stella Monk, MBE

The Movement exists to spread knowledge of the peoples of the Commonwealth and other countries among teachers and children, through school links and individual correspondence. The range for school links is Infant to Secondary. Schools wishing to participate should supply their full name and address, age group, number of pupils and whether girls, boys or mixed. Individual applicants for pen-friends should give their name and address, age and particulars of hobbies and interests. The age range is 9-18. Class links may be made. The only restriction is language: most countries teach English in schools from the age of 14 but under that age only Commonwealth pen friends are available. No charge is made but stamped/addressed envelopes are welcomed.

COMMONWEALTH INDUSTRIES ASSOCIATION LTD

60 Buckingham Gate, London S.W.1 (01-834 4688)

Chairman: The Rt Hon. Robin Turton, MC, MP
Director: Edward Holloway
Secretary: Miss H. Packer
Parliamentary Committee:
Chairman: Sir Ronald Russell, MP
Vice-Chairman: Sir Harmar Nicholls, Bt, JP, MP
Joint Hon. Secretaries: Michael Clark Hutchison, MP; John Farr, MP

The Association was founded in 1926 as the Empire Industries Association, merged with the British Empire League in 1947 and became a company limited by guarantee in 1967. Its affairs are managed by a Council elected by the members. The Association maintains close contact with both Houses of Parliament through a Parliamentary Committee.

The aims are: to strengthen the Commonwealth by means of mutual preferential trade, capital investment, migration and technical and scientific co-operation; to maintain free enterprise as the basis of the United Kingdom's power to compete in world markets; to strengthen the Sterling Area; to ensure a continuing market for Commonwealth goods, foodstuffs and raw materials in the United Kingdom and a corresponding market for United Kingdom goods in all parts of the Commonwealth; to aid the newer Commonwealth nations to develop their own resources; to encourage Commonwealth shipping and air services; to protect United Kingdom industry and agriculture from unfair foreign competition and thus to ensure full employment.

A panel of lecturers and speakers address audiences on these subjects throughout Britain. *Britain and Overseas*, a bi-monthly journal, is sent to members and subscribers and has a wide circulation at home and overseas.

The Association depends entirely on voluntary funds.

COMMONWEALTH INFORMATION CENTRE
Commonwealth Secretariat, Marlborough House, Pall Mall, S.W.1.
(01–839 3411)

The Commonwealth Secretariat maintains an Information Centre and Reading Room on the ground floor of the West Wing of Marlborough House. It is open to the public from 10 a.m. to 5 p.m., Monday to Fridays, throughout the year except during major conferences. The Centre will answer enquiries about the Commonwealth and inter-governmental activities and has, for free distribution, a variety of publications dealing with the Commonwealth.

COMMONWEALTH INSTITUTE

Kensington High Street, London W8 6NQ (01-602 3252)

Chairman of Governors: The Rt Hon. The Lord Garner, GCMG
Director: J. K. Thompson, CMG
Deputy Director: Mrs M. E. Burke
Establishment and Finance Officer: E. E. Crowhurst
Curator: J. H. Swain
Public Relations Officer: J. R. Turner
Chief Education Officer: N. G. Barnett
Librarian: A. J. Horne

The Commonwealth Institute is the successor to the Imperial Institute which was erected at South Kensington as the National and Empire Memorial of the Golden Jubilee of Queen Victoria, by whom it was opened in May 1893. It was renamed Commonwealth Institute by Act of Parliament in 1958 and moved into its present building in High Street, Kensington in 1962.

The original objects of the Imperial Institute were: to promote the utilisation of the commercial and industrial resources of the Empire by the chemical and technical investigation of raw materials and the supply of information relating to such materials and their production; to maintain a comprehensive exhibition illustrating the life, scenery and progress of all the countries of the Empire; and to organise other services designed to spread a knowledge of the life and work of its peoples.

The Institute was an independent organisation governed by Royal Charter until 1902 when a Resolution of the Governing Body that it should become a national property was accepted by the Government, responsibility for management being entrusted to the Board of Trade. In 1907 this responsibility was transferred to the Colonial Office. In 1923 there was a Committee of Enquiry, the result of which was the Imperial Institute Act of 1925, which again transferred control, this time to the Department of Overseas Trade. In 1949 the scientific side of the Institute's work was taken over by the Colonial Office, and the functions of the Institute became purely educational. In 1949, by Order in Council, its control was again transferred, this time to the Ministry of Education. In 1950 another Committee of Enquiry was set up under Lord Tweedsmuir. It reported in 1952 and made far-reaching recommendations for the reorganisation and expansion of the Institute 'to serve as a Commonwealth forum and further mutual understanding amongst the members of the Commonwealth countries by providing facilities for the presentation and exchange of ideas and information'. In July 1953 the Board of Governors was reconstituted by Order in Council under an independent Chairman, the late Viscount Hudson, with a mandate to consider the Tweedsmuir Report and to advise the Minister on the future development of the Institute. During that year a vigorous programme of reconstruction of the gallery exhibitions was put in hand, the emphasis changing from products to people. The name was changed by the Commonwealth Institute Act, 1958. The present Chairman of Governors is Lord Garner, GCMG, and all the Member countries of the Commonwealth are represented on the Board by their High Commissioners in London. In addition, representatives of educational, Commonwealth, commercial and other relevant interests are appointed to the Governing Body by the responsible Minister who is now the Secretary of State for Foreign and Commonwealth Affairs.

The Act of 1958, besides changing the name, authorised the transfer of the Institute to a new building designed to house its exhibitions and educational activities more appropriately and conveniently. This building, completed in the autumn of 1962 and opened by the Queen on 6th November, occupies a $3\frac{1}{4}$ acre site in Kensington High Street immediately to the south of Holland Park. Essentially functional and entirely modern in conception, the new Institute attempts to express visually the Commonwealth of today. Provided by the British Government, the building also incorporates many gifts in kind from other Commonwealth Governments and commercial and industrial sources. The result is regarded as one of London's most impressive examples of contemporary architecture. The distinctive feature is the diamond-shaped main block with its hyperbolic paraboloid roof sheathed with copper from Zambia. This structure accommodates, on three floors, the permanent exhibitions which illustrate, country by country, the life and environment of all the Commonwealth peoples. The cost of these permanent exhibitions is borne by the individual Commonwealth Governments. The individual exhibits are, of course, extremely varied, but among them is a range of dioramas which is almost certainly the finest to be found anywhere in the world.

In a wing adjoining the exhibition galleries there are, besides the administrative offices, a cinema/theatre, an art gallery, a library, a licensed restaurant and a large reception area (The Jehangir Room). The cinema offers programmes, changed weekly, of Commonwealth news and interest films. It is also available in the evenings for entertainments by actors, singers and dancers from Commonwealth countries. The art gallery houses a regular series of temporary exhibitions of the work of Commonwealth artists.

The Institute is open free to the public from 10 a.m. to 5.30 p.m. on weekdays and from 2.30 to 6 p.m. on Sundays. Film shows are given in the cinema at 12.15, 1.15 and 3 p.m. on weekdays, 2.45, 3.30 and 4.25 p.m. on Saturdays and at 3, 3.50 and 4.40 p.m. on Sundays.

The education activities of the Institute are designed to promote knowledge of the peoples of the Commonwealth especially among students and pupils in colleges and schools. Every year well over 100,000 schoolchildren in organised groups visit the exhibition galleries for lessons, many of which are given by the Institute's own teaching staff. Among the many visiting parties are groups of student teachers who come to learn about the facilities of the Institute and to attend short courses in the techniques of museum teaching. A service of Talks to Schools operates throughout the British Isles, and in 1970 7,183 such talks reached a total audience of 600,000. Conferences and courses (72 in 1970) are organised for practising teachers, students in colleges of education and for senior pupils of all types of secondary students. Lectures for senior pupils in secondary schools and students in colleges of education and technology are arranged singly or in series, and the Institute provides specialist lecturers. Teaching aids on loan to teachers and students include filmstrips, slides and tape recordings and also such material as booklets, pictures and samples of products.

Field study courses in overseas Commonwealth countries and educational cruises are organised to provide opportunities of study in greater depth. In 1969 they included a four-week course in South India and Ceylon for 80 teachers and lecturers, and a four-week cruise to the Eastern Caribbean for over 1,000 sixth formers and their teachers. A further cruise to the West Indies was arranged in 1970, this time going west to include Jamaica.

The Institute's Library covers all aspects of the Commonwealth today and of its individual members. Its stock includes many books and journals published in other Commonwealth countries which are not readily available in libraries in Britain. Graded reading lists on the countries of the Commonwealth and on Commonwealth topics are available on request.

The Library is open to the public for reference and provides a loan service to teachers, students in colleges of education and other students at sixth-form level and above. In addition to normal loan facilities, small collections of books will be assembled at the request of those engaged on more intensive study, and issued on extended loan.

A fully illustrated handbook and guide describing the Institute and its educational functions is available at a cost of $17\frac{1}{2}$p from the Institute's bookstall. The bookstall stocks a wide variety of reasonably priced material including pictures, maps, books and booklets and a series of miniature flags of the Commonwealth. A leaflet describing the Education Services is available free of charge.

The Commonwealth Institute, Scotland, with premises at 8 Rutland Square, Edinburgh, is responsible for the work in that country. It operates in harmony with the broad policy determined by the Board of Governors of the Institute in London, but it has its own independent Committee under the Chairmanship of Sir James Henderson, KBE, CMG, who is also a member of the Board in London.

COMMONWEALTH LIAISON COMMITTEE

The Commonwealth Liaison Committee was originally established in 1948 to supplement the existing inter-governmental channels for keeping Commonwealth countries fully informed on matters connected with the European Recovery Programme. From 1949 onwards its functions were expanded so as to cover discussion of financial and economic problems of general interest for all Commonwealth countries. Early in 1955 the Committee took over the remaining functions of the former Sterling Area Statistical Committee. The Commonwealth Liaison Committee does not formulate policy, but provides a forum for the exchange of information on economic matters. As an exception to this, in 1964 the Commonwealth Prime Ministers agreed that the Committee should consider proposals about Commonwealth development projects, administrative training, higher education, the Commonwealth Medical Conference, the Commonwealth Parliamentary Association, the Commonwealth Foundation and Satellite Communications. These proposals were reviewed by Commonwealth

Finance Ministers at their meeting in Kuala Lumpur in September 1964 and were subsequently pursued through other channels as appropriate.

All Commonwealth Governments are members of the Committee. In accordance with the memorandum on the Commonwealth Secretariat agreed by the Commonwealth Prime Ministers at their 1965 meeting, the Commonwealth Secretariat services meetings of the Committee, which take place at Marlborough House.

COMMONWEALTH MEDICAL ADVISORY BUREAU

British Medical Association House, Tavistock Square,

London W.C.1 (01–387 4499)

Medical Director: Dr A. B. Gilmour

The Bureau is maintained by the British Medical Association to welcome doctors visiting the United Kingdom from other parts of the Commonwealth and to give them advice and help during their stay. The Medical Director is assisted by an Advisory Committee which includes among its members representatives of Commonwealth High Commissioners in London and of societies and medical organisations interested in the welfare of the Commonwealth visitors.

The most frequent enquiries concern postgraduate medical education in all its aspects and doctors can be given information about courses of study or introduced to specialists in their own fields of work.

To avoid employment difficulties at a time when there is great competition for all available appointments, the doctor is advised to contact the Bureau well in advance.

COMMONWEALTH MEDICAL ASSOCIATION

British Medical Association House, Tavistock Square, London W.C.1

(01-387 4499)

Joint Presidents: Professor A. A. Sandosham; Dr Gwee Ah Leng
Vice-President: Professor D. E. C. Mekie, OBE
Hon. Secretary/Treasurer: Dr Derek Stevenson

The aims and objectives of the Commonwealth Medical Association are to promote within the Commonwealth the interests of the medical and allied sciences and to maintain the honour and traditions of the profession; to effect the closest possible links between its members; and to disseminate news and information of interest.

Membership is open to the national medical associations of the Commonwealth, and the Republic of Ireland.

The governing body of the Association is its Council to which each member Association is entitled to send one voting delegate.

The Association was formed during the course of the 7th British Commonwealth Medical Conference held in Colombo in November 1962. The Council of the Association meets biennially. In 1966 it decided to establish a Commonwealth Medical Association Travelling Fellowship. The Fellow appointed would be a distinguished physician or teacher who would be invited to visit a number of member Associations with three main purposes: (a) to promote the interests of the Association and to discuss common problems with member Associations; (b) to give lectures to professional meetings and (c) to collect information on behalf of the Council. In addition, the Council decided to continue the issue of periodical news letters edited by the Honorary Secretary/Treasurer, and to invite each member Association to appoint a Liaison Officer to facilitate communication and further the objects of the Commonwealth Medical Association.

THE COMMONWEALTH MIGRATION COUNCIL

60 Buckingham Gate, London S.W.1 (VICtoria 1646/7)

Executive Committee:
Chairman: Sir John Reiss, BEM
Joint Vice-Chairmen: Air Chief Marshal Sir Hugh Lloyd, GBE, KCB, MC, DFC;
Colonel The Lord Barnby, CMG, CBE, MVO;
John Biggs-Davison, MP; Nigel Fisher, MC, MP;
B. Godman-Irvine, MP; Brian Harrison, MP;
Malcolm MacPherson, MBE, MP;
The Lord Winterbottom; John Page, MP;
Miss Margaret Popham, CBE (Hon. Treasurer);
The Rt Hon. Sir David Renton, KBE, TD, QC, MP;
Hon. Secretary: Col. R. F. Wright
Organising Secretary: Dominic Le Foe

The Council was founded by Sir Clifford Heathcote Smith and a few friends shortly after the war and became a Company Limited by Guarantee in 1954.

Briefly, its purpose is to help increase the flow of British migrants to Canada, Australia and New Zealand and to strengthen the ties of the Commonwealth by expanding trade and economic development. It is a voluntary society and receives no grants-in-aid. Amongst its many activities the Council supplies speakers and lecturers, promotes public meetings and discussions, maintains a small reference section and from time to time convenes conferences for societies working in the same field. For the past twelve years it has run a Student Scheme whereby students from British universities are found vacation jobs in Canada, enabling them to stay and study at minimum expense. A *Newsletter* of statistical and economic data, together with comment of the Council, is published ten times a year. There is a strong Parliamentary membership of the Executive for the purpose of promoting Parliamentary interest in its aims and objects.

The Council monitors the Press, and takes steps to correct inaccurate articles relating to the success achieved by individual migrants.

Material is supplied to Press, Radio and TV sources, if the extent of the work justifies it, on a fee basis.

COMMONWEALTH PARLIAMENTARY ASSOCIATION

Houses of Parliament, London S.W.1 (01–930 6240 Ext. 520)

MEMBERS OF GENERAL COUNCIL 1970–71
Chairman: Hon. Tun Tan Siew Sin, SSM, JP, MP,
Minister of Finance, Malaysia
Immediate Past Chairman: Senator the Hon. Sir Alister McMullin, KCMG,
President of the Senate, Commonwealth of Australia
Honorary Treasurer: Mr B. Godman Irvine, MA, United Kingdom
Councillors appointed under Clause 24 of the Constitution:
Hon. M. O. Bash-Taqi, MP, Sierra Leone
Hon. P. A. Kisumo, MP, Minister for Regional Administration
and Development, Tanzania
Dr the Hon. G. S. Dhillon, MP, Speaker of the Lok Sabha, India

Branch Representatives

Australia: Commonwealth, Hon. P. R. Lynch, MP
States: Hon. T. W. Mitchell, MP (Victoria)
Barbados: Senator the Hon. F. G. Smith, QC
Botswana: Hon. M. P. K. Nwako, MP
Britain: Sir Alfred Broughton, MP
Mr B. Godman Irvine, MP
Canada: Federal, Hon. John N. Turner, PC, QC, MP
Provinces: Hon. F. M. Cass, QC, CD, MPP (Ontario)
Ceylon: Hon. S. Tillekeratne, MP; Mr S. Samarasekera, MP
The Gambia: Mr K. Krubally, MP
Ghana: Hon. B. K. Adama, MP; Mr S. A. Okudzeto, MP
Guyana: Hon. H. O. Jack, MP; Mr Derek C. Jagan, MP
India: Union, Shri P. Parthasarathy, MP
States: Shri B. K. Banerjee, MLA
Jamaica: Hon. Roy McNeill, MP; Mr W. O. Isaacs, MP
Kenya: Hon. I. E. Omolo Okero, MP; Hon. A. A. Ochwada, MP
Lesotho: (Branch in abeyance)
Malawi: Hon. A. M. Nyasulu, MP; Mr M. H. Blackwood, CBE, MP
Malaysia: Federal, Hon. Mohamed bin Ujang, AMN, PJK, MP
States: Hon. Tuan Haji Ahmad Razali bin Haji Mohd, Ali, AMN, MP
Malta: Dr the Hon. S. Abela, MP; Dr the Hon. F. Dingli, MP
Mauritius: Hon. K. Sunassee, MLA; Hon. J. H. Ythier, MLA

Nauru: Hon. Kenas Aroi, MP
New Zealand: Mr J. F. Luxton, MP; Mr R. J. Tizard, MP
Nigeria: (Branch in abeyance)
Pakistan: (Branch in abeyance)
Sierra Leone: Hon. J. J. O. Hadson-Taylor, MP; Hon. J. B. Francis, MP
Singapore: Mr Wee Toon Boon, MP; Mr N. Govindasamy, MP
Swaziland: Senator Chief J. M. Mamba
Tanzania: Mr A. S. Maskini, MP; Hon. P. A. Kisumo, MP
Trinidad & Tobago: Mr S. Shah, MP; Mr F. Blackman, MP
Uganda: (Branch in abeyance)
Western Samoa: Hon. Va'ai Kolone, MP
Zambia: Hon. K. H. Nkwabilo, MP; Mr C. Z. Hamusankwa, MP
Bahamas: Hon. A. D. Hanna, MHA
Bermuda: Hon. F. J. Barritt, MCP
Cook Islands: Hon. Tiakana Numanga, MLA
British Honduras, Grenada, St Lucia: Senator the Hon. Winston Whyte
Northern Ireland, Isle of Man, Jersey, Gibraltar: Senator W. H. Krichefski, OBE
Fiji, Northern Territory, Papua & New Guinea: Hon. Loloma I. Livingston, MLC
Dominica, St Vincent, Antigua, St Christopher-Nevis-Anguilla, Montserrat, British Virgin Islands, Cayman Islands: Hon. H. K. Tannis, MP

EXECUTIVE COMMITTEE OF THE GENERAL COUNCIL 1971

Chairman:
Hon. A. G. Montano, MP, Trinidad & Tobago

Ex-officio Members:
The Chairman of the General Council
The Vice-Chairman of the General Council (To be appointed)
The Immediate Past Chairman of the General Council
The Hon. Treasurer of the Association
The three Clause 24 Councillors
Sir Frederic Bennett, MP,
United Kingdom, Hon. Financial Adviser to the Association

Regional Representatives:
Africa: Hon. W. P. Nyirenda, MP, Minister of Education, Zambia.
Asia: Hon. F. R. D. Bandaranaike, MP, Minister of Home Affairs and Local Government, Ceylon.
Australasia: Mr W. F. Nankivell, MP, South Australia.
Canada: Mr J. E. Walker, MP, Canada
South East Asia: Hon. Tun Tan Siew Sin, SSM, JP, MP, Minister of Finance, Malaysia.
United Kingdom and Mediterranean: Hon. Dr Guido DeMarco, MP, Malta
West Indies, Central and South American Mainland:
Mr N. J. Bissember, MP, Guyana
Secretary-General: R. V. Vanderfelt, OBE,
Editor of Publications and Deputy Secretary-General: Ian Grey

The Commonwealth Parliamentary Association was founded at the Coronation of King George the Fifth in 1911 in order to facilitate the exchange of visits and information between those engaged in the parliamentary government of the countries of the Commonwealth. It began with six Branches in Britain and the Dominions and now has over ninety Branches in legislatures of the Commonwealth. These comprise Main Branches, Auxiliary Branches, Affiliated Branches and Subsidiary Branches, the Main Branches being those formed in the Parliaments of the self-governing nations of the Commonwealth, the Auxiliary Branches those in Commonwealth countries which are approaching full self-government, while the Affiliated Branches are mostly in territories which enjoy responsible or representative government or possess legislatures in which there is an 'unofficial majority' and the Subsidiary Branches mostly those in countries where there is still an official majority. There are also State Branches in the States of Australia and of Malaysia, and in the Regions of Nigeria (now in abeyance), and Provincial Branches in the Provinces of Canada, the States of India and the Provinces of Pakistan (now in abeyance).

The activities of the Association have kept pace with its increasing membership. The rooms of the Association in the Houses of Parliament at Westminster have become a meeting place for the legislators of the Commonwealth, and at the United Kingdom Branch in Westminster Hall visiting legislators are given parliamentary and other privileges and are enabled to meet Members of both Houses of the British Parliament. Similar privileges are provided by the Branches overseas to enable visiting legislators to meet and exchange views with their Members.

In the past parliamentary conferences of a plenary character were held at intervals of two years in various capitals of the Commonwealth, but since 1961 they have been held annually. Other Conferences of a regional character are held between representatives of Branches in close proximity. Exchanges of Delegations among Branches are arranged, particularly from and to the United Kingdom Branch. Every year a Parliamentary Seminar is held at Westminster under the joint auspices of the General Council and the United Kingdom Branch, attended by about thirty Members invited from various Commonwealth Legislatures. The Office of the General Council produces a quarterly publication, *The Parliamentarian*, formerly the *Journal of Parliaments of the Commonwealth* which contains articles and reviews of books on parliamentary topics as well as reports of proceedings of special interest in Commonwealth Parliaments. The Office has also published authoritative studies, such as *Payments and Privileges of Commonwealth Parliamentarians* and regularly produces reports of the conference of the Association, and provides special information for Branches and individual Members.

While the work involved in these various activities was, until the year 1948, mostly undertaken by the United Kingdom Branch, the need became apparent for some central organisation to act as a liaison body between the Branches, to edit and issue the publications of the Association, to arrange parliamentary conferences, and to help supply information when and where required. At the Commonwealth Parliamentary Conference in London, held in 1948, it was decided, in accordance with a resolution put forward by the Canadian Branch, to set up a General Council with a Secretariat responsible for establishing and maintaining effective contact with all Branches, for producing and distributing the publications of the Association, and for providing the organising Secretariat for all conferences of the Association. Countries which have Main Branches are represented on the General Council by two members each. Special arrangements are made for the representation of other Branches. At the same Conference the name of the Empire Parliamentary Association was changed to Commonwealth Parliamentary Association.

At the Commonwealth Parliamentary Conference in Kampala in 1967, it was decided, in accordance with a Resolution put forward by the Commonwealth of Australia Branch, to set up an Executive Committee of the General Council. This Committee meets twice a year: once in May or June, and again at the time of the annual Conference and meeting of the General Council.

The Council meets annually. The first meeting was held at Ottawa in 1949 and subsequent meetings at Wellington (1950), Colombo (1951), Ottawa (1952), London (1953), Nairobi and Livingstone (1954), Kingston (Jamaica) (1956), New Delhi (1957), Bridgetown (Barbados) (1959), Canberra (1959), Kampala (Uganda) (1960), London (1961), Lagos (1962), Kuala Lumpur (1963), Montego Bay and Kingston (1964), Wellington (1965), Montreal and Ottawa (1966), Kampala (1967), Nassau (1968), Port-of-Spain (1969) and Sydney and Canberra (1970). The expenses of the Council, including the cost of the publications, are met by parliamentary grants through the Branches. The headquarters of the Association are at Westminster, and the Council's office provides a centre for research and information on current Commonwealth affairs for members of all Branches.

Plenary Parliamentary Conferences of the Association took place on seven occasions between 1916 and 1937, and smaller delegations held conferences before and during the Second World War. Beginning with the London Conference in 1948 sixteen plenary Conferences have been held. The host Branches were United Kingdom (1948), New Zealand (1950), Canada (1952), Union of South Africa, Southern Rhodesia and Kenya (1954), India, Pakistan and Ceylon (1957), Australia (1959), United Kingdom (1961), Nigeria (1962), Malaysia (1963), Jamaica (1964), New Zealand (1965), Canada (1966), Uganda (1967), Bahamas (1968), Trinidad and Tobago (1969), Australian Commonwealth and States (1970). The London Conference in 1961 was formally opened by Her Majesty The Queen. At all of these Conference a frank exchange of views on matters of common interest, *e.g.* Commonwealth co-operation, economic relations, migration, international affairs and defence has taken place.

Invitations have been received to hold future plenary conferences in Zambia (1972), United Kingdom (1973) and Ceylon (1974).

The Executive Committee of the General Council met in Mauritius in 1968, in Gibraltar in 1969 and in Jersey in 1970; the Branches in Sierra Leone and Singapore have indicated their wish to host the Committee in 1971 and 1972 respectively.

A close relationship exists between the Commonwealth Parliamentary Association and the British-American Parliamentary Group at Westminster, which works with a similar group in the Congress of the United States. The latter also constitutes an 'Associated Group' of the Association. In 1952 an Associated Group was formed in the Parliament of the Irish Republic. Delegates from both these countries attended the sessions on international affairs and defence at the Conference at Ottawa in 1952, at Lagos in 1962 and at Nassau in 1968, delegations from the United States attended the sessions on these subjects at the Conferences in New Delhi in 1957, Canberra in 1959, London in 1961, Kingston in 1964, Wellington in 1965, Ottawa in 1966, Nassau in 1968 and Port-of-Spain in 1969.

Presidents and Secretaries of Branches:

UNITED KINGDOM

President: Rt Hon. Lord Hailsham QC (Lord Chancellor); Rt Hon. Selwyn Lloyd, CH, CBE, TD, QC, MP, (Speaker of the House of Commons)
Secretary: P. G. Molloy, MC, Westminster Hall, Houses of Parliament, London

CANADA

Presidents: Senator the Hon. Jean-Paul Deschatelets, PC (Speaker of the Senate); Hon. Lucien Lamoureux, QC, MP (Speaker of House of Commons)
Secretary-Treasurer: I. G. Imrie, House of Commons, Ottawa

ONTARIO

President: Hon. F. McIntosh Cass, QC, MPP, (Speaker of Legislative Assembly)
Secretary: R. G. Lewis, QC (Clerk of Legislative Assembly), Parliament Buildings, Toronto

QUEBEC

President: Hon. Jean-Noel Lavoie, MPQ (President of National Assembly)
Secretary: René Blondin (Secretary-General of National Assembly), Parliament Buildings, Quebec

NOVA SCOTIA

President: Hon. George M. Mirchell, MLA (Speaker of House of Assembly)
Secretary: R. A. Laurence, QC (Clerk of Executive Council), Province House, Halifax

NEW BRUNSWICK

President: (To be elected) (Speaker of Legislative Assembly)
Secretary: Ray W. Dixon (Clerk of Legislative Assembly), Parliament Building, Fredericton

MANITOBA

President: (To be elected) (Speaker of Legislative Assembly)
Secretary: Charland Prud'homme, QC (Clerk of Legislative Assembly), Legislative Buildings, Winnipeg

BRITISH COLUMBIA

President: Hon. W. H. Murray, MLA (Speaker of Legislative Assembly)
Secretary: E. K. DeBeck (Clerk of Legislative Assembly). Parliament Buildings, Victoria

SASKATCHEWAN

President: Hon. J. E. Snedker, MLA (Speaker of Legislative Assembly)
Secretary: G. L. Barnhart (Clerk of Legislative Assembly), Legislative Buildings, Regina

ALBERTA

President: Hon. A. J. Dixon, MLA (Speaker of Legislative Assembly)
Secretary: William H. MacDonald (Clerk of Legislative Assembly), Parliament Buildings, Edmonton

NEWFOUNDLAND

President: Hon. George W. Clarke, MHA (Speaker of House of Assembly)
Secretary: Hugh F. Coady (Clerk of House), House of Assembly, St John's

PRINCE EDWARD ISLAND

President: Hon. Cecil A. Miller, MLA (Speaker of Legislative Assembly)
Secretary: G. Lorne Monkley, Deputy Provincial Secretary's Office, P.O. Box 2000, Charlottetown

COMMONWEALTH OF AUSTRALIA

Presidents: Senator the Hon. Sir Alister McMullin, KCMG (President of Senate); Hon. Sir William Aston, KCMG, MP (Speaker of House of Representatives)
Secretary: A. G. Turner, CBE (Clerk of the House), House of Representatives, Canberra 2600

NEW SOUTH WALES

Presidents: Hon. Sir Harry Budd, MLC (President of Legislative Council); Hon. Sir Kevin Ellis, KBE, MLA (Speaker of Legislative Assembly)
Secretary: I. P. K. Vidler (Clerk of Legislative Assembly), Parliament House, Sydney 2000

VICTORIA

Presidents: Hon. R. W. Garrett, AFC, MLC (President of Legislative Council); Hon. Vernon Christie, MP (Speaker of Legislative Assembly)
Secretary: A. R. McDonnell (Clerk of the Legislative Council), Parliament House, Melbourne 3002

QUEENSLAND

President: Hon. D. E. Nicholson, MLA (Speaker of Legislative Assembly)
Secretary: Cyril George (Clerk of Parliament), Parliament House, Brisbane 4000

SOUTH AUSTRALIA

President: Hon. D. A. Dunstan, QC, MP (Premier)
Secretary: I. J. Ball (Clerk of Parliaments), Parliament House, Adelaide 5000

WESTERN AUSTRALIA

Presidents: Hon. L. C. Diver, MLC (President of Legislative Council); (to be elected, (Speaker of Legislative Assembly)
Secretary: J. B. Roberts, MBE, ED (Clerk of Legislative Council), Parliament House, Perth 6000

TASMANIA

President: Mr L. H. Bessell, MHA
Secretary: G. B. Richards (Clerk of House of Assembly), Parliament House, Hobart 7000

NEW ZEALAND

President: Hon. Sir Roy Jack, MP (Speaker of House of Representatives)
Secretary: H. N. Dollimore, CBE (Clerk of House of Representatives), Parliament House, Wellington

INDIA

President: Dr the Hon. G. S. Dhillon, MP (Speaker of Lok Sabha)
Secretary: S. L. Shakdher (Secretary of Lok Sabha), Parliament House, New Delhi

WEST BENGAL

President: Hon. Bijoy Banerjee, MLA (Speaker of Legislative Assembly)
Secretary: S. Banerjea (Secretary of Legislative Assembly), Calcutta

MAHARASHTRA

Presidents: Hon. V. S. Page, MLC (Chairman of Legislative Council); Hon. T. S. Bharde, MLA (Speaker of Legislative Assembly)
Secretary: S. H. Belavadi (Secretary of Legislature), Council Hall, Bombay

TAMIL NADU

Presidents: Hon. Thiro C. P. Chitrarasu, MhC (Chairman of Legislative Council; Hon. Pulavar K. Govindar, MLA (Speaker of Legislative Assembly)
Secretary: C. D. Natarajan (Secretary of Legislative Assembly), Fort St George, Madras-9

PUNJAB

President: Hon. Sardar Darbara Singh, MBE, MLA (Speaker of Legislative Assembly)
Secretary: Shri Krishan Swaroop (Secretary of Legislative Assembly), Vidhan Bhawan, Chandigarh

MYSORE

Presidents: (To be elected) (Chairman of Legislative Council); Sri S. D. Kothavale, MLA (Speaker of Legislative Assembly)
Secretary: T. Hanumanthappa (Secretary of Legislature), P.O. Box 5074, Bangalore-1

RAJASTHAN

President: Hon. Niranjan Nath Acharya, MLA (Speaker of Legislative Assembly)
Secretary: B. K. D. Badgel (Secretary of Legislative Assembly), Assembly House, Jaipur

GUJARAT

President: Hon. Raghavji T. Leuva, MLA (Speaker of Legislative Assembly)
Secretary: D. G. Desai (Secretary, Legislature Secretariat), New Civil Hospital, (OPD), Ahmedabad-16

ANDHRA PRADESH

Presidents: Hon. Sri B. V. Subba Reddy, MLA (Speaker of Legislative Assembly); Hon. Sri P. Ranga Reddy, MLC (Chairman of Legislative Council)
Secretary: A. Shankar Reddy (Secretary to Legislature), Legislature Department, Hyderabad

HARYANA

President: Brig. Ran Singh (Speaker)
Secretary: R. K. Malhotra (Secretary of Legislative Assembly), Chandigarh.

PAKISTAN

(Branch in abeyance)

WEST PAKISTAN

(Branch in abeyance)

EAST PAKISTAN

(Branch in abeyance)

CEYLON

Presidents: Senator the Hon. A. Ratnayake (President of Senate); Hon. Stanley Tillekeratne, MP (Speaker of House of Representatives)
Secretary: S. S. Wijesinha (Clerk of the House), House of Representatives, Colombo

GHANA

President: Hon. Mr Justice Nii Amaa Ollennu (Speaker of National Assembly)
Secretary: Mr C. A. Lokko (Clerk of National Assembly), Parliament House, Accra

MALAYSIA

Presidents: Hon. Tan Sri Haji Mohammed Noah bin Omar, PMN, SPMJ, DPMB, PIS, JP (President of Senate); Hon. Dato C. M. Yusuf bin Sheikh Abdul Rahman, SPMP, OBE, JP, MP (Speaker of House of Representatives)
Secretary: Ahmad bin Abdullah (Clerk to the House of Representatives and Clerk of Parliament), Parliament House, Kuala Lumpur

SARAWAK

President: Hon. William Tan Ho Choon, JMN, CBE (Speaker of Council Negri)
Secretary: Assim bin Munir (Clerk of Council Negri), The Council Chamber, c/o The Legislature, Kuching

SABAH

President: Hon. Dato Haji Mohd. Kassim bin Haji Hashim, PDK, MLA (Speaker of Legislative Assembly)
Secretary: Enche F. C. Neubronner (Clerk of Legislative Assembly), P.O. Box 1247, Kota Kinabalu

NEGRI SEMBILAN

President: Hon. Inche Ariffin bin Ali, AMN, PJK, MLA (Speaker of Legislative Assembly)
Secretary: Khalil bin Ya'acob (Clerk of Legislative Assembly), Seremban

PAHANG

President: Hon. Enche Awang Ngah bin Tok Muda Haji Ibrahim, MLA (Speaker of Legislative Assembly)
Secretary: Ismail bin Haji Abdullah (Clerk of Legislative Assembly), Pejabat Setia Usaha Kerajaan, Kuantan

PERAK

President: Hon. Enche Mohd. Ali Zaini bin Haji Mohd. Zain, MLA (Speaker of Legislative Assembly)
Secretary: Ahmad bin Mohd. Said (Clerk of Legislative Assembly), Peti Surat 1004, Ipoh

JOHORE

President: Hon. Tuan Syed Mohamed bin Edros, AMN, SMS, PIS, MLA (Speaker of Legislative Assembly)
Secretary: Abdullah bin Mohamed (Clerk of Legislative Assembly), Government Offices Building, Johore Bahru

TONGA

President: Hon. Ma'afu (Speaker of Legislative Assembly)
Secretary: S. P. Vaea (Clerk of Legislative Assembly), Nuku'alofa, Tonga

TRENGGANU

President: Hon. Che Wan Abdul Ghani bin Zainal, SMT, JP, MLA (Speaker of Legislative Assembly)
Secretary: Wan Abdul Manan bin Chik, PJK (Clerk of Legislative Assembly), Pejabat Setia Usaha Kerajaan, Kuala Trengganu

SELANGOR

President: Hon. Dato Haji Harun bin Haji Idris, SMS, MLA (Speaker of Legislative Assemlby
Secretary: Kamarul Bahrim bin Haji Abdul Raot (Speaker of Legislative Assembly), Selangor Secretariat, Kuala Lumpur

KEDAH

President: Tuan Haji Zainuddin bin Haj Haji Din, AMN, JP, MLA (Member of State Executive Council)
Secretary: Hassan bin Aminudin (Clerk of Legislative Assembly), Pejabat Setia Usaha Kerajaan, Alor Star

FEDERAL REPUBLIC OF NIGERIA
(Branch in abeyance)

EASTERN NIGERIA
(Branch in abeyance)

WESTERN NIGERIA
(Branch in abeyance)

NORTHERN NIGERIA
(Branch in abeyance)

MID-WESTERN NIGERIA
(Branch in abeyance)

SIERRA LEONE

President: Hon. Sir Emile Fashole-Luke, KBE (Speaker of House of Representatives)
Secretary: J. W. E. Davies (Acting Clerk of House of Representatives), Freetown

UNITED REPUBLIC OF TANZANIA

President: Hon. Chief A. S. Mkwawa, OBE (Speaker of National Assembly)
Secretary: Y. Osman (Clerk-Assistant of the National Assembly), Box 9133, Dar es Salaam

JAMAICA

Presidents: Senator the Hon. G. S. Ranglin (President of Senate); Hon. E. C. L. Parkinson, QC, MP (Speaker of House of Representatives)
Secretary: H. D. Carberry (Clerk to the Houses), Houses of Parliament, Kingston

TRINIDAD & TOBAGO

Presidents: Senator the Hon. J. H. Maurice (President of Senate); Hon. C. A. Thomasos, MP (Speaker of House of Representatives)
Secretary: G. R. Latour (Clerk of House of Representatives), Red House, Port-of-Spain

UGANDA
(Branch in abeyance)

WESTERN SAMOA

President: Hon. Magele Ate, MP (Speaker of Legislative Assembly)
Secretary: G. A. Fepulea'i (Clerk of Legislative Assembly), P.O. Box 198, Apia.

KENYA

President: Hon. F. M. G. Mati, MP (Speaker of the National Assembly)
Secretary: L. J. Ngugi (Clerk to the National Assembly) P.O. Box 1842, Nairobi

MALAWI

Patron: Dr The Hon. H. Kamuzu Banda (President)
Chairman: Hon. A. M. Nyasulu, MP (Speaker of Parliament)
Secretary: Mr O. S. Mkandawire (Clerk of Parliament), P.O. Box 80, Zomba

MALTA, G.C.

President: Hon. Dr A. Bonnici, MP (Speaker of House of Representatives)
Secretary: M. Gregory (Clerk of the House) House of Representatives, Valletta

ZAMBIA

President: Hon. R. M. Nabulyato (Speaker of National Assembly)
Secretary: N. M. Chibesakunda (Clerk of National Assembly) P.O. Box 1229, Lusaka

SINGAPORE

President: Dr Yeoh Ghim Seng, MP (Speaker of Parliament)
Secretary: P. C. Tan (Clerk-Assistant of Parliament), Parliament House, Singapore -6

GUYANA

President: Hon. Sase Narain, MP (Speaker of National Assembly)
Secretary: F. A. Narain (Clerk of National Assembly), Parliament Office, Georgetown

BOTSWANA

President: Rev. the Hon. A. A. F. Lock, MP, (Speaker of National Assembly)
Secretary: G. Matenge (Clerk of National Assembly), P.O. Box 240, Gaberones

LESOTHO
(Branch in abeyance)

MAURITIUS

President: Hon. Sir Harilal Vaghjee (Speaker of Legislative Assembly)
Secretary: G. T. d'Espaignet (Clerk of Legislative Assembly), Port Louis

GAMBIA

President: Alhaji the Hon. Sir Alieu Jack, MP (Speaker of House of Representatives)
Secretary: B. O. Jobe (Clerk of House of Representatives), Bathurst

BARBADOS

Presidents: Senator the Hon. Sir Stanley Robinson, KB, CBE (President of Senate); Hon. Sir Theodore Brancker, KB, QC, MP (Speaker of Assembly)
Secretary: L. Hutchinson (Librarian and Secretary) House of Assembly, Bridgetown

SWAZILAND

Presidents: Senator The Hon. Sir John Houlton, CSI, CIE (Speaker of Senate); Hon. Ian Aers, OBE (Speaker of House of Assembly)
Secretary: N. L. Dlamini (Clerk of House of Assembly), P.O. Box 448, Mbabane

NAURU

President: Hon. Rev. A. Amram, MP (Speaker of Legislative Council)
Secretary: Mr Patrick D. Cook (Clerk of Parliament Nauru Island)

Presidents and Secretaries of Auxiliary Branches

BAHAMAS

Presidents: Senator the Hon. L. J. Knowles, CBE (President of Senate); Hon. A. R. Braynen, MHA (Speaker of House of Assembly)
Secretary: P. O. Saunders (Chief Clerk, House of Assembly), Nassau

BRITISH HONDURAS

Presidents: Senator the Hon. E. W. E. Francis, OBE (President of Senate); Hon. W. H. Courtenay, OBE, MP (Speaker of National Assembly)
Secretary: S. E. Hulse, MBE (Clerk of National Assembly), Belize City

GRENADA

Presidents: Senator the Hon. G. B. James, MP (President of Senate); Hon. G. E. D. Clyne, MP (Speaker of House of Representatives)
Secretary: C. V. Strachan (Clerk of Parliament), Houses of Parliament, St George's

BERMUDA

Presidents: Hon. George O. Ratterray, CBE, MLC (President of Legislative Council); Hon. Lt. Col. J. C. Astwood, CBE, ED, MHA (Speaker of House of Assembly)
Secretary: R. C. Lowe (Clerk to the Legislature), Hamilton

ST LUCIA

President: Hon. W. St Clair Daniel, JP, MP (Speaker of House of Assembly)
Secretsry: Mrs. U. Raveneau (Clerk of House of Assembly) Castries

COOK ISLANDS

President: Hon. Mrs M. Story, MLA (Speaker of Legislative Assembly)
Secretary: John M. Scott (Clerk of Legislative Assembly), Rarotonga

Affiliated Branches

Antigua; British Solomon Islands; British Virgin Islands; Cayman Islands; Dominica; Fiji; Gibraltar: Isle of Man; Jersey; Montserrat; Northern Ireland; Northern Territory; Papua and New Guinea; St Christopher, Nevis and Anguilla; St Lucia; St Vincent; Seychelles

Subsidiary Branches:

To United Kingdom:
  Falkland Islands
  Gilbert and Ellice
  Islands
  Guernsey
  Hong Kong
  St Helena

COMMONWEALTH PRESS UNION
Bouverie House, 154 Fleet Street, London E.C.4 (01-353 6428/9)

President: Colonel The Lord Astor of Hever
Founder: Sir Harry Brittain, KBE, CMG
Chairman of Council: The Hon. Gavin Astor
Vice-Chairman of Council: The Lord Thomson of Fleet, GBE
Hon. Treasurer: E. G. Benn
Secretary: Lt.-Col. T. Pierce-Goulding, MBE, CD
Assistant Secretary: Mrs M. A. Freegard, MBE

The Commonwealth Press Union was founded (as the Empire Press Union) in 1909. It has over 600 members which include nearly all the important newspapers and periodicals as well as news agencies in Britain and in the Commonwealth overseas. It has autonomous Sections in Canada, Australia, New Zealand, India, Pakistan, Ceylon, Malaysia, Singapore, Ghana, Nigeria, Rhodesia and the West Indies.

The objects of the Union include the defence of Press freedom; cheaper and better telecommunication services; the training, education and exchange of journalists throughout the Commonwealth; and the improvement of reporting facilities for the Commonwealth Press as a whole.

The Union holds an Annual Conference in London at which delegates from overseas take part, and a Quinquennial Conference, the last of which was held in the West Indies in November and December 1965.

The last Quinquennial Conference was held in Scotland in October 1970.

COMMONWEALTH PRODUCERS' ORGANISATION
25 Victoria Street, Westminster, London S.W.1 (01-222 2951)

Chairman: Sir Ronald Russell, MP
Deputy Chairmen: Bernard Braine, MP; R. E. Heanley
Executive Director: S. Stanley-Smith

The Organisation exists to promote the interests of Commonwealth primary producers and the development of reciprocal trade within the Commonwealth. It was established in 1916 as the British Empire Producers' Organisation and consists of full, associate and individual members. It has special overseas links with Australia, New Zealand, the Caribbean, Malaysia, Africa and Cyprus. The services provided by the Organisation include research for producer members, the giving of information and advice and the publication of the bi-monthly *Commonwealth Producer* and of occasional newsletters.

COMMONWEALTH SCHOLARSHIP COMMISSION IN THE UNITED KINGDOM
36 Gordon Square, London WC1H 0PF (01-387 8572)

Chairman: The Rt. Hon. Lord Garner, GCMG
Joint Secretaries: Sir Hugh W. Springer, KCMG, CBEg and E. E. Temple

The Commonwealth Scholarship Commision was constituted by Act of Parliament in December 1959 to administer in Britain the Commonwealth Scholarship and Fellowship Plan, which was drawn up at the First Commonwealth Education Conference held at Oxford in 1959 (*see* Chapter 14 of 1961 edition of the *Commonwealth Relations Office List*). The members, up to fifteen in number, are appointed by the Minister for Overseas Development.

x*

As the British agency for the Commonwealth Scholarship and Fellowship Plan the Commission has responsibility for selecting the recipients (about 600 at present) of Commonwealth Scholarships, Commonwealth Academic Staff Fellowships, Commonwealth Visiting Professorships and Commonwealth Medical Awards offered by the British Government; for placing the selected candidates at universities, or other appropriate institutions in Britain; and for administering their awards while in Britain (but see below regarding welfare, stipends and travel). The Commission also receives applications from candidates in Britain for the awards offered by other Commonwealth Governments and makes nominations for final selection by the awarding authorities in the countries concerned. The Commission is assisted by the British Council in relation to the personal welfare, stipends and travel of award holders. The secretariat of the Commission is provided by the Association of Commonwealth Universities (*q.v.*).

COMMONWEALTH SCIENTIFIC COMMITTEE

Africa House, Kingsway, London WC2B 6BD (01–405 7786/7)

Chairman: Dr R. N. Gonzalez

Members:

Britain	Tanzania
Canada	Jamaica
Australia	Trinidad and Tobago
New Zealand	Uganda
India	Kenya
Pakistan	Malawi
Ceylon	Malta, G.C.
Ghana	Zambia
Malaysia	Singapore
Nigeria	Barbados
Sierra Leone	Mauritius

Secretary: Dr R. Glen

The British Commonwealth Scientific Official Conference held in 1946* set up a Standing Committee, with a Working Party of deputies in London (now known as the Consultative Committee), to follow up the recommendations and decisions of the Conference and to make arrangements for the calling of further Conferences. The Standing Committee as originally constituted consisted of the executive heads of the national research organisations of Commonwealth countries, together with representatives of the Colonial Office.

In 1958 the British Commonwealth Scientific Conference was abolished and the Standing Committee was reconstituted as the Commonwealth Scientific Committee (C.S.C.), assuming the additional functions formerly exercised by the Conference, and retaining the same basis of membership and the same terms of reference, *i.e.*

'To consider the best means of ensuring the fullest possible collaboration between the government civil scientific organisations of the Commonwealth.'

The major function of C.S.C. is to provide information and advice to the Scientific Agencies of developing Commonwealth countries for the planning and guidance of their development and research activities and to the aid authorities

* British Commonwealth Scientific Official Conference, London, 1946. Report of Proceedings Cmd. 6970.

in the Commonwealth donor countries as to the kind and amount of assistance which is required by the Scientific Agencies in developing countries. The Secretary, C.S.C., who is in addition the Scientific Adviser to the Commonwealth Secretary-General, furthers the work of the Committee through periodic visits to member countries providing assistance as required. Secretariat services for C.S.C. and its Consultative Committee are drawn from the Common Services section of the Commonwealth Scientific Liaison Offices (C.S.L.O.). C.S.L.O. operates under the aegis of the C.S.C. as do also the following Commonwealth Committees:

Commonwealth Committee on Mineral Resources and Geology
Permanent Committee of the Commonwealth Collections of Micro-organisms
Commonwealth Committee on Mineral Processing

The C.S.C. meets biennially to discuss further measures of Commonwealth scientific collaboration and of bilateral and multilateral assistance. The last meeting was held in Jamaica in November 1970.

COMMONWEALTH SCIENTIFIC LIAISON OFFICES

Africa House, Kingsway, London WC2B 6BD (01-405 7786/7)

Chief Scientific Liaison Officers:
W. L. Haney (Canada); Dr E. G. Hallsworth (Australia); Dr V. Armstrong (New Zealand)
Secretary: E. D. A. Davies

The Commonwealth Scientific Liaison Offices came into existence in May 1948 as the result of a recommendation of the British Commonwealth Scientific Official Conference held in 1946* that the Scientific Liaison Offices in London of the various Commonwealth countries should occupy a joint headquarters while continuing to function as separate autonomous units.

The functions of the individual Scientific Liaison Offices are dictated by the requirements of their own country, but usually include assistance to their own visiting scientists, exchange of scientific information, dealing with scientific enquiries and reporting on the scientific scene in Britain. They are the scientific advisers to their High Commissioners and represent their countries at meetings of Commonwealth and international organisations, conferences, etc.

The Committee of the Commonwealth Scientific Liaison Offices, consisting of the Chief Scientific Liaison Officers, deals with matters of common concern and controls the activities of a Common Services section which provides secretariat services for the Commonwealth Scientific Committee (C.S.C.) and some of its associated committees, in addition to routine services as required.

C.S.L.O. forms a useful channel through which certain of the recommendations of the C.S.C. can be implemented, and in this respect it is responsible for the maintenance of the Commonwealth Index of Scientific Translations, a check list of scientific translations made in the Commonwealth.

The Commonwealth Geological Liaison Office, maintained by the Commonwealth Committee on Mineral Resources and Geology, is also situated within C.S.L.O. for convenience.

* British Commonwealth Scientific Official Conference, London, 1946. Report of Proceedings Cmd. 6970.

COMMONWEALTH SOCIETY FOR THE DEAF

75 Kinnerton Street, Knightsbridge, London S.W.1 (01-235 8182/3)

President: The Rt Hon. The Earl of Inchcape

Vice-Presidents:

The Secretary of State for Foreign and Commonwealth Affairs, The High Commissioners for Australia, Barbados, Botswana, Canada, Ceylon, Cyprus, Fiji, Ghana, India, Jamaica, Kenya, Lesotho, Malawi, Malaysia, Malta G.C., Mauritius, New Zealand, Federal Republic of Nigeria, Pakistan, Sierra Leone, Swaziland, Tanzania, Trinidad and Tobago, Uganda, Zambia and the Commissioner for the Eastern Caribbean

Chairman: Lady Templer

Vice-Chairmen: Sir John Stow, GCMG, KCVO; Mrs Denys Wrey

Hon. Treasurer: E. F. Miller
Hon. Legal Adviser: D. B. G. Bishop
Chairman of the Education Committee: Dr Alec Hay
Chairman of the Medical Committee: Mr Christopher Holborow, FRCS

Secretary: C. H. F. Blake

This Society was formed in 1959. Its objects are to promote the welfare, education and employment of the deaf throughout the Commonwealth, and to assist and co-operate with all organisations having as their object the prevention and cure of deafness. It encourages the formation of schools for the deaf in areas where none are provided by the local education authorities or other bodies and arranges for the training of specialised teachers. To do this it provides scholarships to universities in Britain for overseas teachers and sends trained teachers of the deaf to places abroad where they are needed. Several Schools for the deaf have been founded in this manner and more are in preparation. The first Seminar for Teachers of the Deaf in Africa was held in Nairobi in July 1968, and a similar seminar was held in Hong Kong in 1971.

It is possible for members of the public to join the Society and contributions may be sent to its headquarters.

COMMONWEALTH WAR GRAVES COMMISSION

32 Grosvenor Gardens, London SW1W 0DZ (01-730 0751)

President: H.R.H. The Duke of Kent, GMCG, GCVO
Chairman: The Secretary of State for Defence
Vice-Chairman: Air Chief Marshal Sir Walter Cheshire, GBE, KCB

Members:

The Minister for Housing and Construction	Sir Robert Black, GCMG, OBE
The High Commissioner for Canada	Verner Wylie
The High Commissioner for the Commonwealth of Australia	Miss Joan Woodgate, CBE
	Sir John Winnifrith, KCB
The High Commissioner for New Zealand	Admiral Sir Frank Twiss, KCB, DSC
The South African Ambassador in London	Edward Gardner, QC, MP
The High Commissioner for India	George Wallace, MP
The High Commissioner for Pakistan	General Sir Noel Thomas, KCB, DSO, MC

Director-General (Secretary to the Commission): W. J. Chalmers, CBE
Director of External Relations and Records (Assistant Secretary to the Commission): P. H. M. Swan
Director of Finance and Establishments (Assistant Secretary to the Commission): A. K. Pallot, CMG
Director of Works: Brigadier K. F. Daniell, CBE
Legal Adviser and Solicitor: H. L. Simmons
Chief Horticultural Officer: W. F. W. Harding, OBE
Private Secretary to Director-General: R. J. Dalley

The Commonwealth (formerly Imperial) War Graves Commission was founded by Royal Charter in 1917 to provide for the permanent marking and care of the graves of officers and men of the Commonwealth Forces who lost their lives in the 1914-1918 War, and to commemorate by name those who had no known grave.

Later, the Commission was empowered at the request of any one of its participating governments to care for the graves of men and women, whether military or civilian, who died outside the period of the two wars and for the graves of Allied or ex-Enemy war dead. By a Supplemental Charter granted in 1940, it was entrusted with the commemoration of the dead of the 1939-1945 War.

A Supplemental Royal Charter dated 8th June 1964 consolidated the provisions of the eight previous Supplemental Charters. The Charters of the Commission now consist of the original Royal Charter and the new Supplemental Charter.

Every one of the fallen is commemorated individually, either by a headstone carved with the symbol of his faith, with his name, rank and regimental badge and with whatever text or personal message his relatives may have wished to add or, if his grave is unknown, by name, rank and unit on one of the memorials to the missing. These headstones and memorials are as enduring as human skill can make them, and the headstones are of uniform shape and size, the same for all ranks and services. The principle of equality of treatment reflecting the sacrifice that all made equally, underlies the whole of the Commission's work. It was first approved by the Imperial War Conference of 1918, which also approved the principle that the cost of the work should be shared proportionately by the participating governments according to the number of their graves. The funds of the Commission are thus now provided by the seven Governments participating in its work: Britain, Canada, Australia, New Zealand, South Africa, India and Pakistan.

The graves of the dead of those Commonwealth countries which had not achieved independent status at the time of the two World Wars are included in the total numbers cared for by the Commission. Many of the governments concerned participate in the Commission's work by arranging for and, in a number of cases, bearing the cost of, maintenance of the Commonwealth war graves in their own territories.

More than one million graves are maintained by the Commission, mainly in war cemeteries, large and small, constructed in some 150 different countries. Three-quarters of a million whose graves are unknown or who were cremated are commemorated by name on memorials built in their honour. These memorials range from small memorials bearing only a few names to great structures such as the Menin Gate at Ypres and the Air Forces Memorial at Runnymede bearing many thousands.

Two central monuments are used in the war cemeteries: the tall stone cross known as the Cross of Sacrifice, which bears upon its shaft a Crusader's sword of bronze, and the altar-like Stone of Remembrance carved with the words 'Their Name Liveth for Evermore'—a symbol generally acceptable to all peoples no matter what their religious faith—which is erected in the larger cemeteries. In each war cemetery or plot is a printed Register of those buried there; it can be found in a bronze box let into the entrance piers or into the wall of a shelter building. Along the lines of headstones are borders of flowers, in a setting of lawns, trees and shrubs.

The Commission's work of commemorating the dead of the two World Wars and of maintaining the war graves and memorials throughout the world is directed from its Head Office in London, to which two Regional Offices and seven independent Area Offices are responsible. A number of Agencies has also been established by agreement with the Governments of certain countries. The Commission's rights in foreign countries are protected by a series of treaties between the foreign governments and the Governments participating in the Commission's work.

The Commission's Regional, Area and Agency Organisation is shown below.

REGIONS
UNITED KINGDOM REGION
40/42 High Street, Maidenhead, Berkshire SL6 1QE

South-Eastern Area	Brookwood	Channel Islands, England, Faroe Islands, Iceland, Isle of Man, Northern Ireland, Republic of Ireland, Scotland, Wales
South-Western Area	Cheltenham	
Central Area	Harrogate	
Northern Area	Glasgow	

EASTERN REGION
B-23, Greater Kailash (Ground Floor), New Delhi (48), India

New Delhi   Burma, China, Hong Kong, India Malaysia (Malaya), Maldive Islands, Nepal, Pakistan, Singapore, Thailand

INDEPENDENT AREAS RESPONSIBLE DIRECT TO HEAD OFFICE

FRANCE AREA
Place du Maréchal Foch 62, Arras, France

France, Monaco, Spain (Bilbao only), Switzerland
(France area maintains liaison with the Gibraltar Agency)

NORTH WEST EUROPE AREA
Elverdinge Straat 82, B-8900 Ieper Belgium

Belgium, Czechoslovakia, Denmark, Germany, Luxembourg, Netherlands, Norway, Poland, Sweden

WESTERN MEDITERRANEAN AREA
Viale Pola 27a/29, Roma, Italy

Algeria, Austria, Hungary, Italy, Malta, Morocco, San Marino, Tunisia

EASTERN MEDITERRANEAN AREA
8 King George II Avenue, Old Phaleron, Athens, Greece

Bulgaria, Cyprus, Greece, Iraq, Iran, Muscat and Oman, Lebanon, Rumania, Syrian Arab Republic, Turkey, Yugoslavia

NEAR EAST AREA
Ramleh War Cemetery, Ramla, Israel

Israel

NORTH AFRICA AREA
Heliopolis War Cemetery, Sharia Nabil el Wakad, Heliopolis, Egypt, United Arab Republic, Libyan Arab Republic, Sudan, United Arab Republic

EAST AFRICA AREA
Standard Bank Chambers, Kimathi Street, Nairobi, Kenya

Democratic Republic of the Congo, Ethiopia, French Territory of the Afars and the Issas, Malagasy Republic, Mauritius, Mozambique, Saudi Arabia, Seychelles, Somali Republic, Southern Yemen, Tanzania (Zanzibar) (East Africa Area maintains liaison with the Kenya, Tanganyika, Uganda, Malawi, Rhodesia and Zambia Agencies)

AGENCIES

Canadian Agency
Veterans' Affairs Building,
Wellington Street,

Ottawa, Ontario K1A OP4, Canada
Canada and The United States of America
The Canadian Agency has certain duties of inspection in the following: Antigua, Argentina, Bahamas, Barbados, Bermuda, Brazil, British Honduras, Chile, Costa Rica, Cuba, Dominica, Falkland Islands, Grenada, Guatemala, Guyana, Honduras, Jamaica, Martinique, Netherlands Antilles, Panama Canal Zone, Peru, Puerto Rica, Trinidad and Tobago, Uruguay, St Kitts-Nevis-Anguilla, St Lucia, St Vincent

Anzac Agency
for the Pacific Region
660-662 Bridge Road, Richmond
Victoria 3121, Australia

Australia, Fiji, Indonesia, Japan, Malaysia (Sabah), New Britain, New Caledonia, New Hebrides, New Ireland, Norfolk Island, North-East New Guinea, Papua, Philippines, Society Islands, Solomon Islands, Tonga, Western Samoa
The Commonwealth war graves in New Zealand are maintained by the New Zealand Department of Internal Affairs

South African Agency
Room 417 (Third Floor),
Central Government Offices,
Cr. Vermeulen and Bosman St.
Pretoria, South Africa

Ceylon Agency
Royal Botanic Gardens,
Peradeniya, Ceylon
Ceylon (Eastern Region maintains liaison)

Kenya Agency
c/o Ministry of Internal Security and Defence
P.O. Box 668, Nairobi, Kenya

Tanganyika Agency
President's Office, Regional Administration
P.O. Box 1949, Dar es Salaam, Tanzania

Uganda Agency
c/o Ministry of Defence
P.O. Box 3798, Kampala, Uganda

Malawi Agency
c/o President's Office of the Government of Malawi, Zomba, Malawi

Rhodesia Agency*
c/o Ministry of Defence,
P.B. 7713, Causeway, Salisbury
Rhodesia

Zambia Agency
c/o Ministry of Defence, P.O. Box 208,
Lusaka, Zambia

Gibraltar Agency
Fortress Headquarters, Gibraltar

N.B. War graves and memorials in Ascension Island, Azores, Botswana, Cameroons, Canary Islands, Cape Verde Islands, Chad, Equatorial Guinea, Gambia, Ghana, Guinea, Ivory Coast, Lesotho, Liberia, Madeira, Mali, Mauretania, Nigeria, Portugal, Popular Republic of the Congo, St Helena, Sengal, Sierra Leone, Spain (excluding Bilbao), Swaziland, the Soviet Union, and Togo are administered direct from the Head Office of the Commission

CONFEDERATION OF BRITISH INDUSTRY OVERSEAS SCHOLARSHIPS

21 Tothill Street, London S.W.1 (01-930 6711)

Director-General: W. O. Campbell Adamson
Chairman of the Scholarships Board: Sir Maurice Fiennes

This scholarships scheme was established in October 1950 by the Federation of British Industries (since embodied in the Confederation of British Industry) to give selected engineering graduates from the Commonwealth and developing countries the best available practical training in British Industry. The scheme is supported by the British Government and in addition to enabling scholars to improve their professional knowledge, has as one of its aims the increase of trade between their countries and Britain.

---

* See Southern Rhodesia chapter in Part V of this Year Book.

Since the scheme started 441 scholars have come to Britain from the following Commonwealth countries: Australia 138, Barbados 1, Ceylon 16, Dominica 1, Ghana 1, Guyana 1, Hong Kong 28, India 65, Jamaica 12, Kenya 2, Malaysia 23, New Zealand 45, Nigeria 22, Pakistan 58, Rhodesia 14, Singapore 2, Trinidad and Tobago 6, Uganda 1 and Zambia 5.

There are two main types of scholarship: Type A for recently graduated engineers and offering training for two years (A1), eighteen months (A2), and one year (A3), and Type C for more experienced engineers offering training for up to one year. Types A1 and A2 also offer paid fares to and from the scholars' country, while Type A3 does so in one direction only.

Prospective applicants can obtain further information from the offices of British High Commissioners or from the Manager, Overseas Scholarships, at the above address.

CONSERVATIVE COMMONWEALTH AND OVERSEAS COUNCIL

32 Smith Square, London S.W.1 (01–222 9000)

President: Rt Hon. Sir Alec Douglas-Home, KT, MP
Chairman: Rt Hon. the Earl of Selkirk, GCMG, GBE, AFC, QC

The Conservative Commonwealth and Overseas Council, founded in 1953, is a voluntary and largely non-Parliamentary body which seeks to contribute to the spread of detailed knowledge on problems of the Commonwealth and of remaining Dependencies. Views expressed in its publications are unofficial so far as the Party is concerned, being those of individuals named or of particular groups. Most of its members have direct experience of current needs and conditions in the various Commonwealth regions. Through their working-groups, they are in close touch with the Parliamentary Foreign and Commonwealth Affairs Committee and with Party spokesmen. A particular purpose is to stimulate thought on essential Commonwealth and related matters beyond the press of immediate issues and where possible to suggest courses of action consistent with enlightened British policy and contemporary Conservative outlook. A private annual conference is held in March/April, with guest speakers, on a yearly theme. General and group meetings are also held throughout the year in London, and provincial groups form and meet according to demand.

CONSERVATIVE OVERSEAS BUREAU

32 Smith Square, London S.W.1 (01–222 9000)
Cables: Constitute, London S.W.1

Chairman: Baroness Emmet of Amberley, JP
Joint Vice-Chairmen:
Patrick Wall, MC, VRD, MP; Rt Hon. the Earl of Selkirk, GCMG, GBE, AFC, QC
Secretary: R. D. Milne
Assistant Secretary: Mrs J. M. Willcox

The Conservative Overseas Bureau, founded in 1949, is the headquarters department of the Conservative Party responsible for the mechanics of its relations with all overseas countries. Its supervisory Committee, reviewed annually, is representative of all sectors of the Party organisation. The Bureau's routine rôle is to deal with the many visitors and tele-/postal requests and representations coming from overseas; its positive work lies particularly in inter-party relations, including overseas parties' requests for policy and organisational information. It services the Commonwealth and Overseas Council (*q.v.*) and the Foreign Affairs Forum for parliamentary candidates. The Bureau joins with other voluntary bodies in helping Overseas students with personal problems and political interests respectively. In conjunction with the External Affairs section of the Conservative Research Department and the Conservative Political Centre (the Party's policy-briefing and publishing branch) it issues a monthly *Overseas Review* (62p. p.a. post free-single Copies 6p.). It also maintains working liaison with diplomatic Missions in London and with similar voluntary bodies. The Bureau arranges for U.K. citizens abroad to enrol in the Party and assists Party members travelling overseas with information contacts.

CONSULTATIVE PANEL FOR SOCIAL DEVELOPMENT

Members:

Dr T. R. Batten
Mrs J. Cockerill
Professor R. P. Dove
Mrs I. L. Curry
R. D. Fairn
H. Houghton, CBE
H. D. Hughes
D. Jones, OBE
Professor L. J. Lewis
Miss E. R. Littlejohn, JP
A. V. S. Lochhead
H. Mason, OBE
Miss M. McCullough

Dr E. O. Mercer, OBE
Professor I. Neustadt
J. K. Owens
Mrs M. L. Kellmer Pringle
Professor R. M. Titmuss
L. E. Waddilove
Professor E. A. O. G. Wedell
Miss J. Whittington, CBE, JP
A. E. Wilson
Professor H. C. Wiltshire
Dame Eileen Younghusband, DBE, JP
P. Zealey, OBE

The Consultative Panel was constituted in April 1965 by the Minister of Overseas Development. Its terms of reference are:

> To act as consultants to the Minister for Overseas Development on any aspect of social development of importance to countries which have requested or may request British technical co-operation or other aid in this field. It is especially concerned with the provision by Britain of advisory services, training facilities and staff.

The Panel has working groups on adult education and literacy, social development training and youth services to which additional members are co-opted.

CORONA CLUB

The Corona Club was founded by Joseph Chamberlain in 1900 to provide an annual opportunity for officers on leave from the Colonies to meet each other and members of the Colonial Office and retired officers of the Colonial Service.

To further this idea an Annual Dinner continues to be held, usually in the second or third week of June. This is attended by serving members on leave from the remaining dependencies, but in particular the occasion has become a reunion for retired members of H.M. Overseas Civil Service, some of whom are now in the Home or Diplomatic Services.

Membership of the club is open to all past and present members of the government service in the dependent territories and of the Office of the Crown Agents for Overseas Governments and Administrations and the former Colonial

Office. It includes many officers who, having served prior to independence in former dependent territories, continue to serve under the new Governments.

The annual subscription to the club is 25p, which goes toward printing, clerical assistance and other necessary expenses, any balance being devoted to reduction of the cost of the dinner. Membership can be secured without annual subscriptions by a single compounded subscription of £2·10.

By courtesy of the Committee of the West Indian Club, 4 Whitehall Court, London S.W.1 arrangements have been made by which serving annual or life members of the Corona Club who are on leave in the United Kingdom can be admitted as Special Temporary Members of the West Indian Club.

The President of the Corona Club is Viscount Boyd of Merton, CH, DL, and the Chairman of the Club Committee is Sir John Macpherson, GCMG. Full particulars of the Club may be obtained from the Hon. Secretary, Mr G. W. Thom, OBE, Overseas Development Administration, Foreign and Commonwealth Office.

COTTON RESEARCH CORPORATION

12 Chantrey House, Eccleston Street, London S.W.1 (01–730 4239)

Chairman: Sir Geoffrey Nye, KCMG, OBE
Vice-Chairman: H. Tonge
Director: M. A. Choyce, OBE
Assistant Director and Secretary: M. H. White

The Cotton Research Corporation was established under Royal Charter and endowed by the British Government in 1921. It provides research and advisory services on cotton growing to developing countries, normally through the Technical Assistance arrangements of the Overseas Development Administration.

Members of the Corporation's team of agricultural scientists work in many cotton growing countries in Africa under long-term agreements with their Governments. Short-term help with cotton growing problems is provided to other countries on request.

The annual membership fee that each country pays (£1,000 to £6,000 according to the size of its cotton crop) entitles it to the full range of services, including spinning and fibre tests in the United Kingdom.

COUNCIL FOR EDUCATION IN THE COMMONWEALTH

Chairmen: Dame Joan Vickers, DBE, MP; Frank Judd, MP
Vice-Chairmen: Robert McLennan, MP; Monty Woodhouse, MP
Hon. Treasurer: Ian A. Ross, FCA, FCIS
(Branketre, 28 Alderton Hill, Loughton, Essex (01-508 1314))
Hon. Secretary: H. R. Rose, BSc(Econ,), FCIS
(29 Portland Place, London W.1 (01-637 0471))
Parliamentary Liaison Officer: Mrs Felicity Bolton, CBE
Research Officer: Roy Manley
Editor of Newsletter: Mrs Helen Pickthorn, 3 Hobury Street, London S.W.10

The Council for Education in the Commonwealth was set up to create an informed public opinion on the problems of education in the Commonwealth, particularly in the less developed territories. It is non-party and draws its members from all parts of the Commonwealth.

The Council holds regular monthly discussion meetings at the House of Commons when Parliament is in session, so that members may hear eminent educationalists, Ministers and others, both from overseas and Britain, take part in discussions, and answer questions.

Various working parties have been established and, as a result of the research and memoranda of these committees, the Council is able to present recommendations to the Ministers concerned, and to raise subjects for mutual discussion through its personal and official contacts.

Suggestions for educational activities or subjects for research are welcomed by the Executive Committee, and should be addressed to the Honorary Secretary in the first instance.

The annual subscription for individual membership of the Council is two pounds. Overseas and provincial members receive a regular Newsletter, keeping them in touch with the Council's activities.

COUNCIL FOR TECHNICAL EDUCATION AND TRAINING FOR OVERSEAS COUNTRIES

Eland House, Stag Place, London S.W.1 (01–834 3665)

Chairman: Sir Frederick Pedler

D. B. Bartlett
Mrs B. Platt
C. R. English
H. W. French
M. L. Herzig
A. MacLennan, CBE
J. Mark, MBE
J. Marsh, CBE
K. Marshall
J. P. Martin-Bates
Miss M. Nicholson

Sir Eric Richardson, CBE
Dr E. F. Schumacher
J G Strachan, CBE
M Dodderidge, OBE
C A Thompson
J. E. C. Thornton, OBE
H. A. Warren, OBE
G. E. Watts, CBE
Miss R. Winslade, OBE
J. T. Young

Secretary: H. M. Collins, OBE
Deputy Secretary: D. R. Day, OBE
Appointments Secretary: Miss J. Pearson

The Council was set up by the Secretary for Technical Co-operation in 1962 with the following terms of reference:

To give advice and expert assistance to Her Majesty's Government and others as may be required with a view to promoting technical and commercial education and training for developing countries, and for this purpose, *inter alia:*

(*a*) to furnish advice and information and to promote contacts between those concerned with such education and training in the United Kingdom and in developing countries;

(*b*) to promote and where appropriate to undertake the recruitment of staff for service overseas in this field; and

(*c*) to facilitate the training and education in the United Kingdom of trainees, teachers and others from developing countries.

It is intended during 1971 to change the Council into a corporate legal entity in order to increase British assistance to developing countries in the fields of management education, industrial training and technical education.

COUNCIL OF COMMONWEALTH MINING AND METALLURGICAL INSTITUTIONS

44 Portland Place, London W.1 (01-580 3802)

Chairman: Sir Ronald Prain, OBE
Vice-Chairman: D. S. Burwood
Hon. Treasurer: A. R. O. Williams, OBE
Hon. Secretary: B. W. Kerrigan

Commonwealth Constituent Bodies:

The Institution of Mining and Metallurgy
The Canadian Institute of Mining and Metallurgy
The Australasian Institute of Mining and Metallurgy
The Mining, Geological and Metallurgical Institute of India
The Institute of Metals
The Institute of Petroleum
The Institution of Metallurgists
The Institution of Mining Engineers
The Iron and Steel Institute
South Wales Institute of Engineers
Geological Society of Australia
The Geological Society of South Africa
The South African Institute of Mining and Metallurgy

The objects of the Council are to convene successive Mining and Metallurgical Congresses as a means of promoting the development of the mineral resources of the world; to foster a high level of technical efficiency amongst the members of the Constituent Institutions and to serve as an organ of intercommunication and co-operation between Constituent Bodies.

COUNCIL OF COMMONWEALTH MUNICIPALITIES

(*British Associates of Commonwealth Local Government Ltd.*)

78 Chandos House, Buckingham Gate, London S.W.1. (01–222 2179)

Joint Presidents: Rt Hon. Geoffrey Rippon, QC, MP; Arthur Skeffington, MP
Vice-Presidents: Rt Hon. Arthur Bottomley, OBE, MP; Sir John Rodgers, Bt, MP
Chairman: Sir Denys Lowson, Bt.
Acting Secretary-General: Charles W. Boreham
Hon. Treasurer: P. T. Lovely

The Council is an all-party organisation formed in 1964 to foster co-operation between local government personalities and authorities in the Commonwealth and to disseminate throughout the world knowledge and information concerning Commonwealth affairs.

COVENTRY OVERSEAS STUDENTS TRUST

Coundon House, Coventry

(Coventry 26163—Students) (Coventry 26199—Warden)

Trustees:

The Lord Bishop of Coventry
A. Allison
R. J. Kerr-Muir
The Earl of March and Kinrara
P. S. Rendall

Warden: D. G. Pettifer

Founded 1962 to set up a community on the pattern of Zebra House, London, for the increasing number of overseas students coming to Coventry to study at the various establishments of further and higher education and to take up traineeships in local firms. First project Coundon House which provides accommodation for 40 students.

CROWN AGENTS FOR OVERSEA GOVERNMENTS AND ADMINISTRATIONS

4 Millbank, London S.W.1 (01-222 7730)

The Crown Agents are the officially appointed business and financial agents for a large number of Governments and Public Authorities. These include independent Governments such as Bahrain, Botswana, Brunei, Ceylon, Cyprus, Fiji, The Gambia, Guyana, Jamaica, Jordan, Kenya, Lesotho, Libyan Arab Republic, Malaysia, Malta, Mauritius, Nigeria, Sierra Leone, Singapore, Swaziland, Tanzania, Tonga, Trinidad and Tobago, Uganda, Western Samoa, People's Democratic Republic of Yemen and Zambia and all the territories overseas under British administration or trusteeship. Other authorities for whom they act include the United Nations, many railway, transport, broadcasting, telecommunications and electrical undertakings, port commissions, universities, currency boards and local government authorities in addition to many development and research bodies. The Office is not a Department of the United Kingdom Government and no vote for it comes before the United Kingdom Parliament. It is self-supporting, its funds being derived from fees charged to its Principals from whom instructions are received direct. The Crown Agents do not act for private individuals or commercial concerns.

DEPARTMENT OF HUMAN NUTRITION

London School of Hygiene and Tropical Medicine,

Keppel Street, London WC1E 7HT (01-636 8636)

Telegrams: Hygower, London W.C.1

Professor-in-charge: Professor J. C. Waterlow, CMG

The main functions of the Department are (i) teaching of nutrition to postgraduate students; (ii) experimental and epidemiological research in nutrition; (iii) to study and exchange information on nutrition particularly in developing countries; (iv) to provide assistance in field work and investigations. Detailed information on teaching activities is provided in the School Syllabus. These include a course for the degree of Master of Science in the University of London and teaching of nutrition in the courses for the Diploma in Tropical Public Health, the Diploma in Clinical Medicine of the Tropics and the Conjoint Board Diploma in Tropical Medicine and Hygiene.

The Department is part of the London School of Hygiene and Tropical Medicine. It co-operates with the Department of Health and Social Security in nutritional investigations in the U.K. and also receives support from the Medical Research Council and from the Wellcome Trust.

DIPLOMATIC AND COMMONWEALTH WRITERS ASSOCIATION OF BRITAIN

President: Christopher Serpell (*B.B.C.*)

Vice-Presidents: John Fisher (*Thomson Newspapers*); Derek Ingram (*Gemini News Service*)

Past Presidents: R. H. C. Steed (*The Daily Telegraph*); Patrick Keatley (*The Guardian*); Richard Kershaw (*BBC 'Panorama'*); John Fisher (*Thomson Newspapers*)

Hon. Secretary: William Wolff (*Daily Mirror*), 33 Holborn, London E.C.1
(353 0246)

Hon. Treasurer: Percy Arnold, Hoseyridge, Westerham, Kent
(Westerham 2322)

Committee:

John Dickie (*Daily Mail*)	Clifford Smith (*BBC*)
J. D. F. Jones (*Financial Times*)	Peter Snow (*ITN*)
Michael Lake (*The Guardian*)	Don Taylor (*New Commonwealth*)
Seaghan Maynes (*Reuters*)	John Tilley (*The Scotsman*)

Administrative Secretary: Miss Sheila Saville,
8 Plender Court, College Place, London N.W.1

The Diplomatic and Commonwealth Writers Association of Britain (formerly The Commonwealth Writers of Britain), was founded in London in 1960 and is an association of British correspondents, specialising in Diplomatic and Commonwealth affairs, of United Kingdom newspapers, periodicals, news agencies and broadcasting services.

There is also an associate membership open to Press Attachés of High Commissions, Embassies and Commissions, and also Public Relations Officers of industries, public corporations and firms with interests overseas.

THE DIRECTORATE OF OVERSEAS SURVEYS

Kingston Road, Tolworth, Surbiton, Surrey (01–337 8661)

Director: D. E. Warren
Deputy Director (Mapping) and Deputy to the Director: A. G. Dalgleish
Deputy Director (Survey): J. W. Wright

The Directorate of Overseas Surveys, part of the Overseas Development Administration of the Foreign and Commonwealth Office, carries out basic survey and mapping for overseas countries and arranges the flying of air photography for survey purposes. It provides expert advice to the Administration and to overseas governments and organisations on technical matters concerned with all aspects of survey and mapping including training, qualifications, equipment and techniques.

The Directorate was set up in 1946, under the Colonial Office, as a central organisation to carry out geodetic and topographic surveys in the dependent territories. This work was financed under Colonial Development and Welfare Funds. From 1960 onwards, as advice and help were being sought by developing countries, whatever their status, arrangements were made for much of the work to be undertaken under Technical Assistance Schemes. In 1961, the Directorate became part of the new Department of Technical Co-operation and in 1964 it joined the Ministry of Overseas Development. In 1964, too, the Land Resources Division absorbed the Overseas Pool of Soil Scientists and embarked on a programme of expansion to enable the Directorate to meet increasing requests for scientific investigations into natural resources until in 1971 the Land Resources Division became a separate unit of the ODA.

Accurate maps of the land and its resources are vital for planning development schemes. Since 1946, the Directorate has mapped over 1,780,000 sq. miles of territory and has re-mapped over 260,000 sq. miles, where rapid development has already rendered the earlier editions out-of-date. It is currently producing maps for Botswana, The Gambia, Ghana, Kenya, Malawi, Nigeria, Sierra Leone, Swaziland, Tanzania, Uganda, Zambia, Malta, British Honduras, British Solomon Islands Protectorate, Gilbert and Ellice Islands, Tonga, Mauritius, the West Indies and Malaysia.

The maps are produced by modern air survey methods. Air photography is flown mainly by British air survey companies under contract. Teams of Directorate surveyors are sent overseas to establish a framework of survey stations on the ground. These stations are permanently marked and co-ordinated, so that they may form a basis for all future local surveys. The maps are plotted at the Headquarters at Tolworth and the plots are then checked and annotated by the local survey department, so that they will be as up-to-date as possible. The maps are finally fair-drawn at Tolworth and most of them are printed for the Directorate by the Ordnance Survey of Great Britain.

Basic mapping is normally at a scale of 1:50,000 in Africa: in some sparsely populated areas it is at 1:100,000 or 1:125,000 and in densely populated development areas it may be at 1:10,000 or 1:25,000. The specification for a particular map series is agreed between the Directorate and the country concerned. In general, 1:50,000 maps cover a $\frac{1}{4}°$ square: they are printed in several colours and show contours, natural and man-made features, and broad categories of vegetation and land use. The Directorate's maps are on sale through the survey authorities of each country and through Edward Stanford, Ltd., 12-14 Long Acre, London WC2 9LP.

The technical libraries at Tolworth provide facilities for the consultation of survey data, air photographs and maps of the countries for which the Directorate has worked. The Information and Liaison Centre disseminates and exchanges information on new techniques and equipment in the fields of survey, photogrammetry and cartography.

Close contact is maintained between the Directorate and survey organisations overseas. This is strengthened by the overseas tours of the Directing Staff and by the Conferences of Commonwealth Survey Officers which are held every four years: the last Conference was held in Cambridge in 1971.

The Directorate provides practical training in cartographic and photogrammetric techniques for technical officers from overseas Government Departments. It also seconds experts to take up temporary appointments with overseas governments and international organisations.

THE EAST AFRICA AND MAURITIUS ASSOCIATION

Stuart House, 1 Tudor Street, London EC4Y 0AD

Chairman: K. D. Brough
Director and Secretary: E. M. Rose, CMG

The Association was formed in 1964 to assist participation in the economic development of the East African countries of Kenya, Tanzania and Uganda by firms and companies from other countries, to the mutual economic advantage of those countries and of its members. The Association's interests were extended to Mauritius in 1966. Membership is not confined to British concerns but only those which are predominantly expatriate are eligible.

ECONOMIC AND SOCIAL COMMITTEE ON OVERSEAS RESEARCH

Chairman: R. S. Porter, OBE

Lord Balogh
Professor R. P. Dore
Professor S. J. Gould
Professor J. L. Joy
Professor A. S. MacKintosh
Professor W. T. Newlyn

Professor Edith Penrose
Professor Dudley Seers
Professor P. P. Streeten
Dr D. S. Thornton
Professor D. Walker

Adviser on Social Development, O.D.A.
Director of the Statistics Division, O.D.A.
Secretary: D. I. Scanlan, MVO, OBE

The Economic and Social Committee on Overseas Research (ESCOR) was set up in 1968 by the then Minister of Overseas Development. Terms of reference are to advise the Minister on economic and social research projects submitted to the Overseas Development Administration, and to stimulate research for the economic and social benefit of the developing countries.

THE ENGLISH-SPEAKING UNION OF THE COMMONWEALTH

37 Charles Street, Berkeley Square, London W1X 8AB
(01–629 0104) (Office)   (01–629 7400) (Club)

(Founded in 1918 and including by merger the Atlantic Union founded in 1897, the American and British Commonwealth Association and Books Across the Sea, both founded in 1941)

Patron: Her Majesty The Queen
President: H.R.H. The Prince Phillip, Duke of Edinburgh, KG, KT, OM, GBE
Founder: Sir Evelyn Wrench, KCMG
Executive Director: Miss K. M. Graham, CBE
Finance Director and Secretary: C. Colbeck, OBE
In co-operation with The English-Speaking Union of the United States
Address: 16 East 69th Street, New York 21, U.S.A.
Telephone: Trafalgar 9–6800

The English-Speaking Union is a world-wide organisation consisting of two autonomous bodies: The English-Speaking Union of the Commonwealth, with its headquarters in London and 50 Branches in Britain, 11 in Canada, 5 in Australia, 6 in New Zealand, 6 in India, 1 in Gibraltar, 1 in Malta, 1 in Bermuda, 1 in Pakistan; and the English-Speaking Union of the United States, with its headquarters in New York and 75 Branches throughout the United States. Membership of the Union at 31st December 1969 was about 22,000 in Britain, over 20,000 in the overseas Commonwealth and 36,500 in the United States.

The Royal Charter of the English-Speaking Union of the Commonwealth lays down its first aim and object as being 'To promote understanding between the English-speaking peoples of the world, and to engage in any educational work designed to further that object'. The Preamble to the Charter expressly defines the English-speaking peoples as 'The peoples, irrespective of language, of the Commonwealth and of the United States of America'.

The English-Speaking Union of the United States shares the objectives of The English-Speaking Union of the Commonwealth.

The two Unions seek to promote interchange, understanding and friendship between the peoples of Britain and the Commonwealth overseas, of the Commonwealth overseas and the United States, and of the United States and Britain. Advice, introductions, hospitality and other assistance are provided by the headquarters and branches of each Union to visitors from other English-speaking countries whether members of the Union or not. Knowledge of the different English-speaking countries is promoted through meetings of the Union, the provision of speakers to other organisations, etc. Subscribing members of the Union from overseas and British members paying a special club rate of subscription have the use of residential club facilities at Concord and Dartmouth House in Charles Street, Berkeley Square, London W.1 and non-residential club facilities in some other centres.

The Commonwealth-American Current Affairs Unit at the London headquarters encourages and assists Branches and other interested organisations to arrange study courses, conferences, etc., on various aspects of Commonwealth and Commonwealth-American affairs. It distributes information material in the form of booklets, briefs or notes on subjects of special concern in these fields.

The Unit arranges monthly gatherings of overseas Commonwealth students, especially from Asia and Africa, and from the U.S.A., to meet the Union's younger members. It also arranges an annual Summer School for Overseas Visitors on "Britain Today", as well as orientation courses and 'Schools' for students in Britain from American universities and High Schools.

The Unit also arranges travel grants each year to enable some 100 Africans from Commonwealth countries studying in Britain to visit the European Continent where they meet French-speaking Africans and are briefed on what Associate membership of the European Economic Community means. These are wholly educational and information visits.

Both at their headquarters and in all their Branches, the two Unions arrange frequent speakers' meetings, sometimes jointly with other interested bodies: at these meetings speakers deal with one aspect or another of some other country of the Commonwealth or the United States of America. Where possible a speaker from the country concerned is secured.

This field offers wide possibilities. For instance, the E-S.U. of America pays the expenses of a limited number of carefully selected speakers to visit the United States for a tour of about a month's duration. On these occasions the speaker has the opportunity of addressing in many cities audiences which include members not only of The English-Speaking Union but of other organisations such as the Council on Foreign Relations, and so on. These speakers are recommended by a Speakers' Advisory Committee in London which is able, and indeed anxious, to include in its recommendations speakers of really high quality from Commonwealth countries other than Britain.

The Union operates a variety of Scholarships, Fellowships and Travel Grants, Exchanges of Students, etc, and co-operates with the Department of Education and Science in the exchange of teachers with the U.S.A.

The Education Department administers the British and American Schoolboy and Schoolgirl scholarships which are offered to boys and girls between the ages of 17 and 18½, who are pupils at British Public and American Independent Schools. The Scholarships provide free board and tuition, parents being required to pay the cost of travel and incidental expenses. Candidates must be recommended by the Principal of their School and are chosen by Selection Committees of the English-Speaking Union.

Programmes of postgraduate fellowships and assistantships, tenable in a wide variety of subjects at certain Canadian and United States Universities are also administered by the Education Department. These are open to British candidates under 30, who are holders of, or candidates for, Honours degrees from British Universities. Under the terms of the assistantships holders spend half of their time teaching or undertaking research for the universities and following a programme of courses for the remainder of the time. In association with the Woodrow Wilson National Fellowship Foundation, full-time teaching posts are negotiated at American Universities and colleges.

Walter Hines Page Travelling Scholarships and Chautauqua Scholarships are offered annually through the Education Department. These are short-term scholarships open to teachers in primary, secondary and technical schools. The Senior Scholarship is offered each year by the English-Speaking Union, and various educational associations offer awards to be competed for between their own members. The holders spend four to eight weeks in the United States studying various aspects of American education, complete hospitality being provided by the English-Speaking Union of the United States, who also arrange the scholars' itineraries.

In London and New York and in a number of branches there are special programmes for Younger Members.

The Page Memorial Library houses an exchange service known as Books Across the Sea. This service, which is operated by a Committee of the Union, aims at promoting mutual understanding by the exchange among countries of the Commonwealth and the United States of America of carefully selected books illustrating some aspect of life in their country of origin. Collections of books are also lent to Public Libraries, Schools and Training Colleges and Universities for varying periods, free of charge apart from the cost of transportation.

The administration of the E-S.U's annual Australian Working Visit for British Undergraduates has been transferred to the Careers Research Advisory Centre in Cambridge. This scheme enables 160 British students to work and travel in Australia during the universities' long vacation. The purpose is to give young British undergraduates with initiative, the opportunity of widening their expersence and contributing to British-Australian understanding and goodwill. The scheme is open to all British students born in and residents of Great Britain studying a full-time degree course at a university in the United Kingdom.

Each year, the English-Speaking Union enables more than 500 people to further their education in another part of the Commonwealth or the United States, and welcomes, assists or advises more than 20,000 Commonwealth and American visitors to its headquarters in London.

THE FAIRBRIDGE SOCIETY

Founder: Kingsley Fairbridge, Rhodes Scholar, Oxford

119/126 N.E. Wing, Bush House, Aldwych, London WC2B 4PY
(01–240 0688/9)

President: H.R.H. The Duke of Gloucester, KG, KT
Chairman: General Sir Rodney Moore, GCVO, KCB, CBE
Director: Maj.-Gen. W. T. Campbell, CBE

The Fairbridge Society was founded in 1909 with the objects of:—

    (a) helping children to start a new life in the Commonwealth, and

    (b) to give the Commonwealth good British migrants.

The Society runs two farm schools in Australia, one at Pinjarra near Perth, Western Australia, and the other at Molong, New South Wales (the latter is not accepting British children at present). It also has two houses for children, one in Tasmania and the other near Adelaide, South Australia, each run by a married couple.

In these schools and houses children are cared for, on an inter-denominational basis, in pleasant surroundings and given the same education and opportunities as other children in the State to enter the careers for which their ambitions and abilities qualify them.

Fairbridge provides after-care up to 21 years of age, and its homes are at all ages 'the home' of all Fairbridgians.

The Society helps families to settle in Australia, especially those deprived of one or other parents, by taking the children into their schools and homes and looking after them until the family can be re-united in a new home in that country.

There is also a scheme to assist teenage boys from 15–16 who wish to learn and take up farming in Australia.

Kingsley Fairbridge Scholarships are also offered to young men and women from Great Britain to qualify at Universities in Australia and Canada for a profession which they may follow in one of those countries.

FARNHAM CASTLE

(*The Centre for International Briefing*)

The Castle, Farnham, Surrey (Farnham 21194)

Registered Office: The Castle, Farnham, Surrey.

Director: M. G. Thornton.

The Centre for International Briefing is an independent organisation founded in 1953. Its purpose is to prepare men and women, by means of short residential Courses and Conferences, to live and work successfully in other countries. The Courses are held every week of the year and, dealing with a separate region each week, cover 70 countries throughout the world. Regular five-day residential Courses are also run, dealing with life in Britain, for the benefit of those from abroad who are temporarily resident in the U.K. A total of about 1,500 men and women attend these Courses and Conferences annually.

THE FAUNA PRESERVATION SOCIETY

c/o Zoological Society of London, Regents Park, London N.W.1 (01–586 0872)

Patron: Her Majesty The Queen
President: The Marquess of Willingdon
Vice-Presidents: Syed Ameer Ali, CIE; Professor Jean G. Baer;
Colonel Mervyn Cowie, CBE, ED; Sir Frank Fraser Darling, DSc, FRSE;
The Rt Hon. Lord Hurcomb, GCB, KBE; Sir Julian Huxley, FRS;
H.H. The Maharaja of Mysore, GCB, GCSI;

Captain C. R. S. Pitman, CBE, DSO, MC; Sir Landsborough Thomson, CB;
Professor Sir Solly Zuckerman, OM, KCB, DSc, FRS;
Chairman of Council: Peter Scott, CBE, DSC
Vice-Chairman: Lord Craigton
Hon. Treasurer: I. D. Malcolmson, TD
Hon. Secretary: R. S. R. Fitter

The aim of the Society is the conservation of wildlife throughout the world. Publication, *Oryx*; three times a year.

THE FEDERATION OF COMMONWEALTH CHAMBERS OF COMMERCE
69 Cannon Street, London E.C.4 (01-248 4444)

President: The Rt Hon. Malcolm J. MacDonald, OM
Chairman of Council: Capt. J. Jeffery, OBE, QC (Canada)
Director: W. J. Luxton, CBE
Secretary: H. E. Nichols

The present Federation of Commonwealth Chambers of Commerce has evolved over the years from the British Imperial Council of Commerce which was established in 1911 and which marked the first institutional step towards the formation of a permanent link between the business communities—through their Chambers of Commerce—in the several parts of the Empire.

Keeping pace with developments in the Commonwealth, this evolution has been particularly fast-moving during the last decade. Over 350 of the larger Chambers of Commerce in the Commonwealth and their national Associations to which they belong are linked through their membership of the Federation.

This membership is representative of leading business opinion in each country and the existence of national committees permits the rapid expression of authoritative national views on matters affecting Commonwealth Trade. Direct participation in the Federation by Companies is encouraged through a system of Associate Membership.

Today the Federation regards the following as being its main objectives:

The promotion of Commonwealth Trade, not only with Commonwealth countries but also with the rest of the world through acting as a linking and liaison organisation and by disseminating information and developing practical contacts between businessmen throughout the Commonwealth.

The organisation of a Congress every two years which provides a forum for debating Commonwealth trade and economic affairs and expressing business opinion and recommendations on current topics.

The development of regular bilateral discussions on matters of mutual concern between representatives of National Associations and their Chambers of Commerce in Commonwealth countries.

THE FRIENDS OF MALTA, G.C.
60 Buckingham Gate, London S.W.1 (01-834 2819)

Vice-Presidents: H.E. The Governor-General of Malta; His Grace The Archbishop of Malta;
The Prime Minister of Malta; H.E. The British High Commissioner in Malta;
The Rt Hon. Lord Carrington, KCMG, MC
Chairman of the Council: Basil M. Lindsay-Fynn
Director-General: John Lloyd

The objects of The Friends of Malta, GC, are to further the welfare of the people of Malta; to help those who, because of the reductions of British Services expenditure, have to adjust themselves to a new way of life; to provide expert advice, free from political bias or influence, on the various problems which have arisen from the economic changes which have taken place in the Islands.

Since formation in 1963, the Society has also helped and encouraged the building of homes at economical rates for young Maltese married couples, and assisted charitable organisations such as homes for the aged, hospitals, and orphanages. They are giving special attention to the problems and needs of young people and they support all those who work for the preservation and protection of the architectural heritage of the Islands.

GENERAL MEDICAL COUNCIL
44 Hallam Street, London WIN 6AE (01–580 7642)

President: Lord Cohen of Birkenhead
Registrar: M. R. Draper

The Council is a statutory body, with 47 members, established under the Medical Acts 1858-1969. Its duties include those of supervising and improving medical education, keeping and publishing a Register of duly qualified doctors, and taking disciplinary action when required in cases of criminal convictions or serious professional misconduct.

The Medical Register is published annually by the Council. The 1971 edition contains the names of 120,641 fully and 5,189 provisionally registered medical practitioners. 'Reciprocity', as respects medical practice and the mutual recognition of qualifications, exists between the United Kingdom and many Commonwealth countries which contain Medical Schools. Delegations from the Council visit Commonwealth countries from time to time.

The Council may also grant temporary registration to Commonwealth or foreign practitioners visiting this country for postgraduate training.

THE GIRL GUIDES ASSOCIATION
17-19 Buckingham Palace Road, London S.W.1 (VICtoria 6242)
Telegrams: Girguides, Sowest, London

General Secretary: Mrs Lysia Whiteaker, MBE

The aim of the Girl Guide Association is to encourage good citizenship by training girls in various skills and crafts, including those related to homemaking, and outdoor activities. The girls are given opportunities to develop initiative and qualities of leadership to enable them to take their place as responsible members of the community with a desire to use their knowledge in the service of others.

The Association has branches in British dependent countries and close links with the movement which is strongly established in all independent countries of the Commonwealth. It assists in the development of Guiding overseas in many ways; by sending experienced trainers to assist local training teams; by extending to adult leaders from overseas all the facilities for training available in the United Kingdom, by participation in Commonwealth Conferences and international gatherings.

GRENFELL ASSOCIATION OF GREAT BRITAIN AND IRELAND

P.O. Box 349, Hope House, 45 Gt. Peter Street, London S.W.1 (01-222 6252)

Patrons: Her Majesty The Queen;
Her Majesty Queen Elizabeth The Queen Mother
Vice-Patrons: The Earl of Elgin and Kincardine, CMG;
The Hon. Sir Leonard Outerbridge, CBE, DSO;
The Rt Hon. Lord Rowallan, KT, KBE; The Rt Hon. Lord St. Just;
The Rt Hon. Lord Tweedsmuir, OBE; The Hon. Campbell Macpherson, OBE
Chairman and Hon. Treasurer: The Rt Hon. Lord Grenfell, TD
Chairman of Council: R. P. Grenfell
Secretary: Miss Shirley Yates

This Association supports the work of the International Grenfell Association in Labrador and Northern Newfoundland, which was formed in 1912. It is also supported by the Canadian and American Associations. Its principal aims are the promotion of spiritual and temporal welfare and the provision of medical and surgical aid to seamen, fishermen, persons engaged in the fishing industry and the inhabitants of the coasts of Northern Newfoundland and Labrador. Over this sub-arctic coastline, the International Grenfell Association operates Hospitals, a Sanatorium, Nursing Stations, Children's Home, Hospital Ships, Air Ambulance Service and other forms of social work. There is a publication entitled *Among The Deep Sea Fishers* which is issued quarterly.

THE HONG KONG ASSOCIATION

18 Diamond House, Hatton Garden, London EC1N 8EB (01-405 2729/6144)

Officers of the Committee:
Hon. President: Sir Alexander Grantham, GCMG
Chairman: J. H. Hamm, OBE
Secretary: E. S. Bush

The objects of the Association are to promote and protect the interests of Hong Kong in the United Kingdom with particular reference to its industry and commerce. In order to facilitate an authoritative exchange of information, a Branch Committee has been established in Hong Kong. Membership is open to companies of all nationalities.

A bulletin is issued to Members every other month.

IMPALA HOUSE

7, 8, 9 Chalcot Square, 30, 32, 34 Chalcot Crescent, Primrose Hill, London, N.W.1 (PRImrose 4643)

Founded in 1961 as a sister foundation to Zebra House (*q.v.*), Impala House provides self-contained flats for married students from the Commonwealth and overseas—and particularly married students with children. Plans are well advanced to expand this very successful community to provide 10 more flats and a day nursery.

IMPERIAL DEFENCE COLLEGE
(see under Royal College of Defence Studies)

INCORPORATED LIVERPOOL SCHOOL OF TROPICAL MEDICINE
Pembroke Place, Liverpool 3 (Royal 7611)
Telegrams: Malaria, Liverpool

Dean: Professor B. G. Maegraith
Secretary: D. J. T. Owen
Administrative Secretary: Mrs L. Proctor

(All enquiries with regard to the Diploma in Tropical Medicine and Hygiene should be made to the Administrative Secretary, School of Tropical Medicine, Pembroke Place, Liverpool 3).

The School was founded in 1898 by the late Sir Alfred Jones, KCMG, a prominent Liverpool shipowner. Its objects are to train medical practitioners proceeding to the tropics, to conduct original research into tropical disease, and to deal with clinical tropical medicine.

Courses of instruction for the Diploma in Tropical Medicine and Hygiene (DTM & H) of the University of Liverpool are held twice yearly during the autumn and Lent terms. Each course lasts approximately three months and comprises lectures and demonstrations on tropical medicine and pathology, bacteriology, parasitology, applied biology, tropical hygiene, practical sanitation, vital statistics, epidemiology and meteorological observations. The Milne medal in tropical medicine and the Warrington Yorke medal in tropical hygiene are awarded on the results of the examination for this diploma. Medical practitioners of any nationality holding qualifications acceptable to the University of Liverpool are admitted to the courses of instruction and examination for the DTM & H. The first course for the Diploma in Tropical Child Health D.T.C.H. of the University of Liverpool began in September 1970. Each course lasts 18 months and consists of a year in-service hospital training followed by six months' instruction in Tropical Medicine and Hygiene in the School of Tropical Medicine. Courses will begin in September each subsequent year. Candidates may be of any nationality and must have had experience in paediatrics for at least a year at Senior House Officer level. There are only six vacancies for the first course. Also six months course, leading to the same Diploma, for Doctors with at least three years post-graduate paediatrics experience. Instruction is also given in applied biology and parasitology to students taking the Diploma in Public Health (Liverpool), and in veterinary applied biology and parsitology to undergraduate students working for the BVSc degree.

In conjunction with other departments of the University, a course leading to the degree of MSc of the University of Liverpool is given in Parasitology and Applied Biology involving man, animals, birds, freshwater fish, marine fish and plants.

Facilities are available to those wishing to carry out research. Clinical facilities are available in the Sir Alfred Jones Ward at the Liverpool Royal Infirmary and in the Tropical Disease Centre, Sefton General Hospital. These clinical units

are visited daily by members of the staff of the School in a consultant capacity.
The School publishes the *Annals of Tropical Medicine and Parasitology*, which
has now reached its sixty-third annual volume.

THE INDIA, PAKISTAN AND BURMA ASSOCIATION

Outer Temple, 222 Strand, London WC2R 1BH (01–353 0571-3)

President: Sir Percival Griffiths, KBE, CIE, ICS (retd).
Vice-Presidents: Sir Paul Chambers, KBE, CB, CIE; Sir Jeremy Raisman, GCMG, GCIE, KCSI
Chairman of the Committee: Sir Hugh Mackay Tallack
Secretary: W. D. Bryden
Adviser (India): Sir Ridgeby Foster
Adviser (Pakistan): R. T. Cochran, CBE

The objects of the Association, formed in 1942 as the India-Burma Association,
are to protect and promote the rights and interests of British associations and
individuals engaged in industrial, commercial or trading enterprises in India,
Pakistan and Burma or in commerce or trade between Britain and those
countries.

THE INDIAN JOURNALISTS' ASSOCIATION

President: Dr Tarapada Basu
Hon. Secretary: B. B. Ray Chaudhuri
Hon. Treasurer: Sunder Kabadi

The address of the present Hon. Secretary is:
35 Grafton Way, London W.1 (EUSton 7942)

The Indian Journalists' Association, which was founded in 1947, exists to safeguard and promote the rights and interests of its members in all matters concerning the collection, transmission and publication of news. It also provides a
common venue for its members and visiting journalists from India to meet and
discuss their mutual problems

The Association is representative of all the main newspaper and news agency
interests in India.

INSTITUTE OF COMMONWEALTH STUDIES
(UNIVERSITY OF LONDON)

27 Russell Square, London WC1B 5DS (01–580 5876)

Director: Professor W. H. Morris-Jones
Secretary: Dr P. H. Lyon
Librarian: Mrs P. Larby

The Institute was established in 1949 to promote advanced study of the Commonwealth. Its field of interest is primarily that of the social sciences and recent
history. It encourages collaboration at postgraduate level between workers
who are employing different techniques of research in the study of Commonwealth problems. It provides a meeting place for both postgraduate students

and members of academic staffs of Universities and research institutions in the United Kingdom and overseas countries of the Commonwealth. Seminars are held for advanced students during the University terms. Admission to them is on recommendation by supervisors of studies or at the discretion of the Director of the Institute. Meetings on current topics are arranged from time to time for members of staff and other specially invited persons.

The library, containing some 55,000 books and papers, places particular emphasis upon primary material relating to government, economic and social development, race relations and demography; and with this object it regularly acquires official publications, statistics, guides to archives, etc., of the United Kingdom and Commonwealth countries. Secondary works on the development of the Commonwealth during the past century are also obtained and a strong bibliographical section has been assembled. Books are for reference only and may not be borrowed.

Particulars of admission and forms of application may be obtained from the Assistant Secretary.

INSTITUTE OF COMMONWEALTH STUDIES
(UNIVERSITY OF OXFORD)

Queen Elizabeth House, 21 St Giles, Oxford (Oxford 52952-4)

Director: P. P. Streeten

The Institute of Commonwealth (formerly Colonial) Studies had its origins as a centre for colonial research in Nuffield College under the direction of Dame Margery Perham. The post-war plans for the training of Colonial Service Officers in Oxford and the increasing interest in comparative overseas studies led in 1947 to the creation by the University of the Committee for Colonial (now Commonwealth) Studies which became responsible for the Institute; the Institute is now largely financed by an annual grant from the General Board.

The Institute is a teaching centre for administrators and diplomats from developing countries and post-graduate students of the University and in collaboration with senior members of the University undertakes research and bibliographical work related to developing countries with special emphasis on the history, politics and economics of the tropical Commonwealth. It also houses the Oxford Colonial Records Project which collects and processes material—mostly unpublished—from personal sources relating to British dependencies and their transition to sovereign independent states.

It has a small library of approximately 20,000 items (including periodicals and newspapers and unpublished materials) which is complementary to the Rhodes House Library (Bodleian). There are also press-cutting files. The library is open to all members of the University and to other recommended students, on application to the Librarian.

The Institute works closely with Queen Elizabeth House and occupies part of its premises in St Giles; and since 1968 the posts of Director of the Institute and Warden of Queen Elizabeth House have been held by the same person.

Y

INSTITUTE OF COMMUNITY STUDIES
18 Victoria Park Square, Bethnal Green, London E2 9PF (01-980 6263)

Directors: M. Young; P. Willmott
Treasurer: H. Dickinson

The Institute, which was founded in 1954, is registered as a charity and is financed mainly from charitable foundations. Its function is to carry out social research which has a bearing on issues of practical policy as well as contributing to basic knowledge about society. Book-length reports are published by Routledge and Kegan Paul in a series of 'Reports of the Institute of Community Studies'. The inquiries are mainly in Britain itself, though there has been some research in African cities.

THE INSTITUTE OF PHYSICS
47 Belgrave Square, London S.W.1 (01–235 6111)

President: Dr J. W. Menter
Executive Secretary: Dr L. Cohen

The aims of the chartered body are the advancement and dissemination of a knowledge of physics, pure and applied, and the elevation of the profession of physicists. Branches throughout the British Isles and in New Zealand and Malaysia.

INSTITUTE OF RURAL LIFE AT HOME AND OVERSEAS
Headquarters: 27 Northumberland Road, New Barnet, Herts (01-440 4165)

President: The Rt Hon. The Lord Tweedsmuir, CBE
Treasurer: The Hon. Sir Geoffrey Gibbs, KCMG
Secretary: Philip Eastman

The Institute was established in 1949 to encourage the wider study and understanding of the countryside and to gain the acceptance of Christian values by those engaged in administration, agriculture, education and social development in rural areas throughout the world. It makes available the knowledge and experience of individuals and organisations concerned with rural questions.

Its members receive a quarterly review—*Rural Life*—and publications dealing with various aspects of rural life. Its programme includes an annual conference and lectures in London. These are open to the public and are designed to provide information on Commonwealth affairs, particularly in the rural context, and to be of use to Government servants, missionaries, and others visiting England from overseas territories.

The Institute is in correspondence with over 200 other Societies, at home and overseas, whose interests lie with one or more of the many aspects of rural life. It has appointed Overseas Correspondents in territories all over the world, with the task of keeping it informed about local rural life problems and developments.

The Institute's income is derived from grants made by the larger missionary societies, and from Trusts and Foundations. The minimum membership subscription is £1·00 per annum. The Rules of the Institute, which is a registered charity, provide for individual and corporate or affiliated membership.

INTERNATIONAL AFRICAN INSTITUTE

London Office: St Dunstan's Chambers, 10-11 Fetter Lane, London EC4A 1BJ

(01–353 4751/52)

Administrative Director: Professor Daryll Forde
Secretary: Mrs Wendy Hardcastle

The Institute was founded in 1926, under the chairmanship of the late Lord Lugard, for the purpose of providing an international centre for the promotion of research and the dissemination of information relating to the cultures, languages and social institutions of African peoples.

With the assistance of grants from the Rockefeller and Ford foundations, the Institute has carried out extensive researches, more particularly into problems arising from the impact of western civilization on African societies. It also organises seminars and other meetings on various aspects of African social studies. Financial support for research projects and publications has been received from the British, French and Belgian Governments, African Governments, the Carnegie Corporation of New York, the Ford Foundation, the Rockefeller Foundation and from UNESCO. The Institute publishes monographs on African ethnology, sociology and linguistics, a series of short accounts of African peoples under the general title *Ethnographic Survey of Africa*, a series of volumes comprising the *Handbook of African Languages*, a quarterly journal *Africa*, and a quarterly *International African Bibliography*. With the assistance of a grant from UNESCO, it publishes *African Abstracts* a quarterly reveiw containing summaries of articles in current periodical literature concerned with African studies. The Institute's Research Information Liaison Unit, assisted by a grant from the Ford Foundation produces an International Register and a series of Bulletins on current Africanist Research. Its library may be used by students and reaserch works at the discretion of the Librarian, and provides bibliographical and other information on request. It includes on its Executive Council representatives of African countries and those having cultural and administrative interests in Africa.

All persons interested in the study of African peoples and their modern development are welcomed as members of the Institite (annual subscription £3).

THE INTER-UNIVERSITY COUNCIL FOR HIGHER EDUCATION OVERSEAS

90–91 Tottenham Court Road, London, W1P 0DT (01–580 6572)
Telegrams: Interuniv London W1P 0DT

Chairman: J. B. Butterworth
Vice-Chairmen: Lord Fulton; Professor C. T. Ingold, CMG

Sir Norman Alexander, CBE
Professor Sir William Melville Arnott
Professor D. G. Austin
Professor G. H. Bell
Sir Kenneth Berrill
Dr C. W. L. Bevan, CBE
Lord Boyle of Handsworth
E. L. Bradby
F. H. Cawson, CBE
Professor W. D. Chesterman

Mrs E. M. Chilver
Sir Derman Christopherson, OBE
Sir Christopher Cox, GCMG
Dr H. S. Darling
Dr C. W. Davidson
Professor J. L. D'Silva
Professor T. A. Dunn
Dr E. G. Edwards
H. Fairhurst
Dr M. R. Gavin, CBE

Professor J. D. Gillett, OBE
Dr J. H. E. Griffiths, OBE
Professor A. J. Haddow
Professor S. E. Hunt
Professor P. A. Huxley
Sir Brynmor Jones
Professor L. Joy
Dr F. J. Llewellyn
Professor D. A. Low
Professor J. A. MacDonald
Professor M. M. Mahood
Dr K. Mellanby, CBE
Professor J. H. Middlemiss, CMG
Lord Morris of Grasmere, KCMG
Professor W. A. Murray
Sir Fraser Noble, MBE
Sir Arthur Norrington
Sir Frederick Pedler
Dame Margery Perham, DCMG, CBE
Dr W. Perry, OBE
G. A. Petch

Professor C. H. Philips, OBE
Dr E. J. Richards, OBE
Professor H. N. Robson
Professor H. Schnieden
Professor V. G. J. Sheddick
Dr A. E. Sloman
Professor J. H. Smith
Professor J. B. Stenlake
Sir Roger Stevens, GCMG
Professor W. A. C. Stewart
Professor M. Swann
Sir James Tait
Frank Thistlethwaite
Professor A. Tropp
Dr F. A. Vick, OBE
Professor E. G. White
Dr C. Whitworth
Professor H. C. Wiltshire
E. M. Wright
Professor F. G. Young
J. Mark, OBE (Assessor for O.D.A.)

Director: R. C. Griffiths
Secretary: I. C. M. Maxwell
Assistant Director: Mrs J. M. Hotchkiss
Assistant Secretaries: K. Lockyer; D. P. Saville; J. M. Theakstone

The Inter-University Council for Higher Education Overseas (entitled until 1955 The Inter-University Council for Higher Education in the Colonies) was constituted in 1946 at the invitation of the Secretary of State for the Colonies, by the universities of the United Kingdom and of the Colonial territories. The Council now consists of one representative of each United Kingdom University, except for the University of London which has two; co-opted members; one representative each of the Standing Committee on Teacher Training of the National Council for the Supply of Teachers Overseas and the Council for Technical Education and Training for Overseas Countries; and the Adviser on Higher Education to the Overseas Development Administration.

Its general purposes are:

(1) to encourage co-operation, in so far as such co-operation is mutually desired, between the universities in the United Kingdom and university institutions in: (*a*) East, West and Central Africa, Botswana, Lesotho and Swaziland, the Sudan, Ethiopia, the West Indies, Guyana, Hong Kong, Malaysia, Singapore, Malta, Mauritius, Papua and New Guinea, the South Pacific; and (*b*) such other countries as may be determined.

(2) generally to assist in the development of higher education in the countries and areas aforesaid.

JEROME HOUSING FELLOWSHIP
19–25 Harrington Gardens, London S.W.7 (FREmantle 2789)

Council:
Chairman: Rory McNeile, FCA

Mrs T. W. Scott (Warden—Impala House)
Mrs Josef Bartosik
Mrs Zivka Lewis (Warden—Jerome House)
Jonathan Lewis, OBE

Sir Dermot Milman, Bt (British Council)
Bodo Slazenger
Peter Comyns (Warden—Zebra House)

Founded in 1964 to provide further accommodation on the same pattern as Zebra and Impala House (*q.v.*). Their first project was the purchase of a well-known hotel in South Kensington, at 19-25 Harrington Gardens, S.W.7, which has been converted into accommodation for 220 students with their wives and families, and which is called Jerome House.

JOINT AFRICA BOARD

25 Victoria Street, Westminster, London S.W.1 (01–222 2951)

Chairman: P. H. B. Wall, MC, VRD, MP
Vice-Chairmen: H. St. L. Grenfell, OBE, MC; The Hon. L. Leathers
Secretary: S. Stanley-Smith

The Board was set up in 1923 as the Joint East African Board by a small group of London businessmen and Members of Parliament interested in East Africa. Its scope was later enlarged and its name changed to the Joint East and Central African Board. Its object is to promote agricultural, commercial and industrial development, African advancement and good relations between the races. In 1965 the name was again changed, to Joint Africa Board, to reflect the concentration of the Board's interests in Central Africa and the neighbouring territories in Southern Africa. The Board is financed by subscriptions. Services offered include the provision of information and advice, approaches to Government Departments and material for debates in Parliament and occasional newsletters to members.

JOINT COMMONWEALTH SOCIETIES' COUNCIL

c/o The Royal Overseas League, Park Place, St James', London S.W.1
(01–493 5051)

Chairman: Rt Hon. The Viscount Boyd of Merton, CH

Members of the Council:
The Royal Commonwealth Society
The Victoria League for Commonwealth Friendship
The Royal Over-Seas League
The English-Speaking Union of the Commonwealth
The Royal Society for India, Pakistan and Ceylon
The Royal African Society
League for the Exchange of Commonwealth Teachers
The British Association of Malaysia and Singapore
London House
The West India Committee
The Pakistan Society
The Commonwealth Section of the Royal Society of Arts
The Women's Corona Society
Commonwealth Youth Exchange Council
Commonwealth Friendship Movement

Hon. Secretary: D. K. Daniels, CBE, The Ranfurly Library Service

The Joint Commonwealth Societies' Council (formerly Conference) was established, with the support of the Secretary of State for Commonwealth Relations, to co-ordinate on general lines the activities of recognised Societies, with the object of avoiding overlapping and duplication of effort. These Societies, which came into being at different times and are non-party and non-sectarian, all have the same general object, namely the promotion of mutual understanding and personal friendship between peoples of the Commonwealth.

Representatives of the Foreign and Commonwealth Office, the Commonwealth Secretariat, the Commonwealth Institute and the British Council attend meetings.

The Council organises joint meetings and ceremonies of a Commonwealth character and the joint entertainment of visitors of note and is responsible for the arrangements for the celebration of Commonwealth Day in London and for the distribution of H.M. The Queen's Commonwealth Day Message.

THE LAND RESOURCES DIVISION

Tolworth Tower, Surbiton, Surrey (01-399 5281)

Director: P. C. Chambers, CBE

Supervision of projects in Latin America, Caribbean and Pacific, carographic arrangements, training and stores: T. I. Rees
Superivision of projects in Africa and Asia, publications, information, research and laboratory services: M. A. Brunt
Tropical Soils Liaison Officer (based at Rothamsted Experimental Station): Dr J. K. Coulter (Telephone Harpenden 4671 ext. 197)

The Land Resources Division of the Foreign and Commonwealth Office Overseas Development Administration was separated in April 1971 from its parent body, the Directorate of Overseas Surveys.

The Division assesses land resources for the governments of developing countries and makes recommendations on the use of these resources for the development of agriculture, livestock husbandry and forestry; it also gives advice on related subjects to overseas governments and organisations, makes scientific personnel available for appointment abroad and provides lectures and training courses in the basic techniques of resource appraisal.

The land resource assessments are normally of an integrated type in which scientists of different disciplines cooperate to study the environment in relation to the ultimate object—effective use of land. The Division consequently employs some 60 scientists trained in geology, geomorphology, climatology, soil science, hydrology, irrigation engineering, ecology, forestry, agriculture, livestock husbandry and agricultural economics.

Three main types of project are undertaken by the Division, representing progressively more detailed levels of study in decreasingly extensive areas: reconnaissance land resource assessments; intensive land resource assessments; and finally development studies of sites selected for specific kinds of land use development after careful consideration of the physical and socio-economic environment.

Ideally, within a given region, the Division prefers to take part in a sequence of the three types of study, leading to the development of the most suitable sites and to assist with agronomic trials and similar detailed investigations which may be needed before planning and development begin.

Resource assessment projects are in progress in The Gambia, Nigeria, Bahamas, British Honduras, British Solomon Islands Protectorate, Nepal and Sabah while project work is approaching completion for Zambia, Botswana, Malawi, Fiji and the Cayman Islands. In addition, staff are seconded to give specialist assistance to overseas governments in Uganda (botany of medicinal plants),

Sabah (cocoa agronomy and development), Swaziland (soil fertility agronomy), Malawi (the development of a soil survey unit and detailed studies for irrigation and special crops) and Windward Islands (banana research and development).

The Division cooperates with many other organisations concerned with developing countries and during recent years members of its staff have served with missions of UDP, FAO, IBRD, SEATO, CENTO and the Commonwealth Development Corporation.

The Division's work forms part of the Overseas Development Administration's aid programme in the natural resources field. It works in liaison with the Departments and Advisers dealing with these resources and with other scientific units of the Administration; for example the Marketing Advisor and scientists of the Tropical Products Institute are currently making a study of meat marketing in The Gambia to which the Division is contributing an assessment of grazing resources.

The work of the Division requires certain complementary and ancillary services, some of which are not available overseas. The Directorate of Overseas Surveys procures air photography used extensively for interpretation purposes in land resource projects and also produces maps initially drawn by the Cartographic Unit of the Division. Much land resource information is supplied to overseas governments in map form.

Soils and leaf samples are analysed at the Division's Tropical Soils Analysis Unit at the Ministry of Agriculture's Agricultural Development Advisory Service's Regional Soil Laboratory at Reading.

A Publications, Information and Bibliographic Service is based on the Division's library at headquarters.

THE LAWN TENNIS ASSOCIATION
Barons Court, West Kensington, London W.14 (01–385 2366)

President: Sir Carl Aarvold, OBE, TD
Chairman of the Council 1971: R. H. Buxton
Honorary Treasurer: H. J. Sargeant
Secretary: S. Basil Reay, OBE

The objects of the Lawn Tennis Association, which was founded in January 1888, are to safeguard the interests of the game, to uphold the rules of lawn tennis and rules and regulations of the International Lawn Tennis Federation, and the regulations for the Davis Cup and Federation Cup Competitions, to take full control of the game of lawn tennis in England, Scotland and Wales, and to promote all international, national, county or junior events held in this country.

The Lawn Tennis Association had responsibility for the rules of lawn tennis until the International Lawn Tennis Federation was founded in 1913. The Championships at Wimbledon are promoted by the Lawn Tennis Association and the All England Lawn Tennis Club.

The following countries in the Commonwealth are affiliated to the L.T.A.— Australia, Canada, India, New Zealand, Pakistan, Guyana, Ceylon, Cyprus, Ghana, Guernsey, Hong Kong, Jamaica, Jersey, Kenya, Malaysia, Malta, Mauritius, Tanzania, Trinidad and Tobago and Uganda.

There is a particularly friendly relationship between the Lawn Tennis Associations in the Commonwealth countries and the British L.T.A.

LEAGUE FOR THE EXCHANGE OF
COMMONWEALTH TEACHERS

124 Belgrave Road, Westminster, London S.W.1 (01–834 0595)

Chairman: Sir Kenneth Bradley, CMG
Vice-Chairman: L. G. A. Saunders
Hon. Treasurer: V. R. Shaw, JP

The League was founded as the League of the Empire in 1901 (later becoming the League of the British Commonwealth and Empire), and assumed its present title in November 1963. Its objects are to promote friendly and educational intercourse between the different countries of the Commonwealth through the Scheme for the Interchange of Teachers. The work of the League is entirely non-political and non-sectarian. Membership is open to anyone on payment of an annual subscription of one guinea. (Life Membership £5).

The League is governed by a Council which comprises the Chairman, Vice-Chairman and other elected members, representatives of the Association of Education Officers, Association of Directors of Education in Scotland, National Union of Teachers, Inner London Teachers' Association, Educational Institute of Scotland, Joint Four Associations, Association of Teachers in Colleges and Departments of Education, High Commissioners Offices of Canada, Australia, New Zealand and Jamaica (elected by overseas teachers on exchange in the United Kingdom) and from time to time includes co-opted members. Representatives from the Department of Education and Science, Scottish Education Department and Ministry of Education for Northern Ireland attend the meetings of the Council and of the Finance and General Purposes Committee.

The Scheme for the Interchange of Teachers was instituted in 1919 for the express purpose of bringing about co-operation in education between the different countries of the Commonwealth at a time when little or no co-operation existed. In the past teachers from Britain have been sent to Canada, Australia, New Zealand, the Rhodesias and, until 1962, to South Africa. Council has decided to extend the scheme to the newer developing countries of the Commonwealth and the first exchange to Jamaica took place in September 1964, with Kenya in January 1969 and Gibraltar in January 1971. Negotiations with other countries are in progress. The exchange is for a period of one educational year.

The League administers the Scheme for the Interchange of Teachers on behalf of the British Government who finance cost of living and travel grants for teachers proceeding from Britain and subsidise the League's administration.

During the year 1970-71 the following exchanges were arranged—Canada 55, Australia 39, New Zealand 17, Kenya 2, Gibraltar 2. Each exchange involves one U.K. and one overseas teacher.

The League works in close co-operation with the Directors of Education in Britain, Australia and New Zealand and with the Canadian Education Association and the Registrars of the various Canadian Provinces. The same applies to the Jamaican Ministry of Education and the Kenyan and Gibraltarian education authorities. The educational authorities in Britain provide advice on the selection of candidates from Britain and on the suitability of schools for the reception of overseas teachers.

LONDON HOUSE

(The Dominion Students' Hall Trust)

Mecklenburgh Square, London W.C.1 (01–837 8888)

London House was founded in 1930 by the late F. C. Goodenough. It is a hall of residence primarily for post-graduate men students from the British Commonwealth, former member countries of the British Commonwealth and the United States of America.

The Building lies on the south side of Mecklenburgh Square and accommodates some 340 students in study bedrooms. Within the building are a chapel, cinema, squash courts and spacious common rooms.

When required professional advice can usually be obtained for residents and a wide programme of sporting, cultural and recreational activities is provided. *(See also* William Goodenough House)

LONDON SCHOOL OF HYGIENE AND TROPICAL MEDICINE

(Incorporating the Ross Institute and the TUC Centenary Institute)

Keppel Street, Gower Street, London WC1E 7HT (01–636 8636)

Telegrams: Hygower, London W.C.1

The Athlone Committee, appointed in 1921 to consider the needs of postgraduate medical education in London, included in its recommendations that an Institute of State Medicine should be established in the University of London. In 1923 the Rockefeller Foundation undertook to provide $2 million for the establishment of an institute of this kind. It was agreed that the Institute should be called a 'School of Hygiene' and that the scope of its work should be 'the maintenance of health and the prevention of diseases in their widest application, not only in temperate but also in tropical and arctic climates'.

The London School of Tropical Medicine had been founded at the Albert Dock Hospital by the Seamen's Hospital Society in 1899. It had been a School of the University since 1905. This School was amalgamated with the new Institute, and in 1924 the first Royal Charter was granted creating a body corporate to be known as The London School of Hygiene and Tropical Medicine. Its new building was opened in 1929.

In 1934 the School was amalgamated with the Ross Institute, the latter retaining its name and its own Committee with responsibility for promoting and encouraging public health measures in the tropics. This work is still financed mainly by industry. In 1968 the Trades Union Congress, to celebrate its own centenary, provided substantial additional funds to expand the Department of Occupational Health into an Institute providing an advisory service to all sections of industry.

Y*

The Bureau of Hygiene and Tropical Diseases, and the Medical Research Council's Environmental Physiology Research Unit and Social Medicine Unit are accommodated within the building.

The Hospital for Tropical Diseases, originally founded by the Seamen's Hospital Society, remains the associated teaching hospital, but is now administered as part of University College Hospital Group. Winches Farm Field Station, near St Albans, provides additional facilities for research students.

The School prepares graduate students, mostly medical graduates, for the following degrees and diplomas of the University of London, courses for which last for an academic year: MSc in Medical Demography, Medical Parasitology, Medical Statistics, Occupational Hygiene, Occupational Medicine, Social Medicine (2-year course); Diplomas in Bacteriology, Clinical Medicine of the Tropics, Nutrition, and Tropical Public Health.

Short courses are offered in Epidemiology and Medical Statistics. A five-month course is offered for those wishing to study for the examination for the Diploma in Tropical Medicine and Hygiene of the Conjoint Board of the Royal Colleges.

Facilities are provided for suitable candidates to study for the degrees of MPhil and PhD.

MALAYSIA HOUSING SOCIETY

17, 18, 19 Upper Montagu Street, London W.1

Committee of Management:
Chairman: Sir William Goode, G CMG

W. H. C. Bailey, CBE	E. D. Shearn
J. H. Keswick, CMG	C. M. Sheridan, CMG, PMN
R. J. McNeile, FCA	Sir Douglas Waring, CBE, PMN
Stafford Northcote	J. H. D. Sibree, MBE, MC

Secretary: Jonathan Lewis, OBE

Set up in 1964 for a similar purpose to Zebra, Impala and Jerome Houses (*q.v.*) but primarily for students from Malaysia, Singapore and the Far East. First project—the purchase of Nos. 15, 17, and 19 Upper Montagu Street, London W.1, to provide married accommodation and some single flatlets. House called *Sentosa House*, which means House of Peace.

THE MALAYSIA-SINGAPORE COMMERCIAL ASSOCIATION (INCORPORATED)

5th Floor, Grand Buildings, Trafalgar Square, London W.C.2 (01–839 6549)

President: A. S. Kinnear
Members of the Council:

W. H. C. Bailey, CBE	M. A. R. Herries, OBE, MC
T. B. Barlow	K. V. J. Jackson
N. H. T. Bennett	H. Karsten, MBE
P. H. Brodie	R. Lamb
J. N. Catchpole	J. H. Sibree, MBE, MC
F. G. Charlesworth	Sir Hugh Mackay-Tallack
H. F. Clements	E. C. Tokeley
R. A. C. Cobley	J. Wilson, CBE
L. H. N. Davies, CMG	

Secretary: W. C. S. Corry, CBE

The Association exists to protect the commercial and other economic interests of the United Kingdom and the Commonwealth in Malaysia and Singapore. Its membership represents a considerable cross-section of British firms and enterprises operating in those countries. Ordinary Membership is open to British subjects and British and Commonwealth firms, and it is incorporated under the Companies Act.

MEDICAL ADVISORY COMMITTEE

Following the publication in March 1963 of the Government Statement on the report of Sir Arthur Porritt's Working Party on medical aid to the developing countries, the Secretary for Technical Co-operation set up a Medical Advisory Committee, consisting of prominent members of various branches of the Medical profession in Britain, of the Dental, Nursing and Auxiliary services, and of the government organisations concerned with technical assistance in medicine. The Committee, of which Sir Brain Windeyer is the Chairman, is now responsible to the Minister for Overseas Development and has the following terms of reference:

(*a*) To review at appropriate intervals the technical assistance provided by the Overseas Development Administration in medical and allied fields, and to make recommendations to the Minister for Overseas Development;

(*b*) By means of sub-committees and panels to assist the O.D.A. in the various aspects of its work in these fields, and to advise on particular problems put to it by the Administration.

The membership of the Medical Advisory Committee is:

Chairman: Sir Brian Windeyer
Deputy Chairman: N. Leach, CMG

Dr F. D. Beddard	Sir John McMichael
Dr J. H. F. Brotherston	Professor B. G. Maegraith, CMG
Sir John Bruce, CBE, TD	Professor J. H. Middlemiss, CMG
Professor G. M. Bull	Sir John Peel, KCVO
Professor C. M. Fleming, CBE	Lord Rosenheim, KBE
Sir George Godber, KCB	Miss B. G. Schofield, OBE
Sir Charles Harris	Sir Herbert Seddon, CMG
Professor F. R. G. Heaf, CMG	Professor A. B. Semple, CBE
Professor Sir Ian Hill, CBE, TD	Dr E. T. C. Spooner, CMG
Professor K. R. Hill	Dr Margaret Suttill
Surgeon Rear-Admiral W. Holgate, CB, OBE	Mr S. F. Taylor
Dr T. C. Hunt, CBE	Professor R. M. Walker, CBE
Mr H. H. Langston	Professor C. A. Wells, CBE
Dr J. M. Liston, CMG	Professor A. W. Woodruff
Sir Hector MacLennan	

The Committee has established permanent panels to consider technical assistance problems in the following fields:

Medical Education
Recruitment of Medical Staff, Visitors and Consultants
Nursing Services
Preventive Medicine, Ancillary Medical Services and Equipment
Dental Services
Associations between British and Overseas Medical Institutions.

NATIONAL COUNCIL FOR THE SUPPLY AND TRAINING OF TEACHERS OVERSEAS

Chairman: Sir William Houghton

Members:

Sir William Alexander
Bailie Mrs. J. M. Dickson
W. Boaden
E. L. Bradby
Professor G. N. Brown
L. W. K. Brown
Alderman S. M. Caffyn, CBE
The Reverend R. F. G. Calder
The Reverend R. Crawford
R. F. Cunningham
The Rev. B. Duffy
W. C. H. Eakin
M. J. Gifford
Dr J. J. Grant, CBE
P. Griffin, MBE
T. Henderson
Miss J. M. S. Hendry
Alderman The Rt. Hon. Lord Heycock, CBE, CSTJ, DL, JP
A. W. S. Hutchings
T. Jardine
D. G. Jarmin

Professor J. Lewis
The Reverend P. Craik MacQuoid
F. M. Newrick
J. C. Nolan
The Reverend G. R. Osborn
E. G. Quigley
C. W. Robert
F. G. Roberts
Canon J. S. Robertson
Dr W. Roy
L. G. A. Saunders
Miss A. C. Shrubsole
C. R. Allison, MA
Professor A. Taylor
H. A. Warren
Dr G. E. Watts, CBE
J. W. Watts
J. Weir, DSO, JP
G. A. Winter
D. P. Williams
Sir Henry P. Wood, CBE

The Council was established in 1960 under the then Minister of Education. Responsibility for its affairs was transferred in 1965 to the Minister for Overseas Development. It consists of 47 members and 9 official assessors. The Council has two Standing Committees, the General Standing Committee which deals with matters arising in connection with any of the Council's functions, other than teacher training, and the Standing Committee for Teacher Training which deals with teacher training in its widest aspects.

The Council brings together representatives of teachers' organisations, local education authorities, recruiting bodies, and interested Government departments for the following purposes:

(a) to keep under review the progress of recruitment to teaching and teacher training posts overseas; together with all aspects of progressive advancement of teacher training in overseas developing countries;

(b) generally to assist the recruitment of teachers for schools and of those concerned with the education and training of teachers for service in the developing countries overseas and the resettlement of both categories on return; and in respect of teacher training to have special reference to the secondment and exchange of staff with developing countries and the promotion of links between colleges of education at home and overseas;

(c) to stimulate in this country interest in education service in the developing countries overseas and to promote a climate of opinion in which periods of service overseas are recognised as an asset to the professional careers of teachers.

The Council is not concerned with posts in university institutions overseas except in relation to teachers in schools, technical colleges and colleges of education in the United Kingdom who wish to take such posts and to teachers in such posts who wish to serve in schools, technical colleges and colleges of education on return to the United Kingdom.

THE NATURAL RUBBER PRODUCERS'
RESEARCH ASSOCIATION
19 Buckingham Street, London WC2N 6EJ (01–930 9314)
Laboratories: 56 Tewin Road, Welwyn Garden City, Herts.
(Welwyn Garden 25474)

Members of the Board:

L. Bateman, CMG, FRS, Chairman
Lew Sip Hon, KMN
(alternate to L. Bateman)
Lim Kim Cheng, Vice-Chairman

L. Mullins, Director of Research
L. H. N. Davis, CMG
H. B. Egmont Hake, CBE

Secretary: P. O. Wickens, JMN

The Natural Rubber Producers' Research Association, incorporated in 1938, is an independent research organisation financed almost wholly by the Malayan Rubber Fund Board, the Malaysian statutory authority responsible for natural rubber research and development. The annual budget of the N.R.P.R.A. is about £500,000.

In conjunction with its sister organisation in Malaysia, the Rubber Research Institute of Malaya, the N.R.P.R.A. carries out a broad range of scientific and technological studies from botany and biochemistry to applied science and engineering, with the objects of improving the qualities of, and increasing industrial demand for, natural rubber. It provides technical and scientific support for the Malayan Rubber Fund Board's Technical Advisory and Consultancy Services in Australia, Austria, Germany, India, Italy, Japan, New Zealand, Spain, the U.K. and the U.S.A.

NEW ZEALAND SOCIETY
54 Regent Street, London W.1 (734 2181)

Patron: H.R.H. The Prince Philip, Duke of Edinburgh, KG, KT, OM, GBE
Vice-Patron: H.E. Sir Denis Blundell, KBE
High Commissioner for New Zealand

Officers 1970/71

President: J. M. Butler
Vice-Presidents: Alan L. Luke; The Very Reverend Martin Sullivan, Dean of St Paul's
Hon. Secretary: V. G. H. Jones
Hon. Treasurer: L. F. Brown

General Committee

Sir Max Brown, KCB, CMG; Dr H. G. Bremner;
P. G. H. Newton, Marshal of the Royal Air Force; Sir Charles Elworthy, GCB, CBE, DSO;
M. H. R. Sandwith; Warren T. Jones; Dr E. H. Sealy; Col. J. I. M. Smail, OBE, MC, TD;
D. M. Dunnet; A. Trevor Campbell (*ex officio*)

The object of the Society is to promote in the United Kingdom the interests of the Dominion of New Zealand and to provide New Zealanders and others interested in New Zealand with opportunities for joining in activities of mutual interest.

Membership is limited to men who are British subjects (a) either New Zealand born or a person who has resided in New Zealand for not less than five years— or (b) a person having business, financial, or personal contacts or interests in New Zealand. There cannot be more (b) category members than there are (a) category members.

The Society was originally formed in 1925 under another name and became the New Zealand Society in 1933 when it inaugurated 6th February as New Zealand Day in the United Kingdom, this date being the anniversary of the signing of the Treaty of Waitangi.

A commemoration service is held annually on New Zealand Day at the Guild Church of St Lawrence Jewry next to the Guildhall and a Commemorative Dinner is also held annually on or near 6th February, usually at the Savoy Hotel.

THE NUFFIELD FOUNDATION

Nuffield Lodge, Regent's Park, London NW1 4RS (01-722 8871)

Director: Dr Clifford Butler, FRS

The Foundation was established in 1943 by Lord Nuffield. At present it makes grants in the following seven fields: Medicine, Biology, Other Sciences, Social Research and Experiment, Care of Old People and Research in Ageing, Education and the Commonwealth Overseas. Many of the grants for the Commonwealth Overseas are for research, but a few are also given for practical projects. The Foundation has also given major support for the establishment in this country of organisations which provide specialised services to meet particular needs overseas.

In addition to its grants, the Foundation has a programme of personal awards. A limited number of fellowships in the humanities and social sciences, medicine, and natural sciences are awarded each year to graduates between the ages of 30 and 40 from the Commonwealth to study in the United Kingdom. Other schemes include fellowships for Pakistani civil servants, Canadian public officials and trade unionists, scholarships for farmers from Australia, Canada and New Zealand, travel grants for Canadian graduates and special study grants for Australians.

Awards for scientists of the Commonwealth Overseas are also made under the Royal Society and the Nuffield Foundation Commonwealth Bursaries scheme.

ORGANISATION OF EMPLOYERS' FEDERATIONS AND EMPLOYERS IN DEVELOPING COUNTRIES—OEF

Progress House, 10 Snow Hill, London EC1A 2EA (01-248 5454)

Cables: Brovemp London EC1A 2EA

President: The Rt Hon. Lord Campbell of Eskan
Chairman: James Campbell, OBE
Vice-Chairman: D. J. Flunder, MC, VRD
Director: L. S. Dixon, ADK
Assistant Director: F. M. Clark
Editor: Mrs V. L. Roberts

The Organisation was founded in 1945 as the Colonial Employers' Federation but adopted its present name in February, 1965. Its aims are to promote the interests of employers in the developing countries of the world and to keep members informed and advise them on all industrial relations matters affecting or likely to affect their interests; to provide information and advice to members on matters coming within the scope of the International Labour Organisation; to take note of legislative measures which may affect or tend to affect the interests of members and to take such steps as appear to be desirable; to promote and encourage consultation between members and to ascertain their views and take such action as may be necessary or expedient to give effect thereto; and to promote and encourage training in the field of industrial relations.

The Organisation has members in over 40 countries, comprising more than 50 federations (including associations of employers and companies) and 65 firms and individual employers having interests in developing countries.

The Council, which meets twice a year, once in London and once in Geneva, is composed of representatives of member associations and trades or industries, and an Executive Committee is elected from Council members at the Annual General Meeting. A Finance and General Purposes Committee is elected from the Executive Committee.

The Organisation publishes a fortnightly newsletter and Occasional Papers on aspects of industrial relations.

The Chairman and the Director have places on the British Government Tripartite Overseas Labour Consultative Committee.

OVERSEA SERVICE COLLEGE
(*see under* FARNHAM CASTLE)

OVERSEAS DEVELOPMENT INSTITUTE LTD
10-11 Percy Street, London WIP OJB (01-637 3622)

President: Sir Leslie Rowan, Chairman, The British Council
Chairman: Trevor E. Peppercorn, Chairman, Triplex Holdings Ltd

Council:

Ronald Archer,
 Unilever Ltd
Richard Bailey,
 Partner, Gibb-Ewbank Industrial Con-
 sultants
J. G. Beevor,
 Director, Glaxo Group Ltd
Kenneth Berill,
 Chairman, University Grants Committee
Lord Blackett,
 Past President, The Royal Society
The Rev. Alan R. Booth,
 Director, Christian Aid
Lord Boyle of Handsworth,
 Vice-Chancellor, Leeds University
Lord Campbell of Eskan,
 President, Booker McConnell Ltd
Lord Caradon,
 Senior Consultant to United Nations
 Development Programme
Geoffrey Chandler,
 Co-ordinator, Group Trade Relations,
 Shell International Petroleum Company
 Ltd
Michael Clapham,
 Deputy Chairman, Imperial Chemical
 Industries Ltd
Ian Cox,
 Formerly Trade Relations Division, Shell
 International Petroleum Company Ltd
A. H. Dutoon,
 Economic Relations Department, British
 Petroleum Company Ltd
Victor Feather,
 General Secretary, Trades Union Congress
Lord Franks,
 Provost, Worcester College, Oxford
Sir Arthur Gaitskell,
 Member of Board, Commonwealth
 Development Corporation
Sir William Gorell Barnes,
 Director, Royal Insurance Company Ltd
The Hon. Sir John Henniker-Major,
 Director-General, The British Council

Professor Sir Joseph Hutchinson,
 Formerly Drapers' Professor of Agri-
 culture, University of Cambridge
Lady Jackson (Barbara Ward),
 Albert Schweitzer Professor of Inter-
 national Economic Development, Colum-
 bia University
A. W. Knight,
 Deputy Chairman, Courtaulds Ltd
Professor Ian Little,
 Professor of the Economics of Under-
 developed Countries, University of Oxford
Sir Arthur Norman,
 Chairman, The De La Rue Company Ltd
Sir Duncan Oppenheim,
 President, British-American Tobacco
 Company Ltd
Sir Ronald Prain,
 Chairman, RST International Metals Ltd
Lord Redcliffe-Maud,
 Master, University College, Oxford
Professor E. A. G. Robinson,
 Emeritus Professor, University of Cam-
 bridge
Sir Eric Roll,
 Director, S. G. Warburg and Company
 Ltd
Sir Frederic Seebohm,
 Chairman, Barclays Bank DCO
Dudley Seers,
 Director, Institute of Development Studies,
 Sussex
Donald Tyerman,
 Director, United City Merchants Ltd
Lord Walston,
 Chairman, The Institute of Race Relations
John Whitehorn,
 Deputy Director-General, Confederation
 of British Industry
Sir Geoffrey Wilson,
 Chairman, The Race Relations Board
The Rt Hon. K. G. Younger,
 formerly Director, The Royal Institute of
 International Affairs

The Overseas Development Institute was founded towards the end of 1960 by a group of people with the belief that the economic development of the countries of Africa, Asia and South America, and their relations with the industrially developed areas of the world, were of crucial importance.

The Institute is financed by donations from British business and by grants from British and American foundations and other sources. It is non-profit-making. Policies are determined by its Council, which is independent and non-governmental.

The main functions of ODI are:

(a) to provide a centre for research in development issues and problems, and to conduct studies of its own;

(b) to be a forum for the exchange of views and information among those, in Britain and abroad, who are directly concerned with overseas development in business, in government, and in other organisations;

(c) to keep the urgency of development issues and problems before the public and the responsible authorities.

ODI carries out research on problems of aid and development overseas, and the results are normally published. Publications have included a comprehensive survey of Britain's aid to developing countries; studies of French, German and Japanese aid; the role of multilateral financial organisations, regional development banks, and the record of consortia and consultative groups; the experiences of various developing countries in the receipt of aid; a handbook on the less developed countries and world trade; a layman's handbook of current information and ideas on overseas poverty and development; a directory of non-commercial organisations in Britain actively concerned in overseas development and training; a study, based on a series of seminars at ODI, on the construction industry in overseas development; a study of the application of science and technology to the economic development of the less developed countries; and periodical reviews of British development policies. In addition to its information work for which new editions of some earlier publications are being prepared, ODI is at present undertaking a major programme of research on rural development in Africa and Asia; a study of the development of indigenous entrepreneurship in Africa, and of the role of external aid agencies in furthering such development; and a study of the structure and procedures for the administration of aid programmes in Britain and other donor countries.

The Institute organises international conferences, working groups to study particular subjects, and it holds seminars and briefing sessions. A conference, jointly sponsored with the U.K. Chapter of the Society of International Development, on Britain, the EEC and the Third World was held in April 1971, the proceedings of which were subsequently published. ODI tries to make it customary for visitors from overseas with a working interest in development to visit the Institute and discuss their problems with the Institute staff or with others invited to meet them.

ODI's meetings fall into three categories: occasional large meetings and conferences held outside the Institute; small meetings at which an expert in the field is provided with a forum for discussion with a specialised audience well informed on the subject; and internal meetings at which staff of the Institute can discuss specific problems of development with visitors, many of whom are from overseas. Attendance at meetings is by invitation. There is no ordinary membership of the Institute.

OVERSEAS DIVISION, BUILDING RESEARCH STATION

Department of the Environment, Building Research Station,

Garston, Watford WD2 7JR (Garston (Herts.) 4040)

Head of Overseas Division and Adviser to the Minister for Overseas Development:
A. T. Pickles, OBE
Deputy Head: W. Kinniburgh

A Colonial Liaison Section was established at the Building Research Station in 1948. This eas expended in 1953 to deal with planning and housing, and renamed the Tropical Division in 1958. In 1966, to reflect the expanded field of work, it became the Overseas Division. The entire cost of this Unit is met by the Foreign and Commonwealth Office (Overseas Development Administration).

The main functions of the Division are:

(*a*) to supply overseas countries with technical information on building, housing and planning;

(*b*) to assist with the solution of specific technical problems and to answer enquiries;

(*c*) to advise the Minister for Overseas Development on building, housing and planning, especially in countries in receipt of British development aid.

Information is provided through seminars, lectures, *Overseas Building Notes*, and other literature on building, housing and planning in tropical and subtropical countries, as well as articles in the technical press.

OVERSEAS SERVICES RESETTLEMENT BUREAU

Eland House, Stag Place, London S.W.1 (01–834 2377)

Director: Sir Edwin Arrowsmith, KCMG
Deputy Heads:
J. S. A. Lewis, OBE   M. R. D. Langley, OBE, MVO
M. J. B. Molohan, CMG, MBE
Liaison Officer: A. H. Pickwoad, OBE
Adviser on Government and Quasi-Government Appointments (Part-time):
Sir George Mallaby, KCMG, OBE
Adviser on Careers in Business (Part-time): G. B. Howard-Rice

The Bureau was set up in 1957 to assist in resettling officers of HMOCS retiring prematurely from the Service as a result of the grant of self-government or independence to dependent territories. Serving officers, once they have exercised their option to retire, may apply to the Bureau for help in finding employment in the United Kingdom or overseas. In mid 1966 its terms of reference were extended and the Bureau's services became available also to people appointed overseas through the Ministry of Overseas Development (now the Overseas Development Administration) and the Crown Agents, provided they had served for a certain minimum period. At the same time officers who had served in non-government posts in the public sector and whose emoluments were met in part by the British Government became eligible to use the Bureau. In addition, as a result of a further extension in 1967 the Bureau's services are now available to certain officers of the Diplomatic Service who are retired before the age of 60.

The Bureau has established contact with a great number of employers in commerce, industry, government and quasi-government organisations covering administrative as well as professional and technical fields. It puts men and women in touch with them and it also offers advice on training courses, the type of work suited to given qualifications, and on all matters relating to the search for suitable employment.

In 1962, an Advisory Council on the OSRB was set up by the then Secretary for Technical Co-operation. In 1964, the Council was reconstituted by the Minister of Overseas Development to advise on the work of the OSRB. The Chairman is the Viscount Boyd of Merton.

OVERSEAS STUDENTS ADVISORY BUREAU
Broadmead House, 21 Paton Street SW1Y 4DR (01-839-5056/9)

Trustees:

Lord Sainsbury (Chairman)
The Rt Hon. Earl of Listowel, PC, GCMG
J. L. Boss
Major D. Buckley, MBE
Lord Douglass
Raymond P. Brookes

David Edwards (Hon. Solicitor)
W. W. Fea, FCA
G. A. Hanscomb
Frank Harcourt-Munning, CBE
Sir Gilbert Rennie, GBE, KCMG, MC

Director: David Grantley

The Overseas Students Advisory Bureau was constituted a Charitable Trust in July 1963.

Funds come from Overseas countries, private and family trusts, local education authorities, colleges and universities, industry and commerce, and private individuals. The annual budget is approximately £7,000. Copies of the Accounts are available on request.

The Bureau's activities are at present limited to placing overseas students, on full-time and sandwich courses at colleges and universities in this country, into practical training vacancies with industry and commerce for vacation, sandwich, and graduate periods.

This work is to be expanded in the financial year starting 1st April 1971 with the help of a grant from the Overseas Development Administration.

OVERSEAS TERRITORIES INCOME TAX OFFICE
26 Grosvenor Gardens, London S.W.1 (01-730 0300 and 0309)

Official Representative: J. E. Comben, OBE

This Office was established in 1942 to act as Agent in the United Kingdom, under Colonial Income Tax legislation, for Commissioners of Income Tax in the various Territories and has continued to act for a number of countries which have since become independent. It deals with the assessment and collection of

Income Tax payable by companies and pensioners resident in the United Kingdom and with general enquiries relating to overseas taxation, including questions of double taxation relief. It also runs training courses for overseas tax officials. It works in close liaison with the Crown Agents for Oversea Governments and Administrations.

The Overseas Development Administration is responsible for the recruitment of the senior staff of the Office, but it draws its finances from the administrations which it serves.

OXFAM
274 Banbury Road, Oxford (Oxford 56777) (Telex: 83610)

Chairman: M. H. Rowntree
Vice-Chairman: Dr F. C. James
Hon. Treasurer: R. H. Langdon-Davies, DFC
Hon. Secretary: R. J. Mullard
Deputy Hon. Secretary: Dr L. Liepmann
Director: H. Leslie Kirkley, CBE

The principal objects of Oxfam are the relief of poverty, distress and suffering in any part of the world—whether due to natural disaster such as famine or earthquake, to war or civil disturbances, or to lack of resources among the people involved.

Ways of achieving these objects include: providing food, healing, clothing, shelter, training and education and promoting research which in turn may help to relieve distress. Help—in the form of money grants and supplies of clothing, food and medicines—is sent to more than 90 countries and distributed to many kinds of agencies, without discrimination on grounds of race, religion, colour or politics. More than half the grants now go to long-term constructive schemes, designed to remove the causes of hunger, and raise living standards in the future.

Oxfam is registered under the Companies Act, 1948 and Charities Act, 1960. Bankers: Barclays Bank Ltd., The Old Bank, High Street, Oxford.

THE PAKISTAN SOCIETY
37 Sloane Street, London S.W.1 (01–235 6905)

Patrons: H.R.H. The Duke of Edinburgh, KG, KT, OM, GBE;
The President of Pakistan

President: H.E. Mr Salman A. Ali, SQA, PFS

Vice-Presidents:
Begum Liaquat Ali Khan, NI;
Field Marshal Sir Claude Auchinleck, GCB, GCIE, CSI, DSO, OBE;
Begum Shaista Ikramullah; Professor Abdus Salam, SPk, FRS;
Sir Frederick Bourne, KCSI, CIE, SPk; The Rt Hon. The Earl of Inchcape;
Lieutenant-General Mohammad Yousuf; Mr Habib Rahimtoola;
His Grace The Duke of Devonshire, PC, MC; Mr A. W. Adamjee, HPk;
Sir Ambrose Dundas, KCIE, CSI
Chairman of Executive Committee: Sir Alexander MacFarquhar, KBE, CIE
Hon. Secretary: Mr L. V. Deane
Hon. Treasurer: Mr C. W. Tassie, OBE

The principal object of the Society, which was founded in 1951, is to increase knowledge in the United Kingdom of the arts, languages, literature, music, history, religions, antiquities, usages, institutions, customs and manners of Pakistan. Membership is open to men and women of all nationalities, there being Life and Ordinary members. In addition, Associate membership is extended to students or persons not resident in Britain, and Corporate membership to business firms and other bodies approved by the Committee. At the beginning of 1971 there were about 900 members, including 80 Corporate members.

Lecture meetings are held each month to which members are entitled to bring friends; the first five Prime Ministers of Pakistan have been among the speakers. The Committee also arranges certain other social functions, including an Annual Dinner; and joint meetings with sister associations are held from time to time. H.R.H. The Duke of Edinburgh was the Guest of Honour at the Annual Dinner in 1960, President Ayub Khan in 1961 and 1966 and H.H. the Aga Khan in 1962. The Society's *Bulletin* is published twice a year.

PERMANENT COMMITTEE OF THE COMMONWEALTH COLLECTIONS OF MICRO-ORGANISMS

Africa House, Kingsway, London WC2B 6BD (01–405 7786/7)

Chairman: Dr S. T. Cowan

Members:

Britain	India
Canada	Pakistan
Australia	Jamaica
New Zealand	

Secretary: Dr J. M. Shewan

A Committee of the British Commonwealth Scientific Official Conference in 1946* recommended that a central Commonwealth organisation should be established for the maintenance of collections of type cultures and micro-organisms. As a result of the Specialist Conference called in 1947† the Commonwealth Collections of Micro-organisms was established to foster the maintenance and extension of existing culture collections and to increase the general availability and use of cultures where necessary.

The central administration takes the form of a Permanent Committee on which each member country is represented, with secretariat services provided by the Commonwealth Scientific Liaison Offices. Institutes maintaining culture collections prepare catalogues in a standard form, whilst Directories and Collections and Lists of Species maintained are published by CSLO through Her Majesty's Stationery Office at regular intervals.

Membership is open to member countries of the Commonwealth Scientific Committee.

---

* British Commonwealth Scientific Official Conference, London 1946. Report of Proceedings, Cmd. 6970.

† Specialist Conference on Culture Collections of Micro-organisms, London, H.M.S.O., 1947.

QUEEN ELIZABETH HOUSE, OXFORD
(Oxford 52952–4)

Warden: P. P. Streeten

Queen Elizabeth House was constituted by Royal Charter in 1954. The new foundation owes its inception to a gift to the University of Oxford by the late Sir Ernest Oppenheimer for the development of Commonwealth and allied studies. It is centrally situated in Oxford in two adjoining houses on long lease from St John's College, one of which dates back to the early seventeenth century.

Under its Charter the House is a corporate body administered by a Governing Body consisting of a President, the Vice-Chancellor *ex-officio* and not more than twelve other members. The President and three members are appointed by Her Majesty's Government with the approval of the University of Oxford, the University appoints three, and the remainder (of whom one is a member of the Governing Body of the Institute of Development Studies at the University of Sussex) are appointed by the Governing Body. The Warden is appointed by the Governing Body with the approval of the Government and the University.

Queen Elizabeth House is a centre for political, economic, social, administrative, historical, legal and other studies affecting countries in the process of development, both within and outside the Commonwealth. It provides a meeting place for persons especially interested in such studies and helps them to obtain access to the academic resources of Oxford. It works in close association with the Oxford Institute of Commonwealth Studies, which is housed in its premises and with which it shares a Warden/Director. It is a focus for development studies conducted at the University of Oxford; and provides residential accommodation for Visiting Fellows and also, where possible, for graduate students, university teachers, and others visiting Oxford for academic purposes from the Commonwealth and developing countries.

The Warden and Sub-Warden teach and conduct research, particularly on the international aspects of development and on the training of diplomats from developing countries. A research project of which the Warden is Chairman of the Steering Committee is studying the impact of private overseas investment on the economics of the less developed countries. Others are concerned with urbanisation, appropriate industrial technologies, rural development, foreign trade and finance for development.

Following an agreement with the University and the then Ministry of Overseas Development, Visiting Fellowships at Queen Elizabeth House have been established to enable senior administrators in government, local authorities or public corporations, university teachers and members of the private sector from countries in receipt of British technical assistance to spend up to three terms residing in the House and undertaking study (on an *ad hominem* basis and not as members of the University) in their particular field. The fellowships began in Trinity Term 1968 and up to twenty can be awarded each year. These awards aim at enabling the potential leaders in developing countries to widen their experience and deepen their professional knowledge.

A one-year course is provided for diplomats—primarily from developing countries—under the aegis of the Oxford University Committee for Commonwealth Studies.

In the vacations special courses, conferences and seminars are organised and facilities are made available for residential courses in co-operation with other bodies. Amongst the former are courses for the Treasury Civil Service College.

RHODES HOUSE, OXFORD

(Oxford 55745)

Rhodes Trustees:

Chairman: Sir George Abell, KCIE, OBE
Sir Kenneth Wheare, CMG, Rector of Exeter
College, Oxford
The Rt Hon. Lord Franks, GCMG, KCB,
CBE, Provost of Worcester College, Oxford
The Viscount Harcourt, KCMG, OBE

J. G. Phillimore, CMG
Professor D. K. Price
Professor W. D. M. Paton, CBE
The Hon. J. F. H. Baring
The Rt Hon. Lord Blake, Provost of the
Queen's College, Oxford

Secretary and Warden of Rhodes House: E. T. Williams, CB, CBE, DSO, DL

Rhodes House is the headquarters of the Rhodes Trust and lies immediately north of Wadham College on land acquired in 1925. The Trustees administer the Scholarships endowed under the 1902 will of the late Cecil Rhodes in accordance with the conditions of the Rhodes Trust Act of 1946. Some seventy Rhodes Scholarships, each of about £1,400 a year, are awarded annually and are tenable at Oxford by men drawn from the following areas: Australia, Bermuda, British Caribbean, Canada, Ceylon, Ghana, India, Jamaica, Malta, Malaysia, New Zealand, Nigeria, Pakistan, Rhodesia, South Africa, Western Germany and the United States of America.

Apart from the Warden's quarters, Rhodes House itself is not residential, the Rhodes Scholars (of whom there are usually some 180 up at Oxford each academic year) being distributed amongst the various men's Colleges of the University. In addition to the public rooms, the Rhodes House Library (Superintendent: L. B. Frewer: Oxford 55762) of American and Commonwealth history, which is an integral part of the Bodleian Library, is housed by the Trustees in Rhodes House.

RHODES MEMORIAL MUSEUM AND COMMONWEALTH CENTRE

South Road, Bishop's Stortford, Herts. (Bishop's Stortford 51746)

Chairman of Management Committee: Lieutenant-Colonel R. J. Venn, TD, DL
Hon. Secretary: Arnold Bullough (Clerk, Bishop's Stortford Urban District Council)

The Rhodes Memorial Museum has existed since 1938 when a Trust was formed to buy the freehold property known as Netteswell House, South Road, Bishop's Stortford, together with the adjoining house. Cecil John Rhodes, who was the son of the vicar, was born at Netteswell House on 5th July 1853 and was educated at the Grammar School in Bishop's Stortford. The money for converting the houses into a Museum was provided by the British South Africa Company, De Beers and Consolidated Goldfields.

In 1963 it was decided to redecorate, re-arrange and extend the Museum for the purpose of providing the first Commonwealth Centre to exist in a provincial town in Britain, and this was opened on 5th December 1963 by His Grace the Duke of Devonshire, MC, Minister of State for Commonwealth Relations. The capital needed for this extension was met largely by a public appeal launched locally and overseas; by donations from Rhodes Scholars throughout the world; by the generosity of mining companies associated with Cecil Rhodes in his lifetime; by donations from several Commonwealth countries; and by the support of the Bishop's Stortford Urban District Council.

The Museum is open from 10.0 a.m. to 4.0 p.m. except on Sundays and Public Holidays on which days it may be possible to obtain admission on application to the caretaker (Mrs A. Forth). Admission is free, a charge being made only in those cases where parties require a special guide.

THE ROYAL AFRICAN SOCIETY
(Incorporated by Royal Charter)
18 Northumberland Avenue, London W.C.2 (01-930 6733)

President: Brian F. Macdona, CBE
Chairman: Sir Arthur Smith
Secretary: Miss H. Heather

The Royal African Society, a non-political organisation, was founded in 1901 in memory of Mary Kingsley, African explorer and writer, to foster and encourage interest in Africa; to form a link between those who are, or have been, concerned with Africa and to assist the study of African affairs in Britain. To further these aims, the Society publishes a quarterly journal *African Affairs* (which is sent free to all members of the Society and can also be purchased separately), arranges monthly lectures, conferences on Africa, social functions and provides access to a reference library and reading room.

While maintaining a scientific outlook, the Society aims specially at keeping the human interest in the forefront.

ROYAL AGRICULTURAL SOCIETY OF THE COMMONWEALTH
Giggs Hill Green, Thames Ditton, Surrey

President: H.R.H. The Prince Philip, Duke of Edinburgh, KG, KT, OM, GBE
Deputy President: Vincent Fairfax, CMG
Honorary Treasurer: John Everall, FRICS
Honorary Secretary: F. R. Francis

The Society, which is in effect a federation of the national agricultural societies within the Commonwealth, came into being at a meeting of representatives of 'Royal' agricultural societies held at the English Royal Show in 1957, and presided over by the Duke of Edinburgh. It was then agreed that the principal object of the Society should be 'to encourage and arrange the interchange of knowledge and experience in the practice and science of agriculture, with a view to improving methods of both crop production and the breeding of livestock, to improving the efficiency of agricultural implements and machinery, and to encouraging the exchange and settlement of young farmers within the Commonwealth.'

Today membership comprises 21 Societies—two in Africa, seven in Australia, one in New Zealand, one in Canada, one in New Guinea, two in the West Indies, one in Mauritius, the four national societies in the United Kingdom representing England, Scotland, Wales and Northern Ireland, the Royal Smithfield Club and the Royal Association of British Dairy Farmers. The membership of the Royal Agricultural Society of Southern Rhodesia is at present held in abeyance due to existing international difficulties. The first Conference was held at Sydney in April 1963, the second at Cambridge in 1965, the third at Toronto in 1967 and the fourth at Nairobi in September 1969. The 1971 Conference will be held in Edinburgh on 18th, 19th and 21st June. An important facet of the Society's work has become the exchange of ideas and information on new techniques, with special reference to agricultural shows, exhibitions, and the needs of the agricultural community. It is now usual for each conference to have as a theme some subject of topical interest and importance, e.g. Animal Health—"Foot and Mouth Disease" and "Brucellosis" in 1969. Printed reports of the conferences are prepared for member-societies and others interested. It has become evident that many of the problems confronting show organisers throughout the world are identical, e.g. the need to make known new breeding techniques for livestock, the requirements of trade exhibitors and the need to present the right image of modern agriculture to the rapidly expanding urban populations.

ROYAL ASIATIC SOCIETY

56 Queen Anne Street, London W1M 9LA (01–935 8944)

President: Professor B. W. Robinson
Director: Dr A. D. H. Bivar
Secretary: Miss D. Crawford

The Royal Asiatic Society was founded in 1823 for the study of the history, sociology, institutions, manners, customs, languages, art, archaeology and literature of Asia. The Society's Library contains about 100,000 books, with Sanskrit, Pali, Hindi, Arabic, Persian, Turkish, Malay, Javanese, Tibetan, Sinhalese, Burmese and Siamese manuscripts. It operates several trust funds for the publication of books on Oriental subjects, and publishes a *Journal*.

ROYAL BOTANIC GARDENS, KEW

Director: Dr J. Heslop-Harrison

During its span of over 200 years, Kew has been closely associated with the development of Commonwealth countries. From a small start in 1759 as the botanic garden of Augusta, Dowager Princess of Wales and mother of King George III, the Royal Gardens at Kew soon became famed for the unrivalled variety of plants collected from many lands. In 1841 control of the Gardens was assumed by the State and increasingly from that time, under successive Directors, Kew supplied the Commonwealth with plants of economic value and with men trained in horticulture.

Kew is renowned as an institution for the study of plants and especially their identification and classification. A large scientific staff is able to avail itself of a herbarium which is without equal in the richness of its collection of preserved plants and its fine botanical library. In addition there is the collection of living plants, some 25,000 species and botanical varieties, which forms the part of the establishment familiarly known to the public as Kew Gardens.

An important task, which has been steadily prosecuted since 1856, has been the compilation of floras of different parts of the Commonwealth. Regional floras now in preparation include those of Tropical East Africa, southern Central Africa, Iraq and Cyprus, while a revision of the Flora of West Tropical Africa is nearing completion.

The identification and classification of plants is aided by a study of their anatomy, cytology, and physiology, and work of this kind is done in the Jodrell Laboratory, a building which was rebuilt and enlarged in 1963-64.

Special interest has always been taken at Kew in the plants of use to man, and much information on the economic properties of plants has been accumulated. Kew has played a notable part in the distribution of useful plants to Commonwealth countries, and this work continues in a modified form to the present. To reduce the risk of carrying harmful pests or disease during the exchange of economic plants, there has been built at Kew a plant quarantine house, financed by Ministry of Overseas Development funds, in which plants in transit from one part of the Commonwealth to another can be grown under supervision for a period of quarantine.

The training of gardeners is a function of Kew and, although most of the students are recruited in this country, some places are taken by men from other parts of the Commonwealth. Men trained at Kew continue to fill a number of posts overseas.

THE ROYAL CENTRAL ASIAN SOCIETY

42 Devonshire Street, London W.1 (01–580 5728)

President: The Earl of Selkirk, PC, GCMG, GBE, AFC
Chairman of Council: Sir Norman Brain, KBE, CMG
Hon. Secretaries: C. Rees Jenkins; S. J. Fulton, CMG; E. H. Paxton
Secretary: Miss M. FitzSimons

The Royal Central Asian Society, founded in 1901, seeks to maintain in Britain a centre for the collection and diffusion of up-to-date information concerning the culture and current affairs of the whole of Asia, and to promote friendship between the peoples of the Commonwealth and the peoples of Asia. The Society has a world-wide membership, and provides a centre in London through which information can be circulated on all aspects of life in those areas, including modern developments. The *Journal* includes reports on the Society's lectures, discussions and papers, and also reviews of books dealing with Asia. A library of 5,000 books, periodicals etc. is available to members.

ROYAL COLLEGE OF DEFENCE STUDIES

(Formerly Imperial Defence College)

Seaford House, 37 Belgrave Square, London S.W.1 (BELgravia 1091)

Secretary: Brigadier F. N. W. Gore, CBE (Rtd)

The College was established in 1927 following the recommendations of a Cabinet Committee in 1922 presided over by the then Mr Winston Churchill. It exists to give selected senior officers and officials of the United Kingdom the opportunity to study in depth with representatives of the Commonwealth and other nations the problems of defence related to international relations and public policy with emphasis on the strategic aspect. The Commandant may be a Serving Officer of four-star rank or a Civilian of corresponding status and there is a Directing Staff of eight members. These appointments are for two years. The present Commandant is the Hon. Alastair Buchan, CBE, MA, until recently the Director of the Institute for Strategic Studies. In addition, there is an Administrative Staff, which includes the Secretary and a Librarian. The College is non-residential and a maximum of seventy-six students can be taken on each course, which lasts a year. The College is financed from public funds with nominal fees for Overseas Commonwealth students, excluding Canada, with whom there are reciprocal arrangements.

THE ROYAL COMMONWEALTH SOCIETY

Northumberland Avenue, London WC2N 5BJ (01-930 6733)

Patrons: Her Majesty The Queen
H.M. Queen Elizabeth The Queen Mother
Grand President: H.R.H. The Duke of Gloucester, KG
Patron of the Companions:
H.R.H. Princess Alexandra The Hon. Mrs Angus Ogilvy, GCVO
President: The Rt Hon. Malcolm MacDonald, OM
Chairman of Central Council: F. H. Tate
Deputy Chairmen:
B. F. Macdona, CBE; Sir Ridgeby Foster
Secretary-General: A. S. H. Kemp, OBE
Hon. Treasurer: D. S. Whatley

Commonwealth Affairs are the business of the Royal Commonwealth Society. For over 100 years it has concerned itself in the evolution, development and relationships of the various lands and peoples, constituting about a quarter of the world, which today makes up the Commonwealth. It is unique in its long record of constancy of purpose, liberal humanity and political and financial independence.

The keynote of its approach is knowledge and understanding. On the one hand the Society's headquarters in London is a centre of study and source of information based on its great Library which has been built up over a century into the finest of its kind in the world. On the other, it is a warm, spacious, well-appointed club and meeting place where all who are interested in any aspect of the Commonwealth can belong—and feel that they belong.

Its members are drawn mainly from business and professional, diplomatic and political, academic and educational fields. They represent almost every race, political persuasion and age-group and the sexes have equal standing. In few other places does the same spirit prevail.

Its range of Commonwealth Affairs include:—

Library—the Commonwealth Library, built up over a century to nearly 400,000 items, ranging from early original documents to this month's books and periodicals, caters equally for the research worker, general reader of history and biography and students of up-to-date political, economic and cultural developments. Fully catalogued. Issues notes on living conditions in many Commonwealth countries.

Journal—an authoritative journal on Commonwealth affairs including articles, book reviews and reports of talks. Alternate months, price 20p, sent free to members.

Lectures—regular lunch-time meetings addressed by distinguished speakers on Commonwealth topics. Library talks. Evening discussion.

Studies Programme—regular conferences for sixth-formers, and other specialised young and adult audiences. World-wide essay and group project competition for school children. Commonwealth Interchange Study Group Operations (CISGO)—intensive study tours of Commonwealth countries for selected young executives in industry, banks and professions.

General—close links with High Commissions, Government, the City and Commonwealth organisations. Contacts in many countries.

Its Club facilities include the use of the Headquarters building which is situated in the heart of London, close to Trafalgar Square. An ideal meeting place and a convenient base for overseas and country members. Bedroom accommodation for seventy. Double rooms with private bathrooms. Club rooms—restaurant and self-service buttery. Two bars, lounges, television, card and billiard rooms. Rooms available for private functions. A varied programme of social events for members.

In addition to the London premises there are branches in the United Kingdom in Bath, Bournemouth, Bristol, Cambridge, Edinburgh, Hove, Liverpool, Oxford, Guernsey and Jersey.

In other countries there are branches in Australia, Bermuda, Canada, Ceylon, Fiji, Kenya, Malaysia, New Zealand, Nigeria and the Commonwealth Society of Singapore. In addition there are Honorary Representatives in these countries and in India and Pakistan, and many other areas of Africa; Atlantic, Caribbean and Americas; Asia and the Pacific; Mediterranean and Europe.

ROYAL COMMONWEALTH SOCIETY FOR THE BLIND

Commonwealth House, Heath Road, Haywards Heath, Sussex

Telephone: Haywards Heath 2424

Telegrams: Comblind Haywards Heath

Patron: Her Majesty The Queen
President: H.R.H. Princess Alexandra The Hon. Mrs. Angus Ogilvy, GCVO
Chairman: Sir Edmund Arrowsmith, KCMG
Director: John Wilson, CBE

The Royal Commonwealth Society for the Blind, under its previous name of British Empire Society for the Blind, was set up as an independent corporation in January 1950, following the report of a joint Committee of the former Colonial Office and the National Institute for the Blind entitled 'Blindness in British African and Middle East Territories'. Its objects are to stimulate official and voluntary action and to take the lead in a movement 'to promote the welfare, education and employment of the blind, and to prevent blindness'. In the current year the Society is funding 160 projects in 34 countries. The Society is under the direction of a Council to which three members are appointed by British Government Departments, and which includes representative members from 17 Commonwealth countries.

Since the Society's inception, local organisations for the blind have been established in 33 countries, Regional Officers have been stationed in Africa, Asia and the West Indies. Medical projects, utilising mobile clinics, have been promoted in many countries where, in 1970, 272,916 eye patients were treated and 39,822 sight-saving operations were performed. Other activities in which the Society has assisted have been the establishment of some 117 schools and training centres, registration of the blind, Braille production, and training in welfare work amongst the blind. It is also working with Governments and organisations in various territories in the prevention of blindness, in the experimental development of new types of training for blind farmers, peasant cultivators and village craftsmen, and in projects of 'open education' whereby blind children are educated in ordinary primary and secondary schools.

It has established a Commonwealth Scholarship Fund to assist those wishing to obtain special qualifications in ophthalmology, to help defray the cost of training blind welfare workers and to provide financial assistance in other deserving cases, e.g. to meet the cost of attendance at a useful international conference or to finance a publication or investigation.

THE ROYAL INSTITUTE OF INTERNATIONAL AFFAIRS

Chatham House, 10 St. James's Square, London S.W.1
(01–930 2233)

Presidents: Rt Hon. The Earl of Avon, KG, MC; Rt Hon. Philip Noel-Baker, MP
Chairman of Council: Lord Trevelyan, GCMG, CIE, OBE, LLD
Vice-Chairman of Council: Michael Howard, MC
Hon. Treasurer: David Rae Smith, MC
Director: Rt Hon. Kenneth Younger
Director of Studies: J. E. S. Fawcett, DSC

The Institute is an unofficial non-partisan organisation founded in 1920 for the the advancement of the sciences of international politics, economics and jurisprudence; the provision of information by Libraries, publications and in other ways; and the encouragement of similar activities within the Commonwealth. The Institute received a Royal Charter under its present title in 1926. It is supported by business and individual subscriptions, grants from Foundations and to a limited extent, by Endowments.

The Institute promotes research in all aspects of international affairs and publishes a wide range of books, pamphlets and two Journals. These are *International Affairs*, a quarterly containing articles and book reviews and a monthly, *The World Today*, containing more topical articles and comment.

The Institute maintains an extensive international Library and Press Archives. It organises a large programme of private meetings, discussions and study groups on current problems for the benefit of its membership which numbers approximately 3,000.

Membership is limited to British and Commonwealth citizens but most of the facilities are available to the guests of members and to visiting scholars of all nationalities.

ROYAL OVER-SEAS LEAGUE
(Incorporated by Royal Charter)

World Headquarters:
Over-Seas House, Park Place, St James's Street, London S.W.1 (01-493 5051)

Telegrams: Ovazeeleag, London S.W.1

Patron: Her Majesty The Queen
Grand President: Admiral of the Fleet The Earl Mountbatten of Burma,
KG, PC, GCB, OM, GCSI, GCIE, GCVO, DSO
President: Sir Angus Gillan, KBE, CMG
Chairman:
Marshal of the Royal Air Force Sir Charles Elworthy, GCB, CBE, DSO, MVO, DFC, AFC
Director-General: Philip Crawshaw, CBE
Secretary: Miss J. Bond

Principal United Kingdom Branches—London, Edinburgh and Belfast (residential accommodation available).

Principal League Branches Overseas—Adelaide, Brisbane, Melbourne, Sydney, Hobart, Edmonton, Vancouver, Victoria, Auckland, Christchurch, Dunedin, Cape Town, Johannesburg, Nairobi, Singapore, Malta.

The Royal Over-Seas League was founded in 1910 by Sir Evelyn Wrench to promote friendship and understanding between the peoples of the Commonwealth and to maintain its traditions by individual service. Membership is open to all British subjects and Commonwealth citizens.

The League sponsors or supports various Commonwealth projects, maintains a special interest in looking after Commonwealth music students in London, is keenly interested in migration and publishes a quarterly journal *Overseas*.

At World Headquarters first-class residential club facilities and bedroom accommodation for 100 members are available. In addition, accommodation for some 40 members is available at the Beresford House Annexe, 1 St. James's Place, a short distance from World Headquarters. This accommodation can be obtained for a longer period than is normally possible at Over-Seas House. A travel and theatre bureau is provided for members, and a comprehensive programme of social and cultural activities is arranged for the benefit of members and their friends.

THE ROYAL SOCIETY FOR INDIA, PAKISTAN AND CEYLON

3 Temple Chambers, Temple Avenue, London E.C.4 (01-353 8515)

Patron: H.M. Queen Elizabeth The Queen Mother
President: The Rt Hon. Lord Butler of Saffron Walden, CH
Deputy President: The Rt Hon. the Earl of Inchcape
Chairman of Council: Sir Harry Greenfield, CSI, CIE
Vice-Chairman: Dr R. Hingorani
Hon. Secretary: J. W. N. Baldock
Hon. Treasurer: J. R. T. Niemeyer, MBE
Secretary: Miss A. M. Armstrong

The Royal Society for India, Pakistan and Ceylon was formed on 1st May 1966, by the amalgamation of the East India Association and the Royal India, Pakistan and Ceylon Society.

The objects of the Society are: to advance the study of the arts, languages, literature, history, religions, antiquities, usages, institutions, customs and manners of India, Pakistan, Ceylon and neighbouring countries; to promote the study and investigation of questions and matters concerning these countries and to make more accessible to the general public a knowledge of all problems and conditions affecting these countries; and to hold meetings and lectures, read papers, hold discussions, produce, publish and circulate any periodicals and literature that may be deemed advisable.

The Society publishes quarterly the *South Asian Review*, available to non-members at 50p. per copy.

ROYAL SOCIETY FOR THE PREVENTION OF CRUELTY TO ANIMALS

105 Jermyn Street, London S.W.1Y 6EG (01-930 0971)

Patrons:
Her Majesty The Queen
Her Majesty Queen Elizabeth The Queen Mother
Her Royal Highness Princess Alice, Countess of Athlone
President: (To be appointed)
Vice-Presidents: The Rt Hon. Lord Greenwood of Rossendale, PC., JP
Lt.-Col. J. C. Lockwood, CBE, JP, TD
The Dowager Viscountess Galway
Control is by a Council with 43 Members,
Chairman of the Council: J. S. Hobhouse, Esq., AFC
Vice-Chairman of the Council: F. F. A. Burden, Esq., MP

Office Bearers appointed by the Council:

Hon. Treasurer:	Harry White, OBE
Deputy Hon. Treasurer:	A. G. B. Scott
Secretary:	Major R. F. Seager
Deputy Secretary:	A. Joiner
Legal Secretary:	R. Murray
Chief Veterinary Officer:	Lieut.-Col. D. I. C. Tennant
Aministration and Finance Officer	P. W. Lloyd

The R.S.P.C.A. was founded in 1824. It became 'Royal' in 1840, when Her Majesty Queen Victoria graciously permitted the use of this title.

The R.S.P.C.A. seeks to promote kindness to animals by education (among children and adults), by surveillance at cattle markets, docks and railway sidings, and by the establishing of clinics where needy people's animals receive free veterinary treatment, and of kennels where accommodation is offered for unwanted animals, thousands of which the Society places annually in good homes.

An important way of promoting kindness is the encouragement of those abroad working for animal welfare. Encouragement takes the form of advice and of supplying literature and the means of relieving animal suffering. Outside England and Wales, the R.S.P.C.A. has branches in many Commonwealth countries; these branches, like those in England and Wales, are autonomous. Outside the Commonwealth, the Society has affiliations in almost every country in the world.

ROYAL SOCIETY OF ARTS
John Adam Street, London W.C.2 (01–839 2366)

Patron: Her Majesty The Queen
President: H.R.H. The Prince Philip, Duke of Edinburgh, KG, KT, OM, GBE
Chairman of Council: Sir James Taylor, MBE
Secretary: G. E. Mercer
Secretary, Commonwealth Section Committee: J. S. Skidmore

The Royal Society of Arts, which was founded in 1754 'for the encouragement of arts, manufactures and commerce', is one of the oldest learned societies in Britain, and has a unique function as an unspecialised and independent organisation.

The Society's activities are multifarious, and include the arranging of authoritative lectures on the wide range of subjects covered by 'arts, manufactures and commerce', the offer of substantial bursaries to students of industrial design, the granting of honours to eminent industrial designers and rewards for seamanship, the holding of exhibitions, and the conducting of examinations, particularly in subjects related to commerce.

Since its beginning the Society has taken an active interest in the affairs of what is now the Commonwealth, and this is today pursued through its Commonwealth Section, which arranges for a number of important papers to be read each year on recent developments overseas. The Section administers the R. B. Bennett Commonwealth Bequest under which a prize of 100 guineas is awarded every third year for an outstanding contribution to the promotion of the arts, agriculture, industry or commerce within the Commonwealth. An award for documentary film production in the Commonwealth is also offered periodically.

Fellows of the Society are to be found in many parts of the world, and through its monthly *Journal* are kept informed of the latest ideas and progress in the fields with which it is concerned.

THE GRAND PRIORY IN THE BRITISH REALM OF THE MOST VENERABLE ORDER OF THE HOSPITAL OF ST JOHN OF JERUSALEM
(The Order of St John)

St John's Gate, Clerkenwell, London E.C.1 (01-253 6644)

Sovereign Head: Her Majesty The Queen
Grand Prior: Field Marshal H.R.H. The Duke of Gloucester,
KG, KT, KP, GCB, GCMG, GCVO
Lord Prior: The Lord Caccia, GCMG, GCVO
Secretary-General: N. C. McClintock

The Order of St John is dedicated to the encouragement and promotion of works of humanity and charity for the relief of persons in sickness, distress, suffering and danger; and the rendering of aid to the sick and wounded in war.

These objects are carried out principally through the two foundations of the Order; the St John Ophthalmic Hospital in Jerusalem and the St John Ambbulance Association and Brigade.

At the St John Ophthalmic Hospital treatment is given free of charge to all who suffer from diseases of the eyes.

THE ST JOHN AMBULANCE ASSOCIATION & BRIGADE

1 Grosvenor Crescent, London S.W.1 (01–235 5231)

Chief Commander and Commissioner-in-Chief:
Lt.-General Sir William Pike, KCB, CBE, DSO
Director-General: Sir Hugh Stevenson, GBE, KCMG, CIE, CVO
Director Overseas: Sir Hilton Poynton, GCMG
Chief Secretary: Brigadier A. Miller, DSO

The St John Ambulance Association and Brigade, originally two separate foundations of the Order, were merged into a single foundation in 1968. The Association was founded by the Order of St John in 1877 to spread the knowledge of First Aid, Nursing, Child Care and Hygiene. Teaching Manuals on these subjects are published in many languages. Classes and examinations are organised with the help of voluntary workers in England, Wales, Northern Ireland and throughout the Commonwealth, as well as in other countries overseas. Successful candidates at examinations are awarded Certificates of which some 14,000,000 have been issued. Specialised courses are held on such subjects as First Aid in Mines and for Air Attendants.

The Brigade was founded in 1887 when holders of Association First Aid Certificates formed themselves into uniformed groups to assist with public duties. There are now units in nearly all countries of the Commonwealth.

The strength of the Brigade, comprising both Ambulance (male) and Nursing (female) members, at present totals 50,000 adults and 56,000 cadets in Britain with 114,000 adults and 48,000 cadets overseas. The hours of public duties in Britain amount to nearly four million yearly and 400,000 cases were treated during 1969.

The work of the Brigade is entirely voluntary and members give their spare time to public duties whenever their services are called upon. They also attend regular lectures and practices in the evenings and a yearly re-examination must be taken by all members.

The services of the Brigade may be utilised by anyone and members undertake a wide variety of duties, ranging from attendance at sporting events, cinema and theatre duty, voluntary escorts by land, sea or air for children and the sick, to the provision of nursing in the home and relief staff for hospitals during emergencies, such as those caused by epidemics, serious rail or air accidents. In natural disasters such as earthquakes, floods and hurricanes, teams of trained St John workers stand ready to assist in relief work and care for the sick and injured, either within their own area or in a nearby territory should the need arise.

The provision, equipment and maintenance of ambulances, beach and road huts, together with the material used for treating casualties, is undertaken by members from their unit funds collected from the public.

There are no distinctions of race, class or creed within the Brigade and anyone who is prepared to train and devote time to this work may join.

There are now Association Centres or Brigade Units or both in nearly all Commonwealth countries, and in some of these the Association and Brigade have been merged as in the United Kingdom. A separate Overseas Branch was established at Headquarters in 1968.

THE SARAWAK ASSOCIATION
Dolphins, Church Road, Great Bookham, Surrey

Patron: His Excellency The Governor of Sarawak
President: Miss H. M. Wallis, MBE
Secretary: J. W. Wilson

The Association was founded on 9th July, 1924 and has some 500 members. Under the Rules of the Association persons who are or who have been connected with Sarawak by official or business relations, or who have lived in Sarawak for not less than one year, are eligible for membership. The objects of the Association are to encourage its members to keep in touch with each other and to acquaint them with all matters of interest relating to Sarawak; to arrange social functions; and generally to further the interests and prosperity of Sarawak. The management of the Association is vested in a Committee consisting of a President and eight elected members.

THE SAVE THE CHILDREN FUND
29 Queen Anne's Gate, London SW1H 9DA (01-930 2461)

Patron: Her Majesty The Queen
President: H.R.H. The Princess Anne
Chairman: The Rt Hon. the Lord Gore-Booth, GCMG, KCVO
Hon. Treasurer: Donald Tyerman, Esq.
Director General: Sir Colin Thornley, KCMG, CVO

The Save the Children Fund is an independent voluntary organisation, professionally staffed and now more than 50 years old, whose purpose is the rescue in disaster and the longer term welfare of needy children, irrespective of nationality, race or religion.

SCF helps children in nearly 50 countries with teams of over 1,000 field workers, including doctors, nurses, welfare workers and administrators. In the United Kingdom its Homes, Clubs and Playgroups meet pressing needs not yet fully provided by public authorities.

The ultimate aims are to create conditions in which children can grow to a healthy maturity and in overseas projects to train local workers, where necessary, in the professional and technical skills required for child welfare. These world-wide operations cost more than £6,000 a day subscribed at home and abroad. Over the years, SCF has raised and spent nearly £30,000,000 and has brought relief, food, care and hope to many millions of children.

SCHOOL OF ORIENTAL AND AFRICAN STUDIES
(University of London)

Malet Street, London WC1E 7HP (01-580 9021/8)

Telegrams: Soasul, London WC1E 7HP

Director: Professor C. H. Philips
Secretary: J. R. Bracken
Administrative Officer: P. W. H. Brown, BA

The School was established in 1916 by Royal Charter and its purposes are to further research in, and to extend the study and knowledge of the languages of

Z

Eastern and African peoples, ancient and modern, and the literature, history. religion, politics, economics, law, customs and art of those peoples. In recent years, increasing attention has been given to the development of the social sciences and five Centres of Area Studies have been established, together with a Contemporary China Institute.

The School is organised in eleven Departments, viz., Geography; Anthropology and Sociology; Economic and Political Studies; History; Law; Phonetics and Linguistics; and Languages and Cultures of: India, Pakistan and Ceylon; South-East Asia and the Islands; Far East; Near and Middle East; Africa. Courses are provided for first and higher degrees of the University of London in many of the principal languages and cultures of Asia and Africa. Instruction in the languages of Asian and African countries can also be given for members of Government departments, the overseas representatives of British industrial and commercial firms and for members of their technical and executive staffs. Such courses may include lectures on the history, culture, religions, customs, laws, geography and other aspects of the area. In addition, seminar courses on the various regions of Asia and Africa are arranged from time to time for staff of Government departments and business executives. These are normally of three or four days' duration, and are aimed to provide up-to-date assessments of political, economic and social developments in the areas concerned against their historical and cultural background. In addition to lectures by authorities on the area, there is considerable scope for discussion.

The School is also engaged in an extensive programme of extra-mural work with schools and colleges of education throughout Britain. This includes the provision of Schoolteacher Fellowships, the arrangement of in-service courses for teachers, general studies courses, conferences and lectures for sixth-formers and for students in colleges of education; also the preparation of bibliographies and of history studies relating to Asia and Africa.

Publications of the School are *The Bulletin of the School of Oriental and African Studies*, the *Calendar* and the *Annual Report of the Governing Body*.

THE SCOUT ASSOCIATION
25 Buckingham Palace Road, London SWIW 0PY (01–834 6005)

Patron: Her Majesty The Queen
President: H.R.H. The Duke of Gloucester, K G
Chief Scout: The Lord Maclean, K T, K B E
Chief Executive Commissioner: K. H. Stevens
Commonwealth Commissioner: C. Dymoke Green, O B E, J P

The aim of the Association is to encourage the physical, mental and spiritual development of young people so that they may take a constructive place in society.

The characteristic method of training the Scout is by admitting him as a member of a fraternity which, guided by adult leadership, is increasingly self-governing in its successive age-groups; by opening to him a succession of congenial activities and achievements in a largely outdoor setting and opportunities of service to others by putting upon him progressively increasing measures of responsibility for himself and others, so that he acquires competence, self-reliance, character, dependability, and powers both of co-operation and of leadership.

The Scout Movement was founded in 1908 by Lord Baden-Powell of Gilwell and rapidly spread to countries outside the United Kingdom. Those in the Commonwealth were branches of the parent association progressing later to a status of autonomy usually at the time of political independence. There are twenty-six overseas branches of the association.

Of the twelve million Scouts in the world more than two million are in the Commonwealth. There is a separate Commonwealth Department at Headquarters with responsibility for liaison with the Independent Commonwealth Countries and the administration of the Overseas Branches which are visited periodically by a Travelling Commissioner.

The Chief Scout, the Lord Maclean, K T, K B E, is also Chief Scout of the Commonwealth and travels extensively to Commonwealth countries.

SOCIETY FOR HEALTH EDUCATION

(formerly British Society for International Health Education)

24 Southwark Street, London S.E.1 (01–407 1815)
Cables: Brithealth, London

Executive Committee:
President: Harald Peake
Chairman: Sir John Peel
Hon. Treasurer: Sir Miles Clifford

Committee Members:
Dr J. H. Briscoe-Smith; Professor J. H. Butterfield; Dr John Fry; Dr J. H. Hunt; Dr H. Jolly; H. S. Magney; Dr Claude Nicol; Sir John Wolfenden
General Secretary: Susan King-Hall
Technical Adviser: Norman Scothe

The Society was founded (as BSIHE) in 1962 to provide assistance for health education overseas and especially in developing countries. It now arranges training courses overseas and in Britain and offers fellowships for post-graduate training in health education. It promotes attention to health education in courses in the U.K. particularly those taken by overseas students and arranges Seminars for them. To date its activities have taken place in the Commonwealth and particularly Africa, but this is not a requirement. It is supported by voluntary donations from members in Britain, Commonwealth and foreign countries and by grants from charitable and other sources.

TROPICAL MEDICINE RESEARCH BOARD

Chairman: Dr G. M. Bull

Members:

Professor Sir William Melville Arnott	Professor J. N. Morris
Dr W. Fox	Professor G. S. Nelson
Dr L. G. Goodwin	Gordon Pringle
Hugh Jolly	Dr R. J. W. Rees
Dr D. J. Lewis	Dr J. H. Walters

Assessors to the Board
Overseas Development Administration
The Chief Medical Adviser (*ex-officio*)
Head of the Science, Technology and Medical Department (*ex-officio*)

The Tropical Medicine Research Board was established in 1960 to succeed the Colonial Medical Research Committee. The Board's terms of reference are:

To advise:

(*a*) the Minister for Overseas Development, through the Medical Research Council, on all medical research overseas or in the United Kingdom financed from the funds of the Overseas Development Administration of the Foreign and Commonwealth Office.

(*b*) the Medical Research Council on all medical research in or for tropical or sub-tropical countries financed from their own budget.

TROPICAL PRODUCTS INSTITUTE

56/62 Gray's Inn Road, London W.C.1 (01–242 5412)

Telegrams: Troprods, Westcent, London

Director: Dr P. C. Spensley
Deputy Director: Dr E. M. Thain
Assistant Director (Analytical, Service and Non-Food Commodities Department):
Dr. A. J. Feuell
Assistant Director (Food Department): Dr N. R. Jones
Assistant Director (Tropical Stored Products Centre): P. E. Wheatley
Assistant Director (Industrial Development Department): F. J. Hall
Assistant Director (Economics Department): Dr R. H. Kirby
Assistant Director (Overseas Operations Secretariat): Dr D. W. Hall

The Tropical Products Institute has its origins in the Scientific and Technical Department of the Imperial Institute and in the Colonial Products Research Council. The former body came into existence in 1894 to provide a scientific advisory service dealing with the natural resources of the British Empire. The Colonial Products Research Council was set up in 1942 to advise the Secretary of State for the Colonies as to the more fundamental research that should be conducted on the plant and animal resources of Colonial territories to help bring about their greater use. In 1953 the work of these two bodies was combined and in 1957 the organisation moved to its present headquarters and adopted the name of Tropical Products Institute. It became a station of the Department of Scientific and Industrial Research in 1959. From 1963, financial responsibility was assumed by the Department of Technical Co-operation until 1st April 1965 when the Institute became an integral part of the Ministry of Overseas Development (now the Overseas Development Administration).

The Tropical Stored Products Centre, another scientific unit of the then Ministry of Overseas Development, was amalgamated with and became a department of TPI in 1967. The Centre originated from a survey carried out in East and Central Africa in 1948-49 by the Head of the Storage Department of the Pest Infestation Laboratory, Slough, after which certain staff in the Laboratory were allocated to overseas storage problems. The Unit that evolved became, in 1963, the TSPC.

The Tropical Products Institute's function is to help developing countries derive greater benefit from their plant and animal resources, principally by assisting with the scientific, technological and economic problems that arise after harvesting.

Laboratory examinations are made and information supplied on products such as essential oils, spices, gums and resins, vegetable oils, waxes, starch and protein foods, drugs and insecticides from plants, fruits, vegetables, edible nuts, fish, fibres, board and paper making materials. Information is also supplied about sources of raw materials, cultural conditions, storage, methods of processing and utilisation, marketing and commercial possibilities of the products. Commercial valuations and assessments of the suitability of materials are also obtained for the benefit of producing countries.

Specifications and estimates of cost are obtained for plant, machinery and equipment which may be required for production and processing overseas. Where suitable processes are not available new processes may be developed at the Institute's engineering laboratories which are situated at Culham, near Abingdon.

The Tropical Stored Products Centre at Slough concentrates on problems of crop storage, particularly the control of insect pests in store and transport and techniques of storage under both simple and more sophisticated conditions. A proportion of the staff is based more or less permanently overseas carrying out investigations lasting several years. Other problems are tackled by carrying out initial investigations in Britain under laboratory conditions with follow-up studies in the countries concerned.

In addition to laboratory investigations arising out of samples received for examination, the Institute as a whole conducts more fundamental studies of tropical plant and animal products with a view to discovering materials which might form the basis of new industries, and facts about existing products or by-products which might benefit industries already in operation.

The Institute's economists are concerned with the various economic problems arising from existing industries in developing countries or in the development of new ones. They conduct market surveys and collect statistical information about tropical plant and animal products and work with other Sections of the Institute on the economic aspects of inquiries received. The economic feasibility of industrial processes based on natural raw materials is studied. Reports produced as a result of all these studies are issued by the Institute and given a wide circulation overseas.

The development work of the Institute involves selecting from work conducted at the Institute or elsewhere (universities etc.) ideas which might beneficially be developed in tropical areas.

Frequent visits abroad are made by senior members of staff conducting experiments in the field, making the facilities of the Institute more widely known and identifying problems with which the Tropical Products Institute might help. Staff are also seconded for longer periods overseas, for instance a marketing expert and a technical editor are working in Zambia, a storage expert in Jamaica and an oilseeds specialist in Sudan. Also, the Institute has an Overseas Representative serving the Caribbean area, based in Barbados.

The Institute awards a small number of extra-mural research contracts to universities, both overseas and in Britain, for work within its field of interest.

Training courses are provided in the various departments for students from overseas, in all aspects of the Institute's work. The trainees are usually graduates who require special training in analytical methods, the use of modern equipment, storage technology and other aspects of work on natural products. Visits to other organisations and short courses may also be arranged when the needs of trainees cannot be met entirely within the Institute.

The Library has one of the finest collections in the world of books and periodicals on tropical agriculture, tropical products and related subjects; it is open to the specialist public and books are lent to other organisations. A technical index, classified under commodities, is available for consultation. The Institute receives about 1,000 inquiries a year, many of which can be answered from information available in the library or based on previous inquiries and the experience of members of the staff. The Institute's primary responsibility is to developing countries, but inquiries on tropical products from British industry are frequently dealt with. The Institute takes part in scientific and technical exhibitions in Britain and overseas. A film on the Institute, called 'Science for the Tropics', is available from British Information Services overseas and from the Institute. International conferences are organised such as the one in 1965 on 'The Oil Palm', in 1967 on 'Essential Oils Production in Developing Countries', and in 1969 on 'Tropical and Sub-Tropical Fruit'. The next will be in 1972 on 'Spices'.

The *Biennial Report* and quarterly journal, *Tropical Science*, are published by H.M.S.O. and the Institute also publishes *Oil Palm News*, *Tropical Stored Products Information* and *Tropical Products Institute Reports* on markets, small industries and technical matters. The latter are listed in *Tropical Science* and a separate twice-yearly list. In addition general brochures and leaflets are available on the work of the Institute, and a booklet on *Training at the Tropical Products Institute*.

TROPICAL SECTION, ROAD RESEARCH LABORATORY

Department of the Environment, Crowthorne, Berkshire RG11 6AU

(Tel. 034-46 3131)

Head of Tropical Section: Dr E. D. Tingle

The appointment in the late 1940s of a Colonial Liaison Officer at the Road Research Laboratory was followed in 1955 by the establishment of the Tropical Section to deal specifically with overseas road problems and to provide technical aid. The section is financed by the Foreign and Commonwealth Office, Overseas Development Administration.

The main functions of the Section are:

(a) to undertake research on road planning and construction in developing countries and to develop improved methods;

(b) to assist with the solution of specific technical problems and to answer enquiries;

(c) to train highway engineers and transport planners;

(d) to advise the Minister for Overseas Development on applications from overseas countries for road development projects.

The results of research are made known through a wide range of publications produced by the Laboratory. Many reports on individual research topics are available free of charge on application to the Laboratory and other more comprehensive publications are available at modest prices from H.M. Stationery Office. Enquiries should be addressed in the first instance to the Director of Road Research at the Laboratory.

TRYPANOSOMIASIS PANEL

Chairman: Professor W. E. Kershaw, VRD

Members:

Dr J. Ford
Dr L. G. Goodwin
Dr F. Hawking
Dr M. Hutchinson
Col. H. W. Mulligan, CMG
Dr T. A. M. Nash, CMG, OBE
Dr B. A. Newton

W. H. Potts
Professor Sir Alexander Robertson, CBE
Professor B. Weitz, OBE
Dr J. Williamson
O.D.A. Chief Medical Adviser (*ex-officio*)
O.D.A. Animal Health Adviser (*ex-officio*)

Secretary: P. G. Ottewill, GM, AFC

Functioning continuously since 1944, when it was set up as the Tsetse Fly and Trypanosomiasis Panel, the terms of reference of the Trypanosomiasis Panel are 'to consider and advise the Minister for Overseas Development on all matters concerning human and animal trypanosomiasis'.

THE VICTORIA LEAGUE FOR COMMONWEALTH FRIENDSHIP

38 Chesham Place, London S.W.1 (01–235 2201/5)

Patrons: Her Majesty The Queen;
Her Majesty Queen Elizabeth The Queen Mother
President: H.R.H. Princess Alice Countess of Athlone, VA, GCVO, GBE
President, Younger Members Group:
H.R.H. The Princess Margaret, Countess of Snowdon, GCVO
Deputy Presidents: Her Grace The Dowager Duchess of Devonshire, GCVO, CBE;
Sir Ivison Macadam, CVO, CBE
Chairman: Allison, Viscountess Dunrossil

Vice-Chairmen:
The Lady Rayleigh; Mrs R. W. K. Edgley;
E. V. Whitcombe, CBE; Mrs S. G. Kelsey, OBE; P. D. Watson, MBE; Mrs P. K. Boulnois
Hon. Treasurer: Sir Issac Wolfson, Bt, FRS, Hon. FRCP, Hon. DCL (Oxon.), Hon. LLD
(London), Hon. LLD (Glasgow)
General Secretary: Vice-Admiral Sir John Gray, KBE, CB

The Victoria League is a voluntary organisation founded in 1901 to further personal friendship between individuals of the Commonwealth irrespective of race, creed or political opinion. There are Victoria Leagues, and Representatives throughout the Commonwealth with a membership of about 30,000.

Hospitality is arranged in private homes for visitors from the Commonwealth. Victoria Leagues overseas are reciprocal. There are Hostels in London and Birmingham for students. Books and newspapers are despatched to other Commonwealth countries, and children are helped to get into touch by correspondence.

The Younger Members Group has an age limit of 18-29 years, and organises its own activities.

Victoria League House in Edinburgh is the Headquarters in Scotland and is residential.

In Canada the Victoria League is affiliated with the Imperial Order Daughters of the Empire.

VOLUNTARY SERVICE OVERSEAS

14 Bishop's Bridge Road, London W.2 (01-262 2611)

Patron: H.R.H. The Prince Philip, Duke of Edinburgh, KG, KT, OM, GBE
Chairman: Rt Hon. Viscount Amory of Tiverton, KG, PC, GCMG, TD
Director: D. H. Whiting, OBE

Voluntary Service Overseas was founded in 1958. The idea behind it was that young men and women from Britain could provide assistance needed in developing countries and would themselves benefit much from acquiring a greater understanding of the peoples with whom they would be working and from the increased breadth of outlook which this would give them.

The aims of VSO are:—

(1) To help the developing nations solve their economic, technical and educational problems.

(2) To improve relationships and break barriers by providing a field in which young people from different environments may work together.

(3) To give to young men and women the opportunity to widen their own sympathies and understanding through service overseas.

VSO tries to supply some of the shortages in manpower of developing countries. Few volunteers are engaged in relief work. Most work on projects where their knowledge or skill can be passed on to others. For this reason most volunteers are involved in some form of instruction; either in the classroom or in technical institutes of every kind. Even those engaged in practical work in such fields as medicine, agriculture or construction work generally act as instructors as well. In all cases volunteers are involved in responsible work which needs doing and cannot be supplied from local resources. It tests their abilities and character, and in return gives them a vivid insight into another country and its problems. At present VSO has 1,500 volunteers at work in 70 countries. About two-thirds of these volunteers are teaching in secondary or technical schools and training colleges, with a few in primary schools or universities. The remainder are engaged in agricultural and veterinary work, forestry, medical duties of all kinds, engineering and building, librarianship and numerous other activities.

Voluteers are provided in response to specific requests from government departments or other public or private authorities overseas. Every request is carefully examined by the VSO staff in the course of regular overseas tours, and by representatives of the British Council, acting as the Overseas Arm of VSO. (In territories where the British Council is not represented their functions are undertaken by officers of the British Embassy, High Commission or colonial government). While volunteers are serving overseas these agents also attend to their welfare and take whatever action is necessary in the case of political or other emergencies.

Volunteers should be citizens of the United Kingdom of Great Britain and Northern Ireland, or of Commonwealth countries, who are domiciled in the United Kingdom.

Minimum period of service: one year. Those who will not be returning to universities or colleges in U.K. (either as undergraduates or post-graduate students) are encouraged to stay for a longer period. Volunteers have the option of extending their service during the first year, so long as they are required.

THE WELLCOME TRUST

52 Queen Anne Street, London W1M 9LA (01-486 4902/5)

Trustees: The Rt Hon. the Lord Franks of Headington (Chairman);
Professor H. Barcroft; Professor Sir John McMichael;
The Rt Hon. the Lord Murray of Newhaven; R. M. Nesbitt;
Professor R. H. S. Thompson
Director: Dr P. O. Williams
Financial Secretary: J. E. K. Clarke
Assistant Directors:
Dr Edda Hanington (Deputy); Dr B. E. C. Hopwood; Dr B. A. Bembridge

The Wellcome Trust was founded by the will of Sir Henry S. Wellcome in 1936. The income is distributed as grants for research in human and animal medicine.

Information about the work of the Trust may be obtained from the Secretariat at 52 Queen Anne Street, London W.1.

THE WEST AFRICA COMMITTEE

Blossoms Inn, 23 Lawrence Lane, London E.C. 2 (01-600 9491/2)

Chairman: W. T. G. Gates, CBE
Adviser: Sir Evelyn Hone, GCMG, CVO, OBE
Secretary: W. G. Syer, CVO, CBE
Assistant Secretary: Group Captain P. R. Magrath

The West Africa Committee has been in existence, as an independent organisation, since May 1956. Its objects are to facilitate effective contribution towards the economic development of the West African countries of Ghana, Nigeria, Sierra Leone and The Gambia by companies and firms from other countries, to the mutual economic advantage of those West African countries and the members. In addition, regular visits are now made to the Ivory Coast.

The Committee has about 170 members, representing trading concerns, banking, industrialists, shipping, airlines, mining, plantations, petroleum industry, insurance and professional firms. Membership is not limited to British concerns, but only those which are predominantly expatriate in character are eligible. Over 20 per cent of the members are from countries other than Britain.

The Committee maintains representatives in Ghana and in Nigeria and its Adviser, Sir Evelyn Hone, the Secretary and Assistant Secretary make periodical visits to West Africa, the Continent, and the U.S.A.

WEST INDIA COMMITTEE

18 Grosvenor Street, London WIX 0HP (01–629 6353 (5 lines))

Telegrams: Carib Estrand London Cables: Carib, London

President: Lord Campbell of Eskan
Chairman: R. M. Hilary, MBE, TD
Secretary: Lt.-Col. M. R. Robinson, DSO

The Committee, which was established about 1750 and incorporated by Royal Charter in 1904, is an association of Commonwealth subjects and companies interested in the West Indies, the Bahamas, Guyana and British Honduras. The object of the West India Committee is to promote the interests of the agricultural and manufacturing industries of those territories, to encourage British investment there and to further their trade and advance the general welfare of their peoples.

Members receive *The West Indies Chronicle*, published monthly.

The Committee's Rooms contain a comprehensive West Indian reference library, where newspapers from most Commonwealth Caribbean countries are available and where general information on the Caribbean is given to enquirers.

WEST INDIAN CLUB LIMITED

18 Northumberland Avenue, London WC2N 5BJ (01–930 1906)

Telegrams: Recital London

Secretary: J. N. D. Bettley

The main object of the Club is to further the interests of the West Indies and Guyana by providing headquarters for associated action, not political, but social.

WILLIAM GOODENOUGH HOUSE

(The Dominion Students' Hall Trust)

Mecklenburgh Square, London WC1N 2AN (01–278 5131)

Chairman of Council of Governors: Sir Frederic Seebohm, TD
Warden: Sir Francis Loyd, KCMG, OBE
Controller: Miss J. S. M. Dannatt, MA

William Goodenough House was opened in 1957 with the object of providing similar accommodation and amenities to London House for women students and married students from the Commonwealth and from the United States of America. There is single accommodation for 113 women students, and self-contained furnished flats for 59 married students. William Goodenough House provides every amenity, with common-rooms, tennis court, piano room, laundry, nursery, etc., and most London House facilities are available to residents, *e.g.* library, squash court, snack bar.

(*See also* London House)

WOMEN'S CORONA SOCIETY

305/311 Wellington House, London SW1E GBG (01-222 2251)

President: The Lady Garner
Deputy President: Mrs A. H. Pike
Chairman, Executive Committee: Mrs C. R. V. Bell, MBE
Hon. Treasurer: Mrs W. F. Farrant
Executive Secretary: Miss M. F. Hardie

The Women's Corona Society is a voluntary and non-political association of women of all races. Membership is open to any woman in active sympathy with the Society's aims. These aims are: to provide a link between women of different countries and to promote friendship and understanding through educational and social activites; to be of service to women moving to countries other than their own; and to promote knowledge of the peoples and cultures of the world, with particular reference to the Commonwealth. The Society has branches and affiliated societies in many countries.

Full particulars of the services and activities of the Society, at Headquarters in London, overseas, and in other parts of Britain, can be obtained from the Executive Secretary. The services in Britain comprise: introductory courses for women going overseas, organized with the support of the Overseas Development Administration, and an information service on overseas living conditions based on members' reports from the countries concerned and on personal contacts with women recently returned; an escort service for overseas members' children travelling through London; advice, help and hospitality for women from overseas in Britain, particularly those here for study or accompanying their husbands on such visits; and Women Speakers for the Commonwealth (recently merged with the Women's Corona Society) which provides a Panel of speakers from all parts of the Commonwealth who will accept engagements with women's clubs, meetings, etc., and give an up-to-date picture of the country from which they come (no charge is made other than for the speaker's out of pocket expenses).

THE WOMEN'S COUNCIL

(*Co-operating with Women of India, Pakistan, Ceylon, Indonesia, Malaysia, Thailand, the Philippines, Japan, Iran, Korea, Sikkim, Nepal, Laos, Lebanon, Viet-Nam, Bahrain, Hong Kong*)

Acting President: The Hon. Lady Egerton
Vice-President: Mrs Hemming
Hon. Vice-Presidents: Lady Gore-Booth; Lady Fry; Lady Lambe
Acting Chairman: Lady Gammans
Hon. Secretary: Mrs Earle
The address of the Hon. Secretary is: 35 St Peter's Square, London W.6

The Women's Council, which is non-political and non-sectarian, developed out of the Women's Advisory Council on Indian Affairs, which was founded over thirty years ago at the time of the first Round Table Conference. Pakistan and Ceylon joined the Women's Council in 1949, Indonesia in 1959, the Federation of Malaya (now Malaysia), Thailand and the Philippines in 1960, Japan and Iran in 1962, Korea in 1963, Sikkim and Nepal in 1964, Laos and Lebanon in 1965, Viet-Nam in 1966, Bahrain in 1967 and Hong Kong in 1969.

The aims of the Women's Council are to promote among British Women's Organisations interest in and knowledge of the affairs of Asian countries, especially as these affect women and their position in public life, to provide for co-operation with organised women in these countries and to promote contacts between British women and women from Asian countries who are resident in or visiting Britain.

It carries out these aims by holding meetings at which leading women from Asia talk about their countries and their work, by giving informal hospitality for visitors from Asia to meet British women with the same interests, by helping Asian women students, by arranging for Asian visitors to attend conferences held by women's and social welfare organisations in Britain, by helping visitors to hear talks on British social services and to visit institutions, by arranging for women speakers from Asia to address British women's organisations, clubs and schools, and by publishing a *Bulletin* containing news from co-operating countries and reports of the Council's activities.

The Women's Council is formally linked with 45 women's organisations in Britain, co-operates with many others and has a large number of individual members. The annual subscription for organisations and individuals, which includes the *Bulletin*, is £1·50.

THE WORLD WILDLIFE FUND
British National Appeal
7–8 Plumtree Court, London E.C.4 (01–353 2615/3789)
President: H.R.H. The Duke of Edinburgh, KG, KT, OM, GBE
Chairman: Peter Scott, CBE, DSC
Administrator: Arnold Thorne

The World Wildlife Fund is an international charitable foundation devoted to the concept that conservation is for the benefit of man. At one end of its scale of activities it is trying to save certain animal and plant species from extinction and at the other end it extends over the whole intricate relationship between water, soil, plants, animals and man himself.

WWF exists to raise voluntary funds through National Appeals in a number of different countries, and after taking the best possible technical advice (provided through the International Union for Conservation of Nature and other qualified agencies) to distribute the money for saving wildlife and wild places, wherever possible through existing organisations. One third of the funds raised by National Appeals is at the disposal of the National Trustees and may be retained for home conservation.

WWF also works in close co-operation with the International Council for Bird Preservation and the Fauna Preservation Society, and so far as conservation in Britain is concerned, with the Council for Nature and the County Naturalists' Trusts.

WWF has its headquarters in Switzerland, and is controlled by a Board of International Trustees with H.R.H. The Prince of the Netherlands as President and Peter Scott as Chairman. The President of the British National Appeal is H.R.H. The Duke of Edinburgh, who is also a member of the Board of International Trustees.

ZEBRA HOUSE COUNCIL
1/3/7 Marloes Road, London W.8 (FREmantle 2127)

Patrons:

Lady Beit
Viscount Chandos, DSO, MC
Lord Fisher of Lambeth, GCVO, RVC, DD
The Rt Hon. Patrick Gordon Walker, MP
Colonel L. van der Post, CBE

Lord Walston
Lord Vernon
Theodore Bull
Oliver Carruthers

Council:

Chairman/Treasurer: Rory McNeile, FCA
Peter Comyns (Warden)
Mrs T. W. Scott (Warden, Impala House)
Mrs Josef Bartosik

Jonathan Lewis, OBE
Mrs Zivka Lewis (Warden, Jerome House)
Sir Dermot Milman, Bart., (British Council)
Bodo Slazanger

Zebra House was founded in 1958 by a small voluntary group concerned about the welfare of Commonwealth students in this country, particularly from Africa and the first house was bought with their own funds. The aim of the Zebra House Council is to provide good accommodation for Commonwealth students at a modest cost, within a student's normal reach. The Council also runs, in Primrose Hill, Regents Park, the first block of flats in London where married students can live with their families—Impala House (*q.v.*).

ZEBRA TRUST

46a Cheval Place, London S.W.7 (KENsington 0852)

Patron:
H.R.H. The Princess Margaret, Countess of Snowdon, GCVO
Chairman: Mr John Phillimore, CMG
Deputy Chairman: Sir Edmund Hall-Patch, GCMG

Council:

Mrs Josef Bartosik
The Hon. Mrs G. G. Marten
Miss Christine Wilkinson
Leonard Beaton
Henry Crookenden
The Viscount Dunrossil
Peter Ensor
Sir Geoffrey de Freitas, KCMG, MP
Guy Hunter
Derek Ingram

Martin Kenyon
Colonel Laurens van der Post, CBE
Jonathan Lewis, OBE (Director)
Rory McNeile, FCA
The Earl of March and Kinrara
Dr R. E. Robinson, CBE, DFC
Francis Sandilands, CBE
R. Shaw-Kennedy, MBE (Treasurer)
John Sutcliffe, MP
John Thirlwell

The Zebra Trust was founded in 1965 to service the Coventry Overseas Students Trust, the Jerome Housing Fellowship, the Malaysia Housing Society and the Zebra House Council (see separate entries), all of which the founders of the Zebra Trust have helped to sponsor. The Zebra Trust also hopes to promote new educational and welfare projects, particularly for the benefit of Commonwealth students at home and overseas. Their latest 'Zebra House' is in Bristol (9 Miles Road, Clifton, Bristol 8).

PART IX

EXTERNAL TRADE OF COMMONWEALTH COUNTRIES

COMMONWEALTH OF AUSTRALIA
July 1969–June 1970
$A million

Exports (f.o.b.)			Imports (f.o.b.)	
Value	% of total		Value	% of total
3,967·1		TOTAL	3,885·0	
		of which:		
483·0	12·2	Britain	845·0	21·8
1,217·1	30·7	Total Commonwealth	1,279·7	32·9
526·6	13·3	U.S.A.	965·0	24·8
1,015·4	25·6	Japan	481·0	12·4
440·6	11·1	E.E.C.	493·0	12·7

Principal Exports: Meat and meat preparations
Dairy products and eggs
Wheat and flour
Wool
Minerals (excluding fuels)

BARBADOS
1969
$E.C. million

Exports + Re-exports (f.o.b.)			Imports (c.i.f.)	
Value	% of total		Value	% of total
74·2		TOTAL	194·6	
		of which:		
27·8	37·5	Britain	56·2	28·9
2·6	3·5	Canada	21·5	11·0
44·6	60·1	Total Commonwealth	108·2	55·6
16·4	22·1	U.S.A.	43·6	22·4
1·7	2·3	E.E.C.	22·7	11·7

Principal Exports: Sugar and molasses
Crustacea and moluscs
Rum

BOTSWANA
1969
Rands million

Exports Value		Imports Value	% of total
13·1	TOTAL of which:	30·8	
	South Africa	.	

Principal Exports: Meat and meat products
Hides and skins

CANADA
1970
$C million

Domestic Exports + Re-exports (f.o.b.)			Imports (mainly f.o.b.)	
Value	% of total		Value	% of total
16,886·0		TOTAL of which:	13,939·0	
1,499·0	8·9	Britain	738·0	5·3
		Total Commonwealth		
2,277·0	13·5	and Preferential	1,359·0	9·7
10,987·0	65·1	U.S.A.	9,905·0	71·1
1,204·0	7·1	E.E.C.	805·0	5·8
795·0	4·7	Japan	582·0	4·2

Principal Exports: Food and beverages (cereals, fish products, whisky)
Timber, wood pulp and newsprint
Non-ferrous ores, metals and alloys
Machinery and transport equipment

CEYLON
1970
Rs. million

Domestic Exports (f.o.b.)			Imports (c.i.f.)	
Value	% of total		Value	% of total
1,995·3		TOTAL	2,313·3	
454·7	22·8	Britain	329·8	14·3
21·1	1·1	India	225·6	9·8
80·0	4·0	Australia	112·2	4·9
761·4	38·2	Total Commonwealth	918·5	39·7
143·8	7·2	U.S.A.	132·1	5·7
251·5	12·6	China	289·3	12·5

Principal Domestic Exports: Tea
Rubber
Dessicated coconut

Republic of Cyprus
1970
£C million

Exports + Re-exports (f.o.b.) Value	% of total		Imports (c.i.f.) Value	% of total
45·2		**TOTAL**	98·2	
		of which:		
17·4	38·4	Britain	28·9	29·4
17·6	35·1	Total Commonwealth	31·7	32·3
13·6	30·1	E.E.C.	27·0	27·5
0·5	1·1	U.S.A.	6·6	6·7

Principal Exports: Fresh fruit and vegetables
Metalliferous ores and metal scrap
Wine

Fiji
1969
Fiji $ million

Exports (f.o.b.) Value	% of total		Imports (c.i.f.) Value	% of total
53·2		**TOTAL**	77·9	
		of which:		
18·4	34·6	Britain	15·4	19·8
5·5	10·3	Australia	19·6	25·2
2·9	5·5	New Zealand	7·2	9·3
		Total Commonwealth		
7·2	3·6	Japan	11·1	14·2
8·4	15·7	U.S.A.	3·7	4·7

Principal Exports: Sugar
Coconut oil
Gold

The Gambia
June 1967–June 1968
£ million

Exports (f.o.b.) Value	% of total		Imports (c.i.f.) Value	% of total
5·4		**TOTAL**	7·4	
		of which:		
3·7	68·9	Britain	3·0	40·8
3·7	69·4	Total Commonwealth	3·7	50·1
0·5	9·0	Netherlands	0·3	3·7
—	—	Japan	1·1	15·1

Principal Exports: Ground nuts (shelled, cake and meal, unrefined oil)

GHANA

1968

New ₵ million

Exports (f.o.b.) Value	% of total		Imports (c.i.f.) Value	% of total
338·8		**TOTAL** *of which:*	314·9	
91·9	27·1	Britain	86·6	27·6
114·1	33·7	Total Commonwealth	107·6	34·3
59·9	17·7	U.S.A.	60·0	19·1
88·3	26·1	E.E.C.	63·9	20·4

1969

396·5	**TOTAL**	357·5

No country breakdown available yet.

Principal Exports: Cocoa
Timber
Gold
Industrial diamonds

GUYANA

1969

$G million

Exports + Re-exports (f.o.b.) Value	% of total		Imports (c.i.f.) Value	% of total
242·0		**TOTAL** *of which:*	235·8	
58·3	24·1	Britain	74·0	31·4
46·5	19·2	Canada	20·0	8·5
88·5	36·6	Total Sterling Area	122·1	51·8
61·0	25·2	U.S.A.	50·4	21·4
11·9	4·9	E.E.C.	23·4	9·9

Principal Exports: Sugar, rice, rum, shrimps
Alumina, bauxite, timber

HONG KONG
1970
HK$ million

Exports f.o.b) Value	% of total		Imports (c.i.f.) Value	% of total
15,430·5		TOTAL *of which:*	17,606·7	
1,556·1	10·1	Britain	1,517·3	8·6
5,434·5	35·2	U.S.A.	2,316·8	13·2
1,571·1	10·2	E.E.C.	1,614·1	9·2
1,076·2	7·0	Japan	4,188·4	23·7
63·9	0·4	China	2,830·4	16·1

Principal Exports: Clothing

Textile yarn fabrics and make-up articles

Miscellaneous manufactured articles: Electric machinery and apparatus

INDIA
April 1969–March 1970
Rs. million

Exports (f.o.b.) Value	% of total		Imports (c.i.f.) Value	% of total
14,132·1		TOTAL *of which:*	15,674·9	
1,650·7	11·7	Britain	1,003·8	6·4
2,379·7	16·8	U.S.A.	4,599·6	29·3
1,005·0	7·1	E.E.C.	1,703·9	10·9
1,793·6	12·7	Japan	668·2	4·3

Principal Exports: Tea

Edible nuts

Cotton and cotton manufactures

Jute manufactures

Animal feeding stuffs

Hides, skins and leather manufactures

JAMAICA
1969
$J million

| *Exports (f.o.b.)* | | | | *Imports (c.i.f.)* | |
Value	% of total			Value	% of total
105·3			TOTAL *of which:*	184·3	
20·6	19·6		Britain	38·7	21·0
17·2	16·3		Canada	17·4	9·5
46·6	44·2		Total Commonwealth	66·9	36·3
38·7	36·7		U.S.A.	77·3	41·9
			E.E.C.		

Principal Exports: Bauxite and alumina
Sugar and molasses
Bananas

KENYA
1970
£K million

| *Exports (f.o.b.)* | | | *Imports (c.i.f.)* | |
Value	% of total		Value	% of total
71·6		TOTAL	142·0	
14·8	20·7	Britain	41·5	29·2
26·3	36·7	Total Commonwealth	32·4	36·9
6·4	8·9	U.S.A.	11·9	8·4
13·3	18·6	E.E.C.	28·7	20·2

Principal Exports: Coffee
Petroleum products
Tea
Maize
Meat and products
Pyrethrum
Sisal

LESOTHO
1969
Rand million

| *Exports* | | *Imports* |
Value		Value
4·1	TOTAL	23·9

No country breakdown available

Principal Exports: Cattle
Diamonds
Wool

MALAWI
1969
£M million

Exports (f.o.b.)				*Imports (f.o.b.)*	
Value	*% of total*			*Value*	*% of total*
22·1		TOTAL		30·7	
		of which:			
		Britain		9·1	29·6
		Zambia		1·3	4·2
		Total Commonwealth			
		Rhodesia		5·2	16·9
		South Africa		4·6	15·0

Principal Exports: Tobacco
Tea
Groundnuts
Maize

MALAYSIA*
1969
$M million

Exports (f.o.b.)				*Imports (c.i.f.)*	
Value	*% of total*			*Value*	*% of total*
4,075·6		TOTAL		2,802·5	
		of which:			
252·9	6·2	Britain		387·6	13·8
793·2	19·5	Singapore		194·8	7·0
		Total Commonwealth			
724·3	17·8	U.S.A.		160·8	5·7
		E.E.C.			
541·6	13·3	Japan		479·6	17·1

Principal Exports: Rubber, Tin, Timber
Palm oil, Iron ore

MALTA
1969
£ million

Exports (f.o.b.)				*Imports (c.i.f.)*	
Value	*% of total*			*Value*	*% of total*
16·0		TOTAL		61·5	
		of which:			
5·5	34·4	Britain		26·2	42·6
6·3	39·4	Total Commonwealth		29·4	47·8
4·1	25·6	E.E.C.		17·7	28·8

Principal Exports: Textile thread, yarns, fabrics and synthetic fibres.
Clothing
Rubber manufactures
Fruit and vegetables

*West Malaysia only

External Trade

MAURITIUS
1969
Rs.M. million

Exports (f.o.b.)			Imports (c.i.f.)	
Value	% of total		Value	% of total
365·3		TOTAL of which:	376·3	
216·1	59·2	Britain	55·5	14·7
63·0	17·2	Canada	1·4	0·4
0·8	0·2	Australia	27·1	7·2
284·0	77·7	Total Commonwealth	129·5	34·4
1·8	0·5	E.E.C.	55·6	14·8
9·5	2·6	South Africa	31·3	8·3
—	—	Burma	7·7	2·0

Principal Exports: Sugar and molasses

NEW ZEALAND
July 1969–June 1970
$NZ million

Exports (f.o.b.)			Imports (c.i.f.)	
Value	% of total		Value	% of total
1,064·8		TOTAL of which:	1,006·0	
383·1	36·0	Britain	289·9	28·8
80·5	7·6	Australia	192·1	19·1
556·1	52·2	Total Commonwealth	590·5	59·0
164·3	15·4	U.S.A.	130·5	13·0
118·9	11·2	E.E.C.	74·4	7·4
106·1	10·0	Japan	85·0	8·4

Principal Exports: Wool, Meat
Dairy products

FEDERAL REPUBLIC OF NIGERIA
1969
£N million

Exports (f.o.b.)			Imports (c.i.f.)	
Value	% of total		Value	% of total
323·2		TOTAL of which:	248·7	
88·0	27·2	Britain	86·3	34·7
102·5	31·7	Total Commonwealth	99·9	40·2
40·0	12·4	U.S.A.	29·3	11·8
113·7	35·2	E.E.C.	62·7	25·2

Principal Exports: Crude petroleum
Cocoa
Groundnuts, Tin
Palm kernels

PAKISTAN
July 1969–June 1970
Rs. million

| *Exports (f.o.b.)* | | | *Imports (c.i.f.)* | |
Value	% of total		Value	% of total
3,271·4		TOTAL *of which:*	5,098·1	
370·0	11·3	Britain	580·0	11·4
906·3	27·7	Total Commonwealth	813·2	16·0
373·1	11·4	U.S.A.	1,371·4	26·9
480·7	14·7	E.E.C.	1,052·6	20·6

Principal Exports: Jute and jute manufactures
Cotton and cotton manufactures
Leather, Rice

SIERRA LEONE
1970
Le million

| *Exports (f.o.b.)* | | | *Imports (c.i.f.)* | |
Value	% of total		Value	% of total
84·2		TOTAL *of which:*	75·3	
57·3	68·1	Britain	28·8	38·2
57·4	68·2	Total Commonwealth	34·6	45·9
8·2	9·7	E.E.C.	16·9	22·4

Principal Exports: Diamonds
Iron ore
Palm kernels

SINGAPORE
1970
S$ million

| *Exports (f.o.b.)* | | | *Imports (c.i.f.)* | |
Value	% of total		Value	% of total
4,755·8		TOTAL *of which:*	7,533·8	
324·5	6·8	Britain	569·1	7·6
688·7	14·5	West Malaysia	1,117·4	14·8
2,273·4	47·8	Total Commonwealth	1,982·7	26·3
527·3	11·1	U.S.A.	814·4	10·8
565·2	11·9	E.E.C.	395·4	5·2
361·5	7·6	Japan	1,458·0	19·4

Principal Exports: Crude rubber
Petroleum and petroleum products
Manufactured articles

SWAZILAND
1969
Rands million

Exports Value % of total			Imports Value % of total	
44·5		TOTAL	37·4	
		of which:		
7·0	15·7	Rep. South Africa	35·0	93·6
13·4	30·1	Britain		

Principal Exports: Iron ore
Asbestos
Forest products
Sugar

UNITED REPUBLIC OF TANZANIA
1970
Tanzanian Shillings, millions

Exports (f.o.b.) Value % of total			Imports (c.i.f.) Value % of total	
1,704·3		TOTAL	1,939·2	
		of which:		
372·0	21·8	Britain	411·2	21·2
925·0	54·3	Total Commonwealth	571·5	29·5
239·9	14·1	E.E.C.	467·5	24·1

Principal Exports: Coffee
Raw Cotton
Diamonds
Sisal
Cloves

TONGA
1969
Tonga $ '000

Exports (f.o.b.) Value % of total			Imports (c.i.f.) Value % of total	
3,339·7		TOTAL	4,788·2	
		of which:		
973·7	29·2	New Zealand	1,593·7	33·3
141·9	4·2	Australia	1,048·1	21·9
48·7	1·5	Britain	568·1	11·9
17·0	0·5	Hong Kong	79·3	1·7
1,216·6	36·4	Total Commonwealth	3,323·2	69·4
34·3	1·0	Fiji	1,108·8	23·2
158·4	4·7	Japan	102·1	2·1
790·7	23·7	E.E.C.	58·2	1·2

Principal Exports: Bananas
Copra
Desiccated coconut

TRINIDAD AND TOBAGO
1969

Exports (*f.o.b.*) T & T$ million   Imports (*c.i.f.*)

Value	% of total		Value	% of total
949·2		**TOTAL**	965·4	
		of which:		
92·7	9·8	Britain	133·7	13·8
101·4	10·7	Total Commonwealth	172·8	17·9
27·2	2·9	E.E.C.	36·2	3·7
450·0	47·4	U.S.A.	141·2	14·6
52·9	5·6	Sweden	1·8	0·2

Principal Exports: Petroleum products
                 Sugar

UGANDA
1970
Ugandan Shillings, million

Exports			Imports	
Value	% of total		Value	% of total
1,740·1		**TOTAL**	865·3	
		of which:		
358·9	20·6	Britain	278·4	32·2
620·6	35·7	Total Commonwealth	385·3	44·5
141·4	8·1	E.E.C.	192·9	22·3
362·5	20·8	U.S.A.	51·5	6·0

Principal Exports: Coffee
                 Cotton
                 Copper
                 Tea
                 Animal feed stuffs

ZAMBIA
1969
Kwacha million

Exports			Imports	
Value	% of total		Value	% of total
766·5		**TOTAL**	311·8	
		of which:		
198·0	25·8	Britain	71·4	22·9
7·7	1·0	South Africa	69·9	22·4
227·3	29·6	Total Sterling Area	196·7	63·1
252·9	33·0	E.E.C.	30·8	9·9
180·3	23·5	Japan	22·6	7·2
8·7	1·1	U.S.A.	30·1	9·6

Principal Export: Copper

COMMONWEALTH PRODUCTION OF SELECTED COMMODITIES

WHEAT PRODUCTION 1970/71(P)	'000 *metric tons*
Canada	9,023
India	20,093
Australia	8,437
Pakistan	7,399
United Kingdom	4,174
New Zealand	†
Kenya	230

MILLED RICE PRODUCTION (1970/71) (P)	'000 *metric tons*
India	42,672
Pakistan	13,553
Ceylon	1,049
Malaysia (est.)	1,351
Australia	164
Guyana	150

BARLEY PRODUCTION (1970)	'000 *metric tons*
United Kingdom	7,496
Canada	7,108
India	2,716
Australia	2,041
New Zealand	156
Cyprus	51
Pakistan	128

CANE SUGAR PRODUCTION (1969/70)	'000 *metric tons* (raw value)
Total Commonwealth	10,528
India	4,634
Australia	2,507
Pakistan	768
Mauritius	611
Jamaica	382
Fiji	350
Guyana	333
Trinidad and Tobago	222
Swaziland	181
Barbados	160
Uganda	151
Other West Indies British Honduras	102
Other	128

† Not available
P Provisional

COFFEE PRODUCTION (1970/71)   '000 *metric tons*

Total Commonwealth	425
Uganda	198
India	75
Kenya	65
Tanzania	60
Other	27

COCOA PRODUCTION (1969/70)   '000 *metric tons*

Total Commonwealth	761
Ghana	409
Nigeria	310
Other	42

TEA PRODUCTION (1970)   '000 *metric tons*

Total Commonwealth	751
India	421
Ceylon	212
Kenya	41
Pakistan	31
Other	45

LEAF TOBACCO PRODUCTION (1969/70)   *million lb.* (*wet weight*)

Total Commonwealth	†
India	746
Pakistan	360
Canada	204

NATURAL RUBBER PRODUCTION (1969)   '000 *metric tons*

Total Commonwealth	1,577
Malaysia	1,279
Ceylon	151
India	80
Nigeria	61
Other	7

COTTON PRODUCTION (1970/71)   '000 *metric tons*

Total Commonwealth	1,721
India	961
Pakistan	564
Tanzania	81
Uganda	79
Nigeria	43
Other	35

† Not available

APPLE PRODUCTION (1969) '000 *metric tons*
Total Commonwealth	000
Canada	497
Australia	423
United Kingdom	418
New Zealand	82
Other	§

PEAR PRODUCTION (1968) '000 *metric tons*
Total Commonwealth	000
Australia	107
United Kingdom	62
Canada	28
Pakistan	00
New Zealand	11

WOOL (RAW) PRODUCTION (1968-69) *million lb. (greasy basis)*
Total Commonwealth	2,944
Australia	1,952
New Zealand	752
United Kingdom	119
India	72
Pakistan	45
Other	24

SISAL PRODUCTION (1969) '000 *metric tons*
Total Commonwealth	259
Tanzania	209
Kenya and Uganda	50

RAW JUTE PRODUCTION (1968-69) '000 *tons*
Total Commonwealth	1,569
Pakistan	1,028
India	541

BUTTER PRODUCTION (1969) '000 *tons*
New Zealand	267 (1)
Australia	196 (2)
Canada	155
United Kingdom	56

BEEF AND VEAL PRODUCTION (1968) '000 *tons*
United Kingdom	891
Australia	890 (2)
Canada	740
New Zealand	339 (1)

---

(1) year ending 31st May   § Nil or negligible
(2) year ending 30th June

ESTIMATES OF GROSS NATIONAL PRODUCTS OF INDEPENDENT COMMONWEALTH COUNTRIES

Country	Year	Estimated Gross National Product at market prices (US$ million)	Estimated G.N.P. per capita (US$)
Australia	1970	35,097	2,550
Barbados	1967	119	480
Botswana	1966	55	95
Canada	1969	70,720	3,350
Ceylon	1969	1,978	160
Cyprus	1969	504	800
Fiji	1970	196	370
The Gambia	1968	35	100
Ghana (1)	1969	2,282	250
Guyana	1970	252	330
India	1969	44,000	80
Jamaica	1969	1,064	620
Kenya	1969	1,432	130
Lesotho	1968	87	85
Malawi	1969	272	60
Malaysia	1969	3,709	350
Malta	1969	212	670
Mauritius	1968	173	220
New Zealand	1970	5,327	2,815
Nigeria	1967	4,603	75
Pakistan	1970	16,419	125
Sierra Leone	1969	379	150
Singapore	1969	1,702	840
Swaziland	1968	64·3	165
Tanzania	1968	909	70
Tonga			
Trinidad and Tobago	1968	748	730
Uganda	1967	890	110
United Kingdom	1969	109,400	1,970
Zambia	1969	1,625	400

(1) G.D.P. at Market Prices

Sources: U.N. Yearbook of National Accounts
U.N. Monthly Bulletin
World Bank Atlas
O.E.C.D.

COMMONWEALTH IMMIGRATION INTO BRITAIN

U NTIL 1962 Britain had freely admitted citizens of other Commonwealth countries for residence and a quarter of the world's population was thus entitled to enter and settle in Britain at will. In the early nineteen-fifties increasing numbers began to exercise this right with the result that by 1961 (in which year an estimated 170,000 immigrants from other Commonwealth countries entered Britain) it became clear that the rate of flow of Commonwealth immigrants was exceeding Britain's capacity to absorb them, particularly since the majority tended to congregate in already over-crowded areas of the country. It was therefore decided reluctantly that immigration would have to be controlled.

COMMONWEALTH IMMIGRANTS ACTS 1962 AND 1968

Part I of the 1962 Act, which came into operation on 1st July 1962, for an initial period of 18 months, subjected to control all Commonwealth citizens except, broadly speaking, those born in the United Kingdom and those holding passports issued by a United Kingdom authority. Part I of the Act has since been extended annually for periods of one year.

During 1967 there was a rapid increase in the number of citizens of the United Kingdom and Colonies of Asian origin coming to this country from East Africa. In order to prevent the immigration policy from being undermined by this influx of people not subject to control under the 1962 Act, the Government regretfully decided it was necessary to introduce immediate legislation. The 1968 Act, which was passed on 1st March 1968, extended immigration control to certain citizens of the United Kingdom and Colonies who do not have a specific connection with the United Kingdom. Its effect is to extend immigration control to citizens of the United Kingdom and Colonies who hold United Kingdom passports issued abroad, unless they—or one of their parents or grandparents—were born or naturalised in the United Kingdom or acquired citizenship of the United Kingdom and Colonies by adoption or registration in the United Kingdom or by registration in what was at the time an independent Commonwealth country.

Under the 1968 Act special vouchers are issued to heads of households whose exemption from immigration control has been ended by the Act and who wish to settle in the United Kingdom. The dependants of a voucher holder are entitled to accompany him to, or join him in, the United Kingdom under the normal rules of immigration control. The annual quota of vouchers has been fixed at 3,000, but this is subject to review in the light of developments. The Government accepts that the United Kingdom is responsible for citizens of the United Kingdom and Colonies who are expelled from or subjected to serious restraints in their country of residence.

Admission may also not be refused to persons holding employment vouchers from the Department of Employment, *bona fide* students or persons who can support themselves without employment (including tourists and visiting business men), except on the grounds of health, security or criminal record. Visitors are normally free to take employment during the period of their visit and students may normally engage in paid employment during their free time, so long as they spend not less than fifteen hours a week in organised daytime study. Besides their power to refuse admission, immigration officers also have power to impose conditions, but conditions limiting the length of stay or prohibiting employment may not be imposed upon employment voucher holders, returning residents or the wives and young children of men to whose stay in the United Kingdom no such conditions attach.

The Acts apply to citizens of the Irish Republic as to the Commonwealth citizens; but in practice there is no control on traffic between the Irish Republic and Britain.

Parts II and III of the 1962 Act came into force on the 31st May 1962 and are permanent legislation. Part II gave power to the Secretary of State for Home Affairs to deport Commonwealth citizens, British Protected Persons and citizens of the Republic of Ireland who are convicted of offences punishable by imprisonment and recommended by a court for deportation. The Immigration Appeals Act 1969 enabled the Secretary of State to make deportation orders without a court recommendation in respect of persons who are liable to deportation under section 6 of the 1962 Act and who fail to comply with the conditions subject to which they were admitted to the United Kingdom. Persons born in the United Kingdom, or whose fathers were born there or who have lived in Britain for more than five years and persons under seventeen years of age are not liable to deportation. Commonwealth High Commissioners in London are informed as soon as it is known that one of their nationals has been recommended for deportation.

Part III of the Act contains ancillary provisions which, *inter alia*, extended the period from one to five years of ordinary residence needed to qualify a citizen of an independent Commonwealth country for registration, and a British Protected Person for naturalisation, as a citizen of the United Kingdom and Colonies.

Statistics for immigration from the Commonwealth show that for the twelve months period ending 31st December 1970 4,098 voucher holders and 32,627 others were admitted for settlement: the figures were published as Cmnd 4620 in March 1971.

EMPLOYMENT VOUCHERS

Vouchers are issued by the Department of Employment at a controlled rate determined from time to time by the Government. Up to 1st June 1971, the rate of issue was 8,500 per year. This figure has now been reduced to 2,700, of which 600 are allocated to the citizens of Malta, in view of the United Kingdom's special obligations to Malta, and 400 to United Kingdom dependent territories, with the proviso that as a general rule no one territory may receive more than half of the 400. Applications for vouchers are placed in two categories: in the first (category A) are placed applications made by an employer in this country who has a specific job to offer to a named Commonwealth citizen, and in the second (category B) applications made by Commonwealth citizens who possess certain special qualifications or skills. If a voucher is issued, it is sent to the immigrant through the appropriate British post in the territory concerned.

Category A

All applications must be made by the prospective employer in the United Kingdom to any local office of the Department of Employment. Except in the cases of citizens of Malta and persons belonging to dependent territories where the nature of the proposed employment is immaterial provided that the vacancy is genuine, vouchers will be issued in respect of the following types of vacancy only:—

(a) those holding professional qualifications and managerial and executive staff;

(b) skilled craftsmen and experienced technicians;

(c) specialised secretarial and clerical staff; and

(d) those coming to do work which, in the opinion of the Secretary of State for Employment, is of substantial economic or social value to the United Kingdom;

Except for Malta and dependent territories, applications in category A will be considered generally on a 'first come, first served' basis subject to the limitation that not more than 15 per cent of the vouchers available for category A will be issued to applicants from any one country. No vouchers will be issued in respect of vacancies for which suitable resident labour is available.

Category B

Applications in this category will be entertained from people with the following qualifications or skills:—

(a) trained nurses;

(b) teachers who are eligible for the status of qualified teacher in this country and possess a teacher training qualification acceptable to the Department of Education and Science;

(c) graduates in science or technology who are likely to be acceptable to employers here; and

(d) non-graduates with certain professional qualifications who have either a firm offer of a job or have had at least two years' experience in suitable employment since qualifying.

Application in category B must be made by the intending immigrant to the nearest British official representative overseas. Qualified doctors and dentists are dealt with outside the voucher scheme, but they must obtain entry certificates in order to gain admission to the United Kingdom.

DEPENDANTS

Wives of Commonwealth citizens resident in the United Kingdom are entitled to admission for settlement provided that they hold a valid entry certificate issued for that purpose, and so are children under the age of sixteen if both parents or the sole surviving parent are resident in the United Kingdom. Such children must also be in possession of an entry certificate. Children aged 16 or 17 have no rights of admission to join parents but are nevertheless freely admitted under the same rules as children under 16. Children aged 18 or over are expected to qualify for admission in their own right, e.g. as voucher holders (though in exceptional cases they may be admitted up to the age of 21 if they are unmarried and fully dependent on their parents and the rest of the family is coming to the United Kingdom). A widowed mother of any age, a widower over 65, or a married couple of whom either is over 65, will normally be admitted if they are wholly or mainly dependent upon children settled in the United Kingdom who are able and willing to support and accommodate them. Other dependants of Commonwealth citizens resident in the United Kingdom may be admitted depending on the circumstances of the individual case. Since 16th May 1969 when Section 20 of the Immigration Appeals Act came into force, entry certificates have been required in all cases where a dependant wishes to settle in the United Kingdom. Dependants whose entry certificate applications have been refused had a right of appeal under special arrangements introduced in advance of the first stage of the statutory appeals system on 1st July 1970.

STUDENTS AND VISITORS

Commonwealth students and visitors continue to be warmly welcomed but as there has been evasion of immigration controls by students and visitors staying on and taking employment, students are admitted for a period limited generally to a year in the first instance and visitors for a period of six months. The initial period for students is extended to cover the full period of their courses in all cases where it is clear that they genuinely intend to continue their studies. The period for visitors is also freely extended if good cause is shown. Applications for an extension of stay may be made to the Immigration and Nationality Department, Home Office, 271 High Holborn, London WC1 7EW.

ENTRY CERTIFICATES

The possession of an entry certificate is mandatory in the case of a Commonwealth citizen seeking entry on the grounds of being a dependant of a person already resident in the United Kingdom and for Commonwealth men seeking settlement on the sole ground of being the husband or fiancé of a woman resident in the United Kingdom. It is also available as a facility to all Commonwealth citizens on application at British Diplomatic Missions overseas. Possession of an entry certificate facilitates entry into Britain and is a virtual guarantee that entry will be permitted. Although the Immigration Officer will presume the holder is qualified for admission, admission may be refused if the holder has obtained the entry certificate by misrepresentation, if his claim to admission has been removed by a change of circumstances or if the Immigration Officer discovers he should be refused admission on medical, criminal or security grounds or because he is subject to a deportation order.

THE APPEALS SYSTEM

In August 1967 the Committee on Immigration Appeals recommended that a system should be established to hear appeals against refusals of entry certificates and refusals of admission and also against deportation orders. The Government announced that this recommendation had been broadly accepted and that legislation would be introduced in due course to enable an appeals system to be set up.

The Immigration Appeals Act 1969 confers on Commonwealth citizens rights of appeal against decisions to exclude or deport them from the United Kingdom and against the refusal to issue an entry certificate or grant an extension of stay.

Corresponding rights are given to aliens under the Aliens (Appeals) Order 1970.

On 1st July 1970 the first stage of the appeals system was implemented giving a statutory right of appeal to all those Commonwealth citizens refused entry certificates and to those already in the United Kingdom refused permission to stay longer. Pending introduction of the second stage of the appeals system those refused admission though in possession of an entry certificate, an employment voucher or a special voucher, have a right of appeal on a non-statutory basis. There are also certain rights of appeal relating to decisions to deport. See Statutory Instrument 1970 No. 791 under the heading Commonwealth Immigrants, The Immigration Appeals Act 1969 (Commencement No. 2) Order 1970, and Statutory Instrument 1970 No. 794 Commonwealth Immigrants, Aliens, The Immigration Appeals (Procedure) Rules 1970.

In accordance with the provisions of the Act the Secretary of State has appointed a panel of adjudicators to hear appeals in the first instance, and an Immigration Appeals Tribunal, whose members are appointed by the Lord Chancellor, has also been constituted to consider appeals against the decisions of adjudicators. A special panel of Tribunal members has been constituted for the purpose of hearing appeals against decisions or actions taken in the interests of national security.

Note: At the time of going to press, the new Immigration Bill is still before Parliament and its final terms are not yet available. Draft immigration rules have been published as Cmnd 4604 and Cmnd 4610 and may be obtained from HMSO, price 12½p. These may not, however, be identical with the rules which finally emerge.

COMMONWEALTH STUDENTS
IN BRITAIN

THE information contained in this chapter has been provided by the British Council and the Association of Commonwealth Universities. Further information about overseas students in Britain may be obtained from the 1971 *Commonwealth Universities Yearbook* and from *Overseas Students in Britain*, Statistical Supplement 1969-70.

Table 1 gives a breakdown of all Commonwealth students in Britain, at universities and other institutions, by category of study*.

Table 2 gives figures relating to university students from other parts of the Commonwealth who were considered to be 'overseas students' in terms of the definition which is now being used for fees purposes. This definition, as set out by the University Grants Committee, is:

A. The following should not be regarded as overseas students:

(i) any student who has been ordinarily resident in the U.K. for at least three years immediately preceding the date his course is, or was, due to begin;

(ii) any student whose parents or one of them have been ordinarily resident in the U.K. for at least three years immediately preceding the date of his course is, or was, due to begin;

(iii) any student who would have been ordinarily resident in the U.K. for at least three years immediately preceding the date his course is, or was, due to begin had he or his parents or one of them not been employed for the time being outside the U.K.;

(iv) any student aged under 21 at the date his course is, or was, due to begin, if he and his parents or one of them have been ordinarily resident in the U.K. for at least one year immediately preceding that date;

(v) any student who for at least one year immediately preceding the date his or her course is, or was, due to begin, has been (a) ordinarily resident (or on a full-time or sandwich course of higher education) in the U.K. and (b) married to a person who has been ordinarily resident in the U.K. for at least three years immediately preceding that date; or

(vi) any student whose parent or spouse is stationed in the U.K. and is recognised by the Foreign and Commonwealth Office as a member of the staff of a diplomatic mission or as a career consular officer.

B. All other students should be regarded for the purpose of fees as overseas students for the duration of their course.

---

* University and technical college figures in this table are also given in terms of the definition now used for fees purposes. This breakdown covers the period 1969–70 as complete figures for 1970–71 for all Tables were not available at the time of going to press (September 1971).

TABLE 1: COMMONWEALTH STUDENTS BY CATEGORY OF STUDY

	Universities (a)			Technical Colleges (b)			Inns of Court (c)	Colleges of Education (d)	Hospitals (e)		Other Institutions incl. Private Colleges (g)	Industry (h)	Business and Professions (j)	Govt. (k)	Grand Totals
	Post Grad.	Under Grad.	Total	Adv.	Non-Adv.	Total	(approx)		Nursing	Others (approx)	(approx)	(approx)	(approx)	(approx)	(approx)
Associated States of the Carribbean:															
Leeward Islands:															
Antigua	4	1	5	2	4	6	9		106					1	127
St Kitts-Nevis-Anguilla	2	5	7	1	4	5	11		116		2				141
Windward Islands:															
Dominica		3	3	2	3	5	6	3	57			1		1	76
Grenada	1	4	5	5	9	14	10	2	245			1		1	278
St Lucia	1	7	8	2	6	8	2	2	60		3				83
Australia	407	68	475	32	44	76	6	2	82		70	6	27		744
Papua and New Guinea	2		2												2
Bahamas	7	16	23	14	17	31	10	12	59	2	5	4	4		150
Barbados	18	19	37	20	32	52	62	7	907	3	11	1	10	12	1,102
Bermuda	4	17	21	5	16	21	5	14	57		6	1	2	1	128
Botswana	3	8	11	4	12	16	1				43				78
British Honduras	2	8	10	8	7	15	4	1	15	1	5	1		3	55
British Solomon Isles	1	1	2		1	1			2						5
British Virgin Islands		1	1												2
Brunei	3	19	22	13	38	51	3		45	12	118			28	289
Canada	827	104	931	50	65	115	13	11	199	1	56		4	1	1,334
Cayman Islands		1	1						1						2
Ceylon	298	104	402	504	244	748	25	3	400		109	158	183	158	2,186
Cyprus	91	188	279	125	763	888	152	12	130		229	63	79	2	1,834
Falkland Islands															
Fiji	9	6	15	8	13	21	4	3	14		13		5	6	81
The Gambia	10	6	16	7	12	19	2	2	22		11			1	74
Ghana	142	82	224	203	173	376	102	6	590	17	115	32	314	18	1,794
Gibraltar	2	23	25	7	9	16	2	53	15	2	3	2		1	119
Gilbert & Ellice Islands				2	3	5			1		2				15
Guyana	21	67	88	56	68	124	46	5	749		19	5	6	3	1,040
Hong Kong	145	239	384	129	526	655	60	14	807	68	348	80	104	13	2,535
India	720	269	989	289	376	665	174	14	304	9	127	83	172	8	2,545
Jamaica	39	57	96	57	93	150	130	10	2,692	13	38	77	47	93	3,346
Kenya	93	354	447	189	624	813	19	15	284	8	117	24	56	19	1,802
Lesotho	5	10	15		6	6		2		5	3		1		33
Malawi	32	46	78	40	45	85	8	5	41	5	20	13	16	9	280
Malaysia	217	480	697	401	597	998	493	18	1,899	25	323	20	160	207	4,840

TABLE 1: COMMONWEALTH STUDENTS BY CATEGORY OF STUDY—*continued*

	(a) Universities			(b) Technical Colleges			(c) Inns of Court (approx)	(d) Colleges of Education	(e) Hospitals		(g) Other Institutions including Private Colleges (approx)	(h) Industry (approx)	(j) Business and Professions (approx)	(k) Govt. (approx)	Grand Totals (approx)
	Post Grad.	Under Grad.	Total	Adv.	Non-Adv.	Total			Nursing	Others (approx)					
Malta	23	25	48	19	6	25	1	6	47		17	3	3	38	188
Mauritius	23	160	183	45	106	151	27	6	1,933	9	19	21	49	6	2,404
Montserrat		1	1						18		1		1		20
New Hebrides								2	8	1					11
New Zealand	155	19	174	19	25	44	3	1	25		34	5	3	1	290
Nigeria	321	208	529	518	382	900	114	44	566	595	395	340	565	335	4,383
Pakistan	754	186	940	172	454	626	190	11	61	1	126	29	186	5	2,175
Rhodesia	97	142	239	39	40	79	12	12	223		23	2	2	1	593
St Helena		2	2						10			2			14
St Vincent	3	2	5	5	4	9	3		223						240
Seychelles	6	13	19	4	6	10	5	4	35						73
Sierra Leone	52	49	101	102	134	236	22	19	159	5	72	6	71	12	603
Singapore	93	152	245	123	172	295	27	5	245		75	4	55	86	1,055
Swaziland	2	12	14	1	6	7	1	4	6	5	41	1	8	5	35
Tanzania	35	182	217	147	391	538	5	9	183		75	14		2	1,106
Trinidad & Tobago	38	70	108	81	147	228	80	6	1,918	12	41			3	2,391
Tonga		3	3			1			11						18
Turks & Caicos Islands															4
Uganda	71	175	246	145	356	501	34	66	145	12	105	17	21	10	1,157
Zambia	27	76	103	40	94	134	6	7	35	4	57	8	39	12	405
Total	4,808	3,688	8,496	3,636	6,333	9,769	1,884	428	15,767	797	2,812	1,030	2,200	1,102	44,285

TABLE 2: STUDENTS FROM OTHER PARTS OF THE COMMONWEALTH ENROLLED FOR FULL-TIME STUDY OR FULL-TIME RESEARCH IN UNIVERSITIES IN BRITAIN 1969-70.

	Total	Male		Female		In College or Hall		In Lodgings, with Friends, etc.		Known to hold an Award: Fellowship Scholarship, Grant, etc.	
Antigua	5	3	(2)	2	(2)	4	(3)	1	(1)	4	(4)
Australia	475	371	(319)	104	(88)	162	(133)	313	(274)	247	(226)
Bahamas	23	16	(7)	7		7	(2)	16	(5)	17	(4)
Barbados	37	27	(14)	10	(4)	11	(5)	26	(13)	29	(16)
Bermuda	21	12	(3)	9	(1)	14	(2)	7	(2)	9	(2)
Botswana	11	10	(2)	1	(1)	8	(3)	3		11	(3)
British Honduras	10	8		2		5		5		8	
British Solomon Islands	2	2	(2)	—		1	(1)	1	(1)	2	(2)
British Virgin Islands	1	—		1	(1)	—		1	(1)	1	(1)
Brunei	22	18	(3)	4		9		13	(3)	17	(2)
Canada	931	764	(695)	167	(132)	236	(184)	695	(643)	486	(458)
Cayman Islands	1	1		—		1		1		1	
Ceylon	402	354	(261)	48	(37)	150	(108)	252	(190)	249	(228)
Cyprus	279	247	(87)	32	(4)	79	(19)	200	(72)	101	(57)
Dominica	3	1		2		2		1		3	
Fiji	15	14	(9)	1		5	(2)	10	(7)	12	(8)
Gambia, The	16	14	(8)	2	(2)	11	(6)	5	(4)	15	(9)
Ghana	224	198	(130)	26	(12)	75	(45)	149	(97)	179	(120)
Gibraltar	25	24	(2)	1		12	(1)	13	(1)	20	(2)
Grenada	5	5	(1)	—		4	(1)	1		3	
Guyana	88	74	(16)	14	(5)	34	(4)	54	(17)	36	(16)
Hong Kong	384	310	(117)	74	(28)	145	(43)	239	(102)	102	(67)
India	989	884	(643)	105	(77)	285	(192)	704	(528)	536	(461)
Jamaica	96	68	(27)	28	(12)	40	(19)	56	(20)	59	(30)
Kenya	447	368	(81)	79	(31)	203	(31)	244	(62)	150	(64)
Lesotho	15	12	(4)	3	(1)	8	(1)	7	(4)	14	(5)
Malawi	78	73	(31)	5	(1)	44	(20)	34	(12)	54	(27)
Malaysia	697	601	(180)	96	(37)	301	(79)	396	(138)	300	(124)
Malta	48	38	(18)	10	(5)	17	(7)	31	(16)	39	(21)
Mauritius	183	154	(20)	29	(3)	83	(10)	100	(13)	97	(15)
Montserrat	1	1		—		1		—		1	
New Zealand	174	150	(131)	24	(24)	48	(43)	126	(112)	106	(98)
Nigeria	529	458	(288)	71	(33)	211	(95)	318	(226)	376	(238)
Pakistan	940	856	(691)	84	(63)	306	(232)	634	(522)	563	(511)
Papua† & New Guinea‡	2	2	(2)	—		1	(1)	1	(1)	2	(2)
Rhodesia	239	198	(83)	41	(14)	106	(29)	133	(68)	149	(67)
St. Helena	2	1	(1)	1	(1)	—		2	(2)	2	(2)
St. Kitts-Nevis	7	5	(1)	2	(1)	6	(2)	1		5	(2)
St. Lucia	8	6	(1)	2		3		5	(1)	7	(1)
St. Vincent	5	5	(3)	—		1	(1)	4	(2)	4	(3)
Seychelles	19	12	(3)	7	(3)	9	(2)	10	(4)	16	(6)
Sierra Leone	101	81	(38)	20	(14)	45	(13)	56	(39)	90	(43)
Singapore	245	202	(73)	43	(20)	128	(40)	117	(53)	104	(54)
Swaziland	14	13	(2)	1		7		7	(2)	11	(1)
Tanzania	217	192	(31)	25	(4)	97	(11)	120	(24)	71	(28)
Tonga	3	3		—		—		3		3	
Trinidad & Tobago	108	85	(32)	23	(6)	37	(8)	71	(30)	48	(24)
Uganda	246	220	(65)	26	(6)	105	(25)	141	(46)	136	(60)
Zambia	103	91	(25)	12	(2)	49	(6)	54	(21)	61	(19)
TOTAL	8496	7252	(4152)	1244	(656)	3116	(1429)	5380	(3379)	4556	(3131)

† Australian Dependent Territory.   ‡ Under Australian Trusteeship.

The numbers in brackets are those of the POSTGRADUATE students included in the previous figure (e.g. of the 3 male students from Antigua, 2 were studying at the postgraduate level).

STUDENTS FROM OTHER PARTS OF THE COMMONWEALTH ENROLLED
FOR FULL-TIME STUDY OR FULL—TIME RESEARCH IN UNIVERSITIES IN
BRITAIN 1969-70 *continued*

	No Award Known		Undergraduate	Postgraduate	Education		Medicine, Dentistry & Health		Engineering & Technology		Agriculture, Forestry & Veterinary Science	
Antigua	1		1	4	3	(3)	—		1		—	
Australia	288	(181)	68	407	30	(27)	38	(36)	54	(50)	12	(11)
Bahamas	6	(3)	16	7	6	(4)	2		—		—	
Barbados	8	(2)	19	18	9	(7)	5		2		—	
Bermuda	12	(2)	17	4	1		3	(2)	2		—	
Botswana	—		8	3	1		—		—		—	
British Honduras	2		10	—	6		3		—		1	
British Solomon Islands	—		—	2	2	(2)	—		—		—	
British Virgin Islands	—		—	1	1	(1)	—		—		—	
Brunei	5	(1)	19	3	4	(2)	1		9		2	
Canada	445	(369)	104	827	40	(39)	30	(25)	121	(109)	10	(10)
Cayman Islands	—		1	—	—		—		1		—	
Ceylon	153	(70)	104	298	16	(15)	47	(40)	125	(55)	25	(25)
Cyprus	178	(34)	188	91	18	(11)	15	(3)	133	(21)	14	(13)
Dominica	—		3	—	2		—		—		—	
Fiji	3	(1)	6	9	4	(4)	2		1	(1)	—	
Gambia, The	1	(1)	6	10	7	(6)	—		1		1	
Ghana	45	(22)	82	142	42	(9)	35	(17)	20	(13)	20	(18)
Gibraltar	5		23	2	2	(1)	7		1		—	
Grenada	2	(1)	4	1	2	(1)	—		2		—	
Guyana	52	(5)	67	21	4	(3)	24		22	(3)	1	
Hong Kong	282	(78)	239	145	19	(11)	57	(6)	135	(53)	1	(1)
India	453	(259)	269	720	56	(26)	56	(41)	468	(319)	16	(16)
Jamaica	37	(9)	57	39	12	(6)	14	(2)	23	(3)	2	
Kenya	297	(29)	354	93	30	(19)	88	(4)	174	(20)	19	(8)
Lesotho	1		10	5	1	(1)	3	(1)	1	(1)	1	(1)
Malawi	24	(5)	46	32	17	(17)	24		11	(2)	3	(2)
Malaysia	397	(93)	480	217	21	(15)	79	(17)	287	(57)	48	(24)
Malta	9	(2)	25	23	9	(6)	6	(4)	2	(1)	2	
Mauritius	86	(8)	160	23	3	(3)	56	(1)	49	(7)	8	(3)
Montserrat	—		1	—	—		1		—		—	
New Zealand	68	(57)	19	155	5	(5)	14	(10)	12	(11)	9	(7)
Nigeria	153	(83)	208	321	64	(37)	49	(26)	147	(60)	32	(31)
Pakistan	377	(243)	186	754	35	(15)	68	(62)	300	(213)	35	(35)
Papua† & New Guinea‡	—		—	2	—		—		—		1	(1)
Rhodesia	90	(30)	142	97	11	(10)	32	(2)	30	(10)	10	(3)
St. Helena	—		—	2	2	(2)	—		—		—	
St. Kitts-Nevis	2		5	2	1	(1)	—		1		—	
St. Lucia	1		7	1	3	(1)	1		1		1	
St. Vincent	1		2	3	1	(1)	1		2		—	
Seychelles	3		13	6	8	(5)	5		—		1	
Sierra Leone	11	(9)	49	52	22	(16)	17	(2)	15	(4)	3	(2)
Singapore	141	(39)	152	93	16	(9)	25	(11)	116	(29)	8	
Swaziland	3	(1)	12	2	3	(1)	1	(1)	2		—	
Tanzania	146	(7)	182	35	2	(2)	48	(6)	101	(6)	10	(6)
Tonga	—		3	—	2		—		—		—	
Trinidad & Tobago	60	(14)	70	38	6	(5)	15		25	(9)	1	(1)
Uganda	110	(11)	175	71	21	(11)	69	(7)	80	(9)	6	(5)
Zambia	42	(8)	76	27	9	(8)	11	(3)	50	(3)	2	(1)
TOTAL	3940	(1677)	3688	4808	579	(368)	952	(329)	2527	(1069)	305	(224)

† Australian Dependent Territory   ‡ Under Australian Trusteeship

The numbers in brackets are those of the POSTGRADUATE students included in the previous figure (e.g
on page 766, of the 3 male students from Antigua, 2 were studying at the postgraduate level).

AA*

STUDENTS FROM OTHER PARTS OF THE COMMONWEALTH ENROLLED FOR FULL—TIME STUDY OR FULL-TIME RESEARCH IN UNIVERSITIES IN BRITAIN 1969-70 continued

	Biological & Physical Sciences	Social, Administrative & Business Studies	Architecture, Town & Country Planning, Home or Hotel Management, etc.	Languages, Literature & Area Studies	Arts other than Languages	Total
Antigua	—	—	—	—	1 (1)	5
Australia	110 (102)	76 (60)	12 (11)	67 (50)	76 (60)	475
Bahamas	2 (2)	10 (1)	—	2	1	23
Barbados	6 (3)	7 (4)	2 (2)	3 (1)	3 (1)	37
Bermuda	5 (1)	4 (1)	—	4	2	21
Botswana	1	8 (2)	—	1 (1)	—	11
British Honduras	—	—	—	—	—	10
British Solomon Islands	—	—	—	—	—	2
British Virgin Islands	—	—	—	—	—	1
Brunei	5 (1)	1	—	—	—	22
Canada	120 (102)	277 (241)	22 (17)	140 (130)	171 (154)	931
Cayman Islands.						1
Ceylon	83 (66)	72 (65)	7 (7)	11 (10)	16 (15)	402
Cyprus	58 (22)	24 (9)	7 (5)	6 (3)	4 (4)	279
Dominica		1	—	—	—	3
Fiji	2 (1)	4 (1)	2 (2)	—	—	15
Gambia, The		4 (2)	1 (1)	1 (1)	1	16
Ghana	46 (34)	37 (31)	4 (4)	9 (8)	11 (8)	224
Gibraltar	6	2	—	7 (1)	—	25
Grenada	1		—	—	—	5
Guyana	13 (2)	14 (7)	1 (1)	9 (5)	—	88
Hong Kong	93 (34)	43 (18)	7 (5)	21 (12)	8 (5)	384
India	187 (160)	101 (73)	13 (11)	55 (45)	37 (29)	989
Jamaica	14 (9)	22 (13)	2 (2)	3	4 (4)	96
Kenya	74 (23)	45 (9)	4 (4)	5 (3)	8 (3)	447
Lesotho	1 (1)	8	—	—	—	15
Malawi	5 (3)	14 (7)	1	1 (1)	2	78
Malaysia	88 (36)	136 (45)	13 (2)	23 (20)	2 (1)	697
Malta	12 (4)	9 (5)	2	4 (3)	2	48
Mauritius	27 (6)	21 (2)	1 (1)	13	5	183
Montserrat						1
New Zealand	43 (42)	40 (33)	2 (2)	25 (23)	24 (22)	174
Nigeria	63 (45)	133 (88)	7 (7)	22 (21)	12 (6)	529
Pakistan	308 (296)	128 (85)	11 (6)	31 (21)	24 (21)	940
Papua† & New Guinea‡	—	1 (1)	—	—	—	2
Rhodesia	36 (13)	75 (34)	2 (1)	14 (9)	29 (15)	239
St. Helena	—	—	—	—	—	2
St. Kitts-Nevis	2 (1)	3	—	—	—	7
St. Lucia	1	—	—	—	1	8
St. Vincent	2 (1)	1 (1)	—	—	—	5
Seychelles	3 (1)	—	—	—	—	19
Sierra Leone	8 (4)	21 (13)	3 (3)	6 (5)	6 (3)	101
Singapore	41 (27)	32 (12)	5 (4)	1 (1)	1	245
Swaziland	—	5	—	—	3	14
Tanzania	30 (7)	17 (4)	4 (1)	2 (1)	3 (2)	217
Tonga	—	1	—	—	—	2
Trinidad & Tobago	30 (9)	23 (11)	1 (1)	5 (2)	2	108
Uganda	28 (19)	25 (11)	3 (1)	5 (4)	9 (4)	246
Zambia	11 (2)	12 (9)	1	1	6 (1)	103
TOTAL	1565 (1079)	1457 (898)	140 (101)	497 (381)	474 (359)	8496

† Australian Dependent Territory.   ‡ Under Australian Trusteeship.

The numbers in brackets are those of the POSTGRADUATE students included in the previous figure (e.g. on page 766, of the 3 male students from Antigua, 2 were studying at the postgraduate level).

TABLE SHOWING DIFFFERENCES IN TIME BETWEEN COMMONWEALTH COUNTRIES

Figures in horizontal columns indicate difference of time between the country shown in left-hand margin and the countries shown (in vertical columns) at the head of the table.

Figures to the left of the diagonal must be added and figures to the right of the diagonal must be subtracted.

SUMMER TIME (DAYLIGHT SAVING)

Since 1918 most cities and towns in Canada have adoped daylight saving for varying periods in the summer months.

In Britain the statutory period of Summer Time is defined in the Summer Time Acts of 1922 and 1925 but under the Summer Time Act 1947 the statutory dates may be varied by Order in Council. As from 31st October 1971, Summer Time will be used for the period between the 3rd Saturday in March, and the 4th Saturday in October.

	Canada (Pacific Time)
Canada (Pacific Time) (W. of 120° W.)	
Canada (Mountain Time) (102° W. to 120° W.)	1
Canada (Central Time) (85° W. (north) or 90° (south) to 102° W.), British Honduras	2
Canada (Eastern Time) (Ottawa and Washington, D.C.) (68° W. to 85° W. (north) or 90° (south)), Jamaica	3
Canada (Atlantic Time) (E. of 68° W.), Barbados, Antigua, Dominica, Grenada, St Christopher/Nevis/ Anguilla, St Lucia, St Vincent, Trinidad and Tobago and Falkland Islands	4
Guyana	4¼
Canada (Newfoundland)	4½
Britain (GMT), Sierra Leone, Ghana, The Gambia	8
Britain (Summer Time), Nigeria, Malta, Gibraltar	9
Cyprus, Malawi, Zambia, Lesotho, Botswana, Swaziland	10
Tanzania, Uganda, Kenya	11
Mauritius, Seychelles	12
Pakistan (West) (Islamabad, Karachi)	13
India, Ceylon	13½
Pakistan (East) (Dacca)	14
Malaysia (Kuala Lumpur), Singapore	15½
Australia (Western Australia) (Perth), Malaysia (Sabah, Sarawak), Brunei	16
Australia (South Australia, Northern Territory)	17½
Australia (Other States including Australian Capital Territory) (Canberra)	18
New Zealand, Fiji	20
Tonga	21

Canada (Mountain Time)	Canada (Central Time)	Canada (Eastern Time)	Canada (Atlantic Time)	Guyana	Canada (Newfoundland)	Britain (GMT)	Britain (Summer Time)	Zambia	East African Community	Mauritius	Pakistan (West)	India
1	2	3	4	4¼	4½	8	9	10	11	12	13	13½
	1	2	3	3¼	3½	7	8	9	10	11	12	12½
1		1	2	2¼	2½	6	7	8	9	10	11	11½
2	1		1	1¼	1½	5	6	7	8	9	10	10½
3	2	1		¼	½	4	5	6	7	8	9	9½
3¼	2¼	1¼	¼		¼	3¾	4¾	5¾	6¾	7¾	8¾	9¼
3½	2½	1½	½	¼		3½	4½	5½	6½	7½	8½	9
7	6	5	4	3¾	3½		1	2	3	4	5	5½
8	7	6	5¾	5½	2	1		1	2	3	4	4½
9	8	7	6	5¾	5½	2	1		1	2	3	3½
10	9	8	7	6¾	6½	3	2	1		1	2	2½
11	10	9	8	7¾	7½	4	3	2	1		1	1½
12	11	10	9	8¾	8½	5	4	3	2	1		½
12½	11½	10½	9½	9¼	9	5½	4½	3½	2½	1½	½	
13	12	11	10	9¾	9½	6	5	4	3	2	1	½
14½	13½	12½	11½	11¼	11	7½	6½	5½	4½	3½	2½	2
15	14	13	12	11¾	11½	8	7	6	5	4	3	2½
16½	15½	14½	13½	13¼	13	9½	8½	7½	6½	5½	4½	4
17	16	15	14	13¾	13½	10	9	8	7	6	5	4½
19	18	17	16	15¾	15½	12	11	10	9	8	7	6½
20	19	18	17	16¾	16½	13	12	11	10	9	8	7½

Pakistan (East)	Malaysia	Australia (Western)	Australia (South)	Australia (Other States)	New Zealand	Tonga	Time Zone Letter	Time Zone Number	(1) Time Zone Chart of the World. Published by the Admiralty 1969. (2) Statistics Section, Economist Dept.
14	15½	16	17½	18	20	21	U	8	Canada (Pacific Time) (West of 120° W.)
13	14½	15	16½	17	19	20	T	7	Canada (Mountain Time) (102° W. to 120° W.)
12	13½	14	15½	16	18	19	S	6	Canada (Central Time) (85° W. north or 90° south to 102° W.)
11	12½	13	14½	15	17	18	R	5	Canada (Eastern Time) (68° W. to 85° W. (north) or 90° (south))
10	11½	12	13½	14	16	17	Q	4	Canada (Atlantic Time) (E. of 68° W.)
9¾	11¼	11¾	13¼	13¾	15¾	16¾	—	3¾	Guyana
9½	11	11½	13	13½	15½	16½	—	3½	Canada (Newfoundland)
6	7½	8	9½	10	12	13	Z	0	Britain (GMT)
5	6½	7	8½	9	11	12	A	— 1	Britain (Summer Time)
4	5½	6	7½	8	10	11	B	— 2	Zambia
3	4½	5	6½	7	9	10	C	— 3	East African Community
2	3½	4	5½	6	8	9	D	— 4	Mauritius
1	2½	3	4½	5	7	8	E	— 5	Pakistan (West)
½	2	2½	4	4½	6½	7½	—	— 5½	India
	1½	2	3½	4	6	7	G	— 7	Pakistan (East)
1½		½	2	2½	4½	5½	—	— 7½	Malaysia
2	½		1½	2	4	5	I	— 9	Australia (Western)
3½	2	1½		½	2½	3½	—	— 9½	Australia (South)
4	2½	2	½		2	3	L	— 10	Australia (Other States)
6	4½	4	2½	2		1	M	— 12	New Zealand
7	5½	5	3½	3	1		—	— 13	Tonga

COMMONWEALTH CURRENCY

The pound sterling is equivalent to US$2·40. The rates of exchange of Commonwealth Countries, Dependent Territories and Associated States quoted below are as at the end of August 1971.

Country	Unit	Approximate Sterling Equivalent new pence*
Australia	Australian Dollar	47
Bahamas (i)	Bahama Dollar	42
Barbados	East Caribbean Dollar (a) ..	21
Bermuda (ii)	Bermuda Pound	42
Botswana	South African Rand	58
British Honduras	British Honduras Dollar ..	25
British Virgin Islands ..	U.S. Dollar	42
Brunei	Brunei Dollar	14
Canada (vii)	Canadian Dollar	41
Ceylon (iii)	Ceylon Rupee	7
Cyprus	Cyprus Pound	100
Falkland Islands	Falkland Islands Pound ..	100
Fiji (iv)	Fiji Dollar	48
The Gambia (viii)	Dalasi	20
Ghana	Cedi	41
Gibraltar	Gibraltar Pound	100
Gilbert and Ellice Islands ..	Australian Pound	47
Guyana	Guyanan Dollar	21
Hong Kong	Hong Kong Dollar	7
India	Indian Rupee	6
Jamaica (v)	Jamaican Dollar (b)	50
Kenya	Kenyan Shilling..	6
Lesotho	South African Rand	58
Malawi (ix)	Kwacha	50
Malaysia	Malaysian Dollar	14
Malta	Maltese Pound	100
Mauritius	Mauritius Rupee	8
New Zealand..	New Zealand Dollar	47
Nigeria	Nigerian Pound..	117
Pakistan	Pakistan Rupee	9
Pitcairn Island	{ Pound Sterling .. .. { New Zealand Dollar.. ..	100 47
St Helena	Pound Sterling	100
Seychelles	Seychelles Rupee	8

* 100 new pence = £1

Country	Unit	Approximate Sterling Equivalent new pence*
Sierra Leone	Leone	50
Singapore	Singapore Dollar	14
Swaziland	South African Rand	58
Tanzania	Tanzanian Shilling	6
Tonga	Pa'anga	47
Trinidad and Tobago ..	Trinidad and Tobago Dollar ..	21
Uganda	Ugandan Shilling	6
Zambia (vi)	Zambian Kwacha	58

(*a*) The East Caribbean Dollar is also used in Antigua, Dominica, Montserrat, St Christopher-Nevis-Anguilla, St Lucia, St Vincent and Grenada.

(*b*) The Jamaican Dollar is also used in the Cayman Islands and the Turks and Caicos Islands.

In the Western Pacific High Commission, comprising the Gilbert and Ellice Islands, the British Solomon Islands and the New Hebrides, Australian decimal currency is used throughout. In the latter, the New Hebrides franc, 100 of which equal one Australian Dollar, is also used.

(i) The Bahamian Dollar was up-valued on 2nd February 1970 to bring it in par with the U.S. Dollar.

(ii) Bermuda has introduced a decimal currency, based on the Bermuda Dollar at a rate of 2·4 to the Bermuda Pound which remains legal tender for the time being.

(iii) Under a certificate scheme effective from 6th May 1968 the Central Bank of Ceylon will buy sterling at Rs.19.20 to the £, compared with the official rate of Rs.14.28.

(iv) Decimal currency since January 1969.

(v) Decimal currency was introduced on 6th September 1969. The Jamaican Dollar is equal to half the old Jamaican pound.

(vi) The Kwacha (equal to 100 Ngwee) was introduced on 16th January 1968. The Zambian Pound remains legal tender until further notice.

(vii) The Canadian Dollar, previously pegged at 92·5 U.S. cents, has been allowed to float since 1st June 1970.

(viii) A decimal currency, the Dalasi (equal to 100 Bututs) has been introduced at a rate of 5 to the Gambia Pound.

(ix) Decimal currency, based on the Kwacha (worth 10 old shillings) was introduced on 15th February 1971

---

* 100 new pence = £1

BRITISH PARLIAMENTARY AND NON-PARLIAMENTARY PAPERS OF COMMONWEALTH INTEREST (1969–71)

L ISTED below are publications issued by, or on sale from, Her Majesty's Stationery Office, relating to the affairs of Commonwealth countries. This list covers the period 1969 to April 1971. Earlier publications are listed in previous editions of this work.

Dates within brackets denote year of publication or date placed on sale. If the date of a report, conference etc. is the same year as publication, the date is not repeated within brackets.

GENERAL

1. AGRICULTURE

Commonwealth Agricultural Bureau. 40th Annual Report of the Executive Council 1968-69, including Reviews of progress in the Agricultural Sciences. Applied Entomology, Animal Breeding, Nutrition, Horticulture and Plantation Crops, Soils. (Chairman: M. K. A. Agyemar). (1969). (SBN 11 880311 5) $9\frac{5}{8} \times 7\frac{1}{4}$ in. (25 × 19 cm.) 104 pp., illus. $37\frac{1}{2}$p.

Commonwealth Agricultural Bureau. 41st Annual Report of the Executive Council 1969-1970. Including Reviews of Progress in the Agricultural Sciences. Biological Control, Dairy Science and Technology, Forestry, Helminthology. (1971) (SBN 11 880315 8). 104 pp.+1 plate. 50p.

Commonwealth Agricultural Bureaux Review Conference, London, 1970. Report of Proceedings. (Cmnd. 4604). (Miscellaneous no. 1 of 1971). (SBN 10 14604 6). 64 pp. 40p.

2. EDUCATION

The Commonwealth Scholarship Commission in the United Kingdom. 9th Annual Report for the year ending Sept. 30, 1968. (1969) (H.C. 191) (SBN 10 219169 7). 72 pp. $42\frac{1}{2}$p.

Commonwealth Scholarship Commission in the United Kingdom. 10th Annual Report for the year ending Sept. 30, 1969. (1970) Overseas Development Administration, Foreign and Commonwealth Office. (SBN 10 215370 1). 76 pp. 45p.

3. DEVELOPMENT AND AID

An Account of the British Aid Programme. Text of United Kingdom Memorandum to the Development Assistance Committee of the Organisation for Economic Co-operation and Development. April 23, 1969. (SBN 11 580038 7). 28 pp. $12\frac{1}{2}$p.

An Account of the British Aid Programme. Text of United Kingdom Memorandum to the Development Assistance Committee of the Organisation for Economic Co-operation and Development. May 20, 1970). (SBN 11 580055 7). 28 pp. $12\frac{1}{2}$p.

British Aid Statistics. 1965 to 1969. With Correction slip. (1970) (SBN 11 580053 0). 104 pp. £2·00.

British Aid Statistics. Statistics of Economic Aid to Developing Countries 1964 to 1968. (1969) (SBN 11 580036 0). $11\frac{3}{4}'' \times 8\frac{1}{4}''$ (30 × 21 cm.) 92 pp. £1·37½.

Colonial Development and Welfare Act. Final return of schemes made and of Loans approved under the Colonial Development Welfare Acts— April 1, 1969 to March 31, 1970. (H.C. 92) (SBN 10 209271 0). 24 pp. 20p.

Colonial Development and Welfare Act. Return of Schemes made and of Loans approved under the Colonial Development and Welfare Acts in the period from April 1, 1968, to March 31, 1969. (H.C. 393) (SBN 10 239369 9). 24 pp. 15p.

Colonial Development and Welfare Acts 1959-1965. Account prepared pursuant to section 8(1) of the Colonial Development and Welfare Act 1959 of the receipts and payments of the Minister of Overseas Development during the year ended 1967-1968 in respect of loans for approved colonial development programmes; together with the Report of the Comptroller and Auditor General thereon. (In continuation of House of Commons Paper No. 48 of 1967-68). (1969) (H.C. 66) (SBN 10 206669 8). 4 pp. 4p.

Colonial Loans Acts 1949, 1952 and 1962. Statement of the total sums issued out of the consolidated Fund at March 31, 1969 in fulfilment of guarantees given by the Treasury in pursuance of Section 1 of the Colonial Loans Act 1952 and Section 1 of the Colonial Loans Act 1962. (H.C. 268) (SBN 10 227969 1). $9\frac{5}{8}'' \times 6''$ (25 × 16 cm.) 4 pp. 4p.

Colonial Loans Acts 1949, 1952 and 1962. Statement of the total sums issued out of the Consolidated Fund at March 31, 1970 in fulfilment of guarantees given by the Treasury in pursuance of Section 1 of the Colonial Loans Act 1962. (H.C. 246) (1970) (SBN 10 224670 x). 4 pp. 4p (5½p).

Commonwealth Development Corporation. Annual Report and Statement of Accounts for year ended 31st December, 1968. (1969) (H.C. 252) (SBN 10 225269 6). 115 pp. 52½p.

Overseas Aid Act 1966. Account prepared pursuant to section 2(4) of the Overseas Aid Act 1966 of the receipts and payments of the Minister of Overseas Development in respect of the Asian Development Bank for the year ended 31st March, 1968; together with the Report of the Comptroller and Auditor General thereon. (1969) (In continuation of House of Commons Paper No. 35 of 1967-68) (H.C. 115) (SBN 10 211569 9). 4 pp. 4p.

Overseas Resources Development. (1969) (SBN 10 313569 3). 6 pp. 5p.

Overseas Resources Development. Ch. 36 (1969) (SBN 10 543669 0). 4 pp. 4p.

Overseas Resources Development Acts 1959 and 1963. Account prepared pursuant to section 19(2) of the Overseas Resources Development Act 1959, of the receipts and payments of the Minister of Overseas Development in respect of the Commonwealth Development Corporation for the year ended 31st March, 1968; together with the Report of the Comptroller and Auditor General thereon. (In continuation of House of Commons Paper No. 13 of 1967-68) (1969) (H.C. 57) (SBN 10 205769 9). 8 pp. 6p.

4. OVERSEAS SERVICES

Diplomatic Service List 1971. Official Year Book. 6th edition. (SBN 11 590104 3). 456 pp. £2·50.

Guide to the Overseas Service (Pensions Supplement) Regulations 1969 and the Pensions Increase Act, 1969. (SBN 11 580034 4). $8\frac{3}{8}'' \times 5\frac{3}{8}''$ (21×14 cm.) 12 pp. 4p.

London Diplomatic List. Alphabetical list of the representatives of Foreign States and Commonwealth countries in London with their names and designations of the persons returned as composing the establishment of their respective offices, Bi-monthly. $22\frac{1}{2}$p.

Public Service Overseas. The Future of the Overseas Service Aid Scheme and other Supplementary arrangements. (1969) (Cmnd. 3994) (SBN 10 139940 5). 12 pp. 9p.

Yearbook of the Commonwealth. 1969. (SBN 11 580002 6*). $9\frac{5}{8}'' \times 6''$ (25×16 cm.) 802 pp.+folded map. Bound. £3·37$\frac{1}{2}$.

Year Book of the Commonwealth 1970. (SBN 11 580037 9) $8\frac{3}{8}'' \times 5\frac{3}{8}''$ (21×14 cm.) 808 pp.+1 folded map. £3·50.

A Year Book of the Commonwealth 1971. 3rd edition. (SBN 11 580051 4). 816 pp.+1 folded map. Bound. £5·24.

5. COMMUNICATIONS

Cumulative Supplement to the 1969 Edition of Signal Letters of U.K. and Commonwealth Ships, prepared by the Registrar-General of Shipping and Seamen. Corrected to June 30, 1969. (Note. No further editions of 'Signal Letters of U.K. and Commonwealth Ships' are to be published. The 1969 edition will not, therefore, now appear nor any further Cumulative Supplements). (SBN 11 720285 1). $9\frac{5}{8}'' \times 6''$ (25×16 cm.). 12 pp. 5p.

Signal Letters of U.K. and Commonwealth Ships prepared by the Registrar-General of Shipping and Seamen. Cumulative Supplement to the 1969 Edition corrected to (Both $9\frac{5}{8}'' \times 6''$ (25×16 cm.)):

March 31, 1969. (SBN 11 720282 7). 8 pp. 5p.

April 30, 1969. (SBN 11 720283 5). 10 pp. 5p.

6. MINING

British Phosphate Commissioners. Report and Accounts for the year ended 30th June, 1968. (Cmnd. 4080). Miscellaneous No. 23 (1969) (SBN 10 140800 5). 9 pp. 9p.

British Phosphate Commissioners Report and Accounts for the year ended June 30, 1969. (1970) (Cmnd. 4500) (Miscellaneous no. 22 of 1970). (SBN 10 145000 1). 8 pp. 7$\frac{1}{2}$p.

7. MIGRATION AND CITIZENSHIP

Commonwealth Citizens: Control after Entry. Draft Immigration Rules. (1969) (Cmnd. 3951) (SBN 10 139510 8). 16 pp. 10p.

Commonwealth Citizens: Control after Entry. Immigration Rules. (1970) (Cmnd. 4295) (SBN 10 142950 9). 16 pp. 10p.

Commonwealth Immigrant Tables. Sample census 1966. (1969) (SBN 11 6900007 5). 292 pp. £3·25.

Commonwealth Immigrants Acts 1962 and 1968. Both 9⅝″ × 6″ (25 × 16 cm.)): Control of Immigration. Statistics 1968. (1969) (Cmnd. 4029) (SBN 10 140290 2). 16 pp. 12½p.

Commonwealth Immigrant Acts 1962 and 1968. Control of Immigration. Statistics 1969. (1970) (Cmnd. 4327) (SBN 143270 4). 16 pp. 12½p.

Commonwealth Immigrants Acts 1962 and 1968. Control of Immigration Statistics 1970. (1971) (Cmnd. 4620). (SON 10 146200 X). 16 pp. 15p.

Commonwealth Immigrants Acts 1962 and 1968. Instruction to Immigration Officers. (1969) (Cmnd. 4051) (SBN 10 140510 3). 2 pp. 2½p.

Commonwealth Immigrants Acts 1962 and 1968. Instruction to Immigration Officers. (1970) (SBN 10 142980 0) 16 pp. 10p.)

Commonwealth Immigration Control. Select Committee on Race Relations and Immigration. 2nd special report. (Inquiry not completed). Together with the minutes of Proceedings. (1970) (SBN 10 228270 6). 12 pp. 9p.

Sample Census 1966. Great Britain, Commonwealth Immigrant Tables. (1969) (SBN 11 690007 5*). 13⅛″ × 8¼″ (33 × 21 cm.) 292 pp. £3·25.

Select Committee on Race Relations and Immigration. Control of Commonwealth Immigration. Minutes of Evidence:
    Nov. 20, 1969. (H.C. 17-i) (SBN 10 271270 7). pp. 33–48. 17½p.
    No. 27, 1969. (H.C. 17-ii) (SBN 10 271470 3). pp. 49–62. 17½p.

Select Committee on Race Relations and Immigration. Session 1969-70. Control of Commonwealth Immigration. 2v. (1971) (H.C. 205-i; H.C. 205-ii) (SBN 10 272071 1 and SBN 10 272071 8). v. 1 £3·30; v. 2 £2·45.

Statistics of persons acquiring citizenship of the United Kingdom and Colonies 1969. (Cmnd. 4451) (SBN 10 144510 5). 12 pp. 12½p.

8. MISCELLANEOUS

Britain's Associated States and Dependencies. March 1969. (SBN 11 700081 7). 7⅛″ × 4¾″ (18 × 12 cm.). 48 pp. 12½p.

Commonwealth Conference 1968. Report (1969) (Cmnd. 3852) (SBN 10 138520 X). 168 pp. 72½p.

The Commonwealth in Brief. 4th Edition. Sept. 1968 (1969) (SBN 11 700067 1). 7⅛″ × 4¾″ (18 × 12 cm.). 48 pp. 7½p.

Commonwealth Prime Ministers' meeting in London. Jan. 7-15, 1969. Final communiqué. (1970) (Cmnd. 3919) (SBN 10 139190 0). 16 pp. 10p.

Commonwealth War Graves Commission—50th Annual Report. (1969) (SBN 11 880412 X). 9⅝″ × 6″ (25 × 16 cm.). 100 pp., illus. 30p.

Conference of Commonwealth Survey Officers. 1967. Held at Leys School, Cambridge from Aug. 12-23, 1967: (Each 11¾″ × 8¼″ (30 × 21 cm)): Report of Proceedings. Parts I and II. (1969) (58-321-67*). 1,052 pp., illus. £12·12½ (includes 2 parts).

Directorate of Overseas Surveys. Annual Report for the year ended March 31, 1968. (1969) (SBN 11 580014 X). 76 pp. +9 folded maps. Illus. 67½p.

Directorate of Overseas Surveys. Annual Report for the year ended March 31, 1969. (1970) (SBN 11 580046 8). 9⅝″ × 6″ (25 × 16 cm.) 76 pp. +4 plates and 9 folded maps. 80p.

Survey of British and Commonwealth Affairs.: Fortnightly. (*Available on Subscription only.* £3·60 *per annum*).

Survey of Current Affairs. (Formerly Survey of British and Commonwealth Affairs). Vol. 1, no. 1, Jan. 1971. (SBN 11 721232 6). £2·85 *per annum*.

REGIONAL

AUSTRALIA

Agreement between the Government of the United Kingdom of Great Britain and Northern Ireland and the Government of the Commonwealth of Australia to provide for the Establishment and Operation in Australia of a Large Optical Telescope. Canberra, September 25, 1969. (The Agreement entered into force on Feb. 22, 1971). (Cmnd. 4622) (Treaty Series no. 19 of 1971). (SBN 10 146220 4). 12 pp. 10p.

BARBADOS

Agreement between the Government of the United Kingdom of Great Britain and Northern Ireland and the Government of Barbados for the Avoidance of Double Taxation and the Prevention of Fiscal Evasion with respect to Taxes on Income and Capital Gains. Bridgetown, Mar. 26, 1970. (The Agreement entered into force on June 26, 1970). (Cmnd. 4496). (Treaty Series 93 of 1970). (SBN 10 144960 7). 20 pp. 12½p.

BERMUDA

Bermuda. Report for the years 1965 and 1966. (1969) (SBN 11 58004 2). 94 pp. Illus. $8\frac{3}{8}'' \times 5\frac{3}{8}''$ (21 × 14 cm.) 52½p.

Bermuda. Report for the year 1967. (1969) (SBN 11 580005 0). $8\frac{1}{2}'' \times 5\frac{1}{2}''$ (22 × 14 cm.) 80 pp. Illus.+1 folded map. 80p.

Bermuda. Report for the year 1968. (1970) (SBN 11 580052 2). 72 pp., illus.+folding map. 80p.

Bermuda. Report for the year 1969. (1971) (SBN 11 580059 X). 84 pp., illus.+1 map. 95p.

Public Officers Agrrement between the Government of the United Kingdom of Great Britain and Northern Ireland and the Government of Bermuda. (1971) (Cmnd. 4638) (SBN 10 146380 4). 8 pp. 7½p.

BOTSWANA

Agreement amending the Arrangement between the Government of the United Kingdom of Great Britain and Northern Ireland and the Government of the Republic of Botswana for the Avoidance of Double Taxation and the Prevention of Fiscal Evasion with Respect to Taxes on Income. Gaberone, April 9, 1970. (The Agreement entered into force on 26 June, 1970). (Cmnd. 4427) (Treaty Series 64 of 1970) (SBN 10 144270 X). 4 pp. 4p.

Exchange of Letters between the Government of the United Kingdom of Great Britain and Northern Ireland and the Government of Botswana for the Provision of Personnel of the United Kingdom Armed Forces to Assist in the Training of the Police Forces of Botswana. Gaberones, Oct. 9, 1968. (The Agreement is deemed to have entered into force on March 1, 1968). (Cmnd. 3937). (Treaty Series 37 of 1969) (SBN 10 139279 9). 8 pp. 6p.

Exchange of Letters between the Government of the United Kingdom of Great Britain and Northern Ireland and the Government of the Republic of Botswana concerning the Guarantee by the United Kingdom and the maintenance of Reserves in Sterling by the Government of Botswana. (Sterling Area Agreement). Gaberones. Sept. 1, 1969. (Cmnd 4224) (Treaty Series 124 of 1969) (SBN 10 142240 7). 4 pp. 4p.

BRITISH ANTARCTIC TERRITORY

The Antarctic Treaty. Recommendations of the fifth Consultative Meeting held at Paris, Nov. 18-29, 1968. (1969) (Cmnd. 3993) (SBN 10 139930 8). 20 pp. 10p.

BRITISH ANTARCTIC SURVEY

Scientific Reports

57 Geology of Adelaide Island. (By G. J. Dewar, BSc, PhD). (1970) (SBN 11 981148 0). 68 pp., illus.+6 folded inserts and 7 plates. £2·75 (£2·81½).

63 Some aspects of the anatomy of the Ross Seal, Ommatophoca rossi (Pinnipedia: Phocidae) (By Judith E. King, B.Sc.) (1970) (SBN 11 980858 7) 11⅞″×9″ (30×23 cm.). 56 pp.+1 folded table and 10 plates, Illus., £2 2s. (£2 3s.)

63 Correction to Plate IX. (1970) (SBN 11 980858 7). Gratis (1½p).

64 Antarctic Moss Flora. I The Geneva Andreaca, Politia, Polytrichum, Psilopilum and Sarconeurum. (By S. W. Orcere, BA, PhD and others). (1970) (SBN 11 98 1076 X). 120 pp. £3·75 (£3·82½).

BRITISH SOLOMON ISLANDS

British Solomon Islands Order 1970. (Foreign Jurisdiction Act 1890) S.I. (1970) 482. (SBN 11 000482 5). 11p.

British Solomon Islands. Report for the year 1967. (1969) (SBN 11 580010 7). 8⅜″×5¾″ (21×14 cm.). 136 pp.+1 folded map, Illus., 50p.

British Solomon Islands. Report for the year 1968. (1970) (SBN 11 580042 5). 144 pp.+10 plates and 1 folded map. 90p.

BRITISH VIRGIN ISLANDS

Report for the years 1965–1969. (1971) (SBN 11 580064 6). 64 pp. 4 plates, 1 folded map. 45p.

BRUNEI

State of Brunei. Annual Report 1967. (1969) (SBN 11 980575 8). 8½″×5½″ (21×13 cm.). 382 pp.+1 folded map, Illus., Bound. 69p.

State of Brunei. Annual Report 1968. (1970) (SBN 11 980939 7). 8⅜″×5⅜″ (21×14 cm.). 348 pp.+10 plates and folded map, Bound. 71p.

CANADA

Exchange of Notes between the Government of the United Kingdom or Great Britain and Northern Ireland and the Government of Canada amending the Annex to the Agreement signed at London on 11 September, 1964 on arrangements regarding the Status of Canadian Forces in Bermuda. London, 16 December 1969/8. Jan. 1970. (The Exchange of Notes entered into force on 8 Jan. 1970). (1970) (Cmnd. 4359) (SBN 10 143590 8). 8 pp. 6p.

Reviews of National Science Policy. Canada. (SBN 11 920232 8). $9\frac{5}{8}'' \times 6''$ (25×16 cm.). 456 pp.+5 folded charts. £4·10.

CEYLON

Exchange of Notes between the Government of the United Kingdom of Great Britain and Northern Ireland and the Government of Ceylon concerning the Payment outside Ceylon of Pensions and Allowances covered by the Public Officers Agreement, 1947. Colombo, June 20, 1969. (Cmnd. 4200) (Treaty Series 118 of 1969) (SBN 10 142000 5). 4 pp. 4p.

Exchange of Notes between the Government of the United Kingdom of Great Britain and Northern Ireland and the Government of Ceylon revising the Route Schedule annexed to the Agreement for Air Services between and beyond their respective territories signed at Colombo on 5 August, 1969. (Cmnd. 4111) (Treaty Series 81 of 1969) (SBN 10 141110 3). 4 pp. 4p.

Ceylon. International Customs Journals. 11th Edition. Year 1969-70. March 1969. (SBN 11 980626 6). $11\frac{3}{4}'' \times 8\frac{1}{8}''$ (30×21cm.). 106 pp. $22\frac{1}{2}$p.

EAST AFRICA

Flora of Tropical East Africa. (Each $9\frac{5}{8}'' \times 6''$ (25×16 cm.)):

Annonaceal (by B. Verdocowl, BSc, PhD, FLS). (1971) (SBN 85592 011 4). 132 pp. Illus. £1·00.

Cabombaceal (by B. Verdcowl, BSc, PhD, FLS). (1971) (SBN 85592 001 7). 4 pp. Illus. 10p.

Flagellariaceal (by D. M. Napper, BSc, FLS). (1971) (SBN 85592 003 3). 4 pp. Illus. 10p.

Gramineae (Part 1) (by W. D. Clayton, PhD, BSc, ARCS, FLS). (1970) (SBN 11 980926 5). $9\frac{5}{8}'' \times 6''$ ($25+16$ cm.). pp. 1–176, Illus. £1·05.

FALKLAND ISLANDS

Falkland Islands and Dependencies. Report for the years 1966 and 1967. (1969) (SBN 11 580013 1). $8\frac{3}{8}'' \times 5\frac{3}{8}''$ (21×14 cm,). 88 pp.+2 folded maps, Illus. $47\frac{1}{2}$p.

Falkland Islands and Dependencies. Report for the years 1968 and 1969. (1971) (SBN 1 1580060 3). 84 pp., illus.+2 folded maps. 55p.

FIJI

Fiji. Annual Report 1968. (1970) (SBN 11 580040 9) 8⅛″ × 5⅞″ (21 × 15 cm.). 160 pp., Illus. + 1 folded map. 17½p.

Fiji Constitutional Conference 1970. Command 4389. 32½p.

Fiji Independence Act 1970. CH 50. (SBN 10 545070 7). 6p.

Fiji. Annual Report 1969. (1970) (SBN 11 580047 6). 164 pp., illus. + 1 folding map. 45p.

Fiji Independence Bill. (1970) (SBN 10 401371 0). 8 pp. 6p.

Fiji National Flag. (1970) (SBN 11 580026 3). 2 pp., illus. 37½p.

Plant diseases of Fiji (by K. M. Graham, BSA (Toronto), PhD (Toronto). Overseas Research Pulbication no. 17, Ministry of Overseas Development. (1971) (SBN 11 880032 9). 280 pp., illus. Bound. £3·50.

Prerogative Order in Council. Fiji (retiring Benefits) Order 1970. Dated May 19, 1970. (SBN 11 700434 0). 16 pp. 10p.

Public Officers Agreement between the Government of the United Kingdom of Great Britain and Northern Ireland and the Government of Fiji, Suva, Oct. 16, 1970. (The Agreement entered into force on signature). (1971) (Cmnd. 4561) (Treaty series 3 of 1971) (SBN 10 145610 7). 8 pp. 7½p.

Report of the Fiji Constitutional Conference 1970. Miscellaneous no. 9. (1970) (Cmnd. 4389) (SBN 10 143890 7). 68 pp. 32½p.

GAMBIA, THE

Republic of The Gambia Act. Ch. 37. (1970) (SBN 10 543770 0). 2 pp. 2½p (4p).

Republic of The Gambia Act 1970. Ch. 43. (SBN 10 544370 0). 2½p.

Republic of The Gambia Bill. (H.L.) (1970) (SBN 10 318770 7). 4pp. 4p (5½p).

GHANA

Agreement between the Government of the United Kingdom of Great Britain and Northern Ireland and the Government of the Republic of Ghana, on Medium-Term Commercial Debts owned by the Government of the Republic of Ghana and Residents of Ghana. Accra, Dec. 17, 1968. (The Agreement entered into force on Jan. 1, 1969). (Cmnd. 3944). (Treaty Series 40 of 1969) (SBN 10 139440 3). 8 pp. 6p.

GIBRALTAR

Gibraltar Constitution Order 1969. (1970) (SBN 11 700429 4). 25p.

Gibraltar. Report for the year 1967. (1970) (SBN 11 580043 3). 8⅜″ × 5⅜″ (21 × 14 cm.). 144 pp., Illus. + 3 folded inserts. 70p.

Prerogative Order in Council. The Gibraltar Constitution Order 1969. May 23, 1969. (With correction slip) (1970) (SBN 11 700429 4) 9⅝″ × 6″ (25 × 16 cm.). 50 pp. 25p.

GILBERT AND ELLICE ISLANDS

Gilbert and Ellice Islands Colony and the Central and Southern Line Islands. Report for the years 1966 and 1967. (1969) (SBN 11 580033 6). $8\frac{1}{8}'' \times 5\frac{3}{8}''$ (21 × 14 cm.). 112 pp., Illus.+1 folded map. 50p.

Gilbert and Ellice Islands Colony and the Central and Southern Line Islands, Annual Report 1968. (1970) (SBN 11 580039 5). $8\frac{3}{8}'' \times 5\frac{3}{8}''$ (21 × 14 cm.). 108 pp., Illus.+1 folded map. 50p.

GRENADA

Grenada. Report for the years 1965 and 1966. (1969) (SBN 11 580012 3). 64 pp., Illus. $8\frac{3}{8}'' \times 5\frac{3}{8}''$ (21 × 14 cm.). 50p.

GUYANA

Guyana Republic Bill (H.L.) (1970) (SBN 10 314070 0). 2 pp. $2\frac{1}{2}$p.

Protocol between the Government of the United Kingdom of Great Britain and Northern Ireland, the Government of Guyana and the Government of Venezuela relative to the Agreement to resolve the Controversy over the Frontier between Venezuela and British Guiana, signed at Geneva on 17 February 1966. Port-of-Spain, June 18, 1970. (The Protocol entered into force on June 18, 1970). (Cmnd. 4446) (Treaty Series 75 of 1970) (SBN 10 144460 5). 8 pp. 6p.

HONG KONG

Hong Kong. Report for the Year 1968. (With correction slip). (1969) (SBN 11 580032 8). 480 pp., Illus. Bound. £1·25.

Hong Kong Annual Report, 1969. (SBN 11 580045 X). 326 pp.+97 pp. plates. Bound. £1·25.

INDIA

India. The Transfer of Power 1942–47. Vol. I. The Cripps Mission. Jan–April 1942. (Editor-in-Chief Nicholas Mansergh, MA, DLitt, Assistant Editor E. W. R. Lunby, MA). (1970) (SBN 11 580016 6). 992 pp.+1 folding map. Bound. £7·00.

JAMAICA

Agreement between the Government of the United Kingdom of Great Britain and Northern Ireland and the Government of Jamaica for Air Services between and beyond their respective territories. Kingston, March 25, 1970. (The Agreement entered into force on March 25, 1970). (Cmnd. 4382) (Treaty Series no. 45 of 1970) (SBN 10 143820 6). 12 pp. 9p. (10½p).

LESOTHO

Agreement amending the Arrangement between the Government of the United Kingdom of Great Britain and Northern Ireland and the Government of the Kingdom of Lesotho for the Avoidance of Double Taxation and the Prevention of Fiscal Evasion with respect to Taxes on Income. Maseru, July 3, 1968. (The Agreement entered into force on March 28, 1969). (Cmnd. 4047). (Treaty Series 69 of 1969) (SBN 10 140470 0). 4 pp. 4p.

Exchange of letters between the Government of the United Kingdom of Great Britain and Northern Ireland and the Government of Lesotho concerning the Guarantee by the United Kingdom and the Maintenance of Reserves in sterling by the Government of Lesotho (Sterling Area Agreement). Maseru, Jan. 6, 1970. (The Agreement entered into force on Jan. 6, 1970). (Cmnd. 4415) (Treaty Series 38 of 1970) (SBN 10 144240 8). 4 pp. 4p.

MALTA

Exchange of Letters between the Government of the United Kingdom of Great Britain and Northern Ireland and the Government of Floriana, Dec. 23, 1968. (Cmnd. 3942). (Treaty Series 34 of 1969) (SBN 10 139420 9). 4 pp.

Malta (Reconstruction) Act 1947. Account 1967-68. Account prepared in pursuance of Section 2(2) of the Malta (Reconstruction) Act, 1947, of the sums issued to the Government of Malta out of the Consolidated Fund under Section 1 in respect of expenses incurred by that government in making good war damage and in carrying out works in connection with general reconstruction and planning, for the period ended March 31, 1968. Presented pursuant to Act 10 and 11 Geo. 6, c. 9, s. 2. (2). (1969) (H.C.P. 455) (SBN 10 245569 4). 4 pp. 4p.

MAURITIUS

Mauritius. Report for the year 1967. (1970) (SBN 11 580041 7) $8\frac{1}{8}'' \times 6\frac{1}{2}''$ (21×17 cm.). 212 pp.+4 plates, maps and 1 folded inset. £1·30.

NEW HEBRIDES

New Hebrides Anglo-French Condominium. Report for the year 1967 and 1968. (1970) (SBN 11 580054 9). 128 pp., illus.+4 plates. 75p.

NEW ZEALAND

Agreement on Social Security between the Government of the United Kingdom of Great Britain and Northern Ireland and the Government of New Zealand. Wellington, June, 19, 1969. (The Agreement entered into force on Jan. 1, 1970). This publication supersedes New Zealand No. 1 (1969). (Cmnd. 4208). (Treaty Series 13 of 1970). (SBN 10 142810 3) 16 pp. 10p.

NIGERIA

Nigeria. Report of Lord Hunt's Mission. The problem of relief in the aftermath of the Nigerian civil war. (1970) (Cmnd. 4275) (SBN 10 142750 6). 16 pp. 10p.

Report of the Observer Team to Nigeria. Sept. 24-Nov. 23, 1968. (Cmnd. 3878) (1969) (SBN 10 138780 6). 36 pp. $17\frac{1}{2}$p.

PITCAIRN ISLAND

Arms. Granted by Royal Warrant dated Nov. 4, 1969. Pitcairn Island (1970) (SBN 11 580019 0) 9⅝″×5″ (25×16 cm.). 52½p.

RHODESIA

A Principle in Torment. 1: The United Nations & Southern Rhodesia. (Sales No. E.69.I.26). (SBN 11 900912 9). 9″×6″ (23×16 cm.). 76 pp. 32½p.
Rhodesia Independence Bill. (1970) (SBN 10 306270 X). 2 pp. 2½p.

ST. HELENA

St. Helena. Report for the Years 1966 and 1967. (1969) (SBN 11 580015 8). 8¾″×5¾″ (21×14 cm.). 78 pp.+2 maps, Illus. 37½p.
Saint Helena. Report for the years 1968 and 1969. (1971) (SBN 1621 580062 X). 84 pp., illus.+4 plates. 55p.

ST. VINCENT

Public Officers Agreement between Her Majesty's Government in the United Kingdom and the Government of Saint Vincent. (1970) (Cmnd. 4257) (SBN 10 142570 8). 6 pp. 6p.
Report on the St. Vincent Constitutional Conference. June 23-27, 1969. (Cmnd. 4116) (SBN 10 141160 X). 32 pp. 15p.

SEYCHELLES

People of the Seychelles. (By B. Benedict). 3rd edition 1970. Overseas Research Publication no. 14. (2BN 11 880413 8). 80 pp.+1 folded map. 75p (77½p).
Prerogative Order in Council. Seychelles (Amendment) Order 1969. (SBN 11 700430 8). 9⅝″×6″ (25×16 cm.). 2 pp. 2½p.
Prerogative Order in Council dated March 24, 1970. The Seychelles (Electoral Provisions) Order 1970. (SBN 11 700432 4) 9⅝″×6″ (25×16 cm.). 4 pp. 4p.
Report of the Seychelles Constitutional Conference. March 9-13, 1970. (Cmnd. 4338) (SBN 10 143380 8). 12 pp. 9pa.
Seychelles. Report for the Years 1967 and 1968. (1970) (SBN 11 260004 2). 8⅛″×6½″ (21×17 em.). 72 pp.+6 plates and 1 folded map. 40p.

SIERRA LEONE

Agreement Amending the Arrangement between the Government of the United Kingdom of Great Britain and Northern Ireland and the Government of Sierra Leone for the Avoidance of Double Taxation and the Prevention of Fiscal Evasion with Respect to Taxes on Income. Freetown, March 18, 1968. (The Agreement entered into force on Jan. 16, 1969). (Cmnd. 3955). (Treaty Series 42 of 1969). (SBN 10 139550 7). 4 pp. 4p.

SINGAPORE

Agreement between the Government of the United Kingdom of Great Britain and Northern Ireland and the Government of the Republic of Singapore for Air Services between and beyond their Respective Territories. Singapore, Jan. 12, 1971. (The Agreement entered into force on Jan. 12, 1971). (Cmnd. 4619) (Treaty Series no. 20 of 1971) (SBN 10 146190 9). 12 pp. 10p (12½p).

SOUTH AND SOUTH EAST ASIA

Colombo Plan for Co-operative Economic Development in South and South-East Asia. 16th Annual Report of the Consultative Committee. Seoul, Oct. 1968. (1969) (Cmnd. 3910) (SBN 10 139100 1). 440 pp. £1·75.

SWAZILAND

Agreement between the Government of the United Kingdom of Great Britain and Northern Ireland and the Government of the Kingdom of Swaziland for the Avoidance of Double Taxation and the Prevention of Fiscal Evasion with respect to Taxes on Income. London, Nov. 26, 1968. (The Agreement entered into force on March 18, 1969). (Cmnd. 4007). (Treaty Series 57 of 1969) (SBN 10 140070 5). 20 pp. 10p.

Swaziland. Report for the year 1966. (1969) (SBN 11 580009 3). 164 pp. +1 folded map, Illus. 8⅜″ × 5⅜″ (21 × 14 cm.). 75p.

TONGA

Termination of United Kingdom Responsibility for the External Relations of Tonga. Nuku' alofa. May 19, 1970. (Cmnd. 4490) (Tonga No. 1, 1970) (SBN 10 144900 3). 4 pp. 5p.

Tonga Act 1970. CH 22. (SBN 10 542270 3). 4p.

Treaty of Friendship between Her Majesty The Queen in respect of the United Kingdom of Great Britain and Northern Ireland and His Majesty the King of Tonga. Nuku'alofa, May 30, 1968. (Instruments of ratification were exchanged on Dec. 5, 1968 and the Treaty entered into force on that date). This publication supersedes "Tonga No. 1 (1968)", Cmnd. 3654. (Cmnd. 3921) (1969) (SBN 10 139210 9). 12 pp. 9p.

Tonga Bill. (H.L.) (1970) (SBN 10 317070 7 7). 4 pp. 4p.

TRINIDAD AND TOBAGO

Double Taxation. Trinidad and Tobago No. 1 (1970). Protocol amending the Agreement between the Government of the United Kingdom of Great Britain and Northern Ireland and the Government of Trinidad and Tobago for the avoidance of Double Taxation and the Prevention of Fiscal Evasion with respect to Taxes on Income, signed at Port of Spain on 29 Dec., 1966. Port of Spain, 10 Dec., 1969. (The Protocol is not in force). (Cmnd. 4285) (SBN 10 142850 2). 8 pp. 6p.

Double Taxation Relief (Taxes on income) (Trinidad and Tobago) Order 1970. S.I. (1970) 483. (SBN 11 000483 3). 5p.

Protocol amending the Agreement between the Government of the United Kingdom of Great Britain and Northern Ireland and the Government of Trinidad and Tobago for the Avoidance of Double Taxation and the Prevention of Fiscal Evasion with respect to Taxes on Income, signed at Port of Spain on Dec. 29, 1966. Port-of-Spain, Dec. 10, 1969. (The Protocol entered into force on March 24, 1970). This publication supersedes Trinidad and Tobago no. 1 (1970), Cmnd. 4285. (Cmnd. 4444) (Treaty Series 70 of 1970) (SBN 10 144440 0). 6 pp. 6p.

WEST INDIES

Caribbean Development Bank. Treaty Series no. 36 (1970). Agreement establishing the Caribbean Development Bank, Kingston, 18 October 1969. (The United Kingdom instrument of retification was deposited on 23 January 1970 and the agreement entered into force on 26 January 1970). This publication supersedes Miscellaneous No. 1 (1970). (Cmnd. 4254) (Cmnd. 4358) (SBN 10 143580 0). 44 pp. 20p.

Report of the Commission of Inquiry appointed by the Governments of the United Kingdom and St Christopher-Nevis-Anguilla to examine the Anguilla Problem. (1970) (Cmnd. 4510) (Miscellaneous No. 23 of 1970) (SBN 10 145100 8). 132 pp. 80p.

Select Committee on Race Relations and Immigration (Sub-Committee A). Control of Immigration. Minutes of Evidence taken in Barbados, St Lucia and Antigua. December 9, 10, and 12, 1969. (1970) (SBN 10 283170 X). pp. 64–124. 40p.

WESTERN PACIFIC HIGH COMMISSION TERRITORIES

Western Pacific Islands (by Austin Coates). (1971) (SBN 11 880428 6). 368 pp., illus. Bound, 32 plates Corona Library. £1·50 (£1·70).

ZAMBIA

Agreement between the Government of the United Kingdom of Great Britain and Northern Ireland and the Government of the Republic of Zambia for Air Services between their respective territories. Lusaka, March 17, 1967, and Exchange of Notes amending the Agreement. Lusaka, Oct. 30, 1968. (The Agreement entered into force on Nov. 1, 1968) This publication supersedes "Zambia no. 1 (1967)" (Cmnd. 3318). (Cmnd. 3939) (Treaty Series 39 of 1969) (SBN 10 139390 3). 12 pp. 9p.

Agreement between the Government of the United Kingdom of Great Britain and Northern Ireland the the Government of the Republic of Zambia supplementary to and amending the Agreement of Nov. 25, 1955 between the Government of the United Kingdom and the Governmentof the Federation of Rhodesia and Nyasaland for the Avoidance of Double Taxation and Prevention of Fiscal Evasion with respect to Taxes on Income. Lusaka, April 6, 1968. (The Agreement entered into force on June 9, 1969). (1970) (Cmnd. 4365) (Tresty Series 37 of 1970) (SBN 10 143650 5). 4 pp. 4p.

APPENDICES

FOREIGN AND COMMONWEALTH OFFICE OVERSEAS DEVELOPMENT ADMINISTRATION

A s MUCH of the work of the Overseas Development Administration is connected with the Commonwealth, it has been thought useful to include information about it and its associated bodies and committees in the Year Book.

In October 1970, a number of changes in the organisation of central government were announced by the new administration. Amongst these was the dissolution of the Ministry of Overseas Development. This was effected in November 1970 and all the functions of the the the Minister of Overseas Development were then transferred by a statutory instrument to the Secretary of State for Foreign and Commonwealth Affairs. The development work of the enlarged Foreign and Commonwealth Office is the charge of a Minister for Overseas Development who has, by delegation from the Secretary of State, full charge of the functional wing known as the Overseas Development Administration of the Foreign and Commonwealth Office. This wing of the Foreign and Commonwealth Office is staffed by the officers of the former Ministry of Overseas Development.

The central purpose of the Overseas Development Administration is to formulate and carry out British policies for helping the developing countries to raise their living standards. In doing this it works in harmony with the policies of other government departments concerned.

The Overseas Development Administration is responsible for: the British economic aid programme as a whole and its detailed composition; the terms and conditions of aid; the size and nature of the programme for each country; the management of financial aid and technical assistance; relations with international aid organisations; the British interest in United Nations programmes of technical assistance; and relations with voluntary bodies concerned with aid and development.

The only exceptions to this are that in relation to dependent territories the Dependent Territories Division of the Foreign and Commonwealth Office remains responsible, in consultation with the Overseas Development Administration for budgetary aid, while the latter, in discharging its responsibility for development aid, acts in agreement with other divisions of the Foreign and Commonwealth Office. The Overseas Development Administration is not responsible for military aid, which remains under the appropriate division of the Foreign and Commonwealth Office.

On the administrative side the Overseas Development Administration is organised into a number of Divisions headed by Under-Secretaries. Of these one deals with general aid policy, finance and the role of private investment in development; another with British relations with the international bodies handling aid and development, and with other aid-giving countries. Others deal with Asia, Africa and the Caribbean and Latin America. The Geographical Departments which form part of these Divisions are responsible for the capital aid and technical assistance programmes to the countries within these regions and for dealing through British diplomatic posts with the governments concerned regarding these programmes.

Other Divisions deal with technical assistance and are responsible with the Overseas Development Administration's professional advisers for organising the resources of Britain to provide this form of aid and for contacts with the many organisations in Britain outside as well as inside the Government which contribute to this. The subjects dealt with include agriculture and other natural resources; science and technology; schools and teacher training; social education; universities and technical education; recruitment for service overseas and the terms and conditions of service of personnel serving abroad; the organisation of training in Britain; voluntary organisations and the young volunteers programme; assistance in the medical field and population control; and Britain's relations with UNESCO and FAO. An Information Department operates outside the divisional organisation concerned with the engagement of consultants for feasibility studies and other assignments.

The economic Planning Staff is responsible for the Overseas Development Administration's work in the economic and statistical fields including the provision of advice, personnel and training where requested by overseas governments. It is divided into three Divisions. Each of the economists in the Geographical Division is responsible for studying the economic problems of a group of recipient countries as a basis for the working out of aid programmes that will best contribute to their economic development. The International Economics Division takes part, from the economic point of view, in the formulation of general aid policies, and undertakes research into economic trends which affect the rate of progress of the developing countries. Both Divisions work closely with the operational departments concerned. The Statistics Division provides statistical services including compilation of statistics of aid.

The Overseas Development Administration has a staff of professional advisers on technical subjects and is also advised by members of organisations partly or wholly financed from its funds. Subjects covered include education, medicine, a wide range in the field of natural resources (including agriculture and geology), engineering, building, social development and a number of others. When engineering advice of a specialist nature is required, which falls outside the fields of its own Advisory staff, such as telecommunications, it is able to call on the experience of the Crown Agents for Oversea Governments and Administrations. Various organisations engaged in the provision of technical assistance are attached to the Overseas Development Administration; they are the Directorate of Overseas Surveys, the Tropical Products Institute, the Land Resources Division and the Centre for Overseas Pest Research.

APPENDIX B

THE COMMONWEALTH
TELEPHONE CABLE PARTNERSHIP

RIOR to 1956, intra-Commonwealth telecommunications had been carried either by submarine telegraph cable or by radio. However, by 1956 the British Post Office had solved the technical problems of using multi-channel submarine telephone cables to carry conversations over long distances and had come to an agreement with the Canadian Overseas Telecommunication Corporation to lay a 60-channel cable between Britain and Canada. It thus became necessary to consider whether this Anglo-Canadian telephone cable (later named CANTAT) should form part of the existing Commonwealth telecommunications system and whether additional intra-Commonwealth telephone cables should be laid. These questions were considered by a Commonwealth Telecommunications Conference held in London in July 1958; and it was recommended to Governments that a Commonwealth round-the-world telephone cable should be laid, section by section, Commonwealth Governments arranging between themselves to construct and finance particular sections as the need arose. The Conference was not able to recommend that these new telephone cables should be brought within the existing Commonwealth Telecommunications Partnership (*q.v.*) but proposed that they should be kept separate and should be operated under separate financial arrangements. These recommendations were endorsed by the Commonwealth Trade and Economic Conference held in Montreal in 1958 and were accepted by Commonwealth Governments.

As a result of the recommendations of the Conference, Britain, Canada, Australia and New Zealand agreed to lay and jointly finance a telephone cable (called COMPAC) across the Pacific from Canada to Australia via Fiji and New Zealand, and set up a Management Committee, consisting of one representative of each Partner, to construct and operate it. Later, Britain, Canada, Australia. New Zealand and Malaysia agreed to extend this cable (called SEACOM) to New Guinea, Hong Kong, Kota Kinabalu and Singapore, and set up a similar Management Committee for the purpose. The CANTAT cable was opened in 1961, COMPAC in 1964 and SEACOM in 1967.

The telephone cables now combine with some micro-wave and tropospheric scatter systems to form the second Wayleave Scheme, which has been administered since 1966 by a unified management, the Commonwealth Cable Management Committee. This Committee consists of representatives from the telecommunications authorities of Britain, Canada, Australia, New Zealand, Malaysia and Singapore and meets from time to time in each of those countries (and Hong Kong). The co-operative financial arrangements of the Second Wayleave Scheme are similar to the wayleave system operated by the Commonwealth Telecommunciations Partnership (*q.v.*).

The departure of South Africa from the Commonwealth and the advent of satellite telecommunications make it now improbable that a round-the-world submarine telephone cable will be completed.

APPENDIX C

COMMONWEALTH
TELECOMMUNICATIONS PARTNERSHIP

THE first submarine telegraph cables linking what are now independent Commonwealth countries were laid by cable companies as commercial ventures and Governments were not directly concerned. However, because the cable companies were unwilling to meet the expense of laying a cable across the Pacific from Canada to Australia, the Governments of Britain, Canada, New Zealand and some of the Australian States agreed—largely as a result of the advocacy over many years of Sandford Fleming of the Canadian Pacific Railways—to subscribe money for a Pacific Telegraph Cable and set up in 1901 a representative Pacific Cable Board to construct and manage the cable, which was laid in 1902.

In 1927 on the recommendation of an Imperial Wireless and Cable Conference, the various cable and wireless interests which then served the Commonwealth, including the Pacific Cable Board, were merged and a single operating Company later to be known as Cable and Wireless Ltd was set up. A representative Imperial Communications Advisory Committee was established to lay down the policy which should be followed by the Company.

In 1945 a Commonwealth Telecommunications Conference recommended that the assets of Cable and Wireless Ltd in the various Commonwealth countries should be nationalised. The recommendation was accepted by the Commonwealth Governments concerned, and in 1948 a Commonwealth Telegraphs Agreement was drawn up to promote and co-ordinate the telecommunications services of the Commonwealth. Under the agreement, which was signed by the Governments of Britain, Canada, Australia, New Zealand, South Africa, India and Southern Rhodesia, the partner Governments agreed to operate their external telecommunications co-operatively with the advice of a Commonwealth Telecommunications Board in London, on which each was to be represented. In addition, a 'wayleave scheme' was eventually adopted under which each partner retains its annual wayleave revenue and incurs payment of common user costs in the same proportion as its wayleave revenue bears to the total wayleave revenue for the partnership. This practice contrasts with normal international telecommunications accounting, whereby a portion of the revenue collected for an international call or message is passed by the originating country to the terminal country (and any transit country concerned). The 1948 agreement was somewhat modified by a second Commonwealth Telegraphs Agreement signed in 1963.

On the recommendation of a further Commonwealth Telecommunications Conference held in 1965 and 1966 the partnership was re-constituted and the Commonwealth Telecommunications Board was replaced by a new Commonwealth Telecommunications Organisation with a Constitution* which provides for periodical Commonwealth Telecommunications Conferences at which any independent Commonwealth Government may be represented, a Commonwealth Telecommunications Council of serving telecommunications officials meeting at

---

* Published in the United Kingdom by HMSO in March 1968 as Command 3547.

least once a year and carrying on its business between meetings by correspondence and a secretariat, the Commonwealth Telecommunications Bureau (*q.v.*), in London.

The Commonwealth Telecommunications Board was accordingly dissolved on 31st March 1969 by an Order-in-Council made under the Commonwealth Telecommunications Act 1968. The Commonwealth Telegraphs Agreements were at the same time terminated and a new financial agreement between the Partner Governments in respect of the wayleave scheme, the Commonwealth Telecommunications Organisation Financial Agreement 1969, became operative.

The present partnership, which is concerned only with the telecommunications assets (principally submarine telegraph cables and radio links, with some submarine telephone cables) of the First Wayleave Scheme, consists of the Governments of Australia, Barbados, Botswana, Canada, Ceylon, Cyprus, The Gambia, Ghana, Guyana, India, Jamaica, Kenya, Malaysia, Malawi, New Zealand, Nigeria, Sierra Leone, Singapore, Tanzania, Trinidad and Tobago, Uganda, Zambia and the United Kingdom.

APPENDIX D

COMMONWEALTH
TELECOMMUNICATIONS BUREAU

28 Pall Mall, London S.W.1 (01-930 4248)

General Secretary: S. N. Kalra

Chief of Systems Division: C. A. R. Anketell
Chief of Operations: T. J. Petry
Chief of Finance: D. Clarke
Chief of Administration: C. A. G. Coleridge, OBE

The Commonwealth Telecommunications Bureau is the Secretariat of the Commonwealth Telecommunications Organisation*.

The Bureau was incorporated in Britain on 8th May 1968 by the Commonwealth Telecommunications Act 1968 and from 1st April 1969 it took over from the Commonwealth Telecommunications Board the administration of the Commonwealth co-operative telecommunications financial arrangements.

The functions of the Bureau are to collect, maintain and disseminate such traffic, rate, routeing and financial data and other information as the Council may determine; to process material for Conferences and meetings of the Council; to perform the accounting and clearing house functions of the Organisation; to maintain and distribute regulations as determined by the Council; and to perform such other duties as the General Secretary may direct.

---

* *See* p. 794.

APPENDIX E

COMMONWEALTH SUGAR AGREEMENT

IN 1951 the Commonwealth Sugar Agreement was concluded between the British Government and sugar industries and exporters in Australia, South Africa, the West Indies and British Guiana, Mauritius and Fiji. British Honduras acceded to the agreement in 1954 and East Africa acceded in 1960. As a result of the withdrawal of South Africa from the Commonwealth the South African industry ceased to be a part of the agreement on 31st December 1961. To ensure an outlet for Swaziland sugar and comparable returns for her producers after that date, a separate bilateral sugar agreement was negotiated between the United Kingdom and South Africa which terminated on 31st December 1964. On 1st January 1965 Swaziland, India and Rhodesia acceded to the agreement when additional allocation of quotas was possible following the end of the agreement with South Africa.

The agreement provides that each exporting territory shall receive the price settled by negotiation as being reasonably remunerative to efficient producers for a specified quantity of sugar sold to Britain (negotiated price quota). The agreement was originally for eight years but, with the exception of 1967, has been consistently extended annually by one year so as to preserve the eight-year term. In 1968, it was amended and made of indefinite duration, with provision for a review every three years, beginning in 1971.

The negotiated price quotas consolidated in 1965 are:

Australia	335,000 long tons tel quel.
British Honduras	20,500
East Africa	7,000
Fiji	140,000
India	25,000
Mauritius	380,000
Swaziland	85,000
West Indies and Guyana	725,000
	1,717,500

(The Rhodesian quota of 25,000 long tons has been placed in suspense until the return of constitutional rule).

The negotiated price for 1969, 1970, and 1971 consists of the following elements:

Basic Price: £43.50 per long ton, 96° Polarisation, f.o.b. and stowed bulk;

For less developed countries (i.e. all but Australia), a special payment consisting of:

(a) a fixed element of £1.50 per long ton, which includes benefits formerly accruing under Colonial Certificated Preference system; and

(b) variable element which varies inversely with the world price on the following scale:

World Price (*free on board ship*)	Variable Element
Less than £31	£2.50
£31 but less than £33	£2.25
£33 ,, ,, ,, £35	£2.00
£35 ,, ,, ,, £37	£1.75
£37 ,, ,, ,, £39	£1.50
£39 and over	Nil

The world price was below £31 during 1969.

The Sugar Board constituted under the Sugar Act, 1956, meets the U.K. commitment for the purchase of negotiated price quota sugar by purchasing at the negotiated price and selling at the world price in the country of origin.

In addition to the United Kingdom commitment to buy specified quantities at reasonable prices the agreement provides for the orderly marketing in the United Kingdom, New Zealand and Canada of supplies in excess of the negotiated price quotas from the exporting countries and in normal times limits the total amounts which can be sold in these markets (including the negotiated price quotas). These totals are the overall agreement quotas.

COMMONWEALTH SUGAR PRODUCTION AND EXPORTS 1969   '000 metric tons raw value

	Production	C.S.A. Negotiated Price Quota*	U.S. Quota*	Other Preferential Markets (Canada, etc.)*	Non-Preferential Markets	Total Exports
Independent Commonwealth Countries						
Australia	2,507	340	193	358	658	1,642
Barbados	161	119	3	7	—	148
Fiji	350	142	41	123	34	339
India	4,634	27	73	63	182	307
Guyana	332	197	112	4	—	301
Jamaica	380	217	65	—	—	173
Trinidad and Tobago	224	139	20	166	2	616
Mauritius	611	386	17	35	—	165
Swaziland	181	88	7		18	
Dependent Commonwealth Countries						
British Honduras	70	21	14	26	—	61
Associated States						
Leeward and Windward Islands (Antigua and St Kitts)	33	35	—	—	—	—

*'000 metric tons tel quel

APPENDIX F

AREAS AND POPULATIONS OF BRITISH DEPENDENT TERRITORIES

Territory	Area including inland waters (sq. miles)	Estimated Mid-year population		Annual rate of increase 1963-68 %
Bahama Islands	5,382	1970	169,000	2·8
Bermuda (i)	21	1969	52,000(i)	1·9
British Honduras	8,867	1969	120,000	3·1
British Solomon Islands	11,500	1968	147,000	1·9
British Virgin Islands	59	1970	10,500	1·9
Cayman Islands	100	1968	9,000	not available
Falkland Islands (ii)	4,618	1968	2,000	not available
Gibraltar	2·3	1969	27,000	0·8
Gilbert and Ellice Islands	342	1968	57,000	3·0
Hong Kong	399	1969	3,990,000	2·3
Montserrat	38	1969	15,000	1·9
New Hebrides	5,700	1968	78,000	2·0
Pitcairn Island (iii)	2	1969	92	not available
St Helena (iv)	47	1968	5,000	not available
Seychelles	145	1969	51,000	1·7
Turks and Caicos Islands	166	1968	6,000	not available

(i) Civil population only.

(ii) Excluding dependencies. Population of South Georgia at the end of 1967 was 22 persons, the other islands are uninhabited.

(iii) The other islands in the group, Henderson, Ducie and Oeno are uninhabited and have an area of approximately 16·5 square miles.

(iv) Excluding dependencies. Ascension, 34 square miles, population 1,486 (640 St Helenians) as at 31st December 1967 and Tristan da Cunha, 38 square miles, population 245 at end of 1967

INDEX

INDEX

N

O

Printed in England for Her Majesty's Stationery Office
by James Townsend & Sons, Ltd., Western Way, Exeter

Dd. 502349 K22 11/71

SBN 11 580065 4*

THE LONDON DIPLOMATIC LIST

An alphabetical list of the representatives of Foreign States and Commonwealth Countries in London, with the names and designations of the persons returned as composing the establishment of their respective offices

Published every two months prices 25p per copy (by post 29½p); for 1972: 26p per copy. Annual subscription £1.83 including postage

Published by

HER MAJESTY'S STATIONERY OFFICE

HMSO

and obtainable from the
Government Bookshops in London
(post orders to PO Box 569, SE1 9NH)
Edinburgh, Cardiff, Belfast, Manchester,
Birmingham and Bristol,
or through booksellers

Journal of Administration Overseas

An authoritative quarterly providing articles on the varied aspects and problems of administration in developing countries, including training, planning, local government, urbanization and social change, public administration and land tenure.
A compact medium for the exchange of ideas, experiences and knowledge. Book reviews, conference reports, quarterly notes on current affairs.

32½p quarterly (by post 35p)
Annual subscription £1·50 including postage

Published by
HER MAJESTY'S STATIONERY OFFICE
and obtainable from the Government Bookshops in London (post orders to P.O. Box 569, SE1 9NH), Edinburgh, Cardiff, Belfast, Manchester, Birmingham and Bristol, or through booksellers

Prospects for Employment Opportunities in the 1970's

Papers and impressions of the 1970 Cambridge Conference

Planners in the 'Seventies' are presented with the unenviable choice of compromise between the economic need for efficiency in production and the pressing political requirement for more employment. Economists, planners and administrators at the 1970 Cambridge Conference on Development sought to provide at least some of the answers to this vital problem.

£2 (by post £2·08½)

ABC of Development Assistance

A glossary of some terms and institutions

Over 200 entries containing definitions of terms and descriptions of British and international organisations connected with overseas development and aid. The index also provides a guide to abbreviations. It is the first glossary of its kind to be published in this country and is intended for non-specialist use.

30p (by post 34½p)

Please send your orders or write for free lists of titles (specifying subject/s) to Her Majesty's Stationery Office, P6A, Atlantic House, Holborn Viaduct, London EC1P 1BN.

Visit your nearest Government Bookshop and see the wide selection on display.

49 High Holborn, London WC1V 6HB
13a Castle Street, Edinburgh EH2 3AR
109 St Mary Street, Cardiff CF1 1JW
80 Chichester Street, Belfast BT1 4JY
Brazennose Street, Manchester M60 8AS
258 Broad Street, Birmingham B1 2HE
50 Fairfax Street, Bristol BS1 3DE

Why do exporters use

The Chartered Bank?

Because it is there.

There. Right on the spot in more than 30 major trading areas of the world. In Europe and America, in the Mediterranean and, of course, the East, where it has been established for over a century and now has more branches than any other British banking group. Whatever your needs—advice on selling or investment abroad, market intelligence or just information on local economic conditions—you can hardly do better than contact the Trade Promotion Department of The Chartered Bank.

THE CHARTERED BANK

Head Office: 38 Bishopsgate, London, EC2N 2AH. Telephone: 01-588 3688
Manchester Office: 58 Spring Gardens, Manchester M60 2AJ. Telephone: 061-834 7244/6
Liverpool Office: 28 Derby House, Exchange Buildings, Liverpool, L2 3QQ
Telephone: 051-236 2262

A MEMBER OF STANDARD AND CHARTERED BANKING GROUP LIMITED